THE HINDUS

ALSO BY WENDY DONIGER

Siva, the Erotic Ascetic
The Origins of Evil in Hindu Mythology
Dreams, Illusion, and Other Realities
Splitting the Difference: Gender and Myth in Ancient Greece and India

TRANSLATIONS:
The Rig Veda
The Laws of Manu
and
Kamasutra

THE
HINDUS

An Alternative History

WENDY DONIGER

THE PENGUIN PRESS

New York

2009

THE PENGUIN PRESS
Published by the Penguin Group
Penguin Group (USA) Inc., 375 Hudson Street, New York, New York 10014, U.S.A. • Penguin Group (Canada),
90 Eglinton Avenue East, Suite 700, Toronto, Ontario, Canada M4P 2Y3 (a division of Pearson Penguin Canada
Inc.) • Penguin Books Ltd, 80 Strand, London WC2R 0RL, England • Penguin Ireland, 25 St. Stephen's Green,
Dublin 2, Ireland (a division of Penguin Books Ltd) • Penguin Books Australia Ltd, 250 Camberwell Road,
Camberwell, Victoria 3124, Australia (a division of Pearson Australia Group Pty Ltd) • Penguin Books India Pvt Ltd,
11 Community Centre, Panchsheel Park, New Delhi – 110 017, India • Penguin Group (NZ), 67 Apollo Drive,
Rosedale, North Shore 0632, New Zealand (a division of Pearson New Zealand Ltd) • Penguin Books (South Africa)
(Pty) Ltd, 24 Sturdee Avenue, Rosebank, Johannesburg 2196, South Africa

Penguin Books Ltd, Registered Offices:
80 Strand, London WC2R 0RL, England

First published in 2009 by The Penguin Press,
a member of Penguin Group (USA) Inc.

1   3   5   7   9   10   8   6   4   2

Copyright © Wendy Doniger, 2009
All rights reserved

Acknowledgments for permission to reprint copyrighted works
appear on page 754.
Illustration credits appear on page 754.

Library of Congress Cataloging-in-Publication Data
Doniger, Wendy.
The Hindus : an alternative history / Wendy Doniger.
p.   cm.
Includes bibliographical references and index.
ISBN 978-159420-205-6
1. Hinduism—Social aspects—History.   2. Women in Hinduism—History.
3. Pariahs in Hinduism—History.
4. Hinduism—Relations.   I. Title.
BL1151.3.D66 2009
294.509—dc22
2008041030

Printed in the United States of America

Designed by Marysarah Quinn

KATHERINE ULRICH—student, friend, editor supreme—

and

WILL DALRYMPLE—inspiration and comrade in the good fight

CONTENTS

INDIA'S MAJOR GEOGRAPHICAL FEATURES

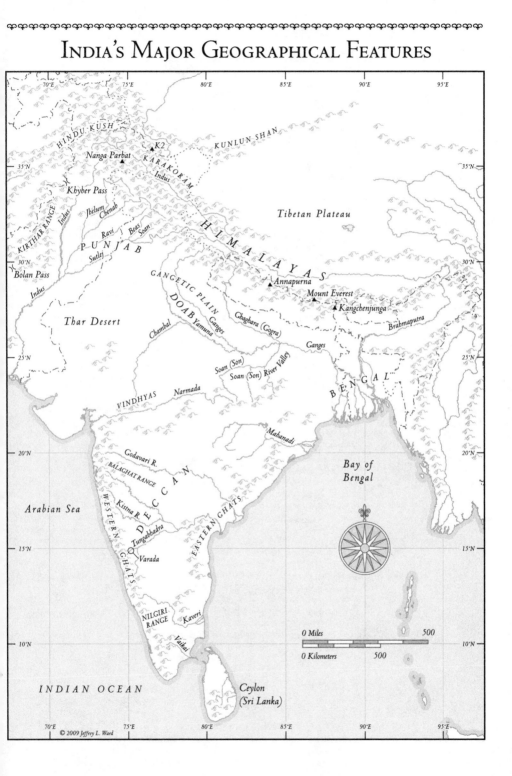

© 2009 Jeffrey L. Ward

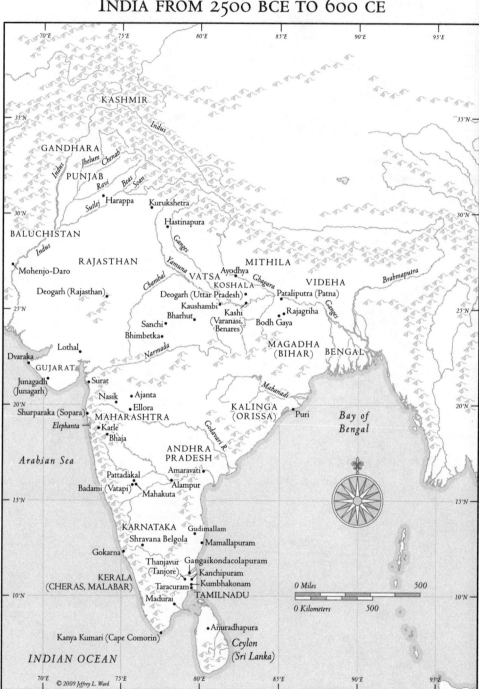

KASHMIR

Indus

GANDHARA

Jhelum *Chenab*

PUNJAB

Ravi *Beas* *Soan*

Indus

Sutlej •Harappa •Kurukshetra

BALUCHISTAN

•Hastinapura

Indus *Ganges*

RAJASTHAN

MITHILA

Yamuna

•Mohenjo-Daro

VATSA •Ayodhya

Chambal KOSHALA *Ghagara* VIDEHA *Brahmaputra*

Deogarh (Rajasthan)•

•Deogarh (Uttar Pradesh) •Pataliputra (Patna)

•Kaushambi *Ganges*

•Bharhut •Kashi •Rajagriha

•Sanchi (Varanasi, •Bodh Gaya

•Bhimbetka Benares)

Narmada MAGADHA BENGAL

•Lothal (BIHAR)

Dvaraka•

GUJARAT •Surat

Junagadh• •Nasik •Ajanta *Mahanadi*

(Junagarh) •Ellora

Shurparaka (Sopara)• KALINGA

Elephanta MAHARASHTRA (ORISSA) •Puri *Bay of*

•Karle *Bengal*

•Bhaja *Godavari R.*

ANDHRA

Arabian Sea PRADESH

•Amaravati

•Pattadakal •Alampur

Badami (Vatapi)•

•Mahakuta

KARNATAKA •Gudimallam

•Shravana Belgola •Mamallapuram

•Gokarna

•Thanjavur •Gangaikondacolapuram

(Tanjore) •Kanchipuram

KERALA •Kumbhakonam

(CHERAS, MALABAR) •Taracuram TAMILNADU

•Madurai

•Anuradhapura

•Kanya Kumari (Cape Comorin) *Ceylon*

(Sri Lanka)

INDIAN OCEAN

0 Miles 500

0 Kilometers 500

© 2009 Jeffrey L. Ward

INDIA FROM 600 CE TO 1600 CE

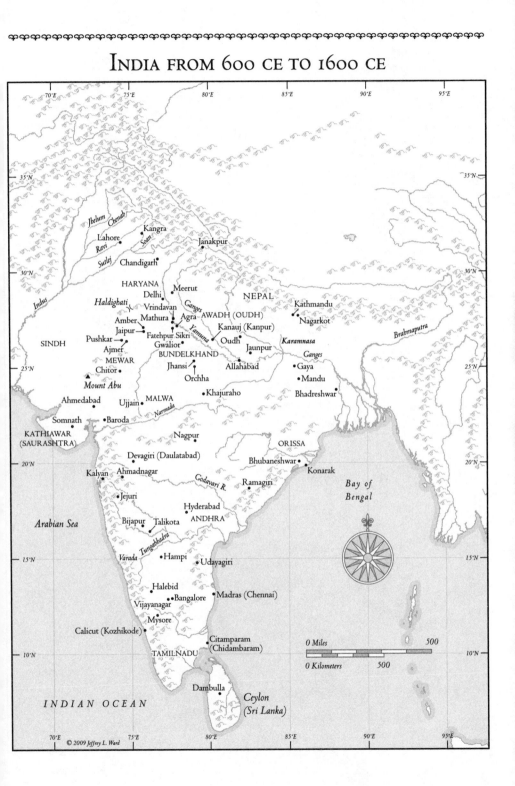

70°E   75°E   80°E   85°E   90°E   95°E

35°N

Jhelum
Chenab
Kangra
Lahore
Ravi
Soan
Janakpur

Sutlej Chandigarh

30°N

HARYANA
Haldighati Delhi Meerut
Vrindavan *Ganges* NEPAL Kathmandu
Amber Mathura Agra AWADH (OUDH) Nagarkot
Jaipur *Yamuna* Kanauj (Kanpur)
Pushkar Fatehpur Sikri Oudh *Karamnasa* *Brahmaputra*
Ajmer Gwalior Jaunpur
MEWAR BUNDELKHAND *Ganges*
Chitor Jhansi Allahabad Gaya
Mount Abu Orchha Mandu
Khajuraho Bhadreshwar
Ahmedabad Ujjain MALWA
Somnath Baroda *Narmada*
KATHIAWAR Nagpur
(SAURASHTRA) ORISSA
Devagiri (Daulatabad) Bhubaneshwar Konarak
Kalyan Ahmadnagar *Godavari R.* Ramagiri **Bay of**
Jejuri Hyderabad **Bengal**
Bijapur Talikota ANDHRA
Varada *Tungabhadra*
Hampi Udayagiri
Halebid
Bangalore Madras (Chennai)
Vijayanagar
Mysore
Calicut (Kozhikode) Citamparam
(Chidambaram)
TAMILNADU

Arabian Sea

SINDH

Indus

25°N

20°N

15°N

0 Miles   500
0 Kilometers   500

10°N

Dambulla Ceylon
(Sri Lanka)

INDIAN OCEAN

70°E   75°E   80°E   85°E   90°E   95°E

© 2009 Jeffrey L. Ward

India from 1600 ce to the Present

KYRGYZSTAN

TAJIKSTAN

AFGHANISTAN

CHINA

Peshawar

Srinagar

JAMMU AND
KASHMIR

HIMACHAL
PRADESH

TIBET

Amritsar

PAKISTAN

PUNJAB

UTTAR-
ANCHAL

HARYANA

Delhi

NEPAL

BHUTAN

Jodhpur

Jaipur

Agra

UTTAR PRADESH

ASSAM
(KAMA-RUPA)

RAJASTHAN

Kanpur
(Kanauj)

Gorakhpur

Gangez

Yamuna

Patna (Pataliputra)

BIHAR

BANGLADESH

Rann of
Kutch

Dhanbad

Serampore
(Srirampur)

Barrackpore

MYANMAR

Ahmedabad

Dewas

Bhopal

MADHYA PRADESH

JHARKHAND

Calcutta (Kolkata)

GUJARAT

Narmada R.

CHHATTISGARH

WEST
BENGAL

Akola

Nagpur

Amaravati

ORISSA

Mahanadi R.

Puri

Bay
of Bengal

Mumbai (Bombay)

MAHARASHTRA

Godavari R.

Adilabad

Poona (Pune)

Hyderabad

Arabian
Sea

GOA

KARNATAKA

ANDHRA
PRADESH

Chandragutti

Bangalore

Chennai (Madras)

Arcot

Pondicherry

KERALA

Keveri R.

Tranquebar

TAMILNADU

Rameshwara

Trivandrum

SRI
LANKA

Indian
Ocean

0 Miles   500

0 Kilometers   500

LIST OF ILLUSTRATIONS

ॐ

THE HINDUS

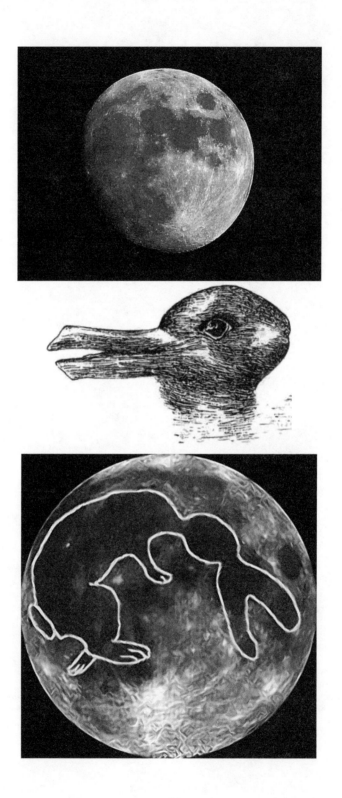

PREFACE:
THE MAN OR THE RABBIT
IN THE MOON

൧

AN ALTERNATIVE HISTORY

The image of the man in the moon who is also a rabbit in the moon, or the duck who is also a rabbit, will serve as a metaphor for the double visions of the Hindus that this book will strive to present.

Since there are so many books about Hinduism, the author of yet another one has a duty to answer the potential reader's Passover question: Why shouldn't I pass over this book, or, Why is this book different from all other books? This book is not a brief survey (you noticed that already; I had intended it to be, but it got the bit between its teeth and ran away from me), nor, on the other hand, is it a reference book that covers all the facts and dates about Hinduism or a book about Hinduism as it is lived today. Several books of each of those sorts exist, some of them quite good, which you might read alongside this one.[1] *The Hindus: An Alternative History* differs from those books in several ways.

First, it highlights a narrative alternative to the one constituted by the most famous texts in Sanskrit (the literary language of ancient India) and represented in most surveys in English. It tells a story that incorporates the narratives of and about alternative people—people who, from the standpoint of most high-caste Hindu males, are alternative in the sense of otherness, people of other religions, or cultures, or castes, or species (animals), or gender (women). Part of my agenda in writing an alternative history is to show how much the groups that conventional wisdom says were oppressed and silenced and played no part in the development of the tradition—women, Pariahs (oppressed castes, sometimes called Untouchables)—did actually contribute to Hinduism. My hope is not to reverse or

[TOP] *The Mark on the Moon,* [MIDDLE] *Wittgenstein's Duck/ Rabbit, and* [BOTTOM] *The Rabbit in the Moon*

misrepresent the hierarchies, which remain stubbornly hierarchical, or to deny that Sanskrit texts were almost always subject to a final filter in the hands of the male Brahmins (the highest of the four social classes, the class from which priests were drawn) who usually composed and preserved them. But I hope to bring in more actors, and more stories, upon the stage, to show the presence of brilliant and creative thinkers entirely off the track beaten by Brahmin Sanskritists and of diverse voices that slipped through the filter, and, indeed, to show that the filter itself was quite diverse, for there were many different sorts of Brahmins; some whispered into the ears of kings, but others were dirt poor and begged for their food every day.

Moreover, the privileged male who recorded the text always had access to oral texts as well as to the Sanskrit that was his professional language. Most people who knew Sanskrit must have been bilingual; the etymology of "Sanskrit" ("perfected, artificial") is based upon an implicit comparison with "Prakrit" ("primordial, natural"), the language actually spoken. This gives me a double agenda: first to point out the places where the Sanskrit sources themselves include vernacular, female, and lower-class voices and then to include, wherever possible, non-Sanskrit sources. The (Sanskrit) medium is not always the message;* it's not all about Brahmins, Sanskrit, the *Gita*. I will concentrate on those moments within the tradition that resist forces that would standardize or establish a canon, moments that forged bridges between factions, the times of the "mixing of classes" (*varna-samkara*) that the Brahmins always tried— inevitably in vain—to prevent.

Second, in addition to focusing on a special group of actors, I have concentrated on a few important actions, several of which are also important to us today: nonviolence toward humans (particularly religious tolerance) and toward animals (particularly vegetarianism and objections to animal sacrifice) and the tensions between the householder life and renunciation, and between addiction and the control of sensuality. More specific images too (such as the transposition of heads onto bodies or the flooding of cities) thread their way through the entire historical fabric of the book. I have traced these themes through the chapters and across the centuries to provide some continuity in the midst of all the flux,[2] even at the expense of what some might regard as more basic matters.

Third, this book attempts to set the narrative of religion within the narrative

---

* To invoke Marshall McLuhan's famous phrase.

of history, as a linga (an emblem of the god Shiva, often representing his erect phallus) is set in a yoni (the symbol of Shiva's consort, or the female sexual organ), or any statue of a Hindu god in its base or plinth (*pitha*). I have organized the topics historically in order to show not only how each idea is a reaction to ideas that came before (as any good old-fashioned philological approach would do) but also, wherever possible, how those ideas were inspired or configured by the events of the times, how Hinduism, always context sensitive,[3] responds to what is happening, at roughly the same moment, not only on the political and economic scene but within Buddhism or Islam in India or among people from other cultures entering India. For Hinduism, positioning kings as gods and gods as kings, seldom drew a sharp line between secular and religious power. In recent years a number of historians of religions, particularly of South Asian religions, have contextualized particular moments in the religious history of the subcontinent.[4] This book attempts to extend that particularizing project to the whole sweep of Indian history, from the beginning (and I do mean the beginning, c. 50,000,000 BCE) to the present. This allows us to see how certain ongoing ideas evolve, which is harder to do with a focus on a particular event or text at a particular moment.

This will not serve as a conventional history (my training is as a philologist, not a historian) but as a book about the evolution of several important themes in the lives of Hindus caught up in the flow of historical change. It tells the story of the Hindus primarily through a string of narratives. The word for "history" in Sanskrit, *itihasa*, could be translated as "That's what happened," giving the impression of an only slightly more modest equivalent of von Ranke's phrase for positivist history: "*Wie es [eigentlich] gewesen ist*" ("The way it [really] happened"). But the *iti* in the word is most often used as the Sanskrit equivalent of "end quote," as in "Let's go [*iti*]," he said. *Itihasa* thus implies not so much what happened as what people *said* happened ("That's what he said happened")—narratives, inevitably subjective narratives. And so this is a history not of what the British used to call maps and chaps (geography and biography) but of the stories in hi-story. It's a kind of narrative quilt made of scraps of religion sewn in next to scraps of social history, a quilt like those storytelling cloths that Indian narrators use as mnemonic devices to help them and the audience keep track of the plot. The narrator assembles the story from the quilt pieces much as the French rag-and-bones man, the *bricoleur*, makes new objects out of the broken-off pieces of old objects (bricolage).[5]

Like any work of scholarship, this book rests on the shoulders of many pygmies as well as giants. I have kept most of the scholarly controversies out of the text, after laying out the rules of the game in these first two chapters of methodological introduction and in the pre-Vedic period (chapters 2 through 4), which might stand as paradigms for what might have been done with all the other chapters, as well as a few other places where the arguments were so loony that I could not resist the temptation to satirize them. Many a "fact" turns out, on closer inspection, to be an argument. There is another story to be told here: how we know what we know, what we used to believe, why we believe what we believe now, what scholars brought up certain questions or gave us the information we now have, what scholars now challenge that information, and what political factors influenced them. Those arguments tell a story that is interesting in itself but to which I merely allude from time to time. I also write in the shadow of a broad scholarship of theories about religion and history, and I will keep that too out of the text. I have tried to avoid setting my opinions against those with whom I disagree or using them as fall guys, beginning an argument by citing the imagined opponent. I have, rather, simply presented each subject in what I believe to be the best scholarly construction, in order to concentrate on the arguments about it within the Hindu texts themselves.

Many crucial questions remain unanswered, and I hope that this book will inspire some readers to go back to the sources and decide for themselves whether or not they agree with me. The relevant materials can be found in the bibliography as well as in the notes for each chapter, which will also provide browsing material for those readers (I confess that I am one of them) who go straight to the back and look at the notes and bibliography first, reading the book like Hebrew, from right to left, to see where the author has been grazing, like dogs sniffing one another's backsides to see what they have eaten lately.*

Sanskritization, Deshification, and Vernacularization

Sanskrit texts from the earliest period assimilated folk texts that were largely oral and composed in languages other than Sanskrit, vernacular languages. But even in the Vedic age, Sanskrit was not what has been called a kitchen language,† not the language in which you said, "Pass the butter."[6] (Actually, Brah-

---

* Other readers, allergic to methodology, should skip straight to chapter 2.
† The term "kitchen language" was, I think, first coined for Afrikaans. But the eleventh-century Indian lexicographer Acharya Yadavaprakasha does actually supply a number of otherwise unattested Sanskrit words for everyday cooking devices (ladles, pots, and so forth), evidence either that some Brahmins *did* speak Sanskrit at home or that Yadavaprakasha was showing off by inventing Sanskrit words for

mins probably did say, "Pass the butter," in Sanskrit when they put butter as an oblation into the fire in the course of the sacrifice, but those same Brahmins would have to have known how to say it in another language as well, in the kitchen.) At the very least, those male Sanskritists had to be bilingual in order to talk to their wives and servants and children.* It was through those interactions that oral traditions got their foot in the Sanskrit door. Henry Higgins, in George Bernard Shaw's *Pygmalion*, is said to be the author of *Spoken Sanskrit*, and many priests and scholars can speak Sanskrit, but no one ever spoke *only* pure Sanskrit. Sanskrit and oral traditions flow back and forth, producing a constant infusion of lower-class words and ideas into the Brahmin world, and vice versa.

It must have been the case that the natural language, Prakrit, and the vernaculars came first, while Sanskrit, the refined, secondary revision, the artificial language, came later. But South Asianists often seem to assume that it is the other way around, that the dialects are "derived from Sanskrit," because Sanskrit won the race to the archives and was the first to be written down and preserved, and we only encounter vernaculars much later. So we say that Sanskrit is older, and the vernaculars younger. But Sanskrit, the language of power, emerged in India from a minority, and at first its power came precisely from its nonintelligibility and unavailability, which made it the power of an elite group.[7] Walt Kelly's Pogo used to use the word "Sam-skrimps" to describe highfalutin double-talk or manipulative twaddle. Many Euro-Americans mispronounce it "Sanscript," implying that it is a language without (*sans*) an (intelligible) script, or "Sand-script," with overtones of ruined cities in the desert or a lost language written in sand.

The sociologist M. N. Srinivas, in 1952, coined the useful term "Sanskritization" to describe the way that Vedic social values, Vedic ritual forms, and Sanskrit learning seep into local popular traditions of ritual and ideology (in part through people who hope to be upwardly mobile, to rise by imitating the manners and habits, particularly food taboos, of Brahmins, and in particular avoiding violence to animals).[8] Indian society, in this view, is a permanent floating game of snakes and ladders (or, perhaps, snakes and ropes, recalling that Ve-

---

objects normally referred to only in the vernaculars. After all, even in the modern period, people called television *dur-darshana,* a made-up Sanskrit neologism for "far-seeing," and it caught on, though *dhumra-varttika* ("smokestick") for "cigarette" did not; people persisted in calling them cigarettes.

* A. K. Ramanujan used to talk of his father's speaking Sanskrit in the front room, his mother's speaking Tamil in the kitchen in the back.

dantic philosophers mistake snakes for ropes and that you can climb up on ropes in the Indian rope trick), which you enter in a state of impurity, gradually advancing over the generations toward the goal of Brahminical purity, trying to avoid the many pitfalls along the way.[9] Tribal groups (Bhils, Gonds, etc.) might undergo Sanskritization in order to claim to be a caste, and therefore, Hindu.[10]

But the opposite of Sanskritization, the process by which the Sanskritic tradition simultaneously absorbs and transforms those same popular traditions, is equally important, and that process might be called oralization, or popularization, or even, perhaps, Deshification (from the "local" or *deshi* traditions) or Laukification, from what Sanskrit calls *laukika* ("of the people" *[loka]*). Let's settle on Deshification. The two processes of Sanskritization and Deshification beget each other. Similarly, through a kind of *identificatio brahmanica*,[11] local gods take on the names of gods in Sanskrit texts: Murukan becomes Skanda, a kind of Sanskritization, while at the same time there is an *identificatio deshika*, by which Sanskrit gods take on the characteristics of local gods, and to the people who worship Murukan, it is Murukan who is absorbing Skanda, not the reverse. "Cross-fertilization" might be a good, equalizing term for the combination of the two processes.

"Written" does not necessarily mean "written in Sanskrit," nor are oral texts always in the vernacular (the *Rig Veda,* after all, was preserved orally in Sanskrit for many centuries before it was consigned to writing). We cannot equate vernacular with oral, for people both write and speak both Sanskrit and the vernacular languages of India, though Sanskrit is written more often than spoken. The distinction between Sanskrit and the vernacular literatures is basically geographical: Though there are regional Sanskrits, the vernaculars, unlike Sanskrit, are defined and named by their place of origin (Bangla from Bengal, Oriya from Orissa, and so forth), while the script in which Sanskrit is most often written allegedly has no particular earthly place of origin (it is called "the [script of the] city of the gods [*deva-nagari*]"). Once people departed from the royal road of Sanskrit literary texts, there were thousands of vernacular paths that they could take, often still keeping one foot on the high road of Sanskrit.

The constant, gradual, unofficial mutual exchange between Sanskrit and the vernacular languages, the cross-fertilization, underwent a dramatic transformation toward the middle of the second millennium: Local languages were now promoted officially, politically, and artistically,[12] replacing the previously fashionable cosmopolitan and translocal language, Sanskrit. Instead of nourishing and supplementing Sanskrit, the vernacular languages as literary languages began to compete with Sanskrit as the language of literary production. This process has been called, in imitation of Srinivas's "Sanskritization" (and in contrast with both Deshification and the more mutually nourishing, two-way process of cross-fertilization) vernacularization, "the historical process of choosing to create a written literature, along with its complement, a political discourse, in local languages according to models supplied by a superordinate, usually cosmopolitan, literary culture,"[13] or "a process of change by which the universalistic orders, formations, and practices of the preceding millennium were supplemented and gradually replaced by localized forms."[14]

The great divide is between written and nonwritten, not between Sanskrit and the vernaculars, particularly as the Sanskrit corpus comes to be Deshified and the vernaculars eventually became Sanskritized themselves, imitating Sanskrit values and conventions, sharing many of the habits of the Sanskrit Brahmin imaginary, such as grammars and lexicons.[15] The bad news is that some of the vernacular literatures are marred by the misogynist and class-bound mental habits of Brahmins, while the good news is that even some Sanskrit texts, and certainly many vernacular texts, often break out of those strictures and incorporate the more open-minded attitudes of the oral vernaculars.

Many ideas, and in particular many narratives, seem to enter Sanskrit literature either from parts of the Sanskrit canon that have fallen away or from non-Sanskrit sources (two entirely nonfalsifiable speculations). It's an old joke among linguists that a language is a dialect with an army,* and this is sometimes used to explain the dominance of Sanskrit texts, since as usual, the victors wrote the history, and in ancient India, they usually wrote it in Sanskrit. (The earliest inscriptions were in Prakrit, not Sanskrit, but from about 150 CE, Sanskrit dominated this field too.) Sanskrit is perched on top of the vernacular literatures like a mahout on an elephant, like Krishna riding on the composite women that form the horse on the jacket of this book.

SELECTIVITY AND SYNECDOCHE

Such a luxurious jungle of cultural phenomena, truly an embarrassment of riches, necessitates a drastic selectivity. I have therefore provided not detailed histories of specific moments but one or two significant episodes to represent

---

* Apparently this was first said in Yiddish, by Max Weinrich, who referred to a dialect with an army and a navy ("*A sprach is a dialekt mit a armee un a flot*").

the broader historical periods in question.[16] The result is not a seamless narrative that covers the waterfront but a pointillist collage, a kaleidoscope, made of small, often discontinuous fragments. Synecdoche—letting one or two moments in history and one or two narratives stand for many—allows us to see alternity in a grain of sand,[17] taking a small piece of human history and using it to suggest the full range of enduring human concerns. These small fragments alternate with a few exemplary narratives quoted in considerable detail, where Hindus speak in their own words (in translation*).

I have tried to balance my translations of the classic, much-translated texts with citations of more obscure, previously unnoticed texts, using as my framework the usual suspects that scholars have rounded up over and over, the basic curry and rice episodes of Hinduism, but moving away quickly, in each chapter, to a handful of lesser-known episodes, things usually left out of survey books on Hinduism. These are not the great imperial moments but episodes that give us an inkling of what religious life was like for some people, including ordinary people, in India long ago. I have also included a few episodes of interaction (both friendly and hostile) between Hindus and non-Hindus in India, such as Buddhists, Jainas, Sikhs, and Muslims, though without paying direct attention to those other religions in their own right. Beginning with a minimal backbone or infrastructure of basic historical events and concepts that many people would agree upon (data never value free but still valuable), we can then move from this point outward to other points, and from social history to literary texts, to search for narratives of and about alternative people. That selectivity makes this book alternative in another sense, in that it leaves wide open a great deal of space for others to select from in writing their histories, alternative to mine. Someone else would make different choices and write a very different book. This is *a* history, not *the* history, of the Hindus.

THEMES AND VARIATIONS

The central actors and their actions are threads around which the great narratives of Hinduism coalesce like crystals in a supersaturated solution. The actors and actions connect in various ways: Sanskrit texts usually regard women and hunted animals as primary objects of addiction, and the senses that cause

---

* All translations from the Sanskrit are my own unless otherwise noted, and I have usually condensed and/or excerpted them, as I have done with citations of other narratives translated from other languages, though I have added nothing that was not in the text.

addiction are likened to horses; animals often represent both women and the lower classes; the tension between sexuality and renunciation results in an ambivalence toward women as mothers and seductresses; and violence is first addressed largely in the form of violence against animals. Violence and tolerance also interact in attitudes not only to other religions but between the upper and lower castes, between men and women, and between humans and animals. I will highlight in each period those moments when intrareligious (including intercaste) or interreligious interactions took place, marked by either tolerance or violence, the deciding factor between the two options often being historical circumstances. Each chapter deals with several themes, but not every chapter has instances of every theme or treats the same theme in the same way (chapter 12 for instance, is about women more than about goddesses, while chapter 14 is about goddesses more than about women), and indeed I have often noted the activities of women in other contexts, without explicitly highlighting their gender. But wherever the evidence allows, I will organize each chapter around these central themes.

(Non)Violence

In the Introduction (chapter 1), I spell out the assumptions behind my attention to history and to the particular actors in this story (women, lower classes and castes, and animals). Here let me just say a few words about the central action: (non)violence.

The term "nonviolence" (*ahimsa*) originally applied not to the relationship between humans but to the relationship between humans and animals. *Ahimsa* means "the absence of the desire to injure or kill," a disinclination to do harm, rather than an active desire to be gentle; it is a double negative, perhaps best translated by the negative "nonviolence," which suggests both mental and physical concern for others. The roots of *ahimsa* may lie in Vedic ritual, in animal sacrifice, in the argument that the priest does not actually injure the animal but merely "pacifies him"; the primary meaning of *ahimsa* is thus to do injury without doing injury, a casuist argument from its very inception. In the *Rig Veda* (the earliest Sanskrit text, from c. 1200 BCE), the word *ahimsa* refers primarily to the prevention of injury or violence to the sacrificer and his offspring, as well as his cattle (10.22.13).[18] The problem is exacerbated by the fact that the verb on which *ahimsa* is based, *han*, is ambiguous, meaning both "to strike or beat" and "to kill." *Ahimsa*, therefore, when applied to cows, to take a case at random, might mean refraining either from beating them or killing them—quite a difference. In any case, *ahimsa* represents not a political doctrine or even a social theory, but the emotion of the horror of killing (or hurting) a living creature, an emotion that we will see attested from the earliest texts.*

Arguments about whether or not to kill, sacrifice, and/or eat animals were often at the heart of interreligious violence, sometimes the grounds on which human beings attacked other human beings (usually with words, though occasionally with blows).† Arjuna, the heroic warrior of the *Mahabharata*, the great ancient Sanskrit poem about a tragic war, excuses the violence of war by saying, "Creatures live on creatures, the stronger on the weaker. The mongoose eats mice, just as the cat eats the mongoose; the dog devours the cat, your majesty, and wild beasts eat the dog. Even ascetics [*tapasas*] cannot stay alive without killing" [12.15.16–24]. The text here justifies human violence by the violence that is rampant in the animal world. Yet the most common sense of *ahimsa* refers to humans' decision to rise above animal violence. Vegetarianism, both as an ideal and as a social fact in India, challenges Arjuna's belief that animals must inevitably feed on one another and attempts to break the chain of alimentary violence simply by affirming that it is not, in fact, necessary to kill in order to eat.

Nonviolence became a cultural ideal for Hindus precisely because it holds out the last hope of a cure, all the more desirable since unattainable, for a civilization that has, like most, always suffered from chronic and terminal violence. Nonviolence is an ideal propped up against the cultural reality of violence. Classical Hindu India was violent in ways both shared with all cultures and unique to its particular time and place, in its politics (war being the raison d'être of every king); in its religious practices (animal sacrifice, ascetic self-torture, fire walking, swinging from hooks in the flesh of the back, and so forth); in its criminal law (impaling on stakes and the amputation of limbs being prescribed punishments for relatively minor offenses); in its hells (cunningly and sadistically contrived to make the punishment fit the crime); and, perhaps at the very heart of it all, in its climate, with its unendurable heat and unpredictable monsoons. Hindu sages

---

* South Asians continue to devise creative ways of addressing this dilemma. In Tibet in the summer of 2006, I met a Buddhist who said that he would eat yak, but not fish, on moral grounds. That is, if you kill a yak, you destroy one soul but feed many people, but you have to kill many fish, and destroy many souls, to feed the same number of people. It occurred to me that it is a good thing that Tibet does not border on whaling waters. This attitude varies by country; Sri Lankan Buddhists opt for fish over large animals.

† As, for instance, in the cow protection riots.

dreamed of nonviolence as people who live all their lives in the desert dream of oases.

It is against this background that we must view the doctrine of nonviolence. The history of Hinduism, as we shall see, abounds both in periods of creative assimilation and interaction and in outbursts of violent intolerance. Sometimes it is possible to see how historical circumstances have tipped the scales in one direction or the other. Sometimes it is not. In their ambivalent attitude to violence, the Hindus are no different from the rest of us, but they are perhaps unique in the intensity of their ongoing debate about it.

THE MAN/RABBIT IN THE MOON

I have organized several of these tensions into dualities, for dualism is an (if not the) Indian way of thinking, as the folklorist A. K. Ramanujan pointed out, speaking of his father: "I (and my generation) was [sic] troubled by his holding together in one brain both astronomy and astrology. I looked for consistency in him, a consistency he didn't seem to care about, or even to think about. . . . 'Don't you know, [he said,] the brain has two lobes?'"[19] But some of the most interesting developments take place in the combinations of the two cultural lobes, whether we define them as Brahmin and non-Brahmin, written and oral, or male and female. One medieval Hindu philosophical text defined a great teacher as someone with the ability to grasp both sides of an argument.[20] It is, I think, no accident that India is the land that developed the technique of interweaving two colors of silk threads so that the fabric is what they call peacock's neck, blue if you hold it one way, green another (or sometimes pink or yellow or purple), and, if you hold it right, both at once.

Another metaphor for this sort of double vision is the dark shape visible on the moon: many Americans and Europeans (for convenience, let us call them Euro-Americans) see the face of a man in the moon (whom some Jewish traditions identify as Cain, cursed to wander), and other cultures see a woman, a moose, a buffalo, a frog, and so forth. But most Hindus (as well as Chinese, Japanese, and Aztecs) see a hare.* (I am calling it a rabbit to avoid the unfortu-

---

* This is not because they see the moon from a different angle; in the Southern Hemisphere this is true, but most of India and all of Japan are in the Northern Hemisphere. From the Northern Hemisphere the eyes are at eleven and one, and the mouth at six; the hare's ears are at between twelve and two, his head at between ten and twelve, his nose pointing at between nine and eleven, and his tail at between four and six.

nate English homonym "hare/hair," another bit of double vision, though calling it a rabbit lands me in the middle of a rock group called the Rabbit in the Moon). The man's right eye can be read as the rabbit's ears, his left eye the rabbit's chest, and his mouth the rabbit's tail. (There was a time, in the 1930s, when some people in India saw the image of Gandhi in the moon.[21]) The Buddhists tell how the moon came to have the mark of a rabbit:

THE RABBIT IN THE MOON

The future Buddha was once born as a rabbit, who vowed that he would give his own flesh to any beggar who came to him, in order to protect the beggar from having to break the moral law by taking animal life. To test him, Indra, the Hindu king of the gods, took the form of a Brahmin and came to him; the rabbit offered to throw himself into a fire and roast himself so that the Brahmin could eat him. Indra conjured up a magical fire; when the rabbit—who first shook himself three times so that any insects that might be on his body would escape death—threw himself into the fire, it turned icy cold. Indra then revealed his identity as Indra, and so that everyone would know of the rabbit's virtue, he painted the sign of a rabbit on the orb of the moon.[22]

The convoluted logic of the rabbit's act of self-violence, in his determination to protect anyone *else* from committing an act of violence against any other animal, is a theme that we will often encounter. The rabbit in the moon is one of so many ideas that Hinduism and Buddhism share.

As an approach to the history of Hinduism, seeing both their rabbit and our man in the moon means maintaining an awareness both of what the tradition says (the insider's view) and of what a very different viewpoint helps us to see (the outsider's view). Hindus may approach their scriptures as a part of their piety or as scholars who study Hinduism as they would study any other human phenomenon, or both simultaneously.* There are certainly things that only a Hindu can know about Hinduism, both factual details of local and private practices and texts and the experiential quality of these and other, better-known religious phenomena. This is what inspires interreligious dialogue, an often interesting and productive conversation between individuals who belong to

---

* This last group represents in many ways the ideal scholars of Hinduism, people like (in my generation) A. K. Ramanujan, Sudhir Kakar, Ashis Nandy, Vasudha Narayanan, and V. Narayana Rao, and, in the younger generation, so many more.

different religions.* But there are also advantages in a more academic approach, such as a religious studies approach, to which the religion of the scholar in question is irrelevant. I would not go so far as some who would insist that a Hindu is *not* the person to ask about Hinduism, as Harvard professor Roman Jakobson notoriously objected to Nabokov's bid for chairmanship of the Russian literature department: "I do respect very much the elephant, but would you give him the chair of zoology?" Nor would I go to the other extreme, to insist that a Hindu is the *only* person to ask about Hinduism. For no single Hindu or, for that matter, non-Hindu can know all of the Hinduisms, let alone represent them. So too there are many different ways of being an academic: Some are careful with their research, others sloppy; some make broad generalizations, while others concentrate on small details.

Nowadays most non-Hindu scholars of Hinduism strike the familiar religious studies yoga posture of leaning over backward, in their attempt to avoid offense to the people they write about. But any academic approach to Hinduism, viewing the subject through the eyes of writers from Marx and Freud to Foucault and Edward Said, provides a kind of telescope, the viewfinder of context, to supplement the microscope of the insider's view, which cannot supply the same sort of context.[23] Always there is bias, and the hope is that the biases of Hindus and non-Hindus will cancel one another out in a well-designed academic study of any aspect of Hinduism. The ancient Persians (according to the Greek historian Herodotus, c. 430 BCE) would debate every important question first drunk, then (on the next day) sober or, as the case may be, first sober, then drunk (1.133). So too, in our scholarly approach, we need to consider the history of Hinduism first from a Hindu viewpoint, then from an academic one. Different sorts of valuable insights may come to individuals both inside and outside the tradition and need not threaten one another. To return to those elephants, you don't have to be an elephant to study zoology, but zoologists do not injure elephants by writing about them. To change the metaphor and apply it more specifically to Hindu texts, a story is a flame that burns no less brightly if strangers light their candles from it.

To return to my central metaphor, once you've seen the rabbit (or hare) in the moon, it's hard to see the man anymore, but the double vision is what we should strive for. This means that when we consider, for instance, the burning of living

---

* This characterizes the "take a Hindu to dinner" approach of such institutions as the one I always think of as the Center for the Prevention of World Religions.

women on the pyres of their dead husbands (which we call suttee, to distinguish it from the woman who commits the act, a woman whom the Hindus call a sati), we must try to see their rabbit, to see the reasons why some Hindus thought (and some continue to think) that it is a good idea for some women to burn themselves to death on their husbands' funeral pyres, while other Hindus strongly disagree. On the other hand, we cannot, and need not, stop seeing our American man (or, perhaps, woman) in the moon: the reasons why many Americans think that suttee is not a good idea at all. The philosopher Ludwig Wittgenstein pointed out that the image of a duck-rabbit (also, actually, a duck-hare) was either a rather smug rabbit or a rather droopy duck[24] but could not be both at once.* But this is precisely the goal that a non-Hindu should have in studying Hinduism: to see in the moon both our man and their rabbit.

You Can't Make an Omelet . . .

Hindus nowadays are diverse in their attitude to their own diversity, which inspires pride in some, anxiety in others. In particular, it provokes anxiety in those Hindus who are sometimes called Hindu nationalists, or the Hindu right, or right-wing Hindus, or the Hindutva ("Hinduness") faction, or, more approximately, Hindu fundamentalists; they are against Muslims, Christians, and the Wrong Sort of Hindus. Their most powerful political organ is the BJP (Bharatiya Janata Party), with its militant branch, the RSS (Rashtriya Swayamsevak Sangh), but they are also involved in groups such as Hindu Human Rights, Vishwa Hindu Parishad, and the ABVP (Akhil Bharatiya Vidyarthi Parishad). I will generally refer to them as the Hindutva faction or the Hindu right. This book is also alternative to the narrative of Hindu history that they tell.

There's a personal story that I should tell about my relationship with this group of Hindus here at the start, in the interest of full disclosure. In the middle of a lecture that I gave in London on November 12, 2003, chaired by William Dalrymple, a man threw an egg at me.[25] (He missed his aim, in every way.) A message that a member of the two-hundred-strong audience posted the next day on a mailing list Web site referred to a passage I had cited from Valmiki's *Ramayana* in which Sita, the wife of Rama, accuses her brother-in-law, Lakshmana, of wanting her for himself. The Web message stated:

---

* Wittgenstein would, I think, have appreciated a more recent double image that has been circulated on the Internet. Close up, it looks like Albert Einstein, but from five feet away, it is the spitting image of Marilyn Monroe.

I was struck by the sexual thrust of her paper on one of our most sacred epics. Who lusted/laid whom, it was not only Ravan who desired Sita but her brother-in-law Lakshman also. Then many other pairings, some I had never heard of, from our other shastras were thrown in to weave a titillating sexual tapestry. What would these clever, "learned" western people be doing for a living if they did not have our shastras and traditions to nitpick and distort?[26]

After a bit more of this, the writer* added:

Her friends and admirers certainly made their applause heard, Muslims among them. In the foyer before the lecture I shook hands and asked a Muslim if he had attended the other lectures in the series and if he was ready for conversion. He said that someone (did he name Vivekananda in the hubbub?) at a similar sort of function had taken off his clothes and asked the audience if they could tell if he was a Hindu or a Muslim.

The deeper political agenda of the author of the posting was betrayed by that second set of remarks, particularly by the gratuitous reference to Muslim conversion, and I am grateful to the unnamed Muslim in this vignette for so aptly invoking the wise words of Vivekananda (or, as the case may more probably be, Kabir). My defense now, for this book, remains what it was in the news coverage then, about the lecture (and the egg):

The Sanskrit texts [cited in my lecture] were written at a time of glorious sexual openness and insight, and I have often focused on precisely those parts of the texts. . . .The irony is that I have praised these texts and translated them in such a way that many people outside the Hindu tradition—people who would otherwise go on thinking that Hinduism is nothing but a caste system that mistreats Untouchables—have come to learn about it and to admire the beauty, complexity and wisdom of the Hindu texts.[27]

---

* The author of the posting was Jitendra Bardwaj, of whom Wikipedia (which may or may not be accurate) says: "Jitendra Bardwaj (born 1937), an independent political campaigner in the United Kingdom, has contested five parliamentary by-elections in what began as an attempt to clear his name after he was convicted of assaulting a police officer outside the Houses of Parliament. As well as campaigning against what he believes is his personal mis-treatment by, and general flaws in, the British legal system, Bardwaj campaigns for the rights of ethnic minorities and for the introduction of Hindu yoga and meditation techniques in British schools."

And, I should have added, the diversity of the Hindu texts. To the accusation that I cited a part of the Hindu textual tradition that one Hindu "had never heard of," my reply is: Yes!, and it's my intention to go on doing just that. The parts of his own tradition that he objected to are embraced by many other Hindus and are, in any case, historically part of the record. One reason why this book is so long is that I wanted to show how very much there is of all that the egg faction would deny. And so I intend to go on celebrating the diversity and pluralism, not to mention the worldly wisdom and sensuality, of the Hindus that I have loved for about fifty years now and still counting.

CHAPTER I
INTRODUCTION: WORKING WITH AVAILABLE LIGHT

ॐ

SEARCHING FOR THE KEY

Someone saw Nasrudin searching for something on the ground.
"What have you lost, Mulla?" he asked. "My key," said the Mulla. So
they both went down on their knees and looked for it. After a time
the other man asked: "Where exactly did you drop it?" "In my own
house." "Then why are you looking here?" "There is more light here
than inside my own house."

Idries Shah (1924–96), citing Mulla Nasrudin
(thirteenth century CE)[1]

This Sufi parable could stand as a cautionary tale for anyone searching for the
keys (let alone the one key) to the history of the Hindus. It suggests that we
may look for our own keys, our own understandings, outside our own houses,
our own cultures, beyond the light of the familiar sources. There's a shortage
of what photographers call available light to help us find what we are looking
for, but in recent years historians have produced studies that provide good
translations and intelligent interpretations of texts in Sanskrit and other Indian
languages and pointers to both texts and material evidence that others had not
noticed before. I have therefore concentrated on those moments that have
been illuminated by the many good scholars whose thick descriptions form an
archipelago of stepping-stones on which a historian can hope to cross the
centuries.

This book tells the story of Hinduism chronologically and historically and
emphasizes the history of marginalized rather than mainstream Hindus. My
aims have been to demonstrate: (1) that Hindus throughout their long history

have been enriched by the contributions of women, the lower castes, and other religions; (2) that although there are a number of things that have been characteristic of many Hindus over the ages (the worship of several gods, reincarnation, karma), none has been true of all Hindus, and the shared factors are overwhelmingly outnumbered by the things that are unique to one group or another; (3) that the greatness of Hinduism—its vitality, its earthiness, its vividness—lies precisely in many of those idiosyncratic qualities that some Hindus today are ashamed of and would deny; and (4) that the history of tensions between the various Hinduisms, and between the different sorts of Hindus, undergirds the violence of the contemporary Indian political and religious scene.

History and diversity—let me lay them out one by one.

HISTORY: AVAILABLE LIGHT

The first European scholars of India believed that Hindus believed that everything was timeless, eternal, and unchanging ("There always was a Veda"), and so they didn't generally value or even notice the ways in which Hindus did in fact recognize change. We now call their attitude Orientalism (a term coined by Edward Said in 1978, in a book by that name), which we may define for the moment—we will return to it when we get to the British Raj—as the love-hate relationship that Europeans had with the Orient for both the right and the wrong reasons—it's exotic, it's erotic, it's spiritual, and it never changes.* Like many of the Indian branch of Orientalists, Europeans picked up this assumption of timeless, unified Hinduism from some Hindus and then reinforced it in other Hindus,² many of whom today regard Hinduism as timeless, though they differ on the actual dating of this timelessness, which (like Hindu scholars of earlier centuries) they tend to put at 10,000 BCE or earlier, while the British generally used to put it much later. The "eternal and unchanging" approach inspired Orientalist philologists to track back to their earliest lair some concepts that do in fact endure for millennia, but without taking into account the important ways in which those concepts changed or the many other aspects of Hinduism that bear little relationship to them.

The so-called central ideas of Hinduism—such as karma, dharma,

---

* Orientalism also underlies the still-widespread misconception that *everything* in India is religious or "spiritual"; often when I mention "South Asian studies" to non-South Asianists, they mishear it as "salvation studies."

samsara—arise at particular moments in Indian history, for particular reasons, and then continue to be alive, which is to say, to change. They remain central, but what precisely they are and, more important, what the people who believe in them are supposed to do about them differ in each era and, within each era, from gender to gender, caste to caste. And many new ideas arise either to replace or, more often, in Hinduism, to supplement or qualify earlier ideas. Some Hindus always knew this very well. Many Hindu records speak of things that happened suddenly, without precedent (*a-purva*, "never before"), right here, right now; they are aware of the existence of local dynasties, of regional gods, of political arrivistes. The Hindu sense of time is intense; the importance of time as an agency of change, the sense that things that happen in the past come to fruition at a particular moment—*now*—pervades the great history (*itihasa*) called the *Mahabharata*. That sense of history is different from ours, as different as Buddhist enlightenment is from the European Enlightenment (what a difference a capital *E* makes). But in India, as in Europe, human beings compose texts at some moment in history, which we strive with varying degrees of success to discover, and those texts continue to develop and to be transformed through commentary, interpretation, and translation.

Hinduism does not lend itself as easily to a strictly chronological account as do some other religions (particularly the so-called Abrahamic religions or religions of the Book, or monotheisms—Judaism, Christianity, Islam), which refer more often to specific historical events. Many central texts of Hinduism cannot be reliably dated even within a century. Since early Buddhism and Hinduism grew up side by side in the same neighborhood, so to speak, historians of Hinduism have often ridden piggyback on historians of Buddhism, a religion that has for the most part kept more precise chronological records; the historians of Buddhism figure out when everything happened, and the historians of Hinduism say, "Our stuff must have happened around then too." Historians of early India have also depended on the kindness of strangers, of foreign visitors to India who left reliably dated (but not always accurately observed) records of their visits.

The chronological framework is largely imperialistic—dates of inscriptions, battles, the endowment of great religious institutions—because those are the things that the people who had the clout to keep records thought was most important. And though we no longer think that kings are all that matter in history (siding more with D. D. Kosambi, who urged historians to ask not who was king but who among the people had a plow), kings (more precisely, rajas) do also still matter. They are, however, no longer all that we would like to know about. The crucial moments for cultural history are not necessarily the great imperial moments, as historians used to think they were, the moments when Alexander dipped his toe into India or the Guptas built their empire. For some of the richest and most original cultural developments take place when there isn't an empire, in the cracks between the great dynastic periods. And although the historical records of inscriptions and coins tell us more about kings (the winners) than about the people (the losers), there are other texts that pay attention to the rest of the populace.

When we cannot date events precisely, we can often at least arrange things in a rough but ready chronological order, though this leads to a house of cards effect when we are forced to reconsider the date of any text in the series. The periodizations, moreover, may give an often false suggestion of causation.* We cannot assume, as philologists have often done, that the texts line up like elephants, each holding on to the tail of the elephant in front, that everything in the Upanishads was derived from the Brahmanas just because some Upanishads cite some Brahmanas. We must also ask how the new text was at least in part inspired by the circumstances of its own time. Why did the Upanishads develop out of the Brahmanas *then*? What about the stuff that isn't in the Brahmanas? "Well (the speculation used to go), maybe they got it from the Greeks; it reminds me of Plato. Or perhaps the Axial Age, sixth century BCE and all that? Or how about this? How about the Indus Valley civilizations? Lots of new ideas must have come from there." Since there is no conclusive evidence for, or against, any of these influences, before we look to Greece we must look to India in the time of the Upanishads to find other sorts of factors that might also have influenced their development—new forms of political organization, taxation, changes in the conditions of everyday life.

Even an imported idea takes root only if it also responds to something already present in the importing culture;[3] even if the idea of reincarnation did come from Greece to India, or from Mesopotamia to both Greece and India (hypotheses that are unlikely but not impossible), we would have to explain why the Indians took up that idea when they did not take up, for instance, Greek ideas about love between men, and then we must note how different the Upa-

---

* One formulation of this assumption is *post hoc, propter hoc* ("after that, because of that"), a phrase that inspired an old British senior common room joke about blaming bad behavior upon drinking an excess of German wine (hock).

nishads are from Plato even in their discussion of ideas that they share, such as reincarnation.

Moreover, to the mix of philology and history we must add another factor, individuality. The question of originality is always a puzzle, in part because we can never account for individual genius; of course ideas don't arise in a vacuum, nor are they nothing but the sum total of ideas that came before them. Individuals have ideas, and those ideas are often quite different from the ideas of other people living at the same time and place. This is particularly important to keep in mind when we search for the voices of marginalized people, who often achieve as individuals what they cannot achieve as a group. People are not merely the product of a zeitgeist; Shakespeare is not just an Elizabethan writer.

In Indian history, individuals have turned the tide of tolerance or violence even against the current of the zeitgeist. The emperors Ashoka and Akbar, for example, initiated highly original programs of religious tolerance, going in the teeth of the practices of their times. Someone with a peculiar, original, individual bent of mind wrote the "There Was Not" (*nasadiya*) hymn of the *Rig Veda*, and the story of Long-Tongue the Bitch in the *Jaiminiya Brahmana*, and the story of Raikva under the cart (one of the earliest homeless people noted in world literature) in the Upanishads. And these individual innovators in the ancient period did not merely compose in Sanskrit. They also lurked in the neglected byways of oral traditions, sometimes in the discourses of women and people of the lower classes, as well as in the broader-based Sanskrit traditions that those local traditions feed. For original ideas are rare both among people who have writing and among those that do not. Public individuals too—such as Ashoka, Akbar, and Gandhi, on the one hand, Aurangzeb, Brigadier General Reginald Dyer, and M. S. Golwalkar, on the other, to take just a few at random—brought about profound transformations in Hinduism.

The question of flourishing is less puzzling than the question of innovation, and we can often ask how a particular king (or political movement, or climactic change) helped the horse sacrifice (or the worship of a goddess or anything else) to survive and thrive. Often history can explain why some ideas take hold and spread while others do not; ideas take root only when they become important to people at a particular time, when they hitch on to something that those people care about. An understanding of the social context of the Upanishads, reintroducing the world into the text, may go a long way to explain not who first thought of the story of Raikva but why the Brahmins were willing to include his story in their texts despite the ways in which it challenged their social order.

MYTH, HISTORY, AND SYMBOLISM

In addition to understanding the history of the texts, we need to understand the relationship between records of historical events and the construction of imaginary worlds as well as the symbolism that often joins them. To begin with the symbolism of physical objects, sometimes a linga is just a linga—or, more often, both a linga and a cigar. Numerous Sanskrit texts and ancient sculptures (such as the Gudimallam linga from the third century BCE) define this image unequivocally as an iconic representation of the male sexual organ in erection, in particular as the erect phallus of the god Shiva. So too a verse from the "Garland of Games" of Kshemendra, a Brahmin who lived in Kashmir in the eleventh century, refers to the human counterpart of the Shiva linga: "Having

The Gudimallam Linga.

locked up the house on the pretext of venerating the linga, Randy scratches her itch with a linga of skin."[4] The first linga in this verse is certainly Shiva's, and there is an implied parallelism, if not identity, between it and the second one, which could be either a leather dildo or its human prototype, attached to a man. And many Hindus have, like Freud, seen lingas in every naturally occurring elongated object, the so-called self-created (*svayambhu*) lingas, including *objets trouvés* such as stalagmites. The linga in this physical sense is well known throughout India, a signifier that is understood across barriers of caste and language, a *linga franca*, if you will.

But other texts treat the linga as an aniconic pillar of light or an abstract symbol of god (the word means simply a "sign," as smoke is the sign of fire), with no sexual reference. To some, the stone lingas "convey an ascetic purity despite their obvious sexual symbolism."[5] There is nothing surprising about this range; some Christians see in the cross a vivid reminder of the agony on Calvary, while others see it as a symbol of their God in the abstract or of Christianity as a religion. But some Hindus who see the linga as an abstract symbol *therefore object* to the interpretations of those who view it anthropomorphically; their Christian counterparts would be people who refuse to acknowledge that the cross ever referred to the passion of Christ. Visitors to the Gudimallam linga in the early twenty-first century noted that while the large linga as a whole remains entirely naked, with all its anatomical detail, the small image of a naked man on the front of the linga was covered with a chaste cloth, wrapped around the whole linga as a kind of total loincloth (or fig leaf) simultaneously covering up the middle of the man in the middle of the linga and the middle of the linga itself. Here is a fine example of a tradition driving with one foot on the brake and the other on the accelerator. We need to be aware of both the literal and symbolic levels simultaneously, as we see both the rabbit and the man in the moon.

Similarly, we have to be careful how we use history and myth to understand one another. In this context I would define a myth as a story that a group of people believe for a long time despite massive evidence that it is not actually true; the spirit of myth is the spirit of Oz: Pay no attention to the man behind the curtain. When we read a text that says that a Hindu king impaled eight thousand Jainas, we need to use history to understand myth—that is, we need to understand why such a text was composed and retold many times; that means knowing the reasons for the tensions between Hindus and Jainas at that time (such as the competition for royal patronage). But we cannot use the myth to reconstruct the actual history behind the text; we cannot say that the text is evidence that a Hindu king actually did impale Jainas. To take another example, when the *Ramayana* speaks of ogres (Rakshasas), it may be simultaneously constructing an imaginary world in which evil forces take forms that can destroy us and using ogres as a metaphor for particular types of human beings. But it does not record an actual event, a moment when people from Ayodhya overcame real people in India (tribals, or Dravidians, or anyone else), nor does the story of the building of the causeway to Lanka mean that Rama and a bunch of monkeys actually built a causeway to (Sri) Lanka. Such myths reveal to us the history of sentiments rather than events, motivations rather than movements.

The history of ideas, even if not a source of "hard" history, is still a very precious thing to have. For stories, and the ideas in stories, do influence history in the other direction, into the future. People who heard or read that story about the impaled Jainas may well have acted differently toward Jainas and/or Hindus (better or worse) as a result. More often than not, we do not know precisely what happened in history, but we often know the stories that people tell about it. As a character in a Garrison Keillor novel remarks, "There are no answers, only stories."[6] In some ways, the stories are not only all that we have access to but all that people at the time, and later, had access to and hence all that drove the events that followed. Real events and sentiments produce symbols, symbols produce real events and sentiments, and real and symbolic levels may be simultaneously present in a single text. Myth has been called "the smoke of history,"[7] and my intention is to balance the smoke of myth with the fire of historical events, as well as to demonstrate how myths too become fires when they do not merely respond to historical events (as smoke arises from fire) but drive them (as fire gives rise to smoke). Ideas are facts too; the belief, whether true or false, that the British were greasing cartridges with animal fat started a revolution in India. For we are what we imagine, as much as what we do.

DIVERSITY

Is there a unique and distinct phenomenon worth naming that covers the religion(s) of the people from the Veda (c. 1200 BCE) to the Hare Krishnas in American airports and that tells us where Hinduism ends and Buddhism begins? It is useful to distinguish the objection that there is no such thing as Hinduism in the sense of a single unified religion, from the objection that the people we call Hindus lack a category, or word, for Hinduism and identify themselves not as Hindus but as Indians or as Bengali Vaishnavas (worshipers of Vishnu, living in Bengal). That is, we may ask: (1) Is there such a thing as Hinduism?; (2) is that the best thing to call it?; and (3) can we do so even if Hindus didn't/don't? These are related but separate questions. Let's consider the phenomenon and the name one by one.

ARE THERE SUCH THINGS AS HINDUS AND HINDUISM?

There are several objections to the use of any single term to denote what, for the sake of argument, we will call Hindus and Hinduism.*

Hindus did not develop a strong sense of themselves as members of a distinct religion until there were other religions against which they needed to define themselves, like the invisible man in the Hollywood film who could be seen only when he was wearing clothing that was not a part of him. Until as late as

---

* One must begin *somewhere*, even with the polluted *H* words, and without the disclaimer of scare quotes to barricade them, like a pair of hands held up for mercy.

the seventeenth century, many Indian rulers used titles that identified them with a divinity or with their preeminence over other rulers or with their personal qualities or with all their subjects, but not merely with the Hindus. Cultures, traditions, and beliefs cut across religious communities in India, and few people defined themselves exclusively through their religious beliefs or practices; their identities were segmented on the basis of locality, language, caste, occupation, and sect.[8] Only after the British began to define communities by their religion, and foreigners in India tended to put people of different religions into different ideological boxes,[9] did many Indians follow suit, ignoring the diversity of their own thoughts and asking themselves which of the boxes they belonged in.[10] Only after the seventeenth century did a ruler use the title Lord of the Hindus (Hindupati).[11]

Indeed most people in India would still define themselves by allegiances other than their religion.[12] The Hindus have not usually viewed themselves as a group, for they are truly a rainbow people, with different colors (*varnas* in Sanskrit, the word that also designates "class"), drawing upon not only a wide range of texts, from the many unwritten traditions and vernacular religions of unknown origins to Sanskrit texts that begin well before 1000 BCE and are still being composed, but, more important, upon the many ways in which a single text has been read over the centuries, by people of different castes, genders, and individual needs and desires. And this intertextuality is balanced by an equally rainbow-hued range of practices, which we might call an interpracticality, on the model of intertextuality, practices that refer to other practices.

Another objection to regarding Hinduism as a monolithic entity is that it is hard to spell out what "they all" believe or do (even if we exclude from "all" people like Shirley MacLaine). There is no single founder or institution to enforce any single construction of *the* tradition, to rule on what is or is not a Hindu idea or to draw the line when someone finally goes too far and transgresses the unspoken boundaries of reinterpretation. Ideas about all the major issues—vegetarianism, nonviolence, even caste itself—are subjects of a debate, not a dogma. There is no Hindu canon. The books that Euro-Americans privileged (such as the *Bhagavad Gita*) were not always so highly regarded by "all Hindus," certainly not before the Euro-Americans began to praise them. Other books have been far more important to certain groups of Hindus but not to others.

One answer to this objection is that like other religions—Christianity, Buddhism, Islam—Hinduism encompasses numerous miscellaneous sects. Religions are messy. But intertextuality (as well as interpracticality) argues for the inclusion of this unruly miscellany under the rubric of Hinduism. The fact that later texts and practices often quote earlier ones, right back to the *Rig Veda*, allows us to call it a single tradition, even though there are many other Hindu texts and practices that have no connection with any Sanskrit text, let alone the Veda. What literary critics call the anxiety of influence[13] works in the other direction in India. The individual artist composing a text or performing a ritual can make innovations, but she demonstrates first her knowledge of the traditions of the past and only then her ability to build upon them and even to reverse them. The assumption is that if she thinks she has an original idea, it means that she has forgotten its source.

Moreover, some of the people we now call Hindus did, when they wanted to, for more than two millennia, find ways to describe themselves as a group, in contrast with Buddhists or Muslims (or particular subsects of Buddhists or Muslims). They called themselves the people of the Veda, or the people who revere the Brahmins who are the custodians of the Veda, or the people who have four classes and four stages of life (*varna-ashrama-dharma*, in contrast with Buddhists). Or they called themselves the Aryas ("nobles"), in contrast with the Dasyus or Dasas ("aliens" or "slaves") or barbarians (*mlecchas*). The texts called the Brahmanas, in the seventh century BCE, define *mlecchas* as people of unintelligible speech, as does a dharma text of the period, which adds that they also eat cow flesh,[14] implying that the Aryas do not. The lawmaker Manu too, in the early centuries CE, treats *mleccha* as a linguistic term, contrasted with Arya (which he correctly regards as a linguistic term) rather than with Dasyu (an ethnic term); those outside the four classes (*varnas*) are aliens (Dasyus), whether they speak barbarian (*mleccha*) languages or Arya languages (10.45). A commentator on Manu, named Medhatithi, glosses *mleccha* with the Sanskrit word *barbara*, cognate with the Greek *barbaroi* ("barbarian," someone who babbles, "*barbarbar*"). No one ever comments on the religious beliefs or practices of these people.

But religious belief and practice are aspects of Hindu identity that both we and they can and do recognize. Caste, the most important of the allegiances by which the people whom we call Hindus do identify themselves most often, is closely regulated by religion. Some people would define a Hindu through exclusion, as someone who doesn't belong to another religion;[15]* officials of the

---

* This seems to me about as useful as the remark (which Aldous Huxley made in *Those Barren Leaves*) that the works of Homer were not written by Homer, but by someone else of the same name.

British Raj used the term "Hindu" to characterize all things in India (especially cultural and religious elements and features found in the cultures and religions of India) that were "not Muslim, not Christian, not Jewish, or, hence, not Western."[16] Taking the opposite tack, the inclusive tack, the Indian Supreme Court, in the Hindu Marriage Act (1955),[17] ruled that any reference to Hindus shall be construed as including "any person who is a Buddhist, Jaina or Sikh by religion," as well as "persons professing the Sikh, Jain or Buddhist religion," a blatant appropriation that most Sikhs, Jains, and Buddhists would resent bitterly.* It also defines a Hindu as someone who is not a Muslim, Christian, Parsi, or Jew, but who is (in addition to a Sikh, Buddhist, or Jaina) one of a rather arbitrary selection of people whose marginality made the court nervous: "any person who is a Hindu by religion in any of its forms or developments, including a Virashaiva, a Lingayat or a follower of the Brahmo, Prarthana or Arya Samaj." Significantly, the definition was needed because different religions have different marriage laws; the horror of miscegenation, always lurking in the Brahmin heart of darkness, was exacerbated by the British legacy within the law code.

But in addition to the circularity, mutual contradictions, and blatant chauvinism of the "not a Muslim" definition, such paraphrases list only other religions available *in India* (they seldom specify "not a Navajo, not a Confucian"); otherwise the word "Hindu" might simply have replaced "gentoo" or "heathen." The political problems that arise from this geographical assumption will resurface below when we consider the word, rather than the concept, "Hinduism."

In what seems to me to be something like desperation, a number of people have defined Hinduism as the religion of people who cannot or will not define their religion. This view was only somewhat sharpened by Sarvepalli Radhakrishnan (president of India from 1962 to 1967), who defined Hinduism as the belief "that truth was many-sided and different views contained different aspects of truth which no one could fully express," which would, I think, make all Unitarians Hindus, or by the militant nationalist B. G. Tilak (1856–1920), who added helpfully that "recognition of the fact that the means to salvation are diverse; and realization of the truth that the number of gods to be worshipped is large, that indeed is the distinguishing feature of Hindu religion."[18]

---

* Though their women might have been grateful to have the daughter's share in the father's property that this progressive legislation granted to Hindu women.

The Supreme Court of India in 1966, and again in 1995, codified and reconfirmed these two nondefinitions of Hinduism.

In 1966 the Indian Supreme Court was called upon to define Hinduism because the Satsangis or followers of Swaminarayan (1780–1830) claimed that their temples did not fall under the jurisdiction of certain legislation affecting Hindu temples. They argued that they were not Hindus, in part because they did not worship any of the traditional Hindu gods; they worshiped Swaminarayan, who had declared that he was the Supreme God. The court ruled against them, citing various European definitions of Hinduism and others, including Radhakrishnan's cited above.[19] But the Satsangis had brought their case to the court in order to challenge the 1948 Bombay Harijan Temple Entry Act, which guaranteed Harijans (Pariahs, Untouchables) access to every Hindu temple; if the Satsangis were not Hindus, this law would not force them to open their doors to Harijans. Thus the legal ruling that defined Hinduism by its tolerance and inclusivism was actually inspired by the desire of certain Hindus to exclude other Hindus from their temples.

THE ZEN DIAGRAM

In answer to several of the objections to the word "Hinduism," some scholars have tried to identify a cluster of qualities each of which is important but not essential to Hinduism; not every Hindu will believe in, or do, all of them, but each Hindu will adhere to some combination of them, as a non-Hindu would not. Scholars differ as to the number and nature of those forms,[20] and we have seen the attempts of the Indian Supreme Court to come up with an inoffensive cluster, but perhaps we can be a little more specific. The elements from which the clusters are formed might include some combination of belief in the Vedas (which excludes Buddhism and Jainism), karma (which does not exclude Buddhism and Jainism), dharma (religion, law, and justice), a cosmology centered on Mount Meru, devotion (bhakti) to one or more members of an extensive pantheon, the ritual offering (*puja*) of fruit and flowers to a deity, vegetarianism as an ideal (though only between about 25 and 40 percent of Indians are actually vegetarian[21]), nonviolence, and blood sacrifice (which may or may not be mutually exclusive). This polythetic approach, which owes much to the concept of family resemblance laid out by the philosopher Wittgenstein,[22] could be represented by a Venn diagram, a chart made of intersecting circles. It might be grouped into sectors of different colors, one for beliefs or practices that some Hindus shared with Buddhists and Jainas, another largely confined to

Hindu texts in Sanskrit, a third more characteristic of popular worship and practice, and so forth. But since there is no single central quality that all Hindus must have, the emptiness in the center, like the still center of a storm, suggests that the figure might better be named a Zen diagram, which is not, as you might think, a Venn diagram with just one ring or one that has an empty ring in the center but one that has no central ring.[23]

There is therefore no central something to which the peripheral people were peripheral. One person's center is another's periphery;[24] all South Asia was just a periphery, for instance, to those Delhi sultans and Mughal emperors who viewed everything from a Central Asian perspective. We may speak of marginalized people in the sense that they have been dispossessed and exploited, but Hinduism has porous margins and is polycentric. The Brahmins had their center, which we will refer to as the Brahmin imaginary, but there were other centers too, alternative centers.

The configuration of the clusters of Hinduism's defining characteristics changes through time, through space, and through each individual.[25] It is constantly in motion, because it is made of people, also constantly in motion. Among the many advantages of the cluster approach is the fact that it does not endorse any single authoritative or essentialist view of what Hinduism is; it allows them all. Any single version of this polythetic polytheism (which is also a monotheism, a monism, and a pantheism), including this one, is no better than a strobe photograph of a chameleon, a series of frozen images giving a falsely continuous impression of something that is in fact constantly changing. Like the man who proudly displayed a roomful of archery targets, each with an arrow in the bull's-eye, but was forced to confess that he had shot the arrows first and then had drawn the targets around them, we can decide what aspects of Hinduism we want to talk about and find the cluster of qualities in which that aspect is embodied—and, if we wish, call it Hinduism. Or backing off ever so slightly, we can speak of beliefs and practices that many Hindus share, which is what I intend to do.

It is often convenient to speak of a Brahmin-oriented quasi-orthodoxy (or orthopraxy—see below), which we might call the Brahmin imaginary or the idealized system of class and life stage (*varna-ashrama-dharma*). But whatever we call this constructed center, it is, like the empty center in the Zen diagram of Hinduisms, simply an imaginary point around which we orient all the actual Hindus who accept or oppose it; it is what Indian logicians call the straw man (*purva paksha*), against whom one argues. The actual beliefs and practices of

Hindus—renunciation, devotion, sacrifice, and so many more—are peripheries that the imaginary Brahmin center cannot hold.

Hindus and Hinduism by Any Other Names[26]

If we can agree that there is something out there worth naming, what shall we call it? The main objections to calling it Hinduism or to calling the people in question Hindus are that those were not always the names that Hindus used for themselves or their religion and that they are geographical names. Let us consider these two objections.

Most of the people we call Hindus call themselves something else, like Golkonda Vyaparis,[27] or, on the rarer occasions when they do regard themselves as a group, refer to themselves not as Hindus but as people with the sorts of definitions that we have just considered (Aryas, people who revere the Veda, who follow the system of class and stage of life, and so forth). Moreover, "Hindu" is not a native word but comes from a word for the "river" (*sindhu*) that Herodotus (in the fifth century BCE[28]), the Persians (in the fourth century BCE), and the Arabs (after the eighth century CE[29]) used to refer to everyone who lived beyond the great river of the northwest of the subcontinent, still known locally as the Sindhu and in Europe as the Indus. James Joyce, in his novel *Finnegans Wake*, in 1939, punned on the word "Hindoo" (as the British used to spell it), joking that it came from the names of two Irishmen, Hin-nessy and Doo-ley: "This is the hindoo Shimar Shin between the dooley boy and the hinnessy."[30] Even Joyce knew that the word was not native to India. It was an outsider's name for the people who inhabited the territory around the Indus River, which the Persians called Hindustan,[31] as did the Mughal emperor Babur in his memoirs in the sixteenth century CE: "Most of the people in Hindustan are infidels whom the people of India call Hindu. Most Hindus believe in reincarnation."[32] It is noteworthy both that Babur singles out reincarnation for the defining belief of Hinduism (one of the circles in our Zen diagram) and that he does not ascribe this belief to *all* Hindus (implicitly acknowledging their diversity). "Hindu" has, however, been an insider's word too for centuries, and it is the word that most Hindus do use now to refer to themselves. And it is not uncommon for one culture to take from another a word to designate a concept for which the original culture had a concept but not a word.

That the word has a geographical basis is, as we have seen, absolutely true. But it is not just the word but the very concept of Hindus and Hinduism that is geographically rooted in history. The textbook of legal code (dharma) attributed to Manu (first century CE) does not use the word "Hindu" but does offer a geographical definition of the people to whom his dharma applies (a definition that, it is worth noting, uses animals to define humans):

> From the eastern sea to the western sea [the Indian Ocean and the Bay of Bengal], the area in between the two mountains [the Himalayas and the Vindhyas] is what wise men call the Land of the Aryas. Where the black antelope ranges by nature, that should be known as the country fit for sacrifices; and beyond it is the country of the barbarians. The twice-born [the upper classes and particularly Brahmins] should make every effort to settle in these countries [2.23–24].

Much has happened since the time when one could define India as the land where the (deer and the) antelope play from sea to shining sea (eastern to western). The belief that all Hindus (should) live in India may have been strong once, though more honored in the breach than in the observance. The Hindus are, after all, one of the great merchant civilizations of the world, and the diaspora is very old indeed. Even Manu merely expresses the pious hope that the upper classes "make every effort" to stay within the boundary lines. Granted, many Hindus did suffer loss of caste status when they headed west across the Indus (particularly under the British Raj). Nevertheless, Hindus spread first through Southeast Asia and later through the British Empire, and they now live all over the world; there are approximately one and a half million Hindus in the United States, some 0.5 percent of the population.

So it has been said for much of Indian history that ideally, all Hindus should live in India. But the corresponding implication, that everyone in India is (or should be) a Hindu, was never true, not true during the millennia of cultures before either the Indus Valley or the Vedas, not true of most of India even after those early settlements of North India, and certainly never true after the rise of Buddhism in the fifth century CE. Nowadays there are still enough Muslims in India—15 percent of the population, almost as many Muslims as in Pakistan[33]— to make India one of the most populous Muslim nations in the world, and Muslim input into Indian culture is far more extensive than the mere numbers would imply. Yet Hindu nationalists have used the geographical implications of the word to equate Hinduism with India and therefore to exclude from the right to thrive in India such people as Muslims and Christians; in 1922, V. D. Savarkar coined the term "Hindutva" to express this equation. But not everyone who uses the word "Hinduism" can be assumed to be in their camp, an assumption that would reduce an intellectual problem to a political problem and a move that we need not make. When we use the word, we can, like Humpty Dumpty, pay it extra, in this case to mean not "the people of India" but the intersecting clusters of Hinduisms outlined above.

What's in a name? We might take a page from Prince and call it "the religion formerly known as Hinduism" or "Hinduism *après la lettre*." Despite the many strikes against the word "Hinduism," Hinduism by any other name would be just as impossible to categorize, and it is still useful to employ *some* word for it. We cannot insist that Hindus rethink the name they want to use for their tradition (as they have renamed not only streets in cities but whole cities, like Madras/Chennai, Bombay/Mumbai, and Calcutta/Kolkata), no matter how recent or troubled the name may be.[34] "Hinduism" is, in any case, the only poker game in town right now;* it is by far the most immediately recognizable word, or even phrase,[35] currently used to describe the Zen diagram of, for want of a better word, Hinduism. In any case, whether or not there really is a Hinduism, there certainly are Hindus.

Sources of Alternative Hinduisms

Different Hindus not only lived different Hinduisms but privileged different aspects of Hinduism, different qualities among the (non)-defining clusters. Scholars too see the Hindu elephant differently depending upon what part of it they grab (to cite the old Indian parable of the blind men: The one with his hands on the tail imagines that the animal is like a rope; on the side, a wall; on the trunk, a snake). Their politics inevitably colors their ideas of what Hinduism is.

In addition to including women's as well as men's voices and Other Ranks as well as Brahmins, Hinduism is composed of local as well as pan-Indian traditions, oral as well as written traditions, vernacular as well as Sanskrit traditions, and nontextual as well as textual sources. The first (often marginalized) elements of each of these pairs tend to reinforce one another, as do the second elements, the dominant elements, but there are important distinctions within each of the two groups. For these contrasting pairs did not translate into

---

* This is the punch line of an old joke, a statement made by a man in response to well-meaning friends who warned him that the reason why he kept losing at poker, week after week, was that the people he played with cheated. It is a remark that could also have been made by Yudhishthira (in the *Mahabharata*), who persisted in playing dice with, and always losing from, people whom he suspected to be cheating or at least knew to be much better players than he was.

polarized groups of people; a single person would often have both halves (as well as non-Hindu traditions) in his or her head; a Brahmin would know the folk traditions, just as, in our world, many people study paleography and then go to church and read Genesis. It is not the case that a puritanical Brahmin studied Manu's dharma texts and a libertine merchant read the *Kama-sutra* (the textbook of the science of erotics); the same man, of either class, might well read dharma with learned men (pandits) by day and the *Kama-sutra* with his mistress by night.

The elite tendencies of written traditions were exacerbated by the climate. The wet heat and the white ants destroyed any written text within a century or two, particularly since vellum was ruled out by the taboo against using animal substances and palm leaf was far more fragile than vellum. So these written texts by definition belonged to the privileged classes; the written texts that survived had to have been copied over and over again by a scribe patronized by someone with money to spare, and the scribe himself was invariably a male of high caste.

Yet oral and written traditions interact throughout Indian history, with oral recitations of written texts and written records of texts recited by people who may or may not have been illiterate. This interaction, which we will note throughout the book, is exemplified by the relationship between writing and reciting in two of the defining texts of Hinduism, the Veda and the *Maha-bharata*.[36] The *Rig Veda* was preserved orally, but it was frozen, every syllable preserved for centuries, through a process of rigorous memorization. There are no variant readings of the *Rig Veda*, no critical editions or textual apparatus. Just the *Rig Veda*. So much for the fluidity of orally transmitted texts. Correspondingly, the expected fixity of written texts dissolves when we look at the history of the reception and transmission of the *Mahabharata*, another enormous Sanskrit text, but one that was preserved both orally and in manuscript. In contrast with the *Rig Veda*, this text changed constantly; it is so extremely fluid that there is no single *Mahabharata;* there are hundreds of *Mahabharata*s, hundreds of different manuscripts and innumerable oral versions. So much for the fixity of written texts.

The relationship between Sanskrit and the other languages of India (the vernaculars) further complicates this picture. Sanskrit is the model for most North Indian languages (and the source of much of their grammar and some of their vocabulary), as Tamil is for the Dravidian languages of the south (such as Telugu, Kannada, and Malayalam). The Sanskrit/Tamil distinction therefore overlaps with the North/South distinction, but we certainly cannot simply equate Sanskrit with North and Tamil with South. Many South Indian ideas—like devotion (*bhakti*), to take a case at random—entered Sanskrit literature, not just Tamil literature, through South Indian Brahmins who wrote in Sanskrit in South India. Not only did southern ideas go north, and vice versa, and not only did Tamil flow into Sanskrit and Sanskrit into Tamil, but Tamil went north, and Sanskrit south.

A similar mutual interpenetration characterizes textual and nontextual sources. The study of Hinduism in the scholarship of Euro-Americans has been overwhelmingly textual; that's one of the characteristics of what we now call Orientalism, the cluster of attitudes that implicated the first European scholars of India in the European colonization of India. The British used texts as a way of disregarding actual Hindu practices and justifying their own imperial project with textual citations. And the Orientalist orientation to texts is the orientation toward Brahmins (and Sanskrit, and writing). More recently, scholars have begun to pay more attention to ritual, archaeology, art history, epigraphy, the records of foreign visitors, and, in the modern period, ethnography, revealing new aspects of a lived religion that is very differently represented in texts. Coins, for instance, tell a story, for money talks in that sense too.

The two sets of sources, textual and nontextual, reveal bits of history to us in different ways, like the lame man riding on the shoulders of the blind man. When it comes to history, you can't trust anyone: The texts lie in one way, while images and archaeology mislead us in other ways. On the one hand, the gods did not fly around in big palaces, as the texts insist that they did, and we cannot know if women really did speak up as Gargi does in the Upanishads, or Draupadi in the *Mahabharata*. On the other hand, the Indus seal we all once interpreted as an ithyphallic Shiva Pashupati is probably just someone sitting cross-legged as South Asians are inclined to do, with a bulging loincloth knot; well, back to the drawing board. Nontextual sources can provide textualists with an occasional shot in the arm, alerting them to what to look for—*in texts*—once they get the idea that they might be there. Texts can do a great deal, with a little help from their nontextual friends.

Texts are still useful in a number of ways. First of all, some of those old Brahmin males knew a hell of a lot of great stories. Second, not all texts were written by Brahmins. Woven into the Brahmin texts, as well as standing alongside them, is another great strand of narratives by that extraordinarily prolific writer Anonymous, who was usually *not* a Brahmin and who should be credited with a great deal of the ancient literature of South Asia. (He—or, just as likely, she—often wrote under the nom de plume of the heavily mythologized authors whom we will soon encounter, people named Vyasa or Valmiki or simply Suta, "the Charioteer Bard.") Third, even those texts that were written by Brahmins were not written (entirely) by Brahmins, nor were all the Brahmins highly literate or elitist; the texts were constantly infused with the contributions of the lower classes and women. Fourth, texts are events too: The Upanishads are part of history as well as imagination. And fifth, texts are also a major source of information about material culture: If we cannot always find the archaeological remains of a plow, we might at least find a text that mentions a plow, just as when we cannot find texts actually written by women, we can at least find references to women, and sympathetic views of their lives, in texts written by men. All these factors greatly expand the caste of characters in ancient Sanskrit texts.

I myself am by both temperament and training inclined to texts. I am neither an archaeologist nor an art historian; I am a Sanskritist, indeed a recovering Orientalist, of a generation that framed its study of Sanskrit with Latin and Greek rather than Urdu or Tamil. I've never dug anything up out of the ground or established the date of a sculpture. I've labored all my adult life in the paddy fields of Sanskrit, and since I know ancient India best, I've lingered in the past in this book longer than an anthropologist might have done, and even when dealing with the present, I have focused on elements that resonate with the past, so that the book is driven from the past, back-wheel-powered.[37] I have also, for most of the same reasons, inclined more toward written, more precisely ancient Sanskrit traditions than oral and vernacular and contemporary ones. But this book is, when all is said and done, and despite my acknowledgment of the baleful influence of text-oriented scholarship, a defense of the richness of texts as the source of information about the sorts of things that some people nowadays assume you need nontextual sources for: women, the lower classes, the way people actually lived.

WOMEN

Women are sometimes said to have been excluded from the ancient Indian texts and therefore to have left no trace, history having been written by the winners, the men. But in fact women made significant contributions to the texts, both as the (usually unacknowledged) sources of many ancient as well as contemporary narratives and as the inspiration for many more. Some Hindu women did read and write, forging the crucial links between vernacular languages and Sanskrit. Women were forbidden to study the most ancient sacred text, the Veda, but the wives, whose presence was required at Vedic rituals, both heard and spoke Vedic verses,[38] and they may well have had wider access to other Sanskrit texts. Later, in the second or third century CE, the *Kama-sutra* tells us not only that women had such access but even that they sometimes commissioned such texts to be written (1.3). Women in Sanskrit plays generally speak only dialects (Prakrits), while men speak only Sanskrit, but since the men and women converse together, generally without translators, the women must understand the men's Sanskrit, and the men the women's dialects. Moreover, some women in plays both speak and write Sanskrit, and some men speak in dialects,* trampling on what is left of the convention. It is a basic principle of one school of Indian logic that something can be prohibited only if its occurrence is possible.[39] The fact that the texts keep shouting that women should not read Vedic texts suggests that women were quite capable of doing so and probably did so whenever the pandits weren't looking. Women as a group have always been oppressed in India (as elsewhere), but individual women have always succeeded in making their mark despite the obstacles.

We can also look for the implied author[40] and identify in men's texts the sorts of things that a woman might have said.[41] Within the Sanskrit texts, women express views of matters as basic as karma in terms quite different from those of men, and these views become even more prominent when women compose their own tales.[42] There is an "ironic" presence of women in the *Mahabharata*, "perhaps beyond earshot, but definitely heard," and their physical absence may lend a kind of invisible luster to the highly visible women in that text.[43] The *Kama-sutra*, in its instructions to the would-be adulterer, presents a strong protofeminist view of what women have to put up with at the hands of inadequate husbands (5.1). Such texts at least keep women in the picture, however biased a picture that may be, until they do finally get to speak as named authors, much later.

Of course, excavating women's voices in male texts must always be qualified by the realization that there may be ventriloquism, misreporting of women, and false consciousness; the male author of the *Kama-sutra* may have sympathy for women but not true empathy; his interest in their thoughts is exploitative,

---

* In Harsha's play *Priyadarshika*, in the senventh century CE, the woman playwright writes in Sanskrit, while the clown, who is not only male but a Brahmin, speaks Prakrit.

though no less accurate for all that. But ventriloquism is a two-way street; there is also a ventriloquism of women's voices in male minds. For even when a male Brahmin hand actually held the pen, as was usually the case no matter what the subject matter was, women's ideas may have gotten into his head. We can never know for sure when we are hearing the voices of women in men's texts, but we can often ferret out (to use an animal metaphor) tracks, what the Hindus call "perfumes" (*vasanas*), that women have left in the literature. A hermeneutic of suspicion, questioning the expressed motivations of the author, is therefore required, but it is still worth reading between the lines, even making the texts talk about things they don't want to talk about. Moreover, texts are not our only source of knowledge of this period; women also left marks, perfumes, that we can find in art and archaeology. We can try to resurrect the women actors in Hindu history through a combination of references to them, both unsympathetic (to see what they had to put up with from some men) and sympathetic (to show that other men did treat them humanely), and moments when we can hear women's own voices getting into the texts and, more rarely, discover actual female authorship.

From Dog Cookers to Dalits

Brahmins may have had a monopoly on liturgical Sanskrit for the performance of certain public rites, but even then the sacrificer uttered some of the ritual words and performed the domestic rites. And the sacrificer need not have been a Brahmin, a member of the highest class; the other two twice-born social classes—warriors/rulers (Kshatriyas) and, below them, merchants, farmers and herders (Vaishyas)—were also initiated and therefore could be sacrificers. The three upper classes were called twice born because of the second birth through the ritual of initiation (the ancient Indian equivalent of becoming born again), in which a man was born (again) as a fully developed member of the community.* The lowest of the four classes, the servants (Shudras), were excluded from these and many other aspects of religious life, but the exclusion of Shudras doesn't automatically make something "Brahminical."

There have been countless terms coined to designate the lowest castes, the dispossessed or underprivileged or marginalized groups, including the tribal peoples. These are the people that Sanskrit texts named by specific castes (Chan-

---

* The term "twice born" (*dvi-ja*) also means a tooth or a bird, each of which undergoes second birth, from the gum or the egg respectively.

dala, Chamara, Pulkasa, etc.) or called Low and Excluded (Apasadas) or Born Last (or Worst, Antyajas) or Dog Cookers (Shva-Pakas*), because caste Hindus thought that these people ate dogs, who in turn ate anything and everything, and in Hinduism, you are what you eat. Much later the British called them Untouchables, the Criminal Castes, the Scheduled (they pronounced it SHED-yuled) Castes, Pariahs (a Tamil word that has found its way into English), the Depressed Classes, and Outcastes. Gandhi called them Harijans ("the People of God"). The members of these castes (beginning in the 1930s and 1940s and continuing now) called themselves Dalits (using the Marathi/Hindi word for "oppressed" or "broken" to translate the British "Depressed"). B. R. Ambedkar (in the 1950s), himself a Dalit, tried, with partial success, to convert some of them to Buddhism. Postcolonial scholars call them (and other low castes) Subalterns. Another important group of oppressed peoples is constituted by the Adivasis ("original inhabitants"), the so-called tribal peoples of India, on the margins both geographically and ideologically, sometimes constituting a low caste (such as the Nishadas), sometimes remaining outside the caste system altogether.

It is important to distinguish among Dalits and Adivasis and Shudras, all of whom have very different relationships with upper-caste Hindus, though many Sanskrit texts confuse them. So too, the Backward Castes, a sneering name that the British once gave to the excluded castes in general, are now regarded as castes separate from, and occasionally in conflict with, certain other Dalit castes; the Glossary of Human Rights Watch defines Backward Castes as "those whose ritual rank and occupational status are above 'untouchables' but who themselves remain socially and economically depressed. Also referred to as Other Backward Classes (OBCs) or Shudras," though in actual practice the OBCs often distinguish themselves from both Dalits and Shudras. All these groups are alike only in being treated very badly by the upper castes; precisely how they are treated, and what they do about it, differs greatly from group to group. All in all, when we refer to all the disenfranchised castes below the three upper classes known as twice born, it is convenient to designate them by the catchall term of Pariahs (a Tamil word—for the caste that beat leather-topped drums—

---

* *Shvan* ("dog") is the source of our "hound," and *paka* (from the Sanskrit *pak/c*, "cook") means ripe, cooked, or perfected and is related to the English term, borrowed from Hindi, "pukka," as in "pukka sahib," "well-ripened/cooked/perfected Englishman."

that finds its way into English) up until the twentieth century and then to call them Dalits.

But whatever we choose to call them, the excluded castes play an important role in the history of the Hindus. Thanks to the Subaltern studies movement, there is a lot more available light for Dalits, particularly in the modern period (from the time of the British); this book aims to contribute to that movement by including more information about Dalits in the ancient period. There have been protests against the mistreatment of the lower castes from a very early age in India, though such protests generally took the form of renouncing caste society and forming an alternative society in which caste was ignored; no actual reforms took place until the nineteenth century and then with only limited success. Much of what I have said about women also applies to Pariahs, and vice versa; Brahmin ventriloquism functions similarly to male ventriloquism, and the lower castes, like women, leave their "perfumes" in upper-caste literature. The positive attitudes to Pariahs in such texts represent a beginning, a prelude to reform; they change the world, even if only by imagining a world in which people treated women or Pariahs better.

The Brahmins did produce a great literature, after all, but they did not compose it in a vacuum. They did not have complete authority or control the minds of everyone in India. They drew upon, on the one hand, the people who ran the country, political actors (generally Brahmins and kings, but also merchants) and, on the other hand, the nonliterate classes. Because of the presence of oral and folk traditions in Sanskrit texts, as well as non-Hindu traditions such as Buddhism and Jainism, Dog Cookers do speak,* not always in voices recorded on a page but in signs that we can read if we try.

For the ancient period, it's often harder to find out who had a plow than to find out, from inscriptions, who endowed what temple. Some people today argue that the Brahmins erased much of the low-caste contribution to Indian culture—erased even their presence in it at all. Certainly the Sanskrit texts stated that the lower castes would pollute any sacred text that they spoke or read, as a bag made of the skin of a dog pollutes milk put into it.[44] But this probably applied only to a limited corpus of texts, Vedic texts, rather than Sanskrit in general. The fact that a sage is punished for teaching the Vedas to the horse-headed gods called the Ashvins, who associate with the class of farmers

---

* Pace Gayatri ("Can the Subaltern Speak?") Spivak.

and herdmen, should alert us to the possibility that teaching the Vedas to the wrong sorts of people might also be a rule honored at least sometimes in the breach as well as in the observance. And we can, as with women's voices, ferret out voices of many castes in the ancient texts, and once we have access to the oral and folk traditions, we can begin to write the alternative narrative with more confidence.

ANIMALS: HORSES, DOGS, AND COWS AS POWER, POLLUTION, AND PURITY

Animals—primarily not only dogs, horses, and cows, but also monkeys, snakes, elephants, tigers, lions, cats, and herons—play important roles in the Hindu religious imaginary, both as actual living creatures and as the key to important shifts in attitudes to different social classes. Yogic postures (*asanas*) and sexual positions, as well as theological schools, are named after animals. Gods become incarnate as animals and have animal vehicles in the human world. The process works in opposite directions at once. On the one hand, the observation of the local fauna provides images with which people may think of their gods; whether or not people get the gods that they deserve, they tend to get the gods (and demons) that their animals deserve—gods inspired by the perceived qualities of the animals. On the other hand, the ideas that people have about the nature of the gods, and of the world, and of themselves will lead them to project onto animals certain anthropomorphic features that may seem entirely erroneous to someone from another culture observing the same animal. And knowing what animals, real live animals, actually appeared in the material culture at a particular time and place helps us place aspects of that culture geographically and sometimes chronologically. Thus animals appear both as objects, in texts about the control of violence against living creatures (killing, eating), and as subjects, in texts where they symbolize people of different classes. Clearly the two—the animals of the terrain and the animals of the mind—are intimately connected, and both are essential to our understanding of Hinduism. If the motto of Watergate was "Follow the money," the motto of the history of Hinduism could well be "Follow the monkey." Or, more often, "Follow the horse."

Three animals—horses, dogs, and cows—are particularly charismatic players in the drama of Hinduism. The mythological texts use them to symbolize power, pollution, and purity, respectively, and link them to three classes of classical Hindu society: Kshatriyas or rulers, particularly foreign rulers (horses), the lower classes (dogs), and Brahmins (cows).* Horses and dogs function in our narrative as marginalized groups on both ends of the social spectrum (foreigners and Pariahs),† while cows are the focus of the ongoing debate about vegetarianism. These three animals pair up first with one and then with another in a complex symbolic dance. Horses and cows provide mirror images of each other's genders. The cow (f.) is the defining gender for the bovine species and the symbol of the good human female (maternal, docile); the negative contrast is provided not by bulls and steers, who have a rather ambivalent status (Shiva's bull, Nandi, is generally docile and benign), but by male buffalo, who have taken over this spot in the paradigm and symbolize evil in both myth and ritual, as well as being often associated with Pariahs. By contrast, the stallion (m.) is the defining gender for equines, mares generally being the symbol of the evil female (oversexed, violent, and Fatally Attractive).[45] Cows and horses can also represent religious contrasts; the Hindu cow and the Muslim horse often appear together on chromolithographs.

Because horses are not native to India and do not thrive there, they must constantly be imported, generally from western and Central Asia.[46] The reasons for this still prevail: climate and pasture.[47] The violent contrast between the hot season and the monsoon makes the soil ricochet between swampy in one season and hard, parched, and cracked in another. The grazing season lasts only from September to May, and even then the grasses are spare and not good for fodder. Moreover, since the best soil is mostly reserved for the cultivation of grains and vegetables to feed a large and largely vegetarian population, there is relatively little room for horses even in those places where more nutritious fodder grasses are found (such as the eastern extensions of the arid zone in the north and northwest of India, particularly in Rajasthan, where horses have in fact been bred successfully for centuries). There is therefore no extensive pasturage, and

---

* The situation is more complex in the *shastras*, which often connect both the horse and the cow with Vaishyas, since that is the class concerned with animal husbandry. But even those texts more often place the horse in the Kshatriya class, as it is used for warfare and royal ceremony rather than for work in the fields. And the cow is the animal given to Brahmins and protected by Brahmins, though frequently coveted and stolen by Kshatriyas.

† Horses and hounds contrast not merely in class but also in philology. The Sanskrit word for a horse (*ashva*) could also be parsed to mean a nondog (*a-shva*). It doesn't really work in the nominative forms by which Indians refer to Sanskrit nouns or in the roots, but it works in the combinatory forms, where *ashvah* loses its final *h* (as in *ashva-medha*, "horse sacrifice") and *shvan/shvaa* loses its *n* or long *a* (as in the compound *shva-paka,* "dog cooker").

horses are stabled as soon as they are weaned, unable to exercise or develop strength and fitness. Here, as elsewhere, wherever conditions are poor for breeding, "a regular injection of suitable horses is vital for the upkeep and improvement of the breed," to keep it from degenerating.[48]

It is therefore part of the very structure of history that India has always had to import horses,[49] which became prized animals, used only in elite royal or military circles. And so the horse is always the foreigner in India, the invader and conqueror, and the history of the horse in India is the history of those who came to India and took power. There is still a Hindi saying that might be translated, "Stay away from the fore of an officer and the aft of a horse" or "Don't get in front of an officer or behind a horse." It dates from a time when petty officials, especially police, revenue collectors, and record keepers, were mounted and everyone else was not. These horsemen were high-handed ("... on your high horse") and cruel, people whom it was as wise to avoid as it was to keep out of the range of those back hooves.

The horse stands as the symbol of the power and aristocracy of the Kshatriyas, the royal warrior class; the horse is the key to major disputes, from the wager about the color of a horse's tail made by the mother of snakes and the mother of birds in the *Mahabharata* (1.17–23) (an early instance of gambling on horses), to heated arguments by contemporary historians about the seemingly trivial question of whether Aryan horses galloped or ambled into the Indus Valley or the Punjab, more than three thousand years ago. Horses continued to be idealized in religion and art, in stark contrast with the broken-down nags that one more often actually encounters in the streets of Indian cities. Under the influence of the Arab and Turkish preference for mares over stallions, the Hindu bias in favor of stallions and against mares gave way to an entire Hindu epic literature that idealized not stallions but mares. Finally, horses are also metaphors for the senses that must be harnessed, yoked through some sort of spiritual and physical discipline such as yoga (a word whose basic meaning is "to yoke," as in "to yoke horses to a chariot").

The cow's purity is fiercely protected by Brahmins and is at the heart of often hotly contested attitudes to food in the history of Hinduism. In the Vedic period, people ate cattle (usually bulls or bullocks or castrated bulls), as they ate all other male sacrificial animals (with the exception of the horse, which was *not* eaten). But though the Vedic people also occasionally ate cows (the female of the species), cows soon became, for most Hindus, cultural symbols of nonviolence and generosity, through the natural metaphor of milking; unlike most animals (but like other lactating female mammals—mares, female camels, buffalo cows, nanny goats), cows can feed you without dying. Cows therefore are, from the earliest texts to the present moment, the object of heated debates about vegetarianism.

At the other end of the animal spectrum are dogs. For caste-minded Hindus, dogs (not significantly gendered like horses and cows) are as unclean as pigs are to Orthodox Jews and Muslims, therefore symbols of the oppressed lowest castes, of the people at the very bottom of human society, indeed outside it, the sorts of people that we call underdogs and Sanskrit authors sometimes called dog cookers.* Dogs are also associated with the Adivasis, the so-called tribal peoples of India. Animal keepers, leatherworkers, people who touch human waste are often referred to as pigs and dogs.† The ancient Indian textbook of political science, the *Artha-shastra*, even suspects dogs of espionage; the author warns the king not to discuss secrets when dogs or mynah birds are present (1.15.4). The mynah bird of course could talk, but the dog? Would he reveal secrets by wagging his tail? (He might recognize a secret agent and blow his cover by not barking in the night.)‡ But texts covertly critical of the caste system reverse the symbolism and speak of breaking the rules for dogs, treating them as if they were not impure. The dog who doesn't bark is about a silence that speaks; it is a good metaphor for the Pariah voice, the dog's voice, that we can sometimes hear only when it does not speak.

The shifting tracks of these animals form a trail of continuity within the diversity of alternative Hinduisms.

PLURALISM AND TOLERANCE[50]

The proliferation of polythetic polytheisms may pose problems for the definition of Hinduism, but they are its glory as a cultural phenomenon. Pluralism and diversity are deeply ingrained in polylithic Hinduism, the Ellis Island of religions; the lines between different beliefs and practices are permeable mem-

---

* Euro-Americans too made this equation, as in the nineteenth-century signs that often proclaimed, NO DOGS OR INDIANS ALLOWED.

† The two species are combined in the German term of insult, *Schweinhund!* ("pig-dog").

‡ · Sherlock Holmes once solved a mystery, the case of Silver Blaze, a racehorse, by using a vital clue of omission. When Inspector Gregory asked Holmes whether he had noted any point to which he would draw the inspector's attention, Holmes replied, "To the curious incident of the dog in the night-time." "The dog did nothing in the night-time," objected the puzzled inspector, the essential straight man for the Socratic sage. "That was the curious incident," remarked Sherlock Holmes. The fact that the dog did not bark when someone entered the house at night was evidence, in this case evidence that the criminal was someone familiar to the dog.

branes. Not only can we see the Hindu traditions as divided among themselves on many central issues throughout history, but we can see what the arguments were on each point, often far more than two views on major questions. The texts wrestle with competing truths, rather than offer pat answers.

One sort of pluralism that has always prevailed in India is what I would call eclectic pluralism, or internal or individual pluralism, a kind of cognitive dissonance,[51] in which one person holds a toolbox of different beliefs more or less simultaneously, drawing upon one on one occasion, another on another.[52] Multiple narratives coexist peacefully, sometimes in one open mind and sometimes in a group of people whose minds may be, individually, relatively closed.* A pivotal example of such individual pluralism can be found in the law text of Manu, which argues, within a single chapter, passionately against and then firmly for the eating of meat (5.26–56). Or as E. M. Forster once put it, "Every Indian hole has at least two exits."[53] When it comes to ritual too, an individual Hindu may worship several different gods on different occasions, to satisfy different needs, on different festival days, in fellowship with different members of the family (a bride will often bring into the home a religion different from that of her husband's), or as a matter of choice as new gods are encountered.

The compound structure of Sanskrit and the fact that most words have several meanings (it used to be said that every Sanskrit word means itself, its opposite, a name of god, and a position in sexual intercourse†) enabled poets to construct long poems that told two entirely different stories at the same time and shorter poems that had multiple meanings, depending on how you divided up the compounds and chose among the various connotations of each word. This poetry, rich in metaphors, could itself stand as a metaphor for the Hindu approach to multivalence.

Eclectic pluralism between religions is more cautious, but it has allowed many an individual, such as a Hindu who worships at a Sufi shrine, to embrace one tradition in such a way as to make possible, if not full engagement with other faiths, at least full appreciation and even admiration of their wisdom and

---

* Contemporary Americans have a somewhat similar sense of the multiplicity of texts and versions of texts through their knowledge of remakes of movies and covers of musical performances.

† This was said at Harvard, when I was there in the sixties, and it seems to have been based on another Orientalist joke sometimes ascribed to Sir Hamilton A. R. Gibb of Oxford and Harvard, that every Arabic word has its primary meaning, then its opposite, then something to do with a camel, and last, something obscene.

power.[54] The sorts of permeable membranes that marked one sort of Hinduism from another also marked Hinduism from other religions; the dialogues were both intrareligious and interreligious. Hinduism interacted creatively with, first, Buddhism and Jainism, then Judaism and Christianity, then Islam and Sikhism, as well as with tribal religions and other imports (such as Zoroastrianism). The interactions were sometimes conscious and sometimes unconscious, sometimes appreciative borrowings and sometimes violent but productive antagonisms (as we will see, for instance, in the sometimes positive and sometimes negative attitudes toward the story of Vishnu's incarnation as the Buddha). In Rohinton Mistry's novel *Such a Long Journey*, there is a wall in Bombay/Mumbai that the neighborhood men persist in peeing and defecating against, creating a stench and a nuisance of flies. The protagonist of the novel hires an artist to paint images of all the religions of the world on the wall, a multireligious polytheistic dialogue of gods and mosques (respecting the Muslim rule against representing figures), so that no one, of any religion, will foul the wall.[55] (It works, for a while, until the city knocks down the wall to widen the road.) This seems to me to be a fine metaphor for both the hopes and the frailty of interreligious dialogue in India.

Hindus, Jainas, and Buddhists all told their own versions of some of the same stories. Hindus and Buddhists (and others) in the early period shared ideas so freely that it is impossible to say whether some of the central tenets of each tradition came from one or the other; often two Hindu versions of the same story, composed in different centuries, have less in common than do a Hindu and a Buddhist version of the same story. The stories change to fit different historical contexts, and often one can date one telling later than another (the language is different, it mentions a later king, and so forth), but where it comes from, and when, nobody knows. Many of the same religious images too were used by Buddhists and Jainas as well as Hindus.[56] To this day Hindus and Christians, or Hindus and Muslims, often worship the same figure under different names; Satya Pir, for instance, is a Muslim holy man (*pir*) who had come, by the eighteenth century, to be identified with a form of the Hindu god Vishnu (Satya Narayana).[57]

The great Indian poet and saint Kabir, who self-consciously rejected both Hinduism and Islam, nevertheless built his own religious world out of what he would have regarded as the ruins of Hinduism and Islam, as did many of the great Sufi saints, at whose shrines many Hindus continue to worship. Building a shrine on the site where a shrine of another tradition used to stand is thus both a metaphor of appreciation and an act of appropriation in India, unhindered by any anxiety of influence.

This open-mindedness was supported by the tendency of Hindus to be more orthoprax than orthodox. That is, most Hindus have not cared about straight opinions (ortho-doxy) nearly so much as they care about straight behavior (ortho-praxy). Although there is a very wide variety of codes of action, each community has a pretty clear sense of what should and shouldn't be done, and some things were Simply Not Done. People have been killed in India because they did or did not sacrifice animals, or had sex with the wrong women, or disregarded the Vedas, or even made use of the wrong sacred texts, but no one was impaled (the Hindu equivalent of burning at the stake) for saying that god was like this rather than like that. Each sect acknowledged the existence of gods other than their god(s), suitable for others to worship, though they might not care to worship them themselves.

Hindus might therefore best be called polydox.[58] Yet renouncers, certain monists, and some of the bhakti sects tended to be more orthodox than orthoprax, and those movements that challenge Brahmins, the Veda, and the values of class and caste are generally called heterodox, or even heretical (*pashanda* or *pakhanda*).[59] The Hindu concept of heresy was thus applied to some people within the Hindu fold, though more often to Buddhists and Jainas.

HYBRIDITY AND MULTIPLICITY

The "solitarist" approach to human identity sees human beings as members of exactly one group, in contrast with the multiple view that sees individuals as belonging to several different groups at once. Visualize our friend the intra-Hinduism Venn/Zen diagram, now in an interreligious guise. The multiple view is both more appropriate and more helpful for people caught up in the confrontation of communities, such as Hindu and Muslim in India.[60]

People sometimes make a further distinction between multiplicity and hybridity. Multiplicity implies a combination in which the contributing elements are theoretically unchanged even when mixed. Hinduism in this sense of multiplicity is perceived to have elements that a Muslim would recognize as Muslim, a Buddhist would recognize as Buddhist, and so forth. An example of religious multiplicity in an individual: On Sunday you go to church and attend a basic Catholic mass much as you would experience it in many (though certainly not all) churches in another city or another country, mutatis mutandis, and on Tuesday you go to a Hindu temple and assist at a ceremony of killing a goat, much as you would experience it in many (though certainly not all) Hindu temples in another city or another country, mutatis mutandis. Hybridity, by contrast, implies fusion. An example of religious hybridity in an individual: On Monday you attend the same sort of basic Catholic mass, but in place of the Eucharist you kill a goat, or you attend the same sort of basic Hindu *puja* but the goddess to whom you pray is Mary, the mother of Jesus, with all her epithets and physical characteristics. The *Oxford English Dictionary* defines "hybrid" as "anything derived from heterogeneous sources, or composed of different or incongruous elements," which, when applied to a community, leaves conveniently open the question of whether those elements remain unchanged. The *OED* definition applies to individuals rather than communities: "the offspring of two animals or plants of different species, or (less strictly) varieties."

Both hybridity and multiplicity can be applied to both communities and individuals. The trouble with both multiplicity and hybridity (as well as syncretism) lies in the assumption that the combinatory elements are separate essences that exist in a pure form before the mix takes place and that the combination either does (for hybrids) or does not (for multiplicities) change them in some way. But there are seldom any pure categories in any human situation, certainly not by the moment when history first catches up with them. Long before 2000 BCE, the Indus Valley Civilization was already a mix of cultures, as was Vedic culture at that time, and eventually the two mixes mixed together, and mixed with other mixes. Hybridity defies binary oppositions and understands reality as a fluid rather than a series of solid, separate boxes.

Hyphens can be read as multiple or as hybrid. The hybrid, hyphenated word "Anglo-Indian" confusingly denotes two opposite sorts of people: The *OED* defines "Anglo-Indian" as "a person of British birth resident, or once resident, in India," or "a Eurasian of India," which is to say either a privileged Englishman ruling "Inja" or a hybrid, an underprivileged person whom the British regarded as the lowest of all castes, a mixed breed.

Hybridity, traditionally, has had the additional disadvantage of carrying a largely negative attitude to the mixing of categories, an attitude that we now regard as reactionary. Thus the hybrid has been despised as a hodgepodge, a mix in which both (or all) of the contributing elements are modified; the *OED* adds, gratuitously, to its definition the phrase, "a half-breed, cross-breed, or mongrel," the racist overtones of its definition echoing the Hindu fear of the mixture of social classes (*varna-samkara*). But nowadays both postcolonial and postmodern thinkers prefer hybrids, define "hybrid" more positively, and indeed argue that we all are hybrids,[61] all always mixed and mixing.[62]

The Parsis ("Persians"—i.e., Zoroastrians) in several communities in India tell a positive story about social hybridity. They say that when the Parsis landed in India, the local Hindu raja sent them a full glass of milk, suggesting that the town was full. The Parsi leader added sugar and returned the glass, indicating that his people could mix among the Arabs and Hindus like sugar in milk, sweetening it but not overrunning it.[63] The metaphor of sugar in milk* suggests the extreme ideal of communal integration, in which individuals change the community by melting into it, flavoring it as a whole with their qualities (Zoroastrianism, or sweetness). The Parsis did not in fact dissolve into Islam and Hinduism; they remained Parsis and indeed were often caught in the crossfire during the riots that followed the Partition of India and Pakistan in 1947. This seems to me the more accurate way to view such cultural mixes: as a suspension of discrete particles rather than a melting pot.

Despite their shortcomings, the concepts of hybridity and multiplicity are useful, if used with care. The phenomenon is basically the same in either case; it's just a matter of points of view, and it doesn't really matter whether you call it multiple or hybrid (or even syncretic). What does matter is how you evaluate the fused mix. Whatever word you use for it, I think it applies to Hinduism, and I think it is a Good Thing.† I once (in a very different context) characterized Hindu mythology as a pendulum of extremes that are never resolved and that are also constantly in motion: "By refusing to modify its component elements in order to force them into a synthesis, Indian mythology celebrates the idea that the universe is boundlessly various, that everything occurs simultaneously, that all possibilities may exist without excluding each other . . . [that] untrammeled variety and contradiction are ethically and metaphysically necessary."[64]

Keeping both extreme swings of the pendulum in mind simultaneously means realizing that an individual actor in the drama of the history of the Hindus may regard herself as a fused hybrid of Muslim and Hindu or as a fused multiple, fully Muslim in some ways and fully Hindu in others, as many Indians have been, throughout history. In either case, there would be no per-

---

* Salt dissolved in water was an ancient Upanishadic metaphor for the complete merging of individual souls in the world soul (*brahman*).
† Indeed, according to the *OED*, even the word "hodgepodge" (or "hotchpotch") originally designated a good thing, the legal combination of diverse properties into a single entity to make possible an equitable division. The earliest attestation is a legal term from 1292.

fectly pure category of Muslim or Hindu anywhere along the line of fusion. Such a person might worship at a Hindu temple on certain days and at a Sufi shrine on others, might read both the Upanishads and the Qu'ran for spiritual guidance, and would celebrate both the great Muslim holy days and the great Hindu festivals.

I would therefore argue for the recognition of the simultaneous presence of a number of pairs of opposites, throughout the history of the Hindus, the both/and view of community. The historiographic pendulum of reconciliation, never resting at the swing either to one side or the other, forces us to acknowledge the existence, perhaps even the authenticity, of the two extremes of various ideas, and also their falseness, as well as the fact that there is no pure moment at either end of the swing, and leave it at that. With apologies to Buddhism, there is no middle way here. Or rather, the middle way has got to take its place alongside all the other, more extreme ways in the Zen diagram.

CHAPTER 2

TIME AND SPACE IN INDIA
50 Million to 50,000 BCE

ॐ

THE BIRTH OF INDIA

The Ganges, though flowing from the foot of Vishnu and through
Siva's hair, is not an ancient stream. Geology, looking further than
religion, knows of a time when neither the river nor the Himalayas
that nourished it existed, and an ocean flowed over the holy places of
Hindustan. The mountains rose, their debris silted up the ocean, the
gods took their seats on them and contrived the river, and the India
we call immemorial came into being.

—E. M. Forster, *A Passage to India* (1924)[1]

TIME

ORIGINS: OUT OF AFRICA

To begin at the beginning:

Once upon a time, about 50 million years ago,[*] a triangular plate of land,
moving fast (for a continent), broke off from Madagascar (a large island lying
off the southeastern coast of Africa) and, "adrift on the earth's mantle,"[2] sailed
across the Indian Ocean and smashed into the belly of Central Asia with such
force that it squeezed the earth five miles up into the skies to form the Himalayan range and fused with Central Asia to become the Indian subcontinent.[3]

---

[*] In the Cretaceous period. The dates are given differently in different sources. Here I am reminded of
the old story about the lady who went to a lecture and heard the lecturer say that the universe was
going to self-destruct in five billion years, at which she fainted. When they asked her why she was so
upset at an event that was five billion years away she heaved a sigh of relief and said, "Oh, thank God. I
thought he said five *million* years."

Or so the people who study plate tectonics nowadays tell us, and who am I to challenge them?* Not just land but people came to India from Africa, much later; the winds that bring the monsoon rains to India each year also brought the first humans to peninsular India by sea from East Africa in around 50,000 BCE.[4] And so from the very start India was a place made up of land and people from somewhere else. So much for "immemorial." Even the ancient "Aryans" probably came, ultimately,[5] from Africa. India itself is an import, or if you prefer, Africa outsourced India.

This prehistoric episode will serve us simultaneously as a metaphor for the way that Hinduism through the ages constantly absorbed immigrant people and ideas and as the first historical instance of such an actual immigration. (It can also be read as an unconscious satire on histories that insist on tracing everything back to ultimate origins, as can the E. M. Forster passage cited at the start.) The narratives that Hindus have constructed about that stage and those actors, narratives about space and time, form the main substance of this chapter. The flood myth, in particular, is about both space (continents sinking) and time (periodic floods marking the aeons). Often unexpressed, always assumed, these narratives are the structures on which all other narratives about history are built. We will then briefly explore the natural features of India—rivers and mountains—that serve not only as the stage on which the drama of history unfolds but as several of the main actors in that drama, for Ganga (the Ganges) and Himalaya appear in the narratives as the wife and father-in-law of the god Shiva, respectively.

GONDWANALAND AND LEMURIA

Francis Bacon was the first to notice, from maps of Africa and the New World first available in 1620, that the coastlines of western Africa and eastern South America matched rather neatly. Scientists in the nineteenth century hypothesized that Antarctica, Australia, Africa, Madagascar, South America, Arabia, and India all were connected in the form of a single vast supercontinent to which an Austrian geologist gave the name of Gondwana or Gondwanaland.

---

* The theory is still generally accepted. Kenneth Chang wrote in the *New York Times*, May 14, 2008, under the headline, DISASTER SET OFF BY COLLIDING LAND MASSES: "The earthquake in the Sichuan Province of China on Monday was a result of a continuing collision between India and Asia. India, once a giant island before crashing into the underside of Asia about 40 million to 50 million years ago, continues to slide north at a geologically quick pace of two inches a year. The tectonic stresses push up the Himalaya Mountains and generate scores of earthquakes from Afghanistan to China."

(He named it after the region of central India called Gondwana—which means "the forest of the Gonds," the Gonds being tribal people of central India— comprising portions of the present states of Madhya Pradesh, Maharashtra, and Andhra Pradesh,[6] the latter a region famous for its enormous rocks, the oldest on the planet.) Scientists then suggested that what were later called continental shifts* began about 167 million years ago (in the mid- to late Jurassic period), causing the eastern part of the continent of Gondwana to separate from Africa and, after a while (about 120 million years ago, in the early Cretaceous period), to move northward. It broke into two pieces. One piece was Madagascar, and the other was the microcontinent that eventually erupted into the Deccan plateau and crashed into Central Asia.† Australian Indologists joke that the Deccan is really part of Australia.[7]

The Gondwanaland story takes us to the farthest limit, the reduction to the absurd, of the many searches for origins that have plagued the historiography of India from the beginning (there, I'm doing it myself, searching for the origins of the myth of origins). Both nineteenth-century scholarship and twenty-first-century politics have taken a preternatural interest in origins. Nineteenth-century scholars who searched for the ur-text (the "original text," as German scholarship defined it), the ur-ruins, the ur-language carried political stings in their tales: "We got there first," "It's ours" (ignoring the history of all the intervening centuries that followed and other legitimate claims). They viewed the moment of origins as if there were a kind of magic Rosetta stone, with the past on one side and the present on the other, enabling them to do a simple one-to-one translation from the past into the present ever after. But even if they could know the ur-past, and they could not (both because logically there is no ultimate beginning for any chain of events and because the data for the earliest periods are at best incomplete and at worst entirely inaccessible), it would hardly provide a charter for the present.

Other scientists in the colonial period agreed about the ancient supercontinent but imagined its disintegration as taking place in the opposite way, not when land (proto-India) broke off from land (Australia/Africa) and moved

---

* The belief that the continents were at one time joined in the geologic past was first set forth in detail in 1912 by Alfred Wegener, a German meteorologist who coined the term "continental shift" to describe it.

† A haunting image of such a continental split occurs in the film *Underground* (1995) when at the end Yugoslavia breaks off and sails away, while people continuing to sing and dance and eat at a wedding are unaware that the little piece of land they are on is sailing away from the mainland, foreshadowing the violent partition of the country, as tragic as the partition of India in 1947.

through water (the Indian Ocean) to join up with other land (Central Asia), but rather when water (the Indian Ocean) moved in over land (a stationary super-continent like Gondwanaland) that was henceforth lost under the waves, like Atlantis. According to this story, water eventually submerged (under what is now called the Indian Ocean) the land that had extended from the present Australia through Madagascar to the present South India.

In 1864 a geologist named that supercontinent Lemuria, because he used the theory to account for the fact that living lemurs were found, in the nineteenth century, only in Madagascar and the surrounding islands, and fossil lemurs were found from Pakistan to Malaya, but no lemurs, living or dead, were found in Africa or the Middle East (areas that would never have been connected to Lemuria as Madagascar and Pakistan presumably once were).[8] Animals, as usual, here define human boundaries, and the myths about those boundaries, as usual, proliferated. In 1876, Ernst Haeckel, a German biologist of a Darwin-ian persuasion, published his *History of Creation*, claiming that the lost continent of Lemuria was the cradle of humankind; in 1885 a British historian argued that the Dravidian languages had been brought to India when the ancestors of the Dravidians came from Lemuria;[9] in 1886 a teenager in California "channeled" voices that suggested that the survivors of Lemuria were living in tunnels under Mount Shasta in California;[10] and in 1888, in *The Secret Doctrine,* Madame Bla-vatsky claimed that certain Indian holy men had shown her a secret book about Lemuria.

This myth nurtured among the colonial powers was then taken up, in the 1890s, by Tamil speakers on the southern tip of South India, who began to re-gard Lemuria as a lost ancestral home from which they all were exiled in India or to argue that the extant India, or Tamil Nadu, or just the southernmost tip of India, Kanya Kumari (Cape Comorin), was all that was left of Lemuria; or that when Lemuria sank, Tamilians dispersed to found the civilizations of Mesopotamia, Egypt, China, the Americas, Europe, and, in particular, the Indus Valley.[11] Nowadays some Tamil separatists want to reverse the process, to de-tach Tamil Nadu from the rest of India, not, presumably, physically, to float back over the Indian Ocean like Gondwanaland in reverse, but politically, in order to recapture the glory of their lost Lemurian past.

The passage from E. M. Forster cited above, "The Birth of India," begins with the Himalayas rising up out of the ocean, Gondwanaland fashion, but then, as it continues, it slips into the other variant, the story of the submersion of Lemuria, and regards that submersion as *preceding* the Gondwanaland episode, pushing back the origins even farther: "But India is really far older. In the days of the prehistoric ocean the southern part of the peninsula already existed, and the high places of Dravidia have been land since land began, and have seen on the one side the sinking of a continent that joined them to Africa, and on the other the upheaval of the Himalayas from a sea."[12] Forster concludes his passage with a third aspect of the myth, its periodicity or cyclicity, its prediction that the flooding of South India will happen again and again: "As Himalayan India rose, this India, the primal, has been depressed, and is slowly re-entering the curve of the earth. It may be that in aeons to come an ocean will flow here too, and cover the sun-born rocks with slime."

So that's how it all began. Or maybe it didn't. Forster of course has the carte blanche of a novelist, but even the plate tectonics people may be building sand castles, for the plate tectonics theory is after all a speculation, albeit a scientific speculation based on good evidence.

Whether or not a subcontinent once shook the dust of Africa off its heels and fused onto Asia, the story of Gondwanaland reminds us that even after the Vedic people had strutted around the Ganges Valley for a few centuries, all they had done was add a bit more to what was already a very rich mix. The multiplicity characteristic of Hinduism results in part from a kind of fusion—a little bit of Ravi Shankar in the night, a Beatle or two—that has been going on for millions of years, as has globalization of a different sort from that which the word generally denotes. The pieces of the great mosaic of Hinduism were put in place, one by one, by the many peoples who bequeathed to India something of themselves, planting a little piece of England, or Samarkand, or Africa, in the Punjab or the Deccan.

Après Moi, le Déluge

Hinduism is so deeply embedded in the land of its birth that we cannot begin to understand its history without understanding something of its geography and in particular the history of representations of its geography. The central trope for both time and space in India is the great flood. The myth of the flood is told and retold in a number of variants, some of which argue for the loss of a great ancient civilization or a fabulous shrine. The telling of a myth of such a flood, building upon a basic story well known throughout India, allows a number of different places to imagine a glorious lost past of which they can still be proud today.

The myth of the flooding of Lemuria, or Dravidia, builds on the traditions of other floods. There is archaeological evidence for the flooding of the Indus Valley cities by the Indus River (c. 2000 BCE), as well as for that of the city of Hastinapura by the Ganges, in about 800 BCE.[13] There is also textual evidence (in the *Mahabharata*) for the flooding of the city of Dvaraka, the city of Krishna, at the westernmost tip of Gujarat, by the Western Ocean (that is, the Arabian Sea),[14] in around 950 BCE. (Sources differ; some say 3102 or 1400 BCE.)[15] The appendix to the *Mahabharata* also tells of the *emergence* of Dvaraka from the ocean in the first place. When Krishna chose Dvaraka as the site for his city, he asked the ocean to withdraw from the shore for twelve leagues to give space for the city; the ocean complied.[16] Since the sea had yielded the land, against nature (like the Netherlands), it would be only fair for it to reclaim it again in the end. Later texts tell of a different sort of bargain: Krishna in a dream told a king to build a temple to him as Jagannatha in Puri, but the ocean kept sweeping the temple away. The great saint Kabir stopped the ocean, which took the form of a Brahmin and asked Kabir for permission to destroy the temple; Kabir refused but let him destroy the temple at Dvaraka in Gujarat. And so he did.[17] Even so, some texts insist that the temple of Krishna in Dvaraka was not flooded; the sea was not able to cover it, "even to the present day,"[18] and the temple, able to wash away all evils, remains there,[19] just as in the periodic flooding of the universe of doomsday, something always survives. (The physical location of the shrine of Dvaraka, at the very westernmost shore of India, where the sun dies every evening, may have inspired the idea that the town was the sacred gate to the world of the dead.[20]) In direct contradiction of the *Mahabharata*'s statement that the entire city was destroyed, these later texts insist that it is still there. Dvaraka is said to exist today in Gujarat, and archaeologists and divers have published reports on what they claim to be its remains.[21]

We may also see here the patterns of the myths of both Lemuria (the ocean submerging Dvaraka) and Gondwana (Dvaraka emerging from the ocean to join onto Gujarat). Other myths too follow in the wake of this one, such as the story that the ocean (called *sagara*) was first formed when the sixty thousand sons of a king named Sagara dug into the earth to find the lost sacrificial horse of their father, who was performing a horse sacrifice.[22] (Some versions say that Indra, the king of the gods, stole the horse.)[23] A sage burned the princes to ashes, and years later Bhagiratha, the great-grandson of Sagara, persuaded the Ganges, which existed at that time only in the form of the Milky Way in heaven, to descend to earth in order to flow over the ashes of his grandfathers and thus purify them so that they could enter heaven; he also persuaded the god Shiva to let the heavenly Ganges River land first on his head and meander through his matted hair before flowing down to the earth, in order to prevent her from shattering the earth by a direct fall out of the sky.[24] According to another text, when Sagara performed the horse sacrifice, the oceans began to overflow and cover all the land with water. The gods asked the great ascetic Parashurama to intercede; he appealed to Varuna (the Vedic god of the waters), who threw the sacrificial vessel far away, causing the waters to recede and thereby creating the western kingdom of Shurparaka.[25] (In a different subtext of this version, when Parashurama was banished from the earth and needed land to live on, Varuna told him to throw his ax as far into the ocean as he could; the water receded up to Gokarna, the place where his ax finally fell, thus creating the land of Kerala.[26])

There are other legends of submerged cities or submerged lands or landmasses.*[27] The cities where the first two assemblies that created Tamil literature were held are said to have been destroyed by the sea.[28] In the seventeenth century, people claimed to be able still to see the tops of a submerged city, temples and all, off the coast of Calicut.[29] For centuries there were said to be seven pagodas submerged off the coast of Mamallipuram, near Madras, and on December 26, 2004, when the great tsunami struck, as the waves first receded about five hundred meters into the sea, Frontline (an Indian news Web site) reported that tourists saw a row of rocks on the north side of the Shore Temple and that behind the Shore Temple in the east, architectural remains of a temple were revealed. "When the waves subsided, these were submerged in the sea again."[30] Archaeologists denied that there could be any submerged temples there.[31] Our knowledge of the long history of the imaginative myth of the submerged Hindu temple inclines us to side with the more skeptical archaeologists.

Behind all these traditions may lie the story of another great flood, first recorded in the *Shatapatha Brahmana* (c. 800 BCE), around the same time as one of the proposed dates for the *Mahabharata* flood, a myth that has also been linked to Noah's Ark in Genesis[32] as well as to stories of the flood that submerged the Sumerian city of Shuruppak and is described in the Gilgamesh epic. Indeed flood myths are found in most of the mythologies of the world: Africa, the Near East, Australia, South Seas, Scandinavia, the Americas, China, Greece. They

---

* For instance, once upon a time all the mountains had wings, but they flew around, bumping into things and generally wreaking havoc. To ground them, Indra cut off their wings, but the god of the wind hid one mountain, Mainaka, in the ocean so that he alone kept his wings.

are widespread because floods are widespread, especially along the great rivers that nurture early civilizations (and even more widespread in the lands watered by the monsoons). There are significant variants: Some cultures give one reason for the flood, some other reasons, some none; sometimes one person survives, sometimes several, sometimes many (seldom none—or who could tell the story?—though the creator sometimes starts from scratch again); some survive in boats, some by other means.[33]

In the oldest extant Indian variant, in the Brahmanas, Manu, the first human being, the Indian Adam, finds a tiny fish who asks him to save him from the big fish who will otherwise eat him. This is an early expression of concern about animals being eaten, in this case by other animals; "fish eat fish," what we call "dog eat dog," is the Indian term for anarchy. The fish promises, in return for Manu's help, to save Manu from a great flood that is to come. Manu protects the fish until he is so big that he is "beyond destruction" and then builds a ship (the fish tells him how to do it); the fish pulls the ship to a mountain, and when the floodwaters subside, Manu keeps following them down. The text ends: "The flood swept away all other creatures, and Manu alone remained here."[34] The theme of "helpful animals" who requite human kindness (think of Androcles and the lion) teaches two morals: A good deed is rewarded, and be kind to (perhaps do not eat?) animals.

Centuries later a new element is introduced into the story of the flood, one so important and complex that we must pause for a moment to consider it: the idea that time is both linear and cyclical. The four Ages of time, or Yugas, are a series named after the four throws of the dice. Confusingly, the number of the Age increases as the numbers of the dice, the quality of life, and the length of the Age decrease: The first Age, the Krita Yuga ("Winning Age") or the Satya Yuga ("Age of Truth"), what the Greeks called the Golden Age (for the four Ages of time, or Yugas, formed a quartet in ancient Greece too), is the winning throw of four, a time of happiness, when humans are virtuous and live for a long time. The second Age, the Treta Yuga ("Age of the Trey"), is the throw of three; things are not quite so perfect. In the third Age, the Dvapara Yuga ("Age of the Deuce"), the throw of two, things fall apart. And the Kali Age is the dice throw of snake eyes, the present Age, the Iron Age, the Losing Age, the time when people are no damn good and die young, and barbarians invade India, the time when all bets are off. This fourth Age was always, from the start, entirely different from the first three in one essential respect: Unlike the other Ages, it is now, it is real. The four Ages are also often analogized to the four legs of dharma visualized as a cow who stands on four legs in the Winning Age, then becomes three-legged, two-legged, and totters on one leg in the Losing Age.

But time in India is not only linear, as in Greece (for the ages steadily decline), but cyclical, unlike Greece (for the end circles back to the beginning again). The cosmos is reborn over and over again, as each successive Kali Age ends in a doomsday fire and a flood that destroys the cosmos but is then transformed into the primeval flood out of which the cosmos is re-created, undergoing a sea change in a new cosmogony.* The idea of circular cosmic time is in part the result of Indian ideas about reincarnation, the circularity of the individual soul. The ending precedes the beginning, but the end and the beginning were always there from the start, before the beginning and after the end, to paraphrase T. S. Eliot.†

In later retellings of the story of the flood, therefore—to return at last to our story— the fish saves Manu from the doomsday flood that comes at the end of the Kali Age, the final dissolution (*pralaya*):

THE FISH AND THE FLOOD

Manu won from the god Brahma, the creator, the promise that he would be able to protect all creatures, moving and still, when the dissolution took place. One day, he found a little fish and saved it until it grew so big that it terrified him, whereupon he realized that it must be Vishnu. The fish said, "Bravo! You have recognized me. Soon the whole earth will be flooded. The gods have made this boat for you to save the great living souls; bring all the living creatures into the boat, and you will survive the dissolution and be king at the beginning of the Winning Age. At the end of the Kali Age, the mare who lives at the bottom of the ocean will open her mouth and a poisonous fire will burst out of her, coming up out of hell; it will burn the whole universe, gods and constellations and all. And then the seven clouds of doomsday will flood the earth until everything is a single ocean. You alone will survive, together with the sun and moon, several gods, and the great religious texts and sciences." And so it happened, and the fish came and saved Manu.[35]

---

* The word for doomsday, or time, or death—Kala—is, like the word for the fourth throw of the dice, derived from the verb *kal*, "to count." The goddess Kali too derives her name from Kala. Kali as in Kali Age is spelled with a short *a* and *i*, whereas the goddess Kali has two long vowels. In the hope of distinguishing them, I will always refer to the latter as the goddess Kali.
† In *Burnt Norton*.

In this text, Manu saves not himself alone but all creatures, and this time the gods, instead of Manu, build the boat. This variant also gives us a much more detailed, and hence more reassuring, image of what is to follow the flood; a new world is born out of the old one. These stories suggest that floods are both inevitable and survivable; this is what happens to the world, yet the world goes on.

More significantly, the myth is now part of the great story of the cycle of time, involving fire as well as water, so that the flood now appears more as a solution than as a problem: It puts out the mare fire that is always on the verge of destroying us. For a mare roams at the bottom of the ocean; the flames that shoot out of her mouth are simultaneously bridled by and bridling the waters of the ocean,[36] like uranium undergoing constant fission, controlled by lithium rods. In several of the myths of her origin, the fire is said to result from the combined fires of sexual desire and the fire of the ascetic repression of sexual desire,[37] or from the fury of the god Shiva when he is excluded from the sacrifice.[38] The submarine mare is (to continue the nuclear metaphor) like a deadly atomic U-boat cruising the deep, dark waters of the unconscious. It should not go unnoticed that the mare is a female, the symbol of all that threatens male control over the internal fires of restrained passions that are always in danger of breaking out in disastrous ways. This delicate balance, this hair-trigger suspension, is disturbed at the end of the Kali Age, the moment of doomsday, when the mare gallops out of the ocean and sets the world on fire, and the newly unchecked ocean leaves its bed and floods the ashes of the universe, which then lie dormant until the next period of creation.[39] And then, like the ashes of Sagara's sons, the ashes of the entire universe are revived as it is reborn. A remnant or seed, a small group of good people, is saved by a fish (usually identified as one of the several incarnations of the great god Vishnu), who pulls a boat to a mountain, where they survive to repeople the universe.[40] (The mountain, the Hindu equivalent of Ararat, is identified with numerous sites throughout India.*) The myth expresses the barely controlled tendency of the universe to autodestruct (and perhaps a kind of prescientific theory of global warming: When it gets hotter, the ice caps will melt, and there will be a flood[41]).

Recent attempts to excavate both Lemuria and the submerged city of Dvaraka,[42] correlated with recent oceanographic work carried out in 1998–99 around the Kerguelen plateau in the southernmost reaches of the Indian Ocean,

---

* Kumbhakonan is one of them; the name is said to derive from the pot (*kumbha*) in which Shiva, not Vishnu, floated the survivors to safety. The mountain is also said to be in Kashmir.

have rekindled speculations about a "lost continent" in the Indian Ocean. What surprised the excavators most was not the enormous plateau that they found in the middle of the Indian Ocean but signs that "near the end of the plateau growth, there is strong evidence of highly explosive eruptions."[43] The volcanic activity of the submarine mare, perhaps?

SPACE

MAPS

So much for origins.

Whatever fused with India had to make its peace with what was already there, its unique climate, fauna, and, eventually, culture. The land and its people transformed all who came to them; they did not simply passively receive the British, or the Mughals before them, let alone the people of the Veda, or that migratory bit of Africa.

Ancient Indian cosmology imagined a flat earth consisting of seven concentric continents, the central one surrounded by the salty ocean and each of the other roughly circular continents surrounded by oceans of other liquids: treacle (molasses), wine, ghee (clarified butter), milk, curds, and freshwater. (This prompted one nineteenth-century Englishman's notorious tirade against "geography made up of seas of treacle and seas of butter."[44]) In the center of the central mainland (the "Plum-tree Continent" or Jambu-Dvipa) stands the cos-

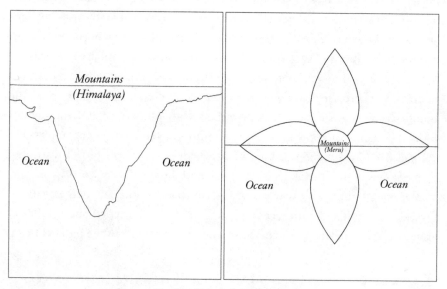

Geographical and Mythological Map of India.

mic mountain Meru, from which four subcontinents radiate out to the east, west, north, and south, like the petals of a lotus; the southernmost petal of this mainland is Bharata-varsha, the ancient Sanskrit name for India. If you bisect the lotus horizontally, you see India as a kite-shaped landmass with mountains in the north and (salt) oceans on all other sides, much as it appears on any Rand McNally map.* The watery world under the earth, which the cobra people (Nagas) inhabit, is also there, in the water table that we encounter every time we sink a well anywhere in the world.

Cosmography and cartography overlie each other, as do the rabbit and the man in the moon, myth and history. It has been rightly remarked that texts are just maps, and map is not territory;[45] but when the maps are big enough, they become territories of their own. There is a shared core underlying both maps and territories, from which myths and political narratives spread out in different directions. There was a flood, and now there is a politically useful myth about it; there is an arrangement of water and land, and there is a politically inspired diagram of it (for different countries draw the borders of Kashmir, to take a case at random, in very different ways). The map of the Plum-tree Continent is to a Rand McNally map as the flood myth is to the geological record. The natural layout of water and land serves as the basis of the myth of a flood and the diagram of the cosmos, which in turn support the construction of a politically useful chart of time and space.

TERRITORY: MOUNTAINS, RIVERS, MONSOON

Many people have imagined the Himalayan Mountains as posing an impregnable barrier, but this image of Inaccessible India is simply a part of the Unchanging India package. India functioned, throughout history, less like Shangri-la than like Heathrow or O'Hare. The Himalayas are indeed high, and no one ever strolled casually across them, but they did not keep people out of India. Alexander the Great managed to get into India over the Himalayan Mountains (probably through the Khyber Pass), horses, mules, camels, and all, and many others followed. Not without reason was the Hindu imagination haunted by the specter of invasion, expressed in the persistent myth of the degenerate Kali Age, a nightmare of barbarian penetration. The physical boundaries of India were as porous as those between its internal belief systems. Silk

---

* Compare the standard map outline of India and the map of Mount Meru and the Plum-tree Continent on page 60.

came from China across the Central Asian silk route (the word for "silk" in Sanskrit is *china*), and just about everyone in the ancient world—beginning with traders from Mesopotamia, Crete, Rome, and Arabia—washed up sooner or later on some coast of India.

So too the Vindhya Mountains form the barrier between North and South India, but the stories about the Vindhyas tell how that barrier was breached, not how it kept people apart: When the Vindhyas began to grow so tall that even the sun had to go around them (just as it circumambulates Mount Meru), the great sage Agastya asked them to bow their heads before him so that he could cross from North to South India (bringing Sanskrit and the Vedas to the Dravidian lands) and to remain that way until he returned; the Vindhyas agreed to this, and since Agastya never returned from South India, where he established the Tamil language, the Vindhyas remain conveniently low.

In South Asia, history flows with the rivers. Three great river systems divide the northern subcontinent: first the Indus ("the River") in Pakistan, with its five tributaries, the rivers of the Punjab (Jhelum, Chenab, Ravi, Beas, and Sutlej) that give the Punjab its name ("Five Waters"); then the Doab or "Two Rivers," the Ganges (Ganga, "Going to Earth" [from heaven, where she is the Milky Way]) and the Yamuna ("Twin Sister," now Jumna) in North India; and then the Brahmaputra ("Son of Brahma") in Bangladesh. All three rivers originate in a single region of southwestern Tibet, their sources so close that they may once have belonged to a single icy lake that was shattered when the piece of Africa that crashed into Central Asia drove off the waters in diverse directions.[46] The Indus flows eighteen hundred miles before it empties into the Arabian sea. The Narmada ("Jester"), the great river that, like the Vindhya Mountains, divides the north from the south, has inspired an extensive mythology that balances that of the Ganges in the north.

What is the relationship between climate and culture in India? Is there some causal link between, on the one hand, "the ambivalent natural environment, where lush harvests coexist with barren soil, drought with flood, feast with famine," and, on the other, the fact that Hindu logicians were the first to posit the coexistence of the elements of contradiction?[47] Other countries have "ambivalent natural environments" too; farmers the world over are at the mercy of the elements. But the violence and uncertainty of the monsoon create an ever-present psychological factor that may well be related to Hindu ideas about the capriciousness and violence of fate and the gods.

Conclusion: Con-fusion

What does the geology of the formation of India tell us about the formation of Hinduism? The answer is suggested by a story that A. K. Ramanujan retold, from Tamil sources:

THE BRAHMIN HEAD AND THE PARIAH BODY

A sage's wife, Mariamma, was sentenced by her husband to death. At the moment of execution she embraced a Pariah woman, Ellamma, for her sympathy. In the fray both the Pariah woman and the Brahmin lost their heads. Later the husband relented, granted them pardon, and restored their heads by his spiritual powers. But the heads were transposed by mistake. To Mariamma (with a Brahmin head and Pariah body) goats and cocks but not buffalo were sacrificed; to Ellamma (Pariah head and Brahmin body) buffalo instead of goats and cocks.[48]

This text is itself an example of what it tells about: It mixes together the story of Mariamma from two different Indian geographical and linguistic traditions, North Indian Sanskrit literature, where she is called Renuka, and South Indian Tamil oral folktales about the origins of two South Indian goddesses.[49] This sort of juxtaposition, in various forms, is widespread in both myth and history, beginning with the piece of Africa stuck onto Central Asia, like a head upon a body, and continuing through all the ideas of women and low castes that get into the heads of Brahmin males. It can stand as a metaphor for all the fusions that make up the rich mix of Hinduism.

The mixing together of various human streams is so basic to the history of Hinduism that the Brahmins could not stop trying, and failing, to prevent it, even as their fear of the powers of the senses to invade the rational control center made them try, also in vain, to control addiction through asceticism. Their ultimate terror was the "confusion" of classes, the miscegenation brought on by the Kali Age. They visualized the mixing of classes as a form of impurity, which should not surprise anyone who has read the British anthropologist Mary Douglas's explanation of the ways that throughout the world, "category errors"—things that do not fall entirely into one class or another—are characterized as dirt and as danger.[50] Brahmins regarded the woman with the Brahmin head and Pariah body—and her twin and partner, with the Pariah head on the Brahmin body— as monstrosities, a double hodgepodge. But from the standpoint of a non-Brahmin, or a scholar of Hinduism, this rich hybrid or multiple mix is precisely what makes Hinduism the cultural masterpiece that it is.

Such a conflation is not a monstrosity, nor is it a mistake—or if it is, it is a *felix culpa*. The transpositions result in two goddesses (read: many Hinduisms), each of whom is far more interesting than the straightforward realignment would have been. Whatever its disparate sources, the resulting creature has an integrity that we must respect, rather like that of my favorite mythical beast, created by Woody Allen, the Great Roe, who had the head of a lion and the body of a lion, but *not the same lion*.[51] The question to ask is not where the disparate elements originated but why they were put together and why kept together. The political implications of regarding Hinduism as either a hodgepodge or, on the other hand, culturally homogeneous or even monolithic are equally distorting; it is always more useful, if a bit trickier, to acknowledge simultaneously the variety of the sources and the power of the integrations. A Hinduism with a Pariah body and a Brahmin head—or, if you prefer, a Pariah head and a Brahmin body—was re-created again and again throughout India history, and these multiple integrities are what this book is about.

CHAPTER 3
CIVILIZATION IN THE INDUS VALLEY
50,000 to 1500 BCE

ॐ

CHRONOLOGY (ALL DATES BCE)

c. 50,000 Stone Age cultures arise

c. 30,000 Bhimbetka cave paintings are made

c. 6500 Agriculture begins

c. 3000 Pastoral nomad societies emerge

c. 2500 Urban societies emerge along the Indus River

c. 2200–2000 Harappa is at its height

c. 2000–1500 Indus civilization declines

"Pashupati" Seal (Seal 420).

In place of an opening epigram, we begin with an image, whose meaning is much disputed, for one of the many challenges of interpreting the Indus Valley Civilization (IVC) lies in deciphering pictures for which we do not know the words. The second challenge is trying to decide what, if anything, of the IVC survives in later Hinduism. For the IVC is older than the oldest extant Hindu texts, the Vedas, and its material remains include many images that may be the earliest-known examples of important Hindu icons that only (re)surface much later.

EARLY HISTORY: BHIMBETKA CAVE PAINTINGS

Much of what we now call Hinduism may have had roots in cultures that thrived in South Asia long before the creation of textual evidence that we can decipher with any confidence. Remarkable cave paintings have been preserved from Mesolithic sites dating from c. 30,000 BCE in Bhimbetka, near present-day Bhopal, in the Vindhya Mountains in the province of Madhya Pradesh.[1] They represent a number of animals that have been identified as deer, boars, elephants, leopards, tigers, panthers, rhinoceroses, antelope, fish, frogs, lizards, squirrels, and birds. One painting seems to depict a man walking a dog on a leash. The animals represented probably existed there (it would be hard for someone who had never seen an elephant to draw a picture of an elephant), though there may be false positives (an artist could have copied someone else's picture of an elephant, and the existence of images of a creature half bull and half man certainly does not prove that such tauranthropoi actually existed). On the other hand, animals that are *not* represented may well also have existed there (the Bhimbetkanese may have had snakes even though they did not make any paintings of snakes); the missing animals may simply have failed to capture the artist's imagination. False negatives in this realm are even more likely than false positives.

Several of the animals in the paintings have horns, like gazelles, and one painting shows people dancing with what may be a unicorn with a close-clipped mane.[2] This possible unicorn continues to tease art historians when it reappears in the IVC.

THE INDUS VALLEY

MATERIAL CULTURE

There were other early settlements in India, notably the culture of Baluchistan, in the westernmost part of what is now Pakistan, dating to before 6000

BCE. But from about 2300 BCE the first urbanization took place, as great cities arose in the valley of the Indus River, 150 miles south of Baluchistan, also in Pakistan. The material remains of this culture, which we call the Indus Valley Civilization or the Harappan Civilization (named after Harappa, one of the two great cities on the Indus, the other being Mohenjo-Daro), present a tantalizing treasure chest of often enigmatic images that hover just beyond our reach, taunting us with what might well be the keys to the roots of Hinduism.

The Indus Valley plain, much like the valleys of the Nile and the Tigris-Euphrates, cradles of Neolithic civilizations, is a semiarid, river-watered region; the "semi" means that on the one hand, the relatively sparse vegetation, not so rich as that of the effluvial plain of the Ganges, for instance, required no iron tools to clear and settle while, on the other hand, the silt from the river floodings provided sufficient natural fertilizer to create the surplus that makes civilization possible.[3] The river was also a channel of trade.

Here's another origin story. In 1856 an English general named Alexander Cunningham, later director general of the archaeological survey of northern India, visited Harappa, where an English engineer named William Brunton was gathering bricks (including what he recognized as bricks from the IVC) as ballast for a railway he was building between Multan and Lahore. Cunningham took note of the site but did nothing about it, and the trains still run on that route, on the main line from Peshawar, on top of a hundred miles of third-millennium BCE bricks. Only after 1917, when an Indian archaeologist found an ancient knife at a place named, significantly, Mound of the Dead (Mohenjo-Daro), and excavations carried out there revealed artifacts identical with those that had been at Harappa, did this civilization begin to be appreciated. Among the treasures that they found were carved stones, flat, rectangular sections of soapstone about the size of a postage stamp, which were used as stamps or seals, as well as sealings (impressions) of such stamps.

The civilization of the Indus Valley extends over more than a thousand sites, stretching over 750,000 square miles, where as many as forty thousand people once lived.[4] Four hundred miles separate the two biggest cities, from Harappa on the Ravi tributary in the north (one of the five rivers of the Punjab) down to Mohenjo-Daro (in the Larkana Valley in Sindh) and on down to the port of Lothal in the delta on the sea. Yet the Indus cities were stunningly uniform and remarkably stable over this wide range, changing little over a millennium, until they begin to crumble near the end. They had trade contacts with Crete, Sumer, and other Mesopotamian cultures, perhaps even Egypt.[5] There are Harappan sites in Oman (on the Arabian Peninsula), and Indus seals show up in Mesopotamia. There was direct contact with Iran, particularly just before the end, a period from which archaeologists have found a very late Indus seal with Indus motifs on one side and Iranian on the other, together with many seals reflecting Central Asian influences.[6] Some Indus images bear a striking resemblance to images from Elam, a part of ancient Iran that was closely linked to adjacent Mesopotamian urban societies.[7] Trade with Central Asia continued in the Indus area even after the demise of the Indus Valley Civilization. In a sense, the Hindu diaspora began now, well before 2000 BCE.

Archaeological evidence suggests that the use of cubical dice began in South Asia and indeed in the IVC.[8] Sir John Hubert Marshall, the director general of the Indian archaeological survey from 1902 to 1931, found many cubical terracotta dice, with one to six dots, at Mohenjo-Daro,[9] and a number of other dice have been identified since then from Harappa and elsewhere, including several of stone (agate, limestone, faience, etc.).[10] This is a fact of great significance in light of the importance of gambling in later Indian civilization, from 1200 BCE.

They had gold, copper, and lead, and they imported bronze, silver, and tin (as well as lapis lazuli and soapstone), but they had no iron; their weapons were made of copper and bronze. There was a huge wheat and barley storage system, and there were household and public drainage works superior to those in parts of the world today, including much of India. Most of the buildings are constructed out of bricks (both sun baked and kiln fired) of remarkably consistent size throughout the extended culture; equally unvarying stone cubes were used to measure weights. The roads too did not just evolve out of deer tracks but were carefully laid out all in the same proportion (streets twice as wide as lanes, avenues twice as wide as streets) and arranged on a grid (north-south or east-west), like the "pink city" of Jaipur in Rajasthan that Maharajah Jai Singh designed and built in the eighteenth century CE. All this uniformity of material culture across hundreds of miles and a great many centuries implies considerable control and planning[11] and suggests, to some scholars, a threat of authoritarian or even totalitarian government. Some speak of the "affluent private residences with bathrooms served by a drainage system," while "the poor, however, lived huddled in slums, the inevitable underclass in a hierarchical system,"[12] and others have seen in the tiny identical houses (protohousing projects? ghettos?) and in the massive government structure, regulating every single brick, an "obsessive uniformity."[13] There is evidence that different professions worked out of distinct areas of the cities, suggesting the existence of something like protocastes.[14] Some scholars have taken the visible signs of an overarching hand of authority and urban planning as evidence of "urbanity, sophistication, well-being, ordered existence."[15] One might also see, in the tiny scale of the seals and the figurines, and in the children's toys, a delicate civilization, whose artwork is fine in both senses—beautiful and small.

PICTURES AND SYMBOLS: THE SEALS AND THE SCRIPT

The civilization of the Indus is not silent, but we are deaf. We cannot hear their words but can see their images.[*]

Most of the seals, which are found throughout the Indus Valley Civilization, are engraved with a group of signs in the Indus script, or a drawing or design, or a combination of these.[16] There are well over two thousand inscriptions, using about four hundred graphemes, and many people have claimed to have deciphered them, often demonstrating truly fantastic flights of imagination, but no one has definitively cracked the code.[17] The individual messages are too short for a computer to decode, and since each seal had a distinctive combination of symbols, there are too few examples of each sequence to provide a sufficient linguistic context. The symbols that accompany a given image vary from seal to seal, so that it's not possible to derive the meaning of the words from the meaning of the images. Many people have speculated that it is an Indo-European language, or a Dravidian language, or a Munda or "Austro-Asiatic" language[18] (supported by the plate tectonics narrative), or not a language at all.[†19] The seals may well have been nothing but devices to mark property in the manner of a signet ring, a stamp of ownership, rather like a bar code,[20] probably made for merchants who used them to brand their wares, signifying nothing but "This is mine." Perhaps the writing is a form of ancient shorthand. Because they present a vivid, highly evocative set of visual symbols, but no text, these images have functioned, for scholars, like Rorschach shapes onto which each interpreter projects his or her own vision of what the hypothetical text should be and should say.[‡] The ambiguity and subjectivity of the interpretation of vi-

---

[*] You can see most of them on the Web site Harappa.com.

[†] The rebuttal to the argument that it is not a language at all is that in some inscriptions the letters all are squeezed together to fit the line at the end, implying that it was written in one direction. If the sequence matters, it's a language.

[‡] The Rorschach test, according to the *Encyclopaedia Britannica*, is "a projective method of psychological testing in which a person is asked to describe what he sees in 10 inkblots, of which some are black or gray and others have patches of colour. The test was introduced in 1921 by the Swiss psychiatrist Hermann Rorschach."

sual images are yet another aspect of the shadow on the moon that is, for some, a rabbit, and for others, a man.

But the images on the seals do make a more general statement that we can decipher, particularly in the realm of flora and fauna. The vast majority of Indus signs can be directly or indirectly related to farming: Typical signs include seeds, fruits, sprouts, grain plants, pulses, trees, farm instruments (hoes, primitive plows, mortars and pestles, rakes, harvesting instruments, etc.), seasonal/celestial or astral signs, and even at times anthropomorphized plowed fields. The images, as well as other archaeological remains, tell us that the winter Indus crop was barley and wheat; the spring crop, peas and lentils; and the summer and the monsoon crops, millets, melons, dates, and fiber plants.[21] They also probably grew rice.[22] They spun, wove, and dyed cotton, probably for the first time on the planet Earth, and may also have been the first to use wheeled transport.[23] They ate meat and fish.[24]

INDUS ANIMALS

Animals, both wild and tame, dominate the representations from the IVC, both on the seals, where they seem to have been drawn from nature, and on figurines, paintings on pottery, and children's toys. These images tell us that tigers, elephants, and one-horned rhinoceroses, as well as buffalo, antelope, and crocodiles, inhabited the forests of this now almost desert region, which then had riverine long grass and open forest country, the natural habitat of tigers and rhinoceroses.[25] (A rhinoceros, a buffalo, and an elephant, all on wheels, were found in a later site in northern Maharashtra, perhaps connected with Harappa.)[26] There are also animal figurines of turtles, hares, monkeys, and birds, and there is a pottery model, 2.9 inches long, of an animal with a long, bushy tail, perhaps a squirrel or a mongoose.[27]

But it is the representations of domesticated animals, as well as the archaeological remains of such animals, that tell us most about the culture of the IVC, in particular about the much-disputed question of its relationship (or lack of relationship) with later Indian cultures such as that of the Vedic peoples. Millennia before the IVC, people in South Asia had hunted a number of animals that later, in the IVC, they bred and domesticated (and sometimes continued to hunt). Before the IVC, they had also domesticated two distinct species of cattle—the humped zebu (*Bos indicus*), with its heavy dewlaps, and a humpless relation of the *Bos primigenius* of West Asia.[28] Zebu and water buffalo (*Bubalus*) were used as draft animals, and elephants (domesticated, more or less) were used for clearing and building.[29] Elephants are not native to the lands found west of central India, but they might have been imported into the Indus Valley.[30]

They had dogs (which may already have been domesticated at Bhimbetka). Marshall, who participated in the first excavations of the site, commented on them at length:

> As would be expected, the dog is common, but all the figures but one are roughly modeled and evidently made by children. That this animal was a pet as well as a guard is proved by some of the figures being provided with collars. We have found a very mutilated figure of a dog with a collar, fastened by a cord to a post, which suggests that house animals were sometimes too fierce to be allowed at large. The one well-made exception . . . almost resembles the English mastiff of to-day.[31]

He also noted a figure of a dog with its tongue hanging out, "a detail seldom shown in a pottery model."[32] The particular breeds of dogs depicted in small statues at the IVC include pariah dogs and, surprisingly, dachshunds.[33]

They had also domesticated camels, sheep, pigs, goats, and chickens. This may have been the first domestication of fowl,* a major contribution to world civilization.[34] Apparently they did not have, or at least think it worthwhile to depict, cats. On seals and pottery, and depicted as figurines, the favorite subject is male animals—most frequently bulls with pendulous dewlaps and big pizzles. There are also short-horned bulls,[35] but in general they went in for horned males: bulls, water buffalo, rams, and others. One scene even depicts a tiger with horns.[36]

By contrast, they do not seem to have found female animals very interesting, and significantly, no figurines of cows have been found.[37] Marshall even comments on this absence, the cow that does not moo in the night, as it were: "The cow, even if it was regarded as sacred, was for some reason, at present unexplained, not represented in plastic form or carved in stone."[38] Of course they must have *had* cows, or they couldn't very well have had bulls (and indeed there is material evidence of cows in the IVC), but the art-historical record tells us that the Indus artists did not use cows as cultural symbols, and why should we assume, with Marshall, that they were sacred? Why, in fact, do archaeologists

---

* It is also possible that fowl were domesticated in several different places.

reach for the word "sacred" every time they find something for which they cannot determine a practical use? (This is a question to which we will return.)

The seals depict animals that have been characterized as being "noted for their physical and sexual prowess—bulls, rhinoceroses, elephants, and tigers—or, as is true of snakes and crocodiles . . . widely regarded as symbols of sexuality, fertility, or longevity."[39] Of course we don't really know how good crocodiles are in bed; our culture thinks of them (or at least their tears and smiles) as symbols of hypocrisy; why should they be symbols of sexuality, and to whom (other than, presumably, other crocodiles)? It has even been suggested that "the present untouchability of dogs could originate from their being sacred [in the IVC] and thus untouchable."[40] The equation of sacrality and untouchability is as unjustified as the assumption that the attitude to dogs did not change in four thousand years.

THE UNICORN (AND OTHER POSSIBLY MYTHICAL BEASTS)

This question of symbolic valence becomes more blatant in the case of more fantastic animals, like unicorns.

The most commonly represented Indus animal, depicted on 1,156 seals and sealings out of a total of 1,755 found at Mature Harappan sites (that is, on 60 percent of all seals and sealings), is "a stocky creature unknown to zoology, with the body of a bull and the head of a zebra, from which head a single horn curls majestically upwards and then forwards."[41] What is this animal? Is it just a two-horned animal viewed from the side or a kind of gazelle with a horn on its nose? Is it a horse with a horn? (It doesn't have the proportions of a horse.) Or a stylized rhinoceros?[42] Or is it, by analogy with its European cousin, a mythical beast? The quasi unicorn always (like other Indus animals sometimes) has a manger in front of him. The manger is sometimes said to have "religious or cultic significance," since one seal shows an image of a unicorn being carried in procession alongside such a manger.[43] Often the manger is called sacred (presumably on the basis of the sacrality of mangers in Christianity).

The unicorn lands us on the horn of a dilemma: Are the animals represented in the art of the IVC religious symbols? Though many Indus animal figurines are simply children's toys, with little wheels on them, scholars persist in investing them with religious meanings. Some of the fossil record too has been invoked as religious testimony. The excavation, in 1929, of twenty severed human skulls "tightly packed together," along with what the excavator interpreted as ritual vessels and the bones of sacrificed animals, has been taken as evidence that human heads were presented to a sacred tree,[44] a scenario reminiscent of the novel *The Day of the Triffids* or the film *The Little Shop of Horrors* ("Feed me! Feed me!" cried the carnivorous plant). And why should an archaeologist have identified the image of a dog threatening a man with long, wavy hair as the hound of Yama, the god of the dead,[45] simply because the dog appears on the burial urns at Harappa? Why can't it just be a dog faithful in death as in life?

Unicorn Seal from Harappa.

And why are the two figures in front of a pair of cobras "a pair of worshipers"?[46] Why not just two, probably nervous blokes? Yet the rest of the scene does indeed suggest something other than common or garden-variety snake charming. The couple with the cobras is kneeling beside a seated figure; another human figure holds back two rearing tigers; a monster half bull and half man attacks a horned tiger. This is not a snapshot of everyday life in the IVC. Scenes and figures such as these may give us glimpses of rituals, of episodes from myth and story, yet we have "nothing to which we can refer these isolated glimpses to give them substance."[47]

Other seals too seem to be telling a story that we cannot quite make out. One scene depicts what has been called "a three-horned deity" (but may just be a guy, or for that matter a gal, in a three-horned hat) apparently emerging from the middle of a tree, while another figure outside the tree is bent "in suppliant posture" with arms raised; a bull stands behind it, and seven girls below them.[48] (This is one of a small number of scenes that occur on seals found in four different cities: Harappa, Kalibangan, Mohenjo-Daro, and Chanhujo-Daro). Another seal depicts a similar scene, this one involving a fig (pipal) tree:* A nude figure with flowing hair and "a horned headdress" (or his own horns?) stands between the upright branches of a pipal tree; another figure,

---

* The spell-check on my Mac tried to correct "pipal" to "papal" throughout, revealing a hitherto unsuspected Eurocentric, indeed philo-Catholic virus deeply programmed into my computer, Microsoft Orientalism.

much like the first but seen from the side, kneels at the base of the tree; a huge goat towers over him from behind. On yet another seal a figure squats among a group of animals on his left, while on his right a tiger is looking upward at a tree in which a man is seated.[49] Something is certainly going on here, but what? A folktale, perhaps? A ritual? These wordless scenes remind me of those contests that magazines run, inviting readers to supply the caption for a cartoon. But a lot more is at stake here than a cartoon.

GENDERED FIGURES

THE LORD OF BEASTS

Marshall began it all, in 1931, in his magisterial three-volume publication, *Mohenjo-Daro and the Indus Civilization*, which devotes five pages of a long chapter entitled "Religion" to seal 420: "There appears at Mohenjo-Daro a male god, who is recognizable at once as a prototype of the historic Siva. . . . The lower limbs are bare and the phallus (*urdhvamedhra*) seemingly exposed, but it is possible that what appears to be the phallus is in reality the end of the waistband."[50] (*Urdhvamedhra* ["upward phallus"] is a Sanskrit term, like the Greek-based English euphemism "ithyphallic," for an erect penis.) The *urdhvamedhra*-or-is-it-perhaps-just-his-waistband-or-the-knot-in-his-dhoti? has come to rival the Vedantic snake-or-is-it-perhaps-just-a-rope? as a trope for the power of illusion and imagination. The image suggested to Marshall an early form of the Hindu god Shiva, and Marshall's suggestion was taken up by several generations of scholars. This was to have far-reaching ramifications, for if this is an image of Shiva, then an important aspect of Hinduism can be dated back far earlier than the earliest texts (the Vedas).

Much was made of this tiny bit of soapstone (remember, the *whole seal* is barely an inch high); the millimeter of the putative erection on this seal has, like the optional inch of Cleopatra's nose, caused a great deal of historical fuss. Scholars have connected the "big-nosed gentleman . . . who sits in the lotus position with an erect penis, an air of abstraction and an audience of animals"[51] with well-known images of the ithyphallic Shiva.[52] The discovery at Indus sites of a number of polished, oblong stones, mostly small but ranging up to two feet in height, and probably used to grind grain, has led some scholars[53] to identify these stones as replicas of the erect phallus (linga) of Shiva and the vagina (yoni) of his consort, and to link these stones with "the later aniconic representations" of Shiva in the form of the linga.[54] Other scholars have suggested that "the Vedic criticism of 'those who worship the phallus'" may refer to this "early Indus cult."[55] There are so many assumptions here that it makes your head spin: that the Indus had a "cult" (a rather pejorative word for a religious sect), that the people of the Veda knew about it, that they disapproved of it instead of assimilating it to their own worship of the phallic Indra—no lawyer would go into court with this sort of evidence.

These all are arguments from hindsight. Marshall identified the figure as Shiva because (1) the Indus figure is seated on a low stool with knees pointed to the sides, feet together at his groin, and arms resting on his knees, a posture that many have identified as yogic (though it is the way that South Asians often sit), and Shiva is the god of yogis; (2) the Indus figure wears a horned headdress (or has horns), perhaps a buffalo mask as well as buffalo horns,[56] just as Shiva wears the horned moon, or a trident, in his hair; [3] in two examples of this scene the Indus figure has faces (or masks?) on the sides as well as the front of his head, while Shiva is often "Five-faced" (*Pancha-mukha*); (4) the figure is flanked by an elephant, a rhinoceros, and a water buffalo; smaller horned animals—antelope or goats—huddle beneath his stool, and he wears a tiger's skin on his torso, while Shiva is called the Lord of Beasts, Pashupati, and wears an animal skin, sometimes of a tiger, sometimes of an elephant;[57] and (5) both figures are ithyphallic.

I bought into the identification with Shiva in 1973,[58] as most scholars have continued to do right up to the present day. Yet many other candidates have also been pushed forward,[59] another good example of the Rorschach (or Rashomon*) phenomenon that produced such rich fantasies about the decipherment of the script. A list of just a few of the figures with which the so-called Lord of Beasts has been identified, a list that the reader should not take seriously but merely skim over to see how creatively scholars can run amok, might run like this (in more or less chronological order):

1. A goddess, on whom the bulge previously identified as an "erect phallus" is nothing but a girdle worn by female IVC figurines.[60]
2. Mahisha, the buffalo demon killed, in later mythology, by the goddess Durga, who is often represented as a riding on a tiger[61] (or a lion).
3. Indra, the Vedic king of the gods,[62] a conclusion supported by taking the first syllables of the Sanskrit words for three of the animals (eliminating

---

* After the Kurosawa film in which several different people present entirely different accounts of the same murder.

the tiger, because it was much larger than the other animals, and the deer, because they are seated apart from the others, and repeating the first syllable of the word for "man," because he was twice as important as the others), so that they spell out *ma-kha-na-sha-na*, an epithet of Indra (though also of Shiva), "destroying the sacrifice."*

4. Rudra, a Vedic prototype of Shiva, surrounded by animals who are incarnations of the Maruts, the storm gods who serve Indra and Rudra.[63]

5. Agni. The pictograms are read to mean "burning in three ways" and so to identify the figure as Agni, the god of fire, who has three forms.[64]

6. A chief named Anil, who ruled over the clans whose totems were the animals on the seal.[65]

7. A "seated" bull.[66]

8. A sage (named Rishyashringa ["Antelope-horned"]) who had a single antelope horn growing out of his forehead (his mother was a white-footed antelope; it's a long story); he appears in the earliest layers of Hindu and Buddhist mythology.[67]

9. Part of "a bull cult, to which numerous other representations of bulls lend substance."[68]

10. A yogic posture,[69] even if the link with Shiva is tenuous.[70]

Most, but not all, of these fantasies assume that the image is a representation of either a priest or a god, more likely a god.[71] In each case, the interpretation was inspired or constrained by the particular historical circumstances and agendas of the interpreter, but I'd love to know what the scholars who came up with these ideas were smoking.

There is, in fact, a general resemblance between this image and later Hindu images of Shiva. The Indus people may well have created a symbolism of the divine phallus, or a horned god, or both. But even if this is so, it does not mean that the Indus images are the source of the Hindu images. We must keep this caution in mind now when we consider the images of women in the IVC.

MOTHERS AND MOTHER GODDESSES

The widespread depiction of women in the IVC artifacts suggests that they were highly valued. In contrast with the predilection for macho animals (in-

---

* As I make it out, it goes: *ma* [*mahisha*, buffalo]-*kha* [*khadga*, rhino]-*na* [*nara*, man]-*sha* [*sharabha*, elephant]-*na* [*nara*, man].

cluding men) on the seals, the many terra-cotta figurines are mostly women, some wearing a wide girdle, a necklace, and an elaborate headdress. They are "Pop-eyed, bat-eared, belted and sometimes mini-skirted."[72] Some of them seem to be pregnant, or to hold, on their breasts or hips, small lumps that might be infants, "evidence perhaps that they expressed a concern for fecundity," a reasonable assumption;[73] they may have been symbols of fecundity in a "loosely structured household cult."[74]

But why assume any cult at all? Why need they symbolize fertility? Or even if they do, why should fertility have to be ritual? (I must confess to having fallen for this too more than a quarter of a century ago: "[S]trong evidence of a cult of the Mother has been unearthed at the pre-Vedic civilization of the Indus Valley [c. 2000 B.C.]."[75] Live and learn.) But not every image is symbolic; not every woman is a goddess. The "prominent and clumsily applied breasts" of these figures have been taken as evidence that they were "fertility symbols,"[76] but they may have been valued simply for what P. G. Wodehouse's Bertie Wooster used to refer to as a "wonderful profile." Big breasts are as useful to courtesans as to goddesses. Are the buxom centerfolds of *Playboy* magazine fertility symbols, or the voluptuous women that Rubens loved to paint? One seal shows a woman, upside down, with a child (or is it a scorpion?) coming out of (or into?) her, between her spread thighs.[77] This has been taken to refer to "a possible Mother Earth myth,"[78] but what was the myth, and is the upside-down woman a goddess, let alone an earth goddess? Why is she not simply a woman giving birth?

Scholars have seen connections between the alleged Lord of Beasts and a goddess, particularly the Hindu goddess who rides on a lion; some (casually conflating lions and tigers) connect the tiger on the seals with Hindu goddesses of a later period or with goddesses of ancient Egypt, the Aegean, Asia Minor, and the whole of West Asia, who were thought to consort with lions, leopards, or panthers.[79] The assumption that the figures of women found at the Indus sites are goddesses is then used to support the argument that the goddesses in later Hinduism—or the minor Vedic goddesses, Yakshinis and Apsarases, as-sociated with trees and water[80]—may be traced back to this early period.[81]

Hindsight speculations about fertility sects associated with female figurines, the bull, the horned deity, and trees like the sacred fig (pipal) are tempting. The seal with the person emerging from the middle of a fig tree may or may not prefigure the later Indian iconography of fig trees and banyan trees.[82] But it is going too far to interpret something so straightforward as a grave containing a male and female skeleton as "possibly the first indication of the well-known Hindu custom of sati" (live widows burning themselves to death on their dead husbands' cremation pyres or entombing themselves in their husband's graves).[83] The couple may simply have been buried side by side, whenever they died.

Some of the figures of well-endowed women are "curiously headless," and in some cases of actual adult burial the feet had been deliberately cut off, a fascinating correspondence, perhaps joined in a Procrustean syndrome. These headless female figures[84] may foreshadow the headless goddesses who people later Hindu mythology, such as the Brahmin woman who exchanged heads with the Pariah woman. (Or is it just that the neck is the thinnest part of such figures and most likely to break?) The prevalence of images of women may well indicate "a greater social presence of the female than in later times, which may also have been a generally more assertive presence."[85]

One tiny (ten-centimeter) bronze image supports the hope that some Indus women did in fact have an "assertive presence" and that is the so-called dancing girl of Mohenjo-Daro, in whom Marshall saw a "youthful impudence." John Keay describes her wonderfully well:

> Naked save for a chunky necklace and an assortment of bangles, this minuscule statuette is not of the usual Indian sex symbol, full of breast and wide of hip, but of a slender nymphet happily flaunting her puberty with delightful insouci-ance. Her pose is studiously casual, one spindly arm bent with the hand resting on a *déhanché* hip, the other dangling so as to brush a slightly raised knee. Slim and attenuated, the legs are slightly parted, and one foot—both are now missing—must have been pointed. . . her head is thrown back as if challenging a suitor, and her hair is somehow dressed into a heavy plaited chignon of peril-ous but intentionally dramatic construction. Decidedly, she wants to be admired; and she might be gratified to know that, four thousand years later, she still is.[86]

Others too admired her "gaunt and boyish femininity," her provocative "foot-less stance, haughty head, and petulantly poised arms,"[87] and found "something endearing" in "the artless pose of an awkward adolescent."[88] She is said to have "proto-Australoid" features that are also attested in skeletons in the Indus Valley.[89] This native girl mocks us, perhaps for our clumsy and arrogant at-tempts to figure out what she, and her compatriots in bronze and clay and soapstone, "mean."

Is Indus Religion a Myth?

The larger archaeological remains are equally ambiguous. Consider the very large swimming pool or bathing tank or public water tank in the citadel at Mohenjo-Daro, approximately forty feet by twenty-three feet and eight feet deep. There are wide steps leading down to it at each end and colonnaded buildings with small rooms around it. From this some have concluded that it was the site of a "Great Bath" where ritual bathing took place as part of a state religion.[90] But all that this structure tells us is that the IVC people liked to bathe, just to get clean or to cool off on hot days or to splash about, same as we do. Cleanliness is next to godliness, but not synonymous with it. The great

Bronze Dancing Girl from Mohenjo-Daro.

attention paid to the sewage system in the IVC suggests a hard-headed approach to hygiene (unless, of course, one wants to view the sewers as sacred underground chambers). Why does the bath have to be a ritual bath?*

The answer is simple enough: because the so-called Great Bath resembles the ritual bathing tanks of Hindu temples that began to appear in the subcontinent in the first few centuries CE[91] and because such a tank reflects a concern with ritual purification through water, an important idea in Hinduism.[92] Four thousand years later, indeed, every temple has its tank. Therefore, the argument goes, the tank must have served the same function in the IVC. Similarly, the so-called College of Priests in Mohenjo-Daro has been taken as evidence for the existence of a widespread priesthood.[93] Well, it's a big building, true, but why couldn't it be a dorm, or a hotel, or a hospital, or even a brothel?

Works of art such as the images on the seals and other artifacts provide

---

* A tongue-in-cheek example of the misinterpretation of plumbing devices, unsupported by texts, as religious objects is David Macaulay's *Motel of the Mysteries* (1979), in which visitors to Earth in 3850, after all civilization has been destroyed, produce a hilarious series of misunderstandings of the material items found in a bathroom: the toilet the Sacred Urn, the toilet seat the Sacred Collar, the toilet paper the Sacred Parchment, a drain plug on a chain the Sacred Pendant. (The television is the Great Altar.) In June 1956, Horace Miner had perpetrated a similar joke in "Body Ritual Among the Nacirema," which *American Anthropologist* printed as a serious article, failing to notice that "Nacirema" is "American" spelled backward.

abundant evidence of imaginative art, perhaps mythological but not necessarily ritual. They may have been purely decorative, or they may illustrate narratives of some sort or convey some sort of symbolic meaning, probably more than one, as symbols often do. But did they necessarily express the symbols of an organized religion? There are no recognizable religious buildings or elaborate burials in the Indus cities ("Clearly, they did not expect huge demands on the dead in the after-life"[94]), no signs of ancestral rituals or "magnificent icons" or any "specially decorated structures." The conclusion is clear enough: "If there were temples they are difficult to identify. . . . The cities may not therefore have been the focus of religious worship."[95] Yet the same fact—that no great temple or center of worship has been found as yet at Mohenjo-Daro—has inspired a very different conclusion: One place where such a structure might have been situated, just east of the bath, has not been excavated because a Buddhist stupa (reliquary mound) stands there, and permission has never been granted to move it.[*96] The stupa is indeed a strong hint that the structure underneath it might have been religious, for Buddhism shares with other religions (including, notably, Hinduism and Islam) the habit of sacred recycling, putting one religious building on the site hallowed by another, the funeral baked meats served cold for the wedding breakfast that follows. And one might argue that it would be odd if given the great regulation and standardization of everything else in public life, the governing powers did not also regulate belief. But all speculations about the role of religion in the lives of the IVC people rest on doubtful retrospective hindsight from Hindu practices many centuries later.[97]

The assumption of a theocratic elite in the IVC underpins the assertion that the images depicted on pictographic seal inscriptions and terra-cotta figures are divinities and that animism, demonic cults, fertility cults, and the worship of natural forces and mother goddesses flourished in the IVC.[98] But surely it's possible that the people of the IVC had no religion at all, in the sense of a state cult or an enforced dogma. Is it possible that this was the first secular state, anticipating the European Enlightenment by four thousand years? Could they have been more like protoatheists than protoyogis? After all, there were many people in later Hinduism who had no use for religion, people such as the Char-

---

[*] Marshall was dying to excavate beneath the stupa but was shackled by the archaeological survey rules. He seriously contemplated (and may actually have tried) lining up all the workmen on the stupa, on the pretext of taking their photograph, in the hope that their weight would bring it down. Personal communication from the Honorable Penelope Chetwode (later Lady Betjeman), to whom Marshall confessed this episode when he was courting her, years later. Wantage, England, 1969.

vakas and the Lokayatas ("Materialists").[99] (If people are going to argue *for* religious meanings from hindsight, one might as well also argue *against* it from hindsight; two can play at that game.) Just as it has been well argued that there is a very good reason why the IVC language remains undeciphered—because the seals may not record any language at all, merely random symbols of ownership[100]—so too we may argue that the other symbols are not part of a coherent religious system but equally random artistic creations.

THE END OF THE INDUS

No one knows how the IVC came to an end. Perhaps it simply ran its course, had its day in the sun, and then the sun, as always, set on that empire. Perhaps it was destroyed by drought. Perhaps the Indus River changed its course, or there was an earthquake.[101] Perhaps massive deforestation degraded the environment. Perhaps the people died of diseases such as severe anemia, as the skeletal remains of what was previously interpreted as a "massacre" suggest.[102] Perhaps it was destroyed by invasions. Last but certainly not least, perhaps it was destroyed by a flood; whatever caused the actual destruction, floods did eventually bury the cities in many layers of Indus mud, which caused both the ground level and the water table to rise by ten meters. Immigrations of new peoples, droughts, deforestation, floods, or alterations in the course of the life-giving river: any of these may have been contributing factors.[103] Whatever the cause, the result was that "on top of the cities, now consigned to oblivion beneath tons of alluvium, other peoples grazed their goats, sowed their seeds and spun their myths. A great civilization was lost to memory."[104] But was it in fact lost?

The flood that may have destroyed the Indus cities may have been the inspiration for the myth of the great flood that is described in the *Shatapatha Brahmana* (c. 800 BCE) and that continues to haunt Hindu mythology to the present day. And it is tempting to argue that some or all of these stories are memories of (if not evidence for) a great flood that destroyed the IVC. But it would be better, I think, to resist that temptation and simply to suggest that present-day scholarly (or nonscholarly) theories of a catastrophic flood at the end of the Indus Valley Civilization were inspired by the myth of the flood, that the scholarly theories themselves are merely the latest variants of the myth of the flood.

TRANSFORMATIONS THROUGH TIME: FAST-FORWARD

Arguments from hindsight pervade the scholarship on the IVC, underpinning correlations between the quasi unicorn and the sage whose mother was an antelope, between the Lord of Beasts on the seal and Shiva, between various images of women and later Hindu goddesses, between the "Great Bath" and the bathing tanks of Hindu temples, between small conical objects that have been interpreted as phallic stones (but may just be pieces used in board games) and the Shiva linga. The obsession with descendants, arguing that the IVC seal can be explained by what we know of Shiva as Lord of Beasts, is the other side of the coin of the obsession with origins, arguing that the figure of Shiva as Lord of Beasts is derived from, and to some extent explained by, the IVC seal. The two approaches scratch each other's backs. The fascination with the IVC comes in part from the intrinsic appeal of its artifacts but also from a perceived need to find *non-Vedic*, indeed *pre-Vedic* sources for most of Hinduism—for Shiva and goddess worship and all the rest of Hinduism that is not attested in the Vedas.

On the other hand, it is always tempting to look for the keys to the IVC where there is available light in later Hinduism, to let Hindu phenomena, which have the context of texts to explain them, illuminate the darkness that surrounds many early Indus images and objects that lack such verbal commentaries. But too often scholars read the Indus images like the pictures in the puzzle books of my youth: How many (Hindu) deer can you see hiding in this (Indus) forest? Throughout this chapter, and indeed throughout this book, I have poured into my ears the wax of pedantic caution, in an attempt (sometimes in vain) to resist the siren song of hindsight. For fig trees, horns, bulls, phalluses, and buxom women do play a central role in later Hinduism, and such images may have been important to Hindus in part because they never lost some of the power they had had in the Indus period. Although these images certainly also occur in many other cultures, the hypothesis that Hinduism inherited them from the Indus seems a more efficient explanation than coincidence or independent origination. Nor is there any likely source (with the possible, but by no means established, exception of Elam) from which the two cultures could have borrowed the same images. It is probable that the forms survived; the mistake is in assuming that the function follows the form. The inhabitants of both Mohenjo-Daro and modern Mumbai had bulls, but they surely had very different ideas about bulls.

It is useful to distinguish hindsight from fast-forwarding. Hindsight often misreads an earlier phenomenon by assuming that it meant then the same thing that it meant later, reading the past through the present, forgetting that we cannot simply lay the present over the past like a plastic map overlay. The false Orientalist assumptions that India was timeless and that the classical texts of the Brahmins described an existing society led to the equally false assumption that the village and caste organization of colonial or even contemporary India was a guide to their historical past.[105]

But at times the atavisms, the modern traces of ancient phenomena, are so striking that it would be perverse to ignore them, and from time to time I have fast-forwarded to note them. We should not impose the meaning of the later icons upon the earlier images, but once we have explored the meaning of the Indus representations within the constrictions of their own limited context, we can go on to speculate on how they may have contributed to the evolution of a later iconography that they sometimes superficially resemble.[106]

For the resemblances between some aspects of the IVC and later Hinduism are simply too stunning to ignore. As the Late Harappan culture declined, its survivors must have carried some of it into the Ganges-Yamuna basin. There are links between archaeological records among the communities of the third millennium BCE, which used only stone and bronze, and the people of the Gangetic plain and the Deccan in around 1000 BCE, who developed the use of iron. At this time, or even a few centuries earlier (in 1500 BCE), the process of urbanization moved gradually south from the Indus cities to the site of Kaushambi, near modern Allahabad in the Gangetic plain, and to the surrounding villages. The material culture does not show continuities; the use of bricks of standard sizes, the geometrical grids, the seals, the sewers, the large urban plan, none of this is preserved.[107] Above all, the technique of administration was lost; not for many centuries would anyone know how to govern such a large community in India. But someone succeeded in preserving on the journey south and east some of the cultural patterns nurtured in the Indus cities, for some of these patterns lived on long after the cities themselves were gone.[108] The Indus civilization may not have simply gone out like the flame of a candle or, at least, not before lighting another candle.

We can see the possible survival, in transformation, of a number of images. The Harappan motif of the fig (pipal)—as a leaf decoration on pottery and as a tree on seals—reappears in the imagery of some later religious sects.[109] There is a conch shell, etched in vermilion, that may well have been used as a libation vessel, just as conch shells, etched in vermilion, are used in Hinduism today. Not only individual images but also aspects of the art forms—especially the

Horse on the Ashokan Column at Sarnath.

so-called animal style, stylized and rounded, with just a few meticulous and suggestive details—seem to have survived. Some of the stylized depictions of the animals on the seals bear a striking resemblance to the depictions of the same animals two thousand years later (and magnified many hundredfold) on the capital plinths of the pillars of Ashoka.[110] These patterns, and the rough outlines of other images that we have considered, perhaps even the stone lingas and the voluptuous women, may have gradually merged with the culture of the people of the Veda.

CHAPTER 4
BETWEEN THE RUINS AND THE TEXT
2000 to 1500 BCE

༄

CHRONOLOGY (ALL DATES BCE)

c. 4000–3000 *Indo-European breaks up into separate languages

c. 2100–2000 Light-spoked chariots are invented

c. 2000–1500 Indus civilization declines

c. 1900 Sarasvati River dries up

c. 1700–1500 Nomads in the Punjab compose the *Rig Veda;* horses arrive in Northwest India

c. 1350 Hittite inscriptions speak about horses and gods

c. 900 The Vedic people move down into the Ganges Valley

VISHNU AND BRAHMA CREATE EACH OTHER

When the three worlds were in darkness, Vishnu slept in the middle of the cosmic ocean. A lotus grew out of his navel. Brahma came to him and said, "Tell me, who are you?" Vishnu replied, "I am Vishnu, creator of the universe. All the worlds, and you yourself, are inside me. And who are you?" Brahma replied, "*I* am the creator, self-created, and everything is inside me." Vishnu then entered Brahma's body and saw all three worlds in his belly. Astonished, he came out of Brahma's mouth and said, "Now, you must enter my belly in the same way and see the worlds." And so Brahma entered Vishnu's belly and saw all the worlds. Then, since Vishnu had shut all the openings, Brahma came out of Vishnu's navel and rested on the lotus.

—*Kurma Purana* (500–800 CE)[1]

THE PROBLEM: THINGS WITHOUT WORDS,
WORDS WITHOUT THINGS

What was the relationship between the people who composed the Vedas (the ancient Sanskrit texts beginning with the *Rig Veda*, in around 1500 BCE) and the people who lived in the Indus River Valley? Where were the people of the Indus Valley Civilization after the end of the IVC? The myth of the mutual creation of the gods Brahma (the creator) and Vishnu (one of the great male gods of Hinduism) provides us with a basic metaphor with which to consider the connections between Vedic and non-Vedic aspects of Hinduism. It is a third way of dealing with false dichotomies: Where the image of the man/rabbit in the moon represented two simultaneous paradigms, and the image of one woman's head on another's body represented the fusion of one culture with another, the mutual creation of Brahma and Vishnu represents such a fusion in which neither can claim priority.

The non-Veda, if I may call it that, has been a largely uncredited partner of Hinduism, for we have heard it only at those relatively late historical moments when it crashed the Sanskrit club. The only way we can tell the story of the literature of the Hindus is to begin with those texts that survived—the Sanskrit texts—but at the same time we must acknowledge, right from the start, from the time of the *Rig Veda*, the presence of something else in these texts, something that is non-Vedic.

Between about 2000 and 1500 BCE, one culture in Northwest India was dying and another was beginning to preserve its poetry. Fade out: Indus Valley Civilization (IVC). Fade in: the Vedas. Each of these cultures may have been in some way a prequel to Hinduism. The objects of the IVC, things without words, give us a certain kind of information about the people who lived there, but no evidence of where the people of the IVC went after the death of their cities (and, presumably, their texts). With the Vedas we have the opposite problem, words without (most) things (just a few pots and an altar or two), and many words *about* things, but without much physical evidence about the daily life of the people who first spoke those words or, again, about where they came from. Before we can begin to talk about people, however, we need to say a word about words, about language, and about the prehistory of the people who composed the *Rig Veda*.

*Indo-Europe, the Land East of the Asterisk

Nineteenth-century German and British linguists, building on some seventeenth-and eighteenth-century hunches,* demonstrated that Vedic Sanskrit was one of the oldest recorded forms of a language family that included ancient Greek and Latin, Hittite (in ancient Anatolia), the Celtic and Norse-Germanic languages, and, ultimately, French, German, Italian, Spanish, English, and all their friends and relations.[2] All these languages are alleged to have run away from the home of a single parent language sometime in the fourth millennium BCE,[3] a language that linguists call Indo-European (or Indo-Germanic or Indo-Aryan—more about the overtones of this word, below), more precisely, *Indo-European. We have no attested examples of that language before the breakup; the *Indo-European speakers almost certainly had no knowledge of writing,[4] and the earliest example of an Indo-European language that we have is a fourteenth-century BCE Anatolian treaty in Hittite that calls on the Hittite version of several Vedic gods: Indra, Mitra, Varuna, and the Ashvins [Nasatyas]). Therefore, an apologetic or apotropaic asterisk usually hovers over the reconstructed, hypothetical (nowadays we would say virtual) forms of Indo-European (or *Proto-Indo-European, as it is usually called, as easy as *PIE) to indicate the absence of any actual occurrences of the word. For instance, linguists use the Latin *equus*, Gallic *epos*, Greek *hippos*, Sanskrit *ashśva*, old English *eoh*, French *cheval*, and so forth, to reconstruct the *PIE word for "horse": *Heḳwo-, or *eḳwos to its pals in the linguists' club. And *deiwos develops into *deus* in Latin, *deva* in Sanskrit, *divo* in Russian, and, eventually, our English "Tues[day]" as well as "divine." Sanskrit and Iranian (or Avestan) formed one of the oldest subfamilies, Indo-Iranian, within this larger group.

How are we to explain the fact (and it is a fact) that people speak one form or another of Indo-European languages from India to Ireland? The hypothesis that a single parent language was the historical source of all the known Indo-European languages is not an observable fact, but linguists regard it as an "inescapable hypothesis."[5] The Indo-European map is linguistic, linking languages

---

* Bishop Walton, in his Introduction to the London Polyglot Bible, in 1672, first noted the connection of Greek and Latin. A Persian grammarian in Delhi in 1720 discovered the Greek and Sanskrit connection. Sir William Jones, in 1788, wrote about common elements in Greek, Roman, and ancient Indian religion and postulated a historical connection. Yet F. Max Müller, who popularized the theory in the nineteenth century, is often given most of the credit.

together in a family (a rather dysfunctional family, but a family) that is distinct from, for instance, Chinese or the Semitic languages (Hebrew, Arabic) or, more significantly for Hinduism, Tamil and the other South Indian languages in the group called Dravidian. The majority of people in India speak an Indo-European language (76 percent), with Dravidian-language speakers accounting for 22 percent, and the remaining 2 percent taken up by Austro-Asiatic, Tibeto-Burman, and tribal languages.

The evidence that the Indo-European languages are related lies primarily in their grammar and vocabulary. Thus the Sanskrit *agni* ("fire") is cognate with Latin *ignis*, English "ignite"; "foot" is *pada* in Sanskrit, *pes, pedis* in Latin, *pied* in French, *Fuss* in German, *foot* in English; and so forth. Many Sanskrit words have English cognates: for example, the Sanskrit *pashu* ("cattle"), preserved in the Latin *pecus*, is embedded in the English "impecunious" ("out of cattle, or low on cash").

But the temptation to draw simple conclusions about nonverbal facts from such verbal correspondences must be resisted; the fact that the word for "hand" is different in most of these languages should not be taken to mean that the Indo-European speakers had feet but not hands. So too, people change while words remain the same; words are often, as the French say, "false friends" (*faux amis*), the same word meaning something different in two different languages, often the very opposite thing. Meanings change in time even within a single culture. Antigods, Asuras (whose name incorporates the word *asu*, "breath"), are the equal and morally indistinguishable elder brothers and rivals of the gods in the Indo-European or at least Indo-Iranian period (when Ahura Mazda, the "great Asura," is the chief god of the Avesta), but they later become totally demonic demons. ("Demons," for that matter, were once benevolent *daimon*s in Greek, before the Christians demonized them, as it were). Sanskrit then created a back formation, taking Asura to mean "non-Sura" (splitting off the initial *a* of *asu* to make an *a* in its privative sense, as in "a-theist") and inventing the word "Suras" (now said to derive from *sura*, "wine") to apply to the wine-drinking gods, the anti-antigods. Although this sort of reasoning might be called etymo-logic, certainly not logic, people persist in using lexicons as the basis of history and in building elaborate theories about social systems and homelands on this flimsy Indo-European linguistic scaffolding.

Indo-European is a language group; technically, there are no Indo-Europeans, merely Indo-European speakers. But since European scholars also assumed, quite reasonably, that wherever the languages went, there had to be people to carry them, Indo-European speakers are often called Indo-Europeans. Moreover, we are able to construct some of Indo-European culture, not merely from isolated words and parallel grammar structures but from the more substantial historical, linguistic, and archaeological evidence. For instance, we know that cattle rustling was the basic trade of all of the Indo-European speakers, from the Celts to the Indians, because closely parallel myths from Greece, India, Iran, northern Europe, the Near East, and Scandinavia allow us to reconstruct a *Proto-Indo-European cattle raiding myth.[6]

Who were these cattle rustlers? More broadly, what is the relationship between the language and the geographical origin and ethnic identity of the *PIE people? Or to put it differently and to limit it to the culture that is the subject of this book . . .

WHERE WERE THE PEOPLE WHO COMPOSED THE VEDAS BEFORE THEY COMPOSED THE VEDAS?

We do not know for sure, but we can guess, and the craze for origins makes us guess. Some guesses make more sense than others. Here are the four most often cited.

FIRST GUESS: THE ARYANS INVADED INDIA FROM *INDO-EUROPE

"Once upon a time," the story goes, "blue-haired, blond-eyed people from the north drove their chariots into India and beat the hell out of the dark-skinned people who lived there." (The northern element was often taken to the extreme. In 1903, Bal Gangadhar Tilak argued, in his *The Arctic Home in the Vedas*, that the Aryans had composed the Vedas at the North Pole and, on the journey south, divided into two branches, one of which went to Europe, the other to India.) Not surprisingly, nineteenth-century European scholars, serving colonial powers, favored theories of cultural interaction involving invasions or colonization, and the theory that the Vedic people invaded India still has general currency. Behind this guess lies the assumption of a diffusionist, centrifugal cultural movement; like an airline hub dispersing planes, the political center sends out armies and imposes its rule on the neighboring lands. The paradigm of this model is Latin, which did indeed diffuse outward from Rome to all the lands that the Romans conquered and that therefore speak the so-called Romance languages. Linguists then constructed, on the Roman model, an earlier family tree of languages diverging from the center, in this case not from Rome but from the Caucasus, somewhere east of the southern Urals, in southeastern Russia, perhaps on the shores of the northern Black Sea or the Sea of Azov.[7] (This is where, as we will see, someone—probably, though not certainly, the *Indo-European people—probably domesticated horses, an event of great significance for the history of Hinduism.) Therefore, the *Indo-European people were also called Caucasians. The mythical land of their family home, recently rechristened Eurostan,[8] might just as well be thought of as *Indo-Europe, the land East of the Asterisk.

According to this scenario, one branch of this group traveled down the east side of the Caspian Sea and continued east through Afghanistan, reaching the Punjab before the middle of the second millennium BCE.[9] But to say that the languages formed a family is *not* to say that the people who spoke them formed a race. There is nothing intrinsically racist about this story of linguistic migration. On the contrary, the eighteenth-century discovery of the Indo-European link was, at first, a preracial discovery of brotherhood; these people are our (linguistic) cousins. But then the nineteenth-century Orientalists, who now had a theory of race to color their perceptions, gave it a distinctly racist thrust. Their attitude to the nineteenth-century inhabitants of India came to something like "Well, they are black, but their skin color is irrelevant; they are white inside, Greek inside, just like us." There were also anti-Semitic implications: One reason why British and German scholars were so happy to discover Sanskrit was that they were delighted to find a language older than Hebrew (which they regarded as, on the one hand, their own language, the language of what they called the Old Testament and, on the other hand, the language of the despised "others," the Jews, for whom the book was the Hebrew Bible). At last, they thought, Hebrew was no longer the oldest language in the world.

Racism quickly came to color the English usage of the Sanskrit word *arya*, the word that the Vedic poets used to refer to themselves, meaning "Us" or "Good Guys," long before anyone had a concept of race. Properly speaking, "Aryan" (as it became in English) designates a linguistic family, not a racial group (just as Indo-European is basically a linguistic rather than demographic term); there are no Aryan noses, only Aryan verbs, no Aryan people, only Aryan-speaking people. Granted, the Sanskrit term does refer to people rather than to a language. But the people who spoke *Indo-European were not a people in the sense of a nation (for they may never have formed a political unity) or a race, but only in the sense of a linguistic community.[10] After all those migrations, the blood of several different races had mingled in their veins.

Nevertheless, the Orientalist version of the Aryan hypothesis boasted not only of the purity of Aryan blood but of the quantity of non-Aryan blood that the Aryans spilled, and this myth was certainly racist. The "invasion of the blonds" story took root and prevailed for many reasons, among them that the British found a history of invasions of India a convenient way to justify their own military conquest of India. And of course the story became an even more racist myth when the Nazis got hold of it and made "Aryan" a word that, like "gay," or "holocaust," or "adult" (in the sense of "pornographic," as in "adult books and films, adult viewing"), no longer means what it once meant.* People always think about race when you say "Aryan," even though you tell them not to; we can't forget what we now know about the word; we can't regain our earlier naiveté. "Hindu" is a somewhat tainted word, but there is no other easy alternative; "Aryan," by contrast, is a *deeply* tainted word, and there are easy alternatives. It is therefore best to avoid using the *A* word, and to call the people who spoke Indo-European languages Indo-European speakers (or, less cumbersome, Indo-Europeans, though this implies an ethnic group).

And since the people who composed the Veda left few archaeological footprints, and all we know for certain about them is that they composed the Veda, let us call its authors, and their community, the Vedic people.

A frequent corollary to the Indo-European invasion theory is the hypothesis that the Vedic people were responsible for the end of the Indus Valley cities. Invasion implies conquest, and who else was there for them to conquer in India? The advocates of this theory cite statements in the Veda about knocking down the fortresses of the barbarians, for the Indus cities did have massive fortification walls.[11] They also cite what they interpret as archaeological evidence of sudden, mass deaths in the Indus Valley, and the verses of the *Rig Veda* that refer to the Dasas as dark-skinned (7.5.3) or dark (1.130.8, 9.41.1, 9.73.5), though the term in question more often refers to evil than to skin color,[12] as well as the one Vedic verse that describes them as snub-nosed ("noseless"†) (5.29.10). Put these data together and you have blond Vedic people responsible for mass death to dark-skinned people in the Indus Valley.

But there is no reason to make this connection. The Vedic people had other

---

* The Nazis also grotesquely distorted, and inverted, both the form and the meaning of the ancient Indian symbol of the swastika, whose Sanskrit name simply meant "a good thing." The swastika has a radically different meaning in Europe and America from the meaning that it had, and still has, inside India. Once we know its Indian origins, we see the swastika with double vision, as we see the duck-rabbit, or the rabbit/man in the moon: It is Vedic and Nazi, recondite and demagogic, at the same time.
† Though the word may mean "mouthless"—i.e., without [our] language.

enemies, and the Indus Valley people had other, more likely sources of destruction, nor is there reliable evidence that their cities were ever sacked.[13] Moreover, it is more likely that the Indo-European incursions came in a series of individual or small group movements, rather than the one, big charge of the light(-skinned) brigade scenario imagined by this first guess.

The smug theory that a cavalcade of Aryans rode roughshod into India, bringing civilization with them, has thus been seriously challenged. The certainty has gone, and new answers have thrown their hats into the ring, just as politically driven as the Aryan invasion theory, and, like most politically driven scholarship (but is there really any other kind?), ranging from plausible (if unsupported) to totally bonkers.

SECOND GUESS: THE CAUCASIANS STROLLED IN FROM THE CAUCASUS

"Once upon a time," the story goes, "people from the north brought their families and their agriculture into India and settled among the people who lived there." The first guess, the Aryan invasion theory, is one of the great testosterone myths: They're guys, they beat everyone up. This second guess, by replacing the word "invasion" with "migration," takes the military triumphalism out of the theory but retains the basic mechanism and the basic structures: Migrants may have brought an Indo-European language into India.[14] This approach accounts for a gradual cultural linguistic infusion into India, still with all the baggage that linguists load onto languages—the social classes, the mythology— and supported by the same linguistic evidence, archaeological evidence (such as burial customs[15]) and pottery that support the invasion theory.[16] Those who hold by either of these two theories (invasion or migration) have recourse to later Indian history. The two powers that built the greatest empires in India, the forces of Central Asian Turks and of the British Raj, first entered India not as military conquerors but as traders and merchants, but in the end, it took force majeure to establish and maintain the control of the subcontinent.

Martin West, a leading scholar of Indo-European languages, disdains the idea that the Indo-European speakers came not as conquerors but as peaceful migrants: "In the last fifty years or so there has been a scholarly reaction against the old idea of militant hordes swarming out of Eurostan with battle-axes held high and occupying one territory after another. It has been fashionable to deride this model and to put all the emphasis on peaceful processes of population and language diffuision."[17] But, he continues, both on the analogy with the way that in observable history, other linguistic groups (such as Arabic, Turkic, Latin,

Celtic, and German, as well as English and Spanish in the New World, which West does not mention) "grew multitudinous and poured across the length and breadth of Europe," and considering the fact that "there are constant references to battles and descriptions of fighting" in Indo-European poetic and narrative traditions, it appears "by no means implausible that similar bouts of aggressive migration in earlier eras played a large part in effecting the Indo-European diaspora." This theory, which is quite plausible, is no longer regarded as PC (in the double sense of "postcolonial" or "politically correct"), because of its political history, and the aptly named Professor West can make it only because he is privileged to belong to a generation of Western (more precisely British) scholars for whom "PC" stands for nothing but "police constable."

THIRD GUESS: THE VEDIC PEOPLE ORIGINATED IN INDIA

"From the dawn of history, *Indo-European speakers lived in India, in the Punjab, where they composed the *Rig Veda*." A stronger version of the theory adds: "They emigrated to Iran (where they composed the *Avesta*), Anatolia (leaving that early Hittite inscription), Greece and Italy (where they incorporated local languages to develop Greek and Latin), and, finally, ancient Britain." (The most extreme version of this guess adds: "All the languages in the world are derived from Sanskrit."[18]) In this view, the Vedic people may have been, rather than invaders (or immigrants) from southern Russia, "indigenous for an unknown period of time in the lower Central Himalayan regions,"[19] particularly in the Punjab. A variant of this argument presupposes not the same centrifugal diffusion that underlies the first two guesses (simply radiating from India instead of the Caucasus) but a centripetal convergence, into India rather than from the Caucasus: Separate languages came together in India, influencing their neighbors to produce a family resemblance; the people who spoke those separate languages came together and then took back home, like souvenirs, bits of one another's languages.

Why couldn't it have happened that way? In reaction to the blatantly racist spin and colonial thrust of the first two guesses, which imply that Europeans brought civilization to India, this theory says, "Look, we in India had civilization before you Europeans did!" (This is certainly true; no matter where they came from or what their relationship was, the people of the Indus were building great cities and the people of the Vedas creating a great literature at a time when the British were still swinging in trees.) And then it goes on to say, "You came from us. The people who created Vedic culture did not enter India; they began in India." As a theory, it is reasonable in itself, but there is considerable evidence against it,[20] and both linguistic and archaeological arguments render it even more purely speculative than the Aryan invasion theory.[21] It has the additional disadvantage of being susceptible to exploitation by the particular brand of Hindu nationalism that wants the Muslims (and Christians) to get out of India: "We were always here, not even just since the *Rig Veda*, but much, much earlier. This land was always ours."

FOURTH GUESS: THE VEDIC PEOPLE LIVED IN THE INDUS VALLEY

"Once upon a time, the people of the Indus Valley Civilization composed the Vedas." The final step is simply to assume that some or all of the inhabitants of the cities of Harappa and Mohenjo-Daro were themselves Indo-European speakers; that the people who built the cities also composed the Vedas,[22] that the Indus civilization itself is the site of the mythological Vedic age.[23] In favor of this is the evidence of some continuity between both the space and the time of the Indus and Vedic civilizations,[24] which almost certainly shared some of the territory of the greater Punjab during some part of the second millennium BCE, as well as a number of cultural features. One variant of this theory argues that (1) since there are Dravidian (and Munda) loan words in the Vedas (which is true), and (2) since the Harappan script is a form of Sanskrit (which is almost certainly not true, and certainly unproved, though reputable scholars as well as cranks have identified the Indus inscriptions as part of "the Indian/Persian/Indo-European religious system and Sanskrit language"[25]), therefore (3) the IVC is a hybrid Sanskrit/Dravidian culture produced by (4) Indo-European speakers who came from Europe to North India to interact with Dravidian speakers from India, starting in the middle of the fourth millennium BCE.[26]

This theory still assumes a migration into India from Europe, but one that is met by an earlier Dravidian presence. Some see in the Indus Valley not merely the seeds of later Hinduism but the very religion described in the almost con-temporaneous *Rig Veda;* they argue, for instance, that the brick platforms found in the Indus were used for Vedic sacrifices.[27] This hybrid is sometimes called the Sarasvati Valley culture, or the Indus-Sarasvati culture, because there were Indus settlements on the Sarasvati River (though it dried up around 1900 BCE) and the *Rig Veda* mentions a Sarasvati River.[28] But even when we grant that some sort of gradual cultural interaction took place, and not simply an invasion, it is not likely that the same people could have built the Indus cities and also composed the *Rig Veda*.

The linguistic and archaeological evidence against this fourth guess is pretty conclusive. It is hard work to fit the ruins of the IVC into the landscape of the *Rig Veda*.[29] The *Rig Veda* does not know any of the places or artifacts or urban techniques of the Indus Valley.[30] None of the things the Veda describes look like the things we see in the archaeology of the Indus. The *Rig Veda* never mentions inscribed seals or a Great Bath or trade with Mesopotamia, despite the fact that it glories in the stuff of everyday life. It never refers to sculptured representations of the human body.[31] It has no words, not even borrowed ones, for scripts or writing, for records, scribes, or letters.[32] After the Indus script, writing was not used again in India until the time of Ashoka, in the third century BCE.

Many of the words that the *Rig Veda* uses for agricultural implements, such as the plow, as well as words for furrow and threshing floor and, significantly, rice, come from non-Sanskritic languages, suggesting that the Vedic people learned much of their agriculture from communities in place in India before they arrived. But the Indus people, who obviously did have plows and mortar, presumably would have had their own words for them. Even in the Vedic period, there was multilingualism. But how could the Vedic people have forgotten about architecture, about bricks, about mortar (let alone about writing)? The answer is simple enough: They had never had them. In the good old days they had always slept on their saddlebags, and once they got to the Punjab they built in wood and straw, like the first two of the three little piggies, not in brick, like the third (and like the Indus people).

It is therefore extremely unlikely that the Indus people composed the *Rig Veda*. The final nail in the coffin of this theory comes not from the rather technical linguistic arguments but from the testimony of animals, particularly horses.

Lions and Tigers and Rhinos, Oh My!

Animals in general provide strong clues; they make suggestions, sometimes overwhelmingly persuasive suggestions, if not airtight proofs. The evidence of animals suggests that the civilizations of the Indus Valley and the Vedas were entirely different, though this does not mean that they did not eventually interact. The *Rig Veda* mentions (here in alphabetical order) ants, antelope, boars, deer, foxes, gazelles, jackals, lions, monkeys, rabbits, rats, quail, and wolves, and other Vedas mention bears, beaver, elk, hares, lynxes, and otters.[33] The *Rig Veda* also mentions lions (10.28.11), though the Vedic people had to invent a word for "lion"[34] (and to borrow a word for "peacock"[35]). (Lions may or may not be depicted in the Indus Valley; there's a figurine that *might* be a lion or a tiger.)

The Vedic people knew the elephant but regarded it as a curiosity; they had to make up a word for it and called it "the wild animal with a hand" *(mriga-hastin)*. But they do not mention tigers or rhinoceroses, animals familiar from the Harappan seals. Nor are there any references to unicorns, mythical or real.[36] The zoological argument from silence ("the lion that didn't roar in the night") is never conclusive (beware the false negative; the absence of evidence is not evidence of absence), but all this suggests that the Vedic people originally lived north of the land where the tiger and the elephant roam, and generally north of the Indus rhinoceroses, on the nonfalsifiable assumption that people who had seen an animal as weird as a rhinoceros would have mentioned it.

TALKING HORSES

Cattle are central to both cultures—though the Indus Valley Civilization favored bulls, the Vedas cows—as well as to many other ancient cultures and therefore of little use as differentiating markers. But the IVC does not seem to know, or care about, the horse, who speaks loudly and clearly in the Vedas (as horses are said to do, beginning in the Vedic tale of the Ashvins—twin horse-headed gods). Let us consider first the possible existence and then the symbolic importance of the horse in each of the two cultures.

On the one hand, wherever Indo-European-speaking cultures have been identified, evidence of horses has been found.[37] This does not in itself prove that an ancient culture with *no* horses is *not* Indo-European,[38] nor does it follow that wherever people had horses, they spoke Indo-European languages. Indo-European culture is contained within the broader range of ancient horse-having cultures, such as China and Egypt. For one thing, the ancestor of the horse, the so-called Dawn Horse, or *Eohippus*, much smaller than the modern horse, lived throughout Europe as well as North America in the Eocene age ("the dawn of time"), some sixty to forty million years ago. The horse was probably domesticated in several places, and it didn't happen all at once even in Central Asia.

Nevertheless, the spread of the Central Asian horse (and, after around 2000 BCE, the chariot, for people rode astride for a long time before they began to drive horses) suggests that in general, when Indo-Aryan speakers arrived somewhere, horses trotted in at the same time, and the archaeological record supports the hypothesis that Indo-European speakers did in fact ride and/or drive, rather than walk, into India. For the horse is not indigenous to India. There is archaeological evidence of many horses in the northwest of the Indian subcontinent only in the second millennium BCE, after the decline of the IVC.

Horse bits and copper and iron objects were used in Maharashtra, and horse paraphernalia (such as bits) south of the Narmada during or after this period suggest an extensive network of horse traders from northwestern India.[39]

By contrast, the absence of a thriving horse population in the IVC, the fact that even adamant opponents of Guesses One and Two must admit that the horse seems not to have played a significant role in the Harappan economy,[40] supports the hypothesis that the Indus Valley people were not Indo-European speakers.[41] Yet the ink was scarcely dry on such statements when people started racing around trying to find horse skeletons in the Indus Valley closet. Now, though it has been asserted with some confidence that no remains of horses have been found anywhere in the Indus Valley culture[42] or, somewhat more tentatively, that "the horse was probably unknown" to the Indus people,[43] there is archaeological evidence for the possible existence of *some* horses in the IVC, if very few. From time to time people have come up with what appear to be the bones of quasihorses, protohorses like the donkey, or the Dawn Horse, or the ass or onager; but horse bones are hard to decipher, and these are much disputed. All in all, there may well have been, here or there in the Indus Valley, a horse that loped in from Central Asia or even West Asia.

But such horses were probably imported, like so many other items, in the course of the vigorous IVC international trade.[44] India's notorious lack of native bloodstock may have been, already in the Indus Valley, as ever after, "the Achilles heel of its ambitious empire-builders."[45] For from the time of the settlements in the Punjab, the Indian love of horses—perhaps imprinted by the early experience of the Indo-Europeans in lands north of India, where horses thrived— was challenged by the simple fact that horses do not thrive on the Indian subcontinent and therefore need to be imported constantly. The evidence for the importing of horses can be used to support Guess One (or at least to counter Guesses Three and Four): The IVC had no horses of its own, so could not have been Indo-European speakers. And so the IVC could have played no part in the most ancient Hindu text, the *Rig Veda*, which is intensely horsey.

But in fact the existence of trade in horses at this time, which seems very likely indeed, can be used to *undercut* rather than support the argument that the Indo-Aryans invaded India on horseback (Guess One), for one could argue that the Vedic people too imported their horses rather than rode (or drove) them in. Assuming that the Indo-Europeans began in India, one can argue that they eventually emigrated to the Caspian and Black Sea coasts and domesticated the horse there, perhaps learning the trick from the natives; then they sent both the horses and the horse-taming knowledge back to their Indian homeland, and that's how horses got into the Vedas.[46] According to this scenario, it was the horses, not the Indo-European-speaking peoples, that were imported. By separating the entrance into India of the people and their horses, hypothesizing that the people came quite early and only later began to import their horses from the Caucasus, once someone *else* had domesticated them,[47] one might still argue for Guess Three (Indo-Europeans first began in India and, later, imported horses) or even for Guess Four (Indo-Europeans began in the IVC and, later, imported horses).

So much for the rather iffy archaeological record of real horses. The cultural use of the horses of the imagination, however, makes a more persuasive argument against Guess Four.

Talking horses, like real horses, are Indo-European but not only Indo-European. Tales of intimate relationships between heroes and their horses are, like the historical mastery of the horse, the common property of Indo-Europeans and the Turkic peoples of Central Asia.[48] A specific historical tradition from Indo-European prehistory is strongly suggested by parallel epithets and other predicates applied to horses in the Greek and Indo-Iranian texts.[49] A fourteenth-century BCE Hittite text on the training of horses uses words of Indo-European provenance. Horses, observed in affectionate, minute, often gory, detail, pervade the poetry of the *Rig Veda*. The Vedic people not only *had* horses but were crazy about horses.

But horses are not depicted at all in the extensive Indus art that celebrates so many other animals. The Indus people were crazy about animals, but not about horses. So widely accepted is the "horse = Indo-European" equation that even when one or two clay figurines that appear to depict horses were found at a few Indus sites, these were said to "reflect foreign travel or imports," though the same arguments for the importing of horses applies to the importing of images of horses and disqualify these figurines as evidence one way or another. But more tellingly, "The horse, the animal central to the Rig Veda, is absent from the Harappan seals"[50] and "unimportant, ritually and symbolically, to the Indus civilization."[51] Such statements too have acted as a gauntlet to provoke rebuttal. Recently an animal on an Indus seal was identified as a horse,[52] but it soon appeared that the seal was upside down, and the animal wasn't a horse at all, but a fabrication, a unicorn bull made to look like a horse—that is, a (real) unicorn masquerading as a (mythical) horse.[53] In Europe, people constructed unicorns by sticking a horn on a horse, either tying a horn onto a real horse or drawing a horn onto a picture of a horse. Only in India does it work the other way around, for on Indus seals, unicorns are real and horses nonexistent.

The absence of representations of horses in the IVC does not mean that they did not have real horses; they might have had them without regarding them as any more worthy of representation than the cows that we know they had and did not depict. Arguments from silence, it will be recalled, may prove to be false negatives, though this particular argument is somewhat supported by the archaeological evidence that there were few, if any, horses. The absence of equine imagery therefore neither proves nor disproves the first three guesses. It does, however, argue strongly against Guess Four, for it is very hard to believe that the hippophiles who composed the Veda would exclude the horse from the stable of animals that they depicted on their seals.

Thus horses do furnish a key to the Indus/Vedic mystery: No Indus horse whinnied in the night. Knowing how important horses are in the Vedas, we may deduce that there was little or no Vedic input into the civilization of the Indus Valley or, correspondingly, that there was little input from the IVC into the civilization of the *Rig Veda*. This does not mean, of course, that the IVC did not contribute in a major way to other, later developments of Hinduism.

An Alternative Answer: Fusion and *Bricolage*

It is therefore unlikely that both the Vedas and Harappa were "a product of the civilization of these two peoples,"[54] but it is more than likely that later Hinduism was a product of both of them, a linguistic and cultural combination of Vedic words and Indus images, as well as other contributions from other cultures. In some areas this combination was a fusion, a melting pot, a hybrid, while in others the elements kept their original shape and behaved more like a tossed salad, a multiplicity. This is of course quite different from saying that the Veda was composed in the Indus Valley cities. But even if the languages and cultures were distinct, as surely they were, people from the two cultures must have met. Ideas already current in India before the entry of the Vedic people or arising outside the Vedic world after that entry may have eventually filtered into Vedic and then post-Vedic Sanskrit literature.[55] (These ideas may have come not only from the IVC but also from the so-called Adivisis or "Original Inhabitants" of India, or from the Munda speakers and Dravidian speakers whose words are already incorporated in the *Rig Veda*, though that is another story.) Survivors of the Indus cities may have taught something of their culture to the descendants of the poets who composed the Vedas. The people of Harappa may have migrated south, so that their culture could have found its way into the strand of Hinduism that arose there.[56] Some elements of pre-Vedic Indo-European civilization may have been taken up by the last inhabitants of the Indus Valley. Some elements of the Indus civilization may have been adopted by the authors of later Vedic literature. Some combination of all of the above seems extremely likely.

A good example of this possible fusion is the case of bricks. The authors of the *Rig Veda* did not know about bricks; their rituals required only small mud altars, not large brick altars. But later, around 600 BCE, when the Vedic people had moved down into the Ganges Valley and their rituals had become more elaborate, they began to build large brick altars. The size of the mud bricks was a multiple or fraction of the height of the patron of the sacrifice, and a fairly sophisticated geometry was developed to work out the proportions.[57] We know that the Indus people had mastered the art of calculating the precise size of bricks, within a system of uniform and proportionate measurement. The use of bricks and the calculations in the Vedic ritual may therefore have come from a Harappan tradition, bypassed the Rig Vedic period, and resurfaced later.[58] This hypothesis must be qualified by the realization that kiln-fired (in contrast with sun-fired) brickwork does not reappear until the last centuries BCE,[59] a long time for that secret to lie dormant. But other aspects of brickmaking, and other ideas, may have been transmitted earlier.

Though the Vedic people told the story of their early life in India, and their descendants controlled the narrative for a very long time, most of what Hindus have written about and talked about and done, from the *Mahabharata* on, has not come from the Veda. In part because of the intertextuality and interpracticality of Hinduism, one text or ritual building on another through the centuries, right back to the Veda, scholars looking at the history of transmission have assumed that the Veda was the base onto which other things were added in the course of Indian history, just as Central Asia was the base that absorbed the impact of that interloping piece of Africa so long ago. And in the textual tradition, at least, this is true enough of the form in which the ideas were preserved, the chain of memorized texts. But from the standpoint of the ideas themselves, it was quite the opposite: The Veda was the newcomer that, like the African island fusing onto a preexisting continental base, combined with a preexisting cultural world consisting perhaps of the Indus Valley, perhaps of any of several other, more widely dispersed non-Vedic cultures.

The non-Veda is the *fons et origo* of Hinduism; new ideas, new narratives, new practices arose in the non-Sanskrit world, found their way into the Sanskrit world, and, often, left it again, to have a second or third or fourth life among the great vernacular traditions of India. These new narratives and practices fitted into the interstices between the plot lines of the great Sanskrit texts, as stories told in response to the protagonists' questions about places encountered on their travels or to illustrate a relevant moral point, or any other reason why. The non-Veda is not one thing but so many things. We have noted, briefly, and can rank in the order that their records appear in history, the existence of at least five cultures: (1) Stone Age cultures in India long before the Indus are the foundation on which all later cultures built. (2) At some point, impossible to fit into a chronology or even an archaeology, come the Adivasis, the "Original Inhabitants" of India, who spoke a variety of languages and contributed words and practices to various strands of Hinduism. Many of them were there long before the IVC and may have been a part of it; many of them have never been assimilated to Hinduism. Next come (3) the Indus civilization and (4) the village traditions that preceded, accompanied, and followed it, and after that (5) the culture of the Vedic people. Along the way, other language groups too, such as (6) the Tamils and other Dravidian speakers,[60] who may or may not have been a part of the IVC, added pieces to the puzzle.

Hinduism, like all cultures, is a *bricoleur*, a rag-and-bones man, building new things out of the scraps of other things. We've seen how the British used the stones of Mohenjo-Daro as ballast for their railway before (and after) they realized what those stones were and that a Buddhist stupa stands over some of the ruins there. So too Hindus built their temples on (and out of) Buddhist stupas as well as on other Hindu temples, and Muslims their mosques on Hindu temples (and Buddhist stupas), often reusing the original stones, new wine in old bottles, palimpsest architecture. In the realm of ideas as well as things, one religion would take up a word or image from another religion as a kind of objet trouvé. There are no copyrights there; all is in the public domain. This is not the hodgepodge that the Hindus and the early Orientalists regarded as dirt, matter out of place, evidence of an inferior status but, rather, the interaction of various different strains that is an inevitable factor in all cultures and traditions, and a Good Thing.

MUTUAL CREATION

A good metaphor for the mutual interconnections between Vedic and non-Vedic aspects of Hinduism is provided by the myth with which this chapter began, "Vishnu and Brahma Create Each Other." Each says to the other, "You were born from me," and both of them are right. Each god sees all the worlds and their inhabitants (including both himself and the other god) inside the belly of the other god. Each claims to be the creator of the universe, yet each contains the other creator. In other versions of this myth, each one calls the other *tata*, a two-way word that a young man can use to call an older man Grandpa, while an older man can use it to call a younger man Sonny Boy; the word actually designates the relationship between young and old.

The myth of Vishnu and Brahma is set at the liminal, in-between moment when the universe has been reduced to a cosmic ocean (dissolution) and is about to undergo a new creation, which in turn will be followed by another dissolution, then another creation, and so on ad infinitum—another series of mutual creations. Vedic and non-Vedic cultures create and become one another like this too throughout the history of Hinduism. This accounts for a number of the tensions that haunt Hinduism throughout its history, as well as for its extraordinary diversity.

CHAPTER 5

HUMANS, ANIMALS, AND GODS IN THE *RIG VEDA*

1500 to 1000 BCE

༺༻

CHRONOLOGY (ALL DATES BCE)

c. 1700–1500 Nomads in the Punjab region compose the *Rig Veda*

c. 1200–900 The Vedic people compose the *Yajur Veda*, *Sama Veda*, and *Atharva Veda*

DIVERSE CALLINGS

Our thoughts bring us to diverse callings, setting people apart:

the carpenter seeks what is broken,

the physician a fracture,

and the Brahmin priest seeks someone who presses soma.

I am a poet; my dad's a physician

and Mom a miller with grinding stones.

With diverse thoughts we all strive for wealth,

going after it like cattle.

Rig Veda (9.112) (c. 1500 BCE)

In this chapter we will encounter the people who lived in the Punjab in about 1500 BCE and composed the texts called the Vedas. We will face the violence embedded in the Vedic sacrifice of cattle and horses and situate that ritual violence in the social violence that it expresses, supports, and requires, the theft of other people's cattle and horses. We will then consider the social world of the Vedas, focusing first on the tension between the Brahmin and royal/martial classes (the first and second classes) and the special position of the fourth and lowest class, the servants; then on other marginalized people; and finally on women. Marginalization also characterizes people of all classes who fall prey to addiction and/or intoxication, though intoxication from the soma plant (pressed to yield juice) is the privilege of the highest gods and Brahmins.

Turning from the people to their gods, we will begin with the pluralism and multiplicity of the Vedic pantheon and the open-mindedness of its ideas about creation. Then we will consider divine paradigms for human priests and kings, the Brahminical god Agni (god of fire) and the royal gods Varuna (god of the waters) and Indra (the king of the gods). We will conclude with ideas about death and reincarnation that, on the one hand, show the same pluralistic range and speculative open-mindedness as the myths of creation and, on the other hand, set the scene for a major social tension among Hindus in centuries to come.

THE TRANSMISSION OF THE *RIG VEDA*

We have just considered at some length the question of the prehistory of the people who composed the *Rig Veda*, people who, sometime around 1500 BCE, in any case probably not earlier than the second millennium BCE,[1] were moving about in what is now the Punjab, in Northwestern India and Pakistan. They lived in the area of the Seven Rivers (Sapta Sindhu), the five tributaries of the Indus plus the Indus itself and the Sarasvati. We can see the remains of the world that the people of the Indus Valley built, but we are blind to the material world of the Vedic people; the screen goes almost blank. The Vedic people left no cities, no temples, scant physical remains of any kind; they had to borrow the word for "mortar."[2] They built nothing but the flat, square mud altars for the Vedic sacrifice[3] and houses with wooden frames and walls of reed stuffed with straw and, later, mud. Bamboo ribs supported a thatched roof. None of this of course survived.

But now at last our sound reception is loud and, for the most part, clear. Those nomads in the Punjab composed poems in an ancient form of Sanskrit; the oldest collection is called the *Rig Veda* ("Knowledge of Verses"). We can hear, and often understand, the words of the Vedas, even though words spoken so long ago are merely clues, not proofs, and interpretation, with all its biases, still raises its ugly head at every turn. The social and material world is vividly present in Vedic texts. What sort of texts are they?

The *Rig Veda* consists of 1,028 poems, often called mantras ("incantations"), grouped into ten "circles" ("mandalas"). (It is generally agreed that the first and last books are later additions, subsequent bookends around books 2–9.) The verses were rearranged for chanting as the *Sama Veda* ("Knowledge of Songs") and, with additional prose passages, for ritual use as the *Yajur Veda* ("Knowledge of Sacrifice"); together they are known as the three Vedas. A fourth, the *Atharva Veda* ("Knowledge of the Fire Priest"), devoted primarily to practical, worldly matters, and spells to deal with them, was composed later, sharing some poems with the latest parts of the *Rig Veda*.

The *Rig Veda* was preserved orally even when the Indians had used writing for centuries, for everyday things like laundry lists and love letters and gambling IOUs.[4] But they refused to preserve the *Rig Veda* in writing.[*] All Vedic rituals were accompanied by chants from the *Sama Veda*, which the priests memorized. The *Mahabharata* (13.24.70) groups people who read and recite the Veda from a written text (rather than memorize it and keep it only in their heads) with corrupters and sellers of the Veda as people heading for hell. A Vedic text states that "a pupil should not recite the Veda after he has eaten meat, seen blood or a dead body, had sexual intercourse, or engaged in writing."[5] It was a powerful text, whose power must not fall into the wrong hands. Unbelievers and infidels, as well as Pariahs and women, were forbidden to learn the Vedas, because they might defile or injure the power of the words,[6] pollute it like milk kept in a bag made of dogskin.

The oral text of the *Rig Veda* was therefore memorized in such a way that no physical traces of it could be found, much as a coded espionage message would be memorized and then destroyed (eaten, perhaps—orally destroyed) before it could fall into the hands of the enemy. Its exclusively oral preservation ensured that the *Rig Veda* could not be misused even in the right hands: you couldn't take the *Rig Veda* down off the shelf in a library, for you had to read it in the company of a wise teacher or guru, who would make sure that you understood its application in your life. Thus the Veda was usually passed down from father to son, and the lineages of the schools or "branches" (*shakhas*) that passed down commentaries "from one to another" (*param-para*) were often also family lineages, patriarchal lineages (*gotras*). Those who taught and learned the *Rig Veda* were therefore invariably male Brahmins in this early period, though later other classes too may have supplied teachers, and from the start those who

---

[*] Daniel H. H. Ingalls, in a talk recorded on film in 1980, remarked that the main thing that kept the authors of the *Mahabharata* from writing it down was the lack of inexpensive writing materials; you could hardly carve it all in rock, and they had not yet discovered the art of writing on palm leaves. This too would have applied to the Veda, but the *Mahabharata* was eventually written down at a time when the Veda was not.

composed the poems may well have been more miscellaneous, even perhaps including some women, to whom some poems are attributed.

The oral nature of the *Rig Veda* (and of the other Vedas too) was expressed in its name; it was called *shruti* ("what is heard"), both because it was originally "heard" (*shruta*) by the human seers to whom the gods dictated it but also because it continued to be transmitted not by being read or seen but by being *heard* by the worshipers when the priests chanted it.[7] The oral metaphor is not the only one—ancient sages also "saw" the Vedic verses—but it does reflect the dominant mode of transmission, orality. It made no more sense to "read" the Veda than it would simply to read the score of a Brahms symphony and never hear it.

Now, one might suppose that a text preserved orally in this way would be subject to steadily encroaching inaccuracy and unreliability, that the message would become increasingly garbled like the message in a game of telephone, but one would be wrong. For the very same sacredness that made it necessary to preserve the *Rig Veda* orally rather than in writing also demanded that it be preserved with meticulous accuracy. People regarded the *Rig Veda* as a revealed text, and one does not play fast and loose with revelation. It was memorized in a number of mutually reinforcing ways, including matching physical movements (such as nodding the head) with particular sounds and chanting in a group, which does much to obviate individual slippage. According to the myth preserved in the tradition of European Indology, when Friedrich Max Müller finally edited and published the *Rig Veda* at the end of the nineteenth century, he asked a Brahmin in Calcutta to recite it for him in Sanskrit, and a Brahmin in Madras, and a Brahmin in Bombay (each spoke a different vernacular language), and each of them said every syllable of the entire text exactly as the other two said it. In fact this academic myth flies in the face of all the available evidence; Müller produced his edition from manuscripts, not from oral recitation. (It is of these manuscripts that Müller remarks, "The MSS. of the Rig-veda have generally been written and corrected by the Brahmans with so much care that there are no various readings in the proper sense of the word."[8]) Yet like many myths, it does reflect a truth: People preserved the *Rig Veda* intact orally long before they preserved it intact in manuscript, but eventually it was consigned to writing (as were the originally oral poems the *Mahabharata* and the *Ramayana*).

Sanskrit, the language of authority, was taken up by the various people in India who spoke other languages. At the same time, Dravidian and Austro-

Asiatic languages (such as the Munda languages) began to enter Vedic Sanskrit. As usual, the linguistic traditions invented one another; Sanskrit influenced Tamil, and Tamil influenced Sanskrit. The Vedic tradition shows its awareness that different groups spoke different languages when it states that the four priests in the horse sacrifice address the horse with four different names, for when it carries men, they call it *ashva* ("horse"); when it carries Gandharvas,* they call it *vajin* ("spirited horse"); for antigods, *arvan* ("swift horse"); and for gods *haya* ("racehorse").[9] Presumably they expect each of these groups to have its own language,[10] which is evidence of a consciousness of multilingualism[11] or multiple dialects.

THE VIOLENCE OF SACRIFICE

Theirs was a "portable religion,"[12] one that they carried in their saddlebags and in their heads. As far as we can reconstruct their rituals from what is, after all, a hymnal, they made offerings to various gods (whom we shall soon encounter below) by throwing various substances, primarily butter, into a fire that flared up dramatically in response. The Vedic ritual of sacrifice (*yajna*) joined at the hip the visible world of humans and the invisible world of gods. The sacrifice established bonds (*bandhus*), homologies between the human world (particularly the components of the ritual) and corresponding parts of the universe. Ritual was thought to have effects on the visible and invisible worlds because of such connections, meta-metaphors that visualize many substances as two things at once—not just a rabbit and a man in the moon, but your eye and the sun.

All the poems of the *Rig Veda* are ritual hymns in some sense, since all were sung as part of the Vedic ceremony, but only some are self-consciously devoted to the meaning of the ritual. The verses served as mantras (words with powers to affect reality) to be pronounced during rituals of various sorts: solemn or semipublic rituals (royal consecrations and sacrifices of the soma plant), life cycle rituals (marriage, funeral, and even such tiny concerns as a baby's first tooth),[13] healing rituals, and both black and white magic spells (such as the ones we will soon see, against rival wives and for healthy embryos). Yet even here pride of place is given to the verbal rather than to the physical aspect of the

---

* Gandharvas (whose name is cognate with *centaur*) are semiequine figures, sometimes depicted in anthropomorphic form (in which case they might well ride horses), sometimes as horse headed or horse torsoed (in which, presumably, they would not).

sacrifice, to poems about the origins and powers of sacred speech (10.71, 10.125). The personal concerns of the priests also inspire considerable interest in the authors of the poems (most of whom were priests themselves): The priest whose patron is the king laments the loss of his royal friend and praises faith and generosity, while other priests, whose tenure is more secure, express their happiness and gratitude (10.33, 101, 117, 133, 141).

Although detailed instructions on the performance of the rituals were spelled out only in the later texts,* the *Rig Veda* presupposes the existence of some protoversion of those texts. There were animal sacrifices (such as the horse sacrifice) and simple offerings of oblations of butter into the consecrated fire. The more violent sacrifices have been seen as a kind of "controlled catastrophe,"[14] on the "quit before you're fired" principle or, more positively, as life insurance, giving the gods what they need to live (soma, animal sacrifices, etc.) in order that they will give us what we need to live.

FAST-FORWARD: THE THREE ALLIANCES

At this point, it might be useful to pause and group ideas about the relationships between humans and gods (and antigods) in the history of Hinduism into three alliances. The three units are not chronological periods but attitudes that can be found, to a greater or lesser degree, across the centuries. It would be foolhardy to tie them to specific times, because attitudes in Hinduism tend to persist from one period to another, simply added on to new ideas that one might have expected to replace them, and archaic ideas are often intentionally resurrected in order to lend an air of tradition to a later text. Nevertheless such a typology has its uses, for each of the three alliances does begin, at least, at a moment that we can date at least relative to the other alliances, and each of them dominates the texts of one of three consecutive periods.

In the first alliance, which might be called Vedic, gods and antigods (Asuras) are opposed to each other, and gods unite with humans against both the antigods, who live in the sky with the gods, and the ogres (Rakshases or Rakshasas), lower-class demons that harass humans rather than gods. The antigods are the older brothers of the gods, the "dark, olden gods" in contrast with "the mortal gods of heaven,"[15] like the Titans of Greek mythology; the Veda still calls the oldest Vedic gods—Agni, Varuna—Asuras. The gods and antigods have the

---

* The Brahmanas tell us a bit more about the rituals, but the detailed instructions only come much later, in the texts called *prayogas*.

same moral substance (indeed the gods often lie and cheat far more than the antigods do; power corrupts, and divine power corrupts divinely); the antigods are simply the other team. Because the players on each side are intrinsically differentiated by their morals, the morals shift back and forth from one category to another during the course of history, and even from one text to another in any single period: As there are good humans and evil humans, so there are good gods and evil gods, good antigods and evil antigods. In the absence of ethical character, what the gods and antigods have is power, which they can exercise at their pleasure. The gods and antigods are in competition for the goods of the sacrifice, and since humans sacrifice to the gods, they are against the antigods, who always, obligingly, lose to the gods in the end. It is therefore important for humans to keep the gods on their side and well disposed toward them. Moreover, since the gods live on sacrificial offerings provided by devout humans, the gods wish humans to be virtuous, for then they will continue to offer sacrifices.

The Vedic gods were light eaters; they consumed only a polite taste of the butter, or the animal offerings, or the expressed juice of the soma plant, and the humans got to eat the leftovers. What was fed to the fire was fed to the gods; in later mythology, when Agni, the god of fire, was impregnated by swallowing semen instead of butter, all the gods became pregnant.[16] Not only did the gods live upon the sacrificial foods, but the energy generated in the sacrifice kept the universe going. The offerings that the priest made into the fire kept the fire in the sun from going out; if no one sacrificed, the sun would not rise each morning. Moreover, the heat (*tapas*) that the priest generated in the sacrifice was a powerful weapon for gods or humans to use against their enemies. Heat is life, in contrast with the coldness of death, and indeed Hindus believe that there is a fire in the belly (called the fire that belongs to all men) that digests all the food you eat, by cooking it (again). When those fires go out, it's all over physically for the person in question, as it is ritually if the sacrificial fires go out; you must keep the sacrificial fire in your house burning and carefully preserve an ember to carry to the new house if you move.

But since antigods had no (legitimate) access to sacrificial *tapas*, the best that they (and the ogres) could do in their Sisyphean attempt to conquer the gods was to interfere with the sacrifice (the antigods in heaven and the ogres on earth) in order to weaken the gods. Though humans served as mere pawns in these cosmic battles, it was in their interest to serve the gods, for the antigods and ogres would try to kill humans (in order to divert the sacrifice from the gods), while the gods, dependent on sacrificial offerings, protected the humans. In the Upanishads, the gods and antigods are still equal enemies, though the antigods make an error in metaphysical judgment that costs them dearly.[17] Throughout the history of Hinduism, beginning in the Vedas, the antigods and ogres often serve as metaphors for marginalized human groups, first the enemies of the Vedic people, then people excluded from the groups that the Brahmins allowed to offer sacrifice. This first Vedic alliance is still a major force in Indian storytelling today, but it was superseded, in some, though not all, ways, by two more alliances.

To fast-forward for just a moment, the second alliance begins in the *Mahabharata* and continues through the Puranas (medieval compendiums of myth and history). In this period, the straightforward Vedic alignment of forces—humans and gods versus antigods and ogres—changed radically, as sacrificial power came to be supplemented and sometimes replaced by ascetic and meditative power. Now uppity antigods and ogres, who offer sacrifices when they have no right to do so or ignore the sacrificial system entirely and generate internal heat (*tapas*) all by themselves, are grouped with uppity mortals, who similarly threaten the gods not with their acts of impiety but, on the contrary, with their excessive piety and must be put back in their place. Often the threatening religious power comes from individual renunciants, a threat to the livelihood of the Vedic ecclesia and an open door to undesirable (i.e., non-Brahmin) types, a kind of wildcat religion or pirated religious power. For like the dangerous submarine mare fire, these individual ascetics generate *tapas* like power from a nuclear reactor or heat in a pressure cooker; they stop dissipating their heat by ceasing to indulge in talking, sex, anger, and so forth; they shut the openings, but the body goes on making heat, which builds up and can all too easily explode. (Later Tantra goes one step further and encourages adepts to increase the heat by generating as well as harnessing unspent desire.)

Old-fashioned sacrifice too now inspires jealousy in the gods, who are, paradoxically, also sacrificers. Indra, who prides himself on having performed a hundred horse sacrifices, frequently steals the stallion of kings who are about to beat his record. (We have seen him do this to King Sagara, resulting in the creation of the ocean.) The result is that now it is the gods, not the antigods, who wish humans to be diminished by evil. The idea that to be too good may be to tempt fate, threaten the gods, or invite the evil eye is widespread, well known from Greek tragedies, which called this sort of presumption hubris (related in concept, though not etymology, to the Yiddish hutzpah). The second alliance is full of humans, ogres, and antigods that are too good for their own good.

The balance of power changed again when, in the third alliance, devotion (bhakti) entered the field, repositioning the Vedic concept of human dependence on the gods so that the gods protected both devoted men and devoted antigods. This third alliance is in many ways the dominant structure of local temple myths even today. But that is getting far ahead of our story.

CATTLE AND HORSES: INDIANS AS COWBOYS

What the Vedic people asked for most often in the prayers that accompanied sacrifice was life, health, victory in battle, and material prosperity, primarily in the form of horses and cows. This sacrificial contract powered Hindu prayers for many centuries, but the relationship with horses and cows changed dramatically even in this early period.

As nomadic tribes, the Vedic people sought fresh pastureland for their cattle and horses.* As pastoralists and, later, agriculturalists, herders and farmers, they lived in rural communities. Like most of the Indo-Europeans, the Vedic people were cattle herders and cattle rustlers who went about stealing other people's cows and pretending to be taking them *back*. One story goes that the Panis, tribal people who were the enemies of the Vedic people, had stolen cows from certain Vedic sages and hidden them in mountain caves. The gods sent the bitch Sarama to follow the trail of the cows; she found the hiding place, bandied words with the Panis, resisted their attempts first to threaten her and then to bribe her, and brought home the cows (10.108).

The Vedic people, in this habit (as well as in their fondness for gambling), resembled the cowboys of the nineteenth-century American West, riding over other people's land and stealing their cattle. The resulting political agendas also present rough parallels (in both senses of the word "rough"): Compare, on the one hand, the scornful attitude of these ancient Indian cowboys (an oxymoron in Hollywood but not in India) toward the "barbarians" (Dasyus or Dasas) whose lands they rode over (adding insult to injury by calling *them* cattle thieves) and, some four thousand years later, the American cowboys' treatment of the people whom they called, with what now seems cruel irony, Indians, such as the Navajo and the Apache. So much for progress. Unlike the American cowboys, however, the Vedic cowboys did not yet (though they would, by the sixth

---

* *Nomas* means "pasture," and a nomad is someone who wanders from pasture to pasture.

century BCE) have a policy of owning and occupying the land, for the Vedic people did not build or settle down; they moved on. They did have, however, a policy of riding over other people's land and of keeping the cattle that they stole from those people. That the word *gavisthi* ("searching for cows") came to mean "fighting" says it all.

The Vedic people sacrificed cattle to the gods and ate cattle themselves, and they counted their wealth in cattle. They definitely ate the beef of steers[18] (the castrated bulls), both ritually and for many of the same reasons that people nowadays eat Big Macs (though in India, Big Macs are now made of mutton); they sacrificed the bulls* (Indra eats the flesh of twenty bulls or a hundred buffalo and drinks whole lakes of soma[19]) and kept most of the cows for milk. One verse states that cows were "not to be killed" (*a-ghnya* [7.87.4]), but another says that a cow should be slaughtered on the occasion of marriage (10.85.13), and another lists among animals to be sacrificed a cow that has been bred but has not calved (10.91.14),[20] while still others seem to include cows among animals whose meat was offered to the gods and then consumed by the people at the sacrifice. The usual meal of milk, ghee (clarified butter), vegetables, fruit, wheat, and barley would be supplemented by the flesh of cattle, goats, and sheep on special occasions, washed down with *sura* (wine) or *madhu* (a kind of mead).

There is a Vedic story that explains how it is that some people stopped killing cows and began just to drink their milk.† The *Rig Veda* only alludes to this story, referring to a king named Prithu, who forced the speckled cow who is the earth to let her white udder yield soma as milk for the gods.[21] But later texts spell it out:

KING PRITHU MILKS THE EARTH

There was a king named Vena who was so wicked that the sages killed him; since he left no offspring, the sages churned his right thigh, from which was born a deformed little man, dark as a burned pillar, who was the ancestor of the Nishadas and the barbarians. Then they churned Vena's right hand, and from him Prithu was born. There was a famine, because the earth was withholding all of her food.

---

* It is most likely that it was the male animal, the bull, that was used for sacrifice, as the males of all the other species of sacrificial animal are explicitly specified, and indeed the "virility" of the sacrificed animals is the point of many myths and ritual texts. Yet it should be noted that the word "go" in Sanskrit (like "cow" in common usage in English) is sexually ambiguous.

† Most horsey nomads drink mare's milk—the Greeks called the Scythian nomads mare milkers—and the Vedic people may have done so before they settled in the Punjab, but milk in the Veda is always cow's milk.

King Prithu took up his bow and arrow and pursued the earth to force her to yield nourishment for his people. The earth assumed the form of a cow and begged him to spare her life; she then allowed him to milk her for all that the people needed. Thus did righteous kingship arise on earth among kings of the lunar dynasty, who are the descendants of Prithu.[22]

This myth, foundational for the dynasty that traces its lineage back to Prithu, is cited in many variants over thousands of years. It imagines a transition from hunting wild cattle (the earth cow) to preserving their lives, domesticating them, and breeding them for milk, in a transition to agriculture and pastoral life. The myth of the earth cow, later the wishing cow (*kama-dhenu*), from whom you can milk anything you desire—not just food but silk cloths, armies of soldiers, anything—is the Hindu parallel to the Roman cornucopia (or the German *Tischlein dech dich*, the table that sets itself with a full table d'hôte dinner on command). Cows are clearly of central economic, ritual, and symbolic importance in the Vedic world.

But the horse, rather than the cow, was the animal whose ritual importance and intimacy with humans kept it from being regarded as food,[23] though not from being killed in sacrifices. Horses were essential not only to drawing swift battle chariots but to herding cattle, always easier to do from horseback in places where the grazing grounds are extensive.[24] And extensive is precisely what they were; the fast track of Vedic life was driven by the profligate grazing habits of horses, who force their owners to move around looking for new grazing land all the time. Unlike cows, horses pull up the roots of the grass or eat it right down to the ground so that it doesn't grow back, thus quickly destroying grazing land, which may require some years to recover; moreover, horses do not like to eat the grass that grows up around their own droppings.[25] The horse in nature is therefore constantly in search of what the Nazis (also justifying imperialistic aggression) called *Lebensraum* ("living space"). It is not merely, as is often argued, that the horse made possible conquest in war, through the chariot; the stallion came to symbolize conquest in war, through his own natural imperialism. And the ancient Indian horse owners mimicked this trait in their horses, at first showing no evidence of any desire to amass property, just a drive to move on, always to move on, to new lands. For the Vedic people probably did then what Central Asians did later: They let the animals roam freely as a herd.[26] But once they began to fence in their horses and kept them from their natural free grazing habits, the need to acquire and enclose new grazing lands became intense, especially when, in the early Vedic period, there was no fodder crop.[27]

THE WIDE-OPEN SPACES

All this land grabbing was supported by a religion whose earliest texts urge constant expansion. The name of the king who hunted the earth cow, Prithu, means "broad," and the feminine form of the word, *Prithivi*, is a word for the whole, broad earth, the natural consort of the king. *Prithu* had the connotation of something very much like "the wide-open spaces." The opposite of the word *prithu* is the word for a tight spot, in both the physical and the psychological sense; that word is *amhas*, signifying a kind of claustrophobia, the uneasiness of being constrained in a small space. (*Amhas* is cognate with our word "anxiety" and the German *Angst*.) In this context, *amhas* might well be translated "Don't fence me in," since it occurs in a number of Vedic poems in which the poet imagines himself trapped in a deep well or a cave, from which he prays to the gods to extricate him. (Sometimes it is the cows who are trapped in the cave, or the waters, or the sun.) Many of the poems take this form; the poet thanks the god for his help in the past ("Remember the time I was in that tight spot, and you got me out?"), reminds him of his gratitude ("And didn't I offer you great vats of soma after that?"), flatters him ("No one but you can do this; you are the greatest"), and asks for a return engagement ("Well, I'm in even worse trouble now; come and help me, I beg you").

Appropriately, it is often the Ashvins who rescue people from such tight spots and bring them back into the good, broad places. For the Ashvins (whose name means "equine") are twin horse-headed gods, animal herders, sons of the divine mare Saranyu (10.17.1–2). The other Vedic gods generally snub the Ashvins, in part because they are physicians (a low trade in ancient India, involving as it does polluting contacts with human bodies) and in part because they persist in slumming, helping out mortals in trouble. The gods denied them access to the ambrosial soma drink until one mortal (a priest named Dadhyanch), for whom the Ashvins had done a favor, reciprocated by whispering to them, through a horse's head he had put on for that occasion to speak to their horse heads, the secret of the soma—literally from the horse's mouth (1.116.12, 1.117.22, 1.84.13–15). Later texts explain that Dadhyanch knew that Indra, the jealous king of the gods, would punish him for this betrayal by cutting off his head, so he laid aside his own head, used a talking horse head to tell the secret, let Indra cut off the horse head, and then put his own back on.[28]

The Horse Sacrifice

Embedded in the tale of Dadhyanch and the Ashvins is the ritual beheading of a horse. One of the few great public ceremonies alluded to in the Vedas is the sacrifice of a horse, by suffocation rather than beheading but followed by dismemberment. There are epigraphical records of (as well as literary satires on) horse sacrifices throughout Indian history. One Vedic poem* describes the horse sacrifice in strikingly concrete, indeed rather gruesome detail, beginning with the ceremonial procession of the horse accompanied by a dappled goat, who was killed with the horse but offered to a different, less important god:

DISMEMBERING THE HORSE

Whatever of the horse's flesh the fly has eaten, or whatever stays stuck to the stake or the ax, or to the hands or nails of the slaughterer—let all of that stay with you even among the gods. Whatever food remains in his stomach, sending forth gas, or whatever smell there is from his raw flesh—let the slaughterers make that well done; let them cook the sacrificial animal until he is perfectly cooked. Whatever runs off your body when it has been placed on the spit and roasted by the fire, let it not lie there in the earth or on the grass, but let it be given to the gods who long for it. . . . The testing fork for the cauldron that cooks the flesh, the pots for pouring the broth, the cover of the bowls to keep it warm, the hooks, the dishes—all these attend the horse. . . . If someone riding you has struck you too hard with heel or whip when you shied, I make all these things well again for you with prayer. . . . The ax cuts through the thirty-four ribs of the racehorse who is the companion of the gods. Keep the limbs undamaged and place them in the proper pattern. Cut them apart, calling out piece by piece. . . . Let not your dear soul burn you as you go away. Let not the ax do lasting harm to your body. Let no greedy, clumsy slaughterer hack in the wrong place and damage your limbs with his knife. You do not really die through this, nor are you harmed. You go to the gods on paths pleasant to go on (1.162).

The poet thus intermittently addresses the horse (and himself) with the consolation that all will be restored in heaven, words in which we may see the first stirrings of ambivalence about the killing of a beloved animal, even in a religious ceremony, an ambivalence that will become much more explicit in the

---

* I will generally render the Vedic poems in prose.

next few centuries. We may see even here a kind of "ritual nonviolence" that is also expressed in a concern that the victim should not bleed or suffer or cry out (one reason why the sacrificial animal was strangled).[29] The euphemism for the killing of the horse, pacifying (*shanti*), further muted the growing uneasiness associated with the killing of an animal. Moreover, unlike cows, goats, and other animals that were sacrificed, many in the course of the horse sacrifice, the horse was not actually eaten (though it was cooked and served to the gods). Certain parts of the horse's carcass (such as the marrow, or the fat from the chest, or the *vapa*, the caul, pericardium, or omentum containing the internal organs) were offered to Agni, the god of the fire, and the consecrated king and the priests would inhale the cooking fumes (regarded as "half-eating-by-smelling" the cooked animal). The gods and priests, as well as guests at the sacrificial feast, ate the cattle (mostly rams, billy goats, and steers); only the gods and priests ate the soma; no one ate the horse. Perhaps the horse was not eaten because of the close relationship that the Vedic people, like most Indo-Europeans,[30] had with their horses, who not only speak, on occasion,[31] but are often said to shed tears* when their owners die.[32]

THE VEDIC PEOPLE

The *Rig Veda* tells us a lot (as in the passage cited at the start of this chapter, a kind of liturgical work song) about family life, about everyday tasks, about craftsmanship, about the materials of sacrifice, and even about diversity. Evidently the rigid hereditary system of the professions characteristic of the caste system was not yet in place now, for the professions at this time varied even within a single family, where a poet could be the son of a physician and a miller. The *Rig Veda* tells us of many professions, including carpenters, blacksmiths, potters, tanners, reed workers, and weavers.[33] But by the end of this period, the class system was in place.

THE FOUR CLASSES AND THE PRIMEVAL MAN

The Vedic people at first distinguished just two classes (*varnas*), their own (which they called Arya) and that of the people they conquered, whom they called Dasas (or Dasyus, or, sometimes, Panis). The Dasas may have been sur-

---

* Drona's horses shed tears when he is about to die (*Mahabharata* 7.192.20); when the Buddha departs, his horse Kanthaka weeps (*Buddhacharita* 6.33–35; 8.3–4, 17); Achilles' horses weep for the death of Patroclus; Brünnhilde's horse Grani hangs his head and weeps over the dead Siegfried.

vivors of early migrations of Vedic people, or people who spoke non-Sanskritic languages, or a branch of the Indo-Iranian people who had a religion different from that of the Vedic people.[34] (In the Indo-Iranian Avesta, *daha* and *dahyu* designate "other people."[35]) The early Veda expresses envy for the Dasas' wealth, which is to say their cattle, but later, "Dasa" came to be used to denote a slave or subordinate, someone who worked outside the family, and the late parts of the Veda mention Brahmins who were "sons of slave women" (Dasi-putra), indicating an acceptance of interclass sexual relationships, if not marriage. We have noted evidence that the Vedic people took significant parts of their material culture from communities in place in India before they arrived, Dasas of one sort or another. The Dasas may also have introduced new ritual practices such as those recorded in the *Atharva Veda*. (The Nishadas, tribal peoples, were also associated with some early rituals.[36])

But the more important social division was not into just two classes (Arya and Dasa, Us and Them) but four. A poem in one of the latest books of the *Rig Veda*, "Poem of the Primeval Man" (Purusha-Sukta [10.90]), is about the dismemberment of the cosmic giant, the Primeval Man (*purusha* later comes to designate any male creature, indeed the male gender), who is the victim in a Vedic sacrifice that creates the whole universe.* The poem says, "The gods, performing the sacrifice, bound the Man as the sacrificial beast. With the sacrifice the gods sacrificed to the sacrifice." Here the "sacrifice" designates both the ritual and the victim killed in the ritual; moreover, the Man is both the victim that the gods sacrificed and the divinity to whom the sacrifice was dedicated— that is, he is both the subject and the object of the sacrifice. This Vedic chicken or egg paradox is repeated in a more general pattern, in which the gods sacrifice to the gods, and a more specific pattern, in which one particular god, Indra, king of the gods, sacrifices (as a king) to himself (as a god). But it is also a tautological way of thinking that we have seen in the myths of mutual creation and will continue to encounter in Hindu mythology.

The four classes of society come from the appropriate parts of the body of the dismembered Primeval Man. His mouth became the priest (the Brahmin, master of sacred speech); all Vedic priests are Brahmins, though not all Brahmins are priests. His arms were the Raja (the Kshatriya, the Strong Arm, the class of warriors, policemen, and kings); his thighs, the commoner (the Vaishya, the fertile producer, the common people, the third estate, who produce the food

---

* This is one of several creation scenarios in the *Rig Veda;* we will see two more below.

for the first two and themselves); and his feet—the lowest and dirtiest part of the body—the servants (Shudras), the outside class within society that defines the other classes. That the Shudras were an afterthought is evident from the fact that the third class, Vaishyas, is sometimes said to be derived from the word for "all" and therefore to mean "everyone," leaving no room for anyone below them—until someone added a class below them.* The fourth social class may have consisted of the people new to the early Vedic system, perhaps the people already in India when the Vedic people entered, the Dasas, from a system already in place in India, or simply the sorts of people who were always outside the system. The final combination often functioned not as a quartet but, reverting to the pattern of Arya and Dasa, as a dualism: all of us (in the first three classes, the twice born) versus all of them (in the fourth class, the non-us, the Others).†

"Poem of the Primeval Man" ranks the kings below the priests. The supremacy of Brahmins was much contested throughout later Hindu literature and in fact may have been nothing but a Brahmin fantasy. Many texts argue, or assume, that Kshatriyas never were as high as Brahmins, and others assume that they always were, and still are, higher than Brahmins. Buddhist literature puts the kings at the top, the Brahmins second,[37] and many characters in Hindu texts also defend this viewpoint.

The French sociologist Georges Dumézil (1898–1986) argued that the *Indo-European speakers had been divided into three social classes or functions: at the top, kings who were also priests, then warriors who were also policemen, and then the rest of the people.[38] Some scholars find this hypothetical division useful; some do not[39] and some think that other cultures too were divided in this way, so that tripartition is not a useful way to distinguish Indo-European culture from any other.‡ (It rather suspiciously resembles the reactionary French ancient regime, which put priests at the top, over aristocrats, and the people in the third group below.) In any case, by the end of the period

---

* Indo-European linguists usually derive "Vaishya" from a different word that means "settlement" or "people who live on the land," but some Sanskrit texts cite the derivation from "all."
† Since the fourth class is also already present in the Veda's Iranian cousin, the Avesta, such a fourth class, consisting primarily of artisans, may in fact have been Indo-European (or at least Indo-Iranian). Yet this Vedic hymn already regards Shudras as outsiders.
‡ The numerous pairings of contrasting terms, such as "mortals and immortals" or "sky and earth" or "creatures two-footed and four-footed," suggest that division into two rather than three is the fundamental structuring principle of Indo-European thought—perhaps of human thought in general. But that is another story.

in which the *Rig Veda* was composed, a fourfold social system that deviates in two major regards from the Dumézilian model was in place: It adds a fourth class at the bottom, and it reverses the status of kings and priests. The kings have come down one rung from their former alleged status of sharing first place with the Brahmins. This, then, would have been one of the earliest documented theocratic takeovers, a silent, totally mental palace coup, the Brahmin forcing the Kshatriya out of first place.

Thus, even in "Poem of the Primeval Man," supposedly postulating a social charter that was created at the very dawn of time and is to remain in place forever after, we can see, in the positioning of the kings in the second rank, movement, change, slippage, progress, or decay, depending upon your point of view. This sort of obfuscation is basic to mythology; the semblance of an unmoving eternity is presented in texts that themselves clearly document constant transformation. "Poem of the Primeval Man" may have been the foundational myth of the Brahmin class, establishing social hierarchies that are unknown to poems from an earlier layer of the *Rig Veda*, such as the poem "Diverse Callings."

One Vedic poem that may incorporate a critique of Brahmins* is a tour de force that applies simultaneously, throughout, to frogs croaking at the start of the rainy season and to Brahmin priests who begin to chant at the start of the rains. It begins:

THE FROGS

After lying still for a year, Brahmins keeping their vow, the frogs have raised their voice that the god of the rainstorm has inspired. When the heavenly waters came upon him, dried out like a leather bag, lying in the pool, then the cries of the frogs joined in chorus like the lowing of cows with calves. As soon as the season of rains has come, and it rains upon them who are longing, thirsting for it, one approaches another who calls to him, "Akh-khala," as a son approaches his father. One greets the other as they revel in the waters that burst forth, and the frog leaps about under the falling rain, the speckled one mingling his voice with the green one. One of them repeats the speech of the other, as a pupil that of a teacher (7.103.1–5).

---

* A possibility supported by analogy with the Greek playwright Aristophanes' comedy *The Frogs*, in which the Dionysian chorus consists entirely of frogs who say, "Brekekekek koax koax," the Greek for "Akh-khala" (which is what frogs say in Sanskrit).

Though this poem may have been a satire, its tone is serious, a metaphor in celebration of a crucial and joyous matter, the arrival of the rains.

Other Others: Marginalizing Intoxication and Addiction

The marginalized people in the lowest social levels of the Veda—Dasas, Shudras—may have included people who were Other not, or not only, in their social class but in their religious practices, such as the wandering bands of warrior ascetics the Vedas refer to as the Vratyas ("People Who Have Taken Vows"), who practiced flagellation and other forms of self-mortification and traveled from place to place in bullock carts.[40] Vratyas were sometimes regarded as inside, sometimes outside mainstream society;[41] the Brahmins sought to bring them into the Vedic system by special purification rituals,[42] and the Vratyas may have introduced some of their own beliefs and practices into Vedic religion.

Or the Others may have been drop-out and turn-on types like the protohippie described in another poem:

THE LONG-HAIRED ASCETIC

Long-Hair holds fire, holds the drug, holds sky and earth. . . . These ascetics, swathed in wind [i.e., naked], put dirty saffron rags on. "Crazy with asceticism, we have mounted the wind. Our bodies are all you mere mortals can see." . . . Long-Hair drinks from the cup, sharing the drug with Rudra (10.136)."

The dirty rags identify these people as either very poor or willingly alienated from social conventions such as dress; that they wear saffron-colored robes may be an early form (hindsight alert!) of the ocher robes that later marked many renunciant groups. Rudra is the master of poison and medicines, but also of consciousness-altering drugs, one of which may have been used here, as such drugs often are, to induce the sensation of flying and of viewing one's own body from outside. Rudra was the embodiment of wildness, unpredictable danger, and fever but also the healer and cooler, who attacks "like a ferocious wild beast" (2.33). He lives on the margins of the civilized world as one who comes from the outside, an intruder, and is excluded from the Vedic sacrifice. He is a hunter. He stands for what is violent, cruel, and impure in the society of gods or at the edge of the divine world.[43]

The *Rig Veda* also tells us of people marginalized not by class or religious practices but by their antisocial behavior under the influence of some addiction.

One Vedic poem lists "wine, anger, dice, or carelessness" as the most likely cause of serious misbehavior (7.86.1–8). Wine and dice are two of the four addictive vices of lust (sex and hunting being the other two), to which considerable attention was paid throughout Indian history. We have seen dice in the Indus Valley Civilization, and we will see gambling with dice remain both a major pastime (along with chariot racing and hunting) and the downfall of kings. Ordinary people as well as kings could be ruined by gambling, as is evident from the stark portrayal of a dysfunctional family in this Vedic poem:

THE GAMBLER

"She did not quarrel with me or get angry; she was kind to my friends and to me. Because of a losing throw of the dice I have driven away a devoted wife. My wife's mother hates me, and my wife pushes me away. The man in trouble finds no one with sympathy. They all say, 'I find a gambler as useless as an old horse that someone wants to sell.' Other men fondle the wife of a man whose possessions have been taken by the plundering dice. His father, mother, and brothers all say of him, 'We do not know him. Tie him up and take him away.' When I swear, 'I will not play with them,' my friends leave me behind and go away. But when the brown dice raise their voice as they are thrown down, I run at once to the rendezvous with them, like a woman to her lover." . . . The deserted wife of the gambler grieves, and the mother grieves for her son who wanders anywhere, nowhere. In debt and in need of money, frightened, he goes at night to the houses of other men. It torments the gambler to see his wife the woman of other men, in their comfortable rooms. But he yoked the brown horses in the early morning, and at evening he fell down by the fire, no longer a man (10.34).

Like a character in a Dostoyevsky novel, the gambler prays not to win but just to stop losing, indeed to stop playing altogether; his inability to stop is likened to a sexual compulsion or addiction. The "brown horses" that he yokes may be real horses or a metaphor for the brown dice; in either case, they destroy him. (The gambler's wife who is fondled by other men reappears in the *Mahabharata* when the wife of the gambler Yudhishthira is stripped in the public assembly.) At the end of the poem, a god (Savitri, the god of the rising and setting sun) warns the gambler, "Play no longer with the dice, but till your field; enjoy what you possess, and value it highly. There are your cattle, and there is your wife."

DRINKING SOMA

Intoxication, though not addiction, is a central theme of the Veda, since the sacrificial offering of the hallucinogenic juice of the soma plant was an element of several important Vedic rituals. The poets who "saw" the poems were inspired both by their meditations and by drinking the soma juice. The poems draw upon a corpus of myths about a fiery plant that a bird brings down from heaven; soma is born in the mountains or in heaven, where it is closely guarded; an eagle brings soma to earth (4.26–7) or to Indra (4.18.13), or the eagle carries Indra to heaven to bring the soma* to humans and gods (4.27.4). This myth points to the historical home of the soma plant in the mountains, probably the mountain homeland of the Vedic people. We do not know for sure what the soma plant was[44] (*pace* a recent lawsuit† over a copyright for it[45]), but we know what it was *not:* It was not ephedra (*Sarcostemma*) or wine or beer or brandy or marijuana or opium.‡ It may have been the mushroom known as the *Amanita muscaria* or fly agaric (called *mukhomor* in Russian, *Pfliegenpilz* in German, *tue-mouche* or *crapaudin* in French).[46] It appears to produce the effects of a hallucinogen (or "entheogen"[47]): "Like impetuous winds, the drinks have lifted me up, like swift horses bolting with a chariot. Yes! I will place the earth here, or perhaps there. One of my wings is in the sky; I have trailed the other below. I am huge, huge! flying to the cloud. Have I not drunk soma? (10.119)." Another soma hymn begins with the same phrase that ends the poem just cited ("Have I not drunk Soma?"), now no longer a question: "We have drunk the soma; we have become immortal; we have gone to the light; we have found the gods. What can hatred and the malice of a mortal do to us now? The glorious drops that I have drunk set me free in wide space (8.48.3)." The feeling of expansiveness, of being set free "in wide space," is not merely a Vedic political agenda, an

---

* In variants from the Indo-European corpus, fire is held within a reed in the Greek myth of Prometheus and brought down from heaven by a firebird in Russian mythology.

† The appeal was rejected because though the claim was that the soma plant was *not* the mushroom *Amanita muscaria*, it never specified what the plant in fact *was*.

‡ Ephedra does not seem to have a sufficiently strong mental effect to have produced the conditions described in the poems. The soma was pressed in the morning and drunk on the same day, thereby eliminating wine and beer (which take longer than that to ferment, even in a hot climate). Palm toddy must be drunk within hours of making it, but toddy is not "pressed," as soma is, nor do coconut palm trees grow in the Punjab. They didn't know about distillation at that time (so much for *daru* or brandy), and they used hemp only to make rope, not marijuana (*bhang*). It wasn't opium; poppies were not grown then in the Punjab.

expression of the lust for those wide-open spaces; it is also a subjective experience of exhilaration and ecstasy. Human poets drink soma only in small quantities and in the controlled context of the ritual. But for the gods who depend upon it, soma can become an addiction (the bolting horses in the hymn cited above recur as a metaphor for senses out of control). Later poets depict Indra, the great soma drinker, as suffering from a bad hangover, in which he cannot stop substances from flowing from all the orifices of his body.[48]

Mrs. Indra and Other Females

The gambler's wife is one of a more general company of long-suffering wives, devoted but often deserted, who people ancient Hindu literature and the society that this literature reflects. In the *Rig Veda*, a text dominated by men in a world dominated by men, women appear throughout the poems as objects. Like the gambler whom Savitri warned, every Vedic man valued equally his two most precious possessions, his cattle and his wife. A man needed a wife to be present when he performed any Vedic sacrifice, though she had to stay behind a screen.[49] Women also appear occasionally as subjects, even as putative authors, of Vedic poems (10.40, 8.91).[50] And women may have had a voice in poems that treat women's interests sympathetically, such as magic spells to incapacitate rival wives and to protect unborn children in the womb (10.184), and in the Vedic ritual that an unmarried virgin performs to get a husband.[51] One of these latter poems is appropriately dedicated to Indrani ("Mrs. Indra"), the wife of Indra (who is, like his Indo-European counterparts—the Greek Zeus and the Norse Odin, German Wotan—a notorious philanderer). It says, in part: "I dig up this plant, the most powerful thing that grows, with which one drives out the rival wife and wins the husband entirely for oneself. I will not even take her name into my mouth; he takes no pleasure in this person. Make the rival wife go far, far into the distance. [She addresses her husband:] Let your heart run after me like a cow after a calf, like water running in its own bed (10.145)." Some spells, like this spell to protect the embryo, are directed against evil powers but addressed to human beings, in this case the pregnant woman: "The one whose name is evil, who lies with disease upon your embryo, your womb, the flesh eater; the one who kills the embryo as it settles, as it rests, as it stirs, who wishes to kill it when it is born—we will drive him away from here. The one who spreads apart your two thighs, who lies between the married pair, who licks the inside of your womb—we will drive him away from here.

The one who by changing into a brother, or husband, or lover lies with you, who wishes to kill your offspring—we will drive him away from here. The one who bewitches you with sleep or darkness and lies with you—we will drive him away from here (10.162)."

There is precise human observation here of what we would call the three trimesters of pregnancy (when the embryo settles, rests, and stirs). Though the danger ultimately comes from supernatural creatures, ogres, such creatures act through humans, by impersonating the husband (or lover! or brother!) of the pregnant woman. This poem provides, among things, evidence that a woman might be expected to have a lover, a suspicion substantiated by a Vedic ritual in which the queen is made to list her lovers of the past year,* though that moment in the ritual may represent nothing more than a "jolt of sexual energy" that the wife, as locus of sexuality, particularly illicit sexuality (since most forms of sex were licit for men), was charged to provide for the ritual.[52] More substantial is the early evidence in this poem of a form of rape that came to be regarded as a bad, but legitimate, form of marriage: having sex with a sleeping or drugged woman. It appears that a woman's brother too is someone she might expect to find in her bed, though the *Rig Veda* severely condemns sibling incest;[53] it is also possible that the brother in question is her husband's brother, a person who, as we shall see, can have certain traditional, though anxiety-producing, connections with his brother's wife.[†]

Women were expected to live on after the deaths of their husbands, as we learn from lines in a funeral hymn addressed to the widow of the dead man: "Rise up, woman, into the world of the living. Come here; you are lying beside a man whose life's breath has gone (10.18)." The poet urges the widow to go on living. Certainly she is not expected to die with her husband, though "lying beside a dead man" may have been a survival from an earlier period when the wife was actually buried with her husband;[54] the *Atharva Veda* regards the practice of the wife's lying down beside her dead husband (but perhaps then getting up again) as an ancient custom.[55] On the other hand, women in the Vedic period may have performed a purely *symbolic* suicide on their husbands' graves, which was later (hindsight alert!) cited as scriptural support for the *actual* self-immolation of widows on their husbands' pyres called suttee.

---

* The *Varuna-praghasa* at the beginning of the rainy season, in which the priest interrogates the queen with a question on the order of "When did you stop beating your wife?"
† It was a man's duty to impregnate his brother's wife, but only if the brother was dead or unable to produce his own heirs.

Several poems explore the relationships between men and women, mortal and immortal. These poems present narratives centering on courtship, marriage, adultery, and estrangement, often in the form of conversations (*akhyanas*) that zero in on the story in medias res, taking it up at a crucial turning point in a plot that we are presumed to know (and that the later commentaries spell out for us).[56] The conversation poems, which often involve goddesses and heavenly nymphs, are particularly associated with fertility and may have been part of a special ritual performance involving actors and dancers.[57] The dialogues with women present situations in which one member of the pair attempts to persuade the other to engage in some sort of sexual activity; sometimes it is the woman who takes the role of persuader,[58] sometimes the man.[59] In general, the mortal women and immortal men are successful in their persuasion, while the quasi-immortal women and mortal men fail.[60]

Apala, a mortal woman, has a most intimate relationship with Indra, as we gather from the story told in the poem attributed to her (a story spelled out by later commentaries) (8.91). She was a young woman whose husband hated her ("Surely we who are hated by our husbands should flee and unite with Indra," v. 4) because she had a skin disease (the ritual makes her "sun-skinned," v. 7). She found the soma plant ("A maiden going for water found soma by the way," v. 1), pressed it in her mouth, and offered it to Indra ("Drink this that I have pressed with my teeth," v. 2). Indra made love to her; she at first resisted ("We do not wish to understand you, and yet we do not misunderstand you," v. 3) and then consented ("Surely he is able, surely he will do it, surely he will make us more fortunate," v. 4). She asked him to cure her and to restore fertility to her father and to his fields ("Make these three places sprout, Indra: my daddy's head and field, and this part of me below the waist," v. 5–6). Indra accomplished this triple blessing ("Indra, you purified Apala three times," v. 7) by a ritual that may have involved drawing Apala through three chariot holes ("in the nave of a chariot, in the nave of the cart, in the nave of the yoke," v. 7), making her slough her skin three times (according to later tradition, the first skin became a porcupine,* the second an alligator, and the third a chameleon[61]).

Apala wants to be "fortunate" (*subhaga*), a word that has three closely linked meanings: beautiful, therefore loved by her husband,† therefore fortunate. In

---

* The porcupine is attested to in India from the time of the *Atharva Veda* through Kipling's Stickly-Prickly (in *Just So Stories*).
† In classical Sanskrit it also means "having a good vagina," which may be a distant but relevant overtone.

other poems, a husband rejects his wife not because she lacks beauty but because he lacks virility (10.40); "fortunate" then assumes the further connotation of having a virile husband.* Finally, it means having a healthy husband, so that the woman does not become a widow. For his failing health too may be the woman's fault; certain women are regarded as dangerous to men. For instance, the blood of the bride's defloration threatens the groom: "It becomes a magic spirit walking on feet, and like the wife it draws near the husband (10.85.29)." The blood spirit takes the wife's form, as the embryo-killing ogre takes the form of her husband/lover/brother. Sex is dangerous.

One long poem (10.85) celebrates the story of the marriage of the moon and the daughter of the sun, and another (10.17.1–2) briefly alludes to the marriage of the sun to the equine goddess Saranyu. But these are not simple hierogamies (sacred marriages), for the celestial gods also share our sexual frailties. To say that a marriage is made in heaven is not necessarily a blessing in the Vedic world; adultery too is made in heaven. (In the *Ramayana* [7.30], Indra's adultery with a mortal woman creates adultery for the first time on earth.) The moon is unfaithful to the sun's daughter when he runs off with the wife of the priest of the gods (Brihaspati) (10.109). And the sun's wife, Saranyu, the daughter of the artisan and blacksmith Tvashtri, gives birth to twins (one of whom is Yama, god of the dead) but then runs away from the sun. She leaves in her place a double of herself, while she herself takes the form of a mare and gives birth to the horse-headed gods, the Ashvins (10.17.1–2).[62] Saranyu belongs to a larger pattern of equine goddesses who abandon their husbands, for while stallions in Vedic ritual thinking are domesticated male animals (*pashu*s), fit for sacrifice, mares belong to an earlier, mythic Indo-European level[63] in which horses were still thought of as wild animals, hunted and perhaps captured but never entirely tamed.

Not all the females in the *Rig Veda* are anthropomorphic. Abstract nouns (usually feminine) are sometimes personified as female divinities, such as Speech (Vach)[64] and Destruction (Nirriti). There are also natural entities with feminine names, such as Dawn and Night and the Waters (including the Sarasvati River) and terrestrial goddesses, such as the nymphs (Apsarases), the forest, and Earth (Prithivi), who is regarded as a mother. And there are divine wives, named after their husbands (Mrs. Indra, Mrs. Surya, Mrs. Rudra, Mrs. Varuna, Mrs. Agni)[65] and at least one divine husband, named after his rather abstract wife: Indra is called the Lord of Shachi (*shachi-pati*), *pati* meaning "husband" or "master"

---

* Impotence is also at issue in other *Rig Vedic* poems (such as 10.86 and 10.102).

(literally "protector") and *shachi* meaning "power" (from the verb *shak* or *shach*). Together, they suggest that Indra is the master of power or married to a goddess named Shachi, which became another name for Indrani. So too later goddesses played the role of the *shakti* (another form derived from the same verb) that empowered the male gods. But no goddesses (except Vach, "Speech") have any part in the sacrifice that was the heart of Vedic religion.[66]

Most Vedic creator gods (like most Vedic gods in general) are male, but one Vedic poem imagines cosmic creation through the down-to-earth image of a female, called Aditi ("Without Limits," "Infinity"), who gives birth to a baby:

ADITI GIVES BIRTH

Let us now speak with wonder of the births of the gods—so that some one may see them when the poems are chanted in this later age. In the earliest age of the gods, existence was born from nonexistence. After this the quarters of the sky, and the earth, were born from her who crouched with legs spread. From female Infinity (Aditi), male dexterity (Daksha) was born, and from male dexterity (Daksha), female infinity (Aditi) was born. After her were born the blessed gods, the kinsmen of immortality (10.72.1–5).

The dominant visual image of this poem is the goddess of infinity, who crouches with legs stretched up (*uttana-pad*), more particularly with knees drawn up and legs spread wide,* a term that designates a position primarily associated with a woman giving birth.[67] This position is later associated with yoga and might have yogic overtones even in this period.

Again we encounter the paradox of mutual creation:† The female principle of infinity and the male principle of virile dexterity create each other as Brahma and Vishnu will later create each other. A Vedic commentary takes pains to explain that for the gods, two births can mutually produce each other.[68] The creator often has the tautological name of "self-existing" or "self-created" (*svay-ambhu*):‡ He creates himself, as does circular time itself, and the cosmos, according to the theory of the four Ages.

---

* Visual depictions of this figure are first attested from the second to the fourth century CE.
† This is an enduring concept in Hinduism; the Marathi saint Tukaram sees the relationship between himself and god in these terms: "There is a whole tree within a seed/ And a seed at the end of each tree/That is how it is between you and me/ One contains the Other."
‡ The *Rig Veda* (10.83.4) applied this name not to a creator but to Manyu, "Anger." By the time of the *Mahabharata*, however, it is an epithet of Manu and then of Brahma.

POLYTHEISM AND KATHENOTHEISM

In the house of the *Rig Veda* there are many divine mansions. We have noted the importance of multiplicity to Hindus and Hinduism, and it begins here. The *Rig Veda* has a kind of polytheism, but one that already has in it the first seeds of what will flower, in the philosophical texts called the Upanishads, into monism (which assumes that all living things are elements of a single, universal substance). A much-quoted line proclaims this singular multiplicity, in a context that is clearly theological rather than philosophical: "They call it Indra, Mitra, Varuna, Agni, and it is the heavenly bird that flies. The wise speak of what is One in many ways; they call it Agni, Yama, Matarishvan" (1.164.46). This is a tolerant, hierarchical sort of devotional polytheism: The worshiper acknowledges the existence, and goodness, of gods other than the god that he or she is addressing at the moment. This creative tension between monism and polytheism extends through the history of Hinduism.

The polytheism of Vedic religion is actually a kind of serial monotheism that Müller named henotheism or kathenotheism, the worship of a number of gods, one at a time, regarding each as the supreme, or even the only, god while you are talking to him. Thus one Vedic poem will praise a god and chalk up to his account the credit for separating heaven and earth, propping them apart with a pillar, but another Vedic poem will use exactly the same words to praise another god. (In addition, each god would have characteristics and deeds that are his alone; no one but Indra cures Apala.) Bearing in mind the way in which the metaphor of adultery has traditionally been used by monotheistic religions to stigmatize polytheism ("whoring after other gods"), and used by later Hinduism to characterize the love of god, we might regard this attitude as a kind of theological parallel to serial monogamy, or, if you prefer, open hierogamos: "You, Vishnu, are the only god I've ever worshiped; you are the only one." "You, Varuna, are the only god I've ever worshiped; you are the only one." "You, Susan, are the only woman I've ever loved; you are the only one." "You, Helen, are the only woman I've ever loved; you are the only one." Vedic kathenotheism made possible a quasihierarchical pantheon; the attitude to each god was hierarchical, but the various competing practical monotheisms canceled one another out, so that the total picture was one of equality; each of several was the best (like the pigs on George Orwell's *Animal Farm*: They're all equal, but some are more equal than others).

This time-sharing property of the Vedic gods is an example of individual pluralism: Each individual worshiper would know, and might use, several different poems to different gods. And the text is intolerant of intolerance. One Rig Vedic poem curses people who accuse others of worshiping false gods or considering the gods useless (7.104.14). When the double negatives in this statement cross one another out, we are left with an extraordinary defense of heretics and atheists. But the broader intellectual pluralism of the Vedas regards the world, or the deity, or truth itself as plural; the Vedas tackle the problem of ontology from several (plural) different angles, branching off from an ancient and still ongoing argument about the way the world *is*, about whether it is basically uniform or basically multiform.

One Vedic poem ends: "Where did this creation come from? The gods came afterward, with the creation of this universe. Who then knows where it came from? Where it came from—perhaps it formed itself, or perhaps it did not—the one who looks down on it, in the highest heaven, only he knows—or perhaps he does not know (10.129)." There is a charming humility and open-mindedness in this poem, which begins, most confusingly, with the statement "There was neither existence nor nonexistence then"—easy enough to say, impossible actually to visualize. Its final phrase ("or perhaps he does not know") seems almost to mock the rhetoric in the line that comes right before it: "—the one who looks down on it, in the highest heaven, only he knows." The poem asks a question about the very nature, perhaps the very existence, of god.

The unanswered cosmic question ("Who really knows?") recurs in the *Rig Veda* in another cosmogonic poem, in which each stanza ends with the questioning refrain: "Who is the god whom we should worship with the oblation?" Thus: "He by whom the awesome sky and the earth were made firm, by whom the dome of the sky was propped up, and the sun, who measured out the middle realm of space—who is the god whom we should worship with the oblation? (10.121)." The Veda shows a tolerance, a celebration of plurality, even in asking unanswerable questions about the beginnings of all things.

Agni, Indra, and Varuna

The great gods of later Hinduism, Vishnu and Shiva (in the form of Rudra), make only cameo appearances in the Veda.[69] By contrast, the most important gods of the Veda, such as Agni, Soma, Indra, and Varuna, all closely tied to the Vedic sacrifice, become far less important in later Hinduism, though they survive as symbolic figures of natural forces: fire, the moon, rain, and the waters, respectively. Other Vedic gods too are personifications of natural forces, particularly solar gods, as Müller rightly noted but overemphasized. (He was mocked for it too; one scholar wrote an article proving that by his own criteria, Max Müller himself was a solar god.[70]) There are exquisite poems to the goddesses Dawn (1.92) and Night (10.127) and to the god Surya, the sun.

But most of the gods, even those representing natural forces, are vividly anthropomorphized. The gods are like us, only more so. They want what we want, things like marriage (and adultery), and fame, and praise. And most of the gods are closely associated with particular social classes: Agni is the Brahmin, Varuna the Brahminical sovereign, Indra the warrior, and the Ashvins the Vaishyas. There are no Shudra gods in the Vedas.

Agni, god of fire, serves as the divine model for the sacrificial priest, the messenger who carries the oblation from humans to the gods, brings all the gods to the sacrifice, and intercedes between gods and humans (1.26.3). When Agni is pleased, the gods become generous. The building of the fire altar is a foundational Vedic ceremony,[71] and the kindling and maintaining of three fires—the household fire (*Garhapatya*), the ceremonial fire (*Dakshina*), and the sacrificial fire (*Ahavaniya*)—were a basic responsibility of every householder.

Agni and Soma connect in many ways. As fire and liquid they are complementary oppositions that unite in the concept of the fiery liquid, the elixir of immortality, or ambrosia; Soma is the fiery fluid and Agni the fluid fire. As ritual elements, the embodiments of the sacrificial fire and the sacrificial drink, they are invoked more than any other gods of the *Rig Veda*. As metaphorical symbols they are the pivot of speculations about the nature of the cosmos. Their mythologies join in the image of the sunbird, a form of Agni (the firebird) who brings Soma to earth (10.123, 177). They are two contrasting sources of the inspiration that enables the Vedic poet to understand the meaning of the sacrifice and of his life: Where Soma is Dionysian, representing the wild, raw, disruptive aspect of rituals, Agni is Apollonian, representing the cultivated, cooked, cultured aspects of rituals. The Vedic sacrifice needs both of them.

Indra, the king of the gods, the paradigmatic warrior, and the god of rain, is (in English) a homonym: He reigns and he rains. As the great soma drinker he appears often in the soma poems, and he is the one who brings Agni back when the antigods (Asuras) steal him (10.51, 124). The poets also praise Indra for freeing the cows that have been stolen and hidden in a cave (3.31, 10.108), but his greatest deed is the killing of the dragon Vritra, who is called a Dasa, and who dams up the waters, causing a drought (1.32). Both Indra and Vritra are drinkers, but Vritra cannot hold his soma as Indra can (on this occasion).

By killing Vritra, Indra simultaneously releases the waters or rains that Vritra has held back and conquers the enemies of the Vedic people, getting back the waters and the cows trapped in the cave.

This myth of dragon slaying, linked to the myth of the cattle raid,[72] is foundational to the Kshatriya class,* as "Poem of the Primeval Man" is for the Brahmin class. Indra's famous generosity—particularly when he is high on soma—and his endearing anthropomorphism emboldened at least one poet to imagine himself in Indra's place (8.14). But these same qualities may have led worshipers even in Vedic times to devalue Indra;† one poem records doubts about his existence: "He about whom they ask, 'Where is he?' or say, 'He does not exist,'—believe in him! He, my people, is Indra (2.12.5)." Yet even that poem ultimately affirms Indra's existence.

Varuna combines aspects of the roles of priest and king. His original function was that of a sky god, in particular the god of the waters in the heavenly vault (Ouranos, also a sky god, is his Greek counterpart). But by the time of the *Rig Veda* Varuna had developed into a god whose primary role was watching over human behavior (as a sky god was well situated to do) and punishing those who violated the sacred law (*rita*) of which Varuna was the most important custodian. He would snare miscreants in his bonds (*pasha*), which often revealed their presence through disease.

One hymn to Varuna is extraordinary in its introspective tone, its sense of personal unworthiness and uncertainty ("What did I do?"):

VARUNA'S ANGER AND MERCY

I ask my own heart, "When shall I be close to Varuna? Will he enjoy my offering and not be provoked to anger? When shall I see his mercy and rejoice?" I ask myself what the transgression was, Varuna, for I wish to understand. I turn to the wise to ask them. The poets have told me the very same thing: "Varuna has been provoked to anger against you." O Varuna, what was the terrible crime for which you wish to destroy your friend who praises you? Proclaim it to me so that I may hasten to prostrate myself before you and be free from error, for you are hard to deceive and are ruled by yourself alone. Free us from the harmful deeds of our fathers and from those that we have committed with our own bodies. The mischief

---

* Indeed, like the cattle raid myth, it is not merely a Vedic but a wider Indo-European myth.
† The Buddhists, in subsequent centuries, often attacked Indra and questioned his existence, and in the *Bhagavata Purana* (10.24.23), when Krishna is fighting against Indra, he dissuades people from praying to Indra for rain, saying, "Clouds driven by mist rain everywhere. What can Indra do?"

was not done by my own free will, Varuna; wine, anger, dice, or carelessness led me astray. The older shares in the mistake of the younger. Even sleep does not avert evil. As a slave serves a generous master, so would I serve the furious god and be free from error (7.86).

The poem assumes that on the one hand, one may not be blamed, or perhaps not entirely blamed, for errors committed under the influence of passionate emotions, and on the other hand, one may be punished not only for conscious errors but also for errors committed unconsciously, in sleep, or even by other people (both one's parents and one's children). The idea that one person can be punished for the crime of another person is the flip side of an idea implicit in the Vedic sacrifice, which the priest performs for the benefit of someone else, the sacrificial patron (*yajamana*, in Sanskrit). This idea becomes much more important in later Hinduism, in texts that characterize the Vedic transaction as one in which the ritual transfers to the sponsor the good karma that the priest generates. Eventually—to fast-forward for a moment—the idea of the transfer of good karma in a ritual act with effects in this life develops into the idea of the moral consequences of any act, not only in this life but also in future lives.

DEATH

Just as the Vedic poets speculate in various contrasting, even conflicting ways about the process of creation, so too do they vary in their speculations about death and in the questions they ask about death. The poets view death and sleep as a part of chaos, in contrast with the ordering of life in the hierarchy of social classes.* Death in the Vedas is something to be avoided as long as possible; one hopes only to escape premature death, never to live forever; the prayer is that people should die in the right order, that children should not die before their parents (10.18.5). Surprisingly for a document so devoted to war and sacrifice, both of which involve killing, the *Rig Veda* actually says relatively little about death. What it does say, however, is comforting: For the virtuous, death is a hazy but pleasant place.

The poet says, speaking of the creator, "His shadow is immortality—and death," and he prays, "Deliver me from death, not from immortality (7.59.12)." By "immortality" the ancient sages meant not an actual eternity of life—even

---

* Some renunciant forms of Hinduism stood this value system on its head and viewed life as a terrifying chaos and death as the liberating peace of perfect order.

the gods do not live forever, though they live much longer than we do, and they never age—but rather a full life span (usually conceived of as seventy or a hundred years). When it comes to the inevitable end of that span, the *Rig Veda* offers varied but not necessarily contradictory images of a rather muted version of life on earth: shade (remember how hot India is), lots of good-looking women (this heaven is imagined by men), and good things to eat and drink. There is also some talk about a deep pit into which evil spirits and ogres are to be consigned forever, but no evidence that human sinners would be sent there (7.104).

The poems also propose many different nonsolutions to the insoluble problem of death, many different ways that the square peg of the fact of death cannot be fitted into the round hole of human rationality. These approaches are often aware of one another; they react against one another and incorporate one another, through the process of intertextuality. And there is general agreement on some points, such as that the dead person would go to the House of Clay, to be punished, or to the World of the Fathers, to be rewarded.[73]

Fast-Forward: Reincarnation

The *Rig Veda* is more concerned with the living than with the dead, as is clear from the way texts address mourners (10.18), but they also address the corpse: "Leaving behind all imperfections, go back home again; merge with a glorious body (10.14.8)." Despite this "glorious body" with which the dead person unites, another poem expresses concern that the old body be preserved and confidence that this will be so. The poem begins by addressing the funeral fire: "Do not burn him entirely, Agni, or engulf him in your flames. Do not consume his skin or his flesh. When you have cooked him perfectly, only then send him forth to the fathers (10.16.1)." Not only is the fire not to destroy the body, but it is to preserve it.* Speaking to the dead man, the poem says: "Whatever the black bird has pecked out of you, or the ant, the snake, or even a beast of prey, may Agni who eats all things make it whole (10.16.6)." (Something very similar was said of and to the sacrificial horse, as we have seen.)

When this poem addresses the dead man, it speaks of the ultimate cosmic dispersal of the old body: "May your eye go to the sun, your life's breath to the wind. Go to the sky or to earth, as is your nature; or go to the waters, if that is your fate. Take root in the plants with your limbs (10.16.3)." (This dismember-

---

* The great French Indologist Louis Renou capriciously translated the idea of being cooked perfectly as *au point*, just as one would say of a good steak.

ment is reversed in "Poem of the Primeval Man" (10.90): "The moon was born from his mind; from his eye the sun was born.") And then it asks Agni to let the dead man "join with a body (10.16.5)."

The fate of the dead was a site of contention that was not tackled head-on until the Upanishads began to meditate philosophically on the ritual and mythology of the Vedas, and it was not fully explored until the full flourishing of Indian philosophy. Yet ever dogged by hindsight, our unshakable bête noire, we might note even in the Vedic poems some rather vague intimations of transmigration.[74] "Take root in the plants with your limbs (10.16.3)" might be a hint of the sort of rebirth in plants that the Upanishads are going to describe in detail, especially when that verse is coupled, later in that same poem, with a rather suggestive, if cryptic, allusion to rebirth: "Let him reach his own descendants, dressing himself in a life span (10.16.5)." This verse can be interpreted to mean that Agni shold let the dead person come back to his former home and to his offspring.[75] The dead in the Upanishads come back to the earth in the form of rain, and that idea may be encoded here too. Though a line in another poem, which expresses several rather different views of the fate of the dead, reverts to the idea of heaven, it also hints at the importance of the record of good deeds—which is to say, good karma: "Unite with the fathers, with Yama [king of the dead], with the rewards of your sacrifices and good deeds, in the highest heaven (10.14.7)." But these are, at best, but the early, murky stirrings of a doctrine that will become clear only in the Brahmanas and Upanishads.

CHAPTER 6
SACRIFICE IN THE BRAHMANAS
800 to 500 BCE

ॐ

CHRONOLOGY (ALL DATES BCE)

1100–1000 Vedic texts mention the Doab (the area between the two [*do*]
rivers [*ab*], the Ganges and the Yamuna)

c. 1000 The city of Kaushambi in Vatsa is founded

c. 950[1] The *Mahabharata* battle is said to have taken place

c. 900 The city of Kashi (Varanasi, Benares) is founded

c. 800–600 The Brahmanas are composed

HUMANS AND CATTLE

In the beginning, the skin of cattle was the skin that humans have
now, and the skin of a human was the skin that cattle have now. Cattle could not bear the heat, rain, flies, and mosquitoes. They went to
humans and said, "Let this skin be yours and that skin be ours."
"What would be the result of that?" humans asked. "You could eat
us," said the cattle, "and this skin of ours would be your clothing."
And so they gave humans their clothing. Therefore, when the sacrificer puts on a red hide, he flourishes, and cattle do not eat him in the
other world; for [otherwise] cattle do eat a human in the other world.

Jaiminiya Brahmana (c. 600 BCE)[2]

Concerns for the relationship between humans and animals, and with retribution in "the other world," are central issues in the Brahmanas. Many new
ideas are introduced in the form of folktales, some of which are alluded to, but
not narrated, in the *Rig Veda*, while others may come from non-Vedic parts of
Indian culture.

THE CITIES ON THE GANGES

Where the *Rig Veda* expressed uncertainty and begged the gods for help, the Brahmanas (mythological, philosophical, and ritual glosses on the Vedas) express confidence that their infallible Vedic verses (mantras) can deal with all dangers. Troubled by the open-ended refrain of the *Rig Vedic* creation poem that could only ask, "Who is the god whom we should honor with the oblation?" the Brahmanas invented a god whose name was the interrogative pronoun Who (*ka*, cognate with the Latin *quis*, French *qui*). One text explained it: The creator asked the god Indra (whose own existence, you may recall, was once in doubt), "Who am I?," to which Indra replied, "Just who you just said" (i.e., "I am Who"), and that is how the creator got the name of Who.[3] So too in one Vedic ceremony,[4] when the ritual subject goes to heaven and comes back again, he must say, on his return, "I am just who I am." Read back into the Vedic poem (as it was in later Vedic commentaries[5]), this resulted in an affirmative statement: "Indeed, Who *is* the god whom we should honor with the oblation," somewhat reminiscent of the famous Abbott and Costello routine "Who's on first?" But this sacerdotal arrogance closed down some of those openings through which fresh theological air had flowed. The question became the answer.

What can account for this dramatic shift in tone, from questions to answers? In part, it was caused by a major change in the living conditions of the authors of these texts. For the Brahmanas were composed during one of the most significant geographical and social shifts in the history of Hinduism, a period that has been called the second urbanization[6] (the first being that of the Indus Valley), a time of social and intellectual transformation so extreme that it could well be called revolutionary. Let us, as usual, ground our discussion of the religious texts in a quick snapshot of the material lives of their authors.

From about 1100 to 1000 BCE, Vedic texts begin to mention the Doab ("Two Waters"), the land between the Ganges and the Yamuna (Jumna), the site of the city of Hastinapur (east of the present Delhi), and the scene in which most of the *Mahabharata* is set. Then, in about 900 BCE, we find references to an area farther down in the western and middle Ganges Valley, where people built palaces and kingdoms. Just as the migrations of the Vedic people into the Punjab probably took place gradually, through several different incursions, so too the move to the Ganges took place incrementally over several centuries. The political changes were correspondingly gradual. Though the Vedas refer to kings, they were really rulers of relatively small, and transitory, political units, numerous small chiefdoms; so too the leaders of the early political units on the Ganges were said to be "kings in name only" (*raja-shabdin*), and a later Buddhist text mocked them, remarking that each one said, "I am the king! I am the king!"[7] Now, however, a few big, powerful kingdoms begin to emerge.

Among the first cities were Kashi, later known as Varanasi (or Benares, the capital of Koshala/Videha), and, southeast of Hastinapur and west of Kashi, the city of Kaushambi (in Vatsa, now Uttar Pradesh), whose stratigraphy suggests a founding date of between 1300 and 1000 BCE.[8] The Brahmanas must have been composed a few centuries after the founding of these cities, for considerable time must have passed since the composition of the *Rig Veda* (even of the first and last books, one and ten, which are already noticeably later than the other eight), since the language of the Brahmanas is significantly different, somewhat like the shift from Beowulf to Chaucer in early English. The Brahmanas cite Vedic verses and explain them, describing the circumstances under which those verses were first created. Not only the language but the nature of the texts changed: Between 1000 and 500 BCE, Vedic rituals spawned more and more commentaries, and by the sixth century BCE the different schools, or branches (*shakha*s), had been well established.[9]

During the first millennium BCE, the Vedic people settled down and built things to last. They continued to move east across North India and to take control of the river trade, forests, and rich deposits of minerals.[10] First they moved east from the Punjab to Magadha (Bihar) and the lower Ganges and later, in a backflow, west from the Ganges to Gujarat. The main crop now shifted from wheat to rice, which yielded a far greater surplus, and they used water buffalo in its cultivation. Eventually they formed cities and states, building urban societies along the Ganges, utilizing the agricultural surplus of wet rice and other crops that benefited from irrigation and control of the river floodings.

They moved partly in search of deposits of iron, which they developed from about 800 BCE (though a better quality was developed by about 600[11]); its use was predominant in the western Ganges plain in the first millennium BCE and spread from the Indo-Gangetic watershed to the confluence of the Ganges and Yamuna.[12] In the *Rig Veda*, the word *ayas* means "bronze"; later the *Atharva Veda* distinguishes red *ayas* ("bronze") from dark *ayas* ("iron"). First used for pins and other parts of horse harnesses, as well as for weapons, iron was not imported but was developed in India, primarily from rich lodes in what is now southern Bihar.[13]

CLASS CONFLICTS

The surplus that became available along the banks of the Ganges meant a new kind of social and economic power. It meant the organization and redistribution of raw materials and the greater stratification of society, in part because the growing of rice is a complex process that requires a higher degree of cooperation than was needed for herding or for simpler forms of agriculture. As labor became more specialized, sharper lines now divided each of the three top classes one from another and divided all of them from the fourth class, of servants.

More extensive kingship also meant more extravagant sacrifices, which in turn required still more wealth. New forms of political and social organization required new forms of ritual specialization. The early cities were ritual complexes, living statements about royal power.[14] The great kingship rituals such as the royal consecration rites and the horse sacrifice responded to a perceived need for an outward justification of the power exercised by "the emerging kingdoms with their increasingly stratified societies and their multi-lingual, multi-cultural and multi-racial populations."[15] The ceremony of royal consecration became a highly elaborate affair, involving a period of symbolic exile, a chariot race, and a symbolic gambling match, all of which were to have long-lasting resonances in the narrative literature. And such complex sacrifices required a more complex math, astronomy, geometry; they also led to a more precise knowledge of animal anatomy.[16] Above all, the importance laid upon the precise words used in the rituals, the mantras, inspired the development of an elaborate system of grammar, which remained the queen of the sciences in India (as theology was for medieval Christianity). The more complex sacrifices also required a more complex priesthood, leading to questions about the qualifications of those claiming the title.

Thus texts of this period define a true Brahmin in terms that transcend birth: "Why do you enquire about the father or the mother of a Brahmin? When you find knowledge in someone, that is his father and his grandfather."[17] And other texts similarly question class lines. One follows the typical Brahmana pattern of explaining the circumstances under which a sage "sees" or "hears" a particular Vedic hymn.

THE SAGES AND THE SON OF A SLAVE WOMAN
Sages performing a sacrifice on the banks of the river Sarasvati drove Kavasha, the son of Ilusha, away from the soma, calling him the son of a slave woman and

saying: "How did he ever come to be consecrated among us? Let him die of thirst, but he must not drink the water of the Sarasvati." When he was alone in the desert, tormented by thirst, he composed a Vedic poem [10.30], and the Sarasvati came to him and surrounded him with her waters. When the sages saw this, they realized, "The gods know him; let us call him back."[18]

In this story, a person from outside the society of the upper classes is assimilated into the inner sanctum of the Vedic priesthood. The sages call him a son of a slave woman, Dasi-putra, a term usually designating the son of a Shudra mother, in this case also the son of a man named Ilusha, presumably a Brahmin.

Shudras and Vaishyas play increasingly important roles in the Brahmanas. The surplus supported kings and an administrative bureaucracy and made a greater demand on the people who produced the wealth, taxation of a portion of the whole crop (according to Manu, a sixth of the crop).[19] The word *bali*, which originally meant (and continued to mean) an offering to gods, now also came to mean a tax paid to kings. This burden alienated at least some of the people, as we learn from one Brahmana:

THE KING EATS THE PEOPLE

"When a deer eats the barley, the farmer does not hope to nourish the animal; when a low-born woman becomes the mistress of a noble man, her husband does not hope to get rich on that nourishment." Now, the barley is the people, and the deer is the royal power; thus the people are food for the royal power, and so the one who has royal power eats the people. And so the king does not raise animals; and so one does not anoint as king the son of a woman born of the people.[20]

Though this text, like most texts of the ancient period, was ultimately passed through a Brahmin filter and therefore surely represents the interests of Brahmins in criticizing the king, it just as surely also captures (if only to use it for Brahminical purposes) the abuse, and the resentment, of people who, not being Brahmins, did not have immediate access to the text. Yet in addition to proclaiming the brutality of the king, it assumes that class lines cannot be crossed, a lowborn man should not allow his wife to have a highborn lover, and a man of the people (a Vaishya) cannot be king.

The sacrifice was far from the only royal concern, as the historian Romila Thapar explains:

The point at which wealth could be accumulated and spent on a variety of adjuncts to authority marked the point at which kingship was beginning to draw on political authority, rather than ritual authority alone. However, the ritual of the sacrifice as a necessary precondition to kingship could not become a permanent feature. Once kingdoms were established there were other demands on the wealth that went to support the kingdoms.[21]

Ritual authority was thus supplemented by other trappings of authority, including armies and tax collectors. These expenses would drain the money that had previously been given to the priests for sacrifices, fueling the growing animosity between rulers and priests, an animosity so central to the history of Hinduism that it has been called "the inner conflict of tradition."[22]

KINGS AND PRIESTS

The move down from the Punjab to the Ganges also sowed the seeds of a problem that was to have repercussions throughout the history of Hinduism: The Vedic people no longer had good grazing lands for their horses, and so it was no longer possible for every member of the tribe to keep a horse. The horse became a rich man's beast, now a hierarchical as well an imperialist animal, but it retained its power as a popular cultural symbol, one whose meaning continued to shift in each new age all through subsequent Indian history. Horses and their power to destroy are at the heart of a story about conflicts between the two upper classes. In battle, the warrior stood on the left of the two-man chariot, holding his bow in one hand and his arrows in the other, while the charioteer, literally the warrior's right-hand man, held the reins in his right hand and a shield in front of both of them with his left hand, so that the archer would have both hands free to shoot. In this story, the king stands in the place of the warrior, holding not a weapon but a whip, while his royal chaplain or domestic priest (Purohita) serves as the charioteer, literally and figuratively holding the reins:

THE KING AND THE PRIEST IN THE CHARIOT

Vrisha was the royal chaplain (Purohita) of Triyaruna, king of the Ikshvakus. Now, in the old days the royal chaplain would hold the reins in the chariot for the king in order to watch out for the king, to keep him from doing any harm. As the two of them were driving along, they cut down with the wheel of the chariot the son of a Brahmin, a little boy playing in the road. One of them [the king] had driven the horses forward, while the other [the priest] had tried to pull them to one side, but they came on so hard that he could not pull them aside. And so they had cut down the boy. They argued with each other about it, and the priest threw down the reins and stepped down from the chariot. The king said, "The one who holds the reins is the driver of the chariot. You are the murderer." "No," said the priest, "I tried to pull back to avoid him, but you drove the horses on. *You* are the murderer." Finally they said, "Let us ask," and they went to ask the Ikshvakus. The Ikshvakus said, "The one who holds the reins is the driver. You are the murderer," and they accused Vrisha, the priest.

He prayed, "Let me get out of this; let me find help and a way out. Let that boy come to life." He saw this mantra [9.65.28–29] and brought the boy to life with it.* . . . For this is a mantra that cures and makes restoration. And it is also a mantra that gives you what you want. Whoever praises with this mantra gets whatever he wants.[23]

The text, right from the start, casts a jaundiced eye upon the king; it assumes that you can't let a king out alone without his keeper, the Brahmin, who goes along "to keep him from doing harm"—that is, from indulging in the royal addictions, here consisting of reckless driving. This is a transformation of the court chaplain's usual task of washing the blood of battle and executions off the king's hands *after* he has sinned.[24] In this case, between the two of them they manage to murder an innocent child, in one of the earliest recorded hit-and-run incidents in history. That child is a Brahmin, related to Vrisha by class; in another variant of this story, the dead boy is actually Vrisha's own son.[25] The jury is hardly impartial, being made up entirely of the king's people, the Ikshvakus, a great northern dynasty, and it is therefore not surprising that they reject the priest's argument that it was all the king's fault, whipping the horses on, and rule that it was the priest's job to rein the horses in. (The text's statement that this incident happened "in the old days" implies that court chaplains no longer drove chariots, if in fact they ever did; the text metaphorically puts the chaplain in the driver's seat or makes him the king's right-hand man, jockeying for power.) The chariot of the senses that a person drives with one (priestly) foot on the brakes and the other (royal) foot on the accelerator is a recurrent image in Hindu philosophy; we have seen a Vedic poem (10.119) in which someone exhilarated (or stoned) on soma says that the drinks have carried him up and

---

* The Vedic mantra that he sees likens Soma to a nimble chariot horse.

away, "Like horses bolting with a chariot."[26] In the Upanishads, as we will soon see, the intellect/charioteer reins in the senses/horses that pull the chariot of the mind.[27] In the *Bhagavad Gita*, the incarnate god Krishna holds the reins for Prince Arjuna, though there Arjuna holds back, and Krishna goads him forward. Charioteers are major players in both the martial and the narrative/philosophical world.

The point of this story of Vrisha seems to be that royal power trumps priestly power in the courts, since the jury is stacked; the only way that the priest can avoid punishment is by using priestly power to erase the entire crime. The mantra that he uses to do this has wider applications; it assures him that he will always get what he wants, even, apparently, when he wants to raise the dead. This same power will belong to the person who hears the story and thus gains access to the mantra known as the "fruits of hearing" (*phala shruti*) that comes at the end of many stories of this type: "Whoever knows this" (*yo evam veda*) gets whatever the protagonist of the story got. (It is guaranteed to work, though it is not foolproof: If you say it and do not get the promised reward, you must have said it wrong somehow.) This is a major innovation of the Brahmana texts: Where the Vedas asked, and hoped, that the gods would help them, the Brahmins of these later texts arrogantly assure the worshiper that they can fix anything.

But the story then goes on to tell us that Vrisha did not get *all* that he wanted; he did not get justice, vindication.

THE FIRE IN THE WOMAN

But Vrisha was angry, and he went to Jana [his father] and said, "They gave a false and prejudiced judgment against me." Then the power went out of the fire of the Ikshvakus: If they placed food on the fire in the evening, by morning it still had not been cooked; and if they placed food on the fire in the morning, the same thing happened to it [by evening]. Then they said, "We have displeased a Brahmin and treated him with dishonor. That is why the power has gone out of our fire. Let us invite him back." They invited him, and he came back, just like a Brahmin summoned by a king. As he arrived, he prayed, "Let me see this power of fire." He saw this mantra and sang it over the fire. Then he saw this: "The wife of Triyaruna is a flesh-eating ghoul [*pishachi*]. She is the one who has covered the fire with a cushion and sits on it." Then he spoke these verses from the *Rig Veda* [5.2.12, 9–10], and as he finished saying them, the power of the fire ran up into her and burned her all up. Then they dispersed that power of the fire properly, here and there [in each house], and the fire cooked for them properly.[28]

The *Rig Veda* verses that Vrisha cites refer, obscurely, to the myth in which Agni, the god of fire, is first lost and then found, which is precisely what has happened (again) here.

This part of the story seems to have little to do with the earlier episode, the fight between the king and his priest. Apparently Vrisha is still full of resentment when he recollects what he (but no one else) regards as the injustice of it all, the insolence of royal office. (The jury's judgment is not, on the face of it, unfair; it is, I should think, reasonable to hold responsible the person who controlled the chariot's brakes.) Yet the fire vanishes immediately after Vrisha seeks help from Jana, his father, and though Jana does nothing explicit to help his son, there are many other stories (some in this same text) in which Agni (who is, after all, a priest himself) vanishes when a priest is offended, and still others in which an offended Brahmin conjures up a demoness (a ghoul [Pishachi], as here, or an ogress [Rakshasi] or a female antigod [Asuri]) to avenge him when he has been harmed. Either or both of these may be implied here. The point of the second half of the story is therefore a warning never to offend a Brahmin.

But the text also makes a gratuitous swipe at the dangerous sexuality of women, for the fire that the queen hides under her lap and that destroys her by entering her between her legs is essential to the life of the whole community, which needs it to cook not only the sacred oblations but all profane food. Both these types of cooking belong to the wife, who cooks the everyday meals and (by her mere presence at the ritual) makes it possible for her husband to offer the oblations into the fire.[29] We will have more occasions to consider the connections between women and fire in Hinduism.

ANIMALS

THE HORSE SACRIFICE REVISITED, I

The Brahmanas now tell us more about the way in which the horse sacrifice, which began as a relatively simple ritual at the time of the *Rig Veda*, developed into a far more complex and expensive ceremony in this later period. The political symbolism of the Vedic horse sacrifice is blatant: The consecrated white stallion was "set free" to wander for a year before he was brought back home and killed, a ritual enactment of the actual equine wandering typical of Vedic culture. During that year the horse was guarded by an army that "followed" him and claimed for the king any land on which he grazed. By the late Vedic period, when the Vedic people had begun to grow fodder crops, the stallion would have been stabled, and a stabled stallion behaves quite differently from one in the wild; he tends to return to the stable where he has been fed. The idea that he will wander away in the Ganges Valley, as he used to do in his salad days up in the Punjab, was by this time an anachronism, a conscious archaism. The king's army therefore drove the horse onward and guided him into the neighboring lands that the king intended to take over. ("Doubtless some manipulated the wandering of the horse to save face," Romila Thapar remarks dryly.[30]) It is not hard to imagine the scene. People would suddenly run out into the fields, shouting, "Get your goddamn horse out of my field; he's trampling the crop," and suddenly a few, or a few hundred, armed men would appear over the brow of the hill and growl, "Say that again?" and the people would reply, "Oh, I beg your pardon, sirs, I didn't realize—do let your lovely horse graze here, and can we bring you a little something for yourselves?" and the soldiers would then claim all the land the horse had grazed. Thus the ritual that presented itself as a casual equine stroll over the king's lands was in fact an orchestrated annexation of the lands on a king's border; a ritual about grazing became a ritual about political aggrandizement. The Vedic drive toward wandering (without settling) had developed into what the Nazis called, euphemistically, incorporation (Anschluss) and nineteenth-century Americans called manifest destiny. No wonder the Sanskrit texts insist that a king had to be very powerful indeed before he could undertake a horse sacrifice, and very few kings did in fact perform this ritual.

In addition to its political purposes, this sacrifice, like most, was designed to restore things that had gone wrong, in this case to restore the king who had been sullied by the bloodshed necessitated by his office. But new things could go wrong during the period when the horse was said to wander freely. So restorations were prescribed if the horse mounted a mare, or became lame, or got sick but not lame, or if the horse's eye was injured or diseased, or if the horse died in water. Finally:

> If the horse should get lost, [the sacrificer] should make a sacrificial offering of three oblations. . . . And even by itself, this ritual finds what has been lost; whatever other thing of his is lost, let him sacrifice with this ritual, and he will surely find it. And if enemies should get the horse, or if the horse should die . . . , they

should bring another horse and consecrate it by sprinkling it with water; this is the restoration for that.[31]

At the end of the ceremony, there is even a restoration for the obscene language that has been an obligatory part of the ritual: "The vital breaths go out of those who speak impure speech in the sacrifice. And so they utter at the end a sweet-smelling mantra, and so they purify their speech and the vital breaths do not go out of them. . . . Thus they purify their speech to keep the gods from going out of the sacrifice."[32] You can fix anything, if you know how and if you are a Brahmin.

DOGS

A dog too played a part in keeping evil out of the sacrifice, and the negative role of the dog is evidence that the lower castes were still essential to the ritual. It may well be that the growing acknowledgment of class distinctions in this period and the formulation of more intense rules of purity and impurity began to find the omnivorous dog a useful symbol of the impure eater, the outsider, in contrast with the noble, herbivorous (i.e., vegetarian) horse. Another factor in the fall of the dog's status may have been the progressive decline of the Vedic gods Indra, Yama, and Rudra, who were associated with dogs.[33]

Early in the ceremony the stallion stood in water. Collateral relatives of the king and queen brought to the stallion a "four-eyed" dog (probably a reference to the two eyes plus the two round marks above the eyebrows that many dogs have to this day). Then, when the dog could no longer touch bottom in the water, the son of a whore killed him with a wooden club, saying, "Off with the mortal! Off with the dog!" For, a Brahmana explained, "Truly the dog is evil, one's fraternal enemy; thus he slays his evil, his fraternal enemy. . . . They say that evil seeks to grasp him who offers the horse sacrifice. He throws the dog beneath the feet of the horse. The horse has a thunderbolt. Thus by a thunderbolt he tramples down evil."[34] The horse then put his right front hoof on the dead dog, while another spell banished any man or dog who might harm the horse.[35] The association of the dog with an unclean woman (the whore whose son kills him) and with feet, as well as explicitly with evil, is an indication of his status as a kind of scapegoat, more precisely a scape-dog, onto whom the sins of the community were transferred. The sacrifice of a "four-eyed dog" at the beginning of the horse sacrifice also takes on deeper meaning when interpreted in the context of the ancient Indian game of dice, for the dice are also said to be four-eyed[36]—that is, marked by four black spots.

Bitches too lose cachet between the *Rig Veda* and the Brahmanas. The *Rig Veda* regarded all dogs as the sons of Indra's beloved brindled bitch Sarama; dogs were called Sons of Sarama (7.55.2–4). In the Brahmanas, Sarama is still a somewhat positive figure; she still finds the cows that the Panis have stolen and resists their bribes of food, as in the earlier text. Indra says, "Since you found our cows, I make your progeny eaters of food," and the brindled dogs who are Sarama's descendants "kill even tigers."[37] But now Sarama eats the amniotic sac that contains the waters—just as dogs (and other animals) do eat the afterbirth—which the text regards as an act of murder. The same ambivalence hedges the curse/boon that her progeny will be omnivorous; it's good to kill tigers but bad to eat the amniotic sac.

Sarama, the ancestress of all dogs, is a good dog, but dogs as a species are bad, for they pollute the oblations by licking them in their attempt to eat them. A number of texts therefore ban dogs from the sacrificial area. The *Rig Veda* warns the sacrificer to keep "the long-tongued dog" away (9.101.1), and the lawbook of Manu (7.21) warns that if the king does not enforce the law, crows will eat the sacrificial cakes and dogs will lick the oblations. Several Brahmanas tell of ways to destroy an ogress named Long-Tongue (Dirgha-jihva), who licks the milk offering and curdles it[38] or licks at the soma all the time.[39] Though she is an ogress (Rakshasi), not specifically called a dog, her name is the name of a dog in the *Rig Veda*, and she does just what dogs are supposed to do: She licks the oblation. This Long-Tongue also just happens to have vaginas on every limb, like another ogress whom Indra destroyed by placing penises on each of his joints and seducing her.[40] And so Indra equips Kutsa's son (Indra's grandson) in the same way. Then:

LONG-TONGUE AND INDRA'S GRANDSON

They lay together. As soon as he had his way with her, he remained firmly stuck in her. He saw these mantras and praised with them, and with them he summoned Indra. Indra ran against her and struck her down and killed her with his thunderbolt that was made of mantras. Whoever praises with these mantras slays his hateful fraternal rivals and drives away all evil demons.[41]

Long-Tongue's long tongue makes her ritually dangerous, and her equally excessive vaginas make her sexually both threatening and vulnerable (eventually immobilized, in an image perhaps suggested by observations of mating dogs, often similarly paralyzed). Despite her grotesque and bestial sexuality, Long-Tongue does no harm, yet she is destroyed. She is more sinned against than sinning. For the point of the Brahmana is that the dangerous bitch (in either canine or human form) is not, ultimately, dangerous—for the man who knows the mantras.

COWS, VEGETARIANISM, AND NONVIOLENCE

Cows are not themselves dangerous (compared with horses and even dogs, not to mention bulls), but they are indirectly responsible for a great deal of trouble in Hinduism. The Brahmanas advise the sacrificer never to stand naked near a cow, for, as we learn from the story that opens this chapter, "Humans and Cattle," the skin of cattle (*pashus*) was once our skin, and (the text continues), if a cow sees you naked, she may run away, thinking, "I am wearing his skin," the implication being that she fears that you might want to take back your skin. The transaction in the other world is here interpreted as the reversal of a reversal: Humans and cattle traded places long ago, and as a result, cattle *willingly* undertook to supply humans with food and clothing but also, apparently, won the boon of eating humans (and, perhaps, flaying them) in the other world. Nakedness, by reducing humans to the level of the beasts, establishes a reciprocal relationship, rendering human beings vulnerable to the sufferings of beasts—being eaten—when they enter the other world.

Another text adds more detail to the basic idea of reciprocity between humans and animals in the other world; it is a long text, and I will just summarize the main points relevant to this discussion. The story concerns Varuna, the Vedic god of the waters and of the moral law, and his son, Bhrigu, who was a famous priest:

VARUNA'S SON GOES TO HELL

Bhrigu, the son of Varuna, thought he was better than his father, better than the gods, better than the other Brahmins. Varuna thought, "My son doesn't know anything. Let's teach him a lesson." He took away his life's breaths, and Bhrigu fainted and went beyond this world to the world beyond. There he saw a man cut another man to pieces and eat him; and then a man eating another man, who was screaming; and then a man eating another man, who was soundlessly screaming. He returned from that world and told Varuna what he had seen. Varuna explained that when people who lack true knowledge and offer no oblations cut down trees for firewood, or cook for themselves animals that cry out, or cook for themselves rice and barley, which scream soundlessly, those trees, and animals, and rice and barley take the form of men in the other world and eat those people in return. "How can one avoid that?" asked Bhrigu. And Varuna replied that you avoid it by putting fuel on the sacred fire and offering oblations.[42]

This text is not just about animals, since trees and barley play an equally important role, but more broadly about all the things used in preparing food (vegetables, animals, and fuel), about consumerism in a very literal sense. Being eaten in the other world is not a punishment for sins but rather a straight reversal of the inevitable (and not condemned) eating in this world. Other Brahmanas confirm this: "Just as in this world men eat cattle and devour them, so in the other world cattle eat men and devour them."[43] And: "Whatever food a man eats in this world, that [food] eats him in the other world."[44] In the Brahmanas, you are, as usual, what you eat, but now in the sense of becoming food for your food.

This experience in the other world is therefore as inevitable as death itself, and just as unpleasant. The soundlessly screaming rice and barley resurfaced in the writings of the great Indian botanist Jagadish Chandra Bose, who moved George Bernard Shaw deeply with his demonstration of an "unfortunate carrot strapped to the table of an unlicensed vivisector."[45] The silent screams in the Sanskrit text have the quality of a nightmare, from which the unconscious Bhrigu flees.

Nowhere, however, does the text suggest that people should stop eating animals (or rice, for that matter). It is possible to avoid the unpleasant consequences of eating; the solution is, as usual in the Brahmanas, to perform the proper rituals, to fix it, to restore anyone who has eaten something alleged to produce unfortunate consequences—if left unrestored. Dangers arise in the context of profane eating and are warded off by sacred feeding (the oblations offered to the gods). Indeed the two are inextricably linked by the belief that it is wrong to take food without offering some, at least mentally, to the gods; in the broadest sense, all human food consists of divine leftovers (later known as *prasad* ["grace"]). The text is not saying, "Do not eat animals, for then they will eat you," but, rather, "Be sure to eat animals in the right way, or they will eat you." One word for "avoidance" (of this retributive devouring) or "restoration" is *nishkriti* ("undoing"), designating a careful plan by which to repair a mistake that will otherwise bring unwanted consequences, as well as the repayment or redemption of a debt and the expiatory payment for an error. The proper sort of "avoidance" makes the meat safe to eat, as if it were kosher or halal. This accomplishes what the Vedic sacrificial priest achieved when he gave the offering first to Agni and only after that invited the people to eat it; in both cases, a preparatory ritual makes the food safe. This sort of "restoration" (also called *prayash-chitta*, often wrongly translated as "expiation") first refers to the measures taken to restore the ritual when it goes wrong (such as fixing the horse in the horse sacrifice). But then it comes to mean the ritual you use to restore something else that might go wrong (the oblation you perform when you eat animals), and finally, the text or the priest tells you how to restore your entire life when it goes wrong (getting rid of your bad karma, making a pilgrimage, surrendering to the god, or whatever else may be prescribed).

The word *ahimsa* ("nonviolence") occurs in the Brahmanas primarily in the sense of "safety," "security." Yet we can also see the stirrings of another, later meaning of *ahimsa*—a desire not to harm animals, as well as an uneasiness about eating animals at all.* Indeed we saw this discomfort even in the *Rig Veda* in the idea of the cow that yields food without being killed, the cow that Prithu milked, and the reassurance that the sacrificial horse doesn't really die. The idea of reversals in the other world was easily ethicized (in Jainism and Buddhism and, later, in Hinduism) into the stricter belief that the best way to avoid being eaten in the other world was not merely to eat animals in the proper (sacrificial) way but to stop eating them altogether. The story of Bhrigu does not yet espouse the ideals of nonviolence or vegetarianism, though it probably contributed to the rise of such doctrines.

For it is evident that people did eat meat, including beef, at this period, though in ways that were becoming increasingly qualified. People ate meat mainly on special occasions, such as rituals or when welcoming a guest or a person of high status.[46] Eating meat in a sacrifice is not the same as eating meat for dinner, and killing too can be dichotomized in this way,† as can the eating of cows versus other sorts of meat, though several texts combine the permission

---

*In *Homo Necans* (1972) Walter Burkert argued that the act of killing the animal in a sacrifice was the survival of a Neolithic hunting ritual expressing grief over the animal's demise. For Burkert, animal sacrifice was a tragic deception, in which the sacrificer assumed that the sacrificial animal consented to being sacrificed. Whether or not Burkert's insights are valid for the Greek evidence, they do seem to be highly relevant to the ancient Indian texts.

†To this day it is often argued in India that the meat of animals killed for the table is poison because such animals die in fear and anger, while animals killed for sacrifice are happy to die, and so their meat is sweet.

for eating meat (including cow) at a sacrifice (where the gods are, after all, the guests) and meat offered to a human guest. "Meat is certainly the best kind of food," says one text.[47] The Brahmanas say that a bull or cow should be killed when a guest arrives, a cow should be sacrificed to Mitra and Varuna, and a sterile cow to the Maruts, and that twenty-one sterile cows should be sacrificed in the horse sacrifice.[48] For "the cow is food."[49] The grammarian Panini, who may have lived as early as the fifth or sixth century BCE, glossed the word goghna ("cowkiller") as "one for whom a cow is killed," that is, a guest (3.4.73).[50] A dharma-sutra from the third century BCE specifies: "The meat of milk cows and oxen may be eaten, and the meat of oxen is fit for sacrifice."[51] This textual evidence is further supported, in this period, by archaeological indications, such as cattle bones found near domestic hearths, bearing marks of having been cut, indicating that their flesh was eaten.[52]

On the other hand, one Brahmana passage forbids the eating of either cow or bull (dhenu or anaduha),* concluding that anyone who did eat them would be reborn as something so strange that people would say, "He committed a sin, he expelled the embryo from his wife." The text then adds, "However, Yajnavalkya said, 'I do eat [the meat of both cow and bull], as long as it's tasty.'"[53] Yajnavalkya was an in-your-face kind of guy. Some people, however, did not eat the meat of cows, as Thapar points out: "This may have contributed to the later attitude of regarding the cow as sacred and inviolable, although association with the sacred need not be explained on rational grounds.... Eventually it became a matter of status to refrain from eating beef and the prohibition was strengthened by various religious sanctions. Significantly, the prohibition was prevalent only among the upper castes."[54] The ambivalence that is embedded in this historical development is not really so hard for us to understand if we cast its light upon our own casual combination of affection for our pets and appetite for filet mignon. We can see here the Indian insight into the conflicted belief that there is a chain of food and eaters (dog eat dog or, in the Indian metaphor, fish eat fish) that both justifies itself and demands that we break out of it: It happens, but it must not happen.[55]

The transformation in attitudes toward eating meat developed at this time in part through the sorts of philosophical considerations evident in the narratives and in part through changes in methods of livestock breeding, grazing

---

* Since only cows and bulls are prohibited, the text may allow for the eating of castrated bulls, steers, or bullocks.

grounds, and ecology as a result of the basic transition into the urban life of the Ganges Valley, as well as by the social tensions exacerbated by these changes. The breeding of animals in an urban setting may have introduced both less humane grazing conditions and a heightened awareness of those conditions (though some urban dwellers may have been, like many contemporary city dwellers, insulated from farming conditions). The new uneasiness about killing animals may also have been a reaction to the increasing number of animals sacrificed in more and more elaborate ceremonies. Sacrifice was still violent, and sacrifice was still power, but a murmur of protest and discontent was growing steadily stronger, soon to find its voice, faintly in the Upanishads and loudly in the *Mahabharata*.

HUMANS AS SACRIFICIAL ANIMALS

The texts of this period regard humans as the pawns of the gods. The Vedas and Brahmanas often list (in addition to human beings, a rule that we consider below) five basic kinds of sacrificial animals, or *pashus*, all male: bull, stallion, billy goat, ram, and ass (or donkey), often divided into three groups, bovines, equines (horse and ass), and extended ovines (sheep and goat). The Rig Vedic "Poem of the Primeval Man" (10.90) tells us: "From that sacrifice in which everything was offered, the melted fat was collected and made into those beasts who live in the air, in the forest, and in villages. Horses were born from it, and those other animals that have two rows of teeth [such as asses]; cows were born from it, and from it goats and sheep were born." These last are the five *pashus*. *Pashus* are generally distinguished from wild animals, who are called *mrigas*, a word derived from the verb "to hunt" (*margayati*, also connected with the noun *marga* ["a trail or path"]), designating any animal that we hunt, particularly a deer. The ancient Indians thus defined animals according to the manner in which they killed them, either in a hunt (*mrigas*) or in a sacrifice (*pashus*). Hunting is one of the vices of addiction, but sacrifice too often becomes excessive, a threat to the gods, who take measures to limit and control it (a feature of the second alliance).

Sometimes a male human being replaces the ass in the list of *pashus*.[56] Were human sacrifices actually performed in ancient India?[57] Perhaps, but certainly no longer at the time of the Vedas, and even for the pre-Vedic period, the scattered evidence sometimes cited to argue for its actual occurrence is not persuasive. Yet the Vedas refer to human sacrifices, and the texts tell you how to do one.[58] Whenever the priests consecrated a Vedic ritual fire altar (*agnicayana*) made of bricks, they placed within it five golden images of the five *pashus*, including a golden man. And archaeological evidence of human skulls and other human bones at the site of such fire altars, together with the bones of a wide variety of other animals, both wild and tame (horses, tortoises, pigs, elephants, bovines, goats, and buffalo), suggests that humans may once actually have been sacrificed in these rituals. The golden man, then, would have replaced a man of flesh and blood.[59] It is also possible that the Vedic horse sacrifice originally involved the sacrifice of a man as well as a horse.[60] But the human sacrifices are never described in anything like the detail of the horse sacrifice, and it is likely that the human victims, like many of the animal victims, were set free after they were consecrated, before the moment when they would have been killed.[61] It may well be that the human sacrifice (*purusha-medha* ["sacrifice of a man"]) was simply a part of the Brahmin imaginary, a fantasy of "the sacrifice to end all sacrifices."[62]

What is most likely is that these texts are saying that human beings are, like all other animals, fit to be sacrificed to the gods, that they are, as it were, the livestock of the gods.[63] What animals are to us, we are to the gods. There was a strong symbolic connection (explicit in many sacrifices and perhaps implicit in all of them) between the ancient Indian human sacrificer and the animal victim. When the sacrificer was initiated, he was consecrated as the victim in the animal sacrifice: "When he performs the animal sacrifice he ransoms himself, a male by means of a male. For the sacrificial victim is a male, and the sacrificer is a male. And this, this flesh, is the best food to eat, and that is how he becomes an eater of the best food to eat."[64] In a sense, every sacrifice ransoms the sacrificer from death.

Even if human sacrifice was not a part of the extant Vedic ritual, it continued to cast its shadow upon that ritual.[65] One Brahmana text arranges the five victims in what seems to be a chronological order:

HOW HUMANS CEASED TO BE SACRIFICIAL BEASTS

In the beginning, the gods used the Man (*purusha*) as their sacrificial beast; when he was used, his sacrificial quality went out of him and entered a horse. They used the horse for their sacrifice; when he was used, his sacrificial quality went out of him and entered a bull. They used the bull for their sacrifice; when he was used, his sacrificial quality went out of him and entered a ram. They used the ram for their sacrifice; when he was used, his sacrificial quality went out of him and entered a billy goat.

They used the billy goat for their sacrifice; when he was used, his sacrificial quality went out of him and entered this earth. The gods searched for it by digging, and they found it; it was this rice and barley. And that is why people even now find rice and barley by digging. And as much virile power as these sacrificial beasts would have for him, that very same amount of virile power is in this oblation of rice for him. And that is how the oblation of rice has the completeness that the fivefold animal sacrifice has.[66]

This text explains how "sacrificeability" travels down the line from the human (male) through the other *pashus* until it lodges in grains (such as rice and barley, which, it may be recalled, "scream soundlessly"), each substituting for the one above it. The sacrificial rice cake is a substitute or symbol (*pratima*) for the animal sacrifice by which the sacrificer redeems himself from the gods.[67] The sacrificial quality that goes from the man to the horse, bull, ram, and goat sets the pattern for the myth in the *Brihadaranyaka Upanishad* (1.4.3–4) in which the father god rapes his daughter, who flees from him in the form of a cow, a mare, a donkey, a goat, and a ewe, only to be caught and raped by him in the form of a bull, stallion, male donkey, goat, and ram.[*] In both of these texts, the first victim in the series is a human being, and the rest of the group consists of the (other) sacrificial animals.

A similar substitution of a plant prevents a human sacrifice in another Brahmana myth: A king's son is to be sacrificed to Varuna; a Brahmin sells his young son Shunahshepha ("Dog Prick," a most unusual name for a Brahmin) as a substitute for the king's son; the Ashvins rescue Shunahshepha by substituting a soma plant for him[†] as the sacrificial offering.[68] This is hardly a brief for human sacrifice; the king obtained the son in the first place only by promising that he would sacrifice him (a self-defeating scenario that we know from Rumpelstiltskin), and Shunahshepha's father is denounced as a monster who has committed an act for which there is no restoration, an act unprecedented even among Shudras. These myths are not historical explanations of a transition from human sacrifice to animal and vegetable sacrifice; they are meditations on the nature of ritual symbolism, explaining how it is that plants or mantras stand for animals, and animals for humans, in the sacrifice.

---

[*] The image of the woman who flees, in vain, from rape by becoming a cow and a mare may also have been inspired by the Vedic myth of Saranyu, who takes the form of a mare to flee from sexual violence but is then raped by the sun when he takes the form of a stallion.

[†] Compare the ram that miraculously appears to save Isaac when Abraham is about to sacrifice him.

An early Upanishad, shortly after the composition of the Brahmanas, spelled out the malevolent implications of the inclusion of humans as sacrificial victims: "Whoever among gods, sages, or men became enlightened became the very self of the gods, and the gods have no power to prevent him. But whoever worships a divinity as other than himself is like a sacrificial animal [*pashu*] for the gods, and each person is of use to the gods just as many animals would be of use to a man. Therefore it is not pleasing to those [gods] that men should become enlightened."[69] Thus, human men and women are the gods' sacrificial sheep.[70] This is the second alliance with a vengeance.

WOMEN

THE HORSE SACRIFICE REVISITED, II

Women played an essential role in the second phase of the horse sacrifice, where the goals of political domination and religious restoration were joined by a third goal, fertility. Four of the king's wives (the chief queen, the favorite wife, the rejected wife, and a fourth wife[71]) mimed* copulation with the stallion, and other women (one maiden and four hundred female attendants) played subsidiary roles.[72] The stallion stood both for the king and for the god (usually Prajapati, the Lord of Creatures, but sometimes Indra),[73] while the queen represented the fertile earth that the king both ruled and impregnated; the ceremony was intended to produce a good crop for the people and offspring for the king.[74] The stallion, generally the right-hand horse of the chariot team,[75] was probably killed, suffocated, before this part of the ceremony. Even in the *Rig Veda* there are hints that the ritual may have included the mimed copulation of the queen with the stallion; one obscene Vedic poem (10.86) may be a satire on the horse sacrifice, with a sexually challenged male monkey playing the role of a mock stallion.[76] But the Brahmanas are the first texts to describe it in any detail; only there is there available light to let us see it clearly.

One text that we have already considered, the text that speaks of the king's eating the people, also glosses several lines from the obscene banter with the queens that accompanies the ritual copulation in the horse sacrifice: " 'The little female bird rocks back and forth as he thrusts the penis into the slit.' Now, that bird is really the people, for the people rock back and forth at the thrust of the

---

* Stephanie Jamison says that the queen did not merely mime copulation, and Jamison is usually right. But in favor of the argument that the queen did *not* actually copulate with the stallion are the considerations that most of the texts instruct the priests to kill the horse first and that the ceremony would be hard to do with a live stallion.

royal power, and the slit is the people, and the penis is the royal power, which presses against the people; and so the one who has royal power is hurtful to the people."[77] On the analogy of the ritual copulation, this text is saying that the king rapes the people. It thus proclaims, in brutal and obscene language, the violence of royal oppression.

Just as evil females (female antigods), in the form of queens or bitches, threatened to destroy the sacrifice (and the sacrificer), so good women (wives) posed a danger to the sacrificer through the likelihood that they would stop being good. This danger affected even the gods:

INDRA'S WIFE AND INDRA'S SON

Kutsa Aurava ("Thigh-born") was made out of the two thighs of Indra. Just as Indra was, so was he, precisely as one would be who is made out of his own self. Indra made him his charioteer. He caught him with his wife, Shachi, the daughter of Puloman, and when he asked her, "How could you do this?" she replied, "I could not tell the two of you apart." Indra said, "I will make him bald, and then you will be able to tell the two of us apart." He made him bald, but Kutsa bound a turban around his head and went to her. This is the turban that charioteers wear.[78]

Mingled in with an arcane etiology (the origins of the turbans of charioteers) is a tale of a wife who fails, or claims to fail, to tell her husband from his son. That Kutsa and Indra are indistinguishable is an idea that begins in the Rig Veda (4.1.10) and is reflected more generally in the Hindu view that the son is made out of the father's self, or actually is that self reborn, and is therefore essentially identical with him.

As wealth accumulates in the Ganges Valley, inheritance becomes an issue, and so does the fidelity of married women. The relatively lax attitude to women in the Rig Veda has largely sunk into the fertile mud of the Ganges Valley; things close down for women, the gates of sexual freedom clang shut. Urbanization gave some women both property rights and more sexual freedom, but that very freedom inspired fears that led others to marry off their daughters at a younger age and to lower the ritual status of married women. We cannot take stories about goddesses (or, for that matter, stories about real women) as information about real women, and attitudes to women are often the inverse of attitudes to goddesses, but changes in what is imagined as possible for goddesses in their anthropomorphic roles as wives and mothers do suggest general shifts in attitudes to women.

We can see hints of the attrition of women's independence in the transformations of the myth of Urvashi. In the *Rig Veda*, Urvashi is a heavenly nymph (Apsaras) and swan maiden who sleeps with King Pururavas and abandons him after bearing him a son; she advises him, as she leaves him forever, that "there are no friendships with women; they have the hearts of jackals (10.95.15)." Like other immortal women who live with mortal men, particularly equine goddesses* (Urvashi is compared with a horse in three verses [10.95.3, 8–9]), she bears him a child and stays with him until he violates his contract with her ("I warned you on that very day, for I knew, but you did not listen to me," she says to him), whereupon she leaves him and the child and returns to her world.[79] The Vedic Urvashi complains that he made love to her too often ("You pierced me with your rod three times a day, and filled me even when I had no desire. I did what you wanted") and against her will ("You who were born to protect have turned that force against me").[80] But when the story is retold in the *Shatapatha Brahmana*, she *begs* Pururavas to make love to her just that often ("You must strike me with the bamboo reed three times a day"), though she has the forethought to add, "But never approach me when I have no desire."[81] The Vedic text implies that his desire is greater than hers, while the Brahmana implies that hers is at least as great, if not greater, an expression of the stereotype of the insatiable woman that will plague Hindu mythology forever after. She threatens to leave him when he fails to keep his promise not to let her look upon him naked. The final transformation is that in the *Rig Veda* he is left longing for her, with a vague promise of reunion in heaven, whereas in the Brahmanas she loves him so much that she not only stays with him but teaches him how to become immortal (a Gandharva). By this time[†] it has become unthinkable that she would leave the father of her child.[82]

DEATH

Sacrifice in the Brahmanas was designed to allay the fear of death, a relatively minor consideration in the *Rig Veda* but a pressing concern in the Brahmanas, for which death became the irritating grain of sand that seeded the pearls of thought. The Vedas spoke of another world to which people were presumably assigned after death, and the Brahmanas maintained and refined this belief:

---

* Such as Saranyu and Sita.
† Though not for long: In the *Mahabharata* (1.92), the goddess of the Ganges, another immortal woman with a mortal husband, not only abandons her husband and children when he violates the contract but kills several of the children.

Through the sacrifice a man could become immortal, for offering sacrifices generated merit that created for the sacrificer a rebirth after death in heaven ("in the
next world"). "Evil Death" is a cliché, an automatic equation throughout this
corpus: Death is evil, and the essence of evil is death.[83] Death is the defining
enemy of the Lord of Creatures (Prajapati), the creator, but also, sometimes,
identical with him or his firstborn son.[84] The Brahmanas attempted to tame
death by gradual degrees, to enable the sacrificer first to live out a full life span,
then to live for a thousand years, and finally to attain a vaguely conceived complete immortality: "Whoever knows this conquers recurring death and attains a
life span; this is freedom from death in the other world and life here."[85]

But there are always nagging doubts that even the perfect ritual cannot really succeed in conquering death. One can never be made entirely safe; the
catch-22 of the sacrificial warrantee is the ever-present danger that one will not
live long enough to complete the sacrifice that will grant immortality. This
danger appears to threaten even the Lord of Creatures. One text tells us that
"even as one might see in the distance the opposite shore, so did he behold the
opposite shore of his own life."[86] For he had already tangled with death: "When
Prajapati was creating living beings, evil death overpowered him. He generated
inner heat for a thousand years, striving to leave that evil behind him, and in
the thousandth year he purified himself entirely; the evil that he washed clean
is his body. But what man could obtain a life of a thousand years? The man who
knows this truth can obtain a thousand years."[87] Prajapati is uniquely qualified
to do this ritual because "he was born with a life of a thousand years."[88] But once
again, "whoever knows this" will, like the god, live long enough to do the ceremony that will let him live forever.

What the authors of these early texts feared was "old age and death" (*jara-
mrityu*).* What they feared most of all was what they called recurrent death, a
series of redeaths (and the rebirths that are preludes to them). For the Brahmanas already mention transmigration:[89] "When they die they come to life again,
but they become the food of this [Death] again and again."[90] To Euro-American
thinkers, reincarnation seems to pose a possible solution to the problem of death:
If what you fear is the cessation of life (we set aside for the moment considerations of heaven and hell), then the belief that you will in fact live again after
you die may be of comfort. How nice to go around again and again, never to be

---

* *Jara* is cognate with the Greek *geron*, *geras*, from which we derive the English "gerontology," and *mrityu* with our "mortal, mortality."

blotted out altogether, to have more and more of life, different lives all the time, perhaps a horse or a dog next time, or an Egyptian queen last time.

But this line of reasoning entirely misses the point of the Hindu doctrine. If it is a terrible thing to grow old and die, once and for all, how much more terrible to do it over and over again. It is like being condemned to numerous life sentences that do not run concurrently. "Recurrent death" may have meant merely a series of ritual deaths within a natural life span[91] or what the poet T. S. Eliot had in mind when he said, "We die to each other daily."* But it probably foreshadowed an actual series of rebirths and redeaths. These were not described in detail until the Upanishads, which transform into a vision of the next life, in *this* world, the things that Bhrigu saw in the other world in the Brahmanas.

The story of Bhrigu's journey to the other world was briefly retold in another Brahmana text[92] in which the boy, now called Nachiketas, annoys his father (now no longer the god Varuna but a human sacrificer who is giving away all that he has) by asking him three times whom he will give *him* to; his exasperated father finally blurts out, "I'll give you to Death!" (in a later version he shouts, "I'll send you to Yama!"—that is, "The devil take you!" or "Go to hell!"[93]), and Nachiketas takes him literally and goes down to the world of the dead. But his father also gives him detailed instructions about what to say and do in the house of Death. Eventually Death offers him three boons, the last of which is that Death teaches Nachiketas how to avoid redeath. And whoever knows the Nachiketas fire and kindles it, the text assures us, conquers redeath. Whereas Bhrigu had a confrontation with animals and learned a lesson about the afterlife from his father, Nachiketas learns the secret from Death himself. And whereas only gods (like Prajapati and Varuna, Bhrigu's father) confronted Death in the first Brahmana text, here a human boy does this and gains not merely a way of eating animals without unfortunate consequences but liberation from death.

FOLKLORE, SACRIFICE, AND DANGER

The story of Bhrigu shares much with other tales of journeys to the underworld,[94] and the text about exchanging skins is one of a number of widely attested folktales about such exchanges and about animals transformed into people and the reverse.[95] The inclusion of folktales in the Brahmanas is an ex-

---

* In *The Cocktail Party.*

ample of the co-opting of alternate histories, of other voices—including non-Brahmin voices—sneaking into the text. The Brahmanas are the vehicle for a great deal of material virtually indistinguishable in tone and basic plot from the stories collected by folklorists in nineteenth-century farmhouses.* The Sanskrit of these passages is much more informal and straightforward, even colloquial, than the technical language in which the rest of the Brahmanas are set.[96] There are several different sorts of Sanskrit in the Brahmanas, each with its own vocabulary, one for mythology, one for philology and etymology, one for ritual instructions, and so forth. And there is one for folklore. Here again the Brahmanas are revolutionary, in opening up the ritual literature to the narration of folktales.

What are these stories doing in these texts, otherwise so dry, so full of abstruse ritual pedantry?[†97] What is such juicy folklore doing in such dusty old ritual attics? Well, the Brahmanas themselves offer many explicit excuses for telling these stories: to restore details omitted in the *Rig Veda* text in question, to gloss an allusion or the special circumstances under which a certain sage saw a poem, or to explain why the sacrifice is done in a certain way.[98] Some authors of the Brahmanas tamper with the tale to make it serve their purposes. Others, however, make no attempt to connect the story with the sacrifice and tamper with it somewhat less; we may assume that these stories represent at least something of the popular, non-Brahmin world.

The deeper reasons for telling the stories, in both instances, are less obvious than the excuses and are more loosely related to the sacrifice; they illuminate certain shadows of the sacrifice, fears that lie behind the sacrifice. In 700 BCE, the only texts that were memorized and preserved were the Brahmanas, and the sacrifice was the focal point for all forms of creative expression. Thus these texts purporting to gloss the sacrifice attracted to themselves, like magnets, everything else that could be dragged in to express the meaning of life in ancient India. Or rather, since the sacrifice was believed to symbolize everything that

---

* "The Three Brothers" (*Jaiminiya Brahmana* 1.184) is Tale Type 654, and the tale of Kutsa and his father follows a pattern best known from Sophocles' Oedipus (Tale Type 921; also T 92.9, T 412).

† For the Brahmanas have long been regarded as the private stock of the most elitist textualists who ever lived. Müller thought the Brahmanas were "simply twaddle, and what is worse, theological twaddle," while Julius Eggeling, who devoted most of his life to translating the *Shatapatha Brahmana*, bemoaned its "wearisome prolixity of exposition, characterised by dogmatic assertion and a flimsy symbolism rather than by serious reasoning." Other scholars called the Brahmanas "an arid desert of puerile speculation," "of sickening prolixity," "filthy," "repulsive," and "of interest only to students of abnormal psychology."

was meaningful in human life, *any* compelling insight into that life would eventually gravitate to the traditional literature that was constantly coalescing around the sacrifice. A certain number of myths were already associated with the sacrifice, as is clear from the tantalizing allusions in the *Rig Veda*, but that text did not have a systematized mythology. The Brahmanas tell many "grand" tales of the victory of gods over antigods, but since they also tell folktales about everyday life, the Vedic ritual cannot be the only key to their meaning.

Yet it is the key to a part of their meaning, for these stories too are connected to the sacrifice on a profound level. In particular, images that express the dangers inherent in death and sex became embedded in narratives about sacrifice since the sacrifice itself (as we saw in the horse sacrifice) is about death and sex. Rituals tend to tame those dangers and to express them in terms of a limited range of human actions, to make them public and to make them safe for the sacrificer; they allow people to order and structure their reactions to these dangers in real life, to create a framework that they can then reintroduce into real experience. Stories about monstrous women help us (especially, but not only, if we are men) to express our nightmares about our mothers (and wives). Participating in the formalized structures of someone else's funeral provides us with a framework within which to contemplate our own death; the "controlled catastrophe" of the sacrifice allowed the sacrificer to offer up a victim who was a substitute for himself, as if to say, "Kill him and not me."

But the ritual itself introduces new dangers and new fears. What happens if something interferes with the ritual so that it doesn't work? We have seen the elaborate countermeasures proposed in response to every foreseeable glitch in the horse sacrifice. The soma sacrifice too, so central to Vedic religion, was threatened by the increasing difficulty of obtaining soma, which grew in the mountains* that the Vedic people had left behind when they moved down to the Ganges.[99] This problem was solved in several ways. There had already been, in the *Rig Veda*, a myth of soma coming from afar. Now the Brahmanas elaborated upon the rituals for buying soma and punishing the soma seller and for deciding what things could be used as substitutes when soma was unavailable; some surrogates may have looked like soma, while others may have had a similar effect.[100] The need for soma surrogates played into one of the ideas underlying the sacrifice itself, that it was, in essence, already a substitute, the victim in

---

* If it was the *Amanita muscaria,* it grew only where there were birch trees.

the sacrifice substituting for the sacrificer. The need for a substitute for the consciousness-altering soma may also have led to the development of other ways of creating unusual psychic states, such as yoga, breath control, fasting, and meditation.

Nor does the danger in the sacrifice come only from the possibility that one may fail to carry out the ritual properly. The power aroused by the correctly performed ritual may get out of hand, for the ritual involves potentially fatal dangers, which compounded the threats to the sacrificer in normal life. These dangers may come from within, from the sacrificer himself, from the pollution inherent in his human vulnerability and mortality, or they may come from the gods.

THE POWERS OF EVIL AND ADDICTION

In the Brahmanas, in a pattern typical of the first alliance, the enemies of the gods (both antigods in the sky and ogres on earth) threaten the sacrifice, break into it, and pollute it from outside. A significant proportion of the energy of the priests was devoted to fending off the antigods and ogres and to repairing the breaks that they made in the sacrifice, and this activity was part of the ritual. But during this period the balance of power shifts to the second alliance, and it is no longer gods and humans against the powers of evil but gods against humans and the (other) powers of evil. The antigods became more like ogres, more clearly distinguished from the gods by evil rather than merely by competition.

Evil originates in the gods themselves and spreads to both antigods and humans. More precisely, it originates in Prajapati, who, as he attempts to create, falls into the grasp of evil. In one myth, a Brahmin rids him of the evil by transforming it into prosperity (Shri) and placing it in cows, in sleep, and in shade.[101] It is rare, however, for evil to be so simply transformed into something good; usually it remains evil and is distributed in that form, to the detriment of those who receive it. Thus, in a kind of reverse savior mythology, the gods create forms of evil—delusion (*moha*), a stain (*kalmasha*), evil *tout court* (*papa*)—that they transfer to humans, who suffer from it forever after. Humans are thus the scapegoats of the gods. In a much-retold myth, Indra becomes infected with Brahminicide—the gold standard of sins—after he kills Vritra (whom the Brahmanas, and all subsequent texts, regard as a Brahmin—a Dasyu Brahmin but a Brahmin). Sometimes Indra gets drunk on soma—his notorious addiction—and on one occasion the Brahminicide flows out of him with the excess soma; from what flows from his nose, a lion arises; from his ears a jackal, from the lower opening of his body, tigers and other wild beasts.[102] Thus the divine hangover leaves us to deal with man-eating beasts.

When Indra kills another enemy, also a Brahmin, he distributes the Brahminicide, with compensations:

INDRA TRANSFERS HIS BRAHMINICIDE

He asked the earth to take a third of his Brahminicide, and in return he promised her that if she should be overcome by digging, within a year the dug-out portion would be filled again; and the third of his Brahminicide that she took became a natural fissure. He asked the trees to accept a third, and promised that when they were pruned, more shoots would spring up; the Brahminicide that they took up became sap. Women took a third of the Brahminicide and obtained the boon of enjoying intercourse right up to the birth of their children; their Brahminicide became the garments stained with menstrual blood.[103]

The boons explain why the distribution is willingly accepted: As long as Indra is polluted, fertility on earth is stymied; it is in the best interests of earth, trees, and women to help Indra out, so that they themselves can remain fertile. (One version of the story inverts the principle and ultimately transfers the sin to abortionists, the enemies of fertility.[104]) But evil cannot be destroyed; the best that one can hope for is to move it to a place where it will do less harm. Therefore the gods in these stories draw evil's fangs by breaking it up, sometimes into three pieces and sometimes into four. Blatant self-interest operates in a variant in which Indra's Brahminicide is "wiped off," as the text puts it, onto people who make offerings without paying the priests;[105] such deadbeats, the bêtes noires of the Brahmin compilers of these texts, are the perfect scapegoats.

Evil on earth in general results from fallout from heaven, from the cosmic struggles of gods and antigods:

GODS, ANTIGODS, HUMANS, AND EVIL

The gods and antigods were striving against one another. The gods created a thunderbolt, sharp as a razor, that was the Man [Purusha]. They hurled this at the antigods, and it scattered them, but then it turned back to the gods. The gods were afraid of it, and so they took it and broke it into three pieces. Then they saw that the divinities had entered humans in the form of Vedic poems. They said, "When this Man has lived in the world with merit, he will follow us by means of sacrifices and good deeds and ascetic heat. We must do something to prevent this.

Let us put evil in him." They put evil in him: sleep, carelessness, anger, hunger, love of dice, desire for women. These are the evils that assail a man in this world. . . . But the gods do not harm the man who knows this, though they do try to destroy the man who tries to harm the man who knows this.[106]

The gods here do not merely accidentally burden humans with evil that they themselves, the gods, cannot manage; they do it purposely, to prevent humans from going to heaven.[*107] And this evil includes two of the four major addictive vices, love of dice and desire for women. The implications of this major shift in the human-divine contract will continue to spread in generations to follow.

Why does this change take place at this moment? The hardening of the lines between states, the beginning of competition for wealth and power, the scramble for the supremacy of the rich Ganges bottomland may have introduced into the myths a more cynical approach to the problem of dealing with evil. And the growth of both power and the abuse of power among the two upper classes may explain why the gods at this time came to be visualized less like morally neutral (if capricious and often destructive) forces of nature—the fire, soma, rain, and rivers of the Veda—or brutal and sensually addicted but fair-minded human chieftains and more like wealthy and powerful kings and Brahmins, selfish, jealous, and vicious.

---

* According to one uncharacteristic story, when the antigods were fighting the gods, the antigods, rather than the gods, put evil into the senses and into the mind; that is why we can see good or evil, speak good or evil, imagine good or evil.

CHAPTER 7

RENUNCIATION IN THE UPANISHADS

600 to 200 BCE

༄

CHRONOLOGY (ALL DATES BCE)

c. 600–500 Aranyakas are composed

c. 500 Shrauta Sutras are composed

c. 500–400 Early Upanishads (*Brihadaranyaka* [BU], *Chandogya* [CU], *Kaushitaki* [KauU]) are composed

c. 500 Pataliputra is founded; Vedic peoples gradually move southward

c. 483 or 410 Siddhartha Gautama, the Buddha, dies

c. 468 Vardhamana Mahavira, the Jina, founder of Jainism, dies

c. 400–1200 Later Upanishads (*Katha* [KU], *Kaushitaki* [KauU], *Shvetashvatara* [SU], and *Mundaka* [MU]) are composed

c. 300 Grihya Sutras are composed

SATYAKAMA'S MOTHER

Once upon a time, Satyakama Jabala said to his mother, Jabala, "Ma'am, I want to live the life of a Vedic student. What is the line of my male ancestors [*gotra*]?" She said to him, "My dear, I don't know the line of your male ancestors. When I was young, I got around a lot, as I was working, and I got you. But my name is Jabala, and your name is Satyakama ['Lover of Truth']. So why don't you say that you are Satyakama Jabala?" Satyakama went to Gautama, the son of Haridrumata, and asked to study with him; when asked about his line of male ancestors he repeated what his mother had said. Gautama replied, "No one who was not a Brahmin would be

able to say that. You have not deviated from the truth, my dear. I
will initiate you."

Chandogya Upanishad (c. 600 BCE)[1]

A woman who is not ashamed to tell her son that she had multiple partners
when she conceived him is one of a number of astonishingly nonconformist
characters, often discussing new ideas about karma and renunciation, whom
we meet in the Upanishads, philosophical texts composed from around the sixth
century BCE.

THE SOCIAL AND POLITICAL WORLD OF THE UPANISHADS

The eastern Ganges at this time, the seventh through the fifth century BCE,
was a place of kingdoms dominated by Magadha, whose capital was Rajagriha,
and Koshala-Videha, whose capital was Kashi (Varanasi, Benares). Trade—
especially of metals, fine textiles, salt, pottery, and, always, horses—flourished,[2]
and the towns were connected by trade routes; all roads led to Kashi. The development of the idea of merit or karma as something "to be earned, accumulated, occasionally transferred and eventually realized"[3] owes much to the
post-Vedic moneyed economy. More generally, where there's trade, people leave
home; new commercial classes emerge; and above all, new ideas spread quickly
and circulate freely. They certainly did so at this time in India, and there was little to stop them: The Vedas did not constitute a closed canon, and there was no
central temporal or religious authority to enforce a canon had there been one.

Commerce was facilitated by the rise of prosperous kingdoms and social
mobility by the rise of great protostates, or oligarchies (*maha-janapadas* or *gana-
sanghas*),[4] governed by Kshatriya clans. One Brahmin source describes these
clans as degenerate Kshatriyas and even Shudras, accusing them of having
ceased to honor the Brahmins or to observe Vedic ritual, worshiping at sacred
groves instead,[5] and of paying short shrift to sacrifices, using their funds for
trade (behavior that goes a long way to explain why the Brahmins called them
Shudras). The clans were said to have just two classes, the ruling families
and the slaves and laborers, an arrangement that would have posed a serious
threat to Brahmin supremacy. Significantly, both Vardhamana Mahavira (also
called the Jina), the founder of Jainism, and Siddhartha Gautama, the founder
of Buddhism, were born into distinguished clans in one of these alternative,
nonmonarchical state systems. Such systems fostered greater personal freedom

and mobility, nurturing individuals as well as social groups—the trader, the shopkeeper, the artisan, the government official.

This rise in individual freedom was, however, offset by the growing bureaucracy and state institutions in both the kingdoms and the oligarchies, which eroded the traditional rural social order and replaced it with new kinds of social control.[6] So too, perhaps in response to the growing social laxity, class lines laid down in texts such as the Brahmanas now began to harden. The first three classes (Brahmin, Kshatriya, and Vaishya) became more sharply delineated not only from the Shudras (the fourth class, below them) but, now, from a fifth category, Pariahs.

A vast transformation of society was taking place in response to the social, economic, and political reorganization of northern South Asia, as small-scale, pastoral chiefdoms gave way to hierarchically ordered settlements organized into states. Students and thinkers moved over a wide geographical area in search of philosophical and theological debate, encountering not merely royal assemblies of Indian thinkers but new peoples and ideas from outside South Asia. Much of the new literature on religious and social law (the Shrauta Sutras and Grihya Sutras) may have been designed to incorporate newcomers or social groups into a ranking system or to accommodate local power relations.[7] The emergent system recognized the authority of village, guild, family, and provincial custom, so long as they did not conflict with some higher authority. Political and intellectual diversity thrived. This may go a long way to explain not where the new ideas in the Upanishads came from but why the Brahmins were willing—perhaps under pressure from other people who had gained access to power—to incorporate these ideas into new texts that were regarded as part of the Vedas, despite the ways in which they contravened the Brahmin imaginary.[8]

THE TEXTUAL WORLD OF THE UPANISHADS

The Upanishads are often referred to as "the end of the Veda" (Vedanta*), for they are the final texts in the body of literature called *shruti* ("what is heard"), unalterable divine revelation, in contrast with the rest of Hindu literature, called *smriti* ("what is remembered"), the tradition attributed to human authors, there-

---

* "Vedanta" also has a second meaning, denoting a particular philosophy, based on commentaries on the Upanishads, that was developed many centuries later by a group of philosophers, of whom Shankara is the most famous.

fore fallible and corrigible. Just as the Brahmanas are, among other things, foot-notes to the Vedas, so the Upanishads began as Cliffs Notes to the Brahmanas, meditations on the meaning of the Vedic rituals and myths. The different Upanishads belong to different branches of the Vedic traditions, different family lineages, but they share so many stories and ideas that they are clearly in conversation with one another.

Bridging these two sets of texts, the Brahmanas and the Upanishads, and actually overlapping with both of them are the Aranyakas ("Jungle Books"), so called presumably because they were composed in the wilderness, or jungle, outside the village; they dealt more with ritual and less with cosmology and metaphysics than the Upanishads did. The early Upanishads (meaning "sitting beside," a name that may refer to the method of placing one thing next to another, making connections, or to pupils sitting beside their teacher) probably[9] were composed in the sixth and fifth centuries BCE.* Again we find a major shift in language, between the Sanskrit of the Brahmanas and that of the Upanishads, not merely in the grammar and vocabulary but also in the style, which is far more accessible, conversational, reader friendly; if we liken the Brahmanas to Chaucer (in their distance from modern English), the Upanishads are like Shakespeare. The grammarian Panini wrote about spoken Sanskrit (*bhasha*), in contrast with Vedic, ritualistic Sanskrit. In North Indian towns and villages, people spoke Prakrits, the "natural" or "unrefined" languages, often regarded as dialects, in contrast with Sanskrit, the "perfected" or "artificial" language. The Buddha, preaching at roughly the time of the Upanishads, was beginning to preach in Magadhi, the local dialect of Magadha, in order to reach a wider audience; the decision to preserve the Buddhist canon in such a dialect, Pali, had an effect much like that of the elimination of Latin from the Catholic mass after Vatican II: It made the liturgy comprehensible to all the Pali-valent Buddhists. The Upanishadic authors too were probably reaching out in that more vernacular direction, stretching the Sanskrit envelope.

Like other great religious reform movements, such as those inspired by Jesus, Muhammad, and Luther, the Upanishads did not replace but merely supplemented the earlier religion, so that just as Catholicism continued to exist alongside Protestantism within Christianity, so Vedic Hinduism (sacrificial,

---

* If the Buddha died in around 400 BCE, as has been recently argued rather persuasively, and if, as seems evident, the Buddha knew at least parts of the early Upanishads (the *Brihadaranyaka*, the *Taittiriya*, and the *Chandogya*), those texts must have been known by about 450 BCE.

worldly) continued to exist alongside Vedantic Hinduism (philosophical, renunciant). The tension between householders and renouncers begins here and
exerts an enormous influence over the subsequent history of the Hindus. But
in Hinduism, unlike Christianity, there never was an official schism. Certain
words from earlier periods—karma, *tapas*—took on new meanings at this
point, though their original meanings never disappeared, resulting in a layering
that served as one of the major sources of multiplicity within Hinduism.

KARMA AND DEATH

Where did the potentially revolutionary ideas of karma and renunciation
come from? We can identify both Vedic and non-Vedic sources. Let's begin
with the Vedic.

In the Upanishads, as in the *Rig Veda*, the body of the dead man returns to
the elements—his eye to the sun, the hair of his body to plants, the hair of his
head into trees, his blood and semen into water, and so forth—but the Upanishadic sages regard this as the beginning, not the end, of the explanation of
death. The sage Yajnavalkya listed the correspondences between the parts of
the body and the cosmos, whereupon his pupil asked, "What happens to the
person then?" The person is the individual soul, the atman, or self, which is
identical with the *brahman*, the world soul (sometimes also called atman, often
transcribed as Atman to distinguish it from the individual soul), as salt becomes
identical with water into which it is dissolved (BU 2.4.12). This is the central
teaching of the Upanishads, a doctrine of pantheism (or panentheism, the world
made of god), most famously expressed in the phrase generally translated "You
are that" (*tat tvam asi*) (CU 6.8.7)[10] In answer to his pupil's question, the Upanishad continues, Yajnavalkya drew him aside in private: "And what did they
talk about? Nothing but karma. They praised nothing but karma. Yajnavalkya
told him: 'A man becomes something good by good karma and something bad
by bad karma' (BU 3.2.13)."

The first and most basic meaning of "karma" is action. The noun "karma"
comes from the verb *kri*, cognate with the Latin *creo*, "to make or do,* to make
a baby or a table or to perform a ritual." It is often contrasted with mind and
speech: One can think, say, or do (*kri*) something, with steadily escalating consequences. The second meaning of "karma" is "ritual action," particularly Vedic
ritual action; this is its primary connotation in the *Rig Veda*. Its third meaning,

---

* In Sanskrit grammar, *karma* is the accusative case.

which begins to be operative in the Upanishads, is "morally charged action, good or bad," a meter that is always running, that is constantly charging something to one's account. And its fourth meaning, which follows closely on the heels of the third, is "morally charged action that has consequences for the soul in the future, that is retributive both within one's life and across the barrier of redeath": You become a sheep that people eat if you have eaten a sheep. (We saw the germ of this theory in the Brahmana descriptions of people soundlessly screaming in the other world and in statements that sacrifice generates merit that guarantees an afterlife in the other world.) In this sense, karma is action whose retributive moral charge determines the nature of your future rebirths. Consequences have consequences, and first thing you know, you're born as a sheep.

Turned on its head, this link led to a fifth meaning of *karma*, not as the cause of future lives but as the result of past lives and the agenda for this life, the inescapable role in life that one was born to play, one's work, or innate activity. Euro-Americans believe too that we often cannot remember the past causes of present circumstances and that the present will influence the future, but the Hindu view differs from this in extending the past and future beyond the boundaries of this life span. F. Scott Fitzgerald, of all people, captured the spirit of karma in the final sentence of *The Great Gatsby:* "So we beat on, boats against the current, borne back ceaselessly into the past." In Hinduism we are also borne back ceaselessly into the future.

The last (sixth) meaning of karma is the implication that good and bad karma may also be transferred from one person to another under certain circumstances, not merely between parents and children (as we saw in the Vedic poem to Varuna) and between sacrificial priest and patron, but between any people who meet. This transfer may take place either intentionally or unintentionally: The dharma texts say that if someone lets a guest depart unfed, the guest will take away the host's good karma and leave behind his own bad karma.[11] In the Brahmana story of Nachiketas, Nachiketas remains in the house of Death for three nights without eating and then tells Death that in effect, on the three nights of fasting he ate "your offspring, your sacrificial beasts (*pashu*s), and your good deeds (*sadhu-krityam*)." This last is an example of the transfer of good karma; unfed, Nachiketas "eats" (which is to say, consumes) Death's good deeds (which is to say, he siphons off Death's good karma) as well as his children and cattle. This blackmail is what forces Death to tell Nachiketas his secrets.

It is not always clear which of these meanings of karma is intended in any particular passage in the Upanishads (or in other texts). Moreover, the idea of karma was certainly not accepted by everyone as the final solution to the problem of death (or the problem of evil); many other, conflicting ideas were proposed and widely accepted, alongside the karma theory.[12]

The Upanishads continue to speak of "recurrent death" (BU 3.2.10, 3.3.2) and now describe the process in cruel detail (BU 4.3.36, 4.4.2). For heaven is no longer the end of the line, as it was in some of the Brahmanas; it is simply another place that eventually everyone leaves. The Upanishads spell out the assumption, sketched in the Brahmanas, that we all are on the wheel of redeath, transmigration (samsara, "flowing around"). From the very start, the idea that transmigration occurred was qualified by two other ideas: that some people wanted to get out of it and that there was a way to do this, a restoration not merely for one of life's mistakes but for life itself, a way to put the fix in on death. When the Upanishads retell the story of Nachiketas, Death explains to the boy the process of dying and going to heaven in much greater detail, and at the end, Nachiketas "became free of old age and death, and so will anyone who knows this teaching (KU 1–2, 6.18)." Significantly, where the Brahmanas promise the conquest of redeath to anyone who knows the ritual, the Upanishad promises it to anyone who knows the teaching, a shift from a way of acting to a way of knowing.

OVERCROWDING AND RECYCLING

The theory of reincarnation, a recycling not of tin cans but of souls, may reflect an anxiety of overcrowding, the claustrophobia of a culture fenced in, a kind of urban Angst (*amhas*). The Upanishadic discussion of the doctrine of transmigration begins when a teacher asks his pupil, "Do you know why the world beyond is not filled up, even when more and more people continuously go there?" and it ends with the statement "As a result, that world up there is not filled up (CU 5.10.8; BU 5.1.1 and 6.2.2)"* The idea of an overcrowded earth is a part of the myth of the four Ages (people live too long in the first Age and become too numerous) and recurs in the *Mahabharata* as a justification for the genocidal war (when the overburdened earth begins to sink beneath the cosmic waters).[13] Is this fear of crowds related to the shock of the new experience of

---

* No one there seems to have thought of asking about the opposite problem, why the world doesn't run out of souls, which constantly leak out of the cycle in both directions, some up to the world of *brahman* and some down to the world of insects. Centuries later Jaina cosmogonies did address this problem.

city life in the Ganges Valley? Were there already slums in Kashi (as there may already have been in Harappa)? If a fear of this sort is what inspired the theory of reincarnation, who precisely was it who was afraid?

The "second urbanization," the spread of paddy rice cultivation into the Ganges Valley, producing a surplus that could support cities, the emergence of societies along the Ganges, created an unprecedented proximity of people. The Greek historian Herodotus, writing in the fifth century BCE, said that the Indians were the most populous country on earth (5.3). Population densities had significantly increased, the result of a combination of the incorporation of indigenous peoples, a soaring birthrate, and the creation of agricultural surpluses.[14] This led to a burgeoning of all the things that people who like to sleep on their saddlebags at night don't like about sleeping indoors, things that are for them a cultural nightmare. The movements to renounce the fleshpots of the Ganges Valley may have been inspired in part by a longing to return to the good old days preserved in the texts, when life was both simpler and freer, more heroic.[15] Such a longing is reflected in the name of the Aranyakas ("Jungle Books"), in the village settings of so much of the Upanishads, and in the forest imagery that abounds in the writings of the early sects, both inside and outside Hinduism. Within the cities the Buddha sat in an isolated spot under a tree to obtain enlightenment, and he first preached in a deer park. The Upanishads seem to have been composed by people who left the settled towns for rustic settings where master and student could sit under some tree somewhere, the ancient Indian equivalent of the bucolic liberal arts college; the renunciants are said to live in the wilderness, in contrast with the conventional Vedic sacrificers who live in villages. No individuals in the Ganges Valley could have remembered the old days up in the Punjab, but there was certainly a group memory, or at least a literary memory, of an idealized time when people lived under the trees and slept under the stars, a cultural memory of wide-open spaces. Many of the old rituals and texts too, such as the tales of cattle raids, no longer made sense but still exerted a nostalgic appeal.

A striking insight into the psychology of the forest dweller stage comes from an unexpected source, Philip Roth's 1998 novel *I Married a Communist*, in a passage describing a shack that the hero, Ira, retreats to in times of trouble:

> The palliative of the primitive hut. The place where you are stripped back to essentials, to which you return—even if it happens not to be where you came from—to decontaminate and absolve yourself of the striving. The place where

you disrobe, molt it all, the uniforms you've worn and the costumes you've gotten into, where you shed your batteredness and your resentment, your appeasement of the world and your defiance of the world, your manipulation of the world and its manhandling of you. The aging man leaves and goes into the woods . . . receding from the agitation of the autobiographical. He has entered vigorously into competition with life; now, becalmed, he enters into competition with death, drawn down into austerity, the final business."[16]

Beneath the specifically American concerns lies an understanding of ways in which, in ancient India too, the forest offers individual purification from the corruption of collective urban life.

The whole tradition was becoming individualistic, not just renunciant; we begin to see a transition from group to individual, a perceived need for personal rituals of transformation, forming a certain sort of person, not just a member of the tribe. At the same time, collective rather than individual choices needed to be made in order to start and maintain alternative societies, such as Buddhism, and monastic communities, as well as to engage in the highly collective enterprise of growing rice.

Reincarnation addressed this social problem and formulated it in terms of individual salvation. It seldom, if ever, occurred to anyone, then or at any time before the nineteenth century in India,* to attempt to change the world; but many people made judgments against it and opted out or tried to solve the problem of suffering within the individual. The new religious movements located the problem of the human condition, of human suffering, within the individual heart and mind (where Freud too located it), rather than in a hierarchical society (where Marx located it). The Upanishads emphasize a more personal religious experience than the one addressed by the Brahmanas.[17] In this way, at least, these movements were individualistic—"Look to your own house" (or, in the Buddha's metaphor, "Get out of your burning house"†)—rather than socially oriented, as nonrenunciant Hinduism was—"Your identity

---

* This was true of premodern Europe as well as India.
† He said this (in the *Lotus Sutra*) in response to people who kept asking for precise details about nirvana (the escape from samsara), as people in a burning house might ask, before agreeing to leave, what sort of house they might get in exchange. The Buddha taught that misery (*duhkha*) is not so much suffering as it is the inevitable loss of happiness, since everything is impermanent (*anicca/anitya*), a problem for which nirvana offered the solution.

is meaningful only as one member of a diverse social body." This in itself was a tremendous innovation.

The Paths of Rebirth and Release

The Upanishads assume, like the Vedas and Brahmanas, that people pass into heaven or hell when they die, but they are far more concerned with the fate of the dead beyond heaven or hell. Here is how the *Brihadaranyaka Upanishad* describes the possible trajectories of people who have died and are being cremated:

THE PATHS OF SMOKE AND FLAME

The people who know this [the Upanishadic doctrine of the identity of the soul and the *brahman*], and the people there in the wilderness who venerate truth as faith—they pass into the flame (of the cremation fire), and thence into the day . . . into the world of the gods, into the sun, and into the region of lightning. A person made of mind comes to the regions of lightning and leads them to the worlds of *brahman*. These exalted people live in those worlds of *brahman* for the longest time. They do not return.

The people who win heavenly worlds, on the other hand, by offering sacrifices, by giving gifts, and by generating inner heat [*tapas*]—they pass into the smoke, and then into the night . . . into the world of the fathers, into the moon. There they become food. There the gods feed on them, as the moon increases and decreases. When that ends, they pass into the sky, then into the wind, then the rain, and then the earth, where they become food. They are offered in the fire of man and are born in the fire of woman. Rising up again to the heavenly worlds, they circle around in the same way.

Those who do not know these two paths, however, become worms, insects, or snakes (BU 6.2.13–16).

This text tells us that people within the Vedic fold at this time had a choice of two ways of being religious.

The people of the wilderness end up in the world of *brahman*, the divine substance of which the universe is composed. *Brahman*, which in the *Rig Veda* designates sacred speech, is the root of a number of words in later Sanskrit distinguished by just one or two sounds (or letters, in English): *brahman* (the divine substance of the universe); Brahma (the creator god); Brahmin or

Brahman (a member of the first or priestly class*); Brahmana (one of a class of texts that follow the Vedas and precede the Upanishads); and Brahma-charin ("moving in *brahman*," designating a chaste student). The world of *brahman* is a world of monism (which assumes that all living things are elements of a single, universal being),[†] sometimes equated with monotheism, in contrast with the world of rebirth, the polytheistic world of sacrifice to multiple gods. The doctrine of the Upanishads is also sometimes characterized as pantheism (in which god is everything and everything is god) or, at times, panentheism (in which god encompasses and interpenetrates the universe but at the same time is greater than and independent of it). It views the very substance of the universe as divine and views that substance and that divinity as unitary. The pluralistic world has a secondary, illusory status in comparison with the enduring, real status of the underlying monistic being.

The people who reach *brahman* have lived in the wilderness, the jungle, either permanently as some sort of forest ascetics or merely on the occasions when they held their religious rituals there. By contrast, the sacrificers, who follow the Vedic path of generosity (to gods and priests or to people more generally) or engage in the ritual practices that generate internal heat (*tapas*), go to heaven but do not stay there; they die again and are reborn. This text does not tell us where these people have lived but a parallel passage in the *Chandogya Upanishad* (5.10.1–8) tells us that the people who devote themselves to giving gifts to gods and to priests (this text specifies the recipients, where the other did not) live in villages. This group no longer generates internal heat as the sacrificers did in the *Brihadaranyaka*, an activity that the *Chandogya* assigns to the people in the wilderness, who venerate (in place of truth, in the *Brihadaranyaka*) internal heat as faith. *Tapas* therefore can belong to either group, for it is a transitional power: For sacrificers, it is the heat that the priest generates in the sacrifice, while for people of the wilderness, it becomes detached from the sacrifice and internalized, just as the sacrifice itself is internalized; now *tapas* is the heat that an individual ascetic generates within himself. The only criterion that

---

* The Sanskrit word for the class I am calling Brahmins is actually *brahmana*, the same word as the name of the texts between the Vedas and Upanishads. To confuse matters further, of the four priests needed to perform certain Vedic sacrifices, one, who just stands around and does nothing but run a full script of the sacrifice in his head, to make sure there are no mistakes, is called the *brahmin* (in Sanskrit), in contrast with the other priests designated by different names.

† The Vedantic philosophers belong, by and large, to the monist tradition.

marks the sacrificers in both texts is their generosity, and the only criterion that marks the people of the wilderness is their life in the wilderness.

The people who reach the moon in the *Brihadaranyaka* are eaten by the gods (as they were eaten by animals in the Other World in the Brahmanas), but the gods in the *Chandogya* merely eat the moon, a more direct way to account for its waning. The *Chandogya* also has a slightly different ending for the second group, the sacrificers who pass through the smoke:

THE THIRD OPTION

They return by the same path by which they came—first to space and to the wind, which turns into smoke and then into a cloud, which then rains down. On earth they grow as rice and barley, plants and trees, sesame and beans, from which it is very difficult to escape. When someone eats that food and sheds his semen, one is born again from him.

Now, people here whose behavior is charming can expect to enter a nice womb, like that of a woman of the Brahmin, Kshatriya, or Vaishya class. But people whose behavior is stinking can expect to enter a nasty womb, like that of a dog, a pig, or a Pariah woman.

And there is a third state, for people who take neither of these paths: They become tiny creatures who go around and around ceaselessly. "Be born! Die!" A person should take measures to avoid that (5.10.1–8).

It is clear from the *Chandogya*, and implicit in the *Brihadaranyaka*, that one does not want to end up in the company of the worms and other tiny creatures in the third state, the place from which no traveler returns. It's better to be a dog.

But it is not so clear from these texts that the path of Vedic gift giving is undesirable, that *everyone* wants to get off the wheel and onto the path of flame. For renouncers, the very idea of good karma is an oxymoron:* Any karma is bad because it binds you to the wheel of rebirth. But the *Chandogya* spells out the belief that for sacrificers, some rebirths are quite pleasant, the reward for good behavior. Their fate corresponds to Yajnavalkya's statement "A man becomes something good by good karma and something bad by bad karma." The *Brihadaranyaka* says much the same thing: "What a man turns out to be depends on how he acts. If his actions [karma] are good, he will turn into something

---

*It is also a palindrome: Do Good's deeds live on? No, Evil's deeds do, O God.

good. If his actions are bad, he will turn into something bad." But then it adds that this applies only to the man who has desires; the man who is freed from desires, whose desires are fulfilled, does not die at all; he goes to *brahman* (BU 4.4.5–6).* So too the funeral ceremonies include instructions that ensure that the dead man will not remain in limbo but will move forward, either to a new life or to final Release (*moksha*) from the cycle of transmigration,[18] further evidence of a deeply embedded tension between the desire to assure a good rebirth and the desire to prevent rebirth altogether. The fear of redeath led to the desire for Release (including Release from the values of Vedic Hinduism), but then the ideal of Release was reabsorbed into Vedic Hinduism and reshaped into the desire to be reborn better, in worldly terms: richer, with more sons, and so forth. These two tracks—one for people who want to get off the wheel of redeath and one for those who don't want to get off the wheel of rebirth—continue as options for South Asians to this day.

The *Kaushitaki Upanishad* describes the fork in the road a bit differently:

THE FINAL EXAM

When people depart from this world, they go to the moon. Those who do not answer the moon's questions become rain, and rain down here on earth, where they are reborn according to their actions [karma] and knowledge—as a worm, an insect, a fish, a bird, a lion, a boar, a rhinoceros, a tiger, a human, or some other creature. Those who answer the moon's questions correctly pass to the heavenly world: They go on the path to the gods, to fire, and finally to *brahman*. On the way, he shakes off his good and bad deeds [karma], which fall upon his relatives: the good deeds on the ones he likes and the bad deeds on the ones he dislikes. Freed from his good and bad deeds, this person, who has the knowledge of *brahman*, goes on to *brahman* (1.1–4a).

The deciding factor here apparently has nothing to do with the sort of worship the dead person engaged in while alive, or whether he lived in the village or the wilderness; there is just one final postmortem exam (proctored by the rabbit in the moon?) that determines everything.† The good and bad deeds weigh in only

---

* Fast-forward alert: This anticipates the notion developed at length in the *Bhagavad Gita*, that acts performed without desire have no karmic effects.
† Rather like the Oxbridge schools exams.

later and then only for the man who gets a first on the exam and proceeds on the path to *brahman* (not, as in the *Chandogya*, for the man on the path of rebirth). Nor does this text spell out what deeds are good, and what bad; that will come in later texts. The important doctrine of the transfer of karma from one person to another is harnessed to the trivial human frailty of liking some relatives and disliking others and caring about the disposal of one's worldly goods (in this case, one's karma). And the worms and insects no longer form a third place of No Exit, but are simply part of the lesser of the only two paths.

THE PATH OF SMOKE: THE PLEASURES OF SAMSARA

The path of smoke, of Vedic generosity, of procreation and samsara survives intact the journey from the Vedas to the Upanishads, though the Upanishads provide very little detail about it, perhaps assuming that everyone knew it because it had been around for centuries. The case in favor of samsara, in its positive aspect of passion, family, love, loss (what Nikos Kazantzakis's Zorba the Greek called "the whole catastrophe"), is strong. The Upanishads reopen some of the options of the Vedas that the Brahmanas closed down and open up other options. Individual texts, as always, often go against the grain of the general zeitgeist.

There's some pretty hot stuff in the Upanishads. The paragraph that introduces the description of the two paths refers to the act of progeneration as an offering in the fire of man and a birth in the fire of woman and analogizes a woman's genitals to the sacrificial fire: Her vulva is the firewood, her pubic hair the smoke, her vagina the flame; the acts of penetration and climax are the embers and the sparks (BU 6.2.13; 6.4.1–3; CU 5.8.1). One text takes the bliss of sexual climax as the closest available approximation to the ineffable experience of deep, dreamless sleep (BU 2.1.19). A woman in her fertile period is described as splendid and auspicious, and her fertility is so important that if she refuses to have sex with her husband at that time, he is advised to bribe her or beat her with a stick or with his fists (BU 6.4.6-7). A more tender attitude is advocated in the mantra that a man should use to make his wife love him, and a more practical one in the mantra for contraception if he does not want her to be pregnant (BU 6.4.9–10), an intention that flies in the face of the dharma texts that insist that the only purpose of sex is procreation.

A remarkably open-minded attitude to women's infidelity is evident in the mantra recommended to make a sexual rival impotent:

MANTRA AGAINST YOUR WIFE'S LOVER

If a man's wife has a lover whom he hates, he should place some fire in an un-baked pot, arrange a bed of reeds in reverse order from the usual way, apply ghee to the tips of the reeds, also in reverse order, and offer them in the fire as he recites this mantra: "You (he names the man) have made an offering in my fire! I take away your out-breath and your in-breath, your sons and livestock, your sacrifices and good works [or good karma], your hopes and plans." If a Brahmin who knows this curses a man, that man will surely leave this world stripped of his virility and his good karma. One should therefore never fool around with the wife of a learned Brahmin who knows this (BU 6.4.12).

In contrast with almost all of later Hinduism, which punished a woman extremely severely for adultery, this text punishes only her partner. Moreover, this punishment is intended (only) for a lover of his wife that the husband hates and therefore not necessarily for a lover that he does not hate, a most permissive qualification, suggestive of a Noel Coward drawing room comedy or a French ménage à trois. The men for whom these mantras are intended would have little use for the path of Release. Their primary concerns were Vedic: family, women, offspring, sons, the lineage of the flesh. For them the sacrifice of semen into a womb was a Vedic sacrifice of butter into the fire; the hated lover is cursed for making such an offering in another man's spousal fire.

THE PATH OF FLAME: *MOKSHA* AND RENUNCIATION

On the other hand, one of the later Upanishads mocks the sacrificial path (MU 1.2.10–11), and other passages in the Upanishads assume, like the Brahmanas, that repeated death is a Bad Thing, that the whips and scorns of time make life a nightmare from which one longs for final Release or freedom (*moksha*), a blessed awakening or, perhaps, a subsidence into a dreamless sleep. The cycle of rebirth was another way of being fenced in (*amhas*), a painfully restricting prison, from which one wanted to break out, to be sprung, which is what *moksha* means; the word is used for the release of an arrow from a bow or of a prisoner from a jail. It is sometimes translated as "Freedom."

Brahman, ineffable, can be described only in the negative: "Not like this, not like that" (*neti, neti*) (BU 4.5.15). Given that the positive goal, what one is going to, *moksha*, is never described, one might at least hope to be told what one was going away from. Precisely what was one freed from? At first, *moksha* meant only freedom from death, a concept firmly grounded within the Vedic sacrificial system that promised the worshiper a kind of immortality. The word appears in the Upanishads in various forms, often as a verb, "to set free." Through the sacrifice, the patron of the sacrifice *frees* himself from the grip of death, the grip of days and nights, the grip of the waxing moon and climbs up to heaven: "It is freedom, complete freedom (BU 3.1.3–6,34–35). Or: "Shaking off evil, like a horse its hair, and *freeing* myself, like the moon from the jaws of the demon of eclipse, I, the perfected self [atman], cast off the imperfect body and attain the world of *brahman* (CU 8.13.1)." *Moksha* sometimes comes to designate Release not merely from death or evil in general but, more specifically, from samsara, from the cycle of rebirth (SU 6.16,18). And then, in later Upanishads, *moksha* is associated with renunciation (*samnyasa*): "The ascetics who have full knowledge of the Vedanta are purified by the discipline of renunciation. In the worlds of *brahman*, at the time of the final end, they become fully immortal and fully *freed* (MU 3.2.6)." And whoever knows this (*yo evam veda*) will realize that unity with *brahman* upon his death and be freed from redeath.

The *Brihadaranyaka* promises freedom from the very things that the Vedic path valued—namely, children and family, the whole catastrophe: "It is when they come to know this self that Brahmins give up the desire for sons, the desire for wealth, and the desire for worlds, and undertake the renunciant life. . . . It was when they knew this that men of old did not desire offspring (BU 3.5.1, 4.4.22)." Such a man no longer amasses karma. He does not think, "I did something good" or "I did something bad," nor is he stained by bad karma/deeds. He is beyond good and evil.* We recognize the confident assurance of the Brahmanas: Even redeath can be fixed, if you know how, but now you do not even have to be a Brahmin to fix it, as long as you have the proper knowledge. This is yet another major innovation.

CONTINUITIES AND DISCONTINUITIES FROM THE VEDAS

The belief that souls are reborn for richer or for poorer, sickness or health, according to their conduct in their previous life, has roots in Vedic ideas of heaven and hell, reward and punishment.[19] So too the idea of the identity of the individual soul (atman) with the world soul (*brahman*) is a natural expansion of the Vedic idea that the individual body is overlaid upon the cosmic body, the eye on the sun, the breath on the wind (although now new questions arise about the

---

* An idea that turned out quite differently when Nietzsche got hold of it.

definition of the self).[20] The initiated Vedic ritual patron practiced a kind of renunciation,[21] and the sacrificer would say a mantra renouncing the fruits of his offerings. Even the idea of the transfer of karma, so central to Buddhism (where it is usually called the transfer of merit), has its roots, as we have seen, in the Vedic poems to the god Varuna (whom the poet asks to forgive him for the sins of his fathers) and in the transfer of evil from gods to humans, in the Brahmanas,[22] though it got an added boost from the growth of a moneyed economy.

The Upanishadic sages take the Vedic themes and run with them in new directions and far. Indeed, they openly challenge the Vedas; one sage quotes the Vedic line about existence coming from nonexistence (10.72.1–5) but then remarks: "How can that possibly be?" and argues instead: "In the beginning, this world was simply what is existent [CU 6.2.2]." The *Rig Veda* passage cited in the *Brihadaranyaka* mentions a slightly different version of the two paths: the path of the fathers and the path of the immortal gods. But in the *Rig Veda*, living creatures on these paths go not through the smoke to the moon or through the flame to the sun, but between the mother (both the female parent and the earth) and the father (both the male parent and the sky) (RV 10.88.15; BU 6.2.2).

Much of Upanishadic thought represents a radical break with the Vedas. Though the realization that each soul was one with the infinite soul was hardly breaking news in the Upanishads, the earlier Vedic sources hardly mention this idea and certainly do not develop it systematically. What was particularly new was the suggestion, only in the later Upanishads, that understanding the equation of atman and *brahman* was a call to action: You must change your life.[*] Most people did not change their lives. But eventually, as the lower classes gained more money, time, and education, some of them had the resources to act on ideas that they might have nourished for a long time and break away from the Vedic world entirely.[23] Aspects of the Upanishads certainly appealed to people who no longer wished, or were never allowed, to play ball with the Brahmins. Although the early Upanishads, as we have seen, regard renunciation as a live option only for *some* people, the later texts, the Renunciation Upanishads (*Samnyasa Upanishads*), encouraged a person heading for the path of Release (or Freedom) to seek *moksha* as soon as possible,[24] to make a vertical takeoff from any point in his life. For such a person, *moksha* is just another word for nothing left to lose.[†]

---

[*] As Rilke imagined the archaic torso of Apollo saying to him: *Du muss dein Leben ändern.*
[†] To paraphrase Janis Joplin.

We have some knowledge of the people who might have contributed these new ideas. The Upanishads refer to already existing renunciants who operated within the Vedic tradition, and Buddhist texts tell us that such people were also there before the time of the Buddha, who, in the story of his enlightenment, meets a sick man, an old man, a dead man, and then a renunciant,[25] perhaps a Vedic renunciant. The fringe mystics that the *Rig Veda* mentions, the Vratyas and the long-haired ascetic, may also have belonged to some of these motley and marginalized Vedic groups. The Upanishads attest to the existence of ascetic traditions that, by the sixth or fifth century BCE, had developed within the bounds of Vedic tradition, though not necessarily within the Brahmin class.[26] Speculation about the nature and purpose of Vedic ritual began eventually, for some thinkers, to subordinate ritual action to spiritual knowledge, which could be attained by asceticism, world renunciation, or the disciplines that came to be known as yoga, designed to transform behavior through their emphasis on re-fining, controlling, and transforming the mind and the body.[27]

Some people rejected the world of heaven that the Vedas promised them but remained within the Hindu fold, on the path to Release; others suspected that the Brahmins could not keep their promises of either path and left the Vedic world entirely, to become Buddhists or Jainas. Some non-Brahmins who were still not ready to leave the Vedic fold entirely may have been reacting against the excesses of the priests, seeking, through asceticism or meditation, freedom from an increasingly regulated society or from a religious life dominated by elaborate and expensive rituals that the Brahmins monopolized.[28] Other non-Brahmins may have been keen to introduce into the Vedic mix ideas, perhaps even ideas about karma and death, that have left no trace elsewhere, while at the same time they hoped in that way to crash the Brahmin party at last. Within Hinduism, the transition was from meditating on the Vedic sacrifice *while* doing it (in the Brahmanas and early Upanishads) to meditating upon the sac-rifice *instead of* doing it (from the time of the Renunciation Upanishads), a move implicit in the renunciation of the householder life.

NON-BRAHMIN SECRETS

The Upanishads attribute some of their new doctrines to an important group of non-Brahmins within the Vedic world, Kshatriyas. It is a king, Jaivali Pravahana of Panchala, who teaches the doctrine of the two paths to the young Brahmin Shvetaketu. In the *Brihadaranyaka,* Shvetaketu approaches the king "while people are waiting upon him," and he later refers to the king (out of his earshot) as a "second-rate prince" (*rajanya-bandhu*). The king insists that both Shvetaketu and his father must beg him to be their teacher, as they do, and before he teaches them, he says, "This knowledge has never before been in the possession of a Brahmin. But I will reveal it to you, to keep you or an ancestor of yours from doing harm to me (BU 6.3.8)." (Note that he still acknowledges the Brahmins' power to curse.) In the *Chandogya*, the king adds, "As a result, throughout the world government has belonged exclusively to royalty (CU 5.3.6)." In the *Kaushitaki*, Shvetaketu's father explicitly regards his royal teacher (another king) as an "outsider," and the king praises the father for swallowing his pride (KauU 1.1–7). The eclectic Upanishadic kings as gurus, such as Janaka of Videha (BU 3.1.1.1, 2.1.1), may have been drawing upon that legacy when they summoned the leading philosophers of their day, holy men of various schools and persuasions (surely including some Brahmins), to compete in their salons and to debate religious questions at royal gatherings.

Of course the kings in these texts may never have existed; they may simply have been dreamed up by Brahmin authors, purely a literary convention, a fantasy.* Texts record sentiments, not events. But it is surely significant that such a positive fantasy, if it is just a fantasy, about royal sages found its way into the texts of the Brahmin imaginary; certainly it is telling that the Upanishads attributed to the Kshatriyas ideas questioning the centrality of the ritual and thus challenging the power of the Brahmins. When the Brahmin Gargya asks King Ajatashatru of Kashi to be his teacher, the king says, "Isn't it a reversal of the norm for a Brahmin to become the pupil of a Kshatriya?" But he does it anyway (BU 2.1.15). These passages may represent a Kshatriya reaction to the Brahmin takeover during the preceding centuries, the period of the Brahmanas.

Nor were Kshatriyas the only non-Brahmins who contributed new ideas to the Upanishads:

RAIKVA, THE MAN UNDER THE CART

King Janashruti was devoted to giving a great deal of everything, especially food, thinking, "People will eat food from me everywhere." One night some wild geese were flying overhead, and one said, "Look, the light of Janashruti fills the sky!" The other replied, "Why speak of Janashruti? For just as the person with the highest throw of the dice wins all the lower throws, Raikva, the gatherer, takes

---

* It is, however, a fantasy supported by Georges Dumézil's arguments for an Indo-European king who was also a priest.

the credit for all the good things that people do. So does anyone who knows what Raikva knows." Janashruti overheard them. He summoned his steward and repeated to him what the geese had said.

The steward searched in vain and said to the king, "Can't find him." The king said, "Look for Raikva in a place where one would search for a non-Brahmin." The steward saw a man under a cart scratching his sores. He approached him respectfully and asked, "Sir, are you Raikva, the gatherer?" The man replied, "Yes, I am." The steward returned to the king and said, "Got him!" Janashruti offered Raikva hundreds of cows and gold if he would teach him the deity that he worshiped, but Raikva refused, saying, "Take them back, Shudra!" When, however, Janashruti offered him all this and his daughter, Raikva lifted up her face and said, "With just this face you could have bought me cheap (CU 4.1–2)."

Janashruti is a rich man and a king. Raikva is, by contrast, evidently a homeless person or a street person. He is also a man who despises cows and gold (two things that Brahmins always like best) and who likes women. It is extremely cheeky of him to call Janashruti a Shudra. Raikva is said to be a gatherer, which may refer to his knack of gathering up everyone else's good karma,* as a successful gambler gathers up the dice of the losers, another early example of the transfer of karma from one person to another. But "gathering" may also refer to Raikva's poverty, for he may have been a gleaner (like Ruth in the Hebrew Bible), gathering up the dregs of the harvest after everyone else has taken the real crop, or even, like so many homeless people, gathering up other people's garbage for his own use. The two meanings work well together: The man who lives on richer people's garbage also lives off their good deeds. (Much later, in the *Mahabharata* [14.90], several people, including a mongoose, tell King Yudhishthira about the great virtue of "the way of gleaning.") At first the steward presumably searches for a Brahmin, for he has to be specifically instructed to search elsewhere. That Janashruti can understand the talking animals (wild geese, which often carry messages in Hindu mythology) is evidence of his high spiritual achievement, but the non-Brahmin Raikva is higher still; his secret knowledge (about the wind and breath as gatherers) trumps Janashruti's ace of Vedic generosity.

---

* The phrase used here is *sadhu-kurvanti*, from the same roots as the *sadhu-krityam* of the Nachiketas story.

An innovator of unknown paternal lineage and hence questionable class appears in the story that immediately follows the tale of Raikva, the story of Satyakama Jabala, the hero of the vignette at the head of this chapter. For Satyakama's mother had slept with many men. ("I got around a lot" [*bahu aham caranti*] has the same double meaning in Sanskrit as it has in English—to move from one place to another and from one sexual partner to another—as well as a third, purely Indian meaning that is also relevant here: to wander as a mendicant.) An ancient Indian text that makes the son of such a woman a spiritual leader is a feminist tract. Such a text also takes truth rather than birth as the criterion of Brahminhood, though it still maintains that only a Brahmin, however defined, may learn the Veda. (Here we may recall the Brahmana statement "Why do you inquire about the father or the mother of a Brahmin? When you find knowledge in someone, that is his father and his grandfather.")[29] Satyakama needs to know his male lineage in order to prove that he was born in a family that has a right to learn the Veda; by conventional rules, he cannot matriculate in Varanasi U and sign up for Upanishads 108 unless he knows who his father is. But this text says it is enough for him to know who he himself is. Eventually Satyakama's teacher sends him out to herd a hundred lean, weak cows. They thrive and increase to a thousand, and after some years the bull speaks to him, and so do the fire, and a goose, and a cormorant, each telling him one foot of the *brahman*, here imagined as a quadruped (CU 4.4–8). His ability to make weak cows into strong cows is a Vaishya trait, but his ability to converse with these animals is a sign of his extraordinary religious talent, rare in any class.

Shramanas and Brahmanas

Though the idea of karma seems to have strong Vedic roots, strong enough that it seems almost inevitable that someone would have come up with it sooner or later (it was, one might say, the karma of the Upanishads to have that idea), ideas such as the identity of the atman with *brahman*, transmigration, and the Release from transmigration through renunciation and asceticism don't have such strong Vedic ties and send us out, like Janashruti's steward, to look for non-Vedic sources.

There were already in existence at this time a number of ascetic movements that were non-Vedic either in coming from some other, indigenous pool of ideas or in rejecting the Vedas, and these movements too may have come into, or influenced, the Upanishads.[30] The karma theory may have developed many of its crucial details within Jainism and moved from there to Buddhism and Hinduism;[31] the Jainas have always taken vegetarianism to the greatest extremes, taking pains to avoid injuring even tiny insects, and this too heavily influenced Hindus. The breakaway groups not only abhorred sacrifice but also rejected the Veda as revelation and disregarded Brahminical teachings and Brahminical claims to divine authority,[32] three more crucial points that distinguished them from Hindus, even from those Hindus who were beginning to take up some of the new doctrines and practices. The Buddhists also denied the existence of an individual soul, scorned the gods (particularly Indra*) as insignificant and/or ridiculous and, like the authors of some of the Upanishads, argued that conduct rather than birth determined the true Brahmin, all significant departures from Hindu doctrines. Moreover, Buddhist monks lived together in monasteries, at first only during the rainy season and later at other times as well, while the Hindu renouncers during this period renounced human companionship too and wandered alone.

A number of groups engaged in friendly intellectual combat at this time. There were probably early adherents of what were to become the six major philosophical schools of Hinduism: Critical Inquiry (Mimamsa), Logic (Nyaya), Particularism (Vaisheshika), Numbers (Sankhya), Yoga, and Vedanta. Ajivikas (contemporaries of the Jainas and Buddhists) rejected free will, an essential component of the doctrine of karma. Lokayatas ("This Worldly" people, also called Materialists and Charvakas, followers of a founder named Charvaka) not only rejected the doctrine of reincarnation (arguing that when the body was destroyed, the spirit that had been created specifically for it dissolved back into nothingness) but believed that physical sense data were the only source of knowledge and that the Vedas were "the prattling of knaves, characterized by the three faults of untruthfulness, internal contradiction, and useless repetition."[33] But most of what we know of the Materialists comes from their opponents and almost surely does not do them justice. Even the permissive *Kama-sutra* (c. second century CE) gives a simplistic version of the Materialist position: "Materialists say: 'People should not perform religious acts, for their results are in the world to come and that is doubtful. Who but a fool would take what is in his own hand and put it in someone else's hand? Better a pigeon today than a peacock tomorrow, and better a copper coin that is certain than a gold coin that is doubtful (1.2.21–23).'" The Materialists, as well as the Nastikas, common or garden-variety atheists (people who say "There is no (*na-asti*) [heaven or gods]"),

---

* This may well have contributed to Indra's fall from popularity within Hinduism too.

were among a number of rebellious intellectual movements that gained momentum in the vigorous public debates of the fifth century BCE.

Renunciants are sometimes called Shramanas ("toilers," designating wanderers, ascetics), in contrast with Brahmanas (the Sanskrit word for Brahmins; the name of Shramanas stuck in part because of the felicitous assonance).* "Shramana" at first often referred to ascetics both within and without the Hindu fold,[34] including Ajivikas, Nastikas, Lokayatas, and Charvakas.[35] But the *Brihadaranyaka* groups Shramanas with thieves, abortionists, Chandalas and Pulkasas (two Pariah groups), and ascetics (BU 4.3.22), and eventually the word "Shramana" came to mean anyone low or vile or, finally, naked.

Shramanas and Brahmins were said to fight like snakes and mongooses[36] or as we would say, like cats and dogs. Many Brahmins loathed the non-Vedic Shramanas (Buddhists and Jainas), who had entirely rejected, in favor of forest meditation, the sacrificial system that was the Brahmin livelihood. But the Shramanas within the Hindu fold, who still paid lip service, at least, to the Vedas and sacrifice but rejected the householder life (also a factor in Brahmin livelihood), were even more loathsome, a fifth column within the ranks. Both Shramanas and Brahmins must have been the source, and the audience, for the Upanishads, some of which they would have interpreted in different ways. Thus Brahmins, or the upper classes more generally, would take "renounce karma" to mean renouncing Vedic ritual, while to the Magadhi crowd that the Buddha preached to, it would have meant renouncing the fruits of actions of all kinds. Largely in response to the Shramana challenge, the Brahmins themselves absorbed a great deal of the renunciant ideal[37] and came to epitomize one sort of renouncer—a paradigm of purity, self-denial, and self-control—even while they excoriated the other sort of renouncer, the low-caste drifter.

But in addition to the Brahminic and Shramanic strains enriching the Upanishads, there was, as always, the great Indian catchall of "local beliefs and customs,"[38] or that ever-ready source of the unknown, the Adivasis or aboriginals, to whom more than one scholar attributes "some more or less universal Hindu beliefs like rebirth and transmigration of the *jiva* [soul] from animal to human existence."[39] There is also always the possibility of infusion of ideas from the descendants of the Indus Valley Civilization, an unknowable pool of what

---

* The Greek historian Megasthenes called them Brahmanes and Sarmanes, and the third-century BCE emperor Ashoka called them Shramanas and Brahmanas or else, significantly, Shramanas and householders.

might be radically different ideas, a tantalizing source that some would, and others would not, distinguish from the Adivasis and Dravidians. But another, better answer for the source of these ideas about individual salvation, better perhaps than a pool whose existence can't be proved, might be simply to admit that some individual, some brilliant, original theologian whose name is lost to us, composed some of the Upanishads. Lining up the usual suspects like this— a natural development from Vedic ideas (no genius required); Kshatriyas; some brilliant person in the Vedic camp; the IVC and its descendants; Adivasis—is often nothing more than confessing, "I can't find it in the Veda."

WOMEN AND OTHER LOWLIFE

The criterion of individual intellectual talent colors an Upanishadic story of a Brahmin with two wives, who are distinguished not by their class (as multiple wives often are) but by their minds:

THE THEOLOGICAL WIFE AND THE WORLDLY WIFE

Yajnavalkya had two wives, Maitreyi and Katyayani. Of the two, Maitreyi was a woman who took part in theological discussions, while Katyayani's understanding was limited to women's affairs. One day, as he was preparing to set out to wander as an ascetic, Yajnavalkya said, "Maitreyi, I am about to go away from this place. So come, let me make a settlement between you and Katyayani." Maitreyi replied, "What is the point in getting something that will not make me immortal? Tell me instead all that you know." Yajnavalkya replied, "I have always been very fond of you, and now you have made me even more so. Come, my dear, and I will explain it to you. But do try to concentrate (BU 4.5; cf. BU 2.4)."

And he explains the doctrine of the self to her and goes away. Katyayani never even appears.* Presumably she (like Martha in the gospel story) takes care of the house (which, also presumably, she will inherit when their husband abandons both wives to take the ascetic path) while the other woman talks theology.

Some women therefore took part in the new theological debates, though none is depicted as an author. Gargi, the feistiest woman in the Upanishads,† is

---

* Katyayani does appear, however, in a much later text (*Skanda Purana* 6.129), in which her jealousy of Maitreyi, Yajnavalkya's favorite, torments her until she performs a particular ritual (*puja*) to Parvati, which makes her equal to Maitreyi in Yajnavalkya's eyes.
† Fast-forward: Gargi is now the name of a woman's college in India and a symbol for women intellectuals.

a staunch defender of Yajnavalkya. On one occasion she questions him about a series of increasingly important worlds, culminating in the worlds of *brahman*. Then Yajnavalkya says, "Don't ask too many questions, Gargi, or your head will shatter apart!" And she shuts up (BU 3.6) (as do, on other occasions, several men who are threatened with having their heads shatter[40]). Another time, she asks Yajnavalkya two questions in front of a group of distinguished Brahmins; she likens herself to "a fierce warrior, stringing his unstrung bow and taking two deadly arrows in his hand, rising to challenge an enemy," an extraordinarily masculine, and violent, simile for a woman. When he answers her, at some length, she cries out, "Distinguished Brahmins! You should count yourselves lucky if you escape from this man without paying him anything more than your respects. None of you will ever defeat him in a theological debate (BU 3.8)." This is one tough lady, cast from the same mold as Urvashi and, later, Draupadi. (A later text even suggests that in addition to his other two wives, Yajnavalkya was also married to Gargi.[41])

Women also had other options. Buddhism offered women security within a socially approved institution as well as a double liberation, on both the worldly and the spiritual planes, glorying in the release not just from rebirth but from the kitchen and the husband.[42] Yet the Buddhists did not value nuns as highly as monks; there is even a tradition that the Buddha himself cautioned against admitting women, which, he warned, would spell the downfall of the order in India within five hundred years,[43] a prophecy that did, more or less, come true.

This period also saw the beginning of the composition of a large literature of supplementary Sanskrit texts, the Shrauta Sutras (c. 500 BCE), which describe the solemn, public rites of the Vedas (the *shruti*), always performed by Brahmins, and the Grihya Sutras (c. 300 BCE), the texts of the household (*griha*), describing the domestic and life cycle rites, often performed by householders who were not necessarily Brahmins. The Grihya Sutras regulated and normalized domestic life, bringing about the penetration of ritual regulation into the daily life of the household, on a scale not seen before. We may look at this development in two different ways, both as a greater power among householders who now had many rituals that they could perform without the help of a Brahmin and as the extension of Brahmin power, through the codification of texts about householders' rituals that had not previously been under Brahmin regulation.[44] While the earlier Shrauta Sutras had made mandatory large-scale ritual performances, in some of which (such as the horse sacrifice) the sacrificer's wife had to be present and even to speak, though not to speak Vedic mantras, the

Grihya Sutras that regulated daily practices to be performed in the home required the more active participation of the sacrificer's wife and other members
of the household. This too may explain the proactive behavior of some of the
women in the Upanishads.

ANIMALS

Low or excluded people are often associated with animals, like Raikva and
Satyakama with geese and bulls, and the fact that certain animals actually proclaim new Upanishadic doctrines tells us something important about the porosity of the class structure in religious circles at this time.

Dogs are satirically transformed from the lowest to the highest caste in an
Upanishadic passage that may have been inspired by the Vedic poem likening
priests (who begin their prayers with the sacred syllable "Om!") to frogs singing
in the rainy season:

THE SONG OF THE DOGS

A group of dogs asked a Vedic priest, "Please, sir, we'd like to find some food by
singing for our supper. We are really hungry." He asked them to return the next
morning, and so the dogs filed in, sliding in slyly as priests slide in slyly in a file,
each holding on to the back of the one in front of him. They sat down together
and began to hum. Then they sang, "Om! Let's eat! Om! Let's drink. Om!
May the gods bring food! Lord of food, bring food! Bring it! Bring it! Om!
(CU 1.12–13)."

Apparently they are rewarded, for the passage concludes with a statement that
anyone who understands the secret meaning of the word "hum" (a meaning
that the text supplies) "will come to own and to eat his own food." To have dogs,
the most impure of animals, impersonate Brahmins makes this remarkable satire, so reminiscent of Orwell's *Animal Farm*, truly bolshie. For dogs are already
stigmatized as eaters of carrion; when someone annoys Yajnavalkya by asking
where the heart is lodged, he replies, impatiently, "In the body, you idiot! If it
were anywhere other than in ourselves, dogs would eat it, or birds would tear
it up (BU 3.9.25)." The author of this text may be poking fun at Brahmins
or pleading for more sympathy for dogs (and therefore for the lower castes), or
both or none of the above.

At the other end of the animal spectrum, the horse's continuing importance
in the Upanishads is a constant reminder of the Kshatriya presence in these

texts. A horse auspiciously opens the very first line of the very first Upanishad: "The head of the sacrificial horse is the dawn; his eye is the sun; his breath the wind; and his gaping mouth the fire common to all men. . . . When he yawns, lightning flashes; when he shakes himself, it thunders; and when he urinates, it rains. His whinny is speech itself (BU 1.1.1)." The Vedic Dawn Horse (*Eohippus*) has cosmic counterparts; his eye is the sun just as, in the funeral hymn in the *Rig Veda*, the eye of the dead man is dispersed (back) to the sun, and the sun is born from the eye of the Primeval Man. The stallion's gaping mouth of flame is later echoed in the submarine mare with fire in her mouth.

Another equine image, the chariot as a metaphor for the control of the senses, familiar from the Brahmana story of Vrisha, reappears now: "A wise man should keep his mind vigilantly under control, just as he would control a wagon yoked to unruly horses (SU 2.9)." A more extended passage explains this metaphor:

> Think of the self as a rider in a chariot that is the body; the intellect is the charioteer, and the mind the reins. The senses are the horses and the paths around them are the objects of the senses. The senses do not obey a man who cannot control his mind, as bad horses disdain the charioteer; such a man continues to be subject to reincarnation. But the senses obey a man whose mind is always under control, as good horses heed the charioteer; such a man reaches the end of the journey (KU 3.3–6).

The senses must be harnessed, yoked, yogaed.* (Sometimes anger rather than desire is the sense that must be controlled, and desire is positioned as the charioteer; desire reins in anger like a charioteer with horses.)[45] For horses, like the senses, straddle the line between wild and tame, always under hair-trigger control like that mare who holds the doomsday flame in her mouth. Indeed the image of the driver of the chariot gives way in later texts to the image of the tiny elephant driver (the mahout) who is barely able to control the enormous rutting elephant on which he rides. Eternal vigilance is the price of *moksha*.

---

* In a parallel image that Plato came up with at roughly the same time (*Phaedrus*, 253D), the horse of the pair that represents the senses is "a crooked, great jumble of limbs . . . companion to wild boasts and indecency. He is shaggy around the ears, deaf as a post, and just barely yields to horse-whip and goad combined."

REBIRTH, NONVIOLENCE, AND VEGETARIANISM

Animals also appear in the lists of unwanted rebirths, in comparison with the two preferable options of rebirth as upper-class humans and Release from rebirth entirely. Dogs in particular represent the horrors of low birth; people who behave badly can expect to enter a nasty womb, like that of a dog. Significantly, the Good Animals, horses and cows, do not appear in the rebirth lists as likely options. One might assume that the belief that we might become reincarnate as animals contributes to the rise of vegetarianism in India, but no sympathy is extended to the animals in the rebirth lists, nor do the early Upanishads betray as many misgivings about eating animals (even reincarnated and/or talking animals) as the Brahmanas did toward the animals in the Other World. Yet the belief that humans and animals were part of a single system of the recycling of souls implies the fungibility of animals and humans and could easily sound a warning: Do not kill/eat an animal, for it might be your grandmother, or your grandchild, or (in the other world) you. For you are who you ate, and you may become whom you eat.

Nonviolence toward animals is mentioned only glancingly, twice, in the early Upanishads and then not as a word (such as *ahimsa*) but as a concept. The *Brihadaranyaka* stipulates that on a particular night, "a man should not take the life of any being that sustains life, not even that of a lizard (BU 1.5.14)." But presumably this is permissible on other nights. And the very last passage of the *Chandogya* states that the man who studies the Veda, becomes a householder, rears virtuous children, reins in his senses, "and refrains from killing any creature except on special occasions"* reaches the world of *brahman* and does not return again (CU 8.15.1). Here nonviolence against animals is specifically connected with the householder life, the path of rebirth, and is qualified in the usual way: There are occasions when it is good to eat animals, such as hospitality to honored guests.[46]

Yet most Indian traditions of reincarnation advise the renouncer to avoid eating meat,[47] and renouncers were likely to be vegetarians; to renounce the flesh is to renounce flesh. Morever, since the renouncer renounces the sacrificial ritual (karma), he thereby loses one of the main occasions when it is legal to kill

---

* Or "except to feed a worthy person" or "except in places specially ordained" or "except at sacrifices." The Sanskrit *anyatra tirtheshu* has all these meanings.

animals.[48] The Brahmanas and Upanishads sow the seeds for the eventual transition away from animal sacrifice. Where Indra in the Vedas ate bulls and buffalo, now the gods neither eat nor drink but become sated by just looking at the soma nectar (CU 3.6.1), just as the king merely smells the odor of the burning marrow in the horse sacrifice. Even in the Vedic ritual, vegetable oblations (rice and barley) were the minimally acceptable lowest form of the sacrificial victim, the *pashu*, but the original animal victim lingers on in the way that the Vedic texts treat even the rice cake like an animal: "When the rice cake [is offered], it is indeed a *pashu* that is offered up. Its stringy chaff, that is the hairs; its husk is the skin; the flour is the blood; the small grains are the flesh; whatever is the best part [of the grain] is the bone."[49]

Gradually many branches of Hinduism banished all animal sacrifices. Though this latter transition is almost always couched in terms of morality (*ahimsa*), there may also have been an element of necessity in it, the need to answer the challenge posed by the antisacrificial polemic of Buddhism and Jainism, which had converted many powerful political leaders. The Buddhists and Jainas too may have had moral reasons to abolish the sacrifice (as they said they did), but they may also have wanted to make a clean break with Hinduism by eliminating the one element by which most Hindus defined themselves, Vedic sacrifice. It was politic too for the Buddhists to promote a religion that did not need Brahmins to intercede for individual humans with gods, indeed that denied the efficacy of gods altogether, and this was the final move that distinguished Buddhists and Jainas from Hindu renunciants, who may not have employed Brahmins themselves but did not deny their authority for others. It was factors such as these, more than compassion for furry creatures, that made Buddhists and Jainas abjure animal sacrifice.* (The stricter *ahimsa* of the Jainas, which forbade them to take any animal life, prevented them from farming, which killed the tiny creatures caught under the plow; they were therefore forced to become bankers and get rich.)

But when we fold this mix back into the broader issues, we must distinguish among killing animals, tormenting animals, sacrificing them, eating them, and, finally, worshiping them. Nonviolence, pacifism, compassion for animals, and

---

* Early Buddhist monks and nuns ate meat but did not kill (or sacrifice) the animals themselves. Nonkilling was a virtue for them, but the Buddha explicitly refused to require monks and nuns to refrain from eating meat.

vegetarianism are not the same thing at all. Indeed Manu equates, in terms of merit, performing a horse sacrifice and abjuring the eating of meat (5.53). It is usual for an individual to eat meat without killing animals (most nonvegetarians, few of whom hunt or butcher, do it every day) and equally normal for an individual to kill people without eating them (what percentage of hit men or soldiers devour their fallen enemies?). We have noted that the horse in the Vedic sacrifice was killed but not eaten. Similarly, vegetarianism and killing may have been originally mutually exclusive; in the earliest period of Indian civilization, in places where there was no standing army, meat-eating householders would, in time of war, like volunteer firemen, become soldiers and consecrate themselves as warriors by giving up the eating of meat.[50] They either ate meat *or* killed.*

In later Hinduism, the strictures against eating and killing continued to work at odds, so that it would have been regarded as better (for most people, in general; the rules would vary according to the caste status of the person in each case) to kill a Pariah than to kill a Brahmin, but better to eat a Brahmin (if one came across a dead one) than to eat a Pariah (under the same circumstances). The degree of purity/pollution in the food that is eaten seems to be an issue distinct from the issue of the amount of violence involved in procuring it. It makes a difference if you find the meat already killed or have to kill it, and this would apply not only to Brahmins versus Pariahs (admittedly an extreme case) but to cows versus dogs as roadkill.

Nevertheless, the logical assumption that any animal that one ate had to have been killed by *someone* led to a natural association between the ideal of vegetarianism and the ideal of nonviolence toward living creatures. And this ideal came to prevail in India, reinforced by the idea of reincarnation. Thus, in the course of a few centuries, the Upanishads took the Vedic depiction of the natural and social orders as determined by power and violence (*himsa*) and reversed it in a 180-degree turn toward nonviolence. The logical link is the realization, so basic to Hinduism in all periods, that every human and every animal dies, that every human and every animal must eat, and that eating requires that someone or something (since vegetables are part of the continuum of life too) must die. The question is simply how one is going to live, and kill to live, until death.

---

* There was also an idea of *tapas*, of controlling the energy in the body through self-denial on the eve of war, that worked by a logic similar to that of the old American tradition of football players' not being allowed to party on the night before the big game.

Fast-Forward

ADDICTION AND RENUNCIATION

One reason why the renunciant movements were accepted alongside the more conventional householder religion was that such movements addressed a problem that was of great concern to the wider tradition, the problem of addiction. A profound psychological understanding of addiction (*sakti*,* particularly excessive attachment, *ati-sakti*†) to material objects and of the true hallmark of addiction, the recurrent failure to give them up even when one wants to give them up—the "just one more and I will stop" scenario—is evident throughout the history of Hinduism. Manu puts it well: "A man should not, out of desire, become addicted to any of the sensory objects; let him rather consider in his mind what is entailed in becoming excessively addicted to them (4.16)." One reaction to this perceived danger was the movement to control addiction through renunciation and/or asceticism, building dikes to hold back the oceanic tides of sensuality. Fasting and vows of chastity were widely accepted, in moderated forms, even among householders.

The Hindu appreciation of the value of exquisite pleasure (*kama*) was balanced by an awareness of the dangers that it posed, when cultivated to the point at which it became a vice (a danger appreciated even by the *Kama-sutra*), and by a number of religious disciplines designed to control the sensual addictions to material objects. Most sorts of renunciation were peaceful, both for the individual renouncer and for the society from which the renouncer withdrew, offsides, hors de combat, while remaining perceived as broadly beneficial to the community at large. But other kinds of renunciation were violent both to the physical body and to the social body, to the world of families. Hinduism was violent not only in its sensuality but in its reaction against that sensuality—violent, that is, both in its addictions and in the measures that it took to curb those addictions (acknowledging, like Dr. Samuel Johnson, that it is easier to abstain than to be moderate).

The senses, as we have seen, were analogized not to unglamorous tame animals like pigs or dogs or to more violent wild animals like lions or crocodiles, but to noble, beautiful, expensive horses. Both the senses and horses were a Good Thing for high-spirited warrior kings (though dangerous even for them;

---

* Not to be confused with *shakti*, a feminine form of power.
† The title of Gandhi's essay on the *Gita* says it is about *asakti-yoga*, usually translated as "selfless action" but more precisely the yoga of nonaddiction.

remember King Triyaruna and his chariot) but not such a Good Thing for more bovine priests and householders whose goal was control. And as Brahmins were perceived (at least by Brahmins) as needed to control kings, so asceticism was thought necessary to rein in the treacherous senses.

Some renouncers chose to marginalize themselves socially in order not to fall prey to the violence and tyranny of the senses—that is, to addiction. At the opposite end from renunciation on the spectrum of sensuality, addiction, like renunciation, served to marginalize upper-caste males and consign them to the ranks of the other marginalized people who are a central concern of our narrative, women and lower castes. Addiction to the vices marginalized some Brahmins and rajas by stripping them of their power and status; kings, at least in stories, lost their kingdoms by gambling or were carried away by hunting and landed in dangerous or polluting circumstances. Hunting was classified as a vice only when it was pursued when there was no need for food, just as gambling became a vice when undertaken independent of a need for money, and sex when there was no need for offspring. Hunting therefore is not a vice for poor people, who hunt for squirrels or whatever they can find to eat, though tribal hunters were regarded as unclean because of their habit of hunting. To some extent, these vices leveled the playing field.

Asceticism and Eroticism

But sensuality continued to keep its foot in the door of the house of religion; the erotic was a central path throughout the history of India. Though asceticism remained alive and well and living in India, in other parts of the forest, householders continued to obey the command to be fruitful and multiply. Material evidence, such as epigraphy, has recently indicated that Hinduism (like Buddhism) on the ground was less concerned with soteriology and more with worldly values than textual scholars have previously assumed. But the religious texts too show this ambivalence. The tension between the two paths, the violent (sacrificial), worldly, materialistic, sensual, and potentially addictive path of smoke and rebirth, on the one hand, and the nonviolent (vegetarian), renunciant, ascetic, spiritual, and controlled path of flame and Release, on the other, was sometimes expressed as the balance between worldly involvement and withdrawal from life, between the outwardly directed drive toward activity (*pravritti*) and the inwardly directed drive toward withdrawal (*nivritti*), between bourgeois householders and homeless seekers, or between traditions that regarded karma as a good or a bad thing, respectively.

From time to time one person or one group raised its voice to accuse the other of missing the point. Hostility was rare but not unknown. One Brahmana depicts the renunciant life in unflattering terms: "Fathers have always crossed over the deep darkness by means of a son, for a son gives a father comfort and carries him across; the self is born from the self. What use is dirt or the black antelope skin [of the ascetic]? What use are beards and asceticism? Brahmins, get a son; that is what people keep saying."[51] The householder's tendency to regard ascetics with a mixture of reverence, envy (perhaps tinged with guilt), pity, and distrust[52] sometimes fueled the widespread image of false ascetics, fake fakirs, and mendacious mendicants, an image just about as old as the tradition of genuine ascetics.[53] The 1891 census listed yogis under "miscellaneous and disreputable vagrants"[54] (think of Raikva), and to this day villagers express "considerable skepticism about yogis in general in Hindu society." Throughout India, people tell stories about yogis who are "mere men" and succumb to temptation by women.[55] The householder could express his ambivalence by honoring "real" ascetics and dishonoring the fakes. Hindus have always been as skeptic as they are omphaloskeptic.

A related tension runs between the vitality of the Hindu sensual and artistic traditions, on the one hand, and the puritanism of many Hindu sects, on the other. It also led to an ongoing ambivalence toward women. Renouncers tended to encourage a virulent loathing and fear of women, while worldly Hindus celebrated women in their sculptures, their poetry, and, sometimes, real life. In addition to various options that were later developed to accommodate *moksha*, one solution was to remove from men entirely the responsibility for the conflict between sexuality and chastity and to project it onto women.[56] For men who took the option of fertility, therefore, women were revered as wives and mothers, while for those who were tempted by chastity, women were feared as insatiable seductresses. This schizoid pattern emerges again and again in attitudes to women throughout the history of Hinduism.

These differences fueled debates on a number of key philosophical and practical issues in Hinduism. For Hindus continue to drive, like King Vrisha in the Brahmana story, with one foot on the accelerator of eroticism and one foot on the brake of renunciation. The tension appears, for instance, in the interaction of two forms of worship: on the one hand, a form that visualizes the god with qualities (*sa-guna*), as an animal, or a man or a woman, with arms and legs and a face, a god that you can tell stories about, a god you can love, a god that becomes incarnate from time to time, assuming an illusory form out of compassion for human beings who need to be able to imagine and love and worship the deity, and, on the other hand, a worship that sees god ultimately without qualities (*nir-guna*), beyond form, ineffable and unimaginable, an aspect of *brahman*. This second viewpoint is often a force for tolerance, rather than difference: If you believe that the deity is ultimately without form, you are less likely to insist on the particular form that you happen to worship or to stigmatize the different form that your neighbor worships. Yet the creative tension between renouncers and Hindus who chose to remain in the thick of human things at times threatened the tolerance and diversity of Hinduism.

We must, in any case, beware of essentializing these oppositions, as the early Orientalists did, as even Karl Marx did, when he characterized Hinduism, in an article in the *New York Tribune*, in June 10, 1853, as "at once a religion of sensualist exuberance, and a religion of self-torturing asceticism; a religion of the Lingam and of the juggernaut; the religion of the Monk, and of the Bayadere [dancing girl]." Rather, we should regard these dichotomies as nothing more than general guidelines or intellectual constructs that help us find our way through the labyrinth of ancient Indian religious groups. Just because the Hindus themselves often formulated their ideas in terms of polar opposites—and they did—there is no reason to believe that these categories corresponded to any sort of lived experience. For though the ideal of renunciation seemed in ways to challenge or even to threaten the traditional Vedic system, it was entirely assimilated by Hinduism, the world's great "have your rice cake and eat it" tradition. To practicing Hindus, it was all part of the same religion, one house with many mansions; their enduring pluralism allowed Hindus to recognize the fissures but to accept them as part of a unified world. In a way somewhat analogous to the attitude of lay Buddhists or Catholics to nuns and monks, many Hindu householders were happy to support renouncers in order to gain secondhand merit from a regimen that they themselves were not willing to undergo, and renouncers were happy to be supported by householders in exchange for their blessings and, sometimes, their teachings. Despite the recurrent conflicts and occasional antagonisms between the two paths, by and large the creative tension between them was peaceful; the two options generally respected each other and lived together happily for centuries, carrying on in tandem. The idea of nonviolence supplemented rather than replaced the Vedic demand for blood sacrifice. Renunciation remained a separate live option alongside the earlier options. Whole groups—the lower castes, for instance—never saw any conflict between the two ideals or simply ignored both. Where a less vigorous, or less tolerant, tradition might have burned the Upanishadic sages at the stake, where most other religions would have either kicked out or swallowed up the antinomian ascetics, Vedic Hinduism moved over to make a place of honor for them.

In general, the followers of the path of Release attached no opprobrium to the path of rebirth. Time and again the road forks, but the two paths continue side by side, sometimes joining, then diverging again, and people can easily leap from one to the other at any moment. Vedic *tapas*, outward-directed heat, seems at first to conflict with Upanishadic *tapas*, inward-directed heat. But ultimately both forms of spiritual heat, as well as erotic heat (*kama*),[57] are aspects of the same human force, simply channeled along different paths. Asceticism ricochets against addiction and back again. Indian logic used as a standard example of inference one that we use too: Where there's smoke, there's fire, smoke being the sign (*linga*, the same word as the "sign" for male gender) of fire. Which is to say, wherever there is the option of transmigration, the path of smoke (samsara), there is also the option of Release from transmigration, the path of fire (*moksha*). Less obvious but equally true: Wherever there is the option of Release from transmigration, fire, there is the option of transmigration, smoke.

CHAPTER 8

THE THREE (OR IS IT FOUR?) AIMS OF LIFE IN THE HINDU IMAGINARY

ॐ

CHRONOLOGY

300–100 BCE The *dharma-sutras* are composed

c. 100 CE Manu composes his *Dharma-shastra*

c. 200 CE Kautilya composes the *Artha-shastra*

c. 300 CE Vatsyayana Mallanaga composes the *Kama-sutra*

THE THREE AIMS

No one enjoyed pleasure just for sexual ecstasy; no one hoarded wealth for the sake of pleasure. No one performed acts of dharma for the sake of wealth; no one committed acts of violence for the sake of dharma.

Ashvaghosha, *Buddhacharita* (first century CE)[1]

In the ideal Hindu world that the poet Ashvaghosha described, none of the three aims is used in the service of the ones below it: Dharma is more important than wealth, which is more important than pleasure (which is more important than mere sexual thrills). The complex hierarchical relationship among the three aims of pleasure, wealth, and dharma is what this chapter is all about. It is an interlude, its subject neither any particular historical period nor any of the main actors in this book (women, low castes, dogs, horses), but certain basic ideas that undergird the practice of Hinduism as well as its historical development. Central among these is the tension between the paths of rebirth and renunciation and between a general dharma that includes renunciation and a specific dharma that often includes violence, both the violence of war and the violence of sacrifice.

THE THREE QUALITIES OF MATTER—PLUS SPIRIT

The Upanishads began to assimilate Release (*moksha*) within an overarching intellectual framework that was only later fully articulated but that had already laid out the basic taxonomies that *moksha* challenged. Alternating with the basic dualisms that we have seen at work, these taxonomies often linked key concepts together in triads, such as the triad of aims in Ashvaghosha's poem, and, later, quartets. "Three" was a kind of shorthand for "lots and lots"; there are three numbers in Sanskrit grammar: one, two, and plural (consisting of all numbers three and above). "Three" also became a symbol for interpenetration, interconnectedness, a collectivity of things that go together, a representation of the multivalent, multifaceted, multiform, multi-whatever-you-like nature of the real phenomenal world.

One basic triad is attested in brief references as early as the *Atharva Veda* and the *Chandogya Upanishad:* that of the three strands or qualities of matter (*gunas*),[2] woven together like the three strands of a braid—lucidity or goodness or intelligibility (*sattva*), energy or activity or passion (*rajas*), and darkness or inertia or entropy (*tamas*).[3] Classical Sankhya philosophy, which provides us with the earliest detailed discussion of the three strands,[4] overlays the initial triad upon several others, such as the classes of gods, humans, and animals-plants, and the three primary colors, not red, blue, and yellow but white (lucidity), red (activity), and black (inertia). So too *sattva* is thought to predominate in cows and Brahmins, *rajas* in horses and Kshatriyas, and *tamas* in dogs and the lower classes.

Enduring triads, besides the three qualities of matter, include the three times (past, present, and future); mind, body, and speech; the three humors of the body (*doshas:* phlegm, bile, and wind); and the three debts that every man owed (study to the sages, funeral offerings to the ancestors, and sacrifice to the gods).[5] There are generally said to be three worlds, usually identified as heaven, earth, and hell in Indo-European texts,[6] then sky, ether, and earth in the *Rig Veda* (which also uses the dual model of sky/heaven and earth), and then, in the Puranas, heaven, earth, and hell again, reverting to the Indo-European model. The expedient of simply adding both the ether *and* hell to the basic pair of sky and earth is not taken, perhaps because the idea of three worlds was already so firmly embedded in Hindu cosmology. The number of worlds remained stable forever—that is, they were never squared, as were other paradigmatic triads that we will soon encounter. Indeed their resistance to quadripartition is one of the props of the argument that triads, rather than quartets, are the basis of Hindu thinking.

Yet other important clusters began as triads and then became quartets.

THE THREE AIMS OF LIFE

One of the most significant shifts from three to four took place within the paradigm of the aims of life (the *purusha-arthas*). Originally they were a triad, dharma, *artha,* and *kama*, known collectively as the Trio (*trivarga*). For assonance, one might call them piety, profit, and pleasure, or society, success, and sex, or duty, domination, and desire. More precisely, dharma includes duty, religion, religious merit, morality, social and ritual obligations, the law, and justice. The *Rig Veda* had spoken of *rita*, a cosmic order that came to mean "truth" and was absorbed by the later concept of ritual dharma in the legal codes. "Dharma" is derived from *dhri*, "to hold fast, to make secure," just as "karma" is derived from *kri*, "to make or do." Dharma holds the universe together; dharma, rather than love, is what makes the world go 'round. Dharma is both the way things are and the way they *should* be.[7] *Artha* is money, political power, and success; it can also be translated as goal or aim (as in the three aims of human life), gain (versus loss), money, the meaning of a word, and the purpose of something. *Kama* represents pleasure and desire, not merely sexual but more broadly sensual—music, good food, perfume, paintings. Every human being was said to have a right, indeed a duty, to all these aims, in order to have a full life.

Sanskrit texts were devoted to each of the three aims; the most famous of these are the dharma text of Manu, the *Artha-shastra* of Kautilya, and the *Kama-sutra* of Vatsyayana. Significantly, there are many texts devoted to dharma, but only one *Artha-shastra* and one *Kama-sutra* survive from the earliest period. Clearly, dharma was both more important and more complex. The codification of dharma at this time is in a sense a reaction to *moksha* (more precisely, to the formulation of *moksha* as an alternative goal). But *moksha* must, of course, also be reacting to dharma (more precisely, to the still uncodified general concept of social order that underlay the Vedas and Brahmanas), for what is it that the renunciant renounces but the householder life, the heart of dharma? Here is another chicken-and-egg process, like Brahma and Vishnu creating each other. No one needed a text to justify the householder life in such detail until some people started saying they didn't want to be householders.

The earliest texts about dharma are the *dharma-sutras*,* from between the third century BCE and the first century CE.[8] Close on their heels came the more elaborate texts known as the *dharma-shastras*, of which the best known is *Manu's Dharma-shastra* (in Sanskrit, the *Manava-dharma-shastra* or *Manu-smriti*, and informally known as *Manu*), probably composed sometime around 100 CE. The text consists of 2,685 verses and calls upon widely dispersed cultural assumptions about psychology, concepts of the body, sex, relationships between humans and animals, attitudes to money and material possessions, politics, law, caste, purification and pollution, ritual, social practice and ideals, world renunciation, and worldly aims. The claims made about the author himself give us a hint of what to expect. Manu is the name of a king (an interesting attribution, given the priestly bias of Manu's text) who is the mythological ancestor of the human race, the Indian Adam. "Manu" means "the wise one." Thus *manava* ("descended from Manu") is a common word for "human" (which, in terms of the lexical meaning of Manu as "wise," might also be the Sanskrit equivalent of *Homo sapiens*). The title therefore conceals a pun: *Manava*, "of Manu," also means "of the whole human race."

The *Artha-shastra*, or textbook on politics, is generally attributed to Kautilya ("Crooked"), the minister of the Mauryan emperor Chandragupta in the fourth century BCE. It may contain material from that period, though it was completed in the early centuries of the Common Era, perhaps by 200 CE. But since we cannot know which parts of it were actually composed in the Mauryan period and tell us what really happened then, and which portions are a later fantasy of what things might have been then, we can't assume that any particular piece is Mauryan. The *Artha-shastra* is a compendium of advice for a king, and though it is often said to be Machiavellian, Kautilya makes Machiavelli look like Mother Teresa. In addition to much technical information on the running of a kingdom, the *Artha-shastra* contains a good deal of thought on the subject of human psychology.

Kautilya has a particularly low opinion of religious sensibilities. He advises the king to go out in public in the company of several friends dressed up as gods, so that his people will see him hobnobbing with them (13.1.3–8); to get a reputation for foreseeing the future by predicting that someone will die and then having him killed (1.11.17–18); to kill an enemy by arranging to have the image

---

* The sutras, or texts consisting of lines "sewn together"—"sutra" being cognate with our "suture"—are the predecessors of the *shastras*.

of a god fall on him (and then presumably proclaiming that the gods killed him) (12.5.1–5); to imitate, in water, the god Varuna or the king of the Cobra People (13.2.16); to play upon people's faith in sacred texts by staging an elaborate charade with a holy man (13.2.1–9); to pretend to be an ogre (13.2.30–37); and to have his agents use the blood of animals to cause a hemorrhage to flow from images of deities in the territory of the enemy and then have other agents declare defeat in battle in consequence of the bleeding of the deity (3.2.27–8). Evidently, Kautilya shared the opinion often attributed to P. T. Barnum that you cannot fool all of the people all of the time, but it isn't necessary. Images of deities (of which we have absolutely no physical evidence in the Mauryan period) play a surprisingly prominent role in legal affairs in this text; there is a specific punishment for people who so forget themselves (*anatmanah*) that they have sex with animals or with images of gods (4.13.28–31) (lingas, perhaps?).*

The *Kama-sutra* was probably composed in the second or third century CE, and is attributed to a man named Vatsyayana Mallanaga, who was almost certainly a real human being (in contrast with the entirely mythical Manu), but about whom we know virtually nothing. Vatsyayana, as an author, is therefore more mythical than Kautilya but less mythical than Manu.

DIVERSITY AMONG THE THREE MAIN TEXTS OF THE THREE AIMS

In a pattern of mutual creation that should by now be familiar, Manu and the *Artha-shastra* quote each other;[9] in particular, Manu borrowed from the *Artha-shastra* the sections pertaining to the king, civil administration, criminal and civil law.[10] The *Artha-shastra*, roughly contemporaneous with several Buddhist texts about kingship,[11] may have contributed to, and taken from, such texts ideas about the importance of taxation and the endowing of stupas/temples. Clearly this is a shared corpus of ideas.†

Yet there are significant differences in the attitudes of the three texts toward religion. *Manu* describes Vedic rituals in great detail but does not mention temples, while both the *Kama-sutra* and the *Artha-shastra* speak of temples and of festivals of the people but make no reference to any Vedic rituals; different texts apparently catered to people who engaged in different religious practices. Kautilya, like Vatsyayana, frequently advises the ruler (as Vatsyayana advises

---

* Women in the *Kama-sutra* have sex with statues, and in the *Narmamala*, as we've seen on page 22, a woman has sex with a linga of leather or skin.
† The *Mahabharata* (13.63) also contains passages of satire on the *Artha-shastra*.

the lover) to make use of, as spies, precisely the people whom Manu specifically outlaws, such as wandering ascetics and wandering nuns (both Buddhist and Hindu).

Renunciants, with no fixed address, are most useful to the *Artha-shastra* political machine, for holy men and women who beg for their living are, along with courtesans, uniquely able to move freely among all levels of society. (Actors too have such freedom, and all the *shastra*s except for the textbook for actors, the *Bharata Natya Shastra*, agree that actors are not to be trusted and that sleeping with the wife of an actor does not count as adultery.) Like the *Artha-shastra*, but perhaps for the opposite reason, the *Kama-sutra* is wary of nuns; it advises a married woman not to hang out with "any woman who is a beggar, a religious mendicant, a Buddhist nun, promiscuous, a juggler, a fortune-teller, or a magician who uses love-sorcery worked with roots (4.1.9)." Manu spends page after page in praise of ascetics, but the *Artha-shastra* has political agents of the king pretend to be wandering ascetics and advises the king to employ genuine ascetics in espionage (1.11.1–20). This surely did further damage to the already poor reputation of many ascetics, whom the *Artha-shastra* further denigrates with tales of false prophets (1.13.15).

The members of the Trio are often said to be separate but equal. Sometimes they work together; thus, for example, one can have sex for the sake of offspring (dharma), for the sake of gaining political power (*artha*), or for sheer pleasure (*kama*), or for some combination of the three (KS 1.5.1–12). Yet the Trio tended to be hierarchized.[12] The *Artha-shastra* and *Kama-sutra* rank dharma first and *kama* last, but Manu, oddly enough, hedges: "Dharma and *artha* are said to be better, or *kama* and *artha*, or dharma alone, or *artha* alone, here on earth. But the fixed rule is that the Trio is best (2.224)." The three aims form a sort of rock-paper-scissors arrangement, in which one is constantly trumping the others in an eternal merry-go-round. Some people attempted to correlate the three aims with the triad of the qualities of matter in a kind of unified field theory, (dharma with *sattva*, *kama* with *rajas*, and *artha* with *tamas*). The members of the Trio are, like the strands of matter, dynamic, inescapably interrelated, and in constantly shifting relationships to one another.

The poet Ashvaghosha was born a Brahmin but converted to Buddhism. He lists the aims in what was generally agreed to be their ascending order of importance: One should not use *artha* for *kama*, since *artha* is more important than *kama*, nor dharma for *artha*, since dharma is more important than *artha*. To supply the first element, *kama*, with a precedent, he invokes an exaggerated, hence less desirable form of the element itself (ecstasy in contrast with mere pleasure), and when he reaches the last aim, dharma, which, to continue the pattern, should not be allowed to compromise a subsequent element higher than itself, he invokes as that subsequent element violence (*himsa*). One might have expected *ahimsa* here, but *himsa*, in its place, evokes the specter of Vedic sacrifice, which makes a very different point: In an ideal (pre-Buddhist) world, no one should perform Vedic sacrifices (involving violence to animals) for the sake of dharma.

Yet even dharma must not be honored at the expense of the other aims. The thirteenth-century commentator on the *Kama-sutra* (1.1.2) tells this story of the interdependence of the three aims, here regarded as divinities:

KING PURURAVAS AND THE THREE AIMS

When King Pururavas went from earth to heaven to see Indra, the king of the gods, he saw Dharma and the others [Artha and Kama] embodied. As he approached them, he ignored the other two but paid homage to Dharma, walking around him in a circle to the right. The other two, unable to put up with this slight, cursed him. Because Kama had cursed him, he was separated from his wife and longed for her in her absence. When he had managed to put that right, then, because Artha had cursed him, he became so excessively greedy that he stole from all four social classes. The Brahmins, who were upset because they could no longer perform the sacrifice or other rituals without the money he had stolen from them, took blades of sharp sacrificial grass in their hands and killed him.

Pururavas, a mortal king, is married to the celestial nymph and courtesan Urvashi. Artha makes Pururavas so greedy that he violates one of the basic principles of dharma—never, ever, steal from Brahmins—and that is his undoing.*

SQUARING THE CIRCLE

The texts we have considered above, and many others, regard the Trio as triple. But sometimes the aims of life are listed not as a Trio but as a quartet (*chatur-varga*), in which the fourth aim is *moksha*. The texts on each of the aims of life do not, by and large, deal with *moksha* when they deal with the other

---

* This story resembles the Greek myth of Paris, who, forced to choose among three goddesses, chose Aphrodite (= Kama) over Hera and Athene (roughly = Dharma and Artha), who cursed him.

three aims, either because they did not take it seriously or, more likely, because they felt it operated in a world beyond the range of their concerns. The three worldly aims of life generally resisted the arriviste renunciant fourth; significantly, Ashvaghosha uses the Trio rather than the quartet in the verse we have cited. To use the Indian metaphor of the Yugas, the dice are loaded three to one in favor of worldliness; *kama*, *artha*, and dharma (as defined in the *dharma-shastras*) are all for householders. Yet *moksha* was far too important to be ignored, and that is where the problems arise. From the time of the Upanishads, the interloping fourth was usually transcendent, the banner of a shift away from worldliness (the path of rebirth) to a life of renunciation and asceticism (the path of Release).

Not surprisingly, the *Kama-sutra* in general gives very short shrift to *moksha* (1.2.4) and even applies the term, surely tongue in cheek, to the courtesan's successful jettisoning ("setting free") of an unwanted lover (6.4.44–5). On the other hand, other texts regard *moksha* as far superior to the other aims, or, rather, in a class apart. Some authors also attempted various unsatisfactory, overlapping correlations between the four aims and other quartets/triads, such as the three (twice born) classes, with *moksha* and dharma for Brahmins; all three of the original Trio for Kshatriyas; and *artha* for Vaishyas. It works better with the colors and qualities: white lucidity for Brahmins, red energy for Kshatriyas, and black torpor for the lower classes. But the matchmaking is generally a doomed attempt to put a square peg in a round hole.

To this basic triad-become-quartet others were soon assimilated.[13] The Vedas are usually regarded as a triad, and many Hindus to this day are named Trivedi ("Knower of Three Vedas"). But the Vedas are also regarded as a quartet, including the *Atharva Veda*, and other Hindus are named Chaturvedi ("Knower of Four Vedas"). (A foolish Brahmin in a seventh-century CE play naively brags that he will be honored even by Brahmins who are Panchavedi, Shadvedi—Knowers of Five Vedas, Six Vedas.[14]) Even the triad of qualities (*gunas*) was squared, when female *prakriti* ("matter, nature," consisting of the three qualities) was contrasted with male *purusha* ("spirit, self, or person"), the transcendent fourth. Similarly, where once the Hindus had formulated a group of three passions—lust (*kama*), anger (*krodha*), and greed (*lobha*, or, in some formulation, fear [*bhaya*])—now a fourth metaphysical, epistemological emotion was added: delusion (*moha*). The new fourth often involved the concept of silence: To the three priests of the sacrifice was added a fourth priest (called the Brahmin) who was merely the silent witness; to the three Vedic modes of experience (waking, dreaming, and dreamless sleep) was added a fourth stage, just called the fourth (*turiya*), a stage of merging completely into *brahman*.[15] When keeping time in music too, Indians count three "heavy" beats and a fourth "empty" beat.[16]

There are also some quartets that never seem to have been triads, such as the four Ages of time, or Yugas, named after the four throws of the dice. Yet the first three ages form one group (Eden, the way it was *in illo tempore*), while the last (the Kali Age) forms the other group (now, reality). The score, as usual, was not four, but three plus one.

FIVE SOLUTIONS TO THE FOURTH ADDITION TO THE THREE AIMS

Hinduism came up with various solutions to the potential conflicts between renunciation and the householder life resulting from the addition of the fourth aim, *moksha*.[17]

First, it was said that the goals of sacrifice and renunciation were to be followed not simultaneously but seriatim, one at a time in sequence. When the aims are four and in sequence, they are sometimes grouped with what came to be known as the four stages of life (*ashrama*s, also, confusingly, the word for a hermitage). But in the earliest texts that mention them (the early *dharma-sutras*), the four *ashrama*s were not stages at all but four options for lifestyles that could be undertaken at any period in a man's life: the chaste student (*brahma-charin*), the householder (*grihastha*), the forest dweller (*vanaprastha*), and the renouncer (*samnyasin*).[18] The system was an attempt, on the part of Brahmins who inclined to renunciation, to integrate that way of life with the other major path, that of the householder. The first *ashrama*, that of the chaste student, always retained its primary meaning of a vow of chastity undertaken *at any time of life*.[19] But by the time of Manu, the four *ashrama*s had become serial (M 6.87–94), rather than choices that one could make at any time. From then on they were generally regarded as stages, and eventually the third stage in the quartet, that of the forest dweller, became highly problematic, especially when attempts were made to distinguish it from the fourth stage, that of the renouncer.[20]

The fourth aim, *moksha*, clearly corresponds to the fourth stage of life, the renouncer's stage, and because of that, scholars have often constructed a false chronology regarding the stages as yet another system of an original three plus a later one. But the first three aims do not correlate so easily with the first three stages. This is how the *Kama-sutra* attempts to put them together and to specify the age at which each should be undertaken:

A man's life span is said to be a full hundred years. By dividing his time, he culti-
vates the three aims in such a way that they enhance rather than interfere with
each other. Childhood is the time to acquire knowledge and other kinds of *artha*,
the prime of youth is for *kama*, and old age is for dharma and *moksha*. Or, because
the life span is uncertain, a man pursues these aims as the opportunity arises, but
he should remain celibate until he has acquired knowledge (1.2.1–6).

The *Kama-sutra* hedges. It speaks of three aims but then sneaks *moksha* in on
the coattails of dharma to include it after all. It does not actually mention the
stages of life (*ashramas*) but speaks instead of childhood (*brahma-charya*, where,
instead of Vedic learning, the boy presumably learns a trade), the prime of
youth (the householder stage), and old age (which might be forest dwelling,
renunciation, or neither, just staying home and getting old). And though the
author assigns (three) ages for the (three, actually four) aims, he then unsays that
division with his remark that one must *carpe* the *diem* at any time. The suggestion that you can indulge in *kama* at any stage of life (except childhood) reflects
(or perhaps even satirizes?) widespread arguments about whether you can engage in renunciation (*samnyasa*) at any stage.[21]

Most Hindus regarded renunciation as something that one did after having
children and grandchildren, a decision often indefinitely postponed while
theoretically extolled. Many Hindus prayed, with St. Augustine, "Make me
chaste, O Lord, but not yet," while for some, the ideal of renunciation, even of
forest-dwelling, functioned as an imagined safety valve to keep them going in
the householder stage: "I can always get out if and when I want to." But making
the fourth aim an optional fourth stage trivialized the claims of the full renunciant philosophy, which was fundamentally opposed to the householder life.
Other resolutions were therefore proposed.

Second was the argument from symbiosis, or plenitude: The two groups of
people, worldly and transcendent, need each other, to compose society as a
whole, the householder to feed the renouncer, the renouncer to bless the householder. There are two forms of immortality, one achieved through one's own
children and one through renunciation.[22] Thus the renouncer's holiness and
knowledge are fed back into the society that supports him,[23] and the paradox
of the renunciant Brahmin is that he must remain outside society in order to be
useful inside.[24]

The third solution was compromise: Sometimes a householder would renounce for a while (following a particular vow) or in some ways (giving up meat

or fasting at regular intervals). The forest-dweller life too, the third stage, was a compromise between the householder and renunciant stages, though, like all compromises, it was hedged with problems.[25]

The fourth solution was identification. Thus it was said that the householder *was* a renouncer if he played his nonrenunciant role correctly, that fulfilling one's worldly obligation was Release (as the god Krishna tells Prince Arjuna in the *Bhagavad Gita*: Do your work well, as a warrior, and you win the merit of renunciation). Thus Manu (5.53) promises that a person who gives up eating meat amasses the same good karma as one who performs a horse sacrifice. A person who understood things properly (*yo evam veda*) could win the merit of the goal he had *not* chosen, even while following the goal he had. It was also said that one must have sons, usually regarded as the goal of the worldly life, to achieve Release. Some Tantrics took this line of argument to the extreme and argued that there was no difference between the apparently opposed paths of Release (*moksha*) and the enjoyment of sensuality (*bhoksha*). So too, in the formulation of the Buddhist philosopher Nagarjuna, the world of rebirth (samsara) was not, as most people thought, the opposite of the world of release from rebirth (nirvana), but the same place. This was a solution that many people gratefully accepted.

The fifth and ultimate Hindu solution was hierarchy, but mutual hierarchy: For some, renunciation outranked family life, and for others, family life outranked renunciation. The drive to hierarchize, throughout classical Hindu thought, rides roughshod over the drive to present equal alternatives or even a serial plan for a well-rounded human life. The *Mahabharata* claims that the three other stages of life cannot surpass that of a good householder,[26] while the reward that most of the *shastra*s promise to the reader/hearer "who knows this" is *moksha*.[27]

RENUNCIATION AND VIOLENCE IN PARTICULAR AND GENERAL DHARMA

We have noted the preeminence of dharma among the three aims both in its status and in the number of texts devoted to it. Dharma is complex, in part because it is a site of contestation between renunciation and violence.

Universal Hindu dharma was an overarching, unitary, nonhierarchical category of the religion for everyone, a shared human aim.[28] This single dharma (sometimes called perpetual dharma [*sanatana dharma*] or dharma held in common [*sadharana dharma*]) involved general moral precepts for all four classes, though different texts had different ideas about what those precepts were. Even a single text, Manu's dharma text, lists them differently in different places. In one verse, "Nonviolence, truth, not stealing, purification, and the suppression of the sensory powers are the dharma of the four classes, in a nutshell (10.63)." Nonviolence also comes first in another, related verse in Manu: "Nonviolence, the suppression of the sensory powers, the recitation of the Veda, inner heat, knowledge, and serving the guru bring about the supreme good (12.83–93; 10.63)." But Manu includes only one of these (suppression of the sensory powers, not nonviolence) in the ten commandments for the top three classes in all four stages of life: "Truth, not stealing, purification, suppression of the sensory powers, wisdom, learning, patience, forgiveness, self-control, and lack of anger (6.91–4)." Significantly, he does not include generosity, the primary Vedic virtue, in any of these lists. The general thought behind all the lists is a vague social ethic.

Indeed, the code was so nebulous that one would not think that as an ideal it would pose a problem for anyone. At the same time, however, each individual was supposed to follow a unique path laid out for him at birth, a path determined primarily by the class and, eventually, the caste (*jati*) into which he was born. This was his own particular dharma, his *sva-dharma*, the job that every man in any particular family was supposed to do, further constrained by such factors as his stage of life and his gender. (I use the male pronoun advisedly; these rules were not meant to apply to women, whose only *sva-dharma* was to obey their husbands, and their only sacrament, marriage.) A person's *sva-dharma* was sometimes called his innate activity (karma in its fifth meaning).

Manu explains how this came about in terms of his own take on the theory of karma, which in his usage means something like assigned work:

THE ORIGIN OF INDIVIDUAL KARMAS
In the beginning the creator made the individual names and individual karmas and individual conditions of all things precisely in accordance with the words of the Veda. And to distinguish karmas, he distinguished right from wrong, and he yoked these creatures with the pairs such as happiness and unhappiness. And whatever karma the Lord yoked each creature to at first, that creature by itself engaged in that very karma as he was created again and again. Harmful or harmless, gentle or cruel, right or wrong, truthful or lying—the karma he gave to each creature in creation kept entering it by itself. Just as the seasons by themselves take on the distinctive signs of the seasons as they change, so embodied beings by themselves take on their karmas, each his own (1.21–30).

The circularity of karma is explicitly set from the time of creation: You must be what you are; you cannot change your qualities. The re-creation of individual characteristics is inevitable, likened to the natural process of the seasons. An individual is born to be a king, or a servant, or, more precisely, in terms of the actuality of caste rather than the theory of class, a potter or a shoemaker. How are their karmas assigned to them? How does Manu know? It's quite simple: He claims to have been an eyewitness, even a participant, in the creation of the world.

The innate characteristics also include what we might regard as individual nature, for which there is another term in Sanskrit, *sva-bhava*. Thus it is the innate, particular nature (*sva-bhava*) of a tiger to be cruel and of a dove to be gentle, just as it is the karma of a tiger to kill and eat smaller animals and of a dove to coo. This too is *sva-dharma*, which is built into you, leaving you few choices in many realms of action, though you have free will in other realms, such as the amassing of karma.

We therefore are trapped within a basic social paradox: If your *sva-dharma* was to be a warrior or a butcher, how were you to reconcile this with the universal dharma that gave pride of place to nonviolence, the stricture against taking life? Hinduism validated the plurality (and the hierarchy) of dharma by endorsing *sva-dharma*, but at the same time, it validated the unity of dharma by endorsing general dharma. As in parliamentary rules of order, the *shastra*s state that the particular rule generally overrides the general rule; *sva-dharma* trumps general dharma. But the larger paradox of absolutism and relativism remained, and there are no easy answers.

CHAPTER 9
WOMEN AND OGRESSES
IN THE *RAMAYANA*
400 BCE to 200 CE

ॐ

CHRONOLOGY

c. 300 BCE–300 CE The *Mahabharata* is composed

c. 200 BCE–200 CE The *Ramayana* is composed

327–25 BCE Alexander the Great invades Northwest South Asia

c. 324 BCE Chandragupta founds the Mauryan dynasty

c. 265–232 BCE Ashoka reigns

c. 250 BCE Third Buddhist Council takes place at Pataliputra

c. 185 BCE The Mauryan dynasty ends

c. 185 BCE Pushyamitra founds the Shunga dynasty

73 BCE The Shunga dynasty ends

c. 150 BCE The monuments of Bharhut and Sanchi are built

c. 166 BCE–78 CE Greeks, Scythians, Bactrians, and Parthians enter India

THE POET, THE HUNTER, AND THE CRANE

After the poet Valmiki learned the story of Rama, he went to bathe in a river. By the river a pair of mating cranes were sweetly singing. A Nishada hunter, hostile and plotting evil, shot down the male of the couple. When the hen saw her mate writhing on the ground, his limbs covered in blood, she cried out words of compassion. And when Valmiki saw that the Nishada had brought down the male crane, he was overcome with compassion, and out of his feeling of compassion he thought, "This was not dharma, to kill a sweetly singing crane for no reason." When he heard the female crane crying, he said, "Nishada, you will never find peace, since you killed the male of

this pair of cranes at the height of his desire." Then Valmiki realized
that he had instinctively spoken in verse, in a meter that he called the
shloka, because it was uttered in sorrow (*shoka*).

Ramayana (400 BCE to 200 CE) (1.2.81.1–17)

This vignette that the *Ramayana* tells about itself weaves together the themes
of dangerous sexuality, the violation of dharma, compassion toward animals,
attitudes toward tribal peoples, and the transmutation of animal passions into
human culture—all central to the concerns of this chapter. At the same time,
the story of Rama and Sita raises new questions about deities who become
human and women who are accused of being unchaste. Where the Brahmanas
documented a period of new, though dispersed, political stability, and the Upanishads gave evidence of a reaction against that very stability, the *Ramayana* (R*)
and the *Mahabharata* (MB), the two great Sanskrit poems (often called epics),
were composed in this period (c. 300 BCE to 300 CE) that saw the rise and fall of
the first great empire in India, followed by a period of chaos that rushed into
the vacuum left by that fall.

NORTH INDIA IN 400 BCE TO 200 CE

This is the moment when we have the first writing that we know how to
decipher,[†] engraved in stone in the form of the Ashokan edicts, as well as other
historical sources—monuments, coins—to supplement our knowledge of the
Sanskrit texts. Another major new source of our knowledge of this period
comes from the reports of Greeks and other visitors. There is also a wealth
of art history, ranging from terra-cotta figures, both human and animal, made
in villages, to polished stone pillars with capitals, for the rich and powerful in
the cities.

We learn from these sources that the extension of agriculture into forested
areas transformed the lives of forest dwellers; that craft specialists often
emerged as distinct social groups; and that the unequal distribution of wealth
sharpened social differences,[1] though new access to economic resources raised
the social position of slaves, landless agricultural laborers, hunters, fishermen
and fisherwomen, pastoralists, peasants, village headmen, craftspeople, and

---

[*] Since the *Ramayana* is the main subject of this chapter, unspecified verse citations refer to that text.
[†] Discounting the still-undeciphered IVC seals.

merchants.[2] In addition to the ongoing tension between Brahmins and Kshatriyas, new tensions arose as the lower classes gained economic and political power and began to challenge the status of the upper classes.*

Just as the doctrines of Buddhism and Hinduism have much in common at this period, so too the same snakes spread their hoods over the heads of the Buddha and Vishnu, the same buxom wood nymphs swing around trees in Hindu and Buddhist shrines, and both traditions carve images of the goddess of luck (Lakshmi).[3] The design of some of the Hindu temples may have borrowed from the Buddhist precedent, for in some of the oldest temples the shrine, with the image in the center, was surrounded by an ambulatory path resembling the path around a stupa. Buddhism and Jainism remained friendly conversation partners, their rivalry with Hinduism often spurring both factions to borrow from each other in a positive way. But the non-Vedic religions also became more competitive, powerful rivals for political patronage as well as for the hearts of men and women, and a source of ideas that challenged the very core of emergent Hinduism. One of those ideas was a more insistent concern for the treatment of animals, leading to a great deal of soul-searching about the meaning of dharma. The attitude to animal sacrifice was also much affected by the rise of the two great male Hindu gods Shiva and Vishnu in sectarian movements that had no use for Vedic ritual.

THE RISE OF THE MAURYAS

Rajagriha (in Magadha, the present-day Bihar) and Kashi (Varanasi, in Koshala), which had come to prominence in the time of the Upanishads, remained great centers of power but were now rivaled by Kaushambi in Vatsa. There were still oligarchies at this time, about whose origins legends now began to circulate. These legends insisted that the founders were of high status but had, for one reason or another, left or been exiled from their homeland.[4] The theme of Kshatriyas in exile is reflected in the narrative of both the *Mahabharata* and the *Ramayana*, whose heroes, before they assume their thrones in the capital cities, are forced to endure long periods of exile in the wilderness, where the plot, as they say, thickens.† But exile is also a part of a much earlier theme embedded in the ceremony of royal consecration,[5] a ritual of the king's exile among

---

* This new social freedom is reflected in the upward mobility of abandoned children like Karna and Vyasa, in the *Mahabharata*.
† The Buddha (another Kshatriya) also left his palace (in his case, voluntarily) and lived in the wilderness for a long time.

the people that is in turn mythologized in the many tales of kings cursed to live among Pariahs.

Magadha controlled the river trade, forests, and rich deposit of minerals; in 321 BCE Pataliputra (the modern Patna), then said to be the world's largest city, with a population of 150,000 to 300,000,[6] became the capital of the first Indian Empire, the Mauryan Empire.[7] In 327 BCE, Alexander the Great managed to get into India over the mountain passes in the Himalayas and crossed the five rivers of the Punjab, no mean accomplishments, though thousands of other visitors to India did it too, before and after him. But his soldiers refused to campaign any farther, and so, in 326, he followed the Indus to its delta and, apparently regarding that as a sufficient accomplishment, went back to Babylon, though not before allegedly slaughtering many Brahmins who had instigated a major rebellion.[8] In India, it seems, he wasn't all that Great.

But the Indo-Greeks remained, primarily but not only in the Gandhara region. They brought with them Roman as well as Greek trade; they imported Chinese lacquer and sent South Indian ivory west to Pompeii. In the Gandhara marketplace, in the northwest, you could buy stone palettes, gold coins, jewelry, engraved gems, glass goblets, and figurines. The art of Gandhara is heavily influenced by Greek tastes, as are the great Buddhist monuments of Bharhut and Sanchi, from the first century BCE, which powerful guilds (*shrenis*) endowed. The Southeast Asia and China trade (both by sea and over the Central Asian silk route) also involved manuscripts, paintings, and ritual objects. The trade in ideas was just as vigorous; Greece imported the teachings of naked philosophers,* and many sects—Materialists, Ajivikas, ascetics, Jainas, and Buddhists—publicly disputed major religious questions.[9]

Out of this culturally supersaturated mix, the Mauryan Empire crystallized. Mahapadma Nanda, the son of a barber (a Shudra of a very low caste indeed, and said, by the Greeks, to have married a courtesan[10]), had founded a short-lived but significant dynasty, the first of a number of non-Kshatriya dynasties, during which he waged a brief vendetta against all Kshatriyas.[11] Chandragupta Maurya usurped the Nanda throne in 321 BCE and began to build a great empire. Buddhist texts say that the Mauryas were Kshatriyas of the clan of Moriyas ("Peacocks") and Shakyas (the clan of the Buddha himself), while Brahmin texts say they were Vaishyas or even Shudras, and heretics. A story goes that a Brahmin named Chanakya ("chickpea"), nicknamed Kautilya

---

* Gymno-sophists, according to Plutarch's *Life of Alexander*.

("Crooked" or "Bent" or "Devious"), was Chandragupta's chief minister and helped him win his empire, advising him not to attack the center of the Nanda Empire but to harass the borders, as a mother would advise a child to eat a hot chapati from the edges. Chanakya is said to be the author of the great textbook of political science, the *Artha-shastra*, which, though it was not completed until many centuries later, may in some ways reflect the principles of Mauryan administration,[12] particularly the widespread use of spies, both foreign and domestic; the Mauryan emperor Ashoka too talks unashamedly about people who keep him informed.[13]

According to Jaina traditions, when Chandragupta, under the influence of a Jaina sage, saw his subjects dying of a famine that he had failed to counteract, he abdicated and fasted to death at Shravana Belgola, in Southwest India. Bindusara succeeded him in 297 BCE. And then Bindusara died, and Ashoka became king, ruling from 265 to 232 BCE and further extending the boundaries of the Mauryan Empire.

THE AFTERMATH OF THE MAURYAS

Let us bracket until the next chapter the details of Ashoka's reign and move on to the subsequent history of this period.

In 183 BCE, Pushyamitra, a Brahmin who was the commander of the army, assassinated the last Maurya (who was allegedly a half-wit), took control of the empire through a palace coup, and founded the Shunga dynasty. Buddhists say that Pushyamitra persecuted Buddhists and gave increasing patronage to Vedic Brahmins, and an inscription proclaims his renewed sponsorship of sacrifices, including not one but two horse sacrifices, by which he established his dynasty. It is possible that Pushyamitra himself* acted as the officiating priest.[14] He is also alleged to have performed a human sacrifice in the city of Kaushambi.[15] Be that as it may, by killing the last Mauryan king, he overthrew a Kshatriya ruler and established a renewed Vedic order. Like the Kshatriya sages of the Upanishads, Pushyamitra reinstated the ancient priest-king model, though from the other direction: Instead of an Upanishadic royal sage—a Kshatriya with the knowledge that Brahmins usually had—he was a warrior priest, a Brahmin who played the role of a king. A passage in a much later text implies that the Shungas were of low birth,[16] but other sources identify Pushyamitra's Shunga

---

* As Napoleon performed his own coronation in 1804.

dynasty as an established Brahmin clan. Whatever his origins, Pushyamitra seems to have established a new Brahmin kingship and reigned for a quarter of a century (c. 185–151 BCE). On these shifting political, religious, and economic sands, Brahmins constituted the most consistently homogeneous group, because of their widespread influence in education and their continuing status as hereditary landholders.[17] Long after many of the Hindu kingdoms had fallen, the Brahmin class within them still survived.

Yet Buddhists thrived, as their sources of income shifted to a wider base. Buddhist monuments depict many scenes of popular devotion and were often financed not by dynastic patronage but by individual benefactors, both monks and nuns within the institutions and, outside, merchants increasingly interested in the security and patronage that religious centers offered in an age of political uncertainty.[18] During this period the whole community—landowners, merchants, high officials, common artisans—funded major Buddhist projects. In Orissa (Kalinga), King Kharavela, a Jaina, published a long autobiographical inscription in which he claims to have supported a Jaina monastery and had Jaina texts compiled and to have respected every sect and repaired all shrines.[19] Women, including women from marginal social positions (such as courtesans), also patronized Buddhists and Jainas. The widespread public recognition of such women both as donors and as renouncers also had an impact on the role of women within Hinduism and on the development of Hindu religious rituals that came to replace the Vedic sacrifice.

Kingdoms now began to dominate the political scene and to have enough of a sense of themselves to be almost constantly at war with one another. The ancient Indian king was called "the one who wants to conquer" (*vijigishu*). That, together with the "circle" theory of politics, according to which the country on your border was your enemy, and your enemy's enemy was your ally, and so forth, made for relentless aggression. Kings killed for thrones; parricide was rampant.[20]

The historian Walter Ruben summarized the period well:

According to Buddhist tradition Bimbisara of Magadha was killed by his son Ajatasatru and the four following kings were also patricides; then the people supplanted this dynasty of murderous despots by electing the minister Sisunaga as king. The last [descendant of Sisunaga] was killed by the first Nanda, allegedly a barber and paramour of the queen. The last Nanda was killed by the Brahmin

Kautalya. The last Maurya was killed by the Brahmin Pushyamitra, founder of the Sunga dynasty. Then followed centuries of war and political trouble caused by foreign invaders from the North-west. . . . Thus, in the course of five hundred years between 500 B.C. and 30 B.C., people in Northern India became accustomed to the idea that it was the right and even the duty of this or that man to assassinate a king. . . . These five hundred years were basic for the evolution of Indian civilization, for the growth of epic and Buddhist literature and for the development of Vaisnava and Saiva mythology and morals.[21]

And with that grim historical prelude, let us consider the story of Rama.

THE TRANSMISSION OF THE *RAMAYANA* AND *MAHABHARATA*

The *Ramayana* may have begun as a story as early as 750 BCE,[22] but it did not reach its present form until between 200 BCE and 200 CE. Its world therefore begins in the North Indian world of the Upanishads (characters such as Janaka of Videha play important roles in both the Upanishads and the *Ramayana*) and continues through the world of the *shastra*s (c. 200 CE). The *Ramayana* and *Mahabharata* mark the transition from the corpus of texts known as *shruti*, the unalterable Vedic canon, to those known as *smriti*, the human tradition. They are religious texts, which end with the "fruits of hearing" them ("Any woman who hears this will bear strong sons," etc.). Hindus from the time of the composition of these poems to the present moment know the characters in the texts just as Euro-Americans, even if they are not religious, know Adam and Eve and Noah's Ark. Hindus can ask, "What would Rama do?" This popularization also means that we now find more input from non-Brahmin authors and that new issues arise regarding the status of the lower classes. We also have more information about women, who, in these stories, at least, are still relatively free, though that freedom is now beginning to be challenged.

The *Ramayana* and *Mahabharata* were probably composed and performed first in the interstices between engagements on a battleground, to an audience that probably consisted largely of Kshatriyas and miscellaneous camp followers. The first bards who recited it were a caste called Charioteers (Sutas), probably but not certainly related to the chariot drivers who appear frequently in narratives, like Vrisha with King Triyaruna. Each Charioteer would have gone into battle with one warrior as a combination chauffeur and bodyguard. And then at night, when all the warriors retired from the field and took off their armor and had their wounds patched and got massaged and perhaps drunk, the bards would tell the stories of their exploits as everyone sat around the campfires. Thus the Charioteer served not just as a driver but as a herald, friend, and confidant, providing the warrior with advice, praise, and criticism.[23] This combination of roles* made the Charioteers, on the one hand, trusted counselors in court circles and, on the other, so far below the courtiers in status (being, through their connection with animals, roughly equivalent to Vaishyas) that when the warrior Karna, in the *Mahabharata*, was thought to be the son of a Charioteer, the princes scorned him.

Later, traveling bards no longer participated in battle, or drove chariots at all, but still recited the great poems in villages and at festivals and still retained their low social status; in addition, priestly singers praised the king in the course of royal sacrifices, while later in the evening the royal bard would sing poems praising the king's accomplishments in war and battle.[24] The *Mahabharata* says that the Charioteers told their stories during the intervals of a great sacrifice, and the audience in this later period would have been, on the one hand, more Brahminical—for the Brahmins were in charge of both the sacrifice and the literature of sacrifice—and, on the other hand, more diverse, as the camp followers would now be replaced by men and women of high as well as low class, who would have been present at the public ceremonies where the tales were recited. At this point the texts were probably circulated orally, as is suggested by their formulaic, repetitious, and relatively simple language.[25]

Later still, the reciters, and improvisers, were probably the Brahmins who were officiating at the sacrifice and recited the *Ramayana* and *Mahabharata* in the interstices between rituals on the sacrificial ground and probably also at shrines (*tirthas*) along pilgrimage routes. These Brahmins eventually committed the texts to writing. Some scholars believe that the texts were composed by Brahmins from the start,[26] Brahmins all the way down. But the Sanskrit tradition itself states unequivocally, and surprisingly, that non-Brahmins, people of low caste, were originally in charge of the care and feeding of the two great Sanskrit poems, which Brahmins took over only sometime later, one of many instances of the contributions of low-caste people to Sanskrit literature. And the

---

* Manu (10.8–12) gave the Charioteers a mythological genealogy of a Brahmin father and a Kshatriya mother, to account for the combination of intellectual and martial skills.

bards really did memorize all of it.*[27] The literate too knew the texts by heart and wrote commentaries on written versions of them.

The texts of the two great poems, originally composed orally, were preserved both orally and in manuscript form for more than two thousand years.† Their oral origins made it possible both for a great deal of folklore and other popular material to find its way into these Sanskrit texts and for the texts to get into the people. Scenarios in the texts may have been re-created in dramatic performance in towns and villages.[28] But the texts were also eventually consigned to writing and preserved in libraries; since the climate and the insects tend to destroy manuscripts, they have to be recopied every two hundred years or so if they are to survive; someone has to choose them and to go to the trouble and expense of having them copied. Buddhism and Jainism had bequeathed to Hinduism, by the seventh century CE, the tradition of gaining merit by having sacred manuscripts copied and donating them to libraries, and that is how these texts were preserved, generating merit for the patrons and income for the scribes.[29]

THE RAMAYANA

Valmiki's Sanskrit *Ramayana*, the oldest-surviving version of the tale, a text of some twenty thousand verses, establishes the basic plot:

RAMA, SITA, AND RAVANA

Ravana, the ogre (Rakshasa) king of Lanka, was a Brahmin and a devotee of Shiva. He had obtained, from Brahma, a boon that he could not be killed by gods or antigods or ogres or any other creatures—though he neglected to mention human beings, as beneath contempt. The god Vishnu therefore became incarnate as a human being, the prince Rama, in order to kill Ravana. Sita, who had been

---

* Fast-forward: They continue to do so; a traveling bard in a village in South India recently told an anthropologist that he knew the whole *Mahabharata* by heart. When the anthropologist asked him how he could possibly remember it, "the minstrel replied that each stanza was written on a pebble in his mind. He simply had to recall the order of the pebbles and 'read' from one after another." In the 1950s, Kamal Kothari sent one of his best singers, from the Langa caste, to adult education classes. He learned to read, but from then on he needed to consult his notes before he sang. As Kothari remarked, "It seems that the illiterate have a capacity to remember in a way that the literate simply do not." Plato, in the *Phaedrus*, remarks that when people have writing, their memories suffer attrition.

† But just as the magic contained in the oral *Rig Veda* contributed to the disinclination to commit it to writing, so too the *Mahabharata*, when converted from its oral to its written form, has potentially inauspicious magic (particularly since it tells of a great holocaust and genocide). For that reason, to this day many people fear to keep complete written texts of it inside their houses.

born from a furrow of the earth, became Rama's wife. When Rama's father, Dasharatha, put Rama's younger brother Bharata on the throne instead of Rama, Rama went into exile in the jungle with Sita and another brother, Lakshmana. Ravana stole Sita and kept her captive on the island of Lanka for many years. With the help of an army of monkeys and bears, in particular the monkey Hanuman, who leaped across to Lanka and then built a causeway for the armies to cross over, Rama killed Ravana and brought Sita back home with him. But when he began to worry about talk that her reputation, if not her chastity, had been sullied by her long sojourn in the house of another man, he forced her to submit to an ordeal by fire. Later he banished her, but she bore him twin sons, who came to him when they were grown. Sita too returned briefly but then disappeared forever back into the earth. Rama ruled for many years, a time of peace and justice.

Rama's brothers are fractional brothers, not even half brothers. The childless king Dasharatha had obtained a magic porridge, infused with the essence of Vishnu, to share among his queens; he gave half to his first wife, Kausalya, who gave birth to Rama; three-eighths to Sumitra, who bore Lakshmana and Shatrughna (each made of three-sixteenths of Vishnu), and one-eighth to Kaikeyi, who bore Bharata.[*]

The *Ramayana*, composed at a time when kingdoms like Videha were becoming powerful in a post-Mauryan era, legitimates monarchy through the vision of the golden age of Ram-raj, Rama's Rule. This vision occurs twice in the *Ramayana*, once at the end of the sixth of the seven books, when Rama and Sita are united after her fire ordeal (6.130)—"There were no widows in distress, nor any danger from snakes or disease; people lived for a thousand years"—and then again at the end of the last book, when Sita has departed forever:

As the glorious and noble Rama ruled, striving for dharma, a long time passed. The bears and monkeys and ogres remained under Rama's control, and he conciliated kings every day. The god of storms rained at the proper time, so that there was abundant food; the skies were clear. Happy, healthy people filled the city and the country. No one died at the wrong time; no living creatures got sick; there was no violation of dharma at all, when Rama ruled his kingdom (7.89.5–10).

---

[*] Other versions of the story divide the fractions slightly differently, but Kausalya always gets half.

This time of peace and prosperity became the template for a kind of theocracy that haunted Indian politics for centuries to come. But the actual historical scene, with its parricides and usurpations, also produced a royal paranoia that is revealed in the underside of Ram-raj, surfacing in palace coups such as the plot to have Bharata take the throne in place of Rama (2.8.18–27) and the machinations of the "bears and monkeys and ogres" that are said to remain under Rama's control in Ram-raj.

THE FORGETFUL AVATAR

Valmiki's Rama usually forgets that he is an incarnate god, an avatar ("crossing down" from heaven to earth) of Vishnu. He genuinely suffers and despairs when he's separated from Sita, as if he had lost touch with the divine foreknowledge that he would win her back. Sometimes Valmiki too treats Rama as a god, sometimes not. For the *Ramayana* is situated on the cusp between the periods in which Rama was first a minor god and then a major god. Hindus in later periods often took the devotion to Rama expressed by Hanuman and Lakshmana as a paradigm for human devotion (bhakti) to a god. Yet in the *Ramayana* these relationships lack the passionate, often violent qualities that characterize the fully developed bhakti of the Tamil texts and the Puranas from the tenth century CE.

As the bhakti movement increasingly imagined a god who combined the awesome powers of a supreme deity with the compassion of an intimate friend, it reinforced the vision of Rama as someone who was both limited by human constraints and aware of his divinity.

Commentators argued that Rama had intentionally become ignorant[30] or that he merely pretended to forget who he was,[31] and in some later retellings, Rama never does forget that he is Vishnu. But it is worth noting that though the *Ramayana* tells a long, detailed story to explain why the monkey Hanuman, the great general of the monkey army, forgets that he has magic powers (to fly, to become very big and very small, etc.), except when he needs them to get to Lanka (7.36), it never explains why it is that Rama (who does not have such magic powers) forgets that he is an incarnation of Vishnu. Both Rama and Krishna (who is an avatar of Vishnu in the *Mahabharata*) flicker between humanity and divinity in spatial as well as temporal terms; they are not only part-time gods but partial or fractional parts of Vishnu, who remains there, fully intact, always a god, while his avatars function on earth, always human. The two avatars are born of human wombs, and when they die, they merge back into Vishnu. Like Rama, Krishna sometimes does, and sometimes does not, act as if he (as well as the people with whom he interacts) knew that he was an avatar of Vishnu.

In a sense, the double nature of incarnation develops in a direct line from the Upanishadic belief that we are all incarnations of *brahman* but subject to the cycle of reincarnation. And some gods appear on earth in disguise already in the Veda, particularly Indra, the great shape shifter, while, later, Shiva often appears briefly in human disguise among mortals in the *Mahabharata*. If you put these ideas together, you end up with an all-powerful god who appears on earth in a complete life span as a human. Why do these two great human avatars appear at this moment in Indian history? Perhaps because an avatar was a way to attach already extant divinities to the growing sect of Vishnu, a way to synthesize previous strands and to appropriate other people's stories. Not only did some of these strands and stories come from Buddhism and Jainism, but the avatar was an answer to one of the challenges that these religions now posed for Hinduism.

For by this time the Buddha and the Jina had successfully established the paradigm of a religious movement centered upon a human being.[*] But Rama and Krishna beat the Buddhists and Jainas at their own game of valorizing the human form as a locus of superhuman wisdom and power, for Rama and Krishna are humans with a direct line to divinity, drawing their power from a god (Vishnu) far greater than any Vedic god and at the same time, through the incarnations, grounded in humanity.

WOMEN: BETWEEN GODDESSES AND OGRESSES

Being human, Rama is vulnerable. Despite his divine reserves, he is tripped up again and again by women—his stepmother Kaikeyi, Ravana's sister the ogress Shurpanakha, and, ultimately, his wife, Sita.

Sita is not only the ultimate male fantasy of the perfect woman but has as her foil a group of women and ogresses who are as Bad as Sita is Good. No one, male or female, could fail to get the point, and no one did. When Rama, the eldest, the son of the oldest queen, Kausalya, is about to ascend the throne, the youngest queen, Kaikeyi, uses sexual blackmail (among other things) to force Dasharatha to put her son, Bharata, on the throne instead and send Rama into exile: She

---

[*] The avatar of Vishnu as the Buddha is an entirely different affair, which does not appear until the Puranas.

locks herself into her "anger room" (India's answer to Lysistrata), puts on filthy clothes, lies down on the ground, and refuses to look at the king or speak to him, and the besotted Dasharatha is powerless to resist her beauty (2.9.16–19). Kaikeyi is the evil shadow of the good queen, Kausalya. But Kaikeyi herself is absolved of her evil by having it displaced onto the old hunchback woman who corrupts Kaikeyi and forces her, against her better judgment, to act as she does. For bringing about the sufferings that will overwhelm Kausalya, Sita curses not Kaikeyi but the hunchback, whose deformation is itself, in the Hindu view, evidence that she must already have committed some serious sin in a previous life. On the other hand, when Shatrughna (Lakshmana's twin brother) abuses the hunchback, he yells curses on Kaikeyi. In this text, even the shadows have shadows.

THE LOSS OF SITA

Sita never dies, but she vanishes four times. First she vanishes when Ravana carries her off, and Rama gets her back. Then she parts from Rama three times, into three natural elements—a fire, the forest, and the earth—as a direct result of that first estrangement: Rama keeps throwing her out now because Ravana abducted her years ago.

First, right after the defeat of Ravana, Rama summons Sita to the public assembly. Then:

SITA ENTERS THE FIRE

Rama said to her: "Doubts have arisen about your behavior. Go, then, wherever you wish. I can have nothing to do with you. What man of good family could take back, simply because his mind was so tortured by longing for her, a woman who had lived in the house of another man? How can I take you back when you have been degraded upon the lap of Ravana? Set your heart on Lakshmana or Bharata, or on Sugriva [the king of the monkeys], or [Ravana's brother] Vibhishana, or whoever will make you happy, Sita. For when Ravana saw your gorgeous body, he would not have held back for long when you were living in his own house." Sita replied to Rama, "You distrust the whole sex because of the way some women behave. If anyone touched my body, it was by force." Then, to Lakshmana: "Build a pyre for me; that is the medicine for this calamity. I cannot go on living, ruined by false accusations." As the fire blazed, she stood before it and said, "As my heart never wavered from Rama, so may the fire, the witness of all people, protect me." And she entered the blaze. As the gods reminded Rama who he was, Fire rose up with Sita in his lap and placed her in the lap of Rama, saying,

"Here is your Sita; there is no evil in her. Though she was tempted and threatened in various ways, she never gave a thought to Ravana. She must never be struck; this I command you." Rama said, "Sita had to enter the purifying fire in front of everyone, because she had lived so long in Ravana's bedrooms. Had I not purified her, good people would have said of me, 'That Rama, Dasharatha's son, is certainly lustful and childish.' But I knew that she was always true to me." Then Rama was united with his beloved and experienced the happiness that he deserved (6.103–6).[32]

"Dasharatha's son is certainly lustful" is a key phrase. Rama knows all too well what people said about Dasharatha; when Lakshmana learns that Rama has been exiled, he says, "The king is perverse, old, and addicted to sex, driven by lust (2.18.3)." Rama says as much himself: "He's an old man, and with me away he is so besotted by Kaikeyi that he is completely in her power, and capable of doing anything. The king has lost his mind. I think sex (*kama*) is much more potent than either *artha* or dharma. For what man, even an idiot like father, would give up a good son like me for the sake of a pretty woman? (2.47.8–10)." Thus Rama invokes the traditional ranking of dharma over sex and politics (*kama* and *artha*) and accuses his father of valuing them in the wrong way, of being addicted to sex. He then takes pains to show that where Dasharatha made a political and religious mistake because he desired his wife too much (*kama* over *artha* and dharma), he, Rama, cares for Sita only as a political pawn and an unassailably chaste wife (*artha* and dharma over *kama*). Rama thinks that sex is putting him in political danger (keeping his allegedly unchaste wife will make the people revolt), but in fact he has it backward: Politics is driving Rama to make a sexual and religious mistake; public concerns make him banish the wife he loves. Rama banishes Sita as Dasharatha has banished Rama. Significantly, the moment when Rama kicks Sita out for the second time comes directly after a long passage in which Rama makes love to Sita passionately, drinking wine with her, for many days on end; the banishment comes as a direct reaction against the sensual indulgence (7.41). Rama's wife is above suspicion, but Rama suspects her. His ambivalence, as well as hers, is expressed in the conflicts between the assertions, made repeatedly by both of them, that Ravana never touched her, that he did but it was against her will, and that physical contact is irrelevant, since she remained true to him in her mind.

When Rama publicly doubts Sita and seems unconcerned about her suffering, the gods ask how he can do this, adding, "Can you not know that you are

the best of all the gods? You are mistreating Sita as if you were a common man."
Rama, uncomprehending, says, "I think of myself as a man, as Rama the son of
King Dasharatha. Tell me who I really am, and who my father is, and where I
come from (6.105.8–10)." Rama is not thinking straight; the gods have to reveal
his avatar to him and use it as an argument to catapult him out of his trivial and
blind attitude to Sita. Later still, when Rama has renounced Sita, and Brahma
has again reminded him that he is Vishnu, Shiva gives Rama and Sita a vision
of the dead Dasharatha, who says to Sita, "My daughter, don't be angry because Rama threw you out. He did this in your own interest, to demonstrate
your purity.* The difficult test of your chastity that you underwent today will
make you famous above all other women. My daughter, you need no instructions about your duty to your husband, but I must tell you that he is the supreme god (6.107.34–35)." And when Sita has vanished again into the earth, this
time for good, and Rama is raging out of control, Brahma comes with all the
gods and says to him, "Rama, Rama, you should not grieve. Remember your
previous existence and your secret plan. Remember that you were born from
Vishnu (7.88)."[33]

Sita walks into fire determined either to kill herself or to win back the right
to go on living with the very much alive Rama. The ordeal is not, however, a
suicide, though she says she "cannot go on living"; on the contrary, it is an antisuttee,[†] in which she enters the fire when her husband is very much alive, not
to join him in heaven (as suttees usually do) but as a kind of threat either to leave
him or to win back the right to go on living with him here on earth.[‡] As a threat
it works: Rama takes her back, and they plan to live happily ever after, a fairy-
tale ending. But we may see a touch of irony in the closing statement that he
"got the happiness that he deserved," for it does not last; the rumors return, and
Rama banishes Sita, though she is pregnant; she goes to Valmiki's hermitage
and gives birth to twin sons. That is the second time Sita leaves him after her
return from Lanka.

Perhaps Valmiki[§] thought there was something unsatisfactory about this

---

* In other retellings of the narrative, too, Rama insists that he merely pretended to subject Sita to an
ordeal and, presumably, pretended to forget that he was a god.
† The *Ramayana* refers to suttee in the story of a prior incarnation of Sita named Vedavati, who tells
Ravana that her mother had burned herself on her husband's funeral pyre (7.17.23).
‡ In later tellings, she really does leave him at this point, but with his connivance, to live in the care of
Fire until long after the battle for Lanka.
§ Or some other poet. The final episode takes place in the last of the seven books of the *Ramayana*,
almost certainly a later addition.

banishment that inspired him to add on another, more final and more noble departure for Sita. It begins years later, when the twins, now grown up, come to Rama's horse sacrifice and recite the *Ramayana*, as Valmiki has taught it to them. The *Ramayana* lays great emphasis on the paternity of Rama's twin sons, on their stunning resemblance to Rama; the crowds of sages and princes at Rama's court "waxed ecstatic as they seemed to drink in with their eyes the king and the two singers. All of them said the same thing to one another: 'The two of them look just like Rama, like two reflections of the same thing. If they did not have matted hair and wear bark garments, we would have no way of distinguishing between the two singers and Rama' (7.85.6–8)." Yet Rama pointedly recognizes them* as "Sita's sons" but not necessarily his own (7.86.2). This is an essential episode, for male identity and female fidelity are the defining desiderata for each human gender in these texts; no one is interested in female identity or male fidelity.[34] These concerns play an important role in the treatment of Sita.

This is the moment when Rama summons Sita again, for the last time, and she herself brings about the final separation:

SITA ENTERS THE EARTH

Rama sent messengers to Valmiki to say, "If she is irreproachable in her conduct and without sin, then let her prove her good faith." Valmiki then came with Sita, and swore by *his* unbroken word of truth that the two boys were Rama's children and that he had seen Sita's innocence in a vision. Rama replied, "I agree entirely; Sita herself assured me before, and I believed her and reinstated her in my house. But there was such public condemnation that I had to send her away. I was absolutely convinced of her innocence, but because I feared the people, I cast her off. I acknowledge these boys to be my sons. I wish to make my peace with the chaste Sita in the middle of the assembly." Then Sita swore, "If, even in thought, I have never dwelt on anyone but Rama, let the goddess Earth receive me." As she was still speaking, a miracle occurred: From the earth there rose a celestial throne supported on the heads of Cobra People [Nagas]; the goddess Earth took Sita in her arms, sat her on that throne, and as the gods watched, Sita descended into the earth.

---

* Did Rama know that Sita was pregnant when he banished her? He seems to allude to her pregnancy in one verse (7.41.22), but as there is no further reference to what would surely have been a very important event, and since some manuscripts omit this verse, it seems unlikely that Rama did know.

His eyes streaming with tears, head down, heartsick, Rama sat there, thoroughly miserable. He cried for a long time, shedding a steady stream of tears, and then, filled with sorrow and anger, he said, "Once upon a time, she vanished into Lanka, on the far shore of the great ocean; but I brought her back even from there; so surely I will be all the more able to bring her back from the surface of the earth (7.86.5–16, 7.87.1–20, 7.88.1–20)."

But he cannot bring her back. When Sita enters the earth, she leaves the king alone, without his queen. She abandons and implicitly blames him when she leaves him, turning this second ordeal (again she asks for a miraculous act to prove her complete fidelity to Rama) into a sacrifice as well as, this time, a permanent exit.

Sita's two ordeals prove her purity, but they are also a supreme, defiant form of protest.[35] Sita is no doormat. She does not hesitate to bully her husband when she thinks that he has made a serious mistake. When Rama tries to prevent her from coming to the forest with him, she says: "What could my father have had in mind when he married me to you, Rama, a woman in the body of a man? What are you afraid of? Don't you believe that I am faithful to you? If you take me with you, I wouldn't dream of looking at any man but you—I'm not like some women who do that sort of thing. But you're like a procurer, Rama, handing me over to other people, though I came to you a virgin and have been faithful to you all this long time." Rama then insists that he had said she couldn't come with him only in order to test her (2.27.3–8, 26). Yeah, sure; she will hear that "testing" line again. Her assertion that Rama is confusing her with other, less faithful women is also one that we will hear again, for she repeats it years later, when Rama accuses her of having been intimate with Ravana.

When they first enter the forest, Sita asks Rama why he carries weapons in this peaceful place, especially when he has adopted the attire (and, presumably, the lifestyle and dharma) of an ascetic.* Rama claims that he needs the weapons to protect her and all the other defenseless creatures in the forest. In an impassioned discourse against violence, Sita tells Rama that she fears he is by nature inclined to violence and that simply carrying the weapons will put wicked thoughts in his mind (3.8.1–29). (Indeed he kills many creatures in the forest, both ogres that deserve it and monkeys that do not. Even the ogress

---

* The god of fire similarly has to remind Arjuna not to take his bow and arrows with him into the forest (MB 17.1.37–40).

Shurpanakha echoes Sita's concerns by querying Rama's apparent commitment to the conflicting dharmas of asceticism and married life [3.16.11].)

THE GODDESS SITA

Sita is not, however, just a woman; she is very much a goddess, though never as explicitly as Rama is a god. In contrast with Rama, whose divinity increases in the centuries *after* the Valmiki text, Sita was a goddess *before* Valmiki composed her story. Sita in the *Ramayana* is an ex-goddess, a human with traces of her former divinity that the story does not erase but largely ignores, whereas Rama is a god in the making, whose moral imperfections leave traces that future generations will scurry to erase. The two meet in passing, like people standing on adjacent escalators, Rama on the way up, Sita on the way down.

One Rig Vedic poem to the deity of the fields analogizes the furrow (which is what the word "Sita" means) to the earth cow who is milked of all foods (RV 4.57.6–7). When Rama weds Sita, he actually marries the earth, as the king always does; the goddess Earth is the consort of every king. But this time he also marries someone explicitly said to be the daughter of the Earth goddess. Sita's birth, even more supernatural than Rama's, is narrated several times.[36] On one occasion, Sita's father, King Janaka of Videha, tells it this way:

THE BIRTH OF SITA

One day in the sacrificial grounds, I saw the ultimate celestial nymph, Menaka, flying through the sky, and this thought came to me: "If I should have a child in her, what a child that would be!" As I was thinking in this way, my semen fell on the ground. And afterward, as I was plowing that field, there arose out of the earth, as first fruits, my daughter, who has celestial beauty and qualities. Since she arose from the surface of the earth, and was born from no womb, she is called Sita, the Furrow.[37]

Rama is well aware of the story. Grieving after Sita has entered the earth, he says to Earth, "You are my own mother-in-law, since, once upon a time, King Janaka drew Sita out of you when he was plowing." More particularly, Sita was born when Janaka was plowing the sacrificial arena, in preparation for the ceremony of royal consecration, and she goes back down to earth during Rama's horse sacrifice; both her birth and her death are framed by sacrifices. Like Rama, Sita becomes incarnate as part of the divine plan to kill Ravana. Sita, not Rama, is primarily responsible for the death of Ravana. Ravana's brother Vibhishana (who eventually abandons Ravana and fights on Rama's side) tries in vain to persuade Ravana to give Sita back to Rama and finally says to Ravana, "Why did you bring here that great serpent in the form of Sita, her breasts its coils, her thoughts its poison, her sweet smile its sharp fangs, her five fingers its five hoods?"[38] Shiva promises the gods that "a woman, Sita the slayer of ogres," will be born, and that the gods will use her to destroy the ogres (6.82.34–37).

At the end of the *Ramayana*, when Sita keeps disappearing and reappearing in a series of epiphanies, she is scorned and insulted until she commits two acts of violence that prove both her purity and her divinity. In this pattern, she resembles a god, particularly Shiva, who vandalizes Daksha's sacrifice when Daksha disdains to invite Shiva to it (MB 12.274). But Sita's story more closely follows the pattern of equine Vedic goddesses like Saranyu and Urvashi: She comes from another world to a mortal king, bears him children (twins, like Saranyu's), is mistreated by him, and leaves him forever, with only the twin children to console him. She can be set free from her life sentence on earth, her contract with a mortal man (Rama), only if he violates the contract by mistreating her.

Male succession is the whole point of the old myth of the equine goddess who comes down to earth to have human children, and female chastity is essential to that succession, another reason for the trials of Sita. Rama experiences the agonies of love in separation (*viraha*) that later characterized the longing for an otiose divinity; in this, as in so much of the plot, Rama is to Sita as a devotee is to a deity. His separation from Sita is also part of the divine plan to destroy Ravana: Long ago, in a battle of gods against antigods, the wife of the sage Bhrigu kept reviving the antigods as fast as the gods could kill them; Vishnu killed her, and Bhrigu cursed Vishnu, saying, "Because you killed a woman, you will be born in the world of men and live separated from your wife for many years (7.51)." So Rama has a previous conviction of abusing women even before he is born on earth. And as we will soon see, he has an even stronger track record for killing ogresses. Rama's mistreatment of Sita creates a problem—the justification of Rama—that inspires later *Ramayanas* to contrive ingenious solutions.

Sita walks out on Rama in the end (as Urvashi does in the Veda but not in the Brahmanas), an extraordinary move for a Hindu wife. Moreover, unlike the paradigmatic good Hindu wife, Sita very definitely is *not* reunited with her husband in heaven. For while she goes down into the earth, returning to her mother, he goes (back) up to heaven when he dies years later, returning to

Vishnu. Both of them revert to their divine status, but in opposite places. When Brahma is chastising Rama for doubting Sita, he reassures Rama that Sita is an incarnation of the goddess Lakshmi and will be reunited with him in heaven (6.105.25–26), but we never see that happen. Rama's return to heaven as Vishnu is described in great detail, and the monkeys revert to their divine form, and everyone you've ever heard of is there to welcome him in heaven (including the ogres), but not Sita (7.100).

Yet the more Sita is a goddess, the more the pattern of the myth of equine goddesses requires her to be mistreated—as if she were nothing but a human woman. Like Urvashi, Sita is treated less like a goddess and more like a mortal as her husband takes over the position of the immortal in the couple. Her banishing is portrayed in entirely mortal terms, and she suffers as a mortal woman. Like Rama, she regards herself as a mortal and forgets her divinity; she says, when she is imprisoned on Lanka, "I must have committed some awful sin in a previous life to have such a cruel life now. I want to die but I can't. A curse on being human, since one can't die when one wants to (5.23.18–20)." Since she (wrongly) thinks she is a mortal, she thinks she cannot die, which goes against common sense; moreover, the ironic implication follows that if she were an immortal (as she is), she could die when she wanted to—precisely what she does in the end when she enters the earth. And just as Rama has to be mortal to kill Ravana, so Sita plays the mortality card in order to resist Ravana and hence to destroy him; Ravana's ogress consorts remind her that she is a human woman, and she acknowledges this fact, incorporating it into her resistance: "A mortal woman cannot become the wife of an ogre (5.22.3, 5.23.3)" (a remark that could also be read as a warning against intercaste marriage).

Sita is subject to mortal desires and delusions and is vulnerable even though she is said to be invulnerable. For instance, Rama insists (when he claims that he knew all along that Sita was chaste and that he made her go through fire only to prove it to everyone else), "Ravana could not even think of raping Sita, for she was protected by her own energy (6.106.15–16)." Yet that very verb, meaning "to rape, violate, or assault," is used when Ravana grabs Sita by the hair (3.50.9), a violation from which her chastity does not in fact protect her. When Ravana plots to capture Sita, he gets the ogre Maricha to take the form of a marvelous golden deer, thickly encrusted with precious jewels, which captivates Sita—the princess in exile is delighted to find that Tiffany's has a branch in the forest—and inspires her to ask Rama to pursue it for her. Lakshmana rightly suspects that it is the ogre Maricha in disguise, and Rama agrees, but

Sita insists that Rama get it for her. The deer leads Rama far away from Sita, and when Rama kills the deer and it assumes its true form as an ogre, Rama realizes that he has been tricked and has thereby lost Sita, whom Ravana (by taking the form of an ascetic and fooling Sita) has captured in Rama's absence (3.40–44). So while Rama ultimately yields to the addiction of hunting, following the deer farther and farther than he knows he should, Sita falls for two illusions (the deer and the ascetic) that make her vulnerable to Ravana and, for many years, lost to Rama.

Shadow Women: Ogresses

When Sita defends herself against accusations that she has broken her marriage vows, and earlier, when she scolds Rama in the forest, she explicitly contrasts herself with "some women" who behave badly, unnamed shadows who may include not only Kaikeyi and the hunchback woman but also, perhaps, the lascivious ogre women as well as mythological women like Ahalya, the archetypal adulteress, whose story the *Ramayana* tells not once but twice.[39] The polarized images of women in the *Ramayana* led to another major split in Hinduism, for though the Brahmin imaginary made Sita the role model for Hindu women from this time forward, other Sanskrit texts as well as many vernacular versions of the *Ramayana* picked up on the shadow aspect of Sita, the passionate, sexual Sita,[40] an aspect that is also embedded in this first text, only partially displaced onto other, explicitly demonic women. Yet the later Brahmin imaginary greatly played down Sita's dark, deadly aspect and edited out her weaknesses to make her the perfect wife, totally subservient to her husband. How different the lives of actual women in India would have been had Sita as she is actually portrayed in Valmiki's *Ramayana* (and in some other retellings) been their official role model. The Valmiki *Ramayana* thus sowed the seeds both for the oppression of women in the dharma-shastric tradition and for the resistance against that oppression in other Hindu traditions.

Rama's nightmare is that Sita will be unchaste, and the sexually voracious ogresses that lurk inside every Good Woman in the *Ramayana* express that nightmare. In a later retelling, the *Bala-Ramayana*, the ogress Shurpanakha takes the form of Kaikeyi, and another ogre takes the form of Dasharatha, and *they* banish Rama; Dasharatha and Kaikeyi have nothing to do with it at all! The entire problem has been projected onto ogres, and the humans remain pure as the driven snow. In Valmiki's text, however, Kaikeyi and Sita still have their inner ogresses within them, expressed as the natural forces that prevent women from realizing the ideal embodied in the idealized Sita. The portrayals of rapacious ogresses hidden inside apparently good women make us see why it was that Sita's chastity became a banner at this time while the other aspects of her character were played down; they help us understand why women came to be repressed so virulently in subsequent centuries: to keep those ogresses shackled.

There are three particularly threatening ogresses in the *Ramayana*. Rama kills the ogress Tataka (1.25.1–14), after a sage reminds him of the mythological precedents for killing a woman (1.24.11–19). Lakshmana cuts off the nose and breasts and ears of Ayomukhi ("Iron Mouth") after she suggests to him, "Let's make love (3.65.7)," and he cuts off the nose and ears of Shurpanakha when she similarly propositions Rama (3.16–17).* This mutilation is the traditional punishment that the dharma texts prescribe for a promiscuous woman, an adulteress.

The mutilation of Shurpanakha is the only assault against a woman that has serious consequences for Rama, because she is Ravana's sister. When she attempts to seduce Rama, he teases her cruelly: "I am already married and couldn't stand the rivalry between co-wives. But Lakshmana is chaste, full of vigor, and has not yet experienced the joys of a wife's company; he needs a consort. You can enjoy him and you won't have any rival (3.17.1–5)." That's when Lakshmana cuts off her nose.† She flees in agony and humiliation and tells Ravana about Sita, praising her beauty and thus triggering the war, for Ravana takes the bait (Sita) as the gods intended from the start. Shurpanakha's attempt to replace Sita in Rama's bed, which Rama and Lakshmana mock, exposes a deep resemblance between the two women and a deep ambiguity in the text's attitude to Sita's sexuality. On the one hand, Sita is the epitome of female chastity. On the other hand, she is, like Shurpanakha, a highly sexual woman,[41] a quality that may explain not only why Ravana desires her but also why he is able to carry her off.

ANIMALS

THE HORSE SACRIFICE

Sita's final disappearance takes place on the occasion of a horse sacrifice. This is appropriate, for she herself lives out the paradigm of an equine goddess,

---

* In Kampan's Tamil version, he cuts off her breasts too.
† Rama's mistreatment of Shurpanakha looks even worse if we compare it with the reception that in the *Mahabharata* (3.13), Bhima (with the support of his family) gives to the ogress Hidimbi when she declares her love for him: He marries her, and she bears him a son.

and she is brought to the horse sacrifice by her twin sons, who are bards, related to the Charioteer bards who perform in the intervals of the ritual. The names of the sons, Kusha and Lava, are the two halves of the noun *kushilava*, designating a wandering bard, as if one son were named "po-" and the other "-et." By coming to Rama's horse sacrifice, Kusha and Lava preserve Rama's family, and as the *kushilava* they preserve the story of Rama's family. So too Valmiki both invents the poetic form, the *shloka*, and raises the poets.

The horse sacrifice plays a crucial role at both ends of the *Ramayana*. At the start King Dasharatha, childless, performs the horse sacrifice not for political and martial aggrandizement but to have a son, another express purpose of the ritual. Yet the list of kings whom he invites to the sacrifice constitutes a roll call for the territories that had better come when he calls them, and it is a wide range indeed, from Mithila and Kashi to the kings of the east and the kings of the south (1.12.17–24). The stallion roams for a year and is killed, together with several aquatic animals, while three hundred sacrificial animals, reptiles, and birds are killed separately. Queen Kausalya herself cuts the stallion open with three knives and then lies with him for one night, as do the two other queens (1.13.27–28). The king smells (but does not eat) the cooked marrow. The sacrifice, described in great detail, is a total success: Vishnu becomes incarnate in Rama and his half brothers.

Years later, after Rama has banished Sita, he resolves to perform a ceremony of royal consecration, but Lakshmana tactfully persuades him to perform, instead, a horse sacrifice, "which removes all sins and is an infallible means of purification (7.84.2–3)." To persuade him, Lakshmana tells him stories of two people who were restored by a horse sacrifice: Indra was purged of Brahminicide after killing a Brahmin antigod,* and a king who had been cursed to become a woman regained his manhood. Thus Rama performs the ceremony to expiate his sins, which are never mentioned, but which surely include his killing of Ravana (a necessary Brahminicide, but Brahminicide nonetheless, for Ravana, though an ogre, is not only a Brahmin but a grandson of Prajapati), corresponding to Indra's killing of several Brahmin antigods, and the banishing of Sita, a sin against a woman that corresponds, roughly, to the error of the king who became a woman. Lakshmana follows the horse as it "wanders" for a year.

---

* The horse sacrifice replaces the distribution of sin that saves Indra in other versions of the myth, both in the Brahmanas and in the *Mahabharata* (12.273.42–45). There a quarter of the Brahminicide goes to the heavenly nymphs, who ask for a way of freeing themselves from it (*moksha*) and are told that their Brahminicide will pass to any man who has sex with menstruating women.

But since Rama has banished Sita, there is no queen to lie down beside the stallion or to bear the king an heir.[*] It is therefore necessary for Sita (and the heir[s]) to return, and they come to the horse sacrifice (7.86–8).

These two horse sacrifices are successfully completed, though the second one is flawed by the absence of the queen, who reappears only to be lost again. This second sacrifice, intended to produce offspring, does so indirectly (by attracting Kusha and Lava), but it is also intended to give the king, through the queen, the fertile powers of the earth.[†] In the end Rama loses both the queen and his connection, through her, with the earth, her mother.

MONKEYS

The central characters of this text—Rama, the perfect prince; Sita, his perfect wife, and Lakshmana, his perfect half brother (later to form the template for the perfect worshiper of the fully deified Rama)—were born to be paradigms, squeaky clean, goody-goodies (or, in the case of the perfectly ogric ogre Ravana, a baddy-baddy). If that were all there were to the *Ramayana*, it would have proved ideologically useful to people interested in enforcing moral standards or in rallying religious fanatics, as, alas, it has proved all too capable of doing to this day in India, but it would probably not have survived as a beloved work of great literature, as it has also done. We have seen how the ogresses express the shadow side of Sita. The bears and monkeys, the two species often said to be closest to the human in both their appearance and their behavior, give the male characters their character. Let us concentrate on the monkeys, as the bears play only a minor role.

Neither so glamorous as horses nor so despised as dogs, the monkeys are the star animal act in the *Ramayana*. The *Ramayana* draws a number of parallels, both explicit and implicit, between the humans and the monkeys.[42] The appropriateness of these parallels is supported by such factors as the human characters' assumption that though they cannot understand the language of the deer (Rama explicitly laments this fact when he runs off after the golden deer that he suspects—rightly—of being an ogre in disguise), they do not comment

---

[*] Only *after* the horse sacrifice are we told of subsequent sacrifices, "He did not chose any wife other than Sita, for a golden image of Janaka's daughter appeared in every sacrifice, fulfilling the purpose of a wife (7.89.4)."
[†] The earth has in fact lost some of its fertility; in the story that Lakshmana tells Rama to persuade him of the efficacy of the horse sacrifice, the story in which Indra transfers his own Brahminicide to several elements, including the earth, Brahminicide takes the form of salt patches in the earth.

on the fact that they can understand the language of monkeys, who are called the deer of the trees. Hanuman not only speaks a human language, but he also speaks Sanskrit. When he approaches Sita on the island of Lanka, he anxiously debates with himself precisely what language he will use to address her: "Since I'm so small, indeed just a small monkey, I'd better speak Sanskrit like a human. I must speak with a human tongue, or else I cannot encourage her. But if I speak Sanskrit like a Brahmin, Sita will think I am Ravana, who can take any form he wants [as she mistook the real Ravana, a notorious shape changer, for a Brahmin sage]. And she'll be terrified and scream, and we'll all be killed." He finally does address her in Sanskrit (he begins to tell a story: "Once upon a time there was a king named Dasharatha . . . "), and she is suitably impressed. She does not scream (5.28.17–23, 5.29.2).

Special monkeys are the sons of gods, as special people are. Sugriva is the son of Surya (the sun god), Valin is the son of Indra (king of the gods), and Hanuman is the son of Vayu, the wind. (Hanuman later became a deity in his own right, worshiped in temples all over India.[43]) But monkeys also unofficially double for each of the major human characters of the *Ramayana*. These monkey doubles are, ironically, more flesh and blood, as we would say, more complex and nuanced, indeed more human than their human counterparts. Or rather, added to those original characters, they provide the ambiguity and ambivalence that constitute the depth and substance of the total character, composed of the original plus the shadow. All the fun is in the monkeys.

After Ravana has stolen Sita, Rama and Lakshmana meet Sugriva, who used to be king of the monkeys and claims that his brother Valin stole his wife and throne. Rama sides with Sugriva and murders Valin by shooting him in the back when he is fighting with Sugriva, an episode that has continued to trouble the South Asian tradition to this very day. Why does Rama kill Valin at all? Apparently because he senses a parallel between his situation and that of Sugriva and therefore sides with Sugriva against Valin. But Rama sides with the wrong monkey. The allegedly usurping monkey, Valin, is, like Rama, the *older* half brother, the true heir; the "deposed" king, Sugriva, the younger brother, originally took the throne (and the monkey queen) from the "usurping" brother, and Valin just took it back. Valin, not Sugriva, is the legal parallel to Rama. Yet Rama sympathizes with Sugriva because each of them has lost his wife and has a brother occupying the throne (and the queen) that was his. The plots are the same, but the villains are entirely different, and this is what Rama fails to notice. Moreover, unlike Sita, but in keeping with Rama's fears about

Sita, Valin's wife was taken by the brother who took the throne. On another occasion, Rama says he would gladly give Sita to Bharata (2.16.33). Does he assume that you get the queen when you get the throne? He kills Valin because the rage and resentment that he *should* feel toward his half brother and father, but does not, are expressed for him by his monkey double—the "deposed" monkey king, Sugriva—and vented by Rama on that double's enemy, Valin. We have noted that when Bharata is given the throne instead of Rama, the half brothers graciously offer each other the kingdom (2.98). But the monkeys fight a dirty battle for the throne, and for the queen too.

Even if we can understand why Rama kills Valin, why does he shoot him in the back? The monkeys' access to human language also grants them access to human ethics, or dharma. The dying Valin reproaches Rama, saying, "I'm just a monkey, living in the forest, a vegetarian. But you are a *man*. I'm a monkey, and it's against the law to eat monkey flesh or wear monkey skin (4.17.26–33)." Rama defends himself against the charge of foul play by saying, "People always use snares and hidden traps to catch wild animals, and there's nothing wrong about this. Even sages go hunting. After all, you're just a monkey, but kings are gods in human form (4.18.34–38)." Rama is on thin ice here; the text judges him to have violated human dharma in his treatment of the monkey. And the monkeys remind him that he is a man (i.e., higher than a monkey), just as the gods elsewhere remind him, when he behaves badly, that he is a god (i.e., higher than a man).

Valin also takes on the displaced force of Rama's suspicions of another half brother, Lakshmana. The text suggests that Rama might fear that Lakshmana might replace him in bed with Sita; it keeps insisting that Lakshmana will *not* sleep with Sita. It doth protest too much. (Recall that when Rama kicks Sita out for the first time and bitterly challenges her to go with some other guy, he lists Lakshmana first of all.)

The tension between the two half brothers, over Sita, is a major motivation for the plot. When Rama goes off to hunt the golden deer and tells Lakshmana to guard Sita, Sita thinks she hears Rama calling (it's a trick) and urges Lakshmana to find and help Rama. Lakshmana says Rama can take care of himself. Sita taunts Lakshmana, saying, "You want Rama to perish, Lakshmana, because of me. You'd like him to disappear; you have no affection for him. For with him gone, what could I, left alone, do to stop you doing the one thing that you came here to do? You are so cruel. Bharata has gotten you to follow Rama, as his spy. That's what it must be. But I could never desire any man but Rama. I would not even touch another man, not even with my foot! (3.43.6–8, 20–24, 34).” Lakshmana gets angry (“Damn you, to doubt me like that, always thinking evil of others, just like a woman [3.43.29])” and stalks off, leaving Sita totally unprotected, and Ravana comes and gets Sita. When Rama returns, Lakshmana reports a slightly different version of what she said to him: “Sita, weeping, said these terrible words to me: ‘You have set your evil heart on me, but even if your brother is destroyed, you will not get me. You are in cahoots with Bharata; you’re a secret enemy who followed us to get me.’” Rama ignores all this and simply says to Lakshmana, “You should not have deserted Sita and come to me, submitting to Sita and to your own anger, just because an angry woman teased you (3.57.14–21).”

But why would Sita have said such a thing if she didn’t fear it on some level? And why would it have made Lakshmana so mad if he did not fear it too? When Rama, hunting for Sita, finds the cloak and jewels that she dropped as Ravana abducted her, he says to Lakshmana, “Do you recognize any of this?” And Lakshmana replies, “I have never looked at any part of Sita but her feet, so I recognize the anklets, but not the rest of her things.” Yet, evidently, Rama had expected him to recognize the jewels that had adorned higher parts of Sita’s body. So too, though the text, insisting on Rama’s infallibility, displaces the error onto Sita and insists that Rama knew it was an ogre all along, the vice of hunting carries him along in its wake nevertheless: Rama follows the ogre as deer too far and so is unable to protect Sita from Ravana, thus inadvertently engineering his own separation from her. Just as Sita was prey to her desire for the deer, and Rama to his desire to hunt it, so Lakshmana too is vulnerable to Sita’s taunts about his desire for her; their combined triple vulnerabilities give Ravana the opening he needs.

At the very end of the *Ramayana*, Rama is tricked into having to kill Lakshmana. This happens as the result of an elaborate (but not atypical, in this text) set of vows and curses. Death incarnate comes to talk with Rama, to remind him that it is time for him to die. Death makes Rama promise to kill anyone who interrupts them; Lakshmana guards the door. An ascetic arrives and threatens to destroy the world if Lakshmana won’t let him see Rama; Lakshmana, caught between a rock and a hard place, chooses the lesser of two evils, his own death rather than the destruction of the world. He interrupts Rama and Death, whereupon Rama says that for Lakshmana, being separated from him (Rama) would be so terrible that it would be the equivalent of death, and so he satisfies the curse by merely banishing Lakshmana, who then commits suicide. Does this episode represent a displaced, suppressed desire of Rama to kill Lakshmana? If so, it is thoroughly submerged, one might even say repressed, on the human plane, but it bursts out in the animal world when Rama kills Valin, the monkey who took away his brother's wife.

This is the sense in which the monkeys are the side shadows of the human half brothers:[44] They suggest what might have been. They function in some ways as the human unconscious; both Valin and Sugriva (4.28.1–8; 4.34.9) are said to be addicted (*sakta*) to sensual behavior, to women, and to drinking. There is no monkey gambling or hunting to speak of, but the monkeys as a group get blind drunk in one very funny scene that resembles a frat party out of control. The monkeys are not merely Valmiki's projections or projections from Rama's mind; they are, rather, parallel lives. The monkey story is not accidentally appended; it is a telling variant of the life of Rama. But it does not mirror that life exactly; it is a mythological transformation, taking the pieces and rearranging them to make a slightly different pattern, as the dreamwork does, according to Freud. Animals often replace, in dreams, people toward whom the dreamer has strong, dangerous, inadmissible, and hence repressed emotions.[45] Or to put it differently, the dreamer displaces emotions felt toward people whom he cannot bear to visualize directly in his dreams and projects those emotions onto animals. In the *Ramayana*, poetry has the function of the dreamwork, reworking the emotions repressed by political concerns (such as the need to deny Rama's all too obvious imperfections) and projecting them onto animals. When Rama's cultural role as the perfect son and half brother prevents him from expressing his personal resentment of his father and half brother, the monkeys do it for him. In the magical world of the monkey forest, Rama's unconscious mind is set free to take the revenge that his conscious mind does not allow him in the world of humans.

TALKING ANIMALS, BESTIAL HUMANS

Monkeys are not the only talking animals who stand in for humans in the *Ramayana*.[46] In a related corpus of myths, hunters mistake people for animals in sexual (or quasisexual) situations. These myths offer yet another set of implicit arguments for the growing movement in favor of vegetarianism.

The underlying theme is the interruption of sexuality. The *Ramayana* briefly narrates such an incident, in the story of Shiva and his wife, Parvati:

THE GODS INTERRUPT SHIVA AND PARVATI

Parvati ("Daughter of the Mountain [Himalaya]") won Shiva's heart and they married. Shiva joyously made love to her night and day—but without ever shedding his semen. The gods were afraid that Shiva and Parvati would produce a child of unbearable power, and so they interrupted them. The god of fire took up Shiva's seed, from which the six-headed god Skanda, general of the gods, was born. But Parvati, enraged, cursed the wives of the gods to be barren forever, since they had thwarted her while she was making love in the hope of bearing a son (1.34–35).

Shiva places his seed in Fire, rather than in Parvati, as an anthropomorphization of the ritual act of throwing an oblation of butter into the consecrated fire that carries the oblation to the gods, acting out the Upanishadic equation of the sexual act and the oblation. The curse of childlessness that the frustrated Parvati gives to the wives of the gods has resonances throughout Hindu mythology. As a result of Parvati's curse, many children of the gods (including Sita) are born from male gods or sages who create children unilaterally merely at the thought, or sight, of a woman, ejaculating into some womb substitute—a flower, a female animal, a river, a furrow—to produce a motherless child, "born of no womb" (a-yoni-ja).[*] Another variant of the interruption theme appears at the end of the Ramayana, in the passage we have just considered, when Lakshmana is forced to interrupt Rama and Death when they are closeted together under strict instructions not to be interrupted. This is the ultimate fatal interruption, interrupting Death himself.

At the same time, interrupted sexuality is often conjoined with the theme of addictive, excessive, careless hunting. Human hunters mistake other humans (or ogres) for animals, particularly when the humans as animals are mating, a mistake that has fatal consequences not only for the human/animals but for the unlucky hunter. In the Mahabharata, Pandu, the father of the heroes, is cursed to die if he makes love with any of his wives, his punishment for having killed, while he was hunting, a sage who had taken the form of a stag and was coupling with a doe[†] and whom Pandu mistook for a stag (1.90.64; 1.109.5–30). So too five years after Dasharatha has banished Rama, he suddenly wakes Kausalya

---

[*] Satyavati and Draupadi are such children, and there are many, many others.
[†] The text says that the sage had taken the form of a deer to mate with his wife in the form of a deer and then that he lived with deer because he shunned humans.

up in the middle of the night and tells her about this episode, which he has only now remembered:

DASHARATHA SHOOTS AN ELEPHANT

"When I was young I was proud of my fame as an archer who could shoot by sound alone. We were not married yet, and it was the rainy season, which excites lust and desire. I decided to take some exercise and went hunting with bow and arrow. I was a rash young man. I heard a noise, beyond the range of vision, of a pitcher being filled with water, which sounded like an elephant in water. I shot an arrow." He had shot an ascetic boy, on whom an aged, blind mother (a Shudra) and father (a Vaishya) depended. The father cursed Dasharatha to end his days grieving for his own son. And as Dasharatha now remembered that curse in bed with Kausalya, he died (2.57.8–38, .58.1–57).

The connection between blindness (aiming by sound alone at the child of sightless parents) and desire (hunting as the equivalent of taking a cold shower to control premarital desire) indicates that desire was already Dasharatha's blind spot long before Kaikeyi manipulated him by locking him out of her bedroom. He is as addicted to sex as he is to hunting.

Another tale in the *Ramayana* also ties together the themes of the interruption of sexuality, the curse of separation from a beloved, and the deadly nature of erotic love but now adds the element of the language of animals, particularly birds:

THE BIRD'S JOKE

A king had been given the boon of understanding the cries of all creatures, but he was warned not to tell anyone about it. Once when he was in bed with his wife, he heard a bird say something funny, and he laughed. She thought he was laughing at her, and she wanted to know why, but he said he would die if he told her. When she insisted that he tell her nevertheless, he sent her away and lived happily without her for the rest of his life (2.32).[47]

Significantly, the man in this story is allowed to understand the speech of animals, and the woman is not. (As the king happens to be the father of Kaikeyi, sexual mischief runs in the family.) This is in keeping with the underlying misogyny of the Sanskrit mythological texts that depict men as more gifted with special powers than women; it may also reflect the sociological fact that men in

India were allowed to read and speak Sanskrit, while in general women were not, as well as the custom of patrilocal marriage, so that a woman often did not speak the language of her husband's family. These stories express the idea that sexuality makes some humans into animals, while language makes some animals into humans.

In the *Mahabharata* a king who has been cursed to become a man-eating ogre devours a sage who is making love to his wife (still in human form), and the wife, furious because she had not yet achieved her sexual goal, curses the king to die if he embraces his own wife (MB 1.173), a combination of Pandu's curse and Parvati's curse of the wives of the gods. Nor are these hunting errors limited to the sexual arena. Krishna, in the *Mahabharata*, dies when a hunter fatally mistakes him for a deer:

THE DEATH OF KRISHNA

Angry sages predicted that Old Age would wound Krishna when he was lying on the ground. Krishna knew that this had to happen that way. Later he realized it was the time to move on, and he obstructed his sensory powers, speech, and mind and lay down and engaged in terminal yoga. Then a fierce hunter named Old Age [Jara] came to that spot greedy for deer and mistook him for a deer and hastily pierced him with an arrow in the sole of his foot. But when he went near him, to take him, the hunter saw that it was a man with four arms, wearing a yellow garment, engaged in yoga. Realizing that he had made a bad mistake, he touched the other man's two feet with his head, his body revealing his distress. Krishna consoled him and then rose up and pervaded the two firmaments with his glory (MB 16.2.10–11, 16.5.18–21).

Three different stories seem to be told here at once. In one, Krishna, a mortal, is wounded by a hunter, like an animal or, rather, as a human mistaken for an animal. In another, Krishna seems to die of old age.[*] In the third story, Krishna, an immortal, decides to leave the world by withdrawing his powers, like a god or a very great yogi. But he didn't need the hunter or old age if he really just died by his own will. Are traces of one story left ghostlike in another?

These stories from the *Mahabharata* argue that humans are different from animals and must rise above animal sexuality and, sometimes, animal violence;

---

[*] The commentator, Nilakantha, says Old Age was not old age but someone of the Kaivarta caste (of fishermen), who just happened to be named Old Age.

the *Ramayana* adds that it is language, particularly poetry, that makes this possible.* The theme of language appears in this corpus on the outside frame of the *Ramayana*, in the vignette of "The Poet, the Hunter, and the Crane" cited at the beginning of this chapter, about the invention of the *shloka* meter (the meter in which both the *Mahabharata* and the *Ramayana* are composed). In that story, the female crane (they are Indian sarus cranes) is so moved at the sight of her dying mate that she utters words of compassion (*karunam giram*). (Some later commentaries suggested that it was the *female* crane who died and the male crane who grieved, foreshadowing the disappearance of Sita and the grief of Rama.[48]) Compassion at the sight of the dying bird inspires Valmiki too to speak. He sees a crane who is killed in a sexual situation, hence separated from his mate, making him cry and inspiring him to invent an unusual language of humans. This story is in many ways the inversion of the story of the king who hears a bird talking when he is in a sexual situation and laughs, exposing him to the danger of death and separating him from his mate.

But it is the grief of the female crane and Valmiki's fellow feeling with her—as well as, perhaps, the touching example of the cranes, who are said to be "singing sweetly" (immediately equated with "at the height of desire") as the hunter strikes—that inspire Valmiki to make his second, more significant utterance; the birdsong turns to compassionate speech and then inspires human poetry. As a result, the Nishada, a member of a tribal group regarded as very low caste, is cursed, and poetry is born. The text treats the Nishada as a nonperson, hostile and evil, a man who violates dharma, kills for no reason, and is cursed to be forever without peace; in direct contrast with the compassionate crane hen and the compassionate poet, the Nishada never speaks. Since the animal he killed was just an animal, not a human in animal form, he receives only a relatively mild punishment—restlessness, perhaps guilt—prefiguring the more serious curse of Dasharatha in the story that is to follow, the tale of the boy mistaken for an elephant. With this link added to the narrative chain, the corpus of stories combines five major themes: succumbing to the lust for hunting; mistaking a human for an animal and killing the "animal"; interrupting the sexual act (by killing one or both of the partners); understanding the language (or song) of animals; and creating a poetic language. Killing an animal interrupts the sexual act, the animal act, killing sex, as it were, and producing in its place the characteristic human act, the making of language.

---

* Indian aesthetic theory had a great deal to say about the transformation of emotion (*rasa*) through art.

What binds the humans and animals together is compassion, a more nuanced form of the guilt and concern for nonviolence that have colored Hindu stories about animals from the start. The *Ramayana* is compassionate and inclusive in its presentation of animals, including Jatayus, an old vulture, a scavenger, who is to birds what dogs are to mammals, normally very inauspicious indeed. But Jatayus bravely attacks Ravana when Ravana is carrying off Sita; when Jatayus lectures Ravana on dharma, Ravana responds by cutting off Jatayus's wings and flying away with Sita, and the dying vulture tells Rama where Ravana has taken Sita. Rama says that he holds the old vulture, Jatayus, in the same esteem that he holds Dasharatha (3.64.26) (which may also be a backhanded indirect dig at Dasharatha), and he buries him with the full royal obsequies as for a father. Rama does, however, use balls of stag's flesh in place of the balls of rice that are usually part of these rituals (3.64.26, 32–33), a reversal of the historical process that led many Hindus to use balls of rice in place of a sacrificial animal.

Another unclean bird plays a role in Rama's story, and that is a crow. When Hanuman visits Sita and asks her for a sign that will prove to Rama that Hanuman has seen her, she tells him of a time when a crow attacked her until his claws dripped with blood; Rama had the power to kill the bird but, in his compassion, merely put out his right eye and sent him away (5.36.10–33). The crows are said to be eaters of offerings, greedy for food, terms often applied to dogs, and Manu (7.21) explicitly links crows and dogs. The crow is a Pariah. Sita compares the crow with Ravana, and the scene foreshadows the abduction of Sita by Ravana. Yet Rama has compassion for the crow, merely taking out his eye, a mutilation that will become part of the vocabulary of bhakti, when a devout worshiper willingly gives his own eye to the god.

Dogs too occupy a moral space here. During the period of Sita's exile, a (talking) dog comes to Rama and complains, first, that dogs are not allowed in palaces or temples or the homes of Brahmins (whereupon Rama invites him into the palace) and, second, that a Brahmin beggar beat him for no reason. Rama summons the Brahmin, who confesses that he struck the dog in anger when he himself was hungry and begging for food; when he told the dog to go away, the dog went only a short distance and stayed there, and so he beat him. Rama asks the dog to suggest an appropriate punishment for the Brahmin, and the dog asks that the Brahmin, whom he describes as filled with anger and bereft of dharma, be made the leader of a Tantric sect. (The dog himself had this position in a former life and regarded it as a guaranteed road to hell.)

This granted, the Brahmin feels certain he has been given a great boon and rides away proudly on an elephant, while the dog goes to Varanasi and fasts to death (7.52).[49] Clearly, the dog is morally superior to the Brahmin, and Rama treats him with great respect throughout this long and rather whimsical episode.

Symbolic Ogres

Dogs in these stories stand both for dogs (a cigar is just a cigar) and sometimes for Pariahs or Nishadas (more than a cigar), often for both at once. Tribal people stand for themselves (a Nishada is just a Nishada), but can Nishadas stand for anyone else? (Apparently not.) On the other hand, can anyone else, besides dogs, stand for Nishadas? More precisely, can ogres stand for Nishadas?

Unlike dogs and Nishadas, ogres and antigods cannot represent themselves because, in my humble opinion, they do not exist; they are imaginary constructions. Therefore they are purely symbolic, and the question is, What do they symbolize? Later in Indian history, they are often said to symbolize various groups of human beings: tribal peoples,[50] foreigners, low castes, Dravidians, South Indians, or Muslims. Various Hindus have named various actual human tribes after ogres and antigods and other mythical beasts (such as Asuras and Nagas), and others have glossed ogres such as the ogress Hidimbi, who marries the human hero Bhima, in the *Mahabharata,* or the Naga princess Ulupi, who marries Arjuna, as symbolic of tribal people who marry into Kshatriya families. One scholar identified the ogres of Lanka as Sinhalese Buddhists, oppressed by hegemonic Brahmins represented by Rama;[51] another argued that the ogres represented the aboriginal population of Australia,[52] a loopy idea that has the single, questionable virtue of correlating well with the Gondwana theory that Australia and India were once linked. Indeed writers have used the ogres as well as other characters of the *Ramayana** throughout Indian history to stand in for various people in various political positions. But what role do the ogres play in Valmiki's *Ramayana*?

There is no evidence that the ogres represent any historical groups of human beings or that the conquest of the ogres of Lanka represents any historical event. On the other hand, just as dogs can symbolize general types of human beings (castes regarded as unclean), so too, particular types of ogres and antigods can symbolize general types of human beings. Ogres and animals belong to social classes (*varnas*), just like human beings; Ravana, a king born of a Brahmin fa-

---

* The monkeys too have been identified with various groups, including the British.

ther and an ogress mother, is often regarded as a Brahmin/Kshatriya/human/ogre mix (though sometimes as a Brahmin, making Rama guilty of Brahminicide), and the vulture Jatayus, a Kshatriya, is buried both as a king and as a vulture (with pieces of meat that would not be given to a king). There are many other Kshatriya ogres and antigods, as well as Brahmin ogres.[53]

Ogres are also symbolic of dark forces outside us that oppress us and sometimes of dark forces within us, the worst parts of ourselves, the shadows of ourselves. In Freudian terms, Ravana is a wonderful embodiment of the ego—proud, selfish, passionate—while Vibhishana (Ravana's pious brother, who sermonizes Ravana and finally defects to Rama) is pure superego, all conscience and moralizing, and Kumbhakarna (Ravana's monstrous brother, who sleeps for years at a time and wakes only to eat and fight) is a superb literary incarnation of the bestial id. The triad is even more significant in Indian terms, in which they might be viewed as representations of the three constituent qualities of matter (the *gunas*): Ravana is *rajas* (energy, passion; ego), Vibhishana *sattva* (lucidity, goodness; superego), and Kumbhakarna *tamas* (entropy, darkness; id).

But the major function of the ogres in the *Ramayana*, apart from their role as the Bad Guys, a role not to be underestimated, is as the projected shadows of individual human figures. Lakshmana says this explicitly to Rama, regarding the ogre Viradha: "The anger I felt towards Bharata because he desired the throne, I shall expend on Viradha (3.2.23)." We have seen how the ogresses cast a shadow on the unrelenting goodness of Sita, and how the monkey brothers illuminate the relationship of the human brothers; the male ogres do much the same. The thorny questions of dharma that the humans express from time to time (in Bharata's outburst, or Sita's scolding) are echoed in the arguments of the monkeys and ogres (when Valin upbraids Rama or Vibhishana preaches to Ravana).

More specifically, just as Rama, Lakshmana, and Bharata form a sort of triad,* so too Ravana, Vibhishana, and Kumbhakarna form a parallel triad.† Ravana remarks, after Kumbhakarna's death, that Kumbhakarna had been his right arm and that Sita is no use to him with Kumbhakarna dead (6.56.7–12), precisely what

---

* Shatrughna, the fourth half brother, is hardly more than the other half of Lakshmana, though he enters the plot near the end.
† Kubera, the fourth half brother, serves, like Shatrughna, a minor function. There is another ogre brother too, Khara, who is killed even before Ravana kidnaps Sita, but the three who fight together at the end form the essential triad.

Rama says about Lakshmana and Sita when he thinks Lakshmana is dead. But the parallels are often contrasting rather than identical: Whereas Lakshmana and Bharata love Rama, both Vibhishana and Kumbhakarna revile Ravana.

THE GOOD OGRE

Some ogres stand for human beings of a particular type rather than a particular class. Some powerful, and often virtuous, ogres and antigods amass great powers through generating inner heat (*tapas*) and usurp the privileges of the gods, following the pattern of the second alliance. The throne of Indra, king of the gods, is made of twenty-four-carat gold, a notorious conductor of heat. When an ascetic on earth generates too much *tapas* through a non-Vedic do-it-yourself religion, the heat rises, as heat is wont to do, and when it gets to Indra's throne, he finds himself literally sitting on a hot seat. At that point he usually sends a celestial nymph (an Apsaras) to seduce the ascetic, to dispel his heat either through desire or through anger.[54]

Ravana is a major player in the second alliance. He wins the boon of near invincibility from Brahma by generating extreme *tapas*. (It is only because Ravana fails to take seriously the fine print in his contract, specifying every creature but humans, that Rama is able to defeat him.) Sita inspires Ravana with both desire and anger. Indeed, in terms of the mythological paradigm, it is Sita, as celestial nymph (or, in Vibhishana's view, great hooded serpent), who defeats Ravana.

Such ogres may stand for humans who, through precisely that sort of religious activity, unmediated by priestly interventions, usurped the privileges of the Brahmins. As shape shifters who pretend to be what they are not, the ascetic ogres are (super)natural metaphors for people who try to become more powerful than they have a right to be, the wildcat yogis who are not members of the Brahmin union. Vibhishana is an early instance of this paradoxical figure. He remains an ogre, indeed becomes king of the ogres after Ravana's death, thus maintaining his own particular dharma, still going into the family business, as it were, but he fights on the side of Rama against Ravana and the other ogres, thus supporting more general dharma (*sadharana dharma*). Maricha, the ogre who takes the form of the golden deer, tries hard, in vain, like Vibhishana, to dissuade Ravana from going after Sita. But Maricha also confesses to Ravana that after an earlier encounter with Rama, he began to practice yoga and meditation and now is so filled with terror of Rama that he sees him everywhere he looks: "This whole wilderness has become nothing but Rama to me; I see him in my dreams, and think of him every time I hear a word that begins with an 'R' (3.38.14–18)." This emotion is what bhakti theologians later describe as "hate-love" (*dvesha-bhakti*), which allows other demonic opponents of the gods (such as Kamsa, the enemy of Krishna) to go straight to heaven when the god in question kills the demon. The reference to the *R* also foreshadows (hindsight alert!) the importance of the name of Rama in later bhakti.

The *Ramayana* does not worry about the paradoxes involved in these clashes between *sva-dharma* and *sadharana dharma*. When the antigod Bali defeats the gods, including Indra, and performs a great sacrifice, in which he gives away anything that anyone asks him for, Vishnu becomes a dwarf and begs as much land as he can cover in three paces; he then strides across the three worlds, which he takes from Bali and gives back to Indra (1.28.3–11). Bali's name, significantly, denotes the offering of a portion of the daily meal—or taxes, the portion of the crop paid to the king. That it is Bali's Vedic virtue of generosity that destroys him may signal a challenge to that entire sacrificial world. But the *Ramayana*, remaining firmly within the second alliance, does not ask why Bali's virtue had to be destroyed. The later Puranas, in retelling this story, will tackle head-on the paradox of the good antigod.

CHALLENGES TO THE CLASS SYSTEM

The gods (and Brahmins) are also threatened from the other side by human beings who are not too good but too bad, including people highly critical of Vedic religion. When Rama is arguing with Bharata about honoring his father's wishes, the Brahmin Jabali presents the atheist position, satirizing the *shraddha*, the ritual of feeding the ancestors, as well as the idea of the transfer of karma: "What a waste of food! Has a dead man ever eaten food? If food that one person eats nourishes another person, then people who journey need never carry provision on the way; his relatives could eat at home for him." He anticipates the Marxist argument too: "The scriptures with their rules were invented by learned men who were clever at getting other people to give them money, tricking the simple-minded. There is no world but this one (2.108.1–17)." When Rama objects violently to this, others assure him that Jabali has presented the atheist argument only to persuade Rama to do what was best for him, that he wasn't really an atheist, that it was all *maya* ("illusion") (2.102.1)." Jabali's argument is the standard Materialist critique of the Veda, as well as the straw man set up in order to be refuted.

A more serious threat to the social order is posed by Shambuka:

RAMA BEHEADS SHAMBUKA

A Brahmin's child died of unknown causes, and the father blamed Rama for failing to maintain dharma, accusing Rama of being guilty of Brahminicide. The sage Narada warned Rama that a Shudra was generating *tapas*, a practice permitted to Shudras only in the Kali Age, and that this violation of dharma was causing disasters such as the death of the child. Rama gave instructions to preserve the child's body in oil. Then he explored the country and found, south of the Vindhyas, a man generating *tapas*, hanging upside down. Rama asked him his class ("Are you a Brahmin, or a Kshatriya, or a Vaishya, or a Shudra?") and the purpose of his *tapas*, and the man replied, "I was born in a Shudra womb, and I am named Shambuka. I am doing this in order to become a god and to conquer the world of the gods." Rama drew his sword from his scabbard and cut off Shambuka's head while he was still talking. And at that very moment, the child came back to life (7.64–67).

Shambuka is upside down, both as a form of *tapas* and because a world in which a Shudra generates *tapas* is topsy-turvy. The central episode of mutilation of an uppity low-caste man is framed, indeed justified, by another story, the stock narrative of a hagiographical miracle, usually used in the service of Brahmins (like Vrisha) rather than of kings, the death and revival of a child. Was there enough pressure on the caste system at the time of the *Ramayana*'s recension to force the narrator to invent this frame to justify Rama's action? Perhaps. We learn nothing at all about Shambuka but his class and the fact that he lives south of the Vindhyas, the no-man's-land of North Indian mythology; he is dehumanized.

Rama also had an uncomfortable relationship with Nishadas, including a hunter named Guha, chief of the Nishadas. When Rama came into the jungle, Guha met him and offered him things to eat and drink; Rama declined for himself, arguing that as an ascetic he could not accept gifts and ate only fruit and roots (an assertion directly contradicted by the fact that after killing the ogre Maricha in the form of a deer, he killed another deer and took home the meat [3.42.21]), but he gladly accepted fodder for the horses, which were the pride of Dasharatha's stable (2.44.15–22). Yet, when Bharata later came looking for Rama, Guha came to meet him too, bringing him fish, flesh, and liquor (2.78.9), and his guide said to Bharata, "He's an old friend of your brother's (2.78.11)." Bharata, unlike Rama, accepted the food, and when Guha told Bharata about his meeting with Rama, he said, "I offered Rama a variety of foods, but Rama refused it all, because he was following the dharma of a Kshatriya, and Kshatriyas must give but never receive (2.82.14)." There are too many excuses, and conflicting excuses at that, to explain why Rama will not eat Guha's food, and the commentaries on this episode are troubled by it.[55]

A famous story about a king's relations with Nishadas and other tribals, as well as Pariahs, is only loosely connected with Rama (it is told to him):

TRISHANKU HALFWAY TO HEAVEN

Vishvamitra was a great and just king. One day he tried to steal from the Brahmin Vasishtha the wish-fulfilling cow, who could produce anything that one asked her for. At Vasishtha's request, she produced armies of Persians and Scythians and Greeks, and then aliens (*mlecchas*) and tribals (Kiratas), who destroyed the king's armies and his sons. Realizing that the power of a Brahmin was greater than that of a Kshatriya, Vishvamitra resolved to become a Brahmin himself. He generated great inner heat but merely became a royal sage, still a Kshatriya.

Meanwhile a king named Trishanku wanted to go to heaven in his own body. Vasishtha told him it was impossible, and Vasishtha's sons in fury cursed Trishanku to become a Pariah (Chandala), black and coarse, wearing iron ornaments, his hair all uncombed, his garlands taken from the cremation ground. His people ran away from him, and he went to Vishvamitra. Vishvamitra promised to help him get to heaven, and to do this, he prepared a great sacrifice for him. When Vedic scholars refused to attend a sacrifice performed by a Kshatriya for a Pariah patron, Vishvamitra cursed them to become reviled, pitiless tribals (Nishadas) and hideous Pariahs (Mushtikas), living on dog meat in cemeteries.

The gods refused to attend the sacrifice, but Vishvamitra used his inner heat to raise Trishanku toward heaven. Indra commanded Trishanku to fall back to earth, but Vishvamitra stopped his fall, so that Trishanku was stuck halfway up in the sky. Vishvamitra created a new set of constellations for him and was about to create a new pantheon of gods as well, but the gods persuaded him to stop. And so Trishanku lives forever like that, upside down, in his alternative universe (1.51–59).

What begins as a conflict between members of the two upper classes leads to an unsatisfactory compromise: Vishvamitra becomes both a Kshatriya and a sage. When he then takes on the entire Brahmin academic establishment and, finally, the gods themselves, this results in yet another uneasy compromise, Trishanku suspended between heaven and earth. Along the way, however, the fallout from these high-class wars creates first a passel of foreigners (the usual Central Asian suspects), then even more alien (*mlecchas*) and tribals, and finally a combination of Pariahs and other tribals. When the dust settles, the moral seems to be that although, as Vishvamitra believes, Brahmins are better than Kshatriyas in some ways (the gods come to their sacrifice), inner heat—the religious power available to non-Brahmins and non-Vedic sacrificers—can do what even sacrifice cannot: Like sacrificial merit, or karma in general, it can be transferred from sacrificer to patron, but unlike them, it can get your body at least halfway to heaven, which the Brahmin Vasishtha said could not be done at all. At least one Kshatriya, moreover, Vishvamitra, makes many Brahmins into Pariahs and forces the gods to meet him literally halfway. This story, well known both in India and in Europe and America,* provides us with yet another vivid image of liminality, fusion, and the partial resolution of irresolvable conflicts.

Just as the alternative universe that Vishvamitra creates is entirely real to Trishanku, so the world of the *Ramayana* that Valmiki created is very real indeed to the many Hindus who have heard it or read it, and Sita and Rama continue to shape attitudes to women and to political conflict in India to this day.

---

* Henry Wadsworth Longfellow, of all people, was inspired by Trishanku:

> *Viswamitra the Magician*
> *By his spells and incantations,*
> *Up to Indra's realms elysian*
> *Raised Trisanku, king of nations.*
>
> *Indra and the gods offended*
> *Hurled him downward, and descending*
> *In the air he hung suspended,*
> *With these equal powers contending.*
>
> *Thus by aspirations lifted,*
> *By misgivings downward driven,*
> *Human hearts are tossed and drifted*
> *Midway between earth and heaven.*

CHAPTER 10

VIOLENCE IN THE
MAHABHARATA

300 BCE to 300 CE

☙

CHRONOLOGY

c. 300 BCE–300 CE The *Mahabharata* is composed

c. 200 BCE–200 CE The *Ramayana* is composed

327–25 BCE Alexander the Great invades Northwest
South Asia

c. 324 BCE Chandragupta founds the Mauryan dynasty

c. 265–232 BCE Ashoka reigns

c. 250 BCE The Third Buddhist Council takes place at Pataliputra

c. 185 BCE The Mauryan dynasty ends

c. 185 BCE Pushyamitra founds the Shunga dynasty

73 BCE The Shunga dynasty ends

c. 150 BCE The monuments of Bharhut and Sanchi are built

c. 166 BCE–78 CE Greeks and Scythians enter India

YUDHISHTHIRA'S DILEMMA

King Yudhishthira walked alone on the path to heaven, never
looking down. Only a dog followed him: the dog that I have already
told you about quite a lot. Then Indra, king of the gods, came to
Yudhishthira in his chariot and said to him, "Get in." Yudhishthira
said, "This dog, O lord of the past and the future, has been constantly
devoted to me. Let him come with me; for I am determined not to
be cruel." Indra said, "Today you have become immortal, like me,
and you have won complete prosperity, and great fame, your majesty,
as well as the joys of heaven. Leave the dog. There is nothing cruel in
that. There is no place for dog owners in the world of heaven; for

evil spirits carry off what has been offered, sacrificed or given as an oblation into the fire, if it is left uncovered and a dog has looked at it. Therefore you must leave this dog, and by leaving the dog, you will win the world of the gods."

Yudhishthira said, "People say that abandoning someone devoted to you is a bottomless evil, equal—according to the general opinion—to killing a Brahmin. I think so too." When the god Dharma, who had been there in the form of the dog, heard these words spoken by Yud-hishthira, the Dharma king, he appeared in his own form and spoke to King Yudhishthira with affection and with gentle words of praise: "Great king, you weep with all creatures. Because you turned down the celestial chariot, by insisting, 'This dog is devoted to me,' there is no one your equal in heaven and you have won the highest goal, of going to heaven with your own body."

> *Mahabharata*, 300 BCE–300 CE (17.2.26, 17.3.1–21)

As the Hindu idea of nonviolence (*ahimsa*) that emerged from debates about eating and/or sacrificing animals was soon taken up in debates about warfare, the resulting arguments, which deeply color the narratives of the *Mahabharata* on all levels, were simultaneously about the treatment of animals, about the treatment of Pariahs symbolized by animals, and about human violence as an inevitable result of the fact that humans are animals and animals are violent. The connection between the historical figure of the Buddhist king Ashoka and the mythological figure of the Hindu king Yudhishthira, and their very similar attempts to mitigate, if not to abolish, violence, particularly violence against animals, are also at the heart of this chapter.

ASHOKA

Ashoka claimed to have conquered most of India, though evidence suggests that he did not venture beyond southern Karnataka to attempt to conquer South India. But in the eighth year of his reign, he marched on Kalinga (the present Orissa) in a cruel campaign that makes Sherman's march look like a children's parade. Afterward he claimed to have been revolted by what he had done, and issued an edict that was carved into the surfaces of rock in several places in India (not including Kalinga, significantly). It is a most remarkable document, allowing us a glimpse into the mind—or, at least, the public mind—

of a ruler who regrets what he regards as a major crime committed in the line of duty. This is how the edict begins:

ASHOKA ON THE ROAD FROM ORISSA

When he had been consecrated eight years, the Beloved of the Gods, the king Piyadasi, conquered Kalinga. A hundred and fifty thousand people were deported, a hundred thousand were killed, and many times that number perished. Afterward, now that Kalinga was annexed, the Beloved of the Gods very earnestly practiced *dhamma*, desired *dhamma* and taught *dhamma*. On conquering Kalinga, the Beloved of the Gods felt remorse, for when an independent country is conquered, the slaughter, death, and deportation of the people are extremely grievous to the Beloved of the Gods and weigh heavily on his mind. What is even more deplorable to the Beloved of the Gods is that those who dwell there, whether Brahmanas, Shramanas, or those of other sects, or householders who show obedience to their superiors, obedience to mother and father, obedience to their teachers, and behave well and devotedly toward their friends, acquaintances, colleagues, relatives, slaves and servants—all suffer violence, murder, and separation from their loved ones. Even those who are fortunate to have escaped and whose love is undiminished suffer from the misfortunes of their friends, acquaintances, colleagues, and relatives. This participation of all men in suffering weighs heavily on the mind of the Beloved of the Gods.[1]

That Ashoka renounced war at this point is perhaps less impressive than it might seem, given that he now already had most of India under his control (or at least more than anyone else had ever had and apparently all that he wanted); he was locking the stable door after the horse was safely tethered in its stall. But his repentance did not mean that he had sworn off violence forever; in this same edict he warns "the forest tribes of his empire" that "he has power even in his remorse, and he asks them to repent, lest they be killed." In another edict he refers, rather ominously, to "the unconquered peoples on my borders" (i.e., not conquered yet?) and acknowledges that they may wonder what he intends to do with/for/to them.[2] He may have hung up his gun belt, but he still had it. What is most remarkable about the inscription about Kalinga, however, is its introspective and confessional tone, its frankness and sincerity, and the decision to carve it in rock—to make permanent, as it were, his realization that military conquest, indeed royal vainglory, was impermanent (*anicca*, in the Buddhist parlance). Here is evidence of an individual who took pains to see that future generations would remember him, and this is a new concept in ancient India.

The *dhamma* to which Ashoka refers in his edict is neither the Buddhist *dhamma* (the Pali word for the teachings of the Buddha in the oldest layer of Buddhist literature) nor Hindu dharma, nor any other particular religion or philosophical doctrine but is, rather, a broader code of behavior, one size fits all, that is implicit in the various good qualities of the people whom he itemizes here as those he regrets having killed, people who might be "Brahmanas, Shramanas [renouncers], or those of other sects." That code of *dhamma* included honesty, truthfulness, compassion, obedience, mercy, benevolence, and considerate behavior toward all, "few faults and many good deeds" (or "little evil, much good") as he summarized it.[3] He urged people to curb their extravagance and acquisitiveness. He founded hospitals for humans and animals and supplied them with medicines; he planted roadside trees and mango groves, dug wells, and constructed watering sheds and rest houses. This idealistic empire was reflected in the perfect world of Rama's Reign (Ram-raj) in the *Ramayana*.

Ashoka made his thoughts known by having them engraved on rocks and, later in his reign, on pillars. These edicts show a concern to conform to the local idiom and context. All in all, nineteen rock edicts and nine pillar edicts, written in the local script, are to be found scattered in more than thirty places throughout India, Nepal, Pakistan, and Afghanistan. The sandstone for the highly polished pillars was quarried at Chunar near Varanasi (Kashi) and shows remarkable technological expertise; averaging between forty and fifty feet in height and weighing up to fifty tons each, the pillars were dragged hundreds of miles to the places where they were erected, all within the Ganges plain, the heart of the empire. Ashoka adapted older, existing pillars that symbolized the pillar that separates heaven and earth and were expressions of an ancient phallic worship of Indra.[4] The lions (symbolizing the Buddha as the emperor) on the capitals of the pillars show Persian influence, for Iranian journeyman carvers came to Ashoka's cosmopolitan empire in search of work after the fall of the Achaemenids. But the bulls and elephants are treated in an unmistakably Indian way,[5] stunningly similar to some of the animals on the Indus seals; the horses too are carved in the distinctive Indian style. Thus the pillar combined, for the first time, the technique of representing animals in a uniquely naturalistic but stylized way that was perfected in 2000 BCE in the Indus Valley, and was the first representation of the horse, an animal that the Indus Valley artisans did not have. Indus form (the Indian style) expressed Indo-European content (the horse). (See the image on page 84.)

Ashoka cared deeply about animals and included them as a matter of course, along with humans, as the beneficiaries of his shade trees and watering places. In place of the royal tradition of touring his kingdom in a series of royal hunts, he inaugurated the tradition of royal pilgrimages to Buddhist shrines, thus substituting a Buddhist (and Hindu) virtue (pilgrimage) for a Hindu vice of addiction (hunting). In one bilingual rock inscription, the Aramaic version says, "Our Lord the king kills very few animals. Seeing this the rest of the people have also ceased from killing animals. Even the activity of those who catch fish has been prohibited."[6] Elsewhere Ashoka urges "abstention from killing and nonviolence [avihimsa] to living beings"[7] and remarks that it is good not to kill living beings.[8]

But he never did discontinue capital punishment or torture or legislate against either the killing or the eating of all animals. This is what he said about his own diet: "Formerly, in the kitchens of the Beloved of the Gods, the king Piyadasi, many hundreds of thousands of living animals were killed daily for meat. But now, at the time of writing of this inscription on dhamma, only three animals are killed [daily], two peacocks and a deer, and the deer not invariably. Even these three animals will not be killed in future."[9] Why go on killing these three? Perhaps because the emperor was fond of roasted peacock and venison.[10] Perhaps he was trying to cut down on meat, the way some chain-smokers try to cut down on cigarettes. And his own particular dhamma became prototypical, since the people are to follow the king's example; the implication was: "This is what I eat in my kitchen; you should eat like that too." But his personal tastes cannot explain the other, longer list (rather approximate in translation, for some of the species are uncertain) of animals that the edicts "protected" from slaughter: parakeets, mynah birds, red-headed ducks, chakravaka geese, swans, pigeons, bats, ants, tortoises, boneless fish, skates, porcupines, squirrels, deer, lizards, cows, rhinoceroses, white pigeons, domestic pigeons, and all four-footed creatures that are neither useful nor edible. Also nanny goats, ewes, and sows lactating or with young, and kids, lambs, and piglets less than six months old. Cocks are not to be made into capons. One animal is not to be fed to another. On certain holy days, fish are not to be caught or sold; on other holy days, bulls, billy goats, rams, boars, and other animals that are usually castrated are not to be castrated; and on still others, horses and bullocks are not to be branded.[11]

What are we to make of these lists? Ashoka is hedging again. He recommends restraint of violence toward living beings in the same breath that he recommends the proper treatment of slaves,[12] but evidently it is all right to kill some of the creatures some of the time. In particular, Ashoka allows for the slaughter of the *pashus*—male goats, sheep, and cattle, the animals most often used both for sacrifice and for food. There is no ecological agenda here for the conservation of wildlife, nor can the lists be explained by the privileging of certain animals for medicinal purposes. What there is is the expression of a man who finds himself between a rock edict and a hard place, a man who has concern for animals' feelings (give them shade, don't castrate them—sometimes) but recognizes that people do eat animals. It is a very limited sort of nonviolence, not unlike that of the Brahmana text that pointed out that eating animals is bad but then let you eat them in certain ways, instead of outlawing it entirely, as one might have expected. Ashoka is the man, after all, who gave up war only after he had conquered all North India.

His attitude to the varieties of religion was similarly politic. As a pluralistic king he had a social ethic that consisted primarily of inclusivity:[13] "Whoever honors his own sect or disparages that of another man, wholly out of devotion to his own, with a view to showing it in a favorable light, harms his own sect even more seriously."[14] Not a word is said about Vedic religion or sacrifice, aside from the casual and entirely neutral references to Brahmanas (Brahmins) along with Shramanas, nor does Ashoka mention class or caste (*varna* or *jati*), aside from that reference to Brahmins. But he does not hesitate to criticize the more popular religion that was the livelihood of lower-class priests: "In illness, at the marriage of sons and daughters, at the birth of children, when going on a journey, on these and on similar occasions, people perform many ceremonies. Women especially perform a variety of ceremonies, which are trivial and useless. If such ceremonies must be performed, they have but small results."[15] Small-time superstition is foolish but harmless, he seems to be saying, with an incidental swipe at women. He approves of public religion, however, and expresses his pride in the increase in displays of heavenly chariots, elephants, balls of fire, and other divine forms,[16] as a means of attracting an audience to create an interest in *dhamma*.[17] This sort of bread and circuses is cynically developed in the *Arthashastra* (13.1.3–8), which devises a number of ingenious things to do with fire and also advises the king to have his friends dress up as gods and let his people see him hanging out with them. It is one of the great pities of human history that Ashoka's program of *dhamma* died with him, in about 232 BCE.

Far more enduring were Ashoka's services to Buddhism, which he spoke of not to the people at large but to other Buddhists. He held the Third Buddhist Council, at Pataliputra, and sent out many missionaries. He built a number of stupas and monasteries. His patronage transformed Buddhism from a small, localized sect to a religion that spread throughout India and far beyond its borders. Both Ashoka and his father, Bindusara, patronized not only Buddhists and Jainas but also the Ajivikas, to whom Ashoka's grandson may have dedicated some caves.[18] The more general program of *dhamma* continued to support all religions, including Hinduism.

Fast-forward: Myths about Ashoka became current shortly after his own time, when Buddhist texts discoursed upon the Kalinga edict, the confession of cruelty, and the subsequent renunciation of cruelty in favor of Buddhism. This resulted in a fantasy that Ashoka killed his ninety-nine brothers to attain the throne and then visited hell, where he learned how to construct a hell on earth, equipped with fiendish instruments of exquisite torture, which he used on anyone who offended him.[19] The mythmaking never stopped. In 2001 a film (*Asoka*, directed by Santosh Sivan) depicted a youthful Ashoka (Shahrukh Khan) who, traveling incognito, meets the regulation heroine in a wet sari under a waterfall (Kareena Kapoor). She is, unbeknownst to him, the queen of Kalinga, also traveling incognita. So when he eventually massacres Kalinga and finds her wandering in despair amid the wide-angle carnage, he is very, very sorry that he has killed all those people. And so, after three hours of nonstop slaughter, in the last two minutes of the film he converts to Buddhism.

THE RISE OF SECTARIAN HINDUISM

Despite (or because of) the rise of Buddhism in this period, both Vedic sacrificers and members of the evolving Hindu sects of Vaishnavas and Shaivas (worshipers of Vishnu and Shiva) found new sponsors among the ruling families and court circles.[20] The keystone for the Brahmin establishment was the new economic power of temple cities.[21] From about 500 BCE, kings still performed Vedic sacrifices to legitimize their kingship,[22] but the sectarian worship of particular deities began partially to replace Vedic sacrifice.[23] As the gods of the Vedic pantheon (Indra, Soma, Agni) faded into the background, Vishnu and Rudra/Shiva, who had played small roles in the Vedas, attracted more and more worshipers. Throughout the *Ramayana* and *Mahabharata*, we encounter people who say they worship a particular god, which is the start of sects and therefore of sectarianism.

Pilgrimage and *puja* are the main forms of worship at this time. Pilgrimage is described at length in the *Mahabharata,* particularly but not only in the "Tour of the Sacred *Tirthas*" (3.80–140). Sacred fords (*tirthas*) are shrines where one can simultaneously cross over (which is what *tirtha* means) the river and the perils of the world of rebirth. As in Ashoka's edicts, the "conquest of the four corners of the earth" (*dig-vijaya*), originally a martial image, is now applied to a grand tour of pilgrimage to many shrines, circling the world (India), always to the right. *Puja* (from the Dravidian *pu* ["flower"])[24] consisted of making an offering to an image of a god (flowers, fruits, sometimes rice), and/or moving a lamp through the air in a circular pattern, walking around the god, and reciting prayers, such as a litany of the names of the god. Krishna in the *Bhagavad Gita*[*] says that pious people offer him a leaf or flower or fruit or water (9.26). Sometimes the image of the god is bathed and dressed, and often the remains of the food that has been offered to the god is then distributed to the worshipers as the god's "favor" or "grace" (*prasada*), a relic of the leftovers (*ucchishta*) from the Vedic sacrifice.

There is rich evidence of the rise of the sectarian gods. The *Mahabharata* includes a Hymn of the Thousand Names of Shiva (13.17), and in 150 BCE Patanjali, the author of the highly influential *Yoga Sutras*, foundational for the Yoga school of philosophy, mentions a worshiper of Shiva who wore animal skins and carried an iron lance. Gold coins from this same period depict Shiva holding a trident and standing in front of a massive bull, presumably the bull that is Shiva's usual vehicle. In the first century BCE, under the Shungas, artisans produced what is generally regarded as the earliest depiction of the god Shiva: a linga just under five feet high, in Gudimallam, in southeastern Andhra Pradesh. (See page 22.) Its anatomical detail, apart from its size, is highly naturalistic, but on the shaft is carved the figure of Shiva, two-armed and also naturalistic, holding an ax in one hand and the body of a small antelope in the other. His thin garment reveals his own sexual organ (not erect), his hair is matted, and he wears large earrings. He stands upon a dwarf. A frieze from the first or second century CE suggests how such a linga might have been worshiped; it depicts a linga shrine under a tree, surrounded by a railing, just like the actual railing that was discovered beneath the floor in which the image was embedded.[25]

The *Mahabharata* tells a story about the circumstances under which Shiva came to be worshiped:

---

[*] Book 6, chapters 23–40 of the *Mahabharata*.

SHIVA DESTROYS DAKSHA'S VEDIC SACRIFICE

Once upon a time, when Shiva was living on Mount Meru with his wife, Parvati, the daughter of the mountain Himalaya, all the gods and demigods thronged to him and paid him homage. The Lord of Creatures named Daksha began to perform a horse sacrifice in the ancient manner, which Indra and the gods attended with Shiva's permission. Seeing this, Parvati asked Shiva where the gods were going, and Shiva explained it to her, adding that the gods had decided long ago not to give him any share in the sacrifice. But Parvati was so unhappy about this that Shiva took his great bow and went with his band of fierce servants to destroy the sacrifice. Some put out the sacrificial fires by dousing them with blood; others began to eat the sacrificial assistants. The sacrifice took the form of a wild animal and fled to the skies, and Shiva pursued it with bow and arrow. The gods, terrified, fled, and the very earth began to tremble. Brahma begged Shiva to desist, promising him a share of the sacrificial offerings forever after, and Shiva smiled and accepted that share (12.274.2–58).

This important myth, retold in various transformations several times in the *Mahabharata*[26] and in other texts through the ages, is in part a historical narrative of what did happen in the history of Hinduism: Shiva was not part of the Vedic sacrifice, and then he became part of the Hindu sacrifice. The gods, particularly Daksha (a creator, mentioned in the *Rig Veda* hymn of Aditi [10.72.1–5]), exclude Shiva from their sacrifice because Shiva is the outsider, the Other, the god to whom Vedic sacrifice is not offered; he is not a member of the club of gods that sacrifice to the gods.[27] He appears to Arjuna, in a pivotal episode of the *Mahabharata*, in the form of a naked Kirata, a tribal hunter (3.40.1–5). The myth of Daksha's sacrifice verifies Shiva's otherness but modifies it so that Shiva is in fact given a share in some sacrifices, still not part of the Vedic world but the supreme god of the post-Vedic world, at least in the eyes of the Shaivas who tell this myth.[28]

In the *Ramayana*, the god Rama is on his way to becoming one of the great gods of sectarian Hinduism. The god Krishna too now enters the world of Sanskrit texts, in the *Mahabharata*. The grammarian Panini, in the fifth century BCE, mentions a Vasudevaka, whom he defines as a devotee (bhakta) of the son of Vasudeva (Krishna), an avatar of Vishnu. This was the time of the beginning of the Bhagavata sects, the worship of Bhagavan, the Lord, a name of Vishnu or Shiva. In 115 BCE, Heliodorus, the son of a Greek from Taxila and himself the Greek ambassador to one of the Shungas,[29] set up a pillar in Besnagar in Madhya Pradesh (not far from the Buddhist stupas at Sanchi), topped by an image of Vishnu's eagle (the Garuda bird) and an inscription. Heliodorus said he had done this in honor of the son of Vasudeva and that he himself was a Bhagavata.[30] This is significant evidence of the conversion of a non-Indian not to Buddhism but to a new form of Hinduism. These are the early stirrings of communal sects that were beginning to supplement, sometimes to replace, the royal and domestic worship of the Vedic gods.

THE ERAS OF THE TWO GREAT POEMS

The *Mahabharata* story may have begun earlier than that of the *Ramayana*, but the text that we have was probably composed in North India between approximately 300 BCE and 300 CE,[*] after the Mauryas and before the Guptas. It therefore shares the general chronology of the *Ramayana*, *entre deux empires*, a time of shifting political and economic power.

The two texts have much in common: They are long poems, in Sanskrit (indeed mostly in the same meter), and both are about war. They quote the same sources and tell many of the same stories. But their differences are more interesting. The geographical setting of the *Mahabharata* signals a time earlier than that of the *Ramayana*. The *Mahabharata* is set in and around the earlier capital of Hastinapur,[†] already a great city in the age of the Brahmanas, instead of the *Ramayana*'s cities of Rajagriha in Magadha and Kashi in Koshala, which were settled later.[31] The *Mahabharata* calls itself the "Fifth Veda" (though so do several other texts) and dresses its story in Vedic trappings (such as ostentatious Vedic sacrifices and encounters with Vedic gods). It looks back to the Brahmanas and tells new versions of the old stories.[32] Indeed, it looks back beyond the Brahmanas to the Vedic age, and may well preserve many memories of that period, and that place, up in the Punjab. The Painted Gray Ware artifacts discovered at sites identified with locations in the *Mahabharata* may be evidence of the reality of the great *Mahabharata* war, which is sometimes supposed to have

---

[*] These dates are much disputed, some scholars emphasizing a much shorter period for the actual recension, with the possibility of single authorship, while others emphasize the longer period and multiple authorship.

[†] The Kuru kings in the *Mahabharata* are said to have later shifted their capital from Hastinapur to Kaushambi because of floods at Hastinapur. Excavations at a village named Hastinapura in Meerut (Uttar Pradesh) have revealed habitations from the twelfth to the seventh centuries BCE, with walls of mud or of mud bricks (sun-fired), or reed walls plastered over with mud; and then, from the sixth to the third centuries BCE, structures of mud brick as well as burned bricks (kiln-fired), and terra-cotta ring wells—all of this a far cry from the fabulous palaces described in the *Mahabharata*.

occurred between 1000 and 400 BCE,[33] usually in 950 BCE, the latter being the most reasonable assertion in light of what we know of Vedic history.[*]

Yet its central plot is really about the building of a great empire far more Mauryan than Vedic. In other ways too it is very much the product of its times, the interregnum between the Mauryan and Gupta empires in the Ganges plain.[34] The text often refers to the quasi-Mauryan *Artha-shastra*, particularly when seeking textual support for hitting a man below the belt or when he's down (10.1.47). The authors react in nuanced ways to the eddying currents of Ashokan Buddhism and the Brahmin ascendancy of the Shungas, striving somehow to tell the story of the destruction and reconstruction of entire groups or classes of people and, at the same time, to reconcile this political flux with the complex values of the emerging dharmas.

Moreover, according to Indian tradition, the *Ramayana* took place in the second age (right after the Golden Age), when the moral life was still relatively intact, while the *Mahabharata* took place later, at the cusp of the third age and the fourth, the Kali Age, when all hell broke loose. The *Ramayana* imagines an age of order preceding that chaos, while the *Mahabharata* imagines the beginning of the breakdown, the planned obsolescence of the moral world. In keeping with the basic Indian belief that time is degenerative, the *Ramayana*, which is more optimistic and imagines a time of peace and prosperity, is said to precede the *Mahabharata*, which is darker and imagines a time of war and the collapse of civilization.

The *Mahabharata* is generally regarded as having reached its final form later than the *Ramayana* but also to have begun earlier; the *Ramayana* is shorter and in many ways simpler, certainly more coherent, but not necessarily chronologically prior. Both texts were in gestation so long, and in conversation during so much of that gestation period, that each of the great poems precedes the other, like Brahma and Vishnu, or dharma and *moksha*. The *Ramayana* cites the *Mahabharata* from time to time, and the *Mahabharata* devotes an entire long section to retelling the *Ramayana* (3.257–75), a version of the story that is probably later than the one told in the *Ramayana* itself.[35] Characters from each make cameo appearances in the other. Intertextuality here hath made its masterpiece; the two texts may have anxiety (*amhas*) about a lot of things but not about influence.[36] There is a famous Sanskrit poem that can be read, depending upon how you divide the compounds and choose among the multiple meanings of the

---

[*] 3012 BCE is also a much-cited date for the battle.

words, to tell the story of either the *Mahabharata* or the *Ramayana*.[37] In many ways, the two stories are two sides of the same coin.

THE INTEGRITY OF THE *MAHABHARATA*

The *Mahabharata* is a text of about seventy-five thousand verses* or three million words, some fifteen times the combined length of the Hebrew Bible and the New Testament, or seven times the *Iliad* and the *Odyssey* combined, and a hundred times more interesting. (The *Ramayana* is about a third of the length of the *Mahabharata*, some twenty thousand verses against the *Mahabharata*'s seventy-five thousand.) The bare bones of the central story (and there are hundreds of peripheral stories too) could be summarized like this, for our purposes:

> The five sons of King Pandu, called the Pandavas, were fathered by gods: Yudhishthira by Dharma, Bhima by the Wind (Vayu), Arjuna by Indra, and the Twins (Nakula and Sahadeva) by the Ashvins. All five of them married Draupadi. When Yudhishthira lost the kingdom to his cousins in a game of dice, the Pandavas and Draupadi went into exile for twelve years, at the end of which, with the help of their cousin the incarnate god Krishna, who befriended the Pandavas and whose counsel to Arjuna on the battlefield of Kurukshetra is the *Bhagavad Gita*, they regained their kingdom through a cataclysmic battle in which almost everyone on both sides was killed.

The *Mahabharata* was retold very differently by all of its many authors in the long line of literary descent. It is so extremely fluid that there is no single *Mahabharata*; there are hundreds of *Mahabharata*s, hundreds of different manuscripts and innumerable oral versions (one reason why it is impossible to make an accurate calculation of the number of its verses). The *Mahabharata* is not contained in a text; the story is there to be picked up and found, salvaged as anonymous treasure from the ocean of story. It is constantly retold and rewritten both in Sanskrit and in vernacular dialects; it has been called "a work in progress,"[38] a literature that "does not belong in a book."[39] The *Mahabharata* (1.1.23) describes itself as unlimited in both time and space—eternal and infinite: "Poets have told it before, and are telling it now, and will tell it again. What is here is also found elsewhere, but what is *not* here is found nowhere else."[40] It

---

* Sometimes said to be a hundred thousand, perhaps just to round it off a bit.

grows out of the oral tradition and then grows back into the oral tradition; it flickers back and forth between Sanskrit manuscripts and village storytellers, each adding new gemstones to the old mosaic, constantly reinterpreting it. The loose construction of the text gives it a quasinovelistic quality, open to new forms as well as new ideas, inviting different ideas to contest one another, to come to blows, in the pages of the text.

Clearly no single author could have lived long enough to put it all together, but that does not mean that it is a miscellaneous mess with no unified point of view, let alone "the most monstrous chaos," "the huge and motley pile," or "gargantuan hodgepodge" and "literary pileup" that scholars have accused it of being.[41] European approaches to the *Mahabharata* often assumed that the collators did not know what they were doing, and, blindly cutting and pasting, accidentally created a monstrosity. But the *Mahabharata* is not the head of a Brahmin philosophy accidentally stuck onto a body of non-Brahmin folklore, like the heads and bodies of the Brahmin woman and the Pariah woman in the story. True, it was like an ancient Wikipedia, to which anyone who knew Sanskrit, or who knew someone who knew Sanskrit, could add a bit here, a bit there. But the powerful intertextuality of Hinduism ensured that anyone who added anything to the *Mahabharata* was well aware of the whole textual tradition behind it and fitted his or her own insight, or story, or long philosophical disquisition, thoughtfully into the ongoing conversation. However diverse its sources, for several thousand years the tradition has regarded it as a conversation among people who know one another's views and argue with silent partners. It is a contested text,[42] a brilliantly orchestrated hybrid narrative with no single party line on any subject. The text has an integrity that the culture supports (in part by attributing it to a single author, Vyasa, who is also a major player in the story) and that it is our duty to acknowledge. The contradictions at its heart are not the mistakes of a sloppy editor but enduring cultural dilemmas that no author could ever have resolved.

THE POLITICAL WORLD OF THE *MAHABHARATA*

The *Mahabharata* challenged the relationships between the two upper classes, only ultimately to reconfirm them. For example, the career of King Pushyamitra, the Brahmin who became a general and reinstated Hinduism over Buddhism in his kingdom, may have inspired an important episode in the *Mahabharata*, the tale of Parashurama ("Rama with an Ax"), the son of a Brahmin father and Kshatriya mother. When a Kshatriya killed Parashurama's father, he avenged the murder by killing the entire class of Kshatriyas, over twenty-one generations. He also avenged the theft of the calf of his father's wishing cow by pursuing the king who stole her, killing him, and taking back the calf (3.116). This variant of the ancient cattle-raiding myth has a Brahmin rather than a Kshatriya protagonist; it turns a famous Kshatriya myth around in order to attack Kshatriya despotism and royal greed and to undo the bifurcation of temporal and spiritual power. The fantasy of Brahmins exterminating Kshatriyas and becoming Kshatriyas (a goal that was also attributed to an early historical king, Mahapadma Nanda) may also have been a projection of Brahmin fears that the Kshatriyas would exterminate Brahmins, by converting to Buddhism or Jainism or by encouraging renunciant Hindu sects.[43]

VIOLENCE OF AND TOWARD ANIMALS

We may see a parallel, perhaps a historical influence, between the ambivalence toward nonviolence (*ahimsa*) expressed in the Ashokan edicts and in the *Mahabharata*.

The *Mahabharata* is about what has been called "grotesque, sanctioned violence,"[44] and violence not only toward animals but among them is a central theme. The assumption that the relationship between the animals themselves was, one might say, red in tooth and claw,* was enshrined in a phrase cited often in both the *Mahabharata* and the *Artha-shastra:* "fish eat fish" (*matsya-nyaya*), the big fish eating the little fish.† In the myth of the flood, the tiny fish asks Manu to save him from the big fish who will otherwise eat him, a literal instance of the metaphor for the vicious, cannibalistic aspect of human nature, the dark things that swim deep in the waters of the unconscious. This image of virtual anarchy was used to justify a law and order agenda and to promote the strict enforcement of restrictive versions of dharma, in order to keep people from behaving like animals. The assertion that without a king wielding punishment the stronger would devour the weaker as big fish eat small fish (or, sometimes, that they would roast them like fish on a spit [Manu 7.20]), is often used as an argument for coercive kingship.

Characters in the *Mahabharata* also, however, sometimes use "fish eat fish" to justify the opposite agenda, anarchy, more precisely the jettisoning of the

---

* Alfred Lord Tennyson, "In Memoriam."
† Perhaps inspired by Asian carp, said to devour all the other fish in the lake.

ancient India equivalent of the Geneva Convention (or the Marquess of Queensberry's rules), on the assumption that people too are animals and cannot be stopped from acting like animals. When Arjuna urges Yudhishthira to action, he says: "I see no being that lives in the world without violence. Creatures exist at one another's expense; the stronger consume the weaker. The mongoose eats mice, just as the cat eats the mongoose; the dog devours the cat, your majesty, and wild beasts eat the dog (12.15)."

Scenes of the violent death of hundreds of animals, like miniatures of the violent death of human beings at the center of the *Mahabharata,* stand like bookends framing the introductory book.[45] It begins with King Janamejaya's attempt to murder all the snakes in the world in revenge for his father's death by snakebite. This is an inverted horse sacrifice, an antisacrifice. The horse, a creature of light, the sky, fire, flying through the air, is the right animal to sacrifice in a Vedic ceremony, while the snake, a creature of darkness, the underworld, water, cold, sliding under the ground, is the wrong animal. To the ancient Indians, a snake sacrifice must have been an abomination,[46] for though Hindus have worshiped snakes from time immemorial, they do so by making small offerings of milk to them, not by killing them. The snake sacrifice in the first book sets the stage for the central *Mahabharata* story. The story of a sacrifice that goes horribly wrong, it is a dark mirror for the *Mahabharata* as a whole, brilliant, sinister, and surreal. For not only is the snake sacrifice the wrong sort of sacrifice to undertake, but Janamejaya's sacrifice is never even completed: Snake after snake is dropped into the fire, writhing in agony, until a sage stops the ritual before the massacre is complete.

And the first book of the *Mahabharata* ends with an attempt by Arjuna, Krishna, and Fire (Agni) to burn up the great Khandava forest, ignoring the plight of the animals that live there: "Creatures by the thousands screamed in terror and were scorched; some embraced their sons or mothers or fathers, unable to leave them. Everywhere creatures writhed on the ground, with burning wings, eyes, and paws (1.217)." Only a few snakes still remained alive when a compassionate sage stopped the snake sacrifice, and only six creatures survived (one snake, four birds, and Maya, the architect of the antigods) when Agni, sated, stopped burning the forest.

YUDHISHTHIRA'S DOG

Stories about animals are sometimes really about animals, the treatment of whom was, as we have seen, both a public concern of rulers and an issue that

Vedic and non-Vedic people often disputed. But stories about animals also function as parables about class tensions in this period.

Take dogs. Hindu dharma forbids Hindus to have any contact with dogs, whom it regards as unclean scavengers, literally untouchable (*a-sprishya*), the parasites of Pariahs who are themselves regarded as parasites. Even Yudhishthira uses dogs as symbols of aggression when he says that humans negotiating peace are like dogs: "tail wagging, a bark, a bark back, backing off, baring the teeth howling, and then the fight begins, and the stronger one wins and eats the meat. Humans are just exactly like that (5.70.70–72)."[47] Even after he has won the war, he says: "We are not dogs, but we act like dogs greedy for a piece of meat (12.7.10)." As for dogs symbolic of low castes, though the *Gita* insists that wise people cast the same gaze on a learned Brahmin, a cow, an elephant, a dog, or a dog cooker (5.18), the *Mahabharata* generally upholds the basic prejudice against dogs, as in this story, which also makes clear the analogy between dogs and upwardly mobile Pariahs:

THE DOG WHO WOULD BE LION

Once there was an ascetic of such goodness that the flesh-eating wild animals—lions and tigers and bears, as well as rutting elephants, leopards, and rhinoceroses—were like his disciples. A dog, weak and emaciated from eating only fruits and roots, like the sage, became attached to him out of affection, tranquil, with a heart like that of a human being. One day a hungry leopard came there and was about to seize the dog as his prey when the dog begged the sage to save him. The sage turned him into a leopard, and then, when a tiger attacked, into a tiger, and then a rutting elephant, and a lion.* Now that he was carnivorous, all the other animals feared him and stayed away, and finally he wanted to eat the sage, who read his thoughts and turned him back into a dog, his own proper form by birth [*jati*]. The dog moped about unhappily until the sage drove him out of the hermitage [12.115–19].

This dog even has a human heart, but he must not be allowed to get ideas above his station. The phrase "his own proper form by birth" (*jati*) can also be translated, "his own proper form by caste," for *jati* means both "birth" and "caste." Both the dog and the sage are all wrong from the very beginning. The dog violates dog dharma by being a vegetarian, whereas he should be a carnivore,

---

* He also becomes a *sharabha*, a fierce mythical beast, variously described.

and the sage is wrong too to protect the dog by making him bigger and bigger instead of, like Manu with the expanding fish, putting him in bigger and bigger places. But the sage does not reciprocate the dog's devotion or attachment to him. Whereas the dog misrecognizes himself as a human, the sage in the end is as cruel as a dog.[48]

A very different point of view is expressed by the tale of a dog with which this chapter began, "Yudhishthira's Dilemma," an episode in which Yudhishthira refuses to go to heaven without the stray dog who has attached itself to him, as the dog who would be lion attached himself to the ascetic—though Yudhishthira's dog proves true to the end. What is most striking about this passage is that the god of Dharma himself becomes incarnate in this animal; it is as if the god of the Hebrew Bible had become incarnate in a pig.*

Dharma uses the dog to make a powerful ethical point; this is surely a way of arguing about the sorts of humans that should or should not go to heaven (a topic that the *Mahabharata* also explicitly addresses) or even, perhaps, by extension, about the castes that should or should not be allowed into temples. All good Hindus go to heaven (in this period), but they do so after dying and being given different, heavenly bodies; Yudhishthira is unique in being given the gift of going to heaven in his own body.[†] Perhaps in acknowledging his bond with animals, treating his dog like "someone who has come to you for refuge" or "a friend," Yudhishthira has somehow preserved the animality of his own body (that very animality denied by the sages, who regard both dogs and women as dirty). And so he enters heaven not merely as a disembodied spirit but as his entire embodied self.[49]

Yudhishthira refuses to abandon a dog who is "devoted" (bhakta) to him; heaven will not be heaven if he cannot bring his dog with him.[‡] The dog, the loyal dog, is, after all, the natural bhakta of the animal kingdom; it's no accident that it's a dog, not, say, a cat, who follows Yudhishthira like that. (Cats, in Hinduism, are depicted as religious hypocrites.[§]) But bhakti at this period meant little more than belonging to someone, being dedicated to someone as a servant

---

* In later Hinduism, Dharma occasionally becomes incarnate as the human equivalent of a dog, a Pariah (Chandala).
† The sage Trishanku tried it and got stuck halfway up.
‡ The anthropologist Elizabeth Marshall Thomas was on the same wavelength when she insisted, in an interview, that there were dogs in heaven. How did she know? she was asked. Because, she replied, otherwise it would not be heaven.
§ The hypocritical cat ascetic is carved on the great frieze at Mamallapuram. (See page 346.)

or loyal friend (or, occasionally, lover, as the term is sometimes also used for carnal love); it did not yet have the specific overtone of passionate love between a god and his devotee that was to become characteristic of a branch of medieval Hinduism. Yet as the word expanded its meaning, the story of Yudhishthira and his dog often came to be read as a model for that sort of devotion.

Indra's argument, that dogs would pollute the sacrificial offerings merely by looking at them, let alone touching them, is a common one. Manu (7.21) warns that if the king did not wield the rod of punishment justly, the dog would lick the oblation and everything would be upside down. In the *Mahabharata* version of the story of Rama and Sita, when Rama throws Sita out for the first time, he compares her, after her sojourn in Ravana's house, to an oblation that a dog has licked (3.275.14). Much of the trouble in the *Mahabharata* begins with a dog who does *not* lick an oblation:

> When Janamejaya and his brothers were performing a sacrifice, a dog, a son of the bitch Sarama, came near. The brothers beat the dog, who ran howling back to his mother and told her that they had beaten him though he had neither looked at nor licked the offerings. Sarama then went to the sacrificial grounds and said to Janamejaya, "Since you beat my son when he had not done anything wrong, danger will befall you when you do not see it coming (1.3.1–18)."

As a result of his prejudiced mistreatment of this pup, Janamejaya soon gets into serious trouble with other animals (snakes). Thus the *Mahabharata* both begins and ends with a story about justice for dogs.

But in Yudhishthira's case the conflict remains unresolved; the text equivocates. The sudden intrusion of the voice of the author in the first person at the beginning of the episode ("the dog that I have already told you about quite a lot [17.2.26]") is highly unusual, almost unprecedented. It is as if the author has anticipated the end of the story and begins to remind the audience that it is just a story—and not only just a story, but just a test (as they used to say of air-raid signals on the radio), one of a series of tests that Dharma set for his son, all of which he passed (17.3.18). For the dog never does go to heaven, never violates Hindu law, because there was no dog; it was all an illusion. In case of a real dog . . . what then? The story shows just how rotten the caste system is but does not change it. No dogs get into heaven.

NONCRUELTY AND NONVIOLENCE

"I am determined not to be cruel," says Yudhishthira. The term that he uses for "not to be cruel" is more literally "not to harm humans [a-nri-shamsa]."* It is a doubly weakened word: a double negative (it doesn't refer to doing something good, just to not doing something bad) and species specific (specifying harm to humans); to apply it to the treatment of an animal is therefore rather forced, given the usual Hindu distinction between cruelty to humans and to animals. The term ("not to be cruel"), which occurs here three times in four verses (17.3.7, 8, 10, and 30), is sometimes translated as "compassion,"† but the usual Sanskrit word for that is *karuna*, a more positive word.[50] Indra praises Yudhishthira for "weep[ing] with" all creatures (*anukrosha*), a word sometimes translated as "compassion," but more than compassion, a vivid form of sympathy. Yudhishthira is damning himself with faint praise if all he can muster up, in place of either "compassion" or "weeping with," is that he doesn't harm humans. He is hedging, just as Ashoka did when he stopped short of embracing nonviolence entirely but merely mitigated some of the brutality to animals in his kingdom.

The issue of noncruelty to animals is a minor variant on the heavier theme of nonviolence (*ahimsa*) toward both animals and humans, in an age when violence—toward humans as well as toward animals—is inevitable. *Ahimsa* ("the absence of the desire to kill") is another of those double negatives, like "noncruelty." (The Indian nationalist leader Bal Gangadhar Tilak [1856–1920] translated *ahimsa*, in the *Gita,* as "harmlessness,"[51] another double negative.) Elsewhere too (3.297.72), Yudhishthira says that noncruelty is the highest dharma. On another occasion, when Yudhishthira threatened to renounce the world, Arjuna had urged him to resign himself to violent action, invoking a host of Vedic gods and one new, sectarian god (Skanda), as well as mongooses and cats and mice, and saying: "People honor most the gods who are killers. Rudra is a killer, and so are Skanda, Indra, Agni, Varuna, Yama. I don't see anyone living in the world with nonviolence (*ahimsa*). Even ascetics (*tapasas*) cannot stay alive without killing (12.15.16, 20–21, 24)." Similarly, Rama, defending himself against charges of foul play against an animal, the monkey Valin, argued: "Even sages go hunting." Arjuna's own consideration of renouncing

---

* Other translators call it "uncruelty," "absence of cruelty," "noninjury," or even "compassion."
† Nilakantha, commenting on the *Mahabharata* in the seventeenth century, glosses "cruelty" as "lack of pity" (*nirdayatvam*); "lack of cruelty," then, which is the form that occurs in the text (*a-nri-shamsya*), would be "pity."

action prompts Krishna's reply in the *Bhagavad Gita*, a text that mentions *ahimsa* only in the course of four lists of conventional virtues (10.5, 13.7, 16.2, and 17.14) and never discusses it.

Many Hindus continued to engage in animal sacrifice at this time, while Buddhists and Jainas and, significantly, an increasing number of Hindus rejected it. Replacing the animal slaughter included in the major Vedic sacrifices,[52] *ahimsa* as a Hindu term claims a space closely associated with Jainism and Buddhism.[53] Yet the Brahmin redactors of the *Mahabharata* created a text that accepted the political implications of the violence of the universe, in part precisely in order to distinguish themselves from the nonviolent Buddhists and Jainas.[54]

Commentators have sometimes regarded Yudhishthira as a Brahmin king (like Pushyamitra) or a Buddhist king (like Ashoka), or both, a Brahminical Ashoka, who is tempted to reject violence much as Ashoka, by the testimony of his edicts, hoped to do.* Yudhishthira's refusal to rule after the war may have been a response to Asoka's thirteenth Major Rock Edict or to legends about Ashoka that circulated after his death.[55] (Aspects of the life and character of Arjuna too may have been created in response to Ashoka.[56])

The *Mahabharata*, like Ashoka, is torn between violence and nonviolence, and occasionally, as in the story of Yudhishthira's dog, rests for a moment in the compromise position of avoiding cruelty. Both Ashoka and Pushyamitra left their marks on Yudhishthira. All three kings responded, in different ways, to the challenge of Buddhists and Jainas, particularly to Jainas, who really *did* preach an uncompromising *ahimsa*. And all three kings created versions of the new *ahimsa* agenda that they could live with, a negotiated peace with both extremes. But nonviolence is not a Buddhist or Jaina monopoly, nor is compassion; everyone was wrestling with these problems at this time, though in different ways, and gradually compassion came to supplement, or sometimes even to replace, generosity (*dana*, "giving") as the primary virtue of householders and sacrificers.

The Brahmins' ultimate credibility as a religious elite depended on disassociating themselves from the direct cruelties of governing,[57] despite their close advisory association with kings. For since the particular dharma, the *sva-dharma*, of Indian kings was inherently violent, they needed royal chaplains to wash off from their hands, every day, the blood of war dead and executed criminals, and

---

* These are not compliments; Yudhishthira is sometimes regarded, rather like Jimmy Carter, as too good to have been a successful ruler or even as a namby-pamby who didn't want to fight. No mother in India nowadays names her son Yudhishthira, as she might name him Arjuna or even Indra.

they had to perform horse sacrifices to make restorations time after time (horse sacrifices that created yet more violence against animals). The ancient composite image of the royal sage or the warrior priest was compromised once and for all by that division of labor, and all of King Yudhishthira's horses and all of his men could not put those images together again.

Even nonviolence could be violent in India; the urge to refrain from killing animals for food, for instance, or to control violent addiction, often burst out in violence against the self. We have seen the tale of the rabbit in the moon, who offered his own flesh to Indra. This is a variant of a much repeated paradigm, the popularity of which shows us how deeply embedded in Hinduism is the ideal of self-sacrifice, often to the point of martyrdom and self-torture. One of the most famous, and often retold,* examples is this one:

KING SHIBI SAVES THE DOVE FROM THE HAWK

The fame of King Shibi's extraordinary generosity reached the gods in heaven, and Indra and Agni decided to put him to the test. Agni assumed the form of a dove, and Indra a hawk, pursuing the dove. The dove flew in terror to Shibi. But the hawk objected, "I live on the meat of small birds; if you deprive me of my food, you are condemning me to death. Is this dharma?" King Shibi asked the hawk if he would accept some other flesh as a substitute. "Hawks eat doves," countered the hawk, but eventually he said, "If you love this dove, cut off a piece of flesh that weighs as much as the dove." Shibi had a scale brought and sliced off pieces of his flesh, but no matter how much he cut, the dove still weighed more. Finally, he climbed into the scale altogether. The hawk revealed that he was Indra and the dove was Agni, and he promised Shibi that his fame would last forever (3.130–31).

The Shylockian precise pound of flesh and the use of hawks and doves to symbolize military aggression and peacefulness are themes that we can recognize from our own world. In the Pali Buddhist version, King Shibi (sometimes called Shivi) vows to give his living heart, his flesh, his blood, or his eyes to anyone who asks for them; Indra, disguised as a blind Brahmin,[†58] asks him for

---

* In a later version (*Markandeya Purana* 3), Indra takes the form of an aged bird with broken wings and asks a sage for human flesh to eat; the sage asks his four sons to supply it (and their blood to drink, for good measure); they refuse and are cursed to become birds with the power of human speech. The sage offers his own flesh to Indra, who reveals that it was of course, just a test.

† In other variants of the *Mahabharata* text, the dove is also said to be a Brahmin.

his eyes, which Shibi has his court physician cut out, causing him excruciating pain, and gives to him; eventually Indra restores Shibi's eyes.[59] The king's indifference to physical pain is both a macho Kshatriya virtue and a badge of ascetic conquest of the body;[60] as a king Shibi draws upon the Kshatriya tradition, in which the warrior Karna, for instance, pretending to be a Brahmin and wrongly believing that he is in fact a Charioteer's son, betrays his hidden Kshatriya blood by remaining silent and motionless while a worm eats right through his thigh. (He does not want to disturb the sleep of his guru, whose head is resting upon Karna's thigh [12.3]).

The logical reductio ad adsurdum of the vegetarian agenda—letting animals eat one's own body, as in the Other World in the Brahmanas—also results from a combination of the bitter realism of the *Mahabharata* and the challenge of nonviolence. The story of Shibi resolves the aporia by the familiar *illusio ex machina:* There was no dove, no hawk; it was just a test. But in a world where there are, after all, hawks who eat doves, a human may avoid personally taking animal life by eating vegetables. Extending *ahimsa* into a universal law, however, a Kantian *sanatana dharma* beyond the human world (taking into account those screaming carrots and the trees soundlessly screaming), would make most creatures starve to death.

SACRIFICE AND ANTISACRIFICE

Nonviolence toward animals clashes head-on with animal sacrifice. The *Mahabharata* says there are seven wild sacrificial beasts (*pashu*s)*—lion, tiger, boar, monkey, bear, elephant, and buffalo—and seven domestic sacrificial beasts, which we know from the Brahmanas: the usual first four—bull, stallion, billy goat, and ram—plus ass, mule (a mixed breed, bred from a horse and a donkey) and a human man (6.5.12–14). But despite including humans as *pashu*s, the text leans over backward to deny human sacrifice. Krishna says to a king who is threatening to sacrifice a number of captive kings, "What pleasure is there for the kings who are anointed and washed like sacrificial beasts in the house of Pashupati? You have captured kings and you want to sacrifice them to Rudra. . . . No one has ever seen a sacrifice of men. So how can you intend to sacrifice men to the god Shiva? How can you give the title of sacrificial beasts to men of the same species as yourself (2.14.18; 2.20.8–11)."

To prevent human sacrifice, the Brahmanas prescribed a course of substitu-

---

*Though these are all animals that other texts call animals to be hunted, *mriga*s.

tions. In the Vedic myth of the sage who used a horse head to tell the Ashvins about the soma,[61] the head of a horse stood in for the head of a human in a sacrificial beheading. In the *Mahabharata*, which rules out human sacrifice, debate centered on the horse sacrifice, the most spectacular of sacrifices, which reaches so high to heaven that it is the first place where the antisacrificial lightning strikes. Daksha's sacrifice is a horse sacrifice, and so is Yudhishthira's.

YUDHISHTHIRA'S HORSE SACRIFICE

After the final, victorious battle, Yudhishthira renounces his previous desire to renounce kingship and decides to perform a spectacular horse sacrifice, making public his serious intentions for the future: to rule with justice as well as with power. But the ritual also looks backward to the past, expiating his sins and exorcising his grief (as Rama's horse sacrifice does for him). For almost everyone has been killed in the great battle; the Pandava brothers remain alive, Pyrrhic victors, to rule their decimated kingdom. Soon even they will die, after most of their remaining comrades kill one another in a stupid drunken brawl.

The great horse sacrifice of Yudhishthira should be a triumphant event. And to a certain extent it is: The consecrated stallion is set free to roam for a year, guarded by Arjuna, who, in the course of his wanderings, fights a number of battles and kills a number of people (despite Yudhishthira's pleas to him to avoid killing whenever possible) until he himself is killed by his son Babhruvahana and revived by Babhuvahana's mother, Chitrangada.[62] Arjuna and the stallion return safely to the capital; three hundred animal victims, including bulls and birds and aquatic animals, are tied to sacrificial stakes. The Brahmins set some of the animals free, "pacify" others, and "take" and "pacify" (i.e., suffocate) the horse. Draupadi lies down beside the suffocated stallion (14.91.2). (Other wives of other Pandavas, including Arjuna's wives Ulupi and Chitrangada, are present but are not said to lie with the stallion.) The Brahmins remove the fat (or marrow) from the horse and boil it; the Pandavas inhale the fumes, which purify them of all evils. (They do not eat the flesh.) The priests offer the remaining pieces of the horse as oblations into the fire. The ceremony is intended not only to purify the Pandavas but to fortify the kingdom for Yudhishthira and to produce an heir for Arjuna, because Draupadi's five children, one born from each husband, all were killed at the end of the great war. The horse therefore stands not only for Yudhishthira but also for Arjuna. Yudhishthira ascends his throne.

But the success of the sacrifice is undermined by a story told right after it ends and the guests depart. A mongoose came out of his hole there and declared, in a human voice, "This whole sacrifice is not equal to one of the grains of barley that were given by a Brahmin who lived by observing the vow of gleaning."* He then told a story about this Brahmin: During a famine he gave his few remaining grains of barley to a guest who turned out to be Dharma in disguise; the gleaner promptly went to heaven, with his family. When the mongoose finished telling this tale, he vanished (14.92–93), and the storyteller concluded, "Indeed, nonhostility [*adroha*] to all creatures, contentment, clean conduct, *tapas*, self-restraint, truthfulness, and generosity all are regarded as equal (14.94.1)." King Janamejaya, listening to the story, then replied, "Kings are addicted to sacrifice, and sages are addicted to inner heat. The Brahmins busy themselves with pacification, tranquilization, and restraint." He went on to argue that since Indra had become ruler of heaven through sacrifice, surely Yudhishthira, who (with Bhima and Arjuna) resembled Indra in wealth and power, was right to perform the horse sacrifice, and the mongoose was wrong to criticize him. The storyteller then told him another story:

INDRA'S ANIMAL SACRIFICE DEBATE

Once upon a time, Indra began a great sacrifice, involving the slaughter of many animals. But as the sacrificial animals [*pashus*] were seized for slaughter, the great sages saw how wretched they were and were overcome by pity (*kripa*). They said to Indra, "This is not the right way to sacrifice. Domestic animals (*pashus*) were not created for sacrifice. This brutality of yours is destructive of dharma, for injury (*himsa*) cannot be called dharma. Sacrifice instead with seeds of grain that have been kept for three years." But Indra, God of a Hundred Sacrifices, in his delusion and pride, did not agree to their words. They put the matter to King Vasu: "What is the ruling about sacrifice? Should it be done with domestic animals that are designated for sacrifice, or with infertile seeds? With horses or with fruits?" King Vasu, without thinking, said, "You can sacrifice with whatever is at hand," and for saying this, which was not true, he went immediately to hell. For a sacrifice performed with materials wrongly obtained, or with an evil mind, does not yield the fruits of dharma. People—Brahmins, Kshatriyas, Vaishyas, and Shudras—do go to heaven by giving away what they have gleaned, and also by compassion to all creatures, and chastity, and sympathy (14.94.1–34).

---

* Perhaps the same vow that Raikva, the gleaner (or gatherer), followed in the Upanishads.

Indra presumably completes his sacrifice, since he disregards the sages' words. But we are told that he did this not out of wisdom but out of his pride and delusion; King Vasu too is punished for disregarding the sages' question. Janamejaya's pluralism (some people have one addiction; others have another) is not the right answer, but the text never tells us what the right answer would be, because there *is* no right answer. These stories cast a serious shadow of doubt on the glory of the horse sacrifice.

So too the unofficial "black" ritual of witchcraft, the snake sacrifice, shadows both of Yudhishthira's official, "white" rituals, the consecration and the horse sacrifice. The *Mahabharata* sees a vice behind every virtue, a snake behind every horse, and a doomsday behind every victory.

CHAPTER 11
DHARMA IN
THE *MAHABHARATA*
300 BCE to 300 CE

࿔

CHRONOLOGY

c. 300 BCE–300 CE The *Mahabharata* is composed

c. 200 BCE–200 CE The *Ramayana* is composed

327–25 BCE Alexander the Great invades Northwest South Asia

c. 324 BCE Chandragupta founds the Mauryan dynasty

c. 265–232 BCE Ashoka reigns

c. 250 BCE The Third Buddhist Council takes place at Pataliputra

c. 185 BCE The Mauryan dynasty ends

c. 185 BCE Pushyamitra founds the Shunga dynasty

73 BCE The Shunga dynasty ends

c. 150 BCE The monuments of Bharhut and Sanchi are built

c. 166 BCE–78 CE Greeks and Scythians enter India

Dharma is subtle.

> *Mahabharata*, passim

THE SUBTLETY OF DHARMA

Some Hindus will tell you that the *Mahabharata* is about the five Pandava brothers, some that it is about the incarnate god Krishna. But most Hindu traditions will tell you that it is about dharma; sometimes they call it a history (*itihasa*), but sometimes a dharma text (*dharma-shastra*). To say that the long sermons on dharma are a digression from the story, a late and intrusive padding awkwardly stuck onto a zippy epic plot, would be like saying that the arias in a Verdi opera are unwelcome interruptions of the libretto; dharma, like the aria, is the centerpiece, for which the narration (the recitative) is merely the frame.

Time and again when a character finds that every available moral choice is the wrong choice, or when one of the good guys does something obviously very wrong, he will mutter or be told, "Dharma is subtle" (*sukshma*), thin and slippery as a fine silk sari, elusive as a will-o'-the-wisp, internally inconsistent as well as disguised, hidden, masked. People try again and again to do the right thing, and fail and fail, until they no longer know what the right thing is. "What is dharma?" asked Yudhishthira, and did not stay for an answer. As one of the early dharma texts put it, "Right and wrong [dharma and *adharma*] do not go about saying, 'Here we are'; nor do gods, Gandharvas, or ancestors say, 'This is right, that is wrong.'"[1] The *Mahabharata* deconstructs dharma, exposing the inevitable chaos of the moral life.

Dharma had already been somewhat codified from between the third and first centuries BCE, when the *dharma-sutras* set forth, in prose, the rules of social life and religious observance.[2] By now the Brahmins were circling the wagons against the multiple challenges of Buddhist *dhamma* (the teachings of the Buddha), Ashokan *Dhamma* (the code carved on inscriptions and preserved in legends), Upanishadic *moksha*, yoga, and the wildfire growth of Hindu sects. Buddhists presented their own ideas about what they called (in Pali) *dhamma*, ideas that overlapped with but were certainly not the same as Hindu ideas about dharma. Before Buddhism became an issue, there had been no need to define dharma in great detail. But now there was such a need, for the Buddha called his own religion the *dhamma*, and eventually dharma came to mean, among other things, one's religion (so that Hindus would later speak of Christianity as the Christian dharma).

Dharma continued to denote the sort of human activity that leads to human prosperity, victory, and glory, but now it also had much more to do. For now the text was often forced to acknowledge the impossibility of maintaining any sort of dharma at all in a world where every rule seemed to be canceled out by another. The narrators kept painting themselves into a corner with the brush of dharma. Their backs to the wall, they could only reach for another story.

THE KARMA OF DHARMA

Dharma is not merely challenged in the abstract; as a god he is also called to account, for even Dharma has karma, in the sense of the moral consequences of his actions. Dharma (which can often best be translated as "justice") at this time was clearly being assailed on all sides by competing agendas that challenged the justice of justice, as this story does:

MANDAVYA AT THE STAKE

There was once a Brahmin named Mandavya, an expert on dharma, who had kept a vow of silence for a long time. One day robbers hid in his house, and when he refused to break his vow to tell the police where they were, and the police then found the robbers hiding there, the king passed judgment on Mandavya along with the thieves: "Kill him." The executioners impaled the great ascetic on a stake. The Brahmin, who was the very soul of dharma, remained on the stake for a long time. Though he had no food, he did not die; he willed his life's breaths to remain within him, until the king came to him and said, "Greatest of sages, please forgive me for the mistake that I made in my delusion and ignorance." The sage forgave him, and the king had him taken down from the stake. But he was unable to pull the stake out, and so he cut it off at its base, thinking it might come in useful for carrying things like flower baskets. And so he went about with the stake still inside him, in his neck, ribs, and entrails, and people used to call him "Tip-of-the-Stake" Mandavya.

Mandavya went to the house of Dharma and scolded him, saying, "What did I do, without knowing what I had done, something so bad that it earned me such retribution?" Dharma said, "You stuck blades of grass up the tails of little butterflies when you were a child, and this is the fruit of that karma." Then Mandavya said, "For a rather small offense you have given me an enormous punishment. Because of that, Dharma, you will be born as a man, in the womb of a Shudra. And I will establish a moral boundary for the fruition of dharma in the world: no sin will be counted against anyone until the age of fourteen (1.101; cf. 1.57.78–71)."

That the Brahmin who knows dharma is mightier than the king should not surprise anyone who has been following the Vedic texts, but that a man who trots around cheerfully with a stake through his intestines is mightier even than the god Dharma himself is worthy of note. The moral law is stupid—children should not be so grotesquely punished for their mischief, even when it involves cruelty to insects—and so the moral law must undergo its own expiation. Dharma, the god, must undergo the curse for miscarriage of dharma. Being born as a human is different both from fathering a child (as Dharma fathers Yudhishthira) and from spinning off an incarnation (as Vishnu does for Rama and Krishna), for when Dharma is born on earth (as Vidura; see below), he ceases to exist in heaven until Vidura dies; that is the nature of the curse. That being born of a Shudra is a terrible curse, one from which you cannot escape in this life, is an attitude that endorses the extant class system. On the other hand, the *Mahabharata* challenges that system by imagining that the moral law might become incarnate in a person born of a woman of the lowest class, a Shudra mother. It also implicitly challenges the ideal of nonviolence toward animals, implying that you can take it too far; people are not the same as animals, and so impaling a butterfly (anally) is not as serious as impaling a man (also anally, by implication).

THE TRANSFER OF KARMA

That even Dharma has karma is an indication of how powerful a force karma had become. Buddhism in this period was already preaching the transfer of merit from one person to another, and early Hindu texts too had hinted at such a possibility. The *Mahabharata* totters on the brink of a full-fledged concept of the transfer of karma, in a passage that takes up the story after Yudhishthira has entered heaven (with Dharma, no longer incarnate as a dog). There he was in for an unpleasant surprise:

YUDHISHTHIRA IN HEAVEN AND HELL

When Yudhishthira, the dharma king, reached the triple-tiered heaven, he did not see his brothers or Draupadi. He asked where his brothers were, and Draupadi, and the gods commanded their messenger to take him to them. The messenger took Yudhishthira to hell, where he saw hideous tortures. Unable to abide the heat and the stench of corpses, he turned to go, but then he heard the voices of his brothers and Draupadi crying, "Stay here, as a favor to us, just for a little while. A sweet breeze from your body wafts over us and brings us relief." Yudhishthira wondered if he was dreaming or out of his mind, but he determined to stay there, to help them.

The gods, with Dharma himself, came to him, and everything disappeared—the darkness, the tortures, everything. Indra said to Yudhishthira, "My son, inevitably all kings must see hell. People who have a record of mostly bad deeds enjoy the fruits of their good deeds first, in heaven, and go to hell afterward. Others experience hell first and go afterward to heaven. You saw hell, and your brothers and Draupadi all went to hell, just in the form of a deception. Come now to heaven." And Dharma said, "I tested you before by taking on the form of a dog, and now this was another test, for you chose to stay in hell for the sake of your brothers." And so Yudhishthira went with Dharma and the gods, and plunged into the heavenly Ganges, and shed his human body. And then he stayed there with his brothers and Draupadi. Eventually, they all reached the worlds beyond which there is nothing (18.1–5).

Yudhishthira's ability to ease his brothers' torments takes the form of a cool, sweet breeze that counteracts the hot, putrid air of hell, through a kind of transfer of merit.* He therefore wants to stay with his brothers in hell, even though he himself does not belong there, just as he wanted to stay with the dog outside heaven, again where he did not belong. Elsewhere in the *Mahabharata* (3.128), when a king wants to take over the guilt of his priest in hell (an interesting role reversal: The priest had sacrificed a child so that the king could get a hundred sons), Dharma protests, "No one ever experiences the fruit of another person's deed." The king, however, insists on living in hell along with the priest for the same term, and eventually both he and the priest go to heaven. He does not save the priest from suffering, but he suffers with him. In the case of Yudhishthira in hell, this time no one tries to persuade him; they all learned how stubborn he was the last time. What, then, is the solution? A sure sign of a moral impasse in any narrative is the invocation of the "it was just a dream" motif at the end, erasing the aporia entirely. Another is the deus ex machina. The *Mahabharata* invokes both here, a double red flag (triple if we count the two gods plus the illusion).

But the illusory cop-out—it wasn't really a dog; it wasn't really hell—is contradicted by the need for people to expiate their sins in a real hell. The heroes go to hell, go to heaven, and in the end go on to worlds "beyond which there is nothing," a phrase that speaks in the tantalizing negatives of the Upanishads and leaves us in the dark about the nature of those worlds. Janamejaya, to whom the story is told, asks a set of questions about the "levels of existence" (*gatis*)—that is, the various sorts of lives into which one can be reborn: "How long did the Pandavas remain in heaven? Or did they perhaps have a place there that would last forever? Or at the end of their karma what level of existence did they reach? (18.5.4–5)." The bard does not really answer these questions, but the reference to the worlds "beyond which there is nothing" and

---

* There is a rough parallel to this idea in the Catholic practice of offering up your suffering to shorten the sentences of souls in purgatory.

the fact that they are not said to be reborn on earth imply that their karma did come to an end, in worlds that are the equivalent of *moksha*. The authors of the *Mahabharata* are thinking out loud, still trying to work it all out. They are keeping their minds open, refusing to reach a final verdict on a subject—the complex function of karma—on which the jury is still out.

DHARMA, MOKSHA, AND BHAKTI IN THE GITA

Dharma needed all the subtlety it could muster to meet the challenges of Buddhism but even more those of *moksha*, which had made major headway since the early Upanishads. Ideas about both dharma and *moksha* had been in the air for centuries, but now they were brought into direct confrontation with each other, in the *Bhagavad Gita*.

The *Gita* is a conversation between Krishna and Arjuna on the brink of the great battle. Krishna had been gracious enough to offer to be Arjuna's charioteer, an inferior position, though appropriate to Krishna's quasi-Brahmin nature.* Arjuna, assailed by many of the doubts that plagued Ashoka,[3] asks Krishna a lot of difficult, indeed unanswerable age-old questions about violence and nonviolence, this time in the context of the battlefield, questioning the necessity of violence for warriors. The sheer number of different reasons that Krishna gives to Arjuna, including the argument that since you cannot kill the soul, killing the body in war (like killing an animal in sacrifice) is not really killing, is evidence for the author's deep disquiet about killing and the need to justify it. The moral impasse is not so much resolved as blasted away when after Krishna has given a series of complex and rather abstract answers, Arjuna asks him to *show* him his true cosmic nature. Krishna shows him his doomsday form, and Arjuna cries out, "I see your mouths with jagged tusks, and I see all of these warriors rushing blindly into your gaping mouths, like moths rushing to their death in a blazing fire. Some stick in the gaps between your teeth, and their heads are ground to powder (11.25–290)." And right in the middle of the terrifying epiphany, Arjuna apologizes to Krishna for all the times that he

---

* As the priest Vrisha had served as the charioteer for King Tryaruna. Closer still, the reader (or hearer) would recall an earlier episode in the *Mahabharata* (in the *Virata Parvan*, book 4), where Arjuna, disguised as an effeminate dancing master, serves as the charioteer for a cowardly prince. In that mock *Gita*, the inversion of power and status (the great warrior as lowly charioteer) foreshadows that of the *Gita*, in which as Arjuna was to the prince, so Krishna is to Arjuna, a creature of great destructive power who velvets his claws for the sake of human affection.

had rashly and casually called out to him, saying, "Hey, Krishna! Hey, pal!" He begs the god to turn back into his pal Krishna, which the god consents to do.

The worshiper (represented by Arjuna) is comforted by the banality, the familiarity of human life, but inside the text, the warrior with ethical misgivings has been persuaded to kill, just as the god kills, and outside the text, the reader or hearer has been persuaded that since war is unreal, it is not evil. And this political message is made palatable by the god's resumption of his role as an intimate human companion. The *Mahabharata* as a whole is passionately against war, vividly aware of the tragedy of war, despite the many statements that violence is necessary. Nor, despite the way that Krishna persuades Arjuna to fight, is the *Gita* used in India to justify war; it is generally taken out of context and used only for its philosophy, which can be used to support arguments for peace, as, notably, in the hands of Gandhi.

Krishna's broader teaching in the *Gita* resolves the tension between dharma and *moksha* by forming a triad with bhakti (worship, love, devotion) as the third member, mediating between the other two terms of the dialectic. When Arjuna can choose neither dharma (he doesn't want to kill his relatives) nor renunciation (he is a Kshatriya), Krishna offers him a third alternative, devotion. The *Gita* sets out a paradigm of three paths (*marga*s) to salvation, also called three yogas: karma (works, rituals), *jnana* (cognate with "knowledge" and "gnosis"), and bhakti (2.49, 3.3). Karma contains within it the worldly Vedic path of rebirth, the world of dharma (here, as elsewhere, functioning as the equivalent of *sva-dharma*), in contrast with *jnana*, which represents the meditational, transcendent Vedantic path of Release, the world of *moksha.** Bhakti bridges the conflicting claims of the original binary opposition between what Luther would have called works (karma) and faith (*jnana*). But each member of the triad of *jnana*, karma, and bhakti was regarded by its adherents as the best, if not the only, path to salvation. One way in which bhakti modifies *moksha* is by introducing into the Upanishadic formula—that you are *brahman* (the divine substance of the universe)—a god with qualities (*sa-guna*) who allows you to love the god without qualities (*nir-guna*). By acting with devotion to Krishna, Arjuna is freed from the hellish consequences of his actions.

---

* The *Gita* also recapitulates the Upanishadic idea of the third path of no return: Krishna says that he hurls cruel, hateful men into demonic wombs in birth after birth, so that they never reach him but go the lowest way to hell (16.19–20).

The *Gita* employs some Buddhist terminology ("nirvana," for instance, the blowing out of a flame, which is a more Buddhist way of saying *moksha*), and Arjuna starts out with what might appear to be a quasi-Buddhist attitude that Krishna demolishes. But "nirvana" is also a Hindu word (found, for example, in the Upanishads), and it is the tension within Hinduism itself that the *Gita* is addressing, the challenge to assimilate the ascetic ideal into the ideology of an upper-class householder.[4] The *Gita*'s brilliant solution to this problem is to urge Arjuna (and the reader/hearer of the *Gita*) to renounce not the actions but their fruits, to live with "karma without *kama*," actions without desires. This is a way to maintain a renouncer's state of mind, a spiritual state of mind, in the midst of material life, a kind of moral Teflon that blocks the consequences of actions. "Karma without *kama*" means not that one should not desire certain results from one's actions, but merely that one should not expect the results (for so much is out of our control) or, more important, regard the results as the point; it's the journey that counts, not where you end up.* In the *Gita*, this means that each of us must perform our own *sva-dharma*—in Arjuna's case, to kill his kinsmen in battle—with the attitude of a renunciant. This is a far cry from the social ethics of Buddhism. "Had the Buddha been the charioteer," says Romila Thapar, "the message would have been different."[5]

CASTE AND CLASS CONFLICTS

The adherence to one's own dharma that the *Gita* preaches is part of a new social system that was taking shape at this time,[6] the system of castes, which could not be neatly and automatically subsumed as subcategories of classes (though Manu tried to do it [10.8–12]). Class (*varna*) and caste (*jati*) began to form a single, though not yet a unified, social system. New communities were beginning to coalesce, their identities defined by a shared occupation and caste status, or by religious sectarian affiliation, or by the use of a particular language.[7] Most of the castes probably derived from clans or guilds, in which, increasingly, families specialized in professions. (The Sanskrit word for caste, *jati*, means "birth.") But other castes might have consisted of alien sects, tribes, and professions, of people of various geographical, sectarian, and economic factions. Now invaders like the Shakas or Kushanas and tribal forest dwellers like the Nishadas, as well as other

---

* Fast-forward: In the 2000 film *The Legend of Bagger Vance,* loosely based on the *Gita,* with golf taking the place of war (though the hero has been traumatized by World War I), the Krishna figure (played by Will Smith) describes to [Ar]Junuh (Matt Damon), for whom he is the caddie (charioteer), the feeling of karma without *kama* as playing in the zone, a great analogy.

groups on the margins of settled society, could also be absorbed into a specific caste (*jati*), often of uncertain class (*varna*), or sometimes into a class, mainly Kshatriya for rulers, seldom Brahmins. Tribes such as Nishadas and Chandalas sometimes seem to have amounted to a fifth *varna* of their own.[8]

The division of society into castes facilitated the inclusion of new cultures and groups of people who could eventually be filed away in the open shelving of the caste system, "slotted into the caste hierarchy, their position being dependent on their occupation and social origins, and on the reason for the induction."[9] This was an effective way to harness the energies and loyalties of skilled indigenous people who were conquered, subordinated, or encroached upon by a society that already observed class distinctions. For while the system of classes (*varnas*) was already a theoretical mechanism for assimilation,[10] the system of castes (*jatis*) now offered the practical reality of a form of integration,[11] from outside the system to inside it. Caste thus paved the way for other conversions, such as that of Hindus to Buddhism or Jainism or to the new non-Vedic forms of Hinduism—renunciant or sectarian.

Many of the assimilated castes were Shudras, who were excluded from participating in the Vedic rituals but often had their own rituals and worshiped their own gods.[12] Below the Shudras were the so-called polluted castes; beside, rather than below them, were the tribals and unassimilated aliens (*mlecchas*). The logic of class placed some tribal groups in a castelike category, albeit one standing outside the caste hierarchy; tribals are relegated not to a distinct level within a vertical structure, but rather to a horizontal annex that could not be integrated into any cubbyhole in the system.[13] But some tribals are peculiarly intimate outsiders, recognized as neighbors whom the system can ultimately assimilate within the system more easily than alien invaders like Turks or Europeans. The system of castes was rationalized through an ideology of purity and pollution that was applied to the subgroups, both ethnic and professional, within the four classes. As some professions were defined as purer than others, the hierarchy took over.

Like the Buddhists and Jainas, many of the new sects disavowed caste or at least questioned its assumptions.[14] At the same time, there was an increasing tendency, which Ashoka did much to popularize, to define a dharma that could be all things to all men, a dharma/*dhamma* so general (*sadharana*, "held in common"), so perpetual (*sanatana*) that it applied to all right-thinking people always, transcending the differences between various sects. And though the Brahmins quickly manipulated the system to keep individuals from moving up in the hierarchy of castes, vertical mobility was possible for the caste as a whole, if the entire group changed its work and, sometimes, its location. In this way, a particular caste might begin as a Shudra caste and eventually become a Brahmin caste. Some of the assimilated castes did become Brahmins, Kshatriyas, or Vaishyas and thus had access to the rites of the twice born. So many kings were of Shudra or Brahmin origin rather than Kshatriyas that by the time the Muslim rulers reached India they found it difficult to make a correct identification of either a class or a caste among their opposite numbers.[15]

The *Mahabharata* both challenges and justifies the entire class structure. The word for "class" (*varna*) here begins to draw upon its other meaning of "color." In the course of one of the long discussions of dharma, one sage says to another: "Brahmins are fair [white], Kshatriyas ruddy [red], Vaishyas sallow [yellow], and Shudras dark [black]." The adjectives can denote either skin color or the four primary colors that are symbolically associated with the four classes,[16] as well as with the three qualities of matter plus yellow (saffron? ocher?) for the transcendent fourth of spirit. In one passage, someone asks a sage a series of questions that show us something of the perceived need, at this time, newly to justify the (mis)treatment of the lower classes:

THE ORIGIN OF CLASS COLORS

"If different colors distinguish different classes among the four classes, how is it that there is a mixture of colors in all classes? Desire, anger, fear, greed, sorrow, worry, hunger, and exhaustion affect all of us. How then are the classes distinguished? Sweat, urine, feces, phlegm, mucus, and blood flow out of all our bodies. How then are the classes distinguished? And how can you tell one class from another among all the species [*jati*] of the countless creatures, moving and still, that have such various colors?" The sage replied: "Actually, there *is* no difference between the classes; this whole universe is made of *brahman*. But when the creator emitted it long ago, actions/karmas divided it into classes. Those Brahmins who were fond of enjoying pleasures, quick to anger and impetuous in their affections, abandoned their own dharma and became Kshatriyas, with red bodies. Those who took up herding cattle and engaged in plowing, and did not follow their own dharma, became yellow Vaishyas. And those who were greedy and fond of violence (*himsa*) and lies, living on all sorts of activities, fallen from purity, became black Shudras. And that's how these actions/karmas split off the Brahmins into a different class, for there was never any interruption of their dharma and their sacrificial rituals (12.181.5–14).

The implication is that in the beginning, everyone had not only the same general physical makeup (the Shylock argument: Cut us and we bleed) and the same general dharma of good behavior, but the same *sva-dharma*, "one's own-dharma," the particular dharma of each class (and, later, each caste), and that that primeval *sva-dharma* was the *sva-dharma* of Brahmins: maintaining dharma and sacrificial rituals. But then each of the other classes voluntarily took up other activities— the Kshatriyas indulged in pleasure and anger (a contradiction of the earlier statement that we all share these emotions), the Vaishyas in commerce, and the Shudras in violent and unclean professions—leaving the Brahmins alone in possession of the original dharma that had been meant for everyone, that had been intended as, in effect, the common (*sadharana*) dharma.

Krishna's declaration to Arjuna in the *Gita* that "it is better to do your own duty poorly than another's well" (echoed in *Manu* [10.97]) ignored the fact that Arjuna's own duty as a warrior would forever doom him to relative inferiority vis-à-vis Brahmins whose *sva-dharma* just happened to conform with the universal dharma that dictated nonviolence. Here is the catch-22 that Manu perpetuates: the hierarchically superior prototype is also the generalizable archetype. Although, in reality, power was largely in the hands of the rulers, the Brahmin imaginary relegated the violent ruler to a place inferior to that of the nonviolent prototype, the Brahmin.

The conversation about the colors thus brings the argument for equality into the open—where it must have been at this time, when various social barriers were being challenged—but the old argument from creation comes to the rescue, and the class differences are affirmed in new ways. Now the class system is not created ab initio, by the gods, as in the Vedic "Poem of the Primeval Man"; now it results from the bad karmic choices of the classes themselves. It's their own damn fault. This is a major transition from authoritative decree to apologia.

THE NISHADAS

The four classes were the central concern of a broader social agenda that included (by excluding) both Pariahs (even lower than the Shudras) and tribal people, epitomized by the Nishadas. A typically cold-blooded disregard of the Nishadas is evident in a story told early in the *Mahabharata*:

THE HOUSE OF LAC

When the Pandavas were still young, and living with their mother, Kunti, their enemies tricked them into staying in a highly combustible house made of lac [a kind of natural resin], which they intended to burn. Yudhishthira decided that they should put six people in the house, set fire to it, and escape. Kunti held a feast to which she invited a hungry Nishada woman and her five sons. The Nishadas got drunk and remained after the other guests had left; the Pandavas set fire to the house and escaped, and when the townspeople found the charred remains of the innocent Nishada woman and her five sons, they assumed that the Pandavas were dead (1.134–37).

Only the single word "innocent" ("without wrongdoing" [1.137.7]) suggests the slightest sympathy for the murdered Nishadas. They are sacrificial substitutes, whom the author of this text treats as expendable because he regards them as subhuman beings. Perhaps their drunkenness (one of the four addictive vices of lust) is meant to justify their deaths.

A somewhat more sympathetic story about Nishadas is the tale of Ekalavya:

EKALAVYA CUTS OFF HIS THUMB

Drona was the Pandavas' archery tutor, and Arjuna was his star pupil. One day a boy named Ekalavya, the son of a tribal Nishada chieftain, came to them. When Drona, who knew dharma, refused to accept the son of a Nishada as a pupil, Ekalavya touched his head to Drona's feet, went out into the jungle, and made a clay image of Drona, to which he paid the respect due a teacher. He practiced intensely and became a great archer. One day the Pandavas went out hunting with their dog. The dog wandered off, came upon Ekalavya, and stood there barking at him until the Nishada shot seven arrows almost simultaneously into the dog's mouth. The dog went whimpering back to the Pandavas, who were amazed and went to find the man who had accomplished this feat. They found him and asked him who he was, and he told them he was the Nishada Ekalavya, a pupil of Drona's.

They went home, but Arjuna kept thinking about Ekalavya, and one day he asked Drona why he had a pupil, the son of a Nishada, who was an even better archer than he, Arjuna. Drona then resolved to do something about this. He took Arjuna with him to see Ekalavya, and when he found him, he said to Ekalavya, "If you are my pupil, pay me my fee right now." Ekalavya, delighted, said, "Command me, my guru. There is nothing I will not give my guru." Drona replied, "Give me your right thumb." When Ekalavya heard this terrible speech from Drona, he kept his promise. His face showed his joy in it, and his mind was entirely resolved to do it. He cut off his thumb and gave it to Drona. And after that, when the Nishada shot an arrow, his fingers were not so quick as before. Arjuna was greatly relieved (1.123.10–39).

This is a brutal story, even for the *Mahabharata*. How are we to understand it? First of all, who is Ekalavya? He is a prince among his own people, but that wins him no points with the Pandava princes. The Nishadas here embrace Hindu dharma and Hindu forms of worship but are still beneath the contempt of the caste system. For such a person to stand beside the Pandava princes in archery classes was unthinkable; that is what Drona, who "knew dharma," realized.

In order to protect both dharma and the reputation of his own world-class archery student, Drona claims his retroactive tuition, the *guru-dakshina*. Of course we are shocked; to add insult to injury, Drona really didn't teach Ekalavya at all and hardly deserves any tuition fees, let alone such a grotesque payment. But where is the author's sympathy? It is hard to be sure. It is arrogant of Ekalavya to push in where he does not belong; he cannot be a noble archer, for he was born into the wrong family for nobility. But Ekalavya does not act arrogant. His outward appearance invokes all the conventional tropes for tribals: he is described as black, wrapped in black deerskin, hair all matted, dressed in rags, his body caked with dirt. He is made of the wrong stuff (or, as we would say, has the wrong genes). He is physically dirt. But his inner soul, reflected in his behavior, is pious and respectful; he does what the teacher tells him to do; not only is he a brilliant archer, but he is honest and humble. To this extent, at least, the *Mahabharata* likes him and presumably pities him; it refers to Drona's command as "terrible" (*daruna*).

Yet the act by which Ekalavya proves his mettle as an archer is one of gratuitous and grotesque cruelty to a dog, the animal that is in many ways the animal counterpart, even the totem, of a Nishada. The dog barks at him, betraying the class attitude that dogs often pick up from their masters; the dog doesn't like the way Ekalavya looks and, probably, smells. Does Ekalavya's unsympathetic treatment of this dog cancel out our sympathy for Ekalavya as the victim of interhuman violence? Does it justify Drona's cruel treatment of him—what goes around comes around, travels down the line—or, at least, remind us of the cruelty inherent in the *sva-dharma* of a hunter? But the text shows no sympathy for the dog and therefore no condemnation of Ekalavya for his treatment of the dog.

Here, as in the tale of Yudhishthira's dog, the story shows just how rotten the caste system is but does not change it. No dogs get into heaven; Ekalavya loses his thumb. I read the text as deeply conflicted; it assumes that this is the way things must be, but it does not like the way things must be. It paints Ekalavya sympathetically despite itself. If we compare this story with the *Ramayana* tale of Shambuka, we can see one significant difference: The central episode of mutilation of an uppity low-caste man is no longer framed and balanced by another story (the revival of a child) or by the interloper's evil goal (usurping the gods' privileges). The basic point is the same as for Shambuka—don't get ideas above your station—but here it is starker, unjustified by anything but uppitiness. And where we learned nothing at all about Shambuka but his class, now Ekalavya's physical repulsiveness is contrasted with his high moral qualities. Is this progress? Perhaps. It shows a more complex view of dharma, though it still upholds that dharma.[17]

In the face of his defense of the class system, the author of this story saw the humanity in Ekalavya, saw that tribals were human beings of dignity and honor. It doesn't necessarily mean that tribals tried to break into the professions of Kshatriyas. Nor does it mean that Kshatriyas went around cutting off the thumbs of tribals. It means that the author of this text imagined the situation and was troubled by it. The people who heard and, eventually, read the text must have seen that too; maybe some of them, as a result, treated the tribals whom they encountered with more humanity. The imagination of a better world may have made it a better world.

Moreover, during the long history of both this story and the story of the Nishada woman and her sons, different people did read the story differently; the reading of the Brahmin imaginary was certainly not the only one. This is a moment that justifies a bit of fast-forwarding. There is a Jaina text from the sixteenth century CE that begins much like the *Mahabharata* story of Ekalavya but then gives the protagonist a different name and a different tribe (a Bhil or Bhilla, even more scorned than a Nishada) and veers in a very different direction:

> In Hastinapura, Arjuna learned the entire science of archery from Drona and
> became as it were another image [*murti*] of Drona, and honored him with many
> gems, pearls, gold, elephants, horses, and so forth. The guru said to him, "Arjuna,
> choose a boon." Arjuna replied, "Sir, if you are satisfied with me, let there be no
> one but me who knows such a science of archery." Thinking, "The words of great

gurus can never fail to come true," Drona agreed. One day, a certain Bhil named Bhimala, living on the banks of the Ganges, came and asked Drona to be his guru; obtaining his promise, he went back to his own place and made an image of Drona out of mud, and honored it with flowers and sandalwood and so forth, and said, "Drona, give me the knowledge of archery," and practiced the science of archery in front of him. And with his mind and heart full of the emotion of passionate devotion to him [bhakti], the Bhil after a certain time became like a second Arjuna.

One day, Arjuna, following Drona, who had gone in front to take a bath in the Ganges, saw that the mouth of his own dog was filled with arrows that had not pierced his upper lip, lower lip, palate, tongue, or teeth. Thinking, "No one but me has such a power," he was amazed, and going forward by following along the arrows from his dog's mouth, he saw Bhimala and asked him, "Who shot these arrows into the dog's mouth?" "I did." "Who is your guru?" The Bhil said, "Drona is my guru." Hearing that, Arjuna reported this to Drona and then said, "Hey, master. If people like you leap over the boundary markers of words, then what can we wretched creatures do?"

Drona went there and asked the Bhil, "Where is your guru?" and the Bhil showed him the representation that he himself had made and told him what he had done, saying, "Arjuna! This is the fruit of my bhakti." But the sneaky, cheating Arjuna said to him, "Bhil, with your great zeal, you must do *puja* with the thumb of your right hand for this Drona whom you met through us." The Bhil said, "Yes," and did it. But then the guru said, "Arjuna! You are a sneaky urban crook, and you have deceived this artless, honest, unsophisticated forest dweller. But by my favor, even without a thumb these people will be able to shoot arrows." And as he said this, the guru gave the Bhil this favor and went back to his own place. And so, even today, a Bhil can shoot arrows using his middle finger and his forefinger.[18]

The entire moral weight has shifted; now it is Arjuna, not Drona, who makes the cruel demand, and Drona who objects to it and who calls Arjuna deceitful and cunning, in contrast with the artless, honest Bhil, who does *not* hurt the dog, as the text takes pains to tell us. Indeed Drona has agreed to be the Bhil's guru at the start and, at the end, grants him superior skill in archery, despite Arjuna's attempts to hobble him. The image of Drona that the Bhil makes of mud is now matched by other flesh and blood images: Arjuna *is* the image of

Drona, and the Bhil *is* the image of Arjuna, hence of Drona, once removed. Altogether, the Bhil, with his grotesque guru gift (no longer a Vedic tuition gift, but a Hindu *puja*), comes off smelling like a rose, and Arjuna, with his gift of gold and precious jewels and horses and elephants, does not.

The forefinger is called the *tarjaniya*, the finger that points, that accuses, and here it points straight at Arjuna. Knowing all this, we can see other possible multiple readings of the story even in the *Mahabharata*. For there is a two-way conversation going on between the Hindu and Jaina texts, an intertextual conversation. The Jaina text quotes the Hindu *Mahabharata*, an example of the widespread intertextuality between religions in India, not just within Hinduism. But Hindus would probably know the Jaina version too, a supposition justifiable on the basis of our understanding of the relationship between Hindus and Jainas at this period, and this may have contributed to the eventual use of the story of Ekalavya by contemporary Hindu Pariahs, for whom he is an important hero.

Whatever the spirit in which the tale of Ekalavya was originally told, it continued to be remembered among people crying out for social reform. A glance at later versions of the same story supports some of the hypothetical meanings that I have hunted out of the original telling and suggests, but certainly does not prove, that the seed of that later response may already have been there in the Sanskrit text (hindsight alert!), or at least that there may have been other readings of this episode besides the original one we have, with other evidence of moral conscience, to bridge the gap between the first recorded telling and later versions that explicitly call out for justice.

Whether the situation was equally encouraging for women is a subject that we must now consider.

WOMEN

The women of the *Mahabharata* are extraordinarily prominent, feisty, and individualistic, in part as a result of changes that were taking place in the social structures at the time of the recension of the text (such as the widespread public recognition of women as donors and renouncers, and their more active role in the *pujas* of sectarian Hinduism), in part as a result of the infusion of the Sanskrit corpus with stories from village and rural traditions that were less hidebound in their attitudes to women. The new attention paid to women in the *Mahabharata* emerges clearly from the stories of the births of both its legendary author, Vyasa, and its heroes:

THE BIRTH OF VYASA

Once a fisherman caught a fish, found a baby girl in its belly, and raised her as his daughter. A powerful Brahmin sage seduced the fisherman's daughter, Satyavati, as she ferried him across the river. She gave birth to her first son, Vyasa, on an island in the river and abandoned him (he had instantly grown to manhood). The sage restored her virginity (and removed her fishy smell) (1.57.32–75).

Vyasa is of mixed lineage, not merely Brahmin and Kshatriya (for though Satyavati's mother was a fish, her father was a king; it's a long story) but human and animal (for his grandparents were a Kshatriya, a female fish, and, presumably, a Brahmin man and woman). This double miscegenation will be repeated several times, always with variations, in this lineage.

The birth of Vyasa's natural sons (Satyavati's grandsons) is more complex and correspondingly more subtly problematic:

THE BIRTH OF VYASA'S CHILDREN

Satyavati later married King Shantanu and gave birth to another son, who became king but died childless, leaving two widows, the Kshatriya princesses Ambika and Ambalika. Satyavati, who did not want the lineage to end, summoned Vyasa to go to the beds of the two widows in order to father children with his half brother's widows. Vyasa was ugly and foul-smelling; his beard was red, his hair orange. Since Ambika closed her eyes when she conceived her son, Dhritarashtra, Vyasa cursed him to be born blind. Ambalika turned pale and conceived Pandu the Pale. When Vyasa was sent to Ambika a second time, she sent in her place a slave girl [*dasi*]. The girl gave Vyasa great pleasure in bed, and he spent the whole night with her; she gave birth to a healthy son, Vidura, but since his mother was not a Kshatriya, he could not be king (1.99–100).

Though Hindu law allows the levirate (*niyoga*), the law by which a brother begets children on behalf of his dead or impotent brother (the *Artha-shastra* [3.4.27–41] says any male in the family can do it), it is often, as here, disastrous.[19] Vyasa appears in the *Mahabharata* as a kind of walking semen bank, the author both of the story of the Pandavas and of the Pandavas themselves (just as Valmiki not only invents the poetic form of the *Ramayana*, the *shloka*, but tells the story and raises, though he does not beget, the poets). The widows reject him because he is old and ugly and smells fishy, a characteristic that he apparently took from his mother when she lost it. He is also the wrong color, and this, plus the mother's temporary pallor, results in the birth of a child, Pandu, who is the wrong color—perhaps an albino, perhaps sickly, perhaps a euphemism for his future impotence.[20] Dhritarashtra's mother-to-be closes her eyes (and, presumably, thinks of Hastinapur), and so her son is blind. A slave girl who functions as a dispensable, low-class stand-in (like the Nishadas burned in the house of lac) gives birth to Vidura, the incarnation of Dharma in fulfillment of Mandavya's curse that he should be born as the son of a Shudra woman. Where Rama and his brothers have different mothers and different wives but share both a single human father and a single divine father, the five Pandavas have one mother (and one wife) and one human father but different divine fathers.

In this disastrous levirate, two wives give birth to three sons (two of whom have, for great-grandparents, a female fish, two Brahmins, and five Kshatriyas, while the third has a Kshatriya, a female fish, two Brahmins, and four slaves. Are you still with me?). In fact the arrangement was originally more symmetrical, for there had been a third woman, Amba,* who had been carried off by Bhishma, yet another son of Satyavati's husband Shantanu (it's another long story†); but she departs before Vyasa arrives on the scene, and she eventually dies in a complex transsexual act of revenge against Bhishma (yet another long story).[21] Ambika's and Ambalika's hatred of their surrogate lover, though much milder than Amba's hatred of Bhishma, results not in their deaths or his but in a confusion over the throne, because the women's recoiling from Vyasa results in physical disabilities in their children that disqualify them from the kingship: blindness, pallor, and low class. This confusion leads to war and ultimately to the destruction of almost all the descendants of Pandu and Dhritarashtra.

The *Mahabharata* goes on to tell us how in the next generation, Pandu was cursed to die if he ever made love with any of his wives, for having mistaken a mating man for a mating stag (1.90.64; 1.109.5–30). Fortunately, Pandu's wife, Kunti, had a mantra that allowed her to invoke gods as proxy fathers of Pandu's

---

* Amba is clearly the basic name, of which Ambika and Ambalika are variants. These are the names of the three queens that Vedic texts describe as pantomiming copulation with the dead stallion who pinch-hits for the king in the horse sacrifice, just as Vyasa is pinch-hitting for his half brother, the dead king.
† The goddess Ganges marries Shantanu but kills the first seven of their children (actually doing them a favor, for they are immortals cursed to be born on earth); like Saranyu, Urvashi, and Sita, she is an immortal woman who leaves her mortal husband when he violates their agreement, in this case by rescuing the eighth child, Bhishma.

sons: Dharma (who fathered Yudhishthira*), the Wind (father of Bhima), and Indra (father of Arjuna) (1.90, 1.101). Kunti then generously lent her mantra to Madri, Pandu's second wife, who invoked the Ashvins to father the twins Nakula and Sahadeva. Years later Pandu seduced Madri one day when he was overcome by desire for her; he died, in fulfillment of the stag's curse and in imitation of the stag's death: a fatal coitus interruptus, the sweet death transformed into a bitter death.

But Kunti had already had one son, secretly, out of wedlock. When she was still a young girl, she had decided to try out her mantra, just fooling around. The sun god, Surya, took her seriously; despite her vigorous protests and entreaties, he raped her and afterward restored her virginity. She gave birth to Karna, whom she abandoned in shame; a Charioteer and his wife adopted him and raised him as their own (1.104; 3.290–94; 5.144.1–9). Karna is in many ways the inverse of Vidura: Where Vidura is an incarnate god, raised royally, and has both a surrogate father (Vyasa) and a surrogate mother (the maid in place of Ambika), Karna is of royal birth, raised as a servant, and has a divine father (Surya), a royal mother (Kunti), and two low-class surrogate parents (the Charioteers).

Beneath the sterile or impotent fathers lie angry women. The lineage of the heroes is a series of seductions and rapes: of Satyavati, Amba, Ambika, Ambalika, Kunti, and Madri. For Satyavati and Kunti, the seducer or rapist restores the woman's virginity afterward, and the resulting children are abandoned, as if to erase the entire incident or at least to exculpate the women.

POLYANDRY

Other events in the lives of these women suggest their unprecedented and, alas, never again duplicated freedom.

Polyandry (multiple husbands) is rampant in the *Mahabharata*, and the text offers us, in four consecutive generations, positive images of women who had several sexual partners (sometimes premarital). Satyavati has two sexual partners (her legitimate husband, Shantanu, and the sage who fathers Vyasa on the island). Ambika and Ambalika have two legitimate partners (the king who dies and Vyasa, through the levirate). Kunti has one husband (Pandu, legitimate but

---

* Thus Dharma is incarnate in one of the three sons of Vyasa in the generation of the fathers (Vidura), and he fathers one of the sons (Yudhishthira) of another of those fathers (Pandu).

unconsummated) and four sexual partners (gods, quasilegitimate). Madri has three partners (Pandu, legitimate and fatally consummated, and two quasi-legitimate gods). Another *Mahabharata* queen, named Madhavi, sells herself to four kings in succession, for several hundred horses each time, and restores her own virginity after each encounter (5.113–17). But the prize goes to Draupadi, who has five legitimate husbands, the five Pandavas. Her polyandrous pentad is truly extraordinary, for though polygyny (multiple wives) was the rule, and men could have several spouses throughout most of Hindu history (as, indeed, each of the Pandavas, except Yudhishthira, had at least one wife in addition to Draupadi; Arjuna had three more), women most decidedly could not. Since there is no other evidence that women at this time actually had multiple husbands, these stories can only be suggestive, if not incontrovertible, evidence either of women's greater sexual freedom or, perhaps, of men's fears of what might happen were women to have that freedom. Draupadi's hypersexuality may simply have validated an ideal that was understood to be out of reach for ordinary women, imagined precisely in order to be disqualified as a viable option. What else, then, can these stories mean?

Hindus at this period were apparently troubled by Draupadi's polyandry, for which the *Mahabharata* gives two different excuses (always a cause for suspicion). First, it says that Arjuna won Draupadi in a contest and brought her home to present her to his mother; as he and his brothers approached the house, they called out, "Look what we got!" and she, not looking up, said, as any good mother would say, "Share it together among you all (1.182)." And so all five brothers married Draupadi. Not content with this rather farfetched explanation, the *Mahabharata* tries again: Vyasa says that all five Pandavas are really incarnations of Indra (which does not contradict the statement that only Arjuna was the *son* of Indra, since as we have seen, these are two different processes: Dharma becomes incarnate in Vidura and fathers Yudhishthira), and Draupadi the incarnation of Shri (the goddess of prosperity, the wife of Indra and of all kings).* Still not satisfied, Vyasa offers a third explanation:

DRAUPADI'S FIVE HUSBANDS

The daughter of a great sage longed in vain for a husband; she pleased the god Shiva, who offered her a boon, and she asked for a virtuous husband. But she

---

* The Puranas (*Markandeya* 5) expand upon this: As a result of his Brahminicide, Indra's power goes into five gods, including him, who father the Pandavas.

asked again and again, five times, and so Shiva said, "You will have *five* virtuous husbands." And that is why she married the five Pandavas. She objected, saying that it is against the law for a woman to have more than one husband, for then there would be promiscuity; moreover, her one husband should have her as a virgin. But Shiva reassured her that a woman is purified every month with her menses and therefore there would be no lapse from dharma in her case, since she had asked repeatedly for a husband. Then she asked him if she could be a virgin again for each act of sexual union, and he granted this too (1.189; 1.1.157).

Like other polyandrous women whose virginities were restored, sometimes after premarital seduction or rape, Draupadi will be restored to purity each month after willing conjugal sex. In this case there is no need to justify or purify her, but there is a perceived need, if she has a different husband each month, to avoid promiscuity—*samkara* ("con-fusion" or "mixing"), the same word that is used for the reprehensible mixture of classes.

The mythological extemporizings were not sufficient to protect Draupadi from frequent slurs against her chastity. When Duryodhana has Draupadi dragged into the assembly hall, much as Rama summons Sita to the public assembly, and Duhshasana attempts to strip her, despite the fact that she is wearing a garment soiled with her menstrual blood (the same blood that was supposed to purify her), the enemies of the Pandavas justify their insults to her by arguing that a woman who sleeps with five men must be a slut (2.61.34–36). Yet all her children are legitimate; they are called the Draupadeyas ("Children of Draupadi") by a matronymic, which may be nothing more than a way of getting around the awkward fact that though she is said to have one son from each husband, people often lose track of which Pandava fathered which son. So too the multiply fathered sons of Kunti are often called Kaunteyas ("Children of Kunti") although they are also called Pandavas, since they have a single legitimate, if not natural, father, Pandu.

The later tradition was not satisfied by any of the official excuses; various retellings in Sanskrit and in vernacular languages during the ensuing, less liberal centuries mocked Draupadi. In one twelfth-century CE text, the evil spirit of the Kali Age incarnate suggests to five gods that are in love with one woman, "Let the five of us enjoy her, sharing her among us, as the five Pandavas did Draupadi."[22] Even the permissive *Kama-sutra* quotes a scholar (or pedant) who said that any married woman who is known to have had five men is "available" (i.e., can be seduced without moral qualms). For "five men or more" (*pancha-*

jana) is an expression for a crowd, a group of people, as in the *panchayat*, the quorum of a village (KS 1.5.30–31). The thirteenth-century CE commentator unpacks the implications: "If, besides her own husband, a woman has five men as husbands, she is a loose woman and fair game for any man who has a good reason to take her. Draupadi, however, who had Yudhishthira and the others as her own husbands, was not fair game for other men. How could one woman have several husbands? Ask the authors of the *Mahabharata*!"

Yet the power of Draupadi's own dharma, her unwavering devotion to her husband(s), is what protects her when Duhshasana tries to strip her; every time he pulls off a her sari, another appears to cover her nakedness, until there is a great heap of silk beside her, and Duhshasana gives up; the implication is that her chastity protects her (2.61.40–45).* The text often reminds us that Draupadi is no mere mortal but a creature from another world; there is a prediction that Draupadi will lead the Kshatriyas to their destruction, fulfilling the gods' intention (1.155). How different the lives of actual women in India would have been had Draupadi, instead of Sita, been their official role model! Many Hindus name their daughters Sita, but few name them Draupadi.

It is always possible that the *Mahabharata* was recording a time when polyandry was the custom (as it is nowadays in parts of the Himalayas), but there is no evidence to support this contention. Indeed Pandu tells Kunti another story explicitly remarking upon an archaic promiscuity that is no longer in effect, pointedly reminding her, and any women who may have heard (or read) the text, that female promiscuity was an ancient option no longer available to them:

THE END OF FEMALE PROMISCUITY

The great sage Shvetaketu was a hermit, people say. Once, they say, right before the eyes of Shvetaketu and his father, a Brahmin grasped Shvetaketu's mother by the hand and said, "Let's go!" The sage's son became enraged and could not bear to see his mother being taken away by force like that. But when his father saw that Shvetaketu was angry he said, "Do not be angry, my little son. This is the eternal dharma. The women of all classes on earth are not fenced in; all creatures behave just like cows, my little son, each in its own class." The sage's son could

---

* Several manuscripts of this passage, as well as many texts composed after the tenth century, remove Draupadi's agency by saying that she called for help from Krishna, who arrived and performed the miracle of the expanding sari. There is a real loss of feminist ground here. In response to the TV *Mahabharata* series, a company marketed the Draupadi Collection of saris, which presumably did *not* stretch infinitely.

not tolerate that dharma and made this moral boundary for men and women on earth, for humans, but not for other creatures. And from then on, we hear, this moral boundary has stood: A woman who is unfaithful to her husband commits a mortal sin that brings great misery, an evil equal to killing an embryo, and a man who seduces another man's wife, when she is a woman who keeps her vow to her husband and is thus a virgin obeying a vow of chastity, that man too commits a mortal sin on earth (1.113.9–20).

What begins as a rape somehow concludes with a law against willing female adultery, as uncontrollable male sexuality is projected onto the control of allegedly oversexed women. Pandu tells this story to Kunti in order to convince her that it *is* legal for her to give him children by sleeping with an appointed Brahmin,* an emergency plan that prompts her then to tell him about the mantra by which she can summon the gods to father her children; he is thus carefully distinguishing the permitted Brahmin from the loose cannon Brahmin in the Shvetaketu story. We recognize Shvetaketu as a hero of the Upanishads, the boy whose father teaches him the doctrine of the two paths; here his father defends promiscuity, using cows as paradigms not, as is usual, of motherly purity, but of bovine license, as cows, of all people, here become the exemplars of primeval female promiscuity. (Perhaps because they are so pure that nothing they do is wrong?)

The *Mahabharata* keeps insisting that all this is hearsay, as if to make us doubt it; it invokes a vivid, quasi-Freudian primal scene to explain a kind of sexual revulsion. A Brahmin's right to demand the sexual services of any woman he fancied[23] evoked violent protest in ancient Indian texts,† and Draupadi herself is subjected to such sexual harassment (unconsummated) on one occasion when she is in disguise as a servant and not recognized as the princess Draupadi (4.21.1–67). We may read the story of Shvetaketu in part as an anti-Brahmin (and anticow purity) tract, depicting, as it does, a Brahmin as sexually out of control, and cows as naturally promiscuous animals, as well as an explicit rejection of archaic polyandry. The *Kama-sutra* (1.1.9) names Shvetaketu as one of its original redactors, and the commentary on that passage cites this *Mahabharata* story to explain how a chaste sage became simultaneously an enemy of male adultery and an authority on sex.

---

* Satyavati too has to tell several stories to Ambika and Ambalika to persuade them to submit to the same sort of levirate.

† A notorious example is the story of Yavakri, who tried to exert this right on the wife of another Brahmin and was murdered by a witch in the form of the wife, conjured up by the Brahmin.

The persistent polyandry in the lineage of the heroines is therefore, I think, a remarkably positive fantasy of female equality, which is to say, a major resistance to patriarchy, and the *Mahabharata* women—Satyavati, Kunti, and Draupadi— are a feminist's dream (or a sexist's nightmare): smart, aggressive, steadfast, eloquent, tough as nails, and resilient. Draupadi, in particular, is unrelenting in her drive to help her husbands regain their kingdom and avenge their wrongs.

Other women in the *Mahabharata* show remarkable courage and intelligence too, but their courage is often used in subservience to their husbands. The wives of the two patriarchs, Pandu and the blind Dhritarashtra, are paradigms of such courage. Gandhari, the wife of Dhritarashtra, kept her eyes entirely blindfolded from the day of her marriage to him, in order to share his blindness. Pandu's widows vied for the privilege of dying on his pyre. When he died, Madri mounted his funeral pyre, for, she insisted, "My desire has not been satisfied, and he too was cheated of his desire as he was lying with me, so I will not cut him off from his desire in the house of death (1.116.26)." This is a most unusual justification for suttee, Madri's intention being not merely to join her husband in heaven (as other suttees will state as their motivation) but to complete the sexual act in heaven. Yet Kunti too wishes to die on Pandu's pyre, without the peculiar justification of coitus interruptus, but simply because she is the first wife. One of them must remain alive to care for both their children; Madri gets her way and mounts the pyre.* Kunti and Gandhari later die alongside Dhritrarashtra in a forest fire from which they make no attempt to escape (15.37). The four wives of Vasudeva (the father of Krishna) immolate themselves on Vasudeva's pyre and join him in heaven; they all were permitted to die because by this time all their children were dead (16.8.16–24).

The association of women with fire is worthy of note. Draupadi, who does *not* die on her husbands' funeral pyres (because [1] she dies before them and [2] they don't *have* funeral pyres; they walk up into heaven at the end of the story), begins rather than ends her life in fire; she is born out of her father's fire altar:

THE BIRTH OF DRAUPADI

Drupada performed a sacrifice in order to get a son who would kill his enemy, Drona. As the oblation was prepared, the priest summoned the queen to receive

---

* The text regards this as Madri's triumph and privilege, but a feminist might wonder if she gets this dubious honor of committing suttee as a punishment for killing Pandu by enticing him (naturally it is the woman's fault) to the fatal coupling.

the oblation and let the king impregnate her, but she took so long to put on her perfume for the occasion that the priest made the oblation directly into the fire, and so the son was born out of the fire, not out of the queen. And after the son came a daughter, Draupadi. A disembodied voice said, "This superb woman will be the death of the Kshatriyas." They called her the Dark Woman (Krishna), because she was dark-skinned (1.155.1–51).

Draupadi, born of fire, is significantly motherless, like Sita, who was born of Earth and returns into the earth, after she has entered fire and come out of it. Like Sita, Draupadi is an elemental goddess who is often called *ayonija* ("born from no womb")[24] and follows her husband(s) to the forest. In Draupadi's case, the absence of the expected mother is balanced by the unexpected presence of the daughter. Unasked for, riding into life on the coattails of her brother, Draupadi went on to become the heart and soul of the Pandavas. She also went on, in India, to become a goddess with a sect of her own, worshiped throughout South India primarily by lower castes, Pariahs, and Muslims.[25] The *Mahabharata* mentions other dark goddesses who may well already have had such sects: the seven or eight "Little Mothers" (Matrikas), dark, peripheral, harmful, especially for children,[26] and the great goddess Kali (Maha-Kali).[27] Indeed Draupadi is closely connected with the dark goddess Kali.[28] As in the stories of the births of Pandu and Draupadi, as well as the origins of class colors, skin color here has a religious significance but no social meaning, positive or negative.

A partial explanation for the *Mahabharata*'s open-minded attitude toward polyandrous women may come from a consideration of the historical context. The text took shape during the Mauryan and immediate post-Mauryan period, a cosmopolitan era that encouraged the loosening of constraints on women in both court and village. The women of the royal family were often generous donors to the Buddhist community,[29] and women from all classes, including courtesans, became Buddhists.[30] The king used women archers for his bodyguards in the palace, and Greek women (Yavanis) used to carry the king's bows and arrows on hunts. Women served as spies. Female ascetics moved around freely. Prostitutes paid taxes. The state provided supervised work, such as spinning yarn, for upper-class women who had become impoverished, widowed, or deserted and for aging prostitutes.* If a slave woman gave birth to her master's

---

* Much of this information about women comes from the *Artha-shastra*, which, if not the Mauryan document that people often assume it is, was nevertheless probably composed in the general period of the composition of the *Mahabharata*, by about 300 CE.

child, both she and the child were immediately released from slavery.[31] Thus women were major players in both Buddhism and Hinduism during this period, and the *Mahabharata* may reflect this greater autonomy. Indeed the tales of polyandry may reflect the male redactors' nightmare vision of where all that autonomy might lead.

THE WORLDS OF THE TWO GREAT POEMS

Indian tradition generally puts the two poems in two different categories: The *Ramayana* is the first poem (*kavya*), and the *Mahabharata* is a history (*itihasa*) or a dharma text.* The *Ramayana* prides itself on its more ornate language, and its central plot occupies most of the text, while the *Mahabharata* reflects the traces of straightforward oral composition and indulges in a great many secondary discussions or narrations only loosely linked to the main plot. The *Mahabharata* at the very end sketches an illusory scene of hell that is an emergency balloon to float it out of a corner it had painted itself into. But the *Ramayana* is about illusion from the very start.

The *Ramayana* tells of a war against foreigners and people of another species, with clear demarcations of forces of good triumphing over evil; the *Mahabharata* is about a bitter civil war with no winners. The *Ramayana* doesn't usually problematize dharma; the *Mahabharata* does, constantly. Where the *Ramayana* is triumphalist, the *Mahabharata* is tragic. Where the *Ramayana* is affirmative, the *Mahabharata* is interrogative.[32] Rama is said to be the perfect man, and his flaws are largely papered over, while the flaws of *Mahabharata* heroes are what the whole thing is about. When Rama's brother Bharata is given the throne that should have been Rama's, each of the brothers, like Alphonse and Gaston in the old story, modestly and generously tries to give the kingdom to the other (R 2.98). In the *Mahabharata*, by contrast, when the succession is in question, the sons of the two royal brothers fight tooth and nail over it. Where the *Ramayana* sets the time of Rama's idyllic rule, the "Ram-Raj," in an idealized, peaceful Mauryan Empire of the future, the *Mahabharata* jumps back in time over the Mauryan Empire to an archaic time of total, no-holds-barred war.

But we cannot say that the *Ramayana* came first, when people still believed

---

* Actually, the *Mahabharata* refers to itself as a "conversation" or "tale" (*akhyana*) more often than an *itihasa*, and occasionally as a poem (*kavya*), just like the *Ramayana*, but it is usually called an *itihasa*. The philosopher Abhinavagupta says that *itihasa* is just another form of *kavya*, and by that definition, the *Mahabharata* is *kavya* too.

in dharma, and then the *Mahabharata* came along and deconstructed it. Nor can we say that the *Mahabharata* first looked the disaster square in the eyes and showed what a mess it was, and then after that the *Ramayana* flinched and cleaned it up, like a gentrified slum or a Potemkin village. Both views exist simultaneously and in conversation: The *Ramayana* says, "There is a perfect man, and his name is Rama," and the *Mahabharata* says, "Not really; dharma is so subtle that even Yudhishthira cannot always fulfill it." Or, if you prefer, the *Mahabharata* says, "Dharma is subtle," and the *Ramayana* replies, "Yes, but not so subtle that it cannot be mastered by a perfect man like Rama."

Each text asks a characteristically different question to prompt the paradigmatic story: The *Ramayana* begins when Valmiki asks the sage Narada, "Is there any man alive who has all the virtues? (R1.1.1–2)," to which the answer is the triumphal, or more or less triumphal, story of Rama. By contrast, embedded inside the *Mahabharata* are two requests by Yudhishthira for a story parallel to his own; when Draupadi has been abducted, he asks if any man was ever unluckier, unhappier than he, whereupon he is told the story of Rama and Sita (3.257–75), and when he has gambled away his kingdom and is in exile, he asks the same question, to which the answer is the story of the long-suffering gambler Nala (3.49.33–34). This contrast between triumph and tragedy could stand for the general tone of the two great poems.

CHAPTER 12

ESCAPE CLAUSES IN THE *SHASTRAS*

100 BCE to 400 CE

༄

CHRONOLOGY

c. 166 BCE–78 CE Greeks (Yavanas), Scythians (Shakas), Bactrians, and Parthians (Pahlavas) continue to enter India

c. 100 CE "Manu" composes his *Dharma-shastra*

c. 78–140 CE Kanishka reigns and encourages Buddhism

c. 150 CE Rudradaman publishes the first Sanskrit inscription, at Junagadh

c. 200 CE Kautilya composes the *Artha-shastra*

c. 300 CE Vatsyayana Mallanaga composes the *Kama-sutra*

RESTORATIONS FOR KILLING A MONGOOSE
OR AN UNCHASTE WOMAN

If a man kills a cat or a mongoose, a blue jay, a frog, a dog, a lizard, an owl, or a crow, he should carry out the vow for killing a Shudra.* For killing a horse, he should give a garment to a Brahmin; for an elephant, five black bulls; for a goat or sheep, a draft ox; for a donkey, a one-year-old calf. To become clean after killing an unchaste woman of any of the four classes, a man should give a Brahmin a leather bag (for killing a Brahmin woman), a bow (for a Kshatriya woman), a billy goat (for a Vaishya woman), or a sheep (for a Shudra woman).

Manu's *Dharma-shastra* (11.132, 137, 139), c. 100 CE

This list (lists being the format of choice for the textbooks known as *shastras*) groups together animals, social classes, and (unchaste) women around the issues

---

* The vow for killing a Shudra is one-sixteenth of the penance for killing a Brahmin, a crime for which various punishments are prescribed (11.73-90, 127).

of killing and restorations for killing, all central issues for the *shastras*. In the long period *entre deux empires*, the formulation of encyclopedic knowledge acknowledged the diversity of opinion on many subjects, while at the same time, some, but not all, of the *shastras* closed down many of the options for women and the lower castes.[1]

The Brahmin imaginary has no canon, but if it did, that canon would be the body of *shastras*, which spelled out the dominant paradigm with regard to women, animals, and castes, the mark at which all subsequent antinomian or resistant strains of Hinduism aimed. The foreign flux, now and at other moments, on the one hand, loosened up and broadened the concept of knowledge, making it more cosmopolitan—more things to eat, to wear, to think about—and at the same time posed a threat that drove the Brahmins to tighten up some aspects of social control.

THE AGE OF DARKNESS, INVASIONS, PARADOX, AND DIVERSITY

Both the diversity encompassed by the *shastras* and their drive to control that diversity are best understood in the context of the period in which they were composed.[2] There were no great dynasties in the early centuries of the Common Era; the Shakas and Kushanas were bluffing when they used the titles of King of Kings and Son of God, on the precedent of the Indo-Greeks. Some Euro-American historians have regarded this period as India's Dark Age, dark both because it lacked the security of a decently governed empire (the Kushanas very definitely did not Rule the Waves) and because the abundant but hard-to-date sources leave historians with very little available light to work with. Some Indian nationalist historians regarded it as the Age of Invasions, the decadent age of non-Indian dynasties, when barbarians (*mlecchas*) continued to slip into India. But it looks to us now rather more like a preimperial Age of Diversity, a time of rich cultural integration, a creative chaos that inspired the scholars of the time to bring together all their knowledge, as into a fortified city, to preserve it for whatever posterity there might be. It all boils down to whether you think confusion (*samkara*) is a Good Thing or a Bad Thing. Political chaos is scary for the orthodox, creative for the unorthodox; what politics sees as instability appears as dynamism in terms of commercial and cultural development.[3] The paradox is that the rule of the "degenerate Kshatriyas" and undistinguished, often non-Indian kings opened up the subcontinent to trade and new ideas.[4] The art and literature of this period are far richer than those of either of the two empires that frame it, the Mauryas and the Guptas.[5]

Buddhist monuments, rather than Hindu, are our main source of the visual record of this period. The gloriously miscellaneous quality of the culture of the time is epitomized in the reliefs on the great Buddhist stupa at Amaravati, in the western Deccan, which depict scenes of everyday life that defy denomination: musicians, dancers, women leaning over balconies, horses cavorting in the street, elephants running amok, bullocks laboring to pull a heavy (but elegant) carriage, ships with sails and oars. In a nice moment of self-referentiality (or infinite regress), there is a scene depicting masons constructing the stupa that depicts a scene of masons constructing the stupa.[6] This sort of self-imaging later became a characteristic of Hindu temples, in which the individual pieces of the temple mirror the grand plan of the whole temple.[7]

There was constant movement, constant trade from Greece, Central Asia, West Asia, the ports of the Red Sea, and Southeast Asia.[8] Trade flowed along the mountainous northern routes through Central Asia and by sea to the great ports of South India. A book with the delicious title of *The Periplus of the Erythraean Sea*, composed by an unnamed Greek in about 80 CE, gave detailed navigational instructions to those planning to sail to what is now Gujarat and thence to gain access to the Deccan, where one could buy and export such delicacies as ginseng, aromatic oils, myrrh, ivory, agate, carnelian, cotton cloth, silk, Indian muslins, yarn, and long pepper. The Indians, for their part, imported "fine wines (Italian preferred), singing boys, beautiful maidens for the harem, thin clothing of the finest weaves, and the choicest ointments." As always, horses were imported from abroad but now were also bred in various parts of India.[9]

In return, Indians traveled to and traded with Southeast Asia and Central Asia,[10] exporting Indian culture to the Mekong Delta, the Malay Peninsula, Sumatra and Sinkiang, to Afghanistan and Vietnam, to the Gobi Desert, on the Silk Route. This economic porosity continued well into the fourth century CE, with trade the one thing that was constant.

Sectarianism Under the Kushanas and Shatavahanas

The Kushanas, nomadic pastoralists, came down from Central Asia into the Indus plain and then along the Ganges plain to Mathura, beyond Varanasi. Like the Vedic people before them, these horsemen herders were also good cavalrymen[11] and, like them, they may well have come as merchants, allies, or even refugees rather than as conquerors. Their empire (from 78 to 144 CE) culminated in the rule of Kanishka (112 to 144 CE)[12] who encouraged a new wave of

Buddhist proselytizing. The Fourth Buddhist Council was held under his patronage, and at his capital at Peshawar an enormous stupa was built, nearly a hundred meters in diameter and twice as high. Some coins of his realm were stamped with images of Gautama and the future Buddha Maitreya. He was the patron of the poet Ashvaghosha, who helped organize the Buddhist Council and composed, among other things, the first Sanskrit drama and a life of the Buddha in Sanskrit poetry.

Yet Kanishka also supported other religions.[13] The Kushana centers of Gandhara and Mathura in the second century CE produced Hindu images that served as paradigms for regional workshops for centuries to follow.[14] A colossal statue of Kanishka has survived, high felt boots and all, though without a head; on the other hand, the Greeks put nothing but heads on their coins.[15] This head-body complementarity, familiar to us from the tale of the mixed goddesses, well expresses the delicate balance of political and religious power during this period. Kanishka's successor issued coins with images of Greek, Zoroastrian, and Bactrian deities, as well as Hindu deities, such as the goddess Uma (Ommo in Bactrian), identified with Parvati, the wife of Shiva, and sometimes depicted together with Shiva. The coins also have images of the goddess Durga riding on her lion and the goddess Shri in a form adapted from a Bactrian goddess.[16] Buddhism and Jainism were still vying, peaceably, with Hinduism.

In 150 CE, Rudradaman, a Shaka king who ruled from Ujjain, published a long Sanskrit inscription in Junagadh, in Gujarat; he carved it, in the palimpsest fashion favored by many Indian rulers (temples on stupas, mosques on temples), on a rock that already held a set of Ashoka's Prakrit Major Rock Edicts. Himself of uncertain class, Rudradaman leaned over backward to praise dharma and pointed out that he had repaired an important Mauryan dam without raising taxes, by paying for it out of his own treasury. He also boasted that he knew grammar, music, the *shastras*, and logic and was a fine swordsman and boxer, an excellent horseman, charioteer, and elephant rider, and a good poet to boot.[17] His is the first substantial inscription in classical Sanskrit (Ashoka and Kanishka had written in various Prakrits, usually Magadhi or Pali). Rudradaman's choice of Sanskrit, underlined by the fact that he wrote right on top of the Prakrit of Ashoka, may have been designed to establish his legitimacy as a foreign ruler, "to mitigate the lamentable choice of parents," as the historian D. D. Kosambi suggested.[18]

The Kushanas gradually weakened, while the Shakas continued to rule until the mid-fifth century CE,[19] but both dynasties left plenty of room for others, such as the Pahlavas (Parthians) in Northwest India and the Shatavahanas, whose capital was at Amaravati in the western Deccan, to spring up too. The Shatavahana rulers made various claims: that they were Brahmins who had intermarried with people who were excluded from the system, that they had destroyed the pride of Kshastriyas, and that they had prevented intermarriage among the four classes.[20] They were orthodox in their adherence to Vedic sacrifice and Vedic gods, and they made land grants to Brahmins, but they also patronized Buddhism, in part because it was more supportive of economic expansion than Hinduism was: It channeled funds into trade instead of sacrifice and waived the caste taboos on food and trade that made it difficult for pious Hindus to travel. (Buddhists, unlike Hindus, proselytized abroad.) Royal grants to Buddhist monasteries would be seed money, quickly matched by donations from private individuals and guilds; the lists of donors in the cave temple inscriptions include weavers, grain merchants, basket makers, leatherworkers, shipping agents, ivory carvers, smiths, salt merchants, and various craftsmen and dealers, some of them even Yavanas (Greeks or other foreigners).

The Shatavahanas completed building the Great Stupa that Ashoka had begun at Amaravati,[21] and mercantile associations living under the Shatavahanas carved out, also in the western Deccan, between about 100 BCE and 170 CE,[22] the magnificently sculpted, generally Buddhist caves of Bhaja, Karle, Nasik, and parts of Ajanta and Ellora. Merchants would cluster around the great Buddhist pilgrimage sites, setting up their bazaars and rest houses, shops and stables.[23] This later became the model for Hindu pilgrimage sites and temples. There are no remains of stone Hindu temples from this period, though the ones that appeared later seem to be modeled on now-lost wooden temples.

The Hindu response to the Buddhist challenge was not only to reclaim dharma from *dhamma* and but to extend it. Dharma in the ritual sutras had been mostly about how to do the sacrifice; the *dharma-shastra*s now applied it to the rest of life, dictating what to eat, whom to marry. So too, while karma in the ritual texts usually designated a ritual act, in the *dharma-shastra*s, as in the *Mahabharata*, it came to be understood more broadly as any morally consequential act binding one to the cycle of death and rebirth. Then there was *moksha* to deal with, not only (as in the earlier period) in the challenge posed by Buddhism and Jainism, but now, in addition, in the more insidious problem posed by the deconstruction of dharma in the *Mahabharata*. The challenge facing not just the Brahmins but everyone else trying to ride the new wave was to factor into the systematizing modes of thought that were already in place the new social elements that were questioning the Brahmin norms. These cultural changes, shaking the security of the orthodox in an age of flux, were tricky for the *dharma-shastra*s to map, let alone attempt to control,[24] and go a long way to explain the hardening of the shastric lines.[25] And so the Brahmins began, once again, to circle their wagons.

SHASTRAS

At the end of the long interregnum, a kind of scholasticism developed that was capable of sorting out all the intervening chaos neatly—or not so neatly. In the first millennium Sanskrit still dominated the literary scene as "the language of the gods," as it had long claimed to be. But now it also became a cosmopolitan language, patronized by a sophisticated community of literati and royalty. It was no longer used only, or primarily, for sacred texts but also as a vehicle for literary and political expression throughout South Asia and beyond.[26] It was now the language of science and art as well as religion and literature, the language, in short, of the *shastra*s.

Shastra means "a text, or a teaching, or a science"; *ashva-shastra* in general is the science of horses, while *the Ashva-shastra* is a particular text* about the science of horses. The word *shastra* comes from the verb *shas*, meaning "to teach or to punish," but it also means "discipline" in the sense of an area of study, such as the discipline of anthropology, thus reflecting both of Michel Foucault's senses of the word. It is related to the verb *shams* ("injure"), which is the root of the noun for "cruelty," and it is probably related to our own "chasten," "chastise," and "chastity," through the Latin *castigare*. Like dharma, the *shastra*s are simultaneously descriptive and proscriptive.

Like the class and caste system itself, the shastric structures were formulated to accommodate diversity. Yet many Brahmins perceived this same diversity as a threat and therefore set out to hierarchize, to put everything in its proper place, to form, to mold, to repress, to systematize—in a word, to discipline (*shas*) the chaos that they saw looming before them. They herded all the new ideas, like so many strange animals, into their intellectual corrals, and they branded them according to their places in the scheme of things. Attitudes toward women and the lower classes hardened in the texts formulated in this period, even while those same texts give evidence, almost against the will of their authors, of an increasingly wide range of human options. It was as if the gathering chaos of

---

* Attributed to Nakula, the Pandava son of one of the twin equine gods, the Ashvins.

the cultural environment had produced an equal and opposite reaction in the Brahmin establishment; one can almost hear the cries for "law and order!"

The spirit was totalizing and cosmopolitan, an attempt to bring together in one place, from all points in India and all levels of society, a complete knowledge of the subject in question. Totality was the goal of the encyclopedic range both of the subject covered in each text (everything you ever wanted to know about X) and of the span of subjects: beginning with the Trio—dharma, politics (*artha*), and pleasure (*kama*)—and going on to grammar, architecture, medicine, dancing and acting, aesthetics in fine art, music, astronomy and astrology, training horses and training elephants, various aspects of natural science and, in particular, mathematics—everything you can imagine and much that you cannot.

The persistent open-endedness, and even open-mindedness, of many of the *shastra*s can be seen in the ways in which they consider variant opinions and offer escape clauses. Each *shastra* quotes its predecessors and shows why it is better than they are (the equivalent of the obligatory review of the literature in a Ph.D. dissertation). The dissenting opinions are cited in the course of what Indian logic called the other side (the "former wing," *purva-paksha*), the arguments that opponents might raise.* They are rebutted one by one, until the author finally gives his own opinion, the right opinion. But along the way we get a strong sense of a loyal opposition and the flourishing of a healthy debate. The *shastra*s are therefore above all dialogical or argumentative.

Take medicine, for instance, known in India as the science of long life (*Ayurveda*). There are a number of medical texts, of which those of Charaka and Sushruta (probably composed in the first and seventh centuries CE, respectively) are the most famous. The medical texts teach how to care for the mind and body in ways that supplement the advice offered, on this same subject, by the *dharma-shastra*s, the teachings of yoga, the Tantras, and other schools of Hinduism. Surgery was generally neglected by Hindu doctors, for reasons of caste pollution, and taken over by Buddhists; the Hindu *shastra*s on medicine derived much of their knowledge of surgery from Buddhist monasteries.[27]

A passage from Charaka is typical of the way that all of the *shastra*s strive to be open-minded and inclusive:

---

* In U.S. law, this is known as a Brandeis brief, which the Supreme Court justice insisted his clerks develop in order to understand the thinking of the opposition.

SECOND, AND THIRD, MEDICAL OPINIONS

Once upon a time, when all the great sages had assembled, a dispute arose about the cause of diseases. One by one the sages stated what each regarded as the cause of disease: the soul, which collects and enjoys karma and the fruits of karma; the mind, when overwhelmed by energy and darkness [*rajas* and *tamas*]; *rasa* [the fluid essence of digested food]; sound and the other objects of the senses; the six elements of matter [earth, water, fire, wind, space, and mind or soul]; one's parents; one's karma; one's own nature; the creator god, Prajapat; and, finally, time.

Now, as the sages were arguing in this way, one of them said, "Don't talk like this. It is hard to get to the truth when people take sides. People who utter arguments and counterarguments as if they were established facts never get to the end of their own side, as if they were going round and round on an oil press. Get rid of this collision of opinions and shake off the darkness of factionalism. Eating bad food is a cause of diseases." But another sage replied, "Sir, physicians have an abundance of different opinions. Not all of them will understand this sort of teaching . . . " (1.1.15.3–34).

Despite the equal time that this passage gives to various approaches, several of which represent major philosophical as well as medical traditions, there is, as always, hierarchy: Not only is the penultimate sage right, and the others presumably wrong, but he even has a riposte ready in anticipation of the fact that they still might not grant that he is right ("It is hard to get to the truth when people take sides"). Yet since they do still refuse to give in to him, the subject remains open after all.

CLASS AND CASTE TAXONOMIES

The rise of myriad small social groups at this time created problems for the taxonomists of the social order. Someone had to put all this together into something like a general theory of human relativity. That someone is known to the Hindu tradition as Manu.

When the authors of the dharma texts set out to reconcile class with caste, they had their work cut out for them. *Varna* and *jati* unite to form the Hindu social taxonomy in much the same way that the Brahmin head and Pariah body (and the Sanskrit and Tamil texts) united to form the two goddesses. Whichever is the older (and there is no conclusive evidence one way or another), *varna* and *jati* had developed independently for some centuries before the *shastras* combined them. But their interconnection was so important to ancient Indian social theory that Manu makes it the very first question that the sages ask him at the start of the book, though he does not give the answer until book ten (of the total of twelve): "Sir, please tell us, properly and in order, the duties of all four classes and also of the people who are born between two classes (1.2)"—that is, of people like the Charioteer caste (Sutas), between Brahmin and Kshatriya.

Manu, elaborating upon a scheme sketched more briefly in the *dharma-sutras* a century or two before him (he takes a relatively brief passage in the *sutras*[28] and unpacks it in forty verses), lays out a detailed paradigm that explains how it is that a Brahmin and a Pariah are related historically. The only trouble is that the authors of the dharma texts made it all up, for there is absolutely no historical evidence that the *jati*s developed out of *varna*s. There are many reasonable explanations of the origins of caste—from professions, guilds, families, tribes outside the Vedic world—and most of them probably have some measure of the whole, more complex truth. Manu's explanation is the only one that is totally off the wall. Still, you have to hand it to him; it's an ingenious scheme: "From a Brahmin man and the daughter of a Shudra, a man of the Nishada caste is born. From a Kshatriya man and the daughter of a Brahmin a man of the Charioteer caste is born. Sons of confused classes are born from a Shudra man with women of the Brahmin class, such as the Chandala, the worst of men (10.8–12)."

And so forth. The Nishadas in these texts form a caste within Hinduism rather than a tribal group outside it, as they do in most of the narrative texts. These all are marriages "against the grain" or "against the current" (literally "against the hair," the wrong way, *pratiloma*, hypogamously), with the man below the woman, in contrast with marriages "with the grain" (the right way, *anuloma*, hypergamously), with the woman below the man. In this paradigm, the higher the wife, and therefore the wider the gap, the lower the mixed offspring. Mind the gap.

So far so good; but clearly only a limited number of castes (several of which we have already encountered) can result from these primary interactions, and there are castes of thousands to be accounted for. So Manu moves on into later generations to explain the origin of other castes: The Chandala, himself born from a Shudra who intermarried with women of higher classes and regarded as the paradigmatic Pariah, becomes the father, through further intermarriage, of even more degraded castes, people whose very essence is a category error squared (10.12, 15, 19, 37–39). (The *Mahabharata* makes the dog cookers descendants of a Chandala man and a Nishadha woman [13.48.10. 21 and .28]). And so on, ad infinitum. Manu's attempt to dovetail castes within the class structure is a masterpiece of taxonomy, though a purely imaginary construct, like a map of the constellations. He created simultaneously a system and a history of the castes.

Despite the purely mythological nature of this charter, some semblance of reality, or at least anthropology, moves into the text when Manu tells us the job descriptions of the first generation of fantasized miscegenation:

> They are traditionally regarded as Dasyus [aliens or slaves], whether they speak barbarian languages or Aryan languages, and they should make their living by their *karmas*, which the twice-born revile: for Charioteers, the management of horses and chariots; for the Nishadas, killing fish. These castes should live near mounds, trees, and cremation grounds, in mountains and in groves, recognizable and making a living by their own karmas [10.45–50].

And reality in all its ugliness takes over entirely in the passage describing the *karmas* of the Chandalas and people of the second generation of miscegenation, and explaining how they are expected to live:

> The dwellings of Chandalas and Dog cookers [*Shva-pakas*] should be outside the village; they must use discarded bowls, and dogs and donkeys should be their wealth. Their clothing should be the clothes of the dead, and their food should be in broken dishes; their ornaments should be made of black iron, and they should wander constantly. A man who carries out his duties should not seek contact with them; they should do business with one another and marry with those who are like them. Their food, dependent upon others, should be given to them in a broken dish, and they should not walk about in villages and cities at night. They may move about by day to do their work, recognizable by distinctive marks in accordance with the king's decrees; and they should carry out the corpses of people who have no relatives; this is a fixed rule. By the king's command, they should execute those condemned to death, and they should take for themselves the clothing, beds and ornaments of those condemned to death (10.51–56).

In later centuries the Pariahs were defined by three factors that we can see *in nuce* here: They are economically exploited, victims of social discrimination, and permanently polluted ritually.[29] The only way out, says Manu, is by "giving up the body instinctively for the sake of a Brahmin or a cow or in the defense of women and children (10.72)." This grand scheme is contradicted by another of Manu's grand schemes; his argument here that the castes came, historically, from the classes conflicts with his statement, elsewhere, that "in the beginning," the creator created all individual things with their own karmas, which sound very much like castes (1.21–30).

Once the castes were created, however they were created, they had to remain separate. The nightmare of personal infection by contact with the wrong castes, particularly with Pariahs, is closely keyed to the terror of the infection of the mind and body by the passions; Manu regards the Pariahs as the Kali Age of the body. The horror of pollution by the lowest castes (the ones who did the dirty work that someone has to do: cleaning latrines, taking out human corpses, dealing with the corpses of cows) most closely approximates the attitude that many Americans had to people with the HIV virus at the height of the AIDS panic: they believed them to be deadly dangerous, highly contagious, and af-flicted as the result of previous evil behavior (drugs or homosexual behavior in the case of AIDS; sins in a former life for caste). Impurity is dangerous; it makes you vulnerable to diseases and to possession by demons. Pollution by contact with Pariahs is regarded as automatic and disastrous, like the bad karma that adheres to you when you mistreat other people.

The same lists, blacklists, as it were, recur in different *shastra*s, lists of people who are to be excluded from various sorts of personal contact: people to whom the Veda should not be taught; women one should not marry; people one should not invite to the ceremony for the dead; people whose food one should not eat; people who cannot serve as witnesses; sons who are disqualified from inheri-tance; the mixed castes, who are excluded from most social contacts; people who have committed the sins and crimes that cause one to fall from caste and thus to be excluded in yet other ways; and, finally, people who have committed the crimes that cause one to be reborn as bad people who are to be excluded.[30] Mad-men and drunkards, adulterers and gamblers, impotent men and lepers, blind men and one-eyed men present themselves as candidates for social inter-course again and again, and are rejected again and again, while other sorts of people are unique to one list or another. Together, and throughout the work as a whole, these disenfranchised groups form a complex pattern of social groups engaged in an elaborate quadrille or square dance, as they advance, retreat, separate, regroup, advance and retreat again.

In dramatic contrast with Manu, neither the *Kama-sutra* nor the *Artha-shastra* says much about either class or caste. The *Artha-shastra* begins with a boilerplate endorsement of the system of the four classes and the four stages of life (1.3.5–12) but seldom refers to classes after that, or to caste as such; it refers, instead, to groups of people distinguished by their professional or religious views, who might have functioned as castes, but Manu cares little about their status. Yet even this text takes care to define common dharma as including *ahimsa*, compassion, and forbearance (just as Manu's *sanatana* or *sadharana dharma* does [6.91–93]) and, just like Manu, warns that everyone must do his *sva-dharma* in order to avoid miscegenation (*samkara*) (1.3.13–15). The *Kama-sutra* ignores caste even when considering marriage (except in one verse), marriage being one of the two places where caste is most important (food being the other). The *Kama-sutra*'s male protagonist may be of any class, as long as he has money (3.2.1); the good life can be lived even by a woman, with money. This is a capital-driven class system, much closer to the American than the British model.

Manu's view of caste became, and remained, the most often cited authority for *varna-ashrama-dharma* (social and religious duties tied to class and stage of life). Over the course of the centuries the text attracted nine complete commentaries, attesting to its crucial significance within the tradition, and other ancient Hindu texts cite it far more frequently than any other *dharma-shastra*. Whether this status extended beyond the texts to the actual use of Manu in legal courts is another matter. But for centuries the text simultaneously mobilized insiders and convinced outsiders that Brahmins really were superior, that status was more important than political or economic power.

Fast-forward: In present-day India, *Manu* remains the basis of the Hindu marriage code, as it defines itself vis-à-vis Muslim or secular (governmental) marriage law. In a contemporary Indian Classic Comic version of the *Maha-bharata*, Pandu cites *Manu* to justify his decision to allow Kunti to be impregnated by five gods.[31] *Manu* remains the preeminent symbol—now a negative symbol—of the repressive caste system: It is *Manu,* more than any other text, that Dalits burn in their protests.[32]

Animals

Manu justifies the law of karma by setting within the creation of the various classes of beings, which he narrates in the very first book, a creation that includes both humans and animals (1.26–50). And when he reverts, in the last book, to the law of karma to explain how, depending on their past actions, people are reborn as various classes of beings, again he speaks of the relationship between humans and animals (12.40–81). Thus animals frame the entire metaphysical structure of Manu. Throughout the intervening chapters, the theme of rebirth in various classes of creatures is interwoven with the problem of killing and eating. More subtle and bizarre relationships between humans and animals are also addressed; there are punishments for urinating on a cow or having sex with female animals (4.52, 11.174).

The same animals and people recur in many different lists, with particular variants here and there; whenever he sets his mind to the problems of evil and violence, Manu tends to round up the usual suspects. Just as madmen, drunkards, and their colleagues recur in the list of people to be rejected, so too dogs, horses, and cows are the basic castes of characters in the theme of killing and eating. And the animals that are the problem are also the solution; various crimes, some having nothing to do with animals, are punished by animals. Thus an adulterous woman is to be devoured by dogs (if her lover is a low-caste man),[33] or paraded on a donkey and reborn as a jackal, and thieves are to be trampled to death by elephants, while cow killing and various other misdemeanors may be expiated by keeping cows company and refraining from reporting them when they pilfer food and water.[34] Unchaste women and Shudras are included among the animals whose murders will be punished, as we saw in the passage that opened this chapter. Manu also refers to the Vedic horse sacrifice as a supreme source of purification and restoration (5.53, 11.261), as indeed it was for both Rama and Yudhishthira. Violations of the taboos of killing and eating (that is, eating, selling, injuring, or killing the wrong sorts of animals) furnish one of the basic criteria for acceptance in or exclusion from society. Thus the distinction between good and bad people, a theme that is the central agenda of the text, is further interwoven into the warp of rebirth and the woof of animals.

WHY YOU MAY, AND MAY NOT, EAT MEAT

The *dharma-shastra*s, like the texts that precede them, wrestle with the question of vegetarianism. The *Kama-sutra*, in the course of a most idiosyncratic definition of dharma, takes meat eating to be a normal part of ordinary life but, at the same time, regards vegetarianism as one of the two defining characteristics of dharma (the other being sacrifice, which often involves the death of animals): Dharma consists in doing things, like sacrifice, that are divorced from material life and refraining from things, like eating meat, that are a part of ordinary life (2.2.7).

In one verse, Manu seems actually to punish a person for *not* eating meat at the proper time: "But when a man who is properly engaged in a ritual does not eat meat, after his death he will become a sacrificial animal during twenty-one rebirths (5.35)." Thus he encourages people to eat meat—if they follow the rules. Elsewhere he describes meat eating too as an addiction that some people cannot give up entirely: "If he has an addiction [to meat], let him make a sacrificial animal out of clarified butter or let him make a sacrificial animal out of flour; but he should never wish to kill a sacrificial animal for no [religious] purpose (5.37)." Clearly Manu has sympathy for the vegetarian with his veggie cutlets, but also for the addicted carnivore.

At first Manu reflects the Vedic view of limited retribution in the Other World: "A twice-born person who knows the rules should not eat meat against the rules, even in extremity; for if he eats meat against the rules, after his death he will be helplessly eaten by those that he ate. 'He whose *meat* in this world do I eat/will in the other world *me eat*.' Wise men say that this is why meat is called meat (5.33.55)." But then Manu switches to the post-Vedic view of transmigration, rather than an Other World, and to vegetarianism with a vengeance:

> As many hairs as there are on the body of the sacrificial animal that he kills for no [religious] purpose here on earth, so many times will he, after his death, suffer a violent death in birth after birth. You can never get meat without violence to creatures with the breath of life, and the killing of creatures with the breath of life does not get you to heaven; therefore you should not eat meat. Anyone who looks carefully at the source of meat, and at the tying up and slaughter of embodied creatures, should turn back from eating any meat (5.38.48–53).

The last line alone expresses actual sympathy for the suffering of the slaughtered animals.

Manu flees from the horns of his dilemma (on one horn, sacrifice; on the other, vegetarianism) to several lists of animals and classes of animals that you can or, on the other hand, cannot eat, lists that rival in unfathomable taxonomic principles not only Deuteronomy but Ashoka's edicts; clearly, you *can* eat a great number of animals, if you know your way around the rules (5.5–25). The authors of *shastras* make many different lists involving animals: classes of beings one should and should not eat; situations in which lawsuits arise between humans and livestock; punishments for people who injure, steal, or kill various animals; animals (including humans) that Brahmins should not sell; and vows of restoration for anyone who has, advertently or inadvertently, injured, stolen,

killed, or eaten (or eaten the excrement of) various animals.[35] The passage with
which this chapter began, "Restorations for Killing a Mongoose or an Unchaste
Woman," spells out one subset of this enormous group, as some animals are
given (presumably to be killed) in restoration for killing other animals or for
killing unchaste, hence subhuman, women.

But in addition to the specific times when it is OK to eat meat—for a
sacrifice, when it has been properly consecrated, when you would otherwise
starve to death (10.105–08), etc.—Manu expresses a general philosophy of
carnivorousness:

> The Lord of Creatures fashioned all this universe to feed the breath of life, and
> everything moving and stationary is the food of the breath of life. Those that do
> not move are food for those that move, and those that have no fangs are food for
> those with fangs; those that have no hands are food for those with hands; and
> cowards are the food of the brave. The eater who eats creatures with the breath of
> life who are to be eaten does nothing bad, even if he does it day after day; for the
> creator himself created creatures with the breath of life, some to be eaten and
> some to be eaters (5.28–30).

Recall the similar verse in the *Mahabharata:* "The mongoose eats mice, just as
the cat eats the mongoose; the dog devours the cat, your majesty, and wild beasts
eat the dog (12.15.21)." Manu's terror of piscine anarchy—"fish eat fish"—is a
direct extension of Vedic assumptions about natural violence. But Manu also
says that "Killing in a sacrifice is not killing. . . . The violence [*himsa*] to those
that move and those that do not move which is sanctioned by the Veda—that
is known as nonviolence [*ahimsa*] (5.39, 44)." By defining the sacrifice as nonviolent, Manu *made* it nonviolent. In this way, he was able to list the Veda and
nonviolence together in his final summary of the most important elements of
the moral life, the basic principles of general and eternal dharma (12.83–93;
6.91–94; 10.63).

The two views, violent and nonviolent, are juxtaposed in an uneasy tension
in the context within which Manu debates most problems, the ritual.[36] Manu
transforms five of the earlier Vedic sacrifices (animal sacrifices in which violence
is assumed) into five Hindu vegetarian sacrifices that avoid violence (3.70–74).
He goes on to argue that these five sacrifices themselves are restorations for the
evils committed by normal householders in "slaughterhouses" where small
creatures are, often inadvertently, killed (an idea that now seems more Jaina

than Hindu but in its day was widely shared): "A householder has five slaughter-houses, whose use fetters him: the fireplace, the grindstone, the broom, the mortar and pestle, and the water jar. The great sages devised the five great sacrifices for the householder to do every day to redeem him from all of these [slaughter-houses] successively (3.68–69)." The justifications of violence in both *Manu* and the *Mahabharata* lie behind a later text in which the Brahmins tell the king, "Violence is everywhere and therefore, whatever the Jaina renouncers say is blind arrogance. Can anyone keep alive without eating? And how is food to be got without violence? Is there anyone on earth who does not have a tendency toward violence? Your majesty! People live by violence alone. . . . If a person thinks of his good qualities and thinks badly of others—then also he commits violence."[37] It is ironic that in this very text, the "violence" of thinking badly of others—what we would call intolerance—is committed against Jaina renouncers, who are (blindly and arrogantly) accused of "blind arrogance."

Manu offers far fewer promeat than antimeat verses (three pro and twenty-five anti). Yet he ends firmly on the fence: "There is nothing wrong in eating meat, nor in drinking wine, nor in sexual union, for this is how living beings engage in life, but disengagement yields great fruit (5.56)." The implication is that these activities are permitted under the specified circumstances, but that even then it is better to refrain from them altogether. Manu's final redaction brings together both a Vedic tradition of sacrifice and violence and a later tradition of vegetarianism and nonviolence. To him goes the credit for synthesizing those traditions and structuring them in such a way as to illuminate his own interpretation of their interrelationship.

This is a dance of the victims and the victimizers. For the same people and animals appear on both sides of the line, and the assertions that certain animals should not be killed and that people who are leprous or blind have no rights are causally related: People who have killed certain animals are reborn as certain animals, but they are also reborn as lepers or blind men. So too not only are there punishments for humans who eat or sell certain animals, but there are also punishments for humans who eat or sell *humans*, including their sons and themselves, or who sell their wives (which Manu both permits and punishes) or drink the milk of women (5.9, 9.46, 174, 11.60, 62).

Finally, Manu invokes the argument from equivalence: "The man who offers a horse sacrifice every year for a hundred years, and the man who does not eat meat, the two of them reap the same fruit of good deeds (5.54)." That is, to sacrifice (to kill an animal) or not to (kill and) eat an animal is the same thing.

And if that fails, Manu invokes the attitude toward substitution that eventually leads to rituals such as "strangling" rice cakes, a clear atavism from an earlier sacrifice of a living creature.[38]

The *Kama-sutra* too regards abstention from meat eating as the paradigmatic act of dharma, yet it notes that people do generally eat meat. Elsewhere too it assumes that the reader of the text will eat meat, as when it recommends, after lovemaking, a midnight supper of "some bite-sized snacks: fruit juice, grilled foods, sour rice broth, soups with small pieces of roasted meats, mangoes, dried meat, and citrus fruits with sugar, according to the tastes of the region (2.10.7–8)." But even Vatsyayana draws the line at dog meat. In arguing that one should not do something stupid just because a text (including his own) tells you to do it, he quotes a verse:

Medical science, for example,
recommends cooking even dog meat,
for juice and virility;
but what intelligent person would eat it? (2.9.42)

It seems, however, that he objects to dog meat on aesthetic rather than dogmatic grounds.

THE CONTROL OF ADDICTION

The Brahmins emitted the *shastra*s, as frightened squid emit quantities of ink, to discipline the addiction that could invade the rational faculties, as the barbarians from the north would invade India in the Kali Age. The *Kama-sutra* shares with both the *Artha-shastra* and Manu (as well as with other important Indian traditions such as yoga) an emphasis on the need for the control of addiction, though each text has its own reasons for this.

The texts often call the four major addictions the vices of lust, sometimes naming them after the activities themselves—gambling, drinking, fornicating, hunting—and sometimes projecting the guilt and blame from the addict onto the objects of addiction: dice, intoxicants (wine, various forms of liquor, as well as marijuana and opium), women (or sex), and wild animals. The addictions are also called the royal vices, and indeed the typical member of the royal or warrior class is "a drinker of wine to the point of drunkenness, a lover of women, a great hunter—killing for sport," as well as a gambler and (beyond the four classical vices) a slayer of men and eater of meat.[39] That is, it was the king's job to indulge in what were, sometimes for him and always for people of other classes, deadly vices. Kings were allowed to have the vices that kill the rest of us, but even kings could be killed by an excess of them; the *Artha-shastra* advises a king to have a secret agent tempt the crown prince with all four vices and another secret agent dissuade him from them (1.1.28–29).* The *Mahabharata* (2.61.20) remarks that the four vices are the curse of a king, and indeed all four play a major part in the *Mahabharata* story: Pandu is doomed by excessive hunting and forbidden sex (book 1); Yudhishthira and Nala are undone by gambling (books 2 and 3); and the entire clan is destroyed by men who break the law against drinking (book 16). The four addictive vices of desire were also associated with violence, in the double sense of releasing pent-up violent impulses and being themselves the violent form of otherwise normal human tendencies (to search for food, take risks, drink, and procreate).

Hunting is the most obscure of the vices to the mind of nonhunting Euro-Americans, but it shares the quality of "just one more"—there are many stories of hunters who kept going even after they knew they should turn back, until they found themselves benighted or in a dangerous place, or both, † as well as the quality of blindness (as in "blind drunk") that makes the hunter mistake a human being for an animal, with disastrous consequences. Both Draupadi (MB 3.248) and Sita (R 3.42) are abducted when their men are away, hunting; King Parikshit, obsessed with hunting, impatiently insults a sage who obstructs his hunt, and is cursed to die (MB 1.26–40); and deer appear to King Yudhishthira in a dream, complaining that their numbers are dwindling because of his family's incessant hunting (MB 3.244).

We have seen the lament of the compulsive gambler, in the *Rig Veda*, and noted the self-destructive gambling of two great kings in the *Mahabharata* (Yudhishthira and Nala). The *Artha-shastra* ranks gambling as the most dangerous vice a king can have, more dangerous than (in descending order) women, drinking, and hunting (8.3.2–6). But gambling, in the form of a game of dice, was an integral part of the ceremony of royal consecration, the metaphor for the disintegrating four Ages, and a central trope for the role of chance in human life. Whereas Einstein remarked that God does not play dice with the

---

* Both Kautilya and Vatsyayana would have loved Nixon, hated Clinton. (Manu would have loathed both of them.)

† The contemporary equivalent might be the *Bonfire of the Vanities* syndrome (from Tom Wolfe's novel), in which rich people in their Mercedes accidentally end up in a really rough part of the Bronx, and the nightmare begins.

universe, Hindu texts state that God—Shiva—does indeed play* dice.[40] The
Vedic consecration ritual includes a ritual dice game of multiple symbolic meanings: the four Ages, the risk implicit in the sacrifice itself, the element of chance
in getting and keeping power, the royal vice of gambling that must be channeled into political daring, and the king's hope of "gathering" in all the winning
throws of all the other players (as Raikva did). The king is regarded as the
maker of the age, and the ceremonial dice game played at his consecration is
said, like the gambling of Shiva in Shaiva mythology, to determine what kind
of cosmic age will come up next: Golden Age or Kali Age.[41]

But one particular king, Yudhishthira, happens to be, as an individual rather
than someone in the office of king, a compulsive and unsuccessful gambler, †
and his enemies take advantage of this: They send in to play against Yudhishthira a man known to be invincible, almost certainly dishonest, and
Yudhishthira gambles away his possessions, then his brothers, himself, and his
wife. Only Draupadi's courage and wit and legal knowledge are able to save
them from slavery, and even so, they lose the kingdom and must go into exile
for twelve years, and remain disguised for a thirteenth. Thus the human vice of
addictive gambling intrudes upon the controlled ritual of gambling.

As for drinking, and intoxication more generally conceived, we have
encountered Indra's colossal hangover in the Brahmanas. There were at least
twelve types of alcohol popular in ancient India: *sura* (also called arrack, made
from coconut or from other fermented fruits or grains, or sugarcane, the
drink most often mentioned, particularly as used by non-Brahmins[42]), *panasa*
(from jackfruit), *draksha* (from grapes, often imported from Rome), *madhuka*
(from honey), *kharjura* (dates), *tala* (palm), *sikhshiva* (sugarcane), *madhvika* (distilled from the flowers of *Mahue longifolia*), *saira* (from long pepper), *arishta*
(from soapberry), *narikelaja* (from coconut), and *maireya* (now called rum).[43]

The *Artha-shastra* advises the king to appoint only teetotaling counselors (to
guard against loose talk) and to keep his sons from liquor, which might make
them cast covetous eyes on his throne (1.5, 2.16). Against enemy princes, however, liquor is a useful weapon: An enemy prince should be weakened by intoxication so that he can be more easily compelled to become an ally (2.17).

Finally, addictive lust. The *Kama-sutra,* working the other side of the street,

---

* Not only that: He cheats and is cheated (and loses to his wife, at that), causing one of their frequent
fights and separations.
† Fast-forward: In the *Amar Chitra Katha* comic book version of the story, Draupadi says that
Yudhishthira was "intoxicated by gambling," conflating two of the vices of lust.

as it were, teaches the courtesans how to create, and manipulate, sexual addiction in others. Advice to the courtesan: "A brief saying sums it up: She makes him love her but does not become addicted to him, though she acts as if she were addicted (6.2.2)." And the clear signs of a man's addiction to her are that "he trusts her with his true feelings, lives in the same way as she does, carries out her plans, is without suspicion, and has no concern for money matters (6.2.73)." Once he is hooked, she can control him: "When a man is too deeply addicted to her, he fears that she will make love with another man, and he disregards her lies. And because of his fear, he gives her a lot (6.4.39–42)." The *Kama-sutra* also offers advice to anyone, male or female, professional or amateur, on the uses of drugs to put lovers in your power (7.1–2).

More generally, renunciants regarded sex as a snare[*] and a delusion,[†] and householder life as a deathtrap. Manu even admits that what makes women so dangerous is the fact that men are so weak:

> It is the very nature of women to corrupt men here on earth; for that reason, circumspect men do not get careless and wanton among wanton women. It is not just an ignorant man, but even a learned man of the world, too, that a wanton woman can lead astray when he is in the control of lust and anger. No one should sit in a deserted place with his mother, sister, or daughter; for the strong cluster of the sensory powers drags away even a learned man (2.213–15).

Manu's entire text is an intricate regimen for the control of the senses, essential for anyone on the path to Release but also a desideratum for people on the path of rebirth. Kautilya, by contrast, tosses off the need for control of the senses with just a few, rather unhelpful lines: "The conquest of the senses arises out of training in the sciences [*vidyas*] and is accomplished by renouncing desire, anger, greed, pride, drunkenness, and exhilaration (1.6.1)." And later: "Absence of training in the sciences is the cause of a person's vices (8.3.1–61)." But Kautilya also prescribes what we would call aversion therapy for a young prince who is addicted to any of the four vices of lust:

> If in the overflowing of adolescence he sets his mind on the wives of other men, the king's agents should turn him off by means of filthy women pretending to be

---

[*] What Shaiva Siddhanta theologians called a *pasha*.
[†] What Kashmiri Shaiva theologians called *maya*.

noble women in empty houses at night.[44] If he lusts for wine, they should turn
him off by a drugged drink [a spiked drink that makes him nauseated]. If he lusts
for gambling, they should have players cheat him. If he lusts for hunting, they
should have him terrified by men pretending to be robbers blocking his path
(1.17.35–38).

The *Kama-sutra* too knows how dangerous the senses can be and likens them,
as usual, to horses: "For, just as a horse in full gallop, blinded by the energy of
his own speed, pays no attention to any post or hole or ditch on the path, so two
lovers blinded by passion in the friction of sexual battle are caught up in their
fierce energy and pay no attention to danger (2.7.33)." How to guard against
that danger? Study the *Kama-sutra*, but also use your head (2.7.34).

In the *Mahabharata*, Nala becomes an addictive gambler only after he has
been possessed by the spirit of the Kali Age, an indication that addiction in
general was perceived as coming from outside the individual. There is no idea
here of an addictive personality; the vices, rather than the people who have
them, are hierarchically ranked. The gambler is not doomed by birth, by his
character; he has somehow fallen into the bad habit of gambling, and if he
made an effort, he could get out of it. Free will, self-control, meditation, controlling the senses: This is always possible. So too there are no alcoholics, just
people who happen, at the moment, to be drinking too much. Anyone exposed
to the objects of addiction is liable to get caught. Sex is the only inborn addiction:
We are all, in this Hindu view, naturally inclined to it, exposed to it all the time,
inherently lascivious.

Manu sums up the shared underlying attitude toward the addictions:

> The ten vices [*vyasanas*] that arise from desire all end badly. Hunting, gambling,
> sleeping by day, malicious gossip, women, drunkenness, music, singing, dancing,
> and aimless wandering are the ten vices born of desire. Drinking, gambling,
> women, and hunting, in that order [i.e., with drinking the worst], are the four
> worst, and, though they are universally addictive, each vice is more serious than
> the one that follows (7.45–53).

Elsewhere (9.235 and 11.55), Manu equates the vice of drinking liquor with the
three major sins of Brahmin killing, theft, and sleeping with the guru's wife.
Those verses assume a male subject, however; drinking by women, by contrast,

Manu associates with the milder habits of keeping bad company, being separated from their husbands, sleeping, living in other people's houses, and aimless wandering (9.13).

The *Artha-shastra* basically agrees with Manu: "Four vices spring from lust—hunting, gambling, women, and drink. Lust involves humiliation, loss of property, and hanging out with undesirable persons like thieves, gamblers, hunters, singers, and musicians. Of the vices of lust, gambling is worse than hunting, women are worse than gambling, drink is worse than women (8.3.2–61)." All this is clear enough; in the *Artha-shastra*, as in *Manu,* drink is the worst vice of lust, women next, then gambling, and hunting the least destructive. But then Kautilya adds, "But gambling is worse than drink—indeed, for a king, it is the worst of the vices (8.3.62–64)," changing the order of vices for a king: Now gambling is the worst, then drink, women, and hunting last.

There was room for an even wider divergence of opinions: A Sanskrit text composed just a bit later (in the fifth or sixth century CE, in Kanchipuram) satirizes both the *Artha-shastra* and *Manu:* A young man whose father had banished him for bad behavior encouraged the king to engage in all the vices; he praised hunting because it makes you athletic, reduces phlegm, teaches you all about animals, and gets you out into the fresh air, and so forth; gambling makes you generous, sharp-eyed, single-minded, keen to take risks; *kama* is the reward for dharma and *artha*, teaches you strategy, and produces offspring (here assumed to be a Good Thing); and drinking keeps you young, uproots remorse, and gives you courage.[45]

Women

WOMEN IN THE *DHARMA-SHASTRAS*

Though women are not the worst of all the addictions, they are the only universal one, and the authors of the *shastra*s apparently found them more fun to write about than any of the others. Manu, in particular, regards women as a sexual crime about to happen: "Drinking, associating with bad people, being separated from their husbands, wandering about, sleeping, and living in other peoples' houses are the six things that corrupt women. Good looks do not matter to them, nor do they care about youth. 'A man!' they say, and enjoy sex with him, whether he is good-looking or ugly (9.12–17)." Therefore men should watch women very carefully indeed: "A girl, a young woman, or even an old woman should not do anything independently, even in her own house. In childhood a woman should be under her father's control, in youth under her husband's, and when her husband is dead, under her sons'. She should not have independence (4.147–49; 9.3)."

This lack of independence meant that in Manu's ideal world, a woman had very little space to maneuver within a marriage, nor could she get out of it: "A virtuous wife should constantly serve her husband like a god, even if he behaves badly, freely indulges his lust, and is devoid of any good qualities. A woman who abandons her own inferior husband . . . is reborn in the womb of a jackal and is tormented by the diseases born of her evil (5.154–64)." And she is not set free from this loser even when he dies:

> When her husband is dead, she may fast as much as she likes, living on auspicious flowers, roots, and fruits, but she should not even mention the name of another man. Many thousands of Brahmins who were chaste from their youth have gone to heaven without begetting offspring to continue the family. A virtuous wife who remains chaste when her husband has died goes to heaven just like those chaste men, even if she has no sons. She reaches her husband's worlds after death, and good people call her a virtuous woman (4.156–66).

Not only may she not remarry, but her *reward* for not remarrying is that she will be her husband's wife in the hereafter, which, "if he behaves badly, freely indulges his lust, and is devoid of any good qualities," may not have been her first choice.

The good news, at least, is that Manu does expect her to live on after her husband dies, not to commit suicide (suttee) on her husband's pyre. Yet Manu's fear that the widow might sleep with another man was an important strand in the later argument that the best way to ensure that the widow never slept with any other man but her husband was to make sure that she died with him. The man of course can and indeed must remarry (4.167–69). All that there is to set against all of this misogyny is Manu's grudging "keep the women happy so that they will keep the men happy" line of argument: "If the wife is not radiant, she does not stimulate the man; and because the man is not stimulated, the making of children does not happen. If the woman is radiant, the whole family is radiant, but if she is not radiant, the whole family is not radiant (3.60–63)." Well, it's better than nothing. I guess.

But we must not forget the gap between the exhortations of the texts and the actual situation on the ground. The records of donations to Buddhist stupas offer strong evidence that contradicts the *dharma-shastras'* denial to women of their rights to such property.[46] In this period, many women used their personal wealth to make grants to Jaina and Buddhist orders. Hindu women too could make donations to some of the new Hindu sects, for they received from their mothers and other female relatives "women's wealth" (*stri-dana*), what Wemmick in Charles Dickens's *Great Expectations* called "portable property," and they were often given a bride-price on marriage, the opposite of dowry (Manu is ambivalent about this), and their children, including daughters, could inherit that (9.131, 191–5). Most often women's wealth consisted of gold jewelry, which they could carry on their bodies at all times. This one claim to independence made Manu nervous; he warns against women hoarding their own movable property without their husbands' permission (9.199).

Manu is the flag bearer for the Hindu oppression of women, but the *shastras* are just as diverse here as they are on other points. The *Artha-shastra* (3.2.31) takes for granted the woman with several husbands, who poses a problem even for the permissive *Kama-sutra* (1.5.30). Kautilya is also more lenient than Manu about divorce and widow remarriage; he gives a woman far more control over her property, which consists of jewelry without limit and a small maintenance (3.2.14); she continues to own these after her husband's death—unless she remarries, in which case she forfeits them, with interest, or settles it all on her sons (3.2.19–34). Thus Kautilya allows women more independence than Manu, but both of them greatly limit women's sexual and economic freedom. Though men controlled land, cattle, and money, women had some other resources. Diamonds have always been a girl's best friend.

WOMEN IN THE *KAMA-SUTRA*

Control of the senses was always balanced by an appreciation for the sensual, and if we listen to the alternative voice of the *Kama-sutra*, we hear a rather different story.

The *Kama-sutra,* predictably, is far more open-minded than Manu about women's access to household funds, divorce, and widow remarriage. The absolute power that the wife in the *Kama-sutra* has in running the household's finances (4.1.1–41) stands in sharp contrast with Manu's statement that a wife "should not have too free a hand in spending (4.150)," and his cynical remark: "No man is able to guard women entirely by force, but they can be safely guarded if kept busy amassing and spending money, engaging in purification, attending to their duties, cooking food, and looking after the furniture

(9.10–11)." And when it comes to female promiscuity, Vatsyayana is predictably light-years ahead of Manu. Vatsyayana cites an earlier authority on the best places to pick up married women, of which the first is "on the occasion of visiting the gods" and others include a sacrifice, a wedding, or a religious festival. More secular opportunities involve playing in a park, bathing or swimming, or theatrical spectacles. More extreme occasions are offered by the spectacle of a house on fire, the commotion after a robbery, or the invasion of the countryside by an army (5.4.42). Somehow I don't think Manu would approve of meeting married women at all, let alone using devotion to the gods as an occasion for it or equating such an occasion with spectator sports like hanging around watching houses burn down.

Here we encounter the paradox of women's voices telling us, through the text, that women had no voices. Vatsyayana takes for granted the type of rape that we now call sexual harassment, as he describes men in power who can take whatever women they want (5.5.7–10). But he often expresses points of view clearly favorable to women,[47] particularly in comparison with other texts of the same era. The text often quotes women in direct speech, expressing views that men are advised to take seriously. The discussion of the reasons why women become unfaithful, for instance, rejects the traditional patriarchal party line that one finds in most Sanskrit texts, a line that punishes very cruelly indeed any woman who sleeps with a man other than her husband. The *Kama-sutra*, by contrast, begins its discussion of adultery with an egalitarian, if cynical, formulation: "A woman desires any attractive man she sees, and, in the same way, a man desires a woman. But after some consideration, the matter goes no farther (5.1.8)." The text does go on to state that women have less concern for morality than men have, and does assume that women don't think about anything but men. And it is written in the service of the hero, the would-be adulterer, who reasons, if all women are keen to give it away, why shouldn't one of them give it to him? But the author empathetically imagines various women's reasons *not* to commit adultery (of which consideration for dharma comes last, as an afterthought), and the would-be seducer takes the woman's misgivings seriously, even if only to disarm her (5.1.17–42). This discussion is ostensibly intended to teach the male reader of the text how to manipulate and exploit such women, but perhaps inadvertently, it also provides a most perceptive exposition of the reasons why inadequate husbands drive away their wives (5.1.51–54).

Such passages may express a woman's voice or at least a woman's point of view. In a culture in which men and women speak to each other (which is to say, in most cultures), we might do best to regard the authors of most texts as andro-gynes, and the *Kama-sutra* is no exception. We can find women's voices, some-times speaking against their moment in history, perhaps even against their author. By asking our own questions, which the author may or may not have considered, we can see that his text does contain many answers to them, embedded in other questions and answers that may have been more meaningful to him.

The *Kama-sutra* assumes a kind of sexual freedom for women that would have appalled Manu but simply does not interest Kautilya. To begin with, the text of the *Kama-sutra* was intended for women as well as men. Vatsyayana ar-gues at some length that some women, at least (courtesans and the daughters of kings and ministers of state) should read his text and that others should learn its contents in other ways, as people in general were expected to know the contents of texts without actually reading them (1.3.1–14). Book 3 devotes one chapter to advice to virgins trying to get husbands (3.4.36–37), and book 4 consists of in-structions for wives (the descriptions of co-wives jockeying for power could have served as the script for the opening of the *Ramayana*). Book 6 is said to have been commissioned by the courtesans of Pataliputra, presumably for their own use.

Vatsyayana is also a strong advocate for women's sexual pleasure. He tells us that a woman who does not experience the pleasures of love may hate her man and may even leave him for another (3.2.35; 4.2.31–35). If, as the context suggests, this woman is married, the casual manner in which Vatsyayana sug-gests that she leave her husband is in sharp contrast with position assumed by Manu. The *Kama-sutra* also acknowledges that women could use magic* to control their husbands, though it regards this as a last resort (4.1.19–21).[48] Vat-syayana also casually mentions, among the women that one might not only sleep with but marry (1.5.22), not only "secondhand" women (whom Manu despises as "previously had by another man") but widows: "a widow who is tormented by the weakness of the senses . . . finds, again, a man who enjoys life and is well endowed with good qualities (4.2.31–34)."

MARRIAGE AND RAPE

The basic agreement of the three principal *shastras*, as well as their divergent emphases, is manifest in their different rankings of the eight forms of marriage that all three list.

---

* This tradition continues in contemporary rural India, where women approve of "positive" magic when it represents powers acquired properly and is used to protect the family or devotional practices.

Let's begin with Manu, who ranks the marriages in this order, each named after the presiding deity or supernatural figure(s):

1. Brahma: A man gives his daughter to a good man he has summoned.
2. Gods: He gives her, in the course of a sacrifice, to the officiating priest.
3. Sages: He gives her after receiving from the bridegroom a cow and a bull.
4. The Lord of Creatures: He gives her by saying, "May the two of you fulfill your dharma together."
5. Antigods: A man takes the girl because he wants her and gives as much wealth as he can to her relatives and to the girl herself.
6. Centaurs (Gandharvas): The girl and her lover join in sexual union, out of desire.
7. Ogres (Rakshasas): A man forcibly carries off a girl out of her house, screaming and weeping, after he has killed, wounded, and broken.
8. Ghouls (Pishachas): The lowest and most evil of marriages takes place when a man secretly has sex with a girl who is asleep, drunk, or out of her mind (3.20.21–36).

Manu insists that the marriages of the ghouls and the antigods should never be performed and that for all classes but Brahmins, the best marriage is when the couple desire each other.[*]

The *Artha-shastra* defines marriages much more briefly, names them differently, and puts them in a different order:

1. Brahma.
2. Lord of Creatures.
3. Sages.
4. Gods.
5. Centaurs.
6. Antigods (receiving a dowry).
7. Ogres (taking her by force).
8. Ghouls (taking her asleep or drunk) (3.2.2–9).

---

[*] He adds that the first six are right for a Brahmin, the last four for a Kshatriya, and these same four, with the exception of the ogre marriage, for a Vaishya or Shudra. Other people say that only one, the ogre marriage, is for a Kshatriya, and only the antigod marriage for a Vaishya and Shudra, while still others say that only the marriages of the centaurs and the ogres are right for rulers.

Kautilya regards the first four as lawful with the sanction of the father of the bride, and the last four with the sanction of her father and the mother, because they are the ones who get the bride-price for her (3.2.10–11). Here, as usual, where Manu's hierarchy depends on class, Kautilya's depends on money. The *Kama-sutra* never lists the marriages at all, nor does it discuss the first four, but it gives detailed instructions on how to manage the three that are ranked last in Manu: the centaur, ghoul, and ogre marriages (3.5.12–30).

A *dharma-sutra* in the third century BCE lists only six forms of marriages;[49] it was left for all three of the later *shastras* to add the two last and worst forms, rape and drugging, a change that signals a significant loss for women. By regarding these two as worse than the other forms of marriage, but not to be ruled out, the *shastras* simultaneously legitimized rape as a form of marriage and gave some degree of legal sanction, retroactively, to women who had been raped. The inclusion of rape in all three lists might be taken as evidence that a wide divergence of customs was actually tolerated in India at that time, though as we have already heard Vatsyayana explicitly state, the fact that something is mentioned in a text is not proof that people should (or do) actually do it. That is, where Manu tells you not to do it and then how to do it, the *Kama-sutra* tells you how to do it and then not to do it. But both instances are evidence that the *shastras* acknowledge the validity, if not the virtue, of practices they do not like.

As for their differences, not surprisingly, the *Kama-sutra* ranks the love match (the centaur wedding of mutual consent) as the best form of marriage ("because it gives pleasure and costs little trouble and no formal courtship, and because its essence is mutual love [3.5.30]"), while Manu ranks it the best for all classes *except Brahmins*, and Kautilya, ever the cynic, ranks it with the bad marriages (though as the best of that second quartet). Clearly there was quite a range of opinions about the way to treat brides at this time, some hearkening back to the earlier freedom of women at the time of the *Mahabharata*, others anticipating the narrowing of women's options in the medieval period.

THE THIRD NATURE: MEN AS WOMEN

One subject on which Manu and Vatsyayana express widely divergent opinions is homosexuality. Classical Hinduism is in general significantly silent on the subject of homoeroticism, but Hindu mythology does drop hints from which we can excavate a pretty virulent homophobia.[50] The dharma textbooks generally ignore, stigmatize, or penalize male homosexual activity: Manu prescribes either loss of caste (11.68) or the mildest of sanctions, a ritual bath (11.174), in dramatic contrast with the heavy penalties, including death, for heterosexual crimes like adultery; the *Artha-shastra* stipulates the payment of just a small fine (3.18.4, 4.13.236). Most Sanskrit texts regard atypical sexual or gender behavior[51] as an intrinsic part of the nature of the person who commits such acts and refer to such a person with the Sanskrit word *kliba,* which has traditionally been translated as "eunuch," but did not primarily mean "eunuch." *Kliba* includes a wide range of meanings under the general rubric of "a man who doesn't do what a man's gotta do," * a man who fails to be a man, a defective male, a male suffering from failure, distortion, and lack. It is a catchall term that the *shastras* used to indicate a man who was in their terms sexually dysfunctional (or in ours, sexually challenged), including someone who was sterile or impotent, a transvestite, a man who had oral sex with other men, who had anal sex, a man with mutilated or defective sexual organs, a man who produced only female children, a hermaphrodite, and finally, a man who had been castrated (for men were castrated in punishment for sexual crimes in ancient India, though such men were not used in harems). "An effeminate man" or, more informally and pejoratively, a "pansy" is probably as close as English can get.

But the *Kama-sutra* departs from this view in significant ways, providing, once again, an alternative view of Hindu social customs. It does not use the pejorative term *kliba* at all, but speaks instead of a "third nature" or perhaps a "third sexuality" in the sense of sexual behavior: *tritiya prakriti,* a term that first appears in this sense in the *Mahabharata. Prakriti* ("nature"; more literally, "what is made before"), from *pra* ("before") and *kri* (the verb "to make"), is a term that we have encountered twice in other forms: as the natural language Prakrit in contrast with the artificial language Sanskrit and as the word for "matter" in contrast with "spirit" (*purusha*).† Here is what the *Kama-sutra* has to say about the third nature:

> There are two sorts of third nature, in the form of a woman and in the form of a
> man. The one in the form of a woman imitates a woman's dress, chatter, grace,
> emotions, delicacy, timidity, innocence, frailty, and bashfulness. The act that is
> done in the sexual organ is done in her mouth, and they call that "oral sex." She

---

* Krishna tells Arjuna, in the *Gita* (2.3), to stop acting like a *kliba*.
† This is a formulation from Sankhya philosophy.

gets her sexual pleasure and erotic arousal as well as her livelihood from this, living like a courtesan. That is the person of the third nature in the form of a woman (2.9.6–11).

The *Kama-sutra* says nothing more about this cross-dressing male, with his stereotypical female gender behavior, but it discusses the fellatio technique of the closeted man of the third nature, who presents himself not as a woman but as a man, a masseur, in considerable sensual detail, in the longest consecutive passage in the text describing a physical act, and with what might even be called gusto (2.9.12–24). Two verses that immediately follow the section about the third nature describe men who seem bound to one another by discriminating affection rather than promiscuous passion (2.9.35–36). These men are called men-about-town, the term used to designate the hetero (or even metro) sexual heroes of the *Kama-sutra*. In striking contrast with workingmen of the third nature, always designated by the pronoun "she" no matter whether she dresses as a man or as a woman, these men who are bound by affection are described with nouns and pronouns that unambiguously designate males, yet they are grouped with women. Vatsyayana remarks casually that some people list a person of the third nature as a "different" sort of *woman* who may be a man's lover (1.5.27). Perhaps, then, they are bisexuals.

Vatsyayana is unique in the literature of the period in describing lesbian activity. He does this at the beginning of the chapter about the harem, in a brief passage about what he calls "Oriental customs" (5.6.2–4). (The use of the term "Oriental," or "Eastern," for what Vatsyayana regards as a disreputable lesbian practice in what was soon to be a colonized part of the Gupta Empire—indeed, the eastern part—suggests that "Orientalism" began not with the British but with the Orientals themselves.) These women use dildos, as well as bulbs, roots, or fruits that have the form of the male organ, and statues of men that have distinct sexual characteristics. But they engage in sexual acts with one another not through the kind of personal choice that drives a man of the third nature, but only in the absence of men, as is sometimes said of men in prison or English boys in boarding schools: "The women of the harem cannot meet men, because they are carefully guarded; and since they have only one husband shared by many women in common, they are not satisfied. Therefore they give pleasure to one another with the following techniques." The commentary makes this explicit, and also helpfully suggests the particular vegetables that one might use: "By imagining a man, they experience a heightened emotion that gives extreme satisfaction. These things have a form just like the male sexual organ: the bulbs of arrowroot, plantain, and so forth; the roots of coconut palms, breadfruit, and so forth; and the fruits of the bottle-gourd, cucumber, and so forth (5.6.2)." One can imagine little gardens of plantain and cucumber being tenderly cultivated within the inner courtyards of the palace. The *Kama-sutra* makes only one brief reference to women who may have chosen women as sexual partners in preference to men (7.1.20; cf. Manu 8.369–70), and it never refers to women of this type as people of a "third nature." Still, here is an instance in which ancient Hindu attitudes to human behavior are far more liberal than those that have prevailed in Europe and America for most of their history.

THE ESCAPE CLAUSE

The *shastra*s present, from time to time, diametrically opposed, even contradictory opinions on a particular subject, without coming down strongly in favor of one or the other. One striking example of an apparent contradiction is Manu's discussion of the levirate (*niyoga*), the law that allows a woman to sleep with her husband's brother when the husband has failed to produce a male heir, a situation that frames the birth of the fathers of the *Mahabharata* heroes. Manu says that you should carry out the *niyoga;* in the next breath, he says that you should not, that it is not recommended, that it is despised (9.56–63, 9.64–68). The commentaries (and later scholars) explicitly regard these two sections as mutually contradictory. But Manu does mean both of them: He is saying that this is what one has to do in extremity, but that it is really a very bad thing to do, and that, if you do it, you should not enjoy it, and you should only do it once. If you have to do it, you must be *very, very careful*.

That is the way in which one should regard other apparent contradictions in Manu, such as the statement (repeated ad nauseam) that one must never kill a Brahmin and the statement: "A man may without hesitation kill anyone who attacks him with a weapon in his hand, even if it is his guru, a child or an old man, or a Brahmin thoroughly versed in the Veda, whether he does it openly or secretly; rage befalls rage (8.350–51)." One can similarly resolve Manu's diatribes against the bride-price with his casual explanations of the way to pay it (3.51–54, 9.93–100, 8.204, 8.366). But it is not difficult to make sense of all this: Ideally, you should not sleep with your brother's wife or kill a Brahmin or accept a bride-price; but there are times when you cannot help doing it, and then Manu is there to tell you how to do it. This is what you do when caught between a rock and a hard place; it is the best you can do in a no-win situation to which there is no truly satisfactory solution.

The Sanskrit term for the rock and the hard place is *apad,* which may be translated "in extremity," an emergency when normal rules do not apply, when all bets are off. *Apad* is often paired with dharma in the phrase *apad-dharma*, the right way to act in an emergency. It is the most specific of all the dharmas, even more specific than one's own dharma (*sva-dharma*), let alone general dharma; indeed, it is the very opposite of *sanatana* or *sadharana dharma*, the dharma for everyone, always. *Apad* is further supplemented by other loophole concepts such as adversity (*anaya*), distress (*arti*), and near starvation (*kshudha*). In a famine a father may kill his son and Brahmins may eat dogs (10.105–08), which would otherwise make them "dog cookers." The polluting power of dogs is over-looked in another context as well: "A woman's mouth is always unpolluted, as is a bird that knocks down a fruit; a calf is unpolluted while the milk is flowing, and a dog is unpolluted when it catches a wild animal (5.130)." That is, since you want to eat the animal that the dog has caught, you need to redefine its mouth as pure, for that occasion.

The emergency escape clause is further bolstered by recurrent references to what is an astonishingly subjective standard of moral conduct (2.6, 12, 223; 4.161, 12.27, 37). Thus the elaborate web of rules, which, if followed to the letter, would paralyze human life entirely, is equally elaborately unraveled by Manu through the escape clauses. Every knot tied in one verse is untied in another verse; the constrictive fabric that he weaves in the central text he unweaves in the subtext of *apad,* as Penelope in Homer's *Odyssey* carefully unwove at night what she had woven in the day.

Other apparent contradictions turn out to be conflations of realistic and idealized approaches to moral quandaries. Idealism, rather than realism, asserts itself in the framework of the *shastras*. But if the *shastras* themselves acknowl-edged the need to escape from the system, how seriously did rank-and-file Hindus take it? Many a young man must have seduced, or been seduced by, his guru's wife. (This situation must have been endemic, given both Manu's para-noid terror of it and its likelihood in a world in which young women married old men who had young pupils.) How likely was such a man, afterward, in punishment, to "sleep on a heated iron bed or embrace a red-hot metal cylin-der . . . or cut off his penis and testicles, hold them in his two cupped hands, and set out toward the south-west region of Ruin, walking straight ahead until he dies (11.104–05)"? Surely none but the most dedicated masochist would turn down the milder alternatives "to dispel the crime of violating his guru's marriage-bed" that Manu, as always, realistically offers: "Or he should restrain his sensory powers and eat very little for three months, eating food fit for an oblation or barley-broth (11.106–07)." How do we know that anyone ever did *any* of this?[*] Who believed the Brahmins? How was Manu used? The *shastra*s were composed by the twice born, for the twice born, and (largely) of the twice born, but "twice born" is a tantalizingly imprecise term. Often it means any of the three upper classes, but usually it means Brahmins alone.

There was a curious lack of communication between theory and practice at this time; the information on pigments and measurements in the *shastra*s on painting and architecture, respectively, do not correspond to the actual pigments and measurements of statuary, nor, on the other hand, is the extraordinary quality of the metal in the famous "Iron Pillar" of Mehrauli supported by the known existence of any treatise on metallurgy.[52] The *Kama-sutra* comments explicitly on this gap between theory and practice, and for Manu there are several quite plausible possible scenarios that will apply in different proportions to different situations: Manu may be describing actual practices that everyone does, or that some people do, that some or all do only because he tells them to, or imagined practices that no one would dream of doing.

Nor was *Manu* the basis on which most Hindus decided what to do and what not to do; local traditions, often functioning as vernacular commentaries on *Manu* (much as case law functions as a commentary on the American Constitution), did that. *Manu* is not so much a law code as it is a second-order reflection on a law code, a meditation on what a law code is all about, on the problems raised by law codes. But in the realm of the ideal, *Manu* is the cornerstone of the Brahmin vision of what human life should be, a vision to which Hindus have always paid lip service and to which in many ways many still genuinely aspire. Like all *shastra*s, it influenced expectations, tastes, and judgments, beneath the level of direct application of given cases. Often it set a mark that no one was expected to hit; sometimes it acknowledged the legitimacy of practices that it did not in fact encourage. The *Kama-sutra* too makes this dis-

---

[*] The specific vows are the Painful Vow of the Lord of Creatures and the Moon Course Vow, which involve skipping certain meals and generally eating very little.

tinction nicely when it argues, in the only verse that appears twice in the text, once in regard to oral sex and once in regard to the use of drugs: "The statement that 'There is a text for this' does not justify a practice (2.9.41; 7.2.55)." The *shastra*s therefore do not tell us what people actually did about anything, but as theoretical treatises they constitute one of the great cosmopolitan scientific literatures of the ancient world.

CHAPTER 13
BHAKTI IN SOUTH INDIA
100 BCE to 900 CE

 confused

CHRONOLOGY[1]

c. 300 BCE Greeks and Ashoka mention Pandyas, Cholas, and Cheras

c. 100 CE Cankam ("assembly") poetry is composed

c. 375 CE Pallava dynasty is founded

c. 550–880 CE Chalukya dynasty thrives

c. 500–900 CE Nayanmar Shaiva Tamil poets live

c. 600–930 CE Alvar Vaishnava Tamil poets live

c. 800 CE Manikkavacakar composes the *Tiruvacakam*

c. 880–1200 CE Chola Empire dominates South India

CAN'T WE FIND SOME OTHER GOD?

I don't call to him as my mother. I don't call to him as my father.
I thought it would be enough to call him my lord—
but he pretends I don't exist, doesn't show an ounce of mercy.
If that lord who dwells in Paccilacciramam, surrounded by pools
filled with geese, postpones the mercies meant for his devotees—
can't we find some other god?

Cuntarar, eighth century CE[2]

The image of god (Shiva, who dwells in Paccilacciramam) as a parent, as a female parent, and finally as an abandoning parent is central to the spirit of bhakti, as is the worshiper's bold and intimate threat to abandon this god, echoing the divine mercilessness even while responding to the divine love. Bhakti, which is more a general religious lifestyle or movement than a specific sect, was a major force for inclusiveness with its antinomian attitudes toward Pariahs and women, yet the violence of the passions that it generated also led to interreligious hostility. This was the third alliance, in which gods were not only on the side of devout human worshipers (as in the first alliance) but also on the side of sinners, some of whom did not worship the god in any of the conventional ways.

TIME AND SPACE, CHRONOLOGY AND GEOGRAPHY

We have now reached a point in the historical narrative where a work of fiction would say, "Meanwhile, back at the ranch" or "In another part of the forest . . ." Until now it has been possible to maintain at least the illusion (*maya*) that there was a single line of development in an intertextual tradition largely centered in North India, a kind of family tree with branches that we could trace one by one, merely stopping occasionally to note the invasion of some South Indian kingdom by a North Indian king or the growing trade between north and south. But now even that illusion evaporates. For Indian history is more like a banyan tree,[3] which, unlike the mighty oak, grows branches that return down to the earth again and again and become the roots and trunks of new trees with new branches so that eventually you have a forest of a banyan tree, and you no longer know which was the original trunk. The vertical line of time is intersected constantly by the horizontal line of space. And so we will have to keep doubling back in time to find out what has been going on in one place while we were looking somewhere else.

Now we must go south.

ANCIENT SOUTH INDIA

To understand the origins of bhakti, we need to have at least a general idea of the world in which bhakti was created, a world in which there was a synthesis between North Indian and South Indian cultural forms, active interaction between several religious movements and powerful political patronage of religion. There was constant contact and trade between North and South India at least by Mauryan times, in the fourth century BCE. South India was known already at the time of the Hebrew Bible (c. 1000 BCE) as a land of riches, perhaps the place to which King Solomon* sent his ships every three years, to bring back gold, silver, ivory, monkeys, and peacocks.[4] The southern trade route brought pearls, shells, and the fine cottons of Madurai to western lands.[5] There was

---

* The reference to Solomon's bringing gold, precious stones, and wood from Ophir (1 Kings 10:11 and 2 Chronicles 9:11) is generally interpreted as a reference to the Malabar coast. Solomon used "ships of Tarshish" to bring peacocks, monkeys, and other treasures every three years (1 Kings 10:21), probably from India, Tarshish being variously identified with places including Crete and India.

bustling contact with Rome (the Romans imported mostly luxury articles: spices, jewels, textiles, ivories, and animals, such as monkeys, parakeets, and peacocks),[6] with China, and with Indianized cultures in Southeast Asia.[7] Oxen and mules were the caravan animals, camels in the desert, and more nimble-footed asses in rough hill terrain.[8] Not horses.

The empires of South India endured far longer than any of the North Indian kingdoms, and some of them controlled, mutatis mutandis, just as much territory. The Greek historian Megasthenes, ambassador to the Mauryan king Chandragupta, in c. 300 BCE, says that the Pandya kingdom (the eastern part of the Tamil-speaking southernmost tip of India) extended to the sea and had 365 villages. Ashoka in his edicts mentions the Pandyas as well as the Cholas (the southern kingdom of Tamil Nadu), the sons of Kerala (the Cheras, on the western coast of South India), and the people on the island now known as Sri Lanka.* The Tamils, in return, were well aware of the Mauryas in particular and North India in general.

The Chola king Rajaraja I (985–1014 CE) carved out an overseas empire. The Cholas were top dogs from the ninth to the early thirteenth century, pushing outward from the Kaveri river basin,[9] attacking their neighbors, Cheras and Pandyas, as well as the present Sri Lanka to the south, and almost continually at war with their neighbors to the north, the Chalukyas. The Chalukya Pulakeshin I (543–566 CE) performed a horse sacrifice and founded a dynasty in Karnataka, with its capital at Vatapi (now Badami); it spread through the Deccan,[10] making treaties with the Cholas, Pandyas, and Cheras.[11] The Cholas finally took over the Chalukya lands in about 880.

In addition to the three great South Indian kingdoms, the Cholas, Pandyas, and Cheras, which endured for centuries, the Pallava dynasty that ruled from Kanchipuram (Kanjeevaram), directly north of the three kingdoms, was a force to be reckoned with from 375 CE on. Pallava ports had been thriving centers of trade with China, Persia, and Rome from Roman times, but the Pallavas achieved some of their greatest works of art and literature in the sixth century CE, after the disintegration of the Gupta Empire; northern artisans contributed to many of the innovations in Pallava Sanskrit literature and temple-based architecture.

---

* In the ancient period this island was called by several other names, including Tamraparni and Singhala-dvipa (later Ceylon). It was probably not identical with the place that the *Ramayana* calls Lanka, though the present island was ultimately named after the *Ramayana*'s Lanka. Nor is there any evidence that the kingdoms mentioned in Ashoka's inscriptions and in the earliest layers of Tamil literature are identical to the later kingdoms of the same name.

EARLY TAMIL BHAKTI LITERATURE

As Pallava and Chola political power and architecture spread, so did bhakti, becoming a riptide that cut across the still-powerful current of Vedic sacrifice, just as *moksha* had done centuries earlier. Beginning among Tamil-literate people,[12] bhakti soon entered the literatures of other Dravidian languages and then reached nonliterate people. It swept over the subcontinent, fertilizing the worship of Krishna at Mathura and of Jagannatha at Puri, as well as widespread traditions of pilgrimage and temple festivals. Always it kept its Tamil character and thus transported Tamil qualities to the north, transforming northern bhakti into a mix of northern and southern, Sanskrit and Tamil forms.[13]

The geographical divide is matched by a major linguistic shift, from Sanskrit and the North Indian vernaculars derived from it (Hindi, Bangla, Marathi, and so forth) to Tamil (a Dravidian language, from a family entirely separate from the Indo-European group) and its South Indian cousins, such as Telugu in Andhra, Kannada in Mysore, and Malayalam in Kerala. Although we have no surviving literature in Tamil until anthologies made in the sixth century CE, other forms of evidence tell us a great deal about a thriving culture in South India, much of it carried on in Tamil, from at least the time of Ashoka, in the third century BCE. As with Sanskrit and the North Indian vernaculars, Tamil was the language of royal decrees and poetry for many centuries before texts in Kannada, Telugu, and Malayalam began to be preserved.

Tamil as a literary language appears to have developed from traditions separate from those of Sanskrit. The inscriptions in Tamil dedications of caves were written in a form of Tamil Brahmi script, probably brought not south from the Mauryan kingdom but north from Sri Lanka.[14] The earliest extant Tamil texts are anthologies of roughly twenty-three hundred short poems probably composed by the early centuries of the Common Era, then anthologized under the Pandyas and later reanthologized under the Cholas in the ninth to thirteenth century.[15] The poems are known in their totality as Cankam ("assembly") poetry, named after a series of three legendary assemblies said to have lasted for a total of 9,990 years long, long ago. The sea is said to have destroyed the cities where the first two assemblies were held, yet another variant of that most malleable of myths, the legend of the flood. "Cankam" is the Tamil transcription of the Sanskrit/Pali word *sangham* ("assembly") and may have been applied to this literature as an afterthought, as a Hindu response to the challenge of Buddhists and Jainas, who termed their own communities *sangham*s. The Cankam anthologies demonstrate an awareness of Sanskrit literature (particularly the *Mahabharata* and *Ramayana*), of the Nandas and Mauryas, and of Buddhists and Jainas.

Brahmins who settled in the South when kingdoms were first established there gradually introduced Sanskrit into the local language and in return learned not only Tamil words but Tamil deities and rituals and much else.[16] This two-way process meant that Tamil forms of religious sentiment moved into Sanskrit (which had had Dravidian loanwords already from the time of the *Rig Veda*) and went north. The Sanskrit Puranas (compendiums of myth and history) arose in the context of the development of kingdoms in the Deccan—Chalukyas and Pallavas in particular.[17] The Tamil "local Puranas" (*sthala puranas*) both echoed the Sanskritic forms and contributed to the contents of the *Bhagavata Purana*, composed in South India.

A few of the Cankam poems are already devoted to religious subjects, singing the praise of Tirumal (Vishnu) and the river goddess Vaikai, or of Murukan, the Tamil god who had by now coalesced with the northern god Skanda, son of Shiva and Parvati. But the overwhelming majority of these first Tamil poems were devoted to two great secular themes, contrasting the intimate emotions of love, the "inner" (*akam*) world, with the virile public world of politics and war, the "outer" (*puram*) world. The poems that praised kings and heroes in the *puram* genre were the basis of later hymns in praise of the gods.

The *akam* poems used geographical landscapes, peopled by animals and characterized by particular flowers, to map the five major interior landscapes of the emotions: love in union (mountains, with monkeys, elephants, horses, and bulls); patiently waiting for a wife (forest and pasture, with deer), anger at infidelity (river valley, with storks, herons, buffalo); anxiously waiting for the beloved (seashore, with seagulls, crocodiles, sharks); separation (desert wasteland, with vultures, starving elephants, tigers, wolves).[18] *Akam* poetry also distinguished seven types of love, of which the first is unrequited love and the last is mismatched love (when the object of desire is too far above the one who desires). The bhakti poets took these secular themes, particularly those involving what Sanskrit poetry called "love in separation" (*viraha*), and reworked them to express the theological anguish of the devotee who is separated from the otiose god, not because the god does not love him in return but because the god is apparently occupied elsewhere.* The assumption seems to be that of the old blues refrain "How can I miss you if you never go away?"

---

* What Homer would have called feasting with the Ethiopians.

Beginning in about 600 CE, the wandering poets and saints devoted to Shiva (the Nayanmars,* traditionally said to number sixty-three) and to Krishna-Vishnu (the twelve Alvars) sang poems in the devotional mode of bhakti. The group of Nayanmars known as the first three (Appar, Campantar, and Cuntarar, sixth to eighth century) formed the collection called the *Tevaram*,[19] which departed from the Cankam style in using a very different Tamil grammar. Nammalvar ("Our Alvar"), the last of the great Alvars, writing in the ninth century, called his work "the sacred spoken word" (*tiruvaymoli*), and Manikkavacakar (late ninth century) called his Shaiva text "the sacred speech" (*Tiruvacakam*).[20] These works were clearly meant to be performed orally, recited, and since the tenth century they have been performed, both in homes and in temples.

Bhakti in the sense of supreme devotion to a god, Shiva, and even to the guru as god, appeared in the *Shvetashvatara Upanishad* (6.23). Ekalavya in the *Mahabharata* demonstrates a kind of primitive bhakti: great devotion to the guru and physical self-violence. The concept of bhakti was further developed in the *Ramayana* and the *Gita*, which established devotion as a third alternative to ritual action and knowledge. But South Indian bhakti ratchets up the emotion from the *Gita*, so that even a direct quotation from the *Gita* takes on an entirely different meaning in the new context, as basic words like *karma* and *bhakti* shift their connotations.

The Tamils had words for bhakti (such as *anpu* and *parru*), though eventually they also came to use the Sanskrit term (which became *patti* in Tamil). But the Tamil poets transformed the concept of bhakti not only by applying it to the local traditions of the miraculous exploits of local saints but by infusing it with a more personal confrontation, an insistence on actual physical and visual presence, a passionate transference and countertransference. A typically intimate and rural note is evident in the Alvars' retelling of the legend in the Valmiki *Ramayana* about a squirrel who assisted Rama in building the bridge to Lanka to rescue Sita; the Alvars add that in gratitude for this assistance, Rama touched the squirrel and imprinted on it the three marks visible on all Indian squirrels today.[†21] The emotional involvement, the pity, desire, and compassion of the bhakti gods causes them to forget that they are above it all,

---

* "Alvar" is both singular and plural; but the singular "Nayanar" forms the plural "Nayanmar."
† A Delhi version of the story makes the squirrel a chipmunk, which Rama stroked, making the stripes. There is also a Muslim version: Muhammad, who was known to be fond of cats, stroked them and made their stripes.

as metaphysics demands, and reduces them to the human level, as mythology demands.

Despite its royal and literary roots, bhakti is also a folk and oral phenomenon. Many of the bhakti poems were based on oral compositions, some probably even by illiterate saints.[22] Both Shaiva and Vaishnava bhakti movements incorporated folk religion and folk song into what was already a rich mix of Vedic and Upanishadic concepts, mythologies, Buddhism, Jainism, conventions of Tamil and Sanskrit poetry, and early Tamil conceptions of love, service, women, and kings,[23] to which after a while they added elements of Islam. This cultural bricolage is the rule rather than the exception in India, but the South Indian use of it is particularly diverse. As A. K. Ramanujan and Norman Cutler put it, "Past traditions and borrowings are thus re-worked into bhakti; they become materials, signifiers for a new signification, as a bicycle seat becomes a bull's head in Picasso. Often the listener/reader moves between the original material and the work before him—the double vision is part of the poetic effect."[24] This too was a two-way street, for just as Picasso imagined someone in need of a bicycle seat using his bull's head for that purpose,[25] so the new bhakti images also filtered back into other traditions, including Sanskrit traditions.

Unlike most Sanskrit authors and Cankam poets, the bhakti poets revealed details of their own lives and personalities in their texts, so that the voice of the saint is heard in the poems. The older myths take on new dimensions in the poetry: "What happens to someone else in a mythic scenario happens to the speaker in the poem."[26] And so we encounter now the use of the first person, a new literary register. It is not entirely unprecedented; we heard some voices, even women's voices (such as Apala's), in direct speech in the *Rig Veda*, and a moment in the *Mahabharata* when the narrator breaks through and reminds the reader, " I have already told you" (about Yudhishthira's dog). But the first person comes into its own in a major way in Cankam poetry and thence in South Indian bhakti.

Sectarian Diversity in South Indian Temples

The growth of bhakti is intimately connected with the burgeoning of sectarian temples. We have seen textual evidence of the growth of sectarianism in the *Mahabharata* and *Ramayana* period, supported by epigraphs and references to temples in texts such as the *Kama-sutra* and the *Artha-shastra*. We have noted the cave temples of Bhaja, Karle, Nasik, Ajanta, and Ellora. And we will soon encounter the sixth-century Vishnu temple in Deogarh in Rajasthan, and other Gupta temples at Aihole, Badami, and Pattadakal. Now is the moment to consider the first substantial *groups* of temples that we can see in the flesh, as it were, in South India, for under the Pallavas, temples began to grow into temple cities.

Building temples may have been, in part, a response to the widespread Buddhist practice of building stupas or to the Jaina and Buddhist veneration of statues of enlightened figures. Hindus vied with Buddhists in competitive fundraising, and financing temples or stupas became a bone of contention. One temple at Aihole, dedicated to a Jaina saint, has an inscription dated 636, which marks this as one of the earliest dated temples in India.[27] The Pallavas supported Buddhists, Jainas, and Brahmins and were patrons of music, painting, and literature. Many craftsmen who had worked on the caves at Ajanta, in the north, emigrated southward to meet the growing demand for Hindu art and architecture in the Tamil kingdoms.[28]

Narasimha Varman I (630–638), also known as Mahamalla or Mamalla ("great wrestler"), began the great temple complex at Mamallapuram that was named after him (it was also called Mahabalipuram); several other Pallavas probably completed it, over an extended period. At Mamallapuram, there is a free-standing Shaiva Shore Temple, a cave of Vishnu in his boar incarnation, an image of Durga slaying the buffalo demon, and five magnificent temples, called chariots (*raths*), all hewn from a single giant stone.* There is also an enormous bas-relief on a sculpted cliff, almost one hundred feet wide and fifty feet high, facing the ocean. The focus of the whole scene is a vertical cleft, in the center, through which a river cascades down, with half cobra figures (Nagas and Naginis) as well as a natural cobra in the midst of it. There are also lots of terrific elephants, deer, and monkeys, all joyously racing toward the descending river. (Real water may have flowed through the cleft at one time.) Sectarian diversity within Hinduism (as Indra and Soma and the Vedic gods were being shoved aside in favor of Vishnu, Shiva, and the goddess) is demonstrated by the dedication of different shrines to different deities and, within the great frieze, by the depiction of both an image of Shiva and a shrine to Vishnu. The frieze also contains a satire on ascetic hypocrisy: The figure of a cat stands in a yogic

---

* The site is generally known as the Five Chariots, but it is sometimes called the Seven Pagodas, and two ancient temples are said still to exist, submerged beneath the ocean, a variant of our old friend the flood myth.

pose, surrounded by mice, one of whom has joined his tiny paws in adoration of the cat; Sanskrit literature tells of a cat who pretended to be a vegetarian ascetic and ate the mice until one day, noting their dwindling numbers, they discovered mouse bones in the cat's feces.[29]

Among many other figures on this frieze is a man standing on one leg in a yogic posture, about whom art historians have argued for many years. Some say he is Arjuna, generating inner heat to persuade Shiva to give him a special weapon, as he does in the *Mahabharata* (3.41). Others say it is the sage Bhagiratha, who also appears in the *Mahabharata* (3.105–08), and in the *Ramayana* (1.42–3), generating inner heat to persuade the heavenly Ganges (the Milky Way) to come to earth to revive the ashes of his grandfathers. The wisest suggestion, I think, is that the frieze represents both at once,[30] that it is a visual form of the usual verbal panegyric, inspired by a great military victory, in 642 CE, by Mahamalla, and that it contains references to both Arjuna and Bhagiratha and to both Shiva and

[TOP] *Great Frieze at Mamallapuram, Descent of the Ganges.* [ABOVE] *The Cat Ascetic.*

Vishnu. This would make it a stone realization of the Sanskrit figure of speech called a *shlesha* ("embrace"), a literary expression that refers to two different stories at once, like the rabbit/man in the moon.

Rajaraja I began building the great temple to Shiva in Thanjavur (called the temple of Brihad-ishvara ["Great Lord"] or Raja-rajeshvara ["the Lord of the King of Kings"]) in 995 but did not live to see it completed in 1012. An inscription credits him with introducing the practice of singing hymns in that temple. One of the largest and tallest temples in all of India, it had a monumental linga in the main shrine and was a major economic venture. Rajaraja donated a great deal of war booty, including the equivalent of 230 kilos of gold, even more silver, and piles and piles of jewels. Villages throughout the Chola kingdom were taxed to support the temple, which gave back some of that wealth by functioning as a bank that made investments and loans to those same villages.[31]

The Chola kingdom was watered by the Kaveri River, sometimes called the Ganges of the South, and indeed the Kaveri basin is to South India what the Ganges basin is to North India. Eventually (in 1023), the Cholas decided to go for the real thing: They hauled quantities of water, presumably in jars, all the way from the Ganges, more than one thousand miles away, to Thanjavur, and so claimed to have re-created the holy land of the north in the middle of Tamil Nadu.[32] The water was presented to King Rajendra (1014–1044) for the ceremonial tank (henceforth known as "the Chola-Ganga") in his capital.[33] The Cholas may have been inspired by a similar project that the Rashtrakutas had undertaken in the eighth century, when they added to the great Shiva temple at Ellora a shrine with images of the three great northern rivers—the Ganges, Yamuna/Jumna, and Sarasvati—and actually brought the waters of these rivers south in large jars.[34] Closer to home, they may have had in mind the real water flowing through the sculpture of the Ganges at Mamallapuram.

The Chola temples were a major source of employment for the community. Engraved on the walls of each temple were the numbers of architects, accountants, guards, and functionaries that it employed, as well as its land revenue.[35] Numerous nonliterate assistants and ordinary laborers worked under the direction of the chief architects and master sculptors who knew the textbooks of architecture and art (the *vastu-shastras* and *shilpa-shastras*).[36] The lists also include the names of numerous temple dancers, some of whom danced only for the god, while others also danced for the king and his friends, and still others were both dancers and high-class courtesans. Dancers are often represented in sculptures on temples.[37]

The temples were not central to all aspects of worship; private worship in the home (*puja*) always remained at the heart of Hinduism, and on the other end of the spectrum, enormous communal festivals (*melas*) marked the religious year for specific areas and, on some occasions, for a great deal of the subcontinent. But temples filled a number of important roles that were covered neither by private *puja* nor by the crush of festivals. One of the innovations of bhakti was to shift the center of public activity from the courts to the temples. Now the temples, not the courts, were the hubs of pilgrimage, meeting places, and markets for souvenirs. Hinduism did *not* kick the moneylenders out of the temples, as some other religions (which shall remain nameless) made a point of doing.

The worlds of the temple radiated outward in concentric circles of temples like the concentric continents in the cosmographic mandala, growing more complex and detailed as they moved away from the core.[38] At the still center was the womb house (*garbha griha*), where the deity was present in a form almost (but not quite) without qualities (*nir-guna*), often a hidden or abstract symbol, a simple image, naked or swathed in thick layers of precious cloth. On the next level, in the chambers around the womb house, there were often friezes or freestanding images of deities, displaying more and more qualities (*sa-guna*), characteristic poses or weapons or numbers of heads or arms. The most extravagant and worldly images appeared on the outer walls of the temple and beyond it on the walls of the entire temple complex, rather like a temple fort, and on those two sets of outer walls artisans carved the more miscellaneous slice-of-life scenes as well as gorgeous women and occasional erotic groups. Just inside and outside the outermost wall, merchants sold the sorts of things that visitors might have wanted to give the deity (fragrant wreaths of flowers, coconuts and bananas and incense and camphor) or to bring home as a holy souvenir.

TEMPLES AND VIOLENCE

The downside of all this architectural glory was that sooner or later a bill was presented; there is no free temple. As endowing temples came in this period to complement and later to replace Vedic sacrifice as the ritual de rigueur for kings, the older triad of king, ritual, and violence was newly configured.

The great temple-building dynasties were people of "charm and cruelty," to borrow a phrase that has been applied to kingdoms in Southeast Asia.[39] Death and taxes were, as always, the standard operating procedure, the death consisting, from Chola times, in a series of martial expeditions to conquer the world (*dig-vijayas*). In 1014, Rajendra I invaded (the present-day) Sri Lanka, sacked Anuradhapura, plundered its stupas, opened relic chambers, and took so much treasure from the Buddhist monasteries that the Buddhist chronicles compared his forces to blood-sucking fiends (*yakkhas*). But Buddhism was not the only Chola target. A western Chalukyan inscription, in the Bijapur district, accuses the Chola army of behaving with exceptional brutality, slaughtering Hindu women, children, and Brahmins and raping high-caste girls.[40] Clearly both of these are heavily slanted evaluations.

Such violence against temples had little, if anything, to do with religious persecution. The Cholas were generally Shaivas, but within their own territories they protected and enriched both Shaiva and Vaishnava temples, as well as Jaina and Buddhist establishments.[41] It was, however, the Cholas' custom to desecrate the temples of their fellow Hindu rivals and to use their own temples to make grandiloquent statements about political power. Plunder was a prime motive for Chola military aggression; Rajaraja looted the Cheras and Pandyas in order to build the Thanjavur temple.*[42] Often the Cholas replaced brick temples with grander stone ones, particularly on their borders with the Rashtrakuta kingdom to the north.[43] Though kings and local rulers maintained large amounts of capital, the temples were the banks of that period, and the invading kings kept knocking off the temples because, as Willie Sutton once said when asked why he robbed banks, "That's where the money is."

The Chalukyas, by contrast, did not destroy the Pallava temples but were content merely to pick up some of the Pallava architectural themes to use in their own capital,[44] importing workmen from both the north and the south. Some of the Chalukya buildings are therefore among the finest extant examples of the southern style, with the enormous front gate (*gopuram*), while others are in the northern style (later epitomized in Khajuraho) and still others in the Orissan style. At first the Chalukyas cut temples right into the rock, but Pulakeshin II (610–642), using local sandstone, built some of the earliest free-standing temples in a new style at Badami and at the neighboring Aihole, Mahakuta, Alampur, and Pattadal.[45] The Chalukya Vikramaditya II (733–746), in 742, left an inscription on the Pallavas' Kailasanatha temple boasting that he had captured it but spared both it and the city, returning the gold that he had taken from the temple. Clearly this was a most unusual thing for a king to do.

---

* A motive not unlike those that drove the pious campagns of Charles Martel and Charlemagne.

KINGSHIP AND BHAKTI

South Indian religion under the Cholas and Pallavas was fueled by royal patronage, and kingship provided one model for bhakti, which, from its very inception, superimposed the divine upon the royal. Some of the early Tamil poems praise the god just as they praise their patron king; you can substitute the word "god" wherever the word "hero" or "king" occurs in some of the early royal panegyrics, and *voilà*, you have a hymn of divine praise.[46] While the secular poems praised the king's ancestors, the bhakti poems praised the god's previous incarnations; the battles of gods and of kings were described in much the same gory detail. But there is a crucial difference: The god offered his suppliants personal salvation as well as the food and wealth that kings usually gave to bards who sought their patronage, spiritual capital in addition to plain old capital.

We have noted the close ties between kingship and devotion in the image of Ram-raj in the *Ramayana,* Rama as king and god. The Cholas regarded themselves as incarnations (not the official avatars but earthly manifestations) of Vishnu but were by and large worshipers of Shiva.* Thus Vishnu (the king), the god manifest within the world, was a devotee of Shiva, the god aloof from the world. As the subject was to the king, so the king was to the god, a great chain of bhakti, all the way down the line, but the king was also identified with the god. The divine married couple, Shiva and Parvati or Sita and Rama, served as a template for the images of a number of kings and their queens† who commissioned sculptures[47] depicting, on one level, the god and his goddess and, on another, the king and his consort.‡ The bronzes commissioned by the Chola kings are the most famous, and surely among the most beautiful, of this genre of the couple standing side by side. Rama and Krishna, the primary recipients of bhakti in North India, were already kings before they were gods; the worship of Rama was by its very nature political from the start. But this was a two-way street, for the rise of bhakti also influenced the way that people treated kings and the games that the kings themselves were able to play.

---

* Temples carved with scenes from the *Ramayana* date from the fifth century CE, but most of the scenes show devotion to Shiva rather than Vishnu.

† Two sisters who were the successive wives of Vikramaditya II (733–746) commissioned two of the great temples at Pattadakal.

‡ Sometimes you can tell if it's a queen or a goddess by counting the arms—four if a goddess, two if a queen—but often the goddess too has just two arms, and then the only clues are the insignia of the goddess.

Sacred places are the counterparts to the king's domain, his capital and his forts.[48] The temple was set up like a palace, and indeed Tamil uses the same word (*koil*, also *koyil* or *kovil*, "the home [*il*] of the king [*ko*]") for both palace and temple. Temples were central to the imperial projects of the upwardly mobile dynasties; every conquering monarch felt it incumbent upon him to build a temple as a way of publicizing his achievement. Brahmins became priests in temples as they had been chaplains to kings. Temples also brought *puja* out of the house and into public life, making group *puja* the center of religious activity, mediating between the house and the palace. These manifestations of the divine were specifically local; the frescoes in the great Thanjavur Brihadishvara temple depicted not just the images of Shiva and Parvati, or of Shiva as Lord of the Dance and Destroyer of the Triple City, images that were known from northern temples, but also scenes from the legends of Shaiva saints (Nayanmars), while other temples did the same for the Vaishnava saints (Alvars).[49] By building temples, making grants for temple rituals, and having the bhakti hymns collected, the Cholas successfully harnessed and institutionalized bhakti. The deep royal connection goes a long way to explaining the ease with which religious stories and images were swept up in political maneuverings throughout the history of Hinduism.

Darshan

A feudal king, subject to a superior ruler, had to appear in person in the court of his overlord, publicly affirming his obedient service through a public demonstration of submission, so that he could see and be seen.[50] So too the temple was both the god's private dwelling and a palace, a public site where people could not only offer *puja* but look at the deity and be looked at by him. Many temples have annual processions in which the central image of the god is taken out and carried around the town in a wooden chariot (*rath*), in clear imitation of a royal procession.

Darshan ("seeing") was the means (known throughout North and South India, from the time of the Alvars and Nayanmars to the present) by which favor passed from one to the other of each of the parties linked by the gaze. One takes darshan of a king or a god, up close and personal. Darshan is a concept that comes to the world of the temple from the world of the royal court. To see the deity, therefore, and to have him (or her) see you was to make possible a transfer of power not unlike the transfer of karma or merit. And this was the intimate transference that South Indian bhakti imagined for the god and the worshiper.[51] Darshan may also have been inspired, in part, by the Buddhist practice of viewing the relics in stupas. But it was also surely a response to the new bhakti emphasis on the aspect of god in the flesh ("right before your eyes" [sakshat]), with flesh and blood qualities (sa-guna), in contrast with the aspect of a god "without qualities" (nir-guna) that the philosophers spoke of.

Artists, both Hindu and Buddhist, have always painted the eyes on a statue last of all, for that is the moment when the image comes to life, when it can see you, and you can no longer work on it; that is where the power begins.[52] Rajasthani storytellers, who use as their main prop a painting of the epic scenes, explained to one anthropologist that once the eyes of the hero were painted in, neither the artist nor the storyteller regarded it as a piece of art: "Instead, it became a mobile temple . . . the spirit of the god was now in residence."[53] The Vedic gods Varuna and Indra were said to be "thousand-eyed," because as kings they had a thousand spies, overseeing justice, and as sky gods they had the stars for their eyes. The sun is also said to be the eye of the sky, of Varuna, and of the sacrificial horse (BU 1.1) and we have noted analogies between human eyes and the sun. Varuna in the Rig Veda (2.27.9) is unblinking, a characteristic that later becomes one of the marks that distinguish any gods from mortals.[54]

In Buddhist mythology (the tale of Kunala[55]), as well as South Indian hagiography (the tale of Kannappar, which we will soon encounter), saints are often violently blinded in martyrdom. The hagiography of the eighth-century Nayanar saint Cuntarar tells us that Shiva blinded him (darshan in its negative form) after he deserted his second wife but restored his vision (darshan in its positive form) when he returned home to her again. Many of Cuntarar's bitterest poems are ascribed to the period of his blindness, including the poem cited at the opening of this chapter, which is in the genre of "blame-praise" or "worship through insult" that also became important (as "hate–devotion") in the Sanskrit tradition. Cuntarar was known for the angry tone of his poems and sometimes called himself "the harsh devotee," though the Tamil tradition called him "the friend of god."[56] His poems, which range from humorous teasing to tragic jeremiads, combined an intimate ridicule of the god with self-denigration.

The sense of personal unworthiness and the desire for the god's forgiveness that we saw in the Vedic poem to Varuna is also characteristic of attitudes toward the bhakti gods, who are, like Varuna, panoptic, as is Shiva in this poem by the twelfth-century woman poet Mahadevi:

People,

male and female,

blush when

a cloth covering their shame comes loose.

When the lord of lives

lives drowned without a face

in the world, how can you be modest?

When all the world is the eye of the lord,

onlooking everywhere, what can you

cover and conceal?[57]

The divine gaze makes meaningless the superficial trappings of both gender ("male and female") and sexuality ("covering their shame").

WOMEN IN SOUTH INDIAN BHAKTI

Gender and sexuality are front and center in bhakti poetry. The gender stereotype of women as gentle, sacrificing, and loving became the new model for the natural worshiper, replacing the gender stereotype of men as intelligent, able to understand arcane matters, and handing down the lineage of the texts. The stereotypes remained the same but were valued differently. And so men imitated women in bhakti, and women took charge of most of the family's religious observances. At the same time, a new image, perhaps even a new stereotype, arose of a woman who defied conventional society in order to pursue her personal religious calling. Only one of the Alvars, in the eighth century, was a woman, Antal, who fantasized about her union with Vishnu as his divine consort until he finally took her as his bride. Her life story is best known of all the Alvars,[58] and many women saints followed her example; her poems express her protest against the oppression of women.[59] Two of the Nayanmars were women whose words were never preserved, one a Pandyan queen and the other the mother of the poet Cuntarar.[60] But a third Nayanmar woman did leave us four poems, Karaikkal Ammaiyar.

Karaikkal Ammaiyar probably lived in the mid-sixth century CE or perhaps in the fifth century.[61] According to Cekkiyar's *Periya Purana* (twelfth century), she was born the beautiful daughter of a wealthy and devout merchant family. Shiva rewarded her devotion by manifesting in her hand delicious mangoes, which magically disappeared. When her husband saw this, he left her. Thinking that he might one day return, she continued her dharmic wifely responsibilities, keeping her husband's house and taking care of herself. One day, however, she discovered that her husband had taken another wife. Feeling that she had no more use for her physical beauty, she begged Shiva to turn her body into a skeleton and made a pilgrimage to Shiva's Himalayan abode, walking the entire way on her hands, feet in the air. Shiva granted her request that she join his entourage as an emaciated ghost or demon (*pey*), singing hymns while Shiva danced in the cremation ground. Eventually she settled in a cremation ground in Alankatu.[62] Four of her poems found a place in the Tamil Shaiva canon, the *Tirumurai*. Here is one:

> She has shriveled breasts
> and bulging veins,
> in place of white teeth
> empty cavities gape.
> With ruddy hair on her belly,
> a pair of fangs, knobby ankles and long shins
> the demon-woman wails at the desolate cremation ground
> where our lord,
> whose hanging matted hair
> blows in all eight directions,
> dances among the flames
> and refreshes his limbs.

His home is Alankatu.[63]

The female saints flagrantly challenge Manu's notorious statement about a woman's constant subservience to her father, husband, and son. They are not usually bound to a man at all, and "It is more common for a married woman saint to get rid of her husband than to endure him."[64] Defying her parents, she may escape marriage in any of several ways. She may become a courtesan, transform herself into an unmarriageable old woman, or terrify her husband by performing miracles (as Karaikkal Ammaiyar does). Or she may become widowed, presumably by chance (though those women saints were capable of almost anything). Widowhood is not normally a fate that any Hindu woman would willingly choose, but in this case the woman would regard herself as married to the god.* Or she may simply renounce marriage, walking out on her husband, leaving him for her true lover, the god. A woman named Dalayi deserted her husband while he was making love to her, at the call of Shiva (a rare reversal of the more usual pattern of the worshiper's interrupting the god when *he* is engaged in lovemaking). Or transgressing the transgression, she may *refuse* to have the god as her lover: The Virashaiva woman saint named Goggavve was so obstinate that she refused to marry the disguised Shiva, even when he threatened to kill her.[65]

The early, secular Tamil male poets often adopted a woman's point of view and a woman's voice. So basic was the woman's voice to the language of bhakti that the bhakti poets took up this convention and developed it into a complex theological argument about men speaking with the voices of women; the fifteenth-century Telugu poet Annamayya wrote many poems in a woman's voice. The female saints of course did not have to undergo any gender conversion (though some of the hagiographies tell of women who, with double-back perversity, "transformed . . . into a male by God's grace.")[66]

In a poem to Krishna, Nammalvar imagines himself as a woman abandoned by Krishna, the Dark One:

Evening has come,
but not the Dark One.
Without him here,
what shall I say?
how shall I survive?
The bulls,
their bells jingling,
have mated with the cows
and the cows are frisky.
The flutes play cruel songs,
bees flutter in the bright
white jasmine
and the blue-black lily.

---

* The Newars of Nepal marry all their young women first to Vishnu as Narayana, making their earthly husbands second husbands—unthinkable for a conventional Hindu woman—and therefore ensuring that they can never be widowed.

The sea leaps into the sky
and cries aloud.[67]

Sometimes the male poet, as worshiper, takes over from the earlier genres of
love poetry (*akam*) the voice of the lovesick heroine, or of her mother, and addresses the lover as the god. Here the male poet assumes the voice of the heroine's mother addressing Rama as destroyer of Lanka:

Like a bar of lac
or wax
thrust into fire
her mind is in peril
and you are heartless.
What shall I do for you,
lord who smashed Lanka,
land ruled by the demon?[68]

The fire that is already a cliché for lovesickness now also represents the fire of
bhakti, and the expectation is that the lover/Rama can save the heroine/worshiper,
as the incarnate god saved Sita from Ravana, but also that he may destroy her, as
he destroyed Ravana, or even perhaps that he may just let her burn, as Rama let
Sita walk into the fire of her ordeal.

Even the thoroughly male god Shiva, whom the poet calls "the lord of meeting rivers," sometimes becomes a woman in Kannada bhakti myth and poetry:

As a mother runs
close behind her child
with his hand on a cobra
or a fire,
the lord of meeting rivers
stays with me
every step of the way
and looks after me.[69]

The poem, quite straightforward, needs no gloss. But a Kannada listener/reader
would hear echoes of this story:

SHIVA AS MIDWIFE

A devotee's daughter was about to give birth to her first child. Her mother
could not cross the flooding Kaveri River and come in time to help her waiting
daughter. So Shiva took the form of the old mother—"back bent like the crescent
moon, hair white as moonlight, a bamboo staff in hand"—and came to her house.
Uma [Parvati, Shiva's wife] and Ganga [the river, often said to be a wife of Shiva]
had been sent ahead with bundles. When labor began, Shiva played midwife; a
boy was born and Mother Shiva cradled and cared for him as if he were Murukan. Soon the floods abated, and the real mother appeared on the doorstep. Shiva
began to slip away. Seeing the two women, the young couple were amazed.
"Which is my mother?" cried the girl. Before her eyes, Shiva disappeared into the
sky like lightning.[70]

"As if he were Murukan" is one of those switchbacks that the mythology of
doubling and impersonation, so dear to Shaiva literature, delights in: A human
woman might indeed treat her grandson like a god (in this case, Murukan,
the son of Shiva), but in this story the god pretends that the child is his very own
son, pretends that he himself is a woman pretending to be Shiva—a double
gender switch too, by the way. Careful, down-to-earth details, such as Shiva's
sending "bundles" on ahead with his two wives, strongly suggest that this is
a story about "women's concerns," surely a place to hear women's voices. Shiva
clearly enjoys being a woman, or else why did he not just stop the river
from flooding so that the real mother could get to her daughter? He wanted to
be there himself, to be intimately involved with this most basic of women's
experiences.

CASTE

PARIAHS

One of the great bhakti legends is the story of the Nayanar saint named Kannappar, told in several texts,[71] perhaps best known from the *Periya Purana* of
Cekkilar, dated to the reign of the Chola king Kulottunka II, 1133–1150 CE:

KANNAPPAR'S EYES

Kannappar was the chief of a tribe of dark-skinned, violent hunters, who lived by
hunting wild animals (with the help of dogs) and stealing cattle. One day he

found Shiva in the jungle; filled with love for the god and pity that he seemed to
be all alone, Kannappar resolved to feed him. So he took pieces of the meat of a
boar that he had killed, tasted each one to make sure it was tender, and brought
the meat to him. He kicked aside, with his foot, the flowers that a Brahmin priest
had left on Shiva's head and spat out on him the water from his mouth. Then he
gave him the flowers that he had worn on his own head. His feet, and his dogs'
paws, left their marks on him. He stayed with him all night, and left at dawn to
hunt again.

The Brahmin priest, returning there, removed Kannappar's offerings and hid
and watched him. In order to demonstrate for the Brahmin the greatness of
Kannappar's love, Shiva caused blood to flow from one of his eyes. To stanch the
flow, Kannappar gouged out his own eye with an arrow and replaced the god's
eye with his. When Shiva made his second eye bleed, Kannappar put his left foot
on Shiva's eye to guide his hand, and was about to pluck out his remaining eye
when Shiva stretched out his hand to stop him, and placed Kannappar at his
right hand.[72]

Kannappar may be a Nishada or some other tribal beyond the Hindu pale; one
Sanskrit version of the story calls him a Kirata. The *Periya Purana* says that his
mother was from the warrior caste of Maravars and his parents had worshiped
Murukan, but Kannappar does not seem to know the rules of Brahmin dharma,
such as the taboo on offering flesh to the gods. (Or with a historian's distance,
we might say that he does not know that high-caste Hindus, like the Brahmin
for whose benefit Shiva stages the whole grisly episode of the eyes, *no longer*
offer flesh to their gods.) He does not know about the impurity of substances,
like spit, that come from the body, the spit that he uses to clean the image as a
mother would use her spit to scrub a bit of dirt off the face of her child. (Or
again, he is unaware of the centuries that have passed since Apala, in the *Rig
Veda*, offered the god Indra the soma plant that she had pressed in her mouth.)
He reverses the proper order of head and foot by putting his foot on the head
of the god instead of his head on the god's foot, the usual gesture of respect.

Kannapar does not understand metaphor: The normal offering to a god is a
flower, perhaps a lotus, and in fact he gives the god flowers (though ones that
have been polluted, in high-caste terms, by being worn on his own head). But
Sanskrit poets often liken beautiful eyes to lotuses, and Kannappar offers the god
the real thing, the eye, the wrong half of the metaphor. Moreover, Kannappar's
gruesome indifference to his self-inflicted pain may have had conscious anteced-

ents in similar acts committed by King Shibi and by Ekalavya, in the *Maha-bharata* (not to mention the blinding of Kunala in the Buddhist tradition).

Many texts retell this story, generally specifying that the form of Shiva that Kannappar found in the forest was a linga and occasionally adding details designed to transform Kannappar from a cattle thief and hunter with dogs (like the Vedic people) into a paradigm of bhakti; thus the animals that he kills are said to be ogres offering their bodies as sacrifice to Shiva.[73] But in the *Periya Purana* his "mistakes" are *felix culpa*s that make possible an unprecedentedly direct exchange of gazes; instead of trading mere glances, he and the god trade their very eyes. This is darshan in its most direct, violent, passionate form.

BRAHMINS

Like the second of the three alliances, in which religious power (conceived of as inner heat) could be generated by individuals without the mediation of Brahmins, the third or bhakti alliance placed the power in the individual and hence by its very nature threatened the hegemony of the Brahmins. Chola records of demands for the lower castes to have equal access to temples further demonstrate that the bhakti movement had originally contained an element of protest against Brahmin exclusivity.[74] As the tale of Kannappar demonstrates so powerfully, some sects of South Indian bhakti regarded non-Brahmins as superior to Brahmins; at the very least, bhakti sometimes sidetracked Brahmin ritual by emphasizing a direct personal relationship between the devotee and the deity.[75] The devotion to the guru that played such a central part in bhakti was also a threat to Brahmins, for the guru was not necessarily a Brahmin. But it did not stop there. As Ramanujan noted, "In the lives of the bhakti saints 'the last shall be first': men wish to renounce their masculinity and to become as women; upper-caste males wish to renounce pride, privilege, and wealth, seek dishonor and self-abasement, and learn from the untouchable devotee."[76] Some bhakti groups cut across political, caste, gender, and professional divisions. Some members were Pariahs, and many were non-Brahmins.

The questioning, if not the rejection, of the hierarchies of gender and caste, coupled with a theology of love, has sometimes inspired an image of the bhakti worshipers as some sort of proto–flower children, Hinduism "lite." But on the one hand, the hierarchical categories are reified even as they are challenged—reversed sometimes, and mocked at other times, but always there. On the other hand, the Brahmin hegemony was still firmly entrenched. Shortly after the tale of Kannappar, the *Periya Purana* tells the story of Tirunalaippovar Nantanar, a

Pariah who went through fire to purify himself since he was not allowed to enter a temple; he was transformed into a Brahmin, a solution that simultaneously vindicates this particular Pariah but enforces the superiority of all Brahmins and upholds the exclusion of Pariahs from temples.[77] Later Nantanar became the hero of tales of caste protest.[78] Like Buddhism and all the other so-called ancient reform movements that protested against the injustice of the Hindu social system, the bhakti movement did not try to change or reform that system itself; reform of caste inequalities came only much later, and even then with only limited success. Rather, bhakti merely created another, alternative system that lived alongside the Brahmin imaginary, a system in which caste injustices were often noted, occasionally challenged, and rarely mitigated.

But unlike the alternative universe that the mythical sage Trishanku created, a double of ours down to the stars and the moon, the bhakti universe was bounded by that permeable membrane so characteristic of Hinduism. The good news about this was that bhakti therefore leaked back into the Brahmin imaginary from time to time, improving the condition of women and the lower castes even there. Although the leaders of many bhakti sects came from the lowest castes, particularly in the early stages of the bhakti movements, high-caste Vaishnavas and Shaivas eventually accepted their literature.[79] But the bad news was that since all permeable membranes are two-way stretches, bhakti also often made concessions to the caste system even within its own ranks—and I do mean ranks. And so what once may have been non-Brahmin texts became tangled in Brahmin values as the price of their admission to the written record. They were compiled in writing long after the period of their oral circulation and compiled in the service of an imperial project of what was essentially Shaiva colonization. Despite the non-Brahminic elements in the bhakti saints of South India, the movement by and large served Brahmin ends.

With the passage of time caste strictures often reasserted themselves; Ramanuja, the philosopher who founded a major Vaishnava bhakti sect, accepted caste divisions in some limited form, and even Chaitanya, a much later Bengali Vaishnava leader, failed to do away with them completely.[80] Nammalvar was from a low-caste farming family; all the hagiographies unanimously declared that he was a Shudra.[81] But the Shri Vaishnava Brahmins who claimed him as a founder were aware of the shadow that this ancestry cast on their legitimacy in the Brahmin imaginary and took various measures to minimize the implications of Nammalvar's low caste. For instance, one hagiographer claimed that the infant Alvar neither ate with nor looked at his family, even refusing the milk of his

Shudra mother's breast,[82] as any self-respecting Brahmin would refuse the food prepared by someone of a lower caste. One step forward, two steps backward.

THE VIOLENCE OF SOUTH INDIAN BHAKTI

Bhakti, like the ascetic movements, was strong on nonviolence to animals, generally (though not always) opposing animal sacrifice (as the story of Kannappar's meat offering demonstrates), but it was not so strong on nonviolence to humans. Love, particularly in the form of desire, can be as violent as hate, as the poet Robert Frost said of fire and ice. The ability to demonstrate indifference to physical pain was an intrinsic part of the narrative traditions of both ascetics (mortifying their flesh in various ways) and warriors, like Shibi and Karna, demonstrating their machismo. But the violence of bhakti was not always directed against the self (Kannappar tearing out his own eye) or the god (Cuntarar threatening Shiva with apostasy). Sometimes the violence was *for* god and, though usually directed against Hindus who refused to worship the god, occasionally in conflict with other religions. The violence inherent in great passion is evident in even the most superficial summary of the acts committed by the Nayanmars in the *Periya Purana*: One or another engages in violent conflicts with Jainas, attempts or commits suicide (in various ways), chops off his father's feet or his wife's hand or a queen's nose or someone else's tongue, slashes his own throat, massacres his relatives, grinds up his own elbow, sets his hair on fire, or kills and/or cooks his/her son.

Bhakti sometimes resulted in physical violence from the god toward the worshiper's family:

CIRUTTONTAR AND THE CURRIED CHILD

A Shaiva ascetic came to Ciruttontar and asked for a little boy to eat, cooked into a curry by the child's parents. Ciruttontar and his wife cut up their only child, a son, and cooked the curry. When they were about to serve it, the guest insisted first that they, too, share the meal and then that they call their son to join them, too. They called him, and he came running in from outside. The ascetic then revealed his true form, as Shiva, in the form of Bhairava, together with Parvati and his sons. He took Ciruttontar and his whole family to Kailasa.[83]

This was just a test, of the type that we know from the testing of Yudhishthira and Shibi in the *Mahabharata*. But it was a gruesome test, even more tragic than the testing of Abraham in the Hebrew Bible (for Ciruttontar's child was actually killed, though later revived) and even more horrible than the trick played on Thyestes in Greek tragedy (whose enemy served him a meal that was made of his sons, though Thyestes did not know it at the time). As in the cases of Yudhishthira and Shibi and Abraham and Job (though not Thyestes), the tragedy proves illusory or, rather, reversible: Just as Job's losses are reversed and Abraham's son is spared at the last minute, Ciruttontar's child comes back to life unharmed. (In some versions of the Ciruttontar story—the tale is told in Telugu, Tamil, and Kannada—different parts of the child's body smell of different spices as he comes running in at the end.) But surely the agony at the moment when the parents thought the child had been cooked for them was very real indeed; that too is bhakti: terrible suffering at the hands of a god. In a text from a later and rather different South Indian tradition, the Virashaiva *Basava Purana*, one of the saints excommunicates Shiva for having forced Ciruttontar to sacrifice his son. That too is bhakti: punishing the god. At the same time, we must not forget the other side of bhakti, the positive emotion of ecstasy, the rapture of being so close to the god.

INTERRELIGIOUS DIALOGUE IN ANCIENT SOUTH INDIA

A poet writing in the eleventh century in Kerala said that in the capital city, "different deities coexisted in peace like wild beasts forgetting their natural animosity in the vicinity of a holy hermitage."[84] But at times they remembered.*

BUDDHISM AND JAINISM

There is a long, sad history of stories of mutual cruelty between Hindus, Buddhists, and Jainas in South India, though there is little evidence that such stories accurately represent actual historical events. The rise of this sort of polemical literature at a time when actual relations between religions were fairly tolerant, on the whole, can perhaps be explained by the fact that Hinduism had to compete, for followers and patrons, with Jainism and Buddhism, both of which were well established in the south well before the time of the Chola ascendancy.[85] Jainism was particularly prominent in Karnataka and the Deccan, and Buddhism, from the time of Ashoka, had been firmly established among the Cholas and the Pandyas. The shift from Vedic sacrifice to other forms of

---

* The relapse into wildness is what dog trainers call "predatory drift": The tamed wild animal suddenly remembers that his companion (another dog) is his natural prey and kills him.

temple-based Hinduism, such as sectarian worship in general and bhakti in particular, meant that ordinary people began using their surplus cash to support religious leaders and institutions other than Vedic priests. The competition for their patronage as well as for royal patronage, sometimes friendly rivalry, sometimes not so friendly, often generated tensions that bhakti intensified rather than alleviated, as it gathered force from the ongoing popular resistance to the ascetic and renunciant traditions, within Hinduism but also in Buddhism and Jainism. Even the bhakti caste reforms may be seen, at least in part, as an attempt to preempt much of the Buddhists' and Jainas' claim to be a refuge from Brahmin authority and caste prejudice.[86] By winning over people of all castes, the Hindu Alvars and Nayanmars may have hoped to stem the growth of Buddhism and Jainism in the South.[87] At times this competition became hostile and broke out in angry rhetoric, especially against Jainas,[88] and in competing propaganda.[89]

The Pallava king Mahendra Varman I (600–630), a Jaina, wrote a Sanskrit comedy, the *Farce of the Drunkard's Games* (*Mattavilasa-prahasana*), about an inebriated Shaiva ascetic who accused a Vaishnava ascetic and a Buddhist monk of stealing the human skull that he used as his begging bowl, a bowl that, they eventually discovered, a stray dog had stolen. The Jainas alone escaped Mahendra's razor-sharp satire, but that was the only blade he ever used against any religious group. The Shaiva saint Appar, who had been a Jaina ascetic, converted to Shaivism, bitterly attacked Jainas (his former people) and Buddhists, and allegedly converted Mahendra Varman from Jainism. But the Pallavas continued to support Buddhists and Brahmins as well as Jainas.

In other parts of India, from time to time, Hindus, especially Shaivas, took aggressive action against Buddhism. At least two Shaiva kings* are reported to have destroyed monasteries and killed monks. The Alvar Tirumankai is said to have robbed a Buddhist monastery, stolen the central image, pounded it into dust, and used the gold for the *gopuram* at Shrirangam.[90] Some of the hymns of both the Alvars and the Nayanmars express strong anti-Buddhist and anti-Jaina sentiments. The *Tiruvatavurar Purana* and *Tiruvilaiyatal Purana* tell this story:

MANIKKAVACAKAR STRIKES THE BUDDHISTS DUMB

Three thousand Buddhist emissaries came from Sri Lanka to the Chola king, who told Manikkavacakar to defeat them in debate and proclaim the truth of the

---

* Mihirakula (early sixth century) and Sasanka (early seventh century).

Shaiva doctrine, whereupon he, the king, would eliminate the Buddhists. After the debate, Manikkavacakar appealed to the goddess Sarasvati to keep the Buddhists from profaning the truth, and she struck them all dumb. When the leader of the Buddhists converted to Shaivism, his daughter regained her ability to speak and began to refute the Buddhists, who converted, adopted the costume of Shaivas, and remained in Citamparam.[91]

Interreligious debate surely hit a low point at that moment. Only in Bihar and Bengal, because of the patronage of the Pala dynasty and some lesser kings and chiefs, did Buddhist monasteries continue to flourish. Buddhism in eastern India was well on the way to being reabsorbed into Hinduism, the dominant religion, when Arabs invaded the Ganges Valley in the twelfth century. After that there were too few Buddhists left to pose a serious challenge, but Jainism remained to fight for its life, and there are many stories about the torture and persecution of Jaina missionaries and rulers in the Tamil kingdom.

In the seventh century the Shaiva saint Tirujnana Campantar, whom the Jainas (according to the Hindus) had attempted to kill, vanquished (also according to the Hindus) the Jainas not in battle but in a contest of miracles and converted the Pandya ruler from Jainism to Shaivism. The *Periya Purana* (which narrates several episodes in which Shaivas confound Buddhists as well as Jainas[92]) tells the story like this:

CAMPANTAR AND THE IMPALED JAINAS

The wicked Jainas, blacker than black, like demons, plotted against Campantar. They set fire to the monastery where he was staying, but Campantar prayed and the fire left the monastery and, instead, attacked the Pandyan king, in the form of a fever. The king said that he would support whichever of the two groups could cure his fever; the Jainas failed, and Campantar cured the king. Then the Jainas proposed that they and Campantar should inscribe the principles of their beliefs on a palm leaf and throw the leaves into a fire; whichever did not burn would be the winner, the true religion. The fire burned up the Jainas' leaf, but not Campantar's. Then the Jainas proposed that they subject another pair of palm leaves to a floating test on the Vaikai River at Madurai. And, they added, "If we lose in the third trial, let the king have us impaled on sharpened stakes." Only the Shaiva texts floated against the current, which washed away the Jaina texts. Eight thousand Jainas impaled themselves upon the stakes.[93]

The king saw which way the holy wind was blowing and went with Campantar. The story of the three miraculous contests is not generally challenged; it is accepted as hagiography and left at that. But the part about the impalings, which does not defy the laws of nature and has been proposed as history, is much disputed.[94] Impaling was, as we saw in the tale of Mandavya, a common punishment in ancient India. But while Campantar himself reviles the Jainas in his own poetry, he doesn't mention the impaling, nor does Appar (usually regarded as slightly older than Campantar), who tells only the story of the three contests, in the early seventh century. References to the impaling begin only centuries later, and this lapse of centuries casts doubt on the historicity of the impaling. Nampi Antar Nampi, in the reign of the Chola king Rajaraja I (985–1014), refers to it, and it is illustrated in a frieze from the reign of Rajaraja II (1150–1173), in the main shrine of the Shiva temple at Taracuram (south of Kumbhakonam, in Thanjavur district, Tamil Nadu).[95] Cekkiyar, the author of the *Periya Purana* version of the story cited above, was known for his anti-Jaina sentiments.[96] Parancoti Munivar reworked the story in his *Tiruvilayatal Purana*, and it is illustrated in paintings in the great tenth-century Brihadishvara temple in Thanjavur.[97] One panel shows Campantar at the left, with the river and the texts upon it; the king and his queen(s) and minister in the middle; the impaled Jainas on the right.[98] The mass execution of Jainas is carved in frescoes on the wall of the Mandapam of the Golden Lily Tank in the temple of the goddess Minakshi in Madurai.

But there is no evidence that any of this actually happened, other than the story, and that story is told, in the ancient sources, only by the tradition that claims to have committed the violence (the Hindus), not by the tradition of the people whom the story regards as the victims (the Jainas). The only historical fact is that there is a strong tradition among Hindus celebrating their belief (right or wrong) that a Hindu king impaled a number of Jainas, that for centuries, Hindus thought that it was something to brag about and to carve on their temples, and to allude to in their poems. Telling this story both generated tension between the communities and reflected already extant tensions.

There are other stories, on both sides. Inscriptions from the sixteenth-century in Andhra Pradesh record the pride that Virashaiva leaders took in beheading white-robed (*shvetambara*) Jainas. They are also said to have converted one temple of five Jinas into a five-linga temple to Shiva, the five lingas replacing the five Jinas, and to have subjected other Jaina temples to a similar fate.[99] An inscription at Ablur in Dharwar praises attacks on Jaina temples in retaliation for Jaina opposition to the worship of Shiva.[100] A dispute is said to have arisen because the Jainas tried to prevent a Shaiva from worshiping his own idol, and in the ensuing quarrel, the Shaivas broke a Jaina idol. When the dispute was brought before the Jaina king Bijjala, he decided in favor of the Shaivas and dismissed the Jainas.[101] This crossover judgment of a Jaina king in favor of Hindus is matched by a case from the fourteenth century in which Jainas who were being harassed by one band of Hindus sought protection from another Hindu ruler.[102] Evidently there were rulers on both sides who could be relied upon to transcend the boundaries of any particular sectarian commitment in order to protect pluralism. A ray of light in a dark story.

Indeed, when conflict arose at this time, it was not generally the Shaivas versus the Jainas (let alone the Vaishnavas), but the Pandyas against the Cholas, and both kings might well be Shaivas or, for that matter, Buddhists. From time to time too, Shaivas tore down Shaiva temples, or Vaishnavas Vaishnava temples, looting the temples and hauling the images home.[103] In other words, as was the case later with the Turkish invasions, warfare had political and economic motives more often than religious ones. Yet the debate between Shaivas and Vaishnavas sometimes became quite heated. Descriptions of intersect discourse are peppered with verbs like "pummel, smash, pulverize," and, above all, "hate."[104]

CHRISTIANITY AND JUDAISM

Jainas and Buddhists had been conversation partners, friend or foe, with Hindus since the sixth century BCE. But from the early centuries CE, the Abrahamic religions joined the conversation, first Christianity, then Judaism, and then Islam.

According to the apocryphal *Acts of St. Thomas* (perhaps from the first century CE), the apostles drew lots and the Apostle Judas Thomas, who was a carpenter, got India. When Jesus appeared to him in a vision that night, Thomas said, "Whithersoever Thou wilt, our Lord, send me; only to India I will not go." Jesus nevertheless eventually indentured him, for twenty pieces of silver, to an Indian merchant, who took him to work on the palace of the ruler of Gandhara, sometime between about 19 and 45 CE.[105] After a second voyage, in 52 CE, Thomas landed in Kerala or Malabar and there established the Syrian Christian community that thrives there today; he then traveled overland to the east coast, where he was martyred in the outskirts of Chennai. As usual, the interchange went in both directions; in exchange for the goods and ideas that the Christians brought to India, they took back, along with Kerala's pepper and cinnamon, always in demand in Rome, equally palatable stories—elements of Ashvaghosha's life of the Buddha (in the second century CE), such as the virgin birth and the temptation by the devil—that may have contributed to narratives of the life of Christ.[106]

Judaism was there in South India too. We have noted Solomon's probable Malabar connections, and according to legends, Jews have resided there since the period of the destruction of the Second Temple (c. 70 CE).[107] The earliest surviving evidence of a Jewish presence, however, is a set of copper plates, dated between 970 and 1035 CE, written in Tamil, and referring to the settlement of Jews in a town north of Cochin, on the Malabar Coast in Kerala; the plates grant one Jacob Rabban various privileges, including the rights to hold a ceremonial parasol and to bear weapons.[108] The Angadi synagogue, the oldest in India, was built in 1344; a second synagogue was constructed in 1489.

ISLAM AND BHAKTI

Islam too was established on the Malabar Coast during this early period. Arabs came to India before there was such a thing as Islam, trading across the Arabian Sea to India's southwest coast, to the cities of the Chalukyas and Cheras, and to Sri Lanka. Arab horses were a major item of trade, imported by land in the north and by sea in the south, to the Kerala coast. Shortly after the Prophet's death, a group of Arabs, whom the Indians called Mapillai ("newly wed grooms" or "sons-in-law"), settled in the northern Malabar area of Kerala; when Arab merchants, newly converted to Islam, arrived there later, they converted many of the Mapillai to Islam, and they have remained there to this day. By the mid-seventh century there were sizable communities of Muslims in most of these ports.[109]

Islam thus came to India when the bhakti movement was first developing, long before Islam became a major force in the Delhi Sultanate in the eleventh century CE. These first Muslims had opportunities both to provide positive inspiration and to excite a response in opposition, to interact with South Indian bhakti on the individual and communal level. A text often appended to the tenth-century Vaishnava *Bhagavata Purana* contains a much-quoted verse that has been used to epitomize the negative relationship between bhakti and Islam. Bhakti herself speaks the verse: "I [Bhakti] was born in Dravida [South India] and grew up in Karnataka. I lived here and there in Maharashtra; and became weak and old in Gujarat. There, during the terrible Kali Age, I was shattered by heretics,* and I became weak and old along with my sons. But after reaching Vrindavana I became young and beautiful again."[110] Who are these heretics (*pakhandas*)?[111] They may very well be Jainas,[112] the traditional enemies of Shaivas in South India, but this is a Vaishnava text and probably northern rather than southern (Vrindavana being the center of pilgrimage for worshipers of Krishna in North India). The "shattering" is not mentioned until Bhakti has moved to North India, to Gujarat (an important Jaina center). Yet the verse has traditionally been interpreted to be referring to Islam, not to Jainism, as the villain of the piece.

At the same time, there were many opportunities for positive interactions between Islam and bhakti in South India. For instance, the idea of "surrender" (*prapatti*), so important to the Shri Vaishnava tradition of South India, may have been influenced by Islam (the very name of which means "surrender"). More generally, the presence of people of another faith, raising awareness of previously unimagined religious possibilities, may have inspired the spread of these new, more ecstatic forms of Hinduism and predisposed conventional Hindus to accept the more radical teachings of the bhakti poets.

PROSELYTIZING

It is not always appropriate to refer to shifts in religious affiliation, between Buddhism, Jainism, and the Vaishnava and Shaiva bhakti sects, as "conversion"; it is generally better to reserve that term for interactions with religions that have jealous gods, like Islam and Christianity. For ordinary people in ancient South India, religious pluralism was more of a supermarket than a battlefield. Laypeople often gave alms to Buddhist monks or, later, prayed to Sufi saints and still visited Hindu temples. But there were some people who really "converted," in the sense of reorienting their entire lives in line with a distinctive worldview and renouncing other competing worldviews; these were the relatively small numbers of monks, nuns, or saints, as well as the members of certain philosophical sects and—the case at hand—some of the more fanatical bhaktas.

Though Buddhism and Jainism were proselytizing religions from the start, Hinduism at first was certainly not; a person had to be born a Hindu to be a Hindu. But the renunciant religions and, after them, some of the heterodox,

---

* There is a pun on "shattered" (khandita) and "heretics" (pakhandas), verse 49.

bhakti, and philosophical sects argued that you might be born one sort of a Hindu and become another sort or even that you could be born a Jaina (or, later, a Muslim or a Protestant) and then belong not to some sort of umbrella Hinduism but to a particular ascetic or bhakti sect. And so some of the bhaktas proselytized like mad, and this made them a threat to the other religions in India in ways that Vedic Hinduism had never been. This zealous proselytizing, I think, justifies the use of the word "conversion" in some instances. The possibility of shifting allegiance entirely, from one Hindu sect to another or even to a non-Hindu religion, may be encoded even in the refrain of the god-mocking poem with which this chapter began: "Can't we find some other god?"

The bhakti authors even mocked their own proselytizing:

SHIVA BECOMES A SHAIVA

A Shaiva saint was a great proselytizer. He converted those of this world by any means whatever—love, money, brute force. One day Shiva came down in disguise to test him, but the devotee did not recognize Shiva and proceeded to convert him, forcing holy ash on the reluctant-seeming god. When his zeal became too oppressive, Shiva tried to tell him who he was, but the baptism of ash was still forced on him. Even Shiva had to become a Shaiva.[113]

The violent power of bhakti, which overcame even the god, transfigured the heart of religion in India ever after.

CHAPTER 14

GODDESSES AND GODS IN THE EARLY PURANAS

300 *to* 600 CE

༯

CHRONOLOGY (ALL DATES CE)

320–550 The Gupta dynasty reigns from Pataliputra

c. 400 Kalidasa writes Sanskrit plays and long poems

405–411 Faxian visits India

455–467 The Huns attack North India

c. 460–77 The Vakataka dynasty completes the caves at Ajanta

350–750 The *Harivamsha* (c. 450) and the early Puranas are composed: *Brahmanda* (350–950), *Kurma* (550–850), *Markandeya* (250–550), *Matsya* (250–500), *Padma* (750–1000), *Shiva* (750–1350), *Skanda* (700–1150), *Vamana* (450–900), *Varaha* (750)

THE FIRE OF SHIVA AND KAMA

Surely the fire of Shiva's anger still burns in you today,

like the fire of the mare in the ocean;

for how else, Kama, could you be so hot

as to reduce people like me to ashes?

Kalidasa, *Shakuntala*,[1] c. 400 CE

The mythology that pits Shiva's ascetic heat against Kama's erotic arrows of flame (Shiva burns Kama's body to ashes, as we shall see) and the ever-present threat of the doomsday mare remain at the heart of both Puranic mythology and Sanskrit court literature sponsored by the rulers of the Gupta Empire. As popular traditions infuse Sanskrit texts and rituals, the sectarian male gods

Shiva and Vishnu* continue to grow in power and complexity, though goddesses now begin to take center stage.

THE AGE OF GOLD

Leaving South India for the north and doubling back a bit in time, we encounter another trunk of the banyan tree that was growing steadily all the time we were sojourning in the south. While the Pallavas and Pandyas and Cholas were sorting one another out, the Gupta Empire, founded by Chandra Gupta I, spread across all of northern and much of central India: the largest empire since the fall of the Mauryas in the third century BCE. The Guptas confused matters by using the second half of the first name of the first Maurya as their dynastic name, so that Chandra Gupta I echoes Chandragupta Maurya, a kind of palimpsest of names. (The Gupta founding date [c. 324 CE] also mirrors the Maurya founding date [c. 324 BCE].) The Guptas wrote over the Mauryas: The Allahabad inscription of 379 CE (detailing the conquest of North India by Samudra Gupta [c. 335–76 CE] and his humiliation of the southern rulers) is a palimpsest written on an Ashokan pillar.[2]

Chandra Gupta II (376–415 CE), inheriting a large empire from his father, Samudra Gupta, completed the Guptas' subjugation of North India (the "conquest of the world," or *dig-vijaya*) and continued his father's policy by extending control over neighboring territories, whether by war or diplomacy (war by other means). The evidence for this control now begins to be quite a bit more substantial than the usual megalomaniac epigraphical chest beating. As there were Greek visitors to the Mauryas, so there are Chinese visitors to the Guptas, whose testimony often substantiates other sources; though they are often no more resistant to local mythmaking than were their Greek predecessors, it is always useful to have a foreign bias to set against the native bias to give us a cross fix.

The Chinese Buddhist Faxian (also spelled Fa Hsien) made a pilgrimage to India in 402 and, after his return to China, translated into Chinese the many Sanskrit Buddhist texts he brought back. He also left detailed descriptions of India, particularly Pataliputra, from 405 to 411, in his "Record of Buddhist Kingdoms." He noted with approval the means for dispensing charity and

---

* We will postpone, until chapter 17, our encounter with the Puranic Vishnu and his avatars and here consider primarily Shiva and the goddesses.

medicine and the free rest houses and hospitals that the emperor maintained. He also corroborated the claim, made in a Gupta inscription, that no one who deserved to be punished was "over-much put to torture";[3] according to Faxian, "Even in cases of repeated rebellion they only cut off the right hand." And, he added, "throughout the country the people kill no living thing nor drink wine, nor do they eat garlic or onions, with the exception of the Chandalas only."[4] (Chandalas are Pariahs.) As usual, the foreigner misinteprets the ideals of non-violence and teetotaling as actual practices. As for class conditions, one of Faxian's few criticisms of the Gupta social system was that the Chandalas were forced to do degrading tasks such as carrying out corpses and had to strike a piece of wood as they entered a town to warn upper-caste people to turn away as they approached.[5] (A later Chinese visitor, Xuan Zang, in the seventh century, observed that executioners and scavengers were forced to live outside the city.)

The Gupta style was imperial, widely exported to make its mark in Southeast Asia as well as South Asia. European historians, themselves imperialists, quite naturally thought that Empire was Good for You, that culture flourished under widespread political consolidation. The extent and the character of the rich Gupta art-historical record inspired European historians to stamp the label of "classical" on the art, architecture, and literature of the Guptas, which they also regarded as "classical" in the sense of "classics": They reminded them of Greek art. They praised the "noble simplicity and quiet grandeur" (Winckelmann) of Gupta art in contrast with the "florid" Hindu temples and texts of subsequent periods that they regarded as decadent.[6] They particularly loved the art of the Gandhara region in the Northwest, which is far more Greek than Indian (lots of drapery on everyone) and which they praised for its anatomical accuracy. They called this the Golden Age of Indian culture, a Eurocentric term, since it was the Greeks who labeled the first age Golden (while the Hindus called it the Winning Age).

MATHEMATICS AND ASTRONOMY

The Gupta court was famous for its "nine gems," the ancient equivalent of MacArthur geniuses, including several scientists who helpfully paid attention to data relevant to their birth dates. The astronomer and mathematician[*] Arya-

---

[*] Mathematics was, and remains, a subject at which Indians excel; the numbers formerly known as Arabic (because they reached Europe only after the Arabs had learned them in India) are now more

bhata,[7] born in 476, was first to calculate the solar year accurately; he also made an explicit statement that the apparent westward motion of the stars is due to the spherical earth's rotation about its axis, and he correctly ascribed the luminosity of the moon and planets to reflected sunlight. His works circulated in the northwest of India and contributed greatly to the development of Islamic astronomy.

The astronomer Varahamihira (505–587) composed a masterful compendium of Greek, Egyptian, Roman, and Indian astronomy; made major advances in trigonometry; and discovered a version of Pascal's triangle. He is also well known for his contributions to iconography and astrology. The mathematician Brahmagupta (598–665) defined zero as the result of subtracting a number from itself. Committed to the theory of the four Ages, he employed Aryabhata's system of starting each day at midnight but rejected Aryabhata's statement that the earth is a spinning sphere. He also dismissed Jaina cosmological views. Like Aryabhata, Brahmagupta profoundly influenced Islamic and Byzantine astronomy. The astronomical and mathematical achievements of the Gupta court show that this period's efflorescence of art and literature—both religious and secular—was part of a broader pattern of creativity and innovation.

Other forms of inventiveness also flourished under the Guptas. Around this time someone in India invented chess. It began as a four-player war game called *chaturanga* ("four-limbs"), a Sanskrit name for a quadripartite battle formation mentioned in the *Mahabharata*. *Chaturanga* flourished in northwestern India by the seventh century and is regarded as the earliest precursor of modern chess because it had two key features found in all later chess variants: Different pieces had different powers (unlike games like checkers and Go), and victory was based on one piece, the king in modern chess. ("Checkmate" is a word derived from the Persian/Arabic *shah-mat* ["the king is dead].") There was therefore an atmosphere in which many branches of learning thrived.

THE AGE OF FOOL'S GOLD?

The dynasty soon gave way to a number of weaker kingdoms and to the Huns, who nipped any subsequent budding Gupta emperors in the bud until the Turks and Sassanian Persians finally stopped them for good.[8] Samudra Gupta had performed a horse sacrifice at which he allegedly gave away ten thousand cows, and his prolific gold coins abound in magnificent horses.[9] But

---

properly known as Hindu-Arabic (and should be still more properly known as Indian-Arabic); they were first attested in the Ashokan inscriptions.

when the Huns severed trade routes in the north, they cut off the vital supply of equine bloodstock overland from central Asia to India. From now on, horses had to be imported to India by sea from Arabia, which made them even more expensive than before and put the Arabs entirely in control of the horse trade. The Guptas' famous gold coinage became first debased, then crudely cast, increasingly stereotyped, scarce, and finally nonexistent,[10] as the empire disintegrated into multiple small kingdoms. But how golden was the Gupta age even in its prime?

Again we encounter a trick of the available light: Because we have Faxian and a lot of inscriptions, we think we know the Guptas, and many historians have been caught up in the spirit of the Guptas' own self-aggrandizement. The Guptas did their boasting in Sanskrit, the language they chose for their courts, a move of conscious archaism. Prior to this, kings had done their boasting in the language that ordinary people spoke, one of the Prakrits, like the Magadhi of the Buddha and of Ashoka. Brahmins had continued to use Sanskrit in such a way that a bilingual literary culture underlay such great texts as the *Mahabharata* and the Puranas, the medieval Sanskrit (and, later, vernacular) compendiums of myth and ritual, which began to be assembled during the Gupta age.[11] The Guptas' use of Sanskrit and patronage of Sanskrit literature also contributed to the Euro-American identification of their age as classical.

But Gupta art, however pretty, was not nearly as imaginative or vigorous as that of the ages that preceded and followed it; it seems lifeless and bloodless, classical in the sense of "boring," in comparison with the earlier Kushana sculpture and, later, the voluptuous statues of the Cholas, the vibrant images of Basohli painting. In my humble opinion, Indian art is better than Greek art and therefore *much* better than art (such as Gupta art) that imitates Hellenistic art (which is second-rate Greek art). The architecture of the first Gupta temples, such as those at Aihole, Badami, and Pattadakal, or the temple of the Ten Avatars (Dashavatara) at Deogarh, in Uttar Pradesh (c. sixth to seventh century), cannot compare with the temples built from the tenth century, the "dazzling ornamented surfaces" of Khajuraho, Konarak, Tanjavur, and Madurai, to name just a few.[12] Other scholars too have judged the Gupta Age to be one of "extraordinary restraint," which eliminated options and alternatives for those "living in the strait-jacket of orthodox Hinduism."[13]

It is a general perversity of Indian history that its greatest architectural monuments—both the great temple clusters and the great palaces and forts—were created not in the centers of power like Pataliputra but in relatively remote provinces, and this is certainly true of the Gupta Age.[14] It was in Ajanta, a fairly remote town in the Deccan, that Harisena of the Vakataka dynasty (c. 460–477), who owed nothing to Gupta patronage—or, more to the point, to Gupta control—completed the great caves whose walls are alive with the first examples of what has been called narrative painting:* scenes depicting the life of the Buddha, his previous lives (Jatakas), a storm at sea, a shipwreck, and the only panoramic battle scene known from ancient India.[15] Great things, golden things, did happen in the Gupta Age, but not always at the hands of the Gupta rulers.

Moreover, the artisans who carved the temples and who ranked socially with musicians and dancing girls, types that always made the Brahmins nervous,[16] did not thrive in this period, as Romila Thapar points out:

> The description of the Gupta period as one of classicism is relatively correct regarding the upper classes, who lived well according to descriptions in their literature and representations in their art. The more accurate, literal evidence that comes from archeology suggests a less glowing life-style for the majority. Materially, excavated sites reveal that the average standard of living was higher in the preceding period.[17]

Yet, as we are about to see, that lower-class majority made its mark upon the upper classes.

FROM THE VILLAGE TO THE COURT: LOST IN TRANSLATION

Sanskrit court poetry drew on earlier Sanskrit texts, as one would expect from the general force of tradition and intertextuality. But it also drew upon folk traditions, as indeed the earlier Sanskrit texts had often done. In translating the plot from one idiom to another, or even from oral/written epic to court dramas, the Gupta poets edited out a great deal, but not all, of the power and dignity of women. One example will stand for many.

The poet Kalidasa, generally regarded as the greatest poet in the Sanskrit tradition, the Shakespeare of India, reworked in his play *Shakuntala* (more precisely "The Recognition of Shakuntala") a story that the *Mahabharata* tells at some length: King Dushyanta encounters Shakuntala in the forest while he

---

* Though narratives were depicted earlier in sculpture, on Buddhist stupas such as Sanchi and Amaravati.

is hunting, killing too many animals and terrifying the rest. He marries her with the ceremony of mutual consent (the Gandharva marriage or marriage of the centaurs) and returns to his court; when she brings their son to him at court, he lies, swearing that he never saw her before, until a disembodied voice from the sky proclaims the child his, and then he says he knew it all along (1.64–69). Dushyanta's cruelty to his sexual partner is foreshadowed by his out-of-control hunting—the two vices are closely connected in the Hindu view—and hardly mitigated by his statement that he rejected Shakuntala because of his fear of public disapproval, an argument that rang equally hollow when Rama used it to reject Sita. Dushyanta is one of a large crowd of *Mahabharata* kings who had children secretly, and Shakuntala one of many women who had them illegitimately.

Whereas the story in the *Mahabharata* is about power and inheritance, Kalidasa turns it into a story about desire and memory. Kalidasa probably had the patronage of the Gupta dynasty, perhaps Chandra Gupta II.* (His poem *The Birth of the Prince,* ostensibly about the birth of the son of Shiva and Parvati— the god Skanda, also called Kumara ["the Youth" or "the Prince"]—may also be an extended pun to celebrate the birth of Kumara Gupta.) The story of Shakuntala was important to the Guptas, for the child of Shakuntala and Dushyanta, named Bharata, was one of the founders of the dynasty that the Guptas claimed for their lineage.† Kalidasa had his work cut out for him to transform Bharata's father from a lying cad‡ to a sympathetic lover,[18] and to give credit where credit's due, he did at least feel that Dushyanta needed some sort of excuse for treating Shakuntala as he did. And so he fell back upon the tried-and-true folk device of the magic ring of memory[19] and the curse of an angry Brahmin (the *presbyter ex machina*): A sage whom Shakuntala neglected in her lovesick distraction put a curse on her, ensuring that the king would forget her until he saw the ring that he (the king) had given her. Shakuntala lost the ring; Dushyanta therefore honestly did not remember her until a fisherman found the ring in a fish that had swallowed it (and was caught and served at Dush-yanta's table). Then Dushyanta was terribly, terribly sorry about it all, and he

---

* The dating of Kalidasa is conjectural, but there is convincing circumstantial evidence to place him during the Gupta period.

† *Bharata* is the word used to designate India in most North Indian languages, to this day.

‡ Fast-forward: In 1938 Akhtar Husain Raipuri translated the play into Urdu. He argued that Kalidasa, being a man of his time and identifying with Brahminical high culture, changed the original epic story in an attempt "to save the king from being seen for what he really was—a man who refused to accept responsibility for seducing an innocent woman" (and, I would add, abandoning her).

searched until he found Shakuntala and his son at last. In this retelling, Shakuntala's mistake (a trivial breach of ascetiquette) injures Dushyanta's mind,
through a kind of transfer of karma, or transitive imagination; it's really all her
fault. Dushyanta suffers for actions committed by someone else, actions of
which he is completely innocent,[20] but of course he is also guilty of an even more
serious forgetfulness than the one that Shakuntala suffers for. At the same time,
the curse on Shakuntala merely activates what is already there *in nuce* in Dushyanta, his forgetfulness. The whole fishy story gets Dushyanta (and Kalidasa)
out of what subsequent Indian scholars recognized as a true moral dilemma.

Shakuntala loses her agency in Kalidasa's hands. In the *Mahabharata* she is
a wise woman who discourses at length on dharma; in Kalidasa she is hardly
more than a child and says little when the king accuses her of lying; indeed most
of her words reach us only because the king tells us she said them. Kalidasa's
Shakuntala, still pregnant, is snatched up by her celestial mother, just as Sita is
after Rama has abandoned her, also pregnant. Indeed the parallels with Sita go
further: Both women are daughters of supernatural women (Shakuntala
the daughter of the celestial nymph Menaka, Sita the daughter of the earth) and
are themselves supernatural (in one reading, Shakuntala is a celestial nymph[21]),
both come from another world to bear the king a son (or sons), and both disappear when the king abuses them. Sisters in the plot, they are also the cousins of
the equine goddesses Saranyu and Urvashi.

Kalidasa's treatment of Shakuntala suggests the declining power and status
of women in this period, though at least some real women exercised considerable power in the highest corridors of Gupta polity. Chandra Gupta I married
a Nepalese (Lichavi) princess, an alliance that extended his territory through
Pataliputra to parts of Nepal; she, and her dowry, were so important that their
son referred to himself as a "son of a Lichavi daughter" rather than of a Gupta
father, and coins showing the king and queen together bear her name as
well as his.[22] Chandra Gupta II arranged a marriage between his daughter
Prabhavati (whose mother was a princess of the Naga people) and Rudrasena
II, king of the Vakatakas, to strengthen his southern flank; when Rudrasena
died, Prabhavati acted as regent for her sons, thereby increasing Gupta influence in the south.

How are we to explain this discrepancy between the literary and political
evidence? General considerations of the relationship between myth and history
operate here: The myths reflect attitudes toward women rather than the actual
history of real women, but they also influence the subsequent actual history of

real women. We might also discount either the political evidence (to argue that the women who were married to the Gupta kings were simply pawns with no real power or that they are the exception to the general rule about the powers of ordinary women) or the literary evidence (to argue that Kalidasa's presentation of women is not typical of attitudes toward women expressed in other literature of this period, such as the Puranas, which we will soon encounter). Both are possible. A third argument, that there is an inverse correlation between the powers of goddesses or supernatural women in texts and natural women on the ground, is one that we will soon consider in the context of *shakti*.

DIVERSITY AND SECTARIAN WORSHIP

In tandem with the general tendency to clamp down on such matters as the rights of women, the narrow-minded attitude to deviation implicit in the concept of heresy took on new power in the Gupta Age.[23] Yet there was a great deal of variation in religious life under the Guptas, in part because the basic political conditions provoked different reactions in different sectors of the population. This had been the case in the centuries preceding the Guptas: The *Ramayana* and the *Mahabharata*, though roughly contemporaneous, had very different attitudes to dharma, as did *Manu* and the *Artha-shastra* and the *Kama-sutra*, also roughly contemporaneous. Such variations were facilitated by the looser political reins of the preimperial age, but under the Guptas too there was room to kick over the traces from time to time. The sectarian diversity of the Guptas, which at times approached a kind of mellow inclusivism, may have been inspired by a need to bring the various sects and religions under the new yoke of empire or simply to differentiate themselves from other rulers, such as those in South India, who were more partisan.

Some Gupta kings sponsored Vishnu and seemed to believe that in return, Vishnu sponsored the Gupta Empire. They put his boar incarnation and the figure of Lakshmi, Vishnu's consort, on their coins and made mythology "a state concern, enlisting particularly Vishnu and his heroic incarnations for their politics."[24] The Allahabad inscription of 379 CE identifies Samudra Gupta with Vishnu.[25] But royal patronage was, all in all, even-handed, and the Gupta kings took the names of various gods; some Guptas leaned one way, some another, and some were pluralistic, but all in all a thousand *pujas* bloomed. And what imperial overlay there was ran pretty thin by the time it trickled down to individual texts, as is evident from the sectarian distribution of the Puranas, some devoted to Shiva, some to Vishnu, some to a goddess, while even a Purana officially devoted to a particular god often devoted considerable space to other gods.[26]

Chandra Gupta II was a devout Hindu, but he also patronized Buddhism and Jainism. In Pataliputra, Faxian witnessed an annual festival in which twenty chariots carrying Buddhist stupas covered with images of the gods and bodhisattvas and figures of the Buddha, all in silver and gold, entered the city after the *brahma-charins* (probably the Brahmins as a whole, not merely the students or the celibates) invited them to do so, an impressive demonstration of ecumenism. Gupta emperors dedicated many Buddhist buildings (stupas, monasteries, and prayer halls), while some of the earliest Hindu temples were built and Hindu icons sculpted during this period (the fifth to eighth centuries). Rock-cut temples and structural temples shared a widely disseminated set of conventions.[27]

The burgeoning religious diversity that the Guptas had encouraged came to an abrupt end when the Huns, who were literal iconoclasts of an extreme sort, especially hostile to Buddhism, began to attack North India in the second half of the fifth century CE; they overran Kashmir and the Punjab and Malwa as far as Gwalior. Buddhism in the Indus basin never recovered from the depredations of the Huns, who killed monks and destroyed monasteries.[28] Adding insult to injury, some Shaiva Brahmins, also hostile to Buddhism, took advantage of the Huns' anti-Buddhism and accepted grants of land from the Huns.[29]

POPULAR TRADITIONS IN THE EARLY SANSKRIT PURANAS: FOUND IN TRANSLATION

The complex interactions between Hindu sects, between Hinduism and Buddhism and Jainism, and between court and village are manifest in various ways in the principal religious texts that developed in this period, the Puranas. Gupta literature came first and reworked folk and epic materials in its own way; then the Puranas came along and reworked both folklore and Gupta literature. The Puranas are far less fastidious than the Vedic texts or even the *Mahabharata*, more relaxed about both language and caste than anything that we have so far encountered. Scholars of Sanskrit poetry poke fun at the bad Sanskrit of the Puranas, which they view as the pulp fiction of ancient India or, as one of my students suggested, the hip-hop of the medieval world,[30] in comparison with court poetry that has the cachet of Shakespeare.

There are often said to be eighteen Puranas and innumerable "Sub-Puranas"

(Upa-puranas), but the lists vary greatly, as do their dates, about which no one is certain,[31] and their contents. The Puranas are not about what they say they are about. They *say* they are about the "Five Signs," which are listed at the start of most Puranas: creation (*sarga*, "emission"), secondary creation (*pratisarga*), the genealogy of gods and kings, the reigns of the Manus (a different mythical Manu was born in each age, to help create the world), and the history of the solar and lunar dynasties. The genealogies of gods, Manus, and kings form an open-ended armature; into these rather vague categories (which some Puranas ignore entirely in any case) individual authors fit what they really want to talk about: the way to live a pious life, and to worship the gods and goddesses. This includes the rituals (*pujas*) that you should perform at home, in the temple, and on special festival days; places to visit on pilgrimage; prayers to recite; and stories to tell and to hear. The closed totality thinking of the *shastras* gives way to open infinity thinking in the Puranas, which often seem to swing at everything that comes across the plate.

Purana means "ancient," and these Sanskrit compendiums of myth and ritual face resolutely back to the hoary past, a conservative stance; the new genre positions itself as age-old, anonymous. It also strikes an imperial stance: The improved communications across the empire and the sense that it was all part of a single cultural unit, from sea to sea (as Manu put it), inspired a kind of literary cosmopolitanism. Kalidasa's poem *The Cloud Messenger* uses the poetic fallacy of a banished lover who enlists a cloud to carry a message to his faraway beloved; it presents a positively imperial survey of the aerial route from Rama-giri (near Nagpur) via Ujjain to Mount Kailasa in the Himalayas.

But the Puranas also provided a Sanskrit medium for popular material transmitted through all classes and places in India, fusing the cosmopolitan, translocal vision of the Gupta court with new local traditions, the praise of the particular *tirtha* in our village, this temple, our river, and instructions on how to worship right here. What set the Puranas apart from one another was primarily the sectarian bias, all the stories (as well as rituals and doctrines) about *our* god, *our* pilgrimage place. Their sectarian view says not "This is the whole world" but "This is our whole world."

The treatment of low castes and especially tribals in the Puranas reflects a nervousness about absorbing these groups into the empire. The early Puranas continued to appropriate popular beliefs and ideas from people of various castes.[32] The very different challenges posed by renunciation, on the one hand, and the luxuriant growth of sectarian diversity, on the other, which the authors of the *dharma-shastra*s worked so hard to reconcile with their own agendas, looked like the chance of a lifetime for the authors of the Puranas. Doctrinally orthoprax Hinduism functioned, as ever, to include everything under the Indian sun. The excluded people (rural storytellers, lower classes, women) who until now had had only episodic success in breaking into Sanskrit literature (Raikva's walk-on part in the Upanishads, Draupadi's embarrassing polyandry) managed now to get major speaking roles. Nurtured first by the patronage of the Guptas and then by the less structured political systems that followed them, the nonhegemonic, non-Vedic traditions supply the major substance of the Puranas.

The growth of temples also led to the greater use of ritual texts, both the Puranas and the texts called *agama*s, which instructed worshipers in the way to perform *puja*s.[33] One of the great innovations of the rise of temple worship is that it eventually made it possible for people who could not read Sanskrit texts to have access to Sanskrit myths and rituals. The images carved on temples brought into the public sphere the mythology of the Puranas. For iconography transcends illiteracy; people get to see the images even if they can't read the texts, and somebody—possibly but not necessarily the priest in the temple—knows the story and tells it. Often someone sitting beside the person reciting the Purana would explain it to those innocent of Sanskrit; these public recitals, collective listenings, were open to everyone, regardless of caste or gender.[34] Moreover, once the images are on the *outsides* of temples, people can see them even if they are Pariahs and not allowed inside the temples. And in return, the temples were part of a system by which folk deities and local religious traditions entered the Brahmin imaginary.

THE BRAHMIN FILTER

The Puranas mediate between the Sanskrit of court poetry and the oral or vernacular traditions. Sometimes, but not always, there was a social and/or economic distance between the classes that produced the vernacular texts, Puranas, and court poetry, but we cannot assume that the Puranas come from poor people. The Puranas cut across class lines and included wealthy merchants among their patrons. One reason why it was possible for the Puranas to assimilate an astonishingly wide range of beliefs and for Hindus to tolerate that range not only within their scriptures and communities but within their own families was their lack of strict orthodoxy. Storytellers smuggled new ideas in under the Brahmin radar, stashing them in older categories, often categories to which the new ideas did not really belong. Significantly, most of the rituals described in the Puranas do not require the mediation of a Brahmin priest;[35] so much for the stranglehold of Brahmin ideology. Moreover, the folk materials made their way into the Sanskrit corpus because the Brahmins were no longer able to ignore them—they were part of such widespread religious movements— and also because the Brahmins, like the privileged in all periods, knew a good thing when they saw it, and these were terrific stories, in many cases the Brahmins' own household stories.

The village traditions and local folk traditions, which the anthropologist Robert Redfield decades ago labeled "little,"[36] in fact constitute most of Hinduism and are one of the main sources even of the so-called pan-Indian traditions (such as the Puranas), which Redfield called the "great" tradition. "Little" carries pejorative as well as geographical connotations, not just small individual villages but a minor, cruder, less civilized tradition beneath scholarly contempt. Yet in terms of both the area that the villages cover in India *as a whole* and their populations (even now 72.2 percent of the national total, according to the 2001 census[37]), not to mention the size of their creative contributions, the terms should really be reversed: the pan-Indian tradition is little, while the village cultures are a (the) great tradition.[38]

What the so-called pan-Indian tradition in effect designates is the lettered, written tradition, the literary tradition, which can claim to be "pan" to the extent that the names of some texts—the Veda, the *Ramayana*—are known all over India (and well beyond), though not everyone in India knows more than an outline of their contents.

We might better use the Sanskrit/Hindi terms and call the local traditions *deshi* or *sthala* (terms meaning "local" or "from our place" or "from our homeland"). The *sthala* Puranas are a genre glorifying not a specific deity but a specific temple or town, usually composed in the vernacular language of that special place. History is local; the texts respond less to the policies of the emperor a thousand miles away than to the mood swings of the local tax collector. The village is also one of the places where we will find the comic vision of the common people, glorying in Hinduism's ability to laugh at its own gods, defying the piety of the more puritanical members of the tradition. The folk tradition in particular takes pleasure in mocking Brahmins. The concepts of the pan-Indian tradition, widely but not universally known to Hindus from all parts of the subcontinent and beyond, and even less universally believed, are embroidered on top of a much larger fabric woven in each local community. Tribal people too were being acculturated into Hindu society during this period, resulting in both their contribution of stories to the Puranas and scattered depictions of them in those texts.[39]

Set against this flow of often non-Brahmin ideas into Sanskrit literature was, however, the final filter of the Sanskrit texts, a Brahmin filter, which tried to domesticate it all, or at the very least to frame it in Brahmin ideology, a process that we have noted even in the transition from the *Mahabharata* to Kalidasa. Brahmins' attitudes to oral folk traditions range from complete ignorance to condemnation but most often amount to appropriating them into their own texts, sometimes in bowdlerized and sanitized forms. Oral (or, better, unwritten) traditions are thus "overwritten" by the literary traditions, which "Hinduize" or "Puranicize" them by consistently changing, in addition to language, food (from meat eating to vegetarianism), caste (from low-caste priests to high Brahmins), and gender (from female storytellers to male).[40] In later centuries we can trace actual transitions from folktales in various vernaculars (such as Tamil, Bangla, Telugu, and Hindi) to Sanskrit versions that the Brahmins thoroughly reworked, but (hindsight alert!) we cannot assume that the same things happened in the same way centuries earlier; there may have been less, or perhaps more, revision then.

For example, if we take a folktale originally told, in Telugu, by a caste of traders and merchants who were "left-hand" (unclean, lower caste), and compare it with the same tale retold, in a Sanskrit Purana, by the same caste when it has moved up to the status of Vaishyas, some things change: In the folk version, the woman protagonist makes decisions for herself as well as for the caste, while in the Sanskrit version, the Brahmin priest makes all the decisions.[41] Yet vast amounts of folklore do slip through the filter and get into the Puranas more or less intact, so that the Brahmin interpretation of the material does not necessarily erase local color and regional flavor. Sometimes the value system survives the journey, like a wine that travels well, and sometimes it does not. But we need not assume that the Brahmin redactors squeezed all the life out of the stories. The Brahmin sieve was not subtle enough to block entirely the currents of folk literature, which flowed in through every opening, particularly in matters concerning goddesses.

Moreover, by this time the Brahmin hold on Sanskrit had begun to be eroded; Vaishyas could read Sanskrit too, and non-Brahmins used Sanskrit in many secular spheres. More to the point, there were many different sorts of Brahmins, Brahmins of various ranks, often distinguished simply by their geographical location or by the degree of their learning, a distinction we saw even in the Brahmanas. Brahmins were not homogeneous; some were more at home with oral presentations than with reading and writing. We have seen that, in the myths, there were Brahmins among the ogres; now there are references to human Brahmins whose ancestors were said to be ogres.[42] So too in actual life there were Shudra Brahmins, *mleccha* Brahmins, Chandala Brahmins, and Nishada Brahmins (who are said to be thieves and fond of fish and meat).[43] Some were very close indeed to the folk sources that they incorporated into the Puranas.

Sectarian Contests

The tensions between the worshipers of Vishnu and Shiva were relatively mild but important enough to be explicitly addressed in narratives. The concept of a trinity, a triumvirate of Brahma, Vishnu, and Shiva (the Trimurti [Triple Form]), which both Kalidasa and the *Markandeya Purana* mention, is a misleading convention. (The triumvirate may have been sustained, though not invented, in response to the Christian trinity.) The idea that Brahma is responsible for creation, Vishnu for preservation or maintenance, and Shiva for destruction does not correspond in any way to the mythology, in which both Vishnu and Shiva are responsible for both creation and destruction and Brahma was not worshiped as the other two were. The fifteenth-century poet Kabir, mocking Hinduism in general, also mocks the idea that the trinity represents the trio of the qualities of matter: Vishnu lucidity (*sattva*), Brahma passion (*rajas*), and Shiva darkness (*tamas*).[44] If one wanted to find a trinity of important deities in Hinduism (as people still do, both as a shortcut through the pantheon and to decorate inclusive wedding invitations), it would be more accurate to speak of Vishnu, Shiva, and Devi, but since there are so many different Vishnus, Shivas, and Devis, even that trinity makes little sense. The relationship between the two major male gods is better viewed as an aspect of Hinduism's penchant for fusing, with Vishnu and Shiva frequently functioning as a pair, often merged as Hari-Hara.

The relative status of the three members of this trinity is explicitly discussed in a myth that begins with an argument between Brahma and Vishnu (a much-told theme of which we have already encountered one variant) and then segues into another popular myth, the tale of Shiva's first appearance out of the linga, in the form of a pillar of fire. Vishnu tells the story:

SHIVA APPEARS OUT OF THE LINGA

Once upon a time, when I had swallowed up the whole triple world in darkness, I lay there alone, with all the creatures in my belly. I had a thousand heads and a thousand eyes, and a thousand feet. Then, all of a sudden, I saw the four-headed Brahma, who said to me, "Who are you? Where do you come from? Tell me, sir. I am the maker of the worlds." I said to him: "*I* am the maker of the worlds, and also the one who destroys them, again and again." As the two of us were talking together in this way, each wishing to get the better of the other, we were amazed to see a flame arising in the north. Its brilliance and power made us cup our hands in reverence and bow to it. The flame grew, and Brahma and I ran up to it. It broke through heaven and earth, and in the middle of the flame we saw a linga, blazing with light. It was indescribable, unimaginable, alternately visible and invisible. At first, it measured just a hand's-breadth, but it kept getting much bigger.

Then Brahma said to me, "Quickly, go down and find out the bottom of this linga. I will go up until I see its top." I agreed. I kept going down for a thousand years, but I did not reach the bottom of the linga, nor did Brahma find its top. We turned back and met again, amazed and frightened; we paid homage to Shiva, saying, "You create the worlds and destroy them. From you all of the goddesses were born. We bow to you."

Then he revealed himself and, filled with pity, laughed, like the roar of thunder, and said, "Don't be afraid. Both of you, eternal, were born from me in the past; Brahma is my right arm, and Vishnu my left arm. I will give you whatever you ask for." Ecstatic, we said, "Let the two of us always be devoted to you." "Yes," said the god of gods, "and create multitudes of progeny." And he vanished.[45]

This myth about the origins of linga worship recognizes it as a new thing, just as the worship of Shiva was a new thing in the myth of Daksha. The author does not try to authenticate the practice by claiming that it was already there in the Vedas; he has a sense of history, of change, of novelty. In the jockeying for power and status among the three gods, Shiva is clearly supreme, in this text, and Vishnu is second to Brahma. (Other variants of the myth reverse the hierarchy and even account for Brahma's historical loss of status altogether: Brahma lies, pretending that he *did* find the end of the linga, and is therefore cursed never to be worshiped again.) By regarding the goddesses as emanations from Shiva, the text subordinates them to him but also emphasizes his connection with them. The hymn of praise for Shiva, which I have greatly abbreviated, is what the worshiper takes away with him or her, a paradigm for the proper worship of the Shiva linga. Here, as so often, beginning with the Vedas, you cannot grasp the power of the text aside from the ritual that is its raison d'être; you have to, as the saying goes, be there.

As the erotic god of the linga as well as the ascetic god of yogis, Shiva straddles the two paths of renunciation and Release. As Lord of the Dance (Nataraja) he dances both the dance of passion (*lasya*) and the dance that destroys the universe (*tandava*).[46] This ambivalence is brilliantly expressed in the myth of Mankanaka:

SHIVA STOPS MANKANAKA FROM DANCING

The sage Mankanaka cut his hand on a blade of sharp *kusha* grass, and plant sap flowed from the wound. Overjoyed, to excess, he started to dance; and everything in the universe danced with him. The gods, alarmed, reported this to Shiva and asked him to stop Mankanaka from dancing. Shiva took the form of a Brahmin and went to him and asked him, "What has occasioned this joy in you, an ascetic?" "Why, Brahmin," said the sage, "don't you see the plant sap flowing from my hand?" The god laughed at him and said, "I am not surprised. Look at this," and he struck his own thumb with the tip of his finger, and ashes shining like snow poured out of that wound. Then Mankanaka was ashamed, and he fell at Shiva's feet and said, "You must be Shiva, the Trident-bearer, first of the gods. Grant me a favor; let my ascetic heat remain intact." Shiva replied, "Your ascetic heat will increase a thousand-fold, and I will dwell in this hermitage with you forever. Any man who bathes in this river and worships me will find nothing impossible to obtain in this world and the other world, and then he will reach the highest place, by my grace."[47]

The mortal ascetic dances with joy when his magic transmutes blood (flowing from a wound made by a blade of the sacred grass that is used in Vedic rituals) into plant sap (a vegetarian move), but his dancing is as excessive as his asceticism was; extreme vegetarianism has turned his very blood to vegetable sap. Shiva uses his own far greater ascetic power to change blood to ashes, the ashes of corpses but also the ashes of the god Kama, whom he has both destroyed and absorbed—the symbol of the seed of life transfixed in death. In this way he teaches the sage that death is more amazing than life. The ending grants a blessing not to the person who hears the story, as earlier texts generally do, but to the person who bathes in this river, the *tirtha*. This is a good example of the transition from a pan-Indian ideal (for the basic text could be recited anywhere) to a more local concentration of sanctity, a particular point of pilgrimage.

PURANIC GODDESSES

The Puranas begin to tell stories about goddesses. Though there are a few independent goddesses in the *Rig Veda*, they are generally personifications of abstract nouns or little more than the wives of their husbands, such as Indrani, "Mrs. Indra," the wife of the god Indra. The births of Draupadi and Sita reveal that they began as goddesses (and Draupadi went on to become a goddess with a sect of her own), though the *Mahabharata* and *Ramayana* treat them by and large as mortal women. Now, however, in the early Puranas, we begin to get a vibrant mythology of independent goddesses.

Though Hindu gods are often grouped under a monotheistic umbrella, so that all gods are said to be aspects of one particular god (sometimes Vishnu, sometimes Shiva) or, more often, aspects of the ineffable monistic *brahman*, people seldom speak of the God, Deva.* Yet though the goddesses of India are equally various, people (both scholars and the authors of Sanskrit texts) often speak of the Goddess, Devi, and tend to treat all the other goddesses as nothing more than aspects of Devi, whereas they all are actually quite different. One gets the impression that in the dark, all goddesses are gray. (So too while gods, ogres, and antigods often have extra heads—Brahma has four, Shiva five, Skanda six, Ravana ten—Puranic goddesses not only seldom have more than one—they have lots of arms, but not heads—but often have less than one; several of them are beheaded. This is a gendered pattern that makes one stop and think.)

I would prefer to treat the Hindu goddesses individually, though reserving the right to generalize about them.

CHANDIKA, THE BUFFALO CRUSHER (MAHISHA-MARDINI)

We will never know for how many centuries she was worshiped in India by people who had no access to Sanskrit texts and whose voices we therefore cannot hear. Kushana coins depict Durga and Parvati, and a Kushana image from

---

* They do speak of the Great God (Mahadeva) and the God (Ishvara), but these are names of one particular god, Shiva, and are not meant to encompass all the varieties of male gods such as Vishnu and Brahma, as the Goddess encompasses all goddesses.

Mathura, perhaps from the second century CE, depicts a tree spirit (Yakshi), perhaps prefiguring Durga, with a cringing dwarf under her feet.* We have noted a few distant early warnings, such as possible sources in the Indus Valley, and there are more substantial hints of the worship of a goddess in the *Mahabharata:* tantalizingly brief references to the seven or eight "Little Mothers" (Matrikas), dark, peripheral, harmful, especially for children, and the Great Kali (Maha-Kali), and to the goddess of Death and Night who appears in a vision in the *Book of the Night Raid*, right before the massacre begins (10.8.64). The *Mahabharata* also tells of gorgeous supernatural women who seduce antigods so that the gods can overpower them; one of these, Mohini, is really just Vishnu in disguise (1.15–17), and the other, Tilottama, is an Apsaras (2.201–2). But these females do not kill the antigods themselves; Mohini merely distracts them so that the gods can steal the soma (back) from them, and Tilottama gets the antigods Sunda and Upasunda to kill each other over her. It remained for the Puranas to tell of a goddess who killed the antigods herself.

Such a goddess, first under the name of Chandika ("the Fierce"†), later often called Durga ("Hard to Get [To]"), bursts onto the Sanskrit scene full grown, like Athene from the head of Zeus, in a complex myth that includes a hymn of a thousand names. Many of the names allude to entire mythological episodes that must have grown onto the goddess, like barnacles on a great ship, gradually for centuries. The founding text is "The Glorification of the Goddess" (*Devi-mahatmya*), a long poem probably interpolated into the *Markandeya Purana* (which also tells a number of other stories about powerful women and goddesses) between the fifth and seventh centuries of the Common Era. It is clear from the complexity of "The Glorification of the Goddess" that it must be a compilation of many earlier texts about the goddess, either from other, lost Sanskrit texts or from lost or never preserved vernacular sources, in Magadhi or Tamil, perhaps. Some of the stories may have come from villages or tribal cultures where the goddess had been worshiped for centuries; early in her history she may have been associated with the periphery of society, "tribal or low-caste peoples who worshiped her in wild places."[48] Yet by the time of the *Markandeya Purana*, goddesses were worshiped in both cities and villages, by people all along the economic spectrum.

"Glorification of the Goddess" is the Devi's "crossover" text, from unknown

---

* In the Dallas Museum of Art.
† The same word that is the basis of the name of the Pariahs called Chandalas.

rituals and local traditions to a pan-Indian Sanskrit text. Why does the *Markan-deya Purana* pay attention to goddesses at this moment? Why now? For one thing, it was a time when devotional texts of all sorts flourished, and since people worshiped Chandika, she too needed to have texts. What may have started out as a local sect began to spread under royal patronage inspired by bhakti. Centuries earlier the Kushanas had put goddesses on their coins; now the stories behind the coins began to circulate too as more valuable narrative currency. At some moment the critical mass of Devi worship forced the Brahmin custodians of Sanskrit narratives to acknowledge it. The Purana goes out of its way to tell us that merchants and kings worshiped her; in the outer frame of the Purana, a sage tells the story of the Goddess of Great Illusion (Maha-maya) to a king who has lost his kingdom and a Vaishya who has lost his wealth and family; at the end of the story the goddess grants each of them what he asks for: The king gets his kingdom (and the downfall of his enemies), while the Vaishya gets not wealth, which he no longer covets, but the knowledge of what he is and what he has (and the downfall of his worldly addictions). Clearly the Vaishya is the man this text greatly prefers.

This is the story it tells about Chandika:

THE KILLING OF THE BUFFALO

Once upon a time, the antigods, led by Mahisha ["Buffalo"], defeated the gods in battle. The gods were so furious that their energies came out of them one by one, and these energies formed the goddess Chandika. The gods also gave her weapons doubled from their own weapons, as well as necklaces and earrings and garlands of lotuses. They gave her a lion for her mount, and the king of snakes gave her a necklace of snakes studded with the large gems that cobras have on their foreheads. When Mahisha, in the form of a water buffalo, saw her, he cried, "Now, who is this?" and he attacked her lion. Eventually, she lassoed him and tied him up. As she cut off the head of the buffalo, he became a lion; as she beheaded the lion, he became a man, with a sword in his hand; then an elephant, and finally a buffalo again. She laughed and drank deep from a divine drink, and her eyes shone red, and the drink reddened her mouth. Then she kicked him on the neck, and as the great antigod came halfway out of the buffalo's open mouth, she cut off his head with her sword.[49]

The final moment in this story is a scene particularly beloved of artists, who often depict Chandika's lion chomping on the buffalo's head while the goddess disposes of the head of the anthropomorphic antigod, who comes out not from the buffalo's mouth but from his neck after he has been beheaded. The goddess rides on a lion, a Vedic animal; in later centuries, when lions become rare in North India, Chandika and other goddesses are often depicted riding on tigers or sometimes just great big pussycats, as depicted by painters and sculptors who have evidently never seen a tiger, let alone a lion. The myth has been convincingly linked to a ritual that has been documented in many parts of India to this day, the ritual sacrifice of a buffalo, often associated with a sect of Draupadi.[50] Goats too and other animals are frequently sacrificed to the goddess Kali; the animal is decapitated, and its blood is offered to her to drink. In some variants of this ritual, a man, dressed either as the buffalo or as a woman, bites the neck and drinks the blood of the sacrificial animal (usually a lamb or a goat).

We can see patriarchal Sanskritic incursions into this early textual version of the myth, the Brahmin filter as always extracting a toll as the story crossed the linguistic border. Chandika's power in this text comes not from within herself but from the energy (*tejas*) of the male gods, as the light of the moon comes from the sun. She is created by re-memberment (the inverse of dismemberments such as that of the Man in "Poem of the Primeval Man"), a not uncommon motif in the ancient texts. Manu, for instance, says (7.3–7) that the first king was created by combining "lasting elements" or "particles" from eight gods.*

A. K. Ramanujan once said that you can divide the many goddesses of India into the goddesses of the tooth and the goddesses of the breast.[51] The goddesses of the breast are wives, more or less subservient to husbands, but they do not usually give birth to children (though they sometimes adopt children). Devi is the Great Mother, but we hear little or nothing about her mythological children; *we* are her children. The tooth goddesses (not at all like tooth fairies) are unmarried, fierce, often out of control. They are killers. They too are generally† barren of children, celibate mothers; indeed some of them wear necklaces made of the heads of children and low-slung belts made of children's hands; with habits like these, it's a very good thing that they *don't* have children of their own. Chandika, whom "Glorification of the Goddess" also calls Ambika ("Little Mother"),‡ is the

---

* The gods are Indra, the Wind, Yama (god of the dead), the Sun, Fire, Varuna (god of the waters), the Moon, and Kubera (god of wealth), often called the eight Guardians of the Directions (east, west, southeast, etc.).
† Durga, in Bengal, is an important exception.
‡ Also the nickname of the queen in Brahmana texts of the horse sacrifice and of one of the grandmothers of the Pandus in the *Mahabharata*.

paradigmatic tooth goddess in India. She is also both the paradigmatic *shakti* ("power") and the paradigmatic possessor of *shakti*.

Shakti is a creative power that generally takes the place of the power to have children; men give birth without women in many myths, while the goddesses, for all their *shakti*, are cursed to be barren. *Shakti* is generally something that a male god, not a goddess, has and that the goddess *is*. One Upanishad depicts Shiva as a magician who produces the world through his *shakti*.[52] Eventually the Puranas used the word to designate the power/wife of any god, often an abstract quantity (a feminine noun in Sanskrit) incarnate as an anthropomorphic goddess. Many female deities, as well as abstract nouns, came to be personified and "wedded" to great gods as their *shakti*s, such as Lakshmi or Shri ("Prosperity"), the wife of Vishnu. Unlike the independent Vedic goddesses Speech and Night, who stand alone, these consort goddesses appear in Sanskrit texts almost exclusively as wives. Shiva, who inherits much of Indra's mythology when Indra fades from the pantheon, also inherits Indra's wife Shachi (a name related to *shakti*), and so, in many texts, Shiva's wife—whether she be Parvati or the goddess Kali or Sati—is the most important *shakti* of all, the role model for the other goddesses who become known as the wives (and *shakti*s) of other gods. In one text, Shiva emits his own *shakti*, who then becomes the Goddess that the gods beg to kill the buffalo.[53]

But the Chandika of "Glorification of the Goddess" is definitively *un*married, independent, a tooth goddess. Shiva is not her husband but merely the messenger that she sends to challenge other rebellious antigods, in the battle that follows immediately after Mahisha's death, nor does she become the wife of Mahisha. Therefore she is not the *shakti* of any particular god, and her *shakti*s, whatever their origins, ultimately belong to no one but herself; they are the *shakti*s of a *shakti*. In the next battle, Chandika emits her own *shakti* (which howls like a hundred jackals) and absorbs all the gods' *shakti*s into her breasts.[54] In its intertextual context, therefore, "Glorification of the Goddess" stands out as a feminist moment framed by earlier and later texts that deny the *shakti* her independence.

The pious hope of goddess feminists, and others, that the worship of goddesses is Good for Women is dashed by observations of India, where the power recognized in goddesses certainly does not necessarily encourage men to grant to women—or women to take from men—political or economic powers. Indeed we can see the logic in the fact that it often works the other way around (the more powerful the goddess, the less power for real women), however much we may deplore it: If women are made of *shakti*—like Chandika, who is her own *shakti*, rather than like Parvati, who is Shiva's *shakti*—and men can only get it by controlling women, women pose a constant threat to men. The conclusion that many men seem to have drawn from this is that women should be locked up and silenced. One defiance of this scenario is the widespread phenomenon of women who are possessed by fierce goddesses, thereby either acquiring or becoming *shakti*s and being empowered to say and do many things otherwise forbidden.[55] But in taking the mythology of goddesses as a social charter, the goddess feminists are batting on a sticky wicca.

SATI, THE WIFE OF SHIVA

One goddess who has played an important role in the lives of real women is Sati, the wife of Shiva, who is occasionally implicated in justifications for the custom of widows immolating themselves on their husbands' pyres, called suttee.

The *Mahabharata* versions of the story of Daksha's sacrifice do not mention Daksha's daughter Sati at all, though sometimes they mention Shiva's other wife, Parvati (who is not related to Daksha in any way, nor does she herself go to the sacrifice, or die, though her wounded amour propre spurs Shiva to break into the sacrifice). At that stage the conflict, about Rudra's non-Vedic status, is just between Daksha and Shiva. Several early Puranas too tell the story of Daksha and Rudra/Shiva without mentioning any wife of Shiva's, or mention her just in passing.[56] Even in versions that name Sati as the daughter of Daksha, the conflict is still primarily between Vaishnava Brahmins and more heterodox Shaivas. This story is narrated in several of the early Puranas:

SATI COMMITS SUICIDE

Daksha, the father of Sati, insulted Shiva by failing to invite him or Sati to a great sacrifice to which everyone else (including Sati's sisters) was invited. Sati, overcome with shame and fury, committed suicide by generating an internal fire in which she immolated herself. Enraged, Shiva came to Daksha's sacrifice, destroyed it, and—after Daksha apologized profusely—restored it.[57]

Sati is not a sati (a woman who commits suttee). Her husband is not dead; indeed, by definition, he can never die. But she dies, usually by fire, and those two textual facts are sometimes taken up as the basis for suttee in later Hindu practice. The compound *sati-dharma* thus has several layers of meaning: it can mean the way that any Good Woman (which is what *sati* means in Sanskrit), particularly a woman true to her husband, should behave, or it can mean the way that this one woman named Sati behaved. Only much later does it come to mean the act of a woman who commits the religious act of suttee, the immolation of a woman on her dead husband's pyre (for which the Sanskrit term was usually "going with" the husband [*saha-gamana*] or "dying after" him [*anu-marana*]).

PARVATI, THE WIFE OF SHIVA

Sati dies and is reborn as Parvati ("Daughter of the Mountain"), the daughter of the great mountain Himalaya, the mountain range where Shiva is often said to live, generally on Mount Kailasa. Parvati is a typical breast goddess, confined and defined by her marriage. But before Parvati could marry Shiva, she had to win him, no easy task, since Shiva had undertaken a vow of chastity. She did it with the help of the god of erotic love, Kama incarnate. The *Mahabharata* refers, briefly, to the encounter between Kama and Shiva, the latter here referred to as a *brahma-charin* (that is, under a vow of celibacy): "Shiva, the great *brahma-charin*, did not give himself over to the pleasures of lust. The husband of Parvati extinguished Kama when Kama attacked him, making Kama bodiless."[58] An inscription of 474 CE refers to the burning of Kama by Shiva,[59] so the story must have been fairly well known by then; Kalidasa tells the story in his poem *The Birth of the Prince*. Here is a slightly fuller Puranic version of the episode:

PARVATI WINS SHIVA

Parvati wished to marry Shiva. She went to Shiva's hermitage and served him in silence; meditating with his eyes shut, he did not notice her. After some time, Indra sent Kama to inspire Shiva with desire for Parvati; Kama shot an arrow at Shiva, and the moment it struck him, Shiva opened his eyes, noticed Parvati, and was ever so slightly aroused. But then he looked farther and saw Kama, his bow stretched for a second shot. Shiva opened his third eye, releasing a flame that burned with the power of his accumulated ascetic heat, and burned Kama to ashes. (Kama continued to function, more effective than ever, dispersed into moonlight and the heady smell of night-blooming flowers; his bow became reincarnate in the arched eyebrows of beautiful women, his arrows in their glances). Shiva then returned to his meditation.

Parvati engaged in fierce asceticism to win Shiva for her husband, fasting, enduring snows in winter, blazing sun in summer. Shiva appeared before her disguised as a *brahma-charin* and tested her by describing all those qualities of Shiva that made him an unlikely suitor, including his antipathy to Kama. When Parvati remained steadfast in her devotion to Shiva, the god revealed himself and asked her to marry him. After the wedding, Kama's widow begged Shiva to revive her husband, and he did so, just in time for the honeymoon.[60]

Himalaya, who is regarded as the source of priceless gems, a king of mountains, disdains Shiva as Daksha had done (though for different reasons), and their fears turn out to be well founded. Shiva is a strange god, the epitome of the sort of person a man would not want his daughter to marry: He is a yogi who has vowed never to marry, he has a third eye in the middle of his forehead, he wanders around naked or wearing nothing but a loincloth woven of living snakes, he has no family, and he lives not in a house but in a cremation ground, smearing his body with the ashes of corpses. It is therefore not surprising that both his potential fathers-in-law object strenuously to him. In one Puranic version of the story, Shiva in disguise tells Parvati's father, Himalaya: "Shiva is an old man, free from passion, a wanderer and a beggar, not at all suitable for Parvati to marry. Ask your wife and your relatives—ask anyone but Parvati."[61] The litany of undesirable qualities is a variant of the genre of "worship by insult" that is both a Tamil and a Sanskrit specialty, and that appears in its darker aspect when Daksha curses Shiva and then worships him for the same qualities for which he had cursed him. Redolent of virility and transgression, Shiva's qualities cast their dark erotic spell on Parvati, as on his worshipers.

The marriage of Shiva and Parvati is celebrated in texts and in ritual hierogamies performed in temples and depicted in paintings and sculptures throughout India. Their marriage is a model of conjugal love, the divine prototype of human marriage, sanctifying the forces that carry on the human race. The marriages of other gods and goddesses too, often local couples celebrated only in one village, constitute a popular theme in temple art and literature, both courtly and vernacular. As in South India, the divine couple often served as a template for the images of kings and their queens who commissioned sculptures depicting, on one level, the god and his goddess, and on another, the king and his consort, or the queen and her consort.

The conflict between Shiva and Kama is only on the surface a conflict between opposites, between an antierotic ascetic power and an antiascetic erotic power. They are two sides of the same coin, two forms of heat, ascetic heat (*tapas*) and erotic heat (*kama*).[62] For it is through his *tapas* that Shiva generates the power that he will use first for his perpetual tumescence and then to produce the seed of a spectacular child. Some variants of the myth express the connection between Kama and *tapas* through an additional episode that brings into this myth a figure that we have encountered before:

THE SUBMARINE MARE

Kama deluded Shiva, arousing him, and when Shiva realized this, he released a fire from his third eye, burning Kama to ashes. But the fire could not return to Shiva, and so when Shiva vanished, the fire began to burn all the gods and the universe. Brahma made the fire into a mare with flames coming out of her mouth. He took her to the ocean and said, "This is the fire of Shiva's anger, which burned Kama and now wants to burn up the entire universe. You must bear it until the final deluge, at which time I will come here and lead it away from you." The ocean agreed to this, and the fire entered the ocean and was held in check.[63]

The fire is not just made of Shiva's anger; it gained special power when it burned Kama, for it absorbed the heat of Kama too. The two fires released by Shiva and Kama meet and produce a fiery weapon of mass destruction that maintains a hair-trigger balance of mutual sublimation. (The *Mahabharata* says that Shiva himself is the mouth of the submarine mare, eating the waters [13.17.54].) But what is repressed must return, and the strain of *tapas* in the tradition is always poised to burst through in any monolithic construction of *kama*, just as *kama* constantly strains to burst out of extreme *tapas*. The three elements—Shiva's anger, Kama's passion, and the mare—are combined in a verse that Dushyanta, madly in love with Shakuntala, addresses to Kama, the verse cited at the start of this chapter. The balanced extremes implicit in this image are also evident from a Sanskrit aphorism about the two excesses (fire and flood) as well as one of the four addictive vices of lust: A king, no matter how physically powerful, should not drink too much, for the mare fire herself was rendered powerless to burn even a blade of grass, because she drank too much.[64]

Parvati's Children

The most serious problem in the marriage of Shiva and Parvati is the lack of any children born of both parents, a lack that is explicitly regarded as problematic by the gods on some occasions and by Parvati on others, but never by Shiva, who, despite his marriage, remains adamantly opposed to having children. Skanda, as we have seen, is born of Shiva alone, an event that triggers Parvati's resentful curse that all the wives of the gods should be barren too. The widespread patriarchal belief that all goddesses are mother goddesses is contradicted by Parvati's curse, as well as by Hindu mythology as a whole. In defiance of her own curse, Parvati in several texts begs Shiva to give her a child, but he never relents. She does *want* to be a mother; it is Shiva, and the gods, who keep her from being one. The closest she comes to motherhood is with Ganesha.

Many different stories are told about the birth of Ganesha, but one of the best known begins with Parvati taking a bath and longing for someone to keep Shiva from barging in on her, as was his habit. (This is yet another example of the *ritus interruptus*, the interruption of a sleeping, meditating, or conferring god or king or of an amorous couple or a bathing woman or goddess.) As she bathes, she kneads the dirt that she rubs off her body into the shape of a child, who comes to life. When Shiva sees the handsome young boy (or when the inauspicious planet Saturn glances at it, in some variants that attempt to absolve Shiva of the inverted Oedipal crime), the child's head falls off; it is eventually replaced with the head of an elephant, sometimes losing part of one tusk along the way.[65] Thus, just as Skanda is the child of Shiva alone, Ganesha is the child of Parvati alone—indeed a child born despite Shiva's negative intervention at several crucial moments. Ganesha's name means "Lord of the Common People" (*gana* meaning the "common people") or "Lord of the Troops" (the *gana*s being the goblin hosts of Shiva, of whom Ganesha is the leader). He is the god of beginnings, always worshiped before any major enterprise, and the patron of intellectuals, scribes, and authors.

Parvati's problematic relationship with her son Viraka ("Little Hero"), usually equated with Skanda, is narrated in several Puranas, of which the earliest is the *Matsya Purana*, dated to the Gupta age, though this passage may be later and is reproduced, with variations, in the still later *Padma* and *Skanda* Puranas:

THE SPLITTING OF GAURI AND THE GODDESS KALI

One day the god Shiva teased his wife, the goddess Parvati, about her dark skin; he called her "Blackie" [Kali] and said that her dark body against his white body was like a black snake coiled around a pale sandalwood tree. When she responded angrily, they began to argue and to hurl insults at each other. Furious, she went away to generate inner heat in order to obtain a fair, golden skin. Her little son Viraka, stammering in his tears, begged to come with her, but she said to him, "This god chases women when I am not here, and so you must constantly guard his door and peep through the keyhole, so that no other woman gets to him."

While she was gone, an antigod named Adi took advantage of her absence to attempt to kill Shiva. He took the illusory form of Parvati and entered Shiva's bedroom, but Shiva, realizing that this was not Parvati but an antigod's magic power of illusion, killed Adi. When the goddess of the wind told Parvati that Shiva had been with another woman, Parvati became furious; in her tortured mind she pictured her son and said, "Since you abandoned me, your mother who loves you so, and gave women an opportunity to be alone with Shiva, you will be born among humans to a mother who is a heartless, hard, numb, cold stone." Her anger came out of her body in the form of a lion, with a huge tongue lolling out of a mouth full of sharp teeth. Then the god Brahma came to her and granted her wish to have a golden body and to become half of Shiva's body, in the form of the androgyne. She sloughed off from her body a dark woman, named the goddess Kali, who went away to live in the Vindhya Mountains, riding on the lion.

Parvati, now in her golden skin [Gauri, "The Fair" or "The Golden"], went home, but her son Viraka, who did not recognize her, stopped her at the door, saying, "Go away! An antigod in the form of the Goddess entered here unseen in order to deceive the god, who killed him and scolded me. So you cannot enter here. The only one who can enter here is my mother, Parvati, who loves her son dearly." When the Goddess heard this, she thought to herself, "It wasn't a woman; it was an antigod. I cursed my son wrongly, when I was angry." She lowered her head in shame and said to her son, "Viraka, I am your mother; do not be confused or misled by my skin; Brahma made me golden. I cursed you when I did not know what had happened. I cannot turn back my curse, but I will say that you will quickly emerge from your human life, with all your desires fulfilled." The Goddess then returned to Shiva, and they made love together for many years.[66]

The goddess Parvati sloughs her black outer sheath (the goddess Kali, often called Kaushika ["the Sheath"]) to reveal her golden inner form (Gauri). (This act of splitting apart reverses the act of coming together that creates the South India goddess from the head of one woman and the body of another.) In the end the golden Gauri, goddess of the breast, has the son, and the dark goddess Kali, very much a tooth goddess, has the toothy lion.

But the original Parvati, who contains both of the other two goddesses in her *in nuce*, is already a cruel mother. Not only does she ignore her son's pitiful pleas as she goes away, abandoning him, but she even throws his words back in his face when she curses him, accusing him of abandoning *her* by failing to restrain his father's sexuality. Viraka fails to recognize her when she returns, mistaking her for a non-Parvati (just as his father had mistaken the antigod for Parvati); his failure to recognize her seems to be superficial—she has changed the color of her skin—but it has deeper, darker overtones, for he believes his mother loves him, and this woman has cursed him (though he does not yet know it); indeed she has cursed him to have (another) unloving mother. The peeled-off goddess Kali is banished to the liminal area of the Vindhya Mountains (the southern region that composers of ancient Sanskrit texts in the north of India regarded as beyond the Hindu pale, the place to dump things that you did not want in the story anymore), and so she is called Vindhya-vasini ("She Who Lives in the Vindhyas"). (The myth may be reversing the historical process, for the goddess Kali may have come *from* the Vindhyas, or from the south in general, into Sanskrit culture.) The remaining golden form, the one that counteracted her son's curse, becomes the female half of the androgyne.

Though Shiva and Parvati are depicted in both sculpture and painting together with Skanda or Ganesha or both, clearly this is not a Leave It to Beaver type of family: Each member is really a separate individual, with a separate prehistory and a separate role in Hindu worship. Nor are they joined together as members of a family usually are: Parvati does not bear the two children that are depicted with her, nor does Shiva father them in the normal way. The family represents, rather, the forces of the universe that humans must sometimes contend with, sometimes call on for help, though they are often clustered together in a group that presents the form, if not the function, of a family. The family is a way of grouping them together in an image that is "with qualities" (*sa-guna*), in this case, the qualities of a human family, while in their more commonly worshiped forms, they are not a family at all.

ANIMALS

VEHICLES

Many Shaiva family portraits include the pets. Skanda has his peacock, Ganesha his bandicoot, Shiva his bull, and Parvati her lion. For this is another way, in addition to full-life avatars and periodic theophanies, in which the Hindu gods become present in our world. Most gods and goddesses (apart from the animal, or animal from the waist or neck down, or animal from the waist or neck up forms of the deities) are accompanied by a vehicle (*vahana*), an animal that serves the deity as a mount. In contrast with the Vedic gods who rode on animals you could ride on (Surya driving his fiery chariot horses, Indra on his elephant Airavata or driving his bay horses), the sectarian Hindu gods sit cross-legged on their animals or ride sidesaddle, with the animals under them presented in profile and the gods full face. Sometimes the animal merely stands beside the deity, both of them stationary.

The Vedic Indra also rode on the Garuda bird, which later became the mount of Vishnu. Garuda is sometimes represented as an eagle from the waist down or the neck up, otherwise anthropomorphic. Some South Indian Vishnu temples have a special landing post for Garuda to alight upon. Shiva's vehicle is the bull Nandi, a symbol of Shiva's masculine power and sexuality; the bull expresses something of the god's own nature as well as his ambivalent relationship to that nature: As the greatest of all ascetics and yogis, Shiva "rides" his own virility in the sense that he controls, harnesses, and tames it. We have met Chandika's lion, and the goddess Kali's lion or tiger (which she sometimes lends to Parvati too). Skanda's vehicle is the peacock, a brilliant choice that needs no explanation for anyone who has ever seen a general in full ceremonial dress, medals and all.

Even some of the half-animal deities have their own entirely animal vehicles: Ganesha's vehicle is an Indian bandicoot or bandicoot rat, a large (six-pound) rodent (the name is derived from the Telugu word for "pig-rat," *pandhikoku*), chosen for Ganesha not because elephants (or even elephant-headed, potbellied, anthropomorphic gods like Ganesha) are likely to canter about on rats, however big, but because rats, like elephants, can get through anything to get what they want, and Ganesha is the remover of obstacles. The bandicoot shares Ganesha's nimbleness of wit, as well as his path-clearing abilities. The rat has now more recently become a mouse, with intellectual pretensions appropriate to Ganesha; there are modern representations of Ganesha in front of a computer with his bandicoot serving as the mouse.[67]

Images of animals are very old indeed in India, as we saw in the Indus Valley, but they may have become newly attractive in the Gupta period because of the need to produce visual representation of icons and emblems to distinguish different gods under sectarianism. The *vahana* is also a vehicle in the sense that a particular drama is sometimes said to be the perfect vehicle for a particular actor, or in the sense of (according to the *Oxford English Dictionary*) "a material embodiment or manifestation, of something." Or perhaps it is a vehicle in the sense that mosquitoes may "carry" malaria. Wherever the animal is found, the deity is also present. Thus the animals carry the gods into our world as a breeze "carries" perfume. This may be seen as a more particularized expression of the basic Hindu philosophy that the ultimate principle of reality (*brahman*) is present within the soul of every living creature (*atman*).

HORSE SACRIFICES

In the horse sacrifice, as we have seen in the ancient texts as well as in the *Mahabharata*, the chief queen pantomimed copulation with the slaughtered stallion, which was said to be both the sacrificing king (to whom he transferred his powers) and a god, usually Prajapati or Indra. Indra is one of several gods designated as the recipients of the horse sacrifice, but he himself not only sacrifices (as the Vedic gods did, in "Poem of the Primeval Man") but is unique in that as a king (albeit of the gods), he is famed for having performed more horse sacrifices than anyone else and is jealous of this world's record (a jealousy that made him steal the hundredth horse of Sagara, whose sons dug out the ocean searching for it). Indra thus (unlike the usual human worshiper, who may combine the roles of sacrificer and victim) normally combines the roles of sacrificer and recipient. That paradox came to the attention of the author of this medieval commentary on the *Ramayana*: "There are two kinds of gods, those who are gods by birth and those who have more recently become gods by means of karma, such as Indra. The gods by birth receive sacrifice but cannot offer sacrifice; the karma gods, like Indra, perform sacrifice and pose obstacles to sacrificers."[68] The higher gods include not only the rest of the Vedic gods but the newer gods, the bhakti gods.

In the *Harivamsha* ("The Dynasty of Vishnu"), an appendix to the *Mahabharata* that functions much like a Purana, Indra combines all three roles: sacrificer, recipient, and victim:

JANAMEJAYA'S HORSE SACRIFICE

Janamejaya was consecrated for the sacrifice, and his queen approached the designated stallion and lay down beside him, according to the rules of the ritual. But Indra saw the woman, whose limbs were flawless, and desired her. He himself entered the designated stallion and mingled with the queen. And when this transformation had taken place, Indra said to the priest in charge of the sacrifice, "This is not the horse you designated. Scram."

The priest, who understood the matter, told the king what Indra had done, and the king cursed Indra, saying, "From today, Kshatriyas will no longer offer the horse sacrifice to this king of the gods, who is fickle and cannot control his senses." And he fired the priests and banished the queen. But then the king of the Gandharvas calmed him down by explaining that Indra had wanted to obstruct the sacrifice because he was afraid that the king would surpass him with the merits obtained from it. To this end, Indra had seized upon an opportunity when he saw the designated horse and had entered the horse. But the woman with whom he had made love in that way was actually a celestial nymph; Indra had used his special magic to make the king think that it was the queen, his wife. The king of the Gandharvas persuaded the king that this was what had happened.[69]

Like his snake sacrifice, Janamejaya's horse sacrifice is interrupted. The *Arthashastra* (1.6.6) remarks that Janamejaya used violence against Brahmins and perished, and a commentator on that text adds that Janamejaya whipped the Brahmins because he suspected them of having violated his queen, though in reality it was Indra who had done it.[70] At the start of this episode, Janamejaya defies Indra implicitly simply by doing the extravagant sacrifice at all, making him the object of the god's jealousy.[71] At the end, he defies Indra explicitly, by excluding him from the sacrifice because the god has spoiled it.

This story of Janamejaya, which *ends* with an exclusion of the deity and a refusal to worship him (reflecting the historical fact that Indra, a Vedic god, was not worshiped any longer in the Puranic period), is thus in many ways an inversion of the story of Daksha, which *begins* with the exclusion of the god Shiva and ends with the promise that Daksha will in fact sacrifice to Shiva, after Shiva has both spoiled and accomplished the sacrifice (reflecting the historical fact that Shiva, a non-Vedic god, was not worshiped until the Puranic period). This inversion was made possible in part because Indra, the god of conventional Vedic religion, the most orthodox of gods, is in many ways the opposite of Shiva, the unconventional outsider.[72]

In the epilogue to the story of Indra and Janamejaya's queen, the king is persuaded (by an appropriately equine figure, a Gandharva, a kind of centaur) that it all was an illusion. This is a common device used to undo what has been done in a myth, as is the device of the magical double that conveniently replaces a woman in sexual danger. (Or who is *said* to have replaced her; is the Gandharva telling the truth?) Here it also recapitulates precisely what the central episode of the myth has just done: It has revealed the illusion implicit in the sacrifice, the illusion that the sacrificial horse is the god Indra and not merely a horse. The horse sacrifice is similarly demystified and satirized in a twelfth-century text in which Kali, the incarnate spirit of the Kali Age, watches the coupling of the sacrificer's wife with the horse of the horse sacrifice and announces, being no pandit, that the person who made the Vedas was a buffoon,[73] which is to say that Kali takes it literally and misses its symbolism. As the cachet of the horse sacrifice and of animal sacrifices in general fell during this period (as satires like this suggest), kings often endowed temples instead of sacrificing horses[74]—sacrificial substitution in a new key.

RESTORING THE *MAHABHARATA*

Puranic rituals often replaced Vedic rituals. We have noted how Vedic rituals were devised to mend the broken parts of human life. Puranic rituals are devised for this too but also to cure the ills of previous ages and, indeed, of previous texts. Though many Puranas offer their hearers/readers Release, most of them are devoted to the more worldly goals of the path of rebirth, and the end of the line is not absorption into *brahman* but an eternity in the heaven of the sectarian god to whom the Purana is devoted. *Moksha* is ineffable, but the texts often describe the bhakti heaven.

The Puranas return to the moral impasses of the *Mahabharata*, some of which were resolved only by the illusion ex machina, and offer new solutions that were not available to the authors of that text. Yudhishthira's dilemma in hell was occasioned by a kind of transfer of merit: Yudhishthira sent a cool breeze to ease the torment of his brothers and Draupadi, as well as a few other relatives. That concept, merely sketched there, is more fully developed a few centuries later in the *Markandeya Purana*:

MERIT TRANSFER IN HELL

Once, when his wife named Fatso [Pivari] had been in her fertile season, King Vipashchit did not sleep with her, as it was his duty to do, but slept instead with his other, beautiful wife, Kaikeyi. He went to hell briefly to expiate this one sin, but when he was about to leave for heaven, the people in hell begged him to stay, since the wind that touched his body dispelled their pain. "People cannot obtain in heaven or in the world of Brahma," said Vipashchit, "such happiness as arises from giving release [nirvana] to suffering creatures." And he refused to leave until Indra agreed to let the king's good deeds [karma] be used to release those people of evil karma from their torments in hell—though they all went from there immediately to another womb that was determined by the fruits of their own karma (14.1–7, 15.47–80).

The episode is clearly based on the *Mahabharata*, and uses some of the same phrases. (It also gives the sexually preferred second wife in this story the name of the sexually preferred second wife in the *Ramayana*, Kaikeyi.) But significantly, the people in hell now are not related to the king in any way; his compassion extends to all creatures. Now also the text begins to speak of Buddhist/Hindu concepts like nirvana and the transfer of karma, making it possible for the real, heaven-bound king to release real sinners from a real hell. Karma and samsara have the last word, though: In the end, having passed through heaven and hell, the sinners are reborn according to their just deserts, a theory that the final chapter of the *Mahabharata* had chosen not to invoke.

The Puranas expand upon the basic *Mahabharata* concept of the time-sharing aspects of heaven and hell, adding psychological details:

> Sometimes a man goes to heaven; sometimes he goes to hell. Sometimes a dead man experiences both hell and heaven. Sometimes he is born here again and consumes his own karma; sometimes a man who has consumed his karma dies and goes forth with just a very little bit of karma remaining. Sometimes he is reborn here with a small amount of good and bad karma, having consumed most of his karma in heaven or in hell. A great source of the suffering in hell is the fact that the people there can see the people who dwell in heaven; but the people in hell rejoice when the people in heaven fall down into hell. Likewise, there is great misery even in heaven, beginning from the very moment when people ascend there, for this thought enters their minds: "I am going to fall from here." And when they see hell they become quite miserable, worrying, day and night, "This is where I am going to go."[75]

The misery of hell is thus somewhat alleviated by schadenfreude, and the pleasures of heaven are undercut by the attitude of Lewis Carroll's White Queen, who cries, "Ouch!" *before* she pricks her finger.[76]

The sins that send you to hell and the virtues that send you to heaven are often described in detail that rivals that of the *shastras*, as the texts seem to vie with one another in imagining gruesome and appropriate punishments to fit the crime. After hearing the spine-curdling descriptions of the tortures of hell, the interlocutor (who is, as in the *Mahabharata*, built into the frame) often asks:

"Isn't there anything that I can do to avoid having that happen to me?" And yes, you will be happy to hear that there is: just as there was a Vedic ritual to protect you, now there is a Puranic ritual, or a Puranic mantra, or a Puranic shrine, or a Puranic pilgrimage, that the text mercifully teaches you right then and there. There are many pilgrimage sites described in the *Mahabharata*, particularly in the great tour of the fords (*tirthas*); but now each Purana plugs one special place.

For the moral dilemma posed by the massacre in the *Mahabharata*, the Puranic solution is a pilgrimage to Prayaga (Allahabad), the junction of the two sacred rivers (the Ganges and the Yamuna), above Varanasi, the site of the greatest annual festival in India, the Kumbha Mela:

AN EXPIATION FOR THE *MAHABHARATA* WAR

When King Yudhishthira and his brothers had killed all the Kauravas, he was overwhelmed by a great sorrow and became bewildered. Soon afterward, the great ascetic Markandeya arrived at the city of Hastinapur. Yudhishthira bowed to the great sage and said, "Tell me briefly how I may be released from my sins. Many men who had committed no offense were killed in the battle between us and the Kauravas. Please tell me how one may be released from the mortal sin that results from acts of violence against living creatures, even if it was done in a former life."

Markandeya said, "Listen, your majesty, to the answer to your question: Going to Prayaga is the best way for men to destroy evil. The god Rudra, the Great God, lives there, as does the self-created lord Brahma, together with the other gods." Yudhishthira said, "Sir, I wish to hear the fruit of going to Prayaga. Where do people who die there go, and what is the fruit of bathing there?"[77]

And the sage obliges him, in considerable detail.

Yudhishthira is haunted by the same problem that troubled Arjuna centuries earlier in the *Gita:* "Many men who had committed no offense were killed in the battle between us and the Kauravas." In the *Mahabharata*, Yudhishthira performed a horse sacrifice to restore himself and the kingdom; in the Puranas, he makes a pilgrimage to Prayaga. The format of this myth—first a statement of a sin (the mess I got myself into), then the promise of a restoration, a solution—is a set piece, new Puranic wine poured into old Brahmana bottles.

The Puranas tackle other *Mahabharata* trouble spots too. In the *Mahabharata*, Balarama is the brother of Krishna, renowned for his physical power and his prowess with the mace. In the Vaishnava Puranas, Balarama becomes far more important and is sometimes regarded as one of the avatars of Vishnu. But he is also a notorious drinker, and the Puranas tell a striking story about this:

A RESTORATION FOR DRUNKENNESS AND MANSLAUGHTER

One day Balarama, the brother of Krishna, got drunk and wandered around, stumbling, his eyes red with drinking. He came to a forest where a group of learned Brahmins were listening to a bard, a Charioteer, reciting stories in the place of a Brahmin. When the Brahmins saw Balarama and realized that he was drunk, they all stood up quickly, all except for the Charioteer. Enraged, Balarama struck the Charioteer and killed him. Then all the Brahmins left the forest, and when Balarama saw how they shunned him and sensed that his body had a disgusting smell, the smell of bloodshed, he realized that he had committed Brahminicide. He cursed his rage, and the wine, and his arrogance, and his cruelty. For restoration, he undertook a twelve-year pilgrimage to the Sarasvati River "against the current," confessing his crime.[78]

Since the Charioteer belongs to a low caste that is said to go "against the current"[79] (born from a father of a caste lower than the mother's), Balarama undertakes the appropriate pilgrimage "against the current"—that is, from the mouth to the source of the Sarasvati River. (Balarama is famous for having altered the course of the Yamuna/Kalindi River.[80]) Yet he understands that he has killed someone who is in some way the equivalent of a Brahmin, not in his caste but perhaps in his knowledge and in his status in the eyes of actual Brahmins, so that in killing him he has committed Brahminicide, and he accuses himself of arrogance for expecting the Charioteer to rise in deference to him. The pilgrimage and confession are his ways of dealing with what he acknowledges as his rage and cruelty, though he curses the wine rather than his own addictive drunkenness. In the Puranas, there is a cure for everything.

CHAPTER 15

SECTS AND SEX IN THE TANTRIC PURANAS AND THE TANTRAS

600 to 900 CE

ॐ

CHRONOLOGY (ALL DATES ARE CE)

550–575 Kalachuris create the cave of Shiva at Elephanta

606–647 Harsha reigns at Kanauj

630–644 Xuan Zang (Hsuan Tsang) visits India

650–800 Early Tantras are composed

765–773 Raja Krishna I creates the Kailasa temple to Shiva at Ellora

900 and 1150 The Chandellas build the temples at Khajuraho

1238–1258 Narasimhadeva I builds the temple of Konarak

WHAT USE ARE IMAGINED IMAGES?

If the shapes that men imagine in their minds could achieve Release for them, then surely men could become kings by means of the kingdom that they get in their dreams. Those who believe that the Lord lives in images made of clay, stone, metal, wood, or so forth and wear themselves out with asceticism without true knowledge—they never find Release. Whether they waste themselves away by fasting, or get potbellies by eating whatever they like, unless they have the knowledge of the ultimate reality—how could they be cured? If people could get Release by performing vows to eat nothing but air, leaves, crumbs, or water, then the serpents and cattle and birds and fish would be Released.

Mahanirvana Tantra[*][1]

---

[*] The *Mahanirvana Tantra* may be as late as the eighteenth century and therefore may incorporate a re-

The texts called the Tantras mock physical icons and dream images, as part of their general challenge to most aspects of conventional Hinduism (including fasting and asceticism), but they go on to replace these physical processes and mental images with ones of their own, produced in Tantric rituals, claiming that they have the power to transform the worshipers into deities. Tantra is one of the many actual peripheries that survive against an imagined non-Tantric center, an all-encompassing religious movement that rivaled Hinduism as a whole and indeed explicitly turned upside down some of the most cherished assumptions of the Brahmin imaginary.

How you define Hindu Tantra is largely predetermined by what you want to say about it; some scholars define it in terms of its theology (connected with goddesses and usually with Shiva, though this is not unique to Tantrism), some its social attitudes (which are generally antinomian, also not unique to Tantrism), and some its rituals (often involving the ingesting of bodily fluids, particularly sexual fluids, which is indeed a Tantric specialty*). Like Hinduism in general, Tantra is best defined through a Zen diagram combining all these aspects.

India in the Time of Harsha

After the Gupta Empire fragmented, in the seventh and eighth centuries CE, once again we enter a period when there is no single political power, which seems to be the default position for most of ancient Indian history; empires are the exception. Again it is a fruitful period of change and creativity, when new castes, sects, and states emerged, and new regional kingdoms.[2] One of these was the kingdom of Harsha, who reigned from 606 to 647. We have far more information about him—more available light—than we have about most kings of this period, largely because of three witnesses. His court poet, Bana, wrote a prose poem about him, the *Harshacharita*, which offers, hidden between the layers of fulsome praise and literary ostentation, quite a lot of information about life as it was lived at Harsha's court. And the Chinese Buddhist traveler Xuan Zang (also spelled Hsuan Tsang, Hiuen Tsiang, Hsuien-tsang, Yuan Chwang), a monk and scholar, inspired by Faxian, who had visited the Guptas two

---

sponse to the British presence in India. Yet both its subject matter and its rhetoric reflect classic Tantric concerns.

* Some people seem to regard anything that has to do with sex in India, or not even only in India, as Tantric, but that way madness lies; Tantra is often, though by no means always, about sex, but sex is certainly not usually about Tantra.

hundred years earlier, visited India between 630 and 644, returning to China
with twenty horses loaded with Buddhist relics and texts. He wrote a long
account of India, including a detailed eyewitness description of Harsha's administration.[3] Since both Bana and Xuan Zang were under Harsha's patronage,
we must take their testimonies with a grain of salt, but much of what each says
is confirmed by the other, as well as by the third, even more biased witness,
Harsha himself, who wrote three Sanskrit plays, two of which describe life
at court.

Harsha came of a powerful family and ruled over the fertile land between
the Ganges and Yamuna rivers, an area that he extended until he ruled the
whole of the Ganges basin (including Nepal and Assam), from the Himalayas
to the Narmada River, besides Gujarat and Saurashtra (the modern Kathiawar). He shifted the center of power from Ujjain and Pataliputra to Kanauj
(near modern Kanpur). After Harsha's initial conquests, there was peace in his
empire. He died without leaving an heir; on his death one of his ministers
usurped the throne. His empire did not survive him.

Harsha was descended from the Guptas through his grandmother, and his
sister, Rajya Sri, was married to the Maukhari king at Kanauj. According to
Bana, after her husband was killed in battle, Rajya Sri was taken hostage. She
escaped and fled to the Vindhyas, where she was about to commit suttee, but
Harsha snatched her from the pyre. She then hoped to become a Buddhist nun,
but Harsha dissuaded her, because through her he could control the Maukhari
kingdom.[4] That Bana regarded the practice of suttee as a serious problem is
apparent from a passage worth quoting at some length:

Life is relinquished quite readily by those overcome by sorrow; but only with
great effort is it maintained when subjected to extreme distress. What is called
"following in death" [anumarana] is pointless. It is a path proper to the illiterate. It
is a pastime of the infatuated. It is a road for the ignorant. It is an act for the rash.
It is taking a narrow view of things. It is very careless. All in all, it is a foolish
blunder to abandon your own life because a father, brother, friend, or husband is
dead. If life does not leave on its own, it should not be forsaken. If you think
about it, you will see that giving up your own life is only an act of self-interest, for
it serves to assuage the unbearable agonies of sorrow that you suffer. It brings no
good whatsoever to the one who is already dead. In the first place, it is not a way
to bring *that* one back to life. Nor is it a way to add to *his* accumulations of merit.
Nor is it a remedy for his possible fall into hell. Nor is it a way to see him. Nor is

it a cause of mutual union. The one who is dead is helpless and is carried off to a different place that is proper for the ripening of the fruit of his actions. As for the person who abandons life—that person simply commits the sin of suicide, and nothing is achieved for either of them. But, living, he can do much for the dead one and for himself by the offering of water, the folding of hands, the giving of gifts, and so forth.[5]

This remarkable statement combines, with no contradiction whatsoever, the religious assumptions of a pious Hindu and a sensible, compassionate, and highly rational argument against the ritual suicide of a widow. This is a valuable piece of evidence of resistance to such ritual immolations during Harsha's reign.*

Harsha was a most cosmopolitan king, known as a patron of the arts and of all religions. Besides the poet Bana and another famous poet, Mayura, he also kept at his court a man named Matanga Divakara, a critic and dramatist who is said either to have come from one of the Pariah castes (a Chandala) or to have been a Jaina.[6] Harsha does not mention temple worship in his plays; he writes, instead, of a spring festival that the whole city participates in, dancing in the streets and sprinkling one another with red dye (as people do during the Holi festival even today), and of an individual *puja* to the god Kama that the queen carries out at a small outdoor shrine.[7] Harsha was a religious eclectic; two of his three plays (the ones about court intrigue) are dedicated to Shiva, while the third, *Nagananda,* invokes the Buddha. But the plot of *Nagananda* is as Hindu as it is Buddhist: A prince gives up his own body to stop a sacrifice of serpents to the mythical Garuda bird, a myth that clearly owes much to the snake sacrifice in the *Mahabharata* as well as to the story of King Shibi (in both Buddhist and Hindu traditions). Xuan Zang noted a movement of nonviolence toward animals during Harsha's reign: Indians are "forbidden to eat the flesh of the ox [or cow],† the ass, the elephant, the horse, the pig, the dog, the fox, the wolf, the lion, the monkey, and all the hairy kind. Those who eat them are despised and scorned."[8]

Harsha may have became a convert to Buddhism in his later life; we know that he sent a Buddhist mission to China and held assemblies at the holy Hindu

---

* So too a late chapter of the *Padma Purana* (perhaps c. 1000 CE) says that Kshatriya women are noble if they immolate themselves, but that Brahmin women may not, and that anyone who helps a Brahmin woman do it is committing Brahminicide (*brahma-hatya*).

† The Chinese character *niu* can mean either "cow" or "ox," as can the Sanskrit word *go.*

site of Prayaga, where donations were made to followers of all sects.[9] During this period Buddhism still thrived in large monasteries in Bihar and Bengal, though it had begun to vanish from South India and was fading in the rest of North India. Xuan Zang says that the king of Sindh was a Shudra, but a good man who revered Buddhism.[10]

TANTRIC PURANAS

PROTO-TANTRIC SHAIVA SECTS

Scholars have scrambled to find the sources of Tantra, the ur-Tantras, during this period, but those sources are numerous, hard to date, and widely dispersed. A number of sects with some Tantric features, though not yet full-blown Tantra, arose in the early centuries of the first millennium CE and later came to be regarded as Tantric—through our bête noire, hindsight. And a number of Shaiva Puranas describe sects that share some, but not all, of the characteristics of Shakta Tantras (that is, Tantras dedicated to the goddess Shakti). Tantric ideas doubtless developed in sources long lost to us, but they appear textually first in the Puranas and after that in the Tantras. We must therefore look to the mythology of Puranas composed during this general period (600 to 900 CE) for the mythological underpinnings of Tantric rituals.

Besides the Puranas, there is scattered textual and epigraphical evidence of movements that may be considered proto-Tantric. In the first century CE, a sage named Lakulisha ("Lord of the Club") founded a sect of Pashupatas, worshipers of Shiva as Lord of Beasts (Pashupati),[11] and in the next centuries more and more people identified themselves as Pashupatas.[12] A Pashupata inscription of 381 CE counts back eleven generations of teachers to Lakulisha.[13] The *Mahabharata* refers to them, but examples of their own texts begin much later.[14] The *Kurma Purana* condemns them, and the *Linga Purana* reflects some of their doctrines.[15] They lived in cremation grounds (hence they were Pariahs, polluted by contact with corpses), and their rituals consisted of offerings of blood, meat, alcohol, and sexual fluids "from ritual intercourse unconstrained by caste restrictions."[16] The imagery of the cremation ground comes from older stories about renouncers and finds its way later into the mythology of Shiva and then into Tantric rituals.

The Pashupatas give a new meaning to passive aggressive; they went out of their way to scandalize respectable folks. The *Pashupata Sutra*, which may be the work of Lakulisha himself, instructs the novice Pashupata to seek the slander

of others by going about like a Pariah (*preta*), snoring, trembling, acting lecher-
ous, speaking improperly, so that people will ill-treat him, and thus he will give
them his bad karma and take their good karma from them,[17] a highly original,
active spin on the usual concept of the intentional transfer of good karma or the
inadvertent accumulation of bad karma. Now we have the intentional transfer
of *bad* karma. For in fact these Pashupatas were perfectly sober and chaste,
merely miming drunkenness and lechery (two of the four addictive vices of lust).
The onlookers were therefore unjustly injuring the Pashupatas, and through this
act their good karma was transferred to the Pashupatas, and the Pashupatas' bad
karma to them.[18] (No one seems to comment on the fact that through their deception, the Pashupatas were harming the onlookers and hence would presumably lose some of their own good karma through this malevolence.)

An early text describes the Pashupatas as wandering, carrying a skull-topped
staff and a begging bowl made of a skull, wearing a garland of human bone,
covered in ashes (the ashes of corpses), with matted hair or shaved head, and
acting in imitation of Rudra (the Vedic antecedent of Shiva).[19] This behavior
closely resembles the vow that Manu prescribes for someone who has killed a
Brahmin: "A Brahmin killer should build a hut in the forest and live there for
twelve years to purify himself, eating food that he has begged for and using the
skull of a corpse as his flag (11.73)." Why was this said to be in imitation of
Rudra/Shiva? Because Shiva was the paradigmatic Brahmin killer, indeed, the
Brahma killer.

SHIVA, THE SKULL BEARER

The Pashupatas were eventually transformed into a sect called the Skull
Bearers (Kapalikas), who no longer followed the philosophy or stigmatizing
behavior of the Pashupatas except for the skull begging bowl and who developed their own texts. Several Puranas tell the myth of the origin of the Skull
Bearers; one version runs like this:

SHIVA BEHEADS BRAHMA

Brahma desired Sarasvati and asked her to stay with him. She said that he would
always speak coarsely. One day when Brahma met Shiva, his fifth head made an
evil sound, and Shiva cut it off. The skull remained stuck fast to his hand, and
though Shiva was capable of burning it up, he wandered the earth with it for the
sake of all people, until he came to Varanasi.[20]

This story may be traced back to the Vedic myth in which Rudra beheads Prajapati to punish him for committing incest with his daughter, Dawn,[21] and to the myth of Indra's pursuit by the female incarnation of Brahminicide, who sticks to him like glue.[22] Already many things have been cleaned up, at least a bit, to the credit of the gods: Brahma now assaults not his own daughter but Sarasvati, who is to become his wife, and who, being the goddess of speech, upbraids him for talking obscenely. Brahma, who often has four heads but is sometimes called Five-Headed (Panchamukha), in this myth is imagined to go from five to four. And now Shiva is not, as in earlier versions, forced helplessly to endure the relentlessly adhesive skull[23] but is entirely in control and submits to the curse "for the sake of all people." This retroactive justification of the god as the power of his sect increases (a transformation that Rama too went through) is an essential move in the theology of the Tantras, as we will see.

Other texts went even further to absolve Shiva of any implication that he might have been punished against his will, by simply removing him from the scene of the crime altogether. One version begins with the familiar tale of Brahma, Vishnu, and the flame linga but then moves on in new directions:

BHAIRAVA BEHEADS BRAHMA

Once when Brahma and Vishnu were arguing about which of them was supreme, a flame linga appeared between them, and from it there emerged a three-eyed man adorned with snakes. Brahma's fifth head called the man his son; thereupon the man, who was Rudra, became angry. He created Bhairava ["The Terrifying One"] and commanded him to punish Brahma. Bhairava beheaded Brahma, for whatever limb offends must be punished. Then Shiva told Bhairava to carry Brahma's skull, and he created a maiden named Brahminicide [Brahma-hatya] and said to her, "Follow Bhairava as he wanders about, begging for alms with this skull and teaching the world the vow that removes the sin of Brahminicide. But when he arrives at the holy city of Varanasi, you must leave him, for you cannot enter Varanasi." And she said, "By serving him constantly under this pretext [of haunting him in punishment], I will purify myself so that I will not be reborn." Then Bhairava entered Varanasi with her still at his left side, and she cried out and went to hell, and the skull of Brahma fell from Bhairava's hand and became the shrine of the Release of the Skull [Kapala-Mochana].[24]

Bhairava first appears as a replacement for Shiva in the Daksha myth, where several texts state that Shiva created him and sent him to do the dirty work of creating mayhem in Daksha's sacrifice.[25] Here he frees Shiva both from the stigma of having committed the original crime of Brahminicide and from submitting to any punishment at all; Shiva creates the avenger himself and even arranges for the punishment incarnate to serve her own vow of penance and find Release. The Release of the Skull thus has a triple meaning; it is the place where Bhairava was released from the skull but also where the skull itself—indeed the very crime of Brahminicide incarnate—was released from its own pollution and became a shrine.* And it is the place of Release (*mochana* is closely related to *moksha*) for those human worshipers who know the myth and/or make a pilgrimage to the shrine. Brahma is saved from the embarrassment of a sexual crime (however bowdlerized) by the substitution of another familiar myth, the myth of the argument between Brahma and Vishnu that we have encountered before. Most important, the myth accounts for the creation of what remains one of the great Shaiva shrines, the Release of the Skull in Varanasi.

The reverse savior myth of Indra's Brahminicide is here reversed back in the other direction so that it becomes a savior myth after all, reformulating the Vedic faith in divine intervention, the worshiper asking the god for help: The god Shiva, or his creature, commits a sin expressly in order to establish a cure for other people who will commit that sin, or other, lesser sins, in the future. According to many versions of the story, Shiva could have rid himself of the skull if he wanted to, but he kept it on his hand until he reached Varanasi, delaying his own salvation, in order to pave the way for humans in need of salvation; his role as savior may have taken on some new qualities at this time as a result of contact with the Mahayana Buddhist ideal of the bodhisattva (potential Buddha) who willingly postpones his own final Release in order to help others to find theirs. Shiva also acts as a savior in the many bhakti myths in which he brings salvation to sinners and in the *Mahabharata* myth of the churning of the ocean: When a fiery poison comes out of the ocean and threatens to burn the universe to ashes (yet another form of the submarine mare fire), Shiva swallows it and holds it forever after in his throat (1.15–17). Shiva's bhakti toward his worshipers also explains why he marries despite his vow to remain

---

* The *Mahabharata* (9.38.1–12) tells another story about the origin of a different shrine called the Release of the Skull, not in Varanasi and not about Shiva: Rama beheaded an ogre whose head accidentally became attached to the thigh of a sage who happened to be wandering in that forest. The sage went on pilgrimages to shrine after shrine and finally was released from the skull at a shrine on the Sarasvati River that henceforth became known as the Release of the Skull.

a chaste yogi forever[26] and, on the other hand, why he persists in generating ascetic heat even when he has decided to marry; in both cases, he does it to keep the universe alive or for the sake of his devotees.[27] The Skull Bearer may also represent a Shaiva response to the avatars of Vishnu. The transition from the pattern of the Indra myth to that of the Shiva myth is made possible by the shift from the second alliance, in which Indra fears or even hates humankind, to the third alliance, the bhakti alliance, in which Shiva loves humankind.

The logic of the myth of a god who commits a sin in order to establish a cure for other people who will commit that sin in the future is made more circular in yet another variant of the story:

THE SKULL BEARER BEHEADS BRAHMA

Once Brahma's fifth head said to Shiva, "Be a Skull Bearer" [Kapalika or Kapalin], addressing Shiva by his future name. Shiva became angry at the word "skull" and cut off the head, which stuck to his hand.[28]

The myth seems aware of the confusion of time cycles, for it notes the incongruity of Brahma's use of Shiva's "future name." Shiva becomes a Skull Bearer because he is a Skull Bearer, apparently deciding to have the game as well as the name. Since the name *is* the person, the word the thing, in the Hindu conception of speech acts such as curses, by naming Shiva, Brahma makes him what he calls him, a Skull Bearer, just as Daksha cursed Shiva to be a heretic because he was one. Shiva, who committed the prototypical Brahminicide—beheading not just any old Brahmin but Brahma himself—also invented the vow to expiate Brahminicide.

Daksha often accuses Shiva and his followers of being, or curses them to be, "Skull Bearers" and "Death Heads" (Kalamukhas).[29] The myth of Daksha sometimes involves the mutual exchange of curses, as the result of which two groups of sages are cursed to become followers of reviled religious sects or false doctrines.[30] Daksha curses all of Shiva's servants to be heretics, Pariahs, beyond the Vedas, and Shiva's servant Nandi (the bull in anthropomorphic form) or Dadhicha curses Daksha and his allies to be hypocrites, false Brahmins,[31] or to be reborn in the Kali Age as Shudras and to go to hell, their minds struck down by evil.[32] Once again the apparent results of the curses are actually their causes: Because Shiva was already a Pariah, denied a share in the sacrifice, Daksha curses him and his followers to be such, and because Daksha heretically denies the true god, Shiva's servant curses him to be a religious hypocrite.

SATI, SECOND TAKE: SHAKTA SHRINES

The story of Sati and Daksha from the early Puranas was now retold, combining that story with the myth in which Shiva wanders with Brahma's head. The result was a myth in which Shiva beheads Daksha and wanders with the corpse of Sati:

SATI'S CORPSE IS DISMEMBERED

Daksha conceived a hatred for Shiva and also for his own daughter Sati, who had married Shiva. Because of her father's offense against her husband, Sati burned her body in the fire of her yoga, to demonstrate Sati-dharma. Then the fire of Shiva's anger burned the triple world, and Shiva beheaded Daksha; eventually, Shiva gave Daksha the head of a goat and revived him. But when Shiva saw Sati being burned in the fire, he placed her on his shoulder and cried out over and over again, "Alas, Sati!" Then he wandered about in confusion, worrying the gods, and Vishnu quickly took up his bow and arrow* and cut away the limbs of Sati, which fell in various places. In each place, Shiva took a different form, and he said to the gods, "Whoever worships the Great Mother with devotion in these places will find nothing unattainable, for she is present in her own limbs. And they will have their prayers answered." And Shiva remained in those places forever, meditating and praying, tortured by separation.[33]

Again, "Sati-dharma" means both what Sati did and what any Good Woman should do. Daksha is beheaded in place of the goat that is the usual sacrificial animal, and when he is revived, he is given the goat's head, for his own is lost. The idea that the sacrifice itself was in essence already a substitute,[34] the victim in the sacrifice substituting for the sacrificer, eventually developed into this myth in which the sacrificer, Daksha, was himself substituted for the goat who was to be the substitute for him, another myth about a sacrifice gone disastrously wrong by being literalized.[†]

---

* In some versions, Vishnu uses his discus (*chakra*), which functions like a combined Frisbee and boomerang: You send it out, and it chops things off and comes back to you.
† Like Janamejaya's sacrifice, in which the god really does replace the sacrificial victim, the horse, as he usually does only metaphorically.

Sati is dismembered, as the Primeval Man was in the Vedas. And just as the place where the skull of Brahma (the antecedent of Daksha[35]) falls becomes the great shrine of the Release of the Skull in Varanasi, so Sati's limbs, as they fall, become the plinths (*pithas*) of pilgrimage shrines,[36] with both Shiva and Sati eternally present to answer prayers. Other texts say that Shiva took the form of a linga in each *pitha*, and the place where her yoni is said to have fallen became the central Tantric shrine in Assam (Kama-rupa).[37]

PROTO-TANTRIC GODDESSES

CHANDIKA/DURGA, SECOND TAKE: SHAKTI BHAKTI

In "Glorification of the Goddess," Chandika was said to have been created from the gods' energies (*tejas*), though she quickly assumed command. Now she is created from her own power, and she is eroticized. Indeed, this process began indirectly even in "Glorification of the Goddess," when, after killing the buffalo, Chandika seduced and killed another antigod:

CHANDIKA SEDUCES AND KILLS SHUMBHA

Shumbha fell madly in love with Chandika and proposed marriage. She replied that she would only marry someone who vanquished her in battle. There was a battle, in which the *shakti*s came out of the gods Brahma, Shiva, Skanda, Vishnu, and Indra to aid her: whatever form, and ornaments, and weapons, and animal vehicles each god had, his *shakti* took that very form. Even Chandika emitted her own *shakti*, howling like a hundred jackals. And after she had absorbed all the gods' *shakti*s, she killed Shumbha.[38]

Shumbha has an ally, Nishumbha, whom Chandika kills too; the names suggest that this myth is modeled on the earlier story of the seduction of the antigods Sunda and Upasunda by the nymph Tilottama, who leaves their killing to the gods. This myth is then a combination of the older theme of "dangerous upstart seduced by nymph" with the new theme of "d.u. killed by goddess." Chandika gives Shumbha death in lieu of sex; he dies in the battle that she demands as a prelude to marriage, a marriage that never happens, and goes straight to heaven, since his love-war relationship with the goddess is regarded as a form of *dvesha-bhakti*, devotion through hatred (as well as love). Though dozens and dozens of antigods who lack Shumbha's passion are vanquished by the gods on every page without seeing the light, his passion makes his death in combat a form of enlightenment, a popular Hindu theme that is foreshadowed by the heaven-guaranteeing heroic battle deaths in the *Mahabharata*.

THE SEDUCTION AND KILLING OF MAHISHA

Most Sanskrit texts play down the erotic relationship between the goddess and the buffalo, and some (beginning with "Glorification of the Goddess") omit it altogether. But other texts revel in it, and it bursts out again and again in the art-historical traditions, in both paintings and sculptures, which emphasize, as do the texts, the extraordinary beauty of Chandika or, rather, of Durga, as she is now usually called. Even "Glorification of the Goddess" tells us that the gods give her some rather good jewelry and specifies that of all the parts of her body made from parts of the gods, her genitals were made of energy itself.[39] But a later Sanskrit text, the *Skanda Purana*, states that Durga was already a powerful goddess when Mahisha defeated the gods and that the gods went to her to beg her for help in dispatching him.[40] Another text from roughly the same period brings out the erotic element more vividly:

CHANDIKA SEDUCES AND KILLS MAHISHA

Mahisha had forced Brahma to promise that if he had to die, it would be at the hands of a woman; he asked this in order to ensure that he would not die, since he regarded it as unthinkable that a mere woman, beneath contempt, should overpower him. The gods created Durga. She enticed Mahisha, who proposed marriage. But she replied that she wanted to kill him, not to sleep with him, that she had become a woman in the first place only in order to kill him; that although she did not appear to be a man, she had a man's nature and was merely assuming a woman's form because he had asked to be killed by a woman. Moreover, she said to Mahisha's messenger, "Your master is a great fool, and certainly no hero, to want to be killed by a woman. For to be killed by one's mistress gives sexual pleasure to a pansy (*kliba*) but misery to a hero." The besotted Mahisha, however, was persuaded by a counselor who suggested that this clearly antierotic speech was the amorous love talk of a passionate woman: "She wishes to bring you into her power by frightening you. This is the sort of indirect speech that enamored women use toward the man they love." Mahisha then dressed up in his best suit and boasted to Durga that he was a man who could make a woman very happy. She laughed and killed him by beheading him.[41]

Mahisha's boon is a variant of Ravana's, narrowing the field of his killer to someone regarded as impossible, a mere woman. And so once again the gods had to create someone to kill the upstart without violating the fine print of the demonic contract. Though Durga here is so beautiful that she inspires the antigod with a destructive erotic passion, she herself is so devoid of erotic feelings that she insists not only that she is a man rather than a woman but that her would-be consort is *not* a man, but a mere pansy. To clinch this argument, she insists that only a pansy would wish to experience a *Liebestod* with a woman. The aggressive woman rides astride the buffalo, and her sexual supremacy is expressed through a martial image: She holds an erect phallic sword in paintings and sculptures depicting the slaying of Mahisha.

The explicit meaning of this image is that the proposed battle is, by implication, a sexual union. But the image also plays upon the notion (which it self-consciously inverts) that every actual sexual act is, by implication, a fatal battle, a notion basic to Indian thinking about the dangers of eroticism and the need for the control, even the renunciation, of sensuality. In a more positive vein, the fact that Mahisha desires to marry and/or battle Durga, despite her clearly antierotic warning, implies that either marriage or battle may be a way of achieving unity; that either may serve as an initiatory death leading to a desired transformation; that strong emotion, be it lust or hatred, seeks a conflict that leads ultimately to the resolution of all conflict in death. It is this deep intertwining of sex and violence that seems to underlie Durga's extraordinary appeal, for she is one of the most popular Hindu deities, worshiped by both men and women.

The image of Durga on top of the helpless Mahisha, placing her feet on shoulders and head as she beheads him or on the back of the cowering buffalo, an image much reproduced in both sculpture and painting, seems to me to be mirrored in the well-known Tantric image of the goddess Kali dancing on the (ithyphallic) corpse of Shiva, with her sword in her hand, often holding in another hand a severed head, an inversion of the myth in which Shiva dances all around India carrying the corpse of Sati. Often the goddess Kali stretches out her tongue to drink the streams of blood spurting from the severed heads or necks; in this she is the descendant of the female antigod Long Tongue in the Brahmanas. Some contemporary Hindu glosses of this icon (particularly in Bengal) attempt to minimize the violence inherent in it; they say, "She sticks out her tongue in shock when she realizes that she is trampling on her own husband," and they say that the severed head represents the severing of the ego, interpretations that reduce the dominating demonic goddess Kali to the properly submissive wife Parvati. But others say that she is the letter *i* that turns the corpse (*shava* in Sanskrit) into Shiva; she brings him to life. Indeed sometimes the Goddess holds the severed head while she straddles a copulating couple.

Whose is the severed head that the goddess holds in many of these icons? Sometimes she herself is headless, Chinnamastaka ("The Severed Head"), and we might think that the head she holds is her own, for it matches her headless body in color and other qualities. One strange variant of the Mahisha myth, which appears in texts in both Sanskrit and Tamil, suggests that the head might be Shiva's. In this myth, after the goddess has killed Mahisha, his head sticks to her hand just as Brahma's head sticks to Shiva's after Shiva beheads Brahma. After bathing in a river shrine (*tirtha*), the goddess discovers that there is a Shiva linga on Mahisha's headless torso—that is, in the place where his head was.[42] In the context of this particular story, the main function of the epiphany is to identify Mahisha as a devotee of Shiva and hence to plunge the goddess into an agony of guilt, necessitating a complex expiation. But in the context of the patterning of the myth as a whole, this linga functions to demonstrate the fusion of Mahisha and Shiva and, moreover, of Mahisha's head and Shiva's phallus.*

Yet another possible victim as donor of the severed head may be the devotee of the goddess. Puranic and Tantric mythology, as well as contemporary local mythology and early Tamil literature, abound in tales of male devotees who cut off their own heads in an act of devotion to Durga, and Mahisha himself is such a devotee.

TANTRICS

With this mythological corpus as a prelude, let us now consider Tantra itself.

The Zen diagram of Tantra (that is, a cluster of qualities, not all of which need be present in any particular text or ritual) includes the worship of the goddess, initiation, group worship, secrecy, and antinomian behavior, particularly sexual rituals and the ingesting of bodily fluids. There are Tantric texts, Tantric rituals, Tantric myths, Tantric art forms, and, above all, Tantric worshipers. There are Tantric mantras (repeated formulas), Tantric yantras (mystical

---

* It is also, by the way, an extraordinarily literal example of what Freud would have called upward displacement.

designs), and Tantras (esoteric texts), as well as Tantric gods and their consorts. Within Hinduism, there are Shaiva, Vaishnava, and Shakta Tantras, as well as Tantras devoted to other gods, and there are, in addition, Buddhist Tantras and some Jaina Tantras; Buddhism and Hinduism once again, as in the Upanishadic period, share a number of features, in this case certain rituals and images.*

Tantra originated, both in Buddhism and in Hinduism, sometime between the sixth and eighth centuries of the Common Era,[43] but it truly hit its stride in the tenth century, having changed significantly in the course of those centuries.[44] In particular, from the tenth century the Tantras were infused with the spirit of bhakti. Tantra probably began in the northern fringes of India, Kashmir, Nepal, Bengal, and Assam—places where Buddhism too flourished—but it soon took hold in central and South India. Something in the social conditions of the time inspired the Tantric innovations, a combination of the growing anti-Brahmin sentiment of some bhakti sects and the impulse, always present from the days of the breakaway Vratya ascetics of the Veda and the extreme renunciants of the later Upanishadic period, to find new religious ways to alter consciousness. In both yoga and Tantra the transformation was controlled by meditation. Similarly, the flying, drug-drinking, long-haired sage of the Veda reappears in the flying, fluid-drinking Tantric.

Much of Tantric ritual took place during secret initiations in relatively remote areas, but these rites were not a particularly well-guarded secret. The secret was that there was no secret.† Tantra and Tantric practices were well publicized, esoteric but not necessarily marginal or even subversive; much of it was public, even royal.[45] Like the sages of the Upanishads, as well as the bhakti movements, Tantrics maintained a close association with kings,‡ who made good use of the Tantras themselves[46] as well as lending to the Tantras the symbolism of kingship. Kings had participated in sexual rituals for many centuries (recall the horse sacrifice), and every king was wedded to at least one goddess, Shri (Good Fortune) or Lakshmi (Good Luck) or Earth itself (Bhu-devi). Moreover, if you transform your body so that you become a god, as Tantrics claimed

---

* Among people who find Tantra shameful, Buddhists say it's Hindu, and Hindus say it's Buddhist (or Tibetan), just as the French used to call syphilis the Spanish disease, the Spanish the Italian disease, and so forth.
† As the French psychoanalyst Jacques Lacan would have argued.
‡ Imagine if the fundamentalists who run so many of the present governments of the world were replaced by Tantrics; now, there's a theocracy for you, to boggle the mind. Or perhaps we should regard Bill Clinton as our first Tantric president.

to do, you are also becoming a king. And Tantra is all about power, and power is catnip for kings.

Using the MO that had served it well for many centuries, the Brahmin imaginary absorbed many of the new sects,[47] but this time it met its match in Tantra.

There are several different sorts of Tantrics. Within the wider landscape of the two paths that had forked apart at the time of the Upanishads, Tantra effected a new resolution. Outside Tantra, Hindu renouncers on the path of Release still hoped for *moksha* at death, by which they meant casting off all constraints of form and individuality to be absorbed in *brahman*. But Hindu householders on the path of rebirth, whose texts were now the Puranas, expected, at death, to be reborn either on earth or—the new option—in the heaven of Shiva or Vishnu or the goddess, from which they would not be reborn again and might even achieve Release; indeed, some Hindus referred to rebirth in such a heaven as a kind of Release. Both groups therefore acknowledged Release as an ultimate goal, but understood it in distinctive ways. Entering this scene, the Tantric "path of mantras," open to both ascetics and householders, promised to grant not only Release (which the Tantras often call nirvana) from the world of transmigration but magical powers (*siddhi*s) and pleasures (*bhoga*s) on the way to Release,[48] thus combining the rewards of the paths of rebirth and Release. The third path, the horrible dead-end reincarnation, mired in the worlds of corals and insects, still threatens the person who neither sacrifices nor meditates, but the Tantric path guarantees to protect the worshiper from that dreadful default. Tantra thus offered the best of both worlds, or, as the Tantric mantra has it, *bhukti-mukti*, *bhoksha-moksha*, or *bhoga-yoga*, "enjoyment-Release," which has been nicely translated as the biunity of "sensual delight and spiritual flight."[49]

Another useful way to view the place of Tantra within the Hinduism of this period would be to divide the options slightly differently, into a devotional world of bhakti (guru/god/goddess) and a philosophical world further divided into Vedanta (meditation) and Tantra (ritual), a triad that comes out of the *Gita* synthesis of devotion, knowledge, and action. This formulation also divides Tantra into its "left-hand" or transgressive traditions (those that violated caste laws of purity—trafficking in blood, death, skulls, sex, all impure) and its "right-hand" or conservative traditions. Most non-Tantric Hindus regard *all* Tantrics as following a left-hand path (*vama*), while the right-hand Tantrics look askance at the Tantrics whom *they* regarded as left-hand, themselves being more right-hand than thou.

TANTRA AS SALVATION IN THE KALI AGE

Shiva's role as a savior is not limited to establishing the sect of the Skull Bearer or the shrine in Varanasi that will save future sinners. In the Shaiva Tantric tradition, Shiva does more; he actively seeks out sinners and instructs them, by teaching them the very doctrines that, in the eyes of someone like Daksha, mark them as Pariahs.

Several Shaiva Puranas disapprove of the Tantras and stand behind "the Vedas," which probably means not actual Vedic sacrifice but "Vedic religion" in the sense of Puranic religion, in this case the worship of Shiva. These Puranas nevertheless assert that Shiva is the author of the Tantras and that the Tantras serve a useful purpose—for some people, but not for *them*. They narrate the tale of a group of sages, cursed to be barred from the use of the Vedas, who were saved by Shiva. How they are cursed takes many forms; sometimes they are the sages who stand with Daksha against Shiva and are cursed in punishment for that. This is one version:

SHIVA TEACHES TANTRIC TEXTS

When Vishnu learned that the sages had been cursed to be outside the pale of the Vedas, he went to Shiva and said, "There is not even a drop of merit in people who are beyond the Vedas. But nevertheless, because of our devotion [bhakti] to them, we must protect them even though they will go to hell. Let us make texts of delusion to protect and delude these evil people." Shiva agreed, and they made the Kapala, Pashupata, Vama ["Left-hand," i.e., Tantric], and other texts. For the sake of the sages, Shiva descended to earth when the force of the curse had come to an end, and he begged alms from those who were outcast, deluding them as he came there adorned with skulls, ashes, and matted hair, saying, "You will go to hell, but then you will be reborn and gradually work your way to the place of merit."[50]

The ambivalent moral status of the sages in this version of the myth is evident from Vishnu's statement: The sages are evil and doomed to hell, but the gods must protect and delude them (an interesting combination) so that they will ultimately find merit. Moreover, even though the doctrines that Shiva teaches them are mediating ones—below the Vedas but above damnation—he cannot teach those doctrines while the sages are still cursed to be heretics (which is what being debarred from the Vedas amounts to in these stories); he must come to them "when the force of the curse had come to an end" to teach them new false texts. That is, they need to have worked off the curse, to have started on the path upward, before he can give them the Tantras.

How can Shiva "protect" the sages by teaching them a new heresy? The "left-hand" doctrines help them by giving them *some* religion, albeit a heresy, since they are denied the Vedas; the heresy serves as a staircase between non-Vedic and Vedic religion,[51] bridging the gap between complete darkness and true religion, purifying them enough so that they can enter the waters of purification. They need an orthodox heresy (an oxymoron, but it fits the situation) to break the ritual chain of impurity. This concept of weaning is expounded by apologists for the Tantras, who argue that Shiva knew that the animal leanings of certain people made them need meat and wine and therefore invented Tantric rites in order gradually to wean them from this pleasure "in associating it with religion," the idea being that it is better to bow to Shiva with your sandals on than never to bow at all.[52] Shudras and the victims of curses are forbidden to study the Vedas; some other people are simply incapable. Out of pity for all of them, Shiva teaches heresy, raising them up "step by step," a doctrine that may have been influenced by the Buddhist idea of skill in means, suiting the teaching to the level of the person to be enlightened. The assumption (often stated explicitly) is that he gives them a religion that is "natural" to them (*sahaja*, "born with" them), that makes use of the things that everyone naturally enjoys—sex, wine, meat. Tantra in this view is Hinduism with training wheels. Thus Shiva makes some people heretics in the first place so that he can ultimately enlighten them. This enlightenment at first appears as a heresy, which they reject, and indeed it is a heresy, in comparison with the ideal, Vedic or Puranic worship. But for some, this heresy is their only salvation, and their own god has created it for a good reason.

The final Puranic rationalization for the Tantras is that heresies taught to heretics make them so evil that they must reach the furthest point of the cycle and then rebound from the extreme, to become good again, to go back to the head of the queue, to go back to GO, like all the creatures of the Kali Age. Indeed the "orthodox heresies" are also justified by the doctrine of the forbidden acts in the Kali Age (*kali-varjya*): Some things that were forbidden in the past (such as Tantric rituals) are permitted now because we are too corrupt to meet the old standards. This argument was then sometimes inverted to argue that some things that were permitted then (such as female promiscuity, or Draupadi's polyandry) are forbidden now for the very same reason: because we are corrupt, in this case too corrupt to commit these acts without being totally destroyed by them.

Tantric Ritual: Fighting Fire with Fire

THE FIVE MS

What *are* these terrible, dangerous things that the Tantric texts taught people to do? Central to Tantric ritual is what the Tantras call the Five Ms, or the Five M Words (since all five terms begin with an *m* in Sanskrit), which might be called, in English, the Five F Words: *madya* (fermented grapes, wine), *mamsa* (flesh, meat), *matsya* (fish), *mudra* (farina), and *maithuna* (fornication). Like so much of Tantra, the Five Ms are an inversion, in this case an inversion of other pentads in more conventional forms of Hinduism. Puranic Hindus ingested the "five products of the cow" (*panchagavya*) to purify themselves of pollution: clarified butter, milk, and yogurt, plus bovine urine and feces.* Tantrism, which accepts this schema, has, in addition, its own version of the five ritual elements, the Five M Words, or, in one variant, the Five Jewels (semen, urine, feces, menstrual blood, and phlegm) or Five Nectars (with marrow in place of phlegm).[53] One Buddhist Tantra further divides flesh (*mamsa*) into Five Meats (beef, dog, elephant, horse, and human flesh), together with Five Ambrosias (semen, urine, feces, blood, and marrow, slightly different from the Five Jewels).[54] All these pentads were probably a deliberate antinomian travesty of the "five products of the cow"; one Tantric text substitutes for the bovine urine and feces the blood and flesh of the cow, a bovicide abomination that deliberately subverted orthodox categories of purity,[55] forcing participants to look beyond the dualities of purity and impurity and the conventions of food and sex that drive so much of Hinduism.[56] One can hardly imagine a more blatant, in-your-face, *maithuna*-you attitude than the one at the heart of this substitution.

The *Mahanirvana Tantra* elaborates upon each of the Five Ms: Wine may be made from sugar (or molasses), rice, honey, or palm tree juice and made by someone of any caste. Meat may be from animals that come from the water, the land, or the sky, and again, it doesn't matter where it comes from or who kills it; the only stipulation is that the animals be male, not female (as is the case for Vedic sacrifices too). Fish are best without bones, though the ones that have lots of bones may also be offered to the goddess if they are very well roasted or fried. The best farina (*mudra*) is made from rice, barley, or "earth-smoke" wheat,

---

* Further still from Tantra, but even more basic to Hinduism (more particularly, to Sankhya), are the five elements, or *tattvas*: earth, fire, water, wind, and space (to which some schools add a sixth, mind or soul).

which is especially nice when fried in butter.[57] And fornication may involve one's own wife, another man's wife, or a woman who belongs to the group in common.

Wine, flesh, and fish were prohibited for high caste Hindus, and there is little debate about the basic lexical connotation or the denotation of these terms,[58] though as we will see, there is much debate about whether they are to be taken literally. But the other two Ms, *mudra* and *maithuna*, have proved more problematic even to define in their primary meanings. *Mudra*, here interpreted as a fourth material article, farina, or parched grain (sometimes kidney beans, or "any cereal believed to possess aphrodisiac properties"[59]), has a primary lexical meaning of "stamp" or "seal" (as in "seal ring"); it also means "signal" or "hand gesture," and may indicate, in some texts, not farina but either of two other Fs: finger positions (physical movements of the hands corresponding to imagined acts) or the female sexual organ, which "seals" the male organ in the sexual act.[60] The uncertainty of the referents of words used in the Tantras compounds the question of their literal or figurative meaning.

As for the last element, *maithuna* is usually translated as sexual intercourse, more literally "pairing," but since all the other terms seem to be material substances, it may mean more precisely "what is derived from sexual intercourse"—that is, the fluids produced in sexual intercourse. This gloss is a bit of a stretch, but it is lexically correct, does assimilate *maithuna* to the other substances consumed as food at the forbidden feast, and has the added virtue of linking the Five Ms with another widely attested characteristic of South Asian Tantra in its earliest documented stage, a ritual in which what Sterling Hayden in *Doctor Strangelove* called "precious bodily fluids" (in this case sexual or menstrual discharge) were swallowed as transformative "power substances."[61]

For the Tantras do say things like "The body of every living creature is made of semen and blood. The [deities] who are fond of sexual pleasure drink semen and blood."[62] Drinking blood and seed together is a very Tantric thing to do. In one of the Puranic antecedents of the Tantras, "Glorification of the Goddess," the goddess Chandika came up against an antigod that was actually named Blood Seed (Raktabija), from every drop of whose blood (or, if you prefer, semen) a new antigod appeared. To conquer him, Chandika created the goddess Kali and instructed her to open wide her mouth and drink the blood as well as the constantly appearing progeny of Blood Seed; then Chandika killed him.[63] The goddess Kali effectively aborts the birth of offspring of Blood Seed by prophylactically swallowing his seed, the drops of his blood.[64] In other

Puranas, the goddess emits multiforms of herself who extend their tongues to lick up each drop of the semen-blood before it can fall to the ground.[65] The long tongue of the goddess Kali, like that of the female antigod Long Tongue, the bitch that licks up the oblations, is the upward displacement of her excessive vaginas, a grotesque nightmare image of the devouring sexual woman, her mouth a second sexual organ.

But it is not semen-blood but female blood (together with male semen rather than male blood) that plays the central role in the Tantras. The menstrual blood of the female participant is connected to the polluting but life-giving blood of the menstruating goddess, which flows to the earth each year,[66] and the blood of her animal victims, decapitated and offered in sacrifice. Not just the goddess, but the Yoginis, a horde of ravishingly beautiful, terrifying, and powerful female deities, participated in the drinking of the sexual fluids. These Yoginis were often placated with blood offerings and animal sacrifices but also propitiated by exchanging sexual fluids with the male practitioners and by consuming those fluids (as well as other prohibited foods). In return the Yoginis granted the practitioners, at the very least, "a powerful expansion of . . . the limited consciousness of the conformist Brahmin practitioner" and, at most, supernatural powers, including the power of flight.[67]

Sanitizing the Symbolism of Tantric Ritual

In protest against these transgressive forms of Tantra, many texts insisted that the ritual instructions were never intended to be followed literally but were purely symbolic. The sanitized interpretation of the Five Ms, for instance, introduced new ritual substitutes, glossing *madya* (wine) as a meditational nectar, *mamsa* (flesh) as the tongue of the practitioner, *matsya* (fish) as his breaths, *mudra* as inner knowledge, and *maithuna* as "supreme essence."[68] We can view the symbolic as a historical development from the actual (as may have been the case with references to human sacrifice at a much earlier period), or we can assume that the ritual was always purely symbolic, never real (like the ogres in the *Ramayana*), or that both were always already present from the start (like the linga that is and is not the phallus of Shiva). We might summarize the question, Did the Tantrics actually have Tantric sex? and respond with three guesses:

FIRST GUESS: They Did.

Variant 1: Once They Did It; Now They Talk About It.

Variant 2: First They Talked About It, and Then They Did It.

SECOND GUESS: It was Always All in Their Heads.

THIRD GUESS: They Always Did It and Imagined It at the Same Time.

Let us consider them one by one.

The historical argument implies that the Hindus themselves bowdlerized their own tradition: "No one is swallowing anything; we're all just meditating." The argument for historical development begins by asserting that Tantra began as a non-Brahmin (sometimes even anti-Brahmin), antihouseholder movement and then was taken up by Brahmins and householders. Since we don't have access to the earliest layers of Tantra, before the extant texts, we can't know who the original worshipers were or what they did then; perhaps they did drink blood at first and then stopped, perhaps not. But we do have Tantric texts that seem to indicate that their authors drank blood and performed the sexual ritual. One can argue that Tantric ritual texts tell us precisely what the practitioners did, and that they mean what they say.[69]

Later, the historical argument continues, many Hindus merely imagined that part of the ritual and/or declared that it never had taken place at all,[70] while Hindus who continued to perform the rituals described them in a code that made it appear that they were merely performing them symbolically. Certain elite Brahmin Tantric practitioners, led by the great systematic and scholastic theologian Abhinavagupta in Kashmir (975–1025 CE), sublimated the ritual into a body of ritual and meditative techniques "that did not threaten the purity regulations required for high-caste social constructions of the self." The Tantra of the cremation ground was cleaned up and housebroken so that it could cross Brahmin thresholds. The theoreticians eliminated the major goal of the unsanitized Tantrics, the consumption of the substances, and kept only the minor goal, the expansion of consciousness, now viewed as the cultivation of a divine state of mind homologous to (rather than actually produced by) the bliss experienced in sexual orgasm. This sanitized High Hindu Tantra was a revisionist transformation "from a kind of doing to a kind of knowing," abstracted into a program of meditation mantras.[71] It led to a split into householder sects, which worshiped Shiva but regarded the ritual texts as merely symbolic meditations, not as prescriptions for action, and more extreme cults, which continued to worship goddesses through rituals involving blood, wine, and erotic fluids, rituals that were entirely real.[72]

The relatively straightforward historical thesis is complicated, or nuanced, by several factors. Even after the period of transition there was still a place in the secret initiations for the consumption of prohibited foods and sexual fluids; the earlier, unreconstructed form of Tantra may also have persisted as a kind of underground river, flowing beneath the new, bowdlerized, dominant form of Tantra. Another sort of compromise consisted in sexual rituals performed only within the confines of *coitus reservatus*, eliminating the release of the fluids. But where some texts speak of meditation instead of *maithuna*, and others talk of *coitus reservatus*, yet others continue to talk about drinking fluids.

A third compromise consisted in performing the original rituals but shifting the goal from the development of magical powers or the transformation of the worshiper to "the transformative psychological effect of overcoming conventional notions of propriety through the consumption of polluting substances."[73] Finally, a system of overcoding may have permitted some high-caste, conformist householder practitioners to have it both ways, to lead a double life by living conventionally while experimenting in secret with Tantric identities; thus they might put on a public face to claim (to eighteenth-century missionaries, for instance) that they were "shocked" (like Claude Rains in *Casablanca*) by Tantric practices, in which they themselves covertly participated.[74]

The bowdlerizing effect may also have been a result of the Tantrics' concern to make crystal clear the line between the use of antinomian elements in the ritual and any sort of casual orgiasticism. That is to say, "Kids, Don't Try This at Home." The original Tantric sources on sexualized ritual seldom mention pleasure, let alone ecstasy, though the later texts do speak of *ananda* (bliss).[75] Indeed the Tantras seem sometimes to lean over backward to be *plus royaliste que le roi* in hedging their sexual ceremonies with secrecy, euphemism, and warnings of danger, realizing that in harnessing sex for their rituals, they are playing with fire. In this, the Tantras share in the more general Hindu cultural awareness of the dangers of sex, which even the *Kama-sutra* emphasizes.

This is a strong argument for the original physical reality of the Tantric substances; why warn people to be careful about them if they don't exist? Wine, for instance, is, like sex, dangerous. The passage in the *Mahanirvana Tantra* glossing the Five Ms includes this caveat: "Meat, fish, parched grain, fruits and roots offered to the divinity when wine is offered are known as the purification [*shuddhi*] of the wine. Drinking wine without this purification, by itself, is like swallowing poison; the person who uses such a mantra becomes chronically ill and soon dies, after living only a short life span."[76] The text, well aware of the fact that intoxicating liquors are one of the addictive vices, returns to this issue later on, taking pains to distinguish the ritual use of wine (which is regarded as a goddess) from casual drinking, which it abhors:

> Mortals who drink wine with the proper rituals and with a well-controlled mind are virtually immortals on earth. But if this Goddess wine is drunk without the proper rituals, she destroys a man's entire intellect, life span, reputation, and wealth. People whose minds are intoxicated from drinking too much wine lose their intelligence, which is the means by which they achieve the four goals of life, and such a man does not know what to do or what not to do; every step he takes results in something that he does not want and that other people do not want. Therefore, the king or the leader of the Tantric group should torture and confiscate the property of a man whom drink has made grotesque, with unsteady speech, feet, or hands, wandering in his wits and out of his mind; and he should heavily fine a man whom drink has made foul-mouthed, crazy, or devoid of shame or fear.[77]

Even wine that has been purified by the ritual is a danger if taken in excess. The social symptoms of alcoholism ("every step he takes results in something that he does not want and that other people do not want") are as closely observed as those in the equally perceptive description of the compulsive gambler in the *Rig Veda*.

Another argument for the historical reality of the left-hand Tantric rituals is the fact that such rituals apparently continue to this day, particularly among the Bauls of Bengal and the Nizarpanths ("Hinduized" Ismai'ilis of western India). An unbroken line of teachers and disciples culminates in present-day living Yoginis, who endure for the most part in the greatly reduced form of aged, poor, widowed, and socially marginalized women, who are sexuality exploited, often accused of practicing witchcraft when an untimely death or some other calamity befalls a village, and still occasionally put to death.[78] At the same time, the bowdlerizing continues too; in modern Kolkata, priests at the Kalighat temple sometimes "Vaishnavize" the goddess Kali by removing reminders of her Tantric background.[79]

In passing, we might consider the variant of the first argument that, in Tantric fashion, reverses it, turning history on its head and arguing that left-hand Tantra was at first just a mental exercise, and then someone took it literally.

(First They Talked About It, and Then They Did It.) This too would account for the two levels of Tantra, and it is logically possible, but there is little historical support for it.

So much for the historical argument that Tantra was a ritual that became, for the dominant culture, a kind of myth (or a myth that became a ritual).

The second argument—that the left-hand Tantric ritual was always just a myth (or It was Always All in Their Heads)—is precisely the viewpoint of the people that those who hold with the historical hypothesis regard as the bowdlerizers, the people who insist that Tantra was never real, that the left-hand Tantric rituals were never actually performed and were only symbolic from the very start. These are probably the majority of educated Hindus today. In keeping with the doctrines of illusion (which were, like Tantra, being developed in eleventh-century Kashmir), this philosophical approach argues that all the Tantric rituals were illusory mental images of rituals that were never real, that Tantric sex was never a ritual but only a myth, as cannibalism has sometimes been thought to be, something that some people thought other people were doing, when in fact no one was doing anything of the sort. This would mean that even the people who wrote the early Tantric texts merely imagined that they were doing what they said they were doing. After all, people have imagined that they have flown to heaven and walked among the gods, so why not imagine that you're drinking your sister's menstrual blood?

But it is also possible that there were two levels of myth and ritual from the start, as there were in the early Upanishads, and this is the third argument: Some people would meditate on the sacrifice *and perform the sacrifice* (or They Always Did It and Imagined It at the Same Time), which also allows for the possibility that others would merely meditate, and still others would merely perform the ritual without meditating. In this view, the two paths of Tantra, meditation and action, *jnana* and karma, lived side by side, like the two paths in the Upanishads, and sometimes even coexisted in a single worshiper. I have argued that stories about Pariahs, goddesses, and antigods may simultaneously reflect actual attitudes to real Pariahs, women, and tribal people and symbolic attitudes to imaginary goddesses, antigods, and, indeed, Pariahs. So too Tantric rituals could be simultaneously real and symbolic. Few would deny that the dominant trend in Tantric interpretation has long been, and remains, metaphorical or metaphysical. But how do we know that the unsanitized school did not interpret their texts, too, metaphorically?

The *Mahanirvana Tantra* recognizes three grades of humans: men who are like beasts, capable only of conventional worship, such as image worship (corresponding perhaps to the third group in the Upanishads, below the main two paths); heroic men, who practice Tantric rituals (the path of rebirth); and godlike men, who practice Tantric meditation, having transcended and internalized Tantric ritual (the path of Release).[80] Yet as we saw in the passage "What Use Are Imagined Images?" this text also seems to mock people who are satisfied with mere mental images of rituals without performing them, to argue that it is better to meditate upon the ritual than to perform the ritual, but only if the worshiper has reached a high level of understanding through *internalizing* the ritual—that is, by performing it many times.

An even closer parallel might be seen in the Upanishadic passage (BU 6.4) in which the worshiper in a sexual embrace with his wife imagines each part of the act as a part of the Vedic offering into the fire, while presumably anyone making the offering into the fire could also imagine each action as its sexual parallel.* Tantra collapses the metaphor and says that the act of intercourse with the ritual female partner is itself a ritual, like making an offering into the fire. Thus the Tantras fold back into the path of Release the Upanishadic sensuality that the Brahmins had filtered out. The *mudra*s, the gestures, may form a mediating bridge between the act actually performed and the mere imagination of the act; they gesture toward the act. This understanding of the multiple layers of ritual symbolism supplements rather than replaces the chronological hypothesis, for if, as appears most likely, both levels were present from the start, historical factors over the centuries may have caused one level, the purely symbolic and mythical, to rise in importance as the other, the unsanitized ritual, lost power and status.

Given the attention that Indian literary and erotic theory pays to double meanings, to the linguistic "embrace" that simultaneously means two different things, it seems wise to assume that the Tantrics too engaged in split-level symbolism. The substances would be both/and as well as neither/nor: both literal and metaphoric, but also neither of these, being signs pointing to a set of meanings—the irrelevance of pollution or the relevance of nonduality—for which the signifiers (in this case, the Five Ms) are arbitrary. What is significant is not whether these antinomian acts were imagined or performed, but that the

---

* This sort of reversal was imagined in an old joke about a Jesuit priest who, when his bishop forbade priests to smoke while meditating, dutifully agreed but argued that surely there would be no objection if he occasionally meditated while he was smoking.

higher-order discourse in which the debate about them took place was of central concern not only to the Tantrics but to mainstream Indian religion.[81]

In part because some people argue that the early Tantrics *never* actually did any of the transgressive things they said they did (the second argument), one might be tempted to insist that they *always* did (the first argument). But the texts, like many, if not most, religious texts, are ambiguous; you can read them to say that they did or that they did not. Thus Tantra was for some people a ritual and for others merely a myth, or for some people a sexual ritual and for others a meditational ritual. And for some, both. Not only does imagination not preclude doing, but doing does not preclude imagination; they can be simultaneous. Tantrics were certainly capable of walking and chewing imaginary gum at the same time.

WHAT'S IN IT FOR THE WOMEN?[82]

Since sex is both dangerous and central to Tantrism (*vama* means both "left-hand" and "a woman," and so to call Tantra the Vama path, as was often done, was to feminize as well as stigmatize it), Tantric sexual rituals, and Tantric women, are very carefully controlled. Many Tantric rituals involve women both as sexual partners and as channelers of the goddess, therefore objects of ritual worship.[83] The centrality of women to Tantric ritual may have had a positive influence on more general attitudes to women during this period, such as Bana's enlightened attitude to the ritual immolation of widows. There is also much talk of *shakti* and goddesses. Where the *Mahabharata* and *Ramayana* and the early Puranas are framed as conversations between two men, one of them a professional narrator (Charioteer), most Shaiva Tantras (and even some of the Vaishnava ones) are framed as dialogues between Shiva and Parvati. But it is by no means clear that Tantra benefited rather than exploited the women involved.

In the central Tantric ceremony, the male Tantric invokes Shiva, who enters him, while his female partner invokes Shiva's *shakti,* the goddess, who enters her. The body of the Tantric thus becomes the icon (*murti*) of the god, and when he unites with his partner, the power of the goddess in her (or in her sexual fluids) unites with his semen and travels up his spine through a series of wheels of power (chakras), or stations of the spine, until they reach the top of his head and produce what is variously described as bliss, complete enlightenment, or Release. The particular power involved in this ritual, called the

Kundalini ("the Coiled One"), takes the form of two channels of bodily fluids imagined in the shape of two serpents, male and female, intertwined around the spine (like the medical caduceus, symbolizing the human body in perfect health). Yoga had already established ways of raising the Kundalini to maintain health and, sometimes, to attain immortality; Tantra added the idea of stirring it up with ritual sex. In Nath versions of Kundalini yoga, the submarine mare is said to be a fire at the base of the spine, homologized with the Kundalini serpent (for horses are often connected with snakes in India). The centrality of semen in this ritual suggests that it was designed for men, though some Indian texts (including medical texts) do assume that women, like men, have semen and can draw it up through the spine to the brain. Some texts go so far as to assume that the male Tantric is able to draw the female's fluid back into his own sexual organ and up his spine, the so-called fountain pen technique.[84]

There is a lot of Tantric talk about how wonderful women are: "Women are gods, women are life, women, indeed, are jewels. One should always associate with women, whether one's own wife or another's. What I have told you is the secret of all the Tantras."[85] Yet there is no evidence that actual Tantric women were equal partners in any sense of the word; to the question What's in it for the women? (once called "the most embarrassing question you can ask any Tantric"[86]), it would appear that the answer is: Not much.[87] Yet though Tantric ritual performance may construct rigid gender roles, it also allows possibilities for the subversions of those roles.[88] Some women found a kind of autonomy, freedom from their families, in the Tantric community, but for the most part the rituals were designed to benefit people who had lingas, not yonis.

Though many Tantrics probably had no concern whatsoever for the way they appeared to others,[89] and most of them were "less concerned with shocking the conventional sensibilities of the wider South Asian society than they were with the transformative effects,"[90] some did seem to thumb their noses at the bourgeois who condemned them. We can see this attitude in the passage with which this chapter began, "What Use Are Imagined Images?" which mocks conventional religion—fasting and the worship of icons. (The extremists among this sort of Tantric were the Aghoris, "to whom nothing is horrible," who would do, or eat, anything at all to cultivate and then to demonstrate their indifference to conventional ideas of pleasure and pain.) Since, as we have seen, texts like the *Kama-sutra* assume that sex and carnivorousness are perfectly normal, you have to go out of your way to make them godlike; hence, for some Tantrics, the ritual involved sex not just with your wife but with your sister and/or a low-caste woman.

The *Mahanirvana Tantra* distinguishes between one's own wife (*svakiya*), who is permitted as a partner for the sexual ritual, and two forbidden women, another man's wife and a woman used in common by the entire group (*sadharana*).* Other Tantric texts from which the author of the *Mahanirvana Tantra* takes pains to distinguish himself permit both one's own wife and another man's wife as partners. (His distaste for these texts is an instance of the sanitizing effect.) The ritual contact with one's own wife involves the use of her "flower," a common euphemism for menstrual blood. The other women present in the ritual are referred to as *shakti*s, a term that may designate the women who are the partners of the other men participating in the ritual.

CASTE INVERSIONS

Tantra combines with the indifference to caste characteristic of many renunciant movements the antipathy to caste characteristic of many bhakti movements.

By the eleventh century the Tantras had been available in Sanskrit for some centuries, and Tantra had filtered into Brahmin circles,[91] particularly in Kashmir (in part through the writings of Abhinavagupta), and into Kashmiri court circles.[92] But this did not by any means limit Tantric audiences to Brahmins; group worship in temples made possible the dissemination of Sanskrit texts to Sanskritless people, and the same would have been true of Tantric circles too. In contrast with the equivocal position of women in Tantra, there is massive evidence that even more than the bhakti movements, Tantra from the very start involved low-caste people. The Tantrics co-opted impurity, using human skulls for their begging bowls, eating nonvegetarian food, and drinking alcohol; they included in their ranks cremation ground ascetics, who were certainly not Brahmins, though not all were from the very lowest castes.[93] Tantra turns Puranic Hindu forms upside down; many of its rituals and myths invert, literally or symbolically, Brahmin concepts of power and pollution.

---

* The terms may be a satire on their use to denote the universal aspect of Hinduism held "in common" by all Hindus in contrast with "one's own" unique dharma.

Some Tantras argue that there are only two castes, male and female; one Purana of a Tantric hue argues that all creatures in the universe are the natural worshipers of Shiva and Parvati, since all males are marked with the sign of the god Shiva (the linga) and join with females, who have what Shiva's consort has, a yoni.[94] In this view, just as our souls (*atmans*) replicate *brahman* within us, so our genitals are semiotic images of the divine, images that we all are born with and always carry on us, as others might acquire and carry a cross or a six-pointed star or, closer to the Tantric home, a Shaiva trident.

Some Tantrics refer to their group as one big happy family, a Kula, and the members of their sect as Kaulas.* The *Mahanirvana Tantra* uses this terminology as it flaunts its inclusion of Pariahs. As usual, Shiva is talking to Parvati:

THE IRRELEVANCE OF CASTE

As the footprints of all living creatures disappear inside the footprint of an elephant, so, all dharmas merge into the Kula dharma. How full of merit are the Kaulas! They are themselves the very forms of places of pilgrimage, who by their mere contact purify aliens, Pariahs, and the vilest people. As all the waters that flow into the Ganges become the Ganges, even so all who join in the Kula practice become Kaulas. As the water that flows into the sea is no longer separated [from the other waters in the sea], even so the people who plunge into the water of the Kula are no longer separated [from the other people in the Kula]. All the two-footed creatures on the surface of the earth, beginning with Brahmins and ending with Pariahs, all become masters in the Kula practice. . . . Any member of the Kula who will not allow into the Kula a Pariah or a foreigner [Yavana, "a Greek"], thinking him low, or a woman, despising her, he, being truly low, goes to the lowest place.[95]

The text assumes that on the one hand, Pariahs and aliens (*mlecchas*) *are* impure, as it boasts that contact with Tantrics will purify them and that most people will *not* treat them (or women) with respect, but also, on the other hand, that they are *not* too low to be allowed into the Tantric circle, and *if* they join the Family, they are to be treated with respect. The primary concern is not to

---

* Kula usually designates "family" in the sense of "good family"; Kulin Brahmins are high-caste Brahmins. To call Tantric groups Kaula is therefore already to mock caste strictures or to use "family" with the sort of irony with which it is used to designate the Mafia. Sometimes Kula refers to one particular branch of Tantrics, sometimes to Tantrics in general.

uplift Pariahs but to extol the power of the Tantras: "If they can save Pariahs, imagine what they will do for a Brahmin!" Thus the text offers evidence of people on both sides of the fight for and against caste.

The Tantras, like some of the Puranas, offer several related arguments to justify, on the one hand, the antinomian nature of certain Tantric texts and rituals and, on the other, the inclusion of people that caste Hindus generally exclude—even certain manifestations of the god Shiva himself. Some Puranas say that Shiva himself is a Pariah, lower than a Shudra,[96] and in vernacular folktales he is often sexually involved with Pariah women.[97] When Shiva appears as the wandering beggar (Bhikshatana-murti), well known from Chola bronzes and stone carvings in temples, he has a bell tied to his leg; as bells were worn by Pariahs in order to warn the upper castes of their approach, the iconography "emphasizes in a way the belief that the god was outside the pale of orthodox Vedism."[98] In this form, as well as in the form of Bhairava, Shiva is often accompanied by a dog, the Pariah of the animal world.

DEAD ANIMALS

The passage with which this chapter begins rejects the "natural" (*sahaja*) path to Release, denying that "the serpents and cattle and birds and fish" are instinctively pious. Yet animals play an essential part in Tantric ritual; the five substances of the cow are the model inverted by the Five Ms (or Five Fs), two of which are animal substances (fish and flesh). Various animals were to be sacrificed to the goddess, including two of the Vedic *pashu*s (goat and sheep) as well as deer, buffalo, pig, porcupine, hare, lizard, tortoise, and rhinoceros. The animal was to be killed with a sharp blow from a knife; then the officiating priest would place a lamp on the head of the animal and offer the head to the goddess.[99]

Despite the linguistic overlay of the Vedic Gayatri hymn* that the priest whispers into the right ear of the animal, the sacrifice is not at all Vedic; it uses non-Vedic as well as Vedic sacrificial animals (omitting cattle and horses but including porcupines), with a non-Vedic laxness (almost any animal will do) and a non-Vedic bluntness (calling a spade a spade when they kill the animal). Moreover, where the Vedic ritual went out of its way to suffocate the animal in

---

* The verse from the *Rig Veda*—3.62.10—that a pious Hindu recites at dawn and that begins "*tat savitur varenyam.*"

order to minimize the spilling of blood, here the blood, so central to Tantra, is the main point of the ritual.

When it comes to vegetarianism, the Tantrics, like other Hindus, compromise: They allow the eating of meat sometimes and with a few restrictions, some of which are the same and some different from those of the Brahmin imaginary:

MEAT NOT TO EAT

Anyone who knowingly eats human flesh or the flesh of a cow will be purified if he fasts for a fortnight; this is the prescribed restoration. A man who has eaten the flesh of an animal that has the form of a man, or the flesh of an animal that eats flesh, may purify himself of this evil by a three-day fast. A man who has eaten food cooked by foreigners, Pariahs, men who are like beasts, or enemies of the Kula—he may become pure by fasting for a fortnight. If he should knowingly eat the leftovers of these people, he should fast for a month; if unknowingly, for a fortnight. If he eats food prepared by lower castes, even once, he should fast for three days to purify himself.

But if food prepared by a man who is like a beast, or by a Pariah or a foreigner, is placed within the Tantric circle or in the hand of a Tantric, one can eat it without incurring any evil. Anyone who eats forbidden food to save his life in time of death or famine, in an emergency, or when it is a matter of life and death does not incur evil. No sins of improper eating count when food is eaten on the back of an elephant, on stones or logs so big that they can only be carried by several men, or where there is no one to notice anything reprehensible. One should not kill animals whose flesh is not to be eaten, or diseased animals, not even for the sake of a divinity; anyone who does this commits an evil act.[100]

This passage has a fairly high-caste orientation. The flesh of cows is as special as that of humans, and the penance for eating either one is the same as the one for eating food prepared by Pariahs, and not nearly as heavy as the penance for eating their leavings. The usual *dharma-shastra* rules for emergencies (anything goes) are here extended rather whimsically to eating on elephants or on very large stones (why?) and rather cynically to moments when no one is looking. But the escape clause of permission to eat animals for religious reasons is here ruled out of court. Indeed, if the meat has a different effect for someone who knowingly eats it, but not for the animal that knows it is being killed for a sacrifice, the mental state of the sacrificer must matter more than that of the animal; eating meat is therefore no longer a moral or medicinal problem but a psychological problem.

The rules for not killing are not as complex as the rules for not eating:

ANIMALS NOT TO KILL

A man who knowingly kills a cow should fast for a month and then eat nothing but crumbs for a month; then for a third month he should eat only food that he has begged for. At the end of the penance, he should shave his head and feed members of the Kula, and both distant and close relatives. If he does it unknowingly, he should do half the penance, and he should not shave or cut his nails or wash his clothes until he has completed his vow. If a cow is killed as a result of lack of care, a Brahmin is purified by fasting for eight days, a Kshatriya for six days, a Vaishya for four, and a Shudra for two.

If anyone willingly kills an elephant, camel, buffalo, or horse, he should fast for three days and then he is free of evil. If he kills a deer, ram, goat, or cat, he should fast for a day; for a peacock, parrot, or goose, he should fast as long as there is daylight. If he kills any other animals that have bones, he should eat no flesh for one night. If he kills living creatures that have no bones, he is purified merely by feeling sorry. Kings who, when they are hunting, kill beasts, fish, or birds do not commit evil, for this is the eternal dharma of kings. But one should always avoid injuring creatures except for the sake of the gods; a man who injures creatures according to the sacred rules is not smeared by evil.[101]

Here, in contrast with the previous passage, there *is* a dispensation for killing for the sake of the gods. And kings are forgiven their hunting, for Tantra is always inclined toward kings. The distinction between knowing and unknowing action, willing and (by implication) unwilling action, is crowned by the unusual acknowledgment of remorse, a factor that is implicit but seldom explicit in earlier texts about vegetarianism; here it is enough merely to be sorry for certain animals that you kill.

SHAIVA TEMPLES, TANTRIC TEMPLES

ELEPHANTA AND ELLORA

Right before, during, and particularly after the reign of Harsha, the great phase of Hindu temple building that has been called the iconic or canonic period began, when structural temples began to supersede excavated ones, and each region developed in a different way.[102] In Maharashtra, the temple to Shiva on the island of Elephanta off the coast of Bombay testifies to the power and prestige of the worship of Shiva at this time and illustrates several of the dominant myths of Shiva, forming a base that the Tantrics often reversed in building their very different rituals and myths. And the Kailasanatha (or Kailasa) temple of Shiva at Ellora demonstrates in stone what Tantra did in ritual: turns conventional Hindu forms on their head.

These two magnificent stone temples capture on the wing the transition between excavated caves and freestanding rock-cut structural temples, for both of them are simultaneously a cave and a temple. Michelangelo once remarked that the form of the figure that he carved out of a stone was already there, hidden within the stone, and all he had to do was to remove those parts of the stone that were *not* a part of the figure. The same explanation could be made for these extraordinary temples: The artisans simply (!) cut into the rock and removed all the earth and stone that were not a part of a massive Hindu temple. They seem at first glance to be purely natural caves, and the convex carvings within them are like the so-called self-created (*svayambhu*) lingas formed of natural rock growths (stalagmites and stalactites) or the temples in Orissa that look, from a distance, like gigantic mushrooms growing there. But then the artistry comes into focus.

Elephanta is almost certainly earlier than Ellora, generally attributed to Krishnaraja I of the Kalachuri dynasty (c. 550–55), who, together with other possible patrons,[103] was a devout member of the Shaiva Pashupata sect that was becoming prominent in this region at this time.[104] The temples were created by carving out rock in such a way as to leave intact the forms of the rows of columns and crossbeams, the internal spaces and the images. Sculptures depict Shiva and Parvati marrying and, later, playing dice; Shiva bringing the Ganges from heaven to earth by letting it flow through his hair, Shiva dancing, Shiva as the great yogic teacher Lakulisha, Shiva impaling an antigod on his trident, Shiva as the androgyne (Ardhanarishvara); and the linga. One scene represents the myth, told in the *Ramayana* (7.16) and elsewhere, in which Ravana, objecting to the lovemaking of Shiva and Parvati on Kailasa, lifted up the mountain, whereupon Shiva simply put his foot down hard on the mountain and imprisoned Ravana under it.

As only 150 miles and two hundred years separate the great Shiva temples at Elephanta and Ellora, it is likely that the artisans of Ellora knew about Elephanta; they certainly adopted techniques from Elephanta, such as the use of basalt. More than thirty temples were carved from the hillside at Ellora between the sixth and ninth centuries CE. The Rashtrakutas built the Kailasanatha temple to Shiva in the eighth century CE, taking over a site where there was already a much smaller cave temple. The Kailasa temple took fifteen years to complete. Many of the craftsmen were imported from the kingdoms of the defeated Chalukyas and Pallavas. As a result, the temple tower resembles the "chariots" at Mamallapuram, and the style of the Kailasanatha temple echoes, though on a far grander scale, aspects of the Pallava shore temple at Mamallapuram built during the same period.

The architects of Ellora excavated the great cave right out of the living basalt of the hillside, leaving, on the floor of the courtyard at the base, freestanding, life-size rock-cut elephants and two massive rock-cut columns, as well as the temple itself, whose tower rises to a height of about ninety feet, or, one might say, whose base is cut down to about ninety feet. The result is an inverted or inside-out temple that one has to climb down into in order to enter, a negative temple like a negative number, turning conventional architectural forms upside down. It solves the problem of decorating the *outside* of a cave. For since worshipers would circumambulate outside the temple (or stupa), people grew to expect temples to have their decorations on the outside. But the early cave temples could be decorated only inside. The solution was to hollow out the hill and *then* build a temple whose outside was inside the hill. The ornate exterior of the mass isolated by the deep trenches, replete with columns and parapets and moldings, becomes an extended trompe l'oeil, or optical illusion, looking as if it had been built *up* like other temples. The artisans also hollowed out the inside (leaving the columns to support it), so that one can also wander inside it just like any other temple. But unlike other temples, this one is a combination of a cave and a mountain.

The temple as a whole was conceived as a replica of the Himalayan peak of Mount Kailasa, the home of the god Shiva.[105] Most of the individual scenes and figures, exquisitely carved, depict Shiva and Parvati, but there is also a magnificent image of Durga killing the buffalo. The artists even went so far as to carve, *under* the temple, at the bottom of the whole colossal edifice, the image of Ravana being trapped by Shiva under Mount Kailasa,[106] a scene also carved at Elephanta. But the Ellora version has a difference, which echoes the bold negative carving of the temple as a whole: The image of Ravana, connected to the mother rock only at his knees and his many arms, is otherwise completely detached from the background and carved in the round.[107] Ravana is thus fi-

The Kailasanatha Temple at Ellora.

nally separated from the rest of the monument and left connected to the dark underworld from which the artists had freed the temple, the "mother rock" that gave birth to everything else but held him back. Later *Ramayanas*, beginning in the Tamil tradition, tell of a shadow Ravana ("Peacock Ravana," Mayili-Ravana) who lived in a shadow universe under the earth,[108] like this Ravana underground at Ellora. We might also see the Kailasa temple as an image of the upside-down world that Trishanku created.

KHAJURAHO AND KONARAK

Two other great temple complexes deserve our consideration here; though both were built somewhat later than the period covered by this chapter, they are best understood in the context of Tantra. The images in the temples of Khajuraho and Konarak are solid evidence of the wide spread of sectarian worship at this time, and some of the Shaiva sects represented there were Tantric.

Khajuraho, the capital of the small kingdom of Bundelkhand that the Chandellas ruled, was a busy cultural center where poets, grammarians, and playwrights rubbed shoulders with affluent Jaina merchants and court officials.[109] Monastic Hindu establishments that arose and grew powerful during this period encouraged the kings to build extravagant temples between 900 and 1150 CE.[110] The great complex of twenty-five temples at Khajuraho and the smaller, exquisite temple in the shape of the chariot of the sun at Konarak, as well as other temples in Bhubaneshwar in Orissa (and in Assam and Katmandu), are noted for the carvings of couples in erotic embraces—often called *maithuna* figures—that decorate their outer walls. Some of the couples are quite demure, gently kissing or fondling each other, but others are in full sexual penetration, "making ingenious love,"[111] some in positions that the *Kama-sutra* warns can only be mastered with practice.

The Temple of the Sun at Konarak, in Orissa, decorated with such figures, was built by the young Narasimhadeva I (1238–58 CE), allegedly to please his mother (a strangely Oedipal gift). It is entirely in the form of a chariot, and the sun is depicted on it in miniature, with his own charioteer driving his seven horses, another instance of the whole replicated within itself. Enormous, three-dimensional animals—kneeling elephants crushing warriors and warhorses overwhelming demons—flank the chariot that is the temple, and a frieze depicting both wild and tame elephants, as well as amorous couples, encloses the lower wall. "Colossal stone wheels, each intricately carved, were positioned along its flanks and a team of massive draught horses, also stone-cut, reared seawards, apparently scuffing and snorting under the strain."[112] Though images carved on the temple show the Man-Lion (Narasimha, one of the avatars of Vishnu) worshiping images of Durga and Jagannatha (another form of Vishnu), it is dedicated to the worship of the sun (Surya), a Vedic god who still had the power to inspire the ruling family to construct this monument.

Less explicit (i.e., noncopulating) erotic figures are carved on many other Hindu temples throughout India. (Even Buddhist stupas are often graced by the buxom tree spirits called Yakshis or Yakshinis and the gorgeous courtesan nymphs called Apsarases.) These more muted erotic scenes are a part of the attempt to represent the whole of the material world on the outer walls of temples, both to celebrate the beauty of the world and, perhaps, to gather up all the sensual forces there so that the worshipers can leave them behind as they progress deeper toward the still center of the temple. Such images promise the worshiper the blessings of fertility as well as eroticism. Three levels of eroticism are depicted with very different degrees of prominence: The sexy women are the largest images; the amorous couples are not nearly so large; and the scenes of group sex, stylized and geometrically arranged, are smaller still. The few obscene friezes are very small indeed and placed at difficult-to-spot places, perhaps a private joke on the part of the sculptors who carved the temples.

The actual *maithuna* couples on Khajuraho and Konarak also partake of these general powers of fertility but may be meant to invoke, in addition, the magical efficacy that the sexual act was supposed to have to protect monuments, which may explain why the erotic images are often placed at the ritually vulnerable parts of temples.[113] Alternatively, the images may have been placed at meeting points of buildings so as to play on "a visual pun between juncture and copulation."[114] The erotic couples on these temples are often said to be Tantric; Khajuraho was an important center for various Tantric sects,[115] and the Chandellas were probably Tantrics.[116] A few friezes at Khajuraho and more in Assam may be specific references to Tantric rituals.[117] For on them, the positioning of the couples (and sometimes groups of three or more) agrees with details of some Tantric texts. Some of the gorgeous women seem to be not Yakshis or Apsarases but Tantric Yoginis, more particularly in some temples the sixty-four Yoginis that the Tantras speak of,[118] some with animal faces.[119] The significant number of Yogini temples constructed between the eighth and twelfth centuries lends weight to the argument that these were the places where Tantric rituals took place.[120] One art historian has commented on the "curious paradox" that some of the temples at Khajuraho "can only be fully appreciated today by being viewed from the air."[121] Were they meant to be viewed by flying Yoginis?

The Chandellas built one temple at Khajuraho at the time of Mahmud of Ghazni's first invasion of India[122] and the Khandariya Mahadeva temple, the greatest of them all, during the subsequent Ghaznavid invasions, though the invading forces never came near Khajuraho. While temples were not necessarily built in response to these invasions (they are equally, if not more, a response to the erosion of Vedic ritual and the rise of new forms of sectarian worship), the building of temples took on new meaning in the presence of Islamic kingdoms and armies. The temple carvings abound in martial themes—warriors, weaponry, elephants, big horses rearing and leaping.[123] To the limited extent that temple building is a political act, these temples eloquently express the Hindu rulers' defiance of the Muslim invaders.[124]

It is perhaps puzzling that though the erotic images on these temples would have been anathema to pious Muslims, they were never the victims of Muslim iconoclasm. They may have been spared because the Ghaznavids did not get to Khajuraho and the Mughals got there only after the Chandellas had deserted the temples, which had then faded from prominence and weren't marked on Aurangzeb's maps.[125] The Orissan temples, as well as the temple of Jagannatha at Puri (built during Muhammad bin Tughluq's reign, in the late tenth to late eleventh centuries),[126] may have escaped because they were too remote to attract Muslim attention. Or could it be that the Muslims, who were, after all, themselves past masters of erotic poetry and painting, cast an appreciative eye upon the carvings and simply rode by?

CHAPTER 16

FUSION AND RIVALRY UNDER THE DELHI SULTANATE

650 to 1500 CE

༺༻

RAMA AND RAHIM

The Hindu says Ram is the beloved, the Turk says Rahim. Then they kill each other.

Kabir, 1398–1448[1]

Even if I am killed, I will not give up repeating the names of Rama and Rahim, which mean to me the same god. With these names on my lips, I will die cheerfully.

Mahatma Gandhi, 1947

The prophetic words of Gandhi, which he spoke just nine months before he was killed, apparently with those names on his lips,* turn the more cynical words of Kabir on their head. It would be good for us to keep the two sides of this paradigm in mind as we consider the history of Hindus among Muslims in India. As Hindus responded to the various cultural transformations wrought by the Muslim presence, new religious ideas also arose to challenge the Brahmin imaginary.

SUNNIS AND SUFIS AND SHAIVAS, OH MY!

In dealing with all but the earliest periods of Indian history, we gave up even the semblance of tracing any single historical center and settled for a selection of peripheries. We still have those peripheries, more than ever, in both the Hindu and the Muslim worlds, though now we also have two moments when there are serious contenders for a center, first the Delhi Sultanate and then the Mughal Empire. But even when there was a center for government, there was never a center for religion. Here, as so often, the main action, and the main evidence, are to be found not so much among the ruins of Delhi and in the chronicles of its sultans as in the records and remains of a dozen other capitals scattered across the subcontinent—Jaunpur, Ahmedabad, Mandu, Chitor, Vijayanagar, Gaur, and many others.[2] Both the Hindu and the Muslim rulers are plural, not only in generally succeeding one another rather quickly but in being very different one from another. The messages from Delhi were therefore very different at different periods, and so were the messages sent back to Delhi.

Just as the term "Hindu" dissolved upon closer examination at the very start of this story, so now does the category of "Muslim." Historians often invoke terms like "Hindu kingdom" in contrast with "Muslim sultanate," but "Hindu" and "Muslim" are seldom the most basic way to distinguish one group from another. For religious differences were often overridden by differences in language, ethnicity, food, clothing, and much more. Most of our sources refer to ethnicities, not to religion; the Hindus generally thought of the Delhi sultans and their people not as Muslims but as Arabs and, later, Turks, often confusing the two groups, calling them all (Arabs as well as Turks) Turks ("Turuskas") and regarding them all, like all non-Hindus, as barbarians (*mlecchas*). The Hindus also had very different attitudes toward the rulers, on the one hand, and

---

* The words are inscribed on a plaque near the place in Delhi where he was shot. There is much dispute as to whether he said "Ram Ram" or "Ram Rahim" when he died.

the resident traders and clerks, on the other; though some Turkish or Arab rulers destroyed Hindu temples, breeding lasting resentment, the ordinary Muslims who worshiped in mosques and Sufi shrines were seldom a problem for Hindus, who had high regard for most Arab and Turkish traders, particularly horse traders.

The terms by which Hindus (more precisely, the people we call Hindus) referred to the people we call Muslims suggest assimilation rather than hostility. The term "Mus-ala-mana" ("one who submits to Allah") is seldom used; this left Hindus the options of designating Muslims by their different ethnic and spatial origins or by using any of several generic terms for non-Hindus. Inscriptions and Sanskrit texts have no single term for the foreigners that the Hindus knew, but use Yavana ("Ionian" or "Greek"), *mleccha* ("barbarian"), and Turuska ("Turk") interchangeably for Greeks, Persians, and Turks. There is irony in the fact that the stereotype of the Turk who destroys temples and idols, appropriates the temple lands of Brahmins, and eats beef became so clichéd, so generalized to the Terrible Other,[3] that the Kashmir chronicle, in 1148 CE, describing a *Hindu* king who plundered temples and had excrement and wine poured over the statues of gods called him a Turk (Turuska).[4]

Some Hindus assimilated the Turks by creating ingenious, and positive, Sanskrit glosses for Arabic words and names: Thus the Ghorids became the Gauri-kula ("family of fair people" or "family of the golden goddess [Parvati]"), sultans became Sura-tranas ("protectors of the gods"), and Muhammad (or Mahmud) became Maha-muda ("great joy"). An inscription, in Sanskrit and Arabic, from 1264 CE about the construction of a mosque in Gujarat, at Somnath (a place of great historical controversy, as we will see), describes the mosque in Hindu terms, as a site of dharma (*dharma-sthana*), where people did *puja* in order to gain merit (*punya karma*).[5] Most significantly, the inscription begins by using the same word* to denote both Shiva and Allah, invoking ("Om! Namah!") Shri Vishvanatha ("Lord of the Universe"), meaning both the Hindu god Shiva as Somanatha and "the divinity to whom those whose prophet (*bodhaka*) was Muhammad were attached (*pratibaddha*)."

On the other side, the Arabs and Turks usually did not think of the Hindus as Hindus;[†] they thought of them as Vaishnavas, or Bengalis, or brilliant artists

---

* The Sanskrit trick of using words with double meanings ("embracing," or *slesha*) was also used in an inscription written for a Muslim ruler under the Delhi Sultanate in 1328 (establishing a garden as a refuge for all animals).
† In part because the Hindus didn't usually call themselves Hindus.

or airheads, as the case might be. Yet they certainly did notice that there were in India people who belonged to religions different from their own, including Buddhists, and they labeled themselves now with a word for Muslim (or, more particularly, Sunni or Sufi), in contrast with the general Hindu sectarian labels (Vaishnava or Shaiva) or, more likely, specific Hindu sects (Virashaiva or Saha-jiya). With this initial caution, let us proceed, still using the indispensable terms "Hindu" and "Muslim" but attempting, wherever possible, to nuance them.

Islam in India Before the Delhi Sultanate

There is abundant and fascinating evidence, an embarrassment of riches, about the relationship between Hindus and Muslims in India from shortly after the time of the Prophet Muhammad, in the seventh century CE. The sources now include many more foreign visitors; in place of the occasional Greeks or Chinese in earlier periods, we now have a full Arabic and Persian historiography, beginning with Al-biruni (973–1048), who came to India, learned Sanskrit, translated Hindu texts, and wrote about the religion (sic: he regarded it as unified) of India. After him came a succession of other great historiographers of India who wrote in Persian and Arabic, such as Ziya'-ud-Din Barani (1285–1357), Abu al-Malik 'Isami (d. 1350), and Ibn Batuta (1304–1368/1377).[6] After the first few more or less contemporary Turko-Persian chroniclers, it was later Arab rather than Turkish historians who generally kept the record of the times (often in retrospect), even for the Turkish rulers.

Islam in India began not with the political conquest of India by Mahmud of Ghazni but much earlier, when the Muslims entered India not as conquerors but as merchants. We have noted the Arab presence in South India from before the time of the Prophet. Before 650, Arabs had made desultory raids by sea on the lower Sind, to protect the trade route carrying Arabian horses to India and Indian spices to Arabia. By 650 Arabs had also reached the Indus River, and though they rarely crossed it,[7] their *ideas* swam across. In the sixty years after Harsha's death in 647, Arabs established a Muslim bridgehead in Sind, a region that the Huns had devastated, Harsha had later infiltrated, and now was largely Buddhist.[8] Then, in around 663, Arab forces crossed the Bolan pass (near Quetta in Pakistan)[9] from Afghanistan into Sind.[10] Peacefully, they traded horses for spices. Only later did the martial invasions come, first by Arabs and then by Turks (from many parts of Central Asia) and Mongols.

In 713, Muhammad ibn Qasim invaded Sind, offering terms of surrender that included a promise to guarantee the safety of Hindu and Buddhist establishments and to allow Brahmin and Buddhist monks to collect alms and temples to receive donations. Hindus and Buddhists were allowed to govern themselves in matters of religion and law; Ibn Qasim's people did not regard non-Muslims as heathens who had to be subdued.[11] He kept his promises, though he did imposed the *jizya*,[12] a tax on male adults who would have been liable to military service if they had been Muslims; non-Muslims were excused from this duty but required instead to pay for their military protection. His forces could not hold Sind, but the soldiers stayed on, intermarried, and brought Muslim teachers and mosques into the subcontinent. At the same time, in the wealthy Gujarati port of Bhadreshwar, the local Jaina rulers, eager to trade with the Arabs, had allowed the resident Ismaili merchants to build mosques in that area.[13]

THE DELHI SULTANATE

Almost three centuries later, the Turks, Persians, and Afghans entered India through the traditional routes of the northwest. On November 27, 1001, the Turkish Mahmud of Ghazni (in Afghanistan) successfully invaded India, near Peshawar. The ruler whom he captured bought his freedom for fifty elephants but acknowledged the loss of caste implicit in capture, abdicated in favor of his son, and climbed on his own funeral pyre.[14] In 1004 Mahmud crossed the Indus, fought again, and established a base in the Punjab, from which he continued to carry out raids; in 1018 he sacked Mathura (a great pilgrimage center on the Yamuna River, for worshipers of Krishna) and then Kanauj (which had been Harsha's capital) and is said to have come away with fifty-three thousand slaves and 350 elephants.[15] Turkish communities were also established in the region of Varanasi and elsewhere.[16] It was a boom area for immigration from Persia and Central Asia, and this greatly added to the cosmopolitanism of the subcontinent, since culture under what became the Ghaznavid Empire in India (that is, the empire ruled by people from Ghazni) was "a blend of Greek philosophy, Roman architecture, Hindu mathematics, and the Persian concept of empire."[17]

For the next four centuries, the northern and central part of the subcontinent saw an almost bewildering array of kings and dynasties, with constant warfare between (and within) them, punctuated by sibling power struggles. From 1192 to 1206 Muhammad of Ghor ruled from his capital at Delhi. One of his successors was a woman named Raziya, who ruled for four years, ending in 1240. She was said to be wise, just, and generous, as well as an effective general, and she brought peace to the country. Disdaining the veil, she went among her people in a cap and coat, like a man. She appointed as her personal attendant an Abyssinian who was probably once a slave and definitely an African.[18] Conspirators captured her, killed her Abyssinian friend, and imprisoned her. She married one of the conspirators and marched with him (and with an army in which there were many Hindus) on Delhi, where she let her ally play the general, badly; she was much more at home than he in the saddle. They were defeated.[19] In 1350, a century after Raziya's death, the historian Isami objected to her blatant interracial liaison,[20] remarking that a woman's place was at her spinning wheel (*charkha*). This may be the earliest reference in India to a spinning wheel, which the Turks apparently imported from Iran. (The sexism they already had in India, thank you.)

Several of Muhammad of Ghor's successors were regarded as slaves,* and their dynasty as a slave dynasty, because they had once been Turkish captives.[21] Ala-ud-din Khalji, an Afghan who ruled from Delhi for twenty years (1296–1316), captured, redeemed, and made a senior commander a Hindu eunuch and slave named Kafur, who converted to Islam.[22] Holy wars (jihads) flared up from time to time, more often politically motivated than religiously inspired, but playing the religion card to rally support, and royal policy toward Hinduism and Islam during these five centuries varied widely. Ala-ud-din sacked and plundered Devagiri but then made peace, married a Maharashtra woman, prohibited the sale and consumption of alcohol, and left the kingdom and its religions otherwise intact.[23] His son is best remembered for parading a line of naked prostitutes on the terraces of the royal palaces and making them pee on the nobles as they entered below.[24]

Then came Muhammad bin Tughluq, whom some regarded as a cruel, bloodthirsty, lunatic tyrant, others as a philosopher king and a genius.[25] He challenged the Muslim *ulama* (the arbiters of Shari'a law, a kind of Muslim conservative supreme court), the intellectual elite, by promoting Indian Muslims of low-caste origin, newcomers to the court,[26] both because he was not a religious bigot and because he saw the advantage of accommodating non-Muslims in India.[27] He took a great interest in Jainas, one of whom was very influential at his court.[28] One thing that can be said of Tughluq is that although many suffered under his rule, at least he was even-handed.[29]

His successor, Feroz Shah Tughluq (1351–1388), desecrated the shrine of

---

* Slaves in ancient India had different rights and restrictions from slaves in Greece, Africa, or America.

Jagannath at Puri, was said to have massacred infidels,[30] and extended the *jizya* to Brahmins (who had been, until then, exempt). On the other hand, Feroz Shah redeemed a number of Hindu slaves as well as an African eunuch slave who founded the Sharqi kingdom of Jaunpur;[31] the eunuch's successors, whom he had to adopt, being unable to beget them, were also of African origin and became a powerful dynasty.[32] The sultanate continued until Babur founded the Mughal Empire in 1526.

In general, the sultanate rulers did not attempt a mass conversion of Hindus,[33] but many Hindus did convert to Islam during this period, usually but not only low-caste laborers and craftspeople and, frequently, captives.[34] On the northwest frontier, some Hindus switched both political allegiance and religion and fought for the Ghaznavids.[35] In the course of conversion, Islamic figures (such as gods and saints) and concepts might be added to Hindu ones, identified with Hindu ones, or, occasionally, taken up in place of Hindu ones, eliminating them from the pantheon.[36]

The Delhi sultans levied the *jizya*, graduated according to income, with exemptions for people at both ends of the social spectrum, the poorest[37] and (until Feroz Shah changed the rule) the purest, the Brahmins.[38] There is also evidence of the existence of a "Turkish" (Turuska) tax, which may have been a poll tax on Muslims in India, a Hindu equivalent of the Muslim *jizya*.[39] Taxes under the Delhi Sultanate seem to have been motivated much more by the need for revenue than by religious sentiments. Some Hindus also responded to the presence of Islam by a series of measures designed to strengthen their own religion, such as enormous land grants to Brahmins, which meant more taxes to generate revenues that could be converted into those grants (exacerbating social oppression and caste discrimination[40]), as well as endowing temples and providing social services on the local level (which mitigated that same oppression and discrimination).

The Brahmins were in a bind: They wanted to keep the barbarians out, but they also had to assimilate and legitimize the foreign rulers in order to keep temporal support for themselves. Their two options for the representation of *mleccha*s were either to legitimize them, as a contingent strategy, or to blame them for the destruction of social order. Within the first option, legitimation, lineages could be appropriated; an inscription from 1369 traces the descent of a sultan from the lineage of the Pandavas in the *Mahabharata*.

As for blame, the Brahmins could always fall back on myths such as the flood, as in a late-fourteenth-century poem from South India that describes the desecrated temples: "Like the Turushkas who know no limits, the Kaveri has forgotten her ancient boundaries and brings frequent destruction with her floods." A Chandella inscription from 1261 speaks of a king who, like Vishnu (in his avatar as the boar), lifted up the earth when it was submerged in an ocean of Turushkas; another calls the Turushkas the great burden of the earth, and likens to Vishnu as the boar the Hindu ruler who conquers them and relieves the earth's burden.[41] But the very same myth is used in reverse in another inscription, from 1491, which depicts Turushkas, Shakas (Scythians), and *mlecchas* as shouldering the great burden of the earth and relieving Vishnu of his worries. It is difficult to argue that chronologically one representation replaces the other.[42] The negative and positive views coexisted, as did the people who held them.

HORSES AND HORSE TRADERS

We have noted the role played by horses in the invasion of India from the time of the Indo-Europeans and Vedic peoples, and then, at regular intervals, by horsemen from Greece, Scythia, and Central Asia. Intimacy with, and mastery of, horses are the common property of Indo-Europeans and the Turkic peoples of Central Asia.[43] We have also noted in passing the constant need for native rulers to import horses into India and the importance of the horse trade in bringing Arabs and Turks (and, with them, Islam) to South India. Horses continued to play a central role in the activities of the Turkic peoples who founded the Delhi Sultanate. Here is also the place, however, to remark upon the importance of elephants,[44] which supplemented horses in essential ways, the tank corps division that supported the cavalry. Elephants were far better suited to the environment, but they were even more expensive than horses (the Mughal emperor Babur complained about how much it cost to feed them: as much as two strings of camels[45]). Together, horses and elephants were simultaneously essential military equipment and luxury status symbols, like Cadillacs and Rolls-Royces.

Central Asia, probably one of the first places where horses were domesticated, produced great horses as well as great horsemen and horse breeders. Mahmud of Ghazni had the advantage of having his forces mounted on Central Asian horses; the most an Indian could hope for in an encounter with them was "perhaps a fleeter horse."[46] Al-biruni remarked that the Turks were famous for their horses, Kandahar (in Afghanistan) for its elephants, and India for its armies.[47] When Muhammad bin Tughluq recruited men from western and

Central Asia, he made them submit to a test of equestrian skill before he signed them on.[48] The Turkish conquerors introduced polo into India in the thirteenth century;[49] Muhammad of Ghor's successor was killed in 1210 when his polo pony fell on him in the course of a game.[50]

Once they got to India, the Turks had to import most of their horses rather than breed them in India. A steady stream of Central Asian imports was "seemingly vital to the virility of Muslim rule."[51] The Deccan sultans and their opposite numbers, the martial Hindu Kshatriyas of Maharashtra and the kings of Vijayanagar, imported Arabian horses on a large scale, "in order to improve the breed of cavalry horses in their own districts."[52] The best horses were imported from Central Asia ("Turki" horses), Iran or Arabia ("Tazi" horses).[53] Marco Polo (1254–1324), who visited India in around 1292, remarked that the Pandyan ruler of Madurai imported two thousand horses a year, "and so do his four brothers."[54] South Indians, particularly in the vicinity of Madurai, still tell stories about the Pandyan kings' energetic importation of horses.[55] There is ample testimony from both foreign* and Indian sources that South Indians imported as many as fourteen thousand horses a year.[56] One of the sixteenth-century South Indian kings of Vijayanagar is reputed to have imported thirteen thousand horses annually for his own personal use and for his officers,[57] and ten thousand Arab and Persian horses were imported into Malabar every year.[58]

Vijayanagar was a conspicuous consumer of foreign imports, including "the desiderata of every Indian army, namely horses, mostly from the Persian Gulf, and some fire-arms." Many horses died onboard ship, for they cannot throw up, and so their seasickness is almost always fatal; they develop severe colic and often die of a twisted gut. Since shipping such fragile and valuable cargo in a pitching ship was a costly and risky venture,[59] to encourage people to undertake the risk of shipping horses who might well die at sea, "it was said that the Vijayanagar rulers would pay even for dead ones."[60] When Vijayanagar was at war with Portugal, the Portuguese monopoly of the horse trade simultaneously deprived Vijayanagar of important revenues and interfered with the supply of remounts.[61]

The need to import horses was exacerbated, according to many foreign observers, from at least the time of the Delhi Sultanate, by the Indian habit of feeding their horses inappropriate foods.[62] Marco Polo insisted that horses in India died from the climate and from unsuitable feeding; even if they bred, they

---

* Portuguese traders like Payez, Nuñez, and Diaz wrote extensively about the horse trade.

produced "nothing but wretched wry-legged weeds."[63] A few centuries later Akbar's historian Abu'l Fazl testified that in addition to grass when available, and hay when there was no grass, horses were fed boiled peas or beans, flour, sugar, salt, molasses, and, to cap it all, ghee.[64] Other sources agree that lacking the right sort of fodder grasses and hay, people in India fed horses mainly wheat, barley, and gram and mixed these grains with all sorts of stuff: cow's milk, coarse brown sugar, sometimes even boiled mutton mixed with ghee,[65] to the horror of Middle Eastern and European visitors.[66]

No oats were grown in India until the nineteenth century. By that time Rudyard Kipling's father, who was a veterinarian, concluded that the Indian diet was detrimental to the horse's liver and caused many diseases and high mortality rates.[67] Much of this criticism, from the Delhi sultans to the Kiplings, smacks of foreign prejudice and imperial self-justification. Surely the foreign horsemen could use their own good horse sense when it came to feeding, as well as bring along some of their own grooms. The ghee mash legend may be one of those canards that just got repeated over and over. On the other hand, people do tend to feed their most precious horses (and dogs) the things that they themselves like best (like chocolates), which often prove disastrous.

The importing of bloodstock was therefore "India's main extravagance."[68] During the sultanate period, Persian and Arabian horses were called *bahri* ("seaborne"), because they were imported, perilously, by sea.[69] Many were brought in overland, but they too underwent hardships and losses. Horses were far too expensive[70] to use as farm animals or beasts of burden, and in any case, the heat and humidity made them fairly useless for that sort of work,[71] which was usually done by water buffalo or oxen. Horses were mostly used for war, as cavalry, supplemented by elephants.[72] Thus the horse remained a Kshatriya animal, with all the negative connotations of that class—power, domination, extortion (by tax collectors who rode into the villages on horseback), death—to which was now added a major new factor: Many of these Kshatriyas were not Hindus but Muslims. Horses therefore both affected the practical relationships between Hindus and Muslims and functioned, in art and literature, as a symbolic gauge of shifting attitudes within those relationships.

Desecration of Temples

As we turn now to less positive aspects of interactions between the Delhi sultans and the Hindus, this is a moment for a hindsight alert: Nowadays the story of Hinduism as told by Hindu nationalists always includes a chapter on the Horrid Things Those Bad Muslims Did. Hindu nationalism has given prominence and importance to stories of victims and victimizers that otherwise would have been just drops in the ocean of vicious battles that have plagued the subcontinent, indeed the planet, for millennia. Yet it is true that some Muslims *did* Do Horrid Things, including that great breeding ground of resentment, the desecration of temples.

The Muslim rulers of India in this period were not all alike in their treatment of Hindu temples. Some Muslim rulers, like some Hindu rulers before them, destroyed Hindu temples.[73] Desecration was not necessarily prompted by bigotry,[74] though some rulers might well have been motivated (or have claimed to be motivated) by religious fanaticism, a hatred of idolatry or polytheism or any religion but Islam. Some, lured by the legendary wealth of the temples,[75] did it to get the plunder, and others went for the temples because as we saw in South India, the temples were the centers of political and economic power. Piety and greed, so often paired, operated here too: Images of gods were made of solid gold,[76] and the temples were also filled with treasures that Hindu rulers had already stolen from *other* Hindu temples and from Buddhist stupas.[77] Moreover, temples were not only places of worship and banks but also political symbols and, at times, military strongholds. They could also be hostages: In parts of Sind in the tenth century, Arab families that ruled what was still a largely non-Muslim population would threaten to vandalize the city's most revered temple whenever "trouble stirred or invasion threatened."[78] Think "marauding nomads" rather than "fanatical Muslims."

Mahmud of Ghazni, an observant Sunni, took a great deal of gold, silver, and precious stones from the images of the Mathura temple in 1004 and then burned it to the ground.[79] In 1026 he attacked the temple of Somanatha (Somnath), which held a famous Shiva linga; this much, at least, seems to be historical fact. Then comes the mythmaking. According to some versions of the story but not others, he stripped the great gilded linga of its gold and hacked it to bits with his sword, sending the bits back to Ghazni, where they were incorporated into the steps of the new Jami Masjid ("Friday Mosque").[80] Triumphalist early Turko-Persian sources paid a great deal of attention to this event; medieval Hindu epics of resistance created a countermythology in which the stolen image came to life and eventually, like a horse returning to the stable, returned to the temple to be reconsecrated;[81] and British historiographers made much of it for their own purposes (such as the claim that they had rescued the Hindus from oppression by Muslims). Other sources, including local Sanskrit inscriptions, biographies of kings and merchants of the period, court epics, and popular narratives that have survived, give their own versions of the event.[82] Here is a good example of history making mythmaking history.

When Muhammad of Ghor routed the Rajputs in 1192, his armies massacred the people and plundered and destroyed many monuments.[83] In Varanasi, according to the rather boasting accounts of some of the Arab chroniclers, his forces demolished the idols in a thousand temples, carted away fourteen hundred camel loads of treasure, and rededicated the temples "to the worship of the true God."[84] They left intact the exquisite Jaina temples carved out of near-translucent white marble between 950 and 1304 CE in Gujarat, most famously at Mount Abu, the exterior of which is rather plain, not unlike a mosque. The plain façade may have been an intentional reversal of the pattern of Hindu temples, which kept the interior plain and saved all the ornamentation for the outer wall, and may have been intended precisely as "a protection against Turko-Afghan attacks."[85]

Ala-ud-din, who had left Devagiri more or less intact in 1296, two years later attacked Somnath (which the Hindus had rebuilt after Mahmud of Ghazni's depredations more than 250 years earlier) and, allegedly, redemolished it, again hammering the (replacement) linga into fragments to pave the ground for Muslim feet, this time in Delhi.[86] (Romila Thapar's study of Somnath[87] documents the Hindu claim that the Muslims destroyed the same shrine again and again.[88]) In Citamparam, Ala-ud-din's forces attacked the Nataraja temple and destroyed the lingas that "the kick of the horse of Islam," as one Indo-Persian poet put it, had not previously attempted to break.[89] Ala-ud-din's successor, the redeemed slave Kafur, conquered Andhra, rich in diamonds, which was ruled by a queen acting as regent for her grandson; he stripped the temple cities of Madurai, Shrirangam, and Citamparam of their solid-gold idols, and carried off 612 elephants and 20,000 horses.[90] The attack on Shrirangam inspired a rich mythology, according to which, when the image of Vishnu as Ranganatha was captured by the sultan's army and taken north, it came to life by night and seduced the sultan's daughter (who, in one account, died of a broken heart and in another was absorbed into the image), and was eventually returned to the Shrirangam temple, often with the help of the theologian Ramanuja. To this day the Ranganatha image receives daily *puja* in the style of the sultan's court, complete with food cooked in the North Indian style.[91]

Some of the theft, rather than destruction, of Hindu images by Muslim conquerors was a kind of recycling, Indian style. Like cannibalism, consuming the parts of someone else's religious monument may either dishonor the source (destroying and desecrating it) or honor it (taking to yourself the power and status of the source). But putting the stones on the ground to be trodden on by people of another religion was unequivocally adding insult to injury. It was the order of the day to destroy other people's religious monuments and steal their treasures; the Muslims had no monopoly on that. The whole basis of Hindu kingship, beginning with the cattle raids of the *Rig Veda*, was the desire for land and plunder. In the sultanate period, an invading army was *expected* to loot the local temple, and when people told stories about invasions, they always mentioned such looting, whether the teller was a court historian or an old fellow in the local toddy shop, and whether the looting had happened or not. Certainly there was exaggeration. With each telling, the temple got richer and richer, and the army had more and more elephants.[92] Not surprisingly, these acts provoked some resistance, and the tall stories provoked both taller deeds and taller stories, such as the claim, made by contemporary Muslim sources, that a Hindu named Bartuh killed 120,000 Muslims in Awadh in Uttar Pradesh in around 1220.[93]

"Here be dragons," the maps of medieval Europe used to say, and a map of medieval India should certainly say, "Here be monsters." The landscape was peopled by inhuman human rulers on both sides. The difference is not merely that some Muslims may have had the additional incentive of iconoclasm but that for the most part during this period the Turks had more power to destroy Hindus than Hindus to destroy Turks. But the will, including, in many quarters, goodwill, was there on both sides.

On the Other Hand . . .

In addition to the monsters on both sides, there were on both sides if not angels at least people who resisted the infinite regress of bloodbaths and retributions, who respected other people's religions or, at the very least, were indifferent to them. Dear reader, you will not be surprised to learn that some of the Delhi sultans were horrible, and others were decent blokes. Some of the Muslim rulers of India have been called "India-oriented, mystical and inclusive," while others were "Mecca-oriented, prophetic and exclusive."[94] The conquests, like most conquests, were pretty brutal: temples sacked, people murdered. But when the battles ended, the conquerors, dramatically outnumbered, had to administer a gigantic territory, and compromises were made. The situation itself was unbalanced; one group had power over the others. But individual rulers shifted the balance for better or for worse. And the same Hindu political theory that caused so much of the trouble ("the country on my border is my enemy; the enemy of my enemy is my friend") also mitigated some of it; the Rashtrakutas, for instance, encouraged Hindu-Muslim relations and protected Muslim merchants, not through any particularly liberal principles of tolerance but because their enemies, the Gurjara Pratiharas, were the enemies of the Arabs of Sind, making said Arabs the Rashtrakutas' natural allies.[95]

In the culture at large, Hindus adopted a number of Muslim social customs. When the royal women of the Turks and the Rajputs first met, the Muslim women did not keep particularly rigidly to purdah; they joined in the drinking parties and literary salons (as we know, for instance, from Babur's memoirs). It was after they had lived in India for a while and encountered the Rajput codes of modesty and honor that the women were more strictly concealed by the curtain of purdah and the zenana (harem) and at the same time also adopted some aspects of the Hindu caste system. Hindu women, in turn, adopted a modified version of the Muslim purdah. What a pity that each side took the worst of both worlds; why not ditch both purdah and caste? How very different world history would have been if they had. Even within these restrictions, however, some women asserted themselves; the ten thousand women allegedly sequestered in the harem of one sultan set up what has been called a feminist republic, with their own administration, militia, manufacturing system, and market.[96]

This was a time when agricultural frontiers expanded, extensive commercial networks developed, gradual technological change took place, and new political and religious institutions (including Hindu ones) developed.[97] Even under Muhammad bin Tughluq, most trade, industry, and financial services remained in Hindu hands, and some Hindu converts to Islam achieved particularly high office. Throughout the Delhi Sultanate, Hindus controlled the royal mints and generally ran the economy. Hindu bankers got rich by helping Muslims, newly arrived from Central Asia, to buy slaves, brocades, jewels, and even horses (previously imported from Central Asia) that they would then present to the sultan. Particularly among working people, among artisans, cultivators, and the commercial and secretarial classes, Indian Muslims and lower-caste Hindus lived and worked together and changed each other.[98] Women circulated like money (as is generally the case); many Muslims took Hindu wives. And when you add in the gardens and melons and fountains that the Mughals gave to

India, not to mention the art and architecture, the picture of cultural exchange brightens considerably.

In dramatic contrast with Buddhism, which was driven out of India by a combination of lack of support, persecution, and the destruction of religious monuments and monasteries (by Hindus as well as Muslims), Hinduism rallied and came back stronger than ever. Though most sultanate rulers condemned idolatry, they did not prevent Hindus from practicing Hinduism. A Hindu inscription of c. 1280 praises the security and bounty enjoyed under the rule of Sultan Balban.[99] In 1326 Muhammad bin Tughluq appointed Muslim officials to repair a Shiva temple so that normal worship could resume, and he stated that anyone who paid the *jizya* could build temples in Muslim territories. Another Delhi sultan, ruling in Kashmir from 1355 to 1373, rebuked his *Brahmin* minister for having suggested that they melt down Hindu and Buddhist images in his kingdom to get the cash.[100]

Indeed, in general, despite the evidence of persecution of varying degrees in different times and places, Hinduism under Islam was alive and well and living in India. The same sultans who, with what Hindus would regard as the left hand, collected the *jizya* and destroyed Hindu temples also, with the right hand, often married Rajput princesses, patronized Hindu artists and Sanskrit scholars, and employed Hindus in the highest offices of state. In Bengal in 1418 a Hindu actually became sultan, Raja Ganesh. His son, converting to Islam, ruled under his father's direction until 1431. He was succeeded by an Arab Muslim, Ala-ud-din Husain (r. 1493–1519), who revered the Vaishnava saint Chaitanya, in return for which the Hindus regarded the sultan as an incarnation of Lord Krishna. On the other hand, during a war, the same Ala-ud-din Husain destroyed a number of temples, particularly in Orissa.[101]

Yogis and other ascetics on the fringes of society appear to have been open to friendly exchanges with Muslims from an early date. The Persian merchant and traveler Buzurg ibn Shahriyar, writing around 953, commented that the Skull Bearer (Kapalika) ascetics of Ceylon "take kindly to Musulmans and show them much sympathy."[102] The Tibetan Buddhist historian Taranath, writing in the thirteenth century, was critical of the Nath yogis for following Shiva rather than the Buddha and for saying "They were not even opposed to the Turuskas [Turks]."[103] A new generation of Indo-Aryan languages, the linguistic and literary ancestors of all the modern North Indian languages, was evolving. The new languages drew their genres, conventions, and themes from both

Muslim literary languages (Persian, Arabic) and Hindu languages—classical (Sanskrit) and vernacular (dialects and Prakrits). Persian and Arabic words and concepts entered the vocabularies of Indian languages at all levels.

SUFISM

Sufism, the mystical branch of Islam, heavily influenced and was influenced by Hinduism. By the middle of the eleventh century Sufis had reached the part of Northwest India that was under Ghaznavid control.[104] Khwaja Muin-ud-din (or Moin-al-din) Chishti is said to have brought to India the Chishti Sufi order; he came to Delhi late in the twelfth century and settled in Pushkar in Ajmer, a place of Hindu pilgrimage.[105] He had many disciples, both Muslim and Hindu. The Chishti Sufi masters were powerful figures in the cultural and devotional life of the Delhi Sultanate (where their followers were often influential members of the court), despite the fact that they regarded "going to the sultan" as the equivalent of "going to the devil."[106]

For many Hindus (though, of course, not for the Sufis themselves), Sufism was Islam lite, or a walking incarnation of interreligious dialogue. Early Indian Sufism proclaimed that Muslims, Christians, Jews, Zoroastrians, and Hindus all were striving toward the same goal and that the outward observances that kept them apart were false. This idea was then incorporated into Hinduism as a major strand of the bhakti movement, which was growing in both power and complexity in this period. In court literature, the Sanskrit theory of the aesthetic emotions (*rasa*), particularly the erotic emotion, fused with the Islamic metaphysics of the love of God to produce a Sufi narrative simultaneously religious and erotic; the Sufi romances made their hero a yogi and their heroine a beautiful Indian woman.[107]

Our main subject here is the Muslim contribution to Hinduism, but we must at least acknowledge, in passing, the flow in the other direction during this period, Hindu influence on Muslim culture. Azad Bilgrami (d. 1785) attempted to prove that India was the true homeland of the Prophet,[108] which is perhaps going too far, but India was indeed the homeland of many important Muslim cultural traditions. One text, *The Pool of Nectar*, which circulated in multiple versions and translations, made available to Muslim readers certain practices associated with the Nath yogis and the teachings known as Hatha Yoga.[109] A school of Kashmiri Sufis, whose members call themselves *rishis* (the name that Hindus use for their pious sages), are strict vegetarians and recite the verses of Lal Ded, a fourteenth-century poet and Hindu holy woman from Kashmir.

Sufis appropriated the Sanskritic poetic language of emotion and devotion from the sects devoted to the worship of Krishna and incorporated much of the philosophy of yoga.

Arabs and Iranians learned much about storytelling in India, and passed on this knowledge to Europeans; many of the same stories are told both in the Hindu *Ocean of the Rivers of Story,* in which the gods are Shiva and Vishnu, and in *The Arabian Nights,* in which there is no god but Allah; some of the stories that these two texts share (such as the plot of Shakespeare's *All's Well That Ends Well*[110]) got to England long before the English got to India. Al-biruni made excellent use of Sanskrit and Indian scholarship[111] and produced a fine study of Hindu culture.[112] The Delhi sultans employed Hindu temple building techniques and Hindu artisans to build their mosques,[113] which was less expensive than outsourcing to Afghanistan. As a result, some mosques are decorated with carved Hindu temple moldings that reveal, in subtle ways, "the unmistakable hand" of Indian artisans.[114] This use of Hindu temple techniques not only gave employment to Hindu artisans but was also much easier on Hindus than the use of the actual stones from Hindu temples to build the mosques.

KABIR

Sufi mysticism heavily influenced the North Indian tradition of bhakti Sants ("saints"), who emphasized the abstract aspect of god "without qualities" (*nirguna*).[115] Many of the Sants who straddled Hinduism and Islam were both low caste and rural, such as Ravidas, who was a Pariah leatherworker (Chamar); Dadu, a cotton carder; Sena, a barber.[116] But not all bhaktas were of low caste; Guru Nanak (who founded Sikhism) was a Kshatriya, and Mirabai a Kshatriya princess. Sants from the thirteenth to seventeenth century in Maharashtra were drawn from all castes.[117]

The most famous of the Sants was Kabir, who was born in Varanasi around the beginning of the fifteenth century into a class of low-caste weavers who had recently converted from Hinduism to Islam.[118] One early hagiography mentions that Kabir had previously worshiped the Shakta goddess, suggesting that Kabir's Muslim family may have converted to Islam from a yogic sect related to the Shaktas, such as the Naths. His mixed birth gave rise to many different stories, some of which attempt to show that Kabir was not really a low-caste Muslim by birth but was adopted by Muslims. Sometimes it is said that Kabir was a Brahmin in a former life or that he was of divine origin but adopted by Muslim weavers of the Julaha caste, who had been Brahmins but had fallen from dharma and become Muslims. Or that he was adopted by Brahmins, worshipers of Shiva, whom some foreigners (perhaps Muslims) forced to drink water from their hands, making them lose caste and become weavers.[119] One version says that a Brahmin widow conceived him immaculately, gave birth to him through the palm of her hand, and set him afloat in a basket on a pond, where a Muslim couple found him and adopted him[120] (an episode that follows the Family Romance pattern of the birth of Karna in the *Mahabharata*), or it is said that the Brahmin widow became pregnant when a famous ascetic blessed her, but she exposed the baby in order to escape dishonor.[121] All these stories attempt to drag Kabir back over the line from Muslim to Hindu.

Kabir is widely believed (on scant evidence) to have become one of the disciples of the Hindu saint Ramananda (c. 1370–1440), who was said to have been a disciple of the philosopher Ramanuja and who preached in Hindustani and had many low-caste disciples. There's a story about Kabir's tricking Ramananda into accepting a Muslim disciple: Kabir lay down across the stairs where Ramananda bathed every morning before dawn; Ramananda tripped over him and cried out, "Ram! Ram!" thus (Kabir argued) transmitting to him Ramananda's own mantra, in effect taking him on as a pupil.[122] This Ram is not Sita's Ram, however, but a god "without qualities" (*nir-guna*), whose name, evoking no story, is complete in itself, a mantra.

Scholars believe that Kabir probably married, and indeed had a son named Kamal, but the Sadhus of the Kabir Panth insist that Kabir was celibate, just as they are.[123] There are, in any case, stories about Kabir and his wife, such as this one.

KABIR, HIS WIFE, AND THE SHOPKEEPER

Kabir had no food to give to the dervishes who came to his house; his wife promised the local shopkeeper that she would sleep with him that night if he gave them the food on credit. When she hesitated to keep her promise, Kabir carried her to the shopkeeper that night, as it was raining and muddy; when the shopkeeper learned of this, he was ashamed, fell at Kabir's feet, gave everything in his shop to the poor, and became a sadhu.[124]

This is also a story about the exploitation of women and the lower castes by men of the higher castes. Despite his casual attitude to his wife's fidelity in this story, Kabir often used a wife's impulse to commit suttee, in order to stay with her husband forever, as a positive metaphor for the worshiper who surrenders his ego to god.[125] And he described Illusion (*maya*) as a seductive woman to whom one becomes addicted and from whom one must break away.[126] Women evidently meant several different things to him.

Kabir preached in the vernacular, insisting, "Sanskrit is like water in a well; the language of the people is a flowing stream." With the social identity of a Muslim and both the earlier family background and the belief system of a Hindu,[127] being a weaver, he wove the woof of Islam onto the warp of Hinduism (or, if you prefer, the reverse) to produce a religion of his own that emphatically distanced itself from both. He once described the two religions, disparagingly, in terms of the animals that Hindus offered to the goddess Kali and that Muslims killed at the end of a pilgrimage: "One slaughters goats, one slaughters cows; they squander their birth in isms."[128] Not surprisingly, both groups attacked him during his life; more surprisingly, both claimed him after his death. For this is the sort of thing that he said:

Who's whose husband? Who's whose wife?
Death's gaze spreads—untellable story.
Who's whose father? Who's whose son?
Who suffers? Who dies? . . . If God wanted circumcision,
why didn't you come out cut?
If circumcision makes you a Muslim,
what do you call your women?
Since women are called man's other half,
you might as well be Hindus. . . .
If putting on the thread makes you a Brahmin,
what does the wife put on?
That Shudra's touching your food, pandit!
How can you eat it?
Hindu, Muslim—where did they come from?
Who started this road?
Look in your heart, send out scouts:
where is heaven?[129]

Religious affiliation was just window dressing, as far as Kabir was concerned:

Veda, Koran, holiness, hell, woman, man. . . .
It's all one skin and bone, one piss and shit,
one blood, one meat. . . .

Kabir says, plunge into Ram!
There: No Hindu. No Turk.[130]

Kabir challenged the authenticity of the amorphous word "Hindu" in part because it was beginning to assume a more solid shape at this time, precisely in contrast with "Turk" (standing for Turks, Arabs, and other non-Hindus).

Kabir regarded caste as irrelevant to liberation,[131] and many stories are told about his challenges to the caste system. For instance:

KABIR AND THE PROSTITUTE

When Kabir became famous, he was mobbed by so many visitors that he had to get rid of them. So he went to the house of a prostitute, put his arm around her neck, grabbed a vessel of holy water as if it were liquor, and drank; then he went to the bazaar with her, and the townspeople laughed at him, and his devotees were very sad. The Brahmins and traders reviled him, saying, "How can low-caste people engage in bhakti? Kabir tried it for just ten days and now has taken up with a prostitute." The king showed him no respect, and everyone was astonished.[132]

The willful seeking of dishonor bears a striking resemblance to the methods used by the Pashupatas, though for an entirely different purpose.

Another story about caste is also a story about talking animals:

KABIR AND THE BUFFALO

One day Kabir and some of his disciples came among Ramanuja's spiritual descendants, all Brahmins who would not eat if even the shadow of a Pariah fell on their cooking places. They did not want Kabir to sit and eat with them. Rather than say this outright, and knowing that low-caste people were forbidden to recite the Veda, they said that only someone who could recite Vedic verses could sit with them. Kabir had a buffalo with him. He put his hand on the buffalo's head and said, "Listen, buffalo! Hurry up and recite some of the Veda!" The buffalo began to recite. Everyone was astonished and begged Kabir to forgive them.[133]

But the strongest testimony to Kabir's attitude to caste comes from his own poetry:

Tell me where untouchability
came from, since you believe in it. . . .
We eat by touching, we wash
by touching, from a touch
the world was born.
So who's untouched? asks Kabir.
Only she
who's free from delusion.[134]

Yet Kabir was not a revolutionary in any political or even social sense. Icono-
clastic, yes; anti-institutional, to be sure; poor and low in status, you bet, but not
concerned about putting an end to poverty. His goal was spiritual rather than
economic or political liberation.[135]

HINDUISM UNDER THE DELHI SULTANATE

Hinduism in this period turned in new directions not only in response to
Islam, though that too, but in response to new developments within the Hindu
world itself, some of which were and some which were not directly influenced
by the Muslim presence. Because of the importance of Vijayanagar and the
abundance of available light there, let us let it stand for all the other Hindu
kingdoms that thrived at this time.

VIJAYANAGAR

Vijayanagar ("City of Victory"), the capital of the last extensive Hindu
empire in India, between the fourteenth and seventeenth centuries, had an
estimated population of five hundred thousand and was the center of a kingdom that controlled most of southern India, from the uplands of the Deccan
plateau to the southernmost tip of the Indian subcontinent, and, at various
times, the Doab, the Deccan, Orissa, and points east and west.

Located just south of the Tungabhadra River in Karnataka, in South India,
Vijayanagar, five kilometers square, was founded in 1336[136] by Harihara I
(r. 1336–1357), a warrior chief from the Sangama dynasty, and Harihara's
brother Bukka (r. 1344–1377). The story goes that that the brothers had been
captured by the army of the Delhi sultan and hauled up to Delhi, where they
converted to Islam and accepted the sultan as their overlord. The Delhi sultan
then sent them back home to pacify the region. Upon their return south, they

promptly shed their allegiance to the sultans, blocked Muslim southward expansion, and were reinstated as Hindus, indeed recognized as reincarnations of Shiva.[137]

Vijayanagar is a sacred site, which many Hindus regarded as the location of the kingdom of the monkey Hanuman, studded with spots identified with specific places mentioned in the *Ramayana*, an identification that didn't politicize the *Ramayana* so much as it *polis*-ized it, turned it into a city-state. Inscriptions, historical narratives, and architectural remains suggest that the concept of Rama as the ideal king, and Ayodhya as the site of the *Ramayana* legend, came alive in central and North India in the twelfth to fourteenth centuries, but only during the Vijayanagar Empire did the cult of Rama become significant at the level of an imperial order.[138] The *Ramayana* had long been an important source for the conceptualization of divine kingship, but now for the first time historical kings identified themselves with Rama and boasted that they had destroyed their enemies as Rama destroyed Ravana; in this way, they would demonize— more precisely, Ravana-ize—their enemies. Scenes from the *Ramayana* appear in temple wall friezes from at least the fifth century CE, but the figure of Rama was not the object of veneration, the actual installed icon, until the sudden emergence of a number of temples at this time.[139] Now Rama and Hanuman became the focus of important sects in northern India, especially around Janakpur, regarded as Sita's birthplace, and Ayodhya in Uttar Pradesh, regarded as Rama's birthplace.

But this was only in part a reaction to the Muslim invasions and the rapid expansion of the Delhi Sultanate. True, Devaraya I (1406–1422) built the first Rama temple at Vijayanagar in the midst of the power struggle with the Delhi sultans. But the story of Rama's defeat of Ravana was celebrated in rituals before the rise of Islam in India, and there are no anti-Muslim statements in any inscriptions relating to the Vijayanagar temples. The fact that Shri Vaishnavas built many of the Rama temples in Vijayanagar,[140] with endowments by a variety of groups, including royal agents, subordinate rulers, private citizens, and merchant guilds, suggests that the cult of Rama had a life of its own, with theological motivations, in addition to its significance for the ideology of kingship.[141]

The Vijayanagar temples may well have been built in part as a response to theological challenges posed by the Jainas, for there was still considerable conflict at this time between Jainas (who were now on the decline) and both Shaivas and Vaishnavas (from the fast-growing sects of Basava and Ramanuja). When the Jainas complained to Bukka I, in 1368 CE at Vijayanagar, about the injustice done to them by the Shri Vaishnavas, the king proclaimed that there was no difference between the Jaina and Vaishnava philosophies and that the Shri Vaishnavas should protect the Jaina tradition.[142] The king would not have to have made an edict urging the Hindus to treat the Jainas well if they hadn't already been treating them badly.

Finally, there was no unified Hindu consciousness in which Rama was personified as a hero against the Muslims. Indeed, one Hindu Sanskrit inscription from the early seventeenth century regards the Lord of Delhi ("Dillishvara") as the ruler of a kingdom just like Ram-raj, the mythical kingdom of Rama.[143] Vijayanagar yields much evidence of Hindu-Muslim synthesis rather than antagonism. The Vijayanagar empire and the sultanates were in close contact and shared many cultural forms; court dancers and musicians often moved easily between the two kingdoms.[144] The kings of Vijayanagar, careless in matters of dharma, used a largely Muslim cavalry, royal fortresses under Brahmin commanders, Portuguese and Muslim mercenary gunners, and foot soldiers recruited from tribal peoples. In 1565, at the battle of Talikota, a confederation of Muslim sultans routed the forces of Vijayanagar and the Nayakas. The usual sacking and slaughter, treasure hunting and pillage of building materials ensued, but without bigotry; the temples were the least damaged of the buildings and were often left intact.[145]

The Nayakas rose to power after Vijayanagar fell in 1565,[146] and they ruled, from Mysore, through the sixteenth and seventeenth centuries. The story of the founding of the Nayaka kingdoms follows lines similar to those of the story of the founding of Vijayanagar: Sent out to pacify the Cholas, the Nayakas double-crossed the Vijayanagar king just as the founding Vijayanagarans had double-crossed the Delhi sultans.[147] What goes around comes around. The Nayakas brought dramatic changes, a renaissance in fifteenth- and sixteenth-century Tamil country and Andhra, ranging from political experimentation and economic and social change to major shifts in concepts of gender.[148]

MOSQUE AND TEMPLE

The Vijayanagar kings used their plunder and tribute for elaborate royal rituals, academic patronage, and trophy temples. The plunder of Hindu temples made possible the building not merely of superb mosques but, indirectly, of superb Hindu temples. Just as Hindu temples had vied, in competitive fund-raising, with Buddhist stupas in South India, so under the sultanate, Muslim and Hindu kings competed in architectural monumentalism, the Muslims inclining toward forts and cities (as well as mosques), the Hindus toward temples, temple complexes, and temple cities (as well as palaces). However different the styles may have been, the two sets of rulers shared the grandiosity; they egged each other on: Godzilla meets King Kong.

There was a break in the building of Hindu temples during each new Muslim invasion, with few new commissions and the loss of some temples that the Muslims destroyed, but then there followed an even greater expansion of art in all fields.[149] Throughout India, Hindu dynasties responded to the entrance of Islam not only by building forts and massing horsemen but by asserting their power through extravagant architecture, most spectacularly at Hampi, Halebid, and Badami. Indeed, the leveling of the sacred monuments at Mathura and Kanauj coincided precisely with the construction of other great dynastic temple complexes.[150] It's a rather backhanded compliment to the Muslims to say that because they tore down so many temples, they paved the way for the Hindus to invent their greatest architecture, but it is also true. For not only is there a balance between the good and bad karma of individual rulers, but the bad things sometimes made possible the good things; the pillage made possible the patronage. In a similarly perverse way, the withdrawal of royal patronage from the temples and Brahmin colleges may have encouraged the spread of new, more popular forms of Hinduism such as bhakti. The dynamic and regenerative quality of Hinduism was never more evident than in these first centuries of the Muslim presence.

Islamic architecture was introduced into India, and welcomed enthusiastically by Hindu builders, long before the establishment of Muslim rule in the thirteenth century. Trade partnerships between the Gujaratis and the Arabs made it possible for Gujarati painters, working under Hindu and Jaina rulers, to absorb Persian and Turkic techniques.[151] Islam gave India not merely the mosque but the mausoleum, the pointed arch, and the high-arching vault, changing the entire skyline of secular as well as sacred architecture—palaces, fortresses, gardens.[152] Mosques also provided a valuable contrast with temples within the landscape of India. The Hindu temple has a small, almost empty space in the still center (the representation of the deity is always there), surrounded by a steadily escalating profusion of detail that makes rococo seem minimalist. But the mosque creates a larger emptiness from its very borders, a space designed not, like the temple, for the home of a deity but for congregational prayer. The mosque, whose serene calligraphic and geometric decoration contrasts with the perpetual motion of the figures depicted on the temple, makes a stand against the chaos of India, creating enforced vacuums that India cannot rush into with all its monkeys and peoples and colors and the smells of the bazaar and, at the same time, providing a flattering frame to offset that very chaos.

Moving Temples: Virashaivas

Sects of renouncers had always followed a religious path away from houses. But now, during this period when so many great temples were being built and the temple rather than the palace or the house was the pivot of the Brahmin imaginary, one large and influential South Indian Hindu sect differed from earlier renouncers in spurning not houses but stone temples, the very temples that were the pride and joy of South Indian rulers and the bastions of the social, economic, and religious order of South India. These were the Lingayats ("People of the Linga") or Virashaivas ("Shiva's Heroes"), also called Charanas ("Wanderers") because they prided themselves on being moving temples, itinerant, never putting down roots.[153] Their founder was Basava (1106–1167), a Brahmin at the court of King Bijjala of Kalyana.[154] Basava preached a simplified devotion: no worship but that of a small linga worn around the neck and no goal but to be united, at death, with Shiva. He rejected the worship of gods that you hock in bad times or hide from robbers (a possible reference to the vulnerability of temple images to invading armies): "How can I feel right about gods you sell in your need, and gods you bury for fear of thieves?"[155]

The only temple you can trust is your own body:

The rich
will make temples for Shiva.
What shall I,
a poor man,
do?

My legs are pillars,
the body the shrine,
the head a cupola
of gold.

> Listen, O lord of the meeting rivers,
>
> things standing shall fall,
>
> but the moving ever shall stay.[156]

And the name "lord of the meeting rivers" resonates, among other things, with the meetings of the community of devotees from every caste and class.[157] "Things standing shall fall" mocks the megalomania of the temple builders.

The Virashaivas were militants who attacked the normative social and cultural order of the medieval south; some people regarded them as heretics, and many classified them as "left-hand" (artisans, merchants, servants) in contrast with "right-hand" (agricultural workers). Legends about the early Virashaivas say that the son of a Pariah married the daughter of a Brahmin; the king condemned both their fathers to death; the Virashaivas rioted against the king and assassinated him; the government attempted to suppress the Virashaivas, but they survived. Basava was against caste and against Brahmins. Muslim social customs, unrestricted by caste, influenced him deeply, and the Virashaivas' rejection of the Brahmin imaginary may be beholden to the influence of Muslim missionaries who were active on India's west coast just when the Virashaiva doctrine was developed there. On the other hand, the threat of Islamic iconoclasm may have been one reason for the widespread use of portable temple images (or portable lingas).[158]

The earlier poems of the Virashaivas were composed in Kannada, but the earliest extant full narrative of the Virashaivas is in Telugu, the thirteenth-century Telugu *Basava Purana* of Palkuriki Somanatha. It is largely a hagiography of Basava, but it is also, in David Shulman's words, "an extraordinarily violent book . . . the Virashaiva heroes are perpetually decapitating, mutilating, or poisoning someone or other—their archenemies, the Brahmins and Jains, or their political rivals, or, with astounding frequency, themselves (usually for some minor lapse in the intensity of their devotion)."[159] Where does this violence come from? We may trace it back to the Tamil saints of the *Periya Purana*, or to the wild followers of Shiva as Virabhadra in Andhra, who represent "an enduring strain of potentially antinomian folk religion that breaks into literary expression under certain historical conditions," such as the political vacuum that existed in twelfth-century Kalyana.[160] Much of the aggression and violence in the *Basava Purana* is directed against conventional religion: The god in the temple *murti* (icon) is so humiliated that he sneaks out the back door; washermen, thieves, and Pariahs win out over the political and religious power mongers. A devotee's dog (actually Shiva disguised in a dog's skin) recites the Veda, shaming the caste-obsessed Brahmins,[161] as the buffalo does, in Kabir's poem; making the interloper a dog instead of a buffalo intensifies the caste issue. Several stories also describe victories over Jainas, some of whom are blinded.[162] Eventually Basava reacted against the Virashaivas' violence and lived his life away from the community he had founded.

MAHADEVYYAKKA: A VIRASHAIVA WOMAN SAINT

In the twelfth century a woman Virashaiva saint named Mahadevyyakka composed poems in Kannada[163] that simultaneously addressed the metaphysics of salvation (including the problem of Maya, ["illusion"]) and the banal problem of dealing with in-laws:

> I have Maya for mother-in-law;
> the world for father-in-law;
> three brothers-in-law, like tigers;
>
> and the husband's thoughts
> are full of laughing women:
>   no god, this man.
>
> And I cannot cross the sister-in-law.
> But I will
> give this working wench the slip
> and go cuckold my husband with Hara, my Lord.[164]

On the banal level, the poem refers to the difficult situation of a woman under the thumb of her mother-in-law in a patrilocal society (which means that you live with your husband's family); "no god, this man" is a direct contradiction of Hindu dharma texts such as that of Manu (5.154), which instructs a woman to treat her husband like a god. There are also more abstract references, some explicit (Maya and the world as mother- and father-in-law), some implicit: The three tigerish brothers-in-law are the three strands of matter (*gunas*), the components of nature that one cannot escape. A. K. Ramanujan sees the husband as symbolic of karma, "the past of the ego's many lives," and the sister-in-law as the binding memory or "perfume" (*vasana*) that clings to karma. None of the people in the poem is related to the speaker/heroine/worshiper by blood; she defies them all, using a vulgar word for "cuckold" that would surely shock them. The poem presents the love of god (Hara, a name of Shiva) as both totally destructive of conventional life and illegitimate, transgressive.[165]

We can reconstruct quite a lot about the life of Mahadevyyakka. She regarded herself as married to Shiva, and tried in vain to avoid marrying Kaushika, a king who fell in love with her. She wrote of this conflict:

> Husband inside,
> lover outside.
> I can't manage them both.
>
> This world
> and that other,
> cannot manage them both.[166]

Eventually she left her husband and wandered naked, clothed only in her hair, like Lady Godiva, until she died, still in her twenties. Ramanujan writes her epitaph: "Her struggle was with her condition, as body, as woman, as social being tyrannized by social roles, as a human confined to a place and a time. Through these shackles she bursts, defiant in her quest for ecstasy."[167] Though hardly a typical woman, Mahadevyyakka nevertheless provides a paradigm precisely for atypicality, for the possibility that a woman might shift the paradigm,* as so many other women have done in the history of Hinduism, so strongly that their lives may have functioned as alternative paradigms for other women.

---

* To use Thomas Kuhn's term for a major change in scientific worldviews.

CHAPTER 17

AVATAR AND ACCIDENTAL GRACE IN THE LATER PURANAS

800 to 1500 CE

ॐ

CHRONOLOGY (ALL DATES ARE CE)

750–1500 Medieval Puranas are composed:

  Agni (850), *Bhagavata* (950), *Bhavishya* (500–1200), *Brahma* (900–1350),

  Brahmavaivarta (1400–1500), *Devibhagavata* (1100–1350), *Garuda* (900),

  Kalika (1350), *Linga* (600–1000), *Mahabhagavata* (1100), *Saura* (950–1150)

1210–1526 The Delhi Sultanate is in power

c. 1200 Early orders of Sufis arise in North India

c. 1200 Virashaivas, including Basava, live in South India

c. 1200 Jayadeva's *Gita Govinda* is composed

c. 1336–1565 Vijayanagar Empire is in its prime

c. 1398–1448 Kabir lives

1469–1539 Guru Nanak founds Sikhism in the Punjab

THE PURANAS TELL IT DIFFERENTLY

Listen to the way Brahma himself tells the story of Prahlada; the
Puranas tell it differently.

Padma Purana, c. 750–1000 CE[1]

The many different ways in which the medieval Puranas tell stories about
animals, women, the lower classes, and other religions are the result of a sudden
burgeoning of the imaginative range of the texts, nurtured in large part by the
ongoing appropriation of ideas from non-Sanskrit, oral, and vernacular cultures. By the ninth century CE, Sanskrit had embraced literary and political as

well as religious realms as a cosmopolitan language that was patronized by the literati and royal courts. Some scholars argue that Sanskrit faded away during this period because "the idiom of a cosmopolitan literature" became somewhat redundant in "an increasingly regionalized world."[2] But it seems to me that the producers of Sanskrit Puranas, regionalized though they most certainly were, responded not by closing up shop but simply doing more and more business as usual, welcoming in regional popular, oral, and vernacular themes and translating them into their own kind of Puranic Sanskrit. It was in this spirit too that they welcomed in regional and popular figures and made them into some of the avatars of Vishnu.

THE AVATARS OF VISHNU

We have already met the first two human avatars of Vishnu, Krishna and Rama, who becaome incarnate on earth to fight against antigods (Asuras) incarnate as humans and against ogres (Rakshasas) who are the enemies of humans. We have also noted, without investigating, a number of references to other avatars that Vishnu had attracted by the early centuries of the Common Era, sometimes said to be six, sometimes eighteen, but usually ten (though not always the same ten*). One of the very few surviving Gupta temples, the temple at Deogarh, in Uttar Pradesh (c. sixth–seventh century CE), is called the Temple of the Ten Avatars (Dashavatara). In the fifteenth century the poet Kabir mocked the ten avatars as "divine malarkey/for those who really know"—that is, for those who know that it is all god's *maya* that Rama appears to marry Sita, and so forth.[3] The Jaina concept of Universal History, which claims nine appearances of a savior in each world epoch, may have played a role in the development of the Hindu schema,[4] for Vishnu too usually has nine avatars in the past, the tenth being (like the Kali Age) reserved for the future (Kalki).

Some of the new avatars were assimilated into the Puranas lists from earlier Sanskrit literature, and all of them entered the ten-avatar structure through the usual processes of Hindu bricolage. The texts often describe the avatars centrifugally, as various functions of the god emanating out of him and expressed as many manifestations (with many arms, many heads). But historically they came into being centripetally, as various gods already in existence were attracted

---

* The *Vayu Purana,* chapter 36, for instance, includes no animal avatars, just six of the usual ten (Man-Lion, Dwarf, Parashurama, Rama, Krsna, and Kalkin) plus Narayana (another form of Vishnu) and three more humans: Dattatreya and Mandhata (with previous histories of their own) and Vyasa (author of the *Mahabharata*).

to Vishnu and attached themselves to him like iron filings to a magnet. Avatars were particularly popular with kings, whose eulogies often sequentially link their conquests or their qualities to avatars—like the boar, he rescured the earth, like Kalki, he repelled the barbarians—perhaps to suggest that the king too was an avatar.

To fast-forward for a moment, Keshab Chunder Sen (1838–1884) in 1882 noted that the succession of Vishnu's avatars could be interpreted as an allegory of the Darwinian evolutionary process, "presciently recognized by ancient Hindu sages and now confirmed by modern science"—that is, an ancient Indian theory that Darwin re-invented.[5] (Sen may or may not have been inspired by the idea of Avataric Evolutionism that Madame Blavatsky discussed in her *Isis Unveiled,* published in 1877.[6]) Since then the ten avatars are often listed beginning with the three least complex life forms and working their way up to humans; sometimes they are also associated with the progression of the ages (Yugas) through time. Thus the list usually goes like this: the fish, the tortoise, the boar, and the Man-Lion (animals, all in the Krita Yuga, the first Age, and all but the Man-Lion aquatic animals); the dwarf, Parashurama, Rama (humans, all in the Treta Yuga, the second Age); Krishna and the Buddha (humans in the Dvapara, the third Age); and Kalki in the Kali Age. But evolutionary theory fits with the Indian theory of the Yugas only if one ignores the little matter of the clash between social evolutionism (things get steadily better) and the Yuga theory of social degeneration (things get steadily worse).

If, however, we take into account the order in which the principal ten figures first surface in texts (including coins and inscriptions), though not necessarily already labeled avatars, let alone historically connected with Vishnu, the list would look more like this: the dwarf (*Rig Veda*); the fish and the boar (Brahmanas); the tortoise, Krishna, Rama, Parashurama, and Kalki (all mentioned in the *Mahabharata*); the Man-Lion and the Buddha (mentioned in the *Vishnu Purana*, c. 400–500 CE).[7] Finally, if we group them according to the main issues with which this book is primarily concerned, the order would be animals (the fish, the boar, the tortoise), women (Krishna/Radha, Rama/Sita), interreligious relations (the Buddha, Kalki*), caste and class (Parashurama, the dwarf, and the Man-Lion). Let us consider them in that order.

---

* A case might well be made for including Kalki as an animal avatar, since he often appears as (though more often with) a white horse, but we will discuss him in the context of interreligious avatars.

ANIMALS

THE FISH (MATSYA)

The myth of the fish and the flood is not originally associated with Vishnu; as we have seen, at first the fish was just a fish. But in the *Mahabharata* (3.185), the fish tells Manu that he is Brahma, Prajapati, the Lord of Creatures, and since the fish expands from a minnow to a kind of whale, and since he is a savior, the Puranas make him one of the avatars of the god Vishnu, who is both an expander (as the dwarf who becomes a giant) and a savior (as Krishna often claims to be).

THE BOAR (VARAHA)

Like the avatar of the fish, the boar avatar was not originally associated with Vishnu; in the Brahmanas, the boar, an amphibious animal, is Prajapati, the Lord of Creatures, who spreads earth out on the waters to make her into a disk and who marries her.[8] The *Vishnu Purana* identifies Prajapati with Narayana (a name of Vishnu).[9] At Udayagiri, in Malwa, a shrine carved out of the rock-face and dated to the opening of the fifth century CE depicts Vishnu's incarnation as the boar, rescuing the earth depicted as a female boar. This may have been a political allegory of Chandra Gupta II's conquest of Malwa,[10] making the image simultaneously Vishnu married to the earth-boar and a king married to the earth goddess.

THE TORTOISE (KURMA)

The tortoise appears in the *Mahabharata* when the gods and antigods decide to churn the ocean of milk to obtain the elixir of immortality, the soma, using Mount Mandara as the churn. All that is said there is: "The gods and antigods said to the king of tortoises, the supreme tortoise, 'You are the one suited to be the resting place for the mountain.' The tortoise agreed, and Indra placed the tip of the mountain on his back, fastening it tightly (1.15–17)." Vishnu is not the tortoise here; indeed he appears in this version of the story in a different form, as the nymph Mohini, who bewitches and seduces the antigods so that they lose their opportunity to drink the soma. But the tortoise goes on to be quite famous in Hindu cosmologies and in images of the myth of the churning, and the Puranas identify the tortoise as an avatar of Vishnu. Usually he is depicted as anthropomorphic from the waist up, tortoise from the waist down, but sometimes simply as a tortoise *tout court*.

Women

krishna (and the women who loved him)

Major changes were beginning to be made in the worship of Krishna at this time. When we meet Krishna in the *Mahabharata,* he is already an adult; the *Harivamsha,* the appendix to the *Mahabharata,* composed a century or two after it (c. 450 CE), gives him a childhood. This childhood may have been derived, in the early centuries CE, from popular, vernacular, non-Brahminical stories about a village boy who lived among the cowherd people,[11] a far cry from the powerful prince Krishna of the *Mahabharata.* In a stroke of genius, the *Harivamsha* put the two mythologies together, the *Mahabharata* story of the prince and the folk/vernacular stories of a cowherd child, by bridging them with a third story, a variant of the story that Freud called the family romance,[12] the myth of a boy of noble blood who is raised by animals, or by the herders of animals, until he grows up and finds his real parents.* The family romance is a ready-made, off-the-rack story right at hand to be picked up and used when there is a sudden need to plug a gaping hole, to construct a childhood for a god who has appeared only as an adult in earlier texts. Once the join was made, the *Harivamsha* quickly absorbed the cowherd mythology and developed it in its own ways. Krishna in the *Mahabharata* was already a double figure, a god pretending to be a prince, but now he was doubly doubled: a god pretending to be a prince pretending to be a cowherd. This opened up the way to the worship of the child Krishna and a theology of the hidden god, revealed through a series of charming miracles that puzzle all but the reader who is in the know.

The *Harivamsha* tells the story of Krishna's birth into his double life:

THE BIRTH OF KRISHNA

The wicked king Kamsa heard a prophecy that the eighth child born of his cousin Devaki and her husband, Vasudeva, would kill Kamsa. He let Devaki live, on condition that Vasudeva would deliver to Kamsa every child she bore, and Kamsa killed seven infants in this way.† Vishnu placed himself in the eighth embryo, and, at his request, the goddess of sleep took the form of the goddess Kali and entered

---

* The pattern applies to Karna, Oedipus, Moses, Cyrus, and, as Alan Dundes has argued persuasively, Jesus. The animals are more prominent in the myths of Tarzan and Kipling's Mowgli.
† There may be an echo here of the *Mahabharata* story in which the Ganges kills the first seven of her children, and only the eighth, Bhishma, is saved.

the womb of Yashoda, the wife of the cowherd Nanda. One night Krishna was born to the princess Devaki and the goddess Kali was born to the cowherd woman Yashoda. Vasudeva carried the infant Krishna to Yashoda and brought the infant girl to Devaki. When Kamsa saw the girl, he dashed her violently to the stone floor. She went to heaven and became an eternal goddess, Kali, to whom sacrifices of animals are made, for she is fond of flesh. And Krishna grew up in the village of cowherds. When he was grown, he killed Kamsa.[13]

Krishna's birth is doubled in yet another way, by the simultaneous birth of Sleep as Kali and the daughter of Devaki as the daughter of Yashoda. The worship of the goddess Kali, a new, specifically Hindu element injected into the basic formula, signals the beginning of a new prominence of women in the worship of Krishna, starting in this text, where Devaki, in a manner reminiscent of Draupadi, harasses her husband, Vasudeva, and forces him to stop saying, "It is all fated," and to do something to save her baby. Indeed bhakti texts generally challenge the more fatalistic construction of karma, believing that people's actions in their current lives can produce good or bad fortune *in this life* and that devotion to the gods, in particular, pays off in this lifetime[14] as well as in the next.

Yashoda and the Gopis

The *Harivamsha* makes Krishna's foster mother, Yashoda, a major character, as does the tenth book of the *Bhagavata Purana,* which bears the imprint of the bhakti wind blowing from the south and develops in glorious detail the other mothers of Krishna, the Gopis or cowherd women, who become his foster mothers and cluster around him in adoration. There are also negative foster mothers: The infant Krishna kills (among many ogres and ogresses) the ogress Putana, who tries to poison him with the milk from her breasts but is killed instead when he sucks out her life's breath with her milk.[15]

The *Bhagavata* also domesticates the myth of looking into the mouth of god (Krishna), which, in the *Gita,* reveals to Arjuna the unbearable image of doomsday. In the Purana, Yashoda looks into the mouth of her toddler Krishna and sees in it the universe and herself (as Brahma sees the universe and himself in Vishnu), a vision that she finds unbearable, just as Arjuna did. In both cases, Krishna grants, in his infinite love, the boon that Arjuna and Yashoda will forget the vision.[16]

GOPIS AS LOVERS

When passion, even religious passion, is the game, the erotic is always a heavy hitter. Krishna in the *Mahabharata* is a prince with many wives, sixteen thousand by some counts, though he had his favorites.* The Puranas depict Krishna as a handsome young man who dances with the many Gopis, the wives of the cowherd men. In the great circle dance in the moonlight (*rasa-lila*), he doubles himself again and again so that each Gopi thinks that Krishna is with her. Similarly, the Gopis double themselves, leaving shadow images of themselves in bed with their unsuspecting husbands. The Gopis are both his mothers and his lovers; the Puranas tend to blur the distinction between the love of Krishna's mothers ("calf love" [*vatsalya*]) and the love of his lovers ("honey-sweet love" [*madhurya*]).[17] Here is yet another example of the astounding Hindu ability to combine ideas that other religions might feel constrained to choose between or at least to keep separate.

RADHA

In later Puranas, one Gopi in particular is the lover of Krishna: Radha, who is virtually unknown to the Sanskrit mythology of Krishna until the seventh century and does not become important to the devotional community until the sixteenth century,[18] when bhakti has feminized sectarianism and made women more important. The story of Krishna and Radha inspired the Sanskrit *Gita Govinda*, "The Song of [Krishna] the Cowherd," by Jayadeva, the court poet of the Bengali King Laksmanasena (c. 1179–1209), an important text for Vaishnava worshipers. Jayadeva's Radha is powerful; Krishna bends down before her and puts her feet on his head. The romance of the two adulterous lovers may owe something to the Persian romances that were becoming known in India through the Muslim presence at this time, in some Sufi sects.[19]

In the *Bhagavata Purana,* Krishna would disappear from the circle dance from time to time, and the Gopis searched for him in an exquisite agony of longing, the great Indian theme of love and separation (*viraha*), here in the familiar bhakti mode of longing for the absent god (the *deus absconditus* or *otiosus*). But in the later Puranas, often under Tantric influences, it was Radha alone with whom the worshiper, male or female, identified. As a Gopi, Radha was

---

* Rukmini, Satyabhama, and Jambavati.

also one of Krishna's foster mothers, a role that she does not entirely abandon when she becomes his lover. In the *Brahmavaivarta Purana,* probably composed in Bengal in the fifteenth or sixteenth century, the mature Radha is put in charge of the infant Krishna, to her intense annoyance; suddenly he turns into a gorgeous young man, with whom she makes love joyously for many days—until he turns back again into a demanding, and wet, infant.[20]

RAMA (AND SITA)

Images from the life of Rama are represented at the Dashavatara temple at Deogarh, though in general there is little evidence of Rama worship in temples at that time (the Gupta period), nor, in dramatic contrast with Krishna, is Rama's story elaborated upon to any significant degree in the early Puranas. But Valmiki's *Ramayana* was not only still widely read in Sanskrit at the time of the later Puranas (800–1500 CE) but was now beginning to be translated into the vernacular literatures, as well as retold in other Sanskrit texts. The *Mahabharata, Harivamsha, Vishnu Purana,* and several other Puranas omit the fire ordeal of Sita entirely,[21] but the fifteenth-century *Adhyatma-Ramayana* used it to exculpate Sita not only from being present in Ravana's home but from the weakness of asking Rama to capture the golden deer for her. This illusory deer, however, may have inspired the *Adhyatma-Ramayana* to create the illusory Sita who now desires the deer:

THE ILLUSORY DEER OF THE ILLUSORY SITA

Rama, knowing what Ravana intended to do, told Sita, "Ravana will come to you disguised as an ascetic; put a shadow [*chaya*] of yourself outside the hut, and go inside the hut yourself. Live inside fire, invisible; when I have killed Ravana, come back to me as you were before." Sita obeyed; she placed an illusory Sita [*maya-sita*] outside and entered the fire. This illusory Sita saw the illusory deer and urged Rama to capture it for her.[22]

Ravana captures the illusory Sita, and Rama then pretends to grieve for Sita, pretends to fight to get her back, and lies to his brother Lakshmana, who genuinely grieves for Sita. Sita herself is never subjected to an ordeal at all; after Ravana has been killed and the false Sita brought back and accused, the illusory Sita enters the fire and vanishes forever, while the real Sita emerges and remains with Rama. Thus the text quells the uneasiness that the reader (or hearer) may well share with Rama at the thought of Sita's living in Ravana's house for so long:

Rama never intended or needed to test Sita (since he knew she wasn't in Ravana's house at all) but had the shadow Sita enter the fire merely in order to bring the real Sita back from the fire, to make her visible again. The shadow Sita protects the real Sita from the trauma of life with Rama as well as with Ravana.

But Rama seems to forget what he has done; he grieves terribly for Sita and orders the shadow Sita into the fire as if she were real. The illusory Sita is part of the greater illusion that Rama, as a great god, is now in charge of; he is play-acting (through his *lila,* his artistic game) the whole time anyway, so why not playact his grief for Sita? Probably in order to maintain the power of the narrative, the author has Rama seem to forget about the shadow at crucial moments; only when the gods come and remind him of his divinity (as they do in the Valmiki text) does Fire (incarnate as the god Agni) return Sita to Rama, remarking, "You made this illusory Sita in order to destroy Ravana. Now he is dead, and that Sita has disappeared."[23] And whereas Sita's desire for the deer in the Valmiki text proves that she can't recognize a substitute deer, in this text she gets a substitute who can't recognize the substitute deer, while Ravana can't recognize the substitute Sita.

The *Brahmavaivarta Purana* develops the idea of the subjectivity of the surrogate Sita, who goes on to have a life of her own as Draupadi, of all people:

> The shadow Sita asked Rama and Fire, "What shall I do?" Fire told her to go to the Pushkara shrine, and there she generated inner heat and was reborn as Draupadi. This shadow, who was in the prime of her youth, was so nervous and excited with lust when she asked Shiva for a husband that she repeated her request five times. And so she obtained five husbands, the five Pandavas.[24]

Fire gives the shadow Sita a sexual future as Draupadi, who, like the shadow Sita, is born of a fire;[25] indeed it may have been the shared theme of birth from fire that attracted Draupadi from her own epic into Sita's story in the other epic, as if Lady Macbeth somehow popped up as a character in *King Lear.*

INTERRELIGIOUS DIALOGUE

THE BUDDHA

The Buddha avatar is mentioned in of the *Mahabharata:*[26] "At the beginning of the Kali Age, Vishnu will become the Buddha, son of Shuddhodana, and he will preach in the Magadha dialect. All men will become bald, like him, and wear the ocher robe, and priests will cease to offer oblations or recite the Veda."[27]

The precise historical detail of preaching in Magadhi, together with the reference to the name of the Buddha's father as it appears in the Pali canon (and in later lists of historical Hindu dynasties[28]), lulls us into a false sense of historical reality—until it gets to the crucial point: "Those who sought refuge with Vishnu [as Buddha] were deluded." The myth of Vishnu's incarnation as the Buddha is established in full detail in the *Vishnu Purana,* represented on the sixth- to seventh-century Dashavatara temple at Deogarh and mentioned in a seventh-century Pallava inscription[29] and an eighth-century Tamil inscription.[30]

The Buddha avatar was not originally, as it might seem at first glance and is often advertised as being, a genuine attempt to assimilate the teachings of the Buddha into Hinduism (though this was certainly done in many other ways). On the contrary, although Vishnu as Buddha expresses the anti-Vedic sentiments that Hindus (rightly) attribute to Buddhists, Jainas, Materialists, and other heretics, he does this in order to destroy the antigods by teaching them an evil doctrine, Buddhism, on the second alliance principle that the gods cannot destroy a virtuous person unless they first corrupt him:

VISHNU AS THE BUDDHA CORRUPTS THE ANTIGODS

The antigods conquered the gods in battle, and the gods went to ask Vishnu for help, saying, "The antigods have stolen our portions of the sacrifices, but they take pleasure in the duties of their own class and they follow the path of the Vedas and are full of inner heat. Therefore we cannot kill them. Please find a way for us to kill them." Then Vishnu emitted from his body a deluding form of his magic power of illusion and said, "This magic deluder will bewitch all the antigods so that they will be excluded from the path of the Vedas and therefore susceptible to slaughter." The gods went back home, and the magic deluder went to the great antigods.

Naked, bald, carrying a bunch of peacock feathers, the magic deluder taught the antigods what he called "the dharma that is the open door to *moksha.*" He said: "This would be dharma, but it would not be dharma. This would give *moksha,* but it would not give *moksha.*" And so on and so forth. Then he put on red robes and spoke to other antigods, saying, "If you wish for heaven or for nirvana, you must stop these evil rites such as killing animals. If an animal slaughtered in the sacrifice is thus promised entry into heaven, why doesn't the sacrificer kill his own father? If the oblation to the ancestors that is eaten by one man satisfies another, then people traveling abroad need not take the trouble to carry food." He caused them all to abandon the dharma of the three Vedas, to be free thinkers, and they became his disciples and persuaded others. The armor of their *sva-dharma* had formerly protected them, but now it was destroyed, and so were they. The gods attacked them and killed them.[31]

The antigods are destroyed because they abandon their antigod *sva-dharma* in order to join the new religious movement. The great deluder, whose defense of nonviolence (*ahimsa*) is here regarded as part of the great lie, is both a Jaina (with peacock feathers) and a Buddhist (in ocher robes); sometimes he is said to be "the Buddha, the son of the Jina."[32] His argument about one man's eating for another is a standard Hindu satire on the heresy of Materialist satire on the Hindu rite of feeding the dead ancestors (*shraddha*); the same argument is used against the Vedas in the Tamil *Nilakeci* (tenth or eleventh century), and the remark about the sacrificer's killing his own father correctly quotes a real argument in a Buddhist Jataka text.[33] Another version of the myth says that Vishnu founded the Materialist and similar sects "for the seeking of liberation through eating flesh, drinking wine, and so forth,"[34] a policy that seems more Tantric than Materialist.

But the conversion of humankind to Buddhism (or Jainism, or Materialism, or Tantrism, or any other heresy) is merely an unfortunate side effect of Vishnu's attack on the antigods, a kind of theological fallout; and the fact that the doctrine is directed against the antigods indicates the degree of anti-Buddhist sentiment that motivated the author of this myth. It is the demonization of Buddhism (as well as the Buddhification of demons). As an unfortunate bit of collateral damage from the wars in heaven, the earth is left with human Buddhists when the gods have succeeded in turning the antigods into Buddhists, like the eucalyptus trees or cane toads that people introduced into new continents in order to destroy something else, not realizing that they would then be stuck with too many eucalyptus trees and cane toads. Similarly, a fierce Hindu goddess (sometimes named Kali) is from time to time created to kill antigods, and she does, but then sometimes she begins to kill the people who created her.[35] There is also a Sanskrit saying: "Like the king's men" (*raja-purusha-nyaya*), referring to the fact that when you call in the soldiers to get rid of bandits who are bothering you, the bandits do go away, but then you are stuck with the often even worse depredations of the soldiers. The corruption of the Buddhists/antigods is stated in terms of orthopraxy (people are made to stop sacrificing), but there is also a touch of orthodoxy: Teach them the wrong belief, and they will do the wrong things.

Yet the spirit of the narrative is more like a playful satire on Buddhism and Jainism than a serious attack. And some of the later Puranas, and other Sanskrit texts of this period, put a positive spin on the Buddha avatar. The *Bhagavata Purana* says that Vishnu became the Buddha in order to protect us from lack of enlightenment and from fatal blunders.[36] The *Varaha Purana* advises the worshiper to worship Kalki when he wants to destroy enemies and the Buddha when he wants beauty.[37] The *Matsya Purana* describes the Buddha as lotus-eyed, beautiful as a god, and peaceful.[38] Kshemendra's eleventh-century "Deeds of the Ten Avatars"[39] and Jayadeva's tenth-century *Gita Govinda* tell the story of the Buddha avatar in a straight, heroic tale based on the standard episodes of Gautama's life as related in the Pali canon, and Jayadeva says that Vishnu became the Buddha out of compassion for animals, to end bloody sacrifices.[40] The *Dashavatara-stotra,* attributed (most probably apocryphally) to Shankara (who was often accused of being a crypto-Buddhist), praises the Buddha avatar.[41] The *Devibhagavata Purana* offers homage to Vishnu, "who became incarnate as the Buddha in order to stop the slaughter of animals and to destroy the sacrifices of the wicked,"[42] adding a moral judgment to Jayadeva's more neutral statement; although the last phrase might be translated "to destroy wicked sacrifices" or taken to imply that all sacrifices are wicked, it is also possible that only wicked (or demonic, or proto-Buddhist) sacrificers, not virtuous Hindu sacrificers, are condemned. These texts may express a Hindu desire to absorb Buddhism in a peaceful manner, both to win Buddhists to the worship of Vishnu and to account for the fact that such a significant heresy could prosper in India.[43] They may also reflect the rising sentiment against animal sacrifice *within Hinduism.* Yet Kabir, in the fifteenth century, mocking the avatars, says, "Don't call the master Buddha/he didn't put down devils."[44] And in some texts and visual depictions, the Buddha is left out of the list of ten avatars; often Balarama, Krishna's brother, takes the Buddha's place.* Hindus spoke in many voices about the Buddha, some positive, some negative, and some indifferent or ambivalent.

The myth of Vishnu as Buddha then ricocheted back into Buddhism in India. For many centuries, Hindus worshiped as a Hindu god the image of the Buddha at the Mahabodhi temple at Bodh Gaya in Bihar (where the Buddha is said to have become enlightened, a major pilgrimage site for Buddhists).[45] And

---

* Outside the Minakshi temple in Madurai is a Vaishnava temple that has Balarama in place of the Buddha.

a legend apparently originating in medieval Sri Lanka refers to ten bodhisatt-vas, one of whom is Vishnu,[46] who is also represented as one of the ten bodhi-sattvas in Sinhalese temples, notably at Dambulla,[47] and becomes the protector of Buddhism throughout Sri Lanka.[48]

We can trace these shifting attitudes through three broad stages. First, Bud-dhism was assimilated into Hinduism in the Upanishads, *Ramayana,* and *Mahabharata.* This was a period of harmony (sometimes competitive, but always civil) among Hindus and Buddhists and Jainas, in actual history, and between gods and humans (the first alliance), in mythology. Then, in the second stage, around the turn of the millennium and after, the Buddhists (in history) became more powerful and were sometimes seen as a threat. The first set of Puranic myths about the Buddha were composed at this time (the Gupta period), when Hinduism was still fighting a pitched battle against Buddhism, Jainism, and other heresies; the scars of the battle may be seen in these Puranic stories that contemptuously denounce the *shastras* of delusion (i.e., the Buddhist and Jaina scriptures) and the people who use them,[49] assimilating this conflict into the pattern of second alliance myths of the corruption of the virtuous antigods.[50]

But then, in the third stage, when Buddhism, though still a force to be reck-oned with in India, was waning, the texts have a more conciliatory attitude, and the Hindus once again acknowledged their admiration of Buddhism. In my-thology, the texts revise the myth of Vishnu as the Buddha to make it generous and tolerant.[51] A Kashmiri king of the tenth century had a magnificent frame made for "an image of the Buddha Avatara," and the image that he used was a Buddha figure that had probably been under worship by Buddhists; this frame may have been made for the Buddhist figure in order to "Hinduize" it,[52] just as the doctrine of the Buddha was placed in the "frame" of Puranic mythology to Hinduize it and as Hindu temples were built on Buddhist stupas and, later, Muslim mosques on Hindu temples.

KALKI

Kalki, usually listed as the final avatar, is the only one yet to come in the future, the messiah who will appear at the end of the present Kali Age, to de-stroy barbarians and atheists (Nastikas). The myth may represent a reaction against the invasion of India by Greeks, Scythians, Parthians, Kushanas, and Huns, but it owes its own conception to those very invaders. For Kalki may have been inspired in part by the future Buddha Maitreya, who will reinstate the norms of Buddhist belief and behavior,[53] though both Kalki and Maitreya might have developed from the image of the purifying savior that the Parthians may have brought into India in the first centuries CE.[54] The idea of the final avatar may have entered India at this time, when millennial ideas were rampant in Europe and Christians were proselytizing in India; the Hindu rider on the white horse may have influenced, or been influenced by, the rider on the white horse in Christian apocalyptic literature,[55] his cloak soaked in blood, sent to put the pagans to the sword. The circularity of historical influence is such that Kalki's purpose is to destroy the barbarian invaders, to raze the wicked cities of the plain that have been polluted by foreign kings, the same horsemen who may have brought the myth of Kalki into India.

Kalki appears first in the *Mahabharata,* after a long description of the horrors of the Kali Age. Then: "A Brahmin by the name of Kalki Vishnuyashas will be born, impelled by Time, in the village of Shambhala." He will be a king, and he will annihilate all the barbarians and destroy the robbers and make the earth over to the twice born at a great horse sacrifice.[56] Nothing is said here about his being an avatar of Vishnu, except that he is named Fame of Vishnu (Vishnu-yashas), and nothing is said about a horse, except for his horse sacrifice. The point about the avatar, but not about the horse, is somewhat clarified in the *Vishnu Purana:*

KALKI WILL KILL THE BARBARIANS

The Scythians, Greeks, Huns, and others will pollute India.[57] Unable to support their avaricious kings, the people of the Kali Age will take refuge in the chasms between mountains, and they will eat honey, vegetables, roots, fruits, leaves, and flowers. They will wear ragged garments made of leaves and the bark of trees, and they will have too many children. No one will live more than twenty-two years. Vedic religion and the dharma of the *shastra*s will undergo total confusion and reversal.

But when the Kali Age is almost over, Vishnu will become incarnate here in the form of Kalki, in the house of the chief Brahmin of the village of Shambala.* He will destroy all the barbarians and Dasyus and men of evil acts and evil thoughts, and he will establish everything, each in its own *sva-dharma.*

And at the end of the Kali Age, the minds of the people will become pure as flawless crystal, and they will be as if awakened at the conclusion of a night. And these men, the residue of humankind, will be the seeds of creatures and will give

---

* This is the first citation of the name Shambala, which was to become an important myth of a lost, magical city in the mountains.

birth to offspring conceived at that very time. And these offspring will follow the ways of the Winning [Krita] Age.[58]

The transition between the end of the Kali Age and the beginning of the Winning Age is usually a cosmological upheaval, fire and flood. Here it is translated into a political upheaval: The barbarians and Dasyus (the old enemies of the Vedic people) are put to the sword. In both cases, however, all the bad people are destroyed and a remnant of good people survives to begin the new world. The doomsday Shaiva mare, with her fire and flood, seems to vanish from the junction of the ages, but at the very end of the passage, the text casually remarks: "Vishnu is the horse's head that lives in the ocean, devouring oblations." So she is there after all.

The Buddha and Kalki appear together in sequence in many of the Puranic lists of avatars and on reliefs of the ten avatars from the Gupta period onward.[59] Vishnu first initiates the Kali Age when he becomes the Buddha to destroy the antigods and make them into heretics, and then, at the end of the Kali Age, he becomes Kalki to destroy both heretics and barbarians. One late Purana makes this connection explicit and sets both Buddha and Kalki in the past, the right time for the Buddha but the wrong time for Kalki:

KALI AND KALKI, BUDDHA AND JINA

At the end of the Kali Age, Adharma and Kali (the incarnation of the Kali Age) were born. Men became lustful, hypocritical and evil, adulterers, drunkards. Ascetics took to houses, and householders were devoid of discrimination. Men abandoned the Vedas and sacrifices, and the gods, without sustenance, sought refuge with Brahma. Then Vishnu was born as Kalki. He levied a great army to chastise the Buddha; he fought the Buddhists, who were led by the Jina, and he killed the Jina and defeated the Buddhists and the barbarians who assisted them. The wives of the Buddhists and barbarians had also taken up arms, but Kalki taught them the paths of karma, *jnana,* and bhakti. He defeated Kali, who escaped to another age.[60]

Kalki comes, as usual, to counteract the doctrines of the Buddhists and Jainas and barbarians. But as time has now passed—the *Kalki Purana* may be as late as the eighteenth century—the barbarians (*mlecchas*)[61] may be Christians or even Muslims. Whoever they are, Kalki teaches their women the three paths of karma, *jnana,* and bhakti, the paths of the *Bhagavad Gita.* This late bhakti text assumes that the women, with their special gift for bhakti, can still be redeemed, if the men cannot. The incarnate Kali Age escapes, because it is inevitable that, after the Winning Age that Kalki here introduces, time will inevitably degenerate, and the Kali Age will be with us again.

KALKI'S HORSE

Eventually Kalki as or with a stallion replaced the underwater mare as the doomsday horse; in later texts, Kalki is said to ride on a horse[62] (a swift horse that the gods give him),[63] and, later still, he himself is said to be a horse or horse-headed. When the Muslim sect of the Imam Shahis reworked the stories of the avatars, Kalki, the tenth avatar, became the imam, who rides on a horse.[64] The horse head may be the result of merging Kalki with earlier equine myths about good horse heads, such as the head of the Upanishadic sacrificial horse and the horse head through which the Vedic Dadhyanch tells the secret of soma to the Ashvins. There is also another good horse-headed Vishnu, Hayagriva ("horse-necked"),* who is sometimes regarded as a separate, minor avatar of Vishnu.[65] In the *Mahabharata* (12.335.1–64), Vishnu takes this form to dive into the ocean to retrieve the Vedas from two antigods who have stolen them; Puranic retellings of the story say that when he resumed his own form, he left the horse head in the ocean, where it becomes our old friend the head of the submarine mare, though now devouring oblations instead of water.[66]

But there are also demonic horses in Vaishnava mythology. A still-later text states that Hayagriva was not a god at all but a horse-headed antigod that had won the boon that only someone horse-headed could kill him, and so when Vishnu was once accidentally beheaded (yes, another story: His head falls into the ocean†), the gods had their blacksmith take an ax, cut the head off a horse, and put it on Vishnu; Vishnu then killed the horse-headed antigod.[67] Krishna also fights with a horse antigod named Keshin ("Long-haired," like the Vedic sage, or here, perhaps, "Long-maned"), whom he kills by wounding him in the mouth and splitting him in half.[68] A Gupta image depicts a young Krishna kicking a horse, presumably the horse antigod Keshin, in the stomach and jamming his elbow in the horse's mouth.[69] The negative image of the Shaiva mare

---

* Hayagriva also becomes a Buddhist deity, but that is another story.
† OK, here is how Vishnu was accidentally beheaded: Vishnu had laughed while looking at Lakshmi's face, and she feared that he thought she was ugly or that he had taken another, more beautiful co-wife. She cursed him to have his head fall off, thinking that having a co-wife would be more painful than being a widow. And so Vishnu's head fell into the ocean.

fire joined to the positive images of Vaishnava horses may have resulted in the ambiguous equine Vaishnava figures of both Keshin and Kalki.

CLASS AND CASTE STRUGGLES

PARASHURAMA

Parashurama ("Rama with an Ax") is not an avatar in the *Mahabharata,* though he is an important figure there in his own right. The son of the insanely jealous Brahmin sage Jamadagni and his Kshatriya wife, Renuka, Parashurama is an awkward interclass mix and gets tragically caught in the crossfire between his parents. One day, as Renuka bathes in the river she catches sight of a king playing in the water with his queen, and she desires him. Her husband, sensing this change, has their son Parashurama, the Lizzie Borden of Hindu mythology (forty whacks and all), behead her. But beheading is seldom fatal in a Hindu myth. Pleased by his son's obedience, Jamadagni offers him a boon, and Parashurama has him bring Renuka back to life (MB 3.116.1–20). (The Tamil version of this story has Parashurama accidentally give his mother the head of a Pariah woman.[70]) Parashurama also requests, and is granted, as an additional boon, "that no one would remember her murder, that no one would be touched by the evil (MB 3.116.21–25)." Thus nothing really happens; at the end, all wrongs are righted. All that is lost when the head has been restored is memory—perhaps not merely the memory of the murder but also the memory of the sexual vision that threatened Renuka's integrity as a chaste wife by threatening to unveil in her the conflicting image of the erotic woman. It is not entirely clear whether the evil consists in the murder or in the original lapse of chastity, nor, therefore, whether Parashurama is asking that his mother, or he himself, or everyone else should never again experience lust.

But Parashurama later lashes out against his mother's class (the whole race of Kshatriyas) and kills them all.[71] What is most puzzling is why this out-of-control boy of mixed birth, who comes from a broken home that he did much to break, is regarded as an appropriate addition to the list of Vishnu's avatars. All he has going for him is a fanatical anti-Kshatriya bias that may have appealed to the Brahmin authors of the Puranas and the irony that he acts like a Kshatriya, not a Brahmin, when he wipes out the Kshatriyas. Perhaps that is enough. Kings invoke him as a role model: "Like Parashurama, he cleansed the earth of his enemies." Like Kalki, Parashurama destroys his own people; where Kalki is modeled on barbarian invaders and kills barbarian invaders, Parashurama is a Kshatriya who kills Kshatriyas.

THE PARADOX OF THE GOOD ANTIGOD

Though the dwarf is the earliest of the avatars, and the Man-Lion the last, they both interact with the paradoxical figure of the good antigod. This figure—first the antigod Bali, whom the dwarf conquers, then Prahlada, whom the Man-Lion saves—seems to be what the anthropologist Mary Douglas would have called a category error, matter out of place: As an antigod he is by definition anti the gods, but he is devoted to, hence pro, at least one god (Indra for Bali, Vishnu for Prahlada). The texts recognize this connection, though they reverse the historical sequence, in making Prahlada Bali's grandfather.

In each of the three alliances, antigods grow strong by amassing the paramount virtue of the period. Thus in the first alliance the antigod Bali poses a threat because he has the Vedic virtue of generosity; in the second alliance, the good antigods in the Buddha myth, as well as ogres like Ravana, have amassed dangerous amounts of inner heat; and in the third alliance, Prahlada becomes a category error through his bhakti to Vishnu. This last instance, however, as we shall see, ultimately offers the solution to the problems of all three alliances.

Humans, not antigods, were the real problem here.[*] The mythology of the good antigod is the Puranas' coded way of talking about the challenge of people born into low castes, hence condemned to do unclean tasks, who nevertheless aspire to a life more in keeping with higher forms of dharma. Most of the Brahmins in charge of Vedic religion would still have nothing to do with such people, but many of the new sects, Puranic or Tantric, were casting about for ways to allow people of all castes to join them without compromising their status as pukka Hindu sects. These myths explore various possible ways of accomplishing this.

At the same time, these are not just stories about human beings interacting; they are also about what they say they are about, the nature of god and salvation. Moreover, a myth that imagines a new relationship between humans and gods makes possible, in turn, new relationships between humans.

THE DWARF (VAMANA)

Very little is said about Vishnu in the *Rig Veda,* but his main appearance is as the protagonist of an important creation myth in which he takes three steps

---

[*] As they are, ultimately, in all aspects of Hinduism, however theological their terms of argument may be.

by which he measures out, and therefore creates, the earthly realms, propping up the sky (1.154.1–6). The Brahmanas tell the story in more detail: "The gods and antigods were at war, and the antigods were winning, claiming the whole world as theirs. The gods asked for a share in the earth, and the antigods, rather jealousy, replied, 'We will give you as much as this Vishnu lies on.' Now Vishnu was a dwarf, but he was also the sacrifice. The gods worshiped with him and obtained this whole earth."[72] In the *Ramayana,* Bali alone, not the antigods in general, poses the threat. The Puranas now make Vishnu a Brahmin as well as a dwarf:

VISHNU BEGS FROM BALI

When the antigod Bali, son of Virochana, controlled all the worlds, Vishnu became incarnate as a dwarf and went where Bali was performing a sacrifice. He became a Brahmin and asked Bali to give him the space that he could cover in three strides. Bali was pleased to do this, thinking that the dwarf was just a dwarf. But the dwarf stepped over the heaven, the sky, and the earth, in three strides, stealing the antigods' prosperity. He sent the antigods and all their sons and grandsons to hell and gave Indra kingship over all the immortals.[73]

The cosmology implicit in the Brahmana myth is stated explicitly in this text: "Vishnu revealed that the whole universe was in his body." Bali is not allowed to excel as a sacrificer; Vishnu sends him to hell, where all antigods, even, or especially, virtuous antigods, belong.

THE MAN-LION (NARASIMHA)

Although the Man-Lion does not appear until the Puranas, the antigods whom he opposes—Prahlada and his father, Hiranyakashipu—have a history that stretches back to the Brahmanas. Prahlada in the Brahmanas and in parts of the *Mahabharata* is a typical, demonic demon—angry, lustful, opposing the gods.[74] But in the *Mahabharata* he becomes a type that we recognize from the second alliance of gods, humans, and antigods, a too-virtuous antigod:

INDRA BEGS FROM PRAHLADA

Prahlada stole Indra's kingdom, and Indra could not get it back because Prahlada was so virtuous. Indra went to Prahlada disguised as a Brahmin, and at Indra's request, Prahlada taught Indra about eternal dharma [*sanatana dharma*]. Pleased with his pupil, Prahlada asked the Brahmin to choose a boon, and Indra as the

Brahmin said, "I wish to have your virtue." Indra left, taking Prahlada's virtue
and dharma with him, and Prahlada's truth followed, and his good conduct, and
his prosperity [Shri] (MB 12.124.19–63).

We recognize here the pattern not only of second alliance myths that assume
the need to steal or corrupt the religious power and/or virtue of anyone who
threatens the gods, but also of a transformation of the pattern of the story of
Ekalavya (who gave his teacher the very essence of what made him great, even
as Prahlada gives his pupil his greatness), with perhaps a bit of a spin taken from
the Tantric Pashupatas who stole the good karma of people whom they tricked
into wronging them. We may also recognize the pattern of the story of Bali (an
antigod whose generosity to Vishnu is his undoing); indeed, in many versions
of the Bali myth, Prahlada, Bali's grandfather, warns Bali that the dwarf is
Vishnu,[75] and in one text, Prahlada complains bitterly that Vishnu as the dwarf
deceived and robbed his grandson Bali, who was "truthful, without desire or
anger, calm, generous, and a sacrificer."[76] (In a late version of the Bali myth that
is even more strongly reminiscent of Ekalavya, Indra himself begs from Bali's
father, Virochana, who generously offers him anything he wants, "Even my
own head," to which Indra without batting an eye replies, "Give me your own
head," and the antigod cuts it off and gives it to him.[77]) The virtue of the antigod
king—his eternal dharma—leads him to lose everything, even his *sva-dharma*
as king of the antigods. The Vedic quality of generosity is still regarded as desirable here, but now we see its disadvantage.

But then the Puranas rewind back to an earlier generation and make the
villain of the piece no longer the virtuous Prahlada but his evil father. Now too
the antigod's opponent is not Indra but Vishnu as the Man-Lion, usually depicted as a lion's head on a man's body, though with many arms, equipped with
terrible claws:

THE MAN-LION KILLS HIRANYAKASHIPU

The antigod Hiranyakashipu obtained a boon from Brahma that he could not be
killed by man or god or beast, from inside or outside, by day or by night, on earth
or in the air, or by any weapon animate or inanimate. Confident of his invulnera-
bility, he began to trouble heaven and earth. His son, Prahlada, on the other hand,
was a fervent devotee of Vishnu. Hiranyakashipu threatened to kill Prahlada,
who insisted nevertheless that Vishnu was the god who pervaded the universe.
Hiranyakashipu kicked a stone pillar and asked: "Is he in this pillar too?" Vishnu

emerged from the pillar in the form of a Man-Lion and disemboweled Hiranyakashipu with his claws, at dusk, on his lap, on the threshold. Then Prahlada became king of the antigods; devoted to Vishnu, he abandoned his antigod nature and sacrificed to the gods.[78]

The more general theme of the antigod who thinks he has a foolproof list of noncombatants but leaves out an essential clause of the contract (humans for Ravana, females for Mahisha) is joined with the theme of the *Mahabharata* tale of Indra and the antigod Vritra (or the antigod Namuchi), who had to be killed at twilight (neither night nor day), on the shore of the ocean (neither on land nor on sea), and with foam (a weapon neither wet nor dry) (MB 12.272–3).

Here Prahlada is a devotee of Vishnu from the start, steadfast despite the threats and attacks by his father, who is furious not because Prahlada is virtuous but merely because he has no respect for his father and the family traditions— that is, because he is violating his *sva-dharma,* a matter of partisan loyalties as well as ethics. Hiranyakashipu tries in vain to have his prodigal son educated in antigod etiquette: rape and pillage. Ultimately, as always, Vishnu kills the antigod, but in the process he upholds bhakti in the face of caste law. Where Vishnu has to cheat Bali by using his virtue against him, now it's OK for Prahlada to be a good antigod. Something has changed. *Sva-dharma* is abolished, while general dharma is preserved and assimilated to bhakti. The texts that tell the story this way do not even bother to explain why the young antigod should serve the gods in the first place, against all laws of antigod nature. By this time, bhakti is taken for granted.

AMAZING GRACE

What made it OK for Prahlada to go against the rules of his birth as an antigod? It required a shift in the shape of the universe.

THE ZERO-SUM WORLD EGG

The basic structures of Hindu cosmology, constantly reinterpreted, served as an armature on which authors in each generation sculpted their musings on the structure of human society. In the *Rig Veda,* the Hindu universe was an egg, the two halves of the eggshell forming heaven and earth, with the sun as the yolk in the middle; it was a sealed, perfectly enclosed space with a given amount of good and evil and a given number of souls. This is why the sage in the Upanishads asks why heaven does not get filled up with all the dead souls going into it. This closed structure began to prove problematic when many Puranic myths acted as or pamphlets for a particular shrine, magnifying its salvific powers, presumably to drum up business by boasting that anyone—even women and people of low castes—could go straight to heaven after any contact with the shrine. In reaction against this, therefore, the gods (read: Brahmins) in some myths worry that so many people are being saved at the new shrines that people in heaven will have to stand with their hands above their heads, like people in a rush-hour subway. To keep heaven a more exclusive club, the gods take measures to destroy the shrines, flooding them or filling them with sand or simply corrupting people (as in the Buddha avatar) so that they stop going to the shrine.[79] Here, as throughout this corpus, we may read these debates about imaginary creatures as paper-thin overlays on the ongoing debate about very real social classes and sectarian and religious conflicts; both Hindu and Muslim rulers did indeed, before, after, and during this period, destroy great Hindu shrines.

Ethically, this is a world of limited good or a zero-sum game: If someone is saved, someone else has to be damned. For Brahmins to be pure, Pariahs have to be impure. This is the jealous world of the second alliance: If you win, I lose. Since evil is a substance, space is a problem. This means, among other things, that evil, once created, cannot get out of the universe; the best you can do is just move it over to some spot where it will do the least possible harm, as the fire that fused Shiva's anger and Kama's erotic power was temporarily stashed in the doomsday mare at the bottom of the ocean.

The good antigod is the figure that ultimately triggers a paradigm shift in this cosmology. At first, he is caught in the clash between a form of general dharma (*sadharana dharma*) and specific dharma (*sva-dharma,* in this case, the duties of an antigod), a conflict that already affects the good ogres such as Vibhishana in the *Ramayana*. One story about a good ogre is based upon a typical myth told at some length in the *Ramayana* (7.5–8), in which an ogre named Sukesha is at first very good (he and his three sons study the Veda and make generous gifts), then good but threatening (they amass great amounts of inner heat and are given boons of invincibility), and finally corrupted by pride (they harass the gods); Vishnu destroys them all in battle and sends them down to hell. When a Purana retells this story, it raises new issues:

THE OGRE SUKESHIN GOES TO HEAVEN

A great ogre named Sukeshin received from Shiva the boon that he could not be conquered or slain. He lived according to dharma, and one day he asked a hermitage full of sages to tell him about dharma. They began by describing the specific dharma of gods (to perform sacrifice), ogres (raping other men's wives, coveting others' wealth, worshiping Shiva), and others. Then they went on to explain general dharma, the tenfold dharma for all classes, such as noninjury, restraint, and generosity. They concluded: "No one should abandon the dharma ordained for his own class and stage of life or his *sva-dharma*."

Sukeshin taught all the ogres about general dharma, and when they practiced it, their brilliant luster paralyzed the sun, moon, and stars; night was like day; owls came out and crows killed them. Then the sun realized the ogres' one weakness: they had abandoned their *sva-dharma,* a lapse that destroyed all their general dharma. Overpowered by anger, the sun shot his rays at them, and their city fell from the sky.

But when Sukeshin saw the city falling, he said, "Honor to Shiva!" and Shiva cast his glance at the sun, which fell from the sky like a stone. The gods propitiated Shiva and put the sun back in his chariot, and they took Sukeshin to dwell in heaven.[80]

The first of the three parts of this myth states the problem: the clash between general and specific dharma. The second defends *sva-dharma,* and the third overrules it, when Sukeshin plays the bhakti card to trump at least some of the aces of the caste system.

At the start, Sukeshin is in a bind: He must not abandon his dharma of rape and pillage, but he must also practice self-restraint (not easily compatible with rape) and generosity (not easily compatible with stealing). The one ray of light in this dark conflict is the fact that the *sva-dharma* of an ogre here apparently includes the worship of Shiva. Sukeshin seizes upon this loophole and proselytizes, with devastating results: Innocent owls die, and the sun is disastrously still. The midnight sun (which drives Scandinavians and Russians to commit suicide in summer) is even worse than the midwinter, when there is no sun; human beings (and, apparently, gods) cannot stand too much light—too much goodness in the wrong place. This is the traditional view: For an ogre, evil is its own reward, and a good ogre (virtuous) is by definition a bad ogre (the white sheep of his family). The jealous sun puts an end to it—but no. The marines land, as the troops of bhakti blow *sva-dharma* out of the water. The solution, however, is implied rather than stated: Sukeshin alone goes to heaven, the token antigod there; the other antigods, whose massive luster caused all the problems, conveniently vanish. Not everyone can go to heaven, it appears. Even with bhakti, at this point, not all are saved; the masses, the lower castes, and unreformed sinners are not saved. Not yet, at any rate.

BLOWING OFF THE ROOF

But later bhakti texts blast through this impasse. The spirit of these texts is what Mircea Eliade celebrated as "breaking open the roof" (*briser le toit*),[81] and the later Puranas did it, cracking open the egg of the closed universe. We have seen one example of this sort of cosmological transformation in two different versions of hell, first with a *Mahabharata* king (Yudhishthira) who cannot transfer his personal good karma and then with a Puranic king (Vipashchit) who can. Now we will encounter a mythology in which, again, sinners are given good karma that they don't deserve, but since now it is a god, rather than a human king, who transfers his powers, his compassion and forgiveness, the god, unlike the king, loses nothing by it, none of his good karma. The world of limited good gives way to a world of infinitely expansible good karma and bhakti; the generous donor keeps it all while the sinners benefit from it too, just as in the avatar the god remains entire in heaven even while he gives a portion of himself to the avatar on earth. Unlike texts such as the *Gita,* these texts are saying that even without bhakti on your part you can be saved from your sins; the god has enough bhakti for both of you.

In several of the late Puranic texts, when a shrine offers universal access to heaven, raising the gods' hackles, Shiva intervenes, preserves or restores the shrine, and takes everyone to "the abode of Brahma."[82] When the god of hell, Yama, complains that women, Shudras, and dog cookers all are going to heaven through one particular shrine, the Shaiva shrine of Somnath, putting Yama out of work, Shiva replies that they all have been purified by the sight of the shrine, and he dismisses Yama without another word.[83] To the complaint that heaven is full of evil people, Shiva simply replies that the people in question are no longer evil, ignoring the other half of the complaint, that heaven is full, or Yama on the dole. (Somnath is, the reader will recall, the temple that Mahmud of Ghazni so notoriously destroyed in 1025, perhaps before this text was composed.) Apparently, Shiva's new heaven cannot be filled; these texts imagine a new heaven that can stretch the envelope to accommodate everyone.[84] Earlier the shape of the universe seemed to constrain the ethical possibilities, but when those possibilities grow intense, the cosmos changes its shape, and this in turn can change the way that human beings treat one another, at least in theory and perhaps in practice. As in the *Gita,* the payoff is still in the next life. Most of these texts are not saying that a Pariah can act like a Brahmin in this life, merely that he too can be freed from this life. But some of them seem to imply that people of all castes can change their forms of worship in *this* life and thus gain a better rebirth. And here again we must acknowledge that these stories are not merely about Pariahs but also about the relationship between all humans and their salvation.

ACCIDENTAL GRACE

Under the combined influence of bhakti, Deshification, and Islam, some texts take the challenge one step further. Now the god to whom the antigod is devoted comes to him and announces that he and all the other antigods are to be taken forever to the heaven of the god, which can accommodate not only all reformed sinners but even *unreformed* sinners too, as well as people of all classes.[85] Indeed this heaven is *particularly* partial to unreformed sinners. This is the culminating myth of the third alliance: The gods love all of us, even the good (hence bad) antigods and, especially, the bad antigods. This is a world of not only unlimited good but undeserved good, of what might be called accidental grace.

We can see a kind of development here. First comes the story of the good bhakta, a good man, a devotee of Shiva, whom Shiva saves from death; there are many stories of this type.[86] Then comes the evil bhakta. The god of death is forced to spare all worshipers of Shiva, even if they are evildoers (or evil thinkers; heretics and liars also go to heaven if they worship Shiva) or antigods who worship Shiva against their *sva-dharma* of being evil;[87] we have seen some of these. Then comes the story of a man who is neither good nor a bhakta:

THE THIEF WHO RANG THE BELL

A thief who killed Brahmins, drank wine, stole gold, and corrupted other men's wives lost everything in a game of dice. That night he climbed on the head of a Shiva-linga and took away the bell [inadvertently ringing it]. Shiva sent his servants to the thief and brought him to Kailasa, where he became a servant of Shiva.[88]

Three of the thief's sins are those of lustful addiction—wine, women, and dice—and the fourth and fifth are the two defining sins of the Brahmin world:

killing Brahmins and stealing (Brahmins') gold. The thief's brush with accidental bhakti does nothing at all to change him; presumably, he goes on dicing, womanizing, and drinking until he dies. Although in some stories the accidental act of worship changes the worshiper, more often the sinners remain unreformed like this and therefore (*sic*) go to heaven.

Here is another story, about a very bad man, this one ironically named Ocean of Virtues (Gunanidhi):

THE ADULTERER WHO LIT A LAMP

Gunanidhi abandoned his wife for a prostitute and went to a temple at night to rob it; he made a new wick for the lamp in order to see what was worth stealing, found the treasure, took it, and then returned to his wicked ways. Years later, when he died, he won deliverance from hell and eternal life in heaven because he had lit a lamp for the god.[89]

(Robbing temples, you will recall, was a very real problem at this time: South Indian kings, Muslim conquerors, everyone was doing it.) Similarly, Devaraja ("King of the Gods"), a thoroughly no-good fellow, accidentally heard the *Shiva Purana* being recited when he was passing by on some foul errand, paid no attention to it at all, but was still saved, by that contact, from the consequences of his sins.[90] Then there was the man of equally dastardly deeds, named Rogue (Kitava), who tripped while hastening to bring flowers to his whore; he fell down, dropped all the flowers, and cried out, "Shiva!"* For offering flowers to Shiva, not only was he saved from being thrown into hell but he was given the throne of Indra, king of the gods, thus fulfilling his name. (He was eventually reborn as the antigod Bali, but that is another story.)[91]

None of these sinners reforms as a result of his accidental encounter with the god; no one sees the light or turns over a new page; all go on whoring, robbing, and so forth until they die, presumably of syphilis, cirrhosis, or impalement. But the mere encounter is enough to save them. The theme of the undeserving devotee implicitly repositions ritualism, even apparently "mindless" ritualism, over bhakti. It argues that feelings, emotions, intentions do not count at all, that certain actions are efficacious in themselves in procuring salvation for the unwitting devotee. You don't even have to know how to do the ritual, but you do it "naturally," almost like the "natural" (*sahaja*) acts of Tantric ritual. In this

---

* As Ramananda cried out the name of Ram when Kabir tripped him.

sense, at least, these stories present a Tantric argument for the efficacy of a ritual useful for sinners in the Kali Age.

These narratives seem counterintuitive and were perceived as perverse by some subsequent Hindu commentators. But where did the idea come from?

Retracing our footsteps, we can see the early stirrings of this concept of the sinner who goes to heaven despite his intentions, in the South Indian idea of "hate-devotion," which takes on new dimensions in the late Puranas. By trying to kill the god, the antigod becomes passionate toward the god, and so the god loves the antigod, with or without repentance.[92] After Krishna killed the ogress Putana ("Stinky"), her body gave off a sweet smell when it burned, for she had been purified by her death at his hands and by suckling him—even though she had done it with the intention of poisoning him. This doctrine, though sometimes challenged in bhakti texts that demanded a conscious turning toward god, was often upheld in texts justifying heresies: "Those who become non-Vedic Pashupatas and decry Vishnu really worship him through the spirit of hatred [*dvesha-buddhi*]."[93] The *Bhagavata Purana* makes explicit the effect of this belief: "Desire, hatred, fear, or love toward the lord, filling the heart with bhakti, destroy all sins and bind one to the lord: The Gopis by desire, Kamsa by fear, the wicked kings by hatred, and his kinsmen by affection were bound to him as we are by bhakti."[94] Other elements too contributed to the development of the idea of accidental grace, such as the Tantric goal of merging with the god by flouting all the rules of conventional dharma.

By the Grace of Dog

In keeping with the other reversals of caste rules, dogs often play important roles in this theology:

THE TRIDENT PAW

An evil thief was killed by the king's men. A dog came to eat him, and accidentally, unthinkingly, the dog's nails made the mark of Shiva's trident on the man's forehead. As a result, Shiva's messengers took the thief to Kailasa.[95]

Now the dog, instead of the sinner, performs an accidental act of worship, as the three scratches of his nails (part of his foot, the lowest part of this lowest of creatures) form the triple lines of Shiva's trident (*trishula*), just as Kannappar's dogs left their paw marks on Shiva, and the natural genitals of male and female Tantrics are read as the signs of Shiva and Parvati. The thief's generosity to the dog is part of his bhakti to the god. The dog who intends to eat the thief (and perhaps succeeds; the text does not say) unthinkingly blesses him. The thief goes to heaven, though the dog does not.

Another dog blesses the sinner who feeds him in a retelling of the story of Kannappar, in the *Skanda Purana:*

THE ACCIDENTALLY FED DOG

Once upon a time there was a certain Kirata named Chanda ["Fierce"], a man of cruel addictions. He killed fish and animals and birds and even Brahmins, and his wife was just like him. One night, on the great Night of Shiva, he spent the night in a *bilva* tree, wide awake, hoping to kill a wild boar. There happened to be a Shiva linga under the tree. The leaves of the *bilva* tree [used in Shiva worship] that the hunter cut off to get a better view fell on the Shiva linga, and mouthfuls of water that he spat out chanced to land there too. And so, unknowingly, he performed a *puja.* His wife too stayed up all night worrying about him, for she feared he had been killed. But she went and found him and brought him food, and while they were bathing before their meal, a dog came and ate all the food. She became angry and started to kill the dog, but Chanda said, "It gives me great satisfaction to know that the dog has eaten the food. What use is this body anyway? Don't be angry." And so he enlightened her.

Shiva sent his messengers with a heavenly chariot to take the Kirata to the world of Shiva, with his wife, because he had worshiped the linga on the Night of Shiva. But the Kirata said, "I am a violent hunter, a sinner. How can I go to heaven? How did I worship the Shiva-linga?" Then they told him how he had cut the *bilva* leaves and put them on the head of the linga, and he and his wife had stayed awake and fasted. And they brought the couple to heaven.[96]

By eating the food, the dog inadvertently causes the Kirata and his wife to give food, a part of the *puja* that, like staying up all night, is prescribed for the Night of Shiva. Thus this story recapitulates and integrates three stories: of linga worship by mouthfuls of unclean food from a hunter (the tale of Kannappar), of inadvertent worship by someone violating Hindu dharma, and of salvation for a man touched by a dog. It also includes the man's wife in the process of his salvation. Luck plays a part too.

The Tantric argument that low people have to have low (or at least very simple and easy) sources of grace underlies a more complex story of salvation by dog, a variant of the myth of the evil king Vena,[97] father of the good king Prithu:

THE DOG THAT BROKE THE CHAIN OF EVIL

As a result of his sins, Vena was born among the barbarians, afflicted with leprosy. He went to purify himself at the shrine of Shiva the Pillar (Sthanu), but the gods forbade him to bathe there. Now, there was a dog there who had been a man in a previous life but had been sinful and hence reborn as a dog. The dog came to the Sarasvati River and swam there, and his impurities were shaken off and his thirst slaked. Then he was hungry and entered Vena's hut; when Vena saw the dog, he was afraid. Vena touched him gently, and the dog showered him with water from the bathing place. Vena plunged into the water, and by the power of the shrine, he was saved. Shiva offered Vena a boon, and Vena said, "I plunged into the lake out of fear of this dog, for the gods forbade me to bathe here. The dog did me a favor, and so I ask you to favor him." Shiva was pleased and promised that the dog would be freed from sin and would go straight to Shiva's heaven. And he promised Vena that he too would go to Shiva's heaven—for a while.[98]

The unclean dog first is cleansed and then transfers the water from his body to that of Vena, by shaking himself (as wet dogs always do); only then does he frighten Vena so much that Vena jumps into the water. I take the text to mean that Vena could jump into the water only after the dog had sprinkled him. He cannot enter the shrine before that, for reasons that are spelled out in another version of the story: As he approaches the shrine of Sthanu, the wind in the sky says, "Do not do this rash deed; protect the shrine. This man is enveloped in an evil so terrible that it would destroy the shrine."[99] This is the catch-22: The sinner would pollute the shrine before the shrine could purify the sinner; the sick man is too sick to take the medicine. The idea of contamination by contact with evil, transfer of evil, a variant of transfer of karma, comes from the zero-sum world of caste pollution; it determines whom you should avoid touching, the basis of the concept of untouchability. By contrast, the world of bhakti brings an open cosmogony and a new vision of the accidental grace of god (and of dog), both a response to and an inspiration for new visions of the grace that is possible for and between all human beings, including those of the excluded social classes. It's a way of making room for people who have been kept outside the system, either by birth or by actions, since actions, as well as birth, can pollute people and marginalize them.

The dog therefore intercedes for the sinner. He makes him a little less polluted, so that he becomes eligible for real purification. Similarly, the heretics to whom Shiva teaches the Tantras need to have worked off the curse, to have started on the path upward, before he can give them the Tantras, and in the view of some non-Tantrics, the Tantras make the Tantrics a little less benighted, so that they become eligible for real religion. Vena is not finished yet; there are other rebirths before he is finally freed. But the dog makes it possible for him to proceed on the path to his salvation. And finally, at the end of the myth, and a millennium or two after Yudhishthira's dog in the *Mahabharata* vanished before he could enter heaven, this dog enters Shiva's heaven.

CHAPTER 18

PHILOSOPHICAL FEUDS IN SOUTH INDIA AND KASHMIR

800 to 1300 CE

CHRONOLOGY (ALL DATES ARE CE)

c. 788–820 Shankara, nondualist philosopher, lives in Kerala
c. 975–1025 Abhinavagupta, Shaiva philosopher, lives in Kashmir
1021 Ghaznavid (Turkish) Muslim capital established at Lahore
c. 1056–1137 Ramanuja, qualified nondualist philosopher, lives in Tamil country
1192 Ghorid Muslim capital established at Delhi
c. 1200 Jayadeva lives in Bengal
1210–1526 The Delhi Sultanate is in power
c. 1238–1317 Madhva, dualist philosopher, lives in Karnataka
c. 1300 Shri Vaishnavas split into Cats and Monkeys

> In those long-gone days the Valley, which is now simply K, had other names. . . . "Kache-Mer" can be translated as "the place that hides a Sea." But "Kosh-mar" . . . was the word for "nightmare."*
>
> Salman Rushdie, *Haroun and the Sea of Stories* (1990)[1]

The sea that Kashmir hides (in this wordplay by Salman Rushdie) is the great Sanskrit Ocean of Story, composed in Kashmir, which Rushdie imagines submerged like other flooded lands in the Indian imagination. Kashmir is also

* Local Kashmiri etymologies include Ka-shush ("to dry up water"), Kashyapa Mir (the lake of the sage Kashyapa) or Kashyapa Meru (Kashyapa's Mount Meru). In English, it is a precious wool whose name means "nothing but money" (cashmere).

the home of several famous debates about the philosophy of illusion, the belief that this world is nothing but a dream—or a nightmare. In this chapter we will consider those debates in narratives about quarrelsome philosophers, philosophical animals, and the recurrent Hindu nightmare of becoming a Pariah or a woman.

PHILOSOPHICAL SCHOOLS

Back to the banyan. Again we must double back to take a look at another branch of that tree, the philosophical branch, returning to the era of the beginning of bhakti in South India and the beginning of the Arab presence in India. The chapters on those two themes also provide the historical background for this chapter, which is about philosophy not as philosophy but as part of Hindu myth and ritual, in part because I am no philosopher and in part because that is not what this book is about, two not unrelated considerations. So I will deal with philosophy only when it gets out of the hands of the philosophers and into the hands of the people who tell stories about the philosophers and incorporate philosophical theories into their myths. For philosophy in India is debated in the worship life of ordinary people.

My focus in this chapter will be on the myths that Hindus told about three great Vedantic philosophers, particularly (continuing the theme of inter- and intrareligious dialogue) stories that the followers of one philosopher told about another philosopher, and on myths that apply the philosophy of illusion to caste and gender and to the householder/renunciant tension, since one of the main arrows in the quiver of renunciation is the argument that the material world is not merely a deathtrap but an *unreal* deathtrap.

Since this approach will ignore many other important philosophical themes, let me at least set the stage by *briefly* outlining the basic positions of the major schools of Hindu philosophy, the six Darshanas or "Points of View." These schools had taken root in earlier centuries but became more fully developed from the twelfth century on, in conversation with one another.

1. Mimamsa ("Critical Inquiry") began with Jaimini (c. 400 BCE) and was devoted to the interpretation of the Vedas, taking the Vedas as the authority for dharma and karma. Jaimini guaranteed the sacrificer life in heaven after death and decreed that women could sacrifice but Shudras could not.[2]

2. Vaisheshika began with Kanada (c. third century BCE), who presented an atomic cosmology, according to which all material objects are made of atoms of the nine elements: the four material elements—earth, water, fire, and air—plus five more abstract elements—space, time, ether, mind, and soul. In this view, god created the world, but not ex nihilo; he simply imposed order on pre-existing atoms. Shankara called the Vaisheshikas half nihilists.[3]

3. Logic and reasoning began with Gautama (c. second century BCE, no relation to the Buddhist Gautama) and was an analytical philosophy basic not only to all later Hindu philosophy but to the scientific literature of the *shastras*.

4. Patanjali's *Yoga-Sutras* (c. 150 BCE) codified yogic practices that had been in place for centuries. Yoga assumes a personal god who controls the process of periodic creation and dissolution and is omniscient and omnipotent. This school emphasized exercises of the mind and the body, "including the very difficult exercise of not exercising them at all."[4] It believed that *moksha* came not from knowledge but from the concentration and discipline of the mind and the body.

5. Sankhya as a philosophy has roots that date from the time of the Upanishads and are important in the *Mahabharata* (especially in the *Gita*) but were first formally codified by Ishvarakrishna (c. third century CE). Sankhya is dualistic, dividing the universe into a male *purusha* (spirit, self, or person) and a female *prakriti* (matter, nature). There are an infinite number of similar but separate *purushas*, no one superior to another.[5] Early Sankhya philosophers argued that god may or may not exist but is not needed to explain the universe; later Sankhya philosophers assumed that god does exist.

6. And then comes Vedanta, the philosophical school that reads the Upanishads through the lens of the unity of the self (*atman*) and the cosmic principle (*brahman*). Often expressed in the form of commentaries on the Upanishads, on the *Gita*, and on Badarayana's *Vedanta-Sutras* (c. 400 BCE), different branches of Vedanta tend to relegate the phenomenal world to the status of an epistemological error (*avidya*), a psychological imposition (*adhyaya*), or a metaphysical illusion (*maya*). Evil too, which the myths struggle to deal with, and, especially, death turn out to be nothing but an illusion.

The great phase of Vedanta began with three great South Indian philosophers, all of whom were Brahmins.[6] A basic schism separated the dualists, who argued that god and the universe (including the worshiper) were of two distinct substances, and the nondualists, who argued that they were of the same substance. Shankara, from Kerala, was a Shaiva exponent of pure nondualism (Advaita) and idealism. Ramanuja, from Kanchipuram (Kanjeevaram), in Tamil country, was a Tamil Vaishnava exponent of qualified nondualism (Vishishta Advaita) and of the religion of the Shri Vaishnavas (see below), who call their tradition the dual Vedanta because it combines the Sanskrit of the Veda with the Tamil of the Alvars.[7] Madhva, also known as Madhvacharya ("Madhva the Teacher"), from Kalyan (in Karnataka), was the founder of the dualist (Dvaita) school of Vedanta. The followers, and opponents, of these three philosophers told many stories about them, from which we can gather some of the human implications of their philosophies and the wide range of diverse voices encoded in them. They were the subjects of a body of mythology in the style of the Puranas, which dramatized their views and assimilated those views to the hagiographic and folk traditions. For their philosophies were not limited to an elite circle of intellectuals but deeply affected devotional Hinduism, trickling down through mythology and folklore.

Vedantic Vendettas in Medieval Narratives

In medieval India, people cared about philosophy enough to fight about it. The "Conquest of the Four Corners of the World" (*dig-vijaya*), originally a royal and military concept, then a metaphor for a great pilgrimage tour, also became the term for the conquest of one philosopher by another.[8] The philosophers fought mostly with words, occasionally with miracles (like the texts that floated upstream in the South Indian contest), more often with (and for) the purses of their patrons, and rarely with fisticuffs. They met on the page or the debating platform, not the battlefield. (Or almost always. It did come to fisticuffs at least once, according to an amazing painting in an illustrated copy of the *Akbarnama*, said to depict "the Emperor Akbar watching a fight between two bands of Hindu devotees at Thaneshwar, Punjab, 1597–8." There is close combat between dozens of yogis and ascetics and devotees of all stripes, shooting arrows from bows and slashing away at one another with swords, knives, and what appears to be anything else at hand.[9])

We have already encountered myths about the preaching of false philosophical and theological doctrines, in the course of Shiva's conflicts with Daksha and Vishnu's avatar as the Buddha. We have traced a rough (and not precisely chronological) progression of the myths of the Buddha avatar through three stages, from the assimilation of Buddhism into Hinduism, to the antagonistic myths of opposition to a Buddhism on the rise, and then to more appreciative myths about a Buddhism on the wane. Now we encounter a fourth stage, in which Buddhism once again contributed in positive ways to the philosophy of idealism in South India and Kashmir (see below), while much of the former animosity against the Buddhists was channeled into animosity against Shankara, in myths modeled in many ways on the myth of Vishnu as the Buddha. Let us consider some of those myths.

SHANKARA STORIES

Shankara's texts speak for his ideas, but the legends about him speak for his life. He is said to have started a reform movement, proposing a moral agenda that could compete with the noble eightfold path of the Buddhists[10] (he was, as we will see, sometimes accused of owing too much to Buddhism) and a philosophy that may have been buoyed up by a need to respond to the monotheist philosophies of Islam. Shankara, regarded as a guru and proselytizer as well as a philosopher, is said to have founded the centers of learning (*matts*) that still thrive in his name in India today; his argument that the phenomenal world of everyday experience and its biological round of birth and death (*samsara*) was ultimately unreal and the source of our bondage was taken as the basis for a monastic or ascetic life of renunciation (*samnyasa*).[11]

But Shankara argued that only Brahmins could renounce,[12] and some of the more general animus against renunciation was channeled into hostility against him. While there had been renouncers in Hinduism since before the time the Upanishads mapped out the path of flame and Release, they lacked the institutional backing to become a major force—until Shankara. But Shankara took the idea of formal monastic orders and institutions from Buddhism and reworked it for Hinduism, an action that stirred up some Brahmins like a saffron flag waved in front of a bull. Ramanuja called Shankara a "crypto-Buddhist" (*prachanna-bauddha*).[13]

Shankara's nondualism was challenged first by Ramanuja's qualified nondualism and, later, by Madhva's dualism; the followers of Madhva argued that Shankara championed monism because he was so stupid that he could only count to one.[14] Nondualism has the disadvantage that you cannot love god or worship god if you *are* god, or if your god is without any qualities (*nir-guna*), a technicality that Shankara allegedly ignored when he wrote the passionate, beautiful poems to Shiva that are attributed to him. Nondualists could get around this by worshiping god with a kind of "as if" for the forms "with qualities" (*sa-guna*): He appears "as if" he were a god with qualities. If, however, you assume that there is a dualism separating you from god and that god has qualities, as Madhva assumes, worship poses no problem.

The hagiographies of Shankara arise at a time when (1) bhakti is rampant, spreading so fast that it even gets into philosophy, like ants at a picnic, and (2) Buddhists and Muslims, as well as Christians in Kerala (Shankara's home territory), are gaining ground. And so, just as the human avatars were in part a response to the human dimension of Buddhism in an earlier age, Shankara, someone who was, like the Buddha (and Muhammad and Jesus), a human founder of a religion, was the answer now.

Born into a high-caste Brahmin family, Shankara taught and debated with many other philosophers. In his journeys throughout India, his biographies claim, he vehemently debated with Buddhists and tried to persuade kings and other influential people to withdraw their support from Buddhist monasteries. One text depicts Shankara as an incarnation of Shiva, sent to earth to combat Vishnu's Buddha avatar:

SHIVA AS SHANKARA VERSUS VISHNU AS BUDDHA

The gods complained to Shiva that Vishnu had entered the body of the Buddha on earth for their sake, but now the haters of religion, despising Brahmins and the dharma of class and stage of life, filled the earth. "Not a single man performs a ritual, for all have become heretics—Buddhists, Kapalikas, and so forth—and so we eat no offerings." Shiva consented to become incarnate as Shankara, to reestablish Vedic dharma, which keeps the universe happy, and to destroy evil behavior.[15]

As usual, the heresy goes too far, destroying the allies as well as the enemies of the gods, and must be combated by the intervention of god.

The myths from this period reveal that it wasn't only non-Hindus in conflict with Shankara; Mimamsa philosophers and other Vedanta schools also apparently had tense relations with Shankara, some of which turned on the question of renouncing desire and sexuality:

SHANKARA AND THE PHILOSOPHER'S WIFE

The Mimamsa philosopher named Mandanamishra had a wife, Bharati, who challenged Shankara to a debate about the art of love, about which he was woefully ignorant, since he had always been chaste, a renouncer. Stymied by a question about sex, he asked for time out and took on the body, but not the soul, of a king who had a large harem, to the relief both of the exhausted king and of the unsatisfied women. After a month of pleasant research and fieldwork, Shankara returned to his philosophical body and won the argument. Both Bharati and her husband then became nondualists.[16]

This tale contrasts sex and renunciation in such a way that the renunciant philosopher is able to have his cake and eat it, to triumph not only in the world of the mind (in which, before this episode begins, he wins a series of debates against the nonrenouncing male Mimamsa philosopher) but in the world of the body, represented by the philosopher's wife (not to mention the harem women who clearly prefer Shankara to the king in bed). This double superiority—for it appears that, like Shiva, this Shankara stored up impressive erotic powers during his years of chastity—rather than the inherent power (or relevance) of nondualism, is apparently what persuades both the philosopher and his wife.

Renunciation took its toll on parents as well as partners, and this story addresses that issue:

SHANKARA AND THE CROCODILE

As a young boy of eight, Shankara is said to have vowed to become a renouncer, to the dismay of his mother, who kept postponing the moment when she would give him her permission. One day while he was bathing in a river a crocodile grabbed his leg. He shouted out, and his mother came to the riverbank. As he was presumably going to die right away, and this was his last chance to achieve Release, the only hope was for him to become a renouncer there and then. His mother agreed, whereupon the crocodile let him go. He became a renouncer but promised his mother he would be with her during her last days and perform her funeral rites, which he did.[17]

This is a story about the need to compromise, to satisfy the concerns of family as well as renunciation—parents want to see their grandchildren—but it is built upon an old story that had been told before to make very different points. The

Rig Veda (10.28.11) mentions crocodiles that drag people away by their legs; the bodhisattva (in a Jataka story carved at Amaravati) and Vishnu[18] are said to have rescued an elephant whose leg had been grabbed by a crocodile, and the Shaiva saint Cuntarar (the same one said to have contested with the Jainas) saves a Brahmin boy from a crocodile. It is easy to see how this story could have been picked up and adapted to the needs of the hagiographers of Shankara.

STORIES OF RAMANUJA AND MADHVA

The chain of sectarian myths does not end with Shankara. Many stories are told about Ramanuja's clash not with disciples of Shankara but with other Shaivas. Ramanuja is said to have challenged the Shaivas in a great temple in Andhra Pradesh; he won not by debate but by the god's action in "picking up and wearing the Vaishnava emblems, while leaving the Shaiva emblems unused on the floor."[19] On another occasion, the Chola king, a Shaiva, tried to make Ramanuja sign a declaration that there was no god but Shiva, but Ramanuja sent two of his disciples, one of them dressed to look like him, in his place; when one of them made a pun on the word "Shiva," the king ordered both men's eyes put out. Ramanuja escaped to Mysore, where he is said to have converted the Hoysala king from Jainism to Shri Vaishnavism and persuaded him to endow a number of Vaishnava temples with lands that had previously belonged to many Jaina temples.

There are also stories of Ramanuja's actions against Muslims, as when he went to Delhi to help recover the lost image of Ranganatha: he found the image, cried, "Beloved son!" and the image jumped into his arms.[20] Ramanuja is also said to have defeated a thousand Jaina ascetics in a debate involving a contest of miracles, whereupon the Jaina monks committed suicide rather than convert.[21] The martyrdom by blinding, the miraculous debate, and the deaths of thousands of Jainas are reminiscent of other South Indian tales told about Shaiva saints, and these about Ramanuja are equally mythological: The historical record documents no mass suicides (or, for that matter, miracles). Most of the kings of that era were not fanatics but supported Shaiva, Vaishnava, Jaina, and Buddhist institutions, nor is there any evidence that the Hoysala king was originally a Jaina or withdrew his supported from the Jainas.[22] But the stories have survived for centuries.

Shankara's followers often came into conflict with the followers of the Vaishnava philosopher Madhva, who is said to have accomplished a number of miracles, some of which were also attributed to Christ in the New Testament:

walking on water,[23] feeding many with a few loaves of bread, calming rough waters, and becoming a "fisher of men."[24] Madhva (or his hagiographers) may have been influenced by Christians, who had been established, since at least the sixth century CE, in Kerala and at Kalyan (in Karnataka), Madhva's birthplace. But it is Buddhism, rather than Christianity, that figures officially in Madhva's conflict with Shaivas. For Madhva placed another new twist on the myth of the Buddha avatar, substituting the Shaiva scriptures for the Buddhist doctrines: Citing a Puranic text in which Shiva agrees to teach false doctrines,[25] Madhva said that Shiva composed the Shaiva scriptures at Vishnu's command, in order to delude humans with false doctrines, to destroy the true religion (the worship of Vishnu), to reveal Shiva, and to conceal Vishnu.[26] And this was just the beginning:[27]

MADHVA VERSUS SHANKARA

At the beginning of the Kali Age, the earth was under the sway of Buddhism. Then an ogre named Manimat was born as a widow's bastard's son, named Sankara [sic]. He seduced the wife of his Brahmin host and made many converts by his magic arts. He studied the *shastra*s with Shiva's blessings. The depraved welcomed him and the antigods hailed him as their savior. On their advice, he joined the Buddhists and taught Buddhism under cover of teaching the Vedanta, and he performed various wicked deeds. His doctrines were like those of the Materialists [Lokayatas], Jainas, and Pashupatas, but more obnoxious and injurious. His followers were tyrannical people who burned down monasteries, destroyed cattle, and killed women and children. He had people whipped because they were not Vedic and converted others by force. When he died, the god of the wind became incarnate as Madhva, to refute the teachings of Manimat-Sankara.[28]

The accusation that Shankara seduced the wife of his Brahmin host may be an allusion to the story of Shankara's vying with the Mimamsa philosopher's wife on the subject of erotic seduction (and using his magic arts to sleep with a king's wives), and the accusation that he pretended to be teaching Vedanta when he taught Buddhism is a product of the recurrent suspicion of Buddhist elements in Shankara's brand of Vedanta. In this text, Manimat joins the already extant Buddhists (instead of founding them, as Vishnu as Buddha does), reverses the incarnation of Shankara (who is now an avatar not of Shiva but of an ogre named Manimat), and is followed by a third avatar, of the god of the wind as

Madhva.* The idea that the gods are sent to corrupt the antigods (as in the myth of the Buddha avatar), combined with the implication that the resulting heretics are antigods (or related to antigods in some way), undergoes a major reversal: The antigods now are not the ones who are corrupted but the ones who do the corrupting. The Madhvas' identification of Shankara as an antigod is particularly harsh in light of the fact that the Madhvas, almost alone among Hindu philosophers, believe that antigods and heretics are doomed to eternal damnation in hell. Finally, this corruption takes place, as usual, in the Kali Age, and the Madhvas take advantage of this to pun on the name of their enemy: Shankara ("he who gives peace," an epithet of Shiva given to many Shaivas) becomes Sankara (also written *sam-kara*), a word that denotes indiscriminate mixture, particularly the breaking down of barriers between classes that is the principal sign of the advent of the Kali Age. In keeping with this name, Sankara is said to be the bastard son of a widow.[29]

MONISM AND CONVERSION IN VEDANTA

One of the philosophical reactions against the excessive hierarchy of the caste system was to devise (or, rather, to revise, for it began in the Upanishads) a philosophical system devoid of hierarchy, indeed of any distinctions at all: monism (which assumes that all living things are elements of a single, universal being). But many of the Vedantic philosophical orders organized themselves into groups that were in fact highly hierarchical (for example, as we have seen, Shankara excluded Shudras) and often intolerant of other orders.

The monistic philosophers asserted that there was one truth, which they knew, and so they proceeded to proselytize. Logically, Hindu universalism (of the sort that assumed that all religions have access to the truth) should have led polytheistic Hindus to the belief that there was no point in trying to convert anyone else to Hinduism, yet this was not always the case. Orthoprax Vedic Hindus certainly made no efforts to proselytize, assuming that you had to be born a Hindu to be a Hindu. But some of the Vedantic Hindus, lapsing into the shadows of orthodoxy,† argued that *their* particular brand of monism was

---

* In the *Mahabharata* (3.157.57–70), Bhima, the son of the god of the wind (Vayu), kills an ogre named Manimat, the ogre who (the followers of Madhva say) was to become Sankara in a later incarnation. According to later followers of Madhva, Madhva himself rewrote and completed this passage of the *Mahabharata*.

† Their renunciant branches also shared with other renunciant orders an emphasis on practices; where orthoprax Hinduism was concerned with regulating the behavior of lay people, renunciant orders (Hindu, Buddhist, or Jaina) focused on the correct practices of monks.

more monistic than thine and did indeed proselytize. And although proselytizing is not in itself necessarily intolerant, it does close the open-ended door of pluralism.

PHILOSOPHICAL ANIMALS

The quarrels of these great South Indian philosophers had repercussions throughout India, particularly in far-off Kashmir. It all began with two South Indian sects that expressed their doctrines primarily through animal metaphors.

SHAIVA SIDDHANTA BEASTS IN A SNARE

One movement for which animal metaphors were central was the Shaiva Siddhanta, which arose at this time in South India to cast a net of theory around some of the unrulier aspects of bhakti. Among other things, it theologized the doctrine of accidental grace.

The philosophy of Shaiva Siddhanta traces its roots back in a general way to the devotional hymns that the Shaiva Nayanmars had written from the fifth to the ninth century. That tradition found its way up to Kashmir, to become one of the elements of Kashmir Shaivism in the ninth century CE. But then Tirumular, a mystic and reformer, is said to have come from Kashmir to South India to found the Shaiva Siddhanta philosophical school, and others* systematized the doctrines of the Nayanmars. The Shaiva Siddhanta in Kashmir had taken elements of Kashmir Tantrism and fused them into a householder's religion,[30] and the Southern Shaiva Siddhantins continued and intensified this transformation. It thrived under royal Hindu patronage and in powerful temple centers, reinfused with Tamil bhakti and transformed, in effect, from a philosophy into a powerful religious culture that thrives there today. Though the Shaiva Siddhantins paid lip service to the Vedas, they rejected caste (or, rather, they were open to everyone but women, children, the old, the mad, and the disabled[31]) and asceticism, and believed, like the Virashaivas, that the body is the true temple of Shiva. Theirs was a separate sect, established in Shaiva temples, into which members had to be initiated.[32] Like other aspects of bhakti, it spread north, reinfusing the Kashmir Shaivism that had in part inspired it.

---

* Bhojadeva (in the eleventh century), Aghorashiva (in the twelfth), and Meykandadevar (in the thirteenth).

In conscious opposition to the idealism and nondualism of both Shankara and Kashmir Shaivism, which regarded god and the soul as one and the universe as illusory, the Shaiva Siddhanta was a realistic and dualistic philosophy. It taught that the lord (*pati*) was not identical with the soul but connected to the soul (*pashu* ["the sacrificial or domesticated animal"]) by a bond (*pasha*), as a leash connects a dog (the ultimate *bhakta*) to its owner. The bond consists of Shiva's will and his power of illusion (*maya*), the illusion made of the universe of all mental and material phenomena—phenomena that, in contrast with the teachings of pure idealism, were real because they were divine.³³ Just as in Tantra Shiva makes some people heretics in the first place so that he can ultimately enlighten them, so in Shaiva Siddhanta he makes people into beasts so that he can release them from the condition of beasts; he deludes people in order to reveal their beast nature, lust and hatred, and then he releases them from that nature. The bond, which was the functional equivalent of bhakti in connecting the worshiper to the god, had negative as well as positive valences.³⁴

The central metaphor of the Shaiva Siddhanta became so well known in Hinduism that it was eventually adopted for uses far from its original meaning for the theologians who coined it, uses such as the literalizing of the metaphor in the actual sacrifice of a beast in a snare. For animal sacrifices continued to take place despite the growing force of the doctrine of nonviolence; the philosopher Madhva (like Manu before him) encouraged Hindus to substitute animals made of dough for real animals in sacrificial rituals,³⁵ and his need to make this suggestion, again, suggests that animals were still being sacrificed. The *Agni Purana* prescribes an animal sacrifice in the course of the initiation of a Vaishnava pupil by his guru, but it cloaks the ritual in euphemisms derived from the Shaiva Siddhanta:

LIBERATING THE BEAST FROM THE SNARE

Enter the temple of worship and worship the image of Vishnu while circumambulating him to the right, saying, "You alone are the refuge for Release from the snares that bind the beasts sunk in the ocean of rebirth; you always look upon your devotees as a cow looks upon her calf. God of gods, have mercy; by your favor, I will release all these beasts that are bound by the snares and bonds of nature." When you have announced this to the lord of gods, have the beasts enter there; purify them with the chants and perfect them with fire. Place them in contact with the image of Vishnu and close their eyes.³⁶

"Close their eyes" is a euphemism for killing the sacrificial animals: the Vedic texts used a different euphemism, speaking of "quieting" the animal. The killing is said to give the beast ultimate Release, here equated with release from the snares (or noose, or bonds) that we know from Shaiva Siddhanta terminology. In this text, however, these philosophies are embodied in an actual rather than a metaphorical beast and a real snare.

Shri Vaishnava Monkeys and Cats

Another South Indian movement, this one devoted to Vishnu rather than Shiva, used an animal analogy, and a maternal metaphor, to express a fork in the road to salvation. This was the Shri Vaishnava sect, which took shape when, in support of the rising sectarian movement of devotion to the child Krishna, Vaishnava theologians in the early medieval period (900–1300 CE) in South India established new scholastic and monastic lineages.[37] In the fourteenth century they branched into the Cat school (Tenkalai, in Tamil) in the south and the Monkey school (Vadakalai) in the north of the Tamil country.[38] Originally a split about a theological belief, epitomized by these two animals, it was caught up into the clash between two separate monastic centers vying for the control of temples, a dispute in which the king played a major adjudicating role:[39] Two Vijayanagara royal agents established the Cat school, and the priest of another king established the Monkey school by setting up a temple at Tirupati.

In the Monkey school, the devotee actively clings to god, who saves him through his grace, just as a baby monkey clings to its mother as she moves through the trees. In the Cat school, by contrast, the devotee is passive and is saved through grace alone, as kittens allow a mother cat to pick them up by the scruffs of their necks and carry them without any effort on their part. Indeed the Cat devotee should not make any effort, should go limp as a kitten, since any effort would simply get in the way of the mother cat. The passive, accidental bhakti of the Cats toward the grace of god was echoed in the doctrine of accidental grace toward unrepentant sinners in the theology of the later Puranas.

Both Cats and Monkeys value bhakti, but less than they value *prapatti* ("surrender"),* an idea that may owe something to the Muslim idea of surrender (which is what *Islam* means). Members of the Monkey school, who regarded

---

* The Shri Vaishnavas identify a number of scenes in the Valmiki *Ramayana* as paradigmatic exemplars of surrender; these include the moments when Lakshmana accompanies Rama to the forest, when Bharata receives Rama's sandals, when the ocean allows Rama to cross over to Lanka, and, especially, the moment when Ravana's brother Vibhishana surrenders politically to Rama.

themselves as twice born people liberated through ritual devotion, sometimes said that the Cat school was designed for the lower castes, because they were not allowed in temples and hence were unable to perform the rituals and could be liberated only through surrender. They therefore regarded Cat bhakti as necessary for those castes, like the Tantras in the Puranic view.

THE SNAKE AND THE ROPE

Another important philosophical animal was the illusory snake that was really a rope. For the Vedantins, the claim that the world is unreal does not mean that it is entirely unreal in the way that the son of a barren woman (a favorite Vedantic example) is unreal. There is, in some sense, a rope, and, at a deeper level, *brahman* does in fact exist. The error lies, rather, in our perception of the rope as something it isn't (the snake).

Unlike other topics that only erudite Indian philosophers wrestled with, illusion got into the very fabric of Hindu culture, so that just about everyone knows about *maya* and the difficulty of telling a snake from a rope. *Maya* (from the verb *ma* ["to make"]) is what is made, artificial, constructed, something that seems to be there but has no substance; it is the path of rebirth, the worship of gods with qualities (*sa-guna*). It is magic, cosmic sleight of hand. *Maya* begins in the earliest text, the *Rig Veda* (1.32) in which the god Indra (the first great magician; magic is called Indra's Net [*indra-jala*]) uses his magic against his equally magical enemy Vritra (for all the antigods are magicians): Indra magically turns himself into the hair of one of his horses' tails, and Vritra magically conjures up a storm. Magic illusions of various sorts play a crucial role in the Valmiki *Ramayana,* in the shadow Sita of later traditions, and in Hindu thinking across the board.

As we have seen, the idea of darshan, of seeing the god and, more important, of knowing that the god sees you, is central to Hinduism and accounts for the extraordinary emphasis on the eyes in Hindu mythology. It was therefore a brilliant move of nondual Vedanta to reverse the valence of vision/sight/gaze by making the image of *false* seeing—of classically mistaking a rope for a snake or a piece of shell for a piece of silver—an enduring trope for the larger mistake of taking the visual world to be the real world. Nondualists imagined gods to be without any visual form or physical qualities (*nir-guna*) but to take on, for various reasons, apparent visual form and physical qualities (*sa-guna*) so that we can worship them. The gods themselves produce the illusion, just as they produce the deluding texts in the story of the Buddha avatar.

The Upanishads speak of four stages of consciousness: waking, dreaming, dreamless sleep, and "the fourth," the supernatural, transcendent state of identity with *brahman*.[40] Waking is the most distorted image of *brahman*, furthest from it; dreaming is a bit better, dreamless sleep better yet. To be enlightened is to realize that the stage of waking is the illusory end of the spectrum and to begin to progress toward the fourth stage. Or to put it differently, to realize that the stage of waking is the illusory end of the spectrum is to realize that dreaming is more real than is conventionally understood.[41] It is no accident that the word *svapna* in Sanskrit means both the physical state of "sleep" (the English word is a cognate of the Sanskrit) and the mental construct of "dream"; there is no difference between matter and mind.

Mistaking one thing for another, such as a rope for a snake, is easily rectified upon closer inspection, but the recollection of our false mental state before we took that second look may trigger our acknowledgment of the far more important mistake that we make all the time, in taking the material world to be real (*brahman*) when it is merely *maya*. When you realize that the snake is not a snake but a rope, you go on to realize that there is not even a rope at all.

ILLUSIONS OF CASTE AND GENDER IN THE *YOGAVASISHTHA*

The philosophy of illusion was developed in a particularly imaginative and brilliant way in the eleventh and twelfth centuries in Kashmir, with heavy input from South India. We have noted the communication back and forth between North and South India in the development of bhakti, Tantra, and the Shaiva Siddhanta. The extreme idealist position in the philosophy of illusion was developed by the Buddhist philosopher Nagarjuna, who is said to have been born a Brahmin in South India, converted to Buddhism, moved to Kashmir (where his school of idealism flourished during the Kushana period), and, when Buddhism came under attack in Kashmir, moved back to South India. Shaiva philosophers in Kashmir combined all these elements, including the Buddhist ideas, with the monistic ideas of Shankara and fused them into a new philosophy of their own, known as Kashmir Shaivism, also called the Recognition (Pratijna) school.[42] A key figure in this movement was the great Shaiva philosopher Abhinavagupta (975–1025), who was also largely responsible for developing the right-hand householder form of Tantrism. Jettisoning the dualism of Shaiva Siddhanta (while retaining much of its ritual), Kashmir Shaivism was relentlessly monistic.

Kashmir Shaivism had died out in Kashmir by the end of the twelfth century, in large part because of a hostile Muslim presence there,[43] and Shaiva

Siddhanta went back south, taking its dualism with it. But other traditions developed in Kashmir in this period not in spite of but because of the foreign presences there. The school of the Muslim philosopher Ibn 'Arabi (1165–1240), who argued that all that is not a part of divine reality is an illusion, is said to have had a major influence on Hindu philosophy at this time, while in return the use of heterosexual love as a symbol for divine love in a few Sufi scriptures from the Mughal period may have been inspired by Kashmiri Tantrism.[44]

Located as it is on the northern border of India, Kashmir is close to the Central Asian strongholds of Buddhism (whose philosophers developed their own major doctrines of illusion) and a number of Muslim (Turkish and Arabic) cultures with highly developed storytelling traditions that rivaled those of ancient India. Eventually a brand of idealist philosophy that was already a mix of Buddhism and Hinduism married a brand of storytelling that was already a mix of Hinduism and Islam, enlivened by a dash of Abhinavagupta's writings on the artistic transformation of the emotions. It was here, therefore, and at this time that the great Indian traditions of storytelling and illusion blossomed in the text of the great *Ocean of Story (Katha-sarit-sagara)* and, above all, in the *Yoga-vasishtha* (in full, the *Yoga-Vasishtha-Maha-Ramayana* or "The Great Story of Rama in Which Vasishtha Teaches His Yoga"). This text heavily influenced the collection of stories often called the *Arabian Nights,* a constantly shifting corpus with narrative traces as early as the tenth century, probably put together in the thirteenth century. Another, later contribution from Hinduism to Islam was made when the great Mughal emperor Akbar had the *Yoga-vasishtha* translated from Sanskrit to Persian; Nizam Panipati dedicated his abridged Persian translation to the crown prince Salim, who (when he became the emperor Jahangir) commissioned a new, illustrated translation.[45] The book became so famous that there were Persian and Arabic satires on it.[46]

That Kashmir Shaivism was called the Recognition school is not irrelevant to the main theme of the *Yoga-vasishtha* narratives, which turn on an individual's recognition of his or her own identity and ontological status. But the glory of the *Yoga-vasishtha* is that it transforms a rather difficult philosophy into a series of engaging narratives.* It all goes back, like so much else, to that fork in the road in the Upanishads. For Vedantic thinkers like Shankara, following the path of Release meant awakening from the dream of the material world to the

---

* George Gamow did the same thing for the speed of light and the quantum factor, in *Mr. Tomkins in Wonderland.*

reality of *brahman*. The twist that the *Yoga-vasishtha* adds is that you cannot wake up from the dream, because it may be someone else's dream.* For householders on the path of rebirth, Release means staying asleep but being aware that you are dreaming. This is also the message of a large corpus of myths in which kings, beginning with Indra, king of the gods, become enlightened, wish to awaken (that is, to renounce material life), but must be persuaded to renounce even the wish to renounce, to remain engaged in life with the major distinction of understanding that it is an illusion. It is a variant of the final advice that Krishna gives to Arjuna in the *Gita* (though the *Yoga-vasishtha* arrives at that point after a very different journey): Continue to act, though with a newly transformed understanding of the unreality of actions and therefore without the desire for the fruits of actions.

The frame story of the *Yoga-vasishtha* presents the text as an episode that Valmiki left out of his version of the *Ramayana;* it claims to fill in the supposed gaps in the older text on which it purports to be based, just as many folk versions of the *Ramayana* actually do.† It frames the story in terms of the ancient tension between the householder life and the truth claims of renunciation. The *Yoga-vasishtha* takes the form of a long conversation between Rama and the sage Vasishtha, at a moment when Rama has returned from a pilgrimage in a state of depression and madness (or so his father and the courtiers describe it): Rama says that anyone who says, "Act like a king," is out of his mind, that everything is unreal, that it is false to believe in the reality of the world, that everything is just the imagination of the mind. Rama's father consults two great sages (always get a second opinion), Vishvamitra and Vasishtha, who assure him that Rama is perfectly right in his understanding of the world, that he has become enlightened, and then offer to cure him.[47] That is, they promise to remove his depression and make him socially functional, while leaving his (correct) metaphysical apprehensions unimpaired.

THE ILLUSION OF GENDER

The *Yoga-vasishtha* tells a tale about another king who returns from renunciation to rule his kingdom and, along the way, realizes the illusory nature of both sex and gender:

---

* The idea that mental constructs are all that we have, and all that is real, is approximated, in our world, by the film *The Matrix* and, to a lesser extent, by *Total Recall.*
† Tom Stoppard's *Rosenkrantz and Guildenstern Are Dead* claims to fill in certain gaps that Shakespeare left in *Hamlet.*

CHUDALA: THE WOMAN WHO PRETENDED TO BE
A MAN WHO BECAME A WOMAN

Queen Chudala and her husband, King Shikhidhvaja, were passionately in love. In time, the queen became enlightened and acquired magic powers, including the ability to fly, but she concealed these powers from her husband, and when she attempted to instruct him, he spurned her as a foolish and presumptuous woman. Eventually the king decided to seek his own enlightenment and withdrew to the forest to meditate; he renounced his throne and refused to let her accompany him but left her to govern the kingdom.

After eighteen years she decided to visit him; she took the form of a young Brahmin boy named Kumbha ["Pot"] and was welcomed by the king, who did not recognize her but remarked that Chudala as Kumbha looked very much like his queen, Chudala. After a while the king became very fond of Chudala as Kumbha, who instructed him and enlightened him, and she began to be aroused by her handsome husband. And so Chudala as Kumbha went away for a while. When she returned, she told the king that a sage had cursed her to become a woman, with breasts and long hair, every night. That night, before the king's eyes, Chudala as Kumbha changed into a woman named Madanika, who cried out in a stammering voice, "I feel as if I am falling, trembling, melting. I am so ashamed as I see myself becoming a woman. Alas, my chest is sprouting breasts, and jewelry is growing right out of my body." Eventually they married and made love all night.

Thus they lived as dear friends during the day and as husband and wife at night. Eventually, the queen changed from Chudala as Kumbha as Madanika to Chudala and told the king all that she had done. He embraced her passionately and said, "You are the most wonderful wife who ever lived!" Then he made love to her all night and returned with her to resume his duties as king. He ruled for ten thousand years and finally attained Release.[48]

Chudala wishes to be her husband's mistress both in the sense of lover and in the sense of teacher, schoolmistress. She has already played the first role but is now denied it, and he refuses to grant her the second role, without relinquishing the first. She succeeds by destabilizing gender through a double gender transformation.

The double woman whom she creates—Chudala as Kumbha as Madanika— is her real self, the negation of the negation of her femininity; the jewelry that actually grows out of her body is what she would have worn as Queen Chudala at the start of the story. This double deception works well enough and may express her full fantasy: to be her husband's intellectual superior under the sun and his erotic partner by moonlight. But since the two roles belong to two different personae, she wants to merge them and to play them both as her original self.

The playful juggling of the genders demonstrates both the unreality of appearances and the falsity of the belief that one gender is better than the other or even different from the other. This extraordinary openness to gender bending in ancient India may be an indirect benefit of the rigid social order: Since other social categories are taken for granted, the text can use them as a springboard for gender role-playing. But the roles, when we look closer, revert to the rigid categories in the end. Chudala has to become a man to teach her husband, and she has to become a woman again to sleep with him. In the Hindu view, Chudala is like a man to begin with, aggressive, resourceful, and wise. Moreover, the relationship between Chudala and the king is never the relationship of a real husband and wife. She is a magician; in other times and places she might have been called a witch. She functions like a Yogini (she can fly) or perhaps even a goddess, giving him her grace and leading him up the garden path of enlightenment, setting up a divine illusion and then revealing herself to him as the gods reveal themselves.

Eventually Chudala repairs the split between *kama* and *moksha* by revealing the illusory nature of both sexual love and renunciation. Like Rama in the frame of the text, the king comes back to his duties as king. As she has gone from female to male to female, he has worked through his own double transformation from *kama* to *moksha* and back to *kama*.

The Illusion of Caste

Two other tales from the *Yogavasishtha* deconstruct caste as the tale of Chudala deconstructs gender, taking as the central, transformative experiences the demotion of first a king and then a Brahmin to Pariahs. The first, the tale of King Lavana, is relatively straightforward, though it begins to challenge the linearity of time and consciousness; the second, the tale of the Brahmin Gadhi, goes further in blurring the line. They are rather long stories, but I will summarize them as briefly as I can, one by one:

LAVANA: THE KING WHO DREAMED HE WAS A PARIAH

There was a king named Lavana, who seemed to fall into a trance one day while gazing at a horse; when he regained his senses, he told this story: "I imagined that

I mounted the horse, which bolted and carried me far away to a village of Pariahs [Chandalas], where the low branch of a tree swept me off the galloping horse. I met a Pariah girl, married her, raised two sons and two daughters with her, and lived there for sixty years; I forgot that I had been a king. Then there was a famine, and as I was about to throw myself into a fire so that my children could eat my flesh and survive, I awoke here on my throne." The courtiers were amazed. The king set out the next day, with his ministers, to find that village again, and he did. He found an old woman there who told him that a king had come there and married her daughter, and then there was a famine and everyone had died. The king returned to his palace.[49]

The king is "carried away" by the bolting horse, a motif taken from the theme of royal addiction to hunting as well as from the recurrent metaphor of a horse as sensuality out of control. The existence of a village, and people, that we at first assume to exist only in the king's imagination but that then leave evidence that others can see (the old woman mentions a number of very specific details from the king's life among the Pariahs) poses a serious challenge to our concept of the limits of the imagination. Lavana seems to seek public corroboration, first in the courtiers and then in the woman in the village, of the truth he knows by himself. The text sets these paradoxes within its own Kashmir Shaiva metaphysics: The mind imposes its idea on the spirit/matter dough of reality, cutting it up as with a cookie cutter, now into stars, now into gingerbread men, now into a palace, now into a village. It makes them, and it finds them already there, like a *bricoleur*, who makes new forms out of objets trouvés. In the end, the king returns to his original life, even though he believes that his other life is just as real (or, as the case may be, unreal); this return is part of the lesson that Rama must also learn.

The theme of the king who becomes, or dreams that he becomes, a Pariah (or vice versa) has an ancient provenance in India.[50] One of the early Upanishads describes the paradigmatic dream in these terms: "When he dreams, he seems to become a great king. Then he seems to become a great Brahmin. He seems to enter into the high and the low."[51] (The "low" would be the Pariah nightmare.) And the theme of kings actually becoming Pariahs or tribals is refracted in the episodes in both the *Mahabharata* and the *Ramayana* in which the king (Yudhishthira, Nala, Rama) is exiled among the common people before he can ascend his throne, to learn how the other half lives. The actual banishment and the dream of banishment are combined in the *Markandeya Purana* tale of King Harishchandra, who is (according to the *Yoga-vasishtha*) Lavana's grand-father:

HARISHCHANDRA: THE KING WHO BECAME A PARIAH
WHO DREAMED HE WAS A PARIAH

King Harishchandra was cursed to become a Chandala, and he lost his wife and son. He lived for years as a Chandala and one night dreamed that he was a Pulkasa [another Pariah caste], born in the womb of a Pulkasa woman; when he was seven years old, some Brahmins, annoyed with him, said, "Behave yourself. Harishchandra annoyed some Brahmins and was cursed to be a Pulkasa." Then they cursed him to go to hell, and he went there for a day and was tortured. He was reborn as a dog, eating carrion and vomit and enduring cold and heat. The dog died and was then reborn as a donkey, an elephant, a monkey, a tortoise, wild boar, porcupine, cock, parrot, crane, and snake. Then he was born as a king who lost his kingdom at dice and lost his wife and son. Finally he awakened, still as a Chandala, working in a cremation ground. One day he met his wife carrying his dead son to be cremated; he and his wife resolved to immolate themselves on their son's pyre. Just then Indra and Dharma came there, revived the son, and took all three of them to heaven.[52]

We can see the seeds of the story of Lavana here, but without the Kashmir Shaiva frame: A curse, rather than a meditation, turns Harishchandra into a real, rather than dreamed, Pariah, though within that real life he also dreams as Lavana dreams. In both stories, the death of the son and the decision to enter the fire trigger the awakening. But in this text, which is framed by samsara and bhakti, the final release is not *moksha* but physical transportation to heaven, the sensuous heaven of Indra. (We can also see a South Indian bhakti thread in the child whom the gods pretend to kill but then revive.) The curse destabilizes caste to a certain extent: If someone can be cursed to become a Pariah, the Pariah you meet might have been a king even in *this* life. The philosophy of illusion further destabilizes it: Not even a curse but just a dream could change you. In either case, caste is not necessarily part of your inalienable substance, the way that the dharma texts say it is.

In the end, Harishchandra and his wife do not return to their original life, as Lavana does, but leave both the earthly dream and the earthly reality, the royal pleasures and the Pariah horrors. In this, they are more Buddhist than Hindu, and indeed the story of Harishchandra may have influenced and/or been influenced by the Buddhist *Vessantara Jataka,* which tells a very similar tale.[53] (Another shared Hindu-Buddhist theme appears when Lavana plans to feed his children on his own flesh, a theme we know from the Hindu-Buddhist stories of the rabbit in the moon and of King Shibi.) The more basic Buddhist paradigm, however, is the life of Gautama Shakyamuni himself, the Buddha, who (according to the Pali texts) leaves his luxurious palace in order to live among the suffering people and never returns; this plot is the very opposite of the Hindu myths of this corpus, in which the king almost always returns.[54]

A nicely self-referential moment occurs when the Brahmins, not recognizing that the Chandala they are talking to is Harishchandra, tell him his own story. But they make him a Pulkasa rather than a Chandala, as Harishchandra himself does in his dream. For the repetitions are never quite alike, and one sort of Pariah may mistake himself (and be mistaken by others) for another sort of Pariah. These variations become more vivid still when the *Yoga-vasishstha* tells a story that both is and is not like the story of Lavana, the story of Gadhi:*

GADHI: THE BRAHMIN WHO DREAMED HE WAS
A PARIAH WHO DREAMED HE WAS A KING

There was a Brahmin named Gadhi, who lost consciousness one day as he bathed in a river; he saw himself reborn as a Pulkasa, within the womb of a Pulkasa woman. He was born, grew up, married, had children, and became old. All of his family died, and he wandered until he came to the city of the Kiras, where the king had died, and the people made him the king. But after eight years an old Pulkasa from the village identified him as a Pulkasa; the people fled from him, and he threw himself into a fire and awoke in the water of the river. He went home and lived as before, until one day another Brahmin came and told him that in the city of the Kiras, a Pulkasa had become king for eight years until he was exposed and killed himself in a fire. Then Gadhi went and found the village and

---

* Gadhi is also the patronymic of Vishvamitra, the king who wanted to become a Brahmin and cursed other sages to become Pariahs. Though this may not be the same man, the name does have that narrative resonance.

the city of the Kiras and found all just as it had been reported. He went back to his life as a Brahmin.[55]

When we set the stories of Lavana and Gadhi side by side, each sheds light on the other, forming a double image of mutually illuminating similes. Lavana is a king who dreams that he is a Pariah and then goes back to being a king. Gadhi is a Brahmin who dreams that he is a Pariah who becomes a king, is unmasked as a Pariah, and turns back into a Brahmin. It might appear that Lavana takes up the Gadhi story at midpoint, a king who remembers that he has been a Pariah. King Lavana travels (or imagines that he travels) to another place, where he lives another life until he awakens again as a king. This also happens to Gadhi, in the middle part of his story, though in the other direction: As a Pariah, he travels to another place and becomes a king. This shared, inverted episode is, however, framed by another in Gadhi's life, in which he dies, is reborn, and experiences an entirely new life, beginning as an embryo. And this frame casts back upon the Lavana story the implication that he too may have a frame, that a Brahmin may have dreamed that he was Lavana who dreamed that he was a Pariah. Gadhi finds out that his memories of the dream were true, but they are not his memories; they belong to someone else. What is real for Lavana becomes a simile for Gadhi, and what is real for Gadhi is merely a simile for Lavana. One man's reality is another man's simile.

The transformations take place differently: King Lavana is never reborn but merely travels to another place; Gadhi, by contrast, does not travel or fall into a trance but actually dies (or imagines that he dies), is reborn, and experiences an entirely new life, beginning as an embryo. On the other hand, Lavana actually succumbs to amnesia and forgets that he was a king, while Gadhi as a Pariah remembers quite well who he was and merely pretends to be a king. The fact that Gadhi is a Brahmin, with special spiritual powers, is highly significant; he remains in mental control throughout and especially at the end, in ways that the king, the victim of his passion (such as his mesmerization by the beauty of the horse), does not. But whatever the status of the protagonist, the text eventually erases the distinction between having an adventure and imagining that you have had an adventure, since in either case the events of the adventure leave physical traces that can be corroborated before witnesses.

The assumptions of Kashmiri Shaiva idealism are very different from those of the average Euro-American reader. More vividly than any argument, the text performs the proposition that our failure to remember our past lives is a more intense form of our failure to recapture our dreams. More than that, it erases the distinction between the reality status of a dreamed (or experienced) episode within a single life and a dreamed (or experienced) episode of total rebirth; the distinction between forgetting that you are a king and pretending to be a king; and, finally, the distinction between the consciousness of a king or Brahmin and a Pariah.

CHAPTER 19

DIALOGUE AND TOLERANCE
UNDER THE MUGHALS

1500 to 1700 CE

ॐ

CHRONOLOGY (ALL DATES CE)

1399 Timur, ruler of Central Asia, destroys Delhi

1526 Babur founds the Mughal Empire

1530–1556 Humayun reigns

1556–1605 Akbar reigns

1605–1627 Jahangir reigns

1627–1658 Shah Jahan reigns

1658–1707 Aurangzeb reigns

1713–1719 Farrukhsiyar reigns

Being aware of the fanatical hatred between Hindus and Muslims, and being convinced that this arose out of mutual ignorance, the enlightened ruler sought to dispel this ignorance by making the books of each religion accessible to the other. He chose the *Mahabharata* to begin with, as this is the most comprehensive and enjoys the highest authority, and arranged for it to be translated by competent men from both religions. In this way he wished to demonstrate to the Hindus that a few of their erroneous practices and superstitions had no basis in their classics, and also to convince the Muslims that it was absurd to ascribe a mere 7,000 years of existence to the world.

Abu'l Fazl (1551–1602)[1]

The enlightened ruler in this passage is Akbar, by far the most pluralist of the Mughal rulers (indeed of most rulers anywhere and anytime in history). His attention to the *Mahabharata* is coupled with his disdain (or that of Abu'l Fazl, his chronicler) for "erroneous" contemporary Hindu practices in contrast with the ancient classics. Other Mughals too valued some aspects of Hinduism very highly, while still others hated the Hindus and regarded their practices as not merely "erroneous" but downright blasphemous. Hinduism continued to agonize over issues of caste and gender, often newly inspired by the Mughal example or the Mughal threat, or both.

THE MUGHALS

Few people have been able to resist the fascination of the Mughals, whose very name comes into English (from a Persian form of "Mongols," sometimes spelled "Mogul") as a word denoting someone of extravagant wealth and power. True, the Mughals had their little ways; they did tend to try to kill (or blind, or lock up) members of their nuclear family rather a lot, and many of them seem to have been drunk and/or stoned most of the time.* Punishment was severe under the Mughals (as it was under the Hindus—and, for that matter, the Europeans—of the period); people were impaled or trampled to death by elephants for a number of crimes and flayed or deprived of hands or feet for relatively minor misdemeanors.[2] But the Mughals also made spectacular contributions to the civilization of the world in general and India and Hinduism in particular. Under the Mughals, industry and trade boomed. Around the court thronged "costumiers, perfumers, gold and silversmiths, jewelers, ivory-carvers, gunsmiths, saddlers, joiners and [an] army of architects, civil engineers, stonemasons and polishers."[3]

Like the Arabs of the Delhi Sultanate, the Turks who became the Mughals were not all the same in their relationship to Hinduism. Some were religious zealots; some didn't care much about religion; some loved Islam but didn't believe that they should impose it on anyone else. Some (notoriously Aurangzeb) were quite (though not unambiguously) horrid; some (most notably Akbar) were quite (though not unambiguously) wonderful; and most of them were a bit of both. And there were many different sorts of Islam—Sunni, Shia, Sufi, and so forth. The Mughals as a group differed from the Delhi sultans as a group: The Mughals ruled longer as individuals and as a dynasty, were more centralized, and held a tighter rein, with more control over more of India; we also have much more available light, much more information, about the

---

* Support for the hypothesis that throughout the world, alcoholism runs in families, through genes and DNA or through the chain reaction of generations.

Mughals. Hinduism too had changed in many important ways since the days of the Delhi Sultanate (new sectarian movements, Tantra, philosophy), so that a different Hinduism now encountered a different Islam.

BABUR THE HORSEMAN AND HORTICULTURALIST

Zahir-ud-din Muhammad, otherwise known as Babur ("the Tiger"), the first great Mughal emperor, traced his descent, on his mother's side, back to Genghis Khan and, on his father's, to Timur the Lame (Tamerlane, in Edgar Allan Poe's epic poem) who, in 1398, led Mongol forces across the Yamuna River and defeated the reigning sultan, massacring or enslaving all the Hindus, sparing only the Muslim quarters of the city. An inauspicious beginning. A century later, in 1484, Babur was born in Ferghana, in the mountains of Central Asia (now Uzbekistan). Despite his Mongol blood, he regarded himself as a Turk, and he was educated in Turki.[4] A stunning mix of elegance and cruelty, Babur constructed gardens and fountains and planted melons wherever he went, a kind of Mughal Johnny Appleseed, but he also knocked down a lot of temples and killed a lot of people. He wrote an extraordinarily intimate, frank, and detailed memoir, the *Baburnama,* from which we can get a vivid sense of the man, from the early days, when he lived a nomadic life, riding his magnificent horse and carrying little with him but a book of poetry, exulting in his freedom.

As soon as he failed to conquer his first target, Timur's old realm of Samarkhand, Babur had set his sights on India, Timur's later conquest; he named his second son Hindal, which is Turkish for "Take India!"[5] But once he actually got there he formed a low opinion of India:

> Hindustan is a place of little charm. There is no beauty in its people, no graceful social intercourse, no poetic talent or understanding, no etiquette, nobility, or manliness. The arts and crafts have no harmony or symmetry. There are no good horses, meat, grapes, melons, or other fruit. There is no ice, cold water, good food or bread in the markets. There are no baths and no madrassas [Muslim schools]. There are no candles, torches, or candlesticks. . . . The one nice aspect of Hindustan is that it is a large country with lots of gold and money.[6]

(He adds, a bit later, "Another nice thing is the unlimited numbers of craftsmen and practitioners of every trade.") Seldom has the nature of a conqueror's interest in the object of his conquest been so nakedly expressed. The lack of good horses was, as we have seen, a perennial problem.

He had relatively little to say about Hinduism: "Most of the people in Hindustan are infidels whom the people of India call Hindu. Most Hindus believe in reincarnation." That's just about it. His interest in rebirth and the related philosophy of karma reemerged on another occasion, when he crossed a river that now forms the border between the Indian states of Uttar Pradesh and Bihar and is called the Karamnasa ("Destroyer of Karma"), sometimes referred to as the Anti-Ganges. Babur remarked of it: "This river is scrupulously avoided by Hindus, and observant Hindus will not cross it. They must board boats and cross its mouth on the Ganges. They believe that the religious merit of anyone touched by its water is nullified The etymology of its name is also said to be derived from this." He objected to both Hindu and Jaina images, especially to a group of idols, some of which were twenty yards tall, "shown stark naked with all their private parts exposed. . . . Urwahi is not a bad place. In fact, it is rather nice. Its one drawback was the idols, so I ordered them destroyed."[7]

His attitude to his own faith was simple and practical; on occasion he used Islamic fervor, which may or may not have been genuine in him, to rally reluctant troops against Rajputs.[8] His dedication to his religion was inseparable from his dedication to his military victories; after one such victory, he wrote this verse: "For the sake of Islam I became a wanderer; I battled infidels and Hindus./ I determined to become a martyr. Thank God I became a holy warrior."[9] His practice of Islam was leavened by his indulgence in the pleasures of the senses: "wines, composing of some very sensual poetry, music, flowers and gardens, women, even a young boy at one time in his youth."[10] Proselytizing and demolishing other people's places of worship were not high on his list of priorities.

Babur is thought to have built several mosques, including the Babri Masjid at Ayodhya, which an inscription attributes to him.* But the pages of the diary covering the period in which such a mosque would have been built, sometime before 1528, are missing, and it is possible that Babur merely renovated an already existing mosque, built sometime after the armies of Muhammad of Ghor reached Ayodhya in 1194.

In 1530, Babur's eldest and favorite son, Humayun, then twenty-two, fell ill and was expected to die. Babur is said to have prayed by Humayun's sickbed

---

* This is the mosque that was later said to have usurped the site of a Rama temple and was torn down by Hindu mobs in 1992.

and transferred his own health to his son (transferring karma, an action more Hindu or Buddhist than Muslim), offering up his own life if Humayun recovered. Humayun recovered and Babur died. He was buried first in a garden at Agra that he himself had designed, and then, as he had wished, he was carried back to Kabul, where he was laid to rest. He had never liked India very much.

HUMAYUN THE ASTRONOMER AND ASTROLOGIST

Humayun, born in 1508 in Kabul, dabbled in astrology and spiritual matters. Neither of these religious interests prevented him from blinding his brother Hindal in retaliation for killing his (Humayun's) spiritual guide.[11] In 1556, as keen on astronomy as on astrology, Humayun tripped going down the stone stairs from his makeshift observatory in Delhi and fell to his death.[12] A messenger hurried to inform his son Akbar, only thirteen years old, that he was now the emperor; in the meantime a man who happened to resemble Humayan (what the Hindus would have called a shadow Humayun) was displayed, on a distant platform, to the anxious crowds.[13]

AKBAR THE TOLERANT

Akbar ruled for half a century. Like his grandfather Babur, Akbar was a fearless and tireless rider,[14] a man of action who killed tigers with spears and was famous for both his courage and his cruelty. When, after a long and bloody battle and siege, Akbar captured the historic fortress of Chitor in Mewar in 1568, he watched the flames consume the women as the men rode out in their own suicidal charge, and then he gratuitously massacred some twenty thousand noncombatants.[15]

In dramatic contrast with Babur, Akbar himself neither read nor wrote. (No one really knows why; he may have been dyslexic, but he may just have been bored with school—a grade school dropout—or a mystic who preferred not to write.[16]) He more than compensated for this, however, by keeping at his court, among his "nine gems," Abu'l Fazl, a great biographer, who wrote both the *Akbar-Nama* (a rather puffed hagiography) and the *Ain-i-Akbari* (a more sober history).

AKBAR'S PLURALISM

Open-minded Hindu and Muslim religious thinkers had engaged in serious interreligious dialogues long before this, as we have seen, but Akbar was the first to put the power of a great empire at the service of pluralism. In 1564 he began to host a series of multireligious theological salons,[17] serving as a source of entertainment and an opportunity to showcase rhetorical talents, much as the Upanishadic kings were depicted as doing two thousand years earlier, though of course with a different range of religious options. In the city that he built at Fatehpur Sikri (near Agra), Akbar constructed a room where religious debates were held on Thursday evenings. At first, the conversations were limited to different Muslim groups (Sunni, Shia, and Ismaili, as well as Sufi); then they were joined by Parsis; then Hindus (Shaiva and Vaishnava bhaktas); disciples of Kabir and probably also of Guru Nanak (Akbar is said to have given the Sikhs the land at Amritsar on which the Golden Temple was later built); Jainas, Jews, and Jesuits. This veritable circus of holy men even included some unholy men—Materialists (Charvakas or Lokayatikas).[18] Or in the immortal (if somewhat overblown) words of Abu'l Fazl: "He sought for truth amongst the dust-stained denizens of the field of irreflection and consorted with every sort of wearers of patched garments such as [yogis, renouncers, and Sufi mystics], and other solitary sitters in the dust and insouciant recluses."[19] Sometimes Akbar wandered incognito through the bazaars and villages, a habit that may have stirred his awareness of or nourished his interest in the religious diversity among his people.

Fatehpur Sikri was the result of Akbar's particular devotion to Sufism; ignoring the Shattaris, who were an important Sufi sect at that time and had influenced earlier Mughals, he had become attached to the Chishtis.[20] In 1569, Akbar visited the Sufi saint Shaikh Salim Chishti, who lived in the village of Sikri. Salim predicted that Akbar would have the son and heir he longed for, and indeed a son (Salim, named after the saint, later to become Jahangir) was born in Sikri that very year. The grateful Akbar immediately made Sikri his capital (renaming it Fatehpur Sikri) and personally directed the building of the Jami Masji (the Friday Mosque) in 1571, as well as other structures that reflect both Hindu aand Muslim architectural influences. But he moved the Mughal capital back to Delhi in 1586, in part because of Fatehpur Sikri's inadequate water supply but also because he was no longer so devoted to the Chishti saint for whom he had chosen the site.

Akbar proclaimed that "the wisdom of Vedanta is the wisdom of Sufism,"[21] and that "all religions are either equally true or equally illusionary."[22] His eclecticism also extended to Christianity, with which he flirted to such a degree that the Portuguese missionaries congratulated themselves that he was on the brink of converting—until they realized that he continued to worship at mosques (and, on occasion, at Hindu temples, as well as participate in Parsi fire rituals[23]). Here, not for the first or last time, Muslim and Hindu pluralism ran up against Christian intolerance. (Indeed, at the very time when Akbar was pursuing these enlightened conversations, the Inquisitions were going on in Europe; Giordano Bruno was burned at the stake in Rome in 1600, "just as Akbar was preaching tolerance of all religions in Agra."[24]) In 1603, Akbar granted the Christians the right to preach, make converts, and build churches. Three sons of Akbar's youngest son, Danyal, were actually christened, although this had been a political ruse, to disqualify the boys from contending for the (Muslim) throne, and they soon reverted to Islam. On one occasion, Akbar proposed to a group of Jesuits and Muslim theologians the test of walking through fire (somewhat like the test that a South Indian Shaiva had proposed to the Jainas) in order to determine which was the true religion. But unlike the Jainas, the Jesuits (in the person of Father Aquaviva) refused. Sometime later Hindus seeking revenge for the destruction of some of their temples by Christian missionaries murdered Aquaviva.

Akbar had a number of wives (usually political rather than romantic alliances), but unlike Henry VIII in a similar pickle, he got his priests to stretch the rules about polygamy.[25] He was less successful in establishing his new religion, his "Divine Faith" (Din-i-Ilahi) with himself at its center—as God or his humble servant? No one has ever been quite sure.[26] Like Ashoka, Akbar carved out his own religion, his own dharma, but with a difference: The rallying call of the new faith—"Allahu Akbar"—was a very serious pun, which could simply be the usual pious invocation affirming that God (Allah) is great (akbar) but in this context suddenly revealed another possible meaning, that Akbar (Akbar) is God (Allah).

In keeping with his pluralism, Akbar's new faith was designed to transcend all sectarian differences and unite his disparate subjects.[27] But it did not have even the limited success that Ashoka's *dhamma* had had. Not surprisingly, some people regarded it as a hodgepodge,[28] but it did not merely peter out with a whimper. "Bang!" went the old elite, the orthodox *ulama,* in revolt against Akbar as a heretic.[29] They issued a fatwa urging all Muslims to rebel, but Akbar rode it out, for the Hindus stood behind him against the Muslim old guard.

HINDUS UNDER AKBAR

The first of the great Mughals to be born in India, Akbar regarded Hindus not as infidels but as subjects. And since some Muslims were his enemies, some

Hindus (the enemies of his enemies) were his friends; he was sheltered by a Hindu king when he had to flee from a powerful Muslim enemy. He married the daughter of the raja of Amber (near Jaipur) and brought the raja, his son, and his grandson (Man Singh) into the Mughal hierarchy as amirs (nobles), his most trusted lieutenants, allowing them to retain their land, their Hinduism, and their caste status. In return, they (and other Rajput princes) provided him with cavalry (a reverse of the usual process whereby Muslims sold horses to Hindus).[30]

Two Hindus, both of whom simultaneously played Brahmin and Kshatriya roles and bridged the social worlds of Hindus and Muslims, were prominent among the inner court circle known as Akbar's nine jewels. One was a Brahmin named Birbal (1528–1583), who was Akbar's minister and a kind of unofficial court jester, inspiring many folktales about his humor and his wit. But he was also an important military leader, and Akbar called him Raja Birbal. The only Hindu to join in Akbar's "Divine Faith,"[31] he died (perhaps as the result of treachery) while he was fighting the Afghans. The other Hindu "jewel" was Todar Mall (also spelled Todar Mal and Todaramalla), a Kshatriya born in Oudh (north of Lucknow), who became Akbar's leading general, finance officer, and then prime minister. Yet he was a pious devotee of Krishna, famous for setting up images of Krishna, and in 1572 he gathered together a group of Varanasi scholars to compose a giant Sanskrit compendium of Hindu culture and learning, the *Todar-ananda* ("Todar's Bliss"). In it he criticized in general the "aliens" (*mlecchas*, surely meaning the Muslims) and in particular the rulers of darkness (*tamas*) (possibly meaning his patron, Akbar). He said that the rising tide of alien culture had inspired him to write the book in order to rescue the Veda when it had been sunk in the ocean of aliens (the old myth of the flooded earth) and to restore the light of empire that had been shut out by the darkness of the rulers in the cruel Kali Age.[32]

Akbar was not always good to Hindus, but he almost always apologized after he had done them harm. He approved the conversion of a temple into a mosque and a Muslim theological school (madrassa). In Nagarkot, near Kangra, during Akbar's reign, Muslim soldiers under Birbal slaughtered two hundred cows and many Hindus and demolished a temple. Local tradition adds that later Akbar made amends and sent a golden umbrella to cover the idol. Akbar also allowed the reconstruction of a Hindu temple built at Kurukshetra, cite of the *Mahabharata* battle, when it had been demolished and a mosque built on its debris.[33] He admitted that in his youth he had forced many Hindus to convert to Islam (he offered life to his first adversaries, after the battle of Panipat in 1556, only if they would convert to Islam[34]), but he later regretted it[35] and went to great lengths to see that Hindus were treated with respect.

He did many good things for Hindus. He abolished the *jizya,* the tax on pilgrims, and other discriminatory measures against Hindus. He ensured that Hindus would have their own laws and their own courts. He celebrated the Hindu festivals of Divali and Dussehra. He put Hindus in charge of almost the entire moneylending system, acknowledging their competence in matters mathematical and financial.[36] The lasting impression that this pro-Hindu policy made on Akbar's Hindu subjects is suggested by the fact that in some of the bardic traditions of Rajasthan, Akbar came to be equated with Rama.[37]

In 1605, a few weeks before Akbar's death, Prince Salim (who was to become Jahangir) inscribed his own genealogy on the Ashokan pillar that Samudra Gupta had already used as a palimpsest; Akbar sent Abu'l Fazl to deal with Jahangir, who had Abu'l Fazl murdered[38] and had the head sent back to him (Salim) in Allahabad.[39] Akbar was understandably infuriated and saddened; a few weeks later he died in Agra.

Jahangir the Alcoholic

Akbar's Rajput bride had given birth to Jahangir (Salim) in 1569. When he grew up, Jahangir murdered, in addition to Abu'l Fazl, several religious leaders, including both the Sikh guru Arjan and the Shi'i Qadi Nurullah Shushtari. He punished an insurgent by serving him the head of his only son, like a melon. Closer to home, when his own son Khusrau waged battle against him, Jahangir had him blinded, remarking that the relationship between father and son was irrelevant to a sovereign. Khusrau's Rajput mother committed suicide.[40]

Jahangir's attitude to Hinduism was disdainfully noninvasive. He talked with Hindu pandits and visited yogis in Peshawar, though he said they "lacked all religious knowledge" and he perceived in their ideas "only darkness of spirit." At Kangra, in the Himalayas, Jahangir demolished a Durga temple, built a mosque at the site, and had a bull slaughtered in the fort, but he didn't demolish the Hindu temple to the goddess Bhawani below the walls of the fort, at the bottom of the hill, which he spoke of in terms of admiration and even affection. Jahangir also left untouched—indeed, had both repaired and extended—the Jwalamukhi ("Mare with Flame in Her Mouth") Temple, "after testing the priests' claim that the fire there was divine and eternal and could not be extinguished by water"—at least, I would add, not until doomsday, when the ocean would extinguish it. Jahangir also allowed a temple to Vishnu's boar avatar to be constructed at Ajmer; he objected not to the temple but to the boar (which was, after all, just a big pig, anathema to Muslims); he spared the temple but destroyed the boar image and threw it into a tank,[41] declaring that it was an example of the "worthless Hindu religion." Still he ordered that no temples be destroyed (though also that no new ones were to be built).[42] Like Babur, he wrote an extensive memoir, but unlike Babur, he took no pleasure in horses. He died in 1627 while traveling from Kashmir to Lahore.

SHAH JAHAN THE BUILDER

Shah Jahan was the third son of Jahangir and the Rajput princess Manmati. He discriminated against non-Muslims and destroyed many Hindu temples, seventy in Varanasi alone. In Kashmir, he demolished an ancient temple at Anantnag ("The Serpent of Infinity," a name of the cosmic cobra that Vishnu rests upon) and renamed the town Islamabad. At Orchha, in Madhya Pradesh, he demolished a temple because it had been built by the grandfather of a Rajput raja who had rebelled against the Mughals.[43] But Shah Jahan was still open to the culture of Hinduism—including Sanskrit poetry—and to some of its people, particularly the rajas. He took a verse that the Sufi poet Amir Khusra (1253–1325), son of a Rajput mother and a Turkic father, had originally composed in praise of India (Khusra's motherland) and had the words inscribed around the roof of the Audience Hall in his Delhi palace: "If there is a heaven on earth, it is here, it is here, it is here." When he built the great Jami Masjid, the Friday Mosque, in Delhi, he included a rather miscellaneous arcade made of disparate columns from twenty-seven demolished Hindu temples.[44] Despite the alleged aniconic nature of Islam, the pillars are still graced with figures, some of Hindu gods, a few of them still with their heads on.

Shah Jahan also built the Shalimar Gardens in Kashmir, the white marble palace in Ajmer, and the high-carat golden, jewel-encrusted Peacock Throne. And when his beloved wife, Mumtaz, died in bearing him their thirteenth child, he built the Taj Mahal in her memory, on the banks of the Yamuna (Jumna) River, on a site bought from a Rajput and made of marble from Rajasthan. His son Aurangzeb imprisoned him across the river, where he could gaze at the Taj Mahal until his death eight years later.

DARA SHIKOH THE MYSTIC SANSKRITIST

Dara Shikoh (also spelled Shukoh) was Shah Jahan's oldest and favorite son, the designated heir. But the orthodox Muslims of the *ulama* distrusted him, for he was a scholar who had argued that "the essential nature of Hinduism was identical with that of Islam,"[45] a pronouncement that orthodox Muslims regarded as heresy.* He consorted with Sufis, Hindus, Christians, and Jews.[46] He learned Sanskrit and translated Sanskrit philosophical texts into Persian.

In 1657, when Shah Jahan was deathly ill, his sons hovered about, as princes are wont to do. Aurangzeb and Dara Shikoh were the main contenders. When Aurangzeb attacked Delhi and imprisoned Shah Jahan in the Agra fort, he killed Dara's sons in front of him,[47] paraded Dara through the streets, had him cut to pieces, and then (according to some stories) had the pieces paraded through the streets.

AURANGZEB THE ZEALOT

Aurangzeb was no more a typical Muslim than Torquemada was a typical Christian. A devout Sunni, he worked hard to repair what he regarded as the damage done by his more tolerant predecessors. In the eloquent words of Bamber Gascoigne, "Akbar [had] disrupted the Muslim community by recognizing that India was not an Islamic country: Aurangzeb disrupted India by behaving as if it were."[48] When Aurangzeb sacked Hyderabad in 1687, he stabled his horses in the Shiite mosques as a deliberate insult to what he regarded as the city's heretics.[49] Thus began twenty years of discrimination against Shiites, Hindus, and Sikhs.

The Sikh support of Dara in the 1658 succession crisis angered Aurangzeb. Moreover, the ninth Sikh guru, Tegh Bahadur, drew large crowds with his preaching and proselytized among Muslims as well as Hindus. Many Muslims converted to Sikhism, so infuriating Aurangzeb that he condemned Tegh Bahadur for blasphemy and executed him. Under Guru Govind Singh, the tenth and last Sikh guru (1666–1708), who insisted that Sikhs leave their hair uncut, carry arms, and use the epithet "Singh" (lion), Sikhism became not merely a movement for religious and social reform but a political and military force to be reckoned with. In 1708, Govind Singh was assassinated while

---

* Perhaps because this was the doctrine of some bhakti sects.

attending the emperor Aurangzeb. This spurred Sikhs, Maharashtrians, and Rajputs to outright defiance.[50]

The Hindus suffered most under Aurangzeb. In 1679, he reimposed the *jizya* on all castes (even the Brahmins, who were usually exempt) and the tax on Hindu pilgrims that Akbar had lifted. He rescinded endowments to temples and to Brahmins, placed heavier duties on Hindu merchants, and replaced Hindus in administration with Muslims. When a large crowd rioted in protests against the *jizya,* he sent in the troops—more precisely, the elephants—to trample them.[51] He put pressure on the Hindus to convert.

Aurangzeb attacked Hyderabad, plundered and desecrated the temples, and killed the Brahmins. He destroyed all newly built or rebuilt Hindu temples and replaced them with mosques; in particular, he replaced the great Vishvanatha Temple in Varanasi and the Keshava Deo Temple at Mathura with two great Aurangzeb mosques and changed the name of Mathura to Islamabad* (as Shah Jahan had done to Anantnag). He also renamed the cave city of Ellora Aurangabad.[52] In several places in Sind, and especially at Varanasi, "Brahmins attracted a large number of Muslims to their discourses. Aurangzeb, in utter disgust, ordered the governors of all these provinces 'to demolish the schools and temples of the infidels and with utmost urgency put down the teaching and the public practices of these religious misbelievers.' "[53] (He particularly hated Varanasi because it was the center of linga worship, which he regarded as the most abominable of all abominations.[54]) He sent someone to Rajasthan to demolish sixty-six temples there.[55]

Yet he financed the maintenance of several other Hindu temples and *matts*, and he even made land grants to some.[56] He destroyed few *old* temples, generally only those that had political or ideological power. Nor, being puritanical and mean in all things and reacting against Shah Jahan's architectural extravagances, did he allow any new mosques to be built (with the exception of the few mosques mentioned above, most of which replaced temples). This led to great hardship for the artisans.[57] Other arts too suffered, as he suppressed poetry and music;[58] dismissed dancers, musicians, and artists from the royal payroll; and hired jurists and theologians in their place.[59] And when he went on to create the post of a *muhtasib,* a censor or guardian of public morality, whose task it was to suppress gambling, blasphemy, alcohol, and opium, the cumulative effect surely acted as a serious wet blanket on both addiction and night life.

---

* Neither of these towns should be confused with the present-day city of Islamabad, capital of Pakistan.

Hindu astrologers had played an important role in the life of the Mughals until Aurangzeb replaced the Hindu astrologers with Muslim ones.[60] Aurangzeb's grandson fought against him on behalf of Hindus. Yet even Aurangzeb had Hindus in his court and ordered his officials to protect Brahmin temple priests who were being harassed, instructing them to leave the Brahmins alone so that they could "pray for the continuance of the Empire."[61] Aurangzeb lived to ninety and died in bed, alone.

When Jahandah Shah took the throne, he immediately reversed all of Aurangzeb's policies that had curbed the pleasures of the flesh. Said to be a frivolous and drunken imbecile, Jahandah Shah surrounded himself with singers, dancers, actors, storytellers, and a notorious mistress, to whom he gave elephants and jewels. Other Mughals of that ilk followed him. Farrukhsiyar took over in 1713 and was murdered in 1719, though not before he carried out a bloody repression of the Sikhs, who continued to harass the Mughals until the British put an end to Mughal rule.[62,]

The Opiates of the Rulers: Addiction to Opium (and Wine)

Aurangzeb's puritanical repressions were in part a response to the history of his family, several of whom suffered from addiction to alcohol and/or drugs, "the bane of the Mughals." They started young; opium was often given to small children to keep them quiet.[63] The addictions of the Mughals may well have reinforced the Hindus' awareness of the dangers of substance abuse.

It all began with Babur, whose memoir (begun when he was barely a teenager) abounds in wine, drugs, and the Mughal equivalent of rock and roll. The drugs included cannabis exported from Kashmir, but the drug of choice was opium, made from poppies grown in Varanasi and one of India's major export products. The opium was usually taken in the form of *ma'jun,* a drug still known today; it was made by pressing dried fruits such as plums, tamarinds, apricots, sometimes also sesame, and mixing the extract with a small amount of opium, somewhat like cognac-filled chocolates or hash brownies, truly a Turkish delight. It was carried on military campaigns and consumed in large amounts at parties, "a socially acceptable recreational drug."[64]

Drugs and drink played a central role in Babur's memoir. A typical early entry:

> We drank until sunset, then got on our horses. The members of the party had
> gotten pretty drunk. . . . Dost-Muhammad Baqir was so drunk that no matter how

Amin-Muhammad Tarkhan and Masti Chuhra's people tried they could not get him on his horse. They splashed water on his head, but that didn't do any good either. Just then a band of Afghans appeared. Amin-Muhammad Tarkhan was so drunk he thought that rather than leaving Dost-Muhammad to be taken by the Afghans we should cut off his head and take it with us. With great difficulty they threw him on his horse and took off. We got back to Kabul at midnight.[65]

Babur was such a great horseman that he could even ride when he was totally stoned: "We drank on the boat until late that night, left the boat roaring drunk, and got on our horses. I took a torch in my hand and, reeling to one side and then the other, let the horse gallop free-reined along the riverbank all the way to camp. I must have been really drunk."[66] This image is also captured by a fine painting entitled *A Drunken Babur Returns to Camp at Night,* from an illustrated copy of the *Babur-nama.*[67] These parties were usually bachelor affairs, royal frat parties, though occasionally women were present.[68] A sure clue that we are dealing here not just with people of privilege having a very good long-running party but with genuine addiction is Babur's frequent (almost always futile) attempts to rein in his drunkenness.[69] Before one great battle, he went on the wagon, and to make sure he would not backslide, he had a quantity of the latest vintage from Ghazni salted for vinegar.[70] When he took the pledge not to drink wine, some of the court copied him and renounced with him, for, he noted, "People follow their kings' religion."[71] But he hated being on the wagon and wrote a charming poem about it, which ended: "People repent, then they give up wine—I gave it up, and now I am repenting!"[72]

There were also excuses to get stoned other than simply wanting to get stoned, another telltale sign of substance abuse: "That night I took some opium for the pain in my ear—the moonlight also induced me to take it. The next morning I really suffered from an opium hangover and vomited a lot. Nevertheless, I went out on a tour of all Man Singh's and Bikramajit's buildings." And: "The weather was so bad that some of us had *ma'jun* even though we had had some the day before."[73] E. M. Forster wrote a wicked satire on the depiction of constant drunkenness, and constant travel, in Babur's memoir: "Was this where the man with the melon fell overboard? Or is it the raft where half of us took spirits and the rest *bhang,*˚ and quarreled in consequence? We can't be

---

˚ Bhang is a preparation of cannabis used in India that does not contain the flowering tops and so is not very strong. It can be smoked or drunk and is used in some Hindu rituals.

sure. Is that an elephant? If so, we must have left Afghanistan. No: we must be in Ferghana again; it's a yak."[74] Here, as so often, you only know where you are by seeing what animals are with you.

None of Babur's successors wrote nearly so vividly about their drinking problems, though as a group they did manage to run up quite a tab. Humayun was an opium addict, particularly fond of *ma'jun;* it is quite possible that his fatal fall down the stairs of his observatory may have been aided and abetted by opium. Akbar drank very rarely, but his first three sons were alcoholics. Murad (Akbar's second son) died of alcoholism, and when Akbar forbade Danyal (his third son, aged thirty-three) to drink wine, Danyal tried to smuggle some in inside a musket; the alcohol dissolved the rust and gunpowder in the musket and killed him.[75]

Jahangir's excessive use of alcohol and opium was thought to have exacerbated his cruelty and vicious temper; his Rajput wife committed suicide by overdosing on opium. He sometimes forced his son Shah Jahan to drink, against his will.[76] Jahangir recorded in detail his own addiction to alcohol, and later opium, and "his apparently half-hearted battle to moderate his consumption."[77] Jahangir was also fascinated by the opium addiction of his friend Inayat Khan and had his portrait painted as he was dying. Jahangir wrote: "Since he was an opium addict and also extremely fond of drinking wine whenever he had the chance, his mind was gradually destroyed."[78]

Nonviolence Mughal Style, Especially Toward Dogs

The vices of the Mughals were not limited to drugs; there was also the vice of hunting, as well as more complicated problems involving animals. There are conflicting strains in the Mughal attitude toward animals. On the one hand, they had a great fascination with and love of animals; the Sufi saints, in particular, were often depicted in the company of tame lions or bears; a tame lion accompanies Akbar's confessor, Shaikh Salim Chishti, in one painting. On the other hand, Muslims often sacrificed animals, including cows, at the end of pilgrimages, and this was a recurrent source of conflict, for many Hindus were, by this time, deeply offended by the sacrifice of cows.[79]

Babur showed no compassion for dogs when he vomited and suspected that someone was trying to poison him: "I never vomited after meals, not even when drinking. A cloud of suspicion came over my mind. I ordered the cook to be held while the vomit was given to a dog that was watched." But he also tortured the cook and had him skinned alive, ordered the taster to be hacked to pieces, and had a woman suspected of complicity thrown under an elephant's feet.[80] So at least the dog was not singled out for mistreatment (and may not even have died; indeed, compared with the cook and taster, the dog got off easy). Akbar, on the other hand, was fond of dogs. He imported them from many countries and admired their courage in attacking all sorts of animals,* even tigers. In contradiction of the teachings of Islam, he regarded neither pigs nor dogs as unclean and kept them in the harem; he also insisted that dogs had ten virtues, any one of which, in a man, would make him a saint. At Akbar's table, some of his friends and courtiers would put dogs on the tablecloth, and some of them went so far as to let the dogs put their tongues into their (the courtiers') mouths, to the horror of Abu'l Fazl.[81] An album published during Akbar's reign shows a Kanphata yogi (a devotee of Shiva) and his dog, with a text that says, "Your dog is better than anything in the world of fidelity."[82]

One story about Akbar and dogs is also a great story about Akbar's religious tolerance. It was told by an Englishman named Thomas Coryat, who traveled to India between 1612 and 1617:

> Ecbar Shaugh [Akbar the Shah] . . . never denied [his mother] any thing but this, that shee demanded of him, that our Bible might be hanged about an asses necke and beaten about the town of Agra, for that the Portugals [Portuguese] tyed [the Qu'ran] about the necke of a dogge and beat the same dogge about the towne of Ormuz. But hee denied her request, saying that, if it were ill in the Portugals to doe so to the Alcoran, being it became not a King to requite ill with ill, for that the contempt of any religion was the contempt of God.[83]

Akbar grants, implicitly, that the dogs insulted the Qu'ran, but he differs from his mother (as he rarely did) in refusing to take revenge, thus short-circuiting the karmic chain of religious intolerance.

NONVIOLENT VOWS OF AKBAR AND JAHANGIR

Dogs' talent for hunting was important to Akbar, who was famous for his own skill, courage, and enthusiasm for the sport. Many pages of the *Ain-i-Akbari* are devoted to hunting tigers and leopards and catching elephants. Yet even there Abu'l Fazl feels it necessary to justify hunting by an argument that it is

---

* Unlike the dog in the *Mahabharata*, who was afraid of a leopard.

not merely, as it might appear, a source of pleasure* but a way of finding out, while traveling incognito, about the condition of the people and the army, taxation, the running of households, and so forth.[84] Moreover, on two separate occasions Akbar himself made vows to limit, if not to give up, hunting, the repeated attempts to give it up being a telltale sign that he, at least, regarded it as an addiction. He made the first vow when his wife was pregnant with his first son, Jahangir, and the embryo seemed to be dying; it happened on a Friday, and Akbar vowed never to hunt with cheetahs on Friday, a vow that he (and Jahangir, in response) kept all his life. This closed off one loophole that he had left in an earlier, limited move toward noninjury, in advising any adherent to his "Divine Faith" (Din-i-ilahi) "not to kill any living creature with his own hand" and not to flay anything: "The only exceptions are in battle and the chase."[85]

On the second occasion, Akbar apparently underwent a conversion experience not unlike that of Ashoka (whom Akbar resembles in other ways too, as we have seen): When Akbar was hunting on April 22, 1578, he looked at the great pile of all the animals that had been killed and suddenly decided to put a stop to it.[86] After that he became a halfhearted vegetarian (also like Ashoka), as we learn from the section of the *Ain-i-Akbari* that records the sayings of Akbar: "Were it not for the thought of the difficulty of sustenance, I would prohibit men from eating meat. The reason why I do not altogether abandon it myself is, that many others might willingly forgo it likewise and be thus cast into despondency." Abu'l Fazl attributes to Akbar a connection between vegetarianism and what a Hindu would have called noncruelty, a connection that Hindus also made: "The compassionate heart of His Majesty finds no pleasure in cruelties. . . . He is ever sparing of the lives of his subjects. . . . His Majesty abstains much from flesh, so that whole months pass away without his touching any animal food."[87]

Abu'l Fazl explicitly attributes much of Akbar's qualified vegetarianism to his affinity with Hinduism, rather disapprovingly (which is a good indication that it is probably true):

> Beef was interdicted, and to touch beef was considered defiling. The reason of this was that, from his youth, His Majesty had been in company with Hindu libertines, and had thus learned to look upon a cow . . . as something holy. Besides, the emperor was subject to the influence of the numerous Hindu princesses of the

---

* The *Kama-sutra* (1.5.4–21) offers a similar set of justifications for adultery.

harem, who had gained so great an ascendancy over him as to make him forswear beef, garlic, onions, and the wearing of a beard.[88]

But since Jainism was also powerful in India at this time, and the Jainas were always more vigorous in their vegetarianism than the Hindus, and since Akbar had been favorably impressed by the Jaina monks in his court and had issued land grants to them as well as to the Hindus, Akbar's change of heart may owe as much to Jainism as to Hinduism.

Jahangir too underwent two conversion experiences about hunting. He had been, if anything, even more obsessed by hunting than Babur and Akbar were, as addicted to hunting as he was to alcohol and opium, and allergic to moderation of any kind. Then, when he took the throne in 1605, he issued a proclamation that no animals should be slaughtered for food, nor any meat eaten, on Thursday (the day of his accession) or Sunday (Akbar's birthday). But he broke this vow by shooting tigers, first in 1610, because (he said) he could not resist his overpowering "liking for tiger-hunting," and again on several other occasions, as late as 1616.[89]

Then, in 1618, when he was fifty, Jahangir made a second vow, to give up shooting "with gun and bullet" and not to injure any living thing with his own hand. His memoir suggests that Jahangir was displacing long-festering feelings of remorse for the murder of Abu'l Fazl, his father's right-hand man. Yet Jahangir rescinded this vow too in 1622, when his own son (the future Shah Jahan) openly turned on him in rebellion, as he himself had turned against Akbar. Instead of taking measures to kill his son, Jahangir started once again to kill animals, another displacement. Since Jahangir did not share his father's great enthusiasm for the Hindus (though he generally continued his father's policies toward them), it is, again, likely that Jainism, which Jahangir had earlier treated with intolerance but later had encouraged with a number of land grants, rather than Hinduism influenced him positively in this instance.[90]

HINDU RESISTANCE: SHIVAJI AND THE MAHARASHTRIANS

Inevitably, there was resistance. The Hindus demolished some mosques and converted them into temples, in the early thirteenth century, after 1540, and again during the reigns of Akbar, Shah Jahan, and Aurangzeb.[91]

The Mughals did not have control of all India; there were major pockets of resistance, including the Punjab under the Sikh gurus, Vijayanagar, the kingdoms in the far south, and, most famously, the Maharashtrians under the command of Shivaji. Even before Shivaji, the Maharashtrians had been a thorn in the Mughal side. In Ahmednagar (the center of power in Maharashtra), the leader of the opposition to the Mughals after 1600 was Malik Ambar, an Abyssinian who had been sold in Baghdad as a slave but became a brilliant military commander and administrator in the Ahmednagar sultanate, dealing equitably with both Hindus and Muslims. He trained mobile Maharashtrian cavalry units and won many victories against Jahangir, until his death in 1626. The most effective cavalry in India belonged to Maharashtra and Mysore, both of which had ready access to the west coast ports and to trade, primarily in horses, from the gulf states.[92]

In 1647, when he was just seventeen years old, Shivaji founded the Maharashtrian kingdom, an unexpected revival of Hindu kingship in the teeth of a powerful Muslim supremacy. When Shivaji captured Bijapur, his men took the treasure, horses, and elephants and enlisted to their side most of the Bijapuri troops, some of whom were Maharashtrians, while some of Shivaji's men were Muslims. In this, as in so much of medieval Indian history, allies and enemies were formed on political and military grounds more often than on religious ones, even for Shivaji, who in later centuries became the hero of Hindu militantism against Muslims. The scourge of Aurangzeb, Shivaji made lavish donations to Brahmins but (according to the Muslim chronicler Khafi Khan) made a point of not desecrating mosques or seizing women. A Maharashtrian Brahmin constructed a Kshatriya genealogy for him that linked him with earlier Rajputs. There are also many legends connecting Shivaji with the Maharashtrian saints Tukaram (1568–1650) and Ramdas (1608–1681). Shivaji died of dysentery in 1680.[93]

In 1688, Aurangzeb captured Shivaji's successor, Shambhaji, and had him tortured and dismembered limb by limb. Shambhaji's brother Rajaram took over until his death, when his senior widow, Tarabai, assumed control in the name of her son, Shambhaji II. In 1714, Shivaji's grandson Shahu appointed as his chief minister a Brahmin who was such a poor horseman that he required a man on each side to hold him in the saddle.[94] The Maharashtrian resistance did not last long after that.

INTERRELIGIOUS DIALOGUE UNDER THE MUGHALS

It is hard to generalize about interreligious relations under all the Mughals; they were so different, Akbar the best (and Dara, though he never got to rule), Aurangzeb the worst, Shah Jahan a mixed bag (he destroyed many Hindu temples, but Mughal officials during his reign participated in Jagannath festivals).[95] But if we do try to generalize, we can say that throughout the Mughal period, official conversions of Hindus to Islam were rare;[96] non-Muslims were not obliged to convert to Islam on entering the Mughal ruling class, and the Mughals generally regarded Islam as their own cultural heritage and did not encourage conversion to Islam among the general population.[97] There is no evidence of massive coercive conversion. Surprisingly little was written about conversion in contemporary sources on either side, suggesting that few regarded it as a major issue. Jahangir did not approve of mass conversions; he punished one Mughal official for converting the son of a defeated Hindu raja.[98] There is evidence of fewer than two hundred conversions under Aurangzeb.

Yet evidently many Hindus did convert, or the Muslim population of India would not have grown as it did. Some Hindus converted for money, some as punishment, some for marriage, some because they believed in it. The sons of a rebellious Rajput were spared on condition of accepting Islam; some refused and chose death instead. One prince converted because he got a tremendous raise in pay by doing so.[99] The Hindu wives of Muslim rulers sometimes converted and even built mosques.[100] A Brahmin who had been appointed to help a theologian of Akbar's court translate the *Atharva Veda* from Sanskrit into Persian ended up converting to Islam. A ruler of Kashmir converted through association with his Muslim minister.[101]

On the other hand, so many Muslims converted to Hinduism that Shah Jahan established a department to deal with it and forbade any proselytizing* by Hindus,[102] and so many conversions took place as the result of intermarriage that Akbar (Akbar!) forbade Hindu women to marry their Muslim lovers; he had the women forcibly removed from their husbands and returned to their birth families. Under Jahangir, twenty-three Muslims in Varanasi fell in love with Hindu women and converted to Hinduism. Under Shah Jahan, Muslim girls in Kashmir married Hindu boys and became Hindu. Muslim women married to Hindu men, and Muslim husbands of Hindu women, sometimes reconverted to Islam. In the fifteenth century the Brahmins thought that there was already a need for conversions back to Hinduism;[103] they overhauled ancient ceremonies designed to reinstate Hindus who had fallen from caste (usually as a result of some ritual impurity) and evolved ceremonies for reconversion,

---

* Most Hindus did not proselytize, but some Vedantic movements and some bhakti sects did.

called purification (*shuddhi*), usually involving both the payment of money and a ritual.

One Portuguese Augustinian friar, Sebastião Manrique, noted the Mughal policy of honoring Hindu law in Bengal between 1629 and 1640, during the reign of Shah Jahan:*

THE CASE OF THE POACHED PEACOCKS

Disguising himself as a Muslim merchant, apparently in order to avoid the hostility that a Christian missionary might expect, Manrique rode on horseback through the monsoon rains and took shelter in the cowshed of a Hindu village. One of his Bengali Muslim attendants caught, killed, and cooked a pair of peacocks; when Manrique learned of this, he feared the wrath of the Hindu villagers and buried the bones and feathers. But the villagers found a few feathers and, armed with bows and arrows, pursued Manrique's company (and their Hindu guide) to the nearby town, where the villagers filed a formal complaint with the Muslim administrator [*shiqdar*] whom the Mughals had put in charge of law and order there. "Evidently aware that to Hindus the peacock was a sacred bird," the administrator threw Manrique *et cie* in jail and, after twenty-four miserable hours, brought them to trial.

The administrator learned who had killed the peacocks and asked him how, being a Bengali and a Muslim, he had dared to kill a living thing in a Hindu district. Manrique answered for his servant, arguing that a Muslim had no need to respect the "ridiculous precepts" of the Hindus; that God nowhere prohibited the killing of such animals but had created them for man's use; and that killing the peacocks did not violate the precepts of the Qur'an. The administrator, however, pointed out that when Akbar had conquered Bengal sixty-four years earlier, he had promised that he and his successors would let Bengalis live under their own customs; the administrator sent the man back to jail, awaiting a sentence that might require whipping and the amputation of his right hand. Manrique bribed the administrator's wife with a piece of Chinese silk taffeta, embroidered with white, pink, and yellow flowers. She persuaded her husband to forgo the amputation and merely subject the man to a whipping.[104]

Though there is significant blurring of the line between the injunction against killing any living thing or only against killing sacred things (peacocks perhaps

---

* I have retold the friar's first-person testimony in the third person.

being sacred to Skanda/Murugan, whose vehicle they are), the main point of this story stands out clearly in either case. Though the Christian was, by his own confession, prepared to mock Hindu sensibilities and to resort to concealment and bribery (which succeeded, in part) to evade them, his expectation that a Muslim judge might share his chauvinism was not justified; like Akbar, whom he invoked, the Muslim administrator respected Hindu law and did not privilege Muslims before the law.

RELIGIOUS FUSION

In the realm of religious texts, both bhakti and Sufism transfused popular literature so thoroughly that it is often hard to tell which tradition is the source of a particular mystical folk song.[105] Much of the poetry written by Muslims, with Muslim names, in Hindi, Bengali (Bangla), Gujarati, Punjabi, and Marathi begins with the Islamic invocation of Allah but goes on to express Hindu content or makes use of Hindu forms, Hindu imagery, Hindu terminology. In return, the sixteenth-century Bangla text entitled *The Ocean of the Nectar of Bhakti,* by the theologian Rupagoswamin, tells the life of Krishna in a form modeled on a Sufi romance.[106] The heroes of the Persian epic the *Shah Nama* and the Sanskrit *Mahabharata* interact in the *Tarikh-i-Farishta,* composed under the Mughals. Hindu-Muslim sects flourished, especially in Bengal, and new Hindu sects emerged, headed by charismatic leaders. Muslims allowed Hindus to perform sacrifices in the ruins of old temples, and many Muslim pilgrims attended the Hindu shrines in Kangra and Mathura.[107]

Syncretism* remained at the heart of Sufism, which in the course of time produced Muslim disciples who had Hindu disciples who had Muslim disciples, and so on, some of whom called God Allah, some Rama or Hari (Vishnu).[108] In Sufi centers, low-caste Hindus, including Pariahs, shared meals with other Hindus as well as with Muslims.[109] A similar synthesis took place in the seventeenth century in "Dakani" poetry composed in Urdu, which blended Islamic and Hindu genres as well as male and female voices, introducing, from the Hindu lyric tradition and the Arabic storytelling tradition, a female narrator.[110] Popular religion often mixed Hindu and Sufi practices together inextricably, to the annoyance of reformers.[111] Many people were Hindu by culture, Muslim by

---

* I use the word with the understanding that it denotes the fusion of a number of religious elements, none of which is in any way a pure essence.

religion, or the reverse. Mughal emperors patronized yoga establishments. Hindus worshiped Sufi Pirs.[112]

Translating Religions

The enrichment of Hinduism by Islam, and Islam by Hinduism, was greatly facilitated by the production of translations, which inspired new, original genres in both cultures. By the time of the Mughals, Indian literature was flourishing in North India in a number of languages: Sanskrit, Persian (the official court language), Arabic, the Turkic languages, and many regional languages, including Sindi, Punjabi, Pashto, and Hindi.[113] In public spheres in South India too, particularly but not only in the Telugu-speaking world, language boundaries were porous both geographically and linguistically, and multiple literary cultures were loosely connected.[114] Urdu ("camp"), a hybrid dialect that Akbar developed in the military encampments, was widely used; it was written in Perso-Arabic script, with much Sanskrit-Hindi syntax and vocabulary.[115] Developed further under Shah Jahan, Urdu became the primary fusion language.

The Mughals extended their patronage to many Hindu scholars and commissioned the translation of many Hindu works from Sanskrit into Arabic and Persian. Already by the eighth century, the collection of animal fables called the *Panchatantra* had been translated into Arabic (known as *The Mirror for Princes* [*Kalila wa Dimna*]), and another version into Persian (entitled *The Lights of Canopus* [*Anvari Suhaili*]). Akbar had Abu'l Fazl translate it into Persian again and also had both the *Mahabharata* and the *Ramayana* translated into Persian.[116] There were Persian translations of the *Harivamsha,* gorgeously illustrated.[117] Jahangir had an abridged translation made of the *Yoga-vasishtha,* and Dara Shikoh himself later translated it again, more fully. Dara also provided the first Persian translation of the Upanishads, which became known in Europe (through a French translation of Dara's Persian) and introduced the British Orientalist William Jones to Indian literature. Thanks to Akbar and Dara, Sanskrit became an important literary language in the Muslim world.[118] The Turkish and Afghan courts of the fourteenth, fifteenth, and sixteenth centuries sponsored a rich and interactive mixture of vernacular and classical or cosmopolitan languages and fostered the growth of regional literature, music, and art.[119] The erotic literature of the Turks and Persians easily assimilated translations of the *Kama-sutra* into Persian, often with wonderful illustrations; the Persian was then translated into European languages.

ARCHITECTURE AND PAINTING

As the Mughals were superb plunderers, so were they superb builders. Their architecture was strongly influenced by Hindu architecture,[120] and in return, Mughal architecture had a vivid impact on many Hindu monuments,[121] inspiring, as in literature, unprecedented Hindu forms.

Babur, who scorned most things Indian, disdained the Indian builders: "A stone mosque was built, but it was not well made. They built it in the Indian fashion."[122] But Akbar, who admired most things Indian, admired its architecture, too; the eclectic architecture of Fatehpur Sikri combined Persian with Hindu and Jaina forms. Akbar employed nearly fifteen hundred stonecutters at Agra.[123] He gave Man Singh permission to erect a number of temples in Vrindaban, built of red sandstone, the material usually reserved for Mughal official architecture; these Hindu temples also had many Mughal architectural features.[124] Since there were no Rama temples in Ayodhya until the sixteenth or seventeenth century, there is some irony in the strong possibility that Babur, whose mosque was to become such a cause célèbre, may have sponsored the first Rama temples in Ayodhya, built when he built the ill-fated Babri Mosque.[125]

In painting too a fusion of Hindu and Muslim forms led to innovations in both cultures. Many paintings on Hindu themes are signed with the names of Muslim artists, and many Hindu miniature paintings were modeled on Persian originals[126] or incorporated composite figures and other fantastic themes from Persian miniatures.[127] Though Indian painters already knew how to illuminate manuscripts with miniatures, the Persians made it a court practice and introduced new techniques and refinements.

As always, the common people of India picked up the tab.[128] The great Mughal monuments were also monuments to Mughal "extravagance and oppression." Though there were no more crop seizures, there was still crippling taxation on peasants and artisans, and the plight of the cultivator was worse than ever, with increased exploitation from above.[129] As there was no free temple, there was certainly no free mosque.

CHAPTER 20
HINDUISM UNDER
THE MUGHALS
1500 to 1700 CE

CHRONOLOGY (ALL DATES ARE CE)

1486–1533 Chaitanya lives

1498–1597 Mirabai lives

1532–1623 Tulsidas lives

1608–1649 Tukaram lives

1622–1673 Kshetrayya lives

> It is a simple fact that contemporary Hinduism as a living practice
> would not be what it is if it were not for the devotional practices ini-
> tiated under Mughal rule.
>
> Amitav Ghosh (1956–)[1]

Hinduisms of various kinds flourished under the Mughals. The production and preservation of a large number of digests, as well as literary and religious texts, during this period suggest that this was another of those periods—we have encountered several—when the presence of foreign cultures in India led many Hindu intellectuals to take pains to preserve their cultural heritage.[2] This was not an unalloyed Good Thing. Some Hindus retreated into more conservative practices lest someone mistake them for Muslims in the dark of cultural fusion. As K. M. Pannikar, prime minister of Bikaner in the 1940s, put it, with benefit of hindsight, "The reaction of Hindu lawgivers to [the Mughal] challenge was in general to make Hinduism more rigid and to re-interpret the rules in such a way as to resist the encroachments of Islam. It is perhaps this defensive attitude toward society that is responsible for the orthodoxy of views which is characteristic of the Dharma Sastra literature of this period."[3]

But in a more positive vein, Hindu kings in medieval India arranged large-scale public debates.[4] Fear of Muslims and a desire to circle the wagons were among the inspirations for this burst of literary and religious activity. Mughal policies that encouraged trade and pilgrimage[5] (in part because several of the Mughals collected taxes on pilgrims) benefited the sacred Vaishnava sites of Ayodhya and Vrindavan. Devotional Vaishnavism flourished under the Mughals in the sixteenth century in ways that are foundational for subsequent Hinduism. The establishment of Muslim rule and the subsequent loss of a political center for Hinduism triggered a shift of focus in Vaishnavism away from the more warriorlike and kingly aspects of Vishnu to those of the passionate god of the forest, the playful, amorous god, Krishna the cowherd.[6] Though the Mughals picked up some aspects of caste, by and large they ignored it, and some Hindus followed their lead and loosened up. Outside the nervous world of the Brahmin imaginary, many good things were happening.

TULSIDAS AND SITA IN NORTH INDIA

Tulsidas (c. 1532/1543–1623), one of the main architects of North Indian Vaishnavism, was close to several movers and shakers at the Mughal court, including Man Singh.[7] His retelling of the *Ramayana* in Hindi, titled "The Holy Lake of the Acts of Rama" (*Ramcaritmanas*), is still read and enacted each year at the "Rama Play" (Ramlila) throughout North India, particularly at Ramnagar near Varanasi. Tulsidas, who composed his poem at a pilgrimage center that had been attacked by Muslims, said that even the Muslims would be saved by Rama's name[8] (rather reminiscent of earlier claims that this or that pilgrimage spot would save even Pariahs). The Brahmins of Varanasi, where the text was composed, are said to have been shocked by the composition of such a text in a vernacular language. They tested it by placing it in the Shiva temple for one night, with the Vedas and Puranas placed on top of it. In the morning Tulsidas's text was on top of them all, legitimizing its authority,[9] like that of the scriptures in the South Indian myth (which texts will float upstream?), buoyancy being, apparently, a sign of sanctity.

Some Brahmins also objected to Tulsidas's challenges to caste. Although by and large Tulsidas toes the Brahmin party line and upholds caste, there are also moments of compassion for Pariahs and tribals, such as this story about a Pariah, told, significantly, through the masking device of an animal:

RAMA AND THE CROW

When Rama was still a little baby, he began to cry when he could not catch the crow that came near him; he pursued the crow no matter how high the bird flew into the air. The crow fell into the child's mouth and watched for thousands of years as Rama was born again and again as a child on earth. Then the child laughed, and the crow fell out of his mouth. Rama granted the terrified crow the boon of eternal devotion to him, and so the crow sings Rama's praises eternally.[10]

The manifestation of god's universal form within an anthropomorphic body, a manifestation that we have seen experienced by Brahma and Vishnu, by Arjuna (in the *Gita*), and by Krishna's mother, is here given to a crow, an unclean scavenger. The caste issue is explicit here: The crow was an uppity Pariah in a former life, until Shiva cursed him to be reborn as a crow. This story stands in marked contrast with Rama's treatment of a crow in Valmiki's *Ramayana,* in which he regards the crow as an enemy and blinds him.

Tulsidas also tackled in his own way the problem of Rama's treatment of Sita. In the centuries that had intervened since Valmiki's *Ramayana,* as Rama had become one of the two great gods of Vaishnavism (Krishna being the other), Sita's fate had become more vexing than ever. Tulsidas dealt with this problem by incorporating into his poem the tradition of the illusory or shadow Sita from earlier Sanskrit texts. Sita enters the fire at the ordeal and "both the shadow form and the stigma of public shame" are consumed in the blazing fire.[11] Thus the Vedantic concept of illusion allows Tulsidas to argue that Rama never intended or needed to test Sita (since he knew she wasn't in Ravana's house at all) but goaded the shadow Sita into undertaking the fire ordeal merely in order to get her into the fire so that he could bring the real Sita back from the fire.[12] And the real Sita then stays with him; Tulsidas omits entirely the episodes in which Sita bears twin sons and enters the earth; the story ends with Rama and Sita together, happily ever after.

CHANDIDAS, CHAITANYA, AND RADHA IN BENGAL

Like Sita, Radha suffered in separation from her beloved (Krishna), but the spirit of Radha's longing in separation was different from Sita's and was interpreted still differently by each of two great medieval Bengali poets, Chandidas and Chaitanya.

In the fourteenth century Bangla poetry of Chandidas, Radha is already married when she goes off with Krishna. (In the sixteenth-century Sanskrit plays of Rupagoswamin, Chaitanya's most famous disciple, Radha is married to Abhimanyu, the son of Arjuna.[13]) Chandidas writes:

Let us not talk of that fatal flute.

It calls a woman away from her home

and drags her by the hair to that Shyam [Krishna].

A devoted wife forgets her spouse

To be drawn like a deer, thirsty and lost.[14]

The legends about Chandidas tell us how the tradition regarded him. His poems say that he was a Brahmin and a village priest who openly declared his love for a low-caste washerwoman named Rami. Legends say that he was dismissed as a priest and fasted to death as a protest but came to life again on the funeral pyre, or that the begum of Gaur took such a fancy to him that her jealous husband, the nawab, had him whipped to death while tied to the back of an elephant.

The Bengali saint Chaitanya (1486–1533) was born into a Brahmin family and received a sound education in the Sanskrit sacred texts. After the death of his father when he was twenty-two, he made a pilgrimage to Gaya to perform the funeral rituals, and there he had a religious experience that inspired him to renounce the world. The world, however, would not renounce him; people flocked to him and joined him in singing songs (*kirtana*) to Krishna and dancing in a kind of trance, as well as repeating the names of Krishna, worshiping temple icons or the tulsi plant (a kind of basil sacred to Vishnu), and retelling Krishna's acts, particularly his loveplay with the cowherd women (Gopis).[15] Chaitanya settled in Orissa in the town of Puri (rather than Vrindavan, the scene of Krishna's youth) at his mother's urging, so that he could more easily stay in touch with her. He had frequent epileptic seizures and may have died by drowning while in a state of religious ecstasy.

Chaitanya and his followers believed that he was an incarnation of Krishna and Radha in one body, where at last the two gods (and Chaitanya) could simultaneously experience the bliss of both sides of the couple in union.[16] The Bengali sect called Sahajiyas ("Naturalists") saw Krishna and Radha united not only in Chaitanya but in every man and every woman; their goal was not to worship or imitate Krishna or Radha, in a dualistic, bhakti sense, but to become them, in a monistic and Tantric sense, to realize both male and female powers within their own bodies.[17] They praised the ideal of love for another man's wife or for a woman of unsuitably low caste, or an unmarried woman's love for a man (for even in texts in which Radha is not anyone else's wife, she is usually not Krishna's wife), because they admired the intensity of such love in the face of social disapproval. The adulterous love between Krishna and Radha or the Gopis made a positive virtue of the addictive vice of lust, coming down solidly on the side of passion and against the control of passion through renunciation; adulterous passion, which had long been the benchmark of what religion was designed to prevent, now became a metaphor for the proper love of god.

Yet unlike the model of Shiva as Skull Bearer, these ideals were never taken as paradigms for an *imitatio dei;* they were theological parables, not licenses to commit adultery. The difference can be accounted for when we consider the radical contrast between the relatively lawless period in which the Kapalikas thrived, not to mention the antinomian nature of their community, and the more tempered and theocratic atmosphere of even the most erotic of the cults of Krishna.

Chaitanya was said to have reconverted the Muslim governor of Orissa back to Hinduism, from which he had converted and to which he had also converted many Pathans (ethnic Afghans).[18] Chaitanya's followers include many groups, beginning with the antinomian Bengali Sahajiyas, who were his contemporaries. His main disciples were the renunciants called Goswamins. One of them, Nityananda, continuing the paradigm, was said to be the incarnation of Balarama, Krishna's brother. In his efforts to convert the Bengali Tantrics, Nityananda is said to have consorted with "prostitutes, drunkards, and others of dubious character," behavior that his followers justified by his association with Balarama, who was known for his excesses.[19] Other Goswamins developed an erotic devotional theology that incorporated still more antinomian and ecstatic Tantric influences and took root among the people known as Bauls.[20]

At the same time, many worshipers in the Chaitanya tradition, recoiling from the antinomian Tantric variations on the theme of Krishna and Radha that had made them the target of social opprobrium,[21] developed a different tradition and went back to the *Gita-Govinda* for their central imagery, emphasizing not the union but the separation (*viraha*) of the two lovers and the suffering of longing for the otiose god, the renunciation rather than the passion of love. Once again, a Tantric tradition had split in two. These Goswamins, anxious to prevent the story of Krishna and Radha from becoming a model for human behavior, hastened to sanitize the myth by reversing the locus of the real people and the shadows; where in earlier texts the Gopis had left shadow images of themselves in bed with their husbansds while they danced with Krishna, now some of the Goswamins specified that the *real* Gopis remained in bed with their husbands and merely sent their shadow doubles to dance with the god.

The quasi-Tantric Bengal traditions debated for centuries whether Krishna and Radha were married or, as they put it, whether Radha was Krishna's wife ("his own" [svakiya]) or his mistress ("someone else's" [parakiya]), and they decided, in 1717, that adulterous love was in fact orthodox.[22]

The question of role models was a pressing one, for in Bengal Vaishnavism the worshiper is inspired to decide not which of the personae dramatis s/he would like to play, but who s/he is: the mother, lover, servant, or friend of Krishna.[23] Bhakti was better suited for women, who could be god's lovers and mothers, the most intimate roles, whereas male worshipers had to pretend to be women (some of them withdrawing to menstruate every month). This gave women a great measure of spiritual authority, though not necessarily practical authority. Rupagosvamin wrote of "the devotion that follows from passion" (raganuga bhakti), in contrast with scriptural devotion (vaidhi bhakti). In the familiar pattern, both paths lead to Krishna.

Yet another branch of Bengali Vaishnavas rejected the renunciation espoused (if one can espouse renunciation) by both the Goswamins and the lineages of the philosophers Ramanuja and Madhva. These were the Radhavallabhas ("Radha's Darlings"), who venerated the householder stage, rejected renunciation, and regarded Krishna not as the supreme deity but as the servant of the goddess Radha. As one British scholar put it, Krishna "may do the coolie-work of building the world, but Radha sits as Queen. He is at best but her Secretary of State."[24] Many of the Bangla verses of Chandidasa and the Maithili verses of Vidyapati (in the fourteen and fifteenth centuries) are written from the standpoint of a Radha who is more powerful than Krishna.

Continuing the Bengali tradition, the celebration of poverty by the poet Ramprasad (1720–1781) served both as solace for other people truly in need and as a metaphor for spiritual poverty, though the upper castes supported Ramprasad quite well and he gave no opposition to caste. His poetry bristles with references to real life: to poverty, farmers, debts, absentee landlords, lawyers, leaking boats, merchants, and traders.[25] Strong Tantric influences are also evident in the wine and drunkenness that pervaded both his poetry and (as the stories go) his life.[26]

TUKARAM'S DOGS IN MAHARASHTRA

Tukaram was a Shudra who lived in Maharashtra from 1608 to 1649. None of his poems were written down in his lifetime; all that we have were later transcribed from oral traditions, along with legends about him. According to one story, which bears a suspicious resemblance to the story of the floating South Indian texts and, closer to home, to the buoyancy of Tulsidas's text, angry Brahmins forced Tukaram to throw all his manuscripts into the river in his native village. Tukaram fasted and prayed, and after thirteen days the sunken notebooks reappeared from the river, undamaged.[27] He married, but since his wife was chronically ill, he took a second wife. When the great famine of 1629 killed his parents, his first wife, and some of his children, he abandoned the householder's life, ignored his debts and the pleas of his (second) wife and his remaining children, and went off into the wilderness. He became a poet, devoted to the god Vitthal, speaking in the idiom that the Marathi poets had fashioned out of the songs that ordinary housewives sang at home and that farmers, traders, craftsmen, and laborers sang at popular religious festivals. Some say he ended his life by throwing himself into the same river where his poems had sunk and reemerged. His poems, which challenge caste and denounce Brahmins, also denounce the ascetic: "He must consume a lot of bhang, and opium, and tobacco;/ But his hallucinations are perpetual."[28]

His poems often imagine the relationship between god and his devotee as the relationship between a secret lover and an adulteress (as many bhakti poets do) or, more unusually, as the violent relationship between a murderer (in this case a Thug, a member of a pack of thieves, stranglers, and worshipers of the goddess Kali) and his victim: "The Thug has arrived in Pandhari./ He will garrotte his victim with the cord of love."[29] He also imagines the divine relationship as a bond between a master and a dog:

GOD'S DOG[*]

I've come to your door
Like a dog looking for a home
O Kind One
Don't drive me away . . .
Says Tuka,
My Master's trained me hard

---

[*] "God's Dog," a short palindrome, could be expanded into another: "Dog as a devil deified lived as a god."

I am allowed to eat
Only out of his own
Hand.[30]

MUGHAL HORSEMEN AND HINDU HORSE GODS

Dogs were one sort of religious symbol; horses were another. And real, as well as symbolic, horses played a major role in Hindu-Muslim relations under the Mughals; horse trading, both literal and figurative, was the common theme. A great deal of the revenue drawn from taxing the peasants was spent on royal horses. In Haridwar, in the Mughal period, the great spring horse fair coincided, not by coincidence, with a famous religious festival that drew thousands of pilgrims to the banks of the Ganges each year. This combination of trade and pilgrimage was widespread; the Maharashtrian and Sikh generals and their troops came to the fairs to pay their devotion at the holy places in the morning and secure a supply of warhorses in the afternoon.[31]

When the Europeans arrived in India in the Mughal period, horses were very expensive animals, the best ones costing up to ten thousand dollars.[32] More than 75 percent of Mughal horses were imported, mostly from Central Asia. Babur seems to have spent more time in the saddle than on the ground, and took a personal interest in the horses.[33] Akbar had 150,000 to 200,000 cavalrymen, plus the emperor's own crack regiment of another 7,000.[34] Abu'l Fazl tells us how important horses were to Akbar, for ruling, conquest, presentation as gifts, and general convenience;[35] Akbar even had luminous polo balls made so that he could play night games.[36] The horses, as always, were mostly imported: "Merchants bring to court good horses from Iraq, Turky, Turkestan . . . Kirghiz, Tibet, Kashmir and other countries. Droves after droves arrive from Turan and Iran, and there are nowadays twelve thousand in the stables of his Majesty."[37]

Abu'l Fazl insists, however, that the best horses of all were bred in India, particularly in the Punjab,* Mewat, Ajmer, and Bengal near Bihar. He continues:

Skilful, experienced men have paid much attention to the breeding of this sensible animal, many of whose habits resemble those of man; and after a short time Hin-

---

* The Punjab still has good grazing; Indian breeders insist, testily, that Pakistan, at the time of partition, got the best grazing land.

dustan ranked higher in this respect than Arabia, whilst many Indian horses cannot be distinguished from Arabs or from the Iraqi breed. There are fine horses bred in every part of the country; but those of Cachh [Kutch] excel, being equal to Arabs. It is said that a long time ago an Arab ship was wrecked and driven to the shore of Cachh; and that it had seven choice horses, from which, according to the general belief, the breed of that country originated.[38]

This, then, is the answer to the apparent contradiction: Indian horses (or, rather, some Indian horses) are Arab horses, and there is no contest.

The Arab horses from Kutch were probably the sires of the most distinctive native Indian breed. Sometime before the eleventh century, a clan of Rajput warriors developed a new breed of warhorses from Arab and Turkmen stock in Marwar (a state whose capital was the city of Jodhpur, the city from which the riding pants and short boots adopted by the British in the nineteenth century take their name). The Marwari is a desert horse with a thick, arched neck, long-lashed eyes, flaring nostrils, and distinctive ears, which curve inward to a sharp point, meeting to form an almost perfect arch at the tips. Aficionados compare the shape of the Marwari's ears to the lyre, to the scorpion's arched stinger, and to the Rajputs' trademark handlebar mustaches, turned upright and set on their thick, bushy ends. (The Kathiawar horse from Gujarat has the same special ears but is not quite so tall or so long.)[39]

Despite these occasional breeding successes, negative factors made the Indian horse into a beast so rarefied that it became more mythical than practical. Ever since the Arabs entered India, then the Turks, and then the Mongols who were to become the Mughals, and despite a few passing references to the Scythians and the British, it has almost always been the Muslims who play the role of good and evil foreign horsemen in the local equine rituals and mythologies of India. These myths and rituals, though not always documented in the Mughal period, are often about the Mughals. The corpus of Hindu myths that depicts the Turks and Arabs bringing horses into India seems to have assimilated the historical experience of the importation of horses not only to the lingering vestiges—the cultural hoofprints, as it were—of Vedic horse myths but also to the cross-cultural theme of magical horses brought from heaven or the underworld.[40]

There are some negative responses too: In the seventeenth century, for instance, a Hindu from Afghanistan insisted that when he died, he wanted to be buried where he couldn't hear the hoof steps of Mughal horses.[41] But despite or because of the political domination that the Mughals maintained, their contribution to the equine legends of Hinduism was generally positive, and the Muslims in the stories are often depicted in a favorable light, both because the Mughals strongly influenced Hindu horse lore and because some Hindus welcomed them as the bearers of the gift of horses. The shadow of the hated and loved Muslim horse may also fall across the highly ambiguous equine figure of Kalki.

Many Hindu rituals involve Muslims and horses. The Muslim saint Alam Sayyid of Baroda was known as the horse saint (Ghore Ka Pir). He was buried with his horse beside him, and Hindus hang images of the horse on trees around his tomb.[42] In Bengal, people offer clay horses to deified Muslim saints like Satya Pir, and Hindus as well as Muslims worship at the shrines of other Muslim "horse saints."[43] Then there is the South Indian Hindu folk hero named Muttal Ravuttan.[44] "Ravuttan" designates a Muslim horseman, a folk memory of the historical figure of the Muslim warrior on horseback, "whether he be the Sufi warrior leading his band of followers or the leader of an imperial army of conquest." At Chinna Salem, Muttal Ravuttan receives marijuana, opium, cigars, and horse gram (*kollu*) for his horse. The offerings are made to an image of him mounted on his horse, sculpted in relief on a stone plaque, or to a clay horse (or horses) standing outside the shrine in readiness for him. The horse is canonically white and is said to be able to fly through the air.[45]

Muslims are deeply involved in the worship of the god Khandoba, an incarnation of Shiva, in Maharashtra, and many of Khandoba's followers have been Muslim horsemen, though it is sometimes said that Aurangzeb was forced to flee from Khandoba's power.[46] In Jejuri, the most famous center of the worship of Khandoba, a Muslim leads the horse in the Khandoba festival and a Muslim family traditionally keeps Khandoba's horses. The worshipers of Khandoba act as the god's horse (occasionally as his dog[47]) by galloping and whipping themselves,[48] and at the annual festival in Jejuri, when, as in many temples, the worshipers carry a portable image of the deity in a palanquin or wheeled cart in procession around the town, devotees possessed by the power of the god move like horses in front of the palanquin.[49] In the myth associated with this ritual, the god Shiva arrives on his bull Nandi[50] before he mounts a horse to fight the demon Mani; some texts say that Nandi turns into the horse,[51] while others[52] say that Shiva ordered the moon to become a horse and, seated on it, cut off the head of the demon.[53] The pan-Indian image of Nandi stands at the bottom of the hill at the shrine of Khandoba; the local horse of Khandoba stands at the top and is regarded as an avatar of Nandi, just as Khandoba is an avatar of Shiva. Both are waiting for Khandoba/Shiva to mount them. Khandoba is not a horse god or a horse; he *rides* a horse, which is, in this context, the very opposite of *being* a horse. In the myth, he rides a demonic horse; in the ritual, he rides his human worshipers. He is the subduer of horses, the tamer of horses. He makes demonic horses, like his worshipers, into divine horses.

THREE TALES OF EQUINE RESURRECTION

A story about horses and Mughals is still prevalent both in oral tradition and in popular printed bazaar pamphlets in Hindi and Punjabi in the great Punjab area—Punjab, Haryana, Himachal Pradesh, and Delhi—where real horses have remained important throughout Indian history. This is the story of Dhyanu Bhagat:

WHY COCONUTS ARE OFFERED TO THE GODDESS

There was once a devotee of the Goddess named Dhyanu Bhagat who lived at the same time as the Mughal emperor Akbar. Once he was leading a group of pilgrims to the Temple of Jvala Mukhi [at Kangra, in Himachal Pradesh] where the Goddess appears in the form of a flame. As the group was passing through Delhi, Akbar summoned Dhyanu to the court, demanding to know who this goddess was and why he worshipped her. Dhyanu replied that she is the all-powerful Goddess who grants wishes to her devotees. In order to test Dhyanu, Akbar ordered the head of his horse to be cut off and told Dhyanu to have his goddess join the horse's head back to its body. Dhyanu went to Jvala Mukhi where he prayed day and night to the Goddess, but he got no answer. Finally, in desperation, he cut off his own head and offered it to the Goddess. At that point, the Goddess appeared before him in full splendor, seated on her lion. She joined his head back to his body and also joined the horse's head back to its body. Then she offered him a boon. He asked that in the future, devotees not be required to go to such extreme lengths to prove their devotion. So, she granted him the boon that from then on, she would accept the offering of a coconut to be equal to that of a head. So, that is why people offer coconuts to the Goddess.[54]

The devouring goddess appears both in the deity who demands blood sacrifices and, at the very start of the story, in the shrine of Jvala Mukhi, the holy place where she takes the form of a flame. For Jvala Mukhi ("Mouth of Fire," a common term for a volcano) is the name of the submarine doomsday mare. In this story about her worship, the heads of the devotee and his horse are not transposed (as they are in Hindu myths about doubly decapitated women and men) but merely removed and restored in tandem, while Dhyanu asks for and receives a boon: that henceforth people can prove their devotion by giving the Goddess coconuts rather than their own heads.

Now, a coconut resembles a human head but does not at all resemble a horse's head. The coconut, as essential to many *puja*s as animals are to a blood sacrifice, is a clue to the fact that this is really a myth about human sacrifice—perhaps a local myth—that has been adapted to take account of the more "Sanskritic" tradition of the horse sacrifice. There are changes: the horse beheaded in the story is not killed in a horse sacrifice, and it is beheaded rather than strangled as the horses in the horse sacrifice generally are (though they are often beheaded in the mythology). We might read this text as a meditation on the historical transition from human sacrifice to Vedic horse sacrifice to contemporary vegetarian *puja,* a progression already prefigured in the Brahmanas. Moreover, coconuts do not grow in the Punjab; the rituals specify that one must use *dry* coconuts for all offerings, presumably because they have traveled all the way from somewhere where they do grow, a long distance. Since these coconuts must be imported, they may therefore represent either the adoption of a myth that is "foreign" (i.e., from another part of India) or a local tradition about a "foreign" ritual that requires *imported* coconuts, appropriate to a ritual about imported horses.

A similar myth collected in Chandigarh substitutes a child for the worshiper himself:

THE HORSE AND THE BOY IN THE CAULDRON

Queen Tara told her husband, King Harichand, of a miracle that the goddess had performed [involving snakes and lizards]. The king asked, "How can I get a direct vision [*pratyakṣ darshan*] of the Mother? I will do anything." Tara told him that it wasn't easy and that he would have to sacrifice his favorite blue horse. He did so. Then she told him to sacrifice his beloved son. He did so. Then she told him to cut up the horse and son and place them in a cauldron and cook them. This he did. She told him to dish out the food on five plates, one for Mata [Mother, the Goddess]), one for himself, one for the horse, one for the son, and one for her. The king, bound to his word, started to eat, but tears welled up in his eyes. The horse and the son both came back to life. Devi appeared on her lion, a direct vision. King Harichand worshipped her and begged for forgiveness. Mata forgave him and then disappeared.[55]

We may see behind this story not merely the Vedic horse sacrifice but the South Indian story of Ciruttontar and the curried child and the well-known Puranic myth of King Harishchandra,[56] whose son died and was eventually restored to him. What has been added is the horse.

A story about a low-caste travesty of a horse sacrifice was recorded in North India during the nineteenth century:

THE HORSE OF LAL BEG, THE SWEEPER

There is a horse miracle story told in connection with Lal Beg, the patron saint of the sweepers, a Pariah caste. The king of Delhi lost a valuable horse, and the sweepers were ordered to bury it, but as the animal was very fat, they proceeded to cut it up for themselves, giving one leg to the king's priest. The king, suspecting what had happened, ordered the sweepers to produce the horse. They were in dismay at the order, but they laid what was left of the animal on a mound sacred to Lal Beg, and prayed to him to save them, whereupon the horse stood up, but only on three legs. So they went to the king and confessed how they had disposed of the fourth leg. The unlucky priest was executed, and the horse soon after died also.[57]

This is a horse sacrifice in the shadow world of the Pariahs, where Vedic traditions turn inside out. True, the horse comes back to life (like the horses in the tales of Dhyanu and Harichand), but not for long, nor does the priest fare well. The point comes through loud and clear: A horse is not a Pariah animal.

EQUINE EPICS

The long struggle and eventual fall of the Rajput kingdoms under the onslaught of the Mughal armies gave rise to a genre of regional, vernacular epics that evolved out of oral narratives in this period, taking up themes from the Sanskrit epics, the *Mahabharata* and *Ramayana,* but transforming them by infusing them with new egalitarian or pluralist themes, such as the figure of the hero's low-caste or Muslim sidekick. The regional epics were nurtured in a culture that combined Afghan and Rajput traditions[58] and much more. They embellish the trope of the end of an era, from the *Mahabharata,* with sad stories of deaths of the last Hindu kings. The bittersweet Pyrrhic victory of the *Mahabharata* heroes here becomes transformed into a corpus of tragic tales of the heroic cultural and martial resistance of the protagonists and their cultural triumph, despite their inevitable martial defeat. As Alf Hiltebeitel puts it, "A

Mahabharata heroic age is thus mapped onto a microheroic age."[59] The Sanskrit epic supplies a pool of symbols,[60] a sea of tropes, characters, and situations that form a kind of "underground pan-Indian folk *Mahabharata*," feeding into a system of texts animated by a combination of Hinduism and Islam.[61] Horses loom large in all of them.

The vernacular equine epics first moved from northwestern and central regions to southern ones and then carried southern religious, martial, and literary tropes back north, in a pattern we recognize from theological and philosophical movements. The irony is that Islamic culture contributed greatly to these grand heroic poems that people composed in response to what they perceived as the fall of a great Hindu civilization at the hands of Muslims. Two among the many heroes of these epics are Gugga and Tej Singh (in Hindi; also called Tecinku in Tamil country and Desingu in Telugu-speaking Andhra).

Gugga (also spelled Guga), a folk god, is said to have been a historical figure who lived, by various accounts, during the reign of Prithvi Raj Chauhan (the last Hindu king of Delhi, c. 1168–1192)[62] or in the time of the last great Mughal, Aurangzeb (1658–1707)—that is, at either end of the Muslim reign. Gugga is a combination of a Muslim fakir (called Gugga Pir or Zahar Pir) and a Chauhan Rajput[63] (that is, a Rajput warrior hero of the Chauhan clan in Rajasthan). According to one version of the story, Gugga, with his famous flying black mare, entered battle and beheaded his two brothers; when his mother disowned him, he converted to Islam and went to Mecca. When Gugga died, the earth opened and received him, still mounted on his mare.[64] Another story tells of Gugga's birth: A great yogi gave some *guggal* (a resinous sap used medicinally) to a Brahmin woman, a woman of a sweeper (Pariah) caste, and a mare, all of whom were impregnated.[65] The horse, the Kshatriya animal par excellence, is here subversively paired with both Brahmins and Pariahs.

Raja Tej Singh was a historical figure, the son of the commander of the fort of Senji under Aurangzeb. When, in 1714, Tej refused to obey a summons from the nawab of Arcot, the deputy of the Mughal ruler (who was then Farrukhsiyar), the nawab waged war against him, in the course of which Tej rode his horse at the head of the nawab's elephant; the horse reared and drummed his hooves on the forehead of the elephant, blunting the Mughal advance. A soldier sliced the hocks of Tej's horse, unseating Tej,[66] who died in the battle, as did his best friend, the Muslim Mahabat Khan. His queen, a beautiful woman aged sixteen or seventeen, "having embraced her husband, ordered with an incredible serenity that the pyre be lit, which was at once done, and she too was burned alive with him."[67] In Tamil and Telugu legend too, Tecinku's best friend was a Muslim, while Tecinku was a devout Vaishnava.[68] Yet despite the friendship between the Muslim and Vaishnava hero, this is not a simple story of communal harmony. Tecinku's Muslim companion is a very Vaishnava sort of Muslim, who prays to both Rama and Allah on several occasions but goes to Vishnu's heaven in the end; Vaishnavism encompasses Islam.[69]

Many of these stories are still told, indeed performed, in Rajasthan today, where the gods' priests and the storytellers (*bhopas*) are drawn from among villagers of the lowest castes.[70] Recently the patron of these performances explained why they were beginning to die out: "When the stories used to be told, everyone had a horse and some cattle. . . . Now, when a *bhopa* tells stories about the beauty of a horse, it doesn't make the same connection with the audience." Yet the epics are surviving in places where "the pastoral context of the story"—of cows and horses and heroic cattle herders—is still intact.[71]

Muslim Mares in Hindu Epics

One strong hint that much of medieval Hindu horse lore comes from Muslims is the gender of the horses. Arab horsemen generally rode mares and told stories about mares, while the Hindus before the Mughal period generally preferred stallions. Vedic symbolism had predisposed Indian horsemen to admire stallions, and Hindu mythology is all about stallions, epitomized by the male horse killed in the horse sacrifice, with all its positive symbolism kept entire (virility, fertility, aggressive volatility). Stallions dominate the depicted Hindu battle scenes, hunting expeditions, and court ceremonies. And there are still tales of Rajput stallions, such as Chetak, a gray stallion that sacrificed his life for Maharana Pratap, the last Rajput to succumb to the Mughals, in the 1576 battle of Haldighati.* The females of the species, on the other hand, mares, are regarded as wild animals never tamed, symbolic of wild women who deceive and leave their husbands, a pattern exacerbated by the image of the submarine mare, symbolic of dangerous lust and anger that will inevitably erupt to destroy the world at doomsday.

A dramatic change takes place in the Hindu equine epics, where many of the horses are good mares, such as Gugga's mare and the celestial mare that the

---

* Fast-forward: The stallion's name lives on in a line of Chetak motorscooters produced by India's Bajaj Auto Ltd.

Telugu hero Peddanna inherits from his foster mother. Dev Narayan, hero of yet another epic, rides a black mare named Tejan.[72] In the epic of Pabuji in Rajasthan, Pabuji has a splendid black mare named Kesar Kalimi ("black saffron"), who dies with him.[73] In some versions, the mare is an incarnation of Pabuji's mother, Kesar Pari ("the saffron nymph"), an Apsaras, who abandons him shortly after his birth but returns to him in the form of a mare when he is twelve. Although Tecinku rides a stallion, Tej in contemporary Hindi folklore rides a mare named Magic Mare (Lila Gori);[74] the force of the mare paradigm in the Hindi version seems to have overridden the earlier and more historical Telugu version, about a stallion.

The many benevolent mares in the oral epics therefore stand in opposition to the enduring Vedic and Puranic stallion tradition, arguing, subversively, for a positive valence for the demonic mare of the Sanskrit epics and Puranas. The authors of the regional equine epics were either ignorant of the Puranic bias against mares (which is unlikely) or chose to ignore it in favor of an imported Arabic pro-mare tradition, a narrative pattern of considerable detail repeated in many different stories.

WOMEN

MUGHAL WIVES (AND SAINTS)

Like mares, women, or at least some women, did rather well under the Mughals. From female Sufi saints[75] and the women of the royal harem down to the wives of the lowest administrators, as we saw in the case of the poached peacocks, women exercised great powers behind the throne.[76] Despite being generally confined in harems guarded by eunuchs, a few princesses had their own libraries, and the women of the harem learned Persian poetry, were often able to sign away land grants (the *uzuk*, the round seal, was kept in the harem), and could have abortions.[77] Though hardly typical (education for girls was rare, and they married too early to have much time for it in any case[78]), these women were at least *possible*, and they expanded the boundaries of the possible for their sisters in their day.

Babur's maternal grandmother managed everything for her young grandson, and his mother accompanied him on many of his campaigns. Hindal's mother, Dildar Begum, restrained him from at least one attack on his brother Humayun, when he was nineteen, by putting on mourning and telling him she was mourning for him, bound as he was on the path of his own destruction.

(He listened then but tried it again later, and Humayun killed him.[*]) Akbar's mother, Hamideh Banu, was in charge of the empire while Akbar went off on military campaigns, and Akbar gave each of his concubines her own house and her own day of the week reserved for him to visit her; he also constructed an entire, strictly regulated city district for the prostitutes, called City of Satan (Shaytanpura). The cash allowances that Akbar's wives received were called pan (betel leaf) money (*barg baha*), a rough equivalent of what Euro-American women used to call pin money. Akbar also had female bodyguards, with archers in the front lines.[79] He took an interest in the education of women and established a school for girls in Fatehpur Sikri.

One woman who opposed Akbar was Chand Bibi ("Lady Chand"), who was regent of Bijapur (1580–1584) and regent of Ahmednagar (1595–1599). A fine horsewoman, who knew many languages (including Arabic, Persian, Turkish, Marathi, and Kannada), she took part in the defense of the fortress of Ahmednagar when forces under orders from Akbar led an attack and siege against it in 1595. But when she began to negotiate a treaty with the Mughals, rumors circulated that she was in league with them, and her own officers murdered her.[80]

One of the few prudent things Jahangir ever did was to marry a very capable woman, Nur Jahan, the thirty-four-year-old widow of one of his Afghan amirs; she was also the daughter of his chief minister (whose large estate she inherited) and sister of his leading general. A first-class rider, polo player, and hunter, she was a "cunning and energetic woman," who exploited the Mughals' weakness for drugs and alcohol. She became the de facto regent on those many occasions when Jahangir was too smashed to function. As Jahangir himself put it, mincing no words, "I have handed the business of government over to Nur Jahan; I require nothing beyond a *ser* of wine and half a *ser* of meat." Coins were struck in her name, and she could sign mandates granting rights. She built many gardens and a gorgeous mausoleum at Agra. She cleverly managed to have her niece (her brother's daughter) Mumtaz Mahal marry Shah Jahan and her own daughter by her first marriage marry one of Shah Jahan's brothers. Other women of Jahangir's harem encouraged the design and building of mosques when he himself did not.[81]

---

[*] History does not record whether or not Dildar Begum resisted the temptation to say, "I told you so, but you never listened to your mother."

Mumtaz Mahal ("the palace favorite") is surely the most famous of the Mughal women, the one for whom Shah Jahan built the Taj Mahal. She was the mother of Dara Shikoh and his older sister, Jahanara. Jahanara was initiated into a Sufi order and wrote about it and about her pilgrimage to the shrine of the Indian Sufi Mu'in ud-Din Chisti in Ajmer; she also wrote a biography of him. She was immensely wealthy, both from half of her mother's fortune and from trading with the Dutch. Jahanara drank wine and inspired many rumors; she was said to have hidden young men in her house, sometimes disguising them in women's clothing and riding with them on an elephant.[82]

Hindu Saints and Antiwives (and Wives)

There was, as we have seen, a great deal of intermarriage between Rajputs and Mughals: Mughal men married Rajput women, and to a lesser extent, Rajput men married Mughal women. Intermarriages of both sorts were also common among the nonroyal classes. Mirza Aziz Koka (governor of Malwa, Akbar's foster brother) wrote a poem comparing the members of the multiethnic harem: "Every man should have four wives: a Persian, with whom he can converse; a woman from Khurusan for the housework; a Hindu woman to raise the children, and one from Transoxiana, whom he can beat as a warning to the others."[83] And Urdu poets composed romantic Hindustani poetry on an ever-popular theme, "Muslim boy meets Hindu girl, with fatal consequences."[84]

Many heroines among the Rajput princesses fought against the Mughals in battle, rather than marry them. Tulsibai, a Maharashtrian woman, led a great army into battle, and Rani Durgawati of Gondwana was famous for her courage. The widow of the Raja of Srinagar ruled with an iron hand during the reign of Shah Jahan; she often ordered the noses to be cut off convicted criminals,[85] a punishment traditionally meted out to unchaste women.

There were also brave women in religious literature of this period, the most famous of whom was Mirabai (c. 1450–1525). According to the earliest version of her life story, she was forced to marry a king's son but preferred the company of wandering mendicants and devotees of Krishna; the king (either her husband or her father-in-law, according to various stories) tried, in vain, to kill her; she left her marriage to join the devotees of Krishna. In later tellings, however (including the Amar Chitra Katha comic book, India's version of Classic Comics), it is her husband's brother who tries to kill her; her husband conveniently dies soon after the marriage, and Mirabai is depicted as "an ideal Hindu wife."

Although her poems are the most quoted and her life story the best known of all the North Indian saints, few of her poems were anthologized in her time. Perhaps this is because her poems mock both marriage and asceticism,[86] leaving her few allies.

Mirabai composed a poem based on a story that Valmiki, Tulsi, and Kabir told about a tribal woman (Shabari) who offered Rama fruit. Mirabai adds a woman's touch. The tribal woman (here a Bhil) first tastes the fruit herself:

> The Bhil woman tasted them, plum after plum,
> and finally found one she could offer him.
> What kind of genteel breeding was this?
> And hers was no ravishing beauty.
> Her family was poor, her caste quite low,
> her clothes a matter of rags.
> Yet Ram took that fruit—that touched, spoiled fruit—
> For he knew that it stood for her love.[87]

Mirabai asks, about the Bhil woman, "What sort of a Veda could she have learned?"

Another poem by Mirabai is about Krishna, whom she calls Mohan ("the deluder"):

> My eyes are greedy. They're beyond turning back.
> They stare straight ahead, friend, straight ahead,
> coveting and coveting still more.
> So here I am, standing at my door
> to get a good look at Mohan when he comes.
> Abandoning my beautiful veil and the modesty
> that guards my family's honor; showing my face.
> Mother-in-law, sister-in-law: day and night they monitor,
> lecturing me about it all and lecturing once again.
> Yet my quick giddy eyes will brook no hindrance.
> They're sold into someone else's hands.
> Some will say I'm good, some will say I'm bad—
> whatever their opinion, I exalt it as a gift,

> But Mira is the lover of her Lord, the Mountain-Lifter.
> Without him, I simply cannot live."[88]

The mother-in-law, a figure who also plagued another woman devotee, Mahadevyyakka, is still around, though no longer analogized to illusion (*maya*); now it is the god himself who is the deluder, capturing Mirabai's eyes in the binding gaze of love (darshan).

There were also a number of women saints in the Maharashtrian tradition, including Muktabai and Janabai, whose verses to the god Vithoba sometimes address him as a woman, Vithabai, and refer to him as a mother, though he is generally male. Yet despite this female presence, other poems about Vithoba project negative images of women, as temptresses who distract men from their path of detachment.[89]

SUTTEE UNDER THE MUGHALS

The fear that widows too might become temptresses was one of the factors that promoted suttee, the Hindu custom of burning the widow with her husband's body.

Akbar opposed suttee but did not abolish it or use the power of the state to suppress it.[90] In 1583, Abu'l Fazl reports, Akbar decreed: "If a Hindu woman wished to be burned with her husband, they should not prevent her, but she should not be forced,"[91] and women who had children were not allowed to burn themselves. Elsewhere Abu'l Fazl quotes Akbar as saying, "It is an ancient custom in Hindustan for a woman to burn herself, however unwilling she may be, on her husband's death and to give her priceless life with a cheerful countenance, conceiving it to be a means of her husband's salvation. It is a strange commentary on the magnanimity of men that they seek their own salvation by means of the self-sacrifice of their wives."[92] Jahangir demanded that any women who intended to commit suttee must come to see him personally, whereupon he promised them gifts and land in order to dissuade them.[93] He also complained bitterly that even Hindu converts to Islam, still marked by "the age of ignorance," persisted in burying* women beside their dead husbands.[94] Under Aurangzeb, a Muslim man dissuaded a Hindu woman from burning herself with her husband's corpse and suggested that she convert to Islam, "which had

---

* Muslims generally buried their dead, instead of burning them as Hindus did.

no provision for this horrendous practice." She did so. But no other man would accept her, as her body was covered with the lesions of leprosy.[95]

Yet the Mughals' hostility to suttee, which some of them regarded as a by-product of Hindu idolatry, was undercut by their deep respect for the values that they thought it represented[96]—courage, loyalty, even love—and Akbar too admired those qualities in the women who committed suttee.[97] A Sufi in the time of Akbar regarded suttee as a example of "burning human love" and used it (as Kabir had done) as a symbol of the affection of the soul toward god.[98] An epidemic of suttees took place in Vijayanagar in the late sixteenth century, when the Deccan sultans destroyed it, and another occurred when the Rajputs fell under the control of the Mughals.[99] When Man Singh died in 1614, six women committed suttee.[100] Clearly whatever Muslim opposition there had been had not made a serious dent in the Hindu commitment to it.

KSHETRAYYA'S COURTESANS IN ANDHRA

Women's voices, produced by men, played a central role in another lineage of devotional poets, who wrote in Telugu from the fifteenth to the eighteenth century in southern Andhra and the Tamil region. The most important of these poets was Kshetrayya, who may have lived in the mid-seventeenth century, under the Nayakas, and who worshiped a form of Krishna that he called Muvva Gopala.[101] His poems imagine a courtesan speaking to her customer, who is not only her lover but also her god and her king. The poems thus function on three levels, uniting the themes of ancient South Indian secular love poetry with *bhakti* poetry that was already simultaneously theological and royal; sex was a metaphor for religion and politics (*kama* for dharma and *artha*), and religion a metaphor for sex and politics (dharma for *kama* and *artha*).

In early bhakti, the god was treated as a king, but Kshetrayya wrote at a time when the king had become a god, when the distinction between the king in his palace and the god in his temple had blurred to the point of disappearance.[102] Money was the main characteristic that they shared; as Ramanujan, Narayana Rao, and Shulman put it, "If a king is a god and if anyone who has money is a king, anyone who has money is also god."[103] God is a customer of the worshiper, just as the worshiper may be the customer of a courtesan.

Kshetrayya's songs survived among courtesans and were performed by male Brahmin dancers who played female roles. We can hear the triple registers in the poems, some of which treat of such down-to-earth matters as a woman's concern to find a drug or a magic potion (both of which were traditionally made out of roots, in India) to abort the child that she conceived from her lover—the king, the god, and her customer:

A MARRIED WOMAN TO HER LOVER

Go find a root or something.
I have no girlfriends here I can trust.

When I swore at you, you didn't listen.
You said all my curses were blessings.
You grabbed me, you bastard,
and had me by force.
I've now missed my period,
and my husband is out of town.
   Go find a root or something.
I have set myself up for blame.
What's the use of blaming you?
I've even lost my taste for food.
What can I do now?
Go to the midwives and get me a drug
before the women begin to talk.
   Go find a root or something.
As if he fell from the ceiling
my husband is suddenly home.
He made love to me last night.
Now I fear no scandal.
All my wishes, Muvva Gopala,
have reached their end,
so, in your image,
I'll bear you a son.
   Go find a root or something.[104]

Abortion is, together with the killing of a Brahmin, the defining mortal sin in the dharma texts. Here, however, abortion is called for because the god has raped the worshiper, with overtones of the king's power to possess sexually any woman in his realm. The mythological possibilities encapsulated in the last two lines—"so, in your image,/I'll bear you a son"—are staggering; the whole my-thology of gods fathering human sons (think of the divine lineages of the *Ma-habharata* heroes!) is cast in a different light, for in the end the woman intends to bear the child, not to have an abortion after all. Sex, religion, and politics mirror one another through a man's imagination of a woman's imagination of god as customer and the poet's vision of the love of god not as a lofty, abstract sentiment but as the most intimate, even sordid, of human concerns.

CHAPTER 21
CASTE, CLASS, AND CONVERSION UNDER THE BRITISH RAJ
1600 to 1900 CE

ॐ

This matter of creeds is like horseflesh. . . . the Faiths are like the horses. Each has merit in its own country.

> Mahbub Ali, in Rudyard Kipling's *Kim,* 1901[1]

The tumult and the shouting dies—
The captains and the kings depart—
Still stands Thine ancient sacrifice,

An humble and a contrite heart.
Lord God of Hosts, be with us yet,
Lest we forget, lest we forget!

Rudyard Kipling, "Recessional," 1897

This chapter will begin with a *very* fast gallop over the perilous steeplechase race known as the British Raj (the two centuries during which India was part of the British Empire), highlighting, like all reportage of equine events, the disastrous falls along the way, particularly those with consequences for religion. There was a chronological divide, between what we might call three waves of the Raj, in imitation of the feminist and cinematic nomenclature. The first wave took place in the eighteenth century, with the first consolidations of the previously scattered European presence in India, and, in scholarship, the discovery of the Indo-European language system; it began with the Black Hole and the subsequent government takeover in 1756. The second wave began in 1813, with the official entrance of Christian missionaries. And the third wave began in 1857–1858, with the aftermath of the event known to the British as the Sepoy, Bengal, or Indian Mutiny; to Indians as the National Uprising or First War of Independence; and to most others as the Insurrection or Great Rebellion,* depending on where you stand. Like the three alliances of Hinduism, the three waves do not replace one another but build up like a palimpsest: The new ones develop, but the old ones remain, so that Rudyard Kipling, for instance, though he lived during the third wave, is really a first wave Anglo-Indian, with a difference.

I will conclude with case studies of two riders in that race, Sir Charles James Napier and Kipling. Kipling's ideas about horses and religion (as in the first passage cited above) are surprisingly pluralistic (as is his attitude to power in the second passage cited above). Then we will, as always, consider the horses. As for Hinduism, I am not even going to try to cover the many texts that were produced, and the many practices that evolved, during this period but will focus on ways in which the British affected Hinduism, for British voices too became part of Hinduism, along with Hindu voices raised in reaction and protest to those British voices. I will leave to the next chapter a discussion of religious reforms among Hindus during this period.

---

* One man's freedom fighter is another man's terrorist.

Early History of the British in India

In the eighteenth century all sorts of Europeans, mainly the Dutch, the Portuguese, the French, and the British, were milling about in India. "The French and Indian Wars" can be read as a kind of historical pun; such wars took place on two continents (North America [1754–1763] and Asia [from 1751 until well into the nineteenth century]) and involved two different sorts of "Indians" but the same sort of British and French. During this period in India, while the Europeans fought one another and the British intrigued among themselves for personal advantage, Mughals killed Mughals, Rajputs killed Rajputs, Mughals killed Rajputs, Rajputs killed Mughals, British killed Mughals and Rajputs, Mughals and Rajputs killed British, and starvation and taxation kept killing the farmers and laborers of India as usual.

At first a commercial rather than political or martial or missionary presence, the East India Company never lost that original priority; it was always there for the cash, not for the glory. Its main trade was in cotton textiles, but it also bought silks, molasses, and saltpeter from Bengal, indigo from Gujarat, and much else.[2] In addition to the private loot systematically grabbed by company officials, there were a number of grants, treaties, agreements, and understandings, which became "the pretext for the assumption of sovereign rights over trade, revenue, law, and land on the part of a monopoly joint stock company that was at the same time systematically violating the terms of its own relationship to the Crown and Parliament of England."[3] Those treaties and agreements, together with the company's military and financial presence, allowed it to take part in the government and to make laws governing the people of India, even though it was a private trading company. When the East India Company declared bankruptcy (though all the members of the company were ostentatiously rich), the British government took over to protect its investment.

British-Mughal Alliances: Nawabs and Nabobs

The Urdu/Hindi word "nawab" designated both native deputy viceroys under the Mughals and independent rulers of Bengal, Oudh, and Arcot. The English called them nabobs (also spelled nawbob, nobob, nahab, and nobab). But then, confusingly, the English spelling (nabob) came to denote Englishmen who made fortunes working for the British East India Company and returned home to purchase seats in Parliament and retire to elegant country homes—or, finally, anyone of great wealth and/or power and/or prominence, just as the

English word "mogul" (from "Mughal") did. The whole lot of them, British and Mughal, were robber barons, all cut from the same (cotton) cloth. Debauched nawabs surrounded themselves with swarms of "eunuchs, courtesans, concubines and catamites," while the nabobs were equally dissolute and in league with the nawabs.[4] Some Hindus thought that the British and the Mughals, nawabs and nabobs, balanced (if they did not cancel out) each other and were equally alien to the rest of the people of India.

The company had native troops to defend it, called sepoys (from *sipahis,* a Turkish word for "soldiers." The rank-and-file sepoys, many of whom were left over from the Mughal armies, were soldiers for hire and had been, in their day, defenders of kings, hardened bandits, grooms for horses and camels, and skilled spies. Often sepoys of the Indian nawabs and maharajas fought against sepoys of the British nabobs; the old sepoy in Kipling's novel *Kim,* written in 1901, was proud to fight for the British and against his own people, whom he regarded as traitors. In battle, sepoys were known to switch sides depending on who they thought was winning the battle, to make sure that they got a share of the spoils of war. Under these circumstances, allegiance was a very slippery thing indeed. The British rank-and-file soldiers usually came from the British or Irish working class and were predominantly unskilled laborers. Most of them were small by today's standards (between five feet two inches and five feet five inches tall), dwarfed by the six-foot-tall sepoy grenadiers. Yet until 1857–1858, though the ratio in the British army was nine Indian soldiers to one British soldier, the British kept the whip hand; they had the guns, as well as an equally powerful weapon, a highly efficient public relations machine that befogged both their own troops and the sepoys. Until 1857.

The First Wave: Conservatives and Orientalists in the British Caste System

Social theories of both race and class propped up the British. Often class trumped race. At a party in 1881 the Prince of Wales insisted that King Kalakaua of Hawaii should take precedence over the crown prince of Germany, his brother-in-law, and when his brother-in-law objected, the prince of Wales offered "the following pithy and trenchant justification: 'Either the brute is a king, or he's a common or garden nigger; and if the latter, what's he doing here?' "[5] Whatever their social origins in Britain, the British generally joined the upper classes when they entered India. They saw the native princes, not the Brahmins, at the top of the multistory Hindu hierarchy and generally treated them as social equals.[6] Kipling's "The Man Who Would Be King" laid bare to the bone all the aristocratic pretensions of the British ruling elite in his unblinking portrait of two lawless scoundrels who came to India precisely in order to throw off the class-bound shackles of their old identity and to get rich, indeed to become kings and even, for a while, gods (to the point of one of them being crucified). The British adventurers in India snubbed everyone but the rajas, for they felt themselves to be rajas, and their political domain became known as the Raj; they called their public court and assembly, the setting for elaborate pomp and circumstance, a durbar, the word that the rajas had used for their own audiences, also known as darshan (the word for a glimpse of a god or a king). Yet it was all pomp and circumstance. Under colonial rule, kingship was moored no longer in power but in a royal ritual devoid of power, a "hollow crown,"[7] and privilege was preserved primarily in pageantry.[8]

The Hindu caste system—more precisely the class system within which the caste system was imperfectly assimilated, awkwardly interleaved—enabled the British to fit into Hinduism as one more Other, another Other. The sahibs (as the British were called and addressed: "sir") belonged to the castes of horsemen who came to India throughout Indian history, beginning with the authors of the *Rig Veda* and continuing through the Kushanas and Scythians and the Mughals/Mongols. Along the lines of the process of assimilation within the caste system, called Sanskritization, this was an instance of Kshatriyazation, assimilation into the class of Kshatriyas, kings and warriors, a term originally applied to certain non-Hindu tribes that came to be regarded as Kshatriyas but later also to the British.

Thus assimilated to the class of some Hindus (the rajas), the British tended to look upon their own people as members of a class so exalted above the Indian rank and file that friendly association with them was taboo.[9] They supported caste in many ways, both because they unconsciously tended to adopt the ideas of social stratification of the people they were ruling and because the Indian caste system echoed their own subtle and deeply entrenched social hierarchy.[10] The British therefore raised the caste consciousness of the Brahmin sepoys of the Bengal army, encouraging them to regard themselves as an elite and to become more particular about the preparation and eating of their food. Thus "notions of caste, which in India had traditionally been relatively fluid, underwent a process of 'Sanskritization,' as the sepoys came to understand such issues being central to their notions of self respect."[11]

Despite their assimilation to a Hindu class, the British tended to prefer the company of Muslims to Hindus for a number of reasons: Muslims were, like them, the rulers of India; they were better horsemen than the Hindus; Islam was a monotheism that revered the Hebrew Bible and the Christian New Testament; and it was quite easy to convert to Islam, much easier than to convert to Hinduism. The native elites (nawabs) collaborated with the British residents (nabobs) so that the latter became part of the Mughal entrepreneurial class; in 1765, one of the last Mughals formally inducted Robert Clive, governor of Bengal from 1755 to 1760, into the Mughal hierarchy as *diwan,* or chancellor, for Bengal.[12]

In the early years of the Raj, British employees of the John Company (as the East India Company was also called) went native in more intimate ways, hanging out in India, as the hippies were to do centuries later. This was the Lawrence of Arabia crowd, the White Mughals (as William Dalrymple calls them) who admired Indian culture in general and Muslim culture in particular. They were equal opportunity thieves, robbers but not racist robbers. Often they married native women—both Muslim and Hindu, both noble and working class—and treated them well, as legitimate wives, regarding their sons as their legitimate heirs and leaving their fortunes to the women and their children. The practice of keeping an Indian mistress was common; one in three wills from Bengal in 1780 to 1785 contains a bequest to Indian wives or companions or their natural children. And surely many more did this off the record. The young company officials had an after-dinner toast that took the traditional popular song "Alas and Alack-the-Day" and turned it into "A Lass and a Lakh [a hundred thousand rupees] a Day," which expressed what had brought most of them to India in the first place. Similarly, the practice of keeping an Indian mistress became so common that Urdu poets in Lucknow changed the old Hindustani romantic formula—"Muslim boy meets Hindu girl with fatal consequences"—to "English boy meets Hindu girl with fatal consequences."[13]

Native women met the British as equals on the royal level. One Maharashtrian leader, Malhar Rao Holkar, whose son and grandson had died, relied on his daughter-in-law, Ahalyabhai, during his lifetime, and after his death in 1766 she took over and ruled Malwa for thirty years of peace and prosperity. She was said to be "an avatar or Incarnation of the Divinity," according to oral traditions collected by the British. She built forts and roads that kept the land secure, and she patronized temples and other religious establishments as far away as Varanasi and Dvaraka (in Gujarat). In 1772 she wrote a letter likening the British embrace to a bear hug: "Other beasts, like tigers, can be killed by might or contrivance, but to kill a bear it is very difficult. It will die only if you kill it straight in the face. Or else . . . the bear will kill its prey by tickling." (Presumably, the "other beasts" were the Muslim enemies of the Maharashtrians; as in Mughal times, the Maharashtrians were major players, who controlled the most territory, revenue, and forces.[14]) Clearly Ahalyabhai had the British number.

This first wave of British colonizers didn't need to erect elaborate barriers to separate themselves from the people of India in order to preserve, or to construct, their identity. They knew who they were: Englishmen with a God-given right to rule. The scholars of this period, the first Orientalists, were genuinely curious about India and open to the possibility that its civilization might have something of value to teach them; they abetted the government indeed, but primarily in their attempts (misguided as some of those turned out to be) to govern India by its own traditional rules. The men of the East India Company in this period often romanticized India; they learned local languages and went native in various ways, adopting local dress (robes and turbans) and furnishing their houses with Indian fabrics and furniture. In matters of religion too, as we will see, the British were open-minded and fair at the start. This batch of British, typified by Warren Hastings (governor-general, 1773–1786), might be called conservative: Like the Mughals, they provided stable government and law and order, did not interfere with local customs and religions, and supported indigenous arts, education, and festivals.

But this was no multicultural Garden of Eden. Even then considerations of social class rather than egalitarianism were what made some Indian women marry the company men, in much the same way as the Mughals had arranged dynastic marriages. And no amount of goodwill could erase the fact that a relatively small group of men had invaded India and were bleeding everyone in it, through heavy financial tolls extracted by a process that was often forcible, violent, and destructive. Moreover, the seeds of the darker sort of Orientalism were sown even now. The early scholars of Hinduism licked their chops at images of Hindu cruelty; one of the earliest European books about India, Abraham Roger's *The Open Door,* published in Leiden in 1651 and more widely disseminated in the French translation of 1670, selected for its few illustrations images of Hindus swinging from hooks and the Juggernaut rolling over Hindu bodies. (Euro-American writers called all sorts of people Juggernauts, including the pope, Napoleon, and Mr. Hyde [the worse half of Dr. Jekyll].) Already tales of madness, out-of-control multiplicity, and brutal sexuality were being nurtured, now simply out of prurience but eventually to justify colonial interventions.

Moreover, however fine that first fancy may or may not have been, it was quickly polluted. A number of factors eroded the genuine goodwill of most of the British in India. Some of the changes in the British attitude to India and Indians were gradual, arising in either England (such as racism[15]) or India (such as resentment). Partly in response to changes in the concept of family and the availability of better living conditions in India, the men brought their women over from England; this not only dampened (though it did not extinguish) the fires of romances between Englishmen and Indian women, but also banished the formerly live-in servants to separate buildings, now that memsahibs (as the wives of sahibs were called) were running the houses. The men withdrew from Indian life; "the club closed its doors to Indians; and the vicar often came to tea."[16] There were also more white women and children there to justify the erection of barriers against unhealthy native influences and to claim to have been massacred when the massacres began. Going native had lost its charm.

The estrangement between rulers and ruled had begun already in the eighteenth century. Eventually, by the early twentieth century, it would have reached that point where the British could speak to Indians only to order them about. In E. M. Forster's novel *A Passage to India* (1924), the wife of the petty bureaucrat in charge of a particular British colony attempts to learn Urdu: "She had learnt the lingo, but only to speak to her servants, so she knew none of the politer forms and of the verbs only the imperative mood."[17] This did not happen only in novels. In India in 1963, I heard a very similar story from Lady Penelope Chetwode, who had grown up in India when her father (Field Marshal Sir Philip Chetwode) was commander in chief there, from 1930 to 1935 (just a decade after the publication of Forster's novel), and had now returned to India to learn Hindi, among other things. When I asked her, "But why are you only learning Hindi now? Didn't you learn it years ago, when you lived in India?" she replied, deadpan, "Yes, of *course*. But we only learned the *imperatives* of all the verbs!"

Anti-British feeling even in the late eighteenth century was strong enough to spawn, and fuel, a number of anti-British myths. The weavers were caught between the rapacity of the Indian agents who served as middlemen and the Englishmen for whom they worked. The British treated the weavers in Bengal so cruelly[18] that they were widely believed, apparently on no evidence, to have cut off the weavers' thumbs,[*] or, on the basis of one piece of dubious evidence, to have so persecuted the winders of silk that they cut off their own thumbs in protest.[19] Weavers' thumbs were not literally cut off, but the myth arose because "worse than that happened to them and to Bengal."[20] The myth of the weavers' thumbs may also have grown out of the famous *Mahabharata* story of the low-caste archer Ekalavya, forced to cut off his right thumb.

Changes in British-Indian relations were precipitated, in part, by a series of violent and dramatic events, reaching a climax in the Rebellion of 1857–1858. But there had been distant early warnings a century before that.

THE BLACK HOLE

One of the great British icons of the historical mythology of the Raj is the Black Hole of Calcutta. To begin with, the British themselves built the Black Hole, the detention cell and barracks' punishment cell of their fort in Calcutta (a city founded by the British, later renamed Kolkata), and that prison was already known by that epithet before the incident in question. But it entered British mythology in 1756, when the Nawab of Bengal, Siraj-ud-daula, attacked Calcutta and Fort William and the British withdrew in panic to their ships, leaving Siraj in charge of the city, which included a number (a much-disputed number) of European men, women, and children who had failed to get away. Siraj put them, unharmed and apparently intending them no harm, into the Black Hole, from which, next morning, twenty-three (a number that is not much disputed) emerged alive, dehydration and suffocation having killed the rest, perhaps another fifty (this is the disputed number). Of course, many more died every day of starvation in India as a result of British policies (or indifference), but since they weren't British, and slow starvation doesn't (unfortunately) make for lurid headlines, those Indian deaths were not a useful political myth for the British. The news of the Black Hole deaths, however, set off a series of self-righteous British reprisals, as each side kept responding to alleged atrocities of the other, upping the ante, a pattern that was to be repeated many times in India, right through the Partition riots. The Black Hole became a rallying call used to justify a number of British aggressions, beginning with Clive's recapture of Cal-

---

[*] This is a persistent myth. Shashi Tharoor (in *India: From Midnight to the Millennium and Beyond,* chapter 1) remarks that "on at least two occasions, the British ordered the thumbs of whole communities of Indian weavers chopped off so that they could not compete with the products of Lancashire."

cutta in 1757 and, by 1765, the British conquest of the rest of Bengal. Near the end of that conquest, in 1764, twenty-four of the company's Indian sepoys had refused orders and been sadistically executed: They were strapped to cannons by their arms, their bellies against the mouths of the guns, which were then fired, "in front of their quaking colleagues."* Clive made about £400,000 sterling on the conquest of Bengal, and his pals made more than £1,250,000.[21] This is a particularly ugly chapter in the history of the Raj.

Over the next century, taxes levied on the company's "subjects" were consistently increased. Like the Mughals, the British collected the tax on pilgrimages to shrines like the Jagannatha temple and so did not interfere with them. But their main taxes were often paid in crops, and they destroyed the surplus that was an essential buffer when the monsoon failed. The money from taxes became the principal source of the Company's income and so the mainstay of what was called the Pax Britannia (British Peace). But as John Keay remarks, "In the experience of most Indians Pax Britannia meant mainly 'Tax Britannica.' "[22] The merchant in Kipling's *Kim* says, "The Government has brought on us many taxes, but it gives us one good thing—the te-rain that joins friends and unites the anxious. A wonderful matter is the te-rain,"[23] and the British boasted that they had given India the great gift of "trains and drains." This argument (later echoed in the "Hitler built the Autobahn and Mussolini made the trains run on time" justification for crimes against humanity) ignored the deep distrust that many Hindus had of both trains and telegraphs. In response, Indians would retort that the main drain was the drain of resources from India to England,[24] which, exacerbated by stockpiling, corrupt distribution, and hoarding by the British, led to widespread famines. This was a Black Hole in the astronomical sense, a negative space into which the riches and welfare of the Indian people vanished without a trace.

Famine and plague (which raged during this period), as always, affected religion. The widespread economic devastation may well account for the increase, at this time, of goddess worship, which generally flourishes during epidemics. When two years of failed monsoon led to the famine of 1750 to 1755, in which a third of the population of Bengal, some ten million people, died, there was a surge in the worship of the goddess Kali in her aspect of Annapurna ("Full of Food").[25] Hard times give rise to hard deities. And it was religion that really soured the Raj.

---

* This incident is often wrongly said to have occurred a century later, during the 1857 uprising.

THE SECOND WAVE: EVANGELICALS AND OPPORTUNISTS AND THE MISSIONARIES

As long as it was just a matter of graft and the lust for power, the British treated the people they robbed as human beings. It was religion that made them treat them like devils. At first the East India Company had adamantly excluded all Christian missionary activity from its territories, demonstrating a sophisticated understanding of what was at stake in the religious debate* and a consciousness of the disadvantages of unnecessarily antagonizing its Indian subjects. In 1793, Charles Cornwallis (Governor-General from 1786 to 1793) made a pact promising not to interfere with the religions of the people of India. The Company continued the patronage accorded by indigenous rulers to many Hindu temples and forbade its Indian troops to embrace Christianity. But when the Company's charter was renewed in 1813, the growing evangelical conscience in England forced it to allow Christian missions to operate in India. The evangelical Clapham Sect in London converted a Governor-General (Sir John Shore, 1793–1798) and a leading Company director and put pressure on the government in Westminster.[26]

Thus the second wave began. In contrast with the conservatives and Orientalists of the first wave, this batch of British might be labeled evangelicals and opportunists, who regarded India as a land of heathens and idolaters in desperate need of being missionized. They met with some degree of success. Tribals converted to Christianity in large numbers because they associated the value system of the Christian missionaries with the power of the British.[27] Some low-caste Hindus converted to avoid the stigma of being Pariahs, though the missionaries, respecting caste, as all religions in India always did, boasted of the number of their Brahmin converts. Other low-caste Hindus converted just for the relief of the soup kitchens, which made upper-caste Hindus call them rice Christians. Hindus of all castes converted as a result of their involvement in government and administration, intermarriage, and change of heart.

Both Hindus and Muslims blamed the government for allowing the mis-

---

* The Anglicans and Dissenters who came to India from Britain in the 1780s, and the Baptists to Orissa in the 1820s, were comparative latecomers. Syrian Christians had been in Kerala since the second century CE, Portuguese Catholics in Goa since the 1600s, and the Jesuit Roberto de Nobili in Tamil country since 1605. The Portuguese promoted Roman Catholic missionary activity from their small coastal settlements in southern India, around Goa, but their Hindu converts were few and generally of low caste. The Danish Protestant settlements in Tranquebar in Tamil Nadu and Serampore in Bengal operated small but not particularly influential missions.

sionaries free rein.[28] The missionaries influenced the government to intervene in Hindu matters; under James Dalhousie (Governor-General from 1847 to 1856), the government passed laws making it possible for Hindu widows to remarry, Hindu converts to Christianity to retain inheritance rights (which, according to Hindu law, they would have lost when they ceased to be Hindus), and castes to mingle in railroad carriages.[29] Evangelical officers favored Christian sepoys, and meddling, arrogant missionaries taught the young Indian students in their schools to be ashamed of their parents' religions.[30] In a move reminiscent of the ambiguous positioning of the Buddha as an avatar of Vishnu, Jesus became one of the avatars in a Christian tract published in Calcutta (and written in Oriya) in 1837, warning the reader that the deity worshiped in the Jagannatha Temple at Puri in Orissa was a degenerate form of the true Jagannatha and exhorting the pilgrim to Puri to "remain a Hindu and also believe in Christ," who is, by implication, the true Jagannatha.[31]

THE THIRD WAVE: UTILITARIANS AND ANGLICISTS AND THE REBELLION/MUTINY OF 1857

The tipping point came in 1857. The eighteenth century saw military incursions, floods, famines, epidemics, political disruptions, and bankrupt treasuries. Great land settlements displaced many landholders, and the confiscation of buildings previously rent-free for religious officials raised hackles in various quarters. The British relationship to Indians changed dramatically after 1813, degenerating into "a compound of cold utilitarian logic, cloying Christian ideology, and molten free-trade evangelism."[32] That Christian ideology made the country a tinderbox of resentment, just waiting for a flame to touch it off.

The flame, the proximate cause of the rebellion, came, in 1857, in the form of a bit of awkwardness about certain cartridges. Religious awkwardness. The British issued a new rifle, the Enfield, for which the cartridges had to be bitten open (since both hands were otherwise occupied; think of John Wayne biting off the tops of those grenades in World War II movies) to pour the powder down the rifle's barrel. Greased cartridges had been first imported in 1853.[33] The sepoys believed, possibly rightly, that these cartridges were greased with a tallow probably containing both pigs' fat and cows' fat (lard and suet, animal fats that were used for a lot of things in the military, and though the fat was more likely to have been mutton fat, it was still anathema to the many vegetarian Brahmins among the sepoys). The one thing that you could say for this arrangement, which would have forced Muslims to eat pork and Hindus to eat beef, is that it was equally disgusting for both groups to bite the bullet, and at least the British could not be accused of favoritism. But the animal grease was not merely disgusting; it would have been spiritually disastrous, bringing instant excommunication and damnation. (Later the British briefly entertained but finally dismissed a suggestion to allow the troops to grease the cartridges with ghee.) From early 1857, "newspapers had made known the general repugnance felt by the Sepoys to the use of the new cartridges."[34] As one contemporary British observer* wrote of the cartridge scandal, "It was so terrible a thing, that, if the most malignant enemies of the British Government had sat in conclave for years, and brought an excess of devilish ingenuity to bear upon the invention of a scheme framed with the design of alarming the Sipáhi [sepoy] mind from one end of India to the other, they could not have devised a lie better suited to the purpose."[35]

The rumors fueled the suspicion that the British had done it on purpose, in order to leave the sepoys no option, if they wanted to save their souls, but conversion to Christianity. When sepoys refused to load the cartridges, they were publicly humiliated, imprisoned, or expelled.[36] Although the British quickly withdrew the offending cartridges, the damage had been done, and the sepoys didn't trust any existing cartridges.[37] In the intense heat of May 9, 1857, eighty-five sepoys in Meerut were arrested for refusing to handle the cartridges. On the next night, other sepoys banded together, massacred the English residents of the town, and marched on Delhi.[38] More sepoys, and more officers, joined the fight, which quickly escalated. Muslims fought on the side of the Hindus, Sikhs hostile to Muslims with the British. Innocent civilians, women and children, were routinely killed by both the British and the Indian troops.[39]

A small British community sought refuge from the rebellion in the local fort at Jhansi, which was ruled by a Maharashtrian queen named Lakshmi Bai, a beautiful young widow who was an accomplished horsewoman. The British refugees were massacred. Lakshmi Bai insisted that she too had been victimized by the sepoys. When a local rival to the throne invaded Jhansi, she claimed loyalty to the British, but they did nothing to help her. When the British laid siege to Jhansi, in 1858, she led her troops into battle, but Jhansi fell. She slipped out in disguise, rode away, and (with the help of a confederate) captured Gwalior. When the British attacked Gwalior, she was shot to death.[40]

---

* Sir John William Kaye, Fellow of the Royal Society, Knight Commander of the Most Exalted Order of the Star of India.

The Jhansi massacre is one of several events that stand out amid a long catalog of deaths and horrors and thus serve as historical pegs upon which people have hung a range of myths and legends that express the emotional impact of the Rebellion. Another concerns Mangal Pandey, a sepoy of the No. 5 Company of the Thirty-fourth Native Infantry at Barrackpore, near Calcutta, who, on March 29, 1857, more than a month before the Rebellion, publicly objected to the cartridges, on religious grounds. Others joined in, all hell broke loose, and Mangal Pandey was executed by hanging on April 8. But subsequent mythologies (and a popular Bollywood film, Ketan Mehta's *Mangal Pandey,* 2005, with Amir Khan as Pandey) have overlaid the events surrounding Mangal Pandey to such an extent that they have almost totally obscured what evidence there is. According to one legend, when a mounted officer rode at him, Pandey fired at him and hit the horse (the first casualty in the Rebellion), unseating the officer.[41] There is also some debate about whether Pandey was under the influence of bhang,[42] opium, alcohol,[43] some combination of all of them, or none. (The hardship caused by a new opium tax was said to be one of the major factors that led to the Rebellion.[44])

Yet another incident, somewhat better authenticated but equally mythologized, concerns a massacre at Kanpur (or Cawnpore, as the British called it, near what was Harsha's Kanauj) on June 27, 1857. When insurgents besieged the British there, General Wheeler accepted terms under which the British would be allowed passage by boat downriver to Allahabad. Some four hundred of the British surrendered; as they boarded boats at Sati-Chaura Ghat, a detachment of sepoys under the command of Nana Sahib, the Indian ruler of Kanpur, ambushed them, and many of them were shot down or drowned. Nana Sahib rescued about two hundred women and children and locked them up in the Bibighar ("Ladies' House"), which was, significantly, a small bungalow where a British officer had once housed his Indian mistress. Many of the captives were suffering from dysentery and cholera.[45] On July 15, troops of Nana Sahib's adopted son attacked the Bibighar, and when the regular soldiers refused to carry out the command to execute them all (a minor rebellion of its own), four or five butchers from the local market slaughtered all who were still alive and threw the body parts down a well. Some historians argue that Nana Sahib intended to use the captives as hostages and did not issue the order for the extermination, while others believe that he panicked, fearing that the British would seize Kanpur, and gave the order. In any case, as Keay describes it, "Their slaughterhouse methods, clumsy rather than sadistic, constituted an atrocity which would haunt the British till the end of their Indian days. For sheer barbarity this 'massacre of the innocents' was rivaled only by the disgusting deaths devised for dozens of equally innocent Indians by way of British reprisal."[46] Though the cartridges were the proverbial straw, the camel (flanked by the cow and pig) was already heavily loaded with economic, social, and political resentments, which continued to fester.

Recognizing the power of the resentments ignited by these events, the British took countermeasures. In 1858 Victoria proclaimed that the British crown was taking over all the rights of the East India Company; she became queen of India.[47] She forced the missionaries to lay off, now more than ever realizing, again, what was at stake in interfering with Hinduism. Acknowledging that the sepoys in 1857–1858 had genuinely feared conversion to Christianity, Queen Victoria's proclamation of 1858 not only curtailed missionary activity but reduced the public funding of mission schools and ordered British officials to abstain from interfering with Indian beliefs and rituals "on the pain of Our highest displeasure."[48] She also specifically disclaimed any "desire to impose Our convictions on any of Our subjects." (Victoria herself has become the religion: She capitalizes "Our" as the missionaries capitalized "God.")

Many of the missionaries had been killed during the Rebellion, but the damage had already been done. While the new official attitude was superficially similar to the earlier hands-off policy toward Hinduism, the sentiments fueling it were very different; whereas the missionaries had attempted to convert the Hindus, now the British as a whole were totally dismissive of them as irredeemable heathens, with no hope of ever becoming human beings. After 1858 the government officials themselves had become more Christian in their scorn for Hindus, whom they avoided as much as possible. Now that they felt that they had a divine mission to rule India and were convinced of Christianity's moral superiority, they lost their earlier toleration, let alone their support, of Indian religions.[49] This third batch, in contrast with the conservatives and Orientalists, together with the evangelicals and opportunists, were Utilitarians and Anglicists, who believed in the superiority of reason and progress and pushed for Western education.

Hindus Under the Raj

What made the sepoys so suspicious of those greased cartridges in the first place? Let us go back and reconsider the shifting winds of religious interactions in the century between 1756 and 1857.

In the first wave (roughly between 1750 and 1813), despite the steadily darkening political scene, the British had respected both Islam and Hinduism and were, in general, blessedly free of religious zeal.[50] In the late eighteenth century a Muslim visitor to India commented with surprise on the respect that the British paid to both Hindus and Muslims—at least to those of a certain respectability:

> They treat the white-beard elders and old-established families, both Muslim and Hindu, courteously and equably, respecting the religious customs of the country and as well the scholars, sayyids, sheikhs and dervishes they come across. . . . More remarkable still is the fact that they themselves take part in most of the festivals and ceremonies of both the Muslims and the Hindus, mixing with the people.[51]

And there were conversations. The medieval Indian tradition of debate in the Mughal court, patronized by rulers and commonly held in the royal darbar (Akbar is the most famous but by no means the only example), was transformed, in the colonial period, first into Muslim-Christian debates, retaining much of the medieval structure and rhetoric,[52] and then, through the end of the nineteenth century, into debates between Hindu court pandits and traveling controversialists. The social context of these debates was radically broadened, now accessible to a much wider literate audience. One missionary remarked that religious debate was a major source of entertainment in India, "and the people will enjoy the triumph as much when a Brahmun falls as when the Christian is foiled."[53] The crowd laughed at the Brahmins and then at the missionaries. This was a self-serving argument, implying that since Hinduism was already a space of debate and entertainment, the missionaries would do no harm,[54] but there was some truth in it.

The conversations, however, often turned into conversions. Religious tensions were greatly exacerbated during this period by what Hindus perceived as attempts to convert them to Islam or Christianity. As we have noted, traditional Hinduism was not a proselytizing religion, though particular renunciant and reform movements within it did increasingly seek converts. Therefore, when Hindus had ceased to be Hindus, often against their will and/or by accident, and wished to return to the fold, it was difficult for them to reconvert back to Hinduism. Indian sepoys lucky enough to survive the First Afghan War, in 1839 (there were enormous sepoy casualties), found when they returned to India that they were ostracized as Pariahs, for in Afghanistan some had been forced to convert to Islam, and in any case they lost caste by crossing the Indus, transgressing the geographical bounds of India, which was against caste law. (Earlier, Hindus had had the right to refuse foreign service on the grounds that they would be polluted if they crossed the sea.[55]) Sometimes they could reconvert by crossing the palms of various priests with silver; previously Hindus had been able to reconvert with the spoils of conquest, but since the sepoys had lost in Afghanistan, there were no spoils.[56] There were also ritual prescriptions, dating back to the first or second century CE, by which an excommunicated man could be purified by performing a vow of restoration,[57] and new reconversion ceremonies were developed out of these prescriptions as well as from prototypes originally designed for reconversion from Islam under the Mughals.

But converts to Christianity, though relatively few in number, posed different theological and political threats. It was primarily the Protestants rather than the Catholics who messed with Hinduism. Catholics, who had been in India for many centuries, recognized and appreciated many of their own traits in Hindus: the many gods corresponding to many saints; the pageantry, color, and occasional brutality of the imagery; the animal sacrifice that could be assimilated to the Paschal Lamb (or, as the case may be, the Paschal goat, still sacrificed in many Indian Catholic communities at Easter). The Protestants admired little in Hinduism but its texts and philosophy. The rest was a lot too much like Catholicism to suit their tastes.

On the eve of the second wave, when the company's charter was about to be renewed, in 1813, Major General Sir Thomas Munro (who served in India from 1789 to 1827, chiefly in Madras) warned the directors of the East India Company about their attitude to the people of India. He spoke like a true man of the first wave, which indeed he was: He had learned Hindi and Persian and was noted for his generous rapport with both humans and horses (an extraordinary equestrian statue of him in Chennai depicts him mounted without saddle or stirrups, which I take to be symbolic of his relaxed attitude to domination*). On this occasion he granted that other conquerors had treated Indians with greater violence and cruelty, "but none has treated them with so much scorn as we, none has stigmatised the whole people as unworthy of trust, as incapable of honesty, and as fit to be employed only where we cannot do without them."[58]

---

* Riding bareback requires, and allows, the rider to sit into the horse and fuse with his movements. The sculptor, Sir Francis Legatt Chantrey, also depicted the Duke of Wellington, in London, without saddle and stirrups.

His words fell on deaf ears. The British applied their scorn both to the people and to their religion. In 1810, Robert Southey (poet laureate of England), who had never been to India, declared, "The religion of the Hindoos ... of all false religions is the most monstrous in its fables, and the most fatal in its effects."[59] In 1813 (the year that the missionaries were let in), William Wilberforce, an abolitionist and member of an evangelical sect, argued in the House of Commons that the need for such missions in India was more important than the abolition of slavery, because "our religion is sublime, pure and beneficent [while] theirs is mean, licentious and cruel"; because Hindu deities are "absolute monsters of lust, injustice, wickedness and cruelty," Hinduism is "the most enormous and tormenting superstition that ever harassed and degraded any portion of mankind," and Hindus therefore "the most enslaved portion of the human race." Hindu science and cosmography came under fire too. In 1835 Thomas Babington Macaulay (the son of an eminent evangelical leader) issued his notorious tirade against "medical doctrines which would disgrace an English farrier, astronomy which would move laughter in girls at an English boarding school, history abounding with kings thirty feet high and reigns thirty thousand years long, and geography made up of seas* of treacle and seas of butter."[60] And that was *before* the Rebellion.

After that, in the third wave, things went from bad to worse. Even the *Bhagavad Gita,* generally so dear to the hearts of European observers of Hinduism, came under fire in the English imaginary. In Forster's *A Passage to India,* the bigoted policeman McBryde, discussing what he regards as the criminal psychology of Indian natives, remarks, "Read any of the Mutiny records; which, rather than the Bhagavad Gita, should be your Bible in this country. Though I'm not sure that the one and the other are not closely connected."[61] This reflected a widespread nineteenth-century canard: The members of one Bengal secret society were alleged to take an oath of allegiance before an image of the goddess Kali, with the *Bhagavad Gita* in one hand and a revolver in the other.[62] A secret police report submitted in 1909 to the chief secretary to the government of Bengal stated that students were initiated into the secret society by taking their oath lying flat on a human skeleton with a revolver in one hand and a *Gita* in the other.[63] This whole scene is suspiciously close to one imagined by the Bengali author Bankimcandra Chatterji in his highly influential 1882 novel *Anandamath* ("The Mission House"). Though Chatterji may have influenced

---

* Those concentric oceans are indeed a part of Hindu cosmology.

the British, it is more likely that they both were reflecting the mythology of the period rather than any real practice. The most infamous players in that mythology were the Thugs, worshipers of the goddess Kali, to whom they were now said to offer British victims; they were probably just *dacoits* who happened to worship in Kali temples.[64] *The Rambles and Recollections* (1844) of Lieutenant Colonel Sir William Henry ("Thuggee") Sleeman of the Bengal army and the Indian Political Service is the proof text of that mythology.

The British brokering of relations between Hindus and Muslims also did considerable damage. A report by Patrick Carnegy in 1870 insisted that Hindus and Muslims used to worship together in the Babri Mosque complex in the nineteenth century until the Hindu-Muslim clashes in the 1850s: "It is said that up to that time Hindus and Mohamedans alike used to worship in the mosque/temple. Since the British rule a railing has been put up to prevent dispute, within which, in the mosque the Mohamedans pray, while outside the fence the Hindus have raised a platform on which they make their offerings."[65] But the report was based on no evidence whatsoever that there had been such disputes or any need to separate the worshipers.[66] And even by this report, the British had put up a railing where none had been, causing the disputes that they were allegedly preventing.

A more positive, though more obviously mythical, story about a similarly dichotomized Hindu/Muslim shrine is told by Forster. The shrine was created when, according to legend, a Muslim saint was beheaded but, having left his head at the top of a hill, contrived somehow to continue to run (in order to accomplish his mother's command) in the form of a headless torso, to the bottom of the hill, where his body finally collapsed. "Consequently there are two shrines to him to-day—that of the Head above and that of the Body below—and they are worshipped by the few Mohammedans who live near, and by Hindus also."[67] This image of the separation of head and body suggests but does not realize the recombinatory quality of Hindu mythologies of such head/body separations. The two shrines remain apart, but both Muslims and Hindus worship in both.

Generally relations between Hindus and Muslims took several turns for the worse under the Raj, in some cases grotesquely twisting the genuine rapprochements that had taken place under the Mughals. In the nineteenth century, certain yogis claimed that Muhammad had been trained by a student of the great Hindu yogi Gorakhnath. They were scrupulous about fasting and ritual prayer when they were with Muslims, and about Hindu customs when with Hindus, eating pork according to the custom of Hindus and Christians, or beef according to the religion of Muslims and others.[68] They argued that the striking resemblance between the Muslim minaret tower and prayer niche, on the one hand, and the Shaiva linga and yoni, on the other, explained both why the prayer niche and minaret were always found together and why Islam had spread so successfully. In this way, they relativized the sacred sources of Islam and subordinated them to Indian figures and categories.[69] On the central Nath temple at Gorakhpur there is a small board explaining that Muhammad was a Nath yogi and that Mecca was a Shaiva center, known in some Puranas as Makheshvara ("Lord of the Sacrifice").[70] The arrogant insult in this wordplay of appropriation was the very opposite of the appreciative attitude that had inspired Hindus under the Delhi Sultanate to coin Sanskrit versions of Arabic titles such as Mohammad (Maha-muda) and Sultan (Sura-trana).

DEEP ORIENTALISM[71]

British attitudes to India, at first appreciative and tolerant (the first wave), then scornful (the second wave) and hostile (the third), were three facets of what we have been calling Orientalism. At the start, I defined "Orientalism" as the love-hate relationship that Europeans had with the Orient for both the right and the wrong reasons, making it in many ways the European inversion of what the Hindus called hate-love (*dvesha-bhakti*): loving India but with a skewed judgment and self-interest that amounted to hate, that distorted the Orientalists' understanding and was often horrendously destructive to the object of their affection.

The early Orientalists were reacting against an early version of what has recently been dubbed (in response to Edward Said's term) Occidentalism, a stereotyped and dehumanized view of the West (more precisely, Europe and America, in contrast with all Asia).[72] The two views share all the stereotypes, which always misrepresent both sides: the East = religion, spirit, nature, the exotic, adventure, danger, Romanticism (including Orientalism), myth, while the West = science, materialism, the city, boredom, comfort, safety, the Enlightenment, logos. The East is feminine, the West male; Eastern males are therefore feminine and impotent,[*] but also oversexed, because the primitive Other is always oversexed.[73] The only difference, and it is crucial, is the value placed on these stereotypes, Romanticism favoring the Eastern values, Enlightenment the Western ones.

---

[*] Nandy glosses *klibatvam* as "male sexual effeminacy."

Before Said's book, in 1978, Indologists of my generation had admired the British scholars who had recorded dialects and folklore that otherwise would have been lost to posterity, established the study of Sanskrit in Europe, and made available throughout India as well as Europe many of the classical texts recorded in that language. We felt indebted to them for our own knowledge of and love of India. But the anti-Orientalist critique changed our way of thinking forever. It taught us that those British scholars too had been caught up in the colonial enterprise, sustained it, fueled it, facilitated it. It taught us about the collusion between academic knowledge and political power, arguing that we too are implicated in that power when we carry on the work of those disciplines. In Kipling's novel *Kim,* spying often masqueraded as anthropology, another form of Orientalism; Kipling made his master spy, Colonel Creighton, an amateur ethnographer.

At the heart of the anti-Oriental enterprise was the argument that scholars, then and now, affect and often harm the people they study. In a delightful satire on Orientalism *avant la lettre,* J. B. S. Haldane (1892–1964), a British geneticist who spent his final years in India and died in Bhubaneshwar in Orissa, stipulated in his will that after his death his body was to be sent to the nearest medical college, so that "some future Indian doctors will have the unusual experience of dissecting a European."[74] This would be a fitting revenge for all the Indians who had been dissected by European Orientalists.

TRANSLATIONS, LOST IN COLONIZATION

At the start the British hoped to govern India by its laws and, as we saw, treated the Indian ruling class, at least, with some respect. As Protestants they preferred texts to practices, and as Orientalists they preferred the glorious past to what they regarded as the sordid present. This was the result of their confrontation of a quandary: How could Europeans continue to revere the culture of the people who had the oldest language in the world, Sanskrit, and presumably the civilization that went with it (closely related to the Greek civilization that the British claimed as their own heritage), at the same time as they were justifying their rule over contemporary Indians on the ground that those Indians were benighted primitives? The answer was a doublethink historical process: For many centuries, as science replaced superstition (the social variant of Darwinian evolution) and Europe was rising up, India was sinking down, as the Brahmins and the hot, wet climate ruined the pristine Vedas and produced the degradation of present-day Hindus (an inversion of the Darwinian hypothesis). The Orientalists needed some fancy footwork to keep these two rivers flowing up and down at the same time (like yogis simultaneously breathing out of one nostril and in through the other), but somehow they managed. The argument was that the Indians were once like us (language) but are no longer like us (intermarriage of Indo-Europeans with indigenous Indians), the resolution of antiquarianism and racism.[75]

The British Orientalists of the first wave reached back into the past, to Sanskrit texts, and began to translate them. (By the third wave, after 1858, the government severed support for the study of Sanskrit and Persian, disparaging the culture even of ancient India.[76]) European translations began in the eighteenth century with a fittingly fraudulent document, the so-called Ezour Veda (presumably a corruption of *Yajur Veda*), a French text in the form of a dialogue between two Vedic sages, one monotheist and one polytheist, who find that the monotheism of "pristine Hinduism" points to Christian truth. The text was, for a while, believed to be the French translation of a document composed in Sanskrit by one Brahmin and translated by another Brahmin in Benares who knew both French and Sanskrit. The Chevalier de Maudave gave a copy to Voltaire in September 1760, claiming to have received it from the hand of the Brahmin translator; Voltaire was deeply impressed by it and cited it often.[77] In 1822, Sir Alexander Johnston claimed to have found, at the French settlement of Pondicherry, in South India, the manuscript copy of the "Ezour Vedam" in French and Sanskrit. His colleague Francis Whyte Ellis then published an article in which he argued that the work was not the French translation of a Sanskrit original but a work entirely composed in 1621 by the Jesuit Roberto de Nobili, who was accused of having written it in order to deceive Brahmins and convert them to Catholicism. Its authorship remains unknown, but it is now certain that it was an original French composition that claimed to be a copy of a lost Sanskrit text.

The first books genuinely translated from Sanskrit to English were Charles Wilkins's 1785 translation of the *Bhagavad Gita,* Sir William Jones's translation of Kalidasa's *Shakuntala* (in 1789), and then, in 1794, Jones's *Laws of Manu.* The statue of Jones in St. Paul's Church in London holds a volume of *Manu* in his hand, thus commemorating *Manu* in a Christian church, an honor accorded him by no Hindu temple, to my knowledge. As chief justice of the High Court of Calcutta, Jones had searched for something that the Hindu witnesses could be sworn in on that would put the fear of god(s) in them, since perjuries were rife. He tried the Ganges River, but when that failed to produce the desired effect, he sought expert counsel from the local learned men, who gave him *Manu* and inspired him to learn Sanskrit.[78] Jones's *Manu* translation became the basis of much of British law in India (including the disastrous treatment of suttee); the text became instrumental in the construction of a complex system of jurisprudence based on the British belief in a unified Hinduism, the privileging of the "classical" language, Sanskrit, over local languages, and the Protestant bias in favor of scripture. In the courts of the Raj (and later independent India), "general law" (based on British law) was supplemented by a "personal law" determined by one's religious affiliation (such as Hindu law). "Hindu law," or rather the British interpretation of Jones's translation of *Manu,* was applied to nearly 80 percent of the population of colonial India in matters of marriage and divorce, legitimacy, guardianship, adoption, inheritance, and religious endowments.

Yet *Manu* had never been used in precisely this way before; the British system completely bypassed the village governing units (called *panchayats*) that actually adjudicated in vernacular languages on the basis of case law built up over many centuries. This is not to say that the British invented *Manu;* it had been (primarily through its many commentaries) an important text both in local law and in the Brahmin imaginary, which still exerted a heavy influence on many Hindus. What the British did was to replace the multiplicity of legal voices and the centuries of case law with a single voice, that of Jones's *Manu.* It was as if U.S. courts had suddenly abandoned case law to rule only by the Constitution.

The translations of the *Bhagavad Gita* had equally long-lasting repercussions. Wilkins's *Gita* had a preface by Warren Hastings,[79] a brute of the first order, who was impeached (though acquitted) on his return to England, in 1793. Gandhi first read the *Gita,* in 1888–1889, in a later translation by Sir Edwin Arnold; the American transcendentalists too, led by Emerson and Thoreau, read and loved the *Gita.* Yet just as *Manu* was not the most important Hindu legal text, so too texts other than the *Gita*—both Sanskrit texts, like the Upanishads and the Puranas, and vernacular texts, such as the Tulsidas and Kampan *Ramayanas,* and, most of all, oral traditions—were what most Hindus actually used in their worship. The highly Anglicized Indian elite followed the British lead and gave the *Gita* a primacy it had not previously enjoyed, though like *Manu,* it had always been an important text. The fraction of Hinduism that appealed to Protestant evangelical tastes at all was firmly grounded in the renunciant path of Release and philosophical monism. The evangelists in India assumed that God had prepared for their arrival by inspiring the Hindus with

a rough form of monotheism, the monism of the Upanishads;* pukka monotheism, in their view, was available to Brahmins but not to the lower castes, who
were fit only for polytheism.[80]

Many highly placed Hindus so admired their colonizers† that in a kind of
colonial and religious Stockholm syndrome, they swallowed the Protestant line
themselves and not only gained a new appreciation of those aspects of Hinduism that the British approved of (the *Gita,* the Upanishads, monism) but became
ashamed of those aspects that the British scorned (much of the path of rebirth,
polytheism, the earthy and erotic aspects) and even developed new forms of
Hinduism, such as the Arya Samaj and Brahmo Samaj, heavily influenced by
British Protestantism. Scholars have noted a pattern in which colonized people
take on the mask that the colonizer creates in the image of the colonized, mim-
icking the colonizer's perception of the colonized.[81] This group of Indians became just what the Anglicists wanted, typified by Macaulay's hope of
developing in India "a class of persons, Indian in blood and colour but English
in taste, in opinion, in morals and in intellect,"[82] or, as Sumit Sarkar has para-
phrased it, "brown in colour but white in thought and taste."[83] Such people are
what present-day South Asians refer to as coconuts, the opposite of the U.S.
term "Oreos" (and with more precise resonances; in Hindu rituals, coconuts are
often offered to gods in place of human heads).

It is one of the great ironies of the history of sexuality that the Victorian
British, of all people, should have had control of India during one of the great
ages of sexual and gender reform, the nineteenth century.[84] When confronting
the earthier aspects of Hinduism, such as the worship of the linga, the British
were not amused.‡ And some nineteenth-century Hindu movements internal-

---

* Many centuries earlier, the early church fathers had attempted in a similar way to justify the stunning
resemblances between the Gospel story and the myths of the pagans that they so despised, such as the
ancient Greek myth of a god who dies and rises from the dead. Clement of Alexandria initiated "The
Thesis of Demonic Imitation," later advanced by Tertullian and Justin, which argued that the demons,
in order to deceive and mislead the human race, took the offensive and suggested to the Greek poets the
plots of the Greek myths, in the hope that this would make the story of Christ appear to be a fable of
the same sort, when it came ("Oh, never mind, it's just another one of those dying and rising gods
again") and so be ignored.
† Hindu admiration for the British took many forms. In 1963, I once went to great trouble and expense
to visit a famous temple to a tiger god in the jungles of Bengal; when I finally got there, I found in the
shrine a red faced sahib with a rifle, the god who was able to kill tigers.
‡ As Queen Victoria is said to have said. One can imagine that, on first hearing the tale of the interruption of the sexual play of Shiva and Parvati, for instance, the average Victorian Orientalist would have
remarked, as a Victorian matron was said to have remarked on emerging from a performance of
Shakespeare's *Antony and Cleopatra,* "How strangely different from the home life of our dear Queen."

ized British Protestant—indeed Victorian—scorn for Hindu eroticism and polytheism. That attitude was simultaneously scornful and prurient: "Look how dirty and naughty these people are. Look! Look!"

There was a rebound Orientalism in the Hindu reaction to the Protestants, as upper-caste Hindus scurried to get the low-caste temple dancers and prostitutes (Devadasis) out of the temples and swept the village sects and stories out of sight, in shame, in shadow. These right-hand Hindus hastened to put Hindu eroticism into a kind of purdah, behind a veil formed of the *Gita* and Indian philosophy and the more Protestant than thou nineteenth-century Hindu reform movements. Some Hindus took pride in every aspect of Hinduism that appealed to Europeans such as Schelling and Goethe and Hegel and to Americans such as Emerson and Thoreau, holding up those parts of their tradition like cover-up Mother Hubbard gowns as if to say, "We are *not* the filthy savages some of you think we are." This sanitized brand of Hinduism is now often labeled *sanatana dharma,* "perpetual, eternal and universal" Hinduism, although that term was previously used in a very different sense, to designate the moral code that applied to everyone, in contrast with the particular moral code for each particular caste. British legislation of all aspects of Hinduism, including sexual aspects, owed as much to Calvin as to Manu. It was a deadly one-two punch. But British prudery was not "simply an exotic attitude forced on an innately sensual subcontinent. The sexual economics of empire were no less complex than any other form of colonial exchange."[85] For some of the British played an important role in revalidating Indian eroticism against the puritanical tradition of the Hindus themselves, translating the *Gita-Govinda* and tracking down and preserving *Kama-sutra* manuscripts in decaying libraries (the first translation of the *Kama-sutra* into English appeared in 1883).[86] Nor are the British alone to blame for the sanitizing of Tantrism or the quasi-Tantric aspects of Hinduism. Long before the British presence in India, from at least the time of Abhinavagupta in the eleventh century, Brahmin, Buddhist, Jaina, and Christian critics X-rated Tantrics in India, and later some orthodox Muslims objected too. The British just made it all worse, so that thenceforth sexuality in India was subjected to the triple whammy of Hindu, Muslim, and Christian Puritanism.

THE TRANSPOSED HEADS, EUROPEAN STYLE

While the British provided the impetus for changes in Hindu law, society, and religion, Hindu art and literature made their impact on Europe. Some forty years after the "Ezour Veda" captivated Voltaire, the myth of the transposed heads of the Brahmin woman and the Pariah woman inspired Goethe (who also went mad for Shakuntala). Working apparently from Richard Iken's translation of a Persian version of a Tamil version of the story,[87] in 1797 Goethe wrote a poem, "The Pariah," which can be summarized as follows (from the moment when the Brahmin woman has lost her magic chastity):

GOETHE'S "THE PARIAH"

She appeared before her husband, who seized his sword and dragged her to the hill of death. [He beheaded her.] His son stood before him and said, "You may be able to kill your wife, but not my mother. A wife is able to follow her beloved spouse through the flames, and a faithful son can also follow his beloved mother." His father said, "Hurry! Join her head to her body, touch her with the sword, and she will come back to you, alive." The son hastened and found the bodies of two women, lying crosswise, and their heads. He seized his mother's head and put it on the nearest headless body. He blessed it with the sword, and it arose, and his mother's dear lips spoke words fraught with horror: "My son, you were too hasty! There is your mother's body, and next to it the impious head of a fallen, condemned woman. Now I am grafted to her body forever, and will live among the gods, wise in thought, wild in action, full of mad, raging lust from the bosom down. As a Brahmin woman, with my head in heaven, I will live as a Pariah on earth. And whoever, Brahmin or Pariah, is overwhelmed by sorrow, his soul wildly riven, will know me if he looks to heaven.[88]

Note the reference to the possibility of suttee (which got into just about everything that any European wrote about India for several centuries, though here it is also the suttee of a son for his mother) and the judgment that the Brahmin woman is wise and loving, while the Pariah woman is wild in action, mad, and raging in lust. Yet the poem concludes that heaven watches over both Brahmin and Pariah, especially when their souls are "riven" as the women in the story are riven. The word "Pariah," originally found in ancient Tamil literature, referring to a particular low caste, then entered German and English in its broader sense. In 1818 the Irish clergyman and dramatist Charles Robert Maturin called all women "These Pariahs of humanity," and in 1823, Michael Beer's play *Der Pariah* likened the Jews to the Pariahs. Goethe's poem became a best seller (and inspired several imitations) in Germany.

The myth of the transposed heads was also picked up in France and, eventually, England and America, undergoing several gender transformations along the way. In 1928, Marguerite Yourcenar published a story in French entitled "Kali Décapitée," republished in 1938 in English ("Kali Beheaded").[89] In her retelling, the goddess Kali's amorous escapades with Pariahs lead the gods to decapitate her; eventually they join her head to the body of a prostitute who has been killed for having troubled the meditations of a young Brahmin. The woman thus formed is a creature who becomes "the seducer of children, the inciter of old men, and the ruthless mistress of the young." In the English edition, Yourcenar explains that she rewrote the ending, "to better emphasize certain metaphysical concepts from which this legend is inseparable, and without which, told in a Western manner, it is nothing but a vague erotic tale placed in an Indian setting."[90] This is a very different story indeed, combining Hindu ideas of caste rebellion (Brahmin women sleeping with Pariahs and disturbing male Brahmins) with misogynist European ideas about feminist rebellion (seducing children, exciting old men).

The Indologist Heinrich Zimmer (1890–1943) knew both the Goethe poem and a different Sanskrit version of the story, in which two men, rather than two women, are decapitated, and the woman, who is the wife of one and the brother of the other, switches the heads when she restores them to life.[91] Zimmer brought the Sanskrit story to the attention of Thomas Mann, who, in 1940, wrote a novella (*The Transposed Heads*) in which the woman, who is married to one of the men and in love with the other, accidentally, or not so accidentally, switches the heads.[92] And in 1954, Peggy Glanville-Hicks wrote an opera based on the Thomas Mann novel, also entitled *The Transposed Heads*. The notes for the 1984 ABC Classics CD of the opera say, "The original source is in the *Bhagavad Gita*," a lovely leftover from the colonial heyday of the *Gita*, when it was regarded as the source of everything Indian. Ms. Glanville-Hicks herself said, "Many of the themes are taken freely and in some cases directly from Hindu folk sources," and she also described the heroine's inadvertent transposition of her lovers' heads as "the greatest Freudian slip of all time."

HOW SIR CHARLES SIND[93]

The best pun in the history of Raj, one that reveals a number of rather serious aspects of colonialism, is attributed to General Sir Charles James Napier.

Napier was born in 1782 and in 1839 was made commander of Sind (or Scinde, as it was often spelled at that time, or Sindh), an area at the western tip of the northwest quadrant of South Asia, directly above the Rann of Kutch and

Gujarat; in 1947 it became part of Pakistan. In 1843, Napier maneuvered to provoke a resistance that he then crushed and used as a pretext to conquer the territory for the British Empire. Mountstuart Elphinstone (formerly Governor of Bombay) likened the British in Sind after the defeat in Afghanistan to "A bully who had been kicked in the streets and went home to beat his wife."[94] The British press described this military operation at the time as "infamous,"[95] a decade later as "harsh and barbarous" and a "tragedy," while the *Bombay Times* accused Napier of perpetrating a mass rape of the women of Hyderabad.[96] The successful annexation of Sind made Napier's name "a household word in England. He received £70,000 as his share of the spoils"[97] and was knighted. In 1851 he quarreled with Dalhousie (the Governor-General) and left India.

In 1844, the following item appeared in a British publication in London, under the title "Foreign Affairs":

PECCAVI

It is a common idea that the most laconic military despatch ever issued was that sent by Caesar to the Horse-Guards at Rome, containing the three memorable words, *"Veni, vidi, vici"* ["I came, I saw, I conquered"], and, perhaps, until our own day, no like instance of brevity has been found. The despatch of Sir Charles Napier, after the capture of Scinde, to Lord Ellenborough, both for brevity and truth, is, however, far beyond it. The despatch consisted of one emphatic word— *"Peccavi,"* "I have Scinde" (*sinned*).

The joke here (well, it's a British joke) depends upon the translation of the Latin word *peccavi,* which is the first person singular of the past tense, active voice, of the verb *pecco, peccare* ("to sin"), from which are derived our English words "impeccable" (someone who never sins) and "peccadillo" (a small sin). Thus the double meaning is "I have sinned" (that is, "I have committed a moral error") and "I have Scinde" (that is, "I have gained possession of a place called Scinde"). Got it?

The story caught on. In a play published in 1852, a character named Sir Peter Prolix recites, at a dinner party, the following doggerel:

What exclaim'd the gallant Napier,
Proudly flourishing his rapier
To the army and the navy,
When he conquered Scinde?—"Peccavi!"[98]

The story has been told and retold in history books ever since. A 1990 biography of Sir Charles actually entitled *I Have Sind* cites it three times,[99] and the *Encyclopaedia Britannica* online (2008) says that Napier "is said to have sent a dispatch consisting of one word, 'Peccavi' (Latin: 'I have sinned'—i.e., 'I have Sind')."

But all evidence indicates that Sir Charles Napier never dispatched such a message. The passage about Caesar and Napier is not from the *Times* of London but from the comic journal *Punch* (1844, v. 6, 209), whose editors evidently made it up and also represented him as confessing that he had sinned in that his actions had raised such a storm of criticism in England.[100] The authors of the *Punch* item may have been inspired by another apocryphal historical anecdote, which was linked with the *peccavi* story as early as 1875 and was in circulation for some time before that; it tells us that someone who had witnessed the defeat of the Spanish Armada announced it with one word: "Cantharides," the Latin and pharmaceutical name of the allegedly aphrodisiac drug known as the Spanish fly.[101] (Another British joke.) So it is not Napier's text, but it is a British text—a lie but a text—with a history of its own; it is a kind of nineteenth-century urban legend, a myth. Salman Rushdie retold the story in *Shame,* referring to his "looking-glass" Pakistan as "Peccavistan," though he calls the story apocryphal, bilingual, and fictional.[102] The shift from the text of history to the hypertext of journalism is significant; the idea of the sin was initially a writer's idea, not a general's. With this in mind, let us unpack the myth a bit more.

Besides the two meanings I've mentioned ("I have conquered a part of India" and "I have committed a moral error"), there is a third, which we discover if we heed the good advice of Marshall McLuhan, who taught us that the medium is the message, for the medium in this case is Latin. That third message signifies something like "Let's say it in Latin, which we Oxbridge types, English upper classes, know, and the natives do not, though they know English, which we taught them." Stephen Jay Gould, who takes the anecdote as history, remarks: "In an age when all gentlemen studied Latin, and could scarcely rise in government service without a boost from the old boys of similar background in appropriate public schools, Napier never doubted that his superiors . . . would properly translate his message and pun: I have sinned."[103] And when Priscilla Hayter Napier told the story (as history, not myth) she remarked, "Possibly this was when he sent his celebrated message—'*Peccavi,*' which, in the Latin every educated man had then at his command, means 'I have sinned.'"[104] Latin here functions as a code that the bearers of the message will not understand. Yet even *Punch,* which invented the story, glossed it in English, realizing that some of its readers might not have been educated in good schools and therefore might not know Latin.

But it is the second meaning of *peccavi*, the meaning of "sin" as moral error, that is most relevant here.* Though Sir Charles apparently never said (or wrote) *peccavi,* he seems to have had a sense that he had sinned in Sind. When he was posted there, he wrote: "We have no right to seize Sind, yet we shall do so and a very advantageous piece of rascality it will be."[105] "Rascality" is a rather flip way to refer to the murder of many people defending their own land, but afterward he wrote, speaking of his ambition, "I have conquered Scinde but I have not yet conquered myself."[106] Napier was also surprisingly sensitive to the disintegration of the sepoy-officer relationship after 1813, when the first wave gave way to the second. Years before 1857, he expressed regret that the older type of officers who "wrestled" with their sepoys were being replaced by men who did not know the sepoys' languages and practices and who readily addressed the latter as "nigger"† or "suwar" (pig).[107] He was also aware of the British complicity in the negative role of caste: "The most important thing which I reckon injurious to the Indian army, is the immense influence given to caste; instead of being discouraged, it has been encouraged in the Bengal army; in the Bombay army it is discouraged; and that army is in better order than the army of Bengal, in which the Brahmins have been leaders in every mutiny."[108]

But Napier was also capable of equivocating, as when he wrote of the Sind campaign: "I may be wrong, but I cannot see it, and my conscience will not be troubled. I sleep well while trying to do this, and shall sleep sound when it is done."[109] This last phrase is almost verbatim what Harry Truman said after the bombing of Hiroshima: "I never lost any sleep over my decision."[110]

SHALLOW ORIENTALISM

The sense of sin is not usually a part of the discussion of the story of Napier in India, but it may indicate a moment when some of the British felt moral ambivalence about their conquest of India and, perhaps, when we ourselves

---

* That a man of great political power might have intended this subtext is suggested by a remark by President William Jefferson Clinton that *Newsweek* (September 21, 1998, 27) chose to reproduce as an enormous headline: I HAVE SINNED. Several South Asianist colleagues of mine have told me that they too thought at that moment of Sir Charles Napier.
† George Treveleyan, in 1865 (*Cawnpore,* 36), wrote: "That hateful word . . . made its first appearance in decent society during the years which immediately preceded the mutiny."

should feel morally ambivalent about the British. The list of massacres and degradations that I selected for my cavalry charge through the history of the Raj, England's greatest hits (in the Mafia sense of hits), is what Indian logicians call the first side (*purva paksha*), establishing good reasons to hate the British. I should like now to try to nuance that view a little, to aim for a more balanced hate-love toward them.

The Freudian and post-Freudian Marxist agendas tell us to look for the subtext, the hidden transcript, the censored text; the Marxist and to some extent the Freudian assumption is that this subtext is less respectable, more self-serving, but also more honest, more real than the surface text. In India the British surface text—"We are bringing civilization to these savages"—reveals a subtext: "We are using military power to make England wealthy by robbing India." But there are more than two layers to any agenda, and we mustn't assume that it's self-interest all the way down. The *peccavi* anecdote suggests that beneath the subtext of self-interest may lie at least a slightly nobler self-perception, a place where guilt is registered. And perhaps, beneath that, there may be yet another layer, an admiration of India, a desire to learn from India, perhaps even a genuine, if misguided, desire to give India something in return, still surviving, bloody but unbowed, from the first wave of Orientalists.

If we ask, What did the Hindus get out of the Raj besides poor? the answer, in part, is the mixed blessing of certain social and legal reforms, which reinforced the native reform movements already under way. Most of the giants of the independence movement—Gandhi, Nehru, Jinnah, Dadabhai Naoroji, and others—studied abroad, generally in London.[111] But they also got, as they did from the Mughals, the complicated legacy symbolized by horses, now more complex than ever.

Horses in Kipling's *Kim*

Horses were, you will not be surprised to learn, a problem for the British in India. Some horses were bred well in India; in 1860 a Captain Henry Shakespear, who had bred horses in the Deccan for many years, insisted that "no foreign horse that is imported into India . . . can work in the sun, and in all weathers, like the horse bred in the Deccan."[112] But the native Indian forces that opposed the British kept most of the best horses for themselves, and only a small fraction of the worst horses reached the horse fairs in the east, where the British were in control.[113] There was therefore, as usual, the problem of importing horses (most of them being shipped in from New South Wales, hence called Walers); shipping such fragile and valuable cargo "in a pitching East Indiaman on a six-month journey halfway round the world" was a costly and risky venture, and British horses became even more scarce, and even more expensive, when so many of them were used in the Napoleonic Wars.[114] (They imported dogs too; one Englishman in 1614 ordered from England mastiffs, greyhounds, spaniels, and small dogs, three of each, cautioning the importer that dogs were difficult to transport.[115]) Occasionally, exporting, rather than importing, horses also became a problem. Sir Charles Napier was crazy about a half-Arabian horse named Blanco, "perfectly white," whom he rode, talked to, and talked about for sixteen years. Sparing no expense, Napier had tried to ship the old horse home like a pensioned-off Indian civil servant, to spend his final days out at grass—good pasturage at last. But Blanco died in the Bay of Biscay while being, against the usual current, exported from Portugal to England.[116]

At the same time, itinerant native horse traders, who were often highway robbers in their spare time (the equine equivalent of used car salesmen), posed an even greater threat as a kind of underground espionage network, a cosmopolitan culture that had its own esoteric language, a mixture of various local dialects combined with a special jargon and an extensive code of hand signs, exchanged during the actual bargaining at the fair, mainly concealed under a handkerchief.[117] In recorded British history, horse breeding, spying, and Orientalism combined in the character of William Moorcroft, a famous equine veterinarian. In 1819, the British sent him to Northwest India, as far as Tibet and Afghanistan, on a quixotic search for "suitable cavalry mounts."[118] Moorcroft had seen mares from Kutch that he thought might be right for the army, and he was granted official permission "to proceed towards the North Western parts of Asia, for the purpose of there procuring by commercial intercourse, horses to improve the breed within the British Province or for military use."[119] But he also collected information on military supplies and political and economic conditions obtaining at the borders of the Raj,[120] and shortly before his mysterious final disappearance in 1824, he was briefly imprisoned in the Hindu Kush on suspicion of being a spy. Moorcroft had delusions of Orientalism; he told a friend that he would have disguised himself "as a Fakeer" rather than give up his plan, and after he was lost, presumed dead, in August 1825, legends circulated about "a certain Englishman named Moorcroft who introduced himself into Lha-Ssa, under the pretence of being a Cashmerian" or who spoke fluent Persian "and dressed and behaved as a Muslim." The final piece of Orientalism in his life was posthumous: From 1834 to 1841 his papers were edited not by a military or political historian but by Horace Hayman Wilson, secretary of the Asiatic Society of Bengal and the Boden Professor of Sanskrit at Oxford. According to his biographer, Moorcroft was thrilled by the stories he heard "from the north-western horse-traders—swarthy, bearded men like Kipling's Mahbub Ali."[121] But Kipling created Mahbub Ali—a Muslim horse trader who works secretly for the master spy Colonel Creighton—fifty years after the publication of Moorcroft's papers, and aspects of the characters of Creighton, Mahbub Ali, and Kim himself may have been inspired by Moorcroft. Kim is the son of a British soldier (a disreputable Irishman named O'Hara, already a marginal figure in the British world, who married an Irish nursemaid), but he masquerades sometimes as a Hindu, sometimes as a Muslim, and Mahbub Ali, a Tibetan lama, and Colonel Creighton all claim him as their son.

Horses are deeply implicated in espionage in Kipling's *Kim,* right from the start. Napier's code message, in the anecdote, was about a war; the very first chapter of *Kim* introduces a message about a war, coded not in Latin but in horses: "[T]he pedigree of the white stallion is fully established." Again, it is a triple code, of which the first two levels are easy enough to crack: Ostensibly, on the first level, it means that the Muslim horse trader Mahbub Ali is able to vouch for a valuable horse that the colonel may buy. The coded message on the second level is that a provocation has occurred that will justify a British attack in Northwest India (much like Napier's).

The third level of signification is more complex. The idea of a pedigree implies that you know the horse when you know its father and mother (or dam and sire); the ideas underlying the breeding of horses, ideas about "bloodlines" and "bloodstock" and Thoroughbreds, also marked the racist theory of the breeding of humans. Kim is said to have "white blood," an oxymoron. The question that haunts the book is, Who are Kim's sire and dam? I need not point out the significance of the color of the stallion in a book by Kipling (who coined the phrase "the white man's burden"). But we might recall that the Vedic stallion of the ancient Hindus, the symbol of expansionist political power, was also white, in contrast with the Dasyus or Dasas, who were said to come from "dark wombs" (RV 2.20.7). British racist ideas, supported by a complex pseudoscientific ideology, rode piggyback on already existing Hindu ideas about dark and light skin conceived without the support of a racist theory like that of the British; one might say that the Indians imagined racism for themselves before the British imagined it against them. The white stallion also implicitly represents

Kim's Irish father in the metaphor that Creighton and Mahbub Ali apply to Kim, behind his back: Kim is a colt that must be gentled into British harness.[122] On the other hand, to Kim's face, Mahbub Ali uses horses as a paradigm for the multiculturalism of Kim's world, which includes not only his English, Indian, and Tibetan Buddhist father figures, but both a good Catholic chaplain and an evil Anglican chaplain, the Bengali Hindu babu named Hurree Chunder Mookerjee and the Jainas of the temple where the lama resides. Kim feels that he is a sahib among sahibs, but he questions his own identity "among the folk of Hind" in terms of religion: "What am I? Mussalman, Hindu, Jain, or Buddhist?" Mahbub Ali's response (in the passage cited at the start of this chapter) is: "This matter of creeds is like horseflesh . . . the Faiths are like the horses. Each has merit in its own country."[123]

KIPLING, THE GOOD BAD POET

Kim's multireligious identity crisis ("What am I? Mussalman, Hindu, Jain, or Buddhist?") is stripped of its multicultural details in the simple question that he asks himself over and over again—"Who is Kim?"—and then, in the final chapter: "I am Kim. I am Kim. And what is Kim?"* Kipling bequeathed this individual quandary of multicultural identity to other novelists too, including Salman Rushdie, who, I think, modeled the hero of *Midnight's Children* on Kim, a boy with English blood who appears to be both Hindu and Muslim. But Rushdie reverses the point about race: The English blood doesn't matter at all, or the Hindu blood; the boy is a Muslim because he is raised as a Muslim. Hari Kunzru too is indebted to Kipling for some elements of the multicultural hero of his novel *The Impressionist,* though he takes the theme in very different directions: Kunzru's hero has an English father and an Indian mother, and he passes for white but loses the white girl he loves, loses her because (final irony) she prefers men of color.

How are we to evaluate the legacy of Kipling, doing justice both to his racism and to his deeply perceptive portrayal of India?

In his surprisingly appreciative essay on *Kim,* Edward Said wrestles with his conflicted feelings about Kipling. On the one hand, Said demonstrates how deeply embedded, indeed coded, in *Kim* is the racist and imperialist view for

---

* If we are still in the market for arcane bilingual language jokes, Kipling may well have known that Kim (short for Kimball) is the interrogative pronoun "what?" in Sanskrit, just as Ka is "who?" The statement "What is Kim?" is therefore just that, a statement rather than a question, and a tautology to boot: What? is What?

which Kipling became notorious. On the other hand, Said speaks of *Kim* as "profoundly embarrassing"[124]—for Said, and for us, for any readers caught between their warm response to the artistry of the book and their revulsion at the racist terminology and ideology. Said speaks of Kipling as "a great artist blinded in a sense by his own insights about India," who sets out to advance an obfuscating vision of imperial India, but "not only does he not truly succeed in this obfuscation, but his very attempt to use the novel for this purpose reaffirms the quality of his aesthetic integrity." Said's ambivalence was matched by that of the poet W. H. Auden, who argued (in his poem "In Memory of W. B. Yeats," 1939) that history would pardon "Kipling and his views," though he later excised those lines from subsequent editions.

Yet Auden's verses are powerful in precisely the way that, George Orwell pointed out, Kipling's own verse is powerful. Auden argued that Kipling would be pardoned "for writing well." Orwell argued that Kipling is a "good bad poet," who wrote the kind of poetry that you would like to forget but that you remember, almost against your will, more easily, and longer, than good poetry.[125] Kipling is "good bad" not merely in his literary qualities but also in his ethical qualities; he is both a racist and not a racist. Mowgli, for instance, the Indian hero of *The Jungle Book,* is portrayed in positive terms to which race is irrelevant. And Kipling, always aware that the "captains and the kings" would depart from India, could have had Charles Napier in mind when he prayed for divine guidance, "lest we forget"—forget, perhaps, the harm that the British had done in India? Rushdie, writing of his ambivalence toward the good and evil Kipling, remarks, "There will always be plenty in Kipling that I find difficult to *forgive*" (as Auden decided not, ultimately, to pardon Kipling), but then he adds: "but there is also enough truth in these stories to make them impossible to ignore."[126]

That truth grew out of a deep knowledge and love of India, where Kipling was born and which he described (in "Mandalay") as "a cleaner, greener land" (than England). Some of his stories can be read as variants on some of the classical texts of Hinduism. "On Greenhow Hill" (1891) is a translation, in the broadest sense, of the story of Yudhishthira and the dog who accompanies him into heaven; in the Kipling story, some Methodists are trying to convert an Irish Catholic to Methodism. They don't like his dog, and tell him that he must give up the dog because he is "worldly and low," and would he let himself "be shut out of heaven for the sake of a dog?" He insists that if the door isn't wide enough for the pair of them, they'll stay outside rather than be parted. And so they let him bring the dog to chapel. In "The Miracle of Puran Bhagat" (1894), a Hindu who becomes a high-ranking civil servant under the British and is even knighted gives it all up to become a renouncer; wild animals befriend him, as he shuns all human life. But he reenters the world when, warned by the animals, he saves a village from a flash flood, giving up his own life in the process. By translating dharma and the householder life into civil service for the Raj, Kipling gives a new twist to the old problem of the tension between renunciation and service to the world. *Kim* is as much about the search for Release from the wheel of samsara as it is about the intensely political and material world of espionage. In the final chapter, the lama's vision of the universe, including himself ("I saw all Hind, from Ceylon in the sea to the Hills. . . . Also I saw the stupid body of Teshoo Lama lying down . . ."), replicates the vision of the universe, and themselves, that Yashoda and Arjuna saw in the mouth of Krishna.

Kim is a novel written about, and out of, the British love of India. In part, of course, that love was like the love of one Englishman, Shakespeare's Henry V, for France: "I love France so well, that I will not part with a village of it; I will have it all mine."[127] But that is not the only kind of love there is, even in the hearts of other dead white males who "loved" the civilizations of people they colonized;[128] Gandhi referred to the British as "those who loved me."[129] The British also loved India for the right reasons, reasons that jump off every page of *Kim:* the beauty of the land, the richness and intensity of human interactions, the infinite variety of religious forms.

CHAPTER 22

SUTTEE AND REFORM
IN THE TWILIGHT
OF THE RAJ
1800 to 1947 CE

꧁

CHRONOLOGY

1772–1833 Rammohun Roy lives; 1828 he founds Brahmo Samaj

1824–1883 Dayananda Sarasvati lives; 1875 he founds Arya Samaj

1869–1948 Mahatma Mohandas Karamchand Gandhi lives

1861–1941 Rabindranath Tagore lives

1919 Amritsar massacre takes place

1947 Independence and Partition happen

[Version A] After they had performed their superstitious ceremonies, they placed the woman on the pile with the corpse, and set fire to the wood. As soon as the flames touched her, she jumped off the pile. Immediately the brahmuns seized her, in order to put her again into the flames: she exclaimed—"Do not murder me! I do not wish to be burnt!" The Company's officers being present, she was brought home safely.

Missionary Register, March 1820[1]

[Version B] What most surprised me, at this horrid and barbarous rite, was the tranquility of the woman, and the joy expressed by her relations, and the spectators. . . . She underwent everything with the greatest intrepidity, and her countenance seemed, at times, to be animated with pleasure, even at the moment when she was ascending the fatal pile.

J. S. Stavorinus (a Dutch admiral who visited Bengal in
1769 and 1770), 1770[2]

WOMEN: SUTTEE UNDER BRITISH EYES

How can the same act, performed by two different women fifty years apart, elicit such contrasting descriptions and responses? Since the first European accounts, both Europeans and Indians have expressed widely differing opinions about the practice that Anglo-Indian English called suttee, the action of certain women in India who were burned alive on the funeral pyres of their dead husbands. (Sanskrit and Hindi texts call the woman who commits the act a sati, "good woman.") Suttee had been around for quite a while before the Raj, as we have seen. Several queens commit suttee in the *Mahabharata,* and the first-century BCE Greek author Diodorus Siculus mentions suttee in his account of the Punjab. In the Buddhist *Vessantara Jataka,* based on a story shared by Hindus and Buddhists, when Vessantara is about to leave his queen and go into exile without her, she protests: "Burning on a fire, uniting in a single flame— such a death is better for me than life without you."[3] This imagery of wives so faithful that (to paraphrase St. Paul) they'd rather burn than unmarry (by being parted from their husbands in the next life) is part of the discourse of marital love even before it becomes a practice or is associated with funeral pyres. Such stories take to the extreme the sort of self-sacrifice normally expressed by relatively milder habits such as following husbands into exile, as both Sita and Draupadi do. On the other hand, a late chapter of the *Padma Purana* (perhaps c. 1000 CE) says that Kshatriya women are noble if they immolate themselves but that Brahmin women may not and that anyone who helps a Brahmin woman do it is committing Brahminicide.[4]

In the Muslim period, the Rajputs practiced *jauhar* (a kind of prophylactic suttee, the wife immolating herself before the husband's expected death in battle), most famously at Chitorgarh, to save women from a fate worse than death at the hands of conquering enemies. Numerous sati stones, memorials to the widows who died in this way, are found all over India; one of the earliest definitively dated records is a 510 CE inscription from Eran, in Madhya Pradesh. Most of the suttees seem to occur at first in royal Kshatriya families and later among Brahmins in Bengal, but women of all castes could do it. In 1823, for example, 234 Brahmin women, 25 Kshatriyas, 14 Vaishyas, and 292 Shudras were recorded as satis.[5]

To a Euro-American, such women are widows, though from the Hindu standpoint, a sati is the opposite of a widow. A widow is a bad woman; since it is a wife's duty to keep her husband alive, it is ultimately her fault if he dies and dishonorable for her to outlive him; to the degree to which she internalizes these traditional beliefs, she suffers both shame and guilt in her widowhood. A sati, by contrast, is a good woman, who remains a wife always and never a widow, since her husband is not regarded as dead until he is cremated (or, occasionally, buried), and she goes with him to heaven.[6]

Different scholars confronting suttee, like the blind men who encountered the elephant in the middle of the room, see a different beast depending on what part they grasp.[7] One[*] calls it a sacrifice and asks: What were the ancient and persistent traditions that drove some widows to do it voluntarily and other men and women to force other widows to do it involuntarily? Another[†] calls it murder and asks: Can suttee be explained by the more general mistreatment of women by men in India, particularly female infanticide and dowry murders of daughters-in-law (killing one wife so that the man can marry another and get another dowry)? Another[‡] calls it widow burning and asks: Why did the British first loudly denounce suttee, then covertly sanction it, and then officially ban it? This chapter will be concerned primarily with this third question, though we cannot ignore the other two and will begin with them. We will then consider similar complexities that dog the Raj record on issues such as cow protection, (non)violence, addiction to opium and alcohol, and the treatment of the lowest castes.

Did She Jump or Was She Pushed?

Eyewitnesses, both English and Indian, speak with different voices, sometimes of coercion—of women who tried to run away at the last minute and were dragged back, held down with bamboo poles, and weighted down with heavy logs designed to keep them from escaping—and sometimes of willing, joyous submission. But the one voice that we most want to hear in this story seems to be missing: the voice of the woman in the fire. To Gayatri Spivak's ovular question, "Can the subaltern speak?" (the subaltern being in this case the disenfranchised woman), my answer is yes. But that does not mean that we can hear her speak. The satis who are said to have wanted to die and succeeded did not live to tell the tale; the balance of extant testimony is therefore intrinsically slanted in favor of those who successfully escaped. Their voices tell us that the widow

---

[*] Catherine Weinberger-Thomas.
[†] Mala Sen.
[‡] Lata Mani.

was forced to do it (by relatives who wanted her jewelry or feared that she would dishonor them by becoming promiscuous) or that she preferred an early, violent death (often very early indeed, as many were widowed in their early teens) to the hardships of the life of a widow in India. Thus, in dramatic contrast with the multivocality of all the other players in this grim drama, almost every widow whose speech is noted by the colonial records is said to have given the same explanation: material suffering. Economic hardships may indeed have contributed to the spread of suttee. But this argument, that suttee occurred because widows had nothing, is contradicted by the argument that it occurred precisely because they had too much; the larger incidence of suttee among the Brahmins of Bengal, particularly from 1680 to 1830, was due indirectly to the Dayabhaga system of law that prevailed in Bengal, where, unlike in most of the rest of India, widows were entitled to their husbands' share of family lands and wealth[8]— wealth that would revert to the sati's husband's family after her death.

There were also religious reasons for a woman, or her relatives, to choose suttee. Many observers, both English and Indian, testified that women insisted on performing suttee, despite serious attempts, by both British officials and Indian relatives, to dissuade them. What was the religious ideology that might have motivated either the woman herself or the people forcing her to do it, or both? A woman might perform such an action for her own, personal, religious reasons (rebirth in heaven, or Release) or nonreligious reasons (depression, guilt, hardship, the desire to honor her husband and her family or to ensure a better life for her children) or involuntarily for someone else's nonreligious reasons (the reasons of her family, forcing her to do it so that they could get her money) or for their religious reasons (to satisfy their own ideas about the afterlife). Some women, as we shall see, even used suttee as a weapon of moral coercion to reform their husbands.

The crass Materialist hypothesis hardly does credit either to these women or to their religion; to argue that all of the satis were coerced, either driven to suicide or simply murdered, makes them victims rather than free agents, victims of male ventriloquism or false consciousness, an uncomfortable position for either a feminist or a relativist to assume. Taking the religious claims seriously gives the satis a marginally greater measure of what feminists call agency and I would call subjective dignity. It views them as individuals who made choices, who believed in what they were doing. The religious goal of some of these women may have been what they said it was: rebirth with their husband in heaven or again on earth or ultimate Release from rebirth. Some of them probably meant it when they said they wanted to die with their husbands (death for a Hindu is a very different prospect than it is for Christians and Jews), and feminists have taught us that it is sexist to disregard women's words.

Every ritual needs its myth, and the image of the suttee as sacrifice is supported by two myths, neither of which in fact describes an act of suttee. The first is the ancient Sanskrit tale of the goddess Sati, who entered a fire that was, significantly, not the pyre of her husband, Shiva, who never dies: She spontaneously ignited herself in protest when her father, Daksha, failed to invite Shiva to his sacrifice. A second myth, often used to justify the claim that a true sati does not suffer, is the tale of Sita, who entered a fire (again, not her husband's pyre) to prove her chastity and felt its flames as cool as sandalwood. The mythology of the ordeal by fire implied that, like Sita, a truly "good woman" would feel no pain (and many of the reports, including British reports, insisted that the women did not feel any pain), proving that she was not guilty of infidelity or any other failure as a wife, and if she did suffer, she was assured, her pain would destroy the bad karma of her evident guilt. But a suttee differs significantly from an ordeal; guilty or innocent, the sati cannot survive. And these myths were twisted into support for the idea of widows' immolation only at a fairly late date, while other mythological women were sometimes taken as paradigmatic satis instead.[9]

Any explanation of suttee must address the essential question of gender. True, there are many instances, in both myth and history, of Hindu men who sacrificed themselves in fire, but not on the pyres of their wives. Why not? The answer to this question must contextualize suttee as an aspect of the more general male desire to control women's sexuality, in which light suttee emerges not merely as a religious tradition but as a crime against women who are the scapegoats of a sexist society. Since Hindu texts blamed women for the sexual weakness of men, one danger posed by a widow was that she was a loose cannon, a hazard both to men and to her family, which she would dishonor were she unfaithful to her dead husband.

The traits of sexism are, however, recognizably cross-cultural; women have been beaten to death by their husbands and even burned alive (sometimes as witches) in countries where there is no suttee mythology of women and fire. To explain why the abuse of women takes the particular form that suttee assumes in India, we must therefore invoke, after all, the powers of a religious mythology of marriage, death, and rebirth. Once again we need a Zen diagram, allowing for the intersection of Materialist, feminist, and religious concerns.

Are we forced, after all, to choose between crass materialism and religious self-justification? I think not. Here we must consider the question of women's subjectivity, the subaltern's voice. These women were not a homogeneous group of mindless victims or soulless fanatics, but individuals who made various choices for various reasons and had many voices and cannot be sorted into two tidy groups of those who jumped and those who were pushed. Some were murdered for land or money or family honor; some sacrificed themselves for religious reasons; some committed suicide out of guilt, despair, or terror. Some resisted, and ran away, and lived to tell the tale; some tried to resist and failed; some tried to die and failed; some were unable to resist; some did not want to resist. What they all had in common is what they reacted to, the culture, the ideal of what a woman should be and do, a story that they all knew, though some believed it and some did not. That culture too was hardly monolithic; the woman who so impressed the Dutch admiral in 1770 was up against forces very different from those faced by the women who grew up singing ballads praising the immolation of entire royal households in Rajasthan or by those who learned on television about the much publicized, and protested, suttee of a woman named Rup Kanwar on September 4, 1987, at Deorala, in Rajasthan.

Rammohun Roy and the Brahmo Samaj

With these issues in mind, we can go back and consider what some people in nineteenth-century India tried to do about suttee.

Raja Rammohun Roy (1774–1833), a Bengali Brahmin who knew Arabic, Persian, Hebrew, Greek, Latin, and Sanskrit, in addition to his native Bangla (Bengali), was a major voice raised in opposition to suttee. Roy read the scriptures of many religions, only to find, he said, that there was not much difference between them. In 1814 he settled in Calcutta, where he was prominent in the movement that advocated education of a Western type, urging Hindus to learn mathematics, natural philosophy, chemistry, anatomy, and "other useful sciences."[10]

Roy always wore the sacred thread that marked him as a Brahmin, and he kept most of the customs of a Brahmin, but his theology was surprisingly eclectic. (He may also have been the first Hindu to use the word "Hinduism," in 1816.[11]) His intense belief in strict monotheism and his aversion to the sort of image worship that characterized Puranic Hinduism (*puja*, temple worship, pilgrimage) began early and may have been derived from a combination of monistic elements of Upanishadic Hinduism, then Islam and, later, eighteenth-century deism (belief in a transcendent Creator God reached through reason), Unitarianism (belief in God's essential oneness), and the ideas of the Freemasons (a secret fraternity that espoused some deistic concepts). He was one of the first upper-class Hindus to visit Europe, where he made a great hit with the intelligentsia of Britain and France. In 1828 he founded the Brahmo Samaj ("Society of God"), based on the doctrines of the Upanishads, several of which he had translated into Bangla in 1825.[12]

Roy wrote two tracts against suttee, publishing each first in Bangla and then in his own English translation. The first was *A Conference between an Advocate for, and an Opponent of the Practice of Burning Widows Alive,* which he published in two parts, in 1818 and 1820.[13] It was written in the form of a dialogue between an advocate and his opponent—the classical Hindu bow to diverse arguments. Roy denounced suttee from the standpoint of scripture and Hindu law,[14] arguing against it even when it was voluntary and, as such, faithful to "the scriptures"; he advocated ascetic widowhood instead.[15] Though he was unwilling to endorse government interference in matters of religion, his writings may have been a major factor prompting the British to take action against suttee in 1829. In 1830 Roy published a tract entitled *Abstract of the Arguments Regarding the Burning of Widows Considered as a Religious Rite* and, later, *Brief Remarks Regarding Modern Encroachments on the Ancient Rights of Females,* a tract on women's rights to property (a right that married women did not have in England until 1882), based on a reading of both the main commentary on *Manu* (by Mitakshara) and Dayabhaga law (the Bengal marriage code).

After Roy's death in 1833, Debendranath Tagore became leader of the Brahmo Samaj and, like Roy, vigorously opposed the practice of suttee, as did his son Rabindranath (though Rabindranath "treated the ideas behind it respectfully").[16] The third leader of the Brahmo Samaj, Keshab Chunder Sen, abolished caste in the society and admitted women as members.

STRANGE BEDFELLOWS

As for the British, on the issue of reform in general and suttee in particular, they were divided in several ways. Edmund Burke, a conservative, insisted that India was fine as it was, admired its religion and customs, and advised a hands-off policy; he sided with Sir William Jones and the Orientalists, who wanted to educate Indians in their own tongues and their own literatures, and he led the move to impeach Warren Hastings. On the other side, James Mill, a liberal, insisted that India suffered from arrested development and that the British had a duty to intervene and interfere; the Utilitarians sided as usual with Anglicists such as Macaulay, who wanted to teach the Indians about European literatures, in European languages, but on this issue of interference, they also sided with the evangelicals. The colonial bureaucrats were divided on the political costs of intervening in suttee, the Baptist missionaries took very different stances in addressing British and Indian audiences, and European eyewitness accounts of widow burning ricocheted between horror and fascination. One can hardly speak of a European consensus.

The two basic factions among the British also aligned themselves along the divide between, on the one hand, the basic terms of Cornwallis's pact in 1793, the promise not to interfere in religion in India (an early antecedent of *Star Trek*'s prime directive), sympathetic to the Orientalist/Conservative position, and, on the other hand, ideas of universal human rights, which often amounted to their desire to bring Enlightenment rationality to India, the Anglicist position (or even to bring Christianity to them, the evangelical position). The debate over whether suttee was religious (which also argued that it was painless; version B, above: She felt no pain, she really believed it, went willingly) or secular political/economic (and therefore painful; version A: They murdered her, presumably for the money, and she fought and screamed) meant that the British were driving with one foot on the brake and one on the accelerator: If suttee was religious, the prime directive would keep the British out; if it was secular, murder was being committed, and it was the duty of the British to prevent the Hindus from burning their women.

The Hindus were also divided in complex ways, and the grounds shifted in the arguments that they made for and against suttee in response to colonial discourse. The British thought that the various Hindu reform movements canceled one another out,[17] but they misunderstood the nature of Hinduism; each side raged on against the other(s), gaining rather than losing strength from the opposition. On one side were those who supported a strict enforcement of the caste system, held on to their old ways, and opposed any change in caste customs, including antisuttee legislation. On another side were the radicals, who included in their ranks both militant Hindus, who advocated violence, and college-educated students who renounced Hinduism, aped the British, became Anglophile Christians, ate beef and drank beer. Somewhere in between the extremes of both Indians and Europeans, Rammohun Roy and the Indian

Liberal movement opposed child marriages and suttee, preached nonviolence, and tried to build a new world that would combine the best of Hindu and Christian/British values.

The national press in India nowadays marches "in lockstep with the colonial legislator who abolished the custom of widow-burning in 1829."[18] Nationalist historians, despite their otherwise anticolonial bias, have accepted this part of the colonial viewpoint, thus aligning themselves with the Christian missionaries, whom they otherwise generally despise. On the left are the new, secular Indian elites, who engage in "internal colonialism" by protesting against the backlash of a Hinduism that they stigmatize as superstitious, socially retrograde, and obscurantist. On the right are the other sort of nationalist who use suttee as the banner of "Hindu-tva" (Hinduness) to oppress not only women but Muslims and dissidents.

Fast-forward: When it comes to suttee, we too are strange bedfellows, caught between two contemporary value systems. On the one hand, the increasingly popular concept of universal human rights challenges previous scholarly attempts to be value free and brings its adherents uncomfortably close to the camp of the British. On the other hand, such values as moral relativism or respect for other cultures condemn the British as white men saving brown women from brown men.*[19] Allan Bloom, in his conservative book *The Closing of the American Mind* (1987), began his attack on moral relativism with the example of suttee: "If I pose the routine questions designed to confute [the students] and make them think, such as, 'If you had been a British administrator in India, would you have let the natives under your governance burn the widow at the funeral of a man who had died?,' they either remain silent or reply that the British should not have been there in the first place."[20] I disagree. Some years ago, when I was invited to teach a class about India to a group of high school students on the South Side of Chicago, I told them about suttee and put Bloom's question to them, and their unanimous reply was: "I would not interfere; I would not mess with someone else's religion." This answer, which shocked me at the time, came, I eventually realized, out of the Chicago students' own experience of identity politics. But moving beyond the chauvinist British attitude (white men saving brown women from brown men) and then also beyond the relativist reaction ("I would not mess with someone else's religion"), we might aspire to a more complex synthesis, balancing our respect for the Hindus as complex

---

* Gayatri Spivak's phrase.

moral beings, many of whom protested against suttee, with our own sense of human rights. The best we can do is to question the deeper motives of the British, the Hindus, and ourselves.

THE RAJ RIDES TO THE RESCUE

Others before Rammohun Roy, including Akbar and Jahangir, had tried in vain to curtail suttee, and the British involvement in such reforms came from such mixed impulses that it was foredoomed to miscarry.

Every British schoolchild was once taught the story: "In 1829 the British government in India put an end to the Hindu practice of suttee, their moral outrage at this barbaric violation of human rights outweighing their characteristic liberal tolerance of the religious practices of people under their benign rule." But almost every element in this credo is false. True, a law was passed in India in 1829 making it illegal for widows to be burned with their husbands, but moral outrage was not the predominant factor in the British decision to outlaw suttee, nor did they succeed in ending it. On the contrary, the fear of offending high-caste Hindus serving in the British army and civil service, and concern about the political costs of legal interdiction, had led the British for many years to sanction suttee under some circumstances (as long as the woman had no children* and persuaded the magistrate that she was acting of her own free will), thus effectively encouraging it by giving it a legal support it had never had before, making it a colonially enhanced atavism.

In 1680 the Governor of Madras prevented the burning of a Hindu widow, and ten years later an Englishman in Calcutta was said to have rescued a Brahmin widow from the flames of her husband's funeral pyre and taken her as his common-law wife.[21] After that the British generally looked the other way where suttee was concerned. The same Orientalist spirit that led the British to mistake the idea for the reality, wrongly assuming that Hindus were following the *dharma-shastras*, led them to believe that they should not hinder but help the Hindus do as their scriptures dictated, and do it *right*. As usual they reached for *Manu*, but when for once he let them down—Manu is big on ascetic widowhood but does not mention suttee—they found some Bengali scholars who argued that the part of *Manu* advocating the burning of widows had somehow been left out of the Bengal manuscripts, so they helpfully put it back in.[22] (Most

---

* The two wives of Pandu in the *Mahabharata*, for example, could not both commit suttee, for one had to remain alive to care for the children.

of the dharma texts do not mention suttee, concentrating instead on ascetic widowhood; several condemn it in no uncertain terms; and a few late commentaries* argue for it.[23]) And so, on April 20, 1813 (the same year the missionaries were allowed in), a British circular proclaimed that suttee was meant to be voluntary and that it would be permitted in cases in which it was countenanced by the Hindu religion and prevented when the religious authorities prohibited it, as when the woman was less than sixteen years old, pregnant, intoxicated (a point worth noting), or otherwise coerced. In fact, there was a dramatic increase in the number of suttees from 1815 to 1818, the first three years of data collection and the first five years after the circular was published; the toll went from 378 to 839 cases. After that, the numbers declined and then fluctuated between 500 and 600. The 1817–1818 cholera epidemic may have increased the numbers, with more men dead and more widows to die with them, or the clerks may have refined their methods of data collection. But there was also a suspicion that the numbers grew because of government intervention: They had authorized it (their work made it seem as if "a legal suttee was better than an illegal one") and given it interest and celebrity (so that, as in the case of Rup Kanwar in 1987, there were copycat suttees).[24]

And when the British did intervene in suttee, the results were often counterproductive. For instance:

THE SLOW-BURNING FIRE

A certain Captain H. D. Robertson, Collector of Poona in 1828, learned that a botched suttee had allowed the pyre to burn too slowly, causing the would-be sati to escape in agony. She requested that they try again; again it was botched; British officers finally intervened, and she died twenty hours later. Robertson investigated and determined that "Hindu scriptures" did stipulate that such slow-burning grass should be used, though it seldom was. He decided that if the British were to insist that this text be obeyed to the letter, the realization that suttee would now invariably produce a slow burn, increasing the agony, would discourage women from undertaking it. But one woman did still commit suttee, despite attempts to dissuade her, and Robertson was zealous in carrying out what he saw as his duty.[25]

---

* One commentary (Apararka on Yajnyavalkya, probably around 1100 CE) says that a widow may burn herself on her husband's pyre if she is impelled by her own deep grief, but she must not be forced.

What Joseph Conrad called the reformer's compassion here went horribly awry.

Finally, in 1829, the year after Robertston's intervention, several years after prominent Brahmins had already spoken up against suttee, and at a time when there were many Indians in the legislature and William Bentinck, an evangelical sympathizer, was Governor-General (1828–1835), the desire to justify their continuing paternalistic rule over Indians whom they characterized as savage children led the British to ban suttee altogether, as well as child marriage, with much self-aggrandizing fanfare.

The British law probably facilitated more women's deaths than it saved, and its main effect was to stigmatize Hinduism as an abomination in Christian eyes.[26] Suttee is a pornographic image, the torture of a woman by fire, hot in every sense of the word. Relatively few women died that way, in contrast with the hundreds, even thousands who died every day of starvation and malnutrition, but suttee had PR value. Thus the Raj had it both ways, boasting both that it did not interfere with other people's religions and that it defended human rights. The debate, in both India and Britain, turned what had been an exceptional practice into a symbol of the oppression of all Indian women and the moral bankruptcy of Hinduism. Nor did the 1829 law, or, for that matter, the new legislation enacted by India after its Independence put an end to it; at least forty widows have burned since 1947, most of them largely ignored until the suttee of Rup Kanwar in 1987 became a cause célèbre, and some even now attested only in obscure local archives.

Romancing Suttee

Some of the British, sympathetic to one Hindu view, compared the satis with Christian martyrs or the heroic suicides at Masada—death rather than dishonor, better dead than red, and so forth. Other Europeans romanticized suttee in other ways. Abraham Roger, in 1670, recorded a local story:

INDRA TESTS A SATI

Indra, the Vedic king of the gods, came to earth as a man and visited a whore, to test her faith. He paid her well and they made love all night. In the morning, he pretended to be dead, and she wished to be burned with him, despite the protests of her parents, who pointed out that she was not even the man's legitimate wife. When the pyre was ready, Indra woke up, announced that it was just a trick, and took her to his heavenly world.[27]

We have seen Indra's tricks before, but this Dutch author apparently has not. He mistakes suttee for the practice of a woman of the night, rather than the act of a chaste wife. Voltaire (who had gotten India wrong before) also seems to have missed the point: In *Zadig* (1747), he imagined a heroine about to commit suttee and suggested the enactment of a law forcing widows to spend an hour with a young man before deciding to sacrifice themselves. And an eighteenth-century French comic opera presented a Frenchman in India whose wife, an Indian woman who was unfaithful to him, feigned drowning in the hope that her husband would throw *himself* on *her* pyre.[28]

Richard Wagner staged suttee in his opera *Götterdämmerung* by having his heroine, Brünnhilde, ride her horse onto the flaming pyre of her beloved Sieg-fried.* In an early draft of the opera (summer of 1856), Brünnhilde spouts a kind of garbled Vedanta (via the philosopher Schopenhauer, who had read Indian philosophy in German): "I leave the Land of Desire, I flee the Land of Illusion forever; I close behind me the open door of eternal Becoming. . . . Freed from rebirth, everything eternal . . . I saw the world end."[29] Thus some Europeans glorified the custom of suttee.

ANIMALS: DAYANAND SARASVATI, THE ARYA SAMAJ, AND COW PROTECTION

Since women and cows are closely linked in the Hindu imaginary, through the trope of purity, let us turn now to the issue of cow protection, which was the banner of the Arya Samaj even as suttee was for the Brahmo Samaj.

Dayanand Sarasvati (1824–1883) was trained as a yogi but steadily lost faith in yoga. He claimed to base his doctrines on the four Vedas as the eternal word of god and judged later Hindu scriptures critically, denouncing image worship, sacrifice, and polytheism. After traveling widely as an itinerant preacher, in 1875 he founded the Arya Samaj, which rapidly gained ground in western India. Dayananda insisted that "those who read or listen to the Bible, Quran, Purana, false accounts, and poetic theory—books of ideas opposed to the Veda—they become sensuous and depraved."[30] The Arya Samaj further developed the ceremony for "reconversion"† (called purification [*shuddhi*]) to bring "back" to the Vedic fold some Muslims who had never been Hindus at all, as

---

* G. B. Shaw remarked, nastily, of Wagner's wife, Cosima, "She is enough to reconcile me to the custom of suttee."
† Fast-forward: The present-day Hindutva movement has reactivated the process of reconversion.

well as to reconvert some recent Hindu converts to Islam.[31] They used the same ceremony to "purify" Pariah castes.[32] And they sought to distinguish themselves, as Aryans, from Hindus, who in their view (as in the British view) practiced a degraded form of Vedic religion.[33]

In 1893 internal disputes caused the Arya Samaj to split into two parties, sometimes called the Flesh-eating and Vegetarian parties. But the issue of vegetarianism arose before that in 1881, when Dayanand published a treatise called *Ocean of Mercy for the Cow* (*go-karuna-nidhi*), and in 1882, when he founded a committee for the protection of cows from slaughter. For the next decade the Arya Samaj established cow protection societies all over British India. The first agitation over cow slaughter in the Raj took place in a Sikh state of the Punjab where cow slaughter had been a capital offense right up to the moment when the British took over.[34] From then on, the issue challenged the legitimacy of British rule, though the immediate violence was directed against Muslims who killed cows, as they did during the Bakr-Id festival and after pilgrimages (though goats could also be sacrificed). The same debate that hedged British interference in suttee (if it was religious, they should not interfere, but if it was secular, they should) also hedged cow protection.[35] In 1888 a British court in Allahabad ruled that a cow was not a sacred object, that Muslims who slaughtered cows could not be held to have insulted the religion of the Hindus, and that police were to protect Muslims who wanted to slaughter cows.

Cow protection societies continued to form the major plank of the Arya Samaj movement in North India, and cow slaughter was specifically used to justify violence against Pariahs and Muslims. Popular ballads and stories highlighted Kshatriya virtues embodied in acts of saving cows from the assaults of Muslim butchers, to whom Pariahs such as Chamars allegedly supplied cows. At the Bakr-Id festival of 1893, riots broke out involving the entire Hindu population of villages, and thousands of people attacked Muslims. In the 1920s, communal riots occurred around symbols of the cow. Cows continued to provide a lightning rod for communal violence from then until the present day.

Violence and Nonviolence

VIOLENCE: DYER AT AMRITSAR

After World War I, India was a different world, but still the iconic massacres, like those surrounding the 1857 Rebellion, continued. It was 1919. There had been fierce protests against British rule, an orgy of arson and violence that left five Europeans dead. The British forbade all meetings and demonstrations.

A peaceful group assembled in Jallianwala Bagh in Amritsar, an open space hemmed in by houses, to celebrate the feast day of Baisakhi. Brigadier General Reginald Dyer marched his troops in and, without any warning, gave the order to fire on the crowd; they ceased firing only when they ran out of ammunition. Because the British were blocking the only gate to the enclosure, the crowd was trapped. More than twelve hundred men, women, and children were seriously wounded, and three to five hundred were killed.

Dyer, who already had a reputation for brutality (he had had prisoners beaten, sometimes in public, and made Indians crawl on the street), was proud of what he had done. The House of Lords passed a measure commending him, and he was designated a "defender of the Empire." Nor was he ever punished.* But Winston Churchill referred to the massacre as "a monstrous event," the British press expressed shocked outrage, and Dyer's action was condemned worldwide. The House of Commons officially censured him, and he resigned in 1920. Tagore returned his Nobel Prize, and Nehru's father abandoned his Savile Row suits and took to wearing Gandhian homespun.[36]

And the rest, as they say, is history: Indian nationalists, under the banner of the Congress Party, succeeded, after decades of often violent Indian protests and equally violent British reprisals (both imprisonments and executions), in winning independence from the British in 1947.

NONVIOLENCE: GANDHI

One of the key figures in the independence movement was Mahatma Gandhi, who reacted to Amritsar with one of his fasts against the British. Pleading for an honorable and equal partnership between Britain and India, held not by force but "by the silken cord of love," he argued: "Fasting can only be resorted to against a lover, not to extort rights but to reform him, as when a son fasts for a father who drinks. My fast at Bombay and then at Bardoli was of that character. I fasted to reform, say, General Dyer, who not only does not love me, but who regards himself as my enemy."[37]

Gandhi frequently used fasting as a weapon to reform (or coerce) others; on one occasion, he fasted to get Congress to agree to regard the Pariahs (whom he called Harijans [People of God]) as a Hindu community, and he succeeded;

---

* Fast-forward: In 1940, in Caxton Hall, in London, an Indian shot to death, in delayed and displaced retribution, Sir Michael O'Dwyer, the lieutenant governor of the Punjab, who had stood by Major Dyer in 1919.

separate Harijan electorates were abolished, and more seats were reserved exclusively for Harijan members.[38] Fasting, in the dharma texts, was usually a restoration for sins and errors, and Gandhi always had a strong sense of his own shortcomings; the fasting dealt with that too. Thus his fasting was intended first to control himself, then to control his own people, getting them to unite in protest but to pull back from violence; and then to control the British, getting them to let him out of jail on several occasions and, eventually, to quit India. He had more success with the British than with his own people.

Drawing on the nonviolent Jaina and Vaishnava traditions of his native Gujarat, Gandhi, who came from a merchant (Baniya) caste, developed the idea of what he called *satya-graha*—"holding firmly on to truth" (*satya,* like *sati,* derived from the verb "to be" in Sanskrit)—first in South Africa, on behalf of the Indian community there, and then in India, on behalf of the Harijans, elevating suffering and denial into a quasireligious discipline, like yoga or meditation.[39] He used fasting as a weapon of the weak[40] against the British, as Indian women had used it against their husbands for centuries (often simultaneously withholding sexual access, locking themselves into the "anger room," as Kaikeyi did in the *Ramayana*). Gandhi said that you cannot fast against a tyrant, that he fasted to "reform those who loved me." Refuting the binary sexual attributes as the British generally applied them to male colonizers and feminized colonized subjects (the Rape of India syndrome), he made female fortitude, self-sacrifice, and self-control the model of national character for both men and women. Thus he invented a gendered nationalism that expressed an androgynous model of virtue,[41] which he regarded as the essence of both bravery—indeed virility—and the female qualities of endurance and nonviolence.

Gandhi was a one-man strange bedfellow. His insistence on celibacy for his disciples caused difficulty among some of them, as did his habit of sleeping beside girls young enough to be called jailbait in the United States, to test and/or prove his celibate control or to stiffen his resolve. But this practice drew not so much upon the Upanishadic and Vaishnava ascetic traditions, which were the source of many of Gandhi's practices, as upon the ancient Tantric techniques of internalizing power, indeed creating magical powers, by first stirring up the sexual energies and then withholding semen.

On the question of eating beef, Gandhi was also ambivalent. As a child he had heard popular poems recited by schoolboys: "Behold the mighty Englishman/He rules the Indian small,/Because being a meat-eater/He is five cubits tall."[42] Thus, in contradiction of the reasons to eat meat outlined in many Hindu texts, Gandhi felt as if the natural order—the laws of violence and power—required him to eat meat in order to defeat the British. But eating meat was not natural for Gandhi, who was raised in a Vaishnava family that practiced strict vegetarianism,[43] in Gujarat, where Jainism was strong.

In the end Gandhi used the image of calf love (*vatsalya*), the love of and for a mother cow, particularly the Earth Cow, Mother Earth, as a key symbol for his imagined Indian nation, and though he also tried to include Muslims in the family, cow protection was a factor in the failure of his movement to attract large-scale Muslim support. His attitude to cows was, however, an essential component of his version of nonviolence (*ahimsa*), which, in Gandhi's hands, came to mean not just opposition to blood sacrifice but what others called passive* nonresistance[44] and I would call passive-aggressive nonresistance, against the British, without spilling their blood any more than an adherent of traditional *ahimsa* would spill the blood of a sacrificial animal.

Gandhi was well aware that there had never been true nonviolence in India (or anywhere else, for that matter). He once remarked, "Indeed the very word, nonviolence, a negative word, means that it is an effort to abandon the violence that is inevitable in life."[45] If you've read this far, you will know that Gandhi could not simply pick up off the rack a nonviolence already perfected by centuries of Hindu meditation; it was a much-disputed concept. Gandhi had to reinvent nonviolence before he could use it in an entirely new situation, as a political strategy, against the British Raj. But he had a rich tradition to draw upon. Writing about the *Gita,* Gandhi granted, "It may be freely admitted that the Gita was not written to establish *ahimsa.* . . . But if the Gita believed in *ahimsa* or it was included in desirelessness, why did the author adopt a warlike illustration? When the Gita was written, although people believed in *ahimsa,* wars were not only not taboo, but no one observed the contradiction between them and *ahimsa.*"[46]

Hindu idealists gladly embraced the Gandhian hope that the Hindus might set an example for the human race in passive resistance, a hope bolstered by their desire to prove to the disdainful British that the Hindus were not the lascivious, bloodthirsty savages depicted in the colonial caricature. Thus an ancient Hindu ideal was appropriated and given new power by Hindus (such as Gandhi) who had been influenced by Western thinkers (such as Tolstoy) who were acquainted with the neo-Vedantins as well as with German idealists who

---

* Gandhi himself resisted the term "passive," arguing that *satya-graha* was an active measure.

had been reading the Upanishads (originally through Persian, Muslim translations), making these ideas more attractive both to Westerners and to Hindus still living under the shadow of Western domination.

But if Gandhi hoped that the ancient Hindu ideal of nonviolence, even in its modern incarnation, would succeed in the postcolonial context, he was whistling in the dark. His method succeeded against the British but could not avert the tragedy of Partition.* Gandhi's nonviolence failed because it did not pay sufficient attention to the other, more tenacious ancient Hindu ideal that had a deeper grip on real emotions in the twentieth century: violence. For as Krishna pointed out in the *Bhagavad Gita,* it is quite possible to adhere to the mental principles of nonviolence while killing your cousins in battle. (Gandhi wrote a translation, into Gujarati, and commentary to the *Gita* in which he interpreted the *Mahabharata* war as symbolic and read metaphorically Krishna's exhortations to Arjuna to kill his enemies.) The Vedantic reverence for nonviolence flowered in Gandhi; the Vedic reverence for violence flowered in the slaughters that followed Partition. Then more active civil disobedience replaced passive noncooperation, and terrorism also increased. On January 30, 1948, Gandhi was shot to death by Nathuram Godse, a Pune Brahmin who had ties with the militant nationalist organization called the RSS (Rashtriya Swayamsevak Sangh, or National Volunteers' Organization).[47]

Taxing Addiction: Alcohol and Adivasis in Gujarat

Gandhi was concerned with control on both the political level (control of violence) and the personal (control of sensuality). The threats to both were united in the British control of Hindu addiction to opium, for opium, along with indigo (the dye used for European uniforms) and tea, was one of the great Raj cash crops.[48] The East India Company forced Indian peasants to cultivate the poppy from which opium is produced,[49] which was then exported to China in exchange for silks and tea (thereby producing opium addicts in China); when the Chinese resisted, the company dispatched its Indian sepoys to fight and die for the company's cause. But not all the opium got to China. In Kipling's *Kim,*

---

* This is not the place to review the history of Partition, but a few basic points might be useful: The former colony was divided into two countries, India, with a Hindu majority, and Pakistan, with a Muslim majority. This was done because many Muslims believed that their interests would not be protected in a majority Hindu country, however secular the government. Hindus and Sikhs moved from what became Pakistan to India, and Muslims from India to Pakistan, a displacement of between ten and twelve million people. Several hundred thousand Hindus and Muslims lost their lives; entire trains pulled into stations across the border filled only with corpses. An untold number of women were raped.

Kim's father dies of opium and the woman he lives with sells it; Kipling speaks of "the opium that is meat, tobacco, and medicine to the spent Asiatic," a tolerant (if racist) attitude that was, oddly enough, shared by some missionaries, who would not begrudge to the desperately poor the pill of opium that was for some, the missionaries said, their only stimulant. But Kipling neglects to mention that opium also meant death for many people. More precisely, it meant death and taxes. Before the British introduced an opium tax for the first time, opium had been untaxed and used fairly cheaply by all classes of people, in both the towns and the villages. The tax didn't make the addicts give it up, but increased their already desperate poverty.[50]

Alcohol was a more pervasive problem than opium and has deeper and more complex roots in Hindu culture, but it too became a political problem under the Raj, also through a new form of taxation in Gujarat in the 1920s. What has been called the Devi movement started in South Gujarat among a group of Adivasis, a tribal group whom caste Hindus in the nineteenth century regarded as non-Hindu because they ate meat (anything but cattle and horseflesh) and drank liquor.[51] (This definition conveniently ignored the fact that many Hindus ate meat and drank liquor, yet reform movements often argued that giving up meat and wine was a way of giving up being a tribal and becoming part of the four-class system.)[52] More precisely, the Adivasis drank toddy (*tadi*), the fermented juice of a palm tree (coconut, palmyra, or date palm; in South Gujarat, it was mostly date palm), and *daru,* made chiefly from the flowers of the mahua tree (*Madhuca indica*) and said to be seven times as strong as toddy (15 to 30 percent alcohol). Both drinks were cheap to make and not very strong.[53] "God gave the Brahmin ghee [clarified butter, used in Vedic sacrifices] and the Bhil [a tribal people] liquor," a local proverb goes, and these Adivasis believed (as the Vedic Indians had) that the gods also enjoyed sharing a drink with them at various rituals. At funerals, the corpse too was given a drink. They drank toddy in part because it was so much cleaner and healthier than water, but they strongly disapproved of addictive drinking.

The Adivasis did not regard women as property but allowed them to divorce, remarry (even if widowed), and commit adultery (which they regarded as an offense but not a grave offense). And they were anti-Brahmin (some even regarded Brahmin killing as an act of merit) and regarded literacy in Hindu texts as "a cultural force which they had always done their best to keep at bay." The Hinduism to which they were exposed in school was primarily Arya Samaj, amounting to devotion to a Hindu deity (in particular Krishna), a daily bath, and no meat, no blood sacrifice, and, worst of all, no *daru* or toddy.

The Adivasis had always made toddy and *daru* privately at home until the late nineteenth century, when the colonial and various princely states, the capitalists who manufactured liquor in central distilleries, and the liquor dealers (who in South Gujarat were almost all Parsis) combined forces to control and tax liquor, just as the British had taxed opium. But toddy is best consumed within hours of fermenting; by storing it until it could be taxed and sold, the British ruined it; by the time it got to the shops it was weak and tasteless, and expensive, and hard to get. The Parsis who sold it came to town "mounted on a fine horse with a gun and a whip"; they raped the Adivasi women and forced the girls into prostitution for touring officials. This happened so often that the Adivasis devised a ceremony of purification for women whom the Parsis had raped. Thus colonial administrators and landed castes took the Adivasis' land, took their crops, took their women, took bribes, and exploited their labor.

Then the goddess arrived. Originally a smallpox deity (called, apotropaically, Sitala ["the Cool"] because she brought fever), she became for the Adivasis a force for social reform and a vehicle for protest against their exploiters, the Parsis. Though the Adivasis had resisted the educational forces of Hinduism and spurned the help of higher political powers when the nationalists had tried to help them, they did not reject the Higher Power of the goddess, in a move that anticipated Alcoholics Anonymous by a decade or two. The goddess possessed certain women and spoke through them, and the women then led demonstrations, courted imprisonment, and persuaded the men to refuse the tax; they held the men to the mark and goaded them on.

Speaking through the women, the Devi persuaded the men to drink tea instead of liquor, which broke their economic bondage to the Parsis. The solidarity that they had formerly expressed in communal drinking bouts they now symbolized by *not* drinking. Though there was a certain amount of recidivism and the occasional great debauch to celebrate a new recruit's final renunciation, by and large it worked. They sang songs (*bhajans*) to Krishna, some of which exhorted them to give up liquor and stand up against the liquor dealers, while other songs (spiked by the words of the Devi herself) commanded them not to become Christians, to resist the missionaries who were active in their district.

This was not Sanskritization. Like many tribals, the Adivasis realized that they would be very low caste if they became Hindus and so did not claim a rank as a caste (though Hindus often regarded them as a caste). Some of them, however, asked to be regarded as Kshatriyas, who could maintain their high status even while indulging in impure practices such as eating meat and addictive vices such as drinking liquor. This is what has been called Rajputization or Kshatriyazation, the upward mobility of castes that do *not* give up their "impure" habits. But the Devi's command to give up toddy and *daru* doubly empowered them by helping them simultaneously to appropriate the "purer" values of the regionally dominant high-caste Hindus and Jainas and to assert themselves against the most rapacious of the local exploiters, the Parsis.

Indeed, as the Devi movement grew in strength, the Adivasis began to treat the Parsis as Pariahs, taunting them that they should go back to Persia, and forcing Parsi women, for the first time in their lives, to do the tasks of scrubbing, sweeping, and washing. Some Adivasis refused to talk with Parsis or even be touched by them, thus, of course, perpetuating the evils of the caste system. Some Parsis and their strongmen, assisted on occasions by tax officials, retaliated by seizing Adivasis, holding them down, and pouring liquor down their throats (thus making them break their vows and become ritually impure once again) or by pouring toddy into village wells so that the Adivasis would be forced to drink alcohol with their water.

The inspiration of the Devi gave the Adivasis the courage to rebel. Unlike the priestly spokesmen of the Hinduism they had avoided in the schools, the Devi did not require them to worship gods like Krishna or Rama (though some of them did) but allowed them to go on worshiping their old gods and goddesses so long as they did not perform blood sacrifice. The goddess often became incarnate in an old buffalo cow who wandered freely from house to house, and one man became richer after the cow defecated* and urinated in his house.[54] But there were, from the start, skeptics who regarded the cow as a public nuisance, beat her away with a stout stick, drove her out of their crops, and sold her at a public auction. And although most of the Adivasis attributed their new social activism to the goddess, they had learned that change was possible and that they could make it happen by their own actions, long after many of them decided that their supposed champion was no more than a figment of the imagination.[55] The Devi took the place of the intellectuals who, in other times and places (Russia in 1917, to take a case at random), came in from outside

---

* The folklore motif "gold from shit" is known from Indian folktales as far away as Kangra, in the foothills of the Himalayas, and was noted by Freud.

to inspire the oppressed peasants to rebel. This was entirely a tribal movement. The myth, once again, made history possible.

The Devi movement was eventually crushed in many places, through the punishment of its leaders. Often the Devi then departed, in a formal ceremony, but sometimes the movement went on without her. In 1922 one reformer managed both to keep the villagers from drinking and to prevent animal sacrifices (by arguing that sacrificial animals and humans had the same souls). The movement became increasingly secular, and increasingly accommodating. As people noticed that those who went on drinking liquor and eating meat did not experience the divine wrath that they had been threatened with, they followed suit, often within a year of the Devi's departure. Sometimes, quitting before she was fired, the Devi possessed a few Adivasis and proclaimed that they could once more eat meat and fish and drink *daru* and toddy.

As a kind of transition between the Devi movement and the nationalist movement that eventually caught up the Adivasis, a deified form of Gandhi replaced the goddess for a while.[56] (The prohibition of alcohol had been high on the list of things* that Gandhi wanted the British to grant.[57]) Some of the Adivasis said that spiders were writing Gandhi's name in cobwebs; they also saw Gandhi in bottles of kerosene, in the rising sun or the moon (a man—a very particular man—instead of a rabbit), and in wells, where the wheel for the bucket became the spinning wheel (*charkha*) that Gandhi was to make so famous. Eventually Gandhi himself put a stop to all this mythologizing of his image.[58]

Gandhi had chosen for the exemplary hero of his paradigm of fasting with love a son who fasts for a father who drinks. But fasting was not the only measure that could be used to control the drinking of a parent or spouse. A far more extreme version of the pressure that women could exert by fasting or withholding sexual access was suttee, a moral control available to women who had no other powers, a desperate but sometimes effective measure. Rajput women in Rajasthan tell this story about their husbands, who, like all Kshatriyas, are expected to drink liquor, but not too much too often:

There was a woman whose husband was fond of liquor and overindulged regularly, causing much strife within the family. One day he was so drunk that he fell

---

* The others included halving the land revenue, protecting Indian cloth, releasing political prisoners, and abolishing the salt tax, this last being the one that Gandhi decided to make a major issue.

off a roof and died. At that time his wife took a vow of suttee. Before immolating herself, she pronounced a curse that from then on no male in the family would be allowed to drink liquor, and since then no one in that household has dared to drink. Even the women gave up drinking alcohol, in order not to tempt their husbands to start again.[59]

Here it was not a goddess but a human sati whom the women called on to protect their families.

Fast-forward: In the 1990s, in Dobbagunta in Andhra Pradesh, rural women attending a literacy class discovered that they all suffered from their husband's addiction to *arak*, the local alcohol. So they launched a campaign to ban it.* The antiliquor campaign spread across the entire state of Andhra Pradesh. This time too there was no Devi.

CASTE

The Devi movement was as much about caste as about addiction. The British, as we have seen, did little to displace caste and much to enforce it, despite the many voices raised in criticism of Hindu injustices. Eventually both the reform movement and the anti-British initiative passed to a new English-educated Indian elite.[60]

THE CHAMARS AND THE SATNAMIS

One Pariah caste whose polluted status was directly connected with cows was the Chamars, a caste of leatherworkers who had always borne the stigma of their traditional caste *sva-dharma* and whose contact with the carcasses of cows excluded them from Hindu temples. But the Chamars in Chattisgarh, in central India, changed their lives in ways that mirror, mutatis mutandis, similar movements throughout India. The Chamars often owned their own land or worked as sharecroppers and farm servants and formed about a sixth of the local population. But in the 1820s, according to Chamar legend, a Chamar farm servant named Ghasidas (c. 1756–1836) threw the images of the gods and goddesses of the Hindu pantheon onto a rubbish heap and rejected the authority of the Brahmins, the temples, and Hindu *puja,* as well as the colonial authority. Ghasidas proclaimed belief only in the formless god without qualities (*nir-*

---

* In 1995, Nupur Basu made an eleven-minute film about this antialcohol campaign in Dobbagunta, titled *Dry Days in Dobbagunta,* about the events in the early 1990s.

guna), called the True Name (*satnam*), thus affiliating himself with the larger sect of Satnamis that had been founded in the eastern Punjab in 1657. Other low castes joined the Satnampanth ("Path of the True Name"). They all abstained from meat, liquor, tobacco, and certain vegetables, generally red vegetables like tomatoes, chilies, and aubergines (well, a sort of purplish red), and red beans, and they used bullocks instead of cows as their farm animals.[61] In this way they simultaneously rejected Brahmins and took on a Brahminical, Sanskritizing, purifying set of values; they became the people they had rebelled against, replicating among themselves the hierarchy that had excluded them.

The Satnamis developed a new mythology, based on their own oral traditions, in which gurus replaced gods as the central figures. These myths were not written down until the late 1920s, and then only by someone who probably sanitized them, appropriating them to the concerns of a largely reformed Brahminical Hinduism. Yet the written forms did not vary significantly from the myths later collected in the oral tradition. We have questioned the pervasiveness of the Brahmin filter for Puranic stories; it may have been equally loosely constructed here, or, on the other hand, the revised written collection may have fed back into the Satnami oral tradition by the time those stories were collected.[62]

There were other filters to which the Satnami tradition was also exposed. In around 1868 the evangelical missionaries began to convert some of the Satnamis to Christianity, reworking the Satnami oral traditions with Christian teachings and forging connections between Ghasidas and the gurus, on the one hand, and Christ and the missionaries, on the other. And, finally, the most bizarre filter of all: In the 1930s, the Satnamis constructed a new genealogy for their group, with Brahmin ancestors, drawing upon *Manu,* of all things, but reversing Manu's arguments, in an attempt to persuade the provincial administration to enter the group as Hindus rather than Harijans in official records, but still to retain the advantages accorded to what were then called the Scheduled Castes (now Dalits). That is, the Satnamis wished to establish their superiority to other castes within the category of Scheduled Castes, once again reproducing the hierarchy. The administration rejected this petition, arguing that all Harijans were Hindus in any case.[63]

In our day, the advantages of what Hindus call reservation (and we call affirmative action), such as the 1980 Mandal Commission, which reserved nearly half of all government and educational places for the underprivileged castes (whom they called Scheduled Castes), has stood Sanskritization on its head, leading to what we might even call Dalitification. Some Brahmins burned themselves to death in protest over the Mandal recommendations, but the conflict between the so-called Other Backward Castes (OBCs) and (other) Scheduled Castes is sometimes greater than the one between Dalits and Brahmins, as castes not particularly disadvantaged in any way often manage to get themselves reclassified as Scheduled so as to win a share of the new opportunities.[64] In Rajasthan, the Gujars (or Gujjars), an Other Backward Caste, clashed with the Meenas (Dalits), because the Gujars wanted a *lower,* Scheduled status. This was precisely the outcome that Gandhi had feared when he insisted that Harijans decline the chance of being a separate electorate. As Gary Tartakov has put it, "It was evil enough that such racializing degradation was claimed by caste Hindus; it was worse that that is what the members of the Schedule Castes and Tribes accepted themselves to be, *if they remained Hindus.*"[65]

The idea that the solution to the problem of the Dalits was precisely not to remain Hindu was one of the strategies adopted by Ambedkar.

UNTOUCHABLES AND DALITS, BUDDHISTS AND AMBEDKAR

Bhimrao Ramji Ambedkar, a Dalit who was one of the group who drafted the Constitution, agreed with Gandhi that Untouchability had to be stopped, but Gandhi thought you could still keep caste, and Ambedkar said you could not. At first, Ambedkar tried to reform Hinduism; he resisted movements that attempted to convert Dalits to Islam or Christianity. Then he reasoned that since the Hindus viewed their tradition as eternal, they regarded basic elements of that tradition, such as class injustice and Untouchability, as eternal too and impossible to eradicate.[66] "Gandhiji," he said, "I have no homeland. How can I call this land my own homeland and this religion my own wherein we are treated worse than cats and dogs, wherein we cannot get water to drink?"[67] In the end he converted to Buddhism, translating the Buddhist concept of individual suffering (*dukka*) into his own awareness of social suffering, discarding a great deal of Buddhism and inserting in its place his own doctrine of social activism. Though he had the good sense to keep a number of Buddhist stories in his platform, one that he did not keep was the story, so basic to the Buddhist tradition, that the future Buddha was confined within a luxurious palace until one day when he had grown up, he went outside and happened to see a sick man, an old man, a dead man, and a renouncer.[68] Ambedkar objected to this story because it "does not appeal to reason" that a twenty-nine-year-old man would not have been exposed to death by then.[69]

Fast-forward: In 1956 five million Dalits, led by Ambedkar, converted to

Buddhism. Ambedkar was concerned that they would still be labeled Untouchables if they demanded places reserved for affirmative action, and we have seen that this has continued to be a problem. On the other hand, he insisted that even when they became Buddhists they should retain the rights that he had fought so hard to win for Dalits.[70] One of his converts said: "My father became a Buddhist in honor of Ambedkar but could not say so openly. I became a Buddhist too, but only orally, because on the forms you have to write down Scheduled Caste. If you are a Buddhist, you can't get the scholarship. But I am proud to follow Ambedkar. Being Scheduled Caste causes inferiority in our minds. To be Buddhist, it makes me feel free!"[71] It is an irony of history that some Dalits nowadays favor the Aryan invasion theory, but add that they, the Dalits, were the original Adivasis there in India before the Aryans rode in, making the Adivasis older in India and therefore, by the Law of Origins, more honorable than the Aryans.

On November 4, 2001, more than fifty thousand Dalits converted to Buddhism in New Delhi. Some converted only as a protest against the mistreatment of Dalits, but others wholeheartedly became practicing Buddhists. On October 14, 2006, the fiftieth anniversary of the conversion of Ambedkar, Dalits again began to convert in large numbers. As a result, the Hindu Nationalist Party reclassified Buddhism and Jainism as branches of the Hindu religion, to prevent the mass conversions of the Dalits from eroding the political fabric, and several states, including Rajasthan and Madhya Pradesh, introduced laws requiring anyone wishing to convert to obtain official permission first. In separate rallies, not connected to the conversion ceremonies, thousands of Dalits attempted to burn the new laws.[72] In November 2006 the government banned a mass conversion rally in Nagpur that aimed at converting one million Dalits to Buddhism; the authorities were said to be under pressure from Hindu nationalists who called the rally a "Christian conspiracy." Defying the ban and the barricades, thousands of Dalits from across India gathered at the Ambedkar Bhawan. But Dalits continue to be oppressed, and to protest their oppression, in India.

HINDUS IN AMERICA

1900–

ॐ

During the Chicago riots in 1968, Allen Ginsberg chanted "om" for seven hours to calm everyone down. At a certain moment, an Indian gentleman had passed him a note telling him his pronunciation was all wrong.[1]

Deborah Baker, *A Blue Hand: The Beats in India*

The question of the degree to which other Americans too have gotten a lot more than the pronunciation of "om" all wrong, and who is the best judge of that, is what drives this chapter.

Reverse Colonization

There are many ramifications of American imperialism in India—the devising of beefless Big Macs, the outsourcing that guarantees an Indian accent on the line when you call to complain about your Visa bill—but here we will concentrate on the reverse flow, the process by which Hindus, and various forms of Hinduism, came to America and colonized it. This was colonization not in the negative and material sense of economic and political exploitation (the old sense, in which the British colonized India), but in a new positive and intellectual sense of making major contributions to American culture. We might call this reverse colonization, reversed in both direction (from rather than to India) and will (voluntary rather than coerced). At the same time, we must consider the more problematic ways in which Americans have appropriated aspects of Hinduism, new ways that retain the bad odor of the old Raj colonization.

Posh and Pukka American Hindus

American Hindus constitute yet another of the many alternative voices of Hindus. They are an important presence in America, where, in 2004, there were 1,478,670 Hindus (0.5 percent of the total population); and in a land where over a quarter of the population has left the religion of its birth, some of them to take on forms of Hinduism, Hindus convert from their religion less than any other religious group and are the best educated and among the richest religious groups (according to one survey).[2] There are more than two hundred Hindu temples in America, three-quarters of them built in the past three decades. In Lilburn, a suburb of Atlanta, Georgia, one of the fastest-growing South Asian communities in the United States raised more than nineteen million dollars to build one of the largest Hindu temples in the world, where about six thousand worshipers come on festival days. Called the Swaminarayan Mandir (the *New York Times* article about the temple defined *mandir,* the Sanskrit word for "temple," as "a Sanskrit word for the place where the mind becomes still and the soul floats freely"), it was modeled on a temple not in India but in London, Raj inspired and already one remove from the mother country.[3]

Long before they came to our shores in large numbers, Hindus contributed many things to American culture, beginning with the very words we speak, some of them transmitted to us through Anglo-Indian words that entered the English dictionary in the eighteenth and nineteenth centuries. An alphabetical list of just a few of such words conjures up a vivid scene: bungalow, calico, candy, cash, catamaran, cheroot, curry, gymkhana, jodhpur, juggernaut, loot, madras, mango, mogul, moola (British slang for "money," ultimately from the Sanskrit *mula,* "root," as in "root of all evil"), mosquito, mulligatawny, pajama,

Pariah, posh,* pukka,† punch,‡ pundit, thug, tourmaline, veranda—why, any writer worth her salt could turn that list into a film script in an hour ("After he lights his cheroot on the veranda of the bungalow, and changes from pukka jodhpurs to posh pajamas . . ."). More recently, words about religion rather than "loot" and "moola" have entered through American rather than British sources, such as dharma from Jack Kerouac's *The Dharma Bums* (more Buddhist than Hindu) as well as yoga and tantra, guru and ashram, and above all, karma.

INTERRELIGIOUS INTERACTIONS IN CHICAGO

We can trace the path of Hindu religious movements more precisely than that of the words; the movements entered through Chicago.

In 1890 an amateur magician published, in the *Chicago Daily Tribune,* a story that put a new twist on the sort of magic trick that had been practiced in India, and reported by gullible visitors to India, for many centuries.[4] Two men, one named Fred S. Ellmore, claimed to have witnessed this scene:

> A fakir drew from under his knee a ball of gray twine. Taking the loose end between his teeth he, with a quick upward motion, tossed the ball into the air. Instead of coming back to him it kept on going up and up until out of sight and there remained only the long swaying end. . . . [A] boy about six years old . . . walked over to the twine and began climbing it. . . . The boy disappeared when he had reached a point thirty or forty feet from the ground. . . . A moment later the twine disappeared.[5]

The two witnesses sketched it (there was the boy on the rope), photographed it (no boy, no rope), and exposed the trick: "Mr. Fakir had simply hypnotized the entire crowd, but he couldn't hypnotize the camera." The story was much retold until, four months later, the newspaper admitted that it had all been a hoax; the author (John Elbert Wilkie) had made up everything, including the telltale name of Fred Sell-more (get it?). And that was the origin of the Indian rope trick—which turns out to have been not Indian, or a rope (twine), or a trick (since it didn't happen).

---

* Popularly said to be derived from the initial letters of the phrase "port outward, starboard home," with reference to the more comfortable (because cooler) and more expensive side for accommodation on ships traveling between Britain and India.

† "Perfected" or "fully developed," from the Sanskrit verb *pach,* "to cook or ripen."

‡ The drink, made of five [*panch*] ingredients.

Then, in 1893, the World's Parliament of Religions brought Vedanta to Chicago. Among the people who attended the event was Swami Vivekananda (1862–1902), a disciple of Ramakrishna Paramahamsa (1834–1886). Ramakrishna, a devotee of Kali at the Temple of Dakshineshvar, north of Kolkata (Calcutta), was a member of neither the Brahmo Samaj (which was represented by B. B. Nagarkar at the World's Parliament) nor the Arya Samaj but attracted a different sort of educated lay follower. His studies and visions had led him to conclude that "all religions are true" but that the religion of each person's own time and place was the best expression of the truth for that person. And his respect for ordinary religious rituals gave educated Hindus a basis on which they could justify the less philosophical aspects of their religion to an Indian consciousness increasingly influenced by Western values.[6]

Vivekananda, Ramakrishna's disciple, was the first in a long line of proselytizing gurus who exported the ideals of reformed Hinduism to foreign soil and, in turn, brought back American ideas that they infused into Indian Vedanta. Influenced by progressive Western political ideas, Vivekananda set himself firmly against all forms of caste distinction and advised people to eat beef.[*] He made a powerful impression at the World's Parliament of Religions in Chicago and returned to India in 1897 with a small band of Western disciples. There he founded the Ramakrishna Mission, whose branches proclaimed its version of Hinduism in many parts of the world. Other Hindu or quasi-Hindu movements also began to thrive in America. Before Vivekananda, Helena Blavatsky, a Russian, had founded the Theosophical Society in New York City in 1875; after she had journeyed to India in 1879, she set up her headquarters at Adyar, near Madras, and from there she and her followers, incorporating aspects of Hinduism into their doctrines, established branches in many cities of India. But the activities of the now Vedanticized Theosophical Society in the United States began only after Vivekananda had paved the way, and it prospered under the leadership of Annie Besant (1847–1933), who founded Theosophical lodges in Europe and the United States.

A second wave of Hindu imports began in the second half of the twentieth century, the age of the Hindu Hippie Heaven. In 1965, in Los Angeles, A. C. Bhaktivedanta (Prabhupada) founded the Hare Krishna movement, officially

---

[*] Dr. Bowers reports: "After the first session of the Parliament of Religions, I went with Vivekananda to the restaurant in the basement of the Art Institute, and I said to him, 'What shall I get you to eat?' His reply was, 'Give me beef!' " (*Outlook,* July 17, 1897).

known as the International Society for Krishna Consciousness (ISKCON) and tracing its lineage back to Chaitanya. In 1974 followers of Swami Muktananda established the Siddha Yoga Dharma Associates (SYDA) Foundation, teaching their version of Kashmir Shaivism. In 1981, Bhagwan Shree Rajneesh (later Osho) moved his headquarters from Poona (later Pune) to Oregon. Shri Shri Ravishankar, Mother Meera, Amritanandamayi Ma, Shri Karunamayi Ma, Sant Rajinder Singh Ji Maharaj, Shri Ma—all these (and many more) have routinely visited the United States, many of them since the eighties, and several of them women. Amritanandamayi Ma, known to her followers as Amma ("Mother"), came from Kerala to the world (arriving in the United States in 1987) and specialized in Vedanta and hugs; from fifteen hundred to nine thousand people attend her programs in the United States (closer to thirty thousand or forty thousand in India).[8] Amma was one of the speakers at the 1993 World's Parliament of Religions in Chicago.

In 1999, a century and a bit after the *first* World's Parliament of Religions, Chicago city officials placed 340 life-size cow statues along city streets. The cows, which had nothing to do with Hinduism (their referents were the [bullish] stock market and the stockyards), were a huge success. They brought Chicago $200 million in additional tourist revenue and $3.5 million for local charities from the auction of the cows when the exhibition ended. Other cities jumped on the animal bandwagon. New York copied the cow idea, working with a Connecticut company, CowParade, which imported the concept from Zurich, where it had originated. Cincinnati commissioned pigs, and Lexington, Kentucky (home of the Derby), went for horses.[9] But during that summer, Chicago was like Calcutta, in this regard at least; everywhere you turned, you met a cow.

A VIRTUAL INDIA IN AMERICA

America often becomes India in other ways too. Sometimes Hindus in America rework local topography, so that the three rivers in Pittsburgh become the Ganges, Yamuna, and Sarasvati, just as South Indian kings had declared that the Kaveri River was the Ganges. Now some have devised a practice of religious outsourcing that lets them bypass American Hinduism entirely, by conducting their worship lives (virtually) in India. The Internet enables them to be in two places at once, a technique that Hindus perfected centuries ago (recall Krishna present to each of the Gopis at the same time, in different places). If you are a Hindu in America, it is now possible for you to make an offering on the banks of the Ganges without leaving Atlanta or wherever you are; you pay someone else in India to do it for you. (This too is an old Indian trick, a form of transferred merit or karma; recall the Hindu satire on the "Buddhist" satire on the Hindu argument that "if the oblation to the ancestors that is eaten by one man satisfies another, then people traveling abroad need not take the trouble to carry food.") One Web site that offers this service is shrikashivishwanath.org; another is www.webdunia.com/kumbhuinfo (written in Hindi and run by the government of the Indian state of Uttar Pradesh); yet another, bangalinet .com/epuja.htm, bills itself as "a home away from home." Eprathana.com will send someone to any temples you choose, and most of them are small local temples, suggesting that people far from home miss the little shrine at the end of the street as much as they miss the big pilgrimage temples.

When you log on to some of these Web sites, you can view various *puja* options, for which you can register online and pay. For instance, you can perform a "virtual *puja*," a cartoon *puja* in which you burn electronic incense and crack open a virtual coconut. If you are unable to make it to the Ganges River for the great festival of the Kumbh Mela or just for the daily absolution of cumulative misdeeds, you log on, fill out a questionnaire (caste, gender, color, body type—slim or portly—and choice of auspicious days), and attach a passport-size photo. On the selected date, you can go to the Web site to see virtual representations of yourself (your photo superimposed on a body chosen to match what you described in the questionnaire) being cleansed in an animated image of the Ganges River. At the same time, someone who is actually (nonvirtually) there at the river dips your actual photo in the actual (nonvirtual) river, which is what makes the ritual work; it can't all be done by mirrors.[10] Recall the Chola and Rashtrakuta kings who brought real Ganges water south to their temples. Here the worshiper is transported, photographically and electronically, to India in order to make contact with the real river.

Thus American Hindus, despite building grandiose temples here, need not replace the traditional sacred places of Hindu ritual practice with new ones in America. "The reach of the local" is extended by new media that allow ritual observance to center on those locales even at a distance. You can have *prasad* (the leftovers from the gods' meal in the temple) delivered to you, in America, from an Indian temple, by courtesy of the Indian postal services. You can hire a Brahmin priest to perform a special sacrifice for you in Varanasi (see www .bhawnayagya.org). You can even have access to the real goddess Kali, the Indian Kali, at Kali Ghat in Kolkata, virtually.

THE AMERICAN APPROPRIATION OF THE *GITA* AND THE GODDESS KALI

But Kali is here too and so is Krishna.

When J. Robert Oppenheimer witnessed the explosion of the first atomic bomb at Los Alamos, on July 16, 1945, he realized that he was part of the myth of doomsday but not his own Jewish doomsday. (The remarks of others present on that occasion, such as General Thomas F. Farrell, also tended to employ mythical and theological eschatological language, but from the Abrahamic traditions.) Oppenheimer, who liked to think that he knew some Sanskrit, and who had a copy of the *Bhagavad Gita* in his pocket at Los Alamos, said that as he watched the bomb go off, he recalled the verse in the Sanskrit text of the *Bhagavad Gita* in which the god Krishna reveals himself as the supreme lord, blazing like a thousand suns. Later, however, when he saw the sinister clouds gathering in the distance, he recalled another verse, in which Krishna reveals that he is death, the destroyer of worlds. Perhaps Oppenheimer's inability to face his own shock and guilt directly, the full realization and acknowledgment of what he had helped create, led him to distance the experience by viewing it in terms of someone else's myth of doomsday, as if to say: "This is some weird Hindu sort of doomsday, nothing we Judeo-Christian types ever imagined." He switched to Hinduism when he saw how awful the bomb was and that it was going to be used on the Japanese, not on the Nazis, as had been intended. Perhaps he moved subconsciously to Orientalism when he realized that it was "Orientals" (Japanese) who were going to suffer.

Oppenheimer was one of the last generation of Americans for whom the *Gita* (flanked by the Upanishads and other Vedantic works) was the central text of Hinduism, as it had been for Emerson, Thoreau, and other transcendentalists of the nineteenth century. For later generations, it was the goddess Kali (flanked by various forms of Tantra) that represented Hinduism. Kali became a veritable archetype for many Jungian, feminist, and New Age writers; Allen Ginsberg depicted Kali as the Statue of Liberty, her neck adorned with the martyred heads of Julius and Ethel Rosenberg.[11] (Paul Engle later said, simultaneously insulting both India and Ginsberg: "He succeeded in doing the heretofore utterly impossible— bringing dirt *to* India."[12])

Soon the goddess Kali became a major Hollywood star. Her career took off with the film *Gunga Din* (1939), in which Sam Jaffe played the title role

(Reginald Sheffield played Rudyard Kipling*), with Cary Grant and Douglas Fairbanks, Jr., buckling their swashes against Kali's dastardly Thug worshipers, led by Eduardo Ciannelli, who usually played Chicago gangsters. (The film begins with a solemn statement: "The portions of this film dealing with the goddess Kali are based on historical fact.") The 1965 Beatles film *Help!* included a satire on *Gunga Din,* with an attempted human sacrifice to an eight-armed Kali-like goddess.† Kali also appeared in *The Golden Voyage of Sinbad* (1974), *Indiana Jones and the Temple of Doom* (1984), and *The Deceivers* (1988), starring Pierce Brosnan as Captain Savage, who ends up converting to the worship of a particularly violent and erotic form of the goddess as queen of the Thugs.[13]

Kali made her mark in American literature too, if literature is the word I want. Roger Zelazny's *Lord of Light* (1967) was a sci-fi novel based on Hindu myths and peopled by Hindu gods, including Kali. Leo Giroux's *The Rishi* (1986) was a lurid novelization of Colonel Sleeman's already insanely lurid *Rambles and Recollections* (1844), updated to Cambridge, Massachusetts, in 1975; gruesome garrotings are carried out ritually at Harvard and MIT, where "a beautiful half-Indian girl is tormented by visions that urge her to participate in the most unspeakable rites," as the jacket blurb promises us. Claudia McKay's *The Kali Connection* (1994) describes an intimate relationship between two women, a reporter and a member of "a mysterious Eastern cult." In *Forever Odd* by Dean Koontz (2005), the villainess, named after the poisonous plant datura, is "a tough, violent phone-sex babe, crazy as a mad cow," "a murderous succubus," and a living incarnation of Kali ("the many-armed Hindu death goddess"). In a story titled "Sweetheart of the Song Tra Bong," in Tim O'Brien's *The Things They Carried* (1990), which really *is* literature, when a nice American girl gets caught up with U.S. commandos in Vietnam, she is seen wearing around her throat an icon of Kali: "a necklace of human tongues. Elongated and narrow, like pieces of blackened leather, the tongues were threaded along

---

* Kipling did not appear in the 1950 movie of *Kim,* in which Errol Flynn played Mahbub Ali and Paul Lukas played the Tibetan monk.
† Kali's role in the 1965 Beatles film was just the beginning. The cover of the Beatles' 1966 album *Sergeant Pepper's Lonely Hearts Club Band* featured, among many others, Mahatma Gandhi, Sri Yukteswar, Sri Lahiri Mahasaya, and Sri Paramahansa Yogananda. George Harrison met Maharishi Mahesh Yogi in England, and in 1968 the Beatles traveled to India, where they met with the maharishi in Rishikesh in a widely reported and famously photographed visit. (*Life* magazine decided that 1968 was the "Year of the Guru.") In 1969, Harrison met with A. C. Bhaktivedanta Swami Prabhupada at John Lennon's estate in Tittenhurst Park and performed his "Hare Krishna Mantra" with the devotees of the London Radha-Krishna Temple.

a length of copper wire, one overlapping the next, the tips curled upward as if caught in a final shrill syllable."[14] Other manifestations of Kali followed apace, further still from the spirit of Hinduism, such as a lunch box on which Kali dances, her lolling tongue suggesting her eagerness to get at the box's contents.

Particularly offensive are the many porn stars who have taken the name of Kali, presumably in vain. One, who admitted that she based her sexual therapy on Masters and Johnson, still claimed that it was Tantric because, she explained helpfully, "Tantra is a Sanskrit word that means expansion of consciousness and liberation of energy. It is about becoming more conscious and when applied in love-making deepens intimacy, intensity and orgasmic orgiastic experience heading in the direction of full body orgasmic feeling."[15] So now you know. Another self-proclaimed Hindu goddess appears on her Web site (which gives new meaning to ".org") dressed as Kali, with sex toys and bondage gear in her many hands.[16] The upscale British superstore Harrods stopped the sale of bikini underwear bearing images of Hindu goddesses (some of it allegedly with Shiva on the crotch) but apologized only after Hindu Human Rights, a group that says it "safeguards the religion and its followers," lodged a formal protest. Another department store had to apologize for selling toilet seats with images of a Hindu deity, and a third for selling slippers with Hindu symbols. An article reporting on these complaints remarked, "A number of designers have been attracted by the richness of Hindu iconography and the fad for exotic ethnic patterns."[17]

Hindu Human Rights also protested against a musical film that the Muslim filmmaker Ismail Merchant was making in 2004, called *The Goddess,* in which the rock singer Tina Turner (allegedly a Buddhist) was to play the role of the goddess Kali (or, according to some reports, Shakti). Merchant and Turner traveled to India to visit a host of holy cities and were blessed by a Hindu priest, and Merchant insisted that, "contrary to the accusations, "nobody is going to sing and dance on the back of a tiger. The Goddess is not going to be half naked or a sex symbol." (He also insisted that the goddess in his film was not just Kali but "Shakti, the universal feminine energy, which is manifest in Kali, Durga, Mother Mary, Wicca, and each and every woman on the planet.") We will never know; Merchant died in May 2005 and apparently didn't finish the film. Nor did Stanley Kubrick live to finish *Eyes Wide Shut* (1991), which aroused the wrath of the American Hindus Against Defamation because the orgy scene in it was accompanied by the chanting of passages from—what else but the *Bhagavad Gita?* Surely the deaths of the two film directors was a coincidence?

Clearly the non-Hindu American image of Kali and other goddesses is very different from her image among Hindus in India.

Twisted in Translation: American Versions of Hinduism

Nor are the goddesses the only Hindu deities appropriated in this way. In Paul Theroux's *The Elephanta Suite* (2007), a shrine to the monkey god Hanuman displaces a Muslim mosque (an inversion of the alleged displacement of a temple to Rama under the mosque at Ayodhya). Hanuman goes to Manhattan in a forthcoming film in which he helps the FBI battle terrorists. "Hanuman is the original superhero. He is thousands of years older than Superman, Spider-Man and Batman. He is a brand to reckon with among Indian children today," said Nadish Bhatia, general manager of marketing at the Percept Picture Company, which coproduced *The Return of Hanuman.* He continued: "Every society is looking for heroes, and we want to make Hanuman global. . . . If the Coca-Cola brand can come to India and connect with our sensibilities, why can't Hanuman go to New York?"[18] Why not indeed?

Sita too has come to New York (and points west). In 2005, Nina Paley (an American woman previously married to a man from Kerala who left her), created an animated film called *Sitayana* (www.sitasingstheblues.com), billed as "The Greatest Break-Up Story Ever Told" and set to the 1920s jazz vocals of Annette Hanshaw. The episode titled "Trial by Fire" is accompanied by the words of the song "Mean to Me" ("Why must you be mean to me? You love to see me cryin' . . ."). Rama lights the fire and kicks Sita into it; she comes out of the fire; he looks puzzled, then sad, then goes down on one knee in supplication; she calls him "dear" (and you see the golden deer) and jumps into his arms. In Alfonso Cuarón's 1995 remake of *A Little Princess,* the young heroine tells the story of the *Ramayana,* in which Sita sees a wounded deer and asks Rama to go and help it . . . not kill it!

Mainstream or counterculture, once Hindu gods had become household words in America, it was open season on them; anyone could say anything at all. Sometimes it takes a very nasty turn: In Pat Robertson's evangelical novel, *The End of the Age* (1995), the Antichrist is possessed by Shiva, has the president murdered by a venomous cobra, becomes president himself, and forces everyone to worship Shiva and thus to be possessed by demons. More often it is just stupid. An ad proclaims, "Many people worship the Buddha. Many people worship chocolate. Now you can do both at the same time." Another advertises "the Food of the Gods: The Chocolate Gods and Chocolate Goddesses . . . Fine

Quality Gourmet Handmade Chocolates that celebrate those gods and goddesses of love and luxury, joy and happiness, compassion, peace and serenity, healing, and fertility of the body and imagination." It was only a matter of time before someone made "Kamasutra Chocolates," replicating the mating couples depicted on the temples at Khajuraho. Even the folksy Ben & Jerry's made a Karamel Sutra ice cream.

The *Kama-sutra* in general has been the occasion for a great deal of lustful marketing and misrepresentation; most people, both Americans and Hindus (particularly those Hindus influenced by British and/or American ideas about Hinduism), think that the *Kama-sutra* is nothing but a dirty book about "the positions." Since there is no trademarked "Kama-sutra" the title is used for a wide array of products. Kama-sutra is the name of a wristwatch that displays a different position every hour. The Red Envelope company advertises a "Kama Sutra Pleasure Box" and "Kama Sutra Weekender Kit," collections of oils and creams packaged in containers decorated with quasi-Hindu paintings of embracing couples. A cartoon depicts "The Kamasutra Relaxasizer Lounger, 165 positions." (A salesman is saying to a customer, "Most people just buy it to get the catalogue."[19]) There are numerous books of erotic paintings and/or sculptures titled *Illustrated Kama-sutras* and cartoon *Kama-sutras,* in one of which the god Shiva plays a central role.[20] The Palm Pilot company made available a Pocket Sutra, "The Kama Sutra in the palm of your hand," consisting of a very loose translation of parts of the text dealing with the positions. A book titled *The Pop Up Kama Sutra* (2003) failed to take full advantage of the possibilities of this genre; the whole couple pops up. In 2000, the *Onion,* a satirical newspaper, ran a piece about a couple whose "inability to execute The Totally Auspicious Position along with countless other ancient Indian erotic positions took them to new heights of sexual dissatisfaction. . . . Sue was unable to clench her Yoni (vagina) tightly enough around Harold's Linga and fell off . . ."[21] Another satire proposes "a *Kama Sutra* that is in line with a postpatriarchal, postcolonial, postgender, and perhaps even postcoital world."[22] *Kama Sutra: The Musical*[23] is the story of a sexually frustrated young couple whose lust life is revitalized by the mysterious arrival of the eighteen-hundred-year-old creator of the Kama Sutra, Swami Comonawannagetonya. The swami reveals to them the titillating secrets that allow any couple to experience all the joys of a totally fulfilling sex life.

"Karma," which Americans often confuse with *kama* (watch your *r*s!), lost most of its meaning in its American avatar (if "avatar" is the word I want; "avatar" has been taken up by computer text messaging, designating the cartoon caricatures of themselves that people use to identify their virtual personae in cyberspace[24]). Take the 1972 *Last Whole Earth Catalog:* "[T] the karma is a little slower when you're not stoned, but it's the same karma and it works the same way." A United Way billboard: "Giving is good karma." And a voluntary organization called getgoodkarma.org welcomes you to Karmalot (get it?), gives you a simplified and entirely non-Hindu version of "what goes around comes around," and signs you up. Other Hindu terms too have become distorted past recognition. In the film *Network* (1976), the character played by Peter Finch, gone stark raving mad, says, "I'm hooked to some great unseen force, what I think the Hindus call Prana." In *Michael Clayton* (2007), both the whistleblower lawyer, when he goes crazy, and Michael Clayton (George Clooney), when he is triumphant, shout, out of the blue, "I'm Shiva, the god of death!" High Sierra markets an Ahimsa Yoga Pack, to go with its Ananda Yoga Duffel. And now there is the American version of Laughter Yoga, which "combines simple laughter exercises and gentle yoga breathing to enhance health and happiness."[25] There's an energy drink called Guru. There's a movement to make yoga an Olympic sport.

American Tantra

Perhaps the greatest distortions occur in the takeover of Tantra, which has become an Orientalist wet dream. The belief that the Tantras are in any way hedonistic or even pornographic, though a belief shared by many Hindus as well as by some Euro-Americans, is not justified; the Upanishads and Puranas—not to mention the *Kama-sutra*—have far more respect for pleasure of all kinds, including sexual pleasure, than do the Tantras. The ceremonial circumstances under which the Tantric sexual ritual took place make it the furthest thing imaginable from the exotic roll in the hay that it is so often, and so simplistically, assumed to be. Yet many people call the *Kama-sutra,* or even *The Joy of Sex,* Tantric. Some (American) Tantric scholars feel that, like Brahmins, they will be polluted by the Dalit types who sensationalize Hinduism, and so, in order to make a sharp distinction between the two castes of Americans who write about Hindus, they censure the sensationalizers even more severely than the revisionist Hindus do. Some have excoriated others who have "cobbled together the pathetic hybrid of New Age 'Tantric sex,' " who "blend together Indian erotics, erotic art, techniques of massage, Ayurveda, and yoga into a single invented tradition," creating a "funhouse mirror world of modern-day Tantra" that is to Indian Tantra what finger-painting is to art.[26]

Does it make it any better, or even worse, that this sort of Tantra is often marketed by Indian practitioners and gurus? For many Indian gurus take their ideas from American scholars of Tantra and sell them to American disciples who thirst for initiation into the mysteries of the East. Here is what might be termed an inverted pizza effect, in which native categories are distorted by nonnative perceptions of them (as pizza, once merely a Neapolitan specialty, became popular throughout Italy in response to the American passion for pizza). The American misappropriation of Indian Tantra (and, to a lesser extent, yoga) has been reappropriated by India, adding insult to injury.

In an earlier age, the native sanitizing tendency was exacerbated by the superimposition of a distorted European image of Tantra—namely, "the sensationalist productions of Christian missionaries and colonial administrators, who portrayed Tantra as little more than a congeries of sexual perversions and abominations."[27] In their attempts to defend Tantra from this sort of Orientalist attack, early-twentieth-century Tantric scholar-practitioners, both Hindu and non-Hindu, emphasized the metaphorical level of Tantra, which then became dominant both in Hindu self-perception and in the European appreciation of Tantra. This school was made famous, indeed notorious, by Arthur Avalon, aka Sir John Woodroffe (1865–1936) and, later, by Agehananda Bharati, aka Leopold Fischer (1923–1991).

Today, too, many scholars both within and without Hinduism insist that the literal level of Tantra (actually drinking the substances) never existed, that Tantra has always been a meditation technique. Indeed we can take the repercussions back several generations and argue that the revisionist Hindu hermeneutic tradition that was favored by Hindus educated in the British tradition since the nineteenth century and prevails in India today began in eleventh century Kashmir, when a major dichotomy took place between the ritual and mythological aspects of Tantra. For Abhinavagupta's version of Tantra was pitched at a leisured Kashmiri class "arguably homologous to the demographics of the twentieth- and twenty-first-century New Age seekers."[28] Moreover, the "no sex, we're meditating" right-hand brand of Tantra that first caught the European eye turned upside down to become the new left-hand brand of Tantra: "No meditating, we're having Tantric sex." As this movement is centered in California (into which, as Frank Lloyd Wright once remarked, everything on earth that is not nailed down eventually slides), we might call it the Californication* of Tantra.

---

* The title of a Showtime TV series.

Thus a major conflict between Hindu and non-Hindu constructions of Hinduism in America operates along the very same fault line that has characterized the major tension within Hinduism for two and a half millennia: worldly versus nonworldly religion, reduced to Tantra versus Vedanta.

HINDU RESPONSES TO THE AMERICANIZATION OF HINDUISM

Not surprisingly, the sensibilities of many Hindus living in America have been trampled into the dust by the marketing of Tantra and other aspects of Hinduism. Web sites and Internet contacts make Hindus in America an often united (though still very diverse) cultural and political presence, which has developed an increasingly active voice in the movement to control the image of Hinduism that is projected in America, particularly in high school textbooks but also in other publications by non-Hindu scholars and in more general popular imagery. The objections include quite reasonable protests against the overemphasis on the caste system, the oppression of women, and the worship of "sacred cows," as well as the unreasonable demand that the textbooks be altered to include such patently incorrect statements as that suttee was a Muslim practice imported into India or that the caste system has never really existed.[29]

American Hindus have tried to challenge and correct what they perceive, often correctly, to be the inaccuracies and exaggerations of Hinduism in American popular culture. In February 1999, when *Xena: Warrior Princess* (1995–2001) aired its "The Way" episode, with guest appearances by both Krishna and Kali, complaints poured in about subjects ranging from the lesbian subtext of the show to the very fact that a television program could portray a Hindu deity as fictional at all. The episode was pulled, revised, and then reissued within six months, this time with a public announcement to appease those who had been offended.[30]

It is useful to sort out three different sorts of Hindu objections to the American appropriation of Hinduism:

1. Americans have gotten Kali and Tantra all wrong.
2. Even when they get Kali and Tantra right, they are wrong, because they have gotten hold of the Wrong Sort of Hinduism; they should have written about the *Bhagavad Gita* and Vedantic philosophy.
3. Even when Americans write about the *Gita,* they are desecrating and exploiting Hinduism, because only Hindus have a right to talk about Hinduism.

There is some truth, and some falsehood, in the first of these assertions, and mostly falsehood in the second and third.

As for the first—that Americans have gotten Kali and Tantra all wrong[*]— if we learn nothing else from the history of Hinduism, we learn that there is seemingly no limit to the variations that Hindus have rung on every aspect of their religion. Authenticity is therefore a difficult concept to apply to any representation of Hinduism, and some of the most outlandish aspects of California Tantra, for instance, closely mirror the antinomianism of medieval Indian Tantra. Yet Hindus throughout Indian history have made the subjective judgment that some (other) Hindus go too far, and it is hard to resist that judgment when confronting much of the Americanization of Hinduism, not to mention the more grotesque misconstructions made by people who have no commitment to any form of Hinduism but simply pick up pieces of the mythology or art and use them for purposes that are, at best, crassly commercial and, at worst, obscene. Hindus too are capable of desecrating Hinduism. In the Bollywood film *God Only Knows* (2004), in which characters speak a bastardized mix of Hindi and English, with (often inaccurate) English subtitles for the English as well as the Hindi, a fake guru goes up to a red fire hydrant with white trim, watches a dog urinate on it (recall the meaning of dogs in Hinduism), sits down beside it, and puts a garland on it, making it into a Shiva linga of the "self-created" genre; people immediately sit down and start worshiping it. I should think that many Hindus found this scene offensive.

The second objection—that America has taken up the Wrong Sort of Hinduism—also has roots in history. We have seen that Hinduism in America began, in the nineteenth century, with a philosophical, colonially venerated (if not generated) Vedanta and *Gita* but was then supplemented, in the mid-twentieth century, by a second phase of Hinduism, a transgressive, counterculture-catalyzed Kali and Tantra, brokered by megagurus (like Rajneesh) whose broad appeal was built largely on their exotic teachings and charismatic presence. Now the pendulum is swinging back again in a third phase, as many Hindus nowadays wish to go back to that first appropriation, or, rather, to an even more ultra-conservative, often fundamentalist form of Hindu devotional monothe-

---

[*] The title of a recent book attacking American scholars of Hinduism, *Invading the Sacred,* may be seen as a delayed riposte to the title of an earlier book protesting the Hinduization of America: Wendell Thomas, *Hinduism Invades America* (New York: Beacon Press, 1931).

ism (though socially they may be more liberal than their parents; women, for instance, play a far more important role in the management of temples in America than they would be allowed to have in most of India).

The latest generation of Hindu immigrants to America have the same sort of traditional and conservative forms of practice and belief that the Indian immigrants in the sixties and seventies, indeed most immigrant communities, had, as well as the same goals: financial stability, education, acculturation, and the preservation of their traditions in some form.[31] Now, however, they have the generational stability and financial backing to voice their opinions forcefully and publicly. Moreover, cut off as they are from the full range of Hindus and Hinduisms that they would experience in India, American-born Hindus are more susceptible to the narrow presentation of Hinduism offered by their relatives and friends.[32]

Unfortunately, the features of Kali and Tantra that most American devotees embrace and celebrate are often precisely the aspects that the Hindu tradition has tried, for centuries, to tone down, domesticate, deny, or censor actively,[33] the polytheistic, magical, fertile, erotic, and violent aspects. American intellectuals and devotees generally turn to Hinduism for theological systems, charismatic figures, and psychophysical practices unavailable in their own traditions, Jewish and Christian traditions that already have, heaven knows, far more boring, monotheistic, rationalizing fundamentalism, as well as violence, than anyone could possibly want.[34] But this Wrong Sort of Hinduism that the generally middle-class and upper-class spokespersons of the present generation condemn has been, throughout the history of Hinduism, and remains every bit as real to many Hindus—particularly but not only only lower-class Hindus and villagers—as any other.

This brings us to the third objection, which is that even when Americans do get Hinduism right, they desecrate and exploit it when they write about it, merely by virtue of being Americans rather than Hindus. This string of assumptions provides a kind of corollary to the first option (that Americans get it wrong). The same words about Hinduism that might be acceptable in the mouth of a Hindu would not be acceptable coming from an American, just as African Americans can use the *n* word in ways that no white person would dare do, and Jews can tell anti-Semitic jokes that they would be very angry indeed to hear from goyim. On the other hand, for Hindus caught up in identity politics, both in America and in India, a Hindu who makes a "wrong" interpretation of Hinduism is even more offensive (because a traitor to his or her own people) than a non-Hindu making the same interpretation.* You're damned if you aren't and damned if you are.

As an American who writes about Hinduism, I am clearly opposed to this third objection, the exclusion of non-Hindus from the study of Hinduism, for reasons that I have already stated. I appreciate the hypersensitivity to exploitation and powerlessness† that is the inevitable aftermath of colonialism, but I believe that one cannot exploit texts and stories in the same way that one exploits people (or textiles or land or precious gems)—or horses.

The beautiful Marwari horses (and the closely related Kathiawars), with their uniquely curved ears, were bred under the Mughals. After independence, thousands of Marwari horses were shot, castrated, or consigned to hard labor as draft animals. Since only Kshatriyas could own or ride them, Marwaris, like so many horses in Indian history, had become a hated symbol of feudalism and oppressive social divisions. But eventually the Indigenous Horse Society of India and the Marwar Horse Society were established and took measures to define the breed and preserve it, making it available to middle-class, as well as royal, breeders.

Without leaving India, the Marwari horses became American movie stars, and they provide a rule-of-ear clue to determine whether a Hollywood film about India was shot in Rajasthan or in the deserts of Lone Pine, California (two hundred miles north of L.A.), for if the horses in the film have those curved ears, the film was shot in India. But Marwari horses now live also in the United States, where there has been, since 2000, a Marwari stud in Chappaquiddick, Massachusetts, reversing the age-old current of the importing of horses into India.[35] There is an element of colonial manipulation here, for Euro-American ideas of breeding, and standards of equine beauty, influenced the choice of horses that were registered as pure Marwaris in India, and if, as seems possible, the best ones are exported, for extravagant prices, to America, the breed in India will be diminished.

---

* I have in mind, in India, Romila Thapar, the historian of India, and the filmmaker Mira Nair and, in America, Vasudha Narayanan and A. K. Ramanujan, scholars of Hinduism, all of whom have been attacked by the Hindutva faction.
† A patent example of this *ressentiment* is the opening paragraph of Rajiv Malhotra's article "Wendy's Children," posted on the Internet in September 2002, which enormously exaggerates my influence in the academic field of the study of Hinduism. I sometimes use that passage as a brief paragraph to give to people who ask for something with which to introduce me at public events, where hype is often called for.

I believe that stories, unlike horses, and like bhakti in the late Puranic tradition, constitute a world of unlimited good, an infinitely expansible source of meaning. An American who retells a Hindu story does not diminish that story within the Hindu world, even to the arguable extent that taking a Hindu statue from Chennai to New York, or an Indian horse from Kathiawar to Chappaquiddick, diminishes the heritage of India. On the contrary, I believe that the wild misconceptions that most Americans have of Hinduism need to be counteracted precisely by making Americans aware of the richness and human depth of Hindu texts and practices, and an American interlocutor is often the best person to build that bridge. Hence this book.

CHAPTER 24

THE PAST IN THE PRESENT

1950--

ॐ

One day, sitting in the Adi-Dravida street, I tackled a group of older
Pallars on the subjects of death, duty, destiny and rebirth of the soul.
In my inadequate Tamil, I asked them where they thought the soul
went after death. . . . The group collapsed in merriment—perhaps as
much at my speech as at the question. Wiping his eyes, the old man
replied, "Mother, we don't know! Do you know? Have you been
there?" I said, "No, but Brahmans say that if people do their duty
well in this life, their souls will be born next time in a higher caste."
"Brahmans say!" scoffed another elder, "Brahmans say anything.
Their heads go round and round!"

> Kathleen Gough, in 1960, writing about the Pallars,
> a caste of Adi-Dravidas ("Original Dravidians"),
> a South Indian term for formerly Untouchable
> castes known elsewhere as Dalits[1]

The subtitle of this chapter might be "Whatever Happened to . . . the Veda,
the *Ramayana?*" Where the previous chapter traced the historical background
of the political situation of Hindus in contemporary America, this chapter con-
siders the relevance of history to the political situation of Hindus in present-day
India. It demonstrates how alive the past is in present-day India, how contemporary events rebound off the wall of the past. We have noted, throughout, the
intertextual links, the way that stories told in the Vedas and Brahmanas are
retold, with variations, in the *Mahabharata,* and the Puranas, and vernacular
traditions. The heads of the Brahmins "go round and round" as the meanings
of the ancient texts are ignored, or inverted, or, in some cases, followed to the
letter. And the diversity of Hinduism extends also to the diversity of the ways
in which the past is used in the present.

I've taken the contemporary instances not in any logical order but following the chronological order of the historical periods described in some (though not all) of the previous chapters, beginning with the Vedas; in all other ways, they are in a random sequence. There is no consistent direction in which events from the ancient past exert their intense influence on the present moment. In some cases there is a transformation; the ancient myth or ritual takes on entirely new meanings or even new forms in the present. In other cases the past clings to its ancient, sometimes now incomprehensible or clearly irrelevant form and resists any change. Women and Dalits gain new powers but are still in many cases shackled to ancient, repressive forms, just as Hinduism in the contemporary period simultaneously reaches out to a new inclusiveness and new possibilities of equality for those who were oppressed in the past, while Hindu nationalists grow in their power to oppose that very inclusiveness. The new myths of women and Dalits may be unearthings or reworkings of ancient tales that were never preserved or entirely new creations, born of the events of our time.

THE RIG VEDA REVISITED AND REVISIONED

BLOODLESS SACRIFICES

The Veda lives on in revisions of the sacrifice. Although a living animal was suffocated in the Vedic sacrifice, in some cases rice cakes were already substituted for the animal victim. The irony is that now throughout India generally only the lower castes perform animal sacrifices (as the Vedic people did), while Brahmins perform vegetarian versions of Vedic sacrifices, often not just for the reasons that we have noted but also precisely in order to distinguish their sacrifices from the village buffalo sacrifice or chicken offered to the goddess—rites, associated with "carnivorous low castes," that they regard as "popular" and "barbaric."[2] Privately performed sacrifices may include real animals, while publicly sponsored sacrifices are less likely to do so.[3] But the flesh-eating Vedic god may still cast his shadow on the vegetarian sacrifice; the whole coconuts that the deity fancies bear a suspicious resemblance to human heads (a resemblance that is sometimes explicitly mentioned in the accompanying liturgy and in myths about human sacrifice).

The Brahmin priest often sacrifices a goat made of dough and papier-mâché, as Madhva advised his followers to do, and several ritual texts allow.[4] In Kerala, Nambuduri Brahmins use rice wrapped in a banana leaf.[5] Often the rice cakes that are used in place of the goat are wrapped in leaves, tied to little leashes, and carefully "suffocated" before they are offered. At some soma sacrifices, pots of ghee are substituted for the animals. A Vedic ritual in Maharashtra in 1992 was largely transformed into a *puja,* with a strongly Arya Samaj flavor; the sponsor was the guru, taking darshan before the image of the god, but a famous Muslim sitar player performed the music.[6] And when a Vedic sacrifice was performed in London in 1996, there was not even a vegetable substitute for the sacrificial beast; the beasts were "entirely imagined." The priest didn't walk around the imaginary victims or tie them to a (real or imaginary) stake, as one would do with a live animal, but he did mime suffocating them and sprinkled water where they should have been. In place of the omentum (which the sacrificier usually smells but does not eat), they used the large wheat rolls called *roti*s.[7] The transformation of a real ritual into an imagined ritual echoes a process that we have noted in the history of Tantra.

In the combinatory form of Hinduism that remains a basic format in India to the present day, the two forms of sacrifice may be performed together. When a Vedic sacrifice was performed in India in 1955, and public protest prevented the sacrificers from slaughtering a goat, another sacrificer protested the revisionist ritual by offering the same sacrifice—with animal victims—on the outskirts of town.[8] Sometimes, "as a concession to mass sentiments," sacrifices using Vedic mantras and rituals are preceded by popular rituals to local deities.[9] Sometimes the distinction is spatial rather than temporal: The deity in the center of the Hindu temple (an aspect of Shiva or Vishnu or a goddess) is often a strict vegetarian who accepts no blood offerings, only rice, or rice cakes, as well as fruits and flowers, while there may be another deity, outside the temple, to whom blood sacrifices are made. Sometimes the vegetarian deity in the inner shrine is a god, and the carnivorous deity outside is a goddess. Similarly, the shrines of goddesses with an *identificatio brahminica* are generally inside the village, while those of mother goddesses who lacked such connections are outside the village.[10]

This arrangement in the structure of the temple translates into a spatial configuration—from outside to inside—what originated as a synchronic opposition (animal versus vegetable sacrifice) and developed into a historical, diachronic transition (vegetables replacing animals). In the outer markets of the temple, one can purchase an image of the deity, or a postcard of the temple, perhaps a cassette of the songs, *bhajan*s, sung to the deity, but also entirely worldly things, cassettes of (pirated) versions of the Rolling Stones, sandals, saris, embroidered shawls, brass pots, statuettes of couples in *Kama-sutra/* Khajuraho positions (thus once again uniting the sacred and the sensual), anything. The ideological conflict endures, in transformation, through both space and time. It also often endures in a linguistic bifurcation, as worshipers gather in the temple to hear someone read a Sanskrit text; some recite it with him; the storyteller or tour guide will then gloss it in the local language, Telugu or Bangla or whatever, and then explain it, perhaps discuss it with them. Then he will read another verse in Sanskrit, and so on. The rich mix of life on the outskirts of a temple is yet another example of the real periphery that the imaginary Brahmin center cannot hold.

VEDIC ANIMALS IN THE NEWS

SACRED COWS

The Vedic idea of a nonviolent sacrifice also affects contemporary attitudes to cows.

The cow is a central issue for the Hindutva faction, whose influence upon all branches of Indian life is sometimes called Saffronization (on the model of Sanskritization), a term with strong echoes of the renunciant branch of Hinduism, whose members wear saffron- or ocher-colored robes. In recent years, some members of the Hindu right have argued, in contradiction of abundant historical evidence to the contrary, that the ancient Indians never ate beef until the Muslims brought this custom to India; they have persecuted Hindus* who have defended the historical record on this point,[11] and they have attempted to use the alleged sanctity of the cow to disenfranchise Muslims, some of whom eat beef and others of whom slaughter cows, both for the Muslim ritual of Bakr-Id and for the many Hindus who do eat beef. The belief that Hindu cows are sacred is supported by no less an authority than the *OED,* which defines the term as, primarily, designating "The cow as an object of veneration amongst Hindus," and cites an 1891 reference from Rudyard Kipling's father (a vet in India), already in the context of Hindu-Muslim conflict: "The Muhammedan . . . creed is in opposition to theirs [*sc.* the Hindus'] and there are rankling memories of a thousand insults to it wrought on the sacred cow."[12] The term became globalized as a metaphor, indeed a backhanded anti-Hindu ethnic slur. In U.S. journalism the term "sacred cow" came to mean "someone who must not be criticized," and in American literature, "An idea, institution, etc., unreasonably

---

* D. N. Jha, the author of *The Myth of the Holy Cow,* which marshaled abundant proof that Hindus did eat beef in the ancient period, was so violently attacked, physically as well as in the press, that he had to have a police escort twenty-four hours a day for several years after his book was published in India.

held to be immune from questioning or criticism." The term designates precisely the sort of fanaticism that characterizes the methods of those who, in the
cow protection movement under the Raj and again in India today, have insisted
that all cows are sacred.

But are cows sacred in India? Or is the idea of a "sacred cow" an Irish bull*
(the old British chauvinist term for an *ox*-y-moron)? People often perform *puja*
to cows, and at many festivals they decorate cows and give them fruits and
flowers, paint their horns beautifully, and place garlands around their necks.
Cows are in many ways special animals. Certainly they are not publicly killed
in India, for it is against the law to kill a cow in several Indian states and
frowned on in others. Cows already in early Sanskrit texts came to symbolize
Brahmins, since a Brahmin without a cow is less than a complete Brahmin, and
killing a cow (except in a sacrifice) was equated with killing a Brahmin.[13]

But "sacred" means a lot more than not to be killed and is, in any case, a
Christian term that can be, at best, vaguely and inadequately applied in India.
Few of us kill, or eat, our children, but no one would argue that they are sacred.
There are few, if any, Hindu cow goddesses or temples to cows.† Hindus do not
always treat cows with respect or kindness; cows are sometimes beaten and
frequently half starved; Hindus will often treat cows in ways that sheltered
Americans, who eat beef that comes neatly wrapped in plastic, regard as cruel.
The conflicting attitudes of reverence and skepticism in the Gujarat peasants
who did, or did not, drive the buffalo cow out of their houses persists in contemporary India. Hindus who would not dream of eating beef often sell old
cows "to the village," ostensibly to let them out to graze on good grass for a
happy old age; but this is often a euphemism for handing them over (surrepti-
tiously) to a middleman who eventually gives them to someone who kills them
and eats them. Sometimes beef, sold as mutton, is eaten by Hindus who may
well be aware of the deception and simply look the other way. But cows are,
officially, not killed or eaten by traditional upper-caste Hindus.

When their owners set the cows free to wander and forage about the streets
after they are milked in the morning, cows contribute to the menageries in the

---

* The *OED* defines "Irish bull" as "A self-contradictory proposition; in mod. use, an expression contain-
ing a manifest contradiction in terms or involving a ludicrous inconsistency unperceived by the speaker.
Now often with epithet *Irish;* but the word had been long in use before it came to be associated with
Irishmen."
† One learns early in this game never to say "never" about anything in India; sooner or later you dis-
cover that everything exists, though you yourself may not yet have come upon it.

middle of great Indian cities, though the mélange of cars, buses, bicycles, motorcycles, rickshaws, pedestrians, and other animals accounts for the bulk of the problem. On the streets of a town like Jaipur one can encounter (in addition to cows) monkeys, pigs, chickens, goats, peacocks, bullocks, water buffalos, dogs, and some old horses, all roaming freely on a single block. Animals and humans are part of the same spectrum, all more important than cars, which have to get out of the way for them. There is total freedom, and therefore total chaos. The whole country is still one big farm, even in the big cities (except on the main roads); people feed the birds and also the cows and sometimes even the dogs. If cows are sacred, then, so are goats and horses and dogs. Or, by the same token, as one non-Brahmin caste argued, dogs and cattle are equally polluted, "the South Indian scavengers par excellence."[14] The more relevant distinction is between these free souls and freeloaders, on the one hand, and, on the other, more valuable animals, such as better horses, camels, and, occasionally, elephants, which are, by contrast with the street animals, carefully tethered and never abused or, of course, eaten.

Dogs Have Their Day

Dogs, by contrast with cows, are supposed to be treated badly and, as we have seen, usually are, but on many occasions, beginning with the myth of Sarama told in the *Rig Veda,* dogs are, perversely, honored. One of those occasions today is the Tantric worship of Shiva in his aspect as Bhairava, who often has the form or face of a dog or a dog as his vehicle. There are Bhairava temples all over India,[15] where people offer *puja* to both statues of dogs and living dogs. In the temple to Kal Bhairava in Varanasi, there are images of Shiva astride a big white dog, as well as black plaster statues of dogs, paintings of dogs, metal dogs, and real live dogs who sleep and wander inside and outside the temple. Pilgrims to Varanasi worship the dogs and decorate them with garlands of Indian doughnuts and other things delicious to dogs, which the dogs of course immediately shake off and eat. All this is evidence either that (some) dogs are more sacred than cows in Hinduism or, perhaps, that Hindu views of animals are far too complex to capture by words like "sacred" or "impure." Other people's zoological taxonomies look bizarre only to people who view them through their own rather ethnocentric lenses.

A number of castes* take hounds with them during their long expeditions

---

* Such as the Kurubas (a shepherd caste) and Kurnis (a weaver caste) of Northern Andhra Pradesh.

when they graze their sheep in mountain forests. They regard dogs as forms of their god, Mallanna (or Mailara), whom hounds follow in his expeditions and who also takes the form of a dog on occasion. In rituals, the priests (or, sometimes, the householders) enact the roles of dogs and drink milk that they regard as fed to Mallanna.[16] Kal Bhairava may be a Sanskritized (and Tantricized) version of this folk god.

The worshipers of the Maharashtrian horseman god Khandoba (a form of Shiva, often assimilated to Mallanna and called Martanda) sometimes act as his dogs and bark in the course of his rituals, as Bhairava is said to have told them to do. These devotees are called Tigers in Marathi and Kannada; it is said that they originally *were* tigers, but that through the darshan of the god Martanda their bodies became human,[17] a fascinating inversion of the *Mahabharata* story about the dog who got into serious trouble by trying to become a tiger. Forest-dwelling Maharashtrian tribal groups like the Warlis worship and propitiate tigers as the "sentinel deities" or guardians of the village boundaries, but the word for tiger can also denote certain fierce domesticated animals—watchdogs, sheepdogs, or hunting dogs of the kind that attend Khandoba.[18] The mixing of "tiger" and "dog" is chronic in myth, ritual, and art; Bhairava's vehicles are occasionally the dog and the tiger or two animals each of which is a mixture of both.

Two pro-dog stories appeared in the news in November 2007, one about Nepal and one about Tamil Nadu. The first reported on a police dog training school in Nepal that trains dogs for rescue and search, for tracking criminals, explosives, and drugs, and for patrol. There are fifty-one dogs, some born on the premises, others from outside. For most of the year the dogs are not well treated, and many are left (like most animals in Indian towns) to forage for themselves and feed on scraps, but for one day a year they are honored and garlanded (presumably with edibles). The article began: "According to the Hindu scripture, the Mahabharat, dogs accompanied Dharmaraj Yudhishthir on his journey to heaven. There is also a Hindu belief that dogs guard the underworld." Aside from giving Yudhishthira more than one dog, this was a good, historical approach, and the article concluded: "It's recognised that no animal has a closer relationship with people."[19] The compassion here is limited to some dogs, some of the time. But it's a start.

The second story, carried by the *Hindustan Times* and CNN from New Delhi is worth reporting in its entirety:

MAN MARRIES DOG

A man in southern India married a female dog in a traditional Hindu ceremony in a bid to atone for stoning two dogs to death, a newspaper reported Tuesday. [Picture: "P. Selvakumar, left, garlands his 'bride,' Selvi."] The 33-year-old man married the sari-draped dog at a temple in the southern state of Tamil Nadu on Sunday after an astrologer said it was the only way to cure himself of a disability, the *Hindustan Times* newspaper reported. P. Selvakumar told the paper that he had been suffering since he stoned two dogs to death and strung them up in a tree 15 years ago. "After that my legs and hands got paralyzed and I lost hearing in one ear," the paper quoted him as saying. Family members chose a stray female dog named Selvi who was then bathed and clothed for the ceremony. The groom and his family then had a feast, while the dog got a bun, the paper said.[20]

Again the special moment of compassion is balanced by a memory of more typical cruelty. And that cruelty endures: Just a few months later officials of the Indian-administered part of Kashmir announced that they had poisoned (with strychnine) five hundred of the hundred thousand stray dogs in Srinagar and intended to kill them all, saying that the dogs posed a risk to humans and made urban life unbearable. When animal rights activists threatened legal action, the officials said they would merely sterilize the dogs, not poison them with strychnine.[21] Sure.

THE UPANISHADS: RENOUNCING RENUNCIATION

The quotation from Kathleen Gough with which this chapter begins reveals a more widespread disregard for *moksha*, indeed for the entire problem of rebirth and transmigration for which *moksha* is said to be the solution. Villagers in 1964 "stubbornly refused to claim that they hoped for, desired, or did anything deliberately to get *moksha*, even in the context of pilgrimage," and one of them challenged the interviewing anthropologist by saying, referring to the *tirtha* shrine as a "crossing place": "Have you ever *seen moksha* at any crossing place?"[22] Chamars (Dalit leatherworkers) in Senapur, Uttar Pradesh, in the 1950s claimed to know nothing about the fate of the soul after death or other ideas related to karma;[23] the Chamars in Chattisgarh, in central India, ignore the more general householder/renouncer opposition.[24] At the other end of the caste spectrum, E. M. Forster, in 1921, recorded a more ambivalent position in the raja of Dewas: "As a boy, he had thought of retiring from the world, and it was an ideal which he cherished throughout his life, and which, at the end, he would have done well to practise. Yet he would condemn asceticism, declare that salvation could not be reached through it, that it might be Vedantic but it was not Vedic, and matter and spirit must both be given their due."[25] Throngs of pilgrims come to Varanasi to die because they believe that they will immediately attain *moksha*. But at the same time, many women on pilgrimage seek not (or not only, or not primarily) Release from the wheel, but a better life and, almost as an afterthought, a better rebirth. For most of them, moreover, *moksha* is something that by definition you can't want; if you want it, then you can't get it.[26]

The *Ramayana*

THE FLAME OF HISTORY AND THE SMOKE OF MYTH

To say (as I do) that the *Ramayana* tells us a great deal about attitudes toward women and tribal peoples in the early centuries CE is a far cry from saying that someone named Rama actually lived in the city now known as Ayodhya and fought a battle on the island now known as Sri Lanka with a bunch of talking monkeys on his side and a ten-headed demon on the other or with a bunch of tribal peoples (represented as monkeys) on his side and a proto-Muslim monster on the other, as some contemporary Hindus have asserted. Rama left no archaeological or inscriptional record. There is no evidence that anyone named Rama did or did not live in Ayodhya; other places too claim him, in South India as well as North India, for the *Ramayana* was retold many times, in many different Indian languages, with significant variations. There is no second Troy here for a Schliemann to come along and discover. Or, rather, there is a second, and a third, and a nineteenth Troy for anyone to discover.

Placing the *Ramayana* in its historical contexts demonstrates that it is a work of fiction, created by human authors who lived at various times, and shows how the human imagination transformed the actual circumstance of the historical period into something far more beautiful, terrible, challenging, and elevating than the circumstances themselves. Indeed one of the advantages of tracing the variants of a myth (such as the flood myth) is that when we encounter it presented as a historical incident (such as the submerging of a causeway to Lanka), we can recognize it as a myth. Texts reveal histories, but we need to find out about those histories and ground them in solid evidence to read against, not into, the texts' narratives. Reconstructing the ways in which human authors constructed the fictional works, in reaction to earlier texts as well as to historical circumstances, reveals their texts as works of art rather than records of actual events.[27]

Yet in a case that began in 1987, a judge in Dhanbad, in Jharkhand (bordering Bihar and Orissa), issued Rama and Hanuman a summons to appear before the court, since the villagers claimed that a 1.4-acre site with two temples dedicated to them belonged to the gods ("Since the land has been donated to the gods, it is necessary to make them a party to the case," said a local lawyer), against the claim of the Hindu priest who ran the temples, who said that the site belonged to him since a former local king had given it to his grandfather. The summons to the two gods was returned to the court as the address was incomplete. Undeterred, the judge issued another summons through the local newspapers.[28] Nor was this a unique incident. Some Hindus assume that the deity enshrined in a temple is the owner of the temple, that a Hindu statue stolen by a non-Hindu will take action against the thief, and that a statue can sue. A famous case involved a statue of Shiva dancing (Nataraja) that sued the Norton Simon Museum in a U.S. court in 1972–1973.[29] "I can only say that Lord Nataraja himself won the case appearing before courts in the form of the idol," said a Tamil Nadu state official.[30]

BABUR'S MOSQUE AT AYODHYA

For many years, some Hindus have argued that Babur's Mosque (also called the Babri Masjid) was built over a temple commemorating the birthplace of Rama in Ayodhya, the city where, according to the *Ramayana,* Rama was born.[31] During the 1980s, as the Hindu right rose slowly to power, Hindu organizations began holding rallies at the site of Babur's Mosque, campaigning for the "rebuilding" of the temple, despite the absence of any evidence to confirm either the existence of the temple or even the identification of the modern town of Ayodhya with its legendary predecessor. Then the *Ramayana* was broadcast on Indian television in 1987–1988, adding fuel to the mythological furor over the Ayodhya mosque. In 1989, during a judicial procedure that resulted in allowing Muslims continuing access to the mosque, against the plea of Hindus who wanted to lock them out, it was said that "a monkey sat atop the court building and when the order was passed it violently shook the flagstaff from which the national tricolour was fluttering."[32] The monkey was presumed to be Hanuman, who has become the mascot of the RSS, the militant wing of the Bharatiya Janata Party (BJP), and whom Forster, in 1921, already referred to as "the Monkey God (Hanuman-who-knocks-down-Europeans)."[33]

In 1989, as a response to the growing agitation over Ayodhya, a group of historians at the Center for Historical Studies at Jawaharlal Nehru University (JNU) released a pamphlet entitled *The Political Abuse of History: Babri-Masjid-Rama-Janma-Bhumi Dispute.* The pamphlet marked the direct intervention of historians in the debate over Ayodhya and was eventually published as an edited volume.[34] The essays all argue that the case for a Rama temple under the mosque is based on myth rather than history.

In 1990 L. K. Advani, the BJP president, put on the saffron robes of a renouncer (or, nowadays, a right-wing Hindu) and posed with a bow and arrow on top of a truck decorated to look like Rama's chariot. He was arrested as he was heading for Ayodhya.[35] Two years later, on December 6, 1992, as the police stood by and watched, leaders of the BJP whipped a crowd of two hundred thousand into a frenzy. Shouting, "Death to the Muslims!" the mob attacked Babur's Mosque with sledgehammers. As the historian William Dalrymple put it, "One after another, as if they were symbols of India's traditions of tolerance, democracy, and secularism, the three domes were smashed to rubble."[36] In the riots that followed, more than a thousand people lost their lives, and many more died in reactive riots that broke out elsewhere in India, first in the immediate aftermath of the destruction of the mosque, then intermittently, and then very seriously again in 2002. Litigation over the site continues. On the site today (as of 2008) nothing but vandalized ruins remains, yet there is intense security (and there have been several attacks to justify such security). Visitors to the site find, in a dark corner of the large, empty space, a small shrine, like a family *puja* closet, with a couple of oleograph pictures of Rama, where a Hindu priest performs a perfunctory *puja.* Nearby, in a BJP tent, is a model of the new temple they intend to build. Whether or not there ever was a Hindu temple there before, there is a temple, however makeshift, there now.

THE CAUSEWAY TO LANKA

Another, more recent example of the political use of the *Ramayana* myth was relatively bloodless but deeply disturbing. It concerned the proposed dredging of a canal through what is called Rama's Bridge, an area of limestone shoals and shallow water between southern India and the north shore of the island now known as Sri Lanka.* In a favorite episode in the *Ramayana,* retold over the

---

* Now, scholarly opinion has differed for the past century on the location of the mythical Lanka, the island to which Ravana brought Sita, and the identification with present-day Sri Lanka is problematic.

centuries, an army of monkeys, led by Hanuman and Rama, build a causeway (or a bridge, though the description sounds much more like a causeway, piling up stones and mortar) over the water to Lanka, a distance said to be a hundred "yokings"* (about a thousand miles)† (R 4.63.17). Rameshwara, a place of pilgrimage in Tamil Nadu, claims to be the place where the causeway was built.

On September 12, 2007, BBC headlines read, HINDU GROUPS OPPOSE CANAL PROJECT, and they told this story:

> Protest rallies have been held across India by hard-line Hindus to campaign against a proposed shipping canal project between India and Sri Lanka. Massive traffic jams were reported in many places and trains delayed in many parts of the country. Protesters say the project will destroy a bridge they believe was built by Hindu God Ram and his army of monkeys. Scientists question the belief, saying it is solely based on the Hindu mythological epic Ramayana. The Sethusamudram Shipping Canal Project proposes to link the Palk Bay with the Gulf of Mannar between India and Sri Lanka by dredging a canal through the shallow sea. This is expected to provide a continuous navigable sea route around the Indian peninsula. Once complete, the canal will reduce the travel time for ships by around 650 km (400 miles) and is expected to boost the economic and industrial development of the region. Hindu activists say dredging the canal will damage the Ram Setu (or Lord Ram's bridge), sometimes also called Adam's Bridge. They say the bridge was built by Lord Ram's monkey army to travel to Sri Lanka and has religious significance. Scientists and archaeologists, however, say there is no scientific

---

The earliest name for this island, judged by Indian and Greek and Latin sources in the third century BCE, is Tamraparni ("with copper leaves"), which Greek geographers called Taprobane. Later, in the early centuries CE, the name more commonly used in South Asia was Sinhala or Sinhala-dvipa ("Lion's Island"). Arabs referred to it as Sarandib or Serendip (from which Horace Walpole coined the term "serendipity" in his 1754 novel *The Three Princes of Serendip*). Later European mapmakers called it Ceylon (a transformation of Sri Lanka), a name still used occasionally for trade purposes. It became Sri Lanka officially in 1972. This chronology of names poses a puzzle for the historian. If the author of the oldest *Ramayana*, c. 200 BCE, was referring to what we now call Sri Lanka, then the name should have been the one by which the island was known then, either Tamraparni or else Sinhala. But since the name used is Lanka, which appears not to have been the name for the island at that time, then perhaps that Lanka was located somewhere other than where Sri Lanka is now. Alternatively, if Lanka in the text is a reference to the present Sri Lanka, then the composition of the Valmiki poem would have to be dated to a much later period, when the island was called Lanka.

* A yoking (*yojana*) is the approximate distance, sometimes said to be ten miles, sometimes fifty, that you can travel without changing and reharnessing horses.
† The present-day Sri Lanka is about nineteen miles from India. If we take a yoking as ten miles, it's a thousand miles from India to the *Ramayana*'s Lanka; if we take a "yoking" as fifty miles, it's five thousand miles to Lanka.

evidence to prove their claim. They say it has never been proved that Lord Ram's monkey army existed at all as described in the Hindu epic Ramayana. The Archaeological Survey of India says the bridge is not a man-made structure, and is just a natural sand formation.[37]

As the historian Romila Thapar pointed out, "All this uncertainty is quite apart from the question of the technical viability of building a bridge across a wide stretch of sea in the centuries BC."[38] There are also other issues here—ecological, economic, sociological, and practical. The Indian Supreme Court determined that the "bridge" was not man-made (or, presumably, monkey-made). West Bengal's Buddhadeb Bhattacharjee argued that the *Ramayana* was "born in the imagination of poets," but Nanditha Krishna, the director of the C. P. Rama-swami Anjar Foundation, countered that the *Ramayana* was not fiction. Advocates for the monkey bridge have cited, in evidence, NASA photos suggesting an underwater bridge (that is, a causeway) between India and Sri Lanka,[39] yet another instance of our old friend the myth of the submerged continent.

Two days later the headline read, REPORT ON HINDU GOD RAM WITHDRAWN, and the BBC news ran this story:

> The Indian government has withdrawn a controversial report submitted in court earlier this week which questioned the existence of the Hindu god Ram. The report was withdrawn after huge protests by opposition parties. . . . In the last two days, the opposition Bharatiya Janata Party (BJP) has launched a scathing attack on the government for questioning the "faith of the million." Worried about the adverse reaction from the majority Hindu population of the country, the Congress Party-led government has now done a U-turn and with-drawn the statement submitted in court. . . . In the meantime, the court has said that dredging work for the canal could continue, but Ram's Bridge should not be touched.

But how are they to avoid touching the mythological bridge?

MANY *RAMAYANAS*

Another major issue here is the question of who has the right to say what the *Ramayana* is and is not. The arguments about this in many ways parallel those about what Hinduism is and is not. The question of when Sita ceases to be Sita is one that different people will answer in different ways. One of the qualities that allow great myths to survive over centuries, among very different cultures, is their ability to stand on their heads (indeed, to turn cartwheels), to invite complete reversals of the political stance taken by the interpretation of the basic plot.[40]

This is certainly true of the political uses of the *Ramayana,* which has been constantly retold in literature and performance throughout India, most famously in the version of Tulsidas in the sixteenth century, which to this day is performed in Varanasi during a festival that lasts for several weeks each winter. Repressive tellings of the myth use the mythological moment of Ram-raj (Rama's reign), as an imagined India that is free of Muslims and Christians and any other Others, in the hope of restoring India to the Edenic moment of the *Ramayana.*

But many subversive tellings cast Ravana and the ogres as the Good Guys (as some of them are, in some ways, even in Valmiki's version) and Rama as the villain of the piece (as he certainly is not, in Valmiki's version). Michael Madhusudan Datta (1824–1873), a Bengali poet who converted to Christianity, wrote a poem, "The Slaying of Meghanada" (1861), based on the Bengali *Ramayana* of the poet Krittibas, but Datta made Ravana the hero and Ravana's son, Meghanada, the symbol of the Hindus oppressed by the British, whom Datta equated with Rama, the villain.[41] Equally subversive was the *Ramayana* that Tamil separatists told in South India in the early twentieth century, casting Ravana as a noble Tamil king who was treacherously murdered by the forces of the evil Rama coming from the north. Both North and South Indians often identified Rama with the north and Ravana with the south, but the north demonized the "Dravidian" Ravana, the south the "Aryan" Rama, through the composition of explicit "counter epics."[42] In a Dalit telling, Sita, on behalf of the ogres, rebukes Rama for killing innocent people.[43]

The *Ramayana* monkeys were already mixed up in colonial history in ways that still resonate. In the nineteenth century some Hindus in North India made monkeys of the British, calling them "red monkeys," and Orissan narratives still depict them as monkeys. Others say that Sita blessed the eighteen million monkeys who had helped Rama, promising them that they would be reborn as the English. A North Indian folktale tells us that two of the monkeys were rewarded with a "white island" in the far west (that is, England, replacing Lanka). From there, it was prophesied, their descendants would rule the world in the Kali Yuga, the dark age that is to end the world,[44] a time when barbarians (i.e., the British) will invade India, the old political myth distilled from the many actual invasions of India by foreign powers. According to a story told in

Maharashtra, when one of Ravana's ogress wives befriended Sita, during her period of captivity in Ravana's harem, Sita promised her that she would be rewarded by being reborn as Queen Victoria.[45]

One device used to accommodate multiple versions of a story is by reference to multiple eras of cosmic development. One Purana refers explicitly to this technique: "Because of the different eras, the birth of Ganesha is narrated in different ways." On another occasion, the bard recites a story in which a sage forgives his enemies; the audience (built into the text) then interrupts, saying, "We heard it told differently. Let us tell you: the sage cursed them in anger. Explain this." And the bard replies, "That is true, but it happened in another era. I will tell you." And he narrates the second version of the story.[46] Another Purana introduces a second variant of another story by remarking, "The Puranas tell it differently."[47]

There has always been a Darwinian force that allows the survival of some tellings rather than others, determined in part by their quality (the ones that are well told and/or that strike a resonant note with the largest audience survive) and in part by their subsidies (the ones with the richest patrons survive). Money still talks (or tells stories), but mass media now can pervert that process; the tellings that survive are often the ones that are cast or broadcast into the most homes, greatly extending the circle of patrons. *Amar Chitra Katha* comic books have flooded the market with bowdlerized versions of many of the great Hindu classics, in a kind of Gresham's law (bad money driving out good) that is not Darwinian at all but merely Adam Smithian, or capitalist.

Over the past few decades the growing scholarly awareness of the many different *Ramayana*s opened out all the different variants, only to have the door slammed shut by Bollywood and television and the comic books, so that most Hindus now know only one single *Ramayana*. The televising of the *Ramayana* (78 episodes, from January 1987 to July 1988) and *Mahabharata* (108 episodes, a holy number, from 1988 to 1990, on Sunday mornings) was a major factor leading to the destruction of Babur's Mosque in 1992. So powerful were the objections to the proposal of Salman Khan, a Muslim (though with a Hindu mother), to play the role of Rama in a 2003 Bollywood production that the film was never made. On the other hand, though the televised *Mahabharata* was based largely on the *Amar Chitra Katha* comic book, the screenwriter was a leftist Muslim, Rahi Masuma Raza, and the opening credits were in English, Hindi, and Urdu—Urdu for a presumed Muslim audience. Lose one, win one—and the *Mahabharata* was always more diverse than the *Ramayana*.

The Internet too has facilitated the mass circulation of stories that substitute for the storyteller's art the power of mass identity politics. Salman Rushdie, in *Midnight's Children,* imagined a private version of radio, a magic ether by which the children born at midnight on the day of India's independence communicated. Now we have that in reality, the Web site, the chat room, the LISTSERV, the blog from outer space. A self-selecting small but vociferous group of disaffected Hindus have used this Indian ether to communicate with one another within what is perceived as a community. This accounts in large part for the proliferation of these groups and for the magnitude of the reaction to any incident, within just a few hours; it's more fun than video games, and a lot more dangerous too. Another radio metaphor comes to mind, from two American films* in which a bomber pilot is instructed to *turn off his radio* as soon as he gets the command to bomb, so that he will not listen to false counterinstructions. It is this tendency to tune out all other messages that characterizes the blog mentality of the Hindu right.

No More *Ramayanas*

The Hindu right objects strenuously, often by smashing bookstores and burning books, to versions of Hindu stories that it does not like, particularly of the *Ramayana,* more particularly to retellings of the *Ramayana* that probe the sensitive subject of Sita's relationship with Lakshmana. Here is a version recorded from the tribal people known as the Rajnengi Pardhan at Patangarh, Mandla District, and published in 1950:

LAKSHMAN AMONG THE TRIBALS

One night while Sita and Rama were lying together, Sita discussed Lakshman very affectionately. She said, "There he is sleeping alone. What is it that keeps him away from woman? Why doesn't he want to marry?" This roused suspicion in Rama's mind. Sita slept soundly, but Rama kept awake the whole night imagining things. Early next morning he sent for Lakshman from his lonely palace and asked him suddenly, "Do you love Sita?" Lakshman was taken aback and could hardly look at his brother. He stared at the ground for a long time and was full of shame. Lakshman gathered wood and built a great fire and shouted, "Set fire to this wood and if I am pure and innocent I will not burn." He climbed onto

---

* Two films made on the same topic in the same year (1964), *Dr. Strangelove* and *Fail Safe,* imagined a doomsday plan (think: Kali Yuga) for American planes to drop atomic bombs on Russia.

the fire holding in his arms a screaming child. Neither of them was even singed. He left Rama and Sita and would not return, though Sita kept trying to lure him back.[48]

Lakshman then went down to the underworld, where he had many adventures. Here Lakshman, rather than Sita, calls for the fire ordeal to prove his chastity, and Rama's jealousy is directed against him, rather than against Sita. The detail of the screaming child may have crept into the story from the traditions of suttee, in which the woman is *not* allowed to enter the fire if she has a child and is often said *not* to scream; here, where the genders are reversed, those tropes seem to be reversed too.

Right up until the present day, stories of this sort have been recorded and published. Then, in 2008, the Delhi University course on Ancient Indian Culture in the BA (honors) program assigned an essay entitled "Three Hundred Ramayanas: Five Examples and Three Thoughts on Translation," by A. K. Ramanujan (1929–1993), who had taught for many years at the University of Chicago and in 1976 had received from the Indian government the honorary title of Padma Sri, one of India's highest honors. Now Hindu organizations voiced objections to the content of some of the narratives Ramanujan had cited, said to be derogatory toward Hindu gods and goddesses:

> [Ramanujan] even sorts out a tale from Santhal folklore and puts forth the greatest outrage to Hindu psyche before the students of literature that Ravan as well as Lakshman both seduced Sita. No one on Earth so far dared to question the character of Sita so brazenly as Shri Ramanujan has done, though all through under the convenient cover of a folklore! . . . The Delhi University for its BA (Hons) second year course has included portions defaming and denigrating the characters of Lord Ram, Hanuman, Lakshman and Sita and projecting the entire episode as fallacious, capricious, imaginary and fake.[49]

The Lakshmana-Sita relationship was also the sore point in my egg-punctuated London lecture in 2003.

On February 25, 2008, a mob of more than a hundred people, organized by the All-India Students' Council (ABVP), linked with the RSS, gathered outside the building of the School of Social Sciences at Delhi University. Eight or ten of them then went inside and ransacked the office of the head of the department of history, breaking the glass panes and damaging books and other objects in the office, as media and the police watched. The group threatened faculty members and warned them of dire consequences.[50] The protesters also carried placards saying, in Hindi, "The university says there were three hundred versions of the Ramayana, not one"—indeed, indeed! In subsequent interviews, one of the protesters said: "These academics don't understand that they are toying with our faith. They have this idea that it's a written story, a literary text, so it doesn't matter if you say there are 3000 versions of it." Though he admitted the plurality of Hindu traditions, he proposed that "every deviant telling," mostly tribal and Dalit, be erased.[51] The bright side of this dark story is that other students organized massive counterprotests, and editorials strongly critical of the attempts to stifle free speech and diversity appeared in several leading papers.[52] One columnist remarked that Ramanujan was "a scholar who did more for Indian culture than all of the ABVP put together," and added: "The violence around this essay was disturbing, as was the complete obtuseness of people who attacked Ramanujan."[53]

Thoroughly Modern Sitas

Over the centuries, Sita's ordeal has proved problematic for different reasons to different South Asians, from pious apologists who were embarrassed by the god's cruelty to his wife, to feminists who saw in Sita's acceptance of the "cool" flames an alarming precedent for suttee, and, most recently, to Hindus who objected to alternate *Ramayana*s that called into question Sita's single-minded devotion to Rama. Some peasant retellings emphasize Sita's anger at the injustices done to her and applaud her rejection of Rama after she has been sent away, while Dalit versions even depict Sita's love for Ravana ("indicating perhaps that this may be a subterranean theme of even the orthodox version in which she is only suspected"). Maharashtra women praise Sita for disobeying Rama, going to the forest with him when he told her not to. In a folk poem from Uttar Pradesh, Sita refuses to go back to Rama even when Lakshsmana has been sent to bring her and instead raises her sons on her own.[54]

Sita has also been made, counterintuitively, into a champion of women's rights. There is a Sita temple without Rama (far more unusual than a Rama temple without Sita) in a village in Maharashtra, commemorating the year in which Sita wandered, pregnant and destitute, after Rama kicked her out; the temple legend states that when Sita came to this village, the villagers refused to give her food, and she cursed them, so that no grain would ever grow in their fields. In recent years a reformer named Sharad Joshi urged the villagers to redress the wrongs that Rama did to Sita and to erase the curse that has kept them from achieving justice or prosperity, by redressing their own wrongs to their own women, whom they have kept economically dependent and power-less. He told them the story of the *Ramayana,* often moving big, burly farmers to tears, and suggested that Valmiki had introduced the injustice to Sita *not* to hold up Sita's suffering as an example for other wives but rather to warn men not to behave like Rama. ("He could have made Ram into as perfect a husband as he was a son. Instead . . . Valmiki wants to show how difficult it is for even supposedly perfect men to behave justly towards their wives.") Finally, he ar-gued that they should not wait for government laws to enforce the economic rights of women but should voluntarily transfer land to their women, thus pay-ing off a long-overdue debt to Sita. Hundreds of Maharashtrian villagers have done this.[55] In contrast with the ambivalent practical effects of powerful goddesses with their shakti, it was Sita's *lack* of power that seems to have done the trick here.

Sita's curse was also felt elsewhere in Maharashtra, at an abandoned Sita temple in Raveri. "Rakshasas built it," the villagers say. After Sita was driven out of Ayodhya, she settled in Raveri and begged for food, house to house, be-cause she had two small babies and could not work. When the villagers refused her (on the ground that such an abandoned woman must be a "bad woman"), she cursed the village so that it could not grow wheat. Activists used this myth to get peasants to put land in the names of the women of their family.[56]

The *Mahabharata*

Shashi Tharoor retold the *Mahabharata* as *The Great Indian Novel,* in which the self-sacrificing Bhishma (the son of Ganga, in the Sanskrit text) becomes Ganga-ji, a thinly veiled form of Gandhi, while Dhritarashtra is Nehru, with his daughter Duryodhani (Indira Gandhi). Karna goes over to the Muslim side and becomes Jinna (where the original Karna sliced his armor off his body, this Karna seizes a knife and circumcises himself) and is eventually exposed as a chauffeur, the "humble modern successor to the noble profession of charioteer-ing." As Tharoor remarks, "It is only a story. But you learn something about a man from the kind of stories people make up about him."[57]

Draupadi and Satyavati

Sita is not alone in serving as a lightning rod for Hindu ideas about female chastity; her *Mahabharata* counterpart, Draupadi, remains equally controversial. One Dalit woman's take on the disrobing scene, in which Karna teases Draupadi, is skeptical: "Now, even with five husbands didn't Draupadi have to worry about Karna Maharaj's intentions?"[58] Dalit women are equally dubious about Satyavati and Kunti: "One agreed to the whims of a rishi in order to remove the bad odour from her body, the other obeyed a mantra! What wonderful gods! What wonderful rishis!"[59] And a popular song among lower-class women in nineteenth-century Calcutta imagined the objections that Ambalika might have expressed when her mother–in-law, Satyavati, insisted that she let Vyasa impregnate her:

> People say
> as a girl you used to row a boat in the river.
> Seeing your beauty, tempted by your lotus-bud,
> the great Parashar stung you,
> and there was a hue and cry:
> You've done it once,
> You don't have anything to fear.
> Now you can do as much as you want to,
> no one will say anything.
> If it has to be done,
> Why don't you do it, mother?[60]

Despite Satyavati's checkered, to say the least, sexual record, this possibility apparently never occurred to Vyasa (in either of his characters, as author of the Sanskrit *Mahabharata* or, within the text, as the grandfather of its heroes), for a very good reason that Ambalika seems to have overlooked: Satyavati is Vyasa's mother.

KUNTI AND THE NISHADAS

The *Mahabharata* story of the burning of the five Nishadas in the house of lac undergoes a major moral reversal in a contemporary retelling by the Bengali feminist novelist Mahashweta Devi (1926–):

> After the war, Kunti retired to the forest to reflect on her past. One day a Nishada woman [a Nishadi] watched with her as the animals fled from a forest fire. The Nishadi asked her if she remembered the house of lac, and an elderly Nishadi and her five young sons, whom she had made senseless with wine while she escaped

with her own sons. Kunti said she did remember, and the Nishadi said that the woman who had been killed was her mother-in-law; she was the widow of one of the five sons. She added that not once in all her reflections did Kunti remember the six innocent lives that had been lost because she wanted to save herself and her sons. As they spoke, the flames of the forest fire came closer to them. The Nishadi escaped to safety, but Kunti remained where she was.[61]

In Vyasa's *Mahabharata,* Kunti does die in a forest fire, but she never does remember the Nishadi. It is the genius of the modern version to unite these two traditional episodes of a woman and fire, a theme with other overtones as well, to make an entirely new point.

The TV *Mahabharata* also expressed a belated sense of guilt on behalf of the Pandavas, taking pains to note that the Nishadas who burned to death in the house of lac had been its architects; that Duryodhana had planned to kill them, in order to silence them; and that the Pandavas knew this and felt that since the Nishadas were going to die anyway, there was no harm in killing them.

EKALAVYA'S THUMB

One particular Nishada, Ekalavya, plays an important role in the life of contemporary Dalits, who make Ekalavya do for them what the myths did not reveal him doing for himself: revolt.[62] One Dalit poet says, "I am conscious of my resolve,/ the worth of the blood of Ekalavya's finger."[63] A movement to gain water rights for Dalits on the Ganges River used the symbol of Ekalavya:

If you had kept your thumb
history would have happened
somewhat differently.
But . . . you gave your thumb
and history also
became theirs.
Ekalavya,
since that day they
have not even given you a glance.
Forgive me, Ekalavya, I won't be fooled now
by their sweet words.
My thumb
will never be broken.[64]

Another poem, by Tryambak Sapkale (born in 1930), a railway ticket taker on the Dhond–Manmad railway line until his retirement, is a kind of extended meditation on an aphorism by the ancient Greek philosopher Archimedes, about a lever and a fulcrum: "Give me a place to stand on, and I can move the earth":

> Eklavya!
> The round earth.
> A steel lever
> In my hand.
> But no leverage?
> O Eklavya,
> You ideal disciple!
> Give me the finger you cut off;
> That will be my fulcrum.[65]

And a final example was composed by Surekha Bhagat, a widow, born in 1949, who is an Ambedkar Buddhist and works in a tuberculosis sanatorium in Buldhana, Maharashtra:

THE LESSON (SABAK)

> First he was flayed
> then he took a chisel in his hand
> knowing that each blow
> would chisel a stanza
> and so he learned it all
> not needing any Dronacharya
> using his own brain
> to become Eklavya.
>
> Since then no one knew
> quite how
> to ask for tuition fees
> so the custom
> of asking for remuneration
> (in honeyed words)
> stopped, but slowly.[66]

The televised *Mahabharata* made a big point of the Ekalavya story, playing it out at great length. There are Ekalavya education foundations in Ahmedabad and Hyderabad. The Ekalavya Ashram in Adilabad, a northern district bordering on Maharashtra, on the banks of the Godavari River, is a nonprofit tribal welfare facility established in 1990. Run by people from the local business community, it serves underprivileged tribal people who cannot afford to educate their children.

SHASTRAS: SEX AND TAXES

The cross-dressing men of the Third Nature in the *Kama-sutra* may be the cultural ancestors of the Hijras of contemporary India, cross-dressing and sometimes castrated male homosexuals, often prostitutes, who worship the goddess Bahuchara Mata.* Perhaps fifty thousand strong in India today,[67] the Hijras descend upon weddings, birth celebrations, and other occasions of fertility, dancing and singing to the beat of drums, offering their blessing or, if they are not paid, their curse, which may take the form of lifting their skirts to display the wound of their castration. Their ambivalent ability to blackmail through a combination of blessing and curse eventually struck a resonant chord with some government agency charged with tax collection. As a result, in 2006 the Municipal Corporation of Patna, the capital of Bihar, one of India's most impoverished states, hired about twenty Hijras to go from shop to shop (later from house to house), asking the owners to pay overdue municipal taxes, which apparently ran into the millions. The new tax collectors met with considerable success from their very first day on the job, often settling the outstanding arrears on the spot; in lieu of salary, they received 4 percent of the amount they collected.[68]

BHAKTI IN SOUTH INDIA: KANNAPPAR'S EYES

Kannappar's eyes, like Ekalavya's thumb, lived on in later parables, entering Indian folklore, both northern and southern, as a symbol of violent self-sacrifice (though Kannappar is seldom invoked in Sanskrit texts, which generally prefer a more muted bhakti). An Englishman living in India told this story about an event in 1986:

---

* Bahuchara, meaning "Getting Around a Lot," is the same phrase that the mother of Satyakama, in the Upanishads, used to refer to her promiscuity.

A village temple was said to have lost its image of Kannappar; it had been stolen some years ago. Now the villagers announced that they planned to renovate the shrine, probably with a new image of Kannappar. But the thief came forward and offered to return the idol. He said that, in the years that had passed since he had stolen the statue, his eyesight had deteriorated to the point where he was almost blind. He knew the story of Kannappar and had attributed his near-blindness to the curse of the saint. Within weeks of returning the statue, his eyesight began to improve and apparently it eventually returned to normal. An iconographer who had heard about this village "miracle" came to inspect the statue and pronounced that it wasn't a Kannappar statue at all. It was another god entirely, one who had no blindness stories in his CV.[69]

One might see in the mistaking of a non-Kannappar statue for a Kannappar statue the mischievousness of the god or the proof of a religious placebo effect, or simply the common confusion between one god and another. Twenty years later, in 2006, the chief education officer in a campaign in India to promote corneal replacements and other medical measures to avoid blindness "recalled that Kannappa Nayanar, a hunter-turned-saint, was the first eye donor."[70]

GODDESSES: HOGWARTS DURGA, MARY, MINAKSHI, AND SANTOSHI MATA

Indian goddesses continue to evolve. At a festival in Kerala, in January 2008, the goddess Bhagavati got on her elephant and visited her "twin sister," the Virgin Mary, at the church down the road.[71] In South Indian rituals, when the goddess Minakshi marries Shiva (a gendered alliance of a local goddess and a pan-Indian male god) and her brother-in-law Vishnu comes to the wedding (a sectarian alliance of Vaishnavas and Shaivas), Vishnu stops along the way to the wedding to see his Muslim mistress (an interreligious alliance); the next morning he is in a much better mood, and that is when his worshipers ask him for favors.[72] The Delhi High Court ruled that it was not plagiarism for a private citizen in Kolkata to use, for his float in Durga Puja, a gigantic marquee of the imaginary castle of Hogwarts, Harry Potter's school, built in canvas and papier-mâché, as well as statues of Rowling's literary characters.[73]

And new goddesses spring full grown from the head of Bollywood. The goddess Santoshi Mata, first worshiped in the 1960s by women in many cities of Uttar Pradesh, has no base in any pan-Indian Puranic myth but suddenly

crossed over into national popularity in 1975, largely as the result of a mythological film, *Jai Santoshi Ma*. The film depicted her birth (from the god Ganesha) and the origin of her worship; during screenings, the theater became a
temple, and women made offerings, *puja*s of fruit and flowers, on the stage in
front of the screen.[74] The medium was certainly the message here. Now worshiped throughout India, Santoshi is propitiated by comparatively simple and
inexpensive rites performed in the home without the intercession of a priest.
She grants practical and obvious blessings, such as a promotion for an over-
worked husband or a new household appliance.

MODERN AVATARS OF THE AVATARS

RADHA THE SOCIAL WORKER

In 1914, a tax officer near Varanasi named Hariaudh published a long poem
entitled "Sojourn of the Beloved" (*Priyapravas*), in which Radha rejects the
sensuality of erotic longing for Krishna, undertakes a vow of virginity, and
dedicates herself to the "true bhakti" of social service. Fusing elements of Western social utilitarianism, bits of Wordsworth and Tagore, and the monistic
Vedanta of Vivekananda, Radha substitutes for each of the nine conventional
types of bhakti a particular type of altruistic good works: The loving service she
would have given to Krishna as his wife is now directed to the "real world"; the
bhakti of being Krishna's servant or slave becomes lifting up the low and fallen
castes; remembering Krishna becomes remembering the troubles of poor, helpless widows and orphans, giving medicine to those in pain, and giving shelter
and dignity to those who have fallen through their karma. Hariaudh sees Radha's vow of virginity as a solution for the perceived problem of improving the
status of Indian women without opening the door to the sexual freedom of
"Westernized" women. His revisionist myth of Radha managed simultaneously
to offend conservative Brahminical Hinduism and to insult the living religious
practices of Hinduism.[75] Not surprisingly, it did not replace the earlier, earthier
version of the story of Radha.

THE GOOD DEMON BALI AND THE EVIL DWARF

In 1885, Jotiba Phule, who belonged to the low caste of gardeners (Malis),
published a Marathi work with an English introduction, in which he radically
reinterpreted Puranic mythology, seeing the various avatars of Vishnu as stages
in the deception and conquest of India by the invading Aryans, and Vishnu's
antigod and ogre enemies as the heroes of the people.[76] Bali, in particular, the

"good antigod" whom the dwarf Vishnu cheated out of his kingdom, was refigured as Bali Raja, the original king of Maharashtra, reigning over an ideal state of benevolent castelessness and prosperity, with Khandoba and other popular gods of the region as his officials.

To this day many Maharashtrian farmers look forward not to Ram Rajya (they regard Rama as a villain) but to the kingdom of Bali,[77] Bali Rajya: "Bali will rise again," and he will recognize the cultivating classes as masters of their own land. Low castes in rural central Maharashtra identify so closely with Bali, a son of the soil, against the dwarf, the archetype of the devious Brahmin, that they regularly greet each other as "Bali." Sometimes they burn the dwarf in effigy.[78]

THE BUDDHA AND KALKI

In 1990, Pakistani textbooks used a garbled version of the myth of the Buddha avatar to support anti-Hindu arguments: "The Hindus acknowledged Buddha as an avatar and began to worship his image. They distorted his teachings and absorbed Buddhism into Hinduism." A Hindu critic then commented on this passage: "The message is oblique, yet effective—that Hinduism is the greatest curse in the subcontinent's history and threatens to absorb every other faith."[79] Vinay Lal's delightful short book on Hinduism identifies President George W. Bush as the contemporary form of Kalki: He spends a lot of time with horses and is going to destroy the world.[80]

THE TAJ MAHAL AND BABUR'S MOSQUE

One advocate of Hindutva has argued, on the basis of absolutely no evidence, that the Taj Mahal, in Agra, is not a Islamic mausoleum but an ancient Shiva temple, which Shah Jahan commandeered from the Maharaja of Jaipur; that the term "Taj Mahal" is not a Persian (from Arabic) phrase meaning "crown of palaces," as linguists would maintain, but a corrupt form of the Sanskrit term "Tejo Mahalaya," signifying a Shiva temple; and that persons connected with the repair and the maintenance of the Taj have seen the Shiva linga and "other idols" sealed in the thick walls and in chambers in a secret red stone story below the marble basement.[81] In 2007, the Taj was closed to visitors for a while because of Hindu-Muslim violence in Agra.[82]

On a more hopeful note, Muslims for many years participated in the Ganesh Puja in Mumbai by swimming the idol out into the ocean at the end of the festival. There are still many instances of this sort of interreligious cooperation, as there have been since the tenth century CE.

The Worship of Other People's Horses

Let us consider the positive contribution of Arab and Turkish horses to contemporary Hindu religious life, particularly in villages. The symbol of the horse became embedded in the folk traditions of India and then stayed there even after its referent, the horse, had vanished from the scene, even after the foreigners had folded their tents and gone away. To this day, horses are worshiped all over India by people who do not have horses and seldom even see a horse, in places where the horse has never been truly a part of the land. In Orissa, terra-cotta horses are given to various gods and goddesses to protect the donor from inauspicious omens, to cure illness, or to guard the village.[83] In Bengal, clay horses are offered to all the village gods, male or female, fierce or benign, though particularly to the sun god, and Bengali parents until quite recently used to offer horses when a child first crawled steadily on its hands and feet like a horse.[84]

In Tamil Nadu today, as many as five hundred large clay horses may be prepared in one sanctuary, most of them standing between fifteen and twenty-five feet tall (including a large base) and involving the use of several tons of stone, brick, and either clay, plaster, or cement.[85] They are a permanent part of the temple and may be renovated at ten- to twenty-year intervals; the construction of a massive figure usually takes between three to six months. (Many of them have the curved Marwari ears.) The villagers say that the horses are ridden by spirit riders who patrol the borders of the villages, a role that may echo both the role of the Vedic horse in pushing back the borders of the king's realm and the horse's association with aliens on the borders of Hindu society. But the villagers do not express any explicit awareness of the association of the horses with foreigners; they think of the horses as their own.

A Marxist might view the survival of the mythology of the aristocratic horse as an imposition of the lies of the rulers upon the people, an exploitation of the masses by saddling them with a mythology that never was theirs nor will ever be for their benefit, a foreign mythology that produces a false consciousness, distorting the native conceptual system, compounding the felony of the invasion itself. A Freudian, on the other hand, might see in the native acceptance of this foreign mythology the process of projection or identification by which one overcomes a feeling of anger or resentment or impotence toward another person by assimilating that person into oneself, *becoming* the other. Myths about oppressive foreigners (and their horses) sometimes became a positive factor in the lives of those whom they conquered or dominated.

When enormous terra-cotta horses are constructed in South India, the choice of medium is both practical (clay is cheap and available) and symbolic. New horses are constantly set up, while the old and broken ones are left to decay and return to the earth of which they were made.[86] Clay, as Stephen Inglis points out, is the right medium for the worship of a creature as ephemeral as a horse— "semi-mythical, temporary, fragile, cyclical (prematurely dying/transforming)."[87] Elsewhere Inglis has described the work of the Velar, the potter caste that makes the horses: "By virtue of being made, of earth, the image is bound to disintegrate and to be reconstituted. . . . The potency of the craft of the Velar lies in impermanence and potential for deterioration, replacement, and reactivization of their services to the divine. . . . The Velar, and many other craftsmen who work with the immediate and ever changing, are . . . specialists of impermanence."[88] The impermanence of the clay horses may also reflect the awareness of the fragility of both horses in the Indian climate and the foreign dynasties that came and, inevitably, went, leaving the legacy of their horses.

MODERN WOMEN

CASTE REFORM AND IMPERMANENCE: THE WOMEN PAINTERS OF MITHILA

The impermanence of the massive clay horses is one facet of a larger philosophy of impermanence in ritual Hindu art.

In many domestic rituals throughout India, women trace intricate designs in rice powder (called *kolam*s in South India) on the immaculate floors and courtyards of houses, and after the ceremony these designs are blurred and smudged into oblivion by the bare feet of the family, or as the women think of it, the feet of the family carry into the house, from the threshold, the sacred material of the design. As David Shulman has written:

> The *kolam* is a sign; also both less and more than a sign. As the day progresses, it will be worn away by the many feet entering or leaving the house. The rice powder mingles with the dust of the street; the sign fails to retain its true form. Nor is it intended to do so, any more than are the great stone temples which look so much more stable and enduring: they too will be abandoned when the moment of their usefulness has passed; they are built not to last but to capture the momentary, unpredictable reality of the unseen.[89]

The material traces of ritual art must vanish in order that the mental traces may remain intact forever. If the megalomaniac patrons of so many now ruined

A Herd of Laughing Clay Horses from a Rural Temple, Madurai District.

Hindu temples smugly assumed that great temples, great palaces, great art would endure forever, their confidence was not shared by the villagers who actually did the building.

The smearing out of the *kolam* is a way of defacing order so that one has to re-create it. The women who make these rice powder designs sometimes explicitly refer to them as their equivalent of a Vedic sacrificial hall (*yajnashala*), which is also entirely demolished after the sacrifice. Their sketches are referred to as "writing," often the only form of writing that for many centuries women were allowed to have, and the designs are merely an aide-mémoire for the patterns that they carry in their heads, as men carry the Vedas. So too, the visual abstraction of designs such as the *kolam* is the woman's equivalent of the abstraction of the Vedic literature, based as it is on geometry and grammar. The rice powder designs are a woman's way of abstracting religious meanings; they are a woman's visual grammar.[90]

Since the fourteenth century, the women of the Mithila region of northern Bihar and southern Nepal have made wall and floor paintings on the occasion of marriages and other domestic rituals.[91] These paintings, inside their homes, on the internal and external walls of their compounds, and on the ground inside

or around their homes, created sacred, protective, and auspicious
spaces for their families and their
rituals. They depicted Durga,
Krishna, Shiva, Vishnu, Hanuman, and other Puranic deities, as
well as Tantric themes, a headless
Kali (or, sometimes, a many-
headed Kali) trampling on Shiva,
or Shiva and Parvati merged as the
androgyne.[92]

The women painters of Mithila
used vivid natural dyes that soon
faded, and they painted on paper,
thin, frail paper. This impermanence did not matter to the artists,
who did not intend the paintings
to last. The *act* of painting was
seen as more important than the
form it took, and they threw away

*Broken Clay Horses from a Rural Temple,
Madurai District.*

elaborately produced marriage sketches when the ceremony was over, leaving
them to be eaten by mice or using them to light fires. Rain, whitewash, or the
playing of children often destroyed frescoes on courtyard walls.[93] To some extent, this is a concept common to many artists, particularly postmodern artists,
such as Christo and Jeanne-Claude, whose temporary installations included
Running Fence, a twenty-four-mile-long white nylon fabric curtain in Northern
California. Such artists are interested in the act of creation, not in preserving
the object that is created. But this ephemerality takes on a more particular
power in the realm of sacred art, even more particularly in the sacred art of
women, who, in contrast with the great granite monomaniac monuments of
men, are primarily involved in producing human services that leave no permanent trace, with one great exception, of course: children.

The impermanence of the paintings in Mithila came up against another
way of valuing art when, in the aftermath of a major earthquake in 1934, William Archer, the local collector, inspecting the damage in Mithila's villages, saw
the wall and floor paintings for the first time and subsequently photographed
a number of them. He and his wife, Mildred, brought them to wider attention

in several publications. In the 1950s and early 1960s, several Indian scholars and artists visited the region and were equally captivated by the paintings. But it was not until 1966, in the midst of a major drought, that the All India Handicrafts Board sent an artist, Baskar Kulkarni, to Mithila to encourage the women to make paintings on paper that they could sell as a new source of family income. They became known popularly as Madhubani paintings.[94]

Although, traditionally, women of several castes painted, Kulkarni was able to convince only a small group of Mahapatra Brahmin and Kayastha (scribe caste) women to paint on paper. By the late 1960s and early 1970s two of these women, Sita Devi and Ganga Devi, were recognized as artists both in India, where they received numerous commissions, and in Europe, Japan, and the United States, where they represented India in cultural fairs and expositions. Their success and active encouragement inspired many other women to paint.

From the mid-1970s women of several other castes, most especially the Dusadhs, a Dalit community, and the Chamars, also began to paint on paper, along with small numbers of men. It is quite likely that they were already painting at the time of the Archers, who, for some reason, wrote only about the higher-caste women. But instead of painting themes from the *Ramayana* and the Puranas, the Dusadh women painted their own folklore, and their high god, Rahu (who causes eclipses of the sun and moon), and their culture hero, Raja Salhesh. Later they also created new techniques and new subject matter and eventually began to depict some of the gods of the upper castes (Krishna, Shiva). Gradually artists of different castes and genders began to borrow themes and styles from one another. Although the images were similar, women of different castes usually developed distinctive styles of painting.[95] Over time, in part because of the greater diversity of people painting, the subject matter of the paintings expanded to include ancient epics, local legends and tales, domestic, rural, and community life, ritual, local, national, and international politics, as well as the painters' own life histories.

Women of the upper castes eventually added to their repertoire various subjects of social critique, including dowry, female abortion, bride burning, suttee, terrorist attacks (such as a painting of the planes about to hit the Twin Towers), and even caste discrimination: A young Brahmin painter, Roma Jha, depicts upper-caste women refusing access to a well to a Dalit woman.[96] The lower-caste women, who depend upon the paintings for their livelihood, generally stick to more traditional themes, but one woman, Dulari Devi, who is of the impoverished Mallah (fisherman) caste, has painted poor women being denied medical treatment, village headmen chasing away women who have come to complain of maltreatment, and rich families locking their houses and escaping from a flood, leaving the poor to weep over their dead.[97]

The paintings are still ephemeral in the lives of the painters, for like all successful art, they leave the atelier and go out into the world. But the paintings are now preserved in books, catalogs, and frames on the walls of houses throughout India and beyond; like the Marwari horses, they now belong to the world. There are troubling aspects about this transaction: Euro-American people have intervened in the lives and art of the people of Mithila, not only reversing the most basic understanding of what it means to them to make art—its impermanence—but changing the medium (encouraging them to use more permanent dyes, less fragile paper, and so forth) and influencing its subject matter. For capitalism inevitably raises its ugly head: The knowledge of what will sell in New York and San Francisco influences the subjects that the women in Mithila choose to paint, just as European standards of equine breeding influenced the choice of horses that were registered as pure Marwaris. This should give us pause, even before we acknowledge that many people besides the painters make money on these transactions. On the other hand, the painters have also made money, money that has freed them from degrading poverty. We may or may not judge that this gain justifies the possible loss of artistic integrity, but in any case it is what has happened and what is happening. At the end of the day the lives of the painters have been enriched by the income from the paintings, and the lives of everyone who has seen the paintings have been enriched by the women of Mithila.

THE BRAHMIN HEAD AND THE DALIT BODY

The princess Renuka (also known as the goddess Mariamma), whose decapitated head took on the body of a decapitated Dalit (Pariah) woman, continues to survive as a goddess in the village of Chandragutti, 240 miles northwest of Bangalore, where a week-long festival dedicated to the Hindu goddess Renukamba ("Mother Renuka") has taken place every year for centuries. The Chandragutti version of the story is that Renukamba's clothes (instead of her head) dropped off as she fled for her life from her murderous husband, and she took refuge in a nearby cave, where she merged with a deity. Each year, thousands of Dalits have taken off their clothes to immerse themselves in the Varada

Medical Services Offered to the Rich but Denied to the Poor.
Painting by Dulari Devi, Madhubani, Bihar.

River, then climbed two and a half miles with their clothes off to offer prayers to the goddess at the hilltop cave temple.

But police banned the nude pilgrimage in 1986 after devotees clashed with members of the Dalit Sangharsha Samiti (DSS), a group advocating the uplifting of lower castes. DSS volunteers, claiming that the ritual was degrading for Dalits, were beaten when they tried to prevent pilgrims from undressing. The worshipers then attacked police and paraded ten police officials, including two women constables, naked along the banks of the river.[98] Complex issues of sexual propriety intersect here with the rights of Dalits, as non-Dalits attempt to prevent Dalits, ostensibly for their own good, from indulging in their own rituals. No longer a question of heads versus bodies, the worship of Renukamba now expresses an ambivalence toward the human body itself, as well as the enduring tension within the social body of caste Hinduism.

CHAPTER 25

INCONCLUSION, OR,
THE ABUSE OF HISTORY

༄

The spirit of broad catholicism, generosity, toleration, truth, sacrifice
and love for all life, which characterizes the average Hindu mind not
wholly vitiated by Western influence, bears eloquent testimony to the
greatness of Hindu culture. . . . The non-Hindu peoples in Hindustan . . . must not only give up their attitude of intolerance and un-
gratefulness towards this land . . . but must . . . stay in the country
wholly subordinated to the Hindu Nation, claiming nothing, deserv-
ing no privileges, far less any preferential treatment—not even citizen's rights.[1]

Madhav Sadashiv Golwalkar (1906–1973)

If I know Hinduism at all, it is essentially inclusive and ever-
growing, ever-responsive. It gives the freest scope to imagination,
speculation and reason.[2] . . . It is impossible to wait and weigh in
golden scales the sentiments of prejudice and superstition that have
gathered round the priests who are considered to be the custodians of
Hinduism.[3]

Mahatma Gandhi (1869–1948)

The statement by Golwalkar, a leader of the chauvinist Hindu organization
known as the RSS (Rashtriya Swayamsevak Sangh), in 1939, reflects a different
sort of cultural schizophrenia from the creative dichotomies that have typified
so much of Hinduism. The first half of his statement seems to me to express
largely valid historical claims, while the political agenda of the second half
contradicts those claims, paradoxically using the justifiable Hindu pride in religious tolerance to justify intolerance. Gandhi, the bane of the RSS, also makes

two points that are, if not contradictory, in considerable tension: He takes the inclusiveness and imagination of Hinduism for granted, but he contrasts that inclusiveness with the attitudes not (like Golwalkar) of the non-Hindus of India but of the Brahmins, whose "prejudices" against both Dalits and Muslims Gandhi protested throughout his life. The boast that Hinduism is tolerant and inclusive has become not only a part of Hindu law but a truism repeated by many Hindus today, yet this does not mean that it is false; it is a true truism, however contradicted it may be by recurrent epidemics of intolerance and exclusion. How are we to understand the balance of these conflicting currents in the history of the Hindus?

Agni, the name of the Vedic god of fire, is also the name of one of India's most powerful nuclear missiles. Pakistan named its missile Ghorid,[4] after Muhammad of Ghor. Why should the two warring South Asian nations reach back into Vedic and eleventh-century history to name their nuclear warheads? What is the relevance of history to religious intolerance?

India is a country where not only the future but even the past is unpredictable.[*] If you have read this far, dear reader, and have plowed through these many pages, and have paid any attention at all, you will have learned at least one important thing. You could easily use history to argue for almost any position in contemporary India: that Hindus have been vegetarians, and that they have not; that Hindus and Muslims have gotten along well together, and that they have not; that Hindus have objected to suttee, and that they have not; that Hindus have renounced the material world, and that they have embraced it; that Hindus have oppressed women and lower castes, and that they have fought for their equality. Throughout history, right up to the contemporary political scene, the tensions between the various Hinduisms, and the different sorts of Hindus, have simultaneously enhanced the tradition and led to incalculable suffering.

The great mystery about the abuse of history is not the abuse itself but the question of why, in such a future-intoxicated age, we still reach for the past (or a past, however confected) to justify the present. "That's history," after all, is an American way of saying, "So what?" But even such American amnesiacs practice a cult of the past with regard to the Constitution and the often unintelligible intentions of the founding fathers, and they have just a few hundred

---

[*] This is a joke that historians of Russia used to make about revisionist Soviet Union historical propaganda during the cold war. Alas, it applies equally well to many revisionists in India today.

years of history. Hindus have thousands, and their concern for history is correspondingly more intense.

We (and by "we" I mean all of us, Hindus and non-Hindus) can of course learn from the errors of the past, though we are often condemned (pace Santayana) to relive it even when we remember it—indeed, sometimes precisely because we (mis)remember it.* And we must be on guard "lest we forget," as Kipling prayed. Often the future is shaped not by what we remember but by what we forget. But we have lost our naive faith in our ability to know our past in any objective way. And memory may not be on our side here; given the tragic power of revenge, sometimes it pays to have a good forgettery.† At the end of the day, individuals and groups will have to make their decisions in the present, as they did in the past, on some basis other than history, such as, given present conditions, what seems most humane, most compassionate, most liberating for the most people *now.*

In the Epilogue to George Bernard Shaw's play *Saint Joan* (1923), Joan cries out: "Must then a Christ perish in torment in every age to save those who have no imagination?" Surely history is one of the most important things for us to imagine and to realize that we are imagining. What an utter waste it would be not to keep using our knowledge of a tradition, such as the Hindu tradition, that is so rich, so brilliantly adaptive. The profuse varieties of historical survivals and transformations are a tribute to the infinite inventiveness of this great civilization, which has never had a pope to rule certain narratives unacceptable. The great pity is that now there are some who would set up such a papacy in India, smuggling into Hinduism a Christian idea of orthodoxy; the great hope lies in the many voices that have already been raised to keep this from happening.

We can learn from India's long and complex history of pluralism not just some of the pitfalls to avoid but the successes to emulate. We can follow, within the myths, the paths of individuals like King Janashruti or Yudhishthira or Chudala or, in recorded history, Ashoka or Harsha or Akbar or Mahadevyyakka or Kabir or Gandhi, or indeed most rank-and-file Hindus, who embodied a truly tolerant individual pluralism. We can also take heart from movements within Hinduism that rejected both hierarchy and violence, such as the bhakti

---

* "Those who cannot remember the past are condemned to repeat it." George Santayana (*The Life of Reason*, 1905).
† As Carl Sandburg once said.

movements that included women and Dalits within their ranks and advocated a theology of love, though here too we must curb our optimism by recalling the violence embedded in many forms of bhakti, and by noting that it was in the name of bhakti to Ram that the militant Hindu nationalists tore down the Babri Mosque. We must look before we leap into history, look at the present, and imagine a better future.

Perhaps we can ride into that future on the glorious horse that graces the jacket of this book. It is an example of the contribution of a foreign culture to Hinduism, since composite animals of this type come from Persia and entered India with the Mughals, and an example of the intersection of court and village, as the image traveled from the Mughal court in Delhi to a village in the state of Orissa, the source of this contemporary example. It is an image of women, almost certainly painted by a man. Depicting the god Krishna as the rider on the horse makes the Muslim image a Hindu image, and the rider on the horse is an enduring Hindu metaphor for the mind controlling the senses, in this case harnessing the sexual addiction excited by naked women. This multivocal masterpiece is, like Hinduism, a collage made of individual pieces that fit together to make something far more wonderful than any of them.

ACKNOWLEDGMENTS

This book is both from and for my students, who inspired me to write it, contributed many thoughts to it, responded incisively to draft after draft that I taught in classes for years and years, asked me questions I couldn't answer, plied me with books and articles I would otherwise have missed, and constituted the ideal audience for it. A few of my students and ex-students also helped me more specifically, and I want to thank them (in alphabetical order) for their ideas: Manan Ahmed on the Delhi Sultanate and the Mughals; Aditya Behl on Sufis; Brian Collins on the *Mahabharata;* Will Elison on the British; Amanda Huffer on contemporary India and America; Rajeev Kinra on the Delhi Sultanate and the Mughals; Ajay Rao on South India; and Arshia Sattar on the *Ramayana.* Others did more extensive work on this book: Jeremy Morse foraged for elusive facts and texts and disciplined the computer when it acted up; Laura Desmond read early drafts of the whole text, talked over each chapter with me, made revolutionizing comments, and provided the background for the chapter on the *shastras*; and Blake Wentworth drew the rabbit on the moon (in the preface), hunted down obscure texts and illustrations, read several drafts of the chapter on bhakti, and taught me a great deal about South India. I am also grateful to Gurcharan Das and to Donna Wulff and her class at Brown University, for their detailed and candid responses to an early draft, and to Mike O'Flaherty for his fastidious proofreading.

Special thanks go to Scott Moyers for his canny advice about the book in its earliest stages; to Lorraine Daston for reading chapter after chapter and responding, as always, with brilliant ideas that would not have occurred to me in a thousand years; to Mike Murphy for the week at Big Sur in which I pulled it all together; to Vanessa Mobley, my patient and supportive editor at Penguin;

and Nicole Hughes, who shepherded me, and the book, through the production labyrinth with tact and skill; to Emma Sweeney, my feisty and energizing agent; and to Richard Rosengarten, dean of the Divinity School of the University of Chicago, for his unflagging interest and encouragement, his faith in me, and his generosity in providing time for me to write and funds for me to pay my student assistants and my special Indological editor, Katherine Eirene Ulrich.

Katherine Ulrich read several long, long drafts, catching many howlers as well as stylistic tics, pinpointing obscurities, suggesting books and articles, challenging unsupported assumptions, and sustaining me with no-nonsense, appreciative, and often hilarious comments. To cap it all, she gave me the image of the composite horse that appears on the jacket of this book, not just finding it but buying it and carrying it back from India for me. This book is dedicated to her and to William Dalrymple, who stood by me at the lecture in London in 2003 when someone threw an egg at me and who then threw down a gauntlet in his subsequent article about the need to tell the history of Hinduism in a new way. I am grateful to him not only for his encouragement but for the example that he sets in his own work, writing about the history of India in a way that brings it alive to readers of all backgrounds and raises the important issues that give such writing its life and meaning.

Truro, August 2008

CHRONOLOGY

✧

BCE

c. 50,000 Stone Age cultures arise

c. 30,000 Bhimbetka cave paintings are made

c. 6500 Agriculture begins

c. 4000–3000 *Indo-European breaks up into separate languages

c. 3000 Pastoral nomad societies emerge

c. 2500 Urban societies merge along the Indus River

c. 2200–2000 Harappa is at its height

c. 2100–2000 Light-spoked chariots are invented

c. 2000–1500 The Indus Valley civilization declines

c. 1900 The Sarasvati River dries up

c. 1700–1500 Horses arrive in Northwest India

c. 1700–1500 Nomads in the Punjab compose the *Rig Veda;* horses arrive in Northwest India

c. 1350 Hittite inscriptions speak about horses and gods

c. 1200–900 The Vedic people compose the *Yajur Veda, Sama Veda,* and *Atharva Veda*

c. 1100–1000 Vedic texts mention the Doab, the area between the Ganges and Yamuna rivers

c. 1000 The city of Kaushambi in Vatsa is founded

c. 950 The *Mahabharata* battle is said to have taken place

c. 900 The city of Kashi (Varanasi, Benares) is founded

c. 900 The Vedic people move down into the Ganges Valley

c. 800–600 The Brahmanas are composed

c. 600–500 Aranyakas are composed

c. 500 Shrauta Sutras are composed

c. 500 Pataliputra is founded; Vedic peoples gradually move southward

c. 500–400 Early Upanishads are composed

c. 483 or 410 Siddhartha Gautama, the Buddha, dies

c. 468 Vardhamana Mahavira, the Jina, founder of Jainism, dies

c. 400–100 Later Upanishads are composed

c. 400–100 Writing is used in the Ganges Valley

c. 327–325 Alexander the Great invades Northwest South Asia

c. 324 Chandragupta founds the Mauryan dynasty

c. 300 *Grihya Sutras* are composed

c. 300–100 *Dharma-Sutras* are composed

c. 300 Greeks and Ashoka mention Pandyas, Cholas, and Cheras

c. 265–232 Ashoka reigns

c. 250 The Third Buddhist Council takes place at Pataliputra

c. 185 The Mauryan dynasty ends

c. 185 Pushyamitra founds the Shunga dynasty

73 The Shunga dynasty ends

c. 166 BCE–78 CE Greeks, Scythians, Bactrians, and Parthians enter India

c. 300 BCE–300 CE The *Mahabharata* is composed

c. 200 BCE–200 CE The *Ramayana* is composed

CE

c. 78–140 Kanishka reigns and encourages Buddhism

c. 100 Cankam ("assembly") poetry is composed

c. 100 "Manu" composes his *Dharma-shastra*

c. 150 The monuments of Bharhut and Sanchi are built

c. 150 Rudradaman publishes the first Sanskrit inscription, at Junagadh

c. 200 Kautilya composes the *Artha-shastra*

c. 300 Vatsyayana Mallanaga composes the *Kama-sutra*

320–550 The Gupta dynasty reigns from Pataliputra

350–750 The early Puranas are composed

c. 375 The Pallava dynasty is founded

c. 400–477 Kalidasa writes Sanskrit plays and long poems

405–411 Faxian visits India
c. 450 The *Harivamsha* is composed
455–467 The Huns attack North India
c. 460–477 The Vakataka dynasty completes the caves at Ajanta
c. 500–900 Nayanmar Shaiva Tamil poets live
550–575 Kalachuris create the cave of Shiva at Elephanta
c. 550–880 Chalukya dynasty thrives
c. 600–930 Alvar Vaishnava Tamil poets live
606–647 Harsha reigns at Kanauj
630–644 Xuan Zang (Hsuan Tsang) visits India
650–800 Early Tantras are composed
c. 650 Arabs reach the Indus
711–715 Arabs invade Northwest India
750–1500 Medieval Puranas are composed
765–773 Raja Krishna I creates the Kailasa temple to Shiva at Ellora
c. 788–820 Shankara, nondualist philosopher, lives in Kerala
c. 800 Manikkavacakar composes the *Tiruvacakam*
c. 880–1200 The Chola Empire dominates South India
900 and 1150 The Chandellas build the temples at Khajuraho
c. 975–1025 Abhinavagupta, Shaiva philosopher, lives in Kashmir
1001 Mahmud of Ghazni (979–1030) raids North India
1021 Ghaznavid (Turkish) Muslim capital established at Lahore
c. 1056–1137 Ramanuja, qualified Dualist philosopher, lives in Tamil country
1192–1206 Muhammad of Ghor establishes Ghorid capital at Delhi
c. 1200 Jayadeva lives in Bengal
1210–1526 The Delhi Sultanate is in power
1325–1351 Muhammad bin Tughluq reigns
c. 1200 Early orders of Sufis arise in North India
c. 1200 Virashaivas, including Basava, live in South India
1238–1258 Narasimhadeva I builds the temple of Konarak
c. 1238–1317 Madhva, dualist philosopher, lives in Karnataka
c. 1300 Shri Vaishnavas split into Cats and Monkeys
c. 1336–1565 Vijayanagar Empire is in its prime
c. 1398–1448 Kabir lives
1399 Timur, ruler of Central Asia, destroys Delhi
1469–1539 Guru Nanak founds Sikhism in the Punjab
1486–1533 Chaitanya lives

1498–1597 Mirabai lives
1526 Babur founds the Mughal Empire
1530–1556 Humayun reigns
1532–1623 Tulsidas lives
1556–1605 Akbar reigns
1600 (December 31) Queen Elizabeth I charters the British East India Company
1605–1627 Jahangir reigns
1608–1649 Tukaram lives
1622–1673 Kshetrayya lives
1627–1658 Shah Jahan reigns
1658–1707 Aurangzeb reigns
1713–1719 Farrukhsiyar reigns
1750–1755 The Bengal Famine causes ten million deaths
1756 The Black Hole of Calcutta causes dozens of deaths
1757 The British East India Company defeats the Muslim rulers in Bengal
1757 First wave of British Raj begins
1765 Robert Clive becomes chancellor of Bengal
1772–1833 Rammohun Roy lives; 1828 founds Brahmo Samaj
1782–1853 Sir Charles James Napier lives
1813 Second wave of British Raj begins
1824–1883 Dayananda Sarasvati; 1875, founds Arya Samaj
1857–1858 The Rebellion, formerly known as the Mutiny, takes place
1857 Third wave of the British Raj begins
1858 The British viceroy officially replaces Mughal rule (and the East India Company)
1863–1902 Swami Vivekananda lives
1865–1936 Rudyard Kipling lives
1869–1948 Mohandas Karamchand Gandhi, known as Mahatma Gandhi, lives
1861–1941 Rabindranath Tagore lives
1875 Helena Blavatsky founds the Theosophical Society
1893 Vivekananda attends the World's Parliament of Religions in Chicago
1897 Vivekananda founds the Vedanta movement in America
1896–1977 A. C. Bhaktivedanta, Swami Prabhupada (founder of ISKCON), lives
1918–2008 Maharishi Mahesh Yogi (founder of Transcendental Meditation) lives
1919 Amritsar massacre takes place
1931–1990 Bhagwan Shree Rajneesh (Osho) lives
1947 Independence; Partition
1970– Hindus in Europe, United States, and Canada start building temples

GUIDE TO PRONUNCIATION AND SPELLING
OF WORDS IN SANSKRIT AND OTHER
INDIAN LANGUAGES

ॐ

Sanskrit vowels are pronounced very much like Italian vowels. The aspirated consonants should be pronounced distinctly: *bh* as in "cab horse," *dh* as in "mad house," *gh* as in "dog house," *ph* as in "top hat," and *th* as in "goat herd."

Traditionally, scholars have used diacriticals to distinguish between long and short vowels and among three different forms of *s* in Sanskrit, as well as to mark other nice points of the orthography of Sanskrit and other Indian languages that are essential for the citation of texts. Increasingly, scholars writing for a wider audience that is blissfully ignorant of any Indian language have omitted the diacriticals and changed two of the *s*'s to *sh*'s (leaving the third an *s tout court*), and this book follows that practice. This may result in some confusion for readers contemplating the spellings of certain words in this book, such as the name of the gods Shiva and Vishnu, and noting that they are sometimes spelled elsewhere—in works cited in my text or bibliography—as Siva and Visnu. I hope and trust that readers will be able to deal with this conflict, and also to distinguish the Kali Age (Kali with short *a* and short *i*) from the goddess Kali (Kālī with long *a* and long *i*).

Many words in modern Indian languages derived from Sanskrit drop the final short *a* of the Sanskrit, so that Rama sometimes becomes Ram, Lakshmana becomes Lakshman, Hastinapura becomes Hastinapur, and Vijayanagara becomes Vijayanagar. ("Dharma" often becomes "dharam.") As for the British distortions of words in Sanskrit and other Indian languages (Hindoo, suttee), they are often bizarre but usually recognizable.

ABBREVIATIONS

ॐ

TEXTS

AS	*Artha-shastra*
BU	*Brihadaranyaka Upanishad*
CU	*Chandogya Upanishad*
KauU	*Kaushitaki Upanishad*
KS	*Kama-sutra*
KU	*Katha Upanishad*
M	*Manava Dharma Shastra (Manu)*
MB	*Mahabharata*
MU	*Mundaka Upanishad*
OED	*Oxford English Dictionary*
R	*Ramayana*
RV	*Rig Veda*
SU	*Shvetashvatara Upanishad*

POLITICAL ORGANIZATIONS

ABVP: Akhil Bharatiya Vidyarthi Parishad (All-India Students' Council)

BJP: Bharatiya Janata Party (Peoples' Party of India)

RSS: Rashtriya Swayamsevak Sangh (National Volunteers' Organization)

VHP: Vishwa Hindu Parishad (World Hindu Council)

GLOSSARY OF TERMS IN INDIAN LANGUAGES
AND NAMES OF KEY FIGURES

ॐ

Abhinavagupta: philosopher of Kashmir Shaivism, 975–1025 CE

Aditi: "Infinity," name of a Vedic goddess of creation, mother of the Adityas, solar gods

Adivasis: "Original inhabitants," indigenous inhabitants of India, tribal peoples

Advaita: nondualism, a philosophical school, propounded by Shankara

Agastya: a mythical sage said to have brought Sanskrit south to the Tamil land and also established Tamil there

Agni: Vedic god of fire (*ignis*)

agrahara: "taking the field," a grant of temple land to Brahmins

ahimsa: nonviolence, literally "a lack of the desire to harm"

akam: word used in Tamil poetry for the interior world, the world of love

Akbar: Mughal emperor, 1556–1605, noted for his religious pluralism

Alvars: Tamil Vaishnava saints

Amba: "Mother," name of a woman in the *Mahabharata* who was reborn as a man; also the name of a goddess

Ambalika: "Dear Little Mother," name of the mother of Pandu in the *Mahabharata*

Ambika: "Little Mother," name of the mother of Dhritarashtra in the *Mahabharata*

apad-dharma: the permissive religious law that prevails in time of emergency

Apala: a woman who pressed soma in her mouth for the god Indra in the *Rig Veda*

Appar: one of the first three Tamil Nayanmar saints, sixth to eighth century

Apsarases: "Gliding in the Waters," celestial nymphs and courtesans

Arjuna: one of the five sons of Pandu in the *Mahabharata*, fathered by the god Indra

Artha-shastra: textbook of political science

Arya Samaj: a religious movement founded by Dayananda Sarasvati in Bengal in 1875

Aryas: "nobles," name by which the Vedic people referred to themselves

Ashoka: Mauryan emperor, 265–232 BCE, author of the first surviving writing in India, edicts in stone

ashrama: a hermitage; also a stage or way of life (there are four: chaste student, householder, forest dweller, renouncer)

Ashvaghosha: a first century CE poet, author of a life of the Buddha

Ashvins: "Horsemen," twin half horse gods, sons of Saranyu and the sun

Asuras: antigods, enemies of the gods in heaven; originally, the older gods

Atharva Veda: the fourth Veda, largely devoted to magic spells

atman: the self, the individual soul, identical with the world soul (atman or *brahman*)

Aurangzeb: a Mughal emperor, 1658–1707 CE, noted for his chauvinism

avatar: a "descent" of a god, particularly an incarnation of the god Vishnu

Avesta: the sacred text of the ancient Iranians

Ayur-veda: the Veda of long life, the science of medicine

Babur: the first Mughal emperor, 1483–1530

Backward Castes: one of many names for the lowest and most oppressed castes

Bali: a demon undone by his generosity to the god Vishnu, who had become incarnate as a dwarf

Bana: a poet in the court of Harsha, author of a biography of Harsha

banyan: a sacred tree that puts down multiple roots

Basava: a Brahmin who founded the Virashaiva movement, c. 1106–1167 CE

Bhagavad Gita: a philosophical text, spoken by the god Krishna to the prince Arjuna, in the *Mahabharata*

Bhagavan: a name of god, Vishnu or Shiva

Bhagavata: a worshiper of the gods Vishnu or Shiva

Bhagiratha: a sage who brought the Ganges down to earth from the Milky Way

bhakta: devotee of a god

bhakti: passionate devotion to a god who returns that love

Bharata: younger brother of Rama; also the name of the son of Shakuntala and Dushyanta and an ancient name of India

Bharata-varsha: the land of India

Bhil, Bhilla: name of a tribal people

Bhima: one of the five sons of Pandu in the *Mahabharata*, fathered by the god Vayu, the wind

Bhishma: celibate son of Satyavati in the *Mahabharata*

Bhrigu: a powerful sage

Brahma: a god, responsible for the task of creation

brahman: the divine substance of the universe

Brahmanas: texts, from c. 800 to 600 BCE, explaining the Vedic rituals

Brahmin: the highest of the four classes, the class from which Vedic priests must come

Brahmo Samaj: a reform movement founded by Rammohun Roy in 1828

bride-price: a reverse dowry, paid by the groom to the family of the bride

Buddhification: casting a non-Buddhist as a Buddhist

Campantar: one of the first three Tamil Nayanmar saints, sixth to eighth century

Cankam: (from Sanskrit *sangham*): early Tamil literary assembly

Chaitanya: Bengali saint, 1486–1533 CE

Chamars: a Dalit caste, leatherworkers

Chandalas: a Dalit caste, workers in cremation grounds

Chandidas: a fourteenth-century CE Bengali poet

Chandika: "The Fierce," a name of the Goddess

Chandra Gupta I: founder of the Gupta Empire in 324 CE

Chandragupta Maurya: founder of the Mauryan Empire in 324 BCE

Charaka: author of a medical textbook

Charioteers (Sutas): a caste of charioteers and bards

Charvakas: Materialists, regarded as the paradigmatic heretics; also called Lokayatas

Cheras: an ancient South Indian kingdom

Cholas: an ancient South Indian kingdom

Clive, Robert: governor of Bengal from 1755–1760; chancellor from 1765

Cuntarar: one of the first three Tamil Nayanmar saints, sixth to eighth century

Dadhyanch: a Vedic sage whose head was replaced with a horse head

Daksha: a Vedic patriarch, father of Sati, who foolishly refused to invite the god Shiva to his sacrifice

Dalit: preferred contemporary word, derived from the Marathi/Hindi word for "oppressed," for the lowest castes, formerly known as Untouchables

Dalitification: the process by which castes claim to be Dalits; the reverse of Sanskritization

darshan: "seeing," the exchange of powerful gazes between god and worshiper, or king and subject

Dasa: "slave," the word that the Vedic Aryas applied to their enemies

Dasyu: another word for "slave"

Deshification: the process by which the Sanskritic tradition absorbs local traditions

Devaki: royal mother of Krishna

dhamma: Pali for the Sanskrit term dharma; Buddhist law, and Ashokan law

dharma: religious law, justice, righteousness. *See also sadharana, sanatana*

dog cooker *shva-paka:* ancient term of opprobrium for Dalit castes

Draupadi: wife of the five Pandava brothers, heroine of the *Mahabharata,* later a goddess

Dravida: Sanskrit word for South India

Dravidian: a language group from South India that includes Tamil, Telugu, Kannada, and Malayalam

Drona: the Pandavas' tutor in martial arts in the *Mahabharata*

Drupada: father of Draupadi in the *Mahabharata*

dualism: the philosophical view that god and the universe, including the worshiper, are of two different substances

Durga: "Hard to Get [to]," a goddess

Dvaita: dualism, a philosophical school, whose most famous proponent was Madhva

Dvapara Yuga: "The Age of the Deuce," the third of the degenerating ages

Dyer, Major Reginald: British officer who gave the command for the massacre at Amritsar

Ekalavya: tribal (Nishada) prince who cut off his thumb at the request of Arjuna and Drona, in the *Mahabharata*

Ellamma: South Indian goddess with the body of a Brahmin woman and the head of a Dalit woman

Fs, the five: elements of Tantric ritual (fish, flesh, fermented grapes, frumentum, and fornication), *see also* Ms, the five

Faxian: Chinese visitor to India in 402 CE

Gandhari: wife of Dhritarashtra, mother of Duryodhana and his brothers, the enemies of the Pandavas, in the *Mahabharata*

Gandharvas: demigods, musicians, associated with fertility and horses; consorts of the Apsarases

Ganga: the Ganges River

Gargi: a feisty woman who interrogates sages in the Upanishads

Garuda: a mythical eagle, the mount of the god Vishnu

Gayatri: name of a meter; of a particularly holy verse in the *Rig Veda;* and of a goddess

Ghasidas: a Chamar who founded a branch of the Satnamis

Gita: short name of the *Bhagavad Gita*

Gonds: a tribal people

Gondwana: a mythical land thought to have been submerged long, long ago

Gugga (also spelled **Guga**): a folk god, said to have been a historical figure; famous for his flying black mare

guna: "quality," term for the three strands of matter in Sankhya philosophy

Guru Nanak: founder of Sikhism, 1469–1539 CE

Hanuman: the monkey ally of Rama in the *Ramayana*

Harappa: ancient city in the Indus Valley, c. 2500 BCE

Harijan: "People of God" (Hari, Vishnu), Gandhi's name for the Dalits

Indra: Veda king of the gods, god of rain, fertility, and war

Indrani: wife of the Vedic god Indra

itihasa: "that's what happened," history

Jabali: a Brahmin who argues for atheism in the *Ramayana*

Jagannatha: "Lord of the Universe," the name of a form of Vishnu, especially in a temple in Puri, Orissa

Jainas: followers of the religion founded by the Jina, in the fifth century BCE

Jambu-dvipa: "the plum tree continent," the ancient name for the subcontinent of India

Janaka: a king of Videha, father of Sita

Janashruti: a king in the Upanishads

Jara: "old age"; also the name of a hunter who kills the incarnate god Krishna

jati: "birth," caste

Jina: Vardhamana Mahavira, founder of Jainism

jizya: tax levied by Muslim rulers on subjects who did not perform military service

Kabir: a poet, c. 1398–1448 CE, whose teachings bridged Hinduism and Islam

Kaikeyi: mother of Bharata in the *Ramayana*, who insisted that Rama be exiled

Kalamukhas: "Death Heads," a sect of antinomian Shaivas

Kali (goddess): "Time" or "Doomsday," goddess of sex and violence and much more

Kali Age (Yuga): the fourth and worst of the ages; the present age

Kalidasa: a Gupta poet, author of *Shakuntala*

Kalinga: the ancient name of Orissa

Kalki: the final avatar of Vishnu, a horse-headed warrior who will kill the barbarians

Kama-sutra: textbook of pleasure, composed by Vatsyayana, third century CE

Kamsa: king who devoted his life to the attempt to kill Krishna

Kannappar: Tamil saint who tore out his eyes for Shiva

Kanphata: "Pierced-Ear," name of a sect of yogis

Kapala-mochana: "The Release of the Skull," the shrine in Varanasi where the skull of Brahma fell from Shiva's hand

Kapalikas: "Skull Bearers," a sect of Shaivas who imitate Shiva's wandering with Brahma's skull

karma: action, or the fruits of action

Karna: illegitimate son of Kunti, raised by low-caste Charioteers, in the *Mahabharata*

kathenotheism: F. Max Müller's term for the worship of one supreme god at a time

Kaula: "belonging to the family [*kula*]," name of a Tantric sect

Kausalya: mother of Rama, in the *Ramayana*

Kautilya: author of the *Artha-shastra*

kavya: poetry

Khandoba: Maharashtrian god associated with dogs

kliba: a sexually challenged man

Krishna: an incarnation of Vishnu, a hero of the *Mahabharata* who grew up among cowherds

Krita Yuga: the first, or Winning Age

Kshatriyas: the class of warriors and kings

Kshetrayya: a poet, 1622–1673 CE, who wrote poems to Krishna in Telugu

Kula: "the family," name for a Tantric sect

Kumbhakarna: "Pot Ear," a brother of Ravana, in the *Ramayana*

Kundalini: "the encircling," name of a coiled spinal power energized through Tantric yoga

Kunti: a wife of Pandu, mother of the Pandavas and of Karna (all fathered by gods), in the *Mahabharata*

Kutsa: a son of Indra, in the Brahmanas

Lakshmana: brother of Rama, in the *Ramayana*

Lakshmi: goddess of fortune, wife of Vishnu and of earthly kings

Lakulisha: "Lord Holding a Club," founder of the Pashupata sect of Shaivas

Lanka: a mythical island ruled by the ogre Ravana

Laukification: the process by which the Sanskritic tradition absorbs popular (*laukika* ["of the people," *loka*]) traditions

left-hand: sinister or unclean, said by Hindus who think they are the right hand, about other Hindus, particularly certain Tantrics

Lemuria: mythical supercontinent said to have once connected India and Australia

linga: "sign," a sign of sex, particularly the male sexual organ, more particularly the sexual organ of the god Shiva; also regarded as an abstract symbol of Shiva

Lingayat: a South Indian sect of Shaivas, also known as Virashaivas and Charanas

Lokayatas: Materialists, also called Charvakas

Ms, the five: the five elements of Tantric ritual (*mansa, matsya, madya, mudra, maithuna*). *See also* Fs, the five

Madhva: a philosopher, c. 1238–1317 CE, in Karnataka, exponent of the Dvaita (dualist) school

Madri: a wife of Pandu in the *Mahabharata;* mother of the twins Nakula and Sahadeva

Mahabharata: the longer of the two great Sanskrit epics, attributed to the sage Vyasa

Mahadevi: "the great goddess"

Mahadevyyakka: twelfth-century CE woman, Virashaiva saint and poet

Mahisha: "the buffalo," a buffalo antigod killed by Durga

Mahisha-mardini: "buffalo crushing," an epithet of Durga

maithuna: "pairing," sexual coupling

Mallanna: a Maharashtrian god who often takes the form of a dog

Mandavya: a sage, unjustly impaled on a stake, in the *Mahabharata*

Manikkavacakar: nineth-century CE Shaiva poet, author of the *Tiruvacakam*

Mankanaka: a sage who danced too much

mamsa: flesh

Manu: a mythical sage, author of a dharma text

Marathas: a people of Maharashtra

Marathi: language of Maharashtra

mare Fire (*Vadava-agni*): submarine fire in the mouth of a mare

Mariamma: South Indian goddess with the head of a Brahmin woman and the body of a Dalit woman

Maricha: ogre ally of Ravana, who takes the form of a deer to delude Sita

Maruts: wind gods

matt: a Hindu theological school

Mauryas: a great dynasty, from 324 to 185 BCE

Meru: the great mountain at the center of the world

Mimamsa: the philosophy of logic

Mirabai: Hindi poet and woman saint, devotee of Krishna, 1498–1597 CE

Mitra: "Friend," a Vedic god closely linked with Varuna

mlecchas: barbarians

Mohenjo-Daro: a great city in the Indus Valley, c. 2500 BCE

moksha: Release, from the circle of transmigration

monism: doctrine that the universe is made of one divine substance

mrigas: wild beasts, in contrast with *pashus,* domesticated or sacrificial beasts; also a word for deer

Mrityu: death

Murukan: South Indian god identified with Skanda

Muttal Ravuttan: a Muslim horseman, a South Indian Hindu folk hero

nabob: name given to British rulers of India

Nachiketas: a boy who goes to the underworld and learns about death, in the Upanishads

Nakula: one of the twin sons of Madri, fathered by the Ashvins, in the *Mahabharata*

Nammalvar ("Our Alvar"): the last of the great Alvars, in the ninth century

Nanda: name of the cowherd who adopts Krishna, in the Puranas

Nandas: dynasty that preceded the Mauryas

Nandin: the bull of the god Shiva, sometimes his doorkeeper or son

Nantanar: in Tamil myth, a Pariah who went through fire to purify himself because he was not allowed to enter a temple

Nara-simha: "Man-Lion," an avatar of Vishnu, savior of Prahlada

Nasatyas: a name of the Ashvins

Nastikas: "people who say, 'It does not exist,'" atheists

nawab: name given to Muslim rulers under the British Raj

Nayakas: dynasty that ruled much of South India, from Mysore, through the sixteenth and seventeenth centuries

Nayanmars: Tamil Shaiva saints (singular is "Nayanar")

nir-guna: "without qualities," the undifferentiated, abstract of the godhead

nirvana: "the blowing out of a flame," release from the circle of transmigration

Nishadas: tribal peoples of ancient India

nondualism: the philosophical view, expounded by Shankara, that god and the universe are made of one substance

Nyaya: logic, a philosophical school

Orientalism: term coined by Edward Said to describe the attitude of Europeans toward "Orientals"

orthopraxy: an emphasis on "straight behavior" rather than "straight thinking" (orthodoxy)

Pahlavas: Sanskrit term for Parthians, the people whose empire occupied all of what is now Iran, Iraq, and Armenia

Pallavas: South Indian dynasty that ruled from Kanchipuram, north of the Cholas, Pandyas, and Cheras, from the fourth through the ninth century CE

Pandavas: the five sons of Pandu, in the *Mahabharata,* in order of birth: Yudhishthira, Bhima, Arjuna, Nakula, and Sahadeva

pandit: a learned man

Pandu: father of the Pandavas, born pale, cursed to die if he begot legal sons

Pandyas: a South Indian dynasty that ruled the eastern part of the southernmost tip of India from the time of Ashoka to well into the sixteenth century

Panis: enemies of the Vedic people, accused of cattle theft

papa: evil

Parashurama: "Rama with an Ax," an avatar of Vishnu

Pariah: Tamil word for a particular low caste of drummers, then extended to all the Dalit castes

Parsis: "Persians," Zoroastrians

Parvati: "Daughter of the Mountain," wife of Shiva

pasha: the "bond" that ties the individual soul (the *pashu* ["beast"]) to the god (*pati* ["protector"]) in the Shaiva Siddhanta philosophy

pashu: domesticated or sacrificial beast

Pashupatas: followers of Shiva Pashupati, "Lord of Beasts," antinomian and cynical

Pataliputra: city on the Ganges, the modern Patna

Periya Purana: a collection of stories about the Tamil Shaiva saints, by Cekkiyar, dated to the reign of the Chola king Kulottunka II, 1133–1150 CE

pitha: plinth or base of statue, particularly of a deity

Prahlada: a virtuous demon, saved from his wicked father by Vishnu in the form of the Man-Lion (Nara-simha)

Prajapati: "Lord of Creatures," the creator in the Vedas

Prakrit: "natural," the actual spoken languages of ancient India, in contrast with Sanskrit

prakriti: "nature," more particularly matter in contrast with spirit (in Sankhya philosophy)

pralaya: dissolution or doomsday

pratiloma: "against the grain"; more literally, "against the hair," said in particular of marriages in which the woman is of a higher caste than the man

Prithivi: "broad," the earth

Prithu: the first king, who tamed the earth

puja: worship, particularly with flowers and fruits, also sometimes with incense and other offerings

pukka: "ripe" or "cooked," perfected

Pulkasa: name of one of the ancient Dalit castes

puram: in Sanskrit, a city or citadel; in Tamil, the public emotion, in contrast with *akam*

Puranas: compendiums of myth, ritual, and history, originally only in Sanskrit, later also in vernacular languages

purdah: the seclusion of women, particularly behind screens in a house or palace

Purohita: a family priest or royal chaplain

purusha: "male," the Primeval Man in the Vedas; later, any male animal; in Sankhya philosophy, spirit, self, or person

purusha-arthas: the three (later four) goals of life for a man

purva paksha: "first wing," statement of the opponent's position at the start of an argument

Pushyamitra: founder of the Shunga dynasty in 185 BCE

Putana: a demoness who tried to kill Krishna

Qualified Nondualism: philosophy taught by Ramanuja, moderating the view that god and the worshiper are of the same substance

Radhakrishnan, Sarvepalli: philosopher, the first president of India, 1888–1975

Raikva: the first homeless person, in the Upanishads

Raj: short for *rajyam* ["kingdom"]; in particular, the British Raj, the British colonization of India

raja: king

rajas: emotion or passion, one of the three *gunas*, or qualities of matter

rajyam: kingdom

Rakshasas: ogres, demonic creatures on earth

Rama: a prince, an avatar of Vishnu, hero of the *Ramayana*

Ramanuja: a philosopher, exponent of Qualified Nondualism, from Tamil Nadu, c. 1056–1137 CE

Ramanujan, Attipat Krishnaswami: poet, linguist, scholar of Tamil, Telugu, and Kannada, 1929–1993

Ramayana: one of the two great ancient Sanskrit epics, the story of Rama, attributed to the poet Valmiki

Ram-raj (Hindi), Rama-rajya (Sanskrit): perfect reign of Rama

Ranke, Leopold von: a positivist German historian, 1795–1886

Ravana: an ogre (Rakshasa), ruler of the island of Lanka, enemy of Rama in the *Ramayana*

Rig Veda: the most ancient sacred text in India, composed c. 1500 BCE

rishi: a sage

Rishyashringa: a sage with a horn on his head, son of a sage and a female antelope

Rudra: "Howler," a wild Vedic god, later a name of the Hindu god Shiva

sadharana dharma: religious law that applies to everyone in common. *See also* dharma

Sagara: a king whose sons dug out the ocean, which is also called *sagara*

sa-guna: "with qualities," the differentiated, visualized aspect of the godhead

Sahadeva: one of the twin sons of Madri, fathered by the Ashvins, in the *Mahabharata*

sahib: "master," honorific title given to British rulers in India during the Raj

Sama Veda: the Veda of hymns arranged for chanting

samkara: mixture, in particular the mixing together of classes and/or castes

samnyasa: renunciation

samsara: the circle of transmigration

sanatana dharma: the eternal religious law. *See also* dharma

Sankhya: a dualistic philosophy, dating from the time of the Upanishads, that divides the universe into a male purusha (spirit, self, or person) and a female prakriti (matter, nature)

Sanskrit: the perfected or artificial language called the language of the gods; the language of the texts of ancient India

Sanskritization: process by which lower castes, imitating Brahmin ways of eating and dressing, raise their status

Santoshi Ma: goddess first worshiped in the 1960s, now extremely popular, largely as the result of a mythological film, *Jai Santoshi Ma*

Sarama: bitch of the god Indra in the *Rig Veda,* who found stolen cows and brought them back

Sarasvati River: once a river in the Punjab, dried up long ago

sati: a good woman, particularly a devoted wife. *See also* suttee

Sati: wife of the god Shiva, daughter of Daksha, who committed suicide

Satnamis: "Path of the True Name," a sect, founded in the eastern Punjab in 1657, that worships gurus rather than gods

sattva: "truth, goodness," one of the three *guna*s or qualities of matter in Sankhya philosophy

Satyavati: daughter of a fisherman, mother of Vyasa and other key figures in the *Mahabharata*

sepoy (from Turkish **sipahi** ["soldier"]): native troop serving the British in India

Shachi: the wife of the god Indra

Shaiva: pertaining to Shiva; a worshiper of Shiva

Shakas: Scythians

shakti: power, particularly female power, more particularly a goddess or the wife of a god

Shankara: a nondualist philosopher from Kerala, c. 788–820 CE

Shantanu: husband of Satyavati and of the Ganges River, father of Bhishma, in the *Mahabharata*

shastras: texts or textbooks, sciences

Shatrughna: one of Rama's three brothers, in the *Ramayana*

Shattaris: Sufi sect

Shiva: the Great God (Mahadeva)

Shivaji: founder of the kingdom of Maharashtra, leader of resistance against the Mughals, 1630–1680 CE

Shrirangam: Vaishnava temple, also known as Tiruvarangam, in Trichi (Tiruchirappalli), on the Kaveri River, in Tamil Nadu; the seat of Ramanuja

Shudras: "servants," the lowest of the four classes (*varna*s) of ancient Indian society

Shunahshepha: boy, in the Brahmanas, whose father tried to sell him to be sacrificed

Shungas: dynasty that ruled North India from 185 to 73 BCE

Shurapanakha: ogress (Rakshasi), sister of Ravana, mutilated by Lakshmana, in the *Ramayana*

Shvetaketu: a sage, in the Upanishads

Sikhs: followers of the religion founded by Guru Nanak, 1469–1539, in the Punjab

Sindhu: "river," Greek and Persian word later used as the basis of the word for the people who lived east of the Indus, the Hindus

Sita: an incarnate goddess, the wife of Rama, in the *Ramayana*

Skanda: a son of Shiva, general of the gods, identified with Murukan in South India

Skull Bearers. *See* **Kapalikas.**

soma: a plant pressed to yield a hallucinogenic fluid, offered to the gods in the Vedas; also a name of the moon

Somanatha (Somnath): a great temple to Shiva, and the city around it, in southwest Gujarat

Sri Lanka: present-day name of the island previously known as Ceylon or Serendip but probably not Lanka

stupas: Buddhist relic mounds

Sufism: a mystical branch of Islam

Sugriva: a monkey king befriended by Rama in the *Ramayana*

Sukeshin: ogre (Rakshasa) devoted to Shiva, in the Puranas

Surya: the sun, a Vedic god

Sushruta: author of a medical text

Sutas: "Charioteers," name of a caste of charioteers and improvisational bards, in ancient India

suttee (from Sanskrit *sati*): the burning of a woman on the pyre of her dead husband; also, the woman who does this

sva-dharma: one's own particular dharma, in contrast with general (*sadharana dharma*)

svayambhu: "self-existent" or "self-created," an epithet of Prajapati and of several other mythical creators; also applied to lingas and other religious symbols that appear in nature, without human agency

Swaminarayan: founder of the Satsangi sect, 1780–1830 CE

tamas: "darkness," one of the three qualities or *guna*s of matter, according to Sankhya philosophy

Tamil: Dravidian language of South India

Tantra: form of Hinduism (also of Buddhism), and the texts and practices of those traditions

tapas: internal heat, generated through rigid self-control of the senses and violent yogic practices

Tej Singh: historical figure, the son of the commander of the fort of Senji under Aurangzeb; also a hero of Hindi folklore

Thapar, Romila: India's greatest living historian of the ancient period

Thompson, Stith: author of a detailed index of the themes in folklore, 1885-1976 CE

Thugs (from the Sanskrit sthaga ["thief," "rogue"]): members of a gang of assassins who worshiped Kali and terrorized the British in India

Tirumal: Tamil name of Vishnu

Tiruvacakam: "the sacred word": a poem in praise of Shiva, composed by Manikkavacakar, c. 800 CE

Treta Yuga: "the Trey," the second of the four degenerating ages (Yugas)

Trimurti: "triple form," the trinity of Brahma, Vishnu, and Shiva

Trishanku: king who tried in vain to get to heaven and remains stuck halfway there

trivarga: "triple path," the three goals of human life (*purusha-artha*s)

Tukaram: antinomian poet saint in Maharashtra, 1608–1649 CE

Tulsidas: poet, author of the Hindi *Ramcharit-manas*, 1532–1623 CE

Tvastri: Vedic architect, blacksmith, and artisan of the gods

twice born (*dvi-ja*): name of the three higher classes (*varna*s) of Hindu society, reborn on their initiation

ulama: conservative ruling body of Islam

Ulupi: a cobra woman married by Arjuna, in the *Mahabharata*

Upanishads: Sanskrit philosophical texts, from c. 500 BCE

Vaishnava: pertaining to Vishnu; a worshiper of Vishnu

Vaishyas: the third of the four classes (*varna*s) of ancient Indian society

Valin: monkey falsely accused of usurping his brother's throne, unfairly killed by Rama, in the *Ramayana*

Valmiki: author of the *Ramayana* and, within it, guardian and tutor of Rama's twin sons

Vama: "left-hand," said of the more antinomian aspects of Hinduism, particularly of Tantrism

Varanasi: name of Kashi, Benares

varna: "color," any of the four social classes of ancient India

varna-ashrama-dharma: the religious law pertaining to social class (*varna*) and stage of life (*ashrama*), often used as a description of Hinduism

varna-samkara: the mixture of classes, miscegenation

Varuna: Vedic god of the sky, the waters, and the moral law

vasana: "perfume," the memory traces left by former lives

Vasudeva: the cowherd who adopts the infant Krishna and raises him, in the Puranas

Vatsyayana: author of the *Kama-sutra*

Vayu: god of the wind

Veda: "knowledge," one of the three (or four) most ancient sacred texts; also used to denote all four Vedas plus the Brahmanas and Upanishads

Vedanta: "end of the Veda," a term for the Upanishads and for the later philosophy based on the Upanishads

Vedantic: pertaining to the Vedanta

Vessantara Jataka: Buddhist text that tells the story of a king, Vessantara, who lost everything he had

Vibhishana: an ogre, the moralistic brother of Ravana, in the *Ramayana*

Vidura: a son of Vyasa born of a servant girl; an incarnation of dharma

viraha: separation, particularly the emotional agony of separation from a lover or from a beloved god

Virashaiva: a sect of Shaivas, also called Lingayats, founded by Basava c. 1106–1167 CE

Virochana: an antigod, father of Bali

Vishnu: a great god

Vitthal: a Maharashtrian god

Vithoba: a Maharashtrian god

Vivekananda: a holy man, one of the founders of the Vedanta movement, who brought Hinduism to Chicago in 1893 CE

Vritra: an antigod, Indra's great enemy, in the Vedas

Vyasa: a sage, author of the *Mahabharata* and of Pandu, Dhritarashtra, and Vidura

Xuan Zang: Chinese visitor to India in the seventh century CE

Yajur Veda: the third Veda, arranged for the sacrifice

Yakshas, Yakshinis: forest and tree spirits, beautiful, able to confer fertility but sometimes malicious

Yashoda: the cowherd woman who adopted Krishna, in the Puranas

Yavakri: a sage who was killed because he raped a Brahmin's wife, in the Brahmanas and the *Mahabharata*

Yavanas: "Ionians," a Sanskrit word first for Greeks, then for any foreigners

yoni: the womb, the partner of the linga

Yudhishthira: oldest son of Pandu, begotten by Dharma

Yuga: an age, one of four periods of time in which everything degenerates

zenana: the part of a house or palace where women are secluded

Zoroastrians: members of a religion derived from the Iranian Avesta, involving the worship of fire

NOTES

PREFACE: THE MAN OR
THE RABBIT IN THE MOON

1. There are some good short introductions (see, in the Bibliography, Hopkins, Kinsley, Knipe), longer reference works (Flood [*Introduction* and *Companion*], Klostermaier, Michaels, Mittal, and Thursby), and books on Hinduism as it is lived today (Narayanan and Hawley). My own version of the history of the Hindus could be used as a basic textbook for a course over a fourteen-week semester: one week of introduction, one of conclusion, and two chapters a week for twelve weeks. I would recommend supplementing it with a good book on Indian history (Keay and Thapar are my favorites), a good survey (such as Flood's or Glucklich's), and a sourcebook (such as my *Textual Sources for the Study of Hinduism*, or *Sources of Indian Tradition* [3rd ed.], or the forthcoming Norton *Anthology of World Religions*). Basham's *The Wonder That Was India* is still unbeatable as a general introduction to the cultures of India.

2. A good model is provided by Richman's *Many Ramayanas* and *Questioning Ramayanas*, which trace the many *Ramayanas* throughout Hindu history.

3. Ramanujan, "Is There an Indian Way of Thinking?"

4. I have in mind works such as those provided by Shulman (et al.) on the Nayakas and Thapar on Somanatha.

5. Lévi-Strauss, *Structural Anthropology*.

6. Tubb, "Barn, Ben, and Begging Bowl: Sanskrit Words and the Things in the World."

7. Narayana Rao, " Hinduism: The Untold Story."

8. Srinivas, *Religion and Society of the Coorgs*.

9. Hardiman, *The Coming of the Devi*, 158.

10. Srinivas, *Social Change*, 7.

11. Kosambi, *Myth and Reality*, 91–92.

12. Pollock, *The Language of the Gods in the World of men*, 283.

13. Ibid., 23.

14. Pollock, "India in the Vernacular Millennium."

15. Pollock, *Literary Cultures in History*.

16. Microhistory, in the hands of a master like Carlo Ginzburg, is another way to excavate these often lost ordinary histories, but microhistory requires a thick description to which a survey such as this cannot aspire.

17. With apologies to William Blake: "To see a world in a grain of sand/And a heaven in a wild flower,/Hold infinity in the palm of your hand/ And eternity in an hour."

18. Schmidt, "The Origin of Ahimsa."

19. Ramanujan, "Is There an Indian Way of Thinking?"

20. Shankara's "Thousand Teachings," 1.6; Mayeda 2.1.6, 212.

21. Hardiman, *The Coming of the Devi*, 51.

22. "Sasa Jataka," *Jataka*, vol. 3, no. 316, 34–38 of PTS.

23. Doniger, *The Implied Spider*, 154-56.

24. Wittgenstein, *Philosophical Investigations*, part II, paragraph xi; citing Jastrow, "The Mind's Eye."

25. Alison Goddard, *Times Higher Education Supplement*, November 21, 2003, "Email Threats and Egg-throwing Spark Fears of Hindu Extremism," See also Edward Rothstein, "The Scholar Who Irked the Hindu Puritains," in "Arts and Ideas," *New York Times*, January 31, 2005 (reprinted as "Daring to Tackle Sex in Hinduism," in *International Herald Tribune*, February 2, 2005); William Dalrymple, "India: The War over History," *New York Review of Books*, Vol. 52, no.6 (April 7, 2005).

26. IndianCivilization@yahoogroups.com; "Jiten Bardwaj" <jiten51@yahoogroups.com. Parts of the message were cited by Goddard, "Email Threats."

27. Goddard, "Email Threats."

CHAPTER 1. INTRODUCTION: WORKING WITH
AVAILABLE LIGHT

1. Idries Shah, *The Exploits of the Incomparable Mulla Nasrudin*, 26. Idries Shah attributes the parable to Mulla Nasrudin.

2. For the idea that the Europeans have taught Hindus to say that India is timeless, see Sedgwick, *Against the Modern World*.

3. Lévi-Strauss, "Split Representation in the Art of Asia and America."

4. *The Narmamala of Ksemendra* 3:44.

5. Hopkins, *The Hindu Religious Tradition*, 9.

6. Keillor, *Pontoon*.

7. Keay, *India*, 2.

8. Thapar, "Imagined Religious Communities," 77.

9. Mishra, "Exit Wounds," 81.

10. Alex von Tunzelmann, *Indian Summer* (Henry Holt, 2007), cited by Mishra, "Exit Wouds,"81.

11. Burghart, "The Category of 'Hindu,'" 264–65.

12. Gottschalk, *Beyond Hindu and Muslim*.

13. Bloom, *The Anxiety of Influence*.

14. Paraskara, *Paraskara grihya sutra* 10.36, cited by Nath, *Puranas and Acculturation*, 202.

15. Michaels, *Hinduism*, 12-14.

16. Frykenberg, "The Emergence of Modern Hinduism," in Sontheimer and Kulke, *Hinduism Reconsidered*, 31.

17. The act can be found at www.sudhirlaw.com/HMA55.htm.

18. Ronojoy Sen, *Legalizing Religion*, 6–38.

19. Ibid.

20. Brian K. Smith, "Exorcising the Transcendent," requires six qualities out of a cluster of nine; Michaels, *Hinduism*, 20, cluster of five.

21. According to the 2004 Survey Report conducted by the Indian Census, 25 percent of persons aged fifteen years and above are reported to be vegetarian. But according to the 2006 the *Hindu*–CNN–IBN State of the Nation Survey, 40 percent of respondents were vegetarian (a figure that includes those who eat eggs), 55 percent of Brahmins are vegetarian, and in landlocked states such as Rajasthan and Haryana, where seafood is not available as a food source, more than 60 percent are vegetarians. Gujarat, the birthplace of Gandhi and home to a sizable Jain population, is predominantly landlocked, but only 45 percent vegetarian.

22. Wittgenstein, *Philosophical Investigations*. Wittgenstein's method was similarly applied to Hinduism by the anthropologist Gabriella Eichinger Ferro-Luzzi, in "The Polythetic Network."

23. Doniger, *The Woman Who Pretended*, 7.

24. J. Z. Smith on center and periphery.

25. Pace Michaels (*Hinduism*), there can be no single "habitus."

26. Doniger, "Hinduism by Any Other Name."

27. Narayana Rao, "Hinduism : The Untold Story" and "Purana as Brahminic Ideology."

28. Herodotus, *History*, 3.97–100. He called them Hindoi.

29. Thapar, *Early History*, 275.

30. Joyce, *Finnegans Wake*, 10.

31. W. C. Smith, *The Meaning and End of Religion*, 30.

32. Babur, *Baburnama*, 352.

33. *Encyclopaedia Britannica*, s.v. India.

34. Hiltebeitel, "Of Camphor and Coconuts," 28.

35. For the usefulness of the word "Hinduism," despite its drawbacks and the subjective nature of its boundaries, see the arguments for the similarly subjective reasons for delineating the elements of a myth, in Doniger, *The Implied Spider*.

36. Doniger O'Flaherty, *Other Peoples' Myths*, chapter 3.

37. There are also more good books about the Mughals and the British, hot topics and topics for which there is more reliable data, than about the ancient period.

38. Jamison, *Sacrificed Wife*, 14; Patton, "If the Fire Goes Out, the Wife Shall Fast."

39. The Mimamnsa school. Julia Leslie, *The Perfect Wife* 3, citing *Shabda* 10.8.10.22: *praptipurvakah pratishedah bhavati*.

40. Wayne Booth's term, in *The Rhetoric of Fiction*.

41. Doniger, *The Implied Spider*.

42. Ramanujan, "Towards a Counter System."

43. Hiltebeitel, *Rethinking the Mahabharata*, 166–67.

44. For this and other definitions of people beyond the Aryan pale in ancient India, see Doniger O'Flaherty, "The Origins of Heresy in Hindu Mythology" and "The Image of the Heretic in the Gupta Puranas."

45. Doniger O'Flaherty, *Women, Androgynes, and Other Mythical Beasts*.

46. Trautmann, cited by Bryant, *The Quest*, 261.

47. Trautmann, ibid., queried this: "It has yet to be determined why exactly India has never been self-sufficient in horses. Climate? A relative scarcity of pasture?" In a word, yes.

48. Gommans, "The Rise of the Indo-Afghan Empire," 70–73.

49. Trautmann, cited by Bryant, *The Quest*, 261.

50. Doniger, "Pluralism and Intolerance in Hinduism"; "Hindu Pluralism and Hindu Intolerance of the Other"; "Tolstoi's Revenge"; "Do Many Heads Necessarily Have Many Minds?"

51. Festinger, *When Prophecy Fails* and *Cognitive Dissonance*.

52. Doniger O'Flaherty, *Women, Androgynes*, 5-7.

53. Forster, *Hill of Devi*, 199.

54. Doniger O'Flaherty, *Other Peoples' Myths*, final chapter.

55. Mistry, *Such a Long Journey*, 183.

56. Orr, "Identity and Divinity."

57. Stewart, "Satya Pír: Muslim Holy Man and Hindu God," 578.

58. Katherine Ulrich's wonderful term.

59. Doniger, "The Origins of Heresy."

60. Sen, *Identity and Violence.*

61. Joh, *Heart of the Cross*, 53–55; Bhabha, *The Location of Culture* 7, 277, 168–69, 256, 19, 296, 360, 240, 322.

62. This phrase is Kristin Bloomer's.

63. Pangborn, *Zoroastrianism: A Beleaguered Faith*, 8; "Sugar in the Milk: A Parsi Kitchen Story," NPR, March 20, 2008:http://www.npr.org/templates/story/story.php?storyId=88505980&sc=emaf.

64. Doniger O'Flaherty, *Siva*, 318.

CHAPTER 2. TIME AND SPACE IN INDIA

1. Forster, *A Passage to India*, chapter 12.

2. Matthiessen, *The Snow Leopard*, 29.

3. This is my paraphrase of the scientific data. Knipe tells a slightly different version of it, *Hinduism*, 2.

4. Wolpert, *A New History*, 6. This was the civilization of the northern Soan River valley.

5. Witzel, "Indocentrism," 348.

6. Suess, *Das Antlitz der Erde [The Face of the Earth]*.

7. Personal communication from Jim Masselos, Sydney, Australia, May 2006.

8. Sclater, "The Mammals of Madagascar."

9. Macleane, *Manual of the Administration of the Madras Presidency*, 1885.

10. Frederick Spencer Oliver, *A Dweller on Two Planets*, wrote the book in 1883–86, died in 1899, and his mother published it in 1905.

11. Sumathi Ramaswamy, "Home Away from Home?," 151 and 155.

12. Forster, *A Passage to India*, 12.

13. Keay, *India*, 4.

14. *Mahabharata* 3.12.13; 16.8.40; Doniger O'Flaherty, *Origins of Evil*, 261–62.

15. Keay, *India*, 4.

16. *Harivamsha* 86.35–53.

17. Lorenzen, *Kabir Legends*, 49, citing Paramananda's *Kabir Manshur*.

18. *Vishnu Purana* 5.38.9-28.

19. *Bhagavata Purana* 11.3.1–28.

20. Kuiper, "The Bliss of Asa," 113.

21. S. R. Rao, *The Lost City of Dvaraka*.

22. Doniger O'Flaherty, *Origins of Evil*, 88, 100. For the identification of the horse with the sacrificer and with Prajapati, see *Shatapatha Brahmana* 13.1.1.1 and 13.2.1.1. For the many variants of the story of Indra's theft of the sacrificial horse of King Sagara, see *Mahabharata* 3.104–08; *Ramayana* 1.38–44; *Vishnu Purana* 4.4.1–33, etc. For a discussion of these stories, see Doniger O'Flaherty, *Women*, 220–22.

23. *Ramayana* 1.37–43; *Shiva Purana* 5.38; *Linga Purana* 1.66; *Vayu Purana* 88; *Brahmanda Purana* 3.46–53; *Vishnu Purana* 4.4; Doniger O'Flaherty, *Siva*, 230, and fn. 88.

24. *Mahabharata* 3.105–8.

25. Janaki, "Parasurama," citing chapters 51–56 of the *Brahmanda Purana*.

26. Ibid., citing the *Keralamahatmya*.

27. *Rig Veda* 2.12.2, *Maitrayani Samhita* 1.12.13, *Mahabharata* 1.21.5. 2.

28. The legend of the *cankam*s is first expressed in Nakkiranar's commentary on the seventh-century *Irayaiyanar Akapporul*.

29. Das Gupta, *Malabar Nation Trade.*

30. *Frontline*, May 7–20, 2005.

31. T. S. Subramanian, in *Frontline*, 22: 2, (Jan., 15–28, 2005).

32. Keay, *India*, 3–5.

33. Dundes, *The Flood Myth.*

34. *Shatapatha Brahmana* 1.8.1.1–6; Doniger O'Flaherty, *Hindu Myths*, 180.

35. *Matsya Purana* 1.11–34; 2.1–19; Doniger O'Flaherty, *Hindu Myths*, 181–4.

36. *Mahabharata* 3.56.4–6, 1.169.16–26; 1.170.1–21; 1.171.1–23.

37. Doniger O'Flaherty, *Siva.*

38. *Mahabharata* 10.18.21.

39. *Matsya Purana* 175.23–63; *Harivamsha* 1.45.20–64; Doniger O'Flaherty, *Women*, 226–72.

40. *Skanda Purana* 7.1.32.1–128, 33.1–103; Doniger O'Flaherty, *Women*, 228–33; *Siva*, 289–92.

41. The idea of a submarine fire is pre-Vedic, Indo-Iranian (West, *Indo-European Poetry*, 270).

42. Sumathi Ramaswamy, *The Lost Land of Lemuria*, 233. According to the note on p. 276, this research was carried out by the Institute of Geophysics at UT-Austin and MIT.

43. MIT Professor Fred Frey, quoted in the MIT news office bulletin, "Team Finds Surprising Volcanic Clues to Indian Ocean Formation," Deborah Halber, News Office, December 8, 1999.

44. Thomas Babington Macaulay in 1835; Keay, *India*, 431.

45. Jonathan Z. Smith, *Map Is Not Territory.*

46. Wolpert, *India*, 5.

47. Ibid., 19–20.

48. Ramanujan, *Speaking of Siva*, 24.

49. Doniger, *Splitting the Difference*, 204–31.

50. Mary Douglas, *Purity and Danger.*

51. Woody Allen, "Fabulous Tales and Mythical Beasts," 193.

CHAPTER 3. CIVILIZATION IN THE INDUS VALLEY

1. Klostermaier, *A Survey*, 34–35.

2. Neumayer, *Prehistoric Indian Rock Paintings;* Vatsyayan, "Prehistoric Paintings."

3. Wolpert, *India*, 10.

4. Flood, *Introduction*, 25.

5. McEvilley, *The Shape of Ancient Thought.*

6. Farmer, "Mythological Functions"; Erdosy, ed., *The Indo-Aryans.*

7. Knipe, *Hinduism*, 22; Parpola, *Deciphering the Indus Script*, 248–50.

8. W. Norman Brown, "The Indian Games of Pachisi, Chaupar, and Chausar," 32–35.
9. Marshall, *Mohenjo-Daro*, pl. CLIII, 7–10 and 551–52.
10. Dales, "Of Dice and Men," 17–18.
11. Keay, *India*, 9
12. Mitter, *Indian Art*, 8.
13. Keay, *India*, 10.
14. Kenoyer, "Socio-Economic Structures of the Indus Civilization"; "Harappan Craft Specialization and the Question of Urban Segregation and Stratification"; "Specialized Crafts and Culture Change."
15. Knipe, *Hinduism*, 20.
16. Hopkins, *The Hindu Religious Tradition*, 6.
17. Possehl, *The Indus Age*.
18. Witzel, cited in Bryant, *The Quest*, 184.
19. Farmer, Sproat, and Witzel, "The Collapse of the Indus-Script Thesis."
20. Keay, *India*, 16.
21. Farmer, "Mythological Functions."
22. Keay, *India*, 26.
23. Ibid., 13
24. K. M. Sen, *Hinduism*,14.
25. Wolpert, *India*, 16.
26. Thapar, *Early India*, 92.
27. Marshall, *Mohenjo-Daro*, 351.
28. Knipe, *Hinduism*, 21.
29. Wolpert *India,* 20.
30. Ibid, 11.
31. Marshall, *Mohenjo-Daro*, 348.
32. Ibid., 352.
33. Bollee, *Gone to the Dogs*, 7.
34. Wolpert, *India*, 20.
35. Hopkins, *The Hindu Religious Tradition*, 5–6.
36. Ibid, 5–8.
37. Ibid., 5.
38. Marshall, *Mohenjo-Daro*, 355.
39. Hopkins, *The Hindu Religious Tradition*, 7.
40. Bollee, *Gone to the Dogs*, 8, citing Marshall.
41. Keay, *India,* 17, quoting Shireen Ratnagar.
42. Thapar, *Early India,* 85.
43. Hopkins, *The Hindu Religious Tradition*, 6.
44. Farmer, "Mythological Functions."
45. Wolpert, *India*, 23, citing M. S. Vats, who directed the latter phase of the Harappan dig.
46. Hopkins, *The Hindu Religious Tradition*, 6–7.
47. Ibid.
48. Wolpert, *India*, 18.
49. Hopkins, *The Hindu Religious Tradition*, 7.
50. Marshall, *Mohenjo-Daro*, 52–56.
51. Keay, *India*, 14.
52. Doniger O'Flaherty, *Siva*.
53. Hopkins, *The Hindu Religious Tradition*, 8.
54. Flood, *Introduction*, 29.
55. Hopkins, *The Hindu Religious Tradition*, 9–10.
56. Knipe, *Hinduism*, 22.
57. Marshall, *Mohenjo-Daro*, 129.
58. Doniger O'Flaherty, *Siva*.
59. A good summary appears in Bryant,

The Quest, 162–64. I am indebted to Brian Collins for rounding up this list and more of them for me.
60. Sullivan, "A Re-examination."
61. Hiltebeitel, "The Indus Valley 'Proto-Shiva' Reexamined."
62. Krishna Rao, *Indus Script Deciphered*.
63. Singh, "Rgvedic Base of the Pasupati Seal of Mohenjo-Daro," citing RV 1.64.
64. S. R. Rao, *Dawn and Devolution of the Indus Civilization*, 288.
65. Fairservis, *The Harappan Civilization and Its Writing*.
66. Parpola, "Deciphering the Indus Script," 248–50.
67. Richter-Ushanas, *The Indus Script and the Rigveda*.
68. Keay, *India*, 14.
69. Thapar, *Early India*, 86.
70. But against this, see Flood, *Introduction*, 28.
71. Hopkins, *The Hindu Religious Tradition*, 6–7.
72. Keay, *India*, 14.
73. Hopkins, *The Hindu Religious Tradition*, 5.
74. Ibid., 9.
75. Doniger O'Flaherty, *Siva*, 238.
76. Keay, *India*, 14.
77. Farmer, "Mythological Functions." Seal H-180-A-B.
78. Ibid.
79. Knipe, *Hinduism*, 21.
80. Thapar, *Early India*, 86.
81. Flood, *Introduction*, 28.
82. Ibid.
83. Wolpert, *India*, 21.
84. Thapar, *Early India*, 94.
85. Ibid.
86. Keay, *India*, 15.
87. Wolpert, *India*, 17.
88. Mitter, *Indian Art,* 8.
89. Keay, *India*, 15.
90. Flood, *Introduction*, 28.
91. Knipe, *Hinduism*, 21.
92. Flood, *Introduction*, 28.
93. Michaels, *Hinduism*, 31.
94. Thapar, *Early India*, 86.
95. Ibid., 85.
96. Wolpert, *India*, 16.
97. Keay, *India*, 14.
98. Michaels, *Hinduism*, 31.
99. Debiprasanna Chattopadhyaya, *Lokayata*.
100. Farmer, Sproat, and Witzel, "The Collapse of the Indus-Script Thesis."
101. Wolpert, *India*, 20.
102. Thapar, *Early India*, 87.
103. Knipe, *Hinduism*, 23
104. Keay, *India*, 5.
105. Metcalf, *A Concise History,* 3.
106. Thapar, *Early India*, 86.
107. Ibid., 88.
108. Hopkins, *The Hindu Religious Tradition*, 8.

109. Thapar, *Early India*, 85.
110. Wolpert, *India*, 17.

CHAPTER 4: BETWEEN THE RUINS AND THE TEXT
1. *Kurma Purana* 1.9.
2. Sir William Jones, "On the Gods of Greece, Italy, and India."
3. West, *Indo-European Poetry and Myth*, 388.
4. Ibid., 386.
5. Ibid., 1.
6. Lincoln, "The Indo-European Cattle-Raiding Myth," 24; also *Priests, Warriors and Cattle*.
7. West, *Indo-European Poetry and Myth*, 191.
8. Ibid., 2.
9. Ibid., 9 and 10.
10. Ibid., 2.
11. But cf. Bryant, *The Quest*, 60–62.
12. Witzel, "Rgvedic History," 325.
13. Thapar, *Early India*, 86–88.
14. Ibid.
15. West, *Indo-European Poetry*, 388.
16. Thapar, *Early India*, 89.
17. West, *Indo-European Poetry*, 447.
18. Witzel, "Indocentrism," 347.
19. Klostermaier, *Hinduism*, 38.
20. Thapar, *Early India*, 86–87.
21. West, *Indo-European Poetry*; Witzel, "Indocentrism."
22. Knott, *Hinduism*, 7, and Flood, *Introduction*, 31, report, but do not endorse, the theory.
23. Hasenpflug ("a retired German defense ministry linguist"), *The Inscriptions of the Indus Civilization*.
24. Klostermaier, *Hinduism*, 36.
25. Hasenpflug, *The Inscriptions of the Indus Civilization*.
26. Subhash C. Kak, cited by Klostermaier, *Hinduism*, 38.
27. David Frawley, cited in ibid.
28. Klostermaier, *Hinduism*, 36.
29. Bryant, *The Quest*, 195.
30. Thapar, *Early India*, 110.
31. Ibid., 109.
32. Keay, *India*, 25.
33. Elst, "Linguistic Aspects," 260 and 262.
34. Ibid., 260.
35. Keay, *India*, 24.
36. Thapar, *Early India*, 109, 113.
37. Flood, *Introduction*, 34.
38. Bryant, *The Quest*, 15, 120.
39. Thapar, *Early India*, 85, 88, 92, 95–96, 107.
40. B. B. Lal, cited by Bryant, *The Quest*, 173.
41. Aasko Parpola, cited by Flood, *Introduction*, 34.
42. Flood, *Introduction*, 34.
43. Keay, *India*, 25.
44. Bryant, *The Quest*, 119-20, 174, 228.
45. Keay, *India*, 25.
46. Elst, cited by Bryant, *The Quest*, 119.
47. Bryant, *The Quest*, 116.

48. West, *Indo-European Poetry*, 467
49. Ibid., 465.
50. Thapar, *Early India*, 109; Flood 34.
51. Thapar, *Early India*, 85.
52. Jha and Rajaram, *The Deciphered Indus Script*.
53. Witzel and Farmer, "Horseplay in Harappa," *Frontline*, October 13, 2000.
54. Subhash C. Kak, cited by Klostermaier, *Hinduism*, 38
55. Flood, *Introduction*, 31.
56. Klostermaier, *Hinduism*, 39.
57. Staal, *Agni*.
58. Thapar, *Early India*, 130.
59. Keay, *India*, 5.
60. Klostermaier, *Hinduism*, 31.

CHAPTER 5: HUMANS, ANIMALS, AND GODS IN THE *RIG VEDA*
1. Thapar, *Early India*, 109. All translations are from Doniger O'Flaherty, *The Rig Veda* and *Hindu Myths*, unless otherwise noted.
2. Keay, *India*, 24.
3. Mitter, *Indian Art*, 9.
4. Doniger O'Flaherty, *Other Peoples' Myths*, chapter 3.
5. *Aitareya Aranyaka* 5.5.3, cited by Staal, "The Concept of Scripture," 122–23.
6. For a discussion of the oral transmission of the *Rig Veda*, see Louis Renou, *The Destiny of the Veda in India*, 25-26 and 84.
7. For a fuller discussion of the relationship between *shruti* and *smriti*, see Brian K. Smith, "Exorcising the Transcendent: Strategies for Defining Hinduism and Religion" and "The Unity of Ritual: The Place of the Domestic Sacrifice in Vedic Ritualism."
8. Müller, *The Rig Veda*, ix.
9. *Taittiriya Samhita* 7.5.25.2.
10. West, *Indo-European Poetry*, 161.
11. Thapar, *Early India*, 113.
12. Romila Thapar's phrase, after George Michell's "portable temple."
13. Jamison, *Sacrificed Wife*, 9.
14. Heesterman, *The Broken World*.
15. William Buck's apt phrases, in his translation of the *Mahabharata*, 9.
16. Doniger O'Flaherty, *Siva*, 96.
17. *Chandogya Upanishad* 8.7–12.
18. West, *Indo-European Poetry*, 246.
19. Ibid.
20. Jamison, *Ravenous Hyenas*, 258–59.
21. RV 10.148.5; 10.94.14; 8.9.10; cf. 1.112.13; 10.123.1–5, 5.52.16 1.84.10–11; 8.6.19, 2.34.2, 5.60.5, 34–36; Doniger O'Flaherty, *Origins of Evil*, 322.
22. *Mahabharata* 12.59.99–128; *Atharva Veda* 8.10.22–29; etc. Doniger O'Flaherty, *Origins of Evil*, 321–48.
23. Doniger O'Flaherty, *Women;* West, *Indo-European Poetry*, 417.

24. Thapar, *Early India*, 115.
25. Gommans, "The Rise of the Indo-Afghan Empire," 71.
26. Ibid., 69.
27. Thapar, *Early India*, 114.
28. *Shatapatha Brahmana* 14.1.1.18–24; Doniger O'Flaherty, *Hindu Myths*, 56–59.
29. Schmidt, "The Origin of Ahimsa."
30. West, *Indo-European Poetry*, 469
31. Ibid., 467.
32. Ibid., 490.
33. Thapar, *Early India*, 116.
34. Parpola, "The Coming of the Aryans to Iran and India."
35. Thapar, *Early India*, 112.
36. Ibid., 122.
37. *Ambatta Sutta* of the *Sutta Nikaya*.
38. Lincoln, *Myth, Cosmos and Society*.
39. West, *Indo-European Poetry*, 100.
40. Flood, *Introduction*, 79.
41. Witzel, "Early Sanskritization."
42. Such as the *vratyastoma*; *Atharva Veda* 15; Nath, *Puranas and Acculturation*, 41.
43. Scheuer, "Rudra-Siva et la destruction du sacrifice."
44. Doniger O'Flaherty, "The Post-Vedic History of the Soma Plant."
45. U.S. Patent and Trademark Office appeal no. 2005-1337, application no. 10/227,006.
46. Wasson, *Soma*; Flood, *Introduction*, 41.
47. As R. Gordon Wasson called it.
48. *Shatapatha Brahmana* 5.5.4.10; Doniger O'Flaherty, *Origins of Evil*, 153.
49. Jamison, *Sacrificed Wife*, 256.
50. Ghosha as the author of 10.40, Apala as the author of 8.91; Doniger O'Flaherty, *The Rig Veda*, 246–46, 256.
51. Jamison, *Sacrificed Wife*.
52. Ibid., 92.
53. For sibling incest, see Yami's unsuccessful attempt to seduce her brother Yama in *Rig Veda* 10.10.
54. West, *Indo-European Poetry*, 500, citing J. P. Mallory, in a section labeled "Suttee."
55. Ibid., citing *Atharva Veda* 18.3.1.
56. Doniger O'Flaherty, *The Rig Veda*, 245–63.
57. RV 10.135, 10.51, 10.124, 4.26–7, 10.108, 10.28, etc.
58. Yami, the twin sister of Yama, in 10.10; Lopamudra, the wife of Agastya, in 1.179.
59. Pururavas, the husband of Urvashi, in 10.95; Doniger O'Flaherty, *The Rig Veda*, 245.
60. Yami is rejected by Yama, Lopamudra by Agastya, Pururavas by Urvashi.
61. Doniger O'Flaherty, *The Rig Veda*, 312. For the porcupine, see *Atharva Veda* 6.13, Shaunaka recension, Bloomfield ed.
62. Doniger, *Splitting the Difference*.
63. Doniger O'Flaherty, *Women*.
64. RV 10.9, 7.49, 10.146, 10.71, 10.125; Doniger

O'Flaherty, *The Rig Veda*, 61–63, 179–182, 199–200, 231–32, 242–45.
65. West, *Indo-European Poetry*, 139.
66. Flood, *Introduction*, 179; West, *Indo-European Poetry*, 139.
67. Bolon, *Forms of the Goddess Lajja Gauri in Indian Art*, figure 52; Kramrisch, "An Image of Aditi-Uttanapad," 259-70.
68. RV 10.72.1–5; O'Flaherty, *The Rig Veda*, 30, 37–40; Sayana on, citing Yaska's *Nirukta* 11.23.
69. Doniger O'Flaherty, *Textual Sources*, 28–29.
70. Dorson, "The Eclipse of Solar Mythology."
71. Staal, *Agni*.
72. Lincoln, "The Indo-European Cattle-Raiding Myth," 18.
73. Thapar, *Early India*, 130.
74. Ibid.
75. Jurewicz, "Prajapati, the Fire and the *pancagnividya*," 188; Gombrich, "Thought on Karma."

CHAPTER 6: SACRIFICE IN THE *BRAHMANAS*

1. The date is sometimes said to be 3102 BCE or 1400 BCE. West, *Indo-European Poetry*, 13; Brockington, *The Sanskrit Epics*.
2. *Jaiminiya Brahmana* 2.182–83; Doniger O'Flaherty, *Tales of Sex and Violence*, 40–42.
3. *Aitareya Brahmana* 3.21.
4. *Shatapatha Brahmana* 1.1.1.6: idam aham ya evaasmi so 'smi.
5. Sayana's commentary on the *Rig Veda* 1.121.
6. Erdosy, *The Indo-Aryans of Ancient South Asia*.
7. Bhandarkar, *Ancient History of India*, 153–54, citing Kautilya and the *Lalita Vistara*.
8. Stein, *A History of India*, 51.
9. Flood, *An Introduction*, 53
10. Mitter, *Indian Art*, 13; Thapar, *Early India*, 109.
11. Thapar, *Early India*, 112
12. Ibid., 89–90.
13. Flood, *An Introduction*, 33; Keay, *India*, 41.
14. Flood, *An Introduction*, 80–81.
15. Witzel, "The Development of the Vedic Canon," 313, 321, 333.
16. Thapar, *Early India*, 130.
17. *Maitrayani Samhita* 4.8.1; *Kathaka Samhita* 30.1.
18. *Aitareya Brahmana* 2.19 (8.1); *Kaushitaki Brahmana* 12.3.
19. Manu 7.130–31.
20. *Shatapatha Brahmana* 13.2.9.6–9; Doniger O'Flaherty, *Textual Sources*, 17–18.
21. Thapar, *Early India*, 129.
22. Heesterman, *The Inner Conflict of Tradition*.
23. *Jaiminiya Brahmana* 3.94-96; Doniger O'Flaherty, *Tales of Sex and Violence*, 81–84.
24. Dumézil, *The Destiny of the Warrior*.
25. *Brihaddevata*; Doniger O'Flaherty, *Tales of Sex and Violence*, 83; Sieg, *Sagenstoffe*,
26. RV 10.119-2-3, 9, 11–12.
27. *Katha Upanishad* 3.3–6.

28. *Jaiminiya Brahmana* 3.94–96; Doniger O'Flaherty, *Tales of Sex and Violence*, 81–84.
29. Jamison, *Sacrificed Wife*.
30. Thapar, *Early India*, 122.
31. *Shatapatha Brahmana* 13.3.8.1–6; Doniger O'Flaherty, *Textual Sources*, 18–19.
32. *Shatapatha Brahmana* 13.2.9.9 and 13.5.2.10; Doniger O'Flaherty, *Tales of Sex and Violence*, 17–18. The mantra is from RV 4.39, a prayer to a racehorse named Dadhikravan.
33. Debroy, *Sarama and Her Children*.
34. *Taittiriya Brahmana* 3.8.4.2; Doniger O'Flaherty, *Textual Sources*, 14–17.
35. Jamison, *Sacrificed Wife*, 78, 99, citing *Maitrayani Samhita* 2.1.19–23 and 3.12.1.
36. White, "Dogs Die," 283–303.
37. *Jaiminiya Brahmana* 2.440–42; Doniger O'Flaherty, *Tales of Sex and Violence*, 97–98.
38. *Kathaka Samhita* 29.1; *Maitrayani Samhita* 3.10.6; *Aitareya Brahmana* 2.22.10.
39. *Jaiminiya Brahmana* 1.161–2; Doniger O'Flaherty, *Tales of Sex and Violence*, 101–02.
40. *Kaushitaki Brahmana* 23.4.
41. *Jaiminiya Brahmana* 1.161–3, Doniger O'Flaherty, *Tales of Sex and Violence*, 101–02.
42. *Jaiminiya Brahmana* 1.42–44, Doniger O'Flaherty, *Tales of Sex and Violence*, 32–34.
43. *Kaushitaki Brahmana* 11.3; Doniger O'Flaherty, *Tales of Sex and Violence*, 39.
44. *Shatapatha Brahmana* 12.9.1.1; Doniger O'Flaherty, *Tales of Sex and Violence*, 40.
45. Nandy, *Exiled at Home,* 47 and 63; Doniger O'Flaherty, *Tales of Sex and Violence*, 36–37.
46. Thapar, *Early India*, 115.
47. *Shatapatha Brahmana* 11.7.1.3; cf. 12.8.3.12.
48. D. N. Jha, *The Myth of the Holy Cow,* 30–36; Keith, *Religion and Philosophy*, 324–26; Heesterman, *The Broken World*, 194, 283, n. 32; Renou, *Vedic India,* 109.
49. D.N. Jha, *The Myth of the Holy Cow*, 47; *Taittiriya Samhita* 5.6.11–20.
50. Cf. *Ashvalayana Grihya-sutra* 1.24, 31–33, for the ritual of killing a cow on the arrival of a guest.
51. *Apastamba Dharmasutra* 1.17.30 31.
52. Thapar, *Early India*, 90.
53. *Shatapatha Brahmama* 3.1.2.21.
54. Thapar, *Early India*, 115.
55. See the introduction, by Wendy Doniger and Brian K. Smith, to *The Laws of Manu*. See also the conflict between sacrifice and nonviolence in Doniger O'Flaherty, *Other Peoples' Myths*, chapter 4.
56. *Atharva Veda* 11.2.9 and 3.10.6, with Sayana's commentary.
57. Doniger O'Flaherty, *Other Peoples' Myths*, chapter 4.
58. *Shatapatha Brahmana* 13.6.1–2; *Vajasaneyi Samhita* 30.1–22; *Taittiriya Brahmana* 3.4.1.1 ff.
59. Sharma, *The Excavations at Kausambi*, 87ff.; Schlinghoff, "Menschenopfer in Kausambi."

60. Sauve, "The Divine Victim"; Willibald Kirfel, "Der Asvamedha und der Purusamedha."
61. Flood, *Introduction*, 41; Heesterman, *The Broken World*, 10.
62. Lincoln, *Myth, Cosmos, and Society*, 183 n.
63. For men as the sacrificial beasts of the gods, see Doniger O'Flaherty, *The Origins of Evil*, 169–73.
64. *Shatapatha Brahmana* 11.7.1.3; *Taittiriya Brahmana* 3.9.17.4–5.
65. See the discussion of human sacrifice in Parpola, "The Pre-Vedic Indian Background," 49–53; Weber, "Purusamedakandha" and "Ueber Menschenopfer"; Wilson, "On the Sacrifice of Human Beings"; Mitra, "On Human Sacrifices."
66. *Shatapatha Brahmana* 1.2.3.6–7; *Aitareya Brahmana* 2.8; Levi, *La doctrine,* 136–37.
67. Eggeling, *Shatapatha Brahmana*, I, 49.
68. *Aitareya Brahmana* 7.13–18; Doniger O'Flaherty, *Textual Sources,* 20–25.
69. *Brihadaranyaka Upanishad* 1.4.10; *Shatapatha Brahmana* 14.4.2.21–22; Doniger O'Flaherty, *Origins of Evil*, 91.
70. Doniger O'Flaherty, *Origins of Evil*, 171–73.
71. *Shatapatha Brahmana* 13.2.8.1–4.
72. Doniger O'Flaherty, *Textual Sources* 14–19.
73. *Taittiriya Samhita* 7.4.19; Doniger O'Flaherty, *Women*, 154–61; *Textual Sources*, 15–19.
74. *Shatapatha Brahmana* 1.9.9.
75. Grottanelli, "Yoked Horses."
76. Doniger O'Flaherty, *The Rig Veda*, 257–263; Jamison, *Sacrificed Wife*, 77–88, further developed this connection between the horse sacrifice and RV 10.86, and showed that the monkey is a mock horse and the poem a mock horse sacrifice.
77. *Shatapatha Brahmana* 13.2.9.6–9; Doniger O'Flaherty, *Textual Sources*, 17–18.
78. *Jaiminiya Brahmana* 3.199–200; Doniger O'Flaherty, *Tales of Sex and Violence*, 75–76.
79. Doniger, *Splitting the Difference*.
80. Doniger O'Flaherty, *The Rig Veda*, 253–56.
81. *Shatapatha Brahmana* 11.5.1.1–17; Doniger O'Flaherty, *Women*, 180–81.
82. Doniger O'Flaherty, *Women*, 180–81.
83. Doniger O'Flaherty, *Textual Sources*, 12–13.
84. Doniger O'Flaherty, *Origins of Evil*, 216–19.
85. *Shatapatha Brahmana* 10.2.6.190.
86. Ibid, 11.1.6.6; Doniger O'Flaherty, *Origins of Evil*, 217; *Textual Sources*, 29–30.
87. *Shatapatha Brahmana* 10.4.4.1-3. Doniger O'Flaherty, *The Origins of Evil*, 217.
88. *Shatapatha Brahmana* 11.1.6.6; Doniger O'Flaherty, *The Origins of Evil,* 217.
89. Tull, *The Vedic Origins of Karma*.
90. *Shatapatha Brahmana* 10.4.4.1–3; Doniger O'Flaherty, *The Origins of Evil*, 217.
91. Tull, *The Vedic Origins of Karma*.
92. *Taittiriya Brahmana* 3.11.8.1–6.
93. *Katha Upanishad* 1–2, 6.18.
94. Tale Type 369, 465C, 466, 812.
95. Thompson, *Motif Index* A 1715.

96. Jamison, *Ravenous Hyenas.*
97. Julius Eggeling, cited in Doniger O'Flaherty, *Tales of Sex and Violence,* 4–5.
98. *Aitareya Brahmana, Maitrayani Samhita, Kathaka Samhita;* Doniger O'Flaherty, *Tales of Sex and Violence,* 12.
99. Doniger O'Flaherty, "The Post-Vedic History."
100. Wasson, *Soma.*
101. *Jaiminiya Brahmana* 2.369–70; Doniger O'Flaherty, *Origins of Evil,* 140.
102. *Shatapatha Brahmana* 5.5.4.10; Doniger O'Flaherty, *Origins of Evil,* 153.
103. *Taittiriya Samhita* 2.5.1.
104. Tale Type 3.2.8.9-12; *Taittiriya Samhita* 4.1.9; *Atharva Veda* 6.113.
105. *Shatapatha Brahmana* 1.2.3.2–4.
106. *Jaiminiya Brahmana* 1.97–98; Doniger O'Flaherty, *Tales of Sex and Violence,* 51–52. Cf. *Chandogya Upanishad* 1.2.1–6.
107. Doniger O'Flaherty, *Origins of Evil.*

CHAPTER 7. RENUNCIATION IN
THE UPANISHADS
1. *Chandogya Upanishad* 4.4; Doniger O'Flaherty, *Textual Studies,* 31–32.
2. Keay, *India,* 52.
3. Ibid., 63.
4. Thapar, *Early India,* 138.
5. Ibid., 148.
6. Gombrich, *Theravada Buddhism,* 51–58.
7. Derrett, *Dharmasastra and Juridical Literature,* 4–5, 11-12
8. This page, and indeed much of my discussion of the history of India during this period, owes much to conversations with Laura Desmond.
9. Gombrich, "Dating the Buddha."
10. Joel Brereton and Patrick Olivelle have argued, fairly convincingly, that it should rather be translated, "And that's how you are." Olivelle, *Early Upanishads.*
11. *Manu* 3.100; cf. 4.201: The same karmic transfers results from bathing in another man's tank without his permission.
12. Doniger O'Flaherty, introductions to *Karma and Rebirth* and to 2nd ed. *Origins of Evil.*
13. Doniger O'Flaherty, *Origins of Evil,* 248–71.
14. Keay, *India,* 49.
15. Fairservis, *Roots;* Zimmerman, *The Jungle.*
16. Roth, *I Married a Communist,* 72.
17. Flood, *Introduction,* 83.
18. Doniger O'Flaherty, *Karma,* 4.
19. Thapar, *Early India,* 130.
20. Ibid., 132.
21. Heesterman, *The Broken World.*
22. Doniger O'Flaherty, *Karma,* introduction.
23. Thapar, *Early India,* 132
24. Olivelle, *Samnyasa Upanishads,* 116, 123,132–33, 137–39, 152, 157–61.
25. Doniger O'Flaherty, *Dreams,* 149–58.

26. Flood, *Introduction,* 87–88, citing Heesterman.
27. Ibid., 53.
28. Thapar, *Early India,* 132.
29. *Maitrayani Samhita* 4.8.1; *Kathaka Samhita* 30.1
30. Flood, *Introduction,* 87.
31. Obeyesekere, *Imagining Karma.*
32. Thapar, *Early India,* 128.
33. Garbe, "Lokayata."
34. Olivelle, *The Ashrama System,* 9–16.
35. Flood, *Introduction,* 81–82; Doniger O'Flaherty, "The Origins of Heresy."
36. Patanjali, cited by Flood, *Introduction,* 82; cf. Thapar, *Early India,* 63.
37. Flood, *Introduction,* 148.
38. Thapar, *Early India,* 131.
39. Klostermaier, *Hinduism,* 34; cf. Flood, *Introduction,* 86.
40. Insler, "The Shattered Head."
41 *Skanda Purana* 1.2.13.62.
42. Thapar, *Early India,* 262.
43. In the Pali canon, the story is preserved in *Anguttara Nikaya* 8.51 and in the Cullavagga section of the *Vinaya.*
44. My insights into early sutras in general, and this paragraph in particular, come from Laura Desmond.
45. *Ramayana* 5.20.3.
46. Olivelle, *Early Upanishads,* 356.
47. West, *Indo-European Poetry,* 22.
48. Biardeau, *Hinduism,* 31.
49. *Aitareya Brahmana* 2.8–9.
50. Heesterman, *The Inner Conflict.*
51. *Aitareya Brahmana* 7.13–18.
52. Madan, *Non-renunciation.*
53. Doniger O'Flaherty, *Siva,* 44–68.
54. Ernst, "Situating Sufism and Yoga."
55. Narayan, *Storytellers, Saints and Scoundrels.*
56. Jamison, *Sacrificed Wife,* 16–17.
57. Doniger O'Flaherty, *Siva.*

CHAPTER 8. THE THREE (OR IS IT FOUR?) AIMS OF
LIFE IN THE HINDU IMAGINARY
1. Ashvaghosha, *Buddhacarita,* 2.14.
2. V. Shekhawat, "Origin and Structure of *Purushartha* Theory."
3. Larson and Bhattacharya, eds., *Samkhya;* Larson, "India Through Hindu Categories."
4.. Larson, *Classical Samkhya.*
5.. Larson and Bhattacharya, eds., *Samkhya.*
6. Gamkrelidze and Ivanov, *Indo-European and the Indo-Europeans,* 408–11.
7. Cf. religion as the model of and the model for, in Geertz, "Religion as a Cultural System."
8. Olivelle, *Dharmasutras,* xxxiii–iv.
9. Cf. M 8.52–57 and AS 3.1.19; M 7.102 and AS 1.4.5; M 7.105 and AS 1.15.60; M 9.280 and AS 4.11.7
10. Olivelle, "Manu and the *Arthasastra*" and Olivelle, Introduction to *Manu,* xx.

11. *Divyavadana*, *Ashokavadana*, and others.
12. Wilhelm, "The Concept of Dharma in Artha and Kama Literature."
13. Brian K. Smith, *Classifying the Universe*.
14. Harsha, *Priyadarshika*, act 2.
15. *Mandukya Upanishad* 3–7.
16. Erdman, "The Empty Beat."
17. Organ, "Three into Four."
18. Olivelle, *The Ashrama System*.
19. Organ, "Three into Four."
20. Doniger O'Flaherty, *Siva*.
21. Doniger, "Three (or More) Forms."
22. Doniger O'Flaherty, *Siva*, 76–77.
23. Dumont, *Homo Hierarchicus*.
24. Heesterman, *The Inner Conflict of Society*.
25. Doniger O'Flaherty, *Siva*.
26. *Mahabharata* 1.187 (three variants of this verse occur at 1.App. I.1.35–36, 1.App. I.5.18–19, and 18.App. I.3.31–32).
27. Krishna, *Indian Philosophy*, chapters 4, to 11.
28. Doniger O'Flaherty, *The Origins of Evil*, 94–97 and 128–31.

CHAPTER 9. WOMEN AND OGRESSES IN
THE *RAMAYANA*
1. Chakravarti, *Themes in Indian History*, 53.
2. Ibid., 68.
3. Michell, *Hindu Art and Architecture*, 40.
4. Thapar, *Early India*, 148.
5. Heesterman, *The Ancient Indian Royal Consecration*.
6. Thapar, *Early India*, 143.
7. Mitter, *Indian Art*, 13.
8. Bosworth, "Calanus and the Brahman Opposition."
9. Mitter, *Indian Art*, 24.
10. Keay, *India*, 78.
11. Ibid., 70.
12. Thapar, *Early India*, 194.
13. Ibid., 200.
14. Mathur, *Art and Culture*, 1–3.
15. Flood, *Introduction*, 51.
16. Bana, *Harshahcarita*.
17. Mann, *The Sources of Social Power*, 359.
18. Keay, *India*, 103.
19. Thapar, *Early India*, 210–12. The inscription is at the Elephant's Cave (Hathigumpha).
20. Hiltebeiteil, *Rethinking*.
21. Ruben, *Ueber die Frage der Objectivität*, 114, cited by Hiltebeitel, *Rethinking*, 177.
22. Pollock, *Ramayana*, vl. 2, 32–33, but cf. Stein, *A History of India*, 51.
23. West, *Indo-European Poetry*, 469.
24. Ibid., 63; *Shatapatha Brahmana* 13.1.5.6.
25. Lord, *The Singer of Tales*.
26. Chakravarti, *Themes in Indian History*, 74.
27. Dalrymple, "Homer in India: Rajasthan's Oral Epics," 54.
28. Flood, *Introduction*, 105.
29. Nath, *Puranas and Acculturation*, 66.

30. Pollock "Atmanam Manusam Manye," 234–35, citing Tryambaka.
31. Ibid., 242, citing Govindaraja.
32. Doniger O'Flaherty, *Dreams*, 92; *Hindu Myths*, 198–204.
33. R, after 7.88, appendix I, no. 13, 21–25; cf. Doniger, *Splitting the Difference*, 9–27.
34. Doniger, *Splitting the Difference*.
35. Grottannelli, "The King's Grace and the Helpless Woman."
36. Grottanelli, "Yoked Horses, Twins, and the Powerful Lady"; Cornelia Dimmitt, "Sita: Fertility Goddess and *Shakti*."
37. R 1.65.11–14, using the alternative lines rejected by the critical edition, including five lines omitted after verse 13ab; Doniger O'Flaherty, *Textual Sources*, 58–59.
38. R, between 6.9 and 6.10, appendix I, no. 3, verses 278–80.
39. Doniger, *Splitting the Difference*, 88–110.
40. Shulman. "Sita and Satakantharavana."
41. Ibid.
42. Masson, "Fratricide and the Monkeys."
43. Lutgendorf, *Hanuman's Tale*.
44. The term "side shadows" was coined by Gary Saul Morson (after Bakhtin), in *Narrative and Freedom*.
45. Jones, *On the Nightmare*. Freud (in *The Interpretation of Dreams*) also wrote about this.
46. Doniger, *The Bedtrick*, 118–22.
47. *Ramayana* passage rejected by critical edition at 2.32, appendix 1, 14, 36–54. Cf. *Jataka* #386 (the *Kharaputta Jataka*) about a cobra woman and talking animals.
48. Masson, "Who Killed Cock Kraunca?"
49. *Ramayana* 7, appendix 1, no. 8, lines 332–465.
50. Nath, *Puranas and Acculturation*, 102.
51. Pollock, *Ramayana*, vol. 3, 69–70, citing Talboys-Wheeler, *The History of India from the Earliest Ages* (1869).
52. Goldman, *Ramayana*, vol. 1, 26, citing Gorresio.
53. Nath, *Puranas and Acculturation*, 39, 103.
54. Doniger O'Flaherty, *Siva*.
55. Pollock, *Ramayana*, vol. 2, 403–04, 470, notes.

CHAPTER 10. VIOLENCE IN THE *MAHABHARATA*
1. 13th Major Rock Edict, trans, Thapar, *Ashoka*, 255–56; Nikam and McKeon, *Edicts*, 27–29; Sircar, *Inscriptions of Asoka*, 50–52.
2. Second separate rock edict; Thapar, *Ashoka*, 258; Nikam, *Edicts*, 53; Sircar, *Inscriptions*, 41-42.
3. 2nd Pillar Edict; Thapar, *Ashoka*, 262; Nikam, *Edicts*, 41; Sircar, *Inscriptions*, 62–63.
4. Irwin, "Ashokan Pillars."
5. Mitter, *Indian Art*, 14–15.
6. Kandahar bilingual rock inscription; Thapar, *Ashoka*, 261.
7. 4th Major Rock Edict, trans. Thapar, *Ashoka*, 251; Nikam McKeon, *Edicts*, 31; Sircar, *Inscriptions*, 42–43.

8. 11th Major Rock Edict, Sircar, *Inscriptions*, 48.
9. 1st Major Rock Edict, trans. Thapar, *Ashoka*, 250. Nikam and McKeon add "daily," to the last line, 55; Sircar, 41, does not.
10. Thapar, *Ashoka*, 203, "his personal preference."
11. 5th Pillar Edict. Nikam and Mckeon, *Edicts*, 56; Sircar, *Inscriptions*, 64–65.
12. 9th Major Rock Edict, Nikam and McKeon, *Edicts*, 46; Sircar, *Inscriptions*, 46–47.
13. Thapar, *Ashoka*, 202.
14. 12th Major Rock Edict, Thapar, *Ashoka*, 255; Nikam and McKeon, *Edicts*, 51–52; Sircar, *Inscriptions*, 49.
15. 9th Major Rock Edict, trans. Thapar, *Ashoka*, 254; Nikam and McKeon, *Edicts*, 46; Sircar, *Inscriptions*, 46–47.
16. Fourth Major Rock Edict, trans. Thapar, *Ashoka*, 251; Nikam and McKeon, *Edicts*, 31; Sircar, *Inscriptions*, 42–43.
17. Thapar, *Ashoka*, 203.
18. Keay, *India*, 104.
19. Ibid., 91.
20. Thapar, *Early India*, 275.
21. Mann, *The Sources of Social Power*, 359.
22. Thapar, *Early India*, 228.
23. Flood, *Introduction*, 103.
24. Nath, *Puranas and Acculturation*, 104.
25. Michell, *Art and Architecture*, 40–43.
26. *Mahabharata* 7.173, 10.18.1–23, 12.343, 13.76.
27. Doniger O'Flaherty, *Origins of Evil*, 278.
28. Flood, *Introduction*, 218–19.
29. Keay, *India*, 108.
30. Flood, *Introduction*, 119
31. Thapar, *Early India*, 139; Chakravarti, *Themes in Indian History*, 74B.
32. Doniger O'Flaherty, *Tales of Sex and Danger*.
33. Kulke and Rothermund, *A History of India*, 45.
34. Gonzalez-Riemann, *The Mahabharata and the Yugas*.
35. Scharf, *Ramopakhayana*.
36. Harold Bloom, *The Anxiety of Influence*.
37. The *Raghavapandaviya* of Dhananjaya.
38. Hiltebeitel, *The Ritual of Battle*, 14–15.
39. Singer, *When a Great Tradition Modernizes*, 75–76.
40. Also *Mahabharata* 1.56.34; cf. 18.5.38: "Whatever is here about dharma, profit, pleasure, and Release . . ."
41. Hermann Oldenberg, as quoted in Sukthankar, *On the Meaning of the Mahabharata*, 1; Hopkins, *Great Epic of India*, 58; John D. Smith, "Old Indian (The Two Sanskrit Epics)," 50.
42. Reich, *A Battlefield of a Text*; "Sacrificial Violence and Textual Battles."
43. Collins, "Violence, Power and Sacrifice in the Indian Context."
44. Fitzgerald, *The Mahabharata*, v. 7, 123.
45. Doniger O'Flaherty, "Horses and Snakes."
46. Van Buitenen, *The Mahabharata*, book 1, 4.
47. Hiltebeitel, *Rethinking the Mahabharata*, 171.
48. Ibid., 200–02.

49. I owe this realization to Lorraine Daston, Berlin, 2002.
50. Houben et al. and Tull, "The Killing That Is Not Killing."
51. Tilak, *Srimad BhagavadGita-Rahasya*, 44.
52. Biardeau, *Hinduism*, 31.
53. Hiltebeitel, *Rethinking the Mahabharatas*, 202–14.
54. Fitzgerald, *The Mahabharata*, 112.
55. Strong, *Ashokvadana*.
56. Selvanayagam, "Asoka and Arjuna."
57. Fitzgerald, *The Mahabharata*, 122.
58. Also in passages rejected, and not even printed as appendices, in the critical edition. See Ulrich, *Divided Bodies*.
59. Jataka 499 and Jatakamala #2.
60. Collins, "Violence, Power and Sacrifice in the Indian Context."
61. RV 1.117.22; *Shatapatha Brahmana* 14.1.1.18–24; Doniger O'Flaherty, *Hindu Myths*, 56–60.
62. Allen, "Why Did Odysseus Become a Horse?," 148.

CHAPTER 11. DHARMA IN THE *MAHABHARATHA*
1. *Apastamba Dharma Sutra* 1.7.20.6.
2. Apastamba and Gautama were probably third century BCE, Baudhayana second century BCE, and Vasistha first century CE; Olivelle, *Dharmasutras*, xxxiii.
3. Selvanayagam, "Ashoka and Arjuna."
4. Flood, *Introduction*, 148.
5. Thapar, *Early India*, 278.
6. Chakravarti, *The Social Dimensions of Early Buddhism;* Gombrich, *Theravada Buddhism*.
7. Thapar, *Early India*, 279
8. Nath, *Puranas and Acculturation*, 27.
9. Thapar, *Early India*, 124.
10. Thapar, *From Lineage to State*, 170.
11. Thapar, *Early India*, 125.
12. Ibid., 124.
13. Ghurye, *The Scheduled Tribes*; Srinivas, *Social Change in Modern India*.
14. Thapar, *Early India*, 126.
15. Keay, *India*, 189.
16. Turner, *The Forest of Symbols*; Brian Smith, *Classifying the Universe*.
17. Brodbeck, "Ekalavya and Mahabharata 1.121–128."
18. Hemavijayagani, *Katharatnakara* 185.20," story no. 163, "The Story of the Bhilla," pp. 185–86.
19. Doniger, *Bedtrick*, 248–54.
20. Doniger and Spinner, "Misconceptions."
21. Doniger, *Splitting the Difference*.
22. *Naishadiyacarita* 17.132.
23. For Yavakri in the *Jaiminiya Brahmana* and *Mahabharata*, see Doniger O'Flaherty, *Tales of Sex and Violence*.
24. Bulcke, "La naissance de Sita"; Dubuisson, "La déesse chevelue."

25. Hiltebeitel, *The Cult of Draupadi*.
26. Kinsley, *Hindu Goddesses*, 107–09, 151–02.
27. *Mahabharata* 12, appendix 1, no. 28, lines 72–75.
28. Kinsley, *The Sword and the Flute;* Hiltebeitel, *The Ritual of Battle*.
29. Thapar, *Early India*, 228.
30. Mitter, *Indian Art*, 16.
31. Thapar, *Early India*, 193.
32. Pathak, "The Things Kings Sing."

CHAPTER 12. ESCAPE CLAUSES IN THE SHASTRAS
1. Much of the background material and a number of insights in this chapter were provided by Laura Desmond. See also Desmond, *Disciplining Pleasure*.
2. Derrett, *Dharmasastra and Juridical Literature*, 4–5, 11–12.
3. Keay, *India*, 101, 104.
4. Thapar, *Early India*, 261
5. Keay, *India*, 102.
6. Ibid., 125.
7. Mitter, *Indian Art*, 45.
8. Thapar, *Early India*, 279
9. AS 2.30.29, 13.2.20, 39–43.
10. Keay, *India*, 104.
11. Thapar, *Early India*, 219.
12. Keay, *India,* 112 .
13. Flood, *Introduction*, 51.
14. Mitter, *Indian Art*, 46–47.
15. Keay, *India,* 112.
16. Thapar, *Early India*, 223.
17. Ibid., 224; Keay, *India*, 131.
18. Kosambi, *An Introduction to the Study of Indian History*, 286.
19. Thapar, *Early India*, 223.
20. Chakravarti, *Themes in Indian History*, 63.
21. Mitter, *Indian Art*, 27.
22. Keay, *India*, 125.
23. Ibid., 127.
24. Thapar, *Early India*, 279.
25. Pollock, "From Discourse of Ritual to Discourse of Power in Sanskrit Culture."
26. Pollock, "India in the Vernacular Millennium."
27. Thapar, *Early India*, 258; Zysk, *Asceticism and Healing*.
28. *Gautama Dharma-sutra* 4.16–18; *Baudhayana Dharma-sutra* 1.16.6–16, 17.1–14.
29. Deliege, *The Untouchables of India*.
30. *Manu* 2.108–16, 3.8–11, 3.127–86, 236–50, 4.205–23, 8.61–88, 9.143–47, 10.5–61, 11.55–71, 12.54–72.
31. *Amar Chitra Katha, Mahabharata* #3, "The Advent of the Kuru Princes," 13, paraphrasing the Sanskrit text, *Mahabharata* 1.111.31, which in turn paraphrases, and indeed reverses the point of, *Manu* 9.158–60.
32. Galanter, *Competing Equalities*.
33. *Gautama Dharmasutra* 22.14.
34. *Manu* 8.370–71, 9.30, 8.34, 11.109–15.

35. *Manu* 4.205–223, 5.5–44, 6.229–240, 8.296–298, 8.324–8, 11.132–44, 10.896–89, 11.54–227.
36. Brian K. Smith, *Reflections on Resemblances, Ritual, and Religion*, 198–99.
37. Veena Das, *Structure and Cognition*, 29, citing the *Dharmaranya Purana*.
38. Doniger and Smith, "Sacrifice and Substitution."
39. Biardeau, *Hinduism*, 64.
40. Doniger O'Flaherty, *Siva*, 223.
41. Heesterman, *The Ancient Indian Royal Consecration*.
42. Tyagi, *Women Workers*, 181.
43. Chand, *Liquor Menace in India*, 3.
44. Wilson, *Charming Cadavers*.
45. Dandin, "The Adventures of the Ten Princes," 13.63–69, trans. Onians.
46. Thapar, *Early India*, 262.
47. Doniger, *The Implied Spider*, chapter 5.
48. Gold, "The 'Jungli Rani' and Other Troubled Wives."
49. *Apastamba Dharmasutra* 2.11.17–20, 2.12.1.
50. Doniger, *Splitting the Difference*.
51. Sweet and Zwilling, "The First Medicalization."
52. Keay, *India*, 154.

CHAPTER 13. BHAKTI IN SOUTH INDIA
1. Blake Wentworth provided the chronology as well as much of the background material on South Indian history and Tamil literature in this chapter. See also Wentworth, *Yearning for a Dreamed Real: The Procession of the Lord in the Tamil Ulas*.
2. Cuntarar, *Patikam* 14, on *Tiruppaccilacciramam*, verse two (of fourteen), trans. David Shulman, in Doniger O'Flaherty, *Textual Sources*, 170.
3. Julius Lipner used this metaphor in his book *Hindus*. Others have used it too, and for good reason.
4. Kulke and Rotermund, *History of India*, 93.
5. Keay, *India,* 119.
6. Thapar, *Early India*, 243.
7. Keay, *India*, 121, 123.
8. Thapar, *Early India* 235.
9. Keay, *India*, 223.
10. Ibid., 168.
11. Mitter, *Indian Art*, 49.
12. Nath, *Puranas and Acculturation*, 176.
13. Keay, *India*, 219.
14. Ibid., 120.
15. Flood, *Introduction*, 128.
16. Thapar, *Early India*, 234.
17. Flood, *Introduction*, 113.
18. Ramanujan, *Interior Landscape*, 110.
19. Flood, *Introduction*, 169.
20. Ramanujan and Cutler, "From Classicism to Bhakti," 244.
21. Flood, *Introduction*, 131. Cf. Narayanan, "The *Ramayana* in the Theology."

22. Ramanujan, "Varieties of Bhakti," 330.
23. Ramanujan and Cutler, "From Classicism to Bhakti," 232.
24. Ibid., 253.
25. Doniger O'Flaherty, *Dreams*, 286, citing Penrose, "In Praise of Illusion," 274.
26. Ramanujan, "The Myths of Bhakti," 298.
27. Keay, *India,* 169. It is also the earliest dated reference to Kalidasa.
28. Mitter, *Indian Art*, 48.
29. *Tantrakhyana* tale no. 1, cited in Doniger and Smith, trans., *The Laws of Manu*, 92.
30. Rabe, "The Mahamallapuram Prasasti."
31. Ibid., 216–18.
32. Ibid., xxviii, 221.
33. Mitter, *Indian Art*, 57–58. It was called Gangaikondacolapuram.
34. Inden, *Imagining India*, 259.
35. Wujastyk, "Change and Continuity."
36. Mitter, *Indian Art*, 45.
37. Ibid., 58–59; Orr, *Donors, Devotees, and Daughters of God.*
38. Doniger O'Flaherty, *Animals in Four Worlds*, 6-7, 8.
39. Sesser, *Travels in Southeast Asia.*
40. Keay, *India,* 216, 220, 223.
41. Carman, *Theology of Ramanuja,* 27.
42. Keay, *India,* 213, 218 quoting G. W. Spencer.
43. Mitter, *Indian Art*, 57–58.
44. Ibid., 54.
45. Ibid., 48; Flood, *Introduction*, 113.
46. Ramanujan and Cutler, "From Classicism to Bhakti," 234, 236.
47. Keay, *India*, 174.
48. Ramanujan and Cutler, "From Classicism to Bhakti," 238–40.
49. Keay, *India*, 219.
50. Ali, *Courtly Culture.*
51. Eck, *Darshan.*
52. Gombrich, "The Buddha's Eye."
53. Dalrymple, "Homer in India," 52.
54. Doniger, *Splitting the Difference.*
55. *Ashokavadana* 27.
56. Shulman, *Songs of the Harsh Devotee.*
57. Ramanujan, *Speaking of Siva*, 131.
58. Hawley and Juergensmeyer, *Songs of the Saints*, 120.
59. Flood, *Introduction*, 131, says she was the daughter of a Brahmin priest; other traditions make her of low caste.
60. Mangaiyarkkarasi was the queen; Isainani Ammaiyar, the mother. Prentiss, "Joyous Encounters," 76.
61. Indira Peterson places her in the fifth century ("Tamil Saiva Hagiography," 194).
62. Cekkiyar *Periya Puranam,* 157–62.
63. Karaikkalammaiyar, *Tiruvalankattu-mutta-tiruppatikam*, trans. Cutler, *Songs of Experience*, 121.
64. Ramanujan, "On Women Saints," 274.

65. Ibid., 271–74.
66. Ibid.
67. Nammalvar, *Tiruvaymoli* 9.9.10; Ramanujan, *Hymns for the Drowning*, 32.
68. Nammalvar, *Tiruvaymoli* 2.4.10; Ramanujan and Cutler, "From Classicism," 249.
69. Basavanna, trans. Ramanujan, *Speaking of Siva*, 71.
70. Shulman, *Tamil Temple Myths*, 314–15, cited by Ramanujan ("Myths of Bhakti," 298–99), who calls it the legend of Matrbhuteshvara (or, in Tamil, Tayumanavar), "he who even became a mother."
71. The story is retold in the Sanskrit *Skanda Purana, Kedara Khanda* 5.111–97, 22.1–64; see Doniger, "The Scrapbook," 66–70.
72. *Periya Purana* 16 (650–830), McGlasham trans. 71–86.
73. Ramanujan, "Myths of bhakti," 306.
74. Keay, *India*, 219.
75. Ibid.
76. Ramanujan, "On Women Saints," 271.
77. *Periya Purana* 24 (1041–1077), McGlasham trans., 103–06.
78. Ebeling, "Another Tomorrow for Nantanar."
79. K. M. Sen, *Hinduism*, 79.
80. Ibid., 81.
81. Flood, *Introduction*, 131.
82. Ramanujan, *Hymns for the Drowning*, xi.
83. Shulman, *Tamil Temple Myths*, 158; *The Hungry God.*
84. M. G. S. Narayanan, *Cultural Symbiosis in Kerala*, xi.
85. Keay, *India,* 219; Flood, *Introduction*, 170.
86. Keay, *India*, 194.
87. Flood, *Introduction*, 131.
88. Keay, *India*, 219
89. Ulrich, "Food Fights."
90. This is part of the guru lineage in the Vadagali tradition and in the hagiography of Tamil saints known as the *Divyasuricharitam*. See Monius, *Imagining a Place for Buddhism.*
91. *Tiruvatavurar Purana,* canto 6, cited by Pope, *The Sacred Kurral*, xxx–xxxii, lxvii–lxxii.
92. *Periya Purana* 34, 2497–2540, 2780–2824, McGlasham trans., 240–243.
93. Ibid., 34, 2576–2753, McGlasham trans.
94. Thapar, *Cultural Transaction*, 17; Marr, "The 'Periya Puranam' Frieze," 278.
95. Marr, "The 'Periya Puranam' Frieze," 268.
96. Monius, "Love, Violence, and the Aesthetics of Disgust," 117, 126, 155.
97. Marr, "The 'Periya Puranam' Frieze," 279.
98. Ibid., 278.
99. Thapar: *Cultural Transaction*, 17–18, citing P. B. Desai, *Jainism in South India*, 82–83, 401–02.
100. Ibid., 18.
101. Goel, *Hindu Temples*, 413, citing the inscription reproduced in *Epigraphica Indica*, vol., 255.
102. Thapar, *Cultural Transaction*, 18; cf. Bukka I

and the Jainas, in Verghese, *Religious Traditions at Vijayanagara*, 121.

103. Davis, *Lives of Indian Images*.

104. *Pidana, mardana, khandana*, and *dvesha*. Ulrich, "Food Fights."

105. This Syriac version of the *Acts of Thomas* is available in Wright, *Apocryphal Acts of the Apostles*, 146–49.

106. Thapar, *Early India*, 25.

107. M. G. S. Narayanan, *Cultural Symbiosis in Kerala*, x, 4.

108. Ibid., 23–30.

109. Keay, *India*, 181.

110. *Bhagavata Mahatmya*, verses 48–49 of chapter 1, citing the *Padma Purana*. See Prentiss, *The Embodiment of Bhakti*, 35.

111. Doniger O'Flaherty, "The Origins of Heresy."

112. Prentiss, *The Embodiment of Bhakti*, 35.

113. Ramanujan, "The Myths of Bhakti," 307.

CHAPTER 14. GODDESSES AND GODS IN THE EARLY PURANAS

1.Kalidasa, *Shakuntala* 3.2 (alternative verse).

2. Mitter, *Indian Art*, 28.

3. Keay, *India*, 145, citing the third Jungadh inscription.

4. Ibid., citing Beal, *Si yu ki* xxxvii–xxxviii.

5. Keay, *India*, 144.

6. Mitter, *Indian Art*, 2.

7. Ibid., 28.

8. Thapar, *Early India*, 287.

9. Keay, *India*, 139.

10. Ibid., 144.

11. Flood, *Introduction*, 113.

12. Mitter, *Indian Art*, 2.

13. Hein, "A Revolution in Krsnaism," 309–10.

14. Keay, *India*, xx.

15. Mitter, *Indian Art*, 30.

16. Ibid., 31.

17. Thapar, *Early India*, 281.

18. Thapar, *Sakuntala*, 256.

19. Doniger, "Jewels of Rejection."

20. Goldman, "Karma, Guilt, and Buried Memories," 423.

21. Thapar, *Sakuntala*, 41.

22. Keay, *India*, 136–37.

23. Doniger O'Flaherty, "The Image of the Heretic."

24. Ramanujan and Cutler, "From Classicism to Bhakti," 232.

25. Thapar, *Early India*, 244.

26. Ibid., 275.

27. Mitter, *Indian Art*, 45–47.

28. Keay, *India*, 158.

29. Thapar, *Early India*, 287.

30. Ben Shonthal's vivid formulation.

31. Nath, *Puranas and Acculturation*, 8.

32. Thapar, *Early India*, 275.

33. Mitter, *Indian Art*, 56.

34. Nath, *Puranas and Acculturation*, 67.

35. Thapar, *Early India*, 275.

36. Redfield, *The Little Community*.

37. www.censusindia.gov.in/Census_Data_2001/India_at_glance/rural.aspx

38. Narayana Rao, "Hinduism: The Untold Story."

39. Nath, *Puranas and Acculturation*.

40. Narayana Rao, "Hinduism: The Untold Story."

41. Narayana Rao, "Purana as Brahminic Ideology," 91–92.

42. *Markandeya Purana* 135.7, 136.36.

43. Nath, *Puranas and Acculturation*, 57, citing *Atri-smirti* (373–83) and Mitakshara.

44. Hess, *The Bijak of Kabir*, 67.

45. *Brahmanda Purana* 1.2.26.10–61.

46. Doniger O'Flaherty, *Women, Androgynes*, 130-48.

47. *Vamana Purana* S.17.2–23.

48. Kinsley, *Hindu Goddesses*.

49. *Markandeya Purana* 82–83.

50. Hiltebeitel, *The Cult of Draupadi*.

51. Doniger O'Flaherty, *Women, Androgynes*, 90–91.

52. *Shvetashvatara Upanishad* 6.23.

53. *Skanda Purana* 1.3.1.10.1–69; Doniger O'Flaherty, *Hindu Myths*, 243.

54. *Markandeya Purana* 85–90.

55. Frederick Smith, *The Self Possessed*.

56. *Varaha Purana* 33.4–15, 25-34; Doniger O'Faherty, *Hindu Myths*, 122.

57. This is the story that Kalidasa alludes to: "Shiva's wife, Sati, the daughter of Daksha, was devoted to her husband and outraged when her father dishonored him. She discarded her body through yoga." *Kumarasambhava* 1.21

58. *Mahabharata* 12.183.10.3–5; cf. 13.17.98, and Nilakantha on 13.17.101.

59. Fleet, *Corpus*, no. 18, 81, pl. XI, 11.21–23.

60. *Brahmanda Purana* 4.11.1–34, 5.30.30–99; cf. *Vamana Purana* 6.26–27, 25.1–20, 31.1–18.

61. *Brahmavaivarta Purana* 4.41.20–26.

62. Doniger O'Flaherty, *Siva*, 226–32.

63. *Shiva Purana* 2.3.20.1–23; Doniger O'Flaherty, *Hindu Myths*, 160.

64. Böhtlingk, *Indische Spruche*, 1, 25, no. 130; Doniger O'Flaherty, *Siva*, 371, n. 220.

65. Courtright, *Ganesha*.

66. *Padma Purana* 1.46.1–32, 47–108,119–21. The same text, with some variations, appears in the *Skanda Purana* 1.2.27–29 (the version translated in Doniger O'Flaherty, *Hindu Myths*, 251–61, and discussed by Doniger, *Bedtrick*, 69–75) and in the *Matsya Purana* 154–57 (the version translated by Shulman in *God Inside Out*, 156).

67. www.specials.rediff.com/getahead/2004/sep/16ga-ganesh.htm.

68. Commentary on *Ramayana* 1.29.6 (Bombay ed.); Doniger O'Flaherty, *Origins of Evil*, 100.

69. *Harivamsha* 118.11–39.

70. Commentary cited by Kangle, *Arthasastra*, 12.

71. Doniger O'Flaherty, *Origins of Evil*, chapter 9.
72. Doniger O'Flaherty, *Siva*, 84–89.
73. *Naishadiyacarita*, canto 17, verse 201.
74. Dirks, "Political Authority and Structural Change,"125–57.
75. *Markandeya Purana* 10.47–87; 12.3–48; 10.88–97; 11.22–32.
76. Lewis Carroll, "Wool and Water," *Through the Looking Glass*.
77. *Kurma Purana* 1.34.5–18.
78. *Markandeya Purana* 6.
79. *Manu* 10.1.1–13.
80. Sanford, "Holi Through Dauji's Eyes."

CHAPTER 15. SECTS AND SEX IN THE TANTRIC PURANAS AND THE TANTRAS
1. *Mahanirvana Tantra* 14.117–21.
2. Thapar, *Early India*, 261.
3. Keay, *India*, 161.
4. Ibid., citing Bana's *Harsha-charita*.
5. Bana, *Kadambari*, trans. Gwendolyn Layne, 174–75.
6. Lévi, *Le théâtre*, 184–95. The Kashmiri historian Rajashekhara, in the ninth century, identified him as a Chandala. Sylvain Lévi identifies him as a Jaina, but his name betrays his low-caste origin.
7. Harsha, *Ratnavali*.
8. Beal, *Si-yu-ki*, 89.
9. Devahuti, *Harsha: A Political Study*, 154–57.
10. Keay, *India*, 182.
11. Mitter, *Indian Art*, 48.
12. Thapar, *Early India*, 275.
13. Ingalls, "Cynics and Pashupatas," 284, citing the Mathara pillar inscription of Chandragupta II, *Epigraphica Indica*, vol. 21, 1–9.
14. Flood (*Introduction*, 155–57) dates the *Pashupata Sutra* to about the ninth century, but Ingalls thought it was the work of Lakulisha, about 100 CE.
15. Mitter, *Indian Art*, 48.
16. Flood, *Introduction*, 165.
17. *Pashupata Sutra* 3.3–19; Ingalls, "Cynics."
18. Lorenzen, *Kabir Legends*, 102, 31–32; *Kapalikas*, 187–88.
19. Flood, *Introduction*, 157.
20. *Shiva Purana, Jnana Samhita*, 49.65–80; Doniger O'Flaherty, *Origins of Evil*, 280.
21. Doniger O'Flaherty, *Siva*, 123–28.
22. Doniger O'Flaherty, *Origins of Evil*, 146–59.
23. Ibid., 277–86.
24. Ibid., 281; *Shiva Purana* 3.8–9.
25. Doniger O'Flaherty, *Siva*, 124.
26. *Siva Purana* 2.2.16.30–36; cf 2.3.24.60–75; 2.4.4.5.
27. *Mahabhagavata Purana* 22.38–39; *Skanda Purana* 1.1.21.15.
28. *Varaha Purana* 97.2–8; Doniger O'Flaherty, *Origins of Evil*, 279.
29. *Skanda Purana* 1.1.1.20–40; *Shiva Purana* 2.2.26–27.

30. Doniger O'Flaherty, *The Origins of Evil*, 272ff.
31. *Shiva Purana* 2.2.26.15–40.
32. *Saura Purana* 7.38–39; *Markandeya Purana* 49.13; *Kurma Purana* 1.15.29–33.
33. *Devibhagavata Purana* 7.30.
34. Doniger and Smith, "Sacrifice and Substitution."
35. Doniger O'Flaherty, *Siva*, 123–29.
36. Flood, *Introduction*, 192.
37. *Devi-bhagavata Purana* 7.30.27–37, 40–50; *Brahmavaivarta Purana* 4.42–43; *Maha-bhagavata Purana* 11–23; *Skanda Purana, Kedara Khanda* 162; Doniger O'Flaherty, *Hindu Myths*, 249–51.
38. *Markandeya Purana* 85–90.
39. *Markandeya Purana* 80.21–44; cf. *Skanda Purana* 3.1.6.8–42; Doniger O'Flaherty, *Hindu Myths*, 240–49.
40. *Skanda Purana* 1.3.1.10.1–60.
41. *Devi-Bhagavata Purana* 5.2–11; Doniger O'Flaherty, *Women, Androgynes*, 82.
42. *Skanda Purana* 1.3.2.18–21.
43. White, *Kiss of the Yogini*, 21.
44. Flood, *Introduction*, 158.
45. White, *Kiss of the Yogini*, 9, 123, 159.
46. Flood, *Introduction*, 158.
47. Ibid., 154.
48. Ibid., 155.
49. Kripal, "Hinduism and Popular Western Culture."
50. *Kurma Purana* 1.16.109–20; Doniger O'Flaherty, *The Origins of Evil*, 310.
51. *Devi-bhagavata Purana* 7.39.26–32.
52. Woodruffe, *Shakti and Shakta*, 570; Doniger O'Flaherty, *The Origins of Evil*, 318.
53. White, *Kiss of the Yogini*, 254, 211.
54. *Mahayoga Tantra*, cited by Wedemeyer, "Beef, Dog," 385.
55. White, *Kiss of the Yogini*, 253.
56. Wedemeyer, "Beef, Dog."
57. *Mahanirvana Tantra* 6.1–20.
58. Flood, *Introduction*, 189.
59. White, *Kiss of the Yogini*, 220.
60. Ibid., 254.
61. Ibid., xiii.
62. Ibid., 72.
63. *Markandeya Purana* 85–90.
64. *Vamana Purana* 44.30–38; *Markandeya Purana* 88.39–61; *Matsya Purana* 179.1–86; O'Flaherty, *Women*, 34.
65. *Padma Purana* 1.46.1–32, 47–108, 119–21; *Skanda Purana* 1.2.27–29 (Doniger O'Flaherty, *Hindu Myths*, 251–61); *Matsya Purana* 154–57.
66. Urban, "Matrix of Power."
67. White, *Kiss of the Yogini*, 68.
68. Ibid., 220.
69. Ibid., 7–8.
70. Ibid., 67.
71. Ibid., 235
72. Flood, *Introduction*, 166.
73. White, *Kiss of the Yogini*, 235.

74. Ibid., 159.
75. Ibid., xii.
76. *Mahanirvana Tantra* 6.20.
77. Ibid., 11.110–20.
78. White, *Kiss of the Yogini,* 77, 268–71.
79. Sanjukta Gupta, "The Domestication of a Goddess," 62.
80. *Mahanirvana Tantra* 6.1–20.
81. Wedemeyer, "Beef, Dog," 392–93.
82. Urban, "What's in It."
83. Flood, *Introduction,* 191.
84. White, *Kiss of the Yogini,* 82.
85. *Yoni Tantra* 7.16b–17b.
86. Bharati, "Making Sense out of Tantrism and Tantrics," 53.
87. Urban, *The Economics of Ecstasy,* 82–90; *Magia Sexualis,* 91–92; *Tantra,* 9–10, 41, 229.
88. Urban, "Matrix of Power."
89. Flood, *Introduction,* 195–96.
90. White, *Kiss of the Yogini,* 253–54.
91. Flood, *Introduction,* 191–92.
92. As the historian Kshemendra reports, in Kashmir in the tenth or eleventh century CE.
93. Flood, *Introduction,* 161.
94. *Skanda Purana* 1.8.18–19.
95. *Mahanirvana Tantra* 14.180–89.
96. *Skanda Purana* 4.2.87–89.
97. Bipradas, *Manasabijay,* 235, cited by Doniger O'Flaherty, *Siva,* 227.
98. Banerjea, *The Development of Hindu Iconography.*
99. *Mahanirvana Tantra* 6.104–19.
100. Ibid., 11.120–30.
101. Ibid., 11.130–43.
102. Mitter, *Indian Art,* 56.
103. Ibid., 48; cf. Dehejia, *Indian Art,* 128.
104. Mitter, *Indian Art,* 48; cf. Dehejia, *Indian Art,* 128–31.
105. Keay, *India,* xxviii.
106. Mitter, *Indian Art,* 53–54.
107. Dehejia, *Indian Art,* 132–33.
108. Doniger O'Flaherty, *Dreams,* 94–95.
109. Mitter, *Indian Art,* 66–67
110. Devangana Desai, *Religious Imagery,* 153.
111. Keay, *India,* 278.
112. Ibid.
113. Michell, *Hindu Art and Architecture,* 30.
114. Mitter, *Indian Art,* 79, citing Michael Meister.
115. Ibid., 68.
116. Flood, *Introduction,* 158.
117. Devangana Desai, *Religious Imagery.*
118. Dehejia, *Yogini, Cult and Temples.*
119. Mitter, *Indian Art,* 81.
120. White, *Kiss of the Yogini,* 12.
121. Mitter, *Indian Art,* 42–43.
122. Keay, *India,* 213.
123. Michell, *Hindu Art and Architecture,* 29.
124. Keay, *India,* 213.
125. Rushdie, "Introduction" to the *Baburnama.*
126. Keay, *India,* 278.

CHAPTER 16. FUSION AND RIVALRY UNDER THE DELHI SULTANATE

1. Hess and Singh, *The Bijak of Kabir,* 42.
2. Keay, *India,* 279.
3. Chattopadhyaya, *Representing the Other,* 29, 43, 89–90.
4. *Rajatarangini* 7.1090–95.
5. Chattopadhyaya, *Representing the Other,* 71
6. Ibn Batuta, *Travels, A.D. 1325–1354 ,* written in the fourteenth century, trans. H. A. R. Gibb.
7. Keay, *India,* 180.
8. Ibid., 167.
9. Ibid., 181.
10. Ibid., 182.
11. Schimmel, *The Empire,* 107.
12. Keay, *India,* 185.
13. Mitter, *Indian Art,* 85.
14. Keay, *India,* 207.
15. Ibid., 209.
16. Ibid., 235, citing Ibn Asir.
17. Mitter, *Indian Art,* 85.
18. Keay, *India,* 245.
19. Ibid., 247.
20. Ibid., 245–47.
21. Ibid., 240.
22. Ibid., 259.
23. Ibid., 255.
24. Ibid., 60.
25. Ibid., 266.
26. Ibid., 270.
27. Ibid., 266, 270–71.
28. "Jains and Hindus Befriended," in Husain's *Tughluq Dynasty.*
29. Keay, *India,* 266.
30. Ibid., 272.
31. Ibid., 274.
32. Ibid., 271–72, 274.
33. Ibid., 181.
34. Ibid., 275.
35. Ibid., 211.
36. Eaton, *The Rise of Islam,* 268–90.
37. Keay, *India,* 235.
38. Ibid., 242.
39. Ibid., 235.
40. Ibid., 225.
41. Doniger O'Flaherty, *Origins of Evil,* 248–71.
42. Chattopadhyaya, *Representing the Other,* 52, 55, 57, 60, 84, 88.
43. West, *Indo-European Poetry,* 467.
44. Digby, *Warhorse and Elephant.*
45. Babur, *Baburnama,* 335.
46. Keay, *India,* 211.
47. Ibid., 189.
48. Ibid., 275.
49. *Encyclopaedia Britannica,* s. v. "polo."
50. Keay, *India,* 240.
51. Ibid., 276–77.
52. Gommans, *The Rise of the Indo-Afghan Empire,* 71.
53. Ibid., 78.

54. Keay, *India*, 277.
55. Stephen Inglis, personal communication, March 26, 1985.
56. Pusalker, *The Struggle for Empire*, 523.
57. Nagaswamy, "Gateway to the Gods."
58. Mookerji, *The History of Indian Shipping*, 195.
59. Leshnik, "The Horse in India," 56.
60. Keay, *India*, 306.
61. Ibid., 306.
62. Subrahmanyam, "The Political Economy of Commerce"; C. Gupta, "Horse Trade in North India."
63. Keay, *India*, 277.
64. Abu'l Fazl, *Ain-i-akbari*, vol. 1, 142.
65. Gommans, *The Rise of the Indo-Afghan Empire*, 72.
66. Ibid., 73.
67. Ibid., 72–73, quoting J. L. Kipling, *Beast and Man in India*, 167–68.
68. Keay, *India*, 276–77.
69. Gommans, *The Rise of the Indo-Afghan Empire*, 74.
70. Polo, *The Travels*, 357; *Marco Polo: The Description of the World*, 174.
71. Gommans, *The Rise of the Indo-Afghan Empire*, 74.
72. Keay, *India*, 288.
73. Eaton, "Temple Desecration in Pre-modern India."
74. Keay, *India*, 288.
75. Mitter, *Indian Art*, 85.
76. Keay, *India*, 188.
77. Ibid.
78. Ibid., 187.
79. Ibid., 207.
80. Ibid., 209.
81. Davis, *Lives of Images*, 90–112.
82. Thapar, *Somanatha*.
83. Keay, *India*, 237.
84. Ibid., 241, citing Ferishta.
85. Mitter, *Indian Art*, 75.
86. Keay, *India*, 257.
87. Thapar, *Somanatha*.
88. Sarkar, *Beyond Nationalist Frames*, 255
89. Davis, *Lives of Images*, 113, citing Amir Khusraw,
90. Keay, *India*, 258, citing Barani.
91. Davis, *Lives of Indian Images*, 133–35.
92. Eaton, "Temple Desecration in Pre-modern India."
93. Keay, *India*, 242.
94. Schimmel, *The Empire*, 107.
95. Keay, *India*, 202.
96. Ibid., 278, 286.
97. Metcalf, *A Concise History*, 3.
98. Ibid., 275, 278.
99. Keay, *India*, 242.
100. Eaton, "Temple Desecration in Pre-Modern India," 303.
101. Ibid., 285, 287, citing Tod, *Annals*, vol. 1, 23.

102. Ernst, "Situating Sufism and Yoga," 24–25, citing Buzurg ibn Shahriyar, *The Book of the Marvels of India*, 132.
103. Ibid., citing *Taranatha's History of Buddhism in India*, 320.
104. Schimmel, *The Empire*, 128.
105. Keay, *India*, 235.
106. Schimmel, *The Empire*, 109.
107. Behl and Weightman, *Madhu Malati*, xiii.
108. Ernst, "Islamization of Yoga," 107.
109. Ibid.
110. Doniger, "The Clever Wife in Indian Mythology."
111. Keay, *India*, 189.
112. Schimmel, *The Empire*, 107.
113. Keay, *India*, 285.
114. Mitter, *Indian Art*, 87–89.
115. Flood, *Introduction*, 144.
116. Amartya Sen, Foreword to K. M. Sen, *Hinduism*, xix, citing K. M. Sen, *Medieval Mysticism of India*, 146–52.
117. Flood, *Introduction*, 142.
118. Ibid., 145.
119. Lorenzen, *Kabir Legends*, 26–27, citing Anantadas, 7, 43–44, 47, citing contemporary oral tradition.
120. Hess, *The Bijak*, 4–5.
121. Lorenzen, *Kabir Legends*, 43–45, 47, citing contemporary oral tradition.
122. Ibid., 3.
123. Ibid., 18–19.
124. Ibid., 50, from the *Dabistan-i-Mazahib*.
125. Nandy, "Sati as Profit Versus Sati as a Spectacle," 136.
126. Kabir, *The Weaver's Songs*, trans. Dharwadkar, 162.
127. Ibid., 10.
128. Hess, *The Bijak*, no. 30, 51.
129. Ibid., no. 84, 69–70.
130. Ibid., no. 75, 67.
131. Flood, *Introduction*, 145.
132. Lorenzen, *Kabir Legends*, 29, citing Anantadas, *Kabir parachai*, 1693 ms. 4.10–15.
133. Ibid., 65, citing Paramananda-das, *Kabir Manshur*.
134. Hess, *The Bijak*, no. 41, 55.
135. Hess, *A Touch of Grace*, xxi.
136. Keay, *India*, 280.
137. Narayana Rao et al. *Textures of Time*.
138. Ajay Rao, "Othering Muslims or Srivaisnava-Saiva Contestation?"
139. Pollock, "Ramayana and Political Imagination in India," 278.
140. Ajay Rao, *Srivaisnava Hermeneutics*.
141. Ajay Rao, "Othering Muslims or Srivaisnava-Saiva Contestation?"
142. Verghese, *Religious Traditions at Vijayanagara*, 121.
143. Chattopadhyaya, *Representing the Other*, 60

144. Wagoner, "Sultan among Hindu Kings," 851–80.
145. Keay, *India,* 303, 305, 307.
146. Mitter, *Indian Art,* 62.
147. Narayana Rao et al., *Textures of Time,* 44–52, 73–77.
148. Ibid.
149. Michell, *Art and Architecture,* 133.
150. Keay, *India,* 179, 212.
151. Mitter, *Indian Art,* 3.
152. Ibid., 86.
153. Ramanujan, *Speaking of Siva.*
154. Flood, *Introduction,* 171.
155. Ramanujan, *Speaking of Siva,* 28.
156. Ibid., 88; "The Myths of Bhakti," 99.
157. Ibid., 297.
158. Davis, *The Lives of Indian Images.*
159. Shulman, untitled review of *Siva's Warriors,* 313.
160. Ibid.
161. Narayana Rao, *Siva's Warriors,* 235.
162. Ibid., 196–201.
163. Ramanujan, "Varieties of Bhakti," 324–31; *Speaking of Siva,* 111–42.
164. Mahadevyyakka 328; Ramanujan, *Speaking of Siva,* 141; "Varieties of Bhakti," 324.
165. Ramanujan, "Varieties of Bhakti," 326.
166. Ramanujan, *Speaking of Siva,* 127.
167. Ibid., 114.

CHAPTER 17. AVATAR AND ACCIDENTAL
GRACE IN THE LATER PURANAS

1. *Padma Purana* 2.1.5.1–35; Doniger O'Flaherty, *Origins of Evil,* 136–37.
2. Pollock, "Sanskrit Literary Culture from the Inside Out," 102.
3. Hess, *The Bijak,* no. 8, 45–46.
4. Kirfel, *Kosmologie.*
5. Thapar, *Early India,* 276.
6. Killingley, "Hinduism, Darwinism and Evolution."
7. *Vayu Purana* 2.36.74.
8. *Taittiriya Samhita* 7.1.5.1; *Shatapatha Brahmana* 14.1.2.11.
9. *Vishnu Purana* 1.4.
10. Mitter, *Indian Art,* 47.
11. Hawley, *Krishna, The Butter Thief.*
12. Rank, *The Myth of the Birth of the Hero;* Dundes, "The Hero Pattern."
13. *Harivamsha* 47–48.
14. Wadley, *Raja Nal,* 193.
15. *Bhagavata Purana* 10.6.
16. Ibid. 10.7.37, 10.13.44.
17. *Brahmavaivarta Purana* 4.15; Doniger O'Flaherty, *Women,* 103–04.
18. Beck, "Krishna as Loving Husband," 71, citing Charlotte Vaudeville.
19. Behl and Weightman, *Madhu Malati.*
20. *Brahmavaivarta Purana* 4.15.

21. Whaling, *The Rise of the Religious Significance of Rama,* 138; Hess, "Rejecting Sita."
22. *Adhyatma-ramayana* 3.7.1–10.
23. Ibid., 6.8.21.
24. *Brahmavaivarta Purana* 2.14.1–59.
25. *Mahabharata* 1.175.
26. The earliest texts that allude to the Buddha avatar may antedate the *Mahabharata* (Banerjea, *The Development of Hindu Iconography,* 392; Schrader, *Introduction,* 43–47), but this has yet to be proved (Klostermaier, *Hinduism,* 58–59).
27. Kumbhakona ed. of *Mahabharata,* 2.348.2; 12, appendix 1, no. 32, lines 1–17; Doniger O'Flaherty, *Origins of Evil,* 188.
28. *Bhavisya Purana* 3.1.6.35–421; Doniger O'Flaherty, *Origins of Evil,* 203.
29. Hazra, *Studies in the Puranic Records,* 88.
30. Krishna Sastri, "Two Statues of Pallava Kings," 5; Doniger O'Flaherty, *Origins of Evil,* 188.
31. *Vishnu Purana* 3.17–18.
32. *Garuda Purana* 1.32.
33. *Bhuridatta Jataka,* no. 543, esp. verses 210–11.
34. *Kalika Purana* 78.206.
35. Doniger O'Flaherty, *Women,* 80–129.
36. *Bhagavata Purana* 6.8.19.
37. *Varaha Purana* 48.22.
38. *Matsya Purana* 47.24, 54.19.
39. Kshemendra, *Dashavatarcharita* 9.1–74.
40. *Gita Govinda* 1.1.9.
41. Krishna Sastri, "Two Statues of Pallava Kings," 5–7.
42. *Devibhagavata Purana* 10.5.13, *dushta-yajna-vighataya.*
43. Glasenapp, *Von Buddha zu Gandhi,* 113.
44. Hess, *The Bijak,* no. 8, 45–46.
45. Basham, *The Wonder,* 309.
46. *Anagatavamsa,* 33–54.
47. Personal communication from Prof. Richard F. Gombrich, Oxford, U.K., 1973.
48. Holt, *The Buddhist Vishnu.*
49. Huntingon, *A Study of Puranic Myth,* 33.
50. Doniger O'Flaherty, *The Origins of Evil,* 179.
51. Ibid., 204–05.
52. Goetz, *Studies in the History and Art,* 77–80, discussing a frame in Srinagar Museum, of Shankara-varman (r. 883–902).
53. Thapar, *Early India,* 277.
54. Basham, *The Wonder,* 309.
55. Revelation 19.11–15.
56. *Mahabharata* 3.188.86–93, 189.1–13.
57. *Vishnu Purana* 4.24.98.
58. Ibid., 5.17.11; 5.18.1–6; cf. *Bhagavata Purana* 6.18.19.
59. Banerjea, *The Development,* 424.
60. *Kalki Purana* 1.1.14–39; 2.6–7, 3.6–7.
61. Sternbach, reveiw of R. C. Hazra.
62. Michell, *Art and Architecture,* 101.
63. *Bhagavata Purana* 12.2.19.
64. Ivanow, "The Sect of Imam Shah in Gujarat," 62–64.

65. *Bhagavata Purana* 8.24.7–57; *Agni Purana* 2.1–17.
66. *Vishnu Purana* 5.17.11; *Bhagavata Purana* 5.18.1–6.
67. *Devibhagavata Purana* 1.5.1–112; Doniger O'Flaherty, *Women,* 224.
68. *Vishnu Purana* 5.6.
69. Michell, *Art and Architecture,* 51.
70. Doniger, *Splitting the Difference,* 204–16.
71. Goldman, "Fathers, Sons, and Gurus."
72. *Shatapatha Brahmana* 1.2.5.1–9.
73. *Vayu Purana* 2.36.74–86.
74. *Taittiriya Brahmana* 1.5.9.1; *Mahabharata* 12.160.26–28.
75. *Harivamsha* 71.48–72, *Vamana Purana* 51, *Matsya Purana* 244–46.
76. *Devibhagavata Purana* 4.15.36–71.
77. *Skanda Purana* 1.1.18.121–29.
78. *Vishnu Purana* 1.15–20; *Bhagavata Purana* 7.1–10.
79. Doniger O'Flaherty, *Origins of Evil,* 248–71.
80. *Vamana Purana* 15–16.
81. Èliade, *Briser le toit de la maison.*
82. *Vamana Purana* S. 24.6–17.
83. *Skanda Purana* 1.1.31.1–78.
84. Doniger O'Flaherty, *Origins of Evil,* 248–72.
85. Doniger O'Flaherty, "Ethical and Non-Ethical Implications," 196–98.
86. Doniger O'Flaherty, *Origins of Evil,* 231–36.
87. *Skanda Purana, Kedara Khanda,* 5.101.
88. Ibid., 8.1–13.
89. *Shiva Purana* 2.1.17.48–2.1.18.39.
90. *Shiva Purana Mahatmya* 2.1–40.
91. *Skanda Purana* 1.1.18.53–120; Doniger O'Flaherty, *Origins of Evil,* 127–28.
92. Doniger O'Flaherty, *Origins of Evil,* 308–09.
93. Hazra, *Studies in the Puranic Records,* 99n.
94. *Bhagavata Purana* 7.1.29–30; 10.44.39.
95. *Skanda Purana, Kedara Khanda,* 5.92–95.
96. Ibid., 33.1–64.
97. Doniger O'Flaherty, *Origins of Evil,* 321–31.
98. *Vamana Purana* S. 26.4–62; 27.1–23.
99. *Skanda Purana* 7.1.336.95–253; cf. *Garuda Purana* 6.4–8.

CHAPTER 18. PHILOSOPHICAL FEUDS IN
SOUTH INDIA AND KASHMIR

1. Rushdie, *Haroun,* 40.
2. *Purva-mimamsa-sutra* 6.1.8 and 6.1.25–38.
3. K. M. Sen, *Hinduism,* 67. He called them *ardha-vainashika,* punning on *vai-sheshika* (people who make distinctions) and *vai-nashika* (people who make extinctions—of religion).
4. Ibid., 69.
5. Ibid., 66.
6. Flood, *Introduction,* 238–46.
7. Ibid., 132.
8. Klostermaier, *Hinduism,* 60; see also the *Sarva-darsanasamgraha* of Madhava (not to be confused with Madhva), a fourteenth-century Advaitia philosopher.

9. Schimmel, *The Empire,* plate 75.
10. Keay, *India,* 194.
11. Kripal, "Hinduism and Popular Western Culture."
12. Shankara's commentary on the *Brihadaranyaka Upanishad* (iii.5.1 and iv.5.15); Lorenzen, *Who Invented Hinduism?,* 121.
13. Ramanuja's commentary on Badarayana's *Brahmasutra* (*Shribhashya* 2.2.27); Isayeva, *Shankara and Indian Philosophy,* 14.
14. Grierson, "Madhvas," 235.
15. *Shankara-dig-vijaya* of Madhava, 1.28–43.
16. *Shankara-dig-vijaya* of Madhava, chapter 9; *Shankara-vijaya* of Anandagiri, 58–59; Ravicandra's commentary on Amaru; Siegel, *Fires of Love,* 4–5.
17. Flood, *Introduction,* 240.
18. Gopinatha Rao, *Elements,* 1.1.266; Narayana Rao and Shulman, *Classical Teluga Poetry* 143–44.
19. Carman, *Theology of Ramanuja,* 43, n. 37.
20. Davis, *Lives of Indian Images,* 133.
21. Carman, *Theology of Ramanuja,* 44, n. 38, 39.
22. Ibid., 45.
23. Narayana Panditacarya, *Madhva-vijaya* 10.8–10.18, 10.27–10.32
24. *Encyclopaedia Britannica* on Madhva.
25. *Varaha Purana* 71.48–62.
26. Madhva, *Brahma-sutra-bhashya* 1.1.1, citing *Varaha Purana* 1.228; cf. Klostermaier, *Hinduism,* 59–60.
27. Doniger O'Flaherty, *Origins of Evil,* 70–72.
28. Narayana Panditacarya, *Manimanjari* 5–8.
29. Doniger O'Flaherty, *Origins of Evil,* 210.
30. Flood, *Introduction,* 166.
31. Ibid., 164.
32. Ibid., 170.
33. Ibid.,162.
34. Doniger O'Flaherty, *Origins of Evil,* 168–73.
35. Lubin, "Veda on Parade," 398.
36. *Agni Purana* 27.17–28.
37. Beck, "Krishna as Loving Husband of God," 70.
38. Flood, *Introduction,* 137.
39. Appadurai, "Kings, Sects and Temples."
40. *Prashna Upanishad* 4.5.
41. Doniger O'Flaherty, *Dreams, Illusion.*
42. Cox, "Saffron in the Rasam."
43. Flood, *Introduction,* 166.
44. Schimmel, *The Empire,* 137.
45. Ibid. 328 and 114; a copy of the gorgeously illustrated translation is one of the treasures of the Chester Beatty Library in Dublin.
46. Personal communication from Muzaffar Alam, Chicago, December 2007.
47. *Yoga-vasishtha* 1.10–11; Doniger O'Flaherty, *Dreams,* 131, 139–40.
48. *Yoga-vasishtha* 6.1.85–08; Doniger O'Flaherty, *Dreams,* 280–81.
49. *Yoga-vasishtha* 3.104–09, 120–21; Doniger O'Flaherty, *Dreams,* 134–35.
50. Doniger O'Flaherty, *Dreams,* 140–45.

51. *Brihadaranyaka Upanishad* 2.1.18.
52. *Markandeya Purana* 8.128.
53. Gombrich and Cone, *The Perfect Generosity,* xxv–xxvi; *Jataka* 547.
54. Doniger O'Flaherty, *Dreams.*
55. *Yoga-vasishtha* 5.44–49; Doniger O'Flaherty, *Dreams* 135–36.

CHAPTER 19. DIALOGUE AND TOLERANCE
UNDER THE MUGHALS
1. Cited by Schimmel, *The Empire,* 113.
2. Ibid., 94–95.
3. Keay, *India,* 322.
4. Ibid., 274, 289.
5. Schimmel, *The Empire,* 24.
6. Babur, *Baburnama,* 353.
7. Ibid., 52, 442, 415, 342.
8. Keay, *India,* 295,
9. Babur, *Baburnama,* 394.
10. Mukhia, *The Mughals,* 18.
11. Schimmel, *The Empire,* 30–31.
12. Keay, *India,* 309.
13. Gascoyne, *The Great Moguls,* 57.
14. Schimmel, *The Empire,* 31.
15. Keay, *India,* 315.
16. Schimmel, *The Empire,* 33.
17. Keay, *India,* 316–17.
18. Amartya Sen, *The Argumentative Indian,* 288, citing Abu'l Fazl.
19. Keay, *India,* 312, citing Abu'l Fazl, *Akbar Nama,* 2, 271–72.
20. Schimmel, *The Empire,* 131.
21. Ibid., 113, citing Akbar.
22. Khan, "Akbar's Personality Traits," 22.
23. Ibid., 36.
24. Amartya Sen, Foreword to K. M. Sen, *Hinduism,* x–xi.
25. Schimmel, *The Empire,* 36, 94, 120–21.
26. Keay, *India,* 317
27. Ibid.
28. Schimmel, *The Empire,* 38.
29. Keay, *India,* 318.
30. Ibid., 312–13.
31. Schimmel, *The Empire,* 111.
32. Wujastyk, "Change and Creativity," 107, 109–10.
33. Mukhia, *The Mughals,* 23.
34. Ibid., 30.
35. Abu'l Fazl, *Ain-i-Akbari,* vol. 3, 181.
36. Schimmel, *The Empire,* 111.
37. Dalrymple, "The Most Magnificent Muslims," 26.
38. Keay, *India,* 327.
39. Findly, "Jahangir's Vow," 249.
40. Schimmel, *The Empire,* 95–96, 109, 148, 328.
41. Mukhia, *The Mughals,* 19, 23–24.
42. Schimmel, *The Empire,* 114.
43. Mukhia, *The Mughals,* 24.
44. Mitter, *Indian Art,* 87.

45. Richards, *The Mughal Empire,* 152.
46. Schimmel, *The Empire,* 116.
47. Ibid., 50.
48. Gascoigne, *The Great Moghuls,* 227.
49. Dalrymple, *White Moghuls,* 110.
50. Keay, *India,* 344–45
51. Ibid., 343.
52. Ibid., 342–43, 349, 356.
53. Mukhia, *The Mughals,* 25.
54. Keay, *India,* 342.
55. Mukhia, *The Mughals,* 24.
56. Ibid., 26.
57. Keay, *India,* 336, 343.
58. Schimmel, *The Empire,* 52.
59. Keay, *India,* 342
60. Schimmel, *The Empire,* 139.
61. Eaton, *Temple Desecration and Indo-Muslim States,* 305.
62. Keay, *India,* 364
63. Schimmel, *The Empire,* 196.
64. Ibid., 103, 196.
65. Babur, *Baburnama,* 298.
66. Ibid., 276.
67. Schimmel, *The Empire,* 277.
68. Babur, *Baburnama,* 300.
69. Ibid., 301.
70. Keay, *India,* 295.
71. Babur, *Baburnama,* 380–82.
72. Schimmel, *The Empire,* 196; cf. *Babur-nama,* 436.
73. Babur, *Baburnama,* 413, 439.
74. Forster, "The Emperor Babur."
75. Schimmel, *The Empire,* 30, 40, 146, 196.
76. Ibid., 41, 45, 96, 198.
77. Findly, "Jahangir's Vow," 247.
78. Schimmel, *The Empire,* 195.
79. Ibid., 12, 128, 137.
80. Babur, *Baburnama,* 372–74.
81. Abu'l Fazl, *Ain-i-Akbari.* vol. 1, 301, 203–4.
82. Karen Rosenberg, "An Emperor's Art: Small, Refined, Jewel Toned," reviewing an exhibition at the Sackler Gallery. *New York Times,* Friday, July 18, 2008.
83. Mukhia, *The Mughals,* 14, citing Thomas Coryat, *English Traveler to India,* 1612–17.
84. Abu'l Fazl, *Ain-i-Akbari,* 292–300.
85. Findly, "Jahangir's Vow," 250, citing Humayun's memoirs.
86. Schimmel, *The Empire,* 10, 36, citing *Akbar-nama* 3 and Bayazid Bayat, *Tarikh-i-Humayun-wa-Akbar,* 74.
87. Abu'l Fazl, *Ain-i-Akbari,* vol. 3 446, 164.
88. Ibid., 202.
89. Findly, "Jahangir's Vow," 247–48.
90. Ibid., 247, 250, 253.
91. Mukhia, *The Mughals,* 26–27.
92. Keay, *India,* 331, 351.
93. Ibid., 338, 350, 398, 533, 354.
94. Ibid., 356, 363
95. Eaton, *Temple Desecration,* 304.

96. Schimmel, *The Empire*, 112.
97. Eaton, *The Rise of Islam*, 183.
98. Mukhia, *The Mughals*, 30
99. Ibid., 30–31, 37.
100. Schimmel, *The Empire*, 112.
101. Mukhia, *The Mughals*, 31.
102. Schimmel, *The Empire*, 114
103. Mukhia, *The Mughals*, 31–32, 35, 28–29.
104. Eaton, *The Rise of Islam*, 180–82.
105. Schimmel, *The Empire*, 113.
106. Haberman, *Bhaktirasamritasindhu*.
107. Mukhia, *The Mughals*, 23–24.
108. N. K. Sen, *Hinduism*, 89, citing the seventeenth-century Sufi Bawr Saheb, his Hindu disciple Biru Saheb, and his Muslim disciple Yari Shah.
109. Schimmel, *The Empire*, 111.
110. Petievich, "Dakani's Radha-Krishna Imagery."
111. Schimmel, *The Empire*, 137.
112. Stewart, "Satya Pir"; *Fabulous Females*.
113. Schimmel, *The Empire*, 17.
114. Narayana Rao, "Multiple Literary Cultures."
115. Keay, *India*, 336.
116. Schimmel, *The Empire*, 238, 241.
117. Michell, *Art and Architecture*, 136–37.
118. Schimmel, *The Empire*, 238, 229.
119. Behl, *Madhu Malati*, xiii.
120. Keay, *India*, 336.
121. Michell, *Art and Architecture*, 141–42.
122. Babur, *Baburnama*, 365.
123. Keay, *India*, 316, 320.
124. Michell, *Art and Architecture*, 138–39.
125. Bakker, *Ayodhya*.
126. Michell, *Art and Architecture*, 134
127. Schimmel, *The Empire*, 282.
128. Ibid., 300.
129. Keay, *India*, 322, 334.

CHAPTER 20. HINDUISM UNDER THE MUGHALS

1. Amitav Ghosh, cited by Rushdie, Introduction to the *Baburnama*, ix.
2. Wujastyk, "Change and Creativity," 110, citing P. V. Kane.
3. Ibid.
4. Olivelle, *Renunciation in Hinduism: A Medieval Debate*.
5. Lutgendorf, *Hanuman's Tale*, 121, citing Bernard S. Cohn.
6. Haberman, *Acting*, 41.
7. Schimmel, *The Empire*, 237.
8. Lutgendorf, *The Life of a Text*, 99.
9. Lamb, "Personalizing the Ramayana," 237.
10. Tulsi, *Ramcaritmanas (The Holy Lake)*, 7.53; Hawley and Juergensmeyer, *Songs of the Saints of India*, 153.
11. *Ramacaritamanasa* of Tulsi Das, 3.23–24, 6.107–108.
12. Ibid., 6.108.7.

13. Beck, "Krishna as Loving Husband," 71.
14. Bhattacharya, *Love Songs of Chandidas*, 107.
15. Flood, *Introduction*, 141.
16. Ibid., 139.
17. Dimock, *Place of the Hidden Moon*.
18. Mukhia, *The Mughals*, 39.
19. Sanford, "Holi Through Dauji's Eyes,"109.
20. Openshaw, *Seeking Bauls of Bengal*.
21. Beck, "Krishna as Loving Husband," 72–73.
22. Ibid., 78.
23. Haberman, *Acting*.
24. Beck, "Krishna as Loving Husband," 76, quoting J. Farquhar in 1917.
25. Nathan and Seely, *Grace and Mercy in Her Wild Hair*.
26. McLean, *Devoted to the Goddess*; McDermott, *Mother of My Heart*.
27. Dilip Chitre, Introduction to Tukaram, *Says Tuka*, ix.
28. Ibid., xix, xiv, 119.
29. Tukaram, *Says Tuka*, 80.
30. Ibid., 86–87.
31. Gommans, *The Rise of the Indo-Afghan Empire*, 82.
32. Digby, *Warhorse and Elephant*.
33. Babur, *Baburnama*, 446 and 463 (trans. Beveridge).
34. Keay, *India*, 325.
35. Abu'l Fazl, *Ain-i-akbari*, vol. 1, 140.
36. Schimmel, *The Empire*, 203.
37. Abu'l Fazl, *Ain-i-akbari*, vol. 1, 140.
38. Ibid.
39. Kelly, *Marwari*.
40. Doniger, " 'I Have Scinde.' "
41. Schimmel, *The Empire*, 52–53.
42. Crooke, *The Popular Religion and Folk-lore of Northern India*, vol. 2, 206; citing Rousselet, "India and Its Native Princes," 116.
43. Asutosh Bhattacarya, *Folklore of Bengal*, 49. Crooke, *The Popular Religion and Folk-lore*, vol. 2, 206.
44. Hiltebeitel, *The Cult of Draupadi*, vol. 1, *Mythologies*, 101–102.
45. Ibid., 118, 122.
46. Sontheimer, "The Mallari/Khandoba Myth," 155, 163.
47. Personal communication from Jack Stanley, Chicago, 1980.
48. Sontheimer, "Folk Hero, King and God."
49. Sontheimer, "Some Incidents in the History of the God Khandoba," 116.
50. Vinakaya, *Sri Mallari Mahatmya*.
51. Sontheimer, "The Mallari/Khandoba Myth," 161.
52. Ibid., n. 16, citing the *Sri Martanda Vijaya* of Gandgadhara, 34.51 ff.
53. Vinakaya, *Sri Mallari Mahatmya*, 13.24.
54. Erndl, *Victory to the Mother*, 46. The story is found in oral tradition and numerous popular pamphlets.

55. Ibid., 96. From a Hindi oral version collected in Chandigarh, 1982–83.

56. Erndl notes, of her contemporary story: "There is a controversy over whether he is the same as King Hariscandra of Ayodhya, an ancestor of Rama, or a local king of Haripur in District Kangra, H.P. [Himachal Pradesh]."

57. Crooke, *The Popular Religion and Folk-lore*, vol. 2, 206; citing *Indian Antiquary*, vol. 11, 325 ff; *Panjab Notes and Queries*, vol. 2.

58. Hiltebeitel, *Rethinking the Mahbharata*, 2.

59. Ibid., 121.

60. Ibid., 45, citing A. K. Ramanujan.

61. Ibid., 299.

62. Temple, *Legends of the Punjab*, vol. 1, 121–209.

63. Steel, "Folklore in the Panjab," 35.

64. Crooke, *The Popular Religion and Folk-lore*, vol. 1, 211–13, citing *Indian Antiquary*, vol. 11, 33 ff; Cunningham, "Archaeological Reports," vol. 17, 159; "Panjab Notes and Queries," vol. 2, 1; John Campbell Oman, *Cults, Customs, and Superstitions* (1908), 68–82.

65. Rose, *A Glossary of the Tribes and Castes*, 179. From Nabha State, a princely Sikh state near the Punjab.

66. Subrahmanyam, "Friday's Child," 80.

67. Ibid., 81, quoting a French eyewitness account of 1714.

68. Ibid., 92–106, citing Arunachalam, *Peeps into Tamil Literature; Desingu Rajan Kathai*, 138 ff.

69. Subrahmanyam, "Friday's Child," 108–09.

70. Dalrymple, "Homer in India," 51.

71. Ibid., 54

72. Joshi, *Painted Folklore and Folklore Painters of India*, 52.

73. Kramrisch, *Unknown India*, 87.

74. Agravat, *Satyavadi Vir Tejapala*.

75. Lopez, *Religions of India in Practice*.

76. Eaton, *The Rise of Islam*, 180–82.

77. Schimmel, *The Empire*, 156, 158, 161.

78. Ibid., 164.

79. Ibid., 144–15, 155–56.

80. Ibid., 143.

81. Ibid., 143, 147–49, 156.

82. Ibid., 151, 153.

83. Ibid., 155.

84. Dalrymple, *White Moghuls*, 34.

85. Schimmel, *The Empire*, 155.

86. Hawley and Juergensmeyer, *Songs of the Saints of India*, 126–27, 120, 132.

87. Ibid., 137.

88. Hawley, *Three Bhakti Voices*, 111.

89. Flood, *Introduction*, 143–44.

90. Nandy, "Sati as Profit," 139, citing V. N. Datta, *Sati*, 13–14.

91. Abu'l Fazl, *Ain-i-Akbari*, vol. 1, 216.

92. Ibid., vol. 3, 449.

93. Nandy, "Sati as Profit," 140.

94. Mukhia, *The Mughals*, 32, citing the *Tuzuk-I Jahangiri*, trans. Alexander Rogers, vol. 2, 180–81.

95. Ibid., 36.

96. Nandy, "Sati as Profit," 140.

97. Schimmel, *The Empire*, 113.

98. Nau'i, *Burning and Melting*.

99. Sangari, "Perpetuating the Myth," 27.

100. Schimmel, *The Empire*, 166.

101. Ramanujan et al., *When God Is a Customer*.

102. Ibid., 23.

103. Ibid., 24.

104. Ibid., 117–18.

CHAPTER 21. CASTE, CLASS, AND CONVERSION UNDER THE BRITISH RAJ

1. Kipling, *Kim*, 191.

2. Keay, *India*, 372.

3. Dirks, *The Scandal of Empire*, xiii.

4. Keay, *India*, 435

5. Ibid., 8, citing Magnus, *King Edward the Seventh*, 217–18.

6. Ibid., 18.

7. Dube, *Untouchable Pasts*, 11, quoting Nick Dirks, *The Hollow Crown*.

8. Keay, *India*, 447

9. Metcalf, *A Concise History*, 483.

10. Cannadine, *Ornamentalism*.

11. Dalrymple, *The Last Mughal*, 135.

12. Keay, *India*, 376, 382.

13. Dalrymple, *White Moghuls*, 33–34.

14. Keay, *India*, 402, 407, 425,

15. Jasanoff, *Edge of Empire*.

16. Keay, *India*, 432

17. Forster, *A Passage to India*, chapter 5.

18. Mukherjee, *The Rise and Fall of the East India Company*, 300–03.

19. Bolts, *Considerations on Indian Affairs*, 194.

20. Ranjit Roy, *The Agony of West Bengal*, 17.

21. Ibid., 389, 392.

22. Ibid., 414.

23. Kipling, *Kim*, chapter 11.

24. Keay, *India*, 450.

25. Klostermaier, *Hinduism*, 291.

26. Ibid., 428–29, 445.

27. Hardiman, *The Coming of the Devi*, 163; Eaton, "Conversion to Christianity Among the Nagas, 1876–1971," 8, 32–33.

28. Spear, *A History of India*, 140.

29. Keay, *India*, 432, 434.

30. James, *Raj*, 237.

31. An anonymous tract called the *Sadsat Jagannatha Brtanta*, cited in Ignatius Soreng, *Odisare o odiya sahitya re Christa dharma* [*Christianity in Orissa and in Oriya Literature*]; Berhampur: Dipti Prakashani, 1998). I am indebted to Siddharth Satpathy for this reference.

32. Keay, *India*, 427,

33. Surendra Nath Sen, *Eighteen Fifty Seven*, 40–45.

34. Gubbins, *An Account of the Mutinies in Oudh*, 24–25.

35. Kaye, *A History of the Sepoy War in India.*
36. Metcalf, *A Concise History of India,* 100.
37. Keay, *India,* 438.
38. Metcalf, *A Concise History of India,* 100.
39. Keay, *India,* 438
40. Ibid., 443.
41. James, *Raj,* 237.
42. Ibid.
43. Rudrangshu Mukherjee, *Mangal Pandey.*
44. Forbes-Mitchell, *Reminiscences of the Great Mutiny.*
45. James, *Raj,* 251.
46. Keay, *India,* 441-42
47. Ibid., 446.
48. Ibid., 445.
49. Ibid., 429, 445-46.
50. Ibid., 425
51. Dalrymple, *White Moghuls,* 166.
52. Powell, *Muslims and Missionaries,* 117. I am indebted to Catherine Adcock for this citation.
53. Sutton, *Orissa and its Evangelization,* 40.
54. I owe this insightful comment, as well as the Sutton citation itself, to Siddharth Satpathy.
55. James, *Raj,* 237.
56. Keay, *India,* 419.
57. Gautama, *Dharma-sutra* 20.10.
58. Moon, *The British Conquest,* 427.
59. Southey, *The Curse of Kehama,* 9.
60. Ibid., 429, 431.
61. Forster, *A Passage to India,* chapter 18.
62. Jaffrelot, *The Hindu Nationalist Movement in India,* 35.
63. Uma Mukherjee, *Two Great Indian Revolutionaries,* 16-17.
64. Urban, *Tantra,* 156-58.
65. Carnegy, *A Historical Sketch of Tehsil Fyzabad;* Narain, *The Ayodhya Temple/Mosque Dispute,* 8-9.
66. Van der Veer, *Religious Nationalism,* 153.
67. Forster, *A Passage to India,* 287.
68. Ernst, "Situating Sufism," 24-25, citing the *Dabistan,* 149-50; translation, 239-40.
69. *Dabistan,* 147, 157; translation, 235, 251.
70. Ernst, "Situating Sufism," 24-25, citing a letter of David DuBois, June 4, 2003.
71. Sheldon Pollock's term; see "Deep Orientalism?: Notes on Sanskrit and Power Beyond the Raj."
72. Buruma and Margalit, *Occidentalism: The West in the Eyes of Its Enemies.*
73. Nandy, *The Intimate Enemy,* 52; Hwang, *M. Butterfly.*
74. Ramachandra Guha, "Sixty Years in Socks,"15.
75. Trautmann, *Aryans and British India.*
76. Keay, *India,* 431.
77. Rocher, *Ezourvedam,* 3, 19. The text was published in *Asiatic Researches,* Royal Asiatic Society, Bengal, 1822.
78. Kapil Raj, "Refashioning Civilities."
79. Flood, *Introduction,* 124.
80. Partha Mitter, "Rammohun Roy and the New Language of Monotheism."
81. Nandy, *The Intimate Enemy;* Doniger, *The Woman Who Pretended.*
82. Keay, *India,* 431.
83. Sumit Sarkar, *Modern India.*
84. Dalrymple, "India: The Place of Sex."
85. McConnachie, *The Book of Love,* 198.
86. Ibid., 197-98.
87. Figueira, "To Lose One's Head for Love."
88. Published in Goethe, *Werke,* 1840, 1.200; here cited from the English translation by Edgar Alfred Bowring, *The Poems of Goethe.*
89. Yourcenar, "Kali Beheaded."
90. Ibid., 146.
91. Doniger, *Splitting the Difference,* 235.
92. Kulkarni, "Darstellung des Eigenen im Kostum des Fremden"; Schulz, "Hindu Mythology in Mann's Indian Legend"; Mahadevan, "Switching Heads and Cultures."
93. Doniger, " 'I Have Scinde.' "
94. Moon, *The British Conquest,* 567-75.
95. The Whig *Morning Chronicle,* cited by Priscilla Napier, *I Have Sind,* 197.
96. Priscilla Napier, *I Have Sind,* xvi.
97. Mehra, *A Dictionary,* 496-97.
98. George Daniel, *Democritus in London,* 51.
99. Priscilla Napier, *I Have Sind,* xv, 160, 197.
100. Keay, *India,* 421.
101. Rowley, *More Puniana,* 166-67.
102. Rushdie, *Shame,* 88.
103. Gould, "To Be a Platypus," 269.
104. Priscilla Napier, *I Have Sind,* 160.
105. Mehra, *A Dictionary,* 497.
106. William Napier, *The Life and Opinions of General Sir Charles James Napier,* vol. 4, 38.
107. David, *The Indian Mutiny,* 34-44; Edwardes, *Red Year: The Rebellion of 1857,* 21-22.
108. Charles Napier, cited in Ball, *The History of the Indian Mutiny,* 36.
109. William Napier, *The Life and Opinions,* vol. 2, 275.
110. Lifton and Mitchell, *Hiroshima in America,* 176.
111. Keay, *India,* 453.
112. Cited by Bryant, *The Quest for the Origins,* 324.
113. Gommans, *The Rise of the Indo-Afghan Empire,* 98.
114. Alder, *Beyond Bokhara,* 50-51.
115. Schimmel, *The Empire,* 101.
116. William Napier, *The Life and Opinions,* vol. 1, 164-66, 186, 346, 351, 385; Priscilla Napier, *I Have Sind,* 58.
117. Gommans, *The Rise of the Indo-Afghan Empire,* 99.
118. Yang, *Bazaar India,* 116.
119. Alder, *Beyond Bokhara,* 105, 209.
120. Yang, *Bazaar India,* 116.
121. Alder, *Beyond Bokhara,* 107, 209, 341, 357-58, 367.

122. Kipling, *Kim,* 161.
123. Ibid., 191.
124. Said, "The Pleasures of Imperialism," 45.
125. Orwell, "Rudyard Kipling," 135.
126. Rushdie, "Kipling," 80; italics added.
127. Shakespeare, *Henry V,* 5.2.182–83.
128. Trautmann, *Aryans,* 15, 18.
129. Gandhi, *Selected Political Writings,* 89.

CHAPTER 22. SUTTEE AND REFORM IN THE
TWILIGHT OF THE RAJ
1. Cited by Mani, *Contentious Traditions,* 172.
2. Cited by Weinberger-Thomas, *Ashes of
Immortality,* 99.
3. *Vessantara Jataka,* 495 (PTS text); Gombrich and
Cone, *The Perfect Generosity.*
4. Dehejia, "The Iconographies of Sati," 52.
5. Mani, *Contentious Traditions,* 22.
6. Hawley, *Sati,* 13.
7. Doniger, "Why Did They Burn?"
8. Courtright, "The Iconographies of Sati," 42.
9. Hawley, *Sati,* 26. Some legal texts (*Shankha* and
Angiras Smritis) use Arundhati instead; Kane,
History, 2.1, 631.
10. K. M. Sen, *Hinduism,* 95–96.
11. Killingley, *Rammohun Roy,* 61.
12. K. M. Sen, *Hinduism,* 95–96.
13. Ibid.
14. Killingley, *Rammohun Roy.*
15. Mani, *Contentious Traditions,* 54–55.
16. Nandy, "Sati as Profit," 137.
17. Keay, *India,* 457.
18. Weinberger-Thomas, *Ashes,* 89.
19. Spivak, "Can the Subaltern Speak?," 297.
20. Allan Bloom, *The Closing,* 26.
21. Woodruff, *The Men Who Ruled India,* 66, 74.
22. Mani, *Contentious Traditions,* 53.
23. Kane, *History,* 2.1.631–33.
24. Mani, *Contentious Traditions,* 21.
25. Weinberger-Thomas, *Ashes of Immortality,*
202–07.
26. Keay, *India,* 429.
27. Figueira, "Die flambierte Frau," 69, citing
Roger, 220–21.
28. Ibid., 58, 61.
29. Ibid., 65, citing Wagner, *Gesammelte Schriften
und Dichtung,* vol. 6, 255–56.
30. Lubin, "Veda on Parade," 389, citing *Samskara-
vidhi* 289–95.
31. Ghai, *Shuddhi Movement in India,* and Jordens,
"Reconversion to Hinduism, the Shuddhi of the
Arya Samaj."
32. Lubin, "Veda on Parade," 389.
33. Jaffrelot, *Hindu Nationalism,* 2007, 31.
34. Van der Veer, *Religious Nationalism,* 91–92.
35. Adcock, *Religious Freedom and Political Culture.*
36. Keay, *India,* 475.
37. Gandhi, in *Young India,* January 5, 1924, 145.
38. Keay, *India,* 492.

39. Ibid., 471.
40. Scott, *Weapons of the Weak.*
41. Nandy, *The Intimate Enemy,* 52 ff.
42. Gandhi, *An Autobiography,* 20–21.
43. Ibid.
44. Hardiman, *The Coming of the Devi,* 209.
45. Gandhi, *The Mind of Mahatma Gandhi,*
265–99.
46. Gandhi, "The Message of the Gita," in Mitchell, *The Bhagavad Gita,* 218–19.
47. Keay, *India,* 487, 514.
48. Ibid., 448.
49. P. J. Marshall, *Bengal,* xiv–xv, 5.
50. Forbes-Mitchell, *Reminiscences of the Great
Mutiny.*
51. Hardiman, *The Coming of the Devi,* 1, 33, 46.
52. Nath, *Puranas and Acculturation,* 145.
53. The material in the next six paragraphs is taken
from Hardiman, *The Coming of the Devi,* particularly 40, 53–54, 82, 99, 104–05, 129, 134, 139–40,
147, 154, 159, 164, 179, 203.
54. Ibid., 41; Kirin Narayan, *Mondays on the Dark
Side of the Moon.*
55. Hardiman, *The Coming of the Devi,* 42, 175, 216.
56. Ibid., 169, 189–90, 200–01.
57. Keay, *India,* 486.
58. Hardiman, *The Coming of the Devi,* 4,
51–52, 170.
59. Harlan, "Perfection and Devotion," 84–85.
60. Keay, *India,* 447.
61. Dube, *Untouchable Pasts,* 115, 260–61,
62. Ibid., 115–16.
63. Ibid., 15.
64. Keay, *India,* 532.
65. Tartakov, "B. R. Ambedkar," 38.
66. Ambedkar, *Why Go for Conversion?,* 10.
67. Omvedt, 43, citing Ambedkar, *Towards an Enlightened India.*
68. Doniger O'Flaherty, *Dreams, Illusion.*
69. Ambedkar, *The Buddha and His Dhamma;*
Tartakov, *B. R. Ambedkar and the Navayana Diksha.*
70. Keer, *Dr. Ambedkar,* 499.
71. Isaacs, *India's Ex-Untouchables,* 46.
72. Justin Huggler, "India's Untouchables Turn to
Buddhism in Protest at Discrimination by Hindus," *Independent,* October 13, 2006.

CHAPTER 23. HINDUS IN AMERICA
1. Baker, *A Blue Hand,* 214–15.
2. Stephen Prothero of Boston University, cited in
"Poll Finds a Fluid Religious Life in U.S.," *New
York Times,* February 26, 2008. Reported by Neela
Banerjea. Report of the Pew Forum on Religion
and Public Life, http://religions.pewforum.org.
3. Brenda Goodman, "In a Suburb of Atlanta, a
Temple Stops Traffic," *New York Times,* June 5,
2007, B1.
4. Siegel, *Net of Magic.*
5. Lamont, *The Rise of the Indian Rope Trick,* 81

6. Kripal, "Western Popular Culture, Hindu Influences On."
7. Vivekananda, *Swami Vivekananda and His Guru*, 25.
8. Huffer, *Guru Movements in a Globalized Framework*.
9. Stephen Kinzer,"Art on Streets Til the Cows Come Home," *New York Times*, August 20, 2001.
10. Vasquez and Marquardt, *Globalizing the Sacred*, 92, 117.
11. Baker, *A Blue Hand*, 146.
12. Ibid., 146, 214–15.
13. Kripal, "Western Popular Culture, Hindu Influences On."
14. O'Brien, "Sweetheart," 110.
15. www.tantricgoddesskali.com.
16. anniesprinkle.org.
17. Rajesh Priyadarhi, on BBC News, June 9, 2004.
18. Rama Lakshmi, "In India, Gods Rule the 'Toon' Universe; Hindu Myth a Fount of Superheroes," *Washington Post Foreign Service*, January 9, 2008, A11.
19. Mr. Boffo cartoon by Joe Martin, Inc., distributed by Universal Press Syndicate, published in the September 29, 2000, *Chicago Tribune*.
20. Tolputt, *The Cartoon Kama Sutra*, and Manara's *Kama Sutra*.
21. "Tantric Sex Class Opens Up Whole New World of Unfulfillment for Local Couple," *Onion* (March 30–April 5, 2000), 8.
22. Spayde, "The Politically Correct Kama Sutra," 56.
23. The musical was conceived by Terry Abrahamson and directed by Arnie Saks, with music by Stephen Joseph.
24. Britt, "Avatar."
25. American School of Laughter Yoga, e-mail advertisement, June 2, 2005.
26. White, *Kiss of the Yogini*, xi.
27. Ibid., xii.
28. Ibid., xii, 109.
29. Statements made in public hearings before the California Board of Education and the Fairfax County School Board between 2000 and 2005.
30. Kripal, "Western Popular Culture, Hindu Influences On."
31. Ibid.
32. Huffer, *Guru Movements*.
33. Exemplified in Krishnan Ramaswamy et al., *Invading the Sacred*.
34. Kripal, "Western Popular Culture, Hindu Influences On."
35. Jason Overdorf, "Saving the Raja's Horse: British Horsewoman Francesca Kelly Brings India's Fiery Marwari to the United States in Hopes of Reviving the Breed." *Smithsonian*, June 2004. See also www.horsemarwari.com and Kelly and Durfee, *Marwari: Legend of the Indian Horse*.

CHAPTER 24. THE PAST IN THE PRESENT
1. Gough, "Harijans in Thanjavur," 234.
2. Lubin, "Veda on Parade," 398.
3. Ibid., 394.
4. Frederick M. Smith, "Indra Goes West," 259–60, citing Madhava.
5. Lubin, "Veda on Parade," 394.
6. Ibid., 393–94; in Solapur in 1978 and in Pune in 1955.
7. Smith, "Indra Goes West," 259.
8. Lubin, "Veda on Parade," 394.
9. K. M. Sen, *Hinduism*, 47.
10. Kosambi, *Myth and Reality*, 91–92.
11. Doniger, "A Burnt Offering." review of D. N. Jha, *The Myth of the Holy Cow*.
12. J. L. Kipling, *Beast & Man in India*, vol. 6, 116.
13. Biardeau, *Hinduism*, 36.
14. Appadurai, "Gastro Politics," 506.
15. White, "Dogs die."
16. Personal communication from Nagaraj Paturi, Chicago, January 2007.
17. Sontheimer, "King of Warriors," 52–53.
18. Elison, "Immanent Domains."
19. BBC news, November 8, 2007.
20. CNN.com Europe, November 13, 2007.
21. *New York Times*, March 7, 2008, "Kashmir: City Plans to Poison 100,000 Dogs"; March 8, 2008, "Kashmir: Strays Saved from Poisoning."
22. Gold, *Fruitful Journeys*, 5.
23. Cohn, "The Changing Status of a Depressed Caste," 285.
24. Dube, *Untouchable Pasts*, 8.
25. Forster, *Hill of Devi*, 176.
26. Ann Grodzins Gold, personal conversation, August 2007.
27. I owe this concern, and much of its wording, to Arshia Sattar, personal communication, August 13, 2006.
28. BBC News, December 7, 2007. The judge was Sunil Kumar Singh.
29. He bought it from New York dealer Ben Heller for David L. Shirey. "Norton Simon Bought Smuggled Idol," *New York Times*, May 12, 1973.
30. Davis, *Lives of Indian Images*, 252, citing N. Vidyasagar, "Back Home—but Not Yet," *Aside*, August 31, 1991.
31. Bakker, *Ayodhya*.
32. S. Balakrishnan, "Ayodhya: The Communal Tinderbox," *Illustrated Weekly of India*, vol. 11, no. 5 (1989), 30.
33. Forster, *Hill of Devi*, 202.
34. Gopal, ed., *Anatomy of a Confrontation*.
35. Keay, *India*, 532.
36. Dalrymple, "India: The War over History."
37. BBC News, September 12, 2007.
38. Romila Thapar, "Opinion," in *The Hindu*, September 28, 2007; reprinted in *Economic and Political Weekly* (September 29, 2007).
39. eol.jsc.nasa.gov/scripts/sseop/photo.pl?mission=STS067&roll=718A&frame=60.

40. Doniger O'Flaherty, *The Implied Spider.*

41. Seely, *The Slaying of Meghanada.*

42. Richman, "E. V. Ramasami's Reading of the Ramayana."

43. Omvedt, *Dalit Visions,* 100–01, citing Madhu Kishwar, in the *Times of India,* January 28, 1993.

44. Van der Veer, *Gods on Earth,* 14.

45. Upasni Baba, *The talks of Sadguru Upasani-Baba Maharaj,* vol. 2B, 542–54.

46. *Shiva Purana* 2.4.13.4, 4.27.23–24; cf. *Ramayana* 7.4.3–4, 7.16.44.

47. *Padma Purana* 2.1.5.1–35; Doniger O'Flaherty, *Origins of Evil,* 136–37.

48. Elwin, *Myths of Middle India,* 65–67.

49. *Hindu Janajagruti Samiti,* January 18, 2008. See http://www.hindujagruti.org/news/3819.html.

50. *Yahoo News,* February 26, 2008.

51. Raghu Karnad, "Unlikely Arrows in Ram's Quiver," *Tehelka Magazine,* New Delhi (March 15, 2008).

52. Mahesh Rangarajan, "Enemies of Open Society Threaten the Idea of India," *Economic and Political Weekly,* February 23, 2008; Ramachandra Guha, "Devotions Destructive and Divine," *The Hindu,* March 2, 2008.

53. Pratap Bhanu Mehta, "Our Freedoms, Your Lordships," *Indian Express,* March 4, 2008.

54. Omvedt, *Dalit Visions,* 31, 101.

55. Kishwar, "Yes to Sita, No to Ram," 300 ff.

56. Omvedt, *Dalit Visions,* 101–02.

57. Tharoor, *The Great Indian Novel,* 141.

58. Omvedt, *Dalit Visions,* 28, translating Tarabai Shinde, *Stri-Purush Tulna,* 6.

59. Ibid.

60. Sumanta Banerjee, "Women's Popular Culture in Nineteenth Century Bengal," in Sangari and Vaid, *Recasting Women,* 138–39.

61. Chakravarti, *Themes in Indian History,* 78, citing the short story entitled "Kunti O Nishadi" by Mahashweta Devi.

62. Omvedt, *Dalit Visions,* 98.

63. Ibid., 78, quoting an untitled poem by Waman Nimbalkar (called "Just Poem"), *Vagartha,* 12 (January 1976), trans. Graham Smith.

64. Ibid., 8, citing Shashikant Hingonekar, "Eka-lavya," *Asmitadarsh,* no. 12 (April–May–June 1989), trans. Gail Omvedt and Bharat Patankar.

65. Anand and Zelliot, *Anthology of Dalit Literature,* 152. This poem (from *Surung*) was translated by Eleanor Zelliot.

66. Surekha Bhagat, "The Lesson." Personal communication from Eleanor Zelliot, 2005.

67. Jaffrey, *The Invisibles;* Nanda, *Neither Man nor Woman.*

68. Associated Press, November 9, 2006.

69. davidgodman.org/interviews/ttimes.shtml.

70. "Detect Eye Defects Early to Avoid Blindness," *The Hindu,* September 8, 2006.

71. Personal communication from William Dalrymple, January 6, 2008.

72. Hudson, "Siva, Minaksi, Visnu."

73. *Indian Express,* October 18, 2007.

74. Kurtz, *All the Mothers Are One,* 18; Lutgendorf, "Who Wants to Be a Goddess? *Jai Santoshi Maa* Revisited."

75. Ritter, "Epiphany in Radha's Arbor," 181–84, 199, 201.

76. Omvedt, *Dalit Visions,* 19–20, citing Jotiba Phule, *Gulamgiri* (in Marathi, with an English introduction), 1885.

77. Ibid., 85.

78. Youngblood, "Cultivating Identity," 275, 319–20.

79. Shekhar Gupta, "Lopsided Lessons," *India Today,* July 31, 1990.

80. Vinay Lal, *Introducing Hinduism,* 93.

81. P. N. Oak, *Tajmahal: The True Story* (1989).

82. Hari Kumar, "After Clashes, Curfew Is Set in Taj Mahal Area," *New York Times,* August 30 2007.

83. Huyler, *Village India,* 162.

84. Asutosh Bhattacarya, *Folklore of Bengal,* 48–49.

85. Inglis, "Night Riders," 298, 302, 304.

86. Kramrisch, *Village India,* 57.

87. Personal communication from Stephen Inglis, January 8, 1987.

88. Inglis, "The Craft of the Velar," 14–19.

89. Shulman, *The King and the Clown,* 3–4.

90. Lynn Hart, paper presented at the South Asian Conference at the University of Wisconsin at Madison, November 8, 1986.

91. Vequaud, *Women Painters of Mithila.*

92. Brown, "Contested Meanings."

93. Vequaud, "The Colors of Devotion."

94. Szanton and Bakshi, *Mithila Painting: The Evolution of an Art Form,* 3–17.

95. Ibid., 31–37.

96. Ibid., 61–67; Szanton, "Mithila Painting: The Dalit Intervention."

97. Ibid., 69–71.

98. "Renuka's Revenge," Reuters report from Bangalore, March 7, 1995; "Naked Worshippers Lay Bare Dignity of Police and Press," *Times* of London, March 15, 1986; cited in full in Doniger, *Splitting the Difference,* 214–216.

CHAPTER 25. INCONCLUSION, OR, THE ABUSE OF HISTORY

1. Golwalkar, *We, Our Nationhood Defined,* 48–49.

2. Gandhi, *The Collected Works,* vol. 25, 178.

3. Tendulkar, *Mahatma,* vol. 2, 286.

4. Keay, *India,* 533

BIBLIOGRAPHY:
WORKS CITED AND CONSULTED

ॐ

SANSKRIT, GREEK, PALI, AND HINDI
TEXTS, BY TITLE

Adhyatma-Ramayana, with the commentaries of
Narottama, Ramavarman, and Gopala
Chakravarti. Calcutta: Metropolitan Printing &
Publishing House, 1935. Calcutta Sanskrit se-
ries, no. 11.

Agni Purana. Poona: Anandasrama Sanskrit
Series, 1957.

Aitareya Brahamana, with the commentary of Sayana. Calcutta: Bibliotheca Indica, 1895.

Anagatavamsa of Kassapa. Ed. J. Minayeff. *Journal
of the Pali Text Society*. London, 1886. Pp. 33–54.

Apastamba Dharma Sutra. Ed. G. Bühler. Bombay:
Bombay Sanskrit Series 44 and 50, 1892–94.

Arthashastra of Kautilya. Ed. and trans. R. P. Kangle. Vol. 1: text. Vol. 2: translation. Bombay:
University of Bombay, 1960.

Atharva Veda, with the commentary of Sayana. 5
vols. Hoshiarpur: Vishveshvaranand Vedic
Research Institute, 1960.

Basava Purana. See Narayana Rao.

Baudhayana Dharma Sutra. Ed. C. Sastri. Benares:
Kashi Sanskrit Series 104, 1934.

Baudhayana Shrauta Sutra of the Taittirya Samhita.
Ed. W. Caland. Vol. 2. Calcutta: Asiatic
Society, 1913.

Bhagavad Gita. In the *Mahabharata*, Poona edition.

Bhagavata Purana. With the commentary of Shri-
dhara. Benares: Pandita Pustakalaya, 1972.

Brahmanda Purana. Bombay: Venkateshvara
Steam Press, 1857.

Brahma-sutra-bhashya of Madhva. Tirupati:
Tirumala-Tirupati-Devasthanena, 1983.

Brahma-sutra-bhashya of Shankara. Bombay:
Nirnaya Sagara Press, 1948.

Brahmavaivarta Purana. Poona: Anandasrama
Sanskrit Series, 1935

Brihaddevata of Shaunaka. Cambridge: Harvard
University Press, 1904.

Buddha-charita of Ashvaghosha. Ed. E. H. Johnston. Calcutta: Panjab University Oriental
Publications, 1935–36.

Caitanya-caritamrita of Krishnadasa Kaviraja.
Trans. Edward Cameron Dimock and Tony K.
Stewart. Cambridge, Mass.: Harvard University
Press, 1999.

Dabistan al-madhahib of Mobad Shah (Muhsin
Fani, attr.) Bombay, 1262/1846. *The Dabistán or
School of Manners*. Trans. David Shea and An-
thony Troyer. Reprint ed. abridged by A. V.
Williams Jackson. Washington, D.C.: M. Wal-
ter Dunne, 1901.

Dasha-kumara-charita of Dandin. Trans. Isabelle
Onians (*What Ten Young Man Did*). New York:
New York University Press, 2005.

Dashavatara-charita of Kshemendra. Bombay:
Kavyamala Series, 1891.

Devibhagavata Purana. Benares: Pandita
Pustakalaya, 1960.

Garuda Purana. Benares: Pandita Pustakalaya,
1969.

Gautama-dharmasutra. New Delhi: Veda Mitra,
1969.

Gita Govinda of Jaydeva. Hyderabad: Sanskrit
Academy Series, 1969.

Hari-vamsha. Poona: Bhandarkar Oriental Research Institute, 1969.

Harsha-charita of Bana. Bombay: Bombay Sanskrit
and Prakrit Series, 1909.

History of Herodotus. Trans. David Grene.
Chicago: University of Chicago Press, 1987.

Jaiminiya Brahmana. Nagpur: Sarasvati-vihara
Series. 1954.

Jatakamala of Aryasuri. Delhi: Motilal Banarsidass,
1971.

Jatakas. [*Jataka Stories*]. Ed. E. B. Cowell. London:
Pali Text Society, 1973.

Kadambari of Banabhatta. *A Classic Story of Magical Transformations*. Trans. and intro. Gwen-

dolyn Layne. New York and London: Garland Publishing, 1991.

Kalika Purana. Ed. Sri Biswanarayan Sastri. Varanasi: Chowkhamba Sanskrit Series Office, 1972.

Kalki Purana. Mathura: Jai Nitai Press, 2006.

Kamasutra of Vatsyayana, with the commentary of Yashodhara. Ed. with the Hindi "Jaya" commentary by Devadatta Shastri. Varanasi: Kashi Sanskrit Series, 1964.

The Kamasutra of Vatsyayana. Trans. Wendy Doniger and Sudhir Kakar. London and New York: Oxford World Classics, 2002.

Kamasutra: The Pop-Up KamaSutra. NewYork: Harry N. Abrahms, 2003.

Kathaka Samhita [Die Samhita der Katha-Sakha]. 3 vols. Leipzig: F. A. Brockhaus, 1900.

Katha-ratnakara of Hemavijayagani. Banasakantha: Omkarasahiyta Nidhi, 1997.

Katha-sarit-sagara [The Ocean of the Rivers of Story]. Bombay: Nirnara Sagara Press, 1930. English translation: *The Ocean of Story.* Ed. N. M. Penzer, trans. C. W. Tawney. 10 vols. London: Chas. J. Sawyer, 1924.

Kaushitaki Brahmana. 3 vols. Calcutta: Bibliotheca Indica, 1903.

Kurma Purana. Varanasi: All-India Kashiraj Trust, 1972.

Linga Purana. Calcutta: Sri Arunodaraya, 1812.

Madhva-vijaya of Narayana Panditacarya. Vishakhapatnam: Shrimadananda Tirtha Publications, 1983.

Mahabhagavata Purana. Bombay: Venkateshvara Steam Press, 1913.

Mahabharata. Poona: Bhandarkar Oriental Research Institute, 1933–69.

Mahabharata, with the commentary of Nilakantha. Bombay: Jagadishvara, 1862.

Mahanirvana Tantra. Madras: Tantrik Texts, 1929.

Maitrayani Samhita. Wiesbaden: R. Steiner, 1970–72 (1881).

Manavadharmasastra [The Laws of Manu]. Trans. Wendy Doniger with Brian K. Smith. Harmondsworth: Penguin Classics, 1991.

Mani-manjari of Narayana Panditacarya. Bombay: Nirnaya Sagara Press, 1912.

Manusmrti. Bombay: Bharatiya Vidya Series, 1972–78.

Naishadiyacarita of Shri Harsha. Bombay: Nirnaya Sagara Press, 1986.

Narmamala of Kshemendra. Ed. and trans. Fabrizia Baldissera. Würzburg: Südasien-Institut, Ergon Verlag, 2005.

Nirukta of Yaska. Ed. Lakshman Sarup. 2 vols. London and New York: Oxford University Press, 1920–27.

Periya Purana of Cekkilar. Trans. Alistair McGlashan (*The History of the Holy Servants of the Lord Siva*). Victoria, B.C.: Trafford Publishing, 2006.

Phaedrus of Plato. Trans. Alexander Nehamas and Paul Woodruff. In Plato, *Complete Works,* ed. John M. Cooper. Indianapolis: Hackett, 1997.

Prabodhachandrodaya of Mahendradatta. Trans. Sita K. Nambiar. Delhi: Motilal Banarsidass, 1971, 1998.

Priyadarshika of Harsha. Ed. M. R. Kale. Bombay: Motilal Banarsidass, 1928.

Purva-mimamsa-sutra. Jaiminiya-mimamsa-bhashyam of Shabarasvamin. Hirayana: Ramlal Kapar, 1986.

Rajatarangini. Ed. and trans. M. A. Stein (*Rajatarangini, or, Chronicle of the Kings of Kashmir*). Leipzig: Otto Harassowitz, 1892.

Ramacaritamanasa of Tulsi Das [*The Holy Lake of the Acts of Rama*]. Trans. R. C. Prasad. Delhi: Motilal Banarsidass, 1990.

Ramayana of Valmiki. Baroda: Oriental Institute, 1960–75.

Ratnavali of Harsa. Ed. Ashokanath Bhattacharya and Maheshwar Das. Calcutta: Modern Book Agency, 1967.

Rig Veda, with the commentary of Sayana. 6 vols. London: Oxford University Press, 1890–92.

Sarvadarshanasamgraha of Madhava. Trans. E. B Cowell and A. E. Gough. London: Trübner, 1914.

Saura Purana. Poona: Anandashrama Sanskrit Series, 1923.

Shakuntala [Abhijnanashakuntalam] of Kalidasa. Bombay: Nirnaya Sagara Press, 1958.

Shankara-dig-vijaya of Madhava. Poona: Bhandarkar Oriental Research Institute, 1915.

Shankara-vijaya of Anandagiri. Ed. J. Tarkapancanana. Calcutta: Bibliotheca Indica, 1868.

Shatapatha Brahmana. Benares: Chowkhamba Sanskrit Series, 1964.

Shiva Purana. Benares: Pandita Pustakalaya, 1964.

Shiva Purana, Dharmasamhita. Bombay, 1884.

Shivalaya Mahatmya of the *Sahyadrikhanda* of the *Skanda Purana.* Ms. in the library of the Royal Asiatic Society in Bombay. Transcribed and trans. Micaela Soar. 1996.

Skanda Purana. Bombay: Shree Venkateshvara Steam Press, 1867.

Taittiriya Brahmana. Ed. Rajendralala Mitra. Calcutta: Bibliotheca Indica, 1859; Delhi: Motilal Banarsidass, 1985.

Taittiriya Samhita. Poona: Anandasrama Sanskrit Series, 1979.

Upadesha-Sahasri of Shankaracārya. *A Thousand Teachings, in Two Parts—Prose and Poetry.* Ed. Jagadananda. 3rd ed. Mylapore, Madras: Sri Ramakrishna Math, 1961.

———. *A Thousand Teachings: The Upadeshasāhasrī of Shankara.* Trans. and ed. Sengaku Mayeda, foreword John M. Koller. Albany: State University of New York Press, 1991.

Upanishads. One Hundred and Eight Upanishads. Bombay: Nirnaya Sagara Press, 1913.

Vajasaneyi Sanhita. Varanasi: Chaukhamba Sanskrit Series, 1972.

Vamana Purana. Benares: All-India Kashiraj, 1968.

Vayu Purana. Poona: Anandasrama Sanskrit Series, 1860.

Vishnu Purana. Calcutta: Sanatana Shastra, 1972.

Yoni Tantra. Trans. Michael Magee. Vol. 2. Harrow, U.K.: Worldwide Tantra Project, 1995.

SECONDARY SOURCES

Adcock, Catherine. *"Religious Freedom and Political Culture: The Arya Samaj in Colonial* North India." Ph.D. dissertation, University of Chicago, 2007.

Agravat, Ram Prakash. *Satyavadi Vir Tejapala.* Jodhapura: Sri Uttama Ashram, Kagamarga, 1973.

Ahmad, Aziz. "Epic and Counter-Epic in Medieval India." *Journal of the American Oriental Society* 83 (1963), 470–76. Reprinted in *India's Islamic Traditions, 711–1750,* ed. Richard M. Eaton. New York: Oxford University Press, 2003. Pp. 37–49.

Alam, Muzaffar. *"Akhlaqui* Norms and Mughal Governance." In Muzaffar Alam et al., eds. *The Making of Indo-Persian Culture: Indian and French Studies.* Delhi and Paris: Manohar and Centre de Sciences Humaines, 2000. Pp. 67–95.

———. "The Culture and Politics of Persian in Precolonial Hinduism." In Pollock, *Literary Cultures,* 131–98.

Alder, Garry. *Beyond Bokhara: The Life of William Moorcroft, Asian Explorer and Pioneer Veterinary Surgeon,1767–1825.* London: Century Publishing, 1985.

Ali, Daud. *Courtly Culture and Political Life in Early Medieval India.* Cambridge, U.K., and New York: Cambridge University Press, 2004.

Ali, M. Athar. "Encounter and Efflorescence: Genesis of the Medieval Civilization." In *Social Scientist* (New Delhi) 1 (1990), 13–28.

Allen, Nick. "Why Did Odysseus Become a Horse?" *Journal of the American Oriental Society* 26:2 (1995), 143–54.

Allen, Woody. "Fabulous Tales and Mythical Beasts." In *Without Feathers.* New York: Random House, 1976. Pp. 76–79.

Ambedkar, B. R. *The Buddha and His Dhamma.* Bombay: Peoples Education Society. 1957.

———. *Towards an Enlightened India.* New Delhi: Penguin Books, 2004.

———. *Why Go for Conversion?* Bangalore: Pariah Sahitya Akademy, 1981.

Anand, Mulk Raj, and Eleanor Zelliot. *An Anthology of Dalit Literature (Poems).* New Delhi: Gyan Publishing House, 1992.

Appadurai, Arjun. "Gastro-Politics in Hindu South Asia." *American Ethnologist* 8:3 (1981), 494–511.

———. "Kings, Sects and Temples in South India, 1350–1700 A.D." *Economic and Social History Review* 14:1 (1977), 47–73.

Arunachalam, M. *Peeps into Tamil Literature: Ballad Poetry.* Tiruchitrambalam: Gandhi Vidyalayam, 1976.

Aurobindo, Sri. *On Yoga. Book One.* Pondicherry: International University Centre Collection, 1958.

Babb, Lawrence A. *Alchemies of Violence: Myths of Identity and the Life of Trade in Western India.* New Delhi: Sage Publications, 2004.

———. "Glancing: Visual Interaction in Hinduism." *Journal of Anthropological Research* 37:4 (Winter 1981), 387–401.

———. *Redemptive Encounters: Three Modern Styles in the Hindu Tradition.* Berkeley: University of California Press, 1986.

———, and Susan S. Wadley, eds. *Media and the Transformation of Religion in South Asia.* Philadelphia: University of Pennsylvania Press, 1995.

Babur. *The Baburnama. Memoirs of Babur, Prince and Emperor.* Trans. Wheeler M. Thackston. Intro. by Salman Rushdie. New York: Modern Library, 2002. Also, trans. A. S. Beveridge. London: Luzac, 1921.

Baker, Deborah. *A Blue Hand: The Beats in India.* New York: Penguin Press, 2008.

Bakker, Hans T. *Ayodhya. The History of Ayodhya from the 7th Century BC to the Middle of the 18th Century.* Amsterdam: John Benjamins, 1986.

———, ed. *Origin and Growth of the Puranic Text Corpus with Special Reference to the Skanda Purana.* Groningen: E. Forsten, 1986; Delhi: Motilal, 2004

Ball, Charles. *The History of the Indian Mutiny Giving a Detailed Account of the Sepoy Insurrection in India; and a Concise History of the Great Military Events Which Have Tended to Consolidate British Empire in Hindostan.* Vol. 1. New Delhi: Master Publishers, n.d. (1859).

Banerjea, Jitendra Nath. *The Development of Hindu Iconography.* Calcutta: University of Calcutta, 1956.

Banerji, S. C. *Studies in the Mahapuranas.* Calcutta: Punthi Pustak, 1991.

Basham, A. L. *The Wonder That Was India.* London: Sidgwick and Jackson, 1954.

———. ed. Kennth G. Zysk. *The Origins and Development of Classical Hinduism.* New York: Beacon Press, 1989.

———, ed. K. Zysk. *The Sacred Cow: The Evolution of Classical Hinduism.* New York: Beacon Press, 1989.

Beal, Samuel, trans. *Si-yu-ki: Buddhist Records of the Western World.* 2 vols. New York: Paragon, 1968.

Beck, Guy L., ed. *Alternative Krishnas: Regional and Vernacular Variations on a Hindu Deity.* Albany, N.Y.: SUNY, 2005.

Behl, Aditya, and Simon Weightman, trans. *Madhu Malati: An Indian Sufi Romance*. Oxford and New York: Oxford University Press, 2000.

Bhabha, Homi. *The Location of Culture*. New York: Routledge, 1994.

Bhagat, Surekha. "The Lesson." In *Vidrokhi Kavita,* ed. Keshav Meshram, 2nd ed., Pune: Continental Prakashan, 1987. Trans. Gauri Deshpande et al.

Bhandarkar, D. R. *Some Aspects of Ancient Hindu Polity*. Benares: Benares Hindu University, 1929.

Bharati, Agehananda. "Making Sense out of Tantrism and Tantrics." *Loka: A Journal of the Naropa Institute* 2 (1976), 53.

Bhattacarya, Asutosh. *Folklore of Bengal*. New Delhi: National Book Trust, 1978.

Bhattacharya, Deben. *Love Songs of Chandidas*. London: Allen and Unwin, 1967.

Bhattacharya, Nagendranath. *History of the Tantric Religion*. Delhi: Munshiram Manoharlal, 1982.

Biardeau, Madeleine. *Hinduism: The Anthropology of a Civilization*. Delhi: Oxford University Press, 1994.

———. *Stories About Posts; Vedic Variations Around the Hindu Goddess*. Chicago: University of Chicago, 2004.

Blackburn, Stuart H., and Peter J. Claus et al. , eds. *Oral Epics in India*. Berkeley and Los Angeles: University of California Press, 1989.

Bloch, Jules. *Les inscriptions d'Asoka*. Paris: Société d'Édition, 1950.

Bloom, Allan, *The Closing of the American Mind*. New York: Simon and Schuster, 1987,

Bloom, Harold. *The Anxiety of Influence: A Theory of Poetry*. New York: Oxford University Press, 1973.

Böhtlingk, Otto. *Indische Sprüche*. St. Petersburg: Akademie der Wissenschaften, 1870.

Bollee, Willem B. *Gone to the Dogs in Ancient India*. München: Bayerische Akademie der Wissenschaften, Philosophisch-Historisch Klasse, Heft 2; Beck, 2006.

Bolon, Carol Radcliffe. *Forms of the Goddess Lajja Gauri in Indian Art*. University Park: Pennsylvania State University Press, 1992.

Bolts, William. "Considerations on Indian Affairs; Particularly Respecting the Present State of Bengal Dependencies." London: 1772. Reprinted in *The East India Company: 1600–1858,* ed. Patrick Tuck. Vol. 3. London and New York: Routledge, 1998.

Booth, Wayne. *The Rhetoric of Fiction*. Chicago: University of Chicago Press, 1961.

Bosworth, A. Brian. "Calanus and the Brahman Opposition." In *Alexander der Grosse: Eine Welteroberung und ihr Hintergrund. Antiquitas*. Reihe 1, Abhandlungen zur alten Geschichte ; Bd. 46. Ed. Wolfgang Will. Bonn: R. Habelt, 1998. Pp. 173–204.

Britt, Aaron. "Avatar." *New York Times Magazine,* August 8, 2008.

Brockington, John L. *The Sanskrit Epics*. Leiden-Boston: Brill, 1998.

———. "The Sanskrit Epics." In Flood, *The Blackwell Companion*, 116–28.

Brodbeck, Simon. "Ekalavya and *Mahabharata* 1.121–128." *International Journal of Hindu Studies* 10:1 (2006), 10–34.

Brooks, Douglas R. *The Secret of the Three Cities: An Introduction to Hindu Sakta Tantrism*. Chicago: University of Chicago Press, 1990.

Brown, Carolyn Henning. "Contested Meanings: Tantra and the Poetics of Mithila Art," *American Ethnologist* 23:4 (November 1996), 717–37.

Brown, W. Norman. "The Indian Games of Pachisi, Chaupar, and Chausar." *Expedition* 6 (1964), 32–35.

Bryant, Edwin F., ed. *Krishna, a Sourcebook*. New York and Oxford: Oxford University Press, 2007.

———. *The Quest for the Origins of Vedic Literature: The Indo-Aryan Migration Debate*. New York and Oxford: Oxford University Press, 2001.

———, and Laurie L. Patton, eds. *The Indo-Aryan Controversy. Evidence and Inference in Indian History*. London: Routledge, 2005.

Buck, William. *Mahabharata*. Berkeley and Los Angel: University of California Press, 1973.

Buettner, Elizabeth. *Empire Families: Britons and Late Imperial India*. Oxford: Oxford University Press, 2004.

Bulcke, Camille. "La naissance de Sita." *Bulletin de l'école française d'extrême orient* 46 (1952), 107–17.

Burghart, Richard. "The Category of 'Hindu' in the Political Discourse of Nepal." In *The Conditions of Listening: Essays on Religion, History and Politics in South Asia*, ed. C. J. Fuller and Jonathan Spencer. Delhi: Oxford University Press, 1996.

Burkert, Walter. *Homo Necans*. Berkeley: University of California Press, 1983.

Buruma, Ian, and Avishai Margalit. *Occidentalism: The West in the Eyes of Its Enemies*. New York: Penguin Press, 2004.

Buzurg, ibn Shahriyar. *The Book of the Marvels of India*. French trans. L. Marcel Devic. 1883–86. (1) English trans. Peter Quennell. New York: Dial Press, 1929.

Cannadine, David. *Ornamentalism: How the British Saw Their Empire*. New York: Penguin Books, 2001.

———, and Simon Price eds. *Rituals of Royalty: Power and Ceremonial in Traditional Societies*. Cambridge, U.K.: Cambridge University Press, 1987.

Carman, John Braisted. *The Theology of Ramanuja: An Essay in Interreligious Understanding*. New Haven and London: Yale University Press, 1974.

Carnegy, P. *A Historical Sketch of Tehsil Fyzabad*. Lucknow: 1870.

Chakrabarti, Kunal. *Themes in Indian History*. Delhi: Oxford Readings in Sociology, Oxford University Press, 2006.

Chakrabarty, Dipesh. *Provincializing Europe*. Princeton, N.J.; Princeton University Press, 2000.

Chakravarti, Ranabir. "Horse Trade and Piracy at Tana (Thana, Maharashtra, India): Gleanings from Marco Polo." *Journal of the Economic and Social History of the Orient* 33:3 (1991), 159–82.

Chakravarti, Uma. *The Social Dimensions of Early Buddhism*. Delhi: Munshiram Manoharlal, 1996.

Chand, Tek. *Liquor Menace in India*. New Delhi: Gandhi Peace Foundation, 1972.

Chatterjee, Indrani. *Gender, Slavery and Law in Colonial India*. New Delhi: Oxford University Press, 1999.

Chatterji, Bankimcandra. *Anandamath, or The Sacred Brotherhood*. Trans. Julius J. Lipner. New York: Oxford University Press, 2005.

Chattopadhyaya, Brajadulal. *Representing the Other? Sanskrit Sources and the Muslims*. Delhi: Manohar, 1998.

Chattopadhyaya, Debiprasad. *Lokayata: A Study in Ancient Indian Materialism*. New Delhi: People's Pub. House, 1959.

———, ed. *Carvaka/Lokayata: An Anthology of Source Materials and Some Recent Studies*. New Delhi: Indian Council of Philosophical Research, 1990.

Chaudhuri, Nirad C. *The Continent of Circe: An Essay on the Peoples of India*. London: Chatto and Windus, 1965.

Clooney, Francis, S. J. "Restoring 'Hindu Theology' as a Category in Indian Intellectual Discourse." In Flood, *The Blackwell Companion*, 447–77.

———, and Tony K. Stewart. "Vaisnava." In Mittal and Thursby, eds. *The Hindu World*, 162–84.

Coburn, Thomas B. "Scripture in India: Towards a Typology of the Word in Hindu Life." *Journal of the American Academy of Religion* 42:3 (September 1984), 435–60.

Cohen, Arthur. *The Myth of the Judeo-Christian Tradition*. New York: Harper and Row, 1970.

Cohn, Bernard S. "The Changing Status of a Depressed Caste." In *An Anthropologist Among the Historians and Other Essays*. Delhi: Oxford University Press, 1992.

Colas, Gerard. "History of Vaisnava Traditions." In Flood, *The Blackwell Companion*, 229–70.

Collen, Lindsey. *The Rape of Sita*. London: Bloomsbury Press, 1993.

Collins, Brian. "Violence, Power and Sacrifice in the Indian Context." Unpublished essay, 2005.

Converse, Hyla S. "An Ancient Sudra Account of the Origin of Castes." *Journal of the American Oriental Society* 114:4 (1994), 642–44.

Courtright, Paul B. *Ganesha: Lord of Obstacles,*

Lord of Beginnings. New York: Oxford University Press, 1989.

———. "The Iconographies of Sati." In Hawley, *Sati*, 27–48

Cox, Whitney. "Saffron in the Rasam." In *Language, Culture and Power*, essays in honor of Sheldon Pollock. Forthcoming.

Crooke, William. *The Popular Religion and Folk-lore of Northern India*. 2 vols. London: Archibald Constable, 1896.

Cutler, Norman. "Tamil Hindu Literature." In Flood, *The Blackwell Companion*, 145–58.

———. "Three Moments in the Genealogy of Tamil Literary Culture." In Pollock, *Literary Cultures*, 271–322.

———. *Songs of Experience: The Poetics of Tamil Devotion*. Bloomington: Indiana University Press, 1987.

Dales, George F. "Of Dice and Men." *Journal of the American Oriental Society* 88:1 (January–March 1968), 14–23.

Dalrymple, William. *The Age of Kali: Indian Travels and Encounters*. NewYork: HarperCollins; Hammersmith: Flamingo, 1999.

———. *City of Djinns*. New York: Penguin, 1993.

———. "Homer in India: Rajasthan's Oral Epics." *New Yorker* (November 20, 2006), 48–55.

———. "India: The Place of Sex." *New York Review of Books* 55:11 (June 26, 2008), 18–21.

———. "India: The War over History." *New York Review of Books* 52:6 (April 7, 2005), 62–65.

———. *The Last Mughal: The Fall of a Dynasty: Delhi, 1857*. New York: Knopf, 2007.

———. "The Most Magnificent Muslims." *New York Review of Books* 54:18 (November 22, 2007), 26–29.

———. *White Moghuls: Love and Betrayal in 18th Century India*. Hammersmith: HarperCollins, Flamingo, 2003.

Dangle, Arjun, ed. *Poisoned Bread: Translations from Modern Marathi Dalit Literature*. Hyderabad: Orient Longman, Ltd., 1992.

Daniel, E. Valentine. *Charred Lullabies: Chapters in an Anthropology of Violence*. Princeton, N.J.: Princeton University Press, 1996.

———. *Fluid Signs: Being a Person the Tamil Way*. Berkeley: University of California Press, 1984.

Daniel, George. *Democritus in London: With the Mad Pranks and Comical Conceits of Motley and Robin Good-Fellow*. London: William Pickering, 1852.

Danielou, Alain. *A Brief History of India*. Rochester, Vt.: Inner Traditions International, 2003.

———. *India, A Civilization of Differences: The Ancient Tradition of Universal Tolerance*. Rochester, Vt.: Inner Traditions, 2003.

———. *Virtue, Success, Pleasure, Liberation: The Four Arms of Life in the Tradition of Ancient India*. Rochester, Vt.: Inner Traditions, 1993.

Das, Veena. *Structure and Cognition*. Delhi: Oxford University Press, 1977.

Das Gupta, Ashin. *Malabar in Asian Trade, 1740–1800*. Cambridge, U.K.: Cambridge University Press, 1967.

Datta, V. N. *Sati: A Historical, Social, and Philosophical Enquiry into the Hindu Rite of Widow Burning*. New Delhi: Manohar, 1987.

David, Saul. *The Indian Mutiny*. New York: Penguin Books, 2003.

Davis, Richard. *Lives of Indian Images*. Princeton, N.J.: Princeton University Press, 1997.

Debroy, Bibek. *Sarama and Her Children: The Dog in Indian Myth*. Delhi: Penguin India, 2008.

Dehejia, Vidya. "The Iconographies of Sati." In Hawley, *Sati*, 49–53.

———. *Indian Art*. London: Phaidon, 1997.

———. "Reading Love Imagery on the Indian Temple." In *Love in Asian Art and Culture*, ed. Karen Sagstetter. Washington, D.C.: Arthur M. Sackler Gallery, Smithsonian Institution, 1998. Pp. 97-113.

———. *Yogini, Cult and Temples: A Tantric Tradition*. Delhi: National Museum, 1986.

Deliege, Robert. *The Untouchables of India*. Oxford, U.K.: Berg, 2001.

Derrett , J. Duncan M. *Dharmasastra and Juridical Literature*. Wiesbaden: Otto Harrassowitz, 1973.

Desai, Devangana. *The Religious Imagery of Khajuraho*. Mumbai: Franco-Indian Research, 1996.

Desai, Mahadev. *The Gospel of Selfless Action or The Gita According to Gandhi*. Translation of the original in Gujarati, with an introduction and commentary. Ahmedabad: Navajivan Publishing House, 1946.

Desmond, Laura. "*Disciplining Pleasure: The Erotic Science of the Kamasutra*." Ph.D. dissertation, University of Chicago, 2009.

Devahuti, D. *Harsha: A Political Study*. Oxford, U.K.: Clarendon, 1970.

Digby, Simon. *Warhorse and Elephant in the Delhi Sultanate*. Oxford, U.K.: Orient Monographs, 1971.

Dimmitt, Cornelia. "Sita: Fertility Goddess and *shakti*." In Hawley and Wulff, *The Divine Consort*, 210–23.

Dimock, Edward C. *The Place of the Hidden Moon: Erotic Mysticism in the Vaisnava-sahajiya Cult of Bengal*. Chicago: University of Chicago Press, 1966, 1989.

Dirks, Nicholas B. *The Hollow Crown: Ethnohistory of an Indian Kingdom*. Ann Arbor: University of Michigan Press, 1993.

———. "Political Authority and Structural Change in Early South Indian History." *Indian Economic and Social History Review* 13:2 (1976), 125–57.

———. *The Scandal of Empire*. Cambridge, Mass.: Harvard University Press, 2006.

Doniger, Wendy. "A Burnt Offering." Review of D. N. Jha, *The Myth of the Holy Cow. Times Literary Supplement* 5183 (August 2, 2002), 9.

———. *The Bedtrick: Tales of Sex and Masquerade*. Chicago: University of Chicago Press, 2000.

———. "The Clever Wife in Indian Mythology." In *Incompatible Visions: South Asian Religions in History and Culture. Essays in Honor of David M. Knipe.*, ed. James Blumenthal. Madison: University of Madison–Wisconsin, Center for South Asia, 2005. Pp. 185–203.

———. "Do Many Heads Necessarily Have Many Minds? Tracking the Sources of Hindu Tolerance and Intolerance." *Parabola* 30:4 (Winter 2005), 10–19.

———. "Hinduism by Any Other Name." *Wilson Quarterly* (July 1991), 35–41.

———. "Hindu Pluralism and Hindu Intolerance of the Other." In *Concepts of the Other in Near Eastern Religions. Israel Oriental Studies*, vol. 14, eds. Ilai Alon, Ithamar Gruenwald, and Itamar Singer. Leiden and New York: E. J. Brill, 1994. Pp. 369–90.

———. "'I Have Scinde': Flogging a Dead (White Male Orientalist) Horse." Presidential Address. *Journal of Asian Studies* 58:4 (November 1999), 940–60. Available online at www.jstor.org/view/00219118/di015153/01p0195c/0

———. *The Implied Spider: Politics and Theology in Myth*. New York: Columbia University Press, 1998.

———. "Jewels of Rejection and Recognition in Ancient India." *Journal of Indian Philosophy* 26 (1998), 435–53.

———. "Shadows of the *Ramayana*." In *The Epic Voice*, ed. Alan D. Hodder and Ralph Meagher. New York: Praeger, 2002.

———. *Splitting the Difference: Gender and Myth in Ancient Greece and India*. Chicago: University of Chicago Press, 1999.

———. "Tolstoi's Revenge: The Violence of Indian Non-Violence." In *Genocide, War, and Human Survival*, ed. Charles B. Strozier and Michael Flynn. Lanham, Md.: Rowman and Littlefield, 1996. Pp. 219–27.

———. "Why Did They Burn?" A review of three books about widow burning, by Lata Mani, Catherine Weinberger-Thomas, and Mala Sen. *Times Literary Supplement* (September 14, 2001), 3–4.

———. *The Woman Who Pretended to Be Who She Was*. New York: Oxford University Press, 2005.

———. "Zoomorphism in Ancient India: Humans More Bestial than the Beasts." In *Thinking with Animals: New Perspectives on Anthropomorphism*, ed. Lorraine Daston and Gregg Mitman. New York: Columbia University Press, 2005. Pp. 17–36.

Doniger O'Flaherty, Wendy. Articles under "Hinduism" in the *New Encyclopaedia Britannica (Macropaedia)*, 15th ed., vol. 20 (1997); articles first published, 1990 printing. "Hinduism: General Nature and Characteristic Features," 519–21; "The History of Hinduism" (with A. L. Basham and J. A. B. van Buitenen), 521–29; "Sacred Texts" (with J. A. B. van Buitenen, Edward C. Dimock, A. L. Basham, and Brian K. Smith), 529–49; "Cultural Expressions: Visual Arts, Theatre, and Dance," (with A. L. Basham and J. A. B. van Buitenen), 554–55; "Bibliography," (with Brian K. Smith), 557–558.

———. *Animals in Four Worlds: Sculptures from India*. Photos Stella Snead; text Wendy Doniger (3–23) and George Michell. Chicago: University of Chicago Press, 1989.

———. *The Cave of Siva at Elephanta*. Photos Carmel Berkson, text Wendy Doniger O'Flaherty, Carmel Berkson, and George Michell. Princeton, N.J.: Princeton University Press, 1983; New Delhi: Oxford University Press, 1987). Introduction (xii–xiii) and "The Myths Depicted at Elephanta" (27–39) by Wendy Doniger O'Flaherty.

———. *Dreams, Illusion, and Other Realities*. Chicago: University of Chicago Press, 1984.

———. "Ethical and Non-Ethical Implications of the Separation of Heaven and Earth in Indian Mythology." In *Cosmogony and Ethical Order: New Studies in Comparative Ethics*. eds. Frank Reynolds and Robin Lovin. Chicago and London: University of Chicago Press, 1985. Pp. 177–99.

———. *Hindu Myths*. Harmondsworth, U.K.: Penguin, 1975.

———. "Hinduism by Any Other Name." *Wilson Quarterly* (July 1991), 35–41.

———. "Horses and Snakes in the Adi Parvan of the *Mahabharata*." In *Aspects of India: Essays in Honor of Edward Cameron Dimock, Jr.*, eds. Margaret Case and N. Gerald Barrier. New Delhi: American Institute of Indian Studies and Manohar, 1986. Pp. 16–44.

———. "The Image of the Heretic in the Gupta Puranas." In *Essays on Gupta Culture*, ed. Bardwell L. Smith. New Delhi: Motilal Banarsidass, 1983. Pp. 107–28.

———, ed., *Karma and Rebirth in Classical Indian Traditions*. Berkeley: University of California Press; Delhi: Motilal Banarsidass, 1980.

———. *The Origins of Evil in Hindu Mythology*. Berkeley: University of California Press, 1976.

———. "The Origins of Heresy in Hindu Mythology," *History of Religions* 10:4 (May 1971), 271–333.

———. *Other Peoples' Myths: The Cave of Echoes*. New York: Macmillan, 1988; Chicago: University of Chicago Press, 1995.

———. "Pluralism and Intolerance in Hinduism." In *Radical Pluralism and Truth: David Tracy and the Hermeneutics of Religion*, eds. Werner G. Jeanrond and Jennifer L. Rike. New York: Crossroads, 1991. Pp. 215–33.

———. *Purana Perennis: Reciprocity and Transformation in Hindu and Jaina Texts*. Albany, N.Y.: SUNY Press, 1993.

———. "The Post-Vedic History of the Soma Plant." In R. Gordon Wasson, *Soma: Divine Mushroom of Immortality*, New York: Harcourt Brace, 1968. Pp. 95–147.

———. *The Rig Veda*. Harmondsworth, U.K.: Penguin Books, 1981.

———. "The Scrapbook of Undeserved Salvation: The *Kedara Khanda* of the *Skanda Purana*." In Doniger O'Flaherty, ed., *Purana Perennis*, 59–83.

———. *Siva, the Erotic Ascetic*. Oxford, U.K.: Oxford University Press, 1973.

———. *Tales of Sex and Violence: Folklore, Sacrifice, and Danger in the Jaiminiya Brahmana*. Chicago: University of Chicago Press, 1985; Delhi: Motilal Banarsidass, 1987.

———. *Textual Sources for the Study of Hinduism*. Manchester, U.K.: Manchester University Press; New Jersey: Barnes and Noble, 1988; Chicago: University of Chicago Press, 1990.

———. *Women, Androgynes, and Other Mythical Beasts*. Chicago: University of Chicago Press, 1980.

———, and Brian K. Smith, "Sacrifice and Substitution: Ritual Mystification and Mythical Demystification." *Numen* 36:2 (December 1989), 190–223.

———, and J. Duncan M. Derrett, eds. *The Concept of Duty in South Asia*. London: School of Oriental and African Studies; Delhi: Vikas Publishing Company; Columbia, Mo: South Asia Books, 1978.

———, and Howard Eilberg-Schwartz. *Off with Her Head! The Denial of Women's Identity in Myth, Religion, and Culture*. Berkeley: University of California Press, 1995.

———, and Brian K Smith, "Sacrifice and Substitution: Ritual Mystification and Mythical Demystification," *Numen* 36:2 (December 1989), 190–223.

———, and Gregory Spinner. "Misconceptions: Female Imaginations and Male Fantasies in Parental Imprinting," *Daedalus* 127:1 (Winter 1998), 97–130.

Dorson, Richard M. "The Eclipse of Solar Mythology." In Thomas A. Sebeok, *Myth: A Symposium*. Bloomington: Indiana University Press, 1958.

Douglas, Mary. *Purity and Danger: An Analysis of Concepts of Pollution and Taboo*. London: Routledge and K. Paul, 1966.

Doyle, Sir Arthur Conan. "Silver Blaze." In *The Annotated Sherlock Holmes*, ed. William S.

Baring-Gould. 2 vols. New York: Clarkson N. Potter, 1967., Vol. 2, 261–81.

Dube, Saurabh. *Untouchable Pasts: Religion, Identity, and Power Among a Central Indian Community, 1780–1950.* Albany, N.Y.: SUNY Press, 1998.

Dubuisson, Daniel. "La déesse chevelue et la reine coiffeuse." *Journal Asiatique* 266 (1978), 291–310.

Dumézil, Georges. *The Destiny of a King.* Trans. Alf Hiltebeitel. Chicago: University of Chicago Press, 1973.

———. *The Destiny of the Warrior.* Trans. Alf Hiltebeitel. Chicago: University of Chicago Press, 1970.

———. "La vache d'abondance et la vache d'empire." Chapter 3, part 5, of *Servius et la Fortune.* Paris: Gallimard, 1943.

Dumont, Louis. *Homo Hierarchicus.* London: Weidenfeld and Nicolson, 1966.

Dundes, Alan, ed. *The Flood Myth.* Berkeley: University of California Press, 1988.

———. "The Hero Pattern and the Life of Jesus." In Otto Rank et al., *In Quest of the Hero.* Princeton, N. J.: Princeton University Press, 1990. 179–223.

Eaton, Richard M. "Conversion to Christianity Among the Nagas, 1876–1971." *Indian Economic and Social History Review* 2:1 (January–March. 1984), 8–33.

———. *The Rise of Islam and the Bengal Frontier, 1204–1760.* Berkeley: University of California Press, 1993.

———. *Temple Desecration and Indo-Muslim States.* New York: Oxford University Press, 1990.

———. "Temple Desecration and Indo-Muslim States." *Journal of Islamic Studies* 11:3 (2000), 283–319.

———. "Temple Desecration in Pre-modern India," *Frontline,* December 22, 2000, 62–70.

Ebeling, Sascha. "Another Tomorrow for Nantanar: The Continuation and Re-Invention of a Medieval South-Indian Untouchable Saint." In *Geschichten und Geschichte: Religiöse Geschichtsschreibung in Asien und ihre Verwertung in der religionshistorischen Forschung,* eds. Peter Schalk, Max Deeg, Oliver Freiberger, and Christoph Kleine. Acta Universitatis Upsaliensis. Uppsala: University of Uppsala. Forthcoming.

Eck, Diana L. *Banaras: City of Light.* New York: Penguin Books, 1983.

———. *Darsan: Seeing the Divine Image in India.* New York: Columbia University Press, 1996.

Edwardes, Michael. *Red Year: The Rebellion of 1857.* London: Cardinal, 1975.

Eggeling, Julius, trans. *Shatapatha Brahmana.* 5 vols. Oxford, U.K.: Oxford University Press, 1882.

Eliade, Mircea. *Briser le toit de la maison. La créativité et ses symboles.* Paris: Gallimard, 1986.

———. *Yoga Immortality and Freedom.* Princeton, N.J.: Bollingen, 1958.

Elison, William. "Immanent Domains: Gods, Laws, and Tribes in Mumbai." Ph.D. dissertation, University of Chicago, 2007.

Elst, Koenraad. "Linguistic Aspects of the Aryan Non-invasion Theory." In Bryant and Patton, eds., *The Indo-Aryan Controversy,* 234–81.

Elwin, Verrier. *Myths of Middle India.* Delhi: Oxford University Press, 1950, 1991.

Embree, Ainslee, ed., *Sources of Indian Tradition.* Vol. 1, 2nd ed. New York: Columbia University Press, 1988.

Erdman, Joan. "The Empty Beat: Khali as a Sign of Time." *American Journal of Semiotics* 1:4 (1982), 21–45.

Erdosy, George. *Urbanisation in Early Historic India.* Oxford, U.K.: BAR, 1988.

———, ed. *The Indo-Aryans of Ancient South Asia: Language, Material Culture, and Ethnicity.* New York: Walter de Gruyter, 1995.

Erndl, Kathleen M. "Sakta." In Mittal and Thursby, eds. *The Hindu World,* 140–61.

———. *Victory to the Mother: The Hindu Goddess of Northwest India in Myth, Ritual, and Symbol.* New York: Oxford University Press, 1993.

Ernst, Carl W. "The Islamization of Yoga in the Amrtakunda Translations," *Journal of the Royal Asiatic Society,* Series 3, 13:2 (2003), 199–226.

———. "Situating Sufism and Yoga." *Journal of the Royal Asiatic Society,* Series 3, 15:1 (2005), 15–43.

Fairservis, Walter. *The Harappan Civilization and Its Writing.* New Delhi: Oxford University Press, 1992.

———. *The Roots of Ancient India: The Archeology of Early Indian Civilization.* Chicago: University of Chicago Press, 1975.

Farmer, Steve. "Mythological Functions of Indus Inscriptions." Paper presented at Harvard University, May 8–10, 2004.

———, Richard Sproat, and Michael Witzel, "The Collapse of the Indus-Script Thesis: The Myth of a Literate Harappan Civilization." *Electronic Journal of Vedic Studies* 11–12 (December 13, 2004), 19–57.

Fazl, Abu'l. *Akbar Nama.* Trans. A. S. Beveridge. Calcutta: Baptist Mission Press, 1907.

———. *Ain-i-Akbari.* Trans. H. Blochmann. Lahore: Qausain, 1975.

Ferro-Luzzi, Gabriella Eichinger. "The Polythetic Network of Tamil Folk Stories." *Asian Folklore Studies* 56: 1 (1997), 109–28. Reprinted in Sontheimer and Kulke, eds., *Hinduism Reconsidered,* 187–95.

Festinger, Leon. *Cognitive Dissonance.*

Washington, D.C.: American Psychological Association, 1999.
———. *When Prophecy Fails.* Minneapolis: University of Minnesota Press, 1956.
Figueira, Dorothy. *Aryans, Jews, and Brahmins: Theorizing Authority Through Myths of Identity.* Albany, N.Y.: SUNY Press, 2002.
———. "Die flambierte Frau. Sati in European Culture." In Hawley, *Sati,* 55–71.
———. "To Lose One's Head for Love: The Myth of the Transposed Heads in Thomas Mann and Marguerite Yourcenar." *Rivista de Letterature moderne e comparate* 3 (1987), 161–73.
Findly, Ellison B. "Jahangir's Vow of Non-Violence." *Journal of the American Oriental Society* 107:2 (April–June 1987), 245–56.
Fitzgerald, James. "The Great Epic of India as Religious Rhetoric: A Fresh Look at the *Mahabharata.*" *Journal of the American Academy of Religion* 51:4 (1983), 611–30.
———. *The Mahabharata, Vol. 7, The Book of the Women and The Book of Peace, Part One.* Trans. ed., and annotated. Chicago: University of Chicago Press, 2004.
———. "Mahabharata." In Mittal and Thursby, eds. *The Hindu World,* 52–74.
Fleet, John Faithful. *Corpus Inscriptionum Indicarum.* Calcutta: Superintendent of Government Printing, 1888.
Flood, Gavin, ed. *The Blackwell Companion to Hinduism.* Oxford, U.K.: Blackwell Publishing, 2003.
———. *An Introduction to Hinduism.* Cambridge, U.K.: Cambridge University Press, 1996, 2004.
———. "The Saiva Traditions." In Flood, *The Blackwell Companion,* 200–28.
———. "Saivism." In Mittal and Thursby, eds. *The Hindu World,* 119–39.
Forbes-Mitchell, William. *Reminiscences of the Great Mutiny 1857–59.* London, New York: Macmillan, 1895.
Forster, E. M. "The Emperor Babur." In *Abinger Harvest.* New York: Harcourt Brace, 1936.
———. *The Hill of Devi.* New York: Harcourt Brace, 1953.
———. *A Passage to India.* New York: Harcourt Brace, 1924.
Frawley, David. *Myth of the Aryan Invasion of India.* Columbia, Mo.: South Asia Books, 1994.
Freeman, Rich. "Genre and Society: The Literary Culture of Premodern Kerala." In Pollock, *Literary Cultures,* 437–503.
———. "The Literature of Hinduism in Malayalam." In Flood, *The Blackwell Companion,* 159–81.
———. "The Teyyam Tradition of Kerala." In Flood, *The Blackwell Companion,* 307–27.
Frykenberg, Robert Erik, ed. *Christians and Missionaries in India.* London: Routledge, 2003.

———. "The Emergence of Modern Hinduism as a Concept and as an Institution: A Reappraisal with Special Reference to South India." In Sontheimer and Kulke, eds. *Hinduism Reconsidered,* 29–49.
Fuller, Chris. *The Camphor Flame: Popular Hinduism and Society in India.* Princeton, N.J.: Princeton University Press, 1992–2004.
Galanter, Marc. *Competing Equalities: Law and the Backward Classes in India.* Berkeley: University of California Press, 1984.
Gamkrelidze, Thomas V., and Vjareslav V. Ivanov. *Indo-European and the Indo-Europeans.* New York: M. de Gruyter, 1995.
Gandhi, Mohandas K. *An Autobiography: The Story of My Experiments with Truth.* Trans. Mahadev Desai. Boston: Beacon Press, 1957.
———. *The Collected Works of Mahatma Gandhi.* Ahmedabad: Navajivan Publishing House, 1958–94.
———. *The Mind of Mahatma Gandhi,* ed. R. K. Prabhu and U. R. Rao. 3rd ed. Ahmedabad: Navajivan Publishing House, 1968.
Garbe, Richard. "Lokayata." In Hastings' *Encyclopedia of Religion and Ethics* (1926), vol. 8, 138.
Gascoigne, Bamber. *The Great Moguls.* New York: Carroll and Graf, 1971, 2002.
Geertz, Clifford. "Religion as a Cultural System." In *The Interpretation of Cultures.* New York: Basic Books, 1973. 3–32.
Ghai, R. H. *Shuddhi Movement in India: A Study of Its Socio-political Dimensions.* New Delhi: Commonwealth Publishers, 1990
Ghose, Rajeshwari, ed. *In Quest of Secular Symbols: Ayodhya and After.* Perth, Australia: Indian Ocean Centre and South Asian Research Unit, Curtin University of Technology, 1996.
Ghurye, G. S. *The Scheduled Tribes.* Bombay: Popular Prakashan, 1963.
Gilmartin, David, and Bruce B. Lawrence. *Beyond Turk and Hindu: Rethinking Religious Identities in Islamicate South Asia.* Gainesville: University Press of Florida, 2000.
Giroux, Leo, Jr. *The Rishi.* London: Grafton Books, 1986.
Glasenapp, Helmuth von. *Von Buddha zu Gandhi.* Wiesbaden: Otto Harassowitz, 1962.
Glucklich, Ariel. *The Strides of Vishnu: Hindu Culture in Historical Perspective.* New York: Oxford University Press, 2008.
Goel, Sita Ram. *Hindu Temples, What Happened to Them.* 2 vols. New Delhi: Voice of India, 1998.
Goethe, Johann Wolfgang von. *Legende.* In *Werke.* New York: D. Appleton and Co., 1840.
———. *The Poems of Goethe. Translated in the Original Metres,* Trans. Edgar Arthur Bowring. London: G. Bell and Sons, 1891.
Goetz, Hermann. *Studies in the History and Art of Kashmir and the Indian Himalaya.* Wiesbaden: Otto Harassowitz, 1969.

Gold, Ann Grodzins. *Fruitful Journeys: The Ways of Rajasthani Pilgrims.* Berkeley: University of California Press, 1988.

———. "The 'Jungli Rani' and Other Troubled Wives in Rajasthani Oral Traditions." In *From the Margins of Hindu Marriage: Essays on Gender, Religion, and Culture,* eds. Lindsey Harlan and Paul B. Courtright. New York: Oxford University Press, 1995. Pp. 119–36.

———. "Sinking Flowers at Hardwar." In *Religion in India,* ed. T. N. Madan. Delhi: Oxford University Press, 1991.

———. "The Tender Trap: Lord Shiva's Wedding in Vernacular Mythology." In *Multiple Histories: Culture and Society in the Study of Rajasthan,* ed. Lawrence A. Babb et al. Jaipur and New Delhi: Rawat Publications, 2002. Pp. 84–116.

Goldman, Robert P. "Fathers, Sons and Gurus: Oedipal Conflict in the Sanskrit Epics." *Journal of Indian Philosophy* 6 (1978), 325–92.

———. *Gods, Priests, and Warriors: The Bhrgus of the Mahabharata.* New York: Columbia University Press, 1977.

———. *The Ramayana of Valmiki,* Vol. 1. Trans. and intro. R. P. Goldman. Princeton, N.J.: Princeton University Press, 1984.

———. "Karma, Guilt, and Buried Memories: Public Fantasy and Private Reality in Traditional India." *Journal of the American Oriental Society* 105:3 (1985), 413–25.

———, and Sally J. Sutherland Goldman. "Ramayana." In Mittal and Thursby, eds. *The Hindu World,* 75–96.

Golwalkar, M. S. *We, Our Nationhood Defined.* Nagpur: Bharat Prakashan, 1939 [1947].

Gombrich, Ernst H. *Art and Illusion.* Princeton, N.J.: Princeton University Press, 1961.

Gombrich, Richard F. "Ancient Indian Cosmology." In *Ancient Cosmologies,* eds. Carmen Blacker and Michael Loewe. London: Allen and Unwin, 1975. Pp. 110–42.

———. "The Buddha's Eye, the Evil Eye, and Dr. Ruelius." In *The Dating of the Historical Buddha/Die Datierung des historischen Buddha,* ed. Heinz Bechert. Part 2. Symposien zur Buddhismusforschung, 4/2; Göttingen: Vandenhoeck & Ruprecht, 1992. Pp. 335–38.

———. "Dating the Buddha: A Red Herring Revealed." In Bechert, ed. *Dating of the Historical Buddha,* 237–59.

———. *Theravada Buddhism, a Social History.* New York: Routledge, 2006.

———. "Thought on Karma." Forthcoming.

———, and Margaret Cone. *The Perfect Generosity of Prince Vessantara: A Buddhist Epic.* Oxford, U.K.: Clarendon Press, 1977.

Gommans, Jos L. "The Horse Trade in 18th Century South Asia." *Journal of the Economic and Social History of the Orient* 37:3 (1994), 228–50.

———. *The Rise of the Indo-Afghan Empire c. 1710–1780.* Leiden, New York, Köln: E. J. Brill, 1995. Pp. 68–101.

Gonda, Jan. *The Ritual Sutras.* Wiesbaden: Otto Harassowitz, 1977.

Gonzalez-Riemann, Luis. *The Mahabharata and the Yugas.* New York: Peter Lang, 2002.

Gopal, Sarvepalli, ed. *Anatomy of a Confrontation: Ayodhya and the Rise of Communal Politics in India.* Delhi: Penguin India, 1991.

Gopinatha Rao, T. *Elements of Hindu Iconography.* Madras: Law Printing House, 1914–16.

Gottschalk, Peter. *Beyond Hindu and Muslim: Multiple Identity in Narratives from Village India.* New York: Oxford University Press, 2005.

Gough, Kathleen. "Harijans in Thanjavur." In *Imperialism and Revolution in South Asia,* ed. Kathleen Gough and H. Sharma. New York: Monthly Review Press, 1973.

Gould, Stephen Jay. "To Be a Platypus." In *Bully for Brontosaurus: Reflections in Natural History.* New York: W. W. Norton, 1991. 269–79.

Grierson, G. A. "Madhavas." In Hastings' *Encyclopedia of Religion and Ethics,* 8:232–35.

Grimes, John A. "Darsana." In Mittal and Thursby, eds., *The Hindu World,* 553–87.

Grottanelli, Cristiano. "The King's Grace and the Helpless Woman: A Comparative Study of the Stories of Ruth, Charila, Sita." *History of Religions* 22:1 (1982), 1–24.

———. "Yoked Horses, Twins, and the Powerful Lady." *Journal of Indo-European Studies* 14:1–2 (Spring 1986), 125–53.

Gubbins, Martin Richard. *An Account of the Mutinies in Oudh, and of the Siege of the Lucknow Residency; with Some Observations on the Conditions of the Province of Oudh, and on the Causes of the Mutiny in the Bengal Army.* London: Richard Bentley, 1858.

Guha, Ranajit. "Experience, Wonder, and the Pathos of Historicality." In Ranajit Guha, ed. *History at the Limit of World History.* New York: Columbia University Press, 2002. Pp. 48–74.

———. "Sixty Years in Socks: How J. B. S. Haldane Became an Indian." *Times Literary Supplement Commentary* (June 16, 2006), 13–15.

Gupta, C. "Horse Trade in North India: Some Reflections of Socio-Economic Life." *Journal of Ancient Indian History* 14 (1983–84), 186–206.

Gupta, Sanjukta. "The Domestication of a Goddess: Carana-tirtha Kalighat, the Mahapitha of Kali." In *Encountering Kali in the Margins, at the Center in the West,* ed. R. F. McDermott and J. J. Kripal. Berkeley: University of California Press, 2003. Pp. 60–79.

Haberman, David L. *Acting as a Way of Salvation: A Study of Raganuga Bhakti Sadhana.* Delhi: Motilal Banarsidass, 1988, 2001.

———. *Journey Through the Twelve Forests: An*

Encounter with Krishna. New York: Oxford University Press, 1994.

———, and Premlata Sharma. *The Bhaktirasamritasindhu of Rupa Goswamin.* Delhi: Motilal Banarsidass, 2002.

Handelman, Don, and David Shulman. *God Inside Out: Siva's Game of Dice.* New York: Oxford University Press, 1997.

Hardiman, David. *The Coming of the Devi: Adivasi Assertion in Western India.* Delhi: Oxford University Press, 1995.

Hardy, Friedhelm. *The Religious Culture of India: Power, Love, and Wisdom.* Cambridge, U.K.: Cambridge University Press, 1994.

———. *Viraha Bhakti: The Early History of Krishna Devotion in South India.* Delhi: Oxford University Press, 1983.

Harlan, Lindsay. "Perfection and Devotion: Sati Tradition in Rajasthan." In Hawley, ed., *Sati,* 84–85.

Harvey, Peter. *Introduction to Buddhist Ethics.* Cambridge, U.K.: Cambridge University Press, 2000.

Hasenpflug, Rainer. *The Inscriptions of the Indus Civilization.* Norderstedt, Germany: Books on Demand Gmbh, 2006.

Hatcher, Brian. "Remembering Rammohan: An Essay on the (Re-)emergence of Modern Hinduism." *History of Religions* 46:1 (2006), 50–80.

Hatley, Shaman. "Mapping the Esoteric Body in the Islamic Yoga of Bengal." *History of Religions* 46:4 (2007), 379–81.

Hawley, John Stratton. *Krishna, The Butter Thief.* Princeton N.J.: Princeton University Press, 1983.

———. *Three Bhakti Voices: Mirabi, Surdas and Kabir in Their Times and Ours.* Delhi: Oxford University Press, 2005.

———, ed. *Sati, the Blessing and the Curse: The Burning of Wives in India.* New York: Oxford University Press, 1994.

———, and Donna Wulff, eds. *The Divine Consort.* Berkeley: University of California Press, 1982.

Hawley, John Stratton, and Mark Juergensmeyer. *Songs of the Saints of India.* Oxford, U.K.: Oxford University Press, 1988.

Hayashi, Takao. "Indian Mathematics." In Flood, *The Blackwell Companion,* 360–75.

Hazra, R. C. *Studies in the Puranic Records of Hindu Rites and Customs.* Dacca: The University, 1940.

Heesterman, Jan C. *The Ancient Indian Royal Consecration.* 's-Gravenage: Mouton, 1957.

———. *The Broken World of Sacrifice.* Chicago: University of Chicago Press, 1992.

———. *The Inner Conflict of Tradition: Essays in Indian Ritual, Kingship, and Society.* Chicago: University of Chicago Press, 1985.

Hein, Norvin. "A Revolution in Krsnaism: The Cult of Gopala." *History of Religions* 25:4 (May 1986), 309–10.

Herman, Arthur. *Influences: How Ancient Hinduism Dramatically Changed Early Christianity.* Stevens Point, Wis.: Cornerstone Press, 2004.

Hess, Linda. "The Poet, the People, and the Western Scholar: Influence of a Sacred Drama and Text on Social Values in Northern India." *Theatre Journal* 40:2 (May 1988), 236–53.

———. "Rejecting Sita: Indian Responses to the Ideal Man's Cruel Treatment of His Ideal Wife." *Journal of the American Academy of Religion* 67:1 (1999), 1–32.

———, and Shukdev Singh, trans. *A Touch of Grace: Songs of Kabir.* Boston: Shambhala,1994.

———. *The Bijak of Kabir.* New York: Oxford University Press, 1983, 2002.

Hiltebeitel, Alf. "Of Camphor and Coconuts." *Wilson Quarterly* (July 1991), 35–41.

———, ed. *Criminal Gods and Demon Devotees.* Albany, N.Y.: SUNY Press, 1989.

———. *The Cult of Draupadi, vol. 1, Mythologies: From Gingee to Kuruksetra.* Chicago: University of Chicago Press, 1988.

———. *The Cult of Draupadi, vol. 2, On Hindu Ritual and the Goddess.* Chicago: University of Chicago Press, 1991.

———. "The Indus Valley 'Proto-Shiva' Reexamined Through Reflections on the Goddess, the Buffalo, and the Symbolism of *Vahanas.*" *Anthropos* 73 (1978), 767–97.

———. *Rethinking India's Oral and Classical Epics: Draupadi Among Rajputs, Muslims, and Dalits.* Chicago: University of Chicago Press, 1999.

———. *Rethinking the Mahabharata: A Reader's Guide to the Education of the Dharma King.* Chicago: University of Chicago Press, 2001.

———. *The Ritual of Battle.* Ithaca, N.Y.: Cornell University Press, 1976.

Holdrege, Barbara A. "Dharma." In Mittal and Thursby, eds. *The Hindu World,* 213–48.

Holt, John Clifford. *The Buddhist Vishnu: Religious Transformation, Politics, and Culture.* New York: Columbia University Press, 2004.

Hopkins, E.W. *The Great Epic of India.* New York: Scribner's, 1901.

Hopkins, Thomas. *The Hindu Religious Tradition.* Encino, Calif.: Dickenson, 1971.

Houben, Jan E. M.; Karel R. van Kooij, and K. R. van Kooij, eds. *Violence Denied: Violence, Non-violence and the Rationalization of Violence in South Asian Cultural History.* Leiden: Brill, 1999.

Hudson, Dennis. "Siva, Minaksi, Visnu—Reflections on a Popular Myth in Madurai." In Stein, ed., *South Indian Temples,* 107–18.

Huffer, Amanda. "Guru Movements in a Globalized Framework: Amritanandamayi Ma's (Amma's) Community of Devotees in the

United States." Ph.D. dissertation, University of Chicago, n.d.

Husain, Agha Mahdi. *Tughluq Dynasty*. Calcutta: Thacker, Spink, 1863.

Huyler, Stephen P. *Village India*. New York: Harry Abrams, 1985.

Hwang, David Henry. *M. Butterfly*. New York: Plume, 1989.

Inden, Ron. *Imagining India*. Oxford, U.K.: Basil Blackwell, 1990.

Inden, Ron, Jon Walters, and Daud Ali, eds., *Querying the Medieval: Texts and the History of Practices in South Asia*. New York: Oxford University Press, 2000.

Ingalls, Daniel H. H. "Cynics and Pasupatas: The Seeking of Dishonor." *Harvard Theological Review* 55:4 (October 1962), 281–98.

Inglis, Stephen. "The Craft of the Velar." *National Council for Education in the Ceramic Arts Journal* 7:7 (1986), 14–19.

———. "Night Riders: Massive Temple Figures of Rural Tamilnadu." In *A Festschrift for Prof. M. Shanmugam Pillai*. Madurai, 1980. Pp. 297–307.

Insler, Stanley. "The Shattered Head Split and the Epic Tale of Sakuntala." *Bulletin d'Etudes Indiennes* 7–8 (1989–90), 97–139.

Irwin, John. "Ashokan Pillars: A Reassessment of the Evidence." *Burlington Magazine* 115 (November 1973), 706–20; 116 (December 1974), 712–27; 117 (October 1975), 631–45.

Isaacs, Harold. *India's Ex-Untouchables*. New York: John Day Company, 1964.

Isayeva, Natalia. *Shankara and Indian Philosophy*. Albany, N.Y.: SUNY Press, 1992.

Ivanow, W. "The Sect of Imam Shah in Gujarat." *Journal of the Bombay Branch of the Royal Asiatic Society*, New Series, 12 (1936), 19–70.

Jaffrelot, Christophe. *The Hindu Nationalist Movement in India*. New York: Columbia University Press, 1996.

———, ed. *Hindu Nationalism: A Reader*. Delhi: Permanent Black, 2007.

Jaffrey, Zia. *The Invisibles: A Tale of the Eunuchs of India*. New York: Pantheon, 1997.

Jagannathan, Shakuntala. *Hinduism: An Introduction*. Mumbai: Vakils, Feffer and Simons, Ltd., 1984.

James, Lawrence. *Raj*. New York: Little, Brown, 1997.

Jamison, Stephanie. *Sacrificed Wife/Sacrificer's Wife: Women, Ritual, and Hospitality in Ancient India*. New York: Oxford University Press, 1996.

———. *The Ravenous Hyenas and the Wounded Sun: Myth and Ritual in Ancient India*. Ithaca, N.Y., and London: Cornell University Press, 1991.

Janaki, K. S. S. "Parasurama." *Purana* 8:1 (1966), 115–39.

Jasanoff, Maya. *Edge of Empire: Lives, Culture, and Conquest in the East, 1750–1850*. New York: Knopf, 2005.

Jastrow, Joseph. "The Mind's Eye." *Popular Science Monthly* 54 (1899), 299–312.

Jha, D. N. *The Myth of the Holy Cow*. London and New York: Verso, 2002.

Jha, N., and N. S. Rajaram. *The Deciphered Indus Script*. New Delhi: Aditya Prakashan, 2000.

Joh, Wonhee Anne. *Heart of the Cross: A Postcolonial Christology*. Louisville and London: Westminster John Knox Press, 2006.

Johnsen, Linda. *The Complete Idiot's Guide to Hinduism*. Indianapolis, Ind.: Alpha Books, 2002.

Johnson, W. J. *The Sauptikaparvan of the Mahabharata*. Oxford, U.K.: Oxford World Classics, Oxford University Press, 1998.

Jones, Ernest. *On the Nightmare*. London: Hogarth Press, 1949.

Jones, Sir William. "On the Gods of Greece, Italy, and India." *Asiatic Researches* (Calcutta: Asiatic Society of Bengal) 1 (1785), 422 ff.

Jordens, J. T. F. "Reconversion to Hinduism, the Shuddhi of the Arya Samaj." In *Religion in South Asia: Religious Conversion and Revival Movements in South Asia in Medieval and Modern Times*, ed. G. Oddie. London: Curzon Press, 1977. Pp. 144–53.

Joshi , Om Prakash. *Painted Folklore and Folklore Painters of India*. Delhi: Concept Publishing Co., 1976.

Joyce, James. *Finnegans Wake*. New York: Viking Press, 1939.

Jurewicz, Joanna. "Playing with Fire: The Pratityasamutpada from the Perspective of Vedic Thought." *Journal of the Pali Text Society* 26 (2000), 77–103.

———. "Prajapati, the Fire and the *Pancagnividya*." In *On the Understanding of Other Cultures*, ed. Piotr Balcerowicz and Marek Mejor. Warsaw: Instytut Orientalistyczny, 2000. Pp. 181–96.

———. "The Rgveda 10, 129: An Attempt of Interpretation." *Cracow Indological Studies*, vol. 1. Proceedings of the International Conference on Sanskrit and Related Studies, September 23–26, 1993. Cracow: Enigma Press, 1995. Pp. 141–49.

Kabir. *The Weaver's Songs*. Trans. Vinay Dharwadkar. New Delhi: Penguin, 2003. *See also* Hess, Linda.

Kaelber, Walter. "Asrama." In Mittal and Thursby, eds. *The Hindu World*, 383–406.

Kak, Subhash. *The Asvamedha: The Rite and Its Logic*. Delhi: Motilal, 2002.

Kakar, Sudhir. *The Colors of Violence: Cultural Identities, Religion, and Conflict*. Chicago: University of Chicago Press, 1996.

Kane, Pandurang Vaman. *History of Dharmasastra*. 5 vols. Poona: Bhandarkar Oriental Research Institute, 1930–62.

Kangle. *See Arthashastra.*

Karve, Iravati. " 'On the Road': A Maharashtrian Pilgrimage." In *The Experience of Hinduism: Essays on Religion in Maharashtra,* eds. Eleanor Zelliot and Maxine Berntsen. Albany, N.Y.: SUNY Press, 1988.

———. *Yuganta: The End of an Epoch.* Poona: Deshmukh Prakashan, 1969.

Kaviraj, Sudipta. "The Two Histories of Literary Culture in Bengal." In Pollock, *Literary Cultures,* 503–67.

Kaye, Sir John William. *A History of the Sepoy War in India, 1857–1858.* 3 vols. London: W. H. Allen, 1865–77.

Keay, John. *India, a History.* New York: Grove Press, 2000.

Keer, Dhananjay. *Dr Ambedkar: Life and Mission.* Bombay: India Printing Works, 1962.

Keillor, Garrison. *Pontoon: A Novel of Lake Woebegone.* New York: Viking, 2007.

Kelly, Francesca, and Dale Durfee. *Marwari: Legend of the Indian Horse.* New Delhi: Prakash Book Depot, 2000.

Kenoyer, Jonathan Mark. "Harappan Craft Specialization and the Question of Urban Segregation and Stratification." *Eastern Anthropologist* 45:1–2 (1992), 39–54.

———. "Interactive Systems, Specialized Crafts and Culture Change: The Indus Valley Tradition and the Indo-Gangetic Tradition in South Asia." In Erdosy, ed., *The Indo-Aryans of Ancient South Asia,* 213–57.

———. "Socio-Economic Structures of the Indus Civilization as Reflected in Specialized Crafts and the Question of Ritual Segregation." In *Old Problems and New Perspectives in the Archaeology of South Asia,* ed. J. M. Kenoyer. Madison, Wis.: Dept. of Anthropology, University of Wisconsin—Madison, 1989. Pp. 183–92.

Khan, Iqtidar Alam. "Akbar's Personality Traits and World Outlook: A Critical Reappraisal." *Social Scientist* 20: 9–10 (September–October 1992), 16–30.

———. "Medieval Indian Notions of Secular Statecraft in Retrospect." *Social Scientist* 14:1 (January 1986), 3–15.

Killingley, Dermot. "Hinduism, Darwinism and Evolution in Late Nineteenth-Century India." In *Charles Darwin's The Origin of Species: New Interdisciplinary Essays,* eds. David Amigoni and Jeff Wallace. New York and Manchester, U.K.: Manchester University Press, 1995.

———. "Kama." In Mittal and Thursby, eds. *The Hindu World,* 264–88.

———. "Modernity, Reform, and Revival." In Flood, *The Blackwell Companion,* 509–25.

———. *Rammohun Roy in Hindu and Christian Tradition.* Newcastle-upon-Tyne, U.K.: Grevatt and Grevatt, 1993.

Kinsley, David. *Hinduism: A Cultural Perspective.*

2nd ed. Englewood Cliffs, N.J.: Prentice Hall, 1982–93.

———. *Hindu Goddesses.* Delhi: Motilal Banarsidass, 1998.

———. *The Sword and the Flute: Kali and Krishna.* Berkeley: University of California Press, 2000.

Kipling, John Lockwood. *Beast and Man in India.* London and New York: Macmillan, 1891.

Kipling, Rudyard. *The Jungle Book.* London: Macmillan, 1894.

———. *Kim.* Edited with intro. and notes, Edward W. Said. Harmondsworth, U.K.: Penguin Books, 1987.

———. "The Miracle of Puran Bhagat." In *The Second Jungle Book.* London: Macmillan, 1894.

———. "On Greenhow Hill." From *Life's Handicap,* 1891. In *The Portable Kipling,* ed. Irving Howe. New York: Viking Penguin, 1982. Pp. 185–86.

———. *Stories and Poems.* New York: Doubleday, 1956.

Kirfel, Willibald. "Der Asvamedha und der Purusamedha." In *Beiträge zur Indische Philologie und Alterthumskunde für Walther Schubring.* Hamburg: Cram; de Gruyter, 1951. Pp. 39–50.

———. *Die Kosmographie der Inder.* Bonn and Leipzig: K. Schroeder, 1920.

Kishwar, Madhu. "Yes to Sita, No to Ram: The Continuing Hold of Sita on Popular Imagination in India." In Richman, ed. *Questioning Ramayanas,* 285–97.

Kloetzli, Randy, and Alf Hiltebeitel. "Kala." In Mittal and Thursby, eds. *The Hindu World,* 553–86.

Klostermaier, Klaus K. *Hinduism: A Short Introduction.* Oxford, U.K.: One World, 1998.

———. "Moksa." In Mittal and Thursby, eds. *The Hindu World,* 288–308.

———. *A Survey of Hinduism.* 2nd ed. Albany, N.Y.: SUNY Press, 1994.

Knapp, Stephen. *Proof of Vedic Culture's Global Existence.* Detroit, Mich.: World Relief Network, 2000.

Knipe, David. *Hinduism.* San Francisco: Harper, 1991.

Knott, Kim. *Hinduism, a Very Short Introduction.* Oxford, U.K.: Oxford University Press. 1998.

Kölver, Bernhard, and Elisabeth Müller-Luckner, eds. *Recht, Staat und Verwaltung im klassischen Indien.* Munich: R. Oldenbourg, 1997.

Koontz, Dean. *Forever Odd.* New York: Bantam Books, 2005.

Kosambi, Damodar Dharmand. "The Autochthonous Element in the Mahabharata." *Journal of the American Oriental Society* 84:1 (January–March 1964), 31–44.

———. *An Introduction to the Study of Indian History.* Bombay: Popular Prakashan, 1956.

———. *Myth and Reality: Studies in the Forma-*

tion of Indian Culture. Bombay: Popular Prakashan, 1962.

Kramrisch, Stella. The Hindu Temple. Columbia, Mo.: South Asia Books, 1991.

———. "An Image of Aditi-Uttanapad." Artibus Asiae 19 (1956).

———. Unknown India: Ritual Art in Tribe and Village. Philadelphia: Philadelphia Museum of Art, 1968.

Kripal, Jeffrey J. Kali's Child: The Mystical and the Erotic in the Life and Teachings of Ramakrishna. Chicago: University of Chicago Press, 1995.

———. "Remembering Ourselves: Some Countercultural Echoes of Contemporary Tantric Studies." Journal of South Asian Religion 1:1 (Summer 2007).

———. "Western Popular Culture, Hindu Influences On." In The Encyclopedia of Hinduism, eds. Denise Cush, Catherine Robinson, and Michael York. London: Routledge/Curzon, 2007.

Krishna, Daya. Indian Philosophy: A Counter-Perspective. Delhi: Oxford University Press, 1986.

Krishna Rao, M. V. N. Indus Script Deciphered. Delhi: Agam Kala Prakashan, 1982.

Kuiper, F. B. J. "The Bliss of Asa." Indo-Iranian Journal 8:2 (1964), 96–129.

Kulkarni, B. B. "Darstellung des Eigenen im Kostum des Fremden, Variationen eines indischen Marchenmotivs in Goethes 'Paria Trilogie'" and Thomas Mann's "Die vertauschten Kopfe." In Akten des VIII Internationaler Germanisten-Kongresses. ed. E. Iwasaki. Munchen: Ludicium Verlag, 1991, 64–70.

Kulke, Hermann, and Dietmar Rothermund. A History of India. London: Routledge, 1986.

———, and Burkhard Schnepel. Jagannatha Revisted: Studying Society, Religion, and the State in Orissa. New Delhi: Manohar, 2001.

Kurtz, Stanley. All the Mothers Are One: Hindu India and the Cultural Reshaping of Psychoanalysis. New York: Columbia University Press, 1992.

Kuruvachira, J. Roots of Hindutva: A Critical Study of Hindu Fundamentalism and Nationalism. Delhi: Media House, 2005.

Lal, Ruby. Domesticity and Power in the Early Mughal World. Cambridge, U.K.: Cambridge University Press, 2005.

Lal, Vinay, and Borin van Loon. Introducing Hinduism. Thriplow, U.K.: Icon Books, Ltd., 2005.

Lamb, Ramdas. "Personalizing the Ramayana: Ramnamis and Their Use of the Ramcaritmanas." In Richman, Many Ramayanas, 235–256.

Lamont, Peter. The Rise of the Indian Rope Trick: How a Spectacular Hoax Became History. New York: Thunder's Mouth Press, 2004.

Larson, Gerald James. Classical Samkhya: An Interpretation of Its History and Meaning. Santa Barbara, Calif.: Ross/Erikson, 1979.

———. "India Through Hindu Categories: A Samkhya Response." Contributions to Indian Sociology 24:1 (1990), 237–39.

———, and Ram Shankar Bhattacharya, eds. Samkhya: A Dualist Tradition in Indian Philosophy. Encyclopedia of Indian Philosophies, Vol. 4. Delhi: Motilal Banarsidass, 1988.

Leshnik, Lawrence S. "The Horse in India." In Symbols, Subsistence and Social Structure: The Ecology of Man and Animal in South Asia, ed. Franklin C. Southworth. Philadelphia: University of Pennsylvania Press, 1977–78. Pp. 56–57.

Leslie, Julia, ed. Myth and Mythmaking: Continuous Evolution in Indian Tradition. London: Curzon, 1996.

Levi, Sylvain. La doctrine du sacrifice dans les Brahmanas. Paris: E. Leroux, 1898.

———. Le Théâtre Indien. Vol. 1, 2nd printing. Paris: Collège de France,1963.

Lévi-Strauss, Claude. "Split Representation in the Art of Asia and America." In Structural Anthropology. Trans. Claire Jacobson and Brooke Grundfest Schoepf. Harmondsworth, U.K.: Penguin Books, 1963. Pp. 245–68.

Lifton, Robert Jay, and Greg Mitchell. Hiroshima in America: Fifty Years in America. New York: Putnam, 1995.

Lincoln, Bruce. "How to Read a Religious Text: Reflections on Some Passages of the Chandogya Upanisad." History of Religions 46:4 (2007), 379–81.

———. "The Indo-European Cattle-Raiding Myth." History of Religions 16:1 (1976), 42-65.

———. Myth, Cosmos, and Society: Indo-European Themes of Creation and Destruction. Cambridge, Mass.: Harvard University Press, 1986.

———. Priests, Warriors and Cattle. A Study in the Ecology of Religions. Berkeley: University of California Press, 1981.

Lindquist, Steven E. "Gender at Janaka's Court: Women in the Brihadaranyaka Upanishad Reconsidered." Journal of Indian Philosophy 36:3 (2008), 405–26.

Lipner, Julius. Hindus: Their Religious Beliefs and Practices. London and New York: Routledge, 1994.

———. "On Hinduism and Hinduisms: The Way of the Banyan." In Mittal and Thursby, eds. The Hindu World, 9–36.

Lopez, Donald S. Religions of India in Practice. Princeton, N.J.: Princeton University Press, 1995.

Lord, Albert Bates. The Singer of Tales. Cambridge, Mass.: Harvard University Press, 1960.

Lorenzen, David N. "Bhakti." In Mittal and Thursby, eds. The Hindu World, 185–212.

———. *Kabir Legends and Anantadas's Kabir Parachay*. Albany, N.Y.: SUNY Press, 1991.

———. *Kapalikas and Kalamukhas, Two Lost Saivite Sects*. Berkeley: Univeristy of California Press, 1972.

———. "Who Invented Hinduism?" *Comparative Studies in Society and History* 41:4 (October 1999), 630–59.

Lubin, Timothy. "Veda on Parade: Revivalist Ritual as Civic Spectacle." *Journal of the American Academy of Religion* 69:2 (June 2001), 377–408.

Ludden, David E. *India and South Asia: A Short History*. Oxford, U.K.: One World Publications, 2002.

———, ed. *Contesting the Nation: Religion, Community, and the Politics of Democracy in India*. Philadelphia: University of Pennsylvania Press, 1996.

Lutgendorf, Philip. *Hanuman's Tale*. New York: Oxford University Press, 2007.

———. *The Life of a Text*. Berkeley: Univeristy of California Press, 1991.

———. "Who Wants to Be a Goddess? *Jai Santoshi Maa* Revisited." *Chakra (Journal of Indian Religions*, Lund University, Sweden) 3 (2005), 72–112.

McConnachie, James. *The Book of Love: In Search of the Kamasutra*. London: Atlantic, 2007.

McCrindle, J. W. *Ancient India as Described in Classical Literature*. Amsterdam: Philo Press, 1975.

———. *Ancient India as Described by Megasthenes and Arrian*. Calcutta: Thacker, Spink, 1877.

McDermott, Rachel Fell. *Mother of My Heart, Daughter of My Dreams*. New York: Oxford University Press, 2001.

———, and Jeffrey J. Kripal. *Encountering Kaloi: In the Margins, at the Center, in the West*. Berkeley: University of California Press, 2003.

McEvilley, Thomas. *The Shape of Ancient Thought: Comparative Studies in Greek and Indian Philosophies*. New York: Allworth Press, 2002.

McGlashan, Alistair. *See Periya Purana*.

McKay, Claudia. *The Kali Connection: A Lynn Evans Mystery*. Chicago: New Victoria Publishers, 1994.

McLean, Malcolm. *Devoted to the Goddess. The Life and Work of Ramprasad*. Albany, N.Y.: SUNY Press, 1998.

Macleane, Charles D., ed. *Manual of the Administration of the Madras Presidency, 1885*. New Delhi: Asian Educational Service, 1982.

Madan, T. N. *Non-renunciation: Themes and Interpretations of Hindu Culture*. Delhi: Oxford University Press, 1987.

———. "The Householder Tradition in Hindu Society." In Flood, *The Blackwell Companion*, 288–305.

Magnus, P. *King Edward the Seventh*. Harmondsworth, U.K.: Penguin, 1967.

Mahadevan, Anand. "Switching Heads and Cultures: Transformation of an Indian Myth by Thomas Mann and Girish Karnad." *Comparative Literature* 54:1 (Winter 2002), 23–42.

Malamoud, Charles. *Cooking the World: Ritual and Thought in Ancient India*. Trans. David White. Delhi: Oxford University Press, 1996.

Malik, Aditya. *Nectar, Gaze, and Poisoned Breath: An Analysis and Translation of the Rajasthani Oral Narrative of Devnarayan*. Oxford, U.K.: Oxford University Press, 2005.

Malleson, Col. G. B. *The Indian Mutiny of 1857*. New Delhi: Rupa and Co. Publishers, 2005 (reprint).

Mallory, J. P. *In Search of the Indo-Europeans: Language, Archeology, and Myth*. London: Thames and Hudson, 1989.

Mani, Lata. *Contentious Traditions: The Debate on Sati in Colonial India*. Berkeley, Los Angeles, London: University of California Press, 1998.

Mann, Michael. *The Sources of Social Power. Vol. 1. A History of Power from the Beginning to A.D. 1760*. Cambridge, U.K.: Cambridge University Press, 1986.

Marr, J. R. "The 'Periya Puranam' Frieze at Taracuram: Episodes in the Lives of the Tamil Saiva Saints." *Bulletin of the School of Oriental and African Studies, University of London*, 42:2 (1979, in Honour of Thomas Burrow), 268–89.

Marriott, McKim. *India Through Hindu Categories*. Newbury Park, Calif.: Sage Publications, 1990.

———. "Varna and Jati." In Mittal and Thursby, eds. *The Hindu World*, 357–82.

Marshall , Sir John. *Mohenjo-Daro and the Indus Civilization. Being an Official Account of Archaeological Excavations at Mohenjo-Daro Carried Out by the Government of India Between the Years 1922 and 1927, with Plan and Map in Colours, and 164 Plates in Collotype*. 3 vols. London: Arthur Probsthain, 1931.

Marshall, Peter J. *Bengal—The British Bridgehead. Eastern India, 1740–1828*. Cambridge, U.K.: Cambridge University Press, 1987.

Martin, Nancy M. "North Indian Hindi Devotional Literature." In Flood, *The Blackwell Companion*, 182–98.

Masson, J. L "Fratricide and the Monkeys: Psychoanalytic Observations on an Episode in the Valmikiramayanam." *Journal of the American Oriental Society* 95 (1975), 454–59.

———. "Hanuman as an Imaginary Companion." *Journal of the American Oriental Society* 101 (1981), 355–60.

———. "Who Killed Cock Kraunca? Abhinavagaputa's Reflections on the Origins of Aesthetic Experience." *Journal of the Oriental Institute* 18 (1969), 207–24

Matchett, Freda. "The Puranas." In Flood, *The Blackwell Companion*, 129–43.

Mathur, Dr. Vijay Kumar. *Art and Culture Under the Shungas*. Delhi: C. P. Gautam, 1996.

Matilal, Bimal K. "In Defence of a Devious Divinity." In *Essays on the Mahabharata*, ed. Arvind Sharma. Leiden: E. J. Brill, 1991. Pp. 413–14.

Matthiessen, Peter. *The Snow Leopard*. New York: Penguin, 1978, 1996.

Mehra, Parshotam. *A Dictionary of Modern Indian History*. Delhi: Oxford University Press, 1985.

Mehta, Atul K. *Hindulogy in America*. Patna, India: Hindulogy Foundation, 2006.

Meister, Michael W. "Giving Up and Taking On: The Body in Ritual." *Res* 41 (Spring 2002: Anthropology and aesthetics), 92–103.

———. "The Hindu Temple: Axis of Access." In *Concepts of Space, Ancient and Modern*, ed. Kapila Vatsyayan. New Delhi: Indira Gandhi National Centre for the Arts, Abhinav Publications, 1991. Pp. 269–80.

———, and M. A. Dhaky. *Encyclopedia of Indian Temple Architecture*. New Delhi: American Institute of Indian Studies; Philadelphia: University of Pennsylvania Press, 1983.

Metcalf, Barbara. "Too Little and Too Much: Reflections on Muslims in the History of India." *Journal of Asian Studies* 54 (1995), 951–67.

———, and Thomas R. Metcalf. *A Concise History of India*. Cambridge, U.K.: Cambridge University Press, 2002.

Michaels, Axel. *Hinduism. Past and Present*. Princeton, N.J.: Princeton University Press, 2004 [Munich 1998].

Michell, George. *Hindu Art and Architecture*. London: Thames and Hudson, 2000.

———. *The Hindu Temple: An Introduction to Its Meaning and Forms*. Chicago: University of Chicago Press, 1977, 1988.

Minkowski, Christopher. "The Interrupted Sacrifice and the Sanskrit Epics." *Journal of Indian Philosophy* 29 (2001), 169–86.

———. "Janamejaya's Sattra and Ritual Structure." *Journal of the American Oriental Society* 109:3 (1989), 420.

Mishra, Pankaj. "Exit Wounds: The Legacy of Indian Partition." *New Yorker* (August 13, 2007), 80–84.

Mistry, Rohinton. *Such a Long Journey*. New York: Knopf, 1991.

Mitchell, Stephen, trans. *The Bhagavad Gita*. New York: Harmony Books, 2000.

Mitra, Rajendralala. "On Human Sacrifices in Ancient India." *Journal of the Asiatic Society of Bengal*, 1876.

Mittal, Sushil, and Gene Thursby, eds. *The Hindu World*. New York and London: Routledge, 2004.

Mitter, Partha. *Indian Art*. Oxford: Oxford University Press, 2001.

———. "Rammohun Roy and the New Language of Monotheism." *History and Anthropology* 3 (1987), 177–208.

Monier-Williams, Sir Monier. *Religious Thought and Life in India*. London: John Murray,1885.

———. *Sanskrit-English Dictionary*. Oxford, U.K.: Clarendon Press, 1872.

Monius, Anne E. *Imagining a Place for Buddhism*. New York: Oxford University Press, 2001.

———. "Love, Violence, and the Aesthetics of Disgust: Saivas and Jains in Medieval South India." *Journal of Indian Philosophy* 32:2–3 (2004), 113–72.

Mookerjee, Ajit. *Tantra Art: Its Philosophy and Physics*. Basel: Ravi Kumar, 1971.

Mookerji, Radhakumud. *The History of Indian Shipping*. Bombay: Longmans, 1912.

Moon, Penderel. *The British Conquest and Dominion of India*. London: Duckworth, 1989.

Morson, Gary Saul. *Narrative and Freedom: The Shadows of Time*. New Haven and London: Yale University Press, 1994.

Mukherjee, Ramkrishna. *The Rise and Fall of the East India Company: A Sociological Appraisal*. New York and London: Monthly Review Press, 1974.

Mukherjee, Rudrangshu. *Mangal Pandey: Brave Martyr or Accidental Hero?* Delhi: Penguin, 2005.

Mukherjee, Uma. *Two Great Indian Revolutionaries: Rash Behari Bose and Jyotindra Nath Mukherjee*. Calcutta: Firma K. L. Mukhopadhyay, 1966.

Mukhia, Harbans. *The Mughals of India*. Malden, Mass.: Blackwell Publishing, 2004.

Müller, Friedrich Max. *Rig Veda*. London, W. H. Allen, 1849–74.

Nagaraj, D. R. "Critical Tensions in the History of Kannada Literary Culture." In Pollock, *Literary Cultures*, 323–82.

Nagaswamy, R. "Gateway to the Gods. 1. Sermons in stone." *UNESCO Courier* (March 1984).

Nanda, Serena. *Neither Man nor Woman*. Belmont, Calif.: Wadsworth Publishing Co., 1990.

Nandy, Ashis. *Exiled at Home: At the Edge of Psychology, The Intimate Enemy, Creating a Nationality*. New Delhi: Oxford University Press, 1980, 2005.

———. *The Intimate Enemy: Loss and Recovery of Self Under Colonialism*. Delhi: Oxford University Press, 1983.

———. "Sati as Profit Versus Sati as a Spectacle." In Hawley, ed., *Sati*, 131–48.

Napier, Priscilla Hayter. *I Have Sind: Charles Napier in India: 1841–1844*. Salisbury, U.K.: Russell, 1990.

Napier, Sir William. *The Life and Opinions of General Sir Charles James Napier*. 4 vols. 2nd ed. London: John Murray, 1857.

Narain, Harsh. *The Ayodhya Temple/Mosque Dispute*. Delhi: Penman, 1993.

Narayan, Kirin, and Urmila Devi Sood. *Mondays on the Dark Side of the Moon*. New York: Oxford University Press, 1997.

———. *Storytellers, Saints and Scoundrels*. Philadelphia: University of Pennsylvania Press, 1989.

Narayana Rao, Velcheru. "Hinduism: The Untold Story." Unpublished ms., 2006.

———. "Multiple Literary Cultures in Telugu: Court, Temple, and Public." In Pollock, *Literary Cultures*, 383–436.

———. "Purana." In Mittal and Thursby, eds. *The Hindu World*, 97–118.

———. "Purana as Brahminic Ideology." In Doniger, ed., *Purana Perennis*, 85–100.

———. "A Ramayana of Their Own." In Richman, ed., *Many Ramayanas*, 114–36.

———, trans., with Gene H. Roghair. *Siva's Warriors. The Basava Purana of Palkuriki Somanatha*. Princeton, N.J.: Princeton University Press, 1990.

———, and David Shulman. *Annamayya: God on the Hill, Temple Poems from Tirupati*. New York: Oxford University Press, 2005.

———. *Classical Telugu Poetry*. Berkeley: University of California Press, 2002.

———, David Shulman, and Sanjay Subrahmaniam. *Textures of Time: Writing History in South India, 1600–1800*. Delhi: Permanent Black, 2001.

Narayanan, M. G. S. *Cultural Symbiosis in Kerala*. Trivandrum: Kerala Historical Society, 1972.

Narayanan, Vasudha. "Gender in a Devotional Universe." In Flood, *The Blackwell Companion*, 569–87.

———. *Hinduism: Origins, Beliefs, Practices, Holy Texts, Sacred Places*. New York: Oxford University Press, 2004.

———. "The *Ramayana* in the Theology and Experience of the Srivaisnava Community." *Journal of Vaisnava Studies* 2:4 (Fall 1994).

Nath, Vijay. *Puranas and Acculturation: A Historico-Anthropological Perspective*. Delhi: Munshiram Manoharlal, 2001.

Nathan, Leonard, and Clinton Seely. *Grace and Mercy in Her Wild Hair*. Boulder, Colo.: Great Eastern, 1982.

Nau'i. *Burning and Melting: Being the Suz-u-Gudaz of Mohammed Riza Nau'i of Khabushan, translated into English by Mirza Y. Dawud of Persia and Ananda K. Coomaraswamy of Ceylon*. London: Luzac and Co., 1912.

Neumayer, E. *Prehistoric Indian Rock Paintings*. Delhi: Oxford University Press, 1983.

Nikam, N. A., and Richard McKeon. *The Edicts of Ashoka*. Chicago: University of Chicago Press, 1959, 1978.

Nilakantha Shastri, K. A. *A Comprehensive History of India*. Vol. 2. *The Mauryas and the Satavahanas*. Delhi: Peoples Publishing House, 1957.

Nizami. *The Story of Layla and Majnun*. New Lebanon, N.Y.: Omega Publications, 1997 [1966].

Obeyesekere, Gananath. *Imagining Karma*. Berkeley: University of California Press, 2002.

O'Brien, Tim. *The Things They Carried*. New York: Broadway Books, 1990.

Olivelle, Patrick. *The Ashrama System: The History and Hermeneutics of a Religious Institution*. New Delhi: Munshiram Manoharlal, 1993.

———, ed. *Between the Empires: Society in India 300 BCE to 400 CE*. New York: Oxford University Press, 2006.

———, ed. and trans. *Dharmasutras*. New York: Oxford University Press, 1999.

———, ed. and trans. *Early Upanishads*. New York: Oxford University Press, 1998.

———. "Manu and the Arthaśāstra: A Study in Śāstric Intertextuality." *Journal of Indian Philosophy* 32 (2004), 281–91.

———. "The Renouncer Tradition." In Flood, *The Blackwell Companion*, 271–88.

———. *Renunciation in Hinduism: A Medieval Debate*. Vienna: Institut für Indologie der Universität Wien, Sammlung De Nobili: Commission agents, Gerold, 1986–87.

———, ed. and trans. *Samnyasa Upanishads. Hindu Scriptures on Asceticism and Renunciation*. New York: Oxford University Press, 1992.

Omvedt, Gail. *Dalit Visions: The Anti-caste Movement and the Construction of an Indian Identity*. New Delhi: Orient Longman, 1995.

Openshaw, Jeanne. *Seeking Bauls of Bengal*. Cambridge, U.K.: Cambridge University Press, 2002.

Organ, Troy. *Hinduism: Its Historical Development*. Woodbury, N.Y.: Barrons Educational Series, Inc., 1974.

———. "Three into Four in Hinduism." *Ohio Journal of Religious Studies* 1 (1973), 7–13.

Orr, Leslie C. *Donors, Devotees, and Daughters of God*. New York: Oxford University Press, 2000.

———. "Identity and Divinity: Boundary-Crossing Goddesses in Medieval South India." *Journal of the American Academy of Religion* 73:1 (March 2005), 9–43.

Orwell, George. "Rudyard Kipling." A review of T. S. Eliot's *A Choice of Kipling's Verse*. In *A Collection of Essays*. Garden City, N.Y.: Doubleday, 1954.

Ostler, Nicholas. *Empires of the Word: A Language History of the World*. New York: Harper Perennial, 2006.

Padoux, André. "Mantra." In Flood, *The Blackwell Companion*, 478–92.

Pangborn, Cyrus R. *Zoroastrianism: A Beleaguered Faith*. New York: Advent Books, 1983.

Parashar, Aloka. *Mlecchas in Early India: A Study in Attitudes Toward Outsiders up to AD 600*. Delhi: Munshiram Manoharlal, 1991.

Parpola, Asko. "The Coming of the Aryans to Iran and India and the Cultural and Ethnic Identity of the Dasas; The Problem of the Aryans and the Soma." *Studia Orientalia* (Helsinki) 64 (1988), 195–302.

———. *Deciphering the Indus Script.* New York: Cambridge University Press,1994.

———. "The Pre-Vedic Indian Background of the Srauta Rituals." In Staal, *Agni,* 2:41–75.

Pathak, Shubha. "The Things Kings Sing: The Religious Ideals of Poetic Rulers in Greek and. Sanskrit Epics." Ph.D. dissertation, University of Chicago, 2006.

Patton, Laurie. "The Cat in the Courtyard: The Performance of Sanskrit and the Religious Experience of Women." In *Women's Lives, Women's Rituals, in the Hindu Tradition*, ed. Tracy Pintchman. New York: Oxford University Press, 2007. Pp. 19–34.

———. "If the Fire Goes Out, the Wife Shall Fast: Notes on Women's Agency in the Asvalayana Grhya Sutra." In *Problems in Vedic and Sanskrit Literature*, ed. Maitreyee Deshpande. Delhi: New Bharatiya Book Corporation, 2004. Pp. 294–305.

———. "The Prostitute's Gold: Women, Religion and Sanskrit in One Corner of India." In *Postcolonialism, Feminism, and Religious Discourse*, ed. Laura E. Donaldson and Kwok Pui-lan. New York and London: Routledge, 2002. Pp. 125–41.

———. "Veda and Upanishad." In Mittal and Thursby, eds. *The Hindu World*, 37–51.

Pennington, Brian K. *Was Hinduism Invented? Britons, Indians, and the Colonial Construction of Religion.* New York: Oxford University Press, 2005.

Peterson, Indira Viswanathan. "Tamil Saiva Hagiography: The Narrative of the Holy Servants (of Siva) and the Hagiographical Project of Tamil Saivism." In *According to Tradition: Hagiographical Writing in India*, eds. Winand M. Callewaert and Rupert Snell. Wiesbaden: Otto Harrassowitz, 1994.

Petievich, Carla. "Dakani's Radha-Krishna Imagery and Urdu Canon Formation." In *The Banyan Tree: Essays on Early Literature in New Indo-Aryan Languages*, ed. Mariola Offredi. Delhi: Manohar, 2000. Pp. 113–28.

Pinney, Chris. *Camera Indica.* Chicago: University of Chicago Press, 1998.

———, with Rachel Dwyer. *Pleasure and the Nation: The History, Politics and Consumption of Public Culture in India.* London: SOAS, 2003.

Pocock, David. "The Evil Eye." In *Religion in India*, ed. T. N. Madan. Oxford, U.K.: Oxford University Press, 1991. Pp. 50–62.

———. "The Anthropology of Time Reckoning." *Contributions to Indian Sociology* 7 (1964), 18–29.

Pollock, Sheldon. "'*Atmanam manusam manye*':

Dharmakutam on the Divinity of Rama." *Journal of the Oriental Institute, Baroda*, 33.3–4 (March–June 1984), 231–43.

———. "The Cosmopolitan Vernacular." *Journal of Asian Studies* 57:1 (February 1998), 6–37.

———. "Deep Orientalism? Notes on Sanskrit and Power Beyond the Raj." In *Orientalism and the Postcolonial Predicament. Perspectives on South Asia*, ed. Carol A. Breckenridge and Peter van der Veer. Philadelphia: University of Pennsylvania Press, 1993. Pp. 76–133.

———. "The Divine King in the Indian Epic." *Journal of the American Oriental Society* 104:3 (1984), 505–28.

———. "The Ends of Man at the End of Premodernity." Gonda Lecture: Royal Netherlands Academy of Arts and Sciences, Amsterdam, 2005.

———. "From Discourse of Ritual to Discourse of Power in Sanskrit Culture." *Journal of Ritual Studies* 4:2 (1990), 315–45.

———. "India in the Vernacular Millennium: Literary Culture and Polity, 1000–1500." *Daedalus* 127:3 (1998).

———. *The Language of the Gods in the World of Men: Sanskrit, Culture, and Power in Premodern India.* Berkeley, Los Angeles, London: University of California Press, 2006.

———, ed. *Literary Cultures in History: Reconstructions from South Asia.* Berkeley, Los Angeles, London: University of California Press, 2003.

———. "Mimamsa and the Problem of History in Traditional India." *Journal of the American Oriental Society* 109.4 [1989], 603–10.

———. *Ramayana of Valmiki.* Trans. and intro. Vols. 2 and 3. Princeton, N.J.: Princeton University Press, 1984.

———. "*Ramayana* and Political Imagination in India." *Journal of Asian Studies* 52:2 (1993), 261–97.

———. "Sanskrit Literary Culture from the Inside Out." In Pollock, *Literary Cultures*, 39–130.

———. "The Theory of Practice and the Practice of Theory in Indian Intellectual History." *Journal of the American Oriental Society* 105 (1985), 499–519.

Polo, Marco. *Marco Polo: The Description of the World*, ed. A. C. Moule and Paul Pelliot. London: George Routledge, 1938.

———. *The Travels of Marco Polo.* Dutton: New York, 1908.

Pope, G. U. *The Tiruvāçagam, or 'Sacred Utterances' of the Tamil Poet, Saint, and Sage Manikkavacakar.* Oxford, U.K.: Oxford University Press, 1900; reprint 1970, University of Madras.

Possehl, Gregory L. *The Indus Age: The Writing System.* Philadelphia: University of Pennsylvania Press, 1997.

Powell, Avril. *Muslims and Missionaries in Pre-Mutiny India*. Richmond, U.K.: Curzon, 1993.

Prentiss, Karen Pechilis. *The Embodiment of Bhakti*. New York: Oxford University Press, 1999.

———. "Joyous Encounters: Tamil Bhakti Poets and Images of the Divine." In *The Sensuous and the Sacred: Chola Bronzes from South India*. New York: American Federation of Arts; Seattle: University of Washington Press, 2002.

Pusalker, A. D. *The Struggle for Empire*. Vol. 5. *The History and Culture of the Indian People*. Bombay: Bharatiya Vidya Bhavan, 1957.

Quigley, Declan. "On the Relationship Between Caste and Hinduism." In Flood, *The Blackwell Companion*, 495–508.

Rabe, Michael D. "The Mahamallapuram Prasasti: A Panegyric in Figure." *Artibus Asiae* (1997), 189–241.

Radhakrishnan, Sarvepalli, and Charles A. Moore. *A Sourcebook in Indian Philosophy*. Princeton, N.J.: Princeton University Press, 1957.

Raj, Kapil. "Refashioning Civilities, Engineering Trust: William Jones, Indian Intermediaries, and the Production of Reliable Knowledge in Late Eighteenth-Century Bengal." In *Relocating Modern Science*. New York: Palgrave/Macmillan, 2007. Pp. 95–138.

Rajagopal, Arvind. *Politics After Television: Religious Nationalism and the Reshaping of the Indian Public*. Cambridge, U.K.: Cambridge University Press, 2001.

Ramanujan, A. K. *The Oxford India Ramanujan*, ed. Molly Daniels-Ramanujan. Delhi: Oxford University Press, 2004.

———. *The Collected Essays of A. K. Ramanujan*, ed. Vinay Dharwadkar. Delhi: Oxford University Press, 1999.

———. *Hymns for the Drowning*. Princeton, N.J.: Princeton University Press, 1981.

———. *The Interior Landscape: Love Poems from a Classical Tamil Anthology*. Bloomington: Indiana University Press, 1967.

———. "Is There an Indian Way of Thinking?" In *The Collected Essays of A. K. Ramanujan*, 34–52.

———. "The Myths of Bhakti." In *The Collected Essays of A. K. Ramanujan*, 293–308.

———. *Speaking of Siva*. London: Penguin, 1973.

———. "Three Hundred Ramayanas: Five Examples and Three Thoughts on Translation." In *The Collected Essays of A. K. Ramanujan*, 131–60.

———. "Towards a Counter-System: Women's Tales." In *The Collected Essays of A. K. Ramanujan*, 429–47.

———. "Varieties of Bhakti." In *The Collected Essays of A. K. Ramanujan*, 324–33.

———. "Repetition in the *Mahabharata*." In *The Collected Essays of A. K. Ramanujan*, 161–83.

———. "On Woman Saints." In *The Collected Essays of A. K. Ramanujan*, 270–78.

———, and Norman Cutler. "From Classicism to Bhakti." In *The Collected Essays of A. K. Ramanujan*, 232–59.

———, Narayana Rao, and David Shulman. *When God Is a Customer*. Berkeley, Los Angeles, London: University of California Press, 1994.

Ramaswamy, Sumathi. "The Goddess and the Nation: Subterfuges of Antiquity, the Cunning of Modernity." In Flood, *The Blackwell Companion*, 551–68.

———. "Home Away from Home? The Spatial Politics of Modern Tamil Identity." In *Religion, Culture, and Politics in India*, eds. Rajendra Vora and Anne Feldhaus. Delhi: Manohar, 2006. Pp. 147–63.

———. *The Lost Land of Lemuria: Fabulous Geographies, Catastrophic Histories*. Berkeley: University of California Press, 2004.

Ram-Prasad, C. "Contemporary Political Hinduism." In Flood, *The Blackwell Companion*, 526–50.

Rank, Otto. *The Myth of the Birth of the Hero*. New York: R. Brunner, 1952.

Rao, Ajay. "Othering Muslims or Srivaisnava-Saiva Contestation? A New Perspective on the Royal Rama Cult at Vijayanagara." Forthcoming.

———. "Srivaisnava Hermeneutics, 1200–1700: The Practice of Reading in an Intellectual Community." Ph.D. dissertation, University of Chicago, 2008.

Rao, S. R. *Dawn and Devolution of the Indus Civilization*. New Delhi: Aditya Prakashan, 1991.

———. *The Lost City of Dvaraka*. New Delhi: Aditya Prakashan, 1999.

Redfield, Robert. *The Little Community*. Chicago: University of Chicago Press, 1960.

Reich, Tamar. "A Battlefield of a Text: Inner Textual Interpretation in the Sanskrit Mahabharata." Ph.D. dissertation, University of Chicago, 1998.

———. "The Sacrifice of Battle and the Battle of Yoga, or: How to Word-Away a Discontented Wife." In *Notes from a Mandala: Essays in the History of Indian Religions in Honor of Wendy Doniger*, ed. Laurie L. Patton and David Haberman. Newark: University of Delaware Press, 2009.

———. "Sacrificial Violence and Textual Battles: Inner Textual Interpretation in the Sanskrit Mahabharata." *History of Religions* 41 (November 2001), 142–69.

Renou, Louis, ed. *The Destiny of the Veda in India*. Delhi: Motilal Banarsidass, 1965.

———. *Hinduism*. New York: George Braziller, 1962.

———. *Vedic India*. Delhi: Indological Bookhouse, 1971.

Richards, John F. *The Mughal Empire*. Cambridge, U.K.: Cambridge University Press, 1993.

Richman, Paula. "E. V. Ramasami's Reading of the Ramayana." In *Many Ramayanas*, 175–201.

———. *Many Ramayanas: The Diversity of Narrative Traditions in South Asia*. Berkeley: University of California Press, 1991.

———. *Questioning Ramayanas*. Berkeley: University of California Press, 2001.

———. "Shifting Terrain: Rama and Odysseus Meet on the London Stage." *Journal of Vaishnava Studies* 12:2 (Spring 2004), 189–99.

Richter-Ushanas, E. *The Indus Script and the Rgveda*. Delhi: Motilal Banarsidass, 1997.

Ritter, Valerie. "Epiphany in Radha's Arbor: Nature and the Reform of Bhakti in Hariaudh's *Priyapravas*." In Beck, *Alternative Krishnas*, 177–208.

Robb, Peter. *A History of India*. Basingstoke, U.K. and New York: Palgrave, 2002.

———, ed. *The Concept of Race in South Asia*. New Delhi: Oxford University Press, 1995.

Rocher, Ludo, ed. and intro. *Ezourvedam: A French Veda of the Eighteenth Century*. Amsterdam and Philadelphia: J. Benjamins Pub. Co., 1984.

Roger, Abraham. *Le théâtre de l'idolatrie ou la porte ouverte*. Amsterdam: J. Schipper, 1670.

Roghair, Gene H. *The Epic of Palnadu*. Oxford, U.K.: Clarendon Press, 1982.

Rose, H. A. *A Glossary of the Tribes and Castes of the Punjab and North-west Frontier Province*. Vol. 1. Lahore: Government Printing House, 1919.

Roth, Philip. *I Married a Communist*. New York: Houghton Mifflin, 1998.

Rowley, Hugh, ed. *More Puniana; or, Thoughts Wise and Other-Why's*. London: Chatto and Windus, 1875.

Roy, Kumkum, Kunal Chakrabarti, and Tanika Sarkar. *The Vedas, Hinduism, Hindutva*. Kolkata: Alpha, 2005.

Roy, Ranjit. *The Agony of West Bengal*. 3rd. ed. Calcutta: New Age Publishers, 1973.

Ruben, Walter. *Ueber die Frage der Objectivität in der Erforschung des altern Indien*. Berlin: Akademie Verlag, 1968.

Rushdie, Salman. *Haroun and the Sea of Stories*. New York: Viking Penguin, 1990.

———. Introduction to *Baburnama*. *See* Babur.

———. "Kipling." In *Imaginary Homelands: Essays and New Criticism 1981–1991*. New York: Penguin Books, 1991.

———. *Shame*. London: Jonathan Cape, 1983.

Said, Edward W. Introduction to Rudyard Kipling, *Kim*. Harmondsworth, U.K.: Penguin Books, 1987. Later published as "The Pleasures of Imperialism" in Edward W. Said, *Culture and Imperialism*. New York: Vintage Books, 1993.

———. *Orientalism*. New York: Vintage Books, 1979.

Sanford, A. Whitney. "Holi Through Dauji's Eyes: Alternate Views of Krishna and Balarama in Dauji." In Beck, *Alternative Krishnas*, 91–112.

Sangari, Kumkum. "Perpetuating the Myth." *Seminar* 342 (1988).

———, and Sudesh Vaid. *Recasting Women: Essays in Colonial History*. Delhi: Kali for Women Press, 1989.

Sarkar, Sumit. *Beyond Nationalist Frames: Postmodernism, Hindu Fundamentalism, History*. Bloomington: Indiana University Press, 2002.

———. *Modern India, 1885–1947*. Delhi: Macmillan, 1983.

Sarma, Deepak, ed. *Hinduism: A Reader*. Oxford, U.K.: Basil Blackwell, 2008.

Sastri, Rao, and Bahadur H. Krishna. "Two Statues of Pallava Kings and Five Pallava Inscriptions in a Rock Temple at Mahabalipuram." *Memoirs of the Archaeological Survey of India*, no. 26, Calcutta, 1926.

Sauve, James L. "The Divine Victim: Aspects of Human Sacrifice in Viking Scandinavia and Vedic India." In *Myth and Law among the Indo-Europeans*, ed. Jaan Puhvel. Los Angeles: University of California Press, 1970. Pp. 173–91.

Sax, William S. *Mountain Goddess: Gender and Politics in a Himalayan Pilgrimage*. New York: Oxford University Press, 1991.

Scharf, Peter. *Ramopakhyana: The Story of Rama in the Mahabharata*. London: Routledge Curzon, 2003.

Scharfe, Helmut. "Artha." In Mittal and Thursby, eds. *The Hindu World*, 249–63.

Scheuer, Jacques. "Rudra-Siva et la destruction du sacrifice," s.v. "Sacrifice," in Yves Bonnefoy, *Dictionnaire des mythologies*, vol. 2, 417–20; "Rudra-Siva and the Destruction of the Sacrifice," in Bonnefoy, *Mythologies*, ed. and trans. Wendy Doniger. Chicago: University of Chicago Press, 1991.

Schimmel, Anne Marie. *The Empire of the Great Mughals: History, Art, and Culture*. London: Reaktion Books, 2004.

Schlinghoff, Dieter. "Menschenopfer in Kausambi." *Indo-Iranian Journal* 11 (1969), 176–98.

Schmidt, Hanns-Peter. "The Origin of Ahimsa." In *Mélanges d'Indianisme à la mémoire de Louis Renou*. Paris: E. de Boccard, 1968. Pp. 625–55.

Schoff, Wilfred H., trans. and ed. *The Periplus of the Erythraean Sea: Travel and Trade in the Indian Ocean by a Merchant of the First Century*. New Delhi: Munshi Ram Manorhar Lal, 1974.

Schrader, F. Otto. *Introduction to the Pancaratra*. Madras: Adyar Library, 1916.

Schulz, Siegfried A. "Hindu Mythology in Mann's Indian Legend." *Comparative Literature*, Vol. 14, No. 2 (Spring, 1962), 129–42.

Schwartzberg, Joseph. *A Historical Atlas of South*

Asia. Chicago: University of Chicago Press, 1978.

Sclater, Philip. "The Mammals of Madagascar." *Quarterly Journal of Science* (1864).

Scott, James C. *Domination and the Arts of Resistance*. New Haven and London: Yale University Press, 1991.

———. *Weapons of the Weak: Everyday Forms of Peasant Resistance*. New Haven and London: Yale University Press, 1985.

Sedgwick, Mark. *Against the Modern World: Traditionalism and the Secret Intellectual History of the Twentieth Century*. Oxford and New York: Oxford University Press, 2004.

Seely, Clinton B., trans. *The Slaying of Meghanada: A Ramayana from Colonial Bengal*. New York: Oxford University Press, 2004.

Selvanayagam, Israel. "Ashoka and Arjuna as Counterfigures Standing on the Field of Dharma: A Historical-Hermeneutical Perspective." *History of Religions* 32:1 (August 1992), 59–75.

Sen, Amartya. *The Argumentative Indian: Writings on Indian History, Culture, and Identity*. New York: Farrar, Straus 2005.

———. Foreword to K. M. Sen, *Hinduism*.

———. *Identity and Violence: The Illusion of Destiny*. New York: Norton, 2006.

Sen, Kshiti Mohan. *Hinduism*. London: Penguin Books, 1961. With a new foreword by Amartya Sen, 2005.

Sen, Mala. *Death by Fire: Sati, Dowry Death, and Female Infanticide in Modern India*. London: Weidenfeld and Nicolson, 2001.

Sen, Ronojoy. "Legalizing Religion: The Indian Supreme Court and Homogenization of the Nation." Ph.D. dissertation, University of Chicago, June 2005.

Sen, Surendra Nath. *Eighteen Fifty Seven*. Delhi: Publications Division, Government of India, 1995.

Sesser, Stan. *Travels in Southeast Asia*. New York: Knopf, 1993.

Sewell, Robert. *A Forgotten Empire: Vijayanagar: A Contribution to the History of India*. London: S. Sonnenschein and Co., 1900.

Shah, Idries. *The Exploits of the Incomparable Mulla Nasrudin*. London: Cape, 1966.

Sharma, Arvind, ed. *Essays on the Mahabharata*. Leiden: E. J. Brill, 1991.

———. *Hinduism and Its Sense of History*. Delhi: Oxford University Press, 2003.

———, ed. *Sati: Historical and Phenomenological Essays*. Delhi: Motilal Banarsidass, 1988.

———, ed. *The Study of Hinduism*. Columbia: University of South Carolina Press, 2003.

Sharma, G. R. *The Excavations at Kausambi (1957–1959)*. Allahabad: University of Allahabad, 1960.

Sharma, Ram Sharan . "The Ayodhya Issue." In *Destruction and Restoration of Cultural Property*,

eds. P. Stone, J. Thomas, and N. Rao. New York: Routledge, 2001. Pp. 127–38.

Shattuck, Cybelle. *Hinduism*. Upper Saddle River, N.J.: Prentice Hall, 1999.

Shaw, Miranda. *Passionate Enlightenment: Women in Tantric Buddhism*. Princeton, N.J.: Princeton University Press, 1994.

Shekhawat, V. "Origin and Structure of *purush-artha* Theory: An Attempt at Critical Appraisal." *Journal of Indian Council of Philosophical Research* 7:1 (1900), 63–73.

Shulman, David. "On Being Human in the Sanskrit Epic: The Riddle of Nala." *Journal of Indian Philosophy* 22 (1994), 1–29.

———. *The Hungry God*. Chicago: University of Chicago Press, 1993.

———. *The King and the Clown in South Asian Myth and Poetry*. Princeton, N.J.: Princeton University Press, 1985.

———. "Sita and Satakantharavana in a Tamil Folk Narrative." *Journal of Indian Folkloristics* 2 (1979), 1–26.

———. *Songs of the Harsh Devotee: The Tevaram of Cuntaramurttinayanar*. Philadelphia: University of Pennsylvania Press, 1990.

———. *Tamil Temple Myths*. Princeton, N.J.: Princeton University Press, 1980.

———. Untitled review of *Siva's Warriors*. *History of Religions* 32:3 (February 1993), 312–14.

———, Velcheru Narayana Rao; and Sanjay Subrahmanyam. *Symbols of Substance: Court and State in Nayaka Period Tamil Nadu*. Delhi: Oxford University Press, 1992.

———, and Deborah Thiagarajan, eds. *Masked Ritual and Performance in South India: Dance, Healing, and Possession*. Ann Arbor: University of Michigan Press, 2006.

Sieg, Emil. *Die Sagenstoffe des Rgveda und die indische Itihasatradition*. Stuttgart: W. Kohlhammer, 1902.

Siegel, Lee. *Fires of Love/ Waters of Peace: Passion and Renunciation in Indian Culture*. Honolulu: University of Hawaii Press, 1983.

———. *Net of Magic: Wonders and Deceptions in India*. Chicago: University of Chicago Press, 1991.

Singer, Milton. *When a Great Tradition Modernizes*. New York: Praeger, 1972.

Singh, S. P. "Rgvedic Base of the Pasupati Seal of Mohenjo-Daro." *Purutattva* 19 (1988–89), 19–26.

Sircar, D. C. *Inscriptions of Asoka*. New Delhi: Publications Division, Government of India, 1957, 1975.

———. *The Sakta Pithas*. Delhi: Motilal Banarsidass, 1973. First published in the *Journal of the Royal Asiatic Society of Bengal* 14:1 (1948), 1–108.

Smith, Brian K. *Classifying the Universe*. New York: Oxford University Press, 1994.

————. "Exorcising the Transcendent: Strategies for Defining Hinduism and Religion." *History of Religions* 27:1 (August 1987), 32–55.

————. *Reflections on Resemblances, Ritual, and Religion*. New York: Oxford University Press, 1989.

————. "The Unity of Ritual: The Place of the Domestic Sacrifice in Vedic Ritualism." *Indo-Iranian Journal* 28 (1985), 79–96.

Smith, David. *Hinduism and Modernity*. Malden, Mass.: Blackwell Publishing, 2003.

Smith, Frederick M. *The Self Possessed*. New York and Oxford: Oxford University Press, 2006.

————. "Indra Goes West: Report on a Vedic Soma Sacrifice in London in July 1996." *History of Religions* 39:3 (February 2000), 247–67.

Smith, John D. *The Epic of Pabuji*. Cambridge, U.K.: Cambridge University Press, 1991.

————. "Old Indian (The Two Sanskrit Epics)." In *Traditions of Heroic and Epic Poetry*. Vol. 1. *The Traditions*, ed. A. T. Hatto. London: Modern Humanities Research Association, 1980.

Smith, Jonathan Z., *Map Is Not Territory*. Chicago: University of Chicago Press, 1993.

Smith, W. C. *The Meaning and End of Religion*. New York: Macmillan, 1962.

Sontheimer, Gunther Dietz. "Folk Hero, King and God: Some Themes According to the Folk and Textual Traditions in the Khandoba cult." Typescript, November 1984.

————. *King of Warriors, Hunters, and Shepherds: Essays on Khandoba*, eds. Anne Feldhaus, Aditya Malik, and Heidrun Brückner. Delhi: Manohar. 1997

————. "The Mallari/Khandoba Myth as Reflected in Folk Art and Ritual." *Anthropos* 79 (1984),155–70.

————. "Some Incidents in the History of the God Khandoba." In *Asie du sud: traditions et changements*, eds. M. Gaborieau and A. Thorner. Paris : Centre national de la recherche scientifique, 1978. Pp. 111–17.

Sontheimer, Gunther D. and Hermann Kulke, eds. *Hinduism Reconsidered*. Delhi: Manohar, 1989.

Southey, Robert. *The Curse of Kehama*. London: Cassell and Company, 1810, 1901.

Spayde, Jon. "The Politically Correct *Kama Sutra*." *The Utne Reader* (November–December 1996), 56–57.

Spear, Percival. *A History of India*. Vol. 2. London: Penguin Books, 1965.

Spivak, Gayatri Chakravorty. "Can the Subaltern Speak?: Speculations on Widow-Sacrifice." *Wedge* 7–8 (1985); reprinted in Cary Nelson and Lawrence Grossberg, eds., *Marxism and the Interpretation of Culture*. Urbana: University of Illinois Press, 1988.

Srinivas, M. N. *Religion and Society Among the Co-orgs of South India*. Oxford, U.K.: Clarendon Press, 1952.

————. *Social Change in Modern India*. Berkeley: University of California Press, 1966.

Staal, Frits, ed. *Agni: The Vedic Ritual of the Fire Altar*. Berkeley: Asian Humanities Press, 1983.

————. "The Concept of Scripture in the Indian Tradition." In *Sikh Studies: Comparative Perspectives on a Changing Tradition*, ed. Mark Juergensmeyer and N. Gerald Barrier. Berkeley: University of California Press, 1979.

————. "The Science of Language." In Flood, *The Blackwell Companion*, 348–59.

Steel, F. A. "Folklore in the Panjab." *Indian Antiquary* 2 (February 1882), 35.

Stein, Burton. *A History of India*. Delhi: Oxford University Press, 1998.

Sternbach, Ludwik. Review of R. C. Hazra, *Studies in the Upapuranas*, in *Journal of the American Oriental Society*, 79:2 (April–June 1959), 126–27.

Stewart, Tony K. *Fabulous Females and Fearless Pirs: Tales of Mad Adventure in Old Bengal*. New York: Oxford University Press, 2004.

————. "Satya Pir: Muslim Holy Man and Hindu God." In *Religions of India in Practice*, ed. Donald S. Lopez, Jr. Princeton, N.J.: Princeton University Press, 1995. Pp. 578–97.

Strong, John S. *The Legend of King Ashoka (Ashokavadana)*. Delhi: Motilal Banarsidas, 2002.

Subrahmanyam, Sanjay. "Friday's Child: Or how Tej Singh Became Tecinkurajan." *Indian Economic Social History Review* 36 (1999), 69–113.

————. *The Political Economy of Commerce: Southern India 1500–1560*. Cambridge, U.K.: Cambridge University Press, 1990. *See also* Narayana Rao, Shulman.

Suess, Eduard. *Das Antlitz der Erde*. Prague: F. Tempsky, 1883–1909.

Sukthankar, V. S. *On the Meaning of the Mahabharata*. Bombay: Asiatic Society of Bombay, 1957.

Sullivan, Herbert P. "A Re-examination of the Religion of the Indus Civilization." *History of Religions* 4:1 (Summer 1964), 115–25.

Sutton, Amos. *Orissa and Its Evangelization Interspaced with Suggestions Respecting the More Efficient Conducting of Indian Missions*. Boston: W. Heath, 1850.

Sweet, Michael J., and Leonard Zwilling. "The First Medicalization: The Taxonomy and Etiology of Queerness in Classical Indian Medicine." *Journal of the History of Sexuality* 3:4 (April 1993), 590–607.

Szanton, David, and Malini Bakshi. *Mithila Painting: The Evolution of an Art Form*. Ethnic Arts Foundation, Pink Mango. 2007.

————. "Mithila Painting: The Dalit Intervention." In *Dalits and Visual Imagery*, ed. Gary

Tartakov. Delhi: Indian Institute of Dalit Studies. Forthcoming.

Talbot, Cynthia. "Inscribing the Other, Inscribing the Self: Hindu-Muslim Identities in Pre-colonial India." *Comparative Studies in Society and History* 37:4 (October 1995), 692–722, reprinted in Richard M. Eaton, ed., *India's Islamic Traditions, 711–1750.* New York: Oxford University Press, 2003. Pp. 83–117.

Taranatha's History of Buddhism in India. Trans. Lama Chimpa and Alaka Chattopadhyaya. Simla: Indian Institute of Advanced Study, 1970.

Tartakov, Gary. "B. R. Ambedkar and the Narayana Diksha." In *Religious Conversion in India: Modes, Motivations and Meanings*, eds. Rowena Robinson and Sathianathan Clarke. New Delhi: Oxford University Press, 2003. Pp. 192–216.

Temple, Sir Richard Carnap. *Legends of the Punjab.* Patiala, Punjab: Language Department, 1962–63.

Tendulkar, D. G. *Mahatma: Life of Mohandas Karamchand Gandhi.* 8 vols. 2nd ed. New Delhi: Publications Division, 1951; Ahmedabad: Navajivan Publishing House, 1960.

Thapar, Romila. *Ashoka and the Decline of the Mauryas.* Oxford, U.K.: Oxford University Press, 1961.

———. *Cultural Transaction and Early India.* Delhi and New York: Oxford University Press, 1994.

———. *Early India: From the Origins to 1300.* London: Penguin, 2002; Berkeley: University of California Press, 2004.

———. "Epic and History: Tradition, Dissent, and Politics in India." *Past and Present* 125 (1989), 3–26.

———. *From Lineage to State.* Bombay: Oxford University Press, 1984.

———. *History and Beyond: Interpreting Early India; Time as a Metaphor of History; Cultural Transaction and Early India; From Lineage to State.* New York: Oxford University Press, 2000.

———. "Imagined Religious Communities: Ancient History and the Modern Search for a Hindu Identity." In *Interpreting Early India.* Delhi: Oxford University Paperbacks, 1993. Pp. 60–88.

———. *Sakuntala: Texts, Readings, Histories.* New Delhi: Kali for Women, 1999.

———. *Somanatha: The Many Voices of a History.* London: Verso, 2005.

Tharoor, Shashi. *The Great Indian Novel.* New York: Arcade, 1989.

———. *India: From Midnight to the Millennium and Beyond.* New York: Arcade Publishing, 2006

Thomas, Rosie. "Indian Cinema: Pleasures and Popularity." *Screen* 26:3–4 (May–August 1985), 116–31.

Thompson, Stith. *Motif Index of Folk-Literature.* Bloomington: Indiana University Press, 1955–58.

Tilak, Bal Gangadhar. *Srimad BhagavadGita-Rahasya or Karma-Yoga-Sastra.* Trans. B. H. Alchandra Sitaram Sukthankar. London: Books from India, 1980.

Tod, James. *Annals and Antiquities of Rajast'han or the Central and Western Rajpoot States of India.* 2 vols. London: Smith, Elder, 1829–32.

Trautmann, Thomas R. *Aryans and British India.* Berkeley: University of California Press, 1997.

———. "Elephants and the Mauryas." In *Indian History and Thought*, ed. S. Muckerjee. Calcutta: Subarnarekha, 1982. Pp. 245–81.

Treveleyan, Sir George. *Cawnpore.* London: Macmillan, 1907 [1865].

Tubb, Gary. "Barn, Ben, and Begging Bowl: Sanskrit Words and the Things in the World." Lecture at the University of Chicago, January 12, 2007.

Tukaram. *Says Tuka.* Trans. Dilip Chitre. Delhi: Penguin India, 1991.

Tull, Herman. "Karma." In Mittal and Thursby, eds. *The Hindu World*, 309–31.

———. "The Killing That Is Not Killing: Men, Cattle, and the Origins of Non-Violence (Ahimsa) in the Vedic Sacrifice." *Indo-Iranian Journal* 39 (1996), 223–44.

———. "F. Max Müller and A. B. Keith: 'Twaddle,' the 'Stupid' Myth, and the Disease of Indology." *Numen* 38:1 (1991), 27–58.

———. "Non Vedic Aryans or Vedic Non Aryans? An Examination of Mahinda Palihawadana's 'The Indra Cult as Ideology: A Clue to Power Struggle in an Ancient Society.'" *Journal of the Institute for the Study of Religion and Culture* (Japan) 6 (1988), 137–47.

———. "The Tale of 'The Bride and the Monkey': Female Insatiability, Male Impotence, and Simian Virility in Indian Literature." *Journal of the History of Sexuality* 3:4 (April 1993), 574–89.

———. *The Vedic Origins of Karma.* Albany, N.Y.: SUNY Press, 1989.

Turner, Victor. *The Forest of Symbols.* Ithaca, N.Y.: Cornell University Press, 1967.

Tyagi, Anil Kumar. *Women Workers in Ancient India.* Delhi: Radha Publications, 1994.

Ulrich, Katherine Eirene. "Divided Bodies: Corporeal and Metaphorical Dismemberment and Fragmentation in South Asian Religions." Ph.D. dissertation, University of Chicago, 2002.

———. "Food Fights: Buddhist, Hindu, and Jain. Dietary Polemics in South India." *History of Religions* 46:4 (2007), 379–81.

Upasni Baba. *The Talks of Sadguru Upasani-Baba*

Maharaj. 4 vols. Sakori, Maharashtra: Shri Upasani Kanyakumari Sthan, 1957.

Urban, Hugh B. *The Economics of Ecstasy: Tantra, Secrecy, and Power in Colonial Bengal*. New York: Oxford University Press, 2005.

———. *Magia Sexualis*. Berkeley: University of California Press, 2006.

———. "Matrix of Power: Tantra, Kingship and Sacrifice in the Worship of Mother Goddess Kamakhya." Lecture at the University of Chicago, March 7, 2005.

———. *Songs of Ecstasy*. New York: Oxford University Press, 2001.

———. *Tantra: Sex, Secrecy, Politics and Power*. Berkeley: University of California Press, 2003.

van Buitenen, J. A. B., ed. and trans. *The Mahabharata*. Chicago: University of Chicago Press, 1973– .

van der Veer, Peter. *Gods on Earth*. London and New Jersey: Athlone Press, 1988.

———. *Imperial Encounters: Religion and Modernity in India and Britain*. Princeton, N.J.: Princeton University Press, 2001.

———, ed. *Religious Nationalism: Hindus and Muslims in India*. Berkeley: University of California Press, 1994

Vasquez, Manuel A., and Marie F. Marquardt. *Globalizing the Sacred: Religion Across the Americas*. New Brunswick, N.J., and London: Rutgers University Press, 2003.

Vatsyayan, Kapila. "Prehistoric Paintings." *Sangeet Natak, Journal of the Sangeet Natak Akademi* (October–December 1981), 5–18.

Vequaud, Yves. "The Colors of Devotion," *Portfolio* (February–March 1980), 62–63.

———. *Women Painters of Mithila*. London: Thames and Hudson, 1977.

Verghese, Anila. *Religious Traditions at Vijayanagara*. Delhi: Manohar, 1995.

Vivekananda. *Swami Vivekananda and His Guru, with Letters from Prominent Americans on the Alleged Progress of Vedantism in the United States*. London and Madras: Christian Literature Society for India, 1897.

Wadley, Suzanne Snow. *Raja Nal and the Goddess: The North Indian Epic Dhola in Performance*. Bloomington: Indiana University Press, 2004.

Wagoner, Philip. "Sultan Among Hindu Kings: Dress, Titles, and the Islamicization of Hindu Culture at Vijayanagara." *Journal of Asian Studies* 55:4 (November 1996), 851–80.

Wasson, R. Gordon. *Soma: Divine Mushroom of Immortality*. New York: Harcourt Brace, 1968.

Weber, Albrecht. "Purusamedha." *Zeitschrift der deutschen Morgenländischen Gesellschaft* 18 (1864), 277–84

———. "Ueber Menschenopfer bei den Indern der vedischen Zeit." *Indische Streifen* 1 (1868), 54–80.

Wedemeyer, Christian. "Beef, Dog, and Other Mythologies: Connotative Semiotics in Mahayoga Tantra Ritual and Scripture." *Journal of the American Academy of Religion* 75:2 (June 2007), 383–417.

Weinberger-Thomas, Catherine. *Ashes of Immortality: Widow-Burning in India*. Chicago: University of Chicago Press, 1999.

Wentworth, Blake. "Yearning for a Dreamed Real: The Procession of the Lord in the Tamil Ulās." Ph.D. dissertation, University of Chicago, 2009.

West, Martin L. *Indo-European Poetry and Myth*. New York: Oxford University Press, 2007.

Whaling, Frank. *The Rise of the Religious Significance of Rama*. Delhi: Motilal Banarsidass, 1980.

White, David Gordon. *The Alchemical Body: Siddha Traditions in Medieval India*. Chicago: University of Chicago Press, 1996.

———. "Dogs Die." *History of Religions* 29:4 (May 1989), 283–303.

———. *Kiss of the Yogini: "Tantric Sex" in Its South Asian Contexts*. Chicago: University of Chicago Press, 2003.

———. *Myths of the Dog Men*. Chicago: University of Chicago Press, 1991.

Wilhelm, Friedrich. "The Concept of Dharma in Artha and Kama Literature." In *The Concept of Duty in South Asia*, eds. Wendy Doniger O'Flaherty and J. Duncan M. Derrett. London: School of Oriental and African Studies, 1978. Pp. 66–79.

Wilson, H. H. "On the Sacrifice of Human Beings as an Element of the Ancient Religion of India." *Journal of the Royal Asiatic Society*, 1852.

Wilson, Liz. *Charming Cadavers*. Chicago: University of Chicago Press, 1996.

Wittgenstein, Ludwig L. *Philosophical Investigations*. Oxford: Blackwell, 1953.

Witzel, Michael. "The Development of the Vedic Canon and Its Schools: The Social and Political Milieu." In *Inside the Texts, Beyond the Texts. New Approaches to the Study of the Vedas*. Harvard Oriental Series. Opera Minora, 2. Cambridge, Mass.: Harvard University Press, 1997. 257–345.

———. "Early Sanskritization. Origins and Development of the Kuru State." In *Recht, Staat und Verwaltung im klassischen Indien*, ed. B. Kölver. München: R. Oldenbourg, 1997. Pp. 27–52.

———. "Indocentrism: Autochthonous Visions of Ancient India." In Bryant and Patton, eds., *The Indo-Aryan Controversy*, 341–404.

———. "Rgvedic History." In Erdosy, ed., *The Indo-Aryans of Ancient South Asia*.

———. "Vedas and Upanishads." In Flood, *The Blackwell Companion*, 68–101.

Witzel, Michael, Steve Farmer, and Romila Thapar. "Horseplay in Harappa." *Frontline,* October 13, 2000, 4–16.

Wolpert, Stanley. *India.* Berkeley: University of California Press, 1991, 1999.

———. *A New History of India.* New York: Oxford University Press, 1977, 2000, 2004.

Woodruff, Philip. *The Men Who Ruled India.* New York: Schocken Books, 1964.

Woodruffe, Sir John George. *Shakti and Shakta.* Madras: Ganesha, 1929.

Wright, William. *Apocryphal Acts of the Apostles* I/II. London and Edinburgh: Williams and Norgate, 1871.

Wujastyk, Dominik. "Change and Creativity in Early Modern Indian Medical Thought." *Journal of Indian Philosophy* 33 (2005), 95–118.

———. "The Science of Medicine." In Flood, *The Blackwell Companion,* 393–409.

Yang, Anand A. *Bazaar India: Markets, Society, and the Colonial State in Gangetic Bihar.* Berkeley: University of California Press, 1998.

Yano, Michio. "Calendar, Astrology, and Astronomy." In Flood, *The Blackwell Companion,* 376–92.

Youngblood, Michael. "Cultivating Identity: Agrarian Mobilization and the Construction of Collective Interest in Contemporary Western India." Ph.D. dissertation, University of Wisconsin—Madison, 2004.

Yourcenar, Marguerite. "Kali Beheaded." In *Oriental Tales.* Trans. Alberto Manguel. New York: Farrar, Straus, 1938. Pp. 119–28.

Zaehner, R. C. *Hinduism.* London: Oxford University Press, 1962.

Zelliott, Eleanor. *From Untouchable to Dalit: Essays on the Ambedkar Movement.* New Delhi: Manohar, 2005.

Zimmermann, Frances. *The Jungle and the Aroma of Meats.* Berkeley: University of California Press, 1987.

Zysk, Kenneth. *Asceticism and Healing in Ancient India.* New York: Oxford University Press, 1991.

PHOTO CREDITS

ᠲᡃ

Jacket: The jacket image reproduces a contemporary mural from Puri, in Orissa, serigraphed on recycled handmade paper, by Santi Arts, India (www.santiarts.com), who have kindly given us permission to reprint it here. It depicts the god Krishna riding on a horse composed of the cowherd women who love him.

p. xviii. J. Jastrow, "The Mind's Eye," *Popular Science Monthly* 54 (1899), 299.

p. 22. Courtesy of Dr. Vandana Sinha, Director (Academic), Center for Art & Archaeology, American Institute of Indian Studies.

p. 65. Courtesy of Harappa.com. Seal held at the National Museum of Pakistan, Karachi. Originally printed in John Hubert Marshall, *Mohenjo-daro and the Indus civilization* (1931).

p. 73. Copyright Harappa Archaeological Research Project, Courtesy Department of Archaeology and Museums, Government of Pakistan, and Harappa .com.

p. 79. Courtesy of the National Museum of India and Greg Possehl.

p. 84. Courtesy of Frederick Asher.

p. 346. Courtesy of Carmel Berkson.

p. 441. Courtesy of Carmel Berkson.

p. 682. Courtesy of Stephen Inglis.

p. 683. Courtesy of Stephen Inglis.

p. 686. Painting by Dulari Devi, Ranti, Madhubani, Bihar, in the collection of Susan S. Wadley. I am grateful to Dulari Devi, Susan S. Wadley, and David Szanton for permission to reproduce it here.

Grateful acknowledgment is made for permission to reprint selections from the following copyrighted works:

Textual Sources for the Study of Hinduism by Wendy Doniger O'Flaherty (University of Chicago Press, 1990). Selection translated by David Shulman. By permission of Wendy Doniger O'Flaherty and David Shulman.

Speaking of Siva, translated with an introduction by A. K. Ramanujan (Penguin Classics, 1973). Copyright © A. K. Ramanujan, 1973. By permission of Penguin Books Ltd, London.

Songs of Experience: The Poetics of Tamil Devotion by Norman Cutler. Copyright © 1987 by Norman Cutler. Reprinted with permission of Indiana University Press.

Hymns for the Drowning: Poems for Visnu by Nammalvar, translated by A. K. Ramanujan (Princeton University Press, 1981). By permission of Molly A. Daniels Ramanujan.

"From Classicism to Bhakti" by A. K. Ramanujan and Norman Cutler from *The Collected Essays of A. K. Ramanujan,* edited by Vinay Dharwadker. Reprinted by permission of Oxford University Press India, New Delhi.

The Bijak of Kabir, translated by Linda Hess (Oxford University Press, 2002). By permission of Linda Hess.

Says Tuka: Selected Poetry of Tukaram, translated by Dilip Chitre (Penguin India, 1991). By permission of Dilip Chitre.

Songs of the Saints of India by John Stratton Hawley and Mark Juergensmeyer. Reprinted by permission of Oxford University Press India, New Delhi.

Three Bhakti Voices: Mirabai, Surdas and Kabir in Their Times and Ours by John Stratton Hawley. Reprinted by permission of Oxford University Press India, New Delhi.

When God Is A Customer: Telugu Courtesan Songs by Ksetrayya and Others, edited and translated by A. K. Ramanujan, Narayana Rao and David Shulman. © 1994 Regents of the University of California. Published by the University of California Press. By permission of the publisher.

Dalit Vision by Gail Omvedt. © Orient Blackswan Pvt, India. By permission of Orient Blackswan.

An Anthology of Dalit Literature by Mulk Raj Anand and Eleanor Zelliot (Gyan Publishing House, 1992). Selection translated by Jayant Karve and Eleanor Zelliot. By permission of Eleanor Zelliot.

Vidrohi Kavita, edited by Keshav Meshram (Continental Prakashan, 1987). Selection translated by Gauri Deshpande and others. By permission of Eleanor Zelliot.

INDEX

Page numbers in *italics* refer to illustrations.

ABOUT THE AUTHOR

ॐ

Wendy Doniger holds two doctorates, in Sanskrit and Indian studies, from Harvard and Oxford. She is the author of several translations of Sanskrit texts and many books about Hinduism, and has taught at the School of Oriental and African Studies at the University of London and at the University of California at Berkeley. She is currently the Mircea Eliade Distinguished Service Professor of the History of Religions at the University of Chicago.